AMERICAN

POLITICAL

THOUGHT

A NORTON ANTHOLOGY

AMERICAN

POLITICAL

THOUGHT

A NORTON ANTHOLOGY

EDITED BY

ISAAC KRAMNICK
Cornell University

THEODORE J. LOWI
Cornell University

W. W. NORTON & COMPANY

New York · London

W. W. Norton & Company has been independent since its founding in 1923, when William Warder Norton and Mary D. Herter Norton first published lectures delivered at the People's Institute, the adult education division of New York City's Cooper Union. The Nortons soon expanded their program beyond the Institute, publishing books by celebrated academics from America and abroad. By mid-century, the two major pillars of Norton's publishing program—trade books and college texts—were firmly established. In the 1950s, the Norton family transferred control of the company to its employees, and today—with a staff of four hundred and a comparable number of trade, college, and professional titles published each year—W. W. Norton & Company stands as the largest and oldest publishing house owned wholly by its employees.

Copyright © 2009 by W. W. Norton & Company, Inc.

All rights reserved
Printed in the United States of America
First Edition

Editor: Ann Shin
Project editor: Rebecca A. Homiski
Production manager: Ben Reynolds
Editorial assistant: Mollie Eisenberg
Manuscript editor: Barbara Curialle
Book design: Jo Anne Metsch
Composition: Binghamton Valley Composition
Index: Aline E. Reynolds
Manufacturing: R. R. Donnelley & Sons—Crawfordsville, IN

Library of Congress Cataloging-in-Publication Data

American political thought : a Norton anthology / edited by Isaac Kramnick,
Theodore J. Lowi.—1st ed.
    p.   cm.
Includes bibliographical references and index.

ISBN 13: 978-0-393-92886-0 (pbk.)

1. United States—Politics and government—Sources.   I. Kramnick, Isaac.
II. Lowi, Theodore J.
JK21.A4625 2009
320.0973—dc22   2008009413

W. W. Norton & Company, Inc., 500 Fifth Avenue, New York, N.Y. 10110
www.wwnorton.com

W. W. Norton & Company Ltd., Castle House, 75/76 Wells Street, London W1T 3QT

5 6 7 8 9 0

CONTENTS

Empire and Race   893

The Contemporary Discourse

PREFACE

This has been a long and pleasant endeavor, over a decade in the making. One editor came to the anthology as a specialist in political theory who was trying to understand European, and especially English, influences on American thought and institutions. The other editor came from the opposite direction—as a specialist on contemporary American institutions—before being drawn toward the history of political thought through a simple question: "How did we get to where we are now?" Each of us discovered through teaching and research that American political institutions are the unique product of the application of political thought to political action, and conversely, that American political thought is uniquely a product of political action. Neither of us could have contemplated a project of this magnitude without the other. Whereas one editor selected, rejected, and classified, the other concentrated on the themes that are developed in the introduction to each part. Our cooperation gave shape to a body of ideas that we can legitimately refer to as American political thought.

We believe that our anthology realizes the dual aspirations we embraced from the start: that it meet the highest standard of pedagogy, and that it make a distinct contribution to the development of a genuine, autonomous American political thought. We concede that our book is a beginning. We endorse a belief attributed to Michelangelo—everyone's model of the heroic creator—that every stone contains the complete statue, revealed once the excess material has been chiseled away. Have we chipped away too much? Or too little? Does the body of the book speak for itself or need more explanation? It can only be a work in progress because, unlike Michelangelo's human figure, the American body politic requires successive evaluation—which could suffice as the very definition of political theory.

Our book is an anthology, which (from the Greek) means a gathering of flowers, or some other desirable item, such as poems. It is designed to please as well as enlighten, by variety as well as by intensity. It aims to meet the needs of teachers with a selection of essential readings not readily available and to categorize and portray them in a pedagogically friendly way. Categorization of the selections by subject matter within recognized historical periods gives students the relevant social and political context while raising questions about continuity and change in political thought and the impact of ideas on institutions and behavior. There is, then, a good deal of political theory implied in selection and organization. We have taken on an additional scholarly challenge by pointing our selections toward questions that engage all serious students of political thought: Is there an American political thought? If so, what is it?

At another level, our anthology has a strong dual theme. The first theme is, as Louis Hartz put it, the "liberal tradition." We have dramatized that theme through the metaphor of "the race of life," which is so often repeated in American political discourse that it lacks a respectable philosophical designation. In our usage, it is the metaphorical rendering of the dual American ideals of competitive individualism and equal opportunity. This theme is inherent in the Lockean social contract with the state to protect private rights. It is found in the dynamic equilibrium of Adam Smith's competition of selfish interests, his "invisible hand," coupled with Max Weber's notion of the Protestant ethic.

The second theme is the "conservative tradition." For all of his important contributions, Hartz did American political thought an injustice by insisting that Lockean liberalism was embraced so thoroughly that in his words "we never had a real conservative tradition." America has a conservative political tradition that is just as broad and deep as the liberal tradition. But the two are rarely in true competition, let alone dialectical tension. They are as ships passing in the day—conservatism being local and parochial, liberalism more cosmopolitan; conservatism concerned with order and obligation, liberalism with consequences and satisfactions. One pursues goodness, the other happiness. We hope that our anthology will help raise the two traditions to the level of mutual recognition, so that a sustained and substantive dialogue between them can begin.

A final pedagogical note for both teachers and students who use this anthology: We have decided in the essays that introduce the book's five parts to eschew the conventional summary of that era's selections. Instead, we offer a short impressionistic essay about the period: additional material for readers and instructors to think about and discuss. We organize these period essays around representative thinkers whom we label "signature" figures from that era.

We dedicate this book to the graduate students who have studied with us these many decades. We hope they carry with them some small part of the Cornell tradition as they teach in colleges and universities around the world. They have learned from us and we from them.

Acknowledgements

Our principal debt is to W. W. Norton publishers, who have permitted us to join the illustrious series of Norton anthologies. The patience of our editors, Steve Dunn and Ann Shin, over more than ten years demonstrates Norton's appreciation that art is not the only thing that is long. Ideas may come in a flash, but they mature not at first but at last. We thank the many scholars who reviewed the manuscript and the table of contents for the publisher. We are particularly thankful to those who helped us craft this anthology, no one more than Clem Fatovic, to whom we are supremely grateful. Others who helped us produce this book are Glenn Altschuler, Sean Boutin, Kristin McKie, Mingus Mapps, Vladimir Micic, and Hong-An Tran. Then there are those with that indispensable "passion for anonymity" who managed not only the vast amount of paper but who managed the two of us: Jackie Pastore and Michael Busch. We also have our wives and families to thank, for their faith that something good would come of all this. And last, we join in recognition of our esteemed colleague, friend, and role model, M. H. "Mike" Abrams, for having been not only an enthusiastic supporter of our project but for having been the godfather of the kind of serious anthology that deserves a place on the shelf of history and criticism.

Toward an American
Political Thought

Amerian political thought is seldom systematic. It avoids formalism
and the abstractions of logical theorizing. Tocqueville sensed this in
his famous 1831 visit. Americans, he wrote,

> have . . . a philosophical method common to the whole people[:] . . . to
> accept tradition only as a means of information . . . [,] to tend to re-
> sults without being bound to means, and to strike through the form to
> the substance. . . . This . . . leads them to condemn forms, which they
> regard as useless and inconvenient veils placed between them and the
> truth.

Tocqueville suggests that Americans, in fact, turn Descartes on his head:
I am, therefore I think.

Near the end of the nineteenth century, Oliver Wendell Holmes, Jr.,
echoed this attitude in his book *The Common Law*, "The life of law has
not been logic: It has been experience. The felt necessities of the time . . .
have a good deal more to do than syllogism in determining the rules by
which men are governed." His view of law also applies to political thought.

Is "American political thought," then, an oxymoron? No. Americans
come to political thought because ideas have consequences. Ideas come
from experience, but they also give meaning to experience so that it can
be cumulated into wisdom, judgment, ethics, and political thought.

American political thought is not a distillation of a definable body of
philosophic sources. Nor is it a product arising directly from the experiences of governing the nation. Conditions do not determine outcomes.
Our theory about how American political thought developed owes more
to Darwin than to Marx. Some ideas find a hospitable environment and
become schools of thought, ideologies, or philosophies. Some ideas begin

big but have a short half-life; others take longer to gel but endure. Some ideas are dead on arrival. Many ideas are called, but few are chosen. It's not easy to predict which ideas will take root. At first blush, Calvinist predestination seems inappropriate in North America because, as the twentieth-century political philosopher George Sabine noted, it takes "the heart out of human effort." But it actually had the opposite effect, becoming, he wrote, an "ethics of action . . . self-control, discipline, and respect for one's comrades in the battle of life." The "battle of life," more often transformed into the "race of life," has been a staple of American political thought for both liberals and conservatives.

Emphasis on action and experience provided an especially hospitable environment for *pragmatism* in America. William James, its most famous disciple, distinguished pragmatism from traditional philosophy. At the beginning of Lecture I of his "Eight Lectures on Pragmatism," he proclaimed to his Harvard audience: "The philosophy which is so important in each of us is not a technical matter; it is our more or less dumb sense of what life honestly and deeply means." Later, he defines "the pragmatic method": "The attitude of looking away from first things, principles, 'categories,' supposed necessities; and of looking towards last things, fruits, consequences, facts."

In his 1955 book *The Liberal Tradition in America*, Louis Hartz called pragmatism "America's great contribution to the philosophic tradition," adding that "in America the devotion to it has been so irrational that it is not recognized for what it is: liberalism." In any event, pragmatism prospered in a hospitable habitat at the same time that Darwinism had become integral to the American intellectual scene.

As Lincoln warned in his Lyceum speech of 1838, post-revolutionary Americans have contempt for forms. Tocqueville noted that Americans saw forms as "veils placed between them and the truth." Forms were too passive for Americans, who replaced form with method. (By method we mean prescribed procedures, the rules of the game.) Hobbes and Locke philosophized about the "social contract," but Americans adapted it for real governments. The "race of life" is itself a method—embedded in the story of the folkways of sportsmanship. Method runs through every feature of American political thought. The Constitution, with its Bill of Rights, does not distribute or allocate rights; nor does it leave individuals free to assert and defend their own. A number of substantive rights are specified in the Bill of Rights, but they are guaranteed by methodological or procedural limitations on the power of government. For example, "due process of law" does not guarantee individuals fair trials; it provides for fair trials by requiring meticulous observance of rules (methods) laid down for proper judicial process. Property, which may be the right most precious to Americans, is protected by the methodological provisions of the Fifth and Fourteenth Amendments. Justice Felix Frankfurter, one of the great theoretical minds ever to serve on the Supreme Court, wrote one of the best generalizations about method in American political thought in 1951: "The validity and moral authority of a conclusion largely depend on the mode by which it was reached." On this matter, liberals and conservatives in America are in lockstep agreement.

Lord, Labor, and Liberty

Method, with all its potential for good, is sterile without substance: the how requires the what. To keep itself from descending into mere opinion, preference, or interest, method must be grounded in philosophy—in principles broader than "the race of life" and above and beyond the mere convenience of the competitors. In American political thought, many principles have emerged, but only a few have been truly significant. As editors, our selections were guided by the substantive principles that seemed to have set the agenda since the settling of America. Our choices were: lord, labor, and liberty. This was not difficult because we encountered these principles repeatedly, albeit in different names and guises, in the bibliography of American intellectual history.

In America, religion came first. Once again Tocqueville sets the terms of discourse: "It must never be forgotten that religion gave birth to Anglo-American society. In the United States, religion is therefore mingled with all the habits of the nation and all the feelings of patriotism, whence it derives a peculiar force."

Nearly two centuries later, annual polls reveal that religion remains more central in American life than in any other industrialized country. Of course, religion itself has changed since Tocqueville's time. As intellectual historian Henry Steele Commager put it, "religion prospered while theology went slowly bankrupt." However, Commager also added, "although the theological implications of Puritanism wore off in the course of the 18th and 19th centuries, many of its moral and political implications persisted." One of the secrets of its persistence was its voluntary removal from direct involvement in politics and government. The Puritan elders sought no theocracy in their towns. The Founders, most of whom believed in some sort of deity, omitted God from the Constitution. And forty years later Tocqueville observed: "The peaceful dominion of religion [can be attributed] mainly to the separation of church and state."

The second persistent theme is, in its origin, close to the first. John Locke, who gave the English-speaking world its theory of property, saw property as derived from labor, which God had required of fallen men. "Whatsoever then [man] removes out of the state that nature [and God] hath provided . . . , he has mixed his labour with and joined it to something that is his own and thereby makes it his property . . . [*excluding*] the common right of other men."

The story of the relationship between work and property and the Calvinism of the Puritans was told well by the German sociologist Max Weber in *The Protestant Ethic and the Spirit of Capitalism* (1905). Adherents of predestination used labor to conquer inner loneliness and achieve success, a sign that the lonely ascetic, who deferred gratification, was chosen for salvation. Although it was a sin to pursue wealth as an end in itself,

> The attainment of [wealth] as a fruit of labour in a calling was a sign of God's blessing. The religious valuation of . . . systematic work in a worldly calling [is] . . . the surest and most evident proof of rebirth and genuine faith . . . an attitude toward life we have here called the spirit of capitalism.

Liberty completes the American trinity. Long before *liberal* became a political term, it referred to a generous disposition and to a particular attitude toward learning—as in liberal arts. A liberal education was designed for Christian "gentlemen," men of independent means, who met others of the same ilk. But the word also came to stand for independence of mind, albeit within the Christian context. Liberal*ism* came along later as the terms *liberal* and *liberty* were being secularized. Property remained essential to liberal and liberty; the Calvinist idea of property as a tangible assurance of salvation was replaced by prosperity as an earthly reward to those successful in the "race of life." This was also called the "pursuit of happiness." But note well the liberal caveats: Happiness is left to all individuals to define and pursue in their own way. And the right to happiness is not substantive but a methodological right to the *pursuit* of happiness.

A liberal society is thus one that is based on wants people define for themselves rather than needs defined by others, derived from some authoritative moral source. In a society built on the pursuit of wants, liberty requires the absence of restraint. This is why the American Bill of Rights dwelled on what governments cannot do: "Congress shall make no law . . . abridging the freedom of speech, or of the press"; "no warrants shall issue, but upon probable cause"; and so on. The Bill of Rights should actually be called the Bill of Liberties.

Liberty is never totally unrestrained; that would amount to anarchy— a return to the state of nature. In fact, liberty assumes a place and population that is governed by public institutions. Liberty assumes that this society is civil because the inhabitants accept certain principles or virtues. This agreement does not suddenly convert liberty into a communitarian or conservative community. A liberal system is liberal by degree, depending on the content of internal and external restraints and the number of citizens that accept them. Those restraints can be based on either secular or sacred sources. It is in this context, then, that liberty completes the trinity of central themes in American political thought.

An anthology of American political thought is very much an exploration of fragmented variations on these themes. Each selection here—whether from activists and practitioners, amateurs and speculators, true citizens and special pleaders, or poets and preachers—is a treasure worth saving, and each can be considered worthy of synthesis by the great philosophic minds yet to come; while we wait, each will tell us about our past and present. Our task as editors is to provide a sense of continuity without imposing a theory of evolution or teleology.

Lincoln and the Race of Life

Because action and ideas are so closely mated in America, we will overlay our sense of continuity on individual examples of action and ideas—both in this general introduction and in the introduction to each part of the book. We begin with Abraham Lincoln, often considered the thinking person's ideal American. Lincoln forged great ideas from action; he was the embodiment of the "liberal tradition" and of Christian virtue. The politician John Hay called him in 1866 "the greatest character since Christ," to which historian Richard Hofstadter added in his 1948 work *American Political Tradition*, "The Lincoln legend gathers strength from its similarity to the Christian theme of vicarious atonement and redemption" combined with "that self-help which Americans have always so admired." This is Lincoln: a man from Illinois by way of Kentucky with a Calvinist zeal for work and deferred gratification. In Hofstadter's account, he combined the Puritan's "intense awareness of humanity and moral responsibility," with a fierce pride as "the exemplar of the self-made man" and a "morbid compulsion for honesty." But he was not an orthodox religious man, at least not in the conventional sense.

Now we can put this heroic character to work. Facing the 160th Ohio Regiment at one of the darkest moments in the Civil War, Lincoln spoke not of slavery or its abolition, but about himself and his success in the "race of life":

> I happen, temporarily, to occupy this White House. I am living witness that any one of your children may look to come here as my father's child has. It is in order that each of you may have, through this free government . . . an open field and a fair chance for your industry, enterprise and intelligence; that you may all have equal privileges in the

race of life. . . . It is for this that the struggle should be maintained. . . .
The nation is worth fighting for, to secure this inestimable jewel.

This reference of the "race of life" echoed Lincon's speech to a joint session of Congress in July 1861, soon after his March 4 inauguration and
the April 12 firing on Fort Sumter: "[The Civil War] is a struggle for
maintaining in the world, that form and substance of government, whose
leading object is to elevate the condition of men, to lift artificial weights
from all shoulders . . . to afford all, an unfettered start, a fair chance, in
the race of life."

Lincoln's use of the metaphor "the race of life" runs through American
political thought and public discourse like few, if any, other ideas. It signifies the fundamental American belief in equal opportunity for competitive individuals. A century after Lincoln, President Lyndon Johnson told
the 1965 graduating class at Howard University that his policy of affirmative action would help provide a "fair race": "You do not take a person,
who for years has been hobbled by chains and liberate him, bringing him
up to the starting line of a race and then say, 'You are free to compete
with all the others,' and still justly believe you have been completely fair."
For Johnson, born in a dirt-poor region of Texas, "the race of life" was no
mere metaphor; it described the ideal of equal opportunity to realize the
American dream. And so it has for many thinkers in our anthology.

Politics is talk, and political talk is filled with metaphors. Metaphors
help establish the terms of discourse, and anyone who can establish the
terms of discourse has the best chance of winning the argument. There is
Plato's cave and Hobbes's Leviathan. There is the body politic and the
marketplace of ideas; the invisible hand and left versus right; scales of
justice, the balance wheel, and checks-and-balances. There is the chain
of being, chain of command, and chains to be broken. The historian Carl
Becker treated metaphors as "magic words," words that do not require
definition "to convey the way things work" or "the way things ought to
be." Since these "magic words" tend to conceal major premises and tacit
prejudices, they should be treated with care, he suggested, in light of the
relevant "climate of opinion."

We see the race of life as a metaphor that survived many climates of
opinion, giving it ultimately a stature as an enduring myth of American liberalism, which operates, according to Holmes, more subtly "than any articulate major premise." The metaphor appeared first in the philosophical
progenitors of liberalism. Thomas Hobbes used it in 1640 in his stark description of a society in *The Elements of Law*, in which all persons are self-
moving, self-directing machines, constantly in motion and competing with
one another for power, wealth, and glory: "the comparison of the life of

man to a race . . . holdeth so well for this purpose. . . . This race we must suppose to have no other goal, nor other garland, but being foremost."

A century later in his *Theory of Moral Sentiments* (1759), Adam Smith characterized life as "a race for wealth and honour and preferments," but added the condition of fair play. Otherwise "merit and abilities" might lose to "flattery and falsehood." But whereas Smith believed self-interest would lead each competitor to play fair, Hobbes in his *Leviathan* (1651) brought in the state as the enforcer of fair play. As Hobbes put it,

> the use of law . . . is not to bind the people from all voluntary action; but to direct and keep them in such a motion, as not to hurt themselves by their own impetuous desires, rashness, or indiscretion; as hedges are set, not to stop Travelers, but to keep them in their way.

Locke followed with a version of Hobbes's "hedges": "The reason why men enter into civil society," he wrote, "is that there may be laws made, and rules set, as guards and fences." Although Locke did not explicitly use the phrase *race of life*, he referred to "the umpirage, which everyone had consented to" when establishing their government.

The race of life is so deeply ingrained in American political language and discourse that it should no longer be treated as merely a metaphor. To layer the metaphors: the race of life is a trigger of political thought, the *in*articulate major premise of what became, in the nineteenth century, a vehicle for liberal political thought—albeit not systematic political thought—for liberals as different as Lincoln and William Graham Sumner.

Liberalism and Conservatism

Concepts, unlike metaphors, require definition. They should be defined not merely by what they include but by what they exclude, which requires some kind of pairing with another concept. Liberalism has its antonym: conservatism. Many of the metaphors used to extend the race of life help define the two concepts in relation to each other. One embraces the race, one the rules; one embraces the motion, one the hedges; one embraces the freedom, one the chains; one the game, one the umpire; one the will, one the ought; one the immediate, one the deferred; one the existential, one the transcendent; one the mechanical, one the organic; one contract, one tradition; one utility, and one morality.

Liberalism and conservatism exist in history. Efforts to explain the two by locating the causes of each, as though they were determined, are faulty; we prefer to try to understand them in terms of their reasons for being. We do agree that the two emerge as equal and opposite reactions to a common experience: the French Revolution and the collapse of the *ancien regime*, and with it, feudalism, aristocracy, monarchy, and state religion. But we insist that the reactions were reasoned efforts to understand and cope with the vast changes that were occurring. For us, the concepts of liberalism and conservatism are hedges that guide us through the multitudes of selections and ideas in the pages to come. Some ideas will not fit comfortably into either category. But, as in the law, those are the "hard cases" that require special attention.

Conservatism came first historically because it was embedded in every aspect of the prevailing but declining feudalist regimes long before it was given so brilliant a definition by the eighteenth-century British thinker Edmund Burke in his *Reflections on the Revolution in France* (1790). Rejecting what he considered Enlightenment hubris, in which human rationality reconstructed the social order in the name of abstract ideas like human rights, Burke urged respect for tradition and experience. Each generation should embrace its linkage to the past. The dominant metaphor of conservatism is the chain, which serves at least three functions. First, it captures the interconnectedness, the linkage of each unit of creation. Second, the linkage is a gradation, with creatures, especially human beings, each in an assigned place. And third, the connection and placements (or rankings or statuses) are morally ordained, by God or by some other transcendent value system, from Plato's Republic to India's caste system. This is hierarchy—morally sanctioned inequality, with a "chain of command" assignment of role and status to each person. Care must be taken here to distinguish this historically grounded concept from a use of the term "conservatism" widely embraced in the second half of the twentieth century as a label for people whose beliefs are truly Adam Smith–type classical liberalism. In fact, former President Herbert Hoover tried for years after his defeat by Roosevelt to take the term *liberal* back from the Democrats because he viewed the Republican party as the true liberal party. In 1945, Hoover gave up: "Let them have the word. It no longer makes sense." However, we will stay close to the original meaning of conservatism and liberalism.

Conservatism, at least in America, has, in fact, embraced the "race of life." The metaphor occurs in Christian scripture, with Paul referring to having "finished the race" and "reached the finish line." But Calvinism established that the fate of each person is determined regardless of effort; predestination drove each Christian to an ascetic life, with hard work and success as an outward sign of grace. This made conservatism, especially in America, as compatible with capitalism as Adam Smith's liberalism. Whatever the accuracy of Max Weber's thesis about the "protestant ethic" and the "spirit of capitalism," the effect is clear: its consonance with capitalism blurred the distinction of conservatism as the antonym of liberalism and encouraged the neglect of conservatism as a distinct "tradition" in America. Another factor that tended to soften the principled distinction between liberalism and conservatism is the posture of most American churches toward separation of church and state. It bears repeating that Tocqueville's conclusion that the centrality of religion in American life was attributable to the separation of church and state was based on his conversations with American clergy. This posture favoring a secular state by such a conservative element in American society certainly reduced the prospect of the kind of radical polarization between clergy and laity found in Europe.

With *The Liberal Tradition in America*, Louis Hartz gave the definitive reading of American liberalism, which he referred to as a "tradition" and not as a philosophy or school of thought. In America, he wrote, "the fundamental social norm of Locke ceased in large part to look like a norm and began, of all things, to look like a sober description of fact." However, whereas Burke and those who followed him provided a list of conservative principles, no equivalent listing was supplied by liberals, perhaps because liberalism is not as programmatic as conservatism. As editors we think it useful, nonetheless, to impose more rigor on liberalism by contriving a dialectical exchange between it and conservatism, even at the risk of oversimplification.

Louis Hartz did the world of intellectual history and political thought a disservice by failing to follow up with a book about the conservative tradition in America. Hartz's book about the liberal tradition is not a half-truth, but, rather, only half of the truth. According to his colleague Judith Shklar, Hartz described an America that marches "single file down a single straight liberal highway," inviting theorists into "compulsive repetition of the same theme." In a startling exercise of circular reasoning, Hartz's one-word explanation for why "we have never had a real conservative tradition" in America, was "unanimity." We are unipolar because we are unanimous; we are unanimous because we are unipolar. Herbert Marcuse, the leftist philosopher of the 1960s, saw this unanimity as "one-dimensional" and explained it as having been accomplished by converting the liberal embrace of tolerance into repression, "repressive tolerance," or "totalitarian democracy." But this was simply a more sophisticated way of overlooking conservatism. Marcuse, Hartz, and many other liberal intellectuals were so intent on explaining "why there is no socialism in America" that they overlooked liberalism's real adversary.

The mistakes of liberal intellectual historians are rooted in their disregard and ignorance of the U.S. Constitution, especially the principle of federalism, and its impact on American politics. Article I, Section 8, and the Tenth Amendment reserve to the states all powers not delegated to the national government. That is a vast territory called by jurists "the police power"—the power of the sovereign to control the health, safety, and morals of the community. The states, then, were responsible for virtually all of the real governing. And, following Chief Justice John Marshall's holding in *Barron v. Baltimore* (1833), the states would not even be limited by the Bill of Rights for much of American history. Thus, there are no national property, marriage and family, divorce, morality, estate or corporate laws, no federal law governing the practice of professions or the conduct of education. There are no national criminal laws, except those concerning federal territories. Under Article I, Section 8, the domain of federal law included the postal service and postal highways, a common currency, control and disposal of public lands, the census, bankruptcy, "internal improvements," tariffs, and international trade. With only slight exaggeration, this is how we can summarize the prerogatives of national government and state government: state power as police power was moral power, power over conduct deemed good or evil in itself; federal power was instrumental power, power over conduct deemed good or bad (injurious) in its consequences.

As this "specialization of function" endured, the states became hospitable to conservatism and the federal government more hospitable to liberalism. This is not to say that conservatives controlled and won every battle in the state legislatures; the state legislatures were highly responsive to their constituencies—including nonconservative social movements—and to the laws they espoused, from abolition to the rights of women, children, disabled workers, veterans, and the destitute. However, every active citizen knew that on all of the most fundamental, divisive moral issues—from marriage and divorce to children and custody, incest, adoption, racial segregation, schooling, and the foundation of property and corporations—going to Washington would have been a colossal waste of time. Conservatives were neither nonpolitical nor irrational. They focused on the centers of power appropriate to their interests: the states and their local government units.

Thus philosophical conservatism was often overlooked and neglected by American intellectuals because they were focused on national matters, lived in metropolitan areas, and worked in urban universities. On the few occasions when great moral issues arose to national attention, conservatives mobilized as a national movement and then disappeared back into their traditional lairs after the crisis. No wonder that liberal intellectuals treated conservatives as sporadic and aberrant, virtually as a symptom of a disease rather than a bona fide American tradition.

In response to this conservative pattern, Hartz conceded that a book should be written—but "in a psychiatric vein." In fact, a group of distinguished scholars did write such a book: *The New American Right* (edited by Daniel Bell, 1955). These scholars characterized conservatism as a social movement; a social movement is by nature radical and sporadic—a social pathology, not an intellectual tradition. A second edition retitled *The Radical Right* came out in 1963. One of the contributors to the volume, Richard Hofstadter, revised his essay to concede that excessive emphasis was put on "the clinical side of the problem." Yet, two years later, Hofstadter used conservatism as a case of "the paranoid style in American politics." Daniel Bell tried to put the matter to rest in *The End of Ideology: The Exhaustion of Political Ideas in the 1950s* (1965), as though conservatism had disappeared following the Goldwater debacle.

Conservatism had simply returned to its traditional habitat in the 1960s. But that tradition would soon change. Conservatism had not been nationalized in the 1930s because conservatives—especially Southern Democrats—had made a Faustian bargain with the New Deal. The bargain went something like this: "You supporters of the New Deal can have your national regulatory standards and your welfare state as long as you design your policies and programs in a way that leaves race, class (labor), and gender issues to the states." Genuine conservatives, Democrat or Republican, were quite comfortable with national government regulation of big corporations. Republican liberals were the opponents of those New Deal regulatory agencies they called the "alphabetocracy." What the conservative Southern Democrats sought and got were regulatory programs that exempted from regulations those industries in the South, such as laundry and textile industries, farm labor, domestic service, and other unskilled trades, whose employees were principally women, blacks, or extremely low-wage workers—male or female, white or black. The original Social Security and welfare programs were designed for stably employed workers and their survivors and not for what policymakers considered the "undeserving poor" such as unwed mothers or the hopelessly unemployed. Moreover, the regulatory and welfare laws were drafted in a manner that left implementation largely to state legislatures and local welfare agencies and gave them tremendous discretion over the level of benefits and the conditions and standards of eligibility. The bargain was not perfect for either side, but it kept the conservatives reasonably capable of maintaining local law and order by keeping people in their proper place.

The Faustian bargain began to break down after passage of the civil rights laws beginning in 1964, the expansion of the welfare state beginning in 1965 with Medicare and Medicaid, and the national expansion of eligibility for benefits ("coverage") coupled with the relative increase in the level of benefits, even making increases automatic by calibrating or "pegging" benefits to inflation (as measured by the Consumer Price Index).

The policy innovations of the decade from 1964 to 1973 culminated with "affirmative action," federal intervention against state efforts to limit opportunities for minority groups and women: *Golberg v. Kelly* (1970) granted protection against state discretion to deny welfare benefits ("entitlements"), and *Roe v. Wade* (1973) established national judicial and congressional power to intervene against state efforts in the highly charged issue of abortion.

These profound policy innovations completed the "Roosevelt Revolution" and produced a new American state. These innovations were also the death-knell of the Democratic party and the hegemony it enjoyed for nearly forty years after 1933. By the end of the 1970s there had been a wholesale exodus of southern conservatives from the Democratic party and the beginning of a vast ideological realignment—if not yet a full realignment—of the partisan affiliations of American voters. More to the point here, there was a national consolidation and reorientation of conservatism. As noted already, conservatives had occasionally mobilized before. But this time was exceptional, in at least three ways. First, the scale of mobilization was broader and deeper than ever before: evangelical Protestants joined with mainstream Protestant conservatives; secular conservatives joined with religious conservatives; conservative Protestants formed a strong coalition with Catholics for the first time in history. A new breed of secular philosophic conservative intellectuals called neoconservatives came forward to become the major theoretical and philosophical source of policy ideas and rationales.

The second exceptional feature of this new conservative mobilization was its discovery of the media of mass communication. Reverend Jerry Falwell was one of dozens of evangelical ministers who broke through the walls of the churches and tabernacles to reach millions of loyal worshippers first via radio, and then television. Focus on the Family was a still larger radio parsonage, with additional sacred muscle in their extensive publishing program. All this was topped by Reverend Pat Robertson's highly popular conservative television talk show, *The 700 Club*. These media outlets gave conservatism a populist base that was the envy of both major political parties.

The third and most important of the unprecedented features of this most recent mobilization of conservatism on a national scale was the institutionalization of its presence in Washington. The Moral Majority, organized by several very secular political entrepreneurs, cemented the evangelicals and fundamentalist Protestants with conservative Catholics and made a place for them inside the Republican party, giving the party a populist base not present since the early twentieth century. Talented neoconservatives earned places of influence as columnists with leading conservative periodicals and as the "conservative voice" on the editorial pages of all the major newspapers. At last conservatism could boast an intellectual elite—many of the neoconservatives having started out on the left as New Deal liberals, communists, and fellow travelers, moving across the spectrum in reaction against Stalinism and then against the American radicalism of the 1960s. Finally, this newly constituted, genuine right wing attracted enough financial support to form think tanks, policy research and propaganda institutes in Washington, to combat the messages of their long-entrenched "liberal enemies." These organizations gave conservatives a national voice they previously lacked. They also provided well-paid jobs for a new generation of intellectuals, a recruitment pool for policy analysis, speech writing, and intelligence jobs in the White House, State and Defense Departments, security agencies, congressional staffs, and, not least, a means of continued employment for conservatives in Washington during dry periods when the other party is in the majority.

This brings the story of conservatism up to date and demonstrates that American political thought is neither monolithic nor homogeneous. For nearly two centuries, these two streams of political thought—liberalism and conservatism—had their own separate domains. Each had its favorable habitat: the nation or the states. But because so many intellectuals operated as though there was only "the liberal tradition," the two streams of thought were as ships giving each other a wide berth, with an occasional shot across the bow that always came as something of a surprise. Without a dynamic, nationwide confrontation, liberalism became less robust toward the end of the New Deal hegemony in the 1960s. Hartz foresaw this in 1955: "I believe that this is the basic ethical problem of a liberal society: Not the danger of the majority which has been its conscious fear, but the danger of unanimity."

The same dilemma beset conservatism, because on matters of morality and social order—where, in the words of former speaker of the House Tip O'Neil, "all politics is local"—it has had no real challenge either. Thanks to American federalism, "we are all liberals, we are all conservatives." Until the very end of the twentieth century there was no genuine American dialectic, and liberalism was the loser in a contest that never took place. With the national mobilization of conservatism and the emergence of key conservative intellectuals, liberalism has been in retreat, with the term *liberal*, the L word, stigmatized in popular literature, mass communications, and political campaigns. Have the outstanding virtues of liberalism—generosity, tolerance, skepticism, scientism, and above all the embrace of individualism and an openness toward any individual choice that does not harm others—been stigmatized beyond redemption? According to hosts of conservatives and many liberals, the answer is verging on yes. In 1987,

the conservative thinker Allan Bloom administered what may be liberalism's last rites:

> Openness used to be the virtue that permitted us to seek the good by
> using reason. It now means accepting everything and denying reason's
> power. The unrestrained and thoughtless pursuit of openness, without
> recognizing the inherent political, social, or cultural problem of open-
> ness as the goal of nature, has rendered openness meaningless. . . .
> Openness, as currently conceived, is a way of making surrender . . .
> look principled.

Or, can liberalism revive and survive the competition of ideas with a sustained argument that can meet Bloom's critique? Liberalism can reverse
its decline only by renewed and reformed self-definition, and that can
only come from confrontation and dialectic. A nationalized conservatism
may turn out to have been the best thing for liberalism and for a more elevated and instructive American political discourse.

BIBLIOGRAPHY

Becker, Carl. *The Heavenly City of the Eighteenth Century Philosophers*. New Haven:
    Yale University Press, 1932.

Bell, Daniel. *The End of Ideology: On the Exhaustion of Political Ideas in the 1950s.*
    New York: Free Press, 1965.

———, ed. *The New American Right*. New York: Criterion Books, 1955.

———, ed. *The Radical Right*. Freeport, N.Y.: Books for Libraries Press, 1963.

Bloom, Alan. *The Closing of the American Mind*. New York: Simon & Schuster, 1987.

Burke, Edmund. *Reflections on the Revolution in France*, edited by J. C. D. Clark.
    Stanford, Calif.: Stanford University Press, 2001.

Commager, Henry Steele. *The American Mind: An Interpretation of American
    Thought as Character Since the 1880s*. New Haven: Yale University Press, 1950.

Frankfurter, Felix. Concurring Opinion in *Joint Anti-Fascist Refugee Committee v. Mc-
    Grath*, 341 U.S. 123 (1951).

Friedman, Lawrence. *A History of American Law*. New York: Simon & Schuster, 1974.

Hartz, Louis. *The Liberal Tradition in America*. New York: Harcourt, Brace, 1955.

Hobbes, Thomas. *The Elements of Law, Natural and Politic*, edited by J.C.A. Gaskin.
    New York: Oxford University Press, 1999.

———. *Leviathan*, edited by Richard E. Flathman and David Johnston. New York:
    Norton, 1997.

Hofstadter, Richard. *The American Political Tradition*. New York: Knopf, 1948.

———. *The Paranoid Style in American Politics*. New York: Knopf, 1965.

Holmes, Oliver Wendell, Jr. *The Common Law*. New York: Dover, 1991.

———. Dissent in *Lochner v. New York*, 198 U.S. 45 (1905).

James, William. "Pragmatism." In *William James, Writings 1902–1910*, edited by Bruce Kuklick. New York: The Library of America, 1984.

Johnson, Lyndon B. "The Howard University Address." In *The Moynihan Report and the Politics of Controversy*, edited by Lee Rainwater and William L. Yancey. Cambridge, Mass.: MIT Press, 1969.

Lincoln, Abraham. *Speeches and Writings, 1859–1865*, edited by Don E. Fehrenbacher. New York: Viking, 1989.

Locke, John. *The Selected Political Writings of John Locke*, edited by Paul E. Sigmund. New York: Norton, 2005.

Marcuse, Herbert. *One-Dimensional Man*. Boston: Beacon Press, 1991.

———. "Repressive Tolerance." In *A Critique of Pure Tolerance*, edited by Robert Paul Wolff et al. Boston: Beacon Press, 1969.

Perry, Lewis. *Intellectual Life in America*. Chicago: University of Chicago Press, 1989.

Sabine, George. *A History of Political Theory*. New York: Henry Holt, 1950.

Shklar, Judith. *Redeeming American Political Thought*. Chicago: University of Chicago Press, 1998.

Smith, Adam. *The Theory of Moral Sentiments*. Mineola, N.Y.: Dover, 2006.

———. *The Wealth of Nations*, introduction by Robert Reich, edited by Edwin Cannon. New York: Modern Library, 2000.

Sumner, William Graham. *What Social Classes Owe Each Other*. New York: Harper, 1920.

Tocqueville, Alexis de. *Democracy in America*, edited by Isaac Kramnick. New York: Norton, 2007.

Weber, Max. *The Protestant Ethic and the Spirit of Capitalism*. New York: Scribner's, 1958.

PART I

COLONIAL

ROOTS

1620–1760

In America, political thought is usually attached to action. Professors and philosophers can be found in these pages after the Civil War, but there were neither independent philosophers nor salaried intellectuals in colonial America. Virtually every group of settlers was guided by a pastor whom they expected to embody purity and piety. But the pastors inclined toward Old Testament tradition. As the historian Edmund S. Morgan put it, the clergy enjoyed "a social and intellectual prestige that enabled them to exert a powerful influence among their people . . . a speaking aristocracy in the face of a silent democracy." However, the great pastors—John Cotton, Roger Williams, Cotton Mather, and Thomas Hooker—were movers but not shapers. They contributed to the growth of political thought in America, but accepted a kind of spiritual and intellectual separation of church and state that left to government the final authority to deal with such issues as drunkenness, theft, and murder. This makes John Winthrop—an early governor of the Massachusetts Bay Colony and a devout Puritan—the perfect signature character of the seventeenth-century colonial period. Winthrop's belief in the social contract between government and the governed was infused with Puritan religious beliefs that eventually gave way, as we shall see, to the liberalism espoused by Benjamin Franklin—our signature figure for the eighteenth century prior to the founding. These two thinkers, and their similarities and differences, are emblematic of the dramatic shift that occurred in American political thought during the colonial period.

Adversity is never sweet, but, in its uses, is often generous. Among the colonies, Virginia, with its milder climate and fertile soil, should have been the American garden of thought. The first Virginian colonists, however, were mainly townsmen and gentlemen who came for instant riches. Although they were to implant the great English common law and to establish the first New World legislature— the General Assembly of Virginia, which first met in the Jamestown church on July 30, 1619—the people of Virginia and of the entire Middle Atlantic land grant would contribute little to American political thought until the eighteenth century. Rocky, frigid New England, it turned out, provided more fertile soil for political thought.

John Winthrop: Puritanism and Politics

We selected John Winthrop as our emblematic representative for the seventeenth century because he embodied the competing forces within these "Pilgrim fathers"—the active versus the contemplative, the cheerful versus the grim. Born in 1588, John Winthrop was the scion of a propertied English family. At fifteen, John was sent to Cambridge University, where, Morgan writes, "he caught the fever of Puritanism." He was the perfect Puritan. He knew he must live in this world and act as though he were one of the chosen, "without taking his mind off God." Consequently, although tempted to prepare for the ministry, he chose to embrace life while pursuing God through work in business and law. Winthrop embodied what the great sociologist Max Weber termed the "Protestant ethic." Through hard work (and the dowries of his first three wives) Winthrop became a lord of the manor, a lawyer and manorial judge.

Radical English Protestant dissenters from the Church of England were severely persecuted by the Anglican clergy and the Stuart Monarchs James I and Charles I in the early seventeenth century, leading many of them to leave the country. The Separatists moved to Holland, then to Plymouth in New England in 1620. Winthrop and the Puritans left England in 1629 still as loyal subjects "with approbation of the King and without repudiating its churches and the Christians in them." Some of the Puritan merchants who had founded the New England Company in 1628 to exploit New World natural resources managed to gain a royal charter from Charles I, with a legal land grant to the newly named Massachusetts Bay Company. The Massachusetts Bay Company was not the first English "joint-stock company"—or corporation—but either by oversight or purposeful neglect, no provision was made in the royal charter for the location of its headquarters, presumed to be somewhere in England. When the company's board (called the General Court) met in secret in the summer of 1629, they chose John Winthrop as their governor and the colony of Massachusetts Bay as their headquarters. In so doing, they had converted a commercial corporate charter into the first truly incorporated government in America. And their first action in Charlestown under Governor Winthrop was to draft and sign a covenant with God to conform to "the rule of the Gospell, . . . and in mutuall love, and respect each to other, so neere as God shall give us grace."

God gave "a speciall Commission" to the Puritans. They were, they believed, God's chosen people, who would bring saintly Protestant rule to the New World. Not only would they build a Christian Commonwealth in Massachusetts, but they also had been called to an "errand in the wilderness," the obligation to work, cultivate, and improve what "lie wasted" there. Should they answer well this call from God, should they fulfill their covenanted godly responsibilities, then Winthrop saw God's "favours" and "blessings" forthcoming. Should they fail, he writes, "The Lord will surely break out in wrathe against us."

The world was watching to see whether God's chosen people succeeded in doing his bidding. From Winthrop comes the earliest and most enduring statement of American righteousness, its sense of its God-given moral mission, unique among nations. In words that would echo through the ages, even into the late twentieth century and President Ronald Reagan's frequent rhetorical use of the passage, Winthrop warned that "wee shall be as a citty upon a Hill, the eies of all people are upon us."

Massachusetts early on developed an interesting notion of citizenship, though the actual word was conspicuous in its absence. In accord with English practice, the charter had placed all corporate power in the hands of the shareholders, called *freemen*. But this meant that anyone, including non-Puritans, could become a freeman by purchasing stock. To prevent this, Winthrop decreed, "No man shall be admitted to the freedome of this body politicke, but such as are members of the churches within the lymitts of the same." This was the way to build the new Jerusalem, a city to serve God, where liberty was defined not as "the liberty to do what he lists" but "liberty maintained and exercised in a way of subjection to authority."

Winthrop's form of rule was not a democracy of the elected but an aristocracy of the elect. Every man in the colony could "take up the privilege of freemanship" if they were also church members. Church members were those self-recognized as the saved, the elect, a substantial subgroup among the far larger group of regular church attendees. Yet, while limiting freemanship to church members, Winthrop was still extending political rights to a far larger proportion of the people than enjoyed such rights in England, or in fact, anywhere in the world.

Since Puritans applied an absolute sense of good and evil to themselves, they were consistent in applying the same viewpoint to their adversaries. And their religious view supported their economic interests. They sought amicable relations with the Indians, but with the intent to exploit. Their profound commitment to the New

Jerusalem, coupled with their economic ambitions and the belief that Indians were an inferior race, turned the Puritans into Christian soldiers bent on conquest, in accord with their sense of superiority as a chosen people. Although there are few detailed accounts of extreme violence against neighboring tribes, there is the most famous case, an eyewitness account in 1636, reported in Bradford's history of Plymouth Plantation, of an attack on a Pequot village on the Mystic River, wiping out about four hundred natives: "a fearful sight . . . streams of blood . . . [B]ut the victory seemed a sweet sacrifice, and they gave praise thereof to God."

It was inevitable that over time the purity of Puritanism would be adulterated. People would become citizens without church membership. Some of the devout, with Cotton Mather and Jonathan Edwards, abandoned the political altogether, in return for purity and charity—what Wilson Carey McWilliams has described as "the first expression of Puritanism as most Americans know it: pietistic morality and vague benevolence." Others, such as Roger Williams and William Penn, recognized the multiplicity of religions; as Williams put it, "[C]onscience is found in all mankind, more or less: in Jews, Turks, Papists, Protestants and pagans." Williams was as orthodox as his Puritan brethren, but this led him in another direction—toward a dualism, to sever "any connection between the world and the spirit." "The testament of Christ," he wrote, "is opposite to the very essentials . . . of a civil magistry, a civil commonwealth or combination of men, which can respect only civil things."

Benjamin Franklin: The Worldly Puritan

Benjamin Franklin, our second signature figure for this epoch, was the model of the self-made man, another case study of the "Protestant ethic": not outwardly pious but bound by inward asceticism—sober, rigidly ethical, dedicated to a life of hard work, never to gamble but always to compete and take risks. Franklin's great business and public service accomplishments, much like those of John Winthrop, did not directly generate any lasting political thought. His contemplative life came mostly out of one project, the modestly titled *Poor Richard's Almanac* (first published in 1732). "Poor Richard" is Benjamin Franklin, and the man and his writing reflect the secularization of seventeenth-century Puritanism.

Although Franklin is much more than a posterboy for emerging bourgeois liberalism in the United States, devoting large chunks of his time to public service and science, the best way to deal with his political (or politically relevant) thought is still to concentrate on some of his epigrams from *Poor Richard's Almanac*.

> Remember, that *time* is money. He that can earn ten shillings a day by his labor, and . . . sits idle, one-half of that day . . . has really spent, or rather thrown away, five shillings besides. Remember, that *credit* is money. . . . Money can beget money, and its offspring can beget more, and so on. . . . He that murders a crown, destroys all that it might have produced, even scores of pounds.
>
> Remember . . . after industry and frugality, nothing contributes more to the raising of a young man in the world than punctuality and justice in all of his dealings. . . . The most trifling actions that affect a man's credit are to be regarded.
>
> For six pounds a year you may have the use of 100 pounds. . . . He that wastes idly a groat's worth of his time per day . . . wastes the privilege of using 100 pounds each day.

More than a "philosophy of avarice," Franklin's worldview is, as Weber put it, "an ethos." The measure, "time is money," is not a morally neutral rationale for Franklin but, according to Weber, "an ethically coloured maxim for the conduct of life." But what makes Franklin an eighteenth-century mutation of seventeenth-century Puritan thought is that work, industry, and frugality and asceticism are not Puritan duties in service to God but have been redefined as Puritan virtues oriented to life on earth, in service to the realization of one's own self, so that "He shall stand [then] before kings." By the eighteenth century, religion had lost its control over politics. The new focus was on the individual. And this is precisely why "Richard's" views are not only so paradigmatic of economic life for Weber, but are also the necessary standard of the good in political life. In insisting that individual acquisition would turn private vice into public virtue, Franklin anticipated Adam Smith's "invisible hand." Franklin was justifying work not as a sign of grace but as an obligation to the self of what work does for those who work. The three values—Lord, labor and liberty—were not turned on their heads but back on their feet: deism, instrumentalism, and individualism.

In this view, the deity is not dead. The Lord still rules the heavens, but *deity* and *deism* were words used by Franklin, Adams, Jefferson, James Wilson, and many others, who, like Adams, were Christian but also deists, in order to distance themselves from orthodoxy. This leads directly to instrumentalism, which has also been labeled pragmatism, utilitarianism, and liberalism. One illustration is a *bon mot* in Franklin's *Autobiography* that "the most acceptable service we render to [God] is doing good to his other children." Another is his concession that although he had no use for evangelical religion, it was "useful for common folk to be believers." This was not cynicism; if Machiavellian, it was nevertheless an extension of his scientific attitude and a genuine expression of Enlightenment thinking: Does it work? How does it work? Does it work well? What are its consequences and their significance? And that leads out of science to philosophy, or at least to political thought. Even when attacking England's harsher policies toward the colonies, Franklin's objection was not the morality of the harshness or lack of representation but that, as he put it, "The ordaining of laws in favour of *one* part of the nation, to the prejudice and oppression of *another*, is certainly the most erroneous and mistaken policy. . . . These measures never fail to create great and violent jealousies and animosities. . . ." So it is that the scholar Clinton Rossiter concludes his characterization of "Franklin as Political Thinker" with "Franklin's supremely practical observation, 'the *Fact* seems sufficient for our purpose, and the *Fact* is notorious.'"

Individualism, for Franklin, was tied more closely to liberty than to equality. Winthrop also stressed liberty over equality. But there the resemblance to Winthrop stops. John Winthrop's liberty was the freedom to obey established authority, both God and governor. There was an individualism inherent in it that could be said to have anticipated the construction embraced by Franklin, because to Winthrop, common persons could become freemen, and freemen were participants in a social contract. But Franklin's Enlightenment sense of individualism marks an important milestone in American political thought, for it strips individual liberty of its religious and corporate freeman restraints and rests it in the English secular tradition of Locke and Hobbes. Nowhere is this more evident than in the youthful Franklin's contribution to the *New England Courant* in 1722 when he offers *Cato's Letters's* canonical liberal argument for freedom of thought.

> Without Freedom of Thought, there can be no such Thing as Wisdom; and no such Thing as publick Liberty without freedom of speech; which is the Right of every Man. . . .
> This sacred Privilege is so essential to free Governments, that Security of Property and the Freedom of Speech always go

together; and in those wretched Countries where a Man cannot call his Tongue his own, he can scarce call any Thing else his own. . . . When Men differ in Opinion, both Sides ought equally to have the Advantage of being heard by the Publick; and that when Truth and Error have fair Play, the former is always an overmatch for the latter. . . .

On the other hand, the year before his death, Franklin refined the Lockean worldview with a very democratic concept of citizenship. In his 1789 "Remarks Respecting Alterations in the Constitution of Pennsylvania" he writes:

The Combinations of Civil Society are not like those of a Set of Merchants, who club their Property in different Proportions . . . and may therefore have some Right to vote . . . in a greater or less Degree according to their respective Contributions; but the important ends of Civil Society . . . remain the same in every Member of the society; and the poorest continues to have an equal Claim to them. . . .

What a dramatic transformation of colonial political thought Franklin represents. In 1722 his unabashed liberalism flew in the face of the still dominant Puritan notions of intellectual and spiritual orthodoxy, even if they shared an emphasis on the work ethic. Sixty-seven years later his egalitarian views went far beyond the beliefs of his fellow founders as they designed a new government. The democratic ideals that Franklin held in 1789 were shared by only some in the Founding period, and even today may not be shared by all Americans.

BIBLIOGRAPHY

Bradford, William. *Of Plymouth Plantation, 1620–1646.* New York: Modern Library, 1981.

Caffrey, Kate. *The Mayflower.* New York: Stein and Day, 1974.

Franklin, Benjamin. *The Writings of Benjamin Franklin,* edited by A. H. Smyth, vol. X. New York: Macmillan, 1905–1907.

Leder, Lawrence H. *America 1603–1789: Prelude to a Nation.* Minneapolis: Burgess Publishing Company, 1972.

McWilliams, Wilson Carrey. *The Idea of Fraternity in America*. Berkeley: University of California Press, 1973.

Miller, Perry. *Errand Into the Wilderness*. Cambridge: Harvard University Press, 1964.

Morgan, Edmund S. *The Puritan Dilemma: The Story of John Winthrop*. Boston: Little, Brown, 1958.

Perry, Lewis. *Intellectual Life in America: A History*. Chicago: University of Chicago Press, 1989.

Rossiter, Clinton Lawrence. *Seedtime of the Republic*. New York: Harcourt, 1953.

Weber, Max. *From Max Weber: Essays in Sociology*, edited by H. H. Gerth and C. Wright Mills. New York: Oxford University Press, 1946.

———.*The Protestant Ethic and the Spirit of Capitalism*, translated by Talcott Parsons. New York: Scribner's, 1958.

Winthrop, John. *The Journal of John Winthrop, 1630–1649*, edited by Richard S. Dunn and Laetitia Yeandle. Cambridge, Mass.: Harvard University Press, 1996.

Puritan Political and
Social Ideals

JOHN WINTHROP

A Model of Christian Charity (1630)

John Winthrop (1588–1649) was born in Suffolk, England. Unlike most of the other leaders of the Massachusetts Bay Colony, Winthrop was not a cleric. He was a lawyer, but his deep religious convictions are evident in this speech, which he likely gave to fellow passengers on board the Arabella at the end of the Atlantic voyage. The Christian commonwealth ideals that Winthrop displayed throughout his leadership of the colony are evident in his assertion here that although social obligations and distinctions are ordained by God, "we must be willing to abridge our selves of our superfluities, for the supply of others necessities." He also explained that the purpose of the Puritan experiment was to serve God and establish "a Citty upon a hill" in the New World.

A MODELL HEREOF.

God Almightie in his most holy and wise providence hath soe disposed of the Condicion of mankinde, as in all times some must be rich some poore, some highe and eminent in power and dignitie; others meane and in subjeccion.

* * *

THE REASON HEREOF.

1. REAS: *First,* to hold conformity with the rest of his workes, being delighted to shewe forthe the glory of his wisdome in the variety and differance of the Creatures and the glory of his power, in ordering all these differences for the preservacion and good of the whole, and the glory of his greatnes that as it is the glory of princes to have many officers, soe this great King will have many Stewards counting himselfe more honoured in dispenceing his guifts to man by man, then if hee did it by his owne immediate hand.

2. REAS: *Secondly,* That he might have the more occasion to manifest the worke of his Spirit: first, upon the wicked in moderateing and restraineing them: soe that the riche and mighty should not eate upp the poore, nor the poore, and dispised rise upp against theire superiours, and shake off theire yoake; 2ly in the regenerate in exerciseing his graces in them, as in the greate ones, theire love mercy, gentlenes, temperance etc., in the poore and inferiour sorte, theire faithe patience, obedience etc:

3. REAS: Thirdly, That every man might have need of others, and from hence they might be all knitt more nearly together in the Bond of brotherly affeccion: from hence it appeares plainely that noe man is made more honourable then another or more wealthy etc., out of any perticuler and singuler respect to himselfe but for the glory of his Creator and the Common good of the Creature, Man; Therefore God still reserves the propperty of these guifts to himselfe as Ezek: 16. 17. he there calls wealthe his gold and his silver etc. Prov: 3. 9. he claimes theire service as his due honour the Lord with thy riches etc. All men being thus (by divine providence) rancked into two sortes, riche and poore; under the first, are comprehended all such as are able to live comfortably by theire owne meanes duely improved; and all others are poore according to the former distribution. There are two rules whereby wee are to walke one towards another: JUSTICE and MERCY. These are allwayes distinguished in theire Act and in theire object, yet may they both concurre in the same Subject in eache respect; as sometimes there may be an occasion of shewing mercy to a rich man, in some sudden danger of distresse, and allsoe doeing of meere Justice to a poor man in regard of some perticuler contract etc. There is likewise a double Lawe by which wee are regulated in our conversacion one towardes another: in both the former respects, the lawe of nature and the lawe of grace, or the morrall lawe or the lawe of the gospell, to omitt the rule of Justice as not propperly belonging to this purpose otherwise then it may fall into consideracion in some perticuler Cases: By the first of these lawes man as he was enabled soe withall [is] commaunded to love his neighbour as himselfe upon this ground stands

all the precepts of the morrall lawe, which concernes our dealings with men. To apply this to the works of mercy this lawe requires two things first that every man afford his help to another in every want or distresse Secondly, That hee performe this out of the same affeccion, which makes him carefull of his owne good according to that of our Saviour Math: [7:12] Whatsoever ye would that men should doe to you. This was practised by Abraham and Lott in entertaineing the Angells and the old man of Gibea.

The Lawe of Grace or the Gospell hath some differance from the former as in these respectes first the lawe of nature was given to man in the estate of innocency; this of the gospell in the estate of regeneracy: 2ly, the former propounds one man to another, as the same fleshe and Image of god, this as a brother in Christ allsoe, and in the Communion of the same spirit and soe teacheth us to put a difference betweene Christians and others. Doe good to all especially to the household of faith; upon this ground the Israelites were to putt a difference betweene the brethren of such as were strangers though not of the Canaanites. 3ly. The Lawe of nature could give noe rules for dealeing with enemies for all are to be considered as friends in the estate of Innocency, but the Gospell commaunds love to an enemy. proofe. If thine Enemie hunger feede him; Love your Enemies doe good to them that hate you Math: 5. 44.

This Lawe of the Gospell propoundes likewise a difference of seasons and occasions there is a time when a christian must sell all and give to the poore as they did in the Apostles times. There is a tyme allsoe when a christian (though they give not all yet) must give beyond theire abillity, as they of Macedonia. Cor: 2. 6. likewise community of perills calls for extraordinary liberallity and soe doth Community in some speciall service for the Churche. Lastly, when there is noe other meanes whereby our Christian brother may be releived in this distresse, wee must help him beyond our ability, rather then tempt God, in putting him upon help by miraculous or extraordinary meanes.

* * *

The diffinition which the Scripture gives us of love is this Love is the bond of perfection. First, it is a bond, or ligament. 2ly, it makes the worke perfect. There is noe body but consistes of partes and that which knitts these partes together gives the body its perfeccion, because it makes eache parte soe contiguous to other as thereby they doe mutually participate with eache other, both in strengthe and infirmity in pleasure and paine, to instance in the most perfect of all bodies, Christ and his church make one body: the severall partes of this body considered aparte before they were united were as disproportionate and as much disordering as soe many contrary quallities or elements but when christ comes and by his spirit and love knitts all these partes to himselfe and each to other, it is become the most perfect and best proportioned body in the world Eph: 4. 16. "Christ by whome all the body being knitt together by every joynt for the furniture thereof according to the effectuall power which is in the measure of every perfeccion of partes a glorious body without spott or wrinckle the ligaments hereof being Christ or his love for Christ is love 1 John: 4. 8. Soe this definition is right Love is the bond of perfeccion.

From hence wee may frame these Conclusions.

1 first all true Christians are of one body in Christ 1. Cor. 12. 12. 13. 17. [27.] Ye are the body of Christ and members of [your?] parte.

2ly. The ligamentes of this body which knitt together are love.

3ly. Noe body can be perfect which wants its propper ligamentes.

4ly. All the partes of this body being thus united are made soe contiguous in a speciall relacion as they must needes partake of each others strength and infirmity, joy, and sorrowe, weale and woe. 1 Cor: 12. 26. If one member suffers all suffer with it, if one be in honour, all rejoyce with it.

5ly. This sensiblenes and Sympathy of each others Condicions will necessarily infuse into each parte a native desire and endeavour, to strengthen defend preserve and comfort the other. * * * It rests now to make some applicacion of this discourse by the present designe which gave the occasion of writeing of it. Herein are 4 things to be propounded: first the persons, 2ly, the worke, 3ly, the end, 4ly the meanes.

1. For the persons, wee are a Company professing ourselves fellow members of Christ, In which respect onely though wee were absent from eache other many miles, and had our imploymentes as farre distant, yet wee ought to account our selves knitt together by this bond of love, and live in the exercise of it, if wee would have comforte of our being in Christ, this was notorious in the practise of the Christians in former times, as is testified of the Waldenses from the mouth of one of the adversaries Aeneas Sylvius, mutuo [solent amare] penè antequam norint, they use to love any of theire owne religion even before they were acquainted with them.

2ly. for the worke wee have in hand, it is by a mutuall consent through a speciall overruleing providence, and a more then an ordinary approbation of the Churches of Christ to seeke out a place of Cohabitation and Consorteshipp under a due forme of Government both civill and ecclesiasticall. In such cases as this the care of the publique must oversway all private respects, by which not onely conscience, but meare Civill pollicy doth binde us; for it is a true rule that perticuler estates cannott subsist in the ruine of the publique.

3ly. The end is to improve our lives to doe more service to the Lord the comforte and encrease of the body of christe whereof wee are members that our selves and posterity may be the better preserved from the Common corrupcions of this evill world to serve the Lord and worke out our Salvacion under the power and purity of his holy Ordinances.

4ly for the meanes whereby this must bee effected, they are 2fold, a Conformity with the worke and end wee aime at, these wee see are extraordinary, therefore wee must not content our selves with usuall ordinary meanes whatsoever wee did or ought to have done when wee lived in England, the same must wee doe and more allsoe where wee goe: That which the most in theire Churches maineteine as a truthe in profession onely, wee must bring into familiar and constant practise, as in this duty of love wee must love brotherly without dissimulation, wee must love one another with a pure hearte fervently wee must beare one anothers burthens, wee must not looke onely on our owne things, but allsoe on the things of our brethren, neither must wee think that the lord will beare with such faileings at our hands as hee dothe from those among whome we have lived. * * *

When God gives a speciall Commission he lookes to have it strictly observed in every Article, when hee gave Saule a Commission to destroy Amaleck hee indented with him upon certaine Articles and because hee failed in one of the least, and that upon a faire pretence, it lost him the kingdome, which should have beene his reward, if hee had observed his Commission: Thus stands the cause betweene God and us, wee are entered into Covenant with him for this worke, wee have taken out a Commission, the Lord hath given us leave to drawe our owne Articles wee have professed to enterprise these Accions upon these and these ends, wee have hereupon besought him of favour and blessing: Now if the Lord shall please to heare us, and bring us in peace to the place wee desire, then hath hee ratified this Covenant and sealed our Commission, [and] will expect a strickt performance of the Articles contained in it, but if wee shall neglect the observacion of these Articles which are the ends wee have propounded, and dissembling with our God, shall fall to embrace this present world and prosecute our carnall intencions, seekeing greate things for our selves and our posterity, the Lord will surely breake out in wrathe against us be revenged of such a perjured people and make us knowe the price of the breache of such a Covenant.

Now the onely way to avoyde this shipwracke and to provide for our posterity is to followe the Counsell of Micah, to doe Justly, to love mercy, to walke humbly with our God, for this end, wee must be knitt together in this worke as one man, wee must entertaine each other in brotherly Affeccion, wee must be willing to abridge our selves of our superfluities, for the supply of others necessities, wee must uphold a familiar Commerce together in all meekenes, gentlenes, patience and liberallity, wee must delight in eache other, make others Condicions our owne, rejoyce together, mourne together, labour, and suffer together, allwayes haveing before our eyes our Commission and Community in the worke, our Community as members of the same body, soe shall wee keepe the unitie of the spirit in the bond of peace, the Lord will be our God and delight to dwell among us, as his owne people and will commaund a blessing upon us in all our wayes, soe that wee shall see much more of his wisdome power goodnes and truthe then formerly wee have beene acquainted with, wee shall finde that the God of Israell is among us, when tenn of us shall be able to resist a thousand of our enemies, when hee shall make us a prayse and glory, that men shall say of succeeding plantacions: the lord make it like that of New England: for wee must Consider that wee shall be as a Citty upon a Hill, the eies of all people are uppon us; soe that if wee shall deale falsely with our god in this worke wee have undertaken and soe cause him to withdrawe his present help from us, wee shall be made a story and a by-word through the world, wee shall open the mouthes of enemies to speake evill of the wayes of god and all professours for Gods sake; wee shall shame the faces of many of gods worthy servants, and cause theire prayers to be turned into Cursses upon us till wee be consumed out of the good land whether wee are goeing: And to shutt upp this discourse with that exhortacion of Moses that faithfull servant of the Lord in his last farewell to Israell Deut. 30. Beloved there is now sett before us life, and good, deathe and evill in that wee are Commaunded this day to love the Lord our God, and to love one another to walke in his wayes and to keepe his Commaundements and his Ordinance, and his lawes, and the Articles of our Covenant with him that wee may live and be multiplyed, and that the Lord our God may blesse us in the land whether wee goe to possesse it: But if our heartes shall turne away soe that wee will not obey, but shall be seduced and worshipp [serve *cancelled*] other Gods our pleasures, and proffitts, and serve them; it is propounded unto us this day, wee shall surely perishe out of the good Land whether wee passe over this vast Sea to possesse it;

> *Therefore lett us choose life,*
> *that wee, and our Seede,*
> *may live; by obeyeing his*
> *voyce, and cleaveing to him,*
> *for hee is our life, and*
> *our prosperity.*

JOHN WINTHROP

Defence of an Order of Court (1637)

During the Antinomian Controversy of 1637, in which the religious dissenter Anne Hutchinson was banished for teaching that individuals could have direct revelations from God, the Massachusetts General Court passed an order that would keep other religious dissenters out of the colony. Winthrop's defense of the court's order is a classic claim that the good of the community is the only legitimate aim and purpose of the state. It was his communitarian conviction that the commonwealth was a kind of family established by the free consent of the people, who had a right to restrict membership to like-minded individuals.

A DECLARATION OF THE INTENT AND EQUITYE OF THE ORDER MADE AT THE LAST COURT, TO THIS EFFECT, THAT NONE SHOULD BE RECEIVED TO INHABITE WITHIN THIS JURISDICTION BUT SUCH AS SHOULD BE ALLOWED BY SOME OF THE MAGISTRATES

For clearing of such scruples as have arisen about this order, it is to be considered, first, what is the essentiall forme of a common weale or body politic such as this is, which I conceive to be this—The consent of a certaine companie of people, to cohabite together, under one government for their mutual safety and welfare.

In this description all these things doe concurre to the well being of such a body, 1 Persons, 2 Place, 3 Consent, 4 Government or Order, 5 Wellfare.

It is clearly agreed, by all, that the care of safety and wellfare was the original cause or occasion of common weales and of many familyes subjecting themselves to rulers and laws; for no man hath lawfull power over another, but by birth or consent, so likewise, by the law of proprietye, no man can have just interest in that which belongeth to another, without his consent.

From the premises will arise these conclusions.

1. No common weale can be founded but by free consent.

2. The persons so incorporating have a public and relative interest each in the other, and in the place of their cohabitation and goods, and laws etc. and in all the means of their wellfare so as none other can claime priviledge with them but by free consent.

3. The nature of such an incorporation tyes every member thereof to seeke out and entertaine all means that may conduce to the wellfare of the bodye, and to keepe off whatsoever doth appeare to tend to theire damage.

4. The wellfare of the whole is [not] to be put to apparent hazard for the advantage of any particular members.

From these conclusions I thus reason.

1. If we heere be a corporation established by free consent, if the place of our cohabitation be our owne, then no man hath right to come into us etc. without our consent.

2. If no man hath right to our lands, our government priviledges etc., but by our consent, then it is reason we should take notice of before we conferre any such upon them.

3. If we are bound to keepe off whatsoever appears to tend to our ruine or damage, then we may lawfully refuse to receive such whose dispositions suite not with ours and whose society (we know) will be hurtfull to us, and therefore it is lawfull to take knowledge of all men before we receive them.

4. The churches take liberty (as lawfully they may) to receive or reject at their discretion; yea particular towns make orders to the like effect; why then should the common weale be denied the like liberty, and the whole more restrained than any parte?

5. If it be sinne in us to deny some men place etc. amongst us, then it is because of some right they have to this place etc. for to deny a man that which he hath no right unto, is neither sinne nor injury.

6. If strangers have right to our houses or lands etc., then it is either of justice or of mercye; if of justice let them plead it, and we shall know what to answer: but if it be only in way of mercye, or by the rule of hospitality etc., then I answer 1st a man is not a fit object of mercye except he be in miserye. 2d. We are not bound to exercise mercye to others to the ruine of ourselves. 3d. There are few that stand in neede of mercye at their first coming hither. As for hospitality, that rule doth not bind further than for some present occasion, not for continual residence.

7. A family is a little common wealth, and a common wealth is a greate family. Now as a family is not bound to entertaine all comers, no not every good man (otherwise than by way of hospitality) no more is a common wealth.

8. It is a generall received rule, * * * it is worse to receive a man whom we must cast out againe, than to denye him admittance.

9. The rule of the Apostle, John 2. 10. is, that such as come and bring not the true doctrine with them should not be received to house, and by the same reason not into the common weale.

10. Seeing it must be granted that there may come such persons (suppose Jesuits etc.) which by consent of all ought to be rejected, it will follow that by this law (being only for notice to be taken of all that come to us, without which we cannot avoyd such as indeed are to be kept out) is no other but just and needfull, and if any should be rejected that ought to be received, that is not to be imputed to the law, but to those who are betrusted with the execution of it. And herein is to be considered, what the intent of the law is, and by consequence, by what rule they are to walke, who are betrusted with the keeping of it. The intent of the law is to preserve the wellfare of the body; and for this ende to have none received into any fellowship with it who are likely to disturbe the same, and this intent (I am sure) is lawful and good. Now then, if such to whom the keeping of this law is committed, be persuaded in theire judgments that such a man is likely to disturbe and hinder the publick weale, but some others who are not in the same trust, judge otherwise, yet they are to follow their owne judgments, rather than the judgments of others who are not alike interested: As in tryall of an offender by jury; the twelve men are satisfied in their consciences, upon the evidence given, that the party deserves death: but there are 20 or 40 standers by, who conceive otherwise, yet is the jury bound to condemn him according to their owne consciences, and not to acquit him upon the different opinion of other men, except theire reasons can convince them of the errour of their consciences, and this is according to the rule of the Apostle. Rom. 14. 5. Let every man be fully persuaded in his own mynde.

If it be objected, that some prophane persons are received and others who are religious are rejected, I answer 1st, It is not knowne that any such thinge has as yet fallen out. 2. Such a practice may be justifiable as the case may be, for younger persons (even prophane ones) may be of lesse danger to the common weale (and to the churches also) than some older persons, though professors of religion: for our Saviour Christ when he conversed with publicans etc. sayeth that such were nearer the Kingdom of heaven than the religious pharisees, and one that is of large parts and confirmed in some erroneous way, is likely to doe more harme to church and common weale, and is of lesse hope to be reclaymed, than 10 prophane persons, who have not yet become hardened, in the contempt of the meanes of grace.

Lastly, Whereas it is objected that by this law, we reject good christians and so consequently Christ himselfe: I answer 1st. It is not knowne that any christian man hath been rejected. 2. a man that is a true christian, may be denied residence among us, in some cases, without rejecting Christ, as admitt a true christian should come over, and should maintain community of goods, or that magistrates ought not to punish the breakers of the first table, or the members of churches for criminal offences: or that no man were bound to be subject to those lawes or magistrates to which they should not give an explicite consent, etc. I hope no man will say, that not to receive such an one were to reject Christ; for such opinions (though being maintained in simple ignorance, they might stand with a state of grace yet) they may be so dangerous to the publick weale in many respects, as it would be our sinne and unfaithfullness to receive such among us, except it were for tryall of theire reformation. I would demand then in the case in question (for it is bootlesse curiosity to refrayne openesse in things publick) whereas it is sayd that this law was made of purpose to keepe away such as are of Mr. Wheelwright his judgment (admitt it were so which yet I cannot confesse) where is the evill of it? If we conceive and finde by sadd experience that his opinions are such, as by his own profession cannot stand with externall peace, may we not provide for our peace, by keeping of [f] such as would strengthen him and infect others with such dangerous tenets? and if we finde his opinions such as will cause divisions, and make people looke at their magistrates, ministers and brethren as enemies to Christ and Antichrists etc., were it not sinne and unfaithfullness in us, to receive more of those opinions, which we already finde the evill fruite of: Nay, why doe not those who now complayne joyne with us in keeping out of such, as well as formerly they did in expelling Mr. Williams for the like, though lesse dangerous? Where this change of theire judgments should arise I leave them to themselves to examine, and I earnestly entreat them so to doe, and for this law let the equally mynded judge, what evill they finde in it, or in the practice of those who are betrusted with the execution of it (*ca.* June 1637).

JOHN WINTHROP

Little Speech on Liberty (1639)

In this speech on the proper relationship between liberty and authority, Winthrop defended himself against accusations that he had exceeded his authority as deputy governor. In doing this he offered what would become a classic distinction between natural and civil liberty. He maintained that any magistrate who faithfully keeps his covenant with the

*people and acts in accordance with God's laws should be free from pop-
ular control.*

I suppose something may be expected from me upon this charge that is
befallen me, which moves me to speak now to you; yet I intend not to in-
termeddle in the proceedings of the court, or with any of the persons concerned therein. Only I bless God that I see an issue of this troublesome
business. I also acknowledge the justice of the court, and, for mine own
part, I am well satisfied, I was publicly charged, and I am publicly and
legally acquitted, which is all I did expect or desire. And though this be sufficient for my justification before men, yet not so before the God who hath
seen so much amiss in my dispensations (and even in this affair) as calls
me to be humble. For to be publicly and criminally charged in this court is
matter of humiliation (and I desire to make a right use of it), notwithstanding I be thus acquitted. If her father had spit in her face should she
not have been ashamed seven days? Shame had lien upon her, whatever the
occasion had been. I am unwilling to stay you from your urgent affairs, yet
give me leave (upon this special occasion) to speak a little more to this assembly. It may be of some good use to inform and rectify the judgments
of some of the people, and may prevent such distempers as have arisen
amongst us. The great questions that have troubled the country are about
the authority of the magistrates and the liberty of the people. It is yourselves who have called us to this office, and, being called by you, we have
our authority from God, in way of an ordinance, such as hath the image of
God eminently stamped upon it, the contempt and violation whereof hath
been vindicated with examples of divine vengeance. I entreat you to consider that, when you choose magistrates, you take them from among yourselves, men subject to like passions as you are. Therefore, when you see
infirmities in us, you should reflect upon your own, and that would make
you bear the more with us, and not be severe censurers of the failings
of your magistrates, when you have continual experience of the like
infirmaties in yourselves and others. We account him a good servant who
breaks not his covenant. The covenant between you and us is the oath you
have taken of us, which is to this purpose, that we shall govern you and
judge your causes by the rules of God's laws and our own, according to our
best skill. When you agree with a workman to build you a ship or house,
etc., he undertakes as well for his skill as for his faithfulness; for it is his
profession, and you pay him for both. But, when you call one to be a magistrate, he doth not profess nor undertake to have sufficient skill for that
office, nor can you furnish him with gifts, etc., therefore you must run the
hazard of his skill and ability. But if he fail in faithfulness, which by his
oath he is bound unto, that he must answer for. If it fall out that the case

be clear to common apprehension, and the rule clear also, if he transgress here, the error is not in the skill, but in the evil of the will: it must be required of him. But if the case be doubtful, or the rule doubtful, to men of such understanding and parts as your magistrates are, if your magistrates should err here, yourselves must bear it.

For the other point concerning liberty, I observe a great mistake in the country about that. There is a twofold liberty, natural (I mean as our nature is now corrupt) and civil or federal. The first is common to man with beasts and other creatures. By this, man as he stands in relation to man simply, hath liberty to do what he lists: it is a liberty to evil as well as to good. This liberty is incompatible and inconsistent with authority, and cannot endure the least restraint of the most just authority. The exercise and maintaining of this liberty makes men grow more evil, and in time to be worse than brute beasts: *omnes sumus licentia deteriores*. This is that great enemy of truth and peace, that wild beast, which all the ordinances of God are bent against, to restrain and subdue it. The other kind of liberty I call civil or federal; it may also be termed moral, in reference to the covenant between God and man, in the moral law, and the politic covenants and constitutions, amongst men themselves. This liberty is the proper end and object of authority, and cannot subsist without it; and it is a liberty to that only which is good, just, and honest. This liberty you are to stand for, with the hazard (not only of your goods, but) of your lives, if need be. Whatsoever crosseth this is not authority, but a distemper thereof. This liberty is maintained and exercised in a way of subjection to authority; it is of the same kind of liberty wherewith Christ hath made us free. The woman's own choice makes such a man her husband; yet, being so chosen he is her lord, and she is to be subject to him, yet in a way of liberty, not of bondage; and a true wife accounts her subjection her honor and freedom, and would not think her condition safe and free but in her subjection to her husband's authority. Such is the liberty of the church under the authority of Christ, her king and husband; his yoke is so easy and sweet to her as a bride's ornaments; and if through forwardness or wantonness, etc., she shake it off, at any time, she is at no rest in her spirit until she take it up again; and whether her lord smiles upon her, and embraceth her in his arms, or whether he frowns or rebukes, or smites her, she apprehends the sweetness of his love in all, and is refreshed, supported, and instructed by every such dispensation of his authority over her. On the other side, ye know who they are that complain of this yoke and say, let us break their bands, etc., we will not have this man to rule over us. Even so, brethren, it will be between you and your magistrates. If you stand for your natural corrupt liberties, and will do what is good in your own eyes, you will not endure the least weight of authority, but will murmur and oppose, and be always striving to shake off that yoke; but if you will be satisfied to enjoy such civil and lawful liberties, such as Christ allows you, then will you quietly and cheerfully submit unto that authority which is set over you, in all the administrations of it, for your good. Wherein, if we fail at any time, we hope we shall be willing (by God's assistance) to hearken to good advice from any of you, or in any other way of God; so shall your liberties be preserved, in upholding the honor and power of authority amongst you.

JOHN COTTON

An Exposition Upon the 13th Chapter of the Revelations (1639)

Like many other Puritans in early America, the distinguished New England minister John Cotton (1584–1652) believed that there should be a close relationship between civil and religious authorities. Even though Cotton insisted that only church members should be allowed to exercise political authority, he argued that religious authorities should be subordinate to their civil counterparts. In this sermon, Cotton considered a theme that would recur throughout the history of American political thought: the proper relationship between liberty and authority. He promoted the principles of limited government as a remedy for the corrupting influence of power.

This may serve to teach us the danger of allowing to any mortall man an inordinate measure of power to speak great things, to allow to any man uncontrollableness of speech, you see the desperate danger of it: Let all the world learn to give mortall men no greater power then they are content they shall use, for use it they will: and unlesse they be better taught of God, they will use it ever and anon, it may be make it the passage of their proceeding to speake what they will: And they that have liberty to speak great things, you will finde it to be true, they will speak great blasphemies. No man would think what desperate deceit and wickednesse there is in the hearts of men: And that was the reason why the Beast did speak such great things, hee might speak, and no body might controll him: What, saith the Lord in *Jer.* 3. 5. *Thou hast spoken and done evill things as thou couldst.* If a Church or head of a Church could have done worse, he would have done it: This is one of the straines of nature, it affects boundlesse liberty, and to runne to the utmost extent: What ever power he hath received, he hath a corrupt nature that will improve it in one thing or other; if he have liberty, he will think why may he not use it. Set up the Pope as Lord Paramount over Kings and Princes, and they shall know that he hath power over them, he will take liberty to depose one, and set up another. Give him power to make Laws, and he will approve, and disprove as he list; what he approves is Canonicall, what hee disproves is rejected: Give him that power, and he will so order it at length, he will make such a State of Religion, that he that so lives and dyes shall never be saved, and all this springs from the vast power that is given to him, and from the deep depravation of nature. Hee will open his mouth, *His tongue is his owne, who is Lord over him,* Psal. 12. 3, 4. It is therefore most wholsome for Magistrates and Officers in Church and Common-wealth, never to affect more liberty and authority then will do them good, and the People good; for what ever transcendant power is given, will certainly over-run those that give it, and those that receive it: There is a straine in a mans heart that will sometime or other runne out to excesse, unlesse the Lord restraine it, but it is not good to venture it: It is necessary therefore, that all power that is on earth be limited, Church-power or other: If there be power given to speak great things, then look for great blasphemies, look for a licentious abuse of it. It is counted a matter of danger to the State to limit Prerogatives; but it is a further danger, not to have them limited: They will be like a Tempest, if they be not limited: A Prince himselfe cannot tell where hee will confine himselfe, nor can the people tell: But if he have liberty to speak great things, then he will make and unmake, say and unsay, and undertake such things as are neither for his owne honour, nor for the safety of the State. It is therefore fit for every man to be studious of the bounds which the Lord hath set: and for the People, in whom fundamentally all power lyes, to give as much power as God in his word gives to men: And it is meet that Magistrates in the Common-wealth, and so Officers in Churches should desire to know the utmost bounds of their own power, and it is safe for both: All intrenchment upon the bounds which God hath not given, they are not enlargements, but burdens and snares; They will certainly lead the spirit of a man out of his way sooner or later. It is wholsome and safe to be dealt withall as God deales with the vast Sea; *Hitherto shalt thou come, but there shalt thou stay thy proud waves:* and therefore if they be but banks of simple sand, they will be good enough to check the vast roaring Sea. And so for Imperiall Monarchies, it is safe to know how far their power extends; and then if it be but banks of sand, which is most slippery, it will serve, as well as any brazen wall. If you pinch the Sea of its liberty, though it be walls of stone or brasse, it will beate them downe: So it is with Magistrates, stint them where God hath not stinted them, and if they were walls of brasse, they would beate them downe, and it is meet they should: but give them the liberty God allows, and if it be but a wall of sand it will keep them: As this liquid Ayre in which we breath, God hath set it for the waters of the Clouds to the Earth; It is a Firmament, it is the Clouds, yet it stands firme enough, because it keeps the Climate where they are, it shall stand like walls of brasse: So let there be due bounds set, and I may apply it to Families; it is good for the Wife to acknowledge all power and authority to the Husband, and for the Husband to acknowledg honour to the Wife, but still give them that which God hath given them, and no more nor lesse: Give them the full latitude that God hath given, else you will finde you dig pits, and lay snares, and cumber their spirits, if you give them lesse; there is never peace where full liberty is not given, nor never stable peace where more then full liberty is granted: Let them be duely observed, and give men no more liberty then God doth, nor women, for they will abuse it: The Devill will draw them, and Gods providence leade them thereunto, therefore give them no more than God gives. And so for children; and servants, or any others you are to deale with, give them the liberty and authority you would have them use, and beyond that stretch not the tether, it will not tend to their good nor yours: And also from hence gather, and goe home with this meditation; That certainly here is this distemper in our natures, that we cannot tell how to use liberty, but wee shall very readily corrupt our selves: Oh the bottomlesse depth of sandy earth! of a corrupt spirit, that breaks over all bounds, and loves inordinate vastnesse; that is it we ought to be careful of. . . .

ROGER WILLIAMS

The Bloudy Tenent of Persecution (1644)

Born in London, England, and educated at Cambridge University, the radical Puritan preacher Roger Williams (1603–1684) arrived in New England in 1630, where he served as a teacher in the Salem Church of Massachusetts. In 1636, he founded the colony of Rhode Island after he was banished from the Massachusetts Bay Colony for spreading dangerous opinions and defying both civil and religious authorities. During a visit to England in 1644, Williams formulated, in The Bloudy Tenent of Persecution, one of the earliest defenses of the doctrines of

religious toleration, freedom of conscience, and the separation of church
and state.

First, that the blood of so many hundred thousand souls of *Protestants* and *Papists*, spilt in the *Wars* of *present* and *former Ages*, for their respective *Consciences*, is not *required* nor *accepted* by *Jesus Christ* the *Prince* of *Peace*.

Secondly, Pregnant *Scriptures* and *Arguments* are throughout the Worke proposed against the *Doctrine* of *Persecution* for *cause* of *Conscience*.

Thirdly, Satisfactorie Answers are given to *Scriptures*, and *objections* produced by Mr. *Calvin, Beza,* Mr. *Cotton,* and the Ministers of the New England Church and others former and later, tending to prove the *Doctrine* of *Persecution* for Cause of *Conscience*.

Fourthly, The *Doctrine* of *Persecution* for cause of *Conscience*, is proved guilty of all the *blood* of the *Soules* crying for *vengeance* under the *Alter*.

Fifthly, All *Civill States* with their *Officers* of *justice* in their respective *constitutions* and *administrations* are proved *essentially* Civil, and therefore not *judges, Governours* or *Defendours* of the *Spirituall* or *Christian* State and *Worship*.

Sixthly, It is the will and command of *God*, that since the comming of his Sonne the *Lord Jesus a permission* of the most *Paganish, Jewish, Turkish* or *Antichristian consciences* and *worships*, be granted to *all* men in all *Nations* and *Countries*: and they are onely to bee *fought* against with that *Sword* which is only (in *Soule matters*) able to conquer to wit the *Sword* of *Gods spirit*, the *Word* of *God*.

Seventhly, the *state* of the Land of *Israel*, the *Kings* and *people* thereof in *Peace & War*, is proved *figurative* and *ceremoniall*, and no *patterne* nor *president* for any *Kingdoms* or *civill state* in the *world* to follow.

Eightly, *God* requireth not an *uniformity* of *Religion* to be *inacted* and *inforced* in any *civill state*; which inforced *uniformity* (sooner or later) is the greatest occasion of *civill Warre, ravishing* of *conscience, persecution* of *Christ Jesus* in his servants, and of the *hypocrisie* and *destruction* of *millions* of *souls*.

Ninthly, In holding an inforced *uniformity* of *Religion* in a *civil state*, we must necessarily *disclaime* our desires and hopes of the *Jews conversion* to *Christ*.

Tenthly, An inforced *uniformity* of *Religion* throughout a *Nation* or *Civil state*, confounds the *Civill* and *Religious*, denies the principles of Christianity and civility, and that *Jesus Christ* is come in the flesh.

Eleventhly, The permission of other *consciences* and *worships* that a state professeth, only can (according to God) procure a firme and lasting *peace,* (good *assurance* being taken according to the *wisdome* of the *civill state* for *uniformity* of *civil obedience* from all sorts).

Twelfthly, lastly, true *civility* and *Christianity* may both flourish in a *State* or *Kingdome,* notwithstanding the *permission* of diverse and contrary *conscience,* either of *Jew* or *Gentile.* . . .

NATHANIEL WARD

The Simple Cobler of Aggawam (1645)

The Ipswich minister Nathaniel Ward (1578–1652) was one of the principal contributors to the Body of Liberties (1641), a codification of colonial law based largely on the common law of England. In this 1645 pamphlet he vehemently rejected Roger Williams's plea for religious toleration for its divisive consequences. Ward also condemned toleration as a thoroughly impious and un-Christian doctrine, and attacked liberty of conscience as a dangerous form of moral relativism that denies the truth of God's word.

Either I am in an Appoplexie, or that man is in a Lethargie, who doth not now sensibly feele God shaking the heavens over his head, and the earth under his feet: The Heavens so, as the Sun begins to turne into darknesse, the Moon into blood, the Starres to fall down to the ground; So that little Light of Comfort or Counsell is left to the sonnes of men: The Earth so, as the foundations are failing, the righteous scarce know where to finde rest, the inhabitants stagger like drunken men: it is in a manner dissolved both in Religions and Relations: And no marvell; for, they have defiled it by transgressing the Lawes, changing the Ordinances, and breaking the Everlasting Covenant. The Truths of God are the Pillars of the world, whereon States and Churches may stand quiet if they will; if they will not, Hee can easily shake them off into delusions, and distractions enough.

* * *

Too many men having not laid their foundations sure, nor ballasted their Spirits deepe with humility and feare, are prest enough of themselves to evaporate their owne apprehensions. Those that are acquainted with Story know, it hath ever beene so in new Editions of Churches: Such as are least able, are most busie to pudder in the rubbish, and to raise dust in the eye of more steady Repayrers. Civill Commotions make roome for uncivill practises: Religious mutations, for irreligious opinions: Change of Aire, discovers corrupt bodies; Reformation of Religion, unsound mindes. Hee that hath any well-faced phansy in his Crowne, and doth not vent it now, fears the pride of his owne heart will dub him dunce for ever. Such a one will trouble the whole *Israel* of God with his most untimely births, though he makes the bones of his vanity stick up, to the view and griefe of all that are godly wise. The devill desires no better sport than to see light heads handle their heels, and fetch their carreers in a time, when the Roofe of Liberty stands open.

The next perplexed Question, with pious and ponderous men, will be: What should bee done for the healing of these comfortlesse exulcerations. I am the unablest adviser of a thousand, the unworthiest of ten thousand; yet I hope I may presume to assert what follows without just offense.

First, such as have given or taken any unfriendly reports of us *New-English,* should doe well to recollect themselves. Wee have beene reputed a Colluvies of wild Opinionists, swarmed into a remote wildernes to find elbow-roome for our Phanatick Doctrines and practices: I trust our diligence past, and constant sedulity against such persons and courses, will plead better things for us. I dare take upon me, to bee the Herauld of *New-England* so farre, as to proclaime to the world, in the name of our Colony, that all Familists, Antinomians, Anabaptists, and other Enthusiasts shall have free Liberty to keepe away from us, and such as will come to be gone as fast as they can, the sooner the better.

Secondly, I dare averre, that God doth no where in his word tolerate Christian States, to give Toleration to such adversaries of his Truth, if they have power in their hands to suppresse them. * * *

If the devill might have his free option, I beleeve he would ask nothing else, but liberty to enfranchize all false Religions, and to embondage the true; nor should hee need: It is much to be feared, that laxe Tolerations upon State-pretences and planting necessities, will be the next subtle Stratagem he will spread to distate the Truth of God and supplant the peace of the Churches. Tolerations in things tolerable, exquisitely drawn out by the lines of the Scripture, and pensill of the Spirit, are the sacred favours of Truth, the due latitudes of Love, the faire Compartments of Christian fraternity: but irregular dispensations, dealt forth by the facilities of men, are the frontiers of error, the redoubts of Schisme, the perillous irritaments of carnall and spirituall enmity.

My heart hath naturally detested foure things: The standing of the Apocrypha in the Bible; Forrainers dwelling in my Countrey, to crowd out native Subjects into the corners of the Earth; Alchymized coines; Tolerations of divers Religions, or of one Religion in segregant shapes:

He that willingly assents to the last, if he examines his heart by daylight, his conscience will tell him, he is either an Atheist, or an Heretique, or an Hypocrite, or at best a captive to some Lust: Poly-piety is the greatest impiety in the world. * * *

Not to tolerate things meerly indifferent to weak consciences, argues a conscience too strong: pressed uniformity in these, causes much disunity: To tolerate more than indifferents, is not to deale indifferently with God: He that doth it, takes his Scepter out of his hand, and bids him stand by. Who hath to doe to institute Religion but God? The power of all Religion and Ordinances, lies in their purity: their purity in their simplicity: then are mixtures pernicious. I lived in a City, where a Papist preached in one Church, a Lutheran in another, a Calvinist in a third; a Lutheran one part of the day, a Calvinist the other, in the same Pulpit: the Religion of that place was but motly and meagre, their affections Leopard-like.

If the whole Creature should conspire to doe the Creator a mischiefe, or offer him an insolency, it would be in nothing more, than in erecting untruths against his Truth, or by sophisticating his Truths with humane medleyes: the removing of some one iota in Scripture, may draw out all the life, and traverse all the Truth of the whole Bible: but to authorise an untruth, by a Toleration of State, is to build a Sconce against the walls of heaven, to batter God out of his Chaire: To tell a practicall lye, is a great sin, but yet transient; but to set up a Theoricall untruth, is to warrant every lye that lyes from its root to the top of every branch it hath, which are not a few.

* * *

That State is wise, that will improve all paines and patience rather to compose, then tolerate differences in Religion. There is no divine Truth, but hath much Celestial fire in it from the Spirit of Truth: nor no irreligious untruth, without its proportion of Antifire from the Spirit of Error to contradict it: the zeale of the one, the virulency of the other, must necessarily kindle Combustions. Fiery diseases seated in the spirit, embroile the whole frame of the body; others more externall and coole, are less dangerous. They which divide in Religion, divide in God; they who divide in him, divide beyond *Genus Generalissimum,* where there is no reconciliation, without atonement; that is, without uniting in him, who is One, and in his Truth, which is also one.

Wise are those men who will be persuaded rather to live within the pale of Truth where they may bee quiet, than in the purliev's, where they are sure to bee hunted ever and anon, doe Authority what it can. Every singular Opinion, hath a singular opinion of itself: and he that holds it, a singular opinion of himself, and a simple opinion of all contra-sentients:

he that confutes him, must confute all three at once, or else he does nothing; which will not be done without more stirre then the peace of the State or Church can indure.

* * *

He that is willing to tolerate any Religion, or discrepant way of Religion, besides his own, unless it be in matters merely indifferent, either doubts of his own, or is not sincere in it.

He that is willing to tolerate any unsound Opinion, that his own may also be tolerated, though never so sound, will for a need hang God's Bible at the Devil's girdle.

Every toleration of false Religions, or Opinions hath as many Errors and Sins in it, as all the false Religions and Opinions it tolerates, and one sound one more.

That State that will give Liberty of Conscience in matters of Religion, must give Liberty of Conscience and Conversation in their Moral Laws, or else the Fiddle will be out of Tune, and some of the strings crack.

He that will rather make an irreligious quarrel with other Religions than try the Truth of his own by valuable Arguments, and peaceable Sufferings; either his Religion, or himself is irreligious.

Experience will teach Churches and Christians, that it is far better to live in a State united, though a little Corrupt, than in a State, whereof some Part is incorrupt, and all the rest divided.

I am not altogether ignorant of the eight Rules given by Orthodox Divines about giving Tolerations, yet with their favour I dare affirm,

That there is no Rule given by God for any State to give an affirmative Toleration to any false Religion, or Opinion whatsoever; they must connive in some Cases, but may not concede in any. * * *

It is said, That Men ought to have Liberty of their Conscience, and that it is Persecution to debar them of it: I can rather stand amazed than reply to this: it is an astonishment to think that the brains of men should be parboiled in such impious ignorance; Let all the wits under the Heavens lay their heads together and find an Assertion worse than this (one excepted) I will Petition to be chosen the universal Idiot of the World. * * *

Hence it is, that God is so jealous of his Truths, that he hath taken order in his due justice: First, that no practical Sin is so Sinful as some error in judgment; no man so accursed with indelible infamy and dedolent impenitency, as Authors of Heresy. Secondly, that the least Error, if grown sturdy and pressed, shall set open the Spittle-door of all the squint-eyed, wry-necked, and brasen-faced Errors that are or ever were of that litter; if they be not enough to serve its turn, it will beget more, though it hath not one crust of reason to maintain them. Thirdly, that that State which will permit Errors in Religion, shall admit Errors in Policy unavoidably.

Fourthly, that that Policy which will suffer irreligious Errors, shall suffer the loss of so much Liberty in one kind or other. ✳ ✳ ✳

It is greatly to be lamented, to observe the wanton fearlessness of this Age, especially of Younger Professors, to greet new Opinions and Opinionists: as if former truths were grown Superannuate, and Sapless, if not altogether antiquate. *Non senescet veritas.* No man ever saw a gray hair on the head or beard of any Truth, wrinkle, or morphew on its face: The bed of Truth is green all the year long. He that cannot solace himself with any saving truth, as affectionately as at the first acquaintance with it, hath not only a fastidious, but an adulterous Heart.

✳ ✳ ✳

That if the State of *England* shall either willingly Tolerate, or weakly connive at such Courses, the Church of that Kingdome will sooner become the Devills Dancing-Schoole, then Gods-Temple: The Civill State a Beare-garden, then an Exchange: The whole Realme a Pais base, then an *England*. And what pity it is, that that Country which hath been the Staple of Truth to all Christendome, should now become the Aviary of Errors to the whole World, let every fearing heart judge.

I take Liberty of Conscience to be nothing but a freedome from sinne, and error. ✳ ✳ ✳ And liberty of Error nothing but a Prison for Conscience. Then small will bee the kindnesse of a State to build such Prisons for their Subjects.

The Scripture faith, there is nothing makes free but Truth, and Truth saith, there is no Truth but One. If the States of the World would make it their sumoperous Care to preserve this One Truth in its purity and Authority it would ease them of all other Politicall cares. I am sure Satan makes it his grand, if not onely task, to adulterate Truth; Falsehood is his sole Scepter, whereby he first ruffled, and ever since ruined the World.

JOHN WISE

A Vindication of the Government of New England Churches (1717)

The Ipswich Congregationalist minister John Wise (1652–1725) was a reformer who had bravely condemned witchcraft prosecutions. His 1717 essay is a theoretically sophisticated defense of self-government relying on scripture and notions of natural law and natural rights to justify democratic principles in both civil and ecclesiastical government. In this selection from what is probably the first serious and extended treatise on political theory to emerge in America, Wise offers the Lockean argument that the only legitimate form of government is one based on the voluntary consent of individuals, who are born free, equal, and independent.

1   I shall consider Man in a state of Natural Being, as a Free-Born Subject under the Crown of Heaven, and owing Homage to none but God himself. It is certain Civil Government in General, is a very Admirable Result of Providence, and an Incomparable Benefit to Mankind, yet must needs be acknowledged to be the Effect of Humane Free-Compacts and not of Divine Institution; it is the Produce of Mans Reason, of Humane and Rational Combinations, and not from any direct Orders of Infinite Wisdom, in any positive Law wherein is drawn up this or that Scheme of Civil Government. Government [says the Lord *Warrington*] is necessary—in that no Society of Men can subsist without it; and that Particular Form of Government is necessary which best suits the Temper and Inclination of a People. Nothing can be Gods Ordinance, but what he has particularly Declared to be such; there is no particular Form of Civil Government described in Gods Word, neither does Nature prompt it. The Government of the *Jews* was changed five Times. Government is not formed by Nature, as other Births or Productions; If it were, it would be the same in all Countries; because Nature keeps the same Method, in the same thing, in all Climates. If a Common Wealth be changed into a Monarchy, is it Nature that forms, and brings forth the Monarch? Or if a Royal Family be wholly Extinct [as in *Noah's* Case, being not Heir Apparent from Descent from *Adam*] is it Nature that must go to work [with the King Bees, who themselves alone preserve the Royal Race in that Empire] to Breed a Monarch before the People can have a King, or a Government sent over them? And thus we must leave Kings to Resolve which is their best Title to their Crowns, whether Natural Right, or the Constitution of Government settled by Humane Compacts, under the Direction and Conduct of Reason. But to proceed under the head of a State of Natural Being, I shall more distinctly Explain the State of Humane Nature in its Original Capacity, as Man is placed on Earth by his Maker, and Cloathed with many Investitures, and Immunities which properly belong to Man separately considered. As,

     1. The Prime Immunity in Mans State, is that he is most properly the Subject of the Law of Nature. He is the Favourite Animal on Earth; in that this Part of Gods Image, *viz.* Reason is Congenate with

his Nature, wherein by a Law Immutable, Instampt upon his Frame, God has provided a Rule for Men in all their Actions; obliging each one to the performance of that which is Right, not only as to Justice, but likewise as to all other Moral Vertues, the which is nothing but the Dictate of Right Reason founded in the Soul of Man. *Molloy, De Mao, Praef*. That which is to be drawn from Mans Reason, flowing from the true Current of that Faculty, when unperverted, may be said to be the Law of Nature; on which account, the Holy Scriptures declare it written on Mens hearts. For being in-dowed with a Soul, you may know from your self, how, and what you ought to act, Rom. 2. 14. *These having not a Law, are a Law to themselves*. So that the meaning is, when we acknowledge the Law of Nature to be the dictate of Right Reason, we must mean that the Understanding of Man is Endowed with such a power, as to be able, from the Contemplation of humane Condition to discover a necessity of Living agreeably with this Law: And likewise to find out some Principle, by which the Precepts of it, may be clearly and solidly Demonstrated. The way to discover the Law of Nature in our own State, is by a narrow Watch, and accurate Contemplation of our Natural Condition, and propensions. Others say this is the way to find out the Law of Nature. *scil*. If a Man any ways doubts, whether what he is going to do to another Man be agreeable to the Law of Nature, then let him suppose himself to be in that other Mans Room; And by this Rule effectually Executed, A Man must be a very dull Scholar to Nature not to make Proficiency in the Knowledge of her Laws. But more Particularly in pursuing our Condition for the discovery of the Law of Nature, this is very obvious to view, *viz*.

1. A Principle of Self-Love, and Self-Preservation, is very predominant in every Mans Being.

2. A Sociable Disposition.

3. An Affection or Love to Man-kind in General. And to give such Sentiments the force of a Law, we must suppose a God who takes care of all Mankind, and has thus obliged each one, as a Subject of higher Principles of Being, then meer Instincts. For that all Law properly considered, supposes a capable Subject, and a Superiour Power; And the Law of God which is Binding, is published by the Dictates of Right Reason as other ways: Therefore says *Plutarch, To follow God and obey Reason is the same thing*. But moreover that God has Established the Law of Nature, as the General Rule of Government, is further Illustrable from the many Sanctions in Providence, and from the Peace and Guilt of Conscience in them that either obey, or violate the Law of Nature. But moreover, the foundation of the Law of Nature with relation to Government, may be thus Discovered. *Scil*. Man is a Creature extreamly desirous of

his own Preservation; of himself he is plainly Exposed to many Wants, unable to secure his own safety, and Maintenance without the Assistance of his fellows; and he is also able of returning Kindness by the further- ance of mutual Good; But yet Man is often found to be Malicious, Inso- lent and easily Provoked, and as powerful in Effecting mischief, as he is ready in designing it. Now that such a Creature may be Preserved, it is necessary that he be Sociable; that is, that he be capable and disposed to unite himself to those of his own species, and to Regulate himself to- wards them, that they may have no fair Reason to do him harm; but rather incline to promote his Interests, and secure his Rights and Con- cerns. This then is a Fundamental Law of Nature, that every Man as far as in him lies, do maintain a Sociableness with others, agreeable with the main end and disposition of humane Nature in general. For this is very apparent, that Reason and Society render Man the most potent of all Creatures. And Finally, from the Principles of Sociableness it follows as a fundamental Law of Nature, that Man is not so Wedded to his own Interest, but that he can make the Common good the mark of his Aim: And hence he becomes Capacitated to enter into a Civil State by the Law of Nature; for without this property in Nature, *viz.* Sociableness, which is for Cementing of parts, every Government would soon moulder and dissolve.

2. The Second Great Immunity of Man is an Orginal Liberty In- stampt upon his Rational Nature. He that intrudes upon this Liberty, Violates the Law of Nature. In this Discourse I shall wave the Consider- ation of Mans Moral Turpitude, but shall view him Physically as a Crea- ture which God has made and furnished essentially with many Enobling Immunities, which render him the most August Animal in the World, and still, whatever has happened since his Creation, he remains at the upper-end of Nature, and as such is a Creature of a very Noble Charac- ter. For as to his Dominion, the whole frame of the Lower Part of the Universe is devoted to his use, and at his Command; and his Liberty un- der the Conduct of Right Reason, is equal with his trust. Which Liberty may be briefly Considered, Internally as to his Mind, and Externally as to his Person.

1. The Internal Native Liberty of Mans Nature in general implies, a faculty of Doing or Omitting things according to the Direction of his Judg- ment. But in a more special meaning, this Liberty does not consist in a loose and ungovernable Freedom, or in an unbounded Licence of Acting. Such Licence is disagreeing with the condition and dignity of Man, and would make Man of a lower and meaner Constitution than Bruit Crea- tures; who in all their Liberties are kept under a better and more Rational

Government, by their Instincts. Therefore as *Plutarch* says, *Those Persons only who live in Obedience to Reason, are worthy to be accounted free: They alone live as they Will, who have Learnt what they ought to Will.* So that the true Natural Liberty of Man, such as really and truely agrees to him, must be understood, as he is Guided and Restrained by the Tyes of Reason, and Laws of Nature; all the rest is Brutal, if not worse.

2. Mans External Personal, Natural Liberty, Antecedent to all Humane parts, or Alliances must also be considered. And so every Man must be conceived to be perfectly in his own Power and disposal, and not to be controuled by the Authority of any other. And thus every Man, must be acknowledged equal to every Man, since all Subjection and all Command are equally banished on both sides; and considering all Men thus at Liberty, every Man has a Prerogative to Judge for himself, *viz.* What shall be most for his Behoof, Happiness and Well-being.

3. The Third Capital Immunity belonging to Mans Nature, is an equality amongst Men; Which is not to be denied by the Law of Nature, till Man has Resigned himself with all his Rights for the sake of a Civil State; and then his Personal Liberty and Equality is to be cherished, and preserved to the highest degree, as will consist with all just distinctions amongst Men of Honour, and shall be agreeable with the publick Good. For Man has a high valuation of himself, and the passion seems to lay its first foundation [not in Pride, but] really in the high and admirable Frame and Constitution of Humane Nature. The Word Man, says my Author, is thought to carry somewhat of Dignity in its sound; and we commonly make use of this as the most proper and prevailing Argument against a rude Insulter, *viz. I am not a Beast or a Dog, but am a Man as well as your self.* Since then Humane Nature agrees equally with all persons; and since no one can live a Sociable Life with another that does not own or Respect him as a Man; It follows as a Command of the Law of Nature, that every Man Esteem and treat another as one who is naturally his Equal, or who is a Man as well as he. There be many popular, or plausible Reasons that greatly Illustrate this Equality, *viz.* that we all Derive our Being from one stock, the same Common Father of humane Race. On this Consideration *Boethius* checks the pride of the Insulting Nobility.

* * *

And also that our Bodies are Composed of matter, frail, brittle, and lyable to be destroyed by thousand Accidents; we all owe our Existence to the same Method of propagation. The Noblest Mortal in his Entrance on to the Stage of Life, is not distinguished by any pomp or of passage from the lowest of Mankind; and our Life hastens to the same General

Mark: Death observes no Ceremony, but Knocks as loud at the Barriers of the Court, as at the Door of the Cottage. This Equality being admitted, bears a very great force in maintaining Peace and Friendship amongst Men. For that he who would use the Assistance of others, in promoting his own Advantage, ought as freely to be at their service, when they want his help on the like Occasions. *One Good turn Requires another,* is the Common Proverb; for otherwise he must need esteem others unequal to himself, who constantly demands their Aid, and as constantly denies his own. And whoever is of this Insolent Temper, cannot but highly displease those about him, and soon give Occasion of the Breach of the Common Peace.

* * *

That it would be the greatest absurdity to believe, that Nature actually Invests the Wise with a Sovereignity over the weak; or with a Right of forcing them against their Wills; for that no Sovereignty can be Established, unless some Humane Deed, or Covenant Precede: Nor does Natural fitness for Government make a Man presently Governour over another; for that as *Ulpian* says, *by a Natural Right all Men are born free;* and Nature having set all Men upon a Level and made them Equals, no Servitude or Subjection can be conceived without Inequality; and this cannot be made without Usurpation or Force in others, or Voluntary Compliance in those who Resign their freedom, and give away their degree of Natural Being. * * *

1. Every Man considered in a Natural State, must be allowed to be Free, and at his own dispose; yet to suit Mans Inclinations to Society; And in a peculiar manner to gratify the necessity he is in of publick Rule and Order, he is Impelled to enter into a Civil Community; and Divests himself of his Natural Freedom, and puts himself under Government; which amongst other things Comprehends the Power of Life and Death over Him; together with Authority to Injoyn him some things to which he has an utter Aversation, and to prohibit him other things, for which he may have as strong an Inclination; so that he may be often under this Authority, obliged to Sacrifice his Private, for the Publick Good. So that though Man is inclined to Society, yet he is driven to a Combination by great necessity. For that the true and leading Cause of forming Governments, and yielding up Natural Liberty, and throwing Mans Equality into a Common Pile to be new Cast by the Rules of fellowship; was really and truly to guard themselves against the Injuries Men were lyable to Interchangeably; for none so Good to Man, as Man, and yet none a greater Enemy. So that,

2. The first Humane Subject and Original of Civil Power is the People. For as they have a Power every Man over himself in a Natural State,

so upon a Combination they can and do bequeath this Power unto others; and settle it according as their united discretion shall Determine. For that this is very plain, that when the Subject of Sovereign Power is quite Extinct, that Power returns to the People again. And when they are free, they may set up what species of Government they please; or if they rather incline to it, they may subside into a State of Natural Being, if it be plainly for the best. * * *

3. The formal Reason of Government is the Will of a Community, yielded up and surrendred to some other Subject, either of one particular Person, or more, Conveyed in the following manner.

Let us conceive in our Mind a multitude of Men, all Naturally Free and Equal; going about voluntarily, to Erect themselves into a new Common-Wealth. Now their Condition being such, to bring themselves into a Politick Body, they must needs Enter into divers Covenants.

1. They must Interchangeably each Man Covenant to joyn in one lasting Society, that they may be capable to concert the measures of their safety, by a Publick Vote.

2. A Vote or Decree must then nextly pass to set up some Particular speecies of Government over them. And if they are joyned in their first Compact upon absolute Terms, to stand to the Decision of the first Vote concerning the Species of Government: Then all are bound by the Majority to acquiesce in that particular Form thereby settled, though their own private Opinion, incline them to some other Model,

3. After a Decree has specified the Particular form of Government, then there will be need of a New Covenant, whereby those on whom Sovereignty is conferred, engage to take care of the Common Peace, and Welfare. And the Subjects on the other hand, to yield them faithful Obedience. In which Covenant is Included that Submission and Union of Wills, by which a State may be conceived to be but one Person. So that the most proper Definition of a Civil State, is this, *viz.* A Civil State is a Compound Moral Person whose Will [United by those Covenants before passed] is the Will of all; to the end it may Use, and Apply the strength and riches of Private Persons towards maintaining the Common Peace, Security, and Well-being of all. Which may be conceived as tho' the whole State was now become but one Man; in which the aforesaid Covenants may be supposed under Gods Providence, to be the Divine *Fiat*, Pronounced by God, let us make Man * * *

1. The Forms of a Regular State are three only, which Forms arise from the proper and particular Subject, in which the Supream Power Resides, As,

1. A Democracy, which is when the Sovereign Power is Lodged in a Council consisting of all the Members, and where every Member has the Priviledge of a Vote. This Form of Government, appears in the greatest part of the World to have been the most Ancient. For that Reason seems to shew it to be most probable, that when Men [being Originally in a condition of Natural Freedom and Equality] had thoughts of joyning in a Civil Body, would without question be inclined to Administer their common Affairs, by their common Judgment, and so must necessarily to gratifie that Inclination establish a Democracy; neither can it be rationally imagined, that Fathers of Families being yet Free and Independent, should in a moment, or little time take off their long delight in governing their own Affairs, and Devolve all upon some single Sovereign Commander; for that it seems to have been thought more Equitable, that what belonged to all, should be managed by all when all had entered by Compact into one Community. * * *

And moreover it seems very manifest that most Civil Communities arose at first from the Union of Families, that were nearly allyed in Race and Blood. And though Ancient Story make frequent mention of Kings, yet it appears that most of them were such that had an Influence rather in perswading, then in any Power of Commanding. * * *

A democracy is then Erected, when a Number of Free Persons, do Assemble together, in Order to enter into a Covenant for Uniting themselves in a Body: And such a Preparative Assembly hath some appearance already of a Democracy; it is a Democracy in *Embrio* properly in this Respect, that every Man hath the Priviledge freely to deliver his Opinion concerning the Common Affairs. Yet he who dissents from the Vote of the Majority, is not in the least obliged by what they determine, till by a second Covenant, a Popular Form be actually Established; for not before then can we call it a Democratical Government, *viz.* Till the Right of Determining all matters relating to the publick Safety, is actually placed in a General Assembly of the whole People; or by their own Compact and Mutual Agreement, Determine themselves the proper Subject for the Exercise of Sovereign Power. And to compleat this State, and render it capable to Exert its Power to answer the End of a Civil State: These Conditions are necessary.

1. That a certain Time and Place be Assigned for Assembling.

2. That when the Assembly be Orderly met, as to Time and Place, that then the Vote of the Majority must pass for the Vote of the whole Body.

3. That Magistrates be appointed to Exercise the Authority of the whole for the better dispatch of Business, of every days Occurrence; who also may with more Mature diligence, search into more Important Affairs;

and if in case any thing happens of greater Consequence, may report it to the Assembly; and be peculiarly Serviceable in putting all Publick Decrees into Execution. Because a large Body of People is almost useless in Respect of the last Service, and of many others, as to the more Particular Application and Exercise of Power. Therefore it is most agreeable with the Law of Nature, that they Institute their Officers to act in their Name, and Stead.

2. The Second Species of Regular Government, is an Aristocracy; and this is said then to be Constituted when the People, or Assembly United by a first Covenant, and having thereby cast themselves into the first Rudiments of a State; do then by Common Decree, Devolve the Sovereign Power, on a Council consisting of some Select Members; and these having accepted of the Designation, are then properly invested with Sovereign Command; and then an Aristocracy is formed. * * *

3. The third species of a regular government is a monarchy, which is settled when the sovereign power is conferred on some one worthy person. It differs from the former because a monarch, who is but one person in natural as well as in moral account, and so is furnished with an immediate power of exercising sovereign command in all instances of government. But the forenamed must needs have particular time and place assigned, but the power and authority is equal in each.

2. Mixed governments, which are various and of diverse kinds (not now to be enumerated) yet possibly the fairest in the world is that which has a regular monarchy (in distinction as to what is despotic) settled upon a noble democracy as its basis. And each part of the government is so adjusted by pacts and laws that renders the whole constitution an Elysium. It is said of the British Empire, "That it is such a monarchy, as that by the necessary subordinate concurrence of the Lords and Commons, in the making and repealing all statutes or acts of Parliament; it has the main advantages of an aristocracy and of a democracy, and yet free from the disadvantages and evils of either. It is such a monarchy, as by most admirable temperament affords very much to the industry, liberty and happiness of the subject, and reserves enough for the majesty and prerogative of any King who will own his people as subjects, not as slaves. It is a Kingdom that, of all the kingdoms of the world, is most like to the Kingdom of Jesus Christ, whose yoke is easy, and burden light." Thus having drawn up this brief scheme concerning Man, and the nature of civil government he is become sole subject of, I shall next proceed to make improvements of the premises to accommodate the main subject under our consideration.

2. I shall now make some improvement of the foregoing principles of civil knowledge, fairly deduced from the Law of Nature. And, I shall

peculiarly refer to ecclesiastical affairs, whereby we may, in probability, discover more clearly the kind and something of the nature of that government which Christ has placed in and over his Church. The learned debates of men and Divine Writ sometimes seem to cast such a grandeur on the Church and its officers as though they stood in peerage with civil empire. But all such expressions must needs be otherwise interpreted. God is the highest Cause that acts by Council, and it must needs be altogether repugnant to think he should forecast and state of this world by no better a scheme, than to order two sovereign powers in the same grand community, which would be like placing two suns in the firmament, which would be to set the universe into a flame; that should such an error happen, one must needs be forthwith extinguished to bring the frame of nature into a just temper and keep it out of harm's way. But to proceed with my purpose, I shall go back upon the civil scheme and inquire after two things: first of rebellion against government in general and then in special; whether any of the aforesaid species of regular government can be predicable of the Church of God on earth.

1. In general concerning rebellion against government, for particular subjects to break in upon regular communities duly established, is from the premises to violate the Law of Nature, and is a high usurpation upon the first grand immunities of Mankind. Such rebels in states and usurpers in churches affront the world with a presumption that the best of the brotherhood are a company of fools and that themselves have fairly monopolized all the reason of Human Nature. Yea, they take upon them the boldness to assume a prerogative of trampling underfoot the natural original equality and liberty of their fellows, for to push the proprietors of settlements out of possession of their old, and impose new schemes upon them, is virtually to declare them in a state of vassalage, or that they were born to, and therefore will the usurper be so gracious as to insure them they shall not be sold at the next market. They must esteem it a favor, for by this time all the original prerogatives of man's nature are intentionally a victim smoking to satiate the usurper's ambition. It is a very tart observation on an English monarch, and where it may by proportion be applied to a subject, must need sink very deep and serve for evidence under this head. It is in the Secret History, says my author, "Where the constitution of a nation is such that the laws of the land are the measures both of the sovereign's command and the obedience of the subjects whereby it is provided that, as the one are not to invade what by concessions and stipulations is granted to the ruler, for the other is not to deprive them of their lawful and determined rights and liberties; then the Prince who strives to subvert the fundamental laws of the society is the traitor and rebel, and not the

people who endeavor to preserve and defend their own." It's very applicable to particular men in their rebellions or usurpations in Church or state.

2. In special I shall now proceed to inquire whether any of the aforesaid species of regular, unmixed governments can, with any good show of reason, be predicable of the Church of Christ on earth. If the Churches of Christ, as churches, are either the object or subject of a sovereign power entrusted in the hands of men, then most certainly one of the forecited schemes of a perfect government will be applicable to it.

Before I pursue the inquiry, it may not be improper to pause and make some caution here by distinguishing between that which may have some resemblance of civil power and the thing itself, and so the power of churches is but a faint resemblance of civil power, it comes in reality nothing near to the thing itself, for the one is truly coercive, the other persuasive, the one is sovereign power, the other is delegated and ministerial. But not to delay, I shall proceed with my inquiry and therein shall endeavor to humor the several great claimers of government in the Church of Christ. * * *

But to abbreviate, it seems most agreeable with the Light of Nature that if there be any of the regular government settled in the Church of God it must needs be

3. A Democracy. This is a form of government which the Light of Nature does highly value and often directs to as most agreeable to the just and natural prerogatives of Human Beings. This was of great account in the early times of the world. And not only so, but upon the experience of several thousand years after the world had been tumbled and tossed from one species of government to another, at a great expense of blood and treasure, many of the wise nations of the world have sheltered themselves under it again, or at least have blended and balanced their governments with it.

It is certainly a great truth that man's original liberty, after it is resigned (yet under due restrictions), ought to be cherished in all wise governments; or otherwise a man, in making himself a subject, he alters himself from a freeman into a slave, which to do is repugnant to the Law of Nature. Also the natural equality of men among men must be duly favored, in that government was never established by God or Nature to give one man a prerogative to insult over another; therefore in a civil, as well as in a natural, state of being, a just equality is to be indulged so far as that every man is bound to honor every man, which is agreeable both with Nature and Religion. The end of all good government is to cultivate humanity and promote the happiness of all and the good of every man in all his rights, his life, liberty, estate, honor, etc. without injury or abuse done to any. Then certainly it cannot easily be thought that a company of men that shall enter into a voluntary compact, to hold all power in their own hands, thereby to use and improve their united force, wisdom, riches and strength for the common and particular good of every member, as is the nature of a democracy; I say it cannot be that this sort of constitution will so readily furnish those in government with an appetite or disposition to prey upon each other or embezzle the common stock, as some particular persons may be apt to do when set off and entrusted with the same power. And, moreover, this appears very natural, that when the aforesaid government or power, settled in all, when they have elected certain capable persons to minister in their affairs, and the said ministers remain accountable to the Assembly, these officers must needs be under the influence of many wise cautions from their own thoughts (as well as under confinement by their commission) in their whole administration: And from thence it must needs follow that they will be more apt and inclined to steer right for the main point, viz., the peculiar good and benefit of the whole and every particular member fairly and sincerely. And why may not these stand for very rational pleas in Church order?

For certainly if Christ has settled any form of power in his Church he has done it for his Church's safety, and for the benefit of every member: Then he must needs be presumed to have made choice of that government as should least expose his people to hazard, either from the fraud or arbitrary measures of particular men. And it is as plain as daylight, there is no species of government like a democracy to attain this end. There is but about two steps from an aristocracy to a monarchy, and from thence but one to a tyranny. An able standing force and an ill-nature, *ipso facto*, turns an absolute monarch into a tyrant. This is obvious among the Roman Caesars and through the world. And all these direful transmutations are easier in Church affairs (from the different qualities of things) than in civil states. For what is it that cunning and learned men can't make the world swallow as an article of their creed if they are once invested with an uncontrollable power, and are to be the standing orators to mankind in matters of faith and obedience?

JONATHAN MAYHEW

A Discourse Concerning Unlimited Submission and Non-Resistance to the Higher Powers (1750)

The Congregational minister Jonathan Mayhew (1720–1766), an advocate of rational religion, served as the pastor of Boston's West Church from 1747 until his death in 1766. Mayhew believed that subjects had a right to resist and overthrow any government that failed to promote the public welfare and preserve fundamental rights. Mayhew delivered this quintessentially Lockean message in a widely circulated sermon that refuted the doctrines of the divine right of kings and unlimited submission to government, derived from Saint Paul in the famous New Testament passage Romans 13:1–7. Mayhew's popular defense of the right of resistance to illegitimate power was highly influential among the American revolutionaries.

R O M. XIII, 1–[7]

1. *Let every soul be subject unto the higher powers. For there is no power but of God: the powers that be are ordained of God.*
2. *Whosoever therefore resisteth the power, resisteth the ordinance of God: and they that resist shall receive to themselves damnation.*
3. *For rulers are not a terror to good works, but to the evil. Wilt thou then not be afraid of the power? Do that which is good, and thou shalt have praise of the same.*
4. *For he is the minister of God to thee for good. But if thou do that which is evil, be afraid; for he beareth not the sword in vain: for he is the minister of God, a revenger to execute wrath upon him that doth evil.*
5. *Wherefore ye must needs be subject, not only for wrath, but also for conscience sake.*
6. *For, for this cause pay you tribute also: for they are God's ministers, attending continually upon this very thing.*
7. *Render therefore to all their dues: tribute to whom tribute is due; custom to whom custom; fear to whom fear; honor to whom honor.*

It is evident that the affair of civil government may properly fall under a *moral* and *religious* consideration, at least so far forth as it relates to the general nature and end of magistracy and to the grounds and extent of that submission which persons of a private character ought to yield to those who are vested with authority. This must be allowed by all who acknowledge the divine original of Christianity. For although there be a sense, and a very plain and important sense, in which Christ's *kingdom is not of this world,* his inspired apostles have, nevertheless, laid down some general principles concerning the office of civil rulers and the duty of subjects, together with the reason and obligation of that duty. And from hence it follows that it is proper for all who acknowledge the authority of Jesus Christ and the inspiration of his apostles to endeavor to understand what is in fact the doctrine which they have delivered concerning this matter. It is the duty of *Christian* magistrates to inform themselves what it is which their religion teaches concerning the nature and design of their office. And it is equally the duty of all *Christian* people to inform themselves what it is which their religion teaches concerning that subjection which they owe to *the higher powers.* It is for these reasons that I have attempted to examine into the Scripture account of this matter, in order to lay it before you with the same *freedom* which I constantly use with relation to other doctrines and precepts of Christianity; not doubting but you will *judge* upon everything offered to your consideration with the same spirit of *freedom* and *liberty* with which it is *spoken.* * * *

The Apostle's doctrine * * * may be summed up in the following observations, viz.:

> That the end of magistracy is the good of civil society, *as such.*
>
> That civil rulers, *as such,* are the ordinance and ministers of God, it being by his permission and providence that any bear rule, and agreeable to his will that there should be *some persons* vested with authority in society, for the well-being of it.
>
> That which is here said concerning civil rulers extends to all of them in common: it relates indifferently to monarchical, republican, and aristocratical government, and to all other forms which truly answer the sole end of government, the happiness of society; and to all the different degrees of authority in any particular state, to inferior officers no less than to the supreme.
>
> That disobedience to civil rulers in the due exercise of their authority is not merely a *political sin* but an heinous *offense against God and religion.*
>
> That the true ground and reason of our obligation to be subject to the *higher powers* is the usefulness of magistracy (when properly

exercised) to human society and its subserviency to the general welfare.

That obedience to civil rulers is here equally required under all forms of government which answer the sole end of all government, the good of society; and to every degree of authority in any state, whether supreme or subordinate.

(From whence it follows,

That if unlimited obedience and nonresistance be here required as a duty under any one form of government, it is also required as a duty under all other forms, and as a duty to subordinate rulers as well as to the supreme.)

And lastly, that those civil rulers to whom the Apostle enjoins subjection are the persons *in possession; the powers that be,* those who are *actually* vested with authority.

There is one very important and interesting point which remains to be inquired into; namely, the *extent* of that subjection *to the higher powers* which is here enjoined as a duty upon all Christians. Some have thought it warrantable and glorious to disobey the civil powers in certain circumstances, and, in cases of very great and general oppression when humble remonstrances fail of having any effect, and when the public welfare cannot be otherwise provided for and secured, to rise unanimously even against the sovereign himself in order to redress their grievances, to vindicate their natural and legal rights, to break the yoke of tyranny, and free themselves and posterity from inglorious servitude and ruin. It is upon this principle that many royal oppressors have been driven from their thrones into banishment, and many slain by the hands of their subjects. * * *

But, in opposition to this principle, it has often been asserted that the Scripture in general (and the passage under consideration in particular) makes all resistance to princes a crime, in any case whatever.—If they turn tyrants and become the common oppressors of those whose welfare they ought to regard with a paternal affection, we must not pretend to right ourselves unless it be by prayers and tears and humble entreaties; and if these methods fail of procuring redress we must not have recourse to any other, but all suffer ourselves to be robbed and butchered at the pleasure of the *Lord's anointed,* lest we should incur the sin of rebellion and the punishment of damnation. For he has God's authority and commission to bear him out in the worst of crimes, so far that he may not be withstood or controlled. Now whether we are obliged to yield such an absolute submission to our prince, or whether disobedience and resistance may not be justifiable in some cases notwithstanding anything in the passage before us, is an inquiry in which we are all concerned; and this is the inquiry which is the main design of the present discourse.

Now there does not seem to be any necessity of supposing that an absolute, unlimited obedience, whether active or passive, is here enjoined merely for this reason, that the precept is delivered in *absolute terms,* without any *exception* or *limitation* expressly mentioned. We are enjoined (ver. 1) to be *subject to the higher powers,* and (ver. 5) to be *subject for conscience sake.* And because these expressions are absolute and unlimited (or, more properly, general), some have inferred that the subjection required in them must be absolute and unlimited also, at least so far forth as to make passive obedience and nonresistance a duty in all cases whatever, if not active obedience likewise. Though, by the way, there is here no distinction made betwixt active and passive obedience; and if either of them be required in an unlimited sense, the other must be required in the same sense also by virtue of the present argument, because the expressions are equally absolute with respect to both. But that unlimited obedience of any sort cannot be argued merely from the indefinite expressions in which obedience is enjoined appears from hence, that expressions of the same nature frequently occur in Scripture, upon which it is confessed on all hands that no such absolute and unlimited sense ought to be put. For example, *Love not the world; neither the things that are in the world; Lay not up for yourselves treasures upon earth; Take therefore no thought for the morrow;* are precepts expressed in at least equally absolute and unlimited terms: but it is generally allowed that they are to be understood with certain restrictions and limitations, some degree of love to the world and the things of it being allowable. Nor, indeed, do the *Right Reverend Fathers in God* and other *dignified clergymen* of the established church seem to be altogether averse to admitting of restrictions in the latter case, how warm soever any of them may be against restrictions and limitations in the case of submission to authority, whether civil or ecclesiastical. It is worth remarking, also, that patience and submission under private injuries are enjoined in much more peremptory and absolute terms than any that are used with regard to submission to the injustice and oppression of civil rulers. Thus, *I say unto you, that ye resist not evil; but whosoever shall smite thee on the right cheek, turn to him the other also. And if any man will sue thee at the law, and take away thy coat, let him have thy cloak also. And whosoever shall compel thee to go a mile with him, go with him twain.* Any man may be defied to produce such strong expressions in favor of a passive and tame submission to unjust, tyrannical rulers as are here used to enforce submission to private injuries. But how few are there that understand those expressions literally? And the reason why they do not is because (with submission to the *Quakers*) common sense shows that they were not intended to be so understood. * * *

There is, indeed, one passage in the New Testament where it may seem, at first view, that an unlimited submission to civil rulers is enjoined: *Submit yourselves to every ordinance of man for the Lord's sake.* ‡ 1 Pet. ii, 13.—To *every ordinance of man.* However, this expression is no stronger than that before taken notice of with relation to the duty of wives: *So let the wives be subject to their own husbands*—IN EVERY THING. But the true solution of this difficulty (if it be one) is *this:* by *every ordinance of man*§ is not meant every command of the civil magistrate without exception, but *every order of magistrates appointed by man,* whether *superior* or *inferior;* for so the Apostle explains himself in the very next words: *Whether it be to the king as supreme, or to governors, as unto them that are sent,* etc. But although the Apostle had not subjoined any such explanation, the reason of the thing itself would have obliged us to limit the expression *every ordinance of man* to such human ordinances and commands as are not inconsistent with the ordinances and commands of God, the supreme lawgiver, or with any other higher and antecedent obligations.

* * *

And if we attend to the nature of the argument with which the Apostle here enforces the duty of submission to *the higher powers,* we shall find it to be such an one as concludes not in favor of submission to all who bear the *title* of rulers in common, but only to those who *actually* perform the duty of rulers by exercising a reasonable and just authority for the good of human society. * * *

It is obvious, then, in general that the civil rulers whom the Apostle here speaks of, and obedience to whom he presses upon Christians as a duty, are *good rulers;* such as are, in the exercise of their office and power, benefactors to society. Such they are described to be throughout this passage. Thus it is said that they are not *a terror to good works but to the evil;* that they are *God's ministers for good, revengers to execute wrath upon him that doth evil; and that they attend continually upon this very thing.* St. *Peter* gives the same account of rulers: they are *for a praise to them that do well, and the punishment of evildoers.* It is manifest that this character and description of rulers agrees only to such as are rulers in fact as well as in name: to such as govern well and act agreeably to their office. And the Apostle's argument for submission to rulers is wholly built and grounded upon a presumption that they do in fact answer this character, and is of no force at all upon supposition to the contrary. If *rulers are a terror to good works and not to the evil;* if they are not *ministers for good to society* but for evil and distress by violence and oppression; if they *execute wrath upon* sober, peaceable persons who do their duty as members of society, and suffer rich and dishonorable knaves to escape with impunity; if, instead of *attending continually upon* the good work of advancing the public welfare, they *attend* only upon the gratification of their own lust and pride and ambition to the destruction of the public welfare—if this be the case, it is plain that the Apostle's argument for submission does not reach them; they are not the same but different persons from those whom he characterizes and who must be obeyed according to his reasoning. ✳ ✳ ✳

If those who bear the title of civil rulers do not perform the duty of civil rulers but act directly counter to the sole end and design of their office; if they injure and oppress their subjects instead of defending their rights and doing them good, they have not the least pretense to be honored, obeyed, and rewarded according to the Apostle's argument. For his reasoning, in order to show the duty of subjection to the *higher powers,* is, as was before observed, built wholly upon the supposition that they do *in fact* perform the duty of rulers. ✳ ✳ ✳

I now add, farther, that the Apostle's argument is so far from proving it to be the duty of people to obey and submit to such rulers as act in contradiction to the public good and so to the design of their office, that it proves *the direct contrary.* For, please to observe, that if the end of all civil government be the good of society, if this be the thing that is aimed at in constituting civil rulers, and if the motive and argument for submission to government be taken from the apparent usefulness of civil authority, it follows that when no such good end can be answered by submission there remains no argument or motive to enforce it; and if instead of this good end's being brought about by submission, a *contrary end* is brought about and the ruin and misery of society effected by it, here is a plain and positive reason against submission in all such cases, should they ever happen. And therefore, in such cases a regard to the public welfare ought to make us withhold from our rulers that obedience and subjection which it would, otherwise, be our duty to render to them. If it be our duty, for example, to obey our King merely for this reason, that he rules for the public welfare (which is the only argument the Apostle makes use of), it follows by a parity of reason that when he turns tyrant and makes his subjects his prey to devour and to destroy instead of his charge to defend and cherish, we are bound to throw off our allegiance to him and to resist, and that according to the tenor of the Apostle's argument in this passage. Not to discontinue our allegiance, in this case, would be to join with the sovereign in promoting the slavery and misery of that society the welfare of which we ourselves as well as our sovereign are indispensably obliged to secure and promote as far as in us lies. It is true the Apostle puts no case of such a tyrannical prince; but by his grounding his argument for submission wholly upon the good of civil society it is plain he implicitly authorizes and even requires us to make resistance whenever this shall be necessary to the public safety and happiness. Let me make use of this easy and familiar *similitude* to illustrate the point in hand. Suppose God requires a family of children to obey their father and not to resist him, and enforces his command with this argument: that the superintendence and care and authority of a just and kind parent will contribute to the happiness of the whole family so that they ought to obey him for their own sakes more than for his. Suppose this parent at length runs distracted, and attempts, in his mad fit, to cut all his children's throats. Now, in this case, is not the reason before assigned why these children should obey their parent while he continued of a sound mind, namely, *their common good*, a reason equally conclusive for disobeying and resisting him since he is become delirious and attempts their ruin? It makes no alteration in the argument, whether this parent properly speaking loses his reason, or does, while he retains his understanding, that which is as fatal in its consequences as anything he could do were he really deprived of it. This similitude needs no formal application. * * *

Thus it appears that the common argument, grounded upon this passage, in favor of universal and passive obedience really overthrows itself by proving too much, if it proves anything at all; namely, that no civil officer is, in any case whatever, to be resisted, though acting in express contradiction to the design of his office; which no man in his senses ever did or can assert.

If we calmly consider the nature of the thing itself, nothing can well be imagined more directly contrary to common sense than to suppose that *millions* of people should be subjected to the arbitrary, precarious pleasure of *one single man* (who has *naturally* no superiority over them in point of authority) so that their estates, and everything that is valuable in life, and even their lives also shall be absolutely at his disposal, if he happens to be wanton and capricious enough to demand them. What unprejudiced man can think that God made ALL to be thus subservient to the lawless pleasure and frenzy of ONE so that it shall always be a sin to resist him! Nothing but the most plain and express revelation from Heaven could make a sober impartial man believe such a monstrous, unaccountable doctrine; and, indeed, the thing itself appears so shocking—so out of all *proportion*, that it may be questioned whether all the *miracles* that ever were wrought could make it credible that this doctrine *really* came from God. At present, there is not the least syllable in Scripture which gives any countenance to it. The hereditary, indefeasible, divine right of kings, and the doctrine of nonresistance, which is built upon the supposition of such a right, are altogether as fabulous and chimerical as transubstantiation or any of the most absurd reveries of ancient or modern visionaries. These notions are fetched neither from divine revelation nor human reason; and if they are derived from neither of those sources, it is not much matter from *whence they come, or whither they go.* Only it is a pity that such doctrines should be propagated in society, to raise factions and rebellions, as we see they have in fact been, both in the *last* and in the *present* REIGN. * * *

We may very safely assert these two things in general without undermining government: One is that no civil rulers are to be obeyed when they enjoin things that are inconsistent with the commands of God. All such disobedience is lawful and glorious, particularly if persons refuse to comply with any *legal establishment of religion,* because it is a gross perversion and corruption (as to doctrine, worship, and discipline) of a pure and divine religion brought from heaven to earth by the *Son of God* (the only King and Head of the *Christian* church) and propagated through the world by his inspired apostles. All commands running counter to the declared will of the Supreme Legislator of heaven and earth are null and void: and therefore disobedience to them is a duty, not a crime. Another thing that may be asserted with equal truth and safety is that no government is to be submitted to at the *expense* of that which is the *sole end* of all government—the common good and safety of society. Because to submit in this case, if it should ever happen, would evidently be to set up the *means* as more valuable and above the *end,* than which there cannot be a greater solecism and contradiction. The only reason of the institution of civil government, and the only rational ground of submission to it, is the common safety and utility. If, therefore, in any case the common safety and utility would not be promoted by submission to government but the contrary, there is no ground or motive for obedience and submission, but for the contrary.

Whoever considers the nature of civil government must, indeed, be sensible that a great degree of *implicit confidence* must unavoidably be placed in those that bear rule. This is implied in the very notion of authority's being originally a *trust,* committed by the people to those who are vested with it as all just and righteous authority is; all besides is mere lawless force and usurpation, neither God nor nature having given any man a right of dominion over any society independently of that society's approbation and consent to be governed by him.—Now as all men are fallible, it cannot be supposed that the public affairs of any state should be always administered in the best manner possible, even by persons of the greatest wisdom and integrity. Nor is it sufficient to legitimate disobedience to the *higher powers* that they are not so administered, or that they are, in some instances, very ill-managed; for upon this principle it is scarcely supposable that any government at all could be supported or subsist. Such a principle manifestly tends to the dissolution of government, and to throw all things into confusion and anarchy.—But it is equally evident, upon the other hand, that those in authority may abuse their *trust* and power *to such a degree* that neither the law of reason nor of religion requires that any obedience or submission should be paid to them; but, on the contrary, that they should be totally *discarded* and the authority which they were before vested with transferred to others, who may exercise it more to those good purposes for which it is given. Nor is this principle, that resistance to the *higher powers* is, in some extraordinary cases, justifiable, so liable to abuse as many persons seem to apprehend it. For although there will be always some petulant, querulous men in every state—men of factious, turbulent, and carping dispositions—glad to lay hold of any trifle to justify and legitimate their caballing against their rulers and other seditious practices; yet there are, comparatively speaking, but few men of this *contemptible character*. It does not appear but that mankind in general have a disposition to be as submissive and passive and tame under government as they ought to be—witness a great, if not the greatest, part of the known world, who are now groaning, but not murmuring, under the heavy yoke of tyranny! While those who govern do it with any tolerable degree of moderation and justice and, in any good measure, act up to their office and character by being public benefactors, the people will generally be easy and peaceable, and be rather inclined to flatter and adore than to insult and resist them. Nor was there ever any *general* complaint against any administration *which lasted long* but what there was good reason for. Till people find themselves greatly abused and oppressed by their governors, they are not apt to complain; and whenever they do, in fact, find themselves thus abused and oppressed, they must be stupid not to complain. To say that subjects in general are not proper judges when their governors oppress them and play the tyrant and when they defend their rights, administer justice impartially, and promote the public welfare, is as great *treason* as ever man uttered: 'tis treason not against one *single* man but the state—against the whole body politic; 'tis treason against mankind; 'tis treason against common sense; 'tis treason against God. And this impious principle lays the foundation for justifying all the tyranny and oppression that ever any prince was guilty of. The people know for what end they set up and maintain their governors; and they are the proper judges when they execute their *trust* as they ought to do it—when their prince exercises an equitable and paternal authority over them; when from a prince and common father he exalts himself into a tyrant; when from subjects and children he degrades them into the class of slaves, plunders them, makes them his prey, and unnaturally sports himself with their lives and fortunes. ∗ ∗ ∗

To conclude: Let us all learn to be *free* and to be *loyal*. Let us not profess ourselves vassals to the lawless pleasure of any man on earth. But let us remember, at the same time, government is *sacred* and not to be *trifled* with. It is our happiness to live under the government of a PRINCE who is satisfied with ruling according to law, as every other *good prince* will. We enjoy under his administration all the liberty that is proper and expedient for us. It becomes us, therefore, to be contented and dutiful subjects. Let us prize our freedom but not *use our liberty for a cloak of maliciousness*. There are men who strike at *liberty* under the term *licentiousness*. There are others who aim at *popularity* under the disguise of *patriotism*. Be aware of both. *Extremes* are dangerous. There is at present amongst *us*, perhaps, more danger of the *latter* than of the *former*. For which reason I would exhort you to pay all due regard to the government over us, to the KING and all in authority, and to lead a *quiet and peaceable* life. And while I am speaking of loyalty to our *earthly prince,* suffer me just to put you in mind to be loyal also to the supreme RULER of the universe, *by whom kings reign and princes decree justice.* To which King eternal, immortal, invisible, even to the ONLY WISE GOD be all honor and praise, DOMINION and thanksgiving, through JESUS CHRIST our LORD. AMEN.

COTTON MATHER

A Christian at His Calling (1701)

Foundational Protestant teachings on the calling are found in this famous 1701 sermon by the influential Boston preacher Cotton Mather (1663–1728). God calls humanity not only to serve him, but also to labor in an occupation that both honors God and serves human society.

What is your OCCUPATION? Genesis, XLVII. 3.

Tis taken for granted then that they had *One.* It was the *Question* that *Pharaoh* put unto the Sons of *Jacob.* And it implies that every true *Israelite* should be able to give a good *Answer* unto such a *Question.* The *Question* which we are now to Discourse upon is, How a Christian may come to give a *Good Answer* unto that *Question?* or, How a Christian may come to give a *Good Account* of his *Occupation* & of his Behaviour in it?

There are *Two Callings* to be minded by *All Christians*. Every Christian hath a GENERAL CALLING, Which is to Serve the Lord Jesus Christ and Save his own Soul in the Services of *Religion* that are incumbent on all the Children of men. God hath *called* us to *Believe* on His *Son,* and *Repent* of our *Sin,* and observe the Sacred Means of our *Communion* with Himself, and bear our *Testimony* to His *Truths* and *Wayes* in the World: And every man in the world should herein conform to the Calls of that God, who *hath called us with this Holy Calling.* But then, every Christian hath also a PERSONAL CALLING; or, a certain *Particular Employment* by which his *Usefulness* in his Neighbourhood is distinguished. God hath made man a *Sociable* Creature. We expect Benefits from *Humane Society.* It is but equal, that *Humane Society* should Receive Benefits from *Us.* We are Beneficial to *Humane Society* by the Works of that Special OCCUPATION in which we are to be employ'd according to the Order of God.

A Christian, at his *Two Callings*, is a man in a Boat, Rowing for Heaven, the *House* which our Heavenly Father hath intended for us. If he mind but one of his *Callings*, be it which it will, he pulls the *Oar* but on *one side* of the Boat, and will make but a poor dispatch to the Shoar of Eternal Blessedness. . . .

BENJAMIN FRANKLIN

The Way to Wealth (1758)

Benjamin Franklin (1706–1790) was the most celebrated American of his day. He achieved fame as a printer, writer, statesman, diplomat, scientist, and inventor after he left his brother's Boston printing shop at the age of seventeen to make a fresh start in Philadelphia. He founded the University of Pennsylvania, the American Philosophical Society, and the first subscription library in America. The following selection is taken from the preface of Poor Richard Improved, *in which a fictitious old man called Father Abraham harangues a crowd with sayings collected from the equally fictitious Poor Richard Saunders. In this assault on the vices of idleness and sloth, Franklin promoted the*

Protestant work ethic with such memorable lines as "Early to bed, and
early to rise, makes a Man healthy, wealthy and wise."

"Friends, says he, and Neighbours, the Taxes are indeed very heavy, and if those laid on by the Government were the only Ones we had to pay, we might more easily discharge them; but we have many others, and much more grievous to some of us. We are taxed twice as much by our *Idleness*, three times as much by our *Pride*, and four times as much by our *Folly*, and from these Taxes the Commissioners cannot ease or deliver us by allowing an Abatement. However let us hearken to good Advice, and something may be done for us; *God helps them that help themselves*, as *Poor Richard* says, in his Almanack of 1733.

It would be thought a hard Government that should tax its People one tenth Part of their *Time*, to be employed in its Service. But *Idleness* taxes many of us much more, if we reckon all that is spent in absolute *Sloth*, or doing of nothing, with that which is spent in idle Employments or Amusements, that amount to nothing. *Sloth*, by bringing on Diseases, absolutely shortens Life. *Sloth, like Rust, consumes faster than Labour wears, while the used Key is always bright*, as *Poor Richard* says. But *dost thou love Life, then do not squander Time, for that's the Stuff Life is made of*, as *Poor Richard* says.—How much more than is necessary do we spend in Sleep! forgetting that *The sleeping Fox catches no Poultry*, and that *there will be sleeping enough in the Grave*, as *Poor Richard* says. If Time be of all Things the most precious, *wasting Time* must be, as *Poor Richard* says, *the greatest Prodigality*, since, as he elsewhere tells us, *Lost Time is never found again*; and what we call *Time-enough, always proves little enough*: Let us then up and be doing, and doing to the Purpose; so by Diligence shall we do more with less Perplexity. *Sloth makes all Things difficult, but Industry all easy*, as *Poor Richard* says; and *He that riseth late, must trot all Day, and shall scarce overtake his Business at Night*. While *Laziness travels so slowly, that Poverty soon overtakes him*, as we read in *Poor Richard*, who adds, *Drive thy Business, let not that drive thee*; and *Early to Bed, and early to rise, makes a Man healthy, wealthy and wise.*

So what signifies *wishing* and *hoping* for better Times. We may make these Times better if we bestir ourselves. *Industry need not wish*, as *Poor Richard* says, and *He that lives upon Hope will die fasting. There are no Gains, without Pains*; then *Help Hands, for I have no Lands*, or if I have, they are smartly taxed. And, as *Poor Richard* likewise observes, *He that hath a Trade hath an Estate*, and *He that hath a Calling, hath an Office of Profit and Honour*; but then the *Trade* must be worked at, and the *Calling* well followed, or neither the *Estate*, nor the *Office*, will enable us to pay our Taxes.—If we are industrious we shall never starve; for, as *Poor Richard* says, *At the working Man's House* Hunger *looks in, but dares not enter.* Nor will the Bailiff or the Constable enter, for *Industry pays Debts, while Despair encreaseth them*, says *Poor Richard.*—What though you have found no Treasure, nor has any rich Relation left you a Legacy, *Diligence is the Mother of Good luck*, as *Poor Richard* says, *and God gives all Things to Industry.* Then *plough deep, while Sluggards sleep, and you shall have Corn to sell and to keep*, says *Poor Dick.* Work while it is called To-day, for you know not how much you may be hindered To-morrow, which makes *Poor Richard* say, *One To-day is worth two To-morrows*; and farther, *Have you somewhat to do To-morrow, do it To-day.* If you were a Servant, would you not be ashamed that a good Master should catch you idle? Are you then your own Master, *be ashamed to catch yourself idle*, as *Poor Dick* says. When there is so much to be done for yourself, your Family, your Country, and your gracious King, be up by Peep of Day; *Let not the Sun look down and say, Inglorious here he lies.* Handle your Tools without Mittens; remember that *the Cat in Gloves catches no Mice*, as *Poor Richard* says. 'Tis true there is much to be done, and perhaps you are weak handed, but stick to it steadily, and you will see great Effects, for *constant Dropping wears away Stones*, and by *Diligence and Patience the Mouse ate in two the Cable*; and *little Strokes fell great Oaks*, as *Poor Richard* says in his Almanack, the Year I cannot just now remember.

Methinks I hear some of you say, *Must a Man afford himself no Leisure?*—I will tell thee, my Friend, what *Poor Richard* says, *Employ thy Time well if thou meanest to gain Leisure*; and *since thou art not sure of a Minute, throw not away an Hour.* Leisure, is Time for doing something useful; this Leisure the diligent Man will obtain, but the lazy Man never; so that, as *Poor Richard* says, a *Life of Leisure and a Life of Laziness are two Things.* Do you imagine that Sloth will afford you more Comfort than Labour? No, for as *Poor Richard* says, *Trouble springs from Idleness, and grievous Toil from needless Ease. Many without Labour, would live by their* Wits *only, but they break for want of Stock.* Whereas Industry gives Comfort, and Plenty, and Respect: *Fly Pleasures, and they'll follow you. The diligent Spinner has a large Shift*; and *now I have a Sheep and a Cow, every Body bids me Good morrow*; all which is well said by *Poor Richard.*

But with our Industry, we must likewise be *steady, settled* and *careful,* and oversee our own Affairs *with our own Eyes*, and not trust too much to others; for, as *Poor Richard* says,

> *I never saw an oft removed Tree,*
> *Nor yet an oft removed Family,*
> *That throve so well as those that settled be.*

And again, *Three Removes is as bad as a Fire*; and again, *Keep thy Shop, and thy Shop will keep thee*; and again, *If you would have your Business done, go; If not, send.* And again,

> He that by the Plough would thrive,
> Himself must either hold or drive.

And again, *The Eye of a Master will do more Work than both his Hands*; and again, *Want of Care does us more Damage than Want of Knowledge*; and again, *Not to oversee Workmen, is to leave them your Purse open.* Trusting too much to others Care is the Ruin of many; for, as the *Almanack* says, *In the Affairs of this World, Men are saved, not by Faith, but by the Want of it*; but a Man's own Care is profitable; for, saith *Poor Dick, Learning is to the Studious*, and *Riches to the Careful*, as well as *Power to the Bold*, and *Heaven to the Virtuous*. And farther, *If you would have a faithful Servant, and one that you like, serve yourself.* And again, he adviseth to Circumspection and Care, even in the smallest Matters, because sometimes *a little Neglect may breed great Mischief*; adding, *For want of a Nail the Shoe was lost; for want of a Shoe the Horse was lost; and for want of a Horse the Rider was lost*, being overtaken and slain by the Enemy, all for want of Care about a Horse shoe Nail.

So much for Industry, my Friends, and Attention to one's own Business; but to these we must add *Frugality*, if we would make our *Industry* more certainly successful. A Man may, if he knows not how to save as he gets, *keep his Nose all his Life to the Grindstone*, and die not worth a *Groat* at last. *A fat Kitchen makes a lean Will*, as *Poor Richard* says; and,

> Many Estates are spent in the Getting,
> Since Women for Tea forsook Spinning and Knitting,
> And Men for Punch forsook Hewing and Splitting.

If you would be wealthy, says he, in another Almanack, *think of Saving as well as of Getting: The* Indies *have not made* Spain *rich, because her* Outgoes *are greater than her* Incomes. Away then with your expensive Follies, and you will not have so much Cause to complain of hard Times, heavy Taxes, and chargeable Families; for, as *Poor Dick* says,

> Women and Wine, Game and Deceit,
> Make the Wealth small, and the Wants great.

And farther, *What maintains one Vice, would bring up two Children.* You may think perhaps, That a *little* Tea, or a *little* Punch now and then, Diet a *little* more costly, Clothes a *little* finer, and a *little* Entertainment now and then, can be no *great* Matter; but remember what *Poor Richard* says, *Many* a Little *makes a Mickle*; and farther, *Beware of* little *Expences; a small Leak will sink a great Ship*; and again, *Who Dainties love, shall Beggars prove*; and moreover, *Fools make Feasts, and wise Men eat them.*

Here you are all got together at this Vendue of *Fineries* and *Knick-nacks.* You call them *Goods,* but if you do not take Care, they will prove *Evils* to some of you. You expect they will be sold *cheap,* and perhaps they may for less than they cost; but if you have no Occasion for them, they must be *dear* to you. Remember what *Poor Richard* says, *Buy what thou hast no Need of, and ere long thou shalt sell thy Necessaries.* And again, *At a great Pennyworth pause a while:* He means, that perhaps the Cheapness is *apparent* only, and not *real;* or the Bargain, by straitning thee in thy Business, may do thee more Harm than Good. For in another Place he says, *Many have been ruined by buying good Pennyworths.* Again, *Poor Richard* says, *'Tis foolish to lay out Money in a Purchase of Repentance;* and yet this Folly is practised every Day at Vendues, for want of minding the Almanack. *Wise Men,* as *Poor Dick* says, *learn by others Harms, Fools scarcely by their own;* but *Felix quem faciunt aliena Pericula cautum.* Many a one, for the Sake of Finery on the Back, have gone with a hungry Belly, and half starved their Families; *Silks and Sattins, Scarlet and Velvets,* as *Poor Richard* says, *put out the Kitchen Fire.* These are not the *Necessaries* of Life; they can scarcely be called the *Conveniencies,* and yet only because they look pretty, how many *want* to *have* them. The *artificial* Wants of Mankind thus become more numerous than the *natural;* and, as *Poor Dick* says, *For one* poor *Person, there are an hundred* indigent. By these, and other Extravagancies, the Genteel are reduced to Poverty, and forced to borrow of those whom they formerly despised, but who through *Industry* and *Frugality* have maintained their Standing; in which Case it appears plainly, that a *Ploughman on his Legs is higher than a Gentleman on his Knees,* as *Poor Richard* says. Perhaps they have had a small Estate left them which they knew not the Getting of; they think *'tis Day, and will never be Night;* that a little to be spent out of *so much,* is not worth minding; (*a Child and a Fool,* as *Poor Richard* says, *imagine* Twenty Shillings *and* Twenty Years *can never be spent*) but, *always taking out of, the Meal-tub, and never putting in, soon comes to the Bottom;* then, as *Poor Dick* says, *When the Well's dry, they know the Worth of Water.* But this they might have known before, if they had taken his Advice; *If you would know the Value of Money, go and try to borrow some;* for, *he that goes a borrowing goes a sorrowing;* and indeed so does he that lends to such People, when he goes *to get it in again.—Poor Dick* farther advises, and says,

>   *Fond Pride of Dress is sure a very Curse;*
>   *E'er Fancy you consult, consult your Purse.*

And again, *Pride is as loud a Beggar as Want, and a great deal more saucy.*
When you have bought one fine Thing you must buy ten more, that your
Appearance may be all of a Piece; but *Poor Dick* says, *'Tis easier to* sup-
press *the first Desire, than to* satisfy *all that follow it.* And 'tis as truly
Folly for the Poor to ape the Rich, as for the Frog to swell, in order to
equal the Ox.

>   *Great Estates may venture more,*
>   *But little Boats should keep near Shore.*

'Tis however a Folly soon punished; for *Pride that dines on Vanity sups on
Contempt*, as *Poor Richard* says. And in another Place, *Pride breakfasted
with Plenty, dined with Poverty, and supped with Infamy.* And after all, of
what Use is this *Pride of Appearance*, for which so much is risked, so
much is suffered? It cannot promote Health, or ease Pain; it makes no Increase of Merit in the Person, it creates Envy, it hastens Misfortune.

>   *What is a Butterfly? At best*
>   *He's but a Caterpillar drest.*
>   *The gaudy Fop's his Picture just,*

as *Poor Richard* says.

   But what Madness must it be to *run in Debt* for these Superfluities!
We are offered, by the Terms of this Vendue, *Six Months Credit*; and
that perhaps has induced some of us to attend it, because we cannot
spare the ready Money, and hope now to be fine without it. But, ah,
think what you do when you run in Debt; *You give to another, Power
over your Liberty.* If you cannot pay at the Time, you will be ashamed to
see your Creditor; you will be in Fear when you speak to him; you will
make poor pitiful sneaking Excuses, and by Degrees come to lose your
Veracity, and sink into base downright lying; for, as *Poor Richard* says,
The second Vice is Lying, the first is running in Debt. And again, to the
same Purpose, *Lying rides upon Debt's Back.* Whereas a freeborn *Englishman* ought not to be ashamed or afraid to see or speak to any Man
living. But Poverty often deprives a Man of all Spirit and Virtue: *'Tis
hard for an empty Bag to stand upright*, as *Poor Richard* truly says. What
would you think of that Prince, or that Government, who should issue
an Edict forbidding you to dress like a Gentleman or a Gentlewoman,
on Pain of Imprisonment or Servitude? Would you not say, that you are

free, have a Right to dress as you please, and that such an Edict would be a Breach of your Privileges, and such a Government tyrannical? And yet you are about to put yourself under that Tyranny when you run in Debt for such Dress! Your Creditor has Authority at his Pleasure to deprive you of your Liberty, by confining you in Goal [*sic*] for Life, or to sell you for a Servant, if you should not be able to pay him! When you have got your Bargain, you may, perhaps, think little of Payment; but *Creditors, Poor Richard* tells us, *have better Memories than Debtors;* and in another Place says, *Creditors are a superstitious Sect, great Observers of set Days and Times.* The Day comes round before you are aware, and the Demand is made before you are prepared to satisfy it. Or if you bear your Debt in Mind, the Term which at first seemed so long, will, as it lessens, appear extreamly short. *Time* will seem to have added Wings to his Heels as well as Shoulders. *Those have a short Lent,* saith *Poor Richard, who owe Money to be paid at Easter.* Then since, as he says, *The Borrower is a Slave to the Lender, and the Debtor to the Creditor,* disdain the Chain, preserve your Freedom; and maintain your Independency: Be *industrious* and *free;* be *frugal* and *free.* At present, perhaps, you may think yourself in thriving Circumstances, and that you can bear a little Extravangance [*sic*] without Injury; but,

> For Age and Want, save while you may;
> No Morning Sun lasts a whole Day,

as *Poor Richard* says—Gain may be temporary and uncertain, but ever while you live, Expence is constant and certain; and *'tis easier to build two Chimnies than to keep one in Fuel,* as *Poor Richard* says. So *rather go to Bed supperless than rise in Debt.*

> Get what you can, and what you get hold;
> 'Tis the Stone that will turn all your Lead into Gold,

as *Poor Richard* says. And when you have got the Philosopher's Stone, sure you will no longer complain of bad Times, or the Difficulty of paying Taxes.

This Doctrine, my Friends, is *Reason* and *Wisdom;* but after all, do not depend too much upon your own *Industry,* and *Frugality,* and *Prudence,* though excellent Things, for they may all be blasted without the Blessing of Heaven; and therefore ask that Blessing humbly, and be not uncharitable to those that at present seem to want it, but comfort and help them. Remember *Job* suffered, and was afterwards prosperous.

And now to conclude, *Experience keeps a dear School, but Fools will learn in no other, and scarce in that;* for it is true, *we may give Advice, but we cannot give Conduct,* as *Poor Richard* says: However, remember this, *They that won't be counselled, can't be helped,* as *Poor Richard* says: And farther, That *if you will not hear Reason, she'll surely rap your Knuckles.*

Thus the old Gentleman ended his Harangue. The People heard it, and approved the Doctrine and immediately practised the contrary, just as if it had been a common Sermon; for the Vendue opened, and they began to buy extravagantly, notwithstanding all his Cautions, and their own Fear of Taxes.—I found the good Man had thoroughly studied my Almanacks, and digested all I had dropt on those Topicks during the Course of Five-and-twenty Years. The frequent Mention he made of me must have tired any one else, but my Vanity was wonderfully delighted with it, though I was conscious that not a tenth Part of the Wisdom was my own which he ascribed to me, but rather the *Gleanings* I had made of the Sense of all Ages and Nations. However, I resolved to be the better for the Echo of it; and though I had at first determined to buy Stuff for a new Coat, I went away resolved to wear my old One a little longer. *Reader,* if thou wilt do the same, thy Profit will be as great as mine.

I am, as ever,

Thine to serve thee,

July 7, 1757.   RICHARD SAUNDERS.

BENJAMIN FRANKLIN

The Art of Virtue (1784)

Franklin's life was a classic example of the American rags-to-riches story. He extolled the virtues of an orderly life and strove for moral perfection through methodical practice. The following selection is from Part Two of Franklin's Autobiography, which he wrote to provide a useful and entertaining moral example of how it is possible to acquire the "habitudes of virtue." It remains to this day the classic American tale of self-creation, of the disciplined formation of the individual self.

I t was about this time I conceiv'd the bold and arduous project of arriving at moral perfection. I wish'd to live without committing any fault at any time; I would conquer all that either natural inclination, custom, or company might lead me into. As I knew, or thought I knew, what was right and wrong, I did not see why I might not always do the one and avoid the other. But I soon found I had undertaken a task of more difficulty than I had imagined. While my care was employ'd in guarding against one fault, I was often surprised by another; habit took the advantage of inattention; inclination was sometimes too strong for reason. I concluded, at length, that the mere speculative conviction that it was our interest to be completely virtuous, was not sufficient to prevent our slipping; and that the contrary habits must be broken, and good ones acquired and established, before we can have any dependence on a steady, uniform rectitude of conduct. For this purpose I therefore contrived the following method.

In the various enumerations of the moral virtues I had met with in my reading, I found the catalogue more or less numerous, as different writers included more or fewer ideas under the same name. Temperance, for example, was by some confined to eating and drinking, while by others it was extended to mean the moderating every other pleasure, appetite, inclination, or passion, bodily or mental, even to our avarice and ambition. I propos'd to myself, for the sake of clearness, to use rather more names, with fewer ideas annex'd to each, than a few names with more ideas; and I included under thirteen names of virtues all that at that time occurr'd to me as necessary or desirable, and annexed to each a short precept, which fully express'd the extent I gave to its meaning.

These names of virtues, with their precepts were:

1 *Temperance.* Eat not to dullness; drink not to elevation.
2 *Silence.* Speak not but what may benefit others or yourself; avoid trifling conversation.
3 *Order.* Let all your things have their places; let each part of your business have its time.
4 *Resolution.* Resolve to perform what you ought; perform without fail what you resolve.
5 *Frugality.* Make no expense but to do good to others or yourself; *i.e.*, waste nothing.
6 *Industry.* Lose no time; be always employ'd in something useful; cut off all unnecessary actions.
7 *Sincerity.* Use no hurtful deceit; think innocently and justly; and, if you speak, speak accordingly.
8 *Justice.* Wrong none by doing injuries, or omitting the benefits that are your duty.
9 *Moderation.* Avoid extreams; forbear resenting injuries so much as you think they deserve.

10 *Cleanliness*. Tolerate no uncleanliness in body, cloaths, or habitation.

11 *Tranquillity*. Be not disturbed at trifles, or at accidents common or unavoidable.

12 *Chastity*. Rarely use venery but for health or offspring, never to dulness, weakness, or the injury of your own or another's peace or reputation.

13 *Humility*. Imitate Jesus and Socrates.

My intention being to acquire the *habitude* of all these virtues, I judg'd it would be well not to distract my attention by attempting the whole at once, but to fix it on one of them at a time; and, when I should be master of that, then to proceed to another, and so on, till I should have gone thro' the thirteen; and, as the previous acquisition of some might facilitate the acquisition of certain others, I arrang'd them with that view, as they stand above. Temperance first, as it tends to procure that coolness and clearness of head, which is so necessary where constant vigilance was to be kept up, and guard maintained against the unremitting attraction of ancient habits, and the force of perpetual temptations. This being acquir'd and establish'd, Silence would be more easy; and my desire being to gain knowledge at the same time that I improv'd in virtue, and considering that in conversation it was obtain'd rather by the use of the ears than of the tongue, and therefore wishing to break a habit I was getting into of prattling, punning, and joking, which only made me acceptable to trifling company, I gave *Silence* the second place. This and the next, *Order*, I expected would allow me more time for attending to my project and my studies. *Resolution*, once become habitual, would keep me firm in my endeavors to obtain all the subsequent virtues; *Frugality* and Industry freeing me from my remaining debt, and producing affluence and independence, would make more easy the practice of Sincerity and Justice, etc., etc. Conceiving then, that, agreeably to the advice of Pythagoras in his Golden Verses, daily examination would be necessary, I contrived the following method for conducting that examination.

I made a little book, in which I allotted a page for each of the virtues. I rul'd each page with red ink, so as to have seven columns, one for each day of the week, marking each column with a letter for the day. I cross'd these columns with thirteen red lines, marking the beginning of each line with the first letter of one of the virtues, on which line, and in its proper column, I might mark, by a little black spot, every fault I found upon examination to have been committed respecting that virtue upon that day.

Form of Pages

	S.	M.	T.	W.	T.	F.	S.
TEMPERANCE.							
Eat Not to Dullness; Drink Not to Elevation.							
T.							
S.	*	*		*		*	
O.	* *	*	*		*	*	*
R.			*			*	
F.		*			*		
I.			*				
S.							
J.							
M.							
C.							
T.							
C.							
H.							

I determined to give a week's strict attention to each of the virtues successively. Thus, in the first week, my great guard was to avoid every the least offense against *Temperance,* leaving the other virtues to their ordinary chance, only marking every evening the faults of the day. Thus, if in the first week I could keep my first line, marked T, clear of spots, I suppos'd the habit of that virtue so much strengthen'd, and its opposite weaken'd, that I might venture extending my attention to include the next, and for the following week keep both lines clear of spots. Proceeding thus to the last, I could go thro' a course compleat in thirteen weeks, and four courses in a year. And like him who, having a garden to weed, does not attempt to eradicate all the bad herbs at once, which would exceed his reach and his strength, but works on one of the beds at a time, and, having accomplish'd the first, proceeds to a second, so I should have, I hoped, the encouraging pleasure of seeing on my pages the progress I made in virtue, by clearing successively my lines of their spots, till in the end, by a number of courses, I should be happy in viewing a clean book, after a thirteen weeks' daily examination. * * *

The precept of *Order* requiring that *every part of my business should have its allotted time*, one page in my little book contain'd the following scheme of employment for the twenty-four hours of a natural day.

THE MORNING.
Question. What good shall
I do this day?

5	Rise, wash, and address *Powerful Goodness!* Contrive day's business, and take the resolution of the day; prosecute the present study, and breakfast.
6	
7	
8	Work.
9	
10	
11	

NOON.

12	Read, or overlook my accounts, and dine.
1	
2	Work.
3	
4	
5	

EVENING.
Question. What good have
I done to-day?

6	Put things in their places. Supper.
7	Music or diversion, or conversation.
8	Examination of the day.
9	

NIGHT.

10	Sleep.
11	
12	
1	
2	
3	
4	

I enter'd upon the execution of this plan for self-examination, and continu'd it with occasional intermissions for some time. I was surpris'd to find myself so much fuller of faults than I had imagined; but I had the satisfaction of seeing them diminish. To avoid the trouble of renewing now and then my little book, which, by scraping out the marks on the paper of old faults to make room for new ones in a new course, became full of holes, I transferr'd my tables and precepts to the ivory leaves of a memorandum book, on which the lines were drawn with red ink, that made a durable stain, and on those lines I mark'd my faults with a black-lead pencil, which marks I could easily wipe out with a wet sponge. After a while I went thro' one course only in a year, and afterward only one in several years, till at length I omitted them entirely, being employ'd in voyages and business abroad, with a multiplicity of affairs that interfered; but I always carried my little book with me.

My scheme of ORDER gave me the most trouble; and I found that, tho' it might be practicable where a man's business was such as to leave him the disposition of his time, that of a journeyman printer, for instance, it was not possible to be exactly observed by a master, who must mix with the world, and often receive people of business at their own hours. *Order*, too, with regard to places for things, papers, etc., I found extreamly difficult to acquire. I had not been early accustomed to it, and, having an exceeding good memory, I was not so sensible of the inconvenience attending want of method. This article, therefore, caused me so much painful attention, and my faults in it vexed me so much, and I made so little progress in amendment, and had such frequent relapses, that I was almost ready to give up the attempt, and content myself with a faulty character in that respect, like the man who, in buying an ax of a smith, my neighbour, desired to have the whole of its surface as bright as the edge. The smith consented to grind it bright for him if he would turn the wheel; he turn'd, while the smith press'd the broad face of the ax hard and heavily on the stone, which made the turning of it very fatiguing. The man came every now and then from the wheel to see how the work went on, and at length would take his ax as it was, without farther grinding. "No," said the smith, "turn on, turn on; we shall have it bright by-and-by; as yet, it is only speckled." "Yes," says the man, *"but I think I like a speckled ax best."* And I believe this may have been the case with many, who, having, for want of some such means as I employ'd, found the difficulty of obtaining good and breaking bad habits in other points of vice and virtue, have given up the struggle, and concluded that *"a speckled ax was best;"* for something, that pretended to be reason, was every now and then suggesting to me that such extream nicety as I exacted of myself might be a kind of foppery in morals, which, if it were known, would make me ridiculous; that a perfect character might be attended with the inconvenience of being envied and hated; and that a benevolent man should allow a few faults in himself, to keep his friends in countnance.

In truth, I found myself incorrigible with respect to Order; and now I am grown old, and my memory bad, I feel very sensibly the want of it. But, on the whole, tho' I never arrived at the perfection I had been so ambitious of obtaining, but fell far short of it, yet I was, by the endeavour, a better and a happier man than I otherwise should have been if I had not attempted it; as those who aim at perfect writing by imitating the engraved copies, tho' they never reach the wish'd-for excellence of those copies, their hand is mended by the endeavor, and is tolerable while it continues fair and legible.

It may be well my posterity should be informed that to this little artifice, with the blessing of God, their ancestor ow'd the constant felicity of his life, down to his 79th year, in which this is written. What reverses may attend the remainder is in the hand of Providence; but, if they arrive, the reflection on past happiness enjoy'd ought to help his bearing them with more resignation. To Temperance he ascribes his long-continued health, and what is still left to him of a good constituion; to Industry and Frugality, the early easiness of his circumstances and acquisition of his fortune, with all that knowledge that enabled him to be a useful citizen, and obtained for him some degree of reputation among the learned; to Sincerity and Justice, the confidence of his country, and the honorable employs it conferred upon him; and to the joint influence of the whole mass of the virtues, even in the imperfect state he was able to acquire them, all that evenness of temper, and that cheerfulness in conversation, which makes his company still sought for, and agreeable even to his younger acquaintance. I hope, therefore, that some of my descendants may follow the example and reap the benefit.

BENJAMIN FRANKLIN

Information to Those Who Would Remove to America (1784)

In response to numerous inquiries from Europeans interested in settling in North America, Franklin set out to correct several misconceptions they might have about the possibility of easy success in America. In an important and prescient text laying out what would become the core of Americans' sense of themselves and their specialness, Franklin explained that everyone must work in America because individuals are valued there for what they do, not for who they are. Consequently, America was a land of "happy Mediocrity" with no extremes of rich or

poor, and no room for the idle rich. Hard work and equal opportunity
are characteristics of American life.

M any Persons in Europe having directly or by Letters, express'd to
the Writer of this, who is well acquainted with North-America,
their Desire of transporting and establishing themselves in that Country;
but who appear to him to have formed thro' Ignorance, mistaken Ideas &
Expectations of what is to be obtained there; he thinks it may be useful,
and prevent inconvenient, expensive & fruitless Removals and Voyages of
improper Persons, if he gives some clearer & truer Notions of that Part of
the World than appear to have hitherto prevailed.

   He finds it is imagined by Numbers that the Inhabitants of North-
America are rich, capable of rewarding, and dispos'd to reward all sorts of
Ingenuity; that they are at the same time ignorant of all the Sciences; &
consequently that strangers possessing Talents in the Belles-Letters, fine
Arts, &c. must be highly esteemed, and so well paid as to become easily
rich themselves; that there are also abundance of profitable Offices to be
disposed of, which the Natives are not qualified to fill; and that having
few Persons of Family among them, Strangers of Birth must be greatly respected, and of course easily obtain the best of those Offices, which will
make all their Fortunes: that the Goverments too, to encourage Emigra-
tions from Europe, not only pay the expence of personal Transportation,
but give Lands gratis to Strangers, with Negroes to work for them, Utensils of Husbandry, & Stocks of Cattle. These are all wild Imaginations;
and those who go to America with Expectations founded upon them, will
surely find themselves disappointed.

   The Truth is, that tho' there are in that Country few People so miserable
as the Poor of Europe, there are also very few that in Europe would be
called rich: it is rather a general happy Mediocrity that prevails. There are
few great Proprietors of the Soil, and few Tenants; most People cultivate
their own Lands, or follow some Handicraft or Merchandise; very few rich
enough to live idly upon their Rents or Incomes; or to pay the high Prices
given in Europe, for Paintings, Statues, Architecture and the other Works
of Art that are more curious than useful. Hence the natural Geniuses that
have arisen in America, with such Talents, have uniformly quitted that
Country for Europe, where they can be more suitably rewarded. It is true
that Letters and mathematical Knowledge are in Esteem there, but they
are at the same time more common than is apprehended; there being
already existing nine Colleges or Universities, viz. four in New-England,
and one in each of the Provinces of New-York, New-Jersey, Pensilvania,
Maryland and Virginia, all furnish'd with learned Professors; besides a
number of smaller Academies: These educate many of their Youth in the

Languages and those Sciences that qualify Men for the Professions of Divinity, Law or Physick. Strangers indeed are by no means excluded from exercising those Professions, and the quick Increase of Inhabitants every where gives them a Chance of Employ, which they have in common with the Natives. Of civil Offices or Employments there are few; no superfluous Ones as in Europe; and it is a Rule establish'd in some of the States, that no Office should be so profitable as to make it desirable. The 36 Article of the Constitution of Pensilvania, runs expresly in these Words: *As every Freeman, to preserve his Independance, (if he has not a sufficient Estate) ought to have some Profession, Calling, Trade or Farm, whereby he may honestly subsist, there can be no Necessity for, nor Use in, establishing Offices of Profit; the usual Effects of which are Dependance and Servility, unbecoming Freemen, in the Possessors and Expectants; Faction, Contention, Corruption, and Disorder among the People. Wherefore whenever an Office, thro' Increase of Fees or otherwise, becomes so profitable as to occasion many to apply for it, the Profits ought to be lessened by the Legislature.*

These Ideas prevailing more or less in all the United States, it cannot be worth any Man's while, who has a means of Living at home, to expatriate himself in hopes of obtaining a profitable civil Office in America; and as to military Offices, they are at an End with the War; the Armies being disbanded. Much less is it adviseable for a Person to go thither who has no other Quality to recommend him but his Birth. In Europe it has indeed its Value, but it is a Commodity that cannot be carried to a worse Market than to that of America, where People do not enquire concerning a Stranger, *What is he?* but *What can he do?* If he has any useful Art, he is welcome; and if he exercises it and behaves well, he will be respected by all that know him; but a mere Man of Quality, who on that Account wants to live upon the Public, by some Office or Salary, will be despis'd and disregarded. The Husbandman is in honor there, & even the Mechanic, because their Employments are useful. The People have a Saying, that God Almighty is himself a Mechanic, the greatest in the Universe; and he is respected and admired more for the Variety, Ingenuity and Utility of his Handiworks, than for the Antiquity of his Family. They are pleas'd with the Observation of a Negro, and frequently mention it, that *Boccarorra* (meaning the Whiteman) make de Blackman workee, make de Horse workee, make de Ox workee, make ebery ting workee; only de Hog. He de Hog, no workee; he eat, he drink, he walk about, he go to sleep when he please, *he libb like a Gentleman.* According to these Opinions of the Americans, one of them would think himself more oblig'd to a Genealogist, who could prove for him that his Ancestors & Relations for ten Generations had been Ploughmen, Smiths, Carpenters, Turners, Weavers, Tanners, or even Shoemakers, & consequently that they were useful Members of Society; than if he could only prove that they were Gentlemen, doing nothing of Value, but living idly on the Labour of others, mere *fruges consumere nati*, and otherwise *good* for *nothing*, till by their Death, their Estates like the Carcase of the Negro's Gentleman-Hog, come to be *cut up*.

With Regard to Encouragements for Strangers from Government, they are really only what are derived from good Laws & Liberty. Strangers are welcome because there is room enough for them all, and therefore the old Inhabitants are not jealous of them; the Laws protect them sufficiently, so that they have no need of the Patronage of great Men; and every one will enjoy securely the Profits of his Industry. But if he does not bring a Fortune with him, he must work and be industrious to live. One or two Years Residence give him all the Rights of a Citizen; but the Government does not at present, whatever it may have done in former times, hire People to become Settlers, by Paying their Passages, giving Land, Negroes, Utensils, Stock, or any other kind of Emolument whatsoever. In short America is the Land of Labour, and by no means what the English call *Lubberland,* and the French *Pays de Cocagne*, where the Streets are said to be pav'd with half-peck Loaves, the Houses til'd with Pancakes, and where the Fowls fly about ready roasted, crying, *Come eat me!*

Who then are the kind of Persons to whom an Emigration to America may be advantageous? and what are the Advantages they may reasonably expect?

Land being cheap in that Country, from the vast Forests still void of Inhabitants, and not likely to be occupied in an Age to come, insomuch that the Propriety of an hundred Acres of fertile Soil full of Wood may be obtained near the Frontiers in many Places for eight or ten Guineas, hearty young Labouring Men, who understand the Husbandry of Corn and Cattle, which is nearly the same in that Country as in Europe, may easily establish themselves there. A little Money sav'd of the good Wages they receive there while they work for others, enables them to buy the Land and begin their Plantation, in which they are assisted by the Good Will of their Neighbours and some Credit. Multitudes of poor People from England, Ireland, Scotland and Germany, have by this means in a few Years become wealthy Farmers, who in their own Countries, where all the Lands are fully occupied, and the Wages of Labour low, could never have emerged from the mean Condition wherein they were born.

From the Salubrity of the Air, the Healthiness of the Climate, the Plenty of good Provisions, and the Encouragement to early Marriages, by the certainty of Subsistance in cultivating the Earth, the Increase of Inhabitants by natural Generation is very rapid in America, and becomes still more so by the Accession of Strangers; hence there is a continual Demand for more Artisans of all the necessary and useful kinds, to supply those Cultivators of the Earth with Houses, and with Furniture & Utensils of the grosser Sorts which cannot so well be brought from Europe. Tolerably good Workmen in any of those mechanic Arts, are sure to find Employ, and to be well paid for their Work, there being no Restraints preventing Strangers from exercising any Art they understand, nor any Permission necessary. If they are poor, they begin first as Servants or Journeymen; and if they are sober, industrious & frugal, they soon become Masters, establish themselves in Business, marry, raise Families, and become respectable Citizens.

Also, Persons of moderate Fortunes and Capitals, who having a Number of Children to provide for, are desirous of bringing them up to Industry, and to secure Estates for their Posterity, have Opportunities of doing it in America, which Europe does not afford. There they may be taught & practice profitable mechanic Arts, without incurring Disgrace on that Account; but on the contrary acquiring Respect by such Abilities. ✳ ✳ ✳

Several of the Princes of Europe having of late Years, from an Opinion of Advantage to arise by producing all Commodities & Manufactures within their own Dominions, so as to diminish or render useless their Importations, have endeavoured to entice Workmen from other Countries, by high Salaries, Privileges, &c. Many Persons pretending to be skilled in various great Manufactures, imagining that America must be in Want of them, and that the Congress would probably be dispos'd to imitate the Princes above mentioned, have proposed to go over, on Condition of having their Passages paid, Lands given, Salaries appointed, exclusive Privileges for Terms of Years, &c. Such Persons on reading the Articles of Confederation will find that the Congress have no Power committed to them, or Money put into their Hands, for such purposes; and that if any such Encouragement is given, it must be by the Government of some separate State. This however has rarely been done in America; and when it has been done it has rarely succeeded, so as to establish a Manufacture which the Country was not yet so ripe for as to encourage private Persons to set it up; Labour being generally too dear there, & Hands difficult to be kept together, every one desiring to be a Master, and the Cheapness of Land enclining many to leave Trades for Agriculture. Some indeed have met with Success, and are carried on to Advantage; but they are generally such as require only a few Hands, or wherein great Part of the Work is perform'd by Machines. Goods that are bulky, & of so small Value as not well to bear the Expence of Freight, may often be made cheaper in the Country than they can be imported; and the Manufacture of such Goods will be profitable wherever there is a sufficient Demand. The Farmers in America produce indeed a good deal of Wool & Flax; and none is exported, it is all work'd up; but it is in the Way of Domestic Manufacture for the

Use of the Family. The buying up Quantities of Wool & Flax with the Design to employ Spinners, Weavers, &c. and form great Establishments, producing Quantities of Linen and Woollen Goods for Sale, has been several times attempted in different Provinces; but those Projects have generally failed, Goods of equal Value being imported cheaper. And when the Governments have been solicited to support such Schemes by Encouragements, in Money, or by imposing Duties on Importation of such Goods, it has been generally refused, on this Principle, that if the Country is ripe for the Manufacture, it may be carried on by private Persons to Advantage; and if not, it is a Folly to think of forceing Nature. Great Establishments of Manufacture, require great Numbers of Poor to do the Work for small Wages; these Poor are to be found in Europe, but will not be found in America, till the Lands are all taken up and cultivated, and the excess of People who cannot get Land, want Employment. The Manufacture of Silk, they say, is natural in France, as that of Cloth in England, because each Country produces in Plenty the first Material: But if England will have a Manufacture of Silk as well as that of Cloth, and France one of Cloth as well as that of Silk, these unnatural Operations must be supported by mutual Prohibitions or high Duties on the Importation of each others Goods, by which means the Workmen are enabled to tax the home-Consumer by greater Prices, while the higher Wages they receive makes them neither happier nor richer, since they only drink more and work less. Therefore the Governments in America do nothing to encourage such Projects. The People by this Means are not impos'd on, either by the Merchant or Mechanic; if the Merchant demands too much Profit on imported Shoes, they buy of the Shoemaker: and if he asks too high a Price, they take them of the Merchant: thus the two Professions are Checks on each other. The Shoemaker however has on the whole a considerable Profit upon his Labour in America, beyond what he had in Europe, as he can add to his Price a Sum nearly equal to all the Expences of Freight & Commission, Risque or Insurance, &c. necessarily charged by the Merchant. And the Case is the same with the Workmen in every other Mechanic Art. Hence it is that Artisans generally live better and more easily in America than in Europe, and such as are good Œconomists make a comfortable Provision for Age, & for their Children. Such may therefore remove with Advantage to America.

In the old longsettled Countries of Europe, all Arts, Trades, Professions, Farms, &c. are so full that it is difficult for a poor Man who has Children, to place them where they may gain, or learn to gain a decent Livelihood. The Artisans, who fear creating future Rivals in Business, refuse to take Apprentices, but upon Conditions of Money, Maintenance or the like, which the Parents are unable to comply with. Hence the Youth are dragg'd up in Ignorance of every gainful Art, and oblig'd to become Soldiers or Servants or Thieves, for a Subsistance. In America the rapid Increase of Inhabitants takes away that Fear of Rivalship, & Artisans willingly receive Apprentices from the hope of Profit by their Labour during the Remainder of the Time stipulated after they shall be instructed. Hence it is easy for poor Families to get their Children instructed; for the Artisans are so desirous of Apprentices, that many of them will even give Money to the Parents to have Boys from ten to fifteen Years of Age bound Apprentices to them till the Age of twenty one; and many poor Parents have by that means, on their Arrival in the Country, raised Money enough to buy Land sufficient to establish themselves, and to subsist the rest of their Family by Agriculture. * * *

The almost general Mediocrity of Fortune that prevails in America, obliging its People to follow some Business for Subsistance, those Vices that arise usually from Idleness are in a great Measure prevented. Industry and constant Employment are great Preservatives of the Morals and Virtue of a Nation. Hence bad Examples to Youth are more rare in America, which must be a comfortable Consideration to Parents. To this may be truly added, that serious Religion under its various Denominations, is not only tolerated but respected and practised. Atheism is unknown there, Infidelity rare & secret, so that Persons may live to a great Age in that Country without having their Piety shock'd by meeting with either an Atheist or an Infidel. And the Divine Being seems to have manifested his Approbation of the mutual Forbearance and Kindness with which the different Sects treat each other, by the remarkable Prosperity with which he has been pleased to favour the whole Country.

Self-Government

The Mayflower Compact (1620)

Before the Pilgrims landed at Plymouth in New England, they pledged to govern themselves according to mutually agreed-on laws. Also known as the Plymouth Combination, the covenant that they signed on the Mayflower was the basis of government in the colony. The actual document was eventually lost, but its historic significance was indelibly captured in 1802 by John Quincy Adams, the future president and a descendant of one of its signers. He described it as the first example of a government created by voluntary consent.

In the Name of God, Amen. We, whose names are underwritten, the Loyal Subjects of our dread Sovereign Lord King James, by the Grace of God, of Great Britain, France, and Ireland, King, Defender of the Faith, etc. Having undertaken for the Glory of God, and Advancement of the Christian Faith, and the Honour of our King and Country, a Voyage to plant the first Colony in the northern Parts of Virginia; Do by these Presents, solemnly and mutually, in the Presence of God and one another, covenant and combine ourselves together into a civil Body Politick, for our better Ordering and Preservation, and Furtherance of the Ends aforesaid: And by Virtue hereof do enact, constitute, and frame, such just and equal Laws, Ordinances, Acts, Constitutions, and Officers, from time to time, as shall be thought most meet and convenient for the general Good of the Colony; unto which we promise all due Submission and Obedience. In Witness whereof we have hereunto subscribed our names at Cape-Cod the eleventh of November, in the Reign of our Sovereign Lord King James, of England, France, and Ireland, the eighteenth, and of Scotland, the fifty-fourth, Anno Domini, 1620.

An Ordinance and Constitution
of the Virginia Company (1621)

The Virginia House of Burgesses established one of the first precedents for self-government in the American colonies. This document is believed to be a reissue of the original instructions that established the Virginia assembly.

An Ordinance and Constitution of the Treasurer Council, and Company in England, for a Council of State and General Assembly.

I To all people, to whom these presents shall come, be seen, or heard, the treasurer, council, and company of adventurers and planters for the city of London for the first colony of Virginia, send greeting. Know ye, that we, the said treasurer, council, and company, taking into our careful consideration the present state of the said colony of Virginia, and intending by the divine assistance, to settle such a form of government there, as may be to the greatest benefit and comfort of the people, and whereby all injustice, grievances, and oppression may be prevented and kept off as much as possible, from the said colony, have thought fit to make our entrance, by ordering and establishing such supreme councils, as may not only be assisting to the governor for the time being, in the administration of justice, and the executing of other duties to this office belonging, but also, by their vigilant care and prudence, may provide, as well for a remedy of all inconveniences, growing from time to time, as also for advancing of increase, strength, stability, and prosperity of the said colony:

II. We therefore, the said treasurer, council, and company, by authority directed to us from his majesty under the great seal, upon mature deliberation, do hereby order and declare, that, from hence forward, there shall be two supreme councils in Virginia, for the better government of the said colony aforesaid.

III. The one of which councils, to be called the council of state (and whose office shall chiefly be assisting, with their care, advice, and circumspection, to the said governor) shall be chosen, nominated, placed, and displaced, from time to time, by us the said treasurer, council and company, and our successors. * * * Which said counsellors and council we earnestly pray and desire, and in his majesty's name strictly charge and command, that (all factions, partialities, and sinister respect laid aside) they bend their care and endeavours to assist the said governor; first and principally, in the advancement of the honour and service of God, and the enlargement of his kingdom against the heathen people; and next, in erecting of the said colony in due obedience to his majesty, and all lawful authority from his majesty's directions; and lastly, in maintaining the said people in justice and christian conversation amongst themselves, and in strength and ability to withstand their enemies. And this council, to be always, or for the most part, residing about or near the governor.

IV. The other council, more generally to be called by the governor, once yearly, and no oftener, but for very extraordinary and important occasions, shall consist for the present, of the said council of state, and of two burgesses out of every town, hundred, or other particular plantation, to be respectively chosen by the inhabitants, which council shall be called The General Assembly wherein (as also in the said council of state) all matter shall be decided, determined, and ordered by the greater part of the voices then present; reserving to the governor always a negative voice. And this general assembly shall have free power, to treat, consult, and conclude, as well of all emergent occasions concerning the publick weal of the said colony and every part thereof, as also to makes ordain, and enact such general laws and orders, for the behoof of the said colony, and the good government thereof, as shall, from time to time, appear necessary or requisite,

V. Whereas in all other things, we require the said general assembly, as also the said council of state, to imitate and follow the policy of the form of government, laws, customs, and manner of trial, and other administration of justice, used in the realm of England, as near as may be even as ourselves, by his majesty's letters patent, are required.

VI. Provided, that no law or ordinance, made in the said general assembly, shall be or continue in force or validity, unless the same shall be solemnly ratified and confirmed, in a general quarter court of the said company here in England, and so ratified, be returned to them under our seal; it being our intent to afford the like measure also unto the said colony, that after the government of the said colony shall once have been well framed, and settled accordingly, which is to be done by us, as by authority derived from his majesty, and the same shall have been so by us declared, no orders of court afterwards, shall bind the said colony, unless they be ratified in like manner in the general assemblies. In witness whereof we have hereunto set our common seal the 24th of July, 1621. . . . .

Charter of the Massachusetts Bay Company (1629)

Unlike the Virginia colony, the colony in Massachusetts Bay was estab-
lished as a joint-stock company chartered in England. Taking advan-
tage of an oversight in the charter that left the location of company
control unspecified, Puritan members of the Massachusetts Bay Com-
pany transferred control from England to the colony. The charter, which
empowered the leaders of the company to make laws and regulations for
the colonists, became the constitution of the Puritan commonwealth led
by John Winthrop.

And further, That the said Governour and Companye, and their Successors, maie have forever one comon Seale, to be used in all
Causes and Occasions of the said Company, and the same Seale may alter, chaunge, breake, and newe make, from tyme to tyme, at their pleasures. And our Will and Pleasure is, and Wee doe hereby for Us, our
Heires and Successors, ordeyne and graunte, That from henceforth for
ever, there shalbe one Governor, one Deputy Governor, and eighteene Assistants of the same Company, to be from tyme to tyme constituted, elected
and chosen out of the Freemen of the saide Company, for the twyme being,
in such Manner and Forme as hereafter in theis Presents is expressed,
which said Officers shall applie themselves to take Care for the best dispo-
seing and ordering of the generall buysines and Affaires of, for, and concerning the said Landes and Premisses hereby mentioned, to be graunted,
and the Plantation thereof, and the Government of the People there.

* * *

And further, Wee will, and by theis Presents, for Us, our Heires and
Successors, doe ordeyne and graunte, That the Governor of the saide
Company for the tyme being, or in his Absence by Occasion of Sicknes or
otherwise, the Deputie Governor for the tyme being, shall have Authoritie
from tyme to tyme upon all Occasions, to give order for the assembling of
the saide Company, and calling them together to consult and advise of
the Bussinesses and Affaires of the saide Company, and that the said Governor, Deputie Governor, and Assistants of the saide Company, for the
tyme being, shall or maie once every Moneth, or oftener at their Pleasures, assemble and houlde and keepe a Courte or Assemblie of themselves, for the better ordering and directing of their Affaires, and that any

seaven or more persons of the Assistants, togither with the Governor, or Deputie Governor soe assembled, shalbe saide, taken, held, and reputed to be, and shalbe a full and sufficient Courte or Assemblie of the said Company, for the handling, ordering, and dispatching of all such Buysinesses and Occurrents as shall from tyme to tyme happen, touching or concerning the said Company or Plantation; and that there shall or maie be held and kept by the Governor, or Deputie Governor of the said Company, and seaven or more of the said Assistants for the tyme being, upon every last Wednesday in Hillary, Easter, Trinity, and Michaelmas Termes respectivelie forever, one greate generall and solemne assemblie, which foure generall assemblies shalbe stiled and called the foure greate and generall Courts of the saide Company.

In all and every, or any of which saide greate and generall Courts soe assembled, Wee doe for Us, our Heires and Successors, give and graunte to the said Governor and Company, and their Successors, That the Governor, or in his absence, the Deputie Governor of the saide Company for the tyme being, and such of the Assistants and Freemen of the saide Company as shalbe present, or the greater nomber of them so assembled, whereof the Governor or Deputie Governor and six of the Assistants at the least to be seaven, shall have full Power and authoritie to choose, nominate, and appointe, such and soe many others as they shall thinke fitt, and that shall be willing to accept the same, to be free of the said Company and Body, and them into the same to admitt; and to elect and constitute such Officers as they shall thinke fitt and requisite, for the ordering, mannaging, and dispatching of the Affaires of the saide Governor and Company, and their Successors; And to make Lawes and Ordinances for the Good and Welfare of the saide Company, and for the Government and ordering of the saide Landes and Plantation, and the People inhabiting and to inhabite the same, as to them from tyme to tyme shalbe thought meete, soe as such Lawes and Ordinances be not contrarie or repugnant to the Lawes and Statuts of this our Realme of England.

And, our Will and Pleasure is, and Wee doe hereby for Us, our Heires and Successors, establish and ordeyne, That yearely once in the yeare, for ever hereafter, namely, the last Wednesday in Easter Tearme, yearely, the Governor, Deputy-Governor, and Assistants of the saide Company and all other officers of the saide Company shalbe in the Generall Court or Assembly to be held for that Day or Tyme, newly chosen for the Yeare ensueing by such greater parte of the said Company, for the Tyme being, then and there present, as is aforesaide. And, if it shall happen the present governor, Deputy Governor, and assistants, by theis presents appointed, or such as shall hereafter be newly chosen into their Roomes, or any of them, or any other of the officers to be appointed for the said

Company, to dye, or to be removed from his or their severall Offices or Places before the saide generall Day of Election (whome Wee doe hereby declare for any Misdemeanor or Defect to be removeable by the Governor, Deputie Governor, Assistants, and Company, or such greater Parte of them in any of the publique Courts to be assembled as is aforesaid) That then, and in every such Case, it shall and maie be lawfull, to and for the Governor, Deputie Governor, Assistants, and Company aforesaide, or such greater Parte of them soe to be assembled as is aforesaide, in any of their Assemblies, to proceade to a new Election of one or more others of their Company in the Roome or Place, Roomes or Places of such Officer or Officers soe dyeing or removed according to their Discretions, And, immediately upon and after such Election and Elections made of such Governor, Deputie Governor, Assistant or Assistants, or any other officer of the saide Company, in Manner and Forme aforesaid, the Authoritie, Office, and Power, before given to the former Governor, Deputie Governor, or other Officer and Officers soe removed, in whose Steade and Place newe shalbe soe chosen, shall as to him and them, and everie of them, cease and determine.

Provided alsoe, and our Will and Pleasure is, That aswell such as are by theis Presents appointed to be the present Governor, Deputie Governor, and Assistants of the said Company, as those that shall succeed them, and all other Officers to be appointed and chosen as aforesaid, shall, before they undertake the Execution of their saide Offices and Places respectivelie, take their Corporal Oathes for the due and faithfull Performance of their Duties in their severall Offices and Places, before such Person or Persons as are by theis Presents hereunder appointed to take and receive the same. * * *

And, further our Will and Pleasure is, and wee doe hereby for Us, our Heires and Successors, ordeyne and declare, and graunte to the saide Governor and Company, and their Successors, That all and every the Subjects of Us, our Heires or Successors, which shall goe to and inhabite within the saide Landes and Premisses hereby mentioned to be graunted, and every of their Children which shall happen to be borne there, or on the Seas in goeing thither, or retorning from thence, shall have and enjoy all liberties and Immunities of free and naturall Subjects within any of the Domynions of Us, our Heires or Successors, to all Intents, Constructions, and Purposes whatsoever, as if they and everie of them were borne within the Realme of England. And that the Governor and Deputie Governor of the said Company for the Tyme being, or either of them, and any two or more of such of the saide Assistants as shalbe thereunto appointed by the saide Governor and Company at any of their Courts or Assemblies to be held as aforesaide, shall and maie at all Tymes, and from tyme to tyme hereafter, have full Power and Authoritie to minister and give the

Oathe and Oathes of Supremacie and Allegiance, or either of them, to all and everie Person and Persons, which shall at any Tyme or Tymes hereafter goe or passe to the Landes and Premisses hereby mentioned to be graunted to inhabite in the same.

And, Wee doe of our further Grace, certen Knowledg and meere Motion, give and graunte to the saide Governor and Company, and their Successors, That it shall and maie be lawfull, to and for the Governor or Deputie Governor, and such of the Assistants and Freemen of the said Company for the Tyme being as shalbe assembled in any of their generall Courts aforesaide, or in any other Courtes to be specially sumoned and assembled for that Purpose, or the greater Parte of them (whereof the Governor or Deputie Governor, and six of the Assistants to be alwaies seaven) from tyme to tyme, to make, ordeine, and establishe all Manner of wholesome and reasonable Orders, Lawes, Statutes, and Ordinances, Directions, and Instructions, not contrairie to the Lawes of this our Realme of England, aswell for setling of the Formes and Ceremonies of Government and Magistracy, fitt and necessary for the said Plantation, and the Inhabitants there, and for nameing and setting of all sorts of Officers, both superior and inferior, which they shall finde needefull for that Governement and Plantation, and the distinguishing and setting forth of the severall duties, Powers, and Lymytts of every such Office and Place, and the Formes of such Oathes warrantable by the Lawes and Statutes of this our Realme of England, as shalbe respectivelie ministred unto them for the Execution of the said severall Offices and Places; as also, for the disposing and ordering of the Elections of such of the said Officers as shalbe annuall, and of such others as shalbe to succeede in Case of Death or Removeall, and ministring the said Oathes to the newe elected Officers, and for Impositions of lawfull Fynes, Mulcts, Imprisonment, or other lawfull Correction, according to the Course of other Corporations in this our Realme of England, and for the directing, ruling, and disposcing of all other Matters and Thinges, whereby our said People, Inhabitants there, may be soe religiously, peaceablie, and civilly governed, as their good Life and orderlie Conversation, maie wynn and incite the Natives of Country, to the Knowledg and Obedience of the onlie true God and Savior of Mankinde, and the Christian Fayth, which in our Royall Intention, and the Adventurers free Profession, is the principall Ende of this Plantation. * * *

And Wee doe further, for Us, our Heires and Successors, give and graunt to the said Governor and Company, and their Successors by theis Presents, that all and everie such Chiefe Comaunders, Captaines, Governors, and other Officers and Ministers, as by the said Orders, Lawes, Statuts, Ordinances, Instructions, or Directions of the said Governor and Company for the Tyme being, shalbe from Tyme to Tyme hereafter

imploied either in the Government of the saide Inhabitants and Plantation, or in the Waye by Sea thither, or from thence, according to the Natures and Lymitts of their Offices and Places respectively, shall from
Tyme to Tyme hereafter for ever, within the Precincts and Partes of Newe
England hereby mentioned to be graunted and confirmed, or in the Waie
by Sea thither, or from thence, have full and Absolute Power and Authoritie to correct, punishe, pardon, governe, and rule all such the Subjects of
Us, our Heires and Successors, as shall from Tyme to Tyme adventure
themselves in any Voyadge thither or from thence, or that shall at any
Tyme hereafter, inhabite within the Precincts and Partes of Newe England aforasaid, according to the Orders, Lawes, Ordinances, Instructions, and Directions aforesaid, not being repugnant to the Lawes and
Statutes of our Realme of England as aforesaid. . . .

WILLIAM PENN

Preface to the First Frame of Government for Pennsylvania (1682)

*The Quaker William Penn (1644–1718) was the namesake and propri-
etor of the American Commonwealth of Pennsylvania, which he hoped
to settle with individuals who shared his political principles and commitment to religious toleration. In his preface to the Pennsylvania constitution, which guaranteed liberty of conscience, Penn explained that
government has a moral purpose best served by a combination of good
laws and good men.*

When the great and wise God had made the world of all of his creatures, it pleased Him to choose man His deputy to rule it, and to
fit him for so great a charge and trust He did not only qualify him with
skill and power but with integrity to use them justly. This native goodness
was equally his honor and his happiness, and whilst he stood here, all
went well; there was no need of coercive or compulsive means. The precept of divine love and truth in his own bosom was the guide and keeper
of his innocency. But lust, prevailing against duty, made a lamentable
breach upon it, and the law that before had no power over him took place
upon him and his disobedient posterity, that such as would not live

conformable to the holy law within should fall under the reproof and correction of the just law without in a judicial administration.

This the apostle teaches in divers of his epistles. "The law," says he, "was added because of transgression." In another place: "knowing that the law was not made for the righteous man but for the disobedient and ungodly, for sinners, for the unholy and profane, for murderers, for whoremongers, for them that defile themselves with mankind, and for men-stealers, for liars, for perjured persons," etc., but this is not all; he opens and carries the matter of government a little farther: "let every soul be subject to the higher powers, for there is no power but of God. The powers that be are ordained of God; whosoever therefore resisteth the power resisteth the ordinance of God. For rulers are not a terror to good works, but to evil. Wilt thou then not be afraid of the power? Do that which is good, and thou shalt have praise of the same." "He is the minister of God to thee for good." "Wherefore ye must needs be subject not only for wrath but for conscience' sake."

This settles the divine right of government beyond exception, and that for two ends: first, to terrify evildoers; secondly, to cherish those that do well; which gives government a life beyond corruption and makes it as durable in the world as good men shall be, so that government seems to me a part of religion itself, a thing sacred in its institution and end. For if it does not directly remove the cause, it crushes the effects of evil, and is as such, though a lower, yet an emanation of the same divine Power that is both author and object of pure religion, the difference lying here, that the one is more free and mental, the other more corporal and compulsive in its operations, but that is only to evildoers, government in itself being otherwise as capable of kindness, goodness, and charity, as a more private society. They weakly err that think there is no other use for government than correction, which is the coarsest part of it; daily experience tells us that the care and regulation of many other affairs more soft and daily necessary make up much the greatest part of government, and which must have followed the peopling of the world, had Adam never fell, and will continue among men on earth under the highest attainments they may arrive at by the coming of the blessed second Adam, the Lord from heaven. Thus much of government in general as to its rise and end.

For particular frames and models, it will become me to say little, and comparatively I will say nothing. My reasons are:

First. That the age is too nice and difficult for it, there being nothing the wits of men are more busy and divided upon. 'Tis true, they seem to agree in the end, to wit, happiness; but in the means they differ, as to divine, so to this human felicity, and the cause is much the same, not always want of light and knowledge, but want of using them rightly. Men side with their passions against their reason, and their sinister interests have so strong a bias upon their minds that they lean to them against the good of the things they know.

Secondly. I do not find a model in the world that time, place, and some singular emergencies have not necessarily altered, nor is it easy to frame a civil government that shall serve all places alike.

Thirdly. I know what is said by the several admirers of monarchy, aristocracy, and democracy, which are the rule of one, a few, and many, and are the three common ideas of government, when men discourse of that subject. But I choose to solve the controversy with this small distinction and it belongs to all three: any government is free to the people under it, whatever be the frame, where the laws rule and the people are a party to those laws, and more than this is tyranny, oligarchy, or confusion.

But lastly, when all is said, there is hardly one frame of government in the world so ill-designed by its first founders that in good hands, [it] would not do well enough, and story tells us, the best in ill ones can do nothing that is great or good; witness the Jewish and Roman states. Governments, like clocks, go from the motion men give them, and as governments are made and moved by men, so by them they are ruined too. Wherefore governments rather depend upon men than men upon governments. Let men be good and the government cannot be bad: if it be ill, they will cure it. But if men be bad, let the government be never so good, they will endeavor to warp and spoil it to their turn.

I know some say, let us have good laws, and no matter for the men that execute them; but let them consider that though good laws do well, good men do better, for good laws want good men, and be abolished or evaded by ill men, but good men will never want good laws nor suffer ill ones. 'Tis true, good laws have some awe upon ill ministers, but that is where they have not power to escape or abolish them and the people are generally wise and good, but a loose and depraved people (which is the question) love laws and an administration like themselves. That, therefore, which makes a good constitution must keep it; viz., men of wisdom and virtue, qualities that, because they descend not with worldly inheritances, must be carefully propagated by a virtuous education of youth, for which afterages will owe more to the care and prudence of founders and the successive magistracy than to their parents for their private patrimonies.

These considerations of the weight of government and the nice and various opinions about it made it uneasy to me to think of publishing the ensuing frame and conditional laws, foreseeing both the censures they will meet with from men of differing humors and engagements and the occasion they may give of discourse beyond my design.

But, next to the power of necessity (which is a solicitor that will take no denial) this induced me to a compliance, that we have (with reverence to God and good conscience to men) to the best of our skill contrived and composed the frame and laws of this government to the great end of all government; viz., to support power in reverence with the people and to secure the people from the abuse of power, that they may be free by their just obedience and the magistrates honorable for their just administration; for liberty without obedience is confusion, and obedience without liberty is slavery. To carry this evenness is partly owing to the constitution and partly to the magistracy. Where either of these fail, government will be subject to convulsions, but where both are wanting, it must be totally subverted; then where both meet, the government is like to endure, which I humbly pray and hope God will please to make the lot of this of Pennsylvania. Amen.

The North Carolina Biennial Act (1715)

*The North Carolina Assembly modeled this act after England's Trien-
nial Act of 1694, which required parliamentary elections every three
years. The North Carolina act expressed the colonial conviction that
frequent meetings of legislative assemblies were necessary for the protection of the people's privileges from overbearing governors, who often
maintained that legislatures could not meet unless summoned.*

ACT RELATING TO THE BIENNIAL AND OTHER ASSEMBLYS AND REGULATING ELECTIONS AND MEMBERS.

Whereas His Excellency the Palatine and the rest of the true and Absolute Lord's Proprietors of Carolina, having duely considered the priviledges and immunities wherewith the Kingdom of Great Brittain is endued and being desirous that this their province may have such as may thereby enlarge the Settlement and that the frequent sitting of Assembly is a principal safeguard of their People's priviledges, have thought fit to enact. And Be It Therefore Enacted by the said Pallatine and Lords Proprietors by and with the advice and consent of this present Grand Assembly now met at Little River for the North East part of the said province:

II. And it is Hereby Enacted that for the due election and Constituting of Members of the Biennial and other Assemblys it shall be lawfull for the Freemen of the respective precincts of the County of Albemarle to meet the first Tuesday in September every two years in the places hereafter mentioned. . . .

III. And Be It Further Enacted that it is and may be lawfull for the inhabitants and freemen in each Precinct in every other County or Counties that now is or shall be hereafter erected in this Government aforesaid to meet as aforesaid at such place as shall be judged most convenient by the Marshall of such county, unless he be otherwise ordered by the special commands of the Governor or Commander in Chief to choose two freeholders out of every precinct in the county aforesaid to sit and vote in the said Assembly.

IV. And Be It Further Enacted that the Burgesses so chosen in each precinct for the Biennial Assembly shall meet and sitt the first Monday in November then next following, every two years, at the same place the Assembly last satt except the Pallatines Court shall by their proclamation published Twenty days before the said meeting appoint some other place and there with the consent and concurrence of the Pallatine Court shall make and ordain such Laws as shall be thought most necessary for the Good of this Government. Provided allways and nevertheless that the Powers granted to the Lord's Proprietors from the Crown of Calling, proroguing and dissolving Assemblys are not hereby meant or intended to be invaded, limited or restrained.

V. And It Is Hereby Further Enacted by the Authority aforesaid that no person whatsoever Inhabitant of this Government born out of the allegiance of His Majesty and not made free; no Negroes, Mulattoes, Mustees or Indians shall be capable of voting for Members of Assembly; and that no other person shall be allowed or admitted to vote for Members of Assembly in this Government unless he be of the Age of one and twenty years and has been one full year in the Government and has paid one year's levy preceding the Election.

VI. And Be It Further Enacted that all persons offering to vote for Members of Assembly shall bring a list to the Marshall or Deputy taking the Pole containing the names of the persons he votes for and shall subscribe his own name or cause the same to be done: And if any such person or persons shall be suspected either by the Marshall or any of the candidates not to be qualified according to the true intent and meaning of this Act, then the Marshall, Deputy Marshall, or other Officer that shall be appointed to take and receive such votes and list—shall have power to administer an oath or attestation to every such suspected person of his qualification and ability to choose Members of Assembly and whether he has not before given in his list at that Election.

VII. And Be It Further Enacted that Every Officer or Marshall which shall admit of or take the vote of any person not truly qualified according to the purport and meaning of this Act (provided the objection be made by any candidate or Inspector) or shall make undue return of any person for Member of Assembly shall forfeit for such vote taken, so admitted and for such Return Twenty pounds to be employed for and towards the building of any Court House, Church or Chapel as the Governor for the time being shall think fitt; but if no such building require it then to the Lord's Proprietors and Twenty Pounds to each person which of right and majority of votes ought to have been returned: to be recovered by Action of Debt, Bill, Plaint or Information in any Court of Record in this Government wherein no Essoign Wager of Law or Protection shall be allowed or admitted.

VIII. And Be It Further Enacted that every Marshall or Officer whose business and duty it is to make returns of Elections of Members of Assembly, shall attend the Assembly the first Three days of their sitting (unless he have leave of Assembly to depart) to inform the Assembly of all matters and disputes as shall arise about Elections and shall show to the Assembly the List of the Votes for every person returned and have made complaints of false returns to the Assembly; every Marshall or other Officer as aforesaid which shall deny or refuse to attend as aforesaid shall forfeit the sum of Twenty pounds to be recovered and disposed of in such manner and form as the Forfeitures before by this Act appointed.

IX. And Be It Further Enacted that whatsoever Member or Representative so elected as aforesaid shall faile in making his personal appearance and giving his attendance at the Assembly precisely on the day limited by the Writt (or on the day appointed for the meeting of the Biennial Assembly, when the election is for the Biennial Assembly) shall be fined for every day's absence during the sitting of the Assembly (unless by disability or other impediment to be allowed by the Assembly) Twenty Shillings to be levied by a Warrant from the Speaker and to be applied to such uses as the Lower House of Assembly shall think fitt.

X. And Be It Further Enacted that every member of Assembly that shall be elected as aforesaid after the Ratifying of this Act shall not be qualified to sitt as a Member in the House of Burgesses before he shall willingly take the Oath of Allegiance and Supremacy the Adjuration Oath and all such other Oathes as shall be ordered and directed to be taken by the Members of Parliament in Great Britain.

XI. And Be It Further Enacted that the quorum of the House of Burgesses for voting and passing of Bills shall not be less than one full half of the House and that no Bills shall be signed and Ratified except there be present Eight of the Members whereof the Speaker to be one. And in case that eight Members shall meet at any Assembly those eight shall have full power to adjourn from day to day till a sufficient number can assemble to transact the Business of the Government.

New Hampshire Assembly on Choosing a Speaker (1748)

This document highlights one of the perennial disputes between colonial assemblies and royal governors. The assembly of New Hampshire invoked English precedents to justify its claim that the choice of a speaker should rest with the legislature rather than the governor, who usually picked a speaker sympathetic to the interests of the Crown. At stake in this controversy was the ability of colonists to govern themselves through their assemblies without interference from Crown officials.

Your Excellency first sent to this House your Direction to Choose a Speaker; we immediately Did it And informed your Excellency what we had done. Your Excellency's next message was to inquire whether the Members as you were pleased to Call them Returned from Chester and South Hampton Voted in the Choice of a Speaker.

To which we Replyd the Gentlemen which Appeared from Chester and South Hampton Did not vote in the Choice of a Speaker.

Then your Excellency was pleased to Send us your Disapprobation of our Choice of a Speaker and to Direct us to proceed to the Choice of Another And to Declare that no Choice would be Approved of Unless the persons who had been Excluded before were admitted to Vote in the new Choice.

To which we Humbly Replyd that as Soon as your Excellency would be pleased to show us your power to Negative a Speaker we would immediately Submit to it and proceed to Another Choice And as Soon as your Excellency would evince to us that the pretended members had a Right to Sit And Vote in this House we would immediately admit them. But till Such Evidence should be produced both in the one Case and the other we Could not See the way Clear to Comply with what your Excellency had Required.

Then your Excellency was pleased to Reply that when your message should be fully obeyed in the Choice of a New Speaker And the two persons from Chester and South Hampton Admitted to Vote in the Second Choice that then you should be Ready to Give us a Satisfactory Answer to things we had a Right to inquire into and not till then.

Thus Stands the Case Between your Excellency and this House And this is the Seventh day Since the Session Commenced without our being permitted to enter upon the Common and ordinary business of the Province Unless we would yield to your Excellency two important points of Priviledge which we were and are full in the opinion your Excellency had no Right to Demand.

After your Excellency was pleased to begin a dispute with us did we not indeavor to shorten it in a Becoming manner.

When your Excellency inquired whether the persons Returned from South Hampton and Chester were admitted to Vote did we not immediately Answer that they were not. Tho perhaps upon a Critical Examination into the Rights of Governours it would be found that your Excellency had no Right to make Such an inquisition yet how Readily did we yield it And here we would humbly ask why your Excellency Chose Rather to inquire whether the persons Returned from Chester and South Hampton Voted than whether the members Sent from Portsmouth and Dover Did— Does not the Question imply that your Excellency apprehended the Chester and South Hampton persons would not be Admitted. And what could such Apprehensions be Grounded on But a Consciousness that your Excellency had no power to impose them upon us.

Then Sir with Respect to the message we Sent to your Excellency Requesting to see your Power for Negativing a Speaker And Admitting the two persons from Chester and South Hampton, Can your Excellency imagine that such a Reply should be Satisfactory to a Senatorian Assembly. Your Excellency Required of us what we thought Unlawfull and therefore we prayed you would show us your Right to Command and promise; As Soon as your Excellency should do so we would immediately Obey— But Lo, what was your Reply—That when your Message is fully obeyed you would give us a Satisfactory Answer to what we had a Right to inquire into. What is this but insisting that we should first take a Leap in the Dark and then your Excellency would Order a Light to be held to us that we might Discern whether we had leaped Right or wrong.

And now Sir with Respect to the authoritys we promised to Suggest and first in Regard to the Power of Negativing a Speaker we find in Bishop Burnets history of his own times that in the year 1679 It was said the House had the Choice of their Speaker in them and that their presenting the Speaker was only a Solemn Shewing him to the King Such as was presenting the Lord Mayor and Sheriffs of London in the Exchequer but that the King was bound to Confirm their Choice—Again The point was Setled that the Right of Electing was in the House and that Confirmation was a thing of Course. Thus far the Bishop. And thus we presume the Case Stands between the King and the House of Commons at this day. If your Excellency Knows it to be otherwise we Beseech you to Communicate it to us that we may Act According to knowledge for We Abjure all implicit faith in Politicks As well as Religion And are resolved to See with our Own Eyes And Act According to our own Understanding.

Again we find a Grant Made to a Governour of a Neighbouring Province by Letters patent from King William and Queen Mary in the third year of their Reign That he with the Council And Assembly should make Orders, Laws, Statutes and Ordinances, Directions and Instructions for the Welfare of the Province and that he the Governour should have a Negative Voice upon all Such Orders, Laws, Statutes and Ordinances and in all Elections and Acts of Government whatsoever to be passed by the General Court or Assembly or in Council. And Tho' this power is Greater than what we think is Contained in your Excellency's Commission yet his Majesty King George the first in the twelfth year of his Reign Explicitly Says that no Provision is made in the Said Letters Patent meaning those above mentioned touching the Nomination and Election of A Speaker nor any reservation made for his being Approved or Disapproved by a Governour.

Upon your Excellency's Considering what we have offered on this Point We humbly hope your Excellency will be pleased to retract your Disapprobation of Our Choice of a Speaker or Shew us that you have a Right to maintain it. As to calling members of Assembly from Unpriviledged places if your Excellency will be Referred to President Cutt's Commission which was the first for this Province it will we apprehend Easily End the Dispute for by it you may See that in the Very first formation And founding this Government the People were Ordered by the King to have a hand in it. And while there was no Assembly yet in the Province and the first was to be called for a first there must be the King Says to the President and Councill that within a Limitted time they shall issue a Summons for Convening a General Assembly Observing such Rules and Methods and Appointing such time and Place of Meeting As the Electors shall think fit. And Agreeable to this in forming the Government of a Neighbouring Province it was Appointed by the Crown that they should have two members from every Town in their first Assembly And that they with the other Branches of the Legislature should Determine what members should be afterwards Sent to Represent the Country Towns and Places.

What we would further add is the Custom and Usage of the Province According to which by your Excellency's commission General Assemblys are to be Called which as we Apprehend has always been that the Admission of Any new member was by Vote or Act of General Assembly And for this we would Refer your Excellency to a Message Sent to your Excellency by a former Assembly when this Same thing was in Dispute About four years ago.

Upon the whole we Say once more if your Excellency will shew us that you have a Power to Negative a Speaker we will proceed to Another Choice And if your Excellency will shew us that you have a Right to introduce Chester and South Hampton Persons into this House Against the Common Custom and Usage of the Province We will admit them. But in Case no Such Evidences are produced:

Voted and Resolved That we do and will Adhere to our Right and Privilege in both those Cases As well as in all other According to the Laws, Usage and Custom of the Province and are fully Determined not to proceed to the Choice of Another Speaker nor to Admit the two persons from Chester and South Hampton aforesaid but upon the Conditions before mentioned. And this we Humbly offer as the final Result of this House Upon these two Points.

PART II

THE FOUNDING

1760–1791

N   ot quite the demigods celebrated in the popular historical imagination, the founders of the new American republic were, by any standards, an exceptional group of men. How, asked the historian Douglass Adair, can we account for such an "explosion of talent . . . [such an] amazing concentration of political ability in this generation born into a tiny nation on the fringe of the Atlantic?" Adair rejects the miraculous, which some have offered as the answer, because it would imply that the Republic was "supernatural . . . a little like the famous virgin birth reported in the New Testament." He preferred a more down-to-earth answer: the quest for *fame*. Fame, he wrote, "is primarily the desire for immortality. Fame defeats that threat of oblivion with which Death confronts every man." Virtually all of that founding generation shared the passion for fame. And from their reading of the classical writers of antiquity, they knew that there was no greater claim to fame than founding nations. They didn't seek *glory*, "an attribute of God." Those who seek glory assume "that He is always watching . . . and that [they] behave with such piety and goodness in rendering homage to Him [that they] will shine with reflections of His glory." From glory to fame—such is the texture of the leap from the colonial to the republican.

The leaders of the American Revolution communicated their political ideas in pamphlets, newspaper articles, broadsides, almanacs, and poems. Official documents were also important channels, including personal letters made public, petitions back to London but circulated at home, and declarations promulgated by local governments and courts. There were also innumerable orations, both sermons and lay speeches, art forms developed during the colonial period. But there were few lengthy and careful, speculative treatises. No single great theorist emerges in this age of revolution and constitution making.

Those who contributed to American political thought at this time were principally men of action. By far the largest numbers were lawyers, followed by ministers, with a sprinkling of merchants and planters. Engaged professionals, then as now, rarely have the time or the inclination to pursue philosophical principles and write treatises.

Whether this American republic was a miracle or a spontaneous inspiration of the race of life that became a race to fame, the explanation has to reside in what the scholar Adrienne Koch has called "the historical uniqueness of the experience open to them."

Was that unique experience a *revolution*? Not if one means by that word its age-old astronomical reference to returning to an original starting point, though recapturing rights of Englishmen lost to George III's taxation policies might qualify here. Nor if one means by revolution the root and branch transformation of society associated with the later French, Russian, and Chinese experiences. By such standards the American experience of 1776–1789 does not qualify as a revolution. The political scientist Samuel Huntington excludes the United States from the "notable examples" of revolution in his study *Political Order in Changing Societies*. The historian Gordon Wood also concludes that "the impulses to revolution in eighteenth-century America bear little or no resemblance to [those of] modern social protests and revolutions," and "the social conditions [lying] behind all revolutions . . . were not present in colonial America."

Long before this verdict from contemporary scholars, the British thinker and politician Edmund Burke supported the American independence movement, which he saw as an effort to conserve the colonists' traditional rights of Englishmen, which were threatened by British policy. In contrast, Burke vilified the French experience, which he saw as truly worthy of the name *revolution*. In the 1830s, Tocqueville expressed the same view: "The great advantage of the Americans is that they have arrived at a state of democracy without having to endure a democratic revolution, and that they are born equal instead of becoming so." Tocqueville's observations became a basis for the thesis of "American exceptionalism" in political institutions and political thought.

All this notwithstanding, Thomas Jefferson saw America founded in a revolution, the revolutionary right of a free people to be rid of a government that destroyed, not secured, a people's inalienable rights. The Declaration of Independence is pure Jefferson, and behind it are the ideas of the English philosopher John Locke. The bulk of the text—almost two thirds of it—is a bill of particulars against the conduct of "the present King of Great Britain." These grievances are presented as "Facts [to] be submitted to a candid world." Eighteen of them are allegations against the conduct of the king, each beginning with "He has . . ." There are nine additional charges against the conduct of the civil and military representatives of the king in the colonies. Independence was declared only after

"We [as subjects of the Crown] have Petitioned for Redress in the most humble terms . . . answered only by repeated injury. . . . We, therefore, . . . are Absolved from all Allegiance to the British Crown."

Jefferson's theory of revolution was based in largest part on the philosophical tradition of natural law, or God's "law of nature," as the source of natural rights, the foundation of individual freedom. A truly free people, Jefferson believed, would claim that their rights came from the Creator and the law of nature, not from the beneficence of political authorities. It was a self-evident truth for Jefferson that a people voluntarily consented to be governed in order to secure these rights, and that they could withdraw this consent if government failed to do what it was created to do.

Jefferson and Madison: America's Architects

Jefferson's political theory was grounded in an absolute, pure embrace of rights, including the right of revolution when rights are deprived. As one of our signature characters of the founding period, Jefferson embodies the preoccupation with individual rights that formed an essential strand of American political thought. Sixty years after 1776, a young Abraham Lincoln sensed the danger of Jefferson's absolute position, and gave warning: "This state of feeling, [this] spirit of our Revolution . . . *must fade, is fading, has faded,* with the circumstances that produced it. . . . Let those materials be molded into . . . a reverence for the Constitution and the laws."

While the Constitutional Convention was meeting in Philadelphia, Jefferson was ambassador to France. When the text of the Constitution reached him in Paris, he was upset over the absence of a bill of rights. Once a commitment to a bill of rights was made— largely in order to get the Constitution ratified in the Virginia state legislature—Jefferson supported the Constitution. And Jefferson even went so far as to cite the *Federalist Papers* as "the best commentary on the principles of government which ever was written."

Yet Jefferson's support for ratification of the Constitution and respect for the *Federalist Papers* should not overshadow the subtle differences between the more radical Jefferson and the more institutionalist James Madison. Whereas Jefferson was the philosopher of civil society, Madison—our second signature character for this period—was a founder of modern state theory. Of course Madison began with civil society and with the assumption that individuals are rational, fully capable of using reason to pursue their own interests. And since men are *not* angels, as Madison wrote in *Federalist* 10, they will pursue their interests singly or in factions "adverse to the rights of other citizens or to the permanent or aggregate interests of the community."

But civil society was for Madison a mere premise. His solution for the "more perfect union," contrary to those of most theorists of his generation, was that democracy in a large territory would be the most successful solution to tyranny because if you "extend the sphere and you take in a greater variety of parties and interests; you make it less probable that a majority of the whole will have a common motive to invade the rights of other citizens" (*Federalist* 10). These dynamics, he added, must operate within a constitutional structure that does not eliminate the causes of factions (a cure worse than the disease) but can control their effects: "The regulation of these various and interfering interests forms the principal task of modern legislation and [at the same time] involves a spirit of party and faction in the necessary and ordinary operations of government." A good constitution fosters good citizenship as a by-product of the competition of self-interested politicians. We call this sublimation, a principle that was very much in the air after the Scottish thinker Adam Smith published in 1776 his classic economic theory of how individual, private interests promote the maximum wealth for the entire nation:

> It is not from the benevolence of the butcher, the brewer, or the baker that we expect our dinner, but from their regard to their own interest. We address ourselves, not to their humanity but to their self-love.
>
> Every individual . . . intends only his own gain, and he is in this . . . *led by an invisible hand to promote an end which was no part of his intention.* . . . [By] pursuing his own interest he frequently promotes that of the society more effectually than when he really intends to promote it.

During the eighteenth century, science and philosophy were synonyms, and Madison in this sense was truly a political scientist. He was the principal architect of the Constitution of 1787, and he wrote the science (or philosophy) of that Constitution: for him it provided the framework for the "race of life," the rules of conduct and, in Hobbes's terms, the hedges containing its pursuit.

The key to the distinction between Jefferson and Madison, and to their distinctive contributions to American political thought, can be located in Jefferson's conception of rights in the Virginia Act for Establishing Religious Freedom and in Madison's conception in the Bill of Rights. The Virginia Act was drafted by Jefferson in 1777 but was not adopted by the state legislature until 1786, under Madison's legislative management. In the Virginia Act as well as in the Declaration of Independence, the rights put forth by Jefferson were few, simple, abstract, universal, and absolute. Add charismatic: Jefferson's rhetoric and intent fit the definition of charisma, "partaking of the divine." Jefferson held "these truths to be self-evident," but he sometimes wavered on this. He also emphasized the divine origin of rights, hoping by this to bring Americans to a stronger commitment to them. More to the point, he tried to head off a repeal of the Virginia statute by the threat of a mass meeting sometime in the future. Jefferson punctuated that with a passionate appeal: "[I]f any act shall hereafter [be] passed to repeal the present or to narrow its operation, such act will be an infringement of natural right"—a not so thinly veiled reminder of the Jeffersonian right of revolution.

Madison's conception of rights is etched in his authorship of the Bill of Rights. The addition of the Bill of Rights was a concession made to the Jeffersonians in order to get the Constitution ratified; it specifies as many as twenty-five rights, which appear as clauses within the first eight amendments. These rights are not considered self-evident; they are not gifts of God or nature, waiting to be discovered.

In this regard Madison's operational approach differs from Jefferson's natural rights approach and that of the other important bills of rights: The French Declaration of the Rights of Man and Citizen (1789) and the English Bill of Rights (1689). Each of these is inspirational, an effort to inculcate a commitment to the principle of individual rights, a commitment deep enough to produce mobilization for collective redress or even revolution if the deprivations are too frequent, too excessive, too widespread. Perhaps an inspirational, natural-law conception of rights was necessary to advance democracy. Nevertheless, the consequences are clear: The natural rights approach puts the advancement and the defense of rights squarely on individual citizens. In contrast, the American Bill of Rights provides a standard and a method—a cause of action—for implementation of claims to rights. The Bill of Rights is built on contract, but it does not assume that the contract is self-enforcing, just as it does not assume that rights are self-evident. The Bill of Rights specifies rights in terms of limitations on the power of government. This makes the contract truly a contract: the government limits its power in exchange for full use of remaining powers. All of the rights conveyed in the Bill of Rights are defined as brakes on government. Madison explained this approach in *Federalist* 51:

> In framing a government which is to be administered by men over men, the great difficulty lies in this: you must first enable the government to control the governed; and in the next place oblige it to control itself. A dependence on the people is, no doubt, the primary control on the government; but experience has taught mankind the necessity of auxiliary precautions.

These differences between Jefferson and Madison have set the terms of American political discourse for over two hundred years. We can characterize their positions best by pushing them to their polar extremes: Jefferson as *radical republican* and Madison as *liberal republican*. Jefferson was radical in his insistence on an ideal, pure standard of rights and his belief in the capacity of American citizens to create a civil society "to secure these rights." Others were still more radical, seeking a community of virtue to save a democracy from its tendency toward what the historian Bernard Bailyn described as "civil disorder and the early assumption of power by a dictator." Yet another category of radical republicans possessed what Gordon Wood labeled "a decidedly reactionary tone . . . [embodying] the ideal of the good society as it had been set forth from antiquity . . . to discover somehow above all the diverse selfish wills the one supreme moral good to which all parts of the body politic must surrender." This could be a religious or secular republic, but its political theory envisions perfectible individuals creating a virtuous community (or civil society).

The liberal republican alternative did not rely upon a community of virtue to solve the problem of governance. Madison's liberalism rejects the Jeffersonian and the more radical republican dependence on the perfectibility of individuals and the moral superiority of the community, substituting for it a faith in science to fashion a "more perfect union." This would be achieved not by requiring the perfection of each individual and community but by taking individuals as they are, putting them in an institutional framework in which "ambition [is] made to counteract ambition," and producing from that an attitude in which "the stronger individuals are prompted, by the uncertainty of their condition, to submit to a government which may protect the weak as well as themselves" (*Federalist* 51).

We are left with a nagging question: would the end of the Founding period and the advent of stable, ordinary politics mean a waning of political thought? Lincoln's admonition to let the spirit of revolution fade into "a reverence for the Constitution and the laws" could, if followed, mean at the very least a decline of political thought into the trivial and the commonplace. The connection between thought and action remained, and the "race of life" continued to drive society, economy, and politics—but race for what? Madison called it ambition, but ambition for what? More competing interests?

Fortunately the Founding was not a fixed position, nor was it Hobbes's hedge, which kept ambition contained. It was a moment in a moving equilibrium, with each succeeding moment another kind of founding worthy of its own discourse, and with each new crisis an opportunity to rewrite the Constitution in small, and sometimes in large, ways. No political prediction was ever more strongly confirmed than Tocqueville's observation that "Scarcely any question arises in the United States that is not resolved, sooner or later, into a judicial question." But this juridical habit of mind was not limited to the judiciary. Tocqueville predicted further that "the language of law" was going to become "a vulgar tongue." But he was using *vulgar* in its original sense as "common and usual," i.e., the everyday vernacular of ordinary citizens. Although judges have indeed been principal sources of American political thought, the Constitution, as a written covenant and an instrument of government, became a cause of action setting the terms of popular discourse. Thus there has never been a lack of opportunity for ordinary citizens to transcend the ordinary in action and thought. That is just another kind of ambition—for fame, the same which spurred the founders.

This should be our standard of judgment as we move from the great ambition of the Founding to the ordinary ambitions of governing. Ambition in thought can transcend the ordinary in action. If there were not moments of transcendence, an account of American political thought could end here. It does not, because the American republic is an experiment, always in search of itself.

BIBLIOGRAPHY

Adair, Douglass. *Fame and the Founding Fathers.* New York: Norton, 1974.

Adams, Henry. *The United States in 1800.* Ithaca, N.Y.: Cornell University Press, 1955.

Bailyn, Bernard. *The Ideological Origins of the American Revolution.* Cambridge, Mass.: Harvard University Press, 1967.

Hamilton, Alexander, John Jay, and James Madison. *The Federalist Papers,* edited by Isaac Kramnick. London: Penguin, 1987.

Koch, Adrienne. *Power, Morals and the Founding Fathers.* Ithaca, N.Y.: Cornell University Press, 1961.

Lincoln, Abraham. "The Perpetuation of Our Political Institutions." Adress before the Young Men's Lyceum of Springfield, Illinois, January 27, 1838. In *Collected Works of Abraham Lincoln,* vol. 1, pp. 108–15. Ann Arbor: University of Michigan Digital Library Production Services, 2001. http://name.umdl.umich.edu/lincoln1.

Smith, Adam. *The Wealth of Nations,* introduction by Robert Reich, edited by Edwin Cannan. New York: Modern Library, 2000.

Tocqueville, Alexis de. *Democracy in America,* edited by Isaac Kramnick. New York: Norton, 2007.

The Political Theory
of the Revolution

JAMES OTIS

The Rights of the British Colonies
Asserted and Proved (1764)

A prominent Boston lawyer and member of the Massachusetts House of Representatives, James Otis (1725–1783) was an early opponent of the Sugar Act and subsequent efforts to tax the colonists without their consent. Relying heavily on Locke's theory of government, Otis argued that all Americans—"black and white"—were entitled to the same rights as Britons in Britain according to both the laws of nature and British law.

The origin of *government* has in all ages no less perplexed the heads of lawyers and politicians, than the origin of *evil* has embarrassed divines and philosophers: And 'tis probably the world may receive a satisfactory solution on *both* those points of enquiry at the *same* time.

The various opinions on the origin of *government* have been reduced to four. (1) That dominion is founded in *Grace*. (2) On *force* or mere *power*. (3) On *compact*. (4) On *property*.

The first of these opinions is so absurd, and the world has paid so very dear for embracing it, especially under the administration of the *Roman pontiffs*, that mankind seem at this day to be in a great measure cured of their madness in this particular; and the notion is pretty generally exploded, and hissed off the stage.

To those who lay the foundation of government in *force* and mere *brutal power*, it is objected; that, their system destroys all distinction between right and wrong; that it overturns all morality, and leaves it to every man to do what is right in his own eyes; that it leads directly to *scepticism*, and ends in *atheism*. When a man's will and pleasure is his only rule and guide, what safety can there be either for him or against him but in the point of a sword?

On the other hand the gentlemen in favor of the *original compact* have been often told that their system is chimerical and unsupported by reason or experience. * * *

With regard to the fourth opinion, that the *dominion is founded in property*, what is it but playing with words? Dominion in one sense of the term is synonymous with property, so one cannot be called the foundation of the other, but as one *name* may appear to be the foundation or cause of another.

Property cannot be the foundation of dominion as synonymous with government; for on the supposition that property has a precarious existence antecedent to government, and tho' it is also admitted that the security of property is one end of government, but that of little estimation even in the view of a *miser* when life and liberty of locomotion and further accumulation are placed in competition, it must be a very absurd way of speaking to assert that *one* end of government is the foundation of government. If the ends of government are to be considered as its foundation, it cannot with truth or propriety be said that government is founded on any *one* of those ends: * * * at least on something else in conjunction. It is however true in fact and *experience*, as the great, the incomparable *Harrington* has most abundantly demonstrated in his *Oceana*, and other divine writings, that Empire follows the balance of *property*. 'Tis also certain that *property* in fact generally confers power, tho' the possessor of it may not have much more wit than a mole or a musquash: And this is too often the cause, that riches are fought after without the least concern about the right application of them. But is the fault in the riches, or the general law of nature, or the unworthy possessor? It will never follow from all this, that government is *rightfully* founded on *property* alone. What shall we say then? Is not government founded on *grace*? No. Nor on *force*? No. Nor on *compact*? Nor *property*? Not altogether on either. Has it *any* solid foundation? any chief corner stone, but what accident, chance, or confusion may lay one moment and destroy the next? I think it has an everlasting foundation in the *unchangeable will of God*, the author of nature, whose laws never vary. The same omniscient, omnipotent, infinitely good and gracious Creator of the universe, who has been pleased to make it necessary that what we call matter should *gravitate*, for the celestial bodies to roll round their axes, dance their orbits, and perform their various revolutions in that beautiful order and concert, which we all admire, has made it *equally* necessary that from *Adam* and *Eve* to these degenerate days, the different sexes should sweetly *attract* each other, form societies of *single* families, of which

larger bodies and communities are as naturally, mechanically, and necessarily combined, as the dew of Heaven and the soft distilling rain is collected by the all enlivening heat of the sun. *Government* is therefore most
evidently founded on the necessities of our nature. It is by no means an
arbitrary thing, depending merely on *compact* or *human* will for its existence. * * *

Let no man think I am about to commence advocate for *despotism*, because I affirm that government is founded on the necessity of our natures;
and that an original supreme Sovereign, absolute, and uncontrollable,
earthly power *must* exist in and preside over every society; from whose
final decisions there can be no appeal but directly to Heaven. * * * I say
supreme absolute power is *originally* and *ultimately* in the people; and
they never did in fact *freely*, nor can they *rightfully* make an absolute, unlimited renunciation of this divine right. It is ever in the nature of the
thing given in *trust*, and on a condition the performance of which no mortal can dispense with; namely, that the person or persons on whom the
sovereignty is conferred by the people, shall incessantly consult *their*
good. Tyranny of all kinds is to be abhorred, whether it be in the hands of
one, or of the few, or of the many. * * *

The *end* of government being the *good* of mankind, points out its great
duties: It is above all things to provide for the security, the quiet, and
happy enjoyment of life, liberty, and property. There is no one act which
a government can have a right to make, that does not tend to the advancement of the security, tranquility, and prosperity of the people. * * *

The form of government is by *nature* and by *right* so far left to the individuals of each society, that they may alter it from a simple democracy
or government of all over all, to any other form they please. * * *

The same law of nature and of reason is equally obligatory on a
democracy, an *aristocracy*, and a *monarchy*: Whenever the administrators,
in any of those forms, deviate from truth, justice and equity, they verge
towards tyranny, and are to be opposed; and if they prove incorrigible,
they will be *deposed* by the people, if the people are not rendered too
abject. * * *

OF COLONIES IN GENERAL

A plantation or colony, is a settlement of subjects, in a *territory disjoined*
or remote from the mother country, and may be made by private adventurers or the public; but in both cases the Colonists are entitled to as *ample* rights, liberties, and priviledges as the subjects of the mother country
are, and in some respects *to more*. * * *

OF THE NATURAL RIGHTS OF COLONISTS

In order to form an idea of the natural rights of the Colonists, I presume it will be granted that they are men, the common children of the same Creator with their brethren of Great Britain. Nature has placed all such in a state of equality and perfect freedom, to act within the bounds of the laws of nature and reason, without consulting the will or regarding the humor, the passions or whims of any other man, unless they are formed into a society or body politic. * * *

By being or becoming members of society, they have not renounced their natural liberty in any greater degree than other good citizens, and if this be taken from them without their consent, they are so far enslaved. * * *

OF THE POLITICAL AND CIVIL RIGHTS OF THE BRITISH COLONIES

I also lay it down as one of the first principles from whence I intend to deduce the civil rights of the British colonies, that all of them are subject to, and dependent on Great Britain; and that therefore as over subordinate governments, the parliament of Great Britain has an undoubted power and lawful authority to make acts for the general good, that by naming them, shall and ought to be equally binding, as upon the subjects of Great Britain within the realm. This principle, I presume will be readily granted on the other side of the Atlantic. It has been practiced upon for twenty years to my knowledge, in the province of the *Massachusetts Bay*; and I have ever received it, that it has been so from the beginning, in this and the sister provinces, thro' the continent. * * *

Every British subject born on the continent of America, or in any other of the British dominions, is by the law of God and nature, by the common law, and by act of parliament, (exclusive of all charters from the Crown) entitled to all the natural, essential, inherent, and inseparable rights of our fellow subjects in Great Britain. Among those rights are the following, which it is humbly conceived no man or body of men, not excepting the parliament, justly, equitably and consistently with their own rights and the constitution, can take away.

1st. *That the supreme and subordinate powers of the legislation should be free and sacred in the hands where the community have once rightfully placed them.*

2dly. *The supreme national legislative cannot be altered justly 'till the commonwealth is dissolved, nor a subordinate legislative taken away without forfeiture or other good cause.* Nor then can the subjects in the subordinate government be reduced to a state of slavery, and subject to the despotic rule of others. A state has no right to make slaves of the conquered. Even when the subordinate right of legislature is forfeited, and so declared, this cannot affect the natural persons either of those who were invested with it, or the inhabitants, so far as to deprive them of the rights of subjects and of men. The colonists will have an equitable right notwithstanding any such forfeiture of charter, to be represented in Parliament, or to have some new subordinate legislature among themselves. It would be best if they had both. Deprived however of their common rights as subjects, they cannot lawfully be while they remain such. A representation in Parliament from the several Colonies, since they are become so large and numerous, as to be called on not to maintain provincial government, civil and military, among themselves, for this they have cheerfully done, but to contribute towards the support of a national standing army, by reason of the heavy national debt, when they themselves owe a large one, contracted in the common cause, can't be thought an unreasonable thing, nor if asked, could it be called an immodest request. * * *

No representation of the Colonies in parliament alone, would however be equivalent to a subordinate legislative among themselves; nor so well answer the ends of increasing their prosperity and the commerce of Great Britain. It would be impossible for the parliament to judge so well, of their abilities to bear taxes, impositions on trade, and other duties and burthens, or of the local laws that might be really needful, as a legislative here.

3rdly. *No legislative, supreme or subordinate, has a right to make itself arbitrary.*

It would be a most manifest contradiction, for a free legislative, like that of Great Britain, to make itself arbitrary.

4thly. *The supreme legislative cannot justly assume a power of ruling by extempore arbitrary decrees, but is bound to dispense justice by known settled rules, and by duly authorized independent judges.*

5thly. *The supreme power cannot take from any man any part of his property, without his consent in person, or by representation.*

6thly. *The legislature cannot transfer the power of making laws to any other hands.*

These are their bounds, which by God and nature are fixed, hitherto have they a right to come, and no further.

1. *To govern by stated laws.*
2. *Those laws should have no other end ultimately, but the good of the people.*

3. *Taxes are not to be laid on the people, but by their consent in person, or by deputation.*
4. *Their whole power is not transferable.*

These are the first principles of law and justice, and the great barriers of a free state, and of the British constitution in particular. I ask, I want no more—Now let it be shown how 'tis reconcilable with principles, or to many other fundamental maxims of the British constitution, as well as the natural and civil rights, which by the laws of their country, all British subjects are entitled to, as their best inheritance and birth-right, that all the northern colonies, who are without one representative in the house of Commons, should be taxed by the British parliament. * * *

I can see no reason to doubt but that the imposition of taxes, whether on trade, or on land, or houses, or ships, on real or personal, fixed or floating property, in the colonies is absolutely irreconcilable with the rights of the colonists as British subjects and as men. I say men, for in a state of nature no man can take my property from me without my consent: if he does, he deprives me of my liberty and makes me a slave. If such a proceeding is a breach of the law of nature, no law of society can make it just. The very act of taxing exercised over those who are not represented appears to me to be depriving them of one of their most essential rights as freemen, and if continued seems to be in effect an entire disfranchisement of every civil right. For what one civil right is worth a rush after a man's property is subject to be taken from him at pleasure without his consent? If a man is not his *own assessor* in person or by deputy, his liberty is gone or lays entirely at the mercy of others. * * *

Now can there be any liberty, where property is taken away without consent? Can it with any colour of truth, justice or equity, be affirmed, that the northern colonies are represented in parliament? Has this whole continent of near three thousand miles in length, and in which and his other American dominions, his Majesty has, or very soon will have, some millions of as good, loyal and useful subjects, white and black, as any in the three kingdoms, the election of one member of the house of commons?

Is there the least difference, as to the consent of the Colonists, whether taxes and impositions are laid on their trade, and other property, by the crown alone, or by the parliament.[?] As it is agreed on all hands, the Crown alone cannot impose them, we should be justifiable in refusing to pay them, but must and ought to yield obedience to an act of parliament, tho' erroneous, 'till repealed.

* * *

To say the parliament is absolute and arbitrary, is a contradiction. The parliament cannot make 2 and 2, 5; Omnipotency cannot do it. The supreme power in a state, is *jus dicere* only;—*jus dare*, strictly speaking, belongs alone to God. Parliaments are in all cases to declare what is for the good of the whole; but it is not the declaration of Parliament that makes it so: There must be in every instance, a higher authority, viz. GOD. Should an act of parliament be against any of *his* natural laws, which are *immutably* true, their declaration would be contrary to eternal truth, equity and justice, and consequently void: and so it would be adjudged by the parliament itself, when convinced of their mistake. Upon this great principle, parliaments repeal such acts, as soon as they find they have been mistaken, in having declared them to be for the public good, when in fact they were not so. When such mistake is evident and palpable * * * the judges of the executive courts have declared the act 'of a whole parliament void.' See here the grandeur of the British constitution! See the wisdom of our ancestors! The supreme *legislative*, and the supreme *executive*, are a perpetual check and balance to each other. If the supreme executive *errs*, it is informed by the supreme legislative in parliament: If the supreme legislative errs, it is informed by the supreme executive in the King's courts of law—Here, the King appears, as represented by his judges, in the highest lustre and majesty, as supreme executor of the commonwealth; and he never shines brighter, but on his Throne, at the head of the supreme legislative. This is government! This, is a constitution! to preserve which, either from foreign or domestic foes, has cost oceans of blood and treasure in every age; and the blood and the treasure have upon the whole been well spent. * * *

We all think ourselves happy under Great Britain. We love, esteem, and reverence our mother country, and adore our King. And could the choice of independency be offered the colonies, or subjection to Great Britain upon any terms above absolute slavery, I am convinced they would accept the latter. * * *

These colonies are and always have been, 'entirely subject to the crown,' in the legal sense of the terms. But if any politician of 'tampering activity, of wrongheaded inexperience, wisted to be meddling,' means, by 'curbing the colonies in time,' and by 'being made entirely subject to the crown;' that this subjection should be absolute, and confined to the crown, he had better have suppressed his wishes. This never will nor can be done, without making the colonists vassals of the crown. * * * A continuation of the same liberties that have been enjoyed by the colonists since the revolution, and the same moderation of government exercised towards them, will bind them in perpetual lawful and willing subjection, obedience and love to Great Britain: She and her colonies will both prosper and flourish: The monarchy will remain in sound health and full vigor at that blessed period, when the proud arbitrary tyrants of the continent shall either unite in the deliverance of the human race, or resign their crowns. Rescued, human nature must and will be, from the general slavery that has so long triumphed over the species. Great Britain has done much towards it: What a Glory will it be for her to complete the work throughout the world! * * *

The sum of my argument is, That civil government is of God: That the administrators of it were originally the whole people: That they might have devolved it on whom they pleased: That this devolution is fiduciary, for the good of the whole; That by the British constitution, this devolution is on the King, lords, and commons, the supreme, sacred, and uncontrollable legislative power, not only in the realm, but thro' the dominions: That by the abdication, the original compact was broken to pieces: That by the revolution, it was renewed, and more firmly established, and the rights and liberties of the subject in all parts of the dominions, more fully explained and confirmed: That in consequence of this establishment, and the acts of succession and union his Majesty GEORGE III is rightful king and sovereign, and with his parliament, the supreme legislative of Great Britain, France and Ireland, and the dominions thereto belonging: That this constitution is the most free one, and by far the best, now existing on earth: That by this constitution, every man in the dominion is a free man: That no parts of his Majesty's dominions can be taxed without their consent: That every part has a right to be represented in the supreme or some subordinate legislature: That the refusal of this, would seem to be a contradiction in practice to the theory of the constitution: That the colonies are subordinate dominions, and are now in such a state, as to make it best for the good of the whole, that they should not only be continued in the enjoyment of subordinate legislation, but be also represented in some proportion to their number and estates, in the grand legislature of the nation: That this would firmly unite all parts of the British empire, in the greatest peace and prosperity; and render it invulnerable and perpetual.

SAMUEL ADAMS

The Rights of the Colonists (1772)

A radical egalitarian and democrat, the Boston brewer Samuel Adams (1722–1803) founded the Non-Importation Association, the Sons of Liberty, and the Committees of Correspondence. He also helped organized the opposition to the Sugar, Stamp, and Townshend acts. Adams was one of the first and most ardent proponents of American independence. Later he served as governor of Massachusetts and as a member of the Continental Congress. Adopted by Boston on November 20, 1772, his statement on the rights of colonists to life, liberty, and property is vintage Locke: it asserts the right of the colonists to government by consent and the protection of property as the foundation of liberty.

ADOPTED BY THE TOWN OF BOSTON, NOVEMBER 20, 1772

The Committee appointed by the Town the second Instant "to State the Rights of the Colonists and of this Province in particular, as Men, as Christians, and as Subjects; to communicate and publish the same to the several Towns in this Province and to the World as the sense of this Town with the Infringements and Violations thereof that have been, or from Time to Time may be made. Also requesting of each Town a free Communication of their Sentiments Reported—

First, a State of the *Rights* of the Colonists and of this Province in particular—

Secondly, A List of the *Infringements*, and Violations of those Rights.—

Thirdly, A Letter of Correspondence with the other Towns.—

1st. Natural Rights of the Colonists as Men.—

Among the Natural Rights of the Colonists are these First. a Right to *Life*; Secondly to *Liberty*; thirdly to *Property*; together with the Right to support and defend them in the best manner they can—Those are evident Branches of, rather than deductions from the Duty of Self Preservation, commonly called the first Law of Nature—

All Men have a Right to remain in a State of Nature as long as they please: And in case of intollerable Oppression, Civil or Religious, to leave the Society they belong to, and enter into another.—

When Men enter into Society, it is by voluntary consent; and they have a right to demand and insist upon the performance of such conditions, And previous limitations as form an equitable *original compact*.—

Every natural Right not expressly given up or from the nature of a Social Compact necessarily ceded remains.—

All positive and civil laws, should conform as far as possible, to the Law of natural reason and equity.—

As neither reason requires, nor religeon permits the contrary, every Man living in or out of a state of civil society, has a right peaceably and quietly to worship God according to the dictates of his conscience.—

"Just and true liberty, equal and impartial liberty" in matters spiritual and temporal, is a thing that all Men are clearly entitled to, by the eternal and immutable laws Of God and nature, as well as by the law of Nations, & all well grounded municipal laws, which must have their foundation in the former.—

In regard to Religeon, mutual tolleration in the different professions thereof, is what all good and candid minds in all ages have ever practiced; and both by precept and example inculcated on mankind: And it is now generally agreed among christians that this spirit of toleration in the fullest extent consistent with the being of civil society "is the chief characteristical mark of the true church" & In so much that Mr. Lock has asserted, and proved beyond the possibility of contradiction on any solid ground, that such toleration ought to be extended to all whose doctrines are not subversive of society. The only Sects which he thinks ought to be, and which by all wise laws are excluded from such toleration, are those who teach Doctrines subversive of the Civil Government under which they live. The Roman Catholicks or Papists are excluded by reason of such Doctrines as these "that Princes excommunicated may be deposed, and those they call *Hereticks* may be destroyed without mercy; besides their recognizing the Pope in so absolute a manner, in subversion of Government, by introducing as far as possible into the states, under whose protection they enjoy life, liberty and property, that solecism in politicks, Imperium in imperio leading directly to the worst anarchy and confusion, civil discord, war and blood shed—

The natural liberty of Men by entring into society is abrid'g'd or restrained so far only as is necessary for the Great end of Society the best good of the whole—

In the state of nature, every man is under God, Judge and sole Judge, of his own rights and the injuries done him: By entering into society, he agrees to an Arbiter or indifferent Judge between him and his neighbours;

but he no more renounces his original right, than by taking a cause out of the ordinary course of law, and leaving the decision to Referees or indifferent Arbitrations. In the last case he must pay the Referees for time and trouble; he should be also willing to pay his Just quota for the support of government, the law and constitution; the end of which is to furnish indifferent and impartial Judges in all cases that may happen, whether civil ecclesiastical, marine or military.—

"The natural liberty of man is to be free from any superior power on earth, and not to be under the will or legislative authority of man; but only to have the law of nature for his rule."—

In the state of nature men may as the *Patriarchs* did, employ hired servants for the defence of their lives, liberty and property: and they should pay them reasonable wages. Government was instituted for the purposes of common defence; and those who hold the reins of government have an equitable natural right to an honourable support from the same principle "that the labourer is worthy of his hire" but then the same community which they serve, ought to be assessors of their pay: Governors have no right to seek what they please; by this, instead of being content with the station assigned them, that of honourable servants of the society, they would soon become Absolute masters, Despots, and Tyrants. Hence as a private man has a right to say, what wages he will give in his private affairs, so has a Community to determine what they will give and grant of their Substance, for the Administration of publick affairs. And in both cases more are ready generally to offer their Service at the proposed and stipulated price, than are able and willing to perform their duty.—

In short it is the greatest absurdity to suppose it in the power of one or any number of men at the entering into society, to renounce their essential natural rights, or the means of preserving those rights when the great end of civil government from the very nature of its institution is for the support, protection and defence of those very rights: the principal of which as is before observed, are life liberty and property. If men through fear, fraud or mistake, should *in terms* renounce and give up any essential natural right, the eternal law of reason and the great end of society, would absolutely vacate such renunciation; the right to freedom being *the gift* of God Almighty, it is not in the power of Man to alienate this gift, and voluntarily become a slave—

2ᵈ. *The Rights of the Colonists as Christians*—

These may be best understood by reading—and carefully studying the institutes of the great Lawgiver and head of the Christian Church: which are to be found closely written and promulgated in the *New Testament*—

By the Act of the British Parliament commonly called the Toleration Act, every subject in England Except Papists &c was restored to, and re-established in, his natural right to worship God according to the dictates of his own conscience. And by the Charter of this Province it is granted ordained and established (that it is declared as an original right) that there shall be liberty of conscience allowed in the worship of God, to all christians except Papists, inhabiting or which shall inhabit or be resident within said Province or Territory. Magna Charta itself is in substance but a constrained Declaration, or proclamation, and promulgation in the name of King, Lord, and Commons of the sense the latter had of their original inherent, indefeazible natural Rights, as also those of free Citizens equally perdurable with the other. That great author that great jurist, and even that Court writer Mr. Justice Blackstone holds that this recognition was justly obtained of King John sword in hand: and peradventure it must be one day sword in hand again rescued and preserved from total destruction and oblivion.—

3^d. *The Rights of the Colonists as Subjects*

A Common Wealth or state is a body politick or civil society of men, united together to promote their mutual safety and prosperity, by means of their union.

The *absolute Rights* of Englishmen, and all freemen in or out of Civil society, are principally, *personal security personal liberty* and *private property*.

All Persons born in the British American Colonies are by the laws of God and nature, and by the Common law of England, *exclusive of all charters from the Crown*, well Entitled, and by the Acts of the British Parliament are declared to be entitled to all the natural essential, inherent & inseperable Rights Liberties and Privileges of Subjects born in Great Britain, or within the Realm. Among those Rights are the following; which no men or body of men, consistently with their own rights as men and citizens or members of society, can for themselves give up, or take away from others.

First, "The first fundamental positive law of all Commonwealths or States, is the establishing the legislative power; as the first fundamental *natural* law also, which is to govern even the legislative power itself, is the preservation of the Society."

Secondly, The Legislative has no right to absolute arbitrary power over the lives and fortunes of the people: Nor can mortals assume a prerogative, not only too high for men, but for Angels; and therefore reserved for the exercise of the *Deity* alone.—

"The Legislative cannot Justly *assume* to itself a power to rule by extempore arbitrary decrees; but it is bound to see that Justice is dispensed, and that the rights of the subjects be decided, by promulgated, standing and known laws, and authorized *independent Judges*;" that is independent as far as possible of Prince or People. *"There shall be one rule of Justice for rich and poor; for the favorite in Court, and the Countryman at the Plough."*

Thirdly, The supreme power cannot Justly take from any man, any part of his property without his consent, in person or by his Representative.—

These are some of the first principles of natural law & Justice, and the great Barriers of all free states, and of the British Constitution in particular. It is utterly irreconcileable to these principles, and to many other fundamental maxims of the common law, common sense and reason, that a British house of commons, should have a right, at pleasure, to give and grant the property of the Colonists. That these Colonists are well entitled to all the essential rights, liberties and privileges of men and freemen, born in Britain, is manifest, not only from the Colony charter, in general, but acts of the British Parliament. The statute of the 13th of George 2. c. 7 naturalizes even foreigners after seven years residence. The words of the Massachusetts Charter are these, "And further our will and pleasure is, and we do hereby for us, our heirs and successors, grant establish and ordain, that all and every of the subjects of us, our heirs and successors, which shall go to and inhabit within our said province or territory and every of their children which shall happen to be born there, or on the seas in going thither, or returning from thence shall have and enjoy, all liberties and immunities of free and natural subjects within any of the dominions of us, our heirs and successors, to all intents constructions & purposes whatsoever as if they and every of them were born within this our Realm of England." Now what liberty can there be, where property is taken away without consent? Can it be said with any colour of truth and Justice, that this Continent of three thousand miles in length, and of a breadth as yet unexplored, in which however, its supposed, there are five millions of people, has the least voice, vote or influence in the decisions of the British Parliament? Have they, all together, any more right or power to return a single number to that house of commons, who have not inadvertently, but deliberately assumed a power to dispose of their lives, Liberties and properties, then to choose an Emperor of China! Had the Colonists a right to return members to the british parliament, it would only be hurtfull; as from their local situation and circumstances it is impossible they should be ever truly and properly represented there. The inhabitants of this country in all probability in a few years will be more numerous, than those of Great Britain and Ireland together; yet it is absurdly expected by the promoters of the present measures, that these, with their posterity to all generations, should be easy while their property, shall be disposed of by a house of commons at three thousand miles distant from them; and who cannot be supposed to have the least care or concern for their real interest: Who have not only no natural care for their interest, but must be *in effect* bribed against it; as every burden they lay on the colonists is so much saved or gained to themselves. Hitherto many of the Colonists have been free from Quit Rents; but if the breath of a british house of commons can originate an act for taking away all our money, our lands will go next or be subject to rack rents from haughty and relentless landlords who will ride at ease, while we are trodden in the dirt. The Colonists have been branded with the odious names of traitors and rebels, only for complaining of their grievances; How long such treatment will, or ought to be born is submitted.

JONATHAN BOUCHER

On Civil Liberty, Passive Obedience, and Non-Resistance (1774)

A stalwart supporter of established authority, the Englishman Jonathan Boucher (1738–1804) served as the rector of Anglican parishes in Virginia and later in Maryland. A fierce critic of the Lockean philosophy of natural rights, Boucher asserted the divine right of kings against American claims to self-government. He vehemently opposed colonial resistance to authority because he believed that it violated religious obligations to obey the law, which was the only genuine foundation for liberty. Boucher was forced to leave Maryland at the outbreak of the American Revolution and returned permanently to England.

Obedience to Government is every man's duty, because it is every man's interest: but it is particularly incumbent on Christians, because (in addition to its moral fitness) it is enjoined by the positive commands of God: and therefore, when Christians are disobedient to human ordinances, they are also disobedient to God. If the form of government under which the good providence of God has been pleased to place us be mild and free, it is our duty to enjoy it with gratitude and with thankfulness; and, in particular, to be careful not to abuse it by licentiousness. If it be less indulgent and less liberal than in reason it ought to be, still it is our duty not to disturb and destroy the peace of the community, by becoming refractory and rebellious subjects, and *resisting the ordinances of God.* However humiliating such acquiescence may seem to men of warm and eager minds, the wisdom of God in having made it our duty is manifest.

For, as it is the natural temper and bias of the human mind to be impatient under restraint, it was wise and merciful in the blessed Author of our religion not to add any new impulse to the natural force of this prevailing propensity, but, with the whole weight of his authority, altogether to discountenance every tendency to disobedience. * * *

* * * To respect the laws, is to respect liberty in the only rational sense in which the term can be used; for liberty consists in a subserviency to law. "Where there is no law," says Mr. Locke, "there is no freedom." The mere man of nature (if such an one there ever was) has no freedom: *all his lifetime he is subject to bondage.* It is by being included within the pale of civil polity and government that he takes his rank in society as a free man.

Hence it follows, that we are free, or otherwise, as we are governed by law, or by the mere arbitrary will, or wills, of any individual, or any number of individuals. And liberty is not the setting at nought and despising established laws—much less the making our own wills the rule of our own actions, or the actions of others—and not bearing (whilst yet we dictate to others) the being dictated to, even by the laws of the land; but it is the being governed by law, and by law only.

* * *

To pursue liberty, then, in a manner not warranted by law, whatever the pretence may be, is clearly to be hostile to liberty: and those persons who thus *promise you liberty,* are themselves *the servants of corruption.*

"Civil liberty (says an excellent writer) is a severe and a restrained thing; implies, in the notion of it, authority, settled subordinations, subjection, and obedience; and is altogether as much hurt by too little of this kind, as by too much of it. And the love of liberty, when it is indeed the love of liberty, which carries us to withstand tyranny, will as much carry us to reverence authority, and to support it; for this most obvious reason, that one is as necessary to the being of liberty, as the other is destructive of it. And, therefore, the love of liberty which does not produce this effect, the love of liberty which is not a real principle of dutiful behaviour towards authority, is as hypocritical as the religion which is not productive of a good life. Licentiousness is, in truth, such an excess of liberty as is of the same nature with tyranny. For, what is the difference betwixt them, but that one is lawless power exercised under pretence of authority, or by persons vested with it; the other, lawless power exercised under pretence of liberty, or without any pretence at all? A people, then, must always be less free in proportion as they are more licentious; licentiousness being not only different from liberty, but directly contrary to it—a direct breach upon it."

True liberty, then, is a liberty to do every thing that is right, and the being restrained from doing any thing that is wrong. So far from our having a right to do every thing that we please, under a notion of liberty, liberty itself is limited and confined—but limited and confined only by laws which are at the same time both it's foundation and it's support. It can, however, hardly be necessary to inform you, that ideas and notions respecting liberty, very different from these, are daily suggested in the speeches and the writings of the times; and also that some opinions on the subject of government at large, which appear to me to be particularly loose and dangerous, are advanced in the sermon now under consideration; and that, therefore, you will acknowledge the propriety of my bestowing some farther notice on them both.

It is laid down in this sermon, as a settled maxim, that the end of government is "the common good of mankind." I am not sure that the position itself is indisputable; but, if it were, it would by no means follow that, "this common good being matter of common feeling, government must therefore have been instituted by common consent." There is an appearance of logical accuracy and precision in this statement; but it is only an appearance. The position is vague and loose; and the assertion is made without an attempt to prove it. If by men's "common feelings" we are to understand that principle in the human mind called common sense, the assertion is either unmeaning and insignificant, or it is false. In no instance have mankind ever yet agreed as to what is, or is not, "the common good." A form or mode of government cannot be named, which these "common feelings" and "common consent," the sole arbiters, as it seems, of "common good," have not, at one time or another, set up and established, and again pulled down and reprobated. What one people in one age have concurred in establishing as the "common good," another in another age have voted to be mischievous and big with ruin. The premises, therefore, that "the common good is matter of common feeling," being false, the consequence drawn from it, viz. that government was instituted by "common consent," is of course equally false.

This popular notion, that government was originally formed by the consent or by a compact of the people, rests on, and is supported by, another similar notion, not less popular, nor better founded. This other notion is, that the whole human race is born equal; and that no man is naturally inferior, or, in any respect, subjected to another; and that he can be made subject to another only by his own consent. The position is equally ill-founded and false both in it's premises and conclusions. In hardly any sense that can be imagined is the position strictly true; but, as applied to the case under consideration, it is demonstrably not true. Man differs from man in every thing that can be supposed to lead to supremacy and subjection, *as one star differs from another star in glory.* It was the purpose of the Creator, that man should be social: but, without government, there can be no society; nor, without some relative inferiority and superiority, can there be any government. A musical instrument composed of chords, keys, or pipes, all perfectly equal in size and power, might as well be expected to produce harmony, as a society composed of members all perfectly equal to be productive of order and peace. If (according to the idea of the advocates of this chimerical scheme of equality) no man could rightfully *be compelled to come in* and be a member even of a government to be formed by a regular compact, but by his own individual consent; it clearly follows, from the same principles, that neither could he rightfully be made or compelled to submit to the ordinances of any government already formed, to which he has not individually or actually consented. On the principle of equality, neither his parents, nor even the vote of a majority of the society, (however virtuously and honourably that vote might be obtained,) can have any such authority over any man. Neither can it be maintained that acquiescence implies consent; because acquiescence may have been extorted from impotence or incapacity. Even an explicit consent can bind a man no longer than he chooses to be bound. The same principle of equality that exempts him from being governed without his own consent, clearly entitles him to recall and resume that consent whenever he sees fit; and he alone has a right to judge when and for what reasons it may be resumed.

Any attempt, therefore, to introduce this fantastic system into practice, would reduce the whole business of social life to the wearisome, confused, and useless talk of mankind's first expressing, and then withdrawing, their consent to an endless succession of schemes of government. Governments, though always forming, would never be completely formed: for, the majority to-day, might be the minority to-morrow; and, of course, that which is now fixed might and would be soon unfixed. Mr. Locke indeed says, that, "by consenting with others to make one body-politic under government, a man puts himself under an obligation to every one of that society to submit to the determination of the majority, and to be concluded by it." For the sake of the peace of society, it is undoubtedly reasonable and necessary that this should be the case: but, on the principles of the system now under consideration, before Mr. Locke or any of his followers can have authority to say that it actually is the case, it must be stated and proved that every individual man, on entering into the social compact, did first consent, and declare his consent, to be concluded and bound in all cases by the vote of the majority. In making such a declaration, he would certainly consult both his interest and his duty; but at the same time he would also completely relinquish the principle of equality, and eventually subject himself to the possibility of being governed by ignorant and corrupt tyrants. Mr. Locke himself afterwards disproves his own position respecting this supposed obligation to submit to the "determination of the majority," when he argues that a right of resistance still exists in the governed; for, what is resistance but a recalling and resuming the consent heretofore supposed to have been given, and in fact refusing to submit to the "determination of the majority?" It does not clearly appear what Mr. Locke exactly meant by what he calls "the determination of the majority": but the only rational and practical public manner of declaring "the determination of the majority," is by law: the laws, therefore, in all countries, even in those that are despotically governed, are to be regarded as the declared "determination of a majority" of the members of that community; because, in such cases, even acquiescence only must be looked upon as equivalent to a declaration. A right of resistance, therefore, for which Mr. Locke contends, is incompatible with the duty of submitting to the determination of "the majority," for which he also contends.

It is indeed impossible to carry into effect any government which, even by compact, might be framed with this reserved right of resistance. Accordingly there is no record that any such government ever was so formed. If there had, it must have carried the seeds of it's decay in it's very constitution. For, as those men who make a government (certain that they have the power) can have no hesitation to vote that they also have the right to unmake it; and as the people, in all circumstances, but more especially when trained to make and unmake governments, are at least as well disposed to do the latter as the former, it is morally impossible that there should be any thing like permanency or stability in a government so formed. Such a system, therefore, can produce only perpetual dissensions and contests, and bring back mankind to a supposed state of nature; arming every man's hand, like Ishmael's, against every man, and rendering the world an *aceldama*, or field of blood.—Such theories of government seem to give something like plausibility to the notions of those other modern theorists, who regard all governments as invasions of the natural rights of men, usurpations, and tyranny. On this principle it would follow, and could not be denied, that government was indeed fundamentally, as our people are sedulously taught it still is, an evil. Yet it is to government that mankind owe their having, after their fall and corruption, been again reclaimed, from a state of barbarity and war, to the conveniency and the safety of the social state: and it is by means of government that society is still preserved, the weak protected from the strong, and the artless and innocent from the wrongs of proud oppressors.

* * *

Of all the theories respecting the origin of government with which the world has ever been either puzzled, amused, or instructed, that of the Scriptures alone is accompanied by no insuperable difficulties.

It was not to be expected from an all-wise and all-merciful Creator, that, having formed creatures capable of order and rule, he should turn them loose into the world under the guidance only of their own unruly wills; that, like so many wild beasts, they might tear and worry one another in their mad contests for preeminence. His purpose from the first, no doubt, was, that men should *live godly and sober lives.* But, such is the sad estate of our corrupted nature, that, ever since the Fall, we have been averse from good, and prone to evil. We are, indeed, so disorderly and unmanageable, that, were it not for the restraints and the terrors of human laws, it would not be possible for us to dwell together. But as men were clearly formed for society, and to dwell together, which yet they cannot do without the restraints of law, or, in other words, without government, it is fair to infer that government was also the original intention of God, who never decrees the end, without also decreeing the means. Accordingly, when man was made, his Maker did not turn him adrift into a shoreless ocean, without star or compass to steer by. As soon as there were some to be governed, there were also some to govern: and the first man, by virtue of that paternal claim, on which all subsequent governments have been founded, was first invested with the power of government. For, we are not to judge of the Scriptures of God, as we do of some other writings; and so, where no express precept appears, hastily to conclude that none was given. On the contrary, in commenting on the Scriptures, we are frequently called upon to find out the precept from the practice. Taking this rule, then, for our direction in the present instance, we find, that, copying after the fair model of heaven itself, wherein there was government even among the angels, the families of the earth were subjected to rulers, at first set over them by God: *for, there is no power, but of God; the powers that be are ordained of God.* The first father was the first king: and if (according to the rule just laid down) the law may be inferred from the practice, it was thus that all government originated; and monarchy is it's most ancient form.

JOHN ADAMS

Novanglus (1775)

Revolutionary leader, diplomat, first vice president, second president of the United States, and cousin of Samuel Adams, John Adams (1735– 1826) was committed to classical republican ideals. Adams responded to loyalist tracts with a series of essays written under the pseudonym "Novanglus." A great admirer of the British constitution and a committed Whig, Adams argued that, because the British government was a republic and not an empire, the colonists were entitled to govern themselves in matters of internal policy.

The whigs allow that, from the necessity of a case not provided for by common law, and to supply a defect in the British dominions, which there undoubtedly is, if they are to be governed only by that law, America has all along consented, still consents, and ever will consent, that parliament, being the most powerful legislature in the dominions, should regulate the trade of the dominions. This is founding the authority of parliament to regulate our trade, upon *compact* and *consent* of the colonies, not upon any principle of common or statute law; not upon any original principle of the English constitution; not upon the principle that parliament is the supreme and sovereign legislature over them in all cases whatsoever. The question is not, therefore, whether the authority of parliament extends to the colonies in any case, for it is admitted by the whigs, that it does in that of commerce; but whether it extends in all cases. * * *

I agree, that "two supreme and independent authorities cannot exist in the same state," any more than two supreme beings in one universe; and, therefore, I contend, that our provincial legislatures are the only supreme authorities in our colonies. Parliament, notwithstanding this, may be allowed an authority supreme and sovereign over the ocean, which may be limited by the banks of the ocean, or the bounds of our charters; our charters give us no authority over the high seas. Parliament has our consent to assume a jurisdiction over them. And here is a line fairly drawn between the rights of Britain and the rights of the colonies, namely, the banks of the ocean, or low-water mark; the line of division between common law, and civil or maritime law. If this is not sufficient,—if parliament are at a loss for any principle of natural, civil, maritime, moral, or common law, on which to ground any authority over the high seas, the Atlantic especially, let the colonies be treated like reasonable creatures, and they will discover great ingenuity and modesty. The acts of trade and navigation might be confirmed by provincial laws, and carried into execution by our own courts and juries, and in this case, illicit trade would be cut up by the roots forever. * * *

The first planters of Plymouth were "our ancestors" in the strictest sense. They had no charter or patent for the land they took possession of; and derived no authority from the English parliament or crown to set up their government. They purchased land of the Indians, and set up a government of their own, on the simple principle of nature; and afterwards purchased a patent for the land of the council at Plymouth; but never purchased any charter for government, of the crown or the king, and continued to exercise all the powers of government, legislative, executive, and judicial, upon the plain ground of an original contract among the independent individuals for sixty-eight years, that is until their incorporation with Massachusetts by our present charter. The same may be said of the colonies which emigrated to Say-Brook, New Haven, and other parts of Connecticut. They seem to have had no idea of dependence on parliament, any more than on the conclave.

* * *

Thus, it appears, that the ancient Massachusettensians and Virginians had precisely the same sense of the authority of parliament, namely,—that it had none at all; and the same sense of the necessity that, by the voluntary act of the colonies—their free, cheerful consent—it should be allowed the power of regulating trade; and this is precisely the idea of the late congress at Philadelphia, expressed in the fourth proposition of their Bill of Rights.

But this was the sense of the parent country, too, at that time; for King Charles II, in a letter to the Massachusetts, after this law had been laid before him, has these words: "We are informed that you have lately made *some good provision* for observing the acts of trade and navigation, which is well pleasing unto us." Had he or his ministers an idea that parliament was the sovereign legislative over the colony? If he had, would he not have censured this law, as an insult to that legislative?

I sincerely hope we shall see no more such round affirmations, that "it was the sense of the parent country and our ancestors, that they were to remain subject to parliament." So far from thinking themselves subject to parliament, it is clear that, during the interregnum, it was their desire and design to have been a free commonwealth, and independent republic; and after the restoration, it was with the utmost reluctance that, in the course of sixteen or seventeen years, they were brought to take the oaths of allegiance; and for some time after this, they insisted upon taking an oath of fidelity to the country, before that of allegiance to the king.

* * *

"If the colonies are not subject to the authority of parliament, Great Britain and the colonies must be distinct states, as completely so as England and Scotland were before the union, or as Great Britain and Hanover are now." There is no need of being startled at this consequence. It is very harmless. There is no absurdity at all in it. Distinct states may be united under one king. And those states may be further cemented and united together by a treaty of commerce. This is the case. We have, by our own express consent, contracted to observe the Navigation Act, and by our implied consent, by long usage and uninterrupted acquiescence, have submitted to the other acts of trade, however grievous some of them may be. This may be compared to a treaty of commerce, by which those distinct states are cemented together, in perpetual league and amity. And if any further ratifications of this pact or treaty are necessary, the colonies would readily enter into them, provided their other liberties were inviolate.

* * *

As to giving his majesty those titles, I have no objection at all; I wish he would be graciously pleased to assume them.

The only proposition in all this writer's long string of pretended absurdities, which he says follows from the position that we are distinct states, is this:—That "as the king must govern each state by its parliament, those several parliaments would pursue the particular interest of its own state; and however well disposed the king might be to pursue a line of interest that was common to all, the checks and control that he would meet with would render it impossible." Every argument ought to be allowed its full weight; and therefore candor obliges me to acknowledge, that here lies all the difficulty that there is in this whole controversy. There has been, from first to last, on both sides of the Atlantic, an idea, an apprehension, that it was necessary there should be some superintending power, to draw together all the wills, and unite all the strength of the subjects in all the dominions, in case of war, and in the case of trade. The necessity of this, in case of war, has been so apparent, that, as has often been said, we have consented that parliament should exercise such a power. In case of war, it has by some been thought necessary. But in fact and experience, it has not been found so. What though the proprietary colonies, on account of disputes with the proprietors, did not come in so early to the assistance of the general cause in the last war as they ought, and perhaps one of them not at all? The inconveniences of this were small, in comparison of the absolute ruin to the liberties of all which must follow the submission to parliament, in all cases, which would be giving up all the popular limitations upon the government. These inconveniences fell chiefly upon New England. She was necessitated to greater exertions; but she had rather suffer these again and again than others infinitely greater. However, this subject has been so long in contemplation, that it is fully understood now in all the colonies; so that there is no danger, in case of another war, of any colony's failing of its duty.

But, admitting the proposition in its full force, that it is absolutely necessary there should be a supreme power, coextensive with all the dominions, will it follow that parliament, as now constituted, has a right to assume this supreme jurisdiction? By no means.

A union of the colonies might be projected, and an American legislature; for, if America has three millions of people, and the whole dominions, twelve millions, she ought to send a quarter part of all the members to the house of commons; and, instead of holding parliaments always at Westminster, the haughty members for Great Britain must humble themselves, one session in four, to cross the Atlantic, and hold the parliament in America.

There is no avoiding all inconveniences in human affairs. The greatest possible, or conceivable, would arise from ceding to parliament power over us without a representation in it. The next greatest would accrue from any plan that can be devised for a representation there. The least of all would arise from going on as we began, and fared well for one hundred and fifty years, by letting parliament regulate trade, and our own assemblies all other matters.

* * *

But perhaps it will be said, that we are to enjoy the British constitution in our supreme legislature, the parliament, not in our provincial legislatures. To this I answer, if parliament is to be our supreme legislature, we shall be under a complete oligarchy or aristocracy, not the British constitution, which this writer himself defines a mixture of monarchy, aristocracy, and democracy. For king, lords, and commons, will constitute one great oligarchy, as they will stand related to America, as much as the decemvirs did in Rome; with this difference for the worse, that our rulers are to be three thousand miles off. The definition of an oligarchy is a government by a number of grandees, over whom the people have no control.

* * *

If our provincial constitutions are in any respect imperfect, and want alteration, they have capacity enough to discern it, and power enough to affect it, without the interposition of parliament. There never was an American constitution attempted by parliament before the Quebec bill, and Massachusetts bill. These are such *samples* of what they may, and probably will be, that few Americans are in love with them. However, America will never allow that parliament has any authority to alter their constitutions at all. She is wholly penetrated with a sense of the necessity of resisting it at all hazards. And she would resist it, if the constitution of the Massachusetts had been altered as much for *the better* as it is for the worse. The question we insist on most is, not whether the alteration is for the better or not, but whether parliament has any right to make any alteration at all. And it is the universal sense of America, that it has none.

* * *

That a representation in parliament is impracticable, we all agree, but the consequence is, that we must have a representation in our supreme legislatures here. This was the consequence that was drawn by kings, ministers, our ancestors, and the whole nation, more than a century ago, when the colonies were first settled, and continued to be the general sense until the last peace; and it must be the general sense again soon, or Great Britain will lose her colonies.

* * *

This writer says, "that in denying that the colonies are annexed to the realm, and subject to the authority of parliament, individuals and bodies of men subvert the fundamentals of government, deprive us of British liberties, and build up absolute monarchy in the colonies."

This is the first time that I ever heard or read that the colonies are annexed to the realm. It is utterly denied that they are, and that it is possible they should be, without an act of parliament and acts of the colonies. Such an act of parliament cannot be produced, nor any such law of any one colony. Therefore, as this writer builds the whole authority of parliament upon this fact, namely,—that the colonies are annexed to the realm, and as it is certain they never were so annexed, the consequence is, that his whole superstructure falls.

When he says, that they subvert the fundamentals of government, he begs the question. We say, that the contrary doctrines subvert the fundamentals of government. When he says, that they deprive us of British liberties, he begs the question again. We say, that the contrary doctrine deprives us of English liberties; as to British liberties, we scarcely know what they are, as the liberties of England and Scotland are not precisely the same to this day. English liberties are but certain rights of nature, reserved to the citizen by the English constitution, which rights cleaved to our ancestors when they crossed the Atlantic, and would have inhered in them if, instead of coming to New England, they had gone to Otaheite or Patagonia, even although they had taken no patent or charter from the king at all. These rights did not adhere to them the less, for their purchasing patents and charters, in which the king expressly stipulates with them, that they and their posterity should forever enjoy all those rights and liberties.

JOHN ADAMS

Thoughts on Government (1776)

In his 1776 pamphlet, Thoughts on Government, Adams summarized the principles of free government he would follow in crafting the Massachusetts Constitution of 1780—the oldest American constitution still in effect. The document is a classic statement of republican political ideals, including the British thinker James Harrington's idea that good government is essentially "an empire of laws, and not of men." Adams's highly influential pamphlet stresses the importance of institutional arrangements, such as the separation of powers, to constitutional government.

My dear Sir: If I was equal to the task of forming a plan for the government of a colony, I should be flattered with your request and very happy to comply with it because, as the divine science of politics is the science of social happiness, and the blessings of society depend entirely on the constitutions of government, which are generally institutions that last for many generations, there can be no employment more agreeable to a benevolent mind than a research after the best.

Pope flattered tyrants too much when he said,

> *For forms of government let fools contest,*
> *That which is best administered is best.*
>   (Essay on Man)

Nothing can be more fallacious than this. But poets read history to collect flowers, not fruits; they attend to fanciful images, not the effects of social institutions. Nothing is more certain from the history of nations and nature of man than that some forms of government are better fitted for being well administered than others.

We ought to consider what is the end of government before we determine which is the best form. Upon this point all speculative politicians will agree that the happiness of the individual is the end of man. From this principle it will follow that the form of government which communicates ease, comfort, security, or, in one word, happiness to the greatest number of persons and in the greatest degree is the best.

All sober inquirers after truth, ancient and modern, pagan and Christian, have declared that the happiness of man, as well as his dignity, consists in virtue. Confucucius, Zoraster, Socrates, Mahomet, not to mention authorities really sacred, have agreed in this.

If this is a form of government, then, whose principle and foundation is virtue, will not every sober man acknowledge it better calculated to promote the general happiness than any other form?

Fear is the foundation of most governments; but it is so sordid and brutal a passion and renders men in whose breasts it predominates so stupid and miserable that Americans will not be likely to approve of any political institution which is founded on it.

Honor is truly sacred but holds a lower rank in the scale of moral excellence than virtue. Indeed, the former is but a part of the latter and consequently has not equal pretensions to support a frame of government productive of human happiness.

The foundation of every government is some principle or passion in the minds of the people. The noblest principles and most generous affections in our nature, then, have the fairest chance to support the noblest and most generous models of government.

A man must be indifferent to the sneers of modern Englishmen to mention in their company the names of Sidney, Harrington, Locke, Milton, Nedham, Neville, Burnet, and Hoadly. No small fortitude is necessary to confess that one has read them. The wretched condition of this country, however, for ten or fifteen years past has frequently reminded me of their principles and reasonings. They will convince any candid mind that there is no good government but what is republican. That the only valuable part of the British constitution is so because the very definition of a republic is "an empire of laws, and not of men." That, as a republic is the best of governments, so that particular arrangement of the powers of society or, in other words, that form of government which is best contrived to secure an impartial and exact execution of the laws is the best of republics.

Of republics there is an inexhaustible variety because the possible combinations of the powers of society are capable of innumerable variations.

As good government is an empire of laws, how shall your laws be made? In a large society inhabiting an extensive country, it is impossible that the whole should assemble to make laws. The first necessary step, then, is to depute power from the many to a few of the most wise and good. But by what rules shall you choose your representatives? Agree upon the number and qualifications of persons who shall have the benefit of choosing or annex this privilege to the inhabitants of a certain extent of ground.

The principal difficulty lies, and the greatest care should be employed, in constituting this representative assembly. It should be in miniature an exact portrait of the people at large. It should think, feel, reason, and act like them. That it may be the interest of this assembly to do strict justice at all times, it should be an equal representation, or, in other words, equal interests among the people should have equal interests in it. Great care should be taken to effect this and to prevent unfair, partial, and corrupt elections. Such regulations, however, may be better made in times of greater tranquility than the present; and they will spring up themselves naturally when all the powers of government come to be in the hands of the people's friends. At present, it will be safest to proceed in all established modes to which the people have been familiarized by habit.

A representation of the people in one assembly being obtained, a question arises whether all the powers of government—legislative, executive, and judicial—shall be left in this body? I think a people cannot be long free, nor ever happy, whose government is in one assembly. My reasons for this opinion are as follow:

1. A single assembly is liable to all the vices, follies, and frailties of an individual—subject to fits of humor, starts of passion, flights of enthusiasm, partialities, or prejudice—and consequently productive of hasty results and absurd judgments. And all these errors ought to be corrected and defects supplied by some controlling power.
2. A single assembly is apt to be avaricious and in time will not scruple to exempt itself from burdens which it will lay without compunction on its constituents.
3. A single assembly is apt to grow ambitious and after a time will not hesitate to vote itself perpetual. This was one fault of the Long Parliament, but more remarkably of Holland, whose assembly first voted themselves from annual to septennial, then for life, and after a course of years, that all vacancies happening by death or otherwise should be filled by themselves without any application to constituents at all.
4. A representative assembly, although extremely well qualified and absolutely necessary as a branch of the legislative, is unfit to exercise the executive power for want of two essential properties, secrecy and dispatch.

5. A representative assembly is still less qualified for the judicial power because it is too numerous, too slow, and too little skilled in the laws.

6. Because a single assembly, possessed of all the powers of government, would make arbitrary laws for their own interest, execute all laws arbitrarily for their own interest, and adjudge all controversies in their own favor.

But shall the whole power of legislation rest in one assembly? Most of the foregoing reasons apply equally to prove that the legislative power ought to be more complex, to which we may add that if the legislative power is wholly in one assembly and the executive in another or in a single person, these two powers will oppose and encroach upon each other until the contest shall end in war, and the whole power, legislative and executive, be usurped by the strongest.

The judicial power, in such case, could not mediate or hold the balance between the two contending powers because the legislative would undermine it. And this shows the necessity, too, of giving the executive power a negative upon the legislative; otherwise this will be continually encroaching upon that.

To avoid these dangers, let a distinct assembly be constituted as a mediator between the two extreme branches of the legislature, that which represents the people and that which is vested with the executive power.

Let the representative assembly then elect by ballot, from among themselves or their constituents or both, a distinct assembly which, for the sake of perspicuity, we will call a council. It may consist of any number you please, say twenty or thirty, and should have a free and independent exercise of its judgment and consequently a negative voice in the legislature.

These two bodies, thus constituted and made integral parts of the legislature, let them unite and by joint ballot choose a governor, who, after being stripped of most of those badges of domination called prerogatives, should have a free and independent exercise of his judgment and be made also an integral part of the legislature. This, I know, is liable to objections; and if you please, you may make him only president of the council, as in Connecticut. But as the governor is to be invested with the executive power with consent of council I think he ought to have a negative upon the legislative. If he is annually elective, as he ought to be, he will always have so much reverence and affection for the people, their representatives and counsellors, that, although you give him an independent exercise of his judgment, he will seldom use it in opposition to the two houses, except in cases the public utility of which would be conspicuous; and some such cases would happen.

In the present exigency of American affairs, when by an act of Parliament we are put out of the royal protection and consequently discharged from our allegiance, and it has become necessary to assume government for our immediate security, the governor, lieutenant-governor, secretary, treasurer, commissary, attorney-general should be chosen by joint ballot of both houses. And these and all other elections, especially of representatives and counsellors, should be annual, there not being in the whole circle of the sciences a maxim more infallible than this, "where annual elections end, there slavery begins."

These great men, in this respect, should be once a year—

> Like bubbles on the sea of matter borne,
> They rise, they break, and to that sea return.

This will teach them the great political virtues of humility, patience, and moderation, without which every man in power becomes a ravenous beast of prey.

This mode of constituting the great offices of state will answer very well for the present; but if by experiment it should be found inconvenient, the legislature may at its leisure devise other methods of creating them; by elections of the people at large, as in Connecticut; or it may enlarge the term for which they shall be chosen to seven years, or three years, or for life; or make any other alterations which the society shall find productive of its ease, its safety, its freedom, or, in one word, its happiness.

A rotation of all offices, as well as of representatives and counsellors, has many advocates and is contended for with many plausible arguments. It would be attended no doubt with many advantages; and if the society has a sufficient number of suitable characters to supply the great number of vacancies which would be made by such a rotation, I can see no objection to it. These persons may be allowed to serve for three years and then be excluded three years, or for any longer or shorter term.

Any seven or nine of the legislative council may be made a quorum for doing business as a privy council, to advise the governor in the exercise of the executive branch of power and in all acts of state.

The governor should have the command of the militia and of all your armies. The power of pardons should be with the governor and council.

Judges, justices, and all other officers, civil and military, should be nominated and appointed by the governor with the advice and consent of council, unless you choose to have a government more popular; if you do, all officers, civil and military, may be chosen by joint ballot of both houses; or, in order to preserve the independence and importance of each house, by ballot of one house concurred in by the other. Sheriffs should be chosen by the freeholders of counties; so should registers of deeds and clerks of counties.

All officers should have commissions under the hand of the governor and seal of the colony.

The dignity and stability of government in all its branches, the morals of the people, and every blessing of society depend so much upon an upright and skillful administration of justice that the judicial power ought to be distinct from both the legislative and executive, and independent upon both, that so it may be a check upon both, as both should be checks upon that. The judges, therefore, should be always men of learning and experience in the laws, of exemplary morals, great patience, calmness, coolness, and attention. Their minds should not be distracted with jarring interests; they should not be dependent upon any man, or body of men. To these ends, they should hold estates for life in their offices; or, in other words, their commissions should be during good behavior and their salaries ascertained and established by law. For misbehavior the grand inquest of the colony, the house of representatives, should impeach them before the governor and council, where they should have time and opportunity to make their defense; but, if convicted, should be removed from their offices and subjected to such other punishment as shall be thought proper.

A militia law requiring all men, or with very few exceptions besides cases of conscience, to be provided with arms and ammunition, to be trained at certain seasons; and requiring counties, towns, or other small districts to be provided with public stocks of ammunition and entrenching utensils and with some settled plans for transporting provisions after the militia, when marched to defend their country against sudden invasions; and requiring certain districts to be provided with field-pieces, companies of matrosses, and perhaps some regiments of light-horse as always a wise institution, and in the present circumstances of our country indispensable.

Laws for the liberal education of youth, especially of the lower class of people, are so extremely wise and useful that to a humane and generous mind no expense for this purpose would be thought extravagant.

The very mention of sumptuary laws will excite a smile. Whether our countrymen have wisdom and virtue enough to submit to them, I know not; but the happiness of the people might be greatly promoted by them, and a revenue saved sufficient to carry on this war forever. Frugality is a great revenue, besides curing us of vanities, levities, and fopperies, which are real antidotes to all great, manly, and warlike virtues.

A constitution founded on these principles introduces knowledge among the people and inspires them with a conscious dignity becoming freemen; a general emulation takes place which causes good humor, sociability, good manners, and good morals to be general. That elevation of sentiment inspired by such a government makes the common people brave and enterprising. That ambition which is inspired by it makes them sober, industrious, and frugal. You will find among them some elegance, perhaps, but more solidity; a little pleasure, but a great deal of business; some politeness, but more civility. If you compare such a country with the regions of domination, whether monarchical or aristocratical, you will fancy yourself in Arcadia or Elysium.

If the colonies should assume governments separately, they should be left entirely to their own choice of the forms; and if a continental constitution should be formed, it should be a congress containing a fair and adequate representation of the colonies and its authority should sacredly be confined to these cases, namely; war, trade, disputes between colony and colony, the post office, and the unappropriated lands of the crown, as they used to be called.

These colonies, under such forms of government and in such a union, would be unconquerable by all the monarchies of Europe.

You and I, my dear friend, have been sent into life at a time when the greatest lawgivers of antiquity would have wished to live. How few of the human race have ever enjoyed an opportunity of making an election of government—more than of air, soil, or climate—for themselves or their children! When, before the present epoch had three millions of people full power and a fair opportunity to form and establish the wisest and happiest government that human wisdom can contrive? I hope you will avail yourself and your country of that extensive learning and indefatigable industry which you possess to assist her in the formation of the happiest governments and the best character of a great people. For myself, I must beg you to keep my name out of sight; for this feeble attempt, if it should be known to be mine, would oblige me to apply to myself those lines of the immortal John Milton in one of his sonnets:

> *I did but prompt the age to quit their clogs*
> *By the known rules of ancient liberty,*
> *When straight a barbarous noise environs me*
> *Of owls and cuckoos, asses, apes, and dogs.*

THOMAS PAINE

Common Sense (1776)

A failure in every other profession he tried, the Englishman Thomas Paine (1737–1809) became spectacularly successful after his arrival in America in November 1774. The radical democrat started out as the editor of the Pennsylvania Magazine and later wrote in support of the revolutionary cause. His most important contribution was the anonymous pamphlet Common Sense, which galvanized support for independence. Pamphlets were important means of mass communication and political argumentation during this period, but this one surpassed all others, selling a total of 500,000 copies, 120,000 of those in the first three months alone. Paine repudiated the British form of government as an outmoded system and intolerable threat to the natural rights of the colonists to rule themselves.

ON THE ORIGIN AND DESIGN OF GOVERNMENT IN GENERAL, WITH CONCISE REMARKS ON THE ENGLISH CONSTITUTION

Some writers have so confounded society with government, as to leave little or no distinction between them; whereas they are not only different, but have different origins. Society is produced by our wants, and government by our wickedness; the former promotes our happiness *positively* by uniting our affections, the latter *negatively* by restraining our vices. The one encourages intercourse, the other creates distinctions. The first is a patron, the last a punisher.

Society in every state is a blessing, but Government, even in its best state, is but a necessary evil; in its worst state an intolerable one: for when we suffer, or are exposed to the same miseries *by a Government*, which we might expect in a country *without Government*, our calamity is heightened by reflecting that we furnish the means by which we suffer. Government, like dress, is the badge of lost innocence; the palaces of kings are built upon the ruins of the bowers of paradise. For were the impulses of conscience clear, uniform and irresistibly obeyed, man would need no other lawgiver; but that not being the case, he finds it necessary to surrender up a part of his property to furnish means for the protection of the rest; and this he is induced to do by the same prudence which in every other case advises him, out of two evils to choose the least. Wherefore, security being the true design and end of government, it unanswerably follows that whatever form thereof appears most likely to ensure it to us, with the least expence and greatest benefit, is preferable to all others.

In order to gain a clear and just idea of the design and end of government, let us suppose a small number of persons settled in some sequestered part of the earth, unconnected with the rest; they will then represent the first peopling of any country, or of the world. In this state of natural liberty, society will be their first thought. A thousand motives will excite them thereto; the strength of one man is so unequal to his wants, and his mind so unfitted for perpetual solitude, that he is soon obliged to seek assistance and relief of another, who in his turn requires the same. Four or five united would be able to raise a tolerable dwelling in the midst of a wilderness, but one man might labour out the common period of life without accomplishing any thing; when he had felled his timber he could not remove it, nor erect it after it was removed; hunger in the mean time would urge him to quit his work, and every different want would call him a different way. Disease, nay even misfortune, would be death; for though neither might be mortal, yet either would disable him from living, and reduce him to a state in which he might rather be said to perish than to die.

Thus necessity, like a gravitating power, would soon form our newly arrived emigrants into society, the reciprocal blessings of which would supercede, and render the obligations of law and government unnecessary while they remained perfectly just to each other; but as nothing but Heaven is impregnable to vice, it will unavoidably happen that in proportion as they surmount the first difficulties of emigration, which bound them together in a common cause, they will begin to relax in their duty and attachment to each other: and this remissness will point out the necessity of establishing some form of government to supply the defect of moral virtue.

Some convenient tree will afford them a State House, under the branches of which the whole Colony may assemble to deliberate on public matters. It is more than probable that their first laws will have the title only of Regulations and be enforced by no other penalty than public disesteem. In this first parliament every man by natural right will have a seat.

But as the Colony encreases, the public concerns will encrease likewise, and the distance at which the members may be separated, will render it too inconvenient for all of them to meet on every occasion as at first, when their number was small, their habitations near, and the public concerns few and trifling. This will point out the convenience of their consenting to leave the legislative part to be managed by a select number chosen from the whole body, who are supposed to have the same concerns at stake which those have who appointed them, and who will act in the same manner as the whole body would act were they present. If the colony continue encreasing, it will become necessary to augment the number of representatives, and that the interest of every part of the colony may be attended to, it will be found best to divide the whole into convenient parts, each part sending its proper number: and that the *elected* might never form to themselves an interest separate from the *electors*, prudence will point out the propriety of having elections often: because as the *elected* might by that means return and mix again with the general body of the *electors* in a few months, their fidelity to the public will be secured by the prudent reflection of not making a rod for themselves. And as this frequent interchange will establish a common interest with every part of the community, they will mutually and naturally support each other, and on this, (not on the unmeaning name of king,) depends the *strength of government, and the happiness of the governed.*

Here then is the origin and rise of government; namely, a mode rendered necessary by the inability of moral virtue to govern the world; here too is the design and end of government, viz. Freedom and security. And however our eyes may be dazzled with show, or our ears deceived by sound; however prejudice may warp our wills, or interest darken our understanding, the simple voice of nature and reason will say, 'tis right.

I draw my idea of the form of government from a principle in nature which no art can overturn, viz. that the more simple any thing is, the less liable it is to be disordered, and the easier repaired when disordered; and with this maxim in view I offer a few remarks on the so much boasted constitution of England. That it was noble for the dark and slavish times in which it was erected, is granted. When the world was overrun with tyranny the least remove therefrom was a glorious rescue. But that it is imperfect, subject to convulsions, and incapable of producing what it seems to promise, is easily demonstrated.

Absolute governments, (tho' the disgrace of human nature) have this advantage with them, they are simple; if the people suffer, they know the head from which their suffering springs; know likewise the remedy; and are not bewildered by a variety of causes and cures. But the constitution of England is so exceedingly complex, that the nation may suffer for years together without being able to discover in which part the fault lies; some will say in one and some in another, and every political physician will advise a different medicine.

I know it is difficult to get over local or long standing prejudices, yet if we will suffer ourselves to examine the component parts of the English constitution, we shall find them to be the base remains of two ancient tyrannies, compounded with some new Republican materials.

First.—The remains of Monarchical tyranny in the person of the King.

Secondly.—The remains of Aristocratical tyranny in the persons of the Peers.

Thirdly.—The new Republican materials, in the persons of the Commons, on whose virtue depends the freedom of England.

The two first, by being hereditary, are independant of the People; wherefore in a *constitutional sense* they contribute nothing towards the freedom of the State.

To say that the constitution of England is an *union* of three powers, reciprocally *checking* each other, is farcical; either the words have no meaning, or they are flat contradictions.

To say that the Commons is a check upon the King, presupposes two things.

First.—That the King is not to be trusted without being looked after; or in other words, that a thirst for absolute power is the natural disease of monarchy.

Secondly.—That the Commons, by being appointed for that purpose, are either wiser or more worthy of confidence than the Crown.

But as the same constitution which gives the Commons a power to check the King by withholding the supplies, gives afterwards the King a power to check the Commons, by empowering him to reject their other bills; it again supposes that the King is wiser than those whom it has already supposed to be wiser than him. A mere absurdity!

There is something exceedingly ridiculous in the composition of Monarchy; it first excludes a man from the means of information, yet empowers him to act in cases where the highest judgment is required. The state of a king shuts him from the World, yet the business of a king requires him to know it thoroughly; wherefore the different parts, by unnaturally opposing and destroying each other, prove the whole character to be absurd and useless.

Some writers have explained the English constitution thus: the King, say they, is one, the people another; the Peers are a house in behalf of the King, the commons in behalf of the people; but this hath all the distinctions of a house divided against itself; and though the expressions be pleasantly arranged, yet when examined they appear idle and ambiguous; and it will always happen, that the nicest construction that words are capable of, when applied to the description of something which either cannot exist, or is too incomprehensible to be within the compass of description, will be words of sound only, and though they may amuse the ear, they cannot inform the mind: for this explanation includes a previous question, viz. *how came the king by a power which the people are afraid to trust, and always obliged to check?* Such a power could not be the gift of a wise people, neither can any power, *which needs checking*, be from God; yet the provision which the constitution makes supposes such a power to exist.

* * *

Wherefore, laying aside all national pride and prejudice in favour of modes and forms, the plain truth is that *it is wholly owing to the constitution of the people, and not to the constitution of the government* that the crown is not as oppressive in England as in Turkey.

An inquiry into the *constitutional errors* in the English form of government, is at this time highly necessary; for as we are never in a proper condition of doing justice to others, while we continue under the influence of some leading partiality, so neither are we capable of doing it to ourselves while we remain fettered by any obstinate prejudice. And as a man who is attached to a prostitute is unfitted to choose or judge of a wife, so any prepossession in favour of a rotten constitution of government will disable us from discerning a good one.

Of Monarchy and Hereditary Succession

Mankind being originally equals in the order of creation, the equality could only be destroyed by some subsequent circumstance: the distinctions of rich and poor may in a great measure be accounted for, and that without having recourse to the harsh ill-sounding names of oppression and avarice. Oppression is often the *consequence*, but seldom or never the *means* of riches; and tho' avarice will preserve a man from being necessitously poor, it generally makes him too timorous to be wealthy.

But there is another and greater distinction for which no truly natural or religious reason can be assigned, and that is the distinction of men into KINGS and SUBJECTS. Male and female are the distinctions of nature, good and bad the distinctions of Heaven; but how a race of men came into the world so exalted above the rest, and distinguished like some new species, is worth inquiring into, and whether they are the means of happiness or of misery to mankind.

In the early ages of the world, according to the scripture chronology there were no kings; the consequence of which was, there were no wars; it is the pride of kings which throws mankind into confusion. Holland, without a king hath enjoyed more peace for this last century than any of the monarchical governments in Europe. Antiquity favours the same remark; for the quiet and rural lives of the first Patriarchs have a happy something in them, which vanishes when we come to the history of Jewish royalty.

Government by kings was first introduced into the world by the Heathens, from whom the children of Israel copied the custom. It was the most prosperous invention the Devil ever set on foot for the promotion of idolatry. The Heathens paid divine honours to their deceased kings, and the Christian World hath improved on the plan by doing the same to their living ones. How impious is the title of sacred Majesty applied to a worm, who in the midst of his splendor is crumbling into dust!

As the exalting one man so greatly above the rest cannot be justified on the equal rights of nature, so neither can it be defended on the authority of scripture; for the will of the Almighty as declared by Gideon, and the prophet Samuel, expressly disapproves of government by Kings. All anti-monarchical parts of scripture, have been very smoothly glossed over in monarchical governments, but they undoubtedly merit the attention of countries which have their governments yet to form. *Render unto Cesar the things which are Cesar's*, is the scripture doctrine of courts, yet it is no support of monarchical government, for the Jews at that time were without a king, and in a state of vassalage to the Romans.

* * *

To the evil of monarchy we have added that of hereditary succession; and as the first is a degradation and lessening of ourselves, so the second, claimed as a matter of right, is an insult and imposition on posterity. For all men being originally equals, no one by birth could have a right to set up his own family in perpetual preference to all others for ever, and tho' himself might deserve some decent degree of honours of his contemporaries, yet his descendants might be far too unworthy to inherit them. One of the strongest natural proofs of the folly of hereditary right in Kings, is that nature disapproves it, otherwise she would not so frequently turn it into ridicule, by giving mankind an *Ass for a Lion*.

Secondly, as no man at first could possess any other public honors than were bestowed upon him, so the givers of those honors could have no power to give away the right of posterity, and though they might say

"We choose you for our head," they could not without manifest injustice to their children say "that your children and your children's children shall reign over ours forever." Because such an unwise, unjust, unnatural compact might (perhaps) in the next succession put them under the government of a rogue or a fool. Most wise men in their private sentiments have ever treated hereditary right with contempt; yet it is one of those evils which when once established is not easily removed; many submit from fear, others from superstition, and the more powerful part shares with the king the plunder of the rest.

This is supposing the present race of kings in the world to have had an honorable origin: whereas it is more than probable, that, could we take off the dark covering of antiquity and trace them to their first rise, we should find the first of them nothing better than the principal ruffian of some restless gang, whose savage manners or pre-eminence in subtilty obtained him the title of chief among plunderers: and who by increasing in power and extending his depredations, overawed the quiet and defenceless to purchase their safety by frequent contributions.

* * *

Yet I should be glad to ask how they suppose kings came at first? The question admits but of three answers, viz. either by lot, by election, or by usurpation. If the first king was taken by lot, it establishes a precedent for the next, which excludes hereditary succession. Saul was by lot, yet the succession was not hereditary, neither does it appear from that transaction that there was any intention it ever should. If the first king of any country was by election, that likewise establishes a precedent for the next; for to say, that the right of all future generations is taken away, by the act of the first electors, in their choice not only of a king but of a family of kings for ever, hath no parallel in or out of scripture but the doctrine of original sin, which supposes the free will of all men lost in Adam; and from such comparison, and it will admit of no other, hereditary succession can derive no glory. For as in Adam all sinned, and as in the first electors all men obeyed; as in the one all mankind were subjected to Satan, and in the other to sovereignty; as our innocence was lost in the first, and our authority in the last; and as both disable us from re-assuming some former state and privilege, it unanswerably follows that original sin and hereditary succession are parallels. Dishonourable rank! inglorious connection! yet the most subtle sophist cannot produce a juster simile.

* * *

But it is not so much the absurdity as the evil of hereditary succession which concerns mankind. Did it ensure a race of good and wise men it would have the seal of divine authority, but as it opens a door to the *foolish*, the *wicked*, and the *improper*, it hath in it the nature of oppression. Men who look upon themselves born to reign, and others to obey, soon grow insolent. Selected from the rest of mankind, their minds are early poisoned by importance; and the world they act in differs so materially from the world at large, that they have but little opportunity of knowing its true interests, and when they succeed to the government are frequently the most ignorant and unfit of any throughout the dominions.

* * *

In short, monarchy and succession have laid (not this or that kingdom only) but the world in blood and ashes. 'Tis a form of government which the word of God bears testimony against, and blood will attend it.

If we enquire into the business of a King, we shall find that in some countries they may have none; and after sauntering away their lives without pleasure to themselves or advantage to the nation, withdraw from the scene, and leave their successors to tread the same idle round. In absolute monarchies the whole weight of business civil and military lies on the King; the children of Israel in their request for a king urged this plea, "that he may judge us, and go out before us and fight our battles." But in countries where he is neither a Judge nor a General, as in England, a man would be puzzled to know what is his business.

The nearer any government approaches to a Republic, the less business there is for a King. It is somewhat difficult to find a proper name for the government of England. Sir William Meredith calls it a Republic; but in its present state it is unworthy of the name, because the corrupt influence of the Crown, by having all the places in its disposal, hath so effectually swallowed up the power, and eaten out the virtue of the House of Commons (the Republican part in the constitution) that the government of England is nearly as monarchical as that of France or Spain. Men fall out with names without understanding them. For 'tis the Republican and not the Monarchical part of the constitution of England which Englishmen glory in, viz. the liberty of choosing an House of Commons from out of their own body—and it is easy to see that when Republican virtue fails, slavery ensues. Why is the constitution of England sickly, but because monarchy hath poisoned the Republic; the Crown hath engrossed the Commons.

In England a King hath little more to do than to make war and give away places; which, in plain terms, is to empoverish the nation and set it together by the ears. A pretty business indeed for a man to be allowed eight hundred thousand sterling a year for, and worshipped into the bargain! Of more worth is one honest man to society, and in the sight of God, than all the crowned ruffians that ever lived. * * *

THOUGHTS ON THE PRESENT STATE
OF AMERICAN AFFAIRS

In the following pages I offer nothing more than simple facts, plain arguments, and common sense: and have no other preliminaries to settle with the reader, than that he will divest himself of prejudice and prepossession, and suffer his reason and his feelings to determine for themselves: that he will put on or rather that he will not put off the true character of a man, and generously enlarge his views beyond the present day.

Volumes have been written on the subject of the struggle between England and America. Men of all ranks have embarked in the controversy, from different motives, and with various designs; but all have been ineffectual, and the period of debate is closed. Arms as the last resource decide the contest; the appeal was the choice of the King, and the Continent has accepted the challenge.

It hath been reported of the late Mr. Pelham (who tho' an able minister was not without his faults) that on his being attacked in the House of Commons on the score that his measures were only of a temporary kind, replied, *"they will last my time."* Should a thought so fatal and unmanly possess the Colonies in the present contest, the name of ancestors will be remembered by future generations with detestation.

The Sun never shined on a cause of greater worth. 'Tis not the affair of a City, a County, a Province, or a Kingdom; but of a Continent—of at least one eighth part of the habitable Globe. 'Tis not the concern of a day, a year, or an age; posterity are virtually involved in the contest, and will be more or less affected even to the end of time by the proceedings now. Now is the seed time of Continental union, faith, and honour. The least fracture now, will be like a name engraved with the point of a pin on the tender rind of a young oak; the wound will enlarge with the tree, and posterity read it in full grown characters.

By referring the matter from argument to arms, a new æra for politics is struck—a new method of thinking hath arisen. All plans, proposals, &c. prior to the 19th of April, *i.e.* to the commencement of hostilities, are like the almanacks of the last year; which tho' proper then, are superceded and useless now. Whatever was advanced by the advocates on either side of the question then, terminated in one and the same point, viz. a union with Great Britain; the only difference between the parties was the method of effecting it; the one proposing force the other friendship; but it hath so far happened that the first hath failed, and the second hath withdrawn her influence.

As much hath been said of the advantages of reconciliation, which like an agreeable dream, hath passed away and left us as we were, it is but right, that we should examine the contrary side of the argument, and enquire into some of the many material injuries which these Colonies sustain, and always will sustain, by being connected with and dependant on Great Britain. To examine that connection and dependance, on the principles of nature and common sense, to see what we have to trust to if separated, and what we are to expect if dependant.

I have heard it asserted by some, that as America hath flourished under her former connection with Great Britain, the same connection is necessary towards her future happiness, and will always have the same effect—Nothing can be more fallacious than this kind of argument:—we may as well assert that because a child has thrived upon milk, that it is never to have meat, or that the first twenty years of our lives is to become a precedent for the next twenty. But even this is admitting more than is true, for I answer, roundly, that America would have flourished as much, and probably much more had no European power taken any notice of her. The commerce by which she hath enriched herself are the necessaries of life, and will always have a market while eating is the custom of Europe.

But she has protected us say some. That she hath engrossed us is true, and defended the Continent at our expense as well as her own is admitted; and she would have defended Turkey from the same motive, viz. for the sake of trade and dominion.

Alas! we have been long led away by ancient prejudices and made large sacrifices to superstition. We have boasted the protection of Great Britain, without considering, that her motive was *interest* not *attachment*; and that she did not protect us from *our enemies on our account*, but from *her enemies* on *her own account*, from those who had no quarrel with us on any *other account*, and who will always be our enemies on the *same account*. Let Britain waive her pretensions to the continent, or the continent throw off the dependance, and we should be at peace with France and Spain were they at war with Britain. The miseries of Hanover['s] last war ought to warn us against connections.

It hath lately been asserted in parliament, that the colonies have no relation to each other but through the Parent Country, *i.e.* that Pennsylvania and the Jerseys, and so on for the rest, are sister Colonies by the way of England; this is certainly a very round-about way of proving relationship, but it is the nearest and only true way of proving enemyship, if I may so call it. France and Spain never were, nor perhaps ever will be our enemies as *Americans*, but as our being the *subjects of Great Britain*.

But Britain is the parent country say some. Then the more shame upon her conduct. Even brutes do not devour their young, nor savages make war upon their families; wherefore, the assertion if true, turns to her reproach; but it happens not to be true, or only partly so, and the phrase, *parent* or *mother country,* hath been jesuitically adopted by the King and his parasites, with a low papistical design of gaining an unfair bias on the credulous weakness of our minds. Europe and not England is the parent country of America. This new World hath been the asylum for the persecuted lovers of civil and religious liberty from *every part* of Europe. Hither have they fled, not from the tender embraces of the mother, but from the cruelty of the monster; and it is so far true of England, that the same tyranny which drove the first emigrants from home, pursues their descendants still. * * *

But admitting, that we were all of English descent, what does it amount to? Nothing. Britain, being now an open enemy, extinguishes every other name and title: and to say that reconciliation is our duty, is truly farcical. The first king of England, of the present line (William the Conqueror) was a Frenchman, and half the Peers of England are descendants from the same country; wherefore, by the same method of reasoning, England ought to be governed by France.

Much hath been said of the united strength of Britain and the Colonies, that in conjunction, they might bid defiance to the world: But this is mere presumption; the fate of war is uncertain, neither do the expressions mean any thing, for this Continent would never suffer itself to be drained of inhabitants, to support the British Arms in either Asia, Africa, or Europe.

Besides, what have we to do with setting the world at defiance? Our plan is commerce, and that well attended to, will secure us the peace and friendship of Europe because it is the interest of all Europe to have America a *free port.* Her trade will always be a protection, and her barrenness of gold and silver secure her from invaders.

I challenge the warmest advocate for reconciliation, to shew, a single advantage that this Continent can reap by being connected with Great Britain. I repeat the challenge, not a single advantage is derived. Our corn will fetch its price in any market in Europe, and our imported goods must be paid for, buy them where we will.

But the injuries and disadvantages which we sustain by that connection, are without number, and our duty to mankind at large, as well as to ourselves, instruct us to renounce the alliance: Because, any submission to, or dependance on Great Britain, tends directly to involve this Continent in European wars and quarrels. [And sets us at variance with nations, who would otherwise seek our friendship, and against whom, we have neither anger nor complaint.] As Europe is our market for trade, we ought to form no partial connection with any part of it. 'Tis the true interest of America, to steer clear of European contentions, which she never can do, while by her dependance on Britain, she is made the makeweight in the scale of British politics.

Europe is too thickly planted with Kingdoms, to be long at peace, and whenever a war breaks out between England and any foreign power, the trade of America goes to ruin, *because, of her connection with Britain.* The next war may not turn out like the last, and should it not, the advocates for reconciliation now, will be wishing for separation then, because neutrality in that case, would be a safer convoy than a man of war. Every thing that is right or reasonable pleads for separation. The blood of the slain, the weeping voice of nature cries, 'TIS TIME TO PART. Even the distance at which the Almighty hath placed England and America, is a strong and natural proof, that the authority of the one over the other, was never the design of Heaven. The time likewise at which the Continent was discovered, adds weight to the argument, and the manner in which it was peopled encreases the force of it.—The Reformation was preceded by the discovery of America; as if the Almighty graciously meant to open a sanctuary to the persecuted in future years, when home should afford neither friendship nor safety.

The authority of Great Britain over this Continent, is a form of government which sooner or later must have an end: and a serious mind can draw no true pleasure by looking forward, under the painful and positive conviction that what he calls "the present constitution," is merely temporary. As parents, we can have no joy, knowing that *this government* is not sufficiently lasting to ensure any thing which we may bequeath to posterity: And by a plain method of argument, as we are running the next generation into debt, we ought to do the work of it, otherwise we use them meanly and pitifully. In order to discover the line of our duty rightly, we should take our children in our hand, and fix our station a few years farther into life; that eminence will present a prospect, which a few present fears and prejudices conceal from our sight.

Though I would carefully avoid giving unnecessary offence, yet I am inclined to believe, that all those who espouse the doctrine of reconciliation, may be included within the following descriptions. Interested men, who are not to be trusted, weak men who *cannot see,* prejudiced men who *will not* see, and a certain set of moderate men who think better of the European world than it deserves; and this last class, by an ill-judged deliberation, will be the cause of more calamities to this continent, than all the other three.

It is the good fortune of many to live distant from the scene of present sorrow; the evil is not sufficiently brought to *their* doors to make *them* feel the precariousness with which all American property is possessed. But let our imaginations transport us a few moments to Boston; that seat of wretchedness will teach us wisdom, and instruct us for ever to renounce a power in whom we can have no trust. The inhabitants of that unfortunate city who but a few months ago were in ease and affluence, have now no other alternative than to stay and starve, or turn out to beg. Endangered by the fire of their friends if they continue within the city, and plundered by government if they leave it. In their present condition they are prisoners without the hope of redemption, and in a general attack for their relief, they would be exposed to the fury of both armies.

Men of passive tempers look somewhat lightly over the offences of Britain, and still hoping for the best, are apt to call out, *Come, come, we shall be friends again for all this.* But examine the passions and feelings of mankind: Bring the doctrine of reconciliation to the touchstone of nature, and then tell me, whether you can hereafter love, honour, and faithfully serve the power that hath carried fire and sword into your land? If you cannot do all these, then are you only deceiving yourselves, and by your delay bringing ruin upon posterity. Your future connection with Britain whom you can neither love nor honor, will be forced and unnatural, and being formed only on the plan of present convenience, will in a little time, fall into a relapse more wretched than the first. But if you say, you can still pass the violations over, then I ask, Hath your house been burnt? Hath your property been destroyed before your face? Are your wife and children destitute of a bed to lie on, or bread to live on? Have you lost a parent or a child by their hands, and yourself the ruined and wretched survivor? If you have not, then are you not a judge of those who have. But if you have, and still can shake hands with the murderers, then are you unworthy the name of husband, father, friend, or lover, and whatever may be your rank or title in life, you have the heart of a coward, and the spirit of a sycophant.

This is not inflaming or exaggerating matters, but trying them by those feelings and affections which nature justifies, and without which, we should be incapable of discharging the social duties of life, or enjoying the felicities of it. I mean not to exhibit horror for the purpose of provoking revenge, but to awaken us from fatal and unmanly slumbers, that we may pursue determinately some fixed object. 'Tis not in the power of England or of Europe to conquer America, if she doth not conquer herself by *delay* and *timidity*. The present winter is worth an age if rightly employed, but if lost or neglected, the whole continent will partake of the misfortune; and there is no punishment which that man doth not deserve, be he, who, or what, or where he will, that may be the means of sacrificing a season so precious and useful.

'Tis repugnant to reason, to the universal order of things, to all examples from former ages, to suppose, that this continent can long remain subject to any external power. The most sanguine in Britain doth not think so. The utmost stretch of human wisdom cannot at this time, compass a plan, short of separation, which can promise the continent even a year's security. Reconciliation is *now* a fallacious dream. Nature hath deserted the connection, and art cannot supply her place. For, as Milton wisely expresses "never can true reconcilement grow where wounds of deadly hate have pierced so deep."

Every quiet method for peace hath been ineffectual. Our prayers have been rejected with disdain; and hath tended to convince us that nothing flatters vanity or confirms obstinacy in Kings more than repeated petitioning—and nothing hath contributed more, than that very measure, to make the Kings of Europe absolute. Witness Denmark and Sweden. Wherefore, since nothing but blows will do, for God's sake let us come to a final separation, and not leave the next generation to be cutting throats under the violated unmeaning names of parent and child.

To say, they will never attempt it again is idle and visionary, we thought so at the repeal of the stamp-act, yet a year or two undeceived us; as well may we suppose that nations which have been once defeated will never renew the quarrel.

As to government matters 'tis not in the power of Britain to do this continent justice: The business of it will soon be too weighty and intricate to be managed with any tolerable degree of convenience, by a power so distant from us; and so very ignorant of us; for if they cannot conquer us, they cannot govern us. To be always running three or four thousand miles with a tale or a petition, waiting four or five months for an answer, which when obtained requires five or six more to explain it in, will in a few years be looked upon as folly and childishness— There was a time when it was proper, and there is a proper time for it to cease.

Small islands not capable of protecting themselves; are the proper objects for government to take under their care: but there is something very absurd, in supposing a Continent to be perpetually governed by an island. In no instance hath nature made the satellite larger than its primary planet, and as England and America with respect to each other reverse the common order of nature, it is evident that they belong to different systems. England to Europe: America to itself.

I am not induced by motives of pride, party or resentment to espouse the doctrine of separation and independence; I am clearly, positively, and conscientiously persuaded that 'tis the true interest of this continent to be so; that every thing short of that is mere patchwork, that it can afford no lasting felicity,—that it is leaving the sword to our children, and shrinking back at a time, when a little more, a little further, would have rendered this continent the glory of the earth. * * *

But the most powerful of all arguments is, that nothing but independance, i.e. a continental form of government, can keep the peace of the Continent, and preserve it inviolate from civil wars. I dread the event of a reconciliation with Britain now, as it is more than probable, that it will be followed by a revolt some where or other, the consequences of which may be far more fatal than all the malice of Britain.

Thousands are already ruined by British barbarity; (thousands more will probably suffer the same fate;) Those men have other feelings than us who have nothing suffered. All they now possess is liberty, what they before enjoyed is sacrificed to its service, and having nothing more to lose, they disdain submission. Besides, the general temper of the Colonies towards a British government will be like that of a youth, who is nearly out of his time; they will care very little about her: And a government which cannot preserve the peace, is no government at all, and in that case we pay our money for nothing; and pray what is it that Britain can do, whose power will be wholly on paper, should a civil tumult break out the very day after reconciliation? I have heard some men say, many of whom I believe spoke without thinking, that they dreaded an independance, fearing that it would produce civil wars: It is but seldom that our first thoughts are truly correct, and that is the case here; for there are ten times more to dread from a patched up connection, than from independance. I make the sufferers case my own, and I protest, that were I driven from house and home, my property destroyed, and my circumstances ruined, that as a man sensible of injuries, I could never relish the doctrine of reconciliation, or consider myself bound thereby.

The Colonies hath manifested such a spirit of good order and obedience to continental government, as is sufficient to make every reasonable person easy and happy on that head. No man can assign the least pretence for his fears, on any other grounds, than such as are truly childish and ridiculous, viz., that one colony will be striving for superiority over another.

Where there are no distinctions, there can be no superiority; perfect equality affords no temptation. The Republics of Europe are all, (and we may say always) in peace. Holland and Switzerland, are without wars, foreign or domestic: Monarchical governments, it is true, are never long at rest; the crown itself is a temptation to enterprising ruffians at home; and that degree of pride and insolence ever attendant on regal authority, swells into a rupture with foreign powers in instances, where a republican government by being formed on more natural principles, would negociate the mistake.

If there is any true cause for fear respecting independance, it is because no plan is yet laid down. Men do not see their way out—Wherefore, as an opening into that business I offer the following hints; at the same time modestly affirming, that I have no other opinion of them myself, than that they may be the means of giving rise to something better. Could the straggling thoughts of individuals be collected, they would frequently form materials for wise and able men to improve into useful matter.

Let the assemblies be annual with a president only. The representation more equal. Their business wholly domestic, and subject to the authority of a Continental Congress.

Let each Colony be divided into six, eight or ten convenient districts, each district to send a proper number of Delegates to Congress, so that each Colony send at least thirty. The whole number in Congress will be at least 390. Each congress to sit and to choose a president by the following method. When the Delegates are met, let a Colony be taken from the whole thirteen Colonies by lot, after which let the Congress choose (by ballot) a president from out of the Delegates of that province. In the next Congress let a Colony be taken by lot from twelve only, omitting that Colony from which the president was taken in the former Congress, and so proceeding on till the whole thirteen shall have had their proper rotation. And in order that nothing may pass into a law but what is satisfactorily just, not less than three fifths of the Congress to be called a majority—He that will promote discord under a government so equally formed as this, would have joined Lucifer in his revolt.

But as there is a peculiar delicacy from whom, or in what manner this business must first arise, and as it seems most agreeable and consistent, that it should come from some intermediate body between the governed and the governors, that is, between the Congress and the People Let a CONTINENTAL CONFERENCE be held in the following manner, and for the following purpose,

A Committee of twenty six members of congress, viz. Two for each Colony. Two Members from each House of Assembly, or Provincial convention; and five Representatives of the people at large, to be chosen in the capital city or town of each Province, for, and in behalf of the whole Province, by as many qualified voters as shall think proper to attend from all parts of the Province for that purpose: or if more convenient, the Representatives may be chosen in two or three of the most populous parts thereof. In this CONFERENCE thus assembled, will be united the two grand principles of business, *knowledge* and *power*. The members of Congress, Assemblies, or Conventions, by having had experience in national concerns, will be able and useful counsellors, and the whole, being impowered by the people, will have a truly legal authority.

The conferring members being met, let their business be to frame a CONTINENTAL CHARTER, or Charter of the United Colonies; (answering, to what is called the Magna Charta of England) fixing the number and manner of choosing Members of Congress, Members of Assembly, with their date of sitting; and drawing the line of business and jurisdiction between them: Always remembering, that our strength and happiness is Continental, not Provincial. Securing freedom and property to all men, and above all things, the free exercise of religion, according to the dictates of conscience; with such other matter as is necessary for a charter to contain. Immediately after which, the said conference to dissolve, and the bodies which shall be chosen conformable to the said charter, to be the Legislators and Governors of this Continent, for the time being: Whose peace and happiness, may GOD preserve. AMEN.

Should any body of men be hereafter delegated for this or some similar purpose, I offer them the following extracts from that wise observer on Governments, Dragonetti. "The science" says he "of the Politician consists in fixing the true point of happiness and freedom. Those men would deserve the gratitude of ages, who should discover a mode of government that contained the greatest sum of individual happiness, with the least national expense."

But where, say some, is the King of America? I'll tell you, Friend, he reigns above, and doth not make havoc of mankind like the Royal Brute of Great Britain. Yet that we may not appear to be defective even in earthly honours, let a day be solemnly set apart for proclaiming the Charter; let it be brought forth placed on the Divine Law, the word of God; let a crown be placed thereon, by which the world may know, that so far as we approve of monarchy, that in America THE LAW IS KING. For as in absolute governments the King is law, so in free countries the law *ought* to be King; and there ought to be no other. But lest any ill use should afterwards arise, let the Crown at the conclusion of the ceremony be demolished, and scattered among the People whose right it is.

A government of our own is our natural right: and when a man seriously reflects on the precariousness of human affairs, he will become convinced, that it is infinitely wiser and safer, to form a constitution of our own, in a cool deliberate manner, while we have it in our power, than to trust such an interesting event to time and chance. If we omit it now, some Massanello may hereafter arise, who laying hold of popular disquietudes, may collect together the desperate and the discontented, and by assuming to themselves the powers of government, may sweep away the liberties of the Continent like a deluge. Should the government of America return again into the hands of Britain, the tottering situation of things will be a temptation for some deseperate adventurer to try his fortune; and in such a case, what relief can Britain give? Ere she could hear the news, the fatal business might be done; and ourselves suffering like the wretched Britons under the oppression of the Conqueror. Ye that oppose independance now, ye know not what ye do: ye are opening a door to eternal tryanny, by keeping vacant the seat of government. There are thousands, and tens of thousands, who would think it glorious to expel from the Continent, that barbarous and hellish power, which hath stirred up the Indians and the Negroes to destroy us; the cruelty hath a double guilt, it is dealing brutally by us, and treacherously by them.

To talk of friendship with those in whom our reason forbids us to have faith, and our affections wounded thro' a thousand pores instruct us to detest, is madness and folly. Every day wears out the little remains of kindred between us and them, and can there be any reason to hope, that as the relationship expires, the affection will encrease, or that we shall agree better, when we have ten times more and greater concerns to quarrel over than ever?

Ye that tell us of harmony and reconciliation, can ye restore to us the time that is past? Can ye give to prostitution its former innocence? Neither can ye reconcile Britain and America. The last cord now is broken, the people of England are presenting addresses against us. There are injuries which nature cannot forgive; she would cease to be nature if she did. As well can the lover forgive the ravisher of his mistress, as the Continent forgive the murders of Britain. The Almighty hath implanted in us these unextinguishable feelings for good and wise purposes. They are the guardians of his image in our hearts. They distinguish us from the herd of common animals. The social compact would dissolve, and justice be extirpated from the earth, or have only a casual existence were we callous to the touches of affection. The robber and the murderer would often escape unpunished, did not the injuries which our tempers sustain, provoke us into justice.

O ye that love mankind! Ye that dare oppose not only the tyranny, but the tyrant, stand forth! Every spot of the old world is over-run with oppression. Freedom hath been hunted round the globe. Asia and Africa have long expelled her.—Europe regards her like a stranger, and England hath given her warning to depart. O! receive the fugitive, and prepare in time an asylum for mankind.

* * *

On these grounds I rest the matter. And as no offer hath yet been made to refute the doctrine contained in the former editions of this pamphlet, it is a negative proof that either the doctrine cannot be refuted, or that the party in favour of it are too numerous to be opposed. *Wherefore*, instead of gazing at each other, with suspicious or doubtful curiosity, let each of us hold out to his neighbour the hearty hand of friendship, and united in drawing a line, which, like an act of oblivion, shall bury in forgetfulness every former dissension. Let the names of whig and tory be extinct; and let none other be heard among us, than those of a *good citizen, an open and resolute friend,* and *a virtuous supporter of the* RIGHTS OF MANKIND, and of the FREE AND INDEPENDENT STATES OF AMERICA.

THOMAS PAINE

The American Crisis, I (1776)

In the years immediately after independence, Paine served in a number of official positions and used his considerable literary talents in a series of essays designed to restore the flagging morale and stiffen the resolve of Americans weary of war. In December 1776, just when it looked as if the American cause was hopeless, he wrote the first of sixteen pamphlets that appeared under the title The American Crisis from 1776 to 1783. Still famous for its stirring opening lines, the first issue appealed to Americans' sense of patriotism and their self-interest in urging them to persevere and remain united in the war effort.

These are the times that try men's souls. The summer soldier and the sunshine patriot will, in this crisis, shrink from the service of their country, but he that stands it *now* deserves the love and thanks of man and woman. Tyranny, like hell, is not easily conquered; yet we have this consolation with us that, the harder the conflict, the more glorious the triumph. What we obtain too cheap, we esteem too lightly; it is dearness only that gives everything its value. Heaven knows how to put a proper price upon its goods, and it would be strange indeed if so celestial an article as freedom should not be highly rated. Britain, with an army to enforce her tyranny, has declared that she has a right (*not only to tax*) but *to bind us in all cases whatsoever;* and if being *bound in that manner* is not slavery, then is there not such a thing as slavery upon earth. Even

the expression is impious, for so unlimited a power can belong only
to God.

* * *

I have as little superstition in me as any man living, but my secret
opinion has ever been and still is that God Almighty will not give up a
people to military destruction or leave them unsupportedly to perish who
have so earnestly and so repeatedly sought to avoid the calamities of war
by every decent method which wisdom could invent. Neither have I so
much of the infidel in me as to suppose that He has relinquished the government of the world and given us up to the care of devils, and as I do not
I cannot see on what grounds the King of Britain can look up to heaven
for help against us; a common murderer, a highwayman, or a house-
breaker has as good a pretense as he. * * *

* * * I turn with the warm ardor of a friend to those who have nobly
stood and are yet determined to stand the matter out; I call not upon a
few but upon all—not on *this* state or *that* state, but on *every* state—up
and help us, lay your shoulders to the wheel, better have too much force
than too little when so great an object is at stake. Let it be told to the
future world that in the depth of winter, when nothing but hope and
virtue could survive, that the city and the country, alarmed at one common danger, came forth to meet and to repulse it. Say not that thousands are gone, turn out your tens of thousands; throw not the burden
of the day upon Providence, but "show your faith by your works," that
God may bless you. It matters not where you live or what rank of life
you hold, the evil or the blessing will reach you all. The far and the near,
the home counties and the back, the rich and the poor will suffer or rejoice alike. The heart that feels not now is dead; the blood of his children will curse his cowardice who shrinks back at a time when a little
might have saved the whole and made *them* happy. I love the man that
can smile in trouble, that can gather strength from distress and grow
brave by reflection. "Tis the business of little minds to shrink, but he
whose heart is firm and whose conscience approves his conduct will
pursue his principles unto death." My own line of reasoning is to myself
as straight and clear as a ray of light. Not all the treasures of the world,
so far as I believe, could have induced me to support an offensive war,
for I think it murder; but if a thief breaks into my house, burns and destroys my property, and kills or threatens to kill me or those that are in
it and to "bind me in all cases whatsoever" to his absolute will, am I to
suffer it? What signifies it to me whether he who does it is a king or a
common man, my countryman or not my countryman; whether it be
done by an individual villain or an army of them? If we reason to the
root of things, we shall find no difference; neither can any just cause be

assigned why we should punish in the one case and pardon in the other. Let them call me rebel and welcome, I feel no concern from it; but I should suffer the misery of devils were I to make a whore of my soul by swearing allegiance to one whose character is that of a sottish, stupid, stubborn, worthless, brutish man. I conceive likewise a horrid idea in receiving mercy from a being who, at the last day, shall be shrieking to the rocks and mountains to cover him and fleeing with terror from the orphan, the widow, and the slain of America.

There are cases which cannot be overdone by language, and this is one. There are persons, too, who see not the full extent of the evil which threatens them; they solace themselves with hopes that the enemy, if he succeed, will be merciful. It is the madness of folly to expect mercy from those who have refused to do justice; and even mercy, where conquest is the object, is only a trick of war; the cunning of the fox is as murderous as the violence of the wolf, and we ought to guard equally against both.

THOMAS JEFFERSON

Declaration of Independence (1776)

The philosopher-statesman Thomas Jefferson (1743–1826) is known as the author of the Declaration of Independence, but the document that announced the political creed of the new nation was actually a collaborative effort. Jefferson—a radical democrat who later became governor of Virginia, ambassador to France, the first secretary of state, the third president of the United States, the leader of the first Republican party, and the founder of the University of Virginia—wrote the first draft of the declaration. Among its many grievances against the British government, it included an indictment against the king for promoting slavery in the colonies, but that was omitted from the final version because of concerns that it might disunite the colonies. Since the colonies had already been at war with Britain for a year by the time the declaration was issued, it was not really addressed to the British government, but instead formalized the existing state of affairs so that the newly independent states would be eligible for aid from France.

The Unanimous Declaration of the
Thirteen United States of America

When, in the Course of human events, it becomes necessary for one people to dissolve the political bands which have connected them with another, and to assume, among the Powers of the earth, the separate and equal station to which the Laws of Nature and of Nature's God entitle them, a decent respect to the opinions of mankind requires that they should declare the causes which impel them to the separation.

We hold these truths to be self-evident, that all men are created equal, that they are endowed by their Creator with certain unalienable Rights, that among these, are Life, Liberty, and the pursuit of Happiness. That, to secure these rights, Governments are instituted among Men, deriving their just Powers from the consent of the governed. That, whenever any form of Government becomes destructive of these ends, it is the Right of the People to alter or to abolish it, and to institute new Government, laying its foundation on such Principles, and organizing its Powers in such form, as to them shall seem most likely to effect their Safety and Happiness. Prudence, indeed, will dictate that Governments long established should not be changed for light and transient causes; and, accordingly, all experience hath shewn, that mankind are more disposed to suffer, while evils are sufferable, than to right themselves by abolishing the forms to which they are accustomed. But, when a long train of abuses and usurpations, pursuing invariably the same Object, evinces a design to reduce them under absolute Despotism, it is their right, it is their duty, to throw off such Government, and to provide, new Guards for their future Security. Such has been the patient sufferance of these Colonies; and such is now the necessity which constrains them to alter their former Systems of Government. The history of the present King of Great Britain is a history of repeated injuries and usurpations, all having in direct object the establishment of an absolute Tyranny over these States. To prove this, let Facts be submitted to a candid world.

He has refused his Assent to Laws the most wholesome and necessary for the public good.

He has forbidden his Governors to pass Laws of immediate and pressing importance, unless suspended in their operation till his Assent should be obtained; and when so suspended, he has utterly neglected to attend to them.

He has refused to pass other Laws for the accommodation of large districts of People, unless those People would relinquish the right of Representation in the legislature; a right inestimable to them and formidable to tyrants only.

He has called together legislative bodies at places unusual, uncomfortable, and distant from the depository of their Public Records, for the sole Purpose of fatiguing them into compliance with his measures.

He has dissolved Representative Houses repeatedly, for opposing, with manly firmness, his invasions on the rights of the People.

He has refused for a long time, after such dissolutions, to cause others to be elected; whereby the Legislative Powers, incapable of Annihilation, have returned to the People at large for their exercise; the State remaining in the mean time exposed to all the dangers of invasion from without, and convulsions within.

He has endeavoured to prevent the Population of these States; for that purpose obstructing the Laws for Naturalization of Foreigners; refusing to pass others to encourage their migrations hither, and raising the conditions of new Appropriations of Lands.

He has obstructed the Administration of Justice, by refusing his Assent to Laws for establishing Judiciary Powers.

He has made Judges dependent on his Will alone, for the tenure of their offices, and the amount and payment of their salaries.

He has erected a multitude of New Offices, and sent hither swarms of Officers to harrass our People, and eat out their substance.

He has kept among us, in times of Peace, Standing Armies, without the Consent of our legislatures.

He has affected to render the Military independent of and superior to the Civil Power.

He has combined with others to subject us to a jurisdiction foreign to our constitution, and unacknowledged by our laws; giving his Assent to their Acts of pretended Legislation:

For quartering large bodies of armed troops among us:

For protecting them, by a mock Trial, from Punishment for any Murders which they should commit on the Inhabitants of these States:

For cutting off our Trade with all parts of the world:

For imposing Taxes on us without our Consent:

For depriving us, in many cases, of the benefits of Trial by Jury:

For transporting us beyond Seas to be tried for pretended offences:

For abolishing the free System of English Laws in a neighbouring province, establishing therein an Arbitrary government, and enlarging its Boundaries, so as to render it at once an example and fit instrument for introducing the same absolute rule into these Colonies:

For taking away our Charters, abolishing our most valuable Laws, and altering fundamentally the Forms of our Governments:

For suspending our own Legislatures, and declaring themselves invested with Power to legislate for us in all cases whatsoever.

He has abdicated Government here, by declaring us out of his protection, and waging War against us.

He has plundered our seas, ravaged our Coasts, burnt our towns, and destroyed the Lives of our People.

He is at this time transporting large Armies of foreign Mercenaries to compleat the works of death, desolation and tyranny, already begun with circumstances of Cruelty and perfidy scarcely paralleled in the most barbarous ages, and totally unworthy the Head of a civilized nation.

He has constrained our fellow Citizens, taken Captive on the high Seas, to bear Arms against their Country, to become the executioners of their friends and Brethren, or to fall themselves by their Hands.

He has excited domestic insurrections amongst us, and has endeavoured to bring on the inhabitants of our frontiers, the merciless Indian Savages, whose known rule of warfare, is an undistinguished destruction of all ages, sexes and conditions.

In every stage of these Oppressions, We have Petitioned for Redress, in the most humble terms: Our repeated Petitions, have been answered only by repeated injury. A Prince, whose character is thus marked by every act which may define a Tyrant, is unfit to be the ruler of a free People.

Nor have We been wanting in attentions to our Brittish brethren. We have warned them from time to time of attempts by their legislature to extend an unwarrantable jurisdiction over us. We have reminded them of the circumstances of our emigration and settlement here. We have appealed to their native justice and magnanimity, and we have conjured them by the ties of our common kindred, to disavow these usurpations, which, would inevitably interrupt our connexions and correspondence. They too have been deaf to the voice of justice and of consanguinity. We must, therefore, acquiesce in the necessity, which denounces our Separation, and hold them, as we hold the rest of mankind, Enemies in War, in Peace Friends.

We, therefore, the Representatives of the united States of America, in GENERAL CONGRESS assembled, appealing to the Supreme Judge of the World for the rectitude of our intentions, DO, in the Name, and by Authority of the good People of these Colonies, solemnly PUBLISH and DECLARE, That these United Colonies are, and of Right, ought to be *Free and Independent States*; that they are Absolved from all Allegiance to the British Crown, and that all political connexion between them and the State of Great Britain, is and ought to be totally dissolved; and that, as FREE and INDEPENDENT STATES, they have full Power to levy War, conclude Peace, contract Alliances, establish Commerce, and to do all other Acts and Things which INDEPENDENT STATES may of right do. AND for the support of this Declaration, with a firm reliance on the protection of divine Providence, we mutually pledge to each other our Lives, our Fortunes, and our sacred Honour.

The Constitution
and Its Critics

The Articles of Confederation (1778)

An initial draft of the first constitution of the newly independent states was introduced almost immediately after the signing of the Declaration of Independence, but the Continental Congress did not adopt the Articles of Confederation until July 9, 1778. This compact declared a set of common objectives, but it preserved the sovereignty and independence of the states and failed to give the national government enough powers over commerce and taxation to achieve common goals. Shortly after its adoption, nationalist leaders proposed revising the Articles to give it more effective powers, but many Americans were reluctant to abandon a decentralized structure they considered indispensable to the preservation of liberty.

To all whom these Presents shall come, we the undersigned Delegates of the States affixed to our Names send greeting. Whereas the Delegates of the United States of America in Congress assembled did on the fifteenth day of November in the Year of our Lord One Thousand Seven Hundred and Seventy seven, and in the Second Year of the Independence of America agree to certain articles of Confederation and perpetual Union between the States of New-hampshire, Massachusetts-bay, Rhode Island and Providence Plantations, Connecticut, New York, New Jersey, Pennsylvania, Delaware, Maryland, Virginia, North-Carolina, South-Carolina and Georgia in the Words following, viz. "Articles of Confederation and perpetual union between the states of Newhampshire, Massachusetts-bay, Rhode Island and Providence Plantations, Connecticut, New York, New Jersey, Pennsylvania, Delaware, Maryland, Virginia, North-Carolina, South-Carolina and Georgia."

Art. I. The Stile of this confederacy shall be "The United States of America."

Art. II. Each state retains its sovereignty, freedom and independence, and every Power, Jurisdiction and right, which is not by this confederation expressly delegated to the United States, in Congress assembled.

Art. III. The said states hereby severally enter into a firm league of friendship with each other, for their common defence, the security of their Liberties, and their mutual and general welfare, binding themselves to assist each other, against all force offered to, or attacks made upon them, or any of them, on account of religion, sovereignty, trade, or any other pretence whatever.

Art. IV. The better to secure and perpetuate mutual friendship and intercourse among the people of the different states in this union, the free inhabitants of each of these states, paupers, vagabonds and fugitives from Justice excepted, shall be entitled to all privileges and immunities of free citizens in the several states; and the people of each state shall have free ingress and regress to and from any other state, and shall enjoy therein all the privileges of trade and commerce, subject to the same duties, impositions and restrictions as the inhabitants thereof respectively, provided that such restriction shall not extend so far as to prevent the removal of property imported into any state, to any other state of which the Owner is an inhabitant; provided also that no imposition, duties or restriction shall be laid by any state, on the property of the united states, or either of them.

If any Person guilty of, or charged with treason, felony, or other high misdemeanor in any state, shall flee from Justice, and be found in any of the united states, he shall upon demand of the Governor or executive power, of the state from which he fled, be delivered up and removed to the state having jurisdiction of his offence.

Full faith and credit shall be given in each of these states to the records, acts and judicial proceedings of the courts and magistrates of every other state.

Art. V. For the more convenient management of the general interest of the united states, delegates shall be annually appointed in such manner as the legislature of each state shall direct, to meet in Congress on the first Monday in November, in every year, with a power reserved to each state, to recall its delegates, or any of them, at any time within the year, and to send other in their stead, for the remainder of the year.

No state shall be represented in Congress by less than two, nor by more than seven Members; and no person shall be capable of being a delegate for more than three years in any term of six years; nor shall any person, being a delegate, be capable of holding any office under the united states, for which he, or another for his benefit receives any salary, fees or emolument of any kind.

Each state shall maintain its own delegates in a meeting of the states, and while they act as members of the committee of the states.

In determining questions in the united states, in Congress assembled, each state shall have one vote.

Freedom of speech and debate in Congress shall not be impeached or questioned in any Court, or place out of Congress, and the members of congress shall be protected in their persons from arrests and imprisonments, during the time of their going to and from, and attendance on congress, except for treason, felony, or breach of the peace.

Art. VI. No state without the Consent of the united states in congress assembled, shall send any embassy to, or receive any embassy from, or enter into any conference, agreement, or alliance or treaty with any King, prince or state; nor shall any person holding any office of profit or trust under the united states, or any of them, accept of any present, emolument, office or title of any kind whatever from any king, prince or foreign state; nor shall the united states in congress assembled, or any of them, grant any title of nobility.

No two or more states shall enter into any treaty, confederation or alliance whatever between them, without the consent of the united states in congress assembled, specifying accurately the purposes for which the same is to be entered into, and how long it shall continue.

No state shall lay any imposts or duties, which may interfere with any stipulations in treaties, entered into by the united states in congress assembled, with any king, prince or state, in pursuance of any treaties already proposed by congress, to the courts of France and Spain.

No vessels of war shall be kept up in time of peace by any state, except such number only, as shall be deemed necessary by the united states in congress assembled, for the defence of such state, or its trade; nor shall any body of forces be kept up by any state, in time of peace, except such number only, as in the judgment of the united states, in congress assembled, shall be deemed requisite to garrison the forts necessary for the defence of such state; but every state shall always keep up a well regulated and disciplined militia, sufficiently armed and accoutred, and shall provide and constantly have ready for use, in public stores, a due number of field pieces and tents, and a proper quantity of arms, ammunition and camp equipage.

No state shall engage in any war without the consent of the united states in congress assembled, unless such state be actually invaded by enemies, or shall have received certain advice of a resolution being formed by some nation of Indians to invade such state, and the danger is so imminent as not to admit of a delay, till the united states in congress assembled can be consulted: nor shall any state grant commissions to any ships or vessels of war, nor letters of marque or reprisal, except it be after a declaration of war by the united states in congress assembled, and then only against the kingdom or state and the subjects thereof, against which war has been so declared, and under such regulations as shall be established by the united states in congress assembled, unless such state be infested by pirates, in which case vessels of war may be fitted out for that occasion, and kept so long as the danger shall continue, or until the united states in congress assembled shall determine otherwise.

Art. VII. When land-forces are raised by any state for the common defence, all officers of or under the rank of colonel, shall be appointed by the legislature of each state respectively by whom such forces shall be raised, or in such manner as such state shall direct, and all vacancies shall be filled up by the state which first made the appointment.

Art. VIII. All charges of war, and all other expences that shall be incurred for the common defence or general welfare, and allowed by the united states in congress assembled, shall be defrayed out of a common treasury, which shall be supplied by the several states, in proportion to the value of all land within each state, granted to or surveyed for any Person, as such land and the buildings and improvements thereon shall be estimated according to such mode as the united states in congress assembled, shall from time to time direct and appoint. The taxes for paying that proportion shall be laid and levied by the authority and direction of the legislatures of the several states within the time agreed upon by the united states in congress assembled.

Art. IX. The united states in congress assembled, shall have the sole and exclusive right and power of determining on peace and war, except in the cases mentioned in the sixth article—of sending and receiving ambassadors—entering into treaties and alliances, provided that no treaty of commerce shall be made whereby the legislative power of the respective states shall be restrained from imposing such imposts and duties on foreigners, as their own people are subjected to, or from prohibiting the exportation or importation of any species of goods or commodities whatsoever—of establishing rules for deciding in all cases, what captures on land or water shall be legal, and in what manner prizes taken by land or naval forces in the service of the united states shall be divided or appropriated—of granting letters of marque and reprisal in times of peace—appointing courts for the trial of piracies and felonies committed on the high seas and establishing courts for receiving and determining finally appeals in all cases of captures, provided that no member of congress shall be appointed a judge of any of the said courts.

The united states in congress assembled shall also be the last resort on appeal in all disputes and differences now subsisting or that hereafter may arise between two or more states concerning boundary, jurisdiction or any other cause whatever; which authority shall always be exercised in the manner following. Whenever the legislative or executive authority or lawful agent of any state in controversy with another shall present a petition to congress, stating the matter in question and praying for a hearing, notice thereof shall be given the order of congress to the legislative or executive authority of the other state in controversy, and a day assigned for the appearance of the parties by their lawful agents, who shall then be directed to appoint by joint consent, commissioners or judge to constitute a court for hearing and determining the matter in question: but if they cannot agree, congress shall name three persons out of each of the united states, and from the list of such persons each party shall alternately strike out one, the petitioners beginning, until the number shall be reduced to thirteen; and from that number not less than seven, nor more than nine names as congress shall direct, shall in the presence of congress be drawn out by lot, and the persons whose names shall be so drawn or any five of them, shall be commissioners or judges, to hear and finally determine the controversy, so always as a major part of the judges who shall hear the cause shall agree in the determination: and if either party shall neglect to attend at the day appointed, without shewing reasons, which congress shall judge sufficient, or being present shall refuse to strike, the congress shall proceed to nominate three persons out of each state, and the secretary of congress shall strike in behalf of such party absent or refusing; and the judgment and sentence of the court to be appointed, in the manner before prescribed, shall be final and conclusive; and if any of the parties shall refuse to submit to the authority of such court, or to appear to defend their claim or cause, the court shall nevertheless proceed to pronounce sentence, or judgment, which shall in like manner be final and decisive, the judgment or sentence and other proceedings being in either case transmitted to congress, and lodged among the acts of congress for the security of the parties concerned: provided that every commissioner, before he sits in judgment, shall take an oath to be administered by one of the judges of the supreme or superior court of the state, where the cause shall be tried, "well and truly to hear and determine the matter in question, according to the best of his judgment, without favour, affection or hope of reward:" provided also that no state shall be deprived of territory for the benefit of the united states.

All controversies concerning the private right of soil claimed under different grants of two or more states, whose jurisdictions as they may respect such lands, and the states which passed such grants are adjusted, the said grants or either of them being at the same time claimed to have originated antecedent to such settlement of jurisdiction, shall on the petition of either party to the congress of the united states, be finally determined as near as may be in the same manner as is before prescribed for deciding disputes respecting territorial jurisdiction between different states.

The united states in congress assembled shall also have the sole and exclusive right and power of regulating the alloy and value of coin struck by their own authority, or by that of the respective states—fixing the standard of weights and measures throughout the united states—regulating the trade and managing all affairs with the Indians, not members of any of the states, provided that the legislative right of any state within its own limits be not infringed or violated—establishing and regulating post-offices from one state to another, throughout all the united states, and exacting such postage on the papers passing thro' the same as may be requisite to defray the expences of the said office—appointing all officers of the land forces, in the service of the united states, excepting regimental officers—appointing all the officers of the naval forces, and commissioning all officers whatever in the service of the united states—making rules for the government and regulation of the said land and naval forces, and directing their operations.

The united states in congress assembled shall have authority to appoint a committee, to sit in the recess of congress, to be denominated "A Committee of the States," and to consist of one delegate from each state; and to appoint such other committees and civil officers as may be necessary for managing the general affairs of the united states under their direction—to appoint one of their number to preside, provided that no person be allowed to serve in the office of president more than one year in any term of three years; to ascertain the necessary sums of Money to be raised for the service of the united states, and to appropriate and apply the same for defraying the public expences—to borrow money, or emit bills on the credit of the united states, transmitting every half year to the respective states an account of the sums of money so borrowed or emitted,—to build and equip a navy—to agree upon the number of land forces, and to make requisitions from each state for its quota, in proportion to the number of white inhabitants in such state; which requisition shall be binding, and thereupon the legislature of each state shall appoint the regimental officers, raise the men and cloath, arm and equip them in a soldier like manner, at the expence of the united states, and the officers and men so cloathed, armed and equipped shall march to the place appointed, and within the time agreed on by the united states in congress assembled: But if the united states in congress assembled shall, on consideration of circumstances judge proper that any state should not raise men, or should raise a smaller number than its quota, and that any other state should raise a greater number of men than the quota thereof, such extra number shall be raised, officered, cloathed, armed and equipped in the same manner as the quota of such state, unless the legislature of such state shall judge that such extra number cannot be safely spared out of the same, in which case they shall raise, officer, cloath, arm and equip as many of such extra number as they judge can be safely spared. And the officers and men so cloathed, armed and equipped, shall march to the place appointed, and within the time agreed on by the united states in congress assembled.

The united states in congress assembled shall never engage in a war, nor grant letters of marque and reprisal in time of peace, nor enter into any treaties or alliances, nor coin money, nor regulate the value thereof, nor ascertain the sums and expences necessary for the defence and welfare of the united states, or any of them, nor emit bills, nor borrow money on the credit of the united states, nor appropriate money, nor agree upon the number of vessels of war, to be built or purchased, or the number of land or sea forces to be raised, nor appoint a commander in chief of the army or navy, unless nine states assent to the same: nor shall a question on any other point, except for adjourning from day to day be determined, unless by the votes of a majority of the united states in congress assembled.

The congress of the united states shall have power to adjourn to any time within the year, and to any place within the united states, so that no period of adjournment be for a longer duration than the space of six Months, and shall publish the Journal of their proceedings monthly, except such parts thereof relating to treaties, alliances or military operations as in their judgment require secresy; and the yeas and nays of the delegates of each state on any question shall be entered on the Journal, when it is desired by any delegate; and the delegates of a state, or any of them, at his or their request shall be furnished with a transcript of the said Journal, except such parts as are above excepted, to lay before the legislatures of the several states.

Art. X. The committee of the states, or any nine of them, shall be authorised to execute, in the recess of congress such of the powers of congress as the united states in congress assembled, by the consent of nine states, shall from time to time think expedient to vest them with; provided that no power be delegated to the said committee, for the exercise of which, by the articles of confederation, the voice of nine states in the congress of the united states assembled is requisite.

Art. XI. Canada acceding to this confederation, and joining in the measures of the united states, shall be admitted into, and entitled to all the advantages of this union: but no other colony shall be admitted into the same, unless such admission be agreed to by nine states.

Art. XII. All bills of credit emitted, monies borrowed and debts contracted by, or under the authority of congress, before the assembling of the united states, in pursuance of the present confederation, shall be deemed and considered as a charge against the united states, for payment and satisfaction whereof the said united states, and the public faith are hereby solemnly pledged.

Art. XIII. Every state shall abide by the determinations of the united states in congress assembled, on all questions which by this confederation are submitted to them. And the Articles of this confederation shall be inviolably observed by every state, and the union shall be perpetual; nor shall any alteration at any time hereafter be made in any of them; unless such alteration be agreed to in a congress of the united states, and be afterwards confirmed by the legislatures of every state.

AND WHEREAS it hath pleased the Great Governor of the World to incline the heart of the legislatures we respectively represent in congress, to approve of, and to authorize us to ratify the said articles of confederation and perpetual union. KNOW YE that we the undersigned delegates, by virtue of the power and authority to us given for that purpose, do by these presents, in the name and in behalf of our respective constituents, fully and entirely ratify and confirm each and every of the said articles of confederation and perpetual union, and all and singular the matters and things therein contained: And we do further solemnly plight and engage the faith of our respective constituents, that they shall abide by the determinations of the united states in congress assembled, on all questions, which by the said confederation are submitted to them. And that the articles thereof shall be inviolably observed by the states we respectively represent, and that the union shall be perpetual. In Witness whereof we have hereunto set our hands in Congress. Done at Philadelphia in the state of Pennsylvania the ninth Day of July in the Year of our Lord one Thousand seven Hundred and Seventy-eight, and in the third year of the independence of America.

ALEXANDER HAMILTON

Letter to James Duane (1780)

Born in the British West Indies, Alexander Hamilton (1757–1804) en-
listed in the Revolutionary War effort and rose through the ranks of the
colonial army to become lieutenant colonel and aide-de-camp to Gen-
eral George Washington in 1777. He later served as a New York dele-
gate to Congress, practiced law in New York, led the effort to create a
stronger centralized government, helped secure ratification of the Con-
stitution, and became the nation's first treasury secretary. Hamilton saw
serious problems with the Articles of Confederation and proposed a con-
stitutional convention to revise them even before the war was over. He
argued that as long as the states retained their independence, the con-
federation would lack the "energy" characteristic of good governments.
In this letter he also outlines his plan for a national bank.

*D*ear Sir,—Agreeably to your request, and my promise, I sit down to
give you my ideas of the defects of our present system, and the
changes necessary to save us from ruin. * * *

The fundamental defect is a want of power in Congress. It is hardly
worth while to show in what this consists, as it seems to be universally acknowledged; or to point out how it has happened, as the only question is
how to remedy it. It may, however, be said that it has originated from
three causes: an excess of the spirit of liberty, which has made the particular states show a jealousy of all power not in their own hands, and this
jealousy has led them to exercise a right of judging, in the last resort, of
the measures recommended by Congress, and of acting according to their
own opinions of their propriety or necessity; a diffidence in Congress of
their own powers, by which they have been timid and indecisive in their
resolutions; constantly making concessions to the States, till they have
scarcely left themselves the shadow of power; a want of sufficient means
at their disposal to answer the public exigencies, and of vigour to draw
forth those means, which have occasioned them to depend on the
States, individually, to fulfil their engagements with the army, the consequence of which has been to ruin their influence and credit with the

army, to establish its dependence on each state, separately, rather than *on them*, that is, than on the whole collectively.

It may be pleaded that Congress had never any definitive powers granted them, and of course could exercise none, could do nothing more than recommend. The manner in which Congress was appointed would warrant, and the public good required, that they should have considered themselves as vested with full power *to preserve the republic from harm*. They have done many of the highest acts of sovereignty, which were always cheerfully submitted to: The declaration of independence, the declaration of war, the levying of an army, creating a navy, emitting money, making alliances with foreign powers, appointing a dictator, etc. All these implications of a complete sovereignty were never disputed, and ought to have been a standard for the whole conduct of administration. Undefined powers are discretionary powers, limited only by the object for which they were given; in the present case, the independence and freedom of America. * * *

But the Confederation itself is defective, and requires to be altered. It is neither fit for war, nor peace. The idea of an uncontrollable sovereignty in each State, over its internal police, will defeat the other powers given to Congress, and make our union feeble and precarious. There are instances, without number, where acts necessary for the general good, and which rise out of the powers given to Congress, must interfere with the internal police of the States; and there are as many instances in which the particular States, by arrangements of internal police, can effectually, though indirectly, counteract the arrangements of Congress. * * *

The Confederation gives the States, individually, too much influence in the affairs of the army. They should have nothing to do with it. The entire formation and disposal of our military forces ought to belong to Congress. It is an essential cement of the union; and it ought to be the policy of Congress to destroy all ideas of State attachments to the army, and make it look up wholly to them. For this purpose all appointments, promotions, and provisions whatsoever, ought to be made by them. It may be apprehended that this may be dangerous to liberty. But nothing appears more evident to me, than that we run much greater risk of having a weak and disunited federal government, than one which will be able to usurp upon the rights of the people. * * *

The forms of our State constitutions must always give them great weight in our affairs, and will make it too difficult to bend them to the pursuit of a common interest, too easy to oppose whatever they do not like, and to form partial combinations, subversive to the general one. There is a wide difference between our situation and that of an empire under one simple form of government, distributed into counties, provinces, or districts, which have no Legislatures, but merely magistratical bodies to execute the laws of a common sovereign. Here the danger is that the sovereign will have too much power, and oppress the parts of which it is composed. In our case, that of an empire composed of confederated States, each with a government completely organized within itself, having all the means to draw its subjects to a close dependence on itself, the danger is directly the reverse. It is that the common sovereign will not have power sufficient to unite the different members together, and direct the common forces to the interest and happiness of the whole. * * * A little time hence, some of the States will be powerful empires; and we are so remote from other nations, that we shall have all the leisure and opportunity we can wish to cut each other's throats. * * *

The Confederation, too, gives the power of the purse too entirely to the State Legislatures. It should provide perpetual funds, in the disposal of Congress, by a land tax, poll tax, or the like. All imposts upon commerce ought to be laid by Congress, and appropriated to their use; for without certain revenues, a government can have no power. That power which holds the purse-strings absolutely, must rule. This seems to be a medium, which, without making Congress altogether independent, will tend to give reality to its authority.

Another defect in our system is want of method and energy in the administration. This has partly resulted from the other defect; but in a great degree from prejudice and the want of a proper executive. Congress have kept the power too much in their own hands, and have meddled too much with details of every sort. Congress is properly a deliberative corps, and it forgets itself when it attempts to play the executive. It is impossible that a body, numerous as it is, constantly fluctuating, can ever act with sufficient decision, or with system. * * *

A single man in each department of the administration * * * would give us a chance of more knowledge, more activity, more responsibility, and, of course, more zeal and attention. Boards partake of a part of the inconveniences of larger assemblies. Their decisions are slower, their energy less, their responsibility more diffused. They will not have the same abilities and knowledge as an administration by single men. Men of the first pretensions will not so readily engage in them, because they will be less conspicuous, of less importance, have less opportunity of distinguishing themselves. * * * All these reasons conspire to give a preference to the plan of vesting the great executive departments of the State in the hands of individuals. As these men will be, of course, at all times under the direction of Congress, we shall blend the advantages of a monarchy and republic in our constitution. * * *

A third defect is, the fluctuating constitution of our army. This has been a pregnant source of evil; all our military misfortunes, three-fourths of our civil embarrassments, are to be ascribed to it. * * *

The imperfect and unequal provision made for the army, is a fourth defect. Without a speedy change, the army must dissolve. It is now a mob rather than an army, without clothing, without pay, without provision, without morals, without discipline. * * *

The present mode of supplying the army, by State purchases, is not one of the least considerable defects of our system. It is too precarious a dependence, because the States will never be sufficiently impressed with our necessities. * * *

These are the principal defects in the present system that now occur to me. * * *

I shall now propose the remedies which appear to me applicable to our circumstances, and necessary to extricate our affairs from their present deplorable situation.

The first step must be to give Congress powers competent to the public exigencies. This may happen in two ways: one by resuming and exercising the discretionary powers I suppose to have been originally vested in them for the safety of the States, and resting their conduct on the candour of their countrymen and the necessity of the conjuncture; the other, by calling immediately a Convention of all the States, with full authority to conclude finally upon a General Confederation, stating to them beforehand, explicitly, the evils arising from a want of power in Congress, and the impossibility of supporting the contest on its present footing, that the delegates may come possessed of proper sentiments, as well as proper authority, to give efficacy to the meeting. Their commission should include a right of vesting Congress with the whole or a proportion of the unoccupied lands, to be employed for the purpose of raising a revenue, reserving the jurisdiction to the States by whom they are granted.

The first plan, I expect, will be thought too bold an expedient by the generality of Congress; and, indeed, their practice hitherto has so riveted the opinion of their want of power, that the success of this experiment may very well be doubted.

I see no objection to the other mode that has any weight in competition with the reasons for it. The Convention should assemble the first of November next. The sooner the better. Our disorders are too violent to admit of a common or lingering remedy. The reasons for which I require them to be vested with plenipotentiary authority are that the business may suffer no delay in the execution, and may, in reality, come to effect. A Convention may agree upon a Confederation; the States, individually, hardly ever will. We must have one, at all events, and a vigorous one, if we mean to succeed in the contest and be happy hereafter. As I said before, to engage the States to comply with this mode, Congress ought to confess to them, plainly and unanimously, the impracticability of supporting our affairs on the present footing, and without a solid coercive union. I ask that the Convention should have a power of vesting the whole or a part of the unoccupied lands in Congress; because it is necessary that body should have some property as a fund for the arrangements of finance; and I know of no other kind that can be given them.

The Confederation, in my opinion, should give Congress a complete sovereignty; except as to that part of internal police which relates to the rights of property and life among individuals, and to raising money by internal taxes. It is necessary that everything belonging to this should be regulated by the State Legislatures. Congress should have complete sovereignty in all that relates to war, peace, trade, finance, and to the management of foreign affairs; the right of declaring war; of raising armies, officering, paying them, directing their motions in every respect; of equipping fleets, and doing the same with them; of building fortifications, arsenals, magazines, &c., &c.; of making peace on such conditions as they think proper; of regulating trade, determining with what countries it shall be carried on; granting indulgences; laying prohibitions on all the articles of export or import; imposing duties, granting bounties and premiums for raising, exporting or importing; and applying to their own use the product of these duties, only giving credit to the States on whom they are raised in the general account of revenues and expense; instituting admiralty courts, &c.; of coining money, establishing banks on such terms, and with such privileges, as they think proper; appropriating funds, and doing whatever else relates to the operations of finance; transacting everything with foreign nations, making alliances, offensive and defensive, treaties of commerce, &c., &c.

The Confederation should provide certain perpetual revenues, productive and easy of collection; a land tax, poll tax, or the like, which, together with the duties on trade, and the unlocated lands, would give Congress a substantial existence, and a stable foundation for their schemes of finance. What more supplies were necessary, should be occasionally demanded of the States, in the present mode of quotas.

The second step I would recommend is, that Congress should instantly appoint the following great officers of State: A Secretary for Foreign Affairs; a President of War; a President of Marine; A Financier; a President of Trade. Instead of this last, a Board of Trade may be preferable, as the regulations of trade are slow and gradual, and require prudence and experience more than other qualities for which boards are very well adapted.

Congress should choose for these offices, men of the first abilities, property, and character, in the Continent; and such as have had the best opportunities of being acquainted with the several branches. * * *

In my opinion, a plan of this kind would be of inconceivable utility to our affairs; its benefits would be very speedily felt. It would give new life and energy to the operations of government. * * *

The minds of the people are prepared for a thing of this kind. * * * It ought, by all means, to be attempted; and Congress should frame a general plan, and press the execution upon the States. * * * When the Confederation comes to be framed, it ought to provide for this, by a fundamental law, and hereafter there would be no doubt of the success. * * *

The advantages of securing the attachment of the army to Congress, and binding them to the service, by substantial ties are immense. We should then, have discipline, an army, in reality, as well as in name. Congress would then have a solid basis of authority and consequence; for, to me, it is an axiom, that in our constitution an army is essential to the American Union. * * *

Concerning the necessity of heavy pecuniary taxes, I need say nothing, as it is a point in which everybody is agreed; nor is there any danger that the product of any taxes raised in this way will overburthen the people, or exceed the wants of the public. * * *

The general idea I have of a plan is, that a respectable man should be appointed by the State in each county to collect the taxes, and form magazines; that Congress should have, in each State an officer to superintend the whole, and that the State collectors should be subordinate and responsible to them. * * *

I know the objections which may be raised to this plan, its tendency to discourage industry and the like. But necessity calls for it. We cannot proceed without it; and less evils must give place to greater. It is, besides, practiced with success in other countries, and why not in this? It may be said, the examples cited are from nations under despotic governments, and that the same would not be practicable with us. But I contend, where the public good is evidently the object more may be effected in governments like ours than in any other. It has been a constant remark that free countries have ever paid the heaviest taxes. The obedience of a free people to general laws, however hard they bear, is ever more perfect than that of slaves to the arbitrary will of a prince. * * *

How far it may be practicable to erect a bank on the joint credit of the public and of individuals can only be certainly determined by the experiment. But it is of so much importance that the experiment ought to be fully tried. * * *

Paper credit never was long supported in any country, on a national scale, where it was not founded on the joint basis of public and private credit. * * * We have seen the effects of it in America, and every successive experiment proves the futility of the attempt. Our new money is depreciating almost as fast as the old, though it has, in some States, as real funds as paper money ever had. The reason is that the moneyed men have not an immediate interest to uphold its credit. They may even, in many ways, find it their interest to undermine it. The only certain manner to obtain a permanent paper credit, is to engage the moneyed interest immediately in it, by making them contribute the whole or part of the stock, and giving them the whole or part of the profits. * * *

And why cannot we have an American bank? Are our moneyed men less enlightened to their own interest, or less enterprising in the pursuit? I believe the fault is in government, which does not exert itself to engage them in such a scheme. It is true the individuals in America are not very rich; but this would not prevent their instituting a bank; it would only prevent its being done with such ample funds as in other countries. Have they not sufficient confidence in the government, and in the issue of the cause? Let the government endeavour to inspire that confidence, by adopting the measures I have recommended, or others equivalent to them. Let it exert itself to procure a solid confederation; to establish a good plan of executive administration; to form a permanent military force; to obtain, at all events, a foreign loan. If these things were in a train of vigorous execution it would give a new spring to our affairs; government would recover its respectability, and individuals would renounce their diffidence. * * *

The first step to establishing the bank, will be to engage a number of moneyed men of influence to relish the project, and make it a business. The subscribers to that lately established, are the fittest persons that can be found; and their plan may be interwoven. * * *

A bank of this kind, even in its commencement, would answer the most valuable purposes to government, and to the proprietors; in its progress the advantages will exceed calculation. It will promote commerce by furnishing a more extensive medium, which we greatly want in our circumstances. I mean a more extensive, valuable medium. We have an enormous nominal one at this time; but it is only a name. * * *

I have only skimmed the surface of the different subjects I have introduced. * * * I am persuaded a solid confederation, a permanent army, a reasonable prospect of subsisting it, would give us treble consideration in Europe, and produce a peace this winter.

If a Convention is called, the minds of all the States and the people ought to be prepared to receive its determinations by sensible and popular writings, which should conform to the views of Congress. There are epochs in human affairs, when *novelty* even is useful. If a general opinion prevails that the old way is bad, whether true or false, and this obstructs or relaxes the operations of the public service, a change is necessary, if it be but for the sake of change. This is exactly the case now. It is an universal sentiment that our present system is a bad one, and that things do not go right on this account. The measure of a Convention would revive the hopes of the people and give a new direction to their passions, which may be improved in carrying points of substantial utility. * * *

And in future, my dear sir, two things let me recommend as fundamental rules of conduct to Congress: to attach the army to them by every motive; to maintain an air of authority (not domineering) in all their measures with the States. The manner in which a thing is done has more influence than is commonly imagined. Men are governed by opinion; this opinion is as much influenced by appearances as by realities. If a government appears to be confident of its own powers, it is the surest way to inspire the same confidence in others. If it is diffident, it may be certain there will be a still greater diffidence in others, and that its authority will not only be distrusted, controverted, but contemned.

I wish, too, Congress would always consider, that a kindness consists as much in the manner as in the thing. The best things, done hesitatingly, and with an ill grace, lose their effect, and produce disgust rather than satisfaction or gratitude. In what Congress have at any time done for the army, they have commonly been too late. They have seemed to yield to importunity, rather than to sentiments of justice, or to a regard to the accommodation of their troops. An attention to this idea is of more importance than it may be thought. I, who have seen all the workings and progress of the present discontents, am convinced that a want of this has not been among the most inconsiderable causes.

The Constitution of the United States (1787)

The efforts to strengthen the national government and to preserve the stability and order of the Union culminated in the Constitutional Convention, which met from May 28 to September 17, 1787, in Philadelphia. George Washington presided over the meetings of the initially fifty-five delegates, whom Thomas Jefferson described as "an assembly of demigods." Thirty-nine of forty-two delegates present at the conclusion of the convention signed the Constitution, which required the ratification of nine states to go into effect. Although nine states ratified the Constitution by June 21, 1788, the subsequent ratification by Virginia and New York several days later ensured the success of the political experiment.

W e the people of the United States, in order to form a more perfect union, establish justice, insure domestic tranquillity, provide for the common defense, promote the general welfare, and secure the blessings of liberty to ourselves and our posterity, do ordain and establish this Constitution for the United States of America.

ARTICLE I

SECTION 1. All legislative powers herein granted shall be vested in a Congress of the United States, which shall consist of a Senate and House of Representatives.

SECTION 2. 1. The House of Representatives shall be composed of members chosen every second year by the people of the several States, and the electors in each State shall have the qualifications requisite for electors of the most numerous branch of the State legislature.

2. No person shall be a representative who shall not have attained to the age of twenty-five years, and been seven years a citizen of the United States, and who shall not, when elected, be an inhabitant of that State in which he shall be chosen.

3. Representatives and direct taxes shall be apportioned among the several States which may be included within this Union, according to their respective numbers, which shall be determined by adding to the whole number of free persons, including those bound to service for a term of years, and excluding Indians not taxed, *three fifths of all other persons*. The actual enumeration shall be made within three years after the first meeting of the Congress of the United States, and within every subsequent term of ten years, in such manner as they shall by law direct. The number of representatives shall not exceed one for every thirty thousand, but each State shall have at least one representative; and until such enumeration shall be made, the State of New Hampshire shall be entitled to choose three, Massachusetts eight, Rhode Island and Providence Plantations one, Connecticut five, New York six, New Jersey four, Pennsylvania eight, Delaware one, Maryland six, Virginia ten, North Carolina five, South Carolina five, and Georgia three.

4. When vacancies happen in the representation from any State, the executive authority thereof shall issue writs of election to fill such vacancies.

5. The House of Representatives shall choose their speaker and other officers; and shall have the sole power of impeachment.

SECTION 3. 1. The Senate of the United States shall be composed of two senators from each State, *chosen by the legislature thereof*, for six years; and each senator shall have one vote.

2. Immediately after they shall be assembled in consequence of the first election, they shall be divided as equally as may be into three classes. The seats of the senators of the first class shall be vacated at the expiration of the second year, of the second class at the expiration of the fourth year, and of the third class at the expiration of the sixth year, so that one third may be chosen every second year; and if vacancies happen by resignation, or otherwise, during the recess of the legislature of any State, the executive thereof may make temporary appointments until the next meeting of the legislature, which shall then fill such vacancies.

3. No person shall be a senator who shall not have attained to the age of thirty years, and been nine years a citizen of the United States, and who shall not, when elected, be an inhabitant of that State for which he shall be chosen.

4. The Vice President of the United States shall be President of the Senate, but shall have no vote, unless they be equally divided.

5. The Senate shall choose their other officers, and also a president *pro tempore*, in the absence of the Vice President, or when he shall exercise the office of the President of the United States.

6. The Senate shall have the sole power to try all impeachments. When sitting for that purpose, they shall be on oath or affirmation. When the President of the United States is tried, the chief justice shall preside: and no person shall be convicted without the concurrence of two thirds of the members present.

7. Judgment in cases of impeachment shall not extend further than to removal from office, and disqualification to hold and enjoy any office of honor, trust or profit under the United States: but the party convicted shall nevertheless be liable and subject to indictment, trial, judgment and punishment, according to law.

SECTION 4. 1. The times, places and manner of holding elections for senators and representatives, shall be prescribed in each State by the legislature thereof; but the Congress may at any time by law make or alter such regulations, except as to the places of choosing senators.

2. The Congress shall assemble at least once in every year, and such meeting shall be on the first Monday in December, unless they shall by law appoint a different day.

SECTION 5. 1. Each House shall be the judge of the elections, returns and qualifications of its own members, and a majority of each shall constitute a quorum to do business; but a smaller number may adjourn from day to day, and may be authorized to compel the attendance of absent members, in such manner, and under such penalties as each House may provide.

2. Each House may determine the rules of its proceedings, punish its members for disorderly behavior, and, with the concurrence of two thirds, expel a member.

3. Each House shall keep a journal of its proceedings, and from time to time publish the same, excepting such parts as may in their judgment require secrecy; and the yeas and nays of the members of either House on any question shall, at the desire of one fifth of those present, be entered on the journal.

4. Neither House, during the session of Congress, shall, without the consent of the other, adjourn for more than three days, nor to any other place than that in which the two Houses shall be sitting.

SECTION 6. 1. The senators and representatives shall receive a compensation for their services, to be ascertained by law, and paid out of the Treasury of the United States. They shall in all cases, except treason, felony, and breach of the peace, be privileged from arrest during their attendance at the session of their respective Houses, and in going to and returning from the same; and for any speech or debate in either House, they shall not be questioned in any other place.

2. No senator or representative shall, during the time for which he was elected, be appointed to any civil office under the authority of the United States, which shall have been created, or the emoluments whereof shall have been increased during such time; and no person holding any office under the United States, shall be a member of either House during his continuance in office.

SECTION 7. 1. All bills for raising revenue shall originate in the House of Representatives; but the Senate may propose or concur with amendments as on other bills.

2. Every bill which shall have passed the House of Representatives and the Senate, shall, before it becomes a law, be presented to the President of the United States; if he approve he shall sign it, but if not he shall return it, with his objections to that House in which it shall have originated, who shall enter the objections at large on their journal, and proceed to reconsider it. If after such reconsideration two thirds of that House shall agree to pass the bill, it shall be sent, together with the objections, to the other House, by which it shall likewise be reconsidered, and if approved by two thirds of that House, it shall become a law. But in all such cases the votes of both Houses shall be determined by yeas and

nays, and the names of the persons voting for and against the bill shall be entered on the journal of each House respectively. If any bill shall not be returned by the President within ten days (Sundays excepted) after it shall have been presented to him, the same shall be a law, in like manner as if he had signed it, unless the Congress by their adjournment prevent its return, in which case it shall not be a law.

3. Every order, resolution, or vote to which the concurrence of the Senate and the House of Representatives may be necessary (except on a question of adjournment) shall be presented to the President of the United States; and before the same shall take effect, shall be approved by him, or being disapproved by him, shall be repassed by two thirds of the Senate and House of Representatives, according to the rules and limitations prescribed in the case of a bill.

SECTION 8. The Congress shall have the power

1. To lay and collect taxes, duties, imposts, and excises, to pay the debts and provide for the common defense and general welfare of the United States; but all duties, imposts, and excises shall be uniform throughout the United States;

2. To borrow money on the credit of the United States;

3. To regulate commerce with foreign nations, and among the several States, and with the Indian tribes;

4. To establish a uniform rule of naturalization, and uniform laws on the subject of bankruptcies throughout the United States;

5. To coin money, regulate the value thereof, and of foreign coin, and fix the standard of weights and measures;

6. To provide for the punishment of counterfeiting the securities and current coin of the United States;

7. To establish post offices and post roads;

8. To promote the progress of science and useful arts, by securing for limited times to authors and inventors the exclusive right to their respective writings and discoveries;

9. To constitute tribunals inferior to the Supreme Court;

10. To define and punish piracies and felonies committed on the high seas, and offenses against the law of nations;

11. To declare war, grant letters of marque and reprisal, and make rules concerning captures on land and water;

12. To raise and support armies, but no appropriation of money to that use shall be for a longer term than two years;

13. To provide and maintain a navy;

14. To make rules for the government and regulation of the land and naval forces;

15. To provide for calling forth the militia to execute the laws of the Union, suppress insurrections and repel invasions;

16. To provide for organizing, arming, and disciplining the militia, and for governing such part of them as may be employed in the service of the United States, reserving to the States respectively, the appointment of the officers, and the authority of training the militia according to the discipline prescribed by Congress;

17. To exercise exclusive legislation in all cases whatsoever, over such district (not exceeding ten miles square) as may, by cession of particular States, and the acceptance of Congress, become the seat of the government of the United States, and to exercise like authority over all places purchased by the consent of the legislature of the State in which the same shall be, for the erection of forts, magazines, arsenals, dockyards, and other needful buildings; and

18. To make all laws which shall be necessary and proper for carrying into execution the foregoing powers, and all other powers vested by this Constitution in the government of the United States, or in any department or officer thereof.

SECTION 9. 1. The migration or importation of such persons as any of the States now existing shall think proper to admit, shall not be prohibited by the Congress prior to the year one thousand eight hundred and eight, but a tax or duty may be imposed on such importation, not exceeding ten dollars for each person.

2. The privilege of the writ of *habeas corpus* shall not be suspended, unless when in cases of rebellion or invasion the public safety may require it.

3. No bill of attainder or *ex post facto* law shall be passed.

4. No capitation, or other direct, tax shall be laid, unless in proportion to the census or enumeration hereinbefore directed to be taken.

5. No tax or duty shall be laid on articles exported from any State.

6. No preference shall be given by any regulation of commerce or revenue to the ports of one State over those of another: nor shall vessels bound to, or from, one State be obliged to enter, clear or pay duties in another.

7. No money shall be drawn from the treasury, but in consequence of appropriations made by law; and a regular statement and account of the receipts and expenditures of all public money shall be published from time to time.

8. No title of nobility shall be granted by the United States: and no person holding any office or profit or trust under them, shall, without the consent of the Congress, accept of any present, emolument, office, or title, of any kind whatever, from any king, prince, or foreign State.

SECTION 10. 1. No State shall enter into any treaty, alliance, or confederation; grant letters of marque and reprisal; coin money; emit bills of credit; make anything but gold and silver coin a tender in payment of debts; pass any bill of attainder, *ex post facto* law, or law impairing the obligation of contracts, or grant any title of nobility.

2. No State shall, without the consent of the Congress, lay any imposts or duties on imports or exports, except what may be absolutely necessary for executing its inspection laws: and the net produce of all duties and imposts laid by any State on imports or exports, shall be for the use of the Treasury of the United States; and all such laws shall be subject to the revision and control of the Congress.

3. No State shall, without the consent of the Congress, lay any duty of tonnage, keep troops, or ships of war in time of peace, enter into any agreement or compact with another State, or with a foreign power, or engage in war, unless actually invaded, or in such imminent danger as will not admit of delay.

ARTICLE II

SECTION 1. 1. The executive power shall be vested in a President of the United States of America. He shall hold his office during the term of four years, and, together with the Vice President, chosen for the same term, be elected as follows:

2. Each State shall appoint, in such manner as the legislature thereof may direct, a number of electors, equal to the whole number of senators and representatives to which the State may be entitled in the Congress: but no senator or representative, or person holding an office of trust or profit under the United States, shall be appointed an elector.

The electors shall meet in their respective States, and vote by ballot for two persons, of whom one at least shall not be an inhabitant of the same State with themselves. And they shall make a list of all the persons voted for, and of the number of votes for each; which list they shall sign and certify, and transmit sealed to the seat of the government of the United States, directed to the president of the Senate. The president of the Senate shall, in the presence of the Senate and House of Representatives, open all the certificates, and the votes shall then be counted. The person having the greatest number of votes shall be the President, if such number be a majority of the whole number of electors appointed; and if there be more than one who have such majority, and have an equal number of votes, then the House of Representatives shall immediately choose by ballot one of them for President; and if no person have a majority, then from the five highest on the list the said House shall in like manner choose the President. But in choosing the President, the votes shall be taken by States, the representation from each State having one vote; a quorum for this purpose shall consist of a member or members from two thirds of the States, and a majority of all the States shall be necessary to a choice. In every case, after the choice of the President, the person having the greatest number of votes of the electors shall be the Vice President. But if there should remain two or more who have equal votes, the Senate shall choose from them by ballot the Vice President.

3. The Congress may determine the time of choosing the electors, and the day on which they shall give their votes; which day shall be the same throughout the United States.

4. No person except a natural born citizen, or a citizen of the United States, at the time of the adoption of this Constitution, shall be eligible to the office of President; neither shall any person be eligible to that office who shall not have attained to the age of thirty-five years, and been fourteen years a resident within the United States.

5. In case of the removal of the President from office, or of his death, resignation, or inability to discharge the powers and duties of the said office, the same shall devolve on the Vice President, and the Congress may by law provide for the case of removal, death, resignation, or inability, both of the President and Vice President, declaring what officer shall then act as President, and such officer shall act accordingly, until the disability be removed, or a President shall be elected.

6. The President shall, at stated times, receive for his services a compensation, which shall neither be increased nor diminished during the period for which he shall have been elected, and he shall not receive within that period any other emolument from the United States, or any of them.

7. Before he enter on the execution of his office, he shall take the following oath or affirmation:—"I do solemnly swear (or affirm) that I will faithfully execute the office of President of the United States, and will to the best of my ability, preserve, protect and defend the Constitution of the United States."

SECTION 2. 1. The President shall be commander in chief of the army and navy of the United States, and of the militia of the several States, when called into the actual service of the United States; he may require the opinion, in writing, of the principal officer in each of the executive departments, upon any subject relating to the duties of their respective offices, and he shall have power to grant reprieves and pardons for offenses against the United States, except in cases of impeachment.

2. He shall have power, by and with the advice and consent of the Senate, to make treaties, provided two thirds of the senators present concur; and he shall nominate, and by and with the advice and consent of the Senate, shall appoint ambassadors, other public ministers and consuls, judges of the Supreme Court, and all other officers of the United States, whose appointments are not herein otherwise provided for, and which shall be established by law: but the Congress may by law vest the appointment of such inferior officers, as they think proper, in the President alone, in the courts of law, or in the heads of departments.

3. The President shall have power to fill up all vacancies that may happen during the recess of the Senate, by granting commissions which shall expire at the end of their next session.

SECTION 3. He shall from time to time give to the Congress information of the state of the Union, and recommend to their consideration such measures as he shall judge necessary and expedient; he may, on extraordinary occasions, convene both Houses, or either of them, and in case of disagreement between them with respect to the time of adjournment, he may adjourn them to such time as he shall think proper; he shall receive ambassadors and other public ministers; he shall take care that the laws be faithfully executed, and shall commission all the officers of the United States.

SECTION 4. The President, Vice President, and all civil officers of the United States, shall be removed from office on impeachment for, and conviction of, treason, bribery, or other high crimes and misdemeanors.

ARTICLE III

SECTION 1. The judicial power of the United States shall be vested in one Supreme Court, and in such inferior courts as the Congress may from time to time ordain and establish. The judges, both of the Supreme and inferior courts, shall hold their offices during good behavior, and shall, at stated times, receive for their services, a compensation, which shall not be diminished during their continuance in office.

SECTION 2. 1. The judicial power shall extend to all cases, in law and equity, arising under this Constitution, the laws of the United States, and treaties made, or which shall be made, under their authority;—to all cases affecting ambassadors, other public ministers and consuls;—to all cases of admiralty and maritime jurisdiction;—to controversies to which the United States shall be a party;—to controversies between two or more States;—between a State and citizens of another State;—between citizens of different States;—between citizens of the same State claiming lands under grants of different States, and between a State, or the citizens thereof, and foreign States, citizens or subjects.

2. In all cases affecting ambassadors, other public ministers and consuls, and those in which a State shall be party, the Supreme Court shall have original jurisdiction. In all the other cases before mentioned, the Supreme Court shall have appellate jurisdiction, both as to law and to fact, with such exceptions, and under such regulations as the Congress shall make.

3. The trial of all crimes, except in cases of impeachment, shall be by jury; and such trial shall be held in the State where the said crimes shall have been committed; but when not committed within any State, the trial shall be at such place or places as the Congress may by law have directed.

SECTION 3. 1. Treason against the United States shall consist only in levying war against them, or in adhering to their enemies, giving them aid and comfort. No person shall be convicted of treason unless on the testimony of two witnesses to the same overt act, or on confession in open court.

2. The Congress shall have power to declare the punishment of treason, but no attainder of treason shall work corruption of blood, or forfeiture except during the life of the person attainted.

ARTICLE IV

SECTION 1. Full faith and credit shall be given in each State to the public acts, records, and judicial proceedings of every other State. And the Congress may by general laws prescribe the manner in which such acts, records and proceedings shall be proved, and the effect thereof.

SECTION 2. 1. The citizens of each State shall be entitled to all privileges and immunities of citizens in the several States.

2. A person charged in any State with treason, felony, or other crime, who shall flee from justice, and be found in another State, shall on demand of the executive authority of the State from which he fled, be delivered up, to be removed to the State having jurisdiction of the crime.

3. No person held to service or labor in one State under the laws thereof, escaping into another, shall, in consequence of any law or regulation therein, be discharged from such service or labor, but shall be

delivered up on claim of the party to whom such service or labor may be due.

SECTION 3. 1. New States may be admitted by the Congress into this Union; but no new State shall be formed or erected within the jurisdiction of any other State; nor any State be formed by the junction of two or more States, or parts of States, without the consent of the legislatures of the States concerned as well as of the Congress.

2. The Congress shall have power to dispose of and make all needful rules and regulations respecting the territory or other property belonging to the United States; and nothing in this Constitution shall be so construed as to prejudice any claims of the United States, or of any particular State.

SECTION 4. The United States shall guarantee to every State in this Union a republican form of government, and shall protect each of them against invasion; and on application of the legislature, or of the executive (when the legislature cannot be convened) against domestic violence.

ARTICLE V

The Congress, whenever two thirds of both Houses shall deem it necessary, shall propose amendments to this Constitution, or, on the application of the legislatures of two thirds of the several States, shall call a convention for proposing amendments, which in either case, shall be valid to all intents and purposes, as part of this Constitution, when ratified by the legislatures of three-fourths of the several States, or by conventions in three fourths thereof, as the one or the other mode of ratification may be proposed by the Congress; Provided that no amendment which may be made prior to the year one thousand eight hundred and eight shall in any manner affect the first and fourth clauses in the ninth section of the first article; and that no State, without its consent, shall be deprived of its equal suffrage in the Senate.

ARTICLE VI

1. All debts contracted and engagements entered into, before the adoption of this Constitution, shall be as valid against the United States under this Constitution, as under the Confederation.

2. This Constitution, and the laws of the United States which shall be made in pursuance thereof; and all treaties made, or which shall be made,

under the authority of the United States, shall be the supreme law of the land; and the judges in every State shall be bound thereby, anything in the Constitution or laws of any State to the contrary notwithstanding.

3. The senators and representatives before mentioned, and the members of the several State legislatures, and all executive and judicial officers, both of the United States and of the several States, shall be bound by oath or affirmation to support this Constitution; but no religious test shall ever be required as a qualification to any office or public trust under the United States.

ARTICLE VII

The ratification of the conventions of nine States shall be sufficient for the establishment of this Constitution between the States so ratifying the same.

Done in Convention by the unanimous consent of the States present the seventeenth day of September in the year of our Lord one thousand seven hundred and eighty-seven, and of the independence of the United States of America the twelfth. In witness whereof we have hereunto subscribed our names.

[Names omitted]

JOHN ADAMS

A Defence of the Constitutions of Government of the United States of America (1787)

Johns Adams was in England when the Constitutional Convention met, but he still had an important influence in debates over the Constitution with the publication of his three-volume study of the state constitutions. Adams explained that his Defence of the Constitutions of Government of the United States of America "contains my confession of political faith," the central doctrine of which was a firm belief in mixed, or balanced, government. Even though many readers interpreted Adams's work as an encomium on the state constitutions, others questioned his commitment to republicanism because he continued

to draw social distinctions between the "well born" and the "people,"
whom he believed to be the "worst" "keepers of their own liberties."

I t is become a kind of fashion among writers, to admit, as a maxim, that if you could be always sure of a wise, active, and virtuous prince, monarchy would be the best of governments. But this is so far from being admissible, that it will forever remain true, that a free government has a great advantage over a simple monarchy. The best and wisest prince, by means of a freer communication with his people, and the greater opportunities to collect the best advice from the best of his subjects, would have an immense advantage in a free state over a monarchy. A senate consisting of all that is most noble, wealthy, and able in the nation, with a right to counsel the crown at all times, is a check to ministers, and a security against abuses, such as a body of nobles who never meet, and have no such right, can never supply. Another assembly, composed of representatives chosen by the people in all parts, gives free access to the whole nation, and communicates all its wants, knowledge, projects, and wishes to government; it excites emulation among all classes, removes complaints, redresses grievances, affords opportunities of exertion to genius, though in obscurity, and gives full scope to all the faculties of man; it opens a passage for every speculation to the legislature, to administration, and to the public; it gives a universal energy to the human character, in every part of the state, such as never can be obtained in a monarchy. ＊ ＊ ＊

There can be no free government without a democratical branch in the constitution. Monarchies and aristocracies are in possession of the voice and influence of every university and academy in Europe. Democracy, simple democracy, never had a patron among men of letters. Democratical mixtures in government have lost almost all the advocates they ever had out of England and America. Men of letters must have a great deal of praise, and some of the necessaries, conveniences, and ornaments of life. Monarchies and aristocracies pay well and applaud liberally. The people have almost always expected to be served gratis, and to be paid for the honor of serving them; and their applauses and adorations are bestowed too often on artifices and tricks, on hypocrisy and superstition, on flattery, bribes, and largesses. It is no wonder then that democracies and democratical mixtures are annihilated all over Europe, except on a barren rock, a paltry fen, an inaccessible mountain, or an impenetrable forest. The people of England, to their immortal honor, are hitherto an exception; but, to the humiliation of human nature, they show very often that they are like other men. The people in America have now the best opportunity and the greatest trust in their hands, that Providence ever committed to so small a number, since the transgression of the first pair; if they betray their trust, their guilt will merit even greater punishment than other nations have suffered, and the indignation of Heaven. If there is one certain truth to be collected from the history of all ages, it is this; that the people's rights and liberties, and the democratical mixture in a constitution, can never be preserved without a strong executive, or, in other words, without separating the executive from the legislative power. If the executive power, or any considerable part of it, is left in the hands either of an aristocratical or a democratical assembly, it will corrupt the legislature as necessarily as rust corrupts iron, or as arsenic poisons the human body; and when the legislature is corrupted, the people are undone. * * *

By the authorities and examples already recited, you will be convinced that three branches of power have an unalterable foundation in nature; that they exist in every society natural and artificial; and that if all of them are not acknowledged in any constitution of government, it will be found to be imperfect, unstable, and soon enslaved; that the legislative and executive authorities are naturally distinct; and that liberty and the laws depend entirely on a separation of them in the frame of government; that the legislative power is naturally and necessarily sovereign and supreme over the executive; and, therefore, that the latter must be made an essential branch of the former, even with a negative, or it will not be able to defend itself, but will be soon invaded, undermined, attacked, or in some way or other totally ruined and annihilated by the former. * * *

Marchamont Nedham lays it down as a fundamental principle and an undeniable rule, "that the people, (that is, such as shall be successively chosen to represent the people,) are the best keepers of their own liberties, and that for many reasons. First, because they never think of usurping over other men's rights, but mind which way to preserve their own."

Our first attention should be turned to the proposition itself,—"The people are the best keepers of their own liberties."

But who are the people?

"Such as shall be successively chosen to represent them."

Here is a confusion both of words and ideas, which, though it may pass with the generality of readers in a fugitive pamphlet, or with a majority of auditors in a popular harangue, ought, for that very reason, to be as carefully avoided in politics as it is in philosophy or mathematics. If by *the people* is meant the whole body of a great nation, it should never be forgotten, that they can never act, consult, or reason together, because they cannot march five hundred miles, nor spare the time, nor find a space to meet; and, therefore, the proposition, that they are the best keepers of their own liberties, is not true. They are the worst conceivable; they are no keepers at all. They can neither act, judge, think, or will, as a body politic or corporation. If by *the people* is meant all the inhabitants of a single city, they are not in a general assembly, at all times, the best keepers of their own liberties, nor perhaps at any time, unless you separate from them the executive and judicial power, and temper their authority in legislation with the maturer counsels of the one and the few. If it is meant by *the people*, as our author explains himself, a representative assembly, "such as shall be successively chosen to represent the people," still they are not the best keepers of the people's liberties or their own, if you give them all the power, legislative, executive, and judicial. They would invade the liberties of the people, at least the majority of them would invade the liberties of the minority, sooner and oftener than an absolute monarchy, such as that of France, Spain, or Russia, or than a well-checked aristocracy, like Venice, Bern, or Holland.

An excellent writer has said, somewhat incautiously, that "a people will never oppress themselves, or invade their own rights." This compliment, if applied to human nature, or to mankind, or to any nation or people in being or in memory, is more than has been merited. If it should be admitted that a people will not unanimously agree to oppress themselves, it is as much as is ever, and more than is always, true. All kinds of experience show, that great numbers of individuals do oppress great numbers of other individuals; that parties often, if not always, oppress other parties; and majorities almost universally minorities. All that this observation can mean then, consistently with any color of fact, is, that the people will never unanimously agree to oppress themselves. But if one party agrees to oppress another, or the majority the minority, the people still oppress themselves, for one part of them oppress another.

"The people never think of usurping over other men's rights."

What can this mean? Does it mean that the people never unanimously think of usurping over other men's rights? This would be trifling; for there would, by the supposition, be no other men's rights to usurp. But if the people never, jointly nor severally, think of usurping the rights of others, what occasion can there be for any government at all? Are there no robberies, burglaries, murders, adulteries, thefts, nor cheats? Is not every crime a usurpation over other men's rights? Is not a great part, I will not say the greatest part, of men detected every day in some disposition or other, stronger or weaker, more or less, to usurp over other men's rights? There are some few, indeed, whose whole lives and conversations show that, in every thought, word, and action, they conscientiously respect the rights of others. There is a larger body still, who, in the general tenor of their thoughts and actions, discover similar principles and feelings, yet frequently err. If we should extend our candor so far as to own, that the majority of men are generally under the dominion of benevolence and good intentions, yet, it must be confessed, that a vast majority frequently transgress; and, what is more directly to the point, not only a majority, but almost all, confine their benevolence to their families, relations, personal friends, parish, village, city, county, province, and that very few, indeed, extend it impartially to the whole community. Now, grant but this truth, and the question is decided. If a majority are capable of preferring their own private interest, or that of their families, counties, and party, to that of the nation collectively, some provision must be made in the constitution, in favor of justice, to compel all to respect the common right, the public good, the universal law, in preference to all private and partial considerations.

The proposition of our author, then, should be reversed, and it should have been said, that they mind so much their own, that they never think enough of others. Suppose a nation, rich and poor, high and low, ten millions in number, all assembled together; not more than one or two millions will have lands, houses, or any personal property; if we take into the account the women and children, or even if we leave them out of the question, a great majority of every nation is wholly destitute of property, except a small quantity of clothes, and a few trifles of other movables. Would Mr. Nedham be responsible that, if all were to be decided by a vote of the majority, the eight or nine millions who have no property, would not think of usurping over the rights of the one or two millions who have? Property is surely a right of mankind as really as liberty. Perhaps, at first, prejudice, habit, shame or fear, principle or religion, would restrain the poor from attacking the rich, and the idle from usurping on the industrious; but the time would not be long before courage and enterprise would come, and pretexts be invented by degrees, to countenance the majority in dividing all the property among them, or at least, in sharing it equally with its present possessors. Debts would be abolished first; taxes laid heavy on the rich, and not at all on the others; and at last a downright equal division of every thing be demanded, and voted. What would be the consequence of this? The idle, the vicious, the intemperate, would rush into the utmost extravagance of debauchery, sell and spend all their share, and then demand a new division of those who purchased from them. The moment the idea is admitted into society, that property is not as sacred as the laws of God, and that there is not a force of law and public justice to protect it, anarchy and tyranny commence. If "THOU SHALT NOT COVET," and "THOU SHALT NOT STEAL," were not commandments of Heaven, they must be made inviolable precepts in every society, before it can be civilized or made free.

If the first part of the proposition, namely, that "the people never think of usurping over other men's rights," cannot be admitted, is the second, namely, "they mind which way to preserve their own," better founded?

There is in every nation and people under heaven a large proportion of persons who take no rational and prudent precautions to preserve what they have, much less to acquire more. Indolence is the natural character of man, to such a degree that nothing but the necessities of hunger, thirst, and other wants equally pressing, can stimulate him to action, until education is introduced in civilized societies, and the strongest motives of ambition to excel in arts, trades, and professions, are established in the minds of all men. Until this emulation is introduced, the lazy savage holds property in too little estimation to give himself trouble for the preservation or acquisition of it. In societies the most cultivated and polished, vanity, fashion, and folly prevail over every thought of ways to preserve their own. They seem rather to study what means of luxury, dissipation, and extravagance they can invent to get rid of it.

"The case is far otherwise among kings and grandees," says our author, "as all nations in the world have felt to some purpose."

That is, in other words, kings and grandees think of usurping over other men's rights, but do not mind which way to preserve their own. It is very easy to flatter the democratical portion of society, by making such distinctions between them and the monarchical and aristocratical; but flattery is as base an artifice, and as pernicious a vice, when offered to the people, as when given to the others. There is no reason to believe the one much honester or wiser than the other; they are all of the same clay; their minds and bodies are alike. The two latter have more knowledge and sagacity, derived from education, and more advantages for acquiring wisdom and virtue. As to usurping others' rights, they are all three equally guilty when unlimited in power. No wise man will trust either with an opportunity; and every judicious legislator will set all three to watch and control each other. We may appeal to every page of history we have hitherto turned over, for proofs irrefragable, that the people, when they have been unchecked, have been as unjust, tyrannical, brutal, barbarous, and cruel, as any king or senate possessed of uncontrollable power. The majority has eternally, and without one exception, usurped over the rights of the minority. * * *

Though we allow benevolence and generous affections to exist in the human breast, yet every moral theorist will admit the selfish passions in the generality of men to be the strongest. There are few who love the public better than themselves, though all may have some affection for the public. We are not, indeed, commanded to love our neighbor better than ourselves. Self-interest, private avidity, ambition, and avarice, will exist in every state of society, and under every form of government. A succession of powers and persons, by frequent elections, will not lessen these passions in any case, in a governor, senator, or representative; nor will the apprehension of an approaching election restrain them from indulgence if they have the power. The only remedy is to take away the power, by controlling the selfish avidity of the governor, by the senate and house; of the senate, by the governor and house; and of the house, by the governor and senate. Of all possible forms of government, a sovereignty in one assembly, successively chosen by the people, is perhaps the best calculated to facilitate the gratification of self-love, and the pursuit of the private interest of a few individuals; a few eminent conspicuous characters will be continued in their seats in the sovereign assembly, from one election to another, whatever changes are made in the seats around them; by superior art, address, and opulence, by more splendid birth, reputations, and connections, they will be able to intrigue with the people and their leaders, out of doors, until they worm out most of their opposers, and introduce their friends; to this end, they will bestow all offices, contracts, privileges in commerce, and other emoluments, on the latter and their connections, and throw every vexation and disappointment in the way of the former, until they establish such a system of hopes and fears throughout the state, as shall enable them to carry a majority in every fresh election of the house. The judges will be appointed by them and their party, and of consequence, will be obsequious enough to their inclinations. The whole judicial authority, as well as the executive, will be employed, perverted and prostituted to the purposes of electioneering. No justice will be attainable, nor will innocence or virtue be safe, in the judicial courts, but for the friends of the prevailing leaders; legal prosecutions will be instituted and carried on against opposers, to their vexation and ruin; and as they have the public purse at command, as well as the executive and judicial power, the public money will be expended in the same way. No favors will be attainable but by those who will court the ruling demagogues in the house, by voting for their friends and instruments; and pensions and pecuniary rewards and gratifications, as well as honors and offices of every kind, will be voted to friends and partisans. The leading minds and most influential characters among the clergy will be courted, and the views of the youth in this department will be turned upon those men, and the road to promotion and employment in the church will be obstructed against such as will not worship the general idol. Capital characters among the physicians will not be forgotten, and the means of acquiring reputation and practice in the healing art will be to get the state trumpeters on the side of youth. The bar, too, will be made so subservient, that a young gentleman will have no chance to obtain a character or clients, but by falling in with the views of the judges and their creators. Even the theatres, and actors and actresses, must become politicians, and convert the public pleasures into engines of popularity for the governing members of the house. The press, that great barrier and bulwark of the rights of mankind, when it is protected in its freedom by law, can now no longer be free; if the authors, writers, and printers, will not accept of the hire that will be offered them, they must submit to the ruin that will be denounced against them. The presses, with much secrecy and concealment, will be made the vehicles of calumny against the minority, and of panegyric and empirical applauses of the leaders of the majority, and no remedy can possibly be obtained. In one word, the whole system of affairs, and every conceivable motive of hope and fear, will be employed to promote the private interests of a few, and their obsequious majority; and there is no remedy but in arms. Accordingly we find in all the Italian republics the minority always were driven to arms in despair. * * *

* * * To expect self-denial from men, when they have a majority in their favor, and consequently power to gratify themselves, is to disbelieve all history and universal experience; it is to disbelieve Revelation and the Word of God, which informs us, the heart is deceitful above all things, and desperately wicked. There have been examples of self-denial, and will be again; but such exalted virtue never yet existed in any large body of men, and lasted long; and our author's argument requires it to be proved, not only that individuals, but that nations and majorities of nations, are capable, not only of a single act, or a few acts, of disinterested justice and exalted self-denial, but of a course of such heroic virtue for ages and generations; and not only that they are capable of this, but that it is probable they will practise it. There is no man so blind as not to see, that to talk of founding a government upon a supposition that nations and great bodies of men, left to themselves, will practise a course of self-denial, is either to babble like a new-born infant, or to deceive like an unprincipled impostor. * * *

It is pretended by some, that a sovereignty in a single assembly, annually elected, is the only one in which there is any responsibility for the exercise of power. In the mixed government we contend for, the ministers, at least of the executive power, are responsible for every instance of the exercise of it; and if they dispose of a single commission by corruption, they are responsible to a house of representatives, who may, by impeachment, make them responsible before a senate, where they may be accused, tried, condemned, and punished by independent judges. But in a single sovereign assembly, each member, at the end of his year, is only responsible to his constituents; and the majority of members who have been of one party, and carried all before them, are to be responsible only to their constituents, not to the constituents of the minority who have been overborne, injured, and plundered. And who are these constituents to whom the majority are accountable? Those very persons, to gratify whom they have prostituted the honors, rewards, wealth, and justice of the state. These, instead of punishing, will applaud; instead of discarding, will reëlect, with still greater eclat, and a more numerous majority; for the losing cause will be deserted by numbers. And this will be done in hopes of having still more injustice done, still more honors and profits divided among themselves, to the exclusion and mortification of the minority. It is then astonishing that such a simple government should be preferred to a mixed one, by any rational creature, on the score of responsibility.

There is, in short, no possible way of defending the minority, in such a government, from the tyranny of the majority, but by giving the former a negative on the latter,—the most absurd institution that ever took place among men. As the major may bear all possible relations of proportion to the minor part, it may be fifty-one against forty-nine in an assembly of a hundred, or it may be ninety-nine against one only. It becomes therefore necessary to give the negative to the minority, in all cases, though it be ever so small. Every member must possess it, or he can never be secure that himself and his constituents shall not be sacrificed by all the rest. This is the true ground and original of the *liberum veto* in Poland; but the consequence has been ruin to that noble but ill-constituted republic. One fool, or one knave, one member of the diet, which is a single sovereign assembly, bribed by an intriguing ambassador of some foreign power, has prevented measures the most essential to the defence, safety, and existence of the nation. Hence humiliations and partitions! This also is the reason on which is founded the law of the United Netherlands, that all the seven provinces must be unanimous in the assembly of the states-general; and all the cities and other voting bodies in the assemblies of the separate states. Having no sufficient checks in their uncouth constitution, nor any mediating power possessed of the whole executive, they have been driven to demand unanimity instead of a balance. And this must be done in every government of a single assembly, or the majority will instantly oppress the minority. But what kind of government would that be in the United States of America, or any one of them, that should require unanimity, or allow of the *liberum veto*? It is sufficient to ask the question, for every man will answer it alike. * * *

* * * It is agreed that the people in their assemblies, tempered by another coequal assembly and an executive coequal with either, are the best keepers of their liberties. But it is denied that in one assembly, collective or representative, they are the best keepers. It may be reasonably questioned, whether they are not the worst; because they are as sure to throw away their liberties, as a monarch or a senate untempered are to take them; with this additional evil, that they throw away their morals at the same time; whereas monarchs and senates sometimes by severity preserve them in some degree. In a simple democracy, the first citizen and the better sort of citizens are part of the people, and are equally "concerned" with any others "in the point of liberty." But is it clear that in other forms of government "the main interest and concernment, both of kings and grandees, lies either in keeping the people in utter ignorance what liberty is, or else in allowing and pleasing them only with the name and shadow of liberty instead of the substance?" It is very true that knowledge is very apt to make people uneasy

under an arbitrary and oppressive government. But a simple monarch or a sovereign senate which is not arbitrary and oppressive, though absolute, if such cases can exist, would be interested to promote the knowledge of the nation. It must, however, be admitted, that simple governments will rarely if ever favor the dispersion of knowledge among the middle and lower ranks of people. But this is equally true of simple democracy. The people themselves, if uncontrolled, will never long tolerate a freedom of inquiry, debate, or writing; their idols must not be reflected on, nor their schemes and actions scanned, upon pain of popular vengeance, which is not less terrible than that of despots or sovereign senators.

* * * The way to secure liberty is to place it in the people's hands, that is, to give them a power at all times to defend it in the legislature and in the courts of justice. But to give the people, uncontrolled, all the prerogatives and rights of supremacy, meaning the whole executive and judicial power, or even the whole undivided legislative, is not the way to preserve liberty. In such a government it is often as great a crime to oppose or decry a popular demagogue, or any of his principal friends, as in a simple monarchy to oppose a king, or in a simple aristocracy the senators. The people will not bear a contemptuous look or disrespectful word; nay, if the style of your homage, flattery, and adoration, is not as hyperbolical as the popular enthusiasm dictates, it is construed into disaffection; the popular cry of envy, jealousy, suspicious temper, vanity, arrogance, pride, ambition, impatience of a superior, is set up against a man, and the rage and fury of an ungoverned rabble, stimulated underhand by the demagogic despots, breaks out into every kind of insult, obloquy, and outrage, often ending in murders and massacres, like those of the De Witts, more horrible than any that the annals of despotism can produce.

It is indeed true, that "the interest of freedom is a virgin that every one seeks to deflour; and like a virgin it must be kept, or else (so great is the lust of mankind after dominion) there follows a rape upon the first opportunity." From this it follows, that liberty in the legislature is "more secure in the people's than in any other hands, because they are most concerned in it:" provided you keep the executive power out of their hands entirely, and give the property and liberty of the rich a security in a senate, against the encroachments of the poor in a popular assembly. Without this the rich will never enjoy any liberty, property, reputation, or life, in security. The rich have as clear a right to their liberty and property as the poor. It is essential to liberty that the rights of the rich be secured; if they are not, they will soon be robbed and become poor, and in their turn rob their robbers, and thus neither the liberty or property of any will be regarded. * * *

* * * Is it not an insult to common sense, for a people with the same breath to cry *liberty*, an *abolition of debts*, and *division of goods*? If debts

are once abolished, and goods are divided, there will be the same reason for a fresh abolition and division every month and every day. And thus the idle, vicious, and abandoned, will live in constant riot on the spoils of the industrious, virtuous, and deserving. "Powerful and crafty underminers" have nowhere such rare sport as in a simple democracy or single popular assembly. Nowhere, not in the completest despotisms, does human nature show itself so completely depraved, so nearly approaching an equal mixture of brutality and devilism, as in the last stages of such a democracy, and in the beginning of that despotism that always succeeds it.

ALEXANDER HAMILTON, JOHN JAY, AND JAMES MADISON

The Federalist Papers (1787–1788)

The ratification struggle in New York was expected to be critical to the success of the Constitution, so Hamilton enlisted the aid of the Virginian James Madison (1751–1836) and the New Yorker John Jay (1745–1829) in formulating a defense of the Constitution. No one was better qualified to assist Hamilton than Madison, who had studied the history and theory of confederations in preparation for the Constitutional Convention and contributed more than any other member to the final product. Written under the pseudonym "Publius," the first of the Federalist Papers appeared in the Independent Journal on October 27, 1787. Although they were written to influence the debate in New York, the essays were reprinted in other states during the ratification struggle as well. Jefferson considered the Federalist Papers "the best commentary on the principles of government which ever was written."

ALEXANDER HAMILTON

Federalist 1: Introduction

The first number of the Federalist stressed the importance of ratification to the preservation of the Union. In addition to laying out the plan for the rest of the papers, Hamilton clarified the central theoretical questions

*that the struggle over ratification seemed to pose: whether a "science of
politics" was possible, whether "reflection and choice" or "accident and
force" would determine the fate of government in America.*

To the People of the State of New York:
        After an unequivocal experience of the inefficiency of the subsisting federal government, you are called upon to deliberate on a new Constitution for the United States of America. The subject speaks its own importance; comprehending in its consequences nothing less, than the existence of the UNION, the safety and welfare of the parts of which it is composed, the fate of an empire in many respects the most interesting in the world. It has been frequently remarked that it seems to have been reserved to the people of this country, by their conduct and example, to decide the important question, whether societies of men are really capable or not of establishing good government from reflection and choice, or whether they are forever destined to depend for their political constitutions on accident and force. If there be any truth in the remark, the crisis at which we are arrived may with propriety be regarded as the era in which that decision is to be made; and a wrong election of the part we shall act may, in this view, deserve to be considered as the general misfortune of mankind.

The This idea will add the inducements of philanthropy to those of patriotism, to heighten the solicitude which all considerate and good men must feel for the event. Happy will it be if our choice should be directed by a judicious estimate of our true interests, unperplexed and unbiased by considerations not connected with the public good. But this is a thing more ardently to be wished than seriously to be expected. The plan offered to our deliberations affects too many particular interests, innovates upon too many local institutions, not to involve in its discussion a variety of objects foreign to its merits, and of views, passions, and prejudices little favorable to the discovery of truth.

Among the most formidable of the obstacles which the new Constitution will have to encounter may readily be distinguished the obvious interest of a certain class of men in every State to resist all changes which may hazard a diminution of the power, emolument, and consequence of the offices they hold under the State establishment; and the perverted ambition of another class of men, who will either hope to aggrandize themselves by the confusions of their country, or will flatter themselves with fairer prospects of elevation from the subdivision of the empire into several partial confederacies than from its union under one government.

It is not, however, my design to dwell upon observations of this nature. I am well aware that it would be disingenuous to resolve indiscriminately the opposition of any set of men (merely because their situations might subject them to suspicion) into interested or ambitious views. Candor will oblige us to admit that even such men may be actuated by upright intentions; and it cannot be doubted that much of the opposition which has made its appearance, or may hereafter make its appearance, will spring from sources, blameless, at least, if not respectable—the honest errors of minds led astray by preconceived jealousies and fears. So numerous indeed and so powerful are the causes which serve to give a false bias to the judgment, that we, upon many occasions, see wise and good men on the wrong as well as on the right side of questions of the first magnitude to society. This circumstance, if duly attended to, would furnish a lesson of moderation to those who are ever so much persuaded of their being in the right in any controversy. And a further reason for caution, in this respect, might be drawn from the reflection that we are not always sure that those who advocate the truth are influenced by purer principles than their antagonists. Ambition, avarice, personal animosity, party opposition, and many other motives not more laudable than these, are apt to operate as well upon those who support as those who oppose the right side of a question. Were there not even these inducements to moderation, nothing could be more ill-judged than that intolerant spirit which has, at all times, characterized political parties. For in politics, as in religion, it is equally absurd to aim at making proselytes by fire and sword. Heresies in either can rarely to be cured by persecution.

And yet, however just these sentiments will be allowed to be, we have already sufficient indications that it will happen in this as in all former cases of great national discussion. A torrent of angry and malignant passions will be let loose. To judge from the conduct of the opposite parties, we shall be led to conclude that they will mutually hope to evince the justness of their opinions, and to increase the number of their converts by the loudness of their declamations and the bitterness of their invectives. An enlightened zeal for the energy and efficiency of government will be stigmatized as the offspring of a temper fond of despotic power and hostile to the principles of liberty. And overscrupulous jealousy of danger to the rights of the people, which is more commonly the fault of the head than of the heart, will be represented as mere pretense and artifice, the stale bait for popularity at the expense of the public good. It will be forgotten, on the one hand, that jealousy is the usual concomitant of love, and that the noble enthusiasm of liberty is apt to be infected with a spirit of narrow and illiberal distrust. On the other hand, it will be equally forgotten that the vigor of government is essential to the security of liberty; that, in the contemplation of a sound and well-informed judgment, their interest can never be separated; and that a dangerous ambition more often lurks behind the specious mask of zeal for the rights of the people than under the forbidding appearance of zeal for the firmness and efficiency of government. History will teach us that the former has been found a much more certain road to the introduction of despotism than the latter, and that of those men who have overturned the liberties of republics, the greatest number have begun their career by paying an obsequious court to the people; commencing demagogues, and ending tyrants.

In the course of the preceding observations, I have had an eye, my fellow-citizens, to putting you upon your guard against all attempts, from whatever quarter, to influence your decision in a matter of the utmost moment to your welfare, by any impressions other than those which may result from the evidence of truth. You will, no doubt, at the same time have collected from the general scope of them, that they proceed from a source not unfriendly to the new Constitution. Yes, my countrymen, I own to you that, after having given it an attentive consideration, I am clearly of opinion it is your interest to adopt it. I am convinced that this is the safest course for your liberty, your dignity, and your happiness. I affect not reserves which I do not feel. I will not amuse you with an appearance of deliberation when I have decided. I frankly acknowledge to you my convictions, and I will freely lay before you the reasons on which they are founded. The consciousness of good intentions disdains ambiguity. I shall not, however, multiply professions on this head. My motives must remain in the depository of my own breast. My arguments will be open to all, and may be judged of by all. They shall at least be offered in a spirit which will not disgrace the cause of truth.

I propose, in a series of papers, to discuss the following interesting particulars:—*The utility of the UNION to your political prosperity—The insufficiency of the present Confederation to preserve that Union—The necessity of a government at least equally energetic with the one proposed, to the attainment of this object—The conformity of the proposed Constitution to the true principles of republican government—Its analogy to your own State constitution—*and lastly, *The additional security which its adoption will afford to the preservation of that species of government, to liberty, and to property.*

In the progress of this discussion I shall endeavor to give a satisfactory answer to all the objections which shall have made their appearance, that may seem to have any claim to your attention.

It may perhaps be thought superfluous to offer arguments to prove the utility of the UNION, a point, no doubt, deeply engraved on the hearts of the great body of the people in every State, and one which, it may be imagined, has no adversaries. But the fact is that we already hear it whispered in the private circles of those who oppose the new Constitution, that the thirteen States are of too great extent for any general system, and that we must of necessity resort to separate confederacies of distinct portions of the whole. This doctrine will, in all probability, be gradually propagated, till it has votaries enough to countenance an open avowal of it. For nothing can be more evident to those who are able to take an enlarged view of the subject than the alternative of an adoption of the new Constitution or a dismemberment of the Union. It will therefore be of use to begin by examining the advantages of that Union, the certain evils, and the probable dangers, to which every State will be exposed from its dissolution. This shall accordingly constitute the subject of my next address.

ALEXANDER HAMILTON

Federalist 9: The Utility of the Union as a Safeguard Against Domestic Faction and Insurrection

In this paper Hamilton laid the foundations for a theory of federalism. Political theorists had long argued that a small territory was essential to republican government, but the Constitution would establish a government that stretched across an extensive territory. Anti-Federalists feared that the Constitution would do away with the states, which were regarded as the embodiments of republican government. Relying heavily on the arguments of the respected French political writer Montesquieu (1689–1755), Hamilton argued that the new system of government posed no threat to the states because it created a confederate republic that made the states "constituent parts of the national sovereignty."

A firm Union will be of the utmost moment to the peace and liberty of the States, as a barrier against domestic faction and insurrection. It is impossible to read the history of the petty republics of Greece and Italy without feeling sensations of horror and disgust at the distractions with which they were continually agitated, and at the rapid succession of revolutions by which they were kept in a state of perpetual vibration between the extremes of tyranny and anarchy. If they exhibit occasional calms, these only serve as short-lived contrasts to the furious storms that are to succeed. If now and then intervals of felicity open to view, we behold them with a mixture of regret arising from the reflection that the pleasing scenes before us are soon to be overwhelmed by the tempestuous waves of sedition and party rage. If momentary rays of glory break forth from the gloom, while they dazzle us with a transient and fleeting brilliancy, they at the same time admonish us to lament that the vices of government should pervert the direction and tarnish the luster of those bright talents and exalted endowments for which the favored soils that produced them have been so justly celebrated.

From the disorders that disfigure the annals of those republics the advocates of despotism have drawn arguments, not only against the forms of republican government, but against the very principles of civil liberty. They have decried all free government as inconsistent with the order of society, and have indulged themselves in malicious exultation over its friends and partisans. Happily for mankind, stupendous fabrics reared on the basis of liberty, which have flourished for ages, have, in [a] few glorious instances, refuted their gloomy sophisms. And, I trust, America will be the broad and solid foundation of other edifices, not less magnificent, which will be equally permanent monuments of their errors.

But it is not to be denied that the portraits they have sketched of republican government were too just copies of the originals from which they were taken. If it had been found impracticable to have devised models of a more perfect structure, the enlightened friends to liberty would have been obliged to abandon the cause of that species of government as indefensible. The science of politics, however, like most other sciences, has received great improvement. The efficacy of various principles is now well understood, which were either not known at all, or imperfectly known to the ancients. The regular distribution of power into distinct departments; the introduction of legislative balances and checks; the institution of courts composed of judges holding their offices during good behavior; the representation of the people in the legislature by deputies of their own election: these are wholly new discoveries, or have made their principal progress towards perfection in modern times. They are means, and powerful means by which the excellences of republican government may be retained and its imperfections lessened or avoided. To this catalogue of circumstances that tend to the amelioration of popular systems of civil government, I shall venture, however novel it may appear to some, to add one more, on a principle which has been made the foundation of an objection to the new Constitution; I mean the ENLARGEMENT of the ORBIT within which such systems are to revolve, either in respect to the dimensions of a single State, or to the consolidation of several smaller States into one great Confederacy. The latter is that which immediately concerns the object under consideration. It will, however, be of use to examine the principle in its application to a single State, which shall be attended to in another place.

The utility of a Confederacy, as well to suppress faction and to guard the internal tranquillity of States, as to increase their external force and security, is in reality not a new idea. It has been practiced upon in different countries and ages, and has received the sanction of the most approved writers on the subjects of politics. The opponents of the plan proposed have, with great assiduity, cited and circulated the observations of Montesquieu on the necessity of a contracted territory for a republican government. But they seem not to have been apprised of the sentiments of that great man expressed in another part of his work, nor to have adverted to the consequences of the principle to which they subscribe with such ready acquiescence.

When Montesquieu recommends a small extent for republics, the standards he had in view were of dimensions far short of the limits of almost every one of these States. Neither Virginia, Massachusetts, Pennsylvania, New York, North Carolina, nor Georgia can by any means be compared with the models from which he reasoned and to which the terms of his description apply. If we therefore take his ideas on this point as the criterion of truth, we shall be driven to the alternative either of taking refuge at once in the arms of monarchy, or of splitting ourselves into an infinity of little jealous, clashing, tumultuous commonwealths, the wretched nurseries of unceasing discord, and the miserable objects of universal pity or contempt. Some of the writers who have come forward on the other side of the question seem to have been aware of the dilemma; and have even been bold enough to hint at the division of the larger States as a desirable thing. Such an infatuated policy, such a desperate expedient, might, by the multiplication of petty offices, answer the views of men who possess not qualifications to extend their influence beyond the narrow circles of personal intrigue, but it could never promote the greatness or happiness of the people of America.

Referring the examination of the principle itself to another place, as has been already mentioned, it will be sufficient to remark here that, in the sense of the author who has been most emphatically quoted upon the occasion, it would only dictate a reduction of the SIZE of the more considerable MEMBERS of the Union, but would not militate against their being all comprehended in one confederate government. And this is the true question, in the discussion of which we are at present interested.

So far are the suggestions of Montesquieu from standing in opposition to a general Union of the States, that he explicitly treats of a CONFEDERATE REPUBLIC as the expedient for extending the sphere of popular government, and reconciling the advantages of monarchy with those of republicanism.

"It is very probable" (says he), "that mankind would have been obliged at length to live constantly under the government of a single person, had they not contrived a kind of constitution that has all the internal advantages of a republican, together with the external force of a monarchial government. I mean a CONFEDERATE REPUBLIC.

"This form of government is a convention by which several smaller *states* agree to become members of a larger *one,* which they intend to form. It is a kind of assemblage of societies that constitute a new one, capable of increasing, by means of new associations, till they arrive to such a degree of power as to be able to provide for the security of the united body.

"A republic of this kind, able to withstand an external force, may support itself without any internal corruptions. The form of this society prevents all manner of inconveniences.

"If a single member should attempt to usurp the supreme authority, he could not be supposed to have an equal authority and credit in all the confederate states. Were he to have too great influence over one, this would alarm the rest. Were he to subdue a part, that which would still remain free might oppose him with forces independent of those which he had usurped, and overpower him before he could be settled in his usurpation.

"Should a popular insurrection happen in one of the confederate states, the others are able to quell it. Should abuses creep into one part, they are reformed by those that remain sound. The state may be destroyed on one side, and not on the other; the confederacy may be dissolved, and the confederates preserve their sovereignty.

"As this government is composed of small republics, it enjoys the internal happiness of each; and with respect to its external situation, it is possessed, by means of the association, of all the advantages of large monarchies."

I have thought it proper to quote at length these interesting passages, because they contain a luminous abridgment of the principal arguments in favor of the Union, and must effectually remove the false impressions which a misapplication of other parts of the work was calculated to make. They have, at the same time, an intimate connection with the more immediate design of this paper; which is, to illustrate the tendency of the Union to repress domestic faction and insurrection.

A distinction, more subtle than accurate, has been raised between a *Confederacy* and a *consolidation* of the States. The essential characteristic of the first is said to be the restriction of its authority to the members in their collective capacities, without reaching to the individuals of whom they are composed. It is contended that the national council ought to have no concern with any object of internal administration. An exact equality of suffrage between the members has also been insisted upon as a leading feature of a confederate government. These positions are, in the main, arbitrary; they are supported neither by principle nor precedent. It has indeed happened that governments of this kind have generally operated in the manner which the distinction, taken notice of, supposes to be inherent in their nature; but there have been in most of them extensive exceptions to the practice, which serve to prove, as far as example will go, that there is no absolute rule on the subject. And it will be clearly shown, in the course of this investigation, that, as far as the principle contended for has prevailed, it has been the cause of incurable disorder and imbecility in the government.

The definition of a *Confederate Republic* seems simply to be "an assemblage of societies," or an association of two or more states into one state. The extent, modifications, and objects of the federal authority are mere matters of discretion. So long as the separate organization of the members be not abolished; so long as it exists, by a constitutional necessity, for local purposes; though it should be in perfect subordination to the general authority of the union, it would still be, in fact and in theory, an association of states, or a confederacy. The proposed Constitution, so far from implying an abolition of the State governments, makes them constituent parts of the national sovreignty, by allowing them a direct representation in the Senate, and leaves in their possession certain exclusive and very important portions of sovereign power. This fully corresponds, in every rational import of the terms, with the idea of a federal government.

JAMES MADISON

Federalist 10: The Same Subject Continued

Madison addressed the problem of factions in the tenth paper, which many consider to be one of the most important American contributions to Western political thought. Madison turned conventional political thinking on its head by arguing that an extended sphere of government actually refines the quality of representation in government and neutralizes factions without threatening liberty. It is also in this paper that Madison characterized the United States as a republic because it was a representative system of government, as opposed to a pure democracy, which he considered vulnerable to the "mischief of factions."

Among the numerous advantages promised by a well-constructed union, none deserves to be more accurately developed than its tendency to break and control the violence of faction. The friend of popular governments never finds himself so much alarmed for their character and fate as when he contemplates their propensity to this dangerous vice. He will not fail, therefore, to set a due value on any plan which, without violating the principles to which he is attached, provides a proper cure for it. The instability, injustice, and confusion introduced into the public councils have, in truth, been the mortal diseases under which popular governments have everywhere perished; as they continue to be the favorite and fruitful topics from which the adversaries to liberty derive their most specious declamations. The valuable improvements made by the American constitutions on the popular models, both ancient and modern, cannot certainly be too much admired; but it would be an unwarrantable partiality, to contend that they have as effectually obviated the danger on this side as was wished and expected. Complaints are everywhere heard from our most considerate and virtuous citizens, equally the friends of public and private faith and of public and personal liberty, that our governments are too unstable; that the public good is disregarded in the conflicts of rival parties; and that measures are too often decided, not according to the rules of justice, and the rights of the minor party, but by the superior force of an interested and overbearing majority. However anxiously we may wish that these complaints had no foundation, the evidence of known facts will not permit us to deny that they are in some degree true. It will be found, indeed, on a candid review of our situation, that some of the distresses under which we labor have been erroneously charged on the operation of our governments; but it will be found, at the same time, that other causes will not alone account for many of our heaviest misfortunes; and, particularly, for that prevailing and increasing distrust of public engagements, and alarm for private rights, which are echoed from one end of the continent to the other. These must be chiefly, if not wholly, effects of the unsteadiness and injustice with which a factious spirit has tainted our public administrations.

By a faction, I understand a number of citizens, whether amounting to a majority or minority of the whole, who are united and actuated by some common impulse of passion, or of interest, adverse to the rights of other citizens or to the permanent and aggregate interests of the community.

There are two methods of curing the mischiefs of faction: the one, by removing its causes; the other, by controlling its effects.

There are again two methods of removing the causes of faction: the one, by destroying the liberty which is essential to its existence; the other, by giving to every citizen the same opinions, the same passions, and the same interests.

It could never be more truly said than of the first remedy, that it was worse than the disease. Liberty is to faction what air is to fire, an aliment without which it instantly expires. But it could not be less folly to abolish liberty, which is essential to political life, because it nourishes faction, than it would be to wish the annihilation of air, which is essential to animal life, because it imparts to fire its destructive agency.

The second expedient is as impracticable as the first would be unwise. As long as the reason of man continues fallible, and he is at liberty to exercise it, different opinions will be formed. As long as the connection subsists between his reason and his self-love, his opinions and his passions will have a reciprocal influence on each other; and the former will be objects to which the latter will attach themselves. The diversity in the faculties of men, from which the rights of property originate, is not less an insuperable obstacle to a uniformity of interests. The protection of these faculties is the first object of government. From the protection of different and unequal faculties of acquiring property, the possession of different degrees and kinds of property immediately results; and from the influence of these on the sentiments and views of the respective proprietors ensues a division of the society into different interests and parties.

The latent causes of faction are thus sown in the nature of man; and we see them everywhere brought into different degrees of activity, according to the different circumstances of civil society. A zeal for different opinions concerning religion, concerning government and many other points, as well of speculation as of practice; an attachment to different leaders ambitiously contending for pre-eminence and power, or to persons of other descriptions whose fortunes have been interesting to the human passions, have, in turn, divided mankind into parties, inflamed them with mutual animosity, and rendered them much more disposed to vex and oppress each other, than to co-operate for their common good. So strong is this propensity of mankind to fall into mutual animosities, that where no substantial occasion presents itself, the most frivolous and fanciful distinctions have been sufficient to kindle their unfriendly passions and excite their most violent conflicts. But the most common and durable source of factions has been the various and unequal distribution of property. Those who hold and those who are without property have ever formed distinct interests in society. Those who are creditors and those who are debtors fall under a like discrimination. A landed interest, a manufacturing interest, a mercantile interest, a moneyed interest, with many lesser interests, grow up of necessity in civilized nations, and divide them into different classes, actuated by different sentiments and views. The regulation of these various and interfering interests forms the principal task of modern legislation, and involves the spirit of party and faction in the necessary and ordinary operations of the government.

No man is allowed to be a judge in his own cause; because his interest would certainly bias his judgment and, not improbably, corrupt his integrity. With equal, nay, with greater reason, a body of men are unfit to be both judges and parties at the same time; yet what are many of the most important acts of legislation, but so many judicial determinations, not indeed concerning the rights of single persons, but concerning the rights of large bodies of citizens? and what are the different classes of legislators, but advocates and parties to the causes which they determine? Is a law proposed concerning private debts?—it is a question to which the creditors are parties on one side, and the debtors on the other. Justice ought to hold the balance between them. Yet the parties are, and must be, themselves the judges; and the most numerous party, or, in other words, the most powerful faction, must be expected to prevail. Shall domestic manufactures be encouraged, and in what degree by restrictions on foreign manufactures? are questions which would be differently decided by the landed and the manufacturing classes, and probably by neither with a sole regard to justice and the public good. The apportionment of taxes on the various descriptions of property is an act which seems to require the most exact impartiality; yet there is, perhaps, no legislative act in which greater opportunity and temptation are given to a predominant party, to trample on the rules of justice. Every shilling with which they overburden the inferior number is a shilling saved to their own pockets.

It is in vain to say that enlightened statesmen will be able to adjust these clashing interests and render them all subservient to the public good. Enlightened statesmen will not always be at the helm; nor, in many cases, can such an adjustment be made at all, without taking into view indirect and remote considerations, which will rarely prevail over the immediate interest which one party may find in disregarding the rights of another or the good of the whole.

The inference to which we are brought is that the causes of faction cannot be removed, and that relief is only to be sought in the means of controlling its effects.

If a faction consists of less than a majority, relief is supplied by the republican principle, which enables the majority to defeat its sinister views by regular vote. It may clog the administration, it may convulse the society; but it will be unable to execute and mask its violence under the forms of the Constitution. When a majority is included in a faction, the form of popular government, on the other hand, enables it to sacrifice to its ruling passion or interest both the public good and the rights of other citizens. To secure the public good, and private rights, against the danger of such a faction, and at the same time to preserve the spirit and the form of popular government, is then the great object to which our inquiries are directed. Let me add that it is the great *desideratum*, by which alone this form of government can be rescued from the opprobrium under which it has so long labored, and be recommended to the esteem and adoption of mankind.

By what means is this object attainable? Evidently by one of two only. Either the existence of the same passion or interest in a majority, at the same time, must be prevented; or the majority, having such coexistent passion or interest, must be rendered, by their number and local situation, unable to concert and carry into effect schemes of oppression. If the impulse and the opportunity be suffered to coincide, we well know that neither moral nor religious motives can be relied on as an adequate control. They are not found to be such on the injustice and violence of individuals, and lose their efficacy in proportion to the number combined together; that is, in proportion as their efficacy becomes needful.

From this view of the subject it may be concluded that a pure democracy, by which I mean a society consisting of a small number of citizens, who assemble and administer the government in person, can admit of no cure for the mischiefs of faction. A common passion or interest will, in almost every case, be felt by a majority of the whole; a communication and concert results from the form of government itself; and there is nothing to check the inducements to sacrifice the weaker party or an obnoxious individual. Hence it is that such democracies have ever been spectacles of turbulence and contention; have ever been found incompatible with personal security, or the rights of property, and have in general been as short in their lives as they have been violent in their deaths. Theoretic politicians, who have patronized this species of government, have erroneously supposed that by reducing mankind to a perfect equality in their political rights, they would at the same time be perfectly equalized and assimilated in their possessions, their opinions, and their passions.

A republic, by which I mean a government in which the scheme of representation takes place, opens a different prospect, and promises the cure for which we are seeking. Let us examine the points in which it varies from pure democracy, and we shall comprehend both the nature of the cure and the efficacy which it must derive from the union.

The two great points of difference between a democracy and a republic are: First, the delegation of the government, in the latter, to a small number of citizens elected by the rest; secondly, the greater number of citizens, and greater sphere of country, over which the latter may be extended.

The effect of the first difference is, on the one hand, to refine and enlarge the public views, by passing them through the medium of a chosen body of citizens, whose wisdom may best discern the true interest of their country, and whose patriotism and love of justice will be least likely to sacrifice it to temporary or partial considerations. Under such a regulation, it may well happen that the public voice, pronounced by the representatives of the people, will be more consonant to the public good than if pronounced by the people themselves, convened for the purpose. On the other hand, the effect may be inverted. Men of factious tempers, of local prejudices, or of sinister designs, may by intrigue, by corruption, or by other means, first obtain the suffrages, and then betray the interests of the people. The question resulting is, whether small or extensive republics are most favorable to the election of proper guardians of the public weal; and it is clearly decided in favor of the latter by two obvious considerations.

In the first place, it is to be remarked that, however small the republic may be, the representatives must be raised to a certain number, in order to guard against the cabals of a few; and that, however large it may be, they must be limited to a certain number, in order to guard against the confusion of a multitude. Hence, the number of representatives in the two cases not being in proportion to that of the constituents, and being proportionally greatest in the small republic, it follows that if the proportion of fit characters be not less in the large than in the small republic, the former will present a greater option, and consequently a greater probability of a fit choice.

In the next place, as each representative will be chosen by a greater number of citizens in the large than in the small republic, it will be more difficult for unworthy candidates to practise with success the vicious arts, by which elections are too often carried; and the suffrages of the people, being more free, will be more likely to centre in men who possess the most attractive merit and the most diffusive and established characters.

It must be confessed that in this as in most other cases, there is a mean, on both sides of which inconveniences will be found to lie. By enlarging too much the number of electors, you render the representative too little acquainted with all their local circumstances and lesser interests; as by reducing it too much, you render him unduly attached to these, and too little fit to comprehend and pursue great and national objects. The federal Constitution forms a happy combination in this respect; the great and aggregate interests being referred to the national, the local and particular to the State, legislatures.

The other point of difference is, the greater number of citizens and extent of territory which may be brought within the compass of republican than of democratic government; and it is this circumstance principally which renders factious combinations less to be dreaded in the former, than in the latter. The smaller the society, the fewer probably will be the distinct parties and interests composing it; the fewer the distinct parties and interests, the more frequently will a majority be found of the same party; and the smaller the number of individuals composing a majority, and the smaller the compass within which they are placed, the more easily will they concert and execute their plans of oppression. Extend the sphere, and you take in a greater variety of parties and interests; you make it less probable that a majority of the whole will have a common motive to invade the rights of other citizens; or if such a common motive exists, it will be more difficult for all who feel it to discover their own strength, and to act in unison with each other. Besides other impediments, it may be remarked that where there is a consciousness of unjust or dishonorable purposes, communication is always checked by distrust, in proportion to the number whose concurrence is necessary.

Hence it clearly appears that the same advantage which a republic has over a democracy, in controlling the effects of faction, is enjoyed by a large over a small republic—is enjoyed by the Union over the States composing it. Does the advantage consist in the substitution of representatives, whose enlightened views and virtuous sentiments render them superior to local prejudices, and to schemes of injustice? It will not be denied that the representation of the Union will be most likely to possess these requisite endowments. Does it consist in the greater security afforded by a greater variety of parties, against the event of any one party being able to outnumber and oppress the rest? In an equal degree does the increased variety of parties, comprised within the Union, increase this security. Does it, in fine, consist in the greater obstacles opposed to the concert and accomplishment of the secret wishes of an unjust and interested majority? Here, again, the extent of the Union gives it the most palpable advantage.

The influence of factious leaders may kindle a flame within their particular States, but will be unable to spread a general conflagration through the other States. A religious sect may degenerate into a political faction in a part of the confederacy; but the variety of sects dispersed over the entire face of it must secure the national councils against any danger from that source. A rage for paper money, for an abolition of debts, for an equal division of property, or for any other improper and wicked project will be less apt to pervade the whole body of the Union than a particular member of it; in the same proportion as such a malady is more likely to taint a particular county or district than an entire State.

In the extent and proper structure of the Union, therefore, we behold a republican remedy for the diseases most incident to republican government. And according to the degree of pleasure and pride we feel in being republicans, ought to be our zeal in cherishing the spirit and supporting the character of federalists.

ALEXANDER HAMILTON

Federalist 23: The Necessity of a Government at Least Equally Energetic with the One Proposed

One of the chief complaints against the Articles of Confederation was its inability to secure the purposes of the Union. In this essay Hamilton made a forceful case for a powerful and energetic government capable

*of dealing with unforeseeable emergencies and crises. Vigorously deny-
ing that the government should be limited in its ability to protect the
community, Hamilton stated that "the means ought to be proportioned
to the end" for government to be effective.*

The necessity of a Constitution, at least equally energetic with the
one proposed, to the preservation of the Union, is the point at the
examination of which we are now arrived.

This inquiry will naturally divide itself into three branches—the objects to be provided for by the federal government, the quantity of power
necessary to the accomplishment of those objects, the persons upon
whom that power ought to operate. Its distribution and organization will
more properly claim our attention under the succeeding head.

The principal purposes to be answered by union are these—the common defence of the members; the preservation of the public peace, as well
against internal convulsions as external attacks; the regulation of commerce with other nations and between the States; the superintendence of
our intercourse, political and commercial, with foreign countries.

The authorities essential to the common defence are these: to raise
armies; to build and equip fleets; to prescribe rules for the government of
both; to direct their operations; to provide for their support. These powers ought to exist without limitation, *because it is impossible to foresee or
define the extent and variety of national exigencies, or the correspondent
extent and variety of the means which may be necessary to satisfy them.*
The circumstances that endanger the safety of nations are infinite, and
for this reason no constitutional shackles can wisely be imposed on the
power to which the care of it is committed. This power ought to be coextensive with all the possible combinations of such circumstances; and
ought to be under the direction of the same councils which are appointed
to preside over the common defence.

This is one of those truths which, to a correct and unprejudiced mind,
carries its own evidence along with it; and may be obscured, but cannot
be made plainer by argument or reasoning. It rests upon axioms as simple
as they are universal; the *means* ought to be proportioned to the *end*; the
persons, from whose agency the attainment of any *end* is expected, ought
to posses the *means* by which it is to be attained.

Whether there ought to be a federal government intrusted with the
care of the common defence, is a question in the first instance, open for
discussion; but the moment it is decided in the affirmative, it will follow,
that the government ought to be clothed with all the powers requisite to
complete execution of its trust. And unless it can be shown that the circumstances which may affect the public safety are reducible within cer-

tain determinate limits; unless the contrary of this position can be fairly and rationally disputed, it must be admitted, as a necessary consequence that there can be no limitation of that authority which is to provide for the defence and protection of the community, in any matter essential to its efficacy—that is, in any matter essential to the *formation, direction* or *support* of the NATIONAL FORCES.

Defective as the present Confederation has been proved to be, this principle appears to have been fully recognized by the framers of it; though they have not made proper or adequate provision for its exercise. Congress have an unlimited discretion to make requisitions of men and money; to govern the army and the navy; to direct their operations. As their requisitions are made constitutionally binding upon the States, who are in fact under the most solemn obligations to furnish the supplies required of them, the intention evidently was, that the United States should command whatever resources were by them judged requisite to the "common defence and general welfare." It was presumed that a sense of their true interests, and a regard to the dictates of good faith, would be found sufficient pledges for the punctual performance of the duty of the members to the federal head.

The experiment has, however, demonstrated that this expectation was ill-founded and illusory; and the observations, made under the last head, will, I imagine, have sufficed to convince the impartial and discerning, that there is an absolute necessity for an entire change in the first principles of the system; that if we are in earnest about giving the Union energy and duration, we must abandon the vain project of legislating upon the States in their collective capacities; we must extent the laws of the federal government to the individual citizens of America; we must discard the fallacious scheme of quotas and requisitions, as equally impracticable and unjust. The result from all this is that the Union ought to be invested with full power to levy troops; to build and equip fleets; and to raise the revenues which will be required for the formation and support of an army and navy, in the customary and ordinary modes practised in other governments.

If the circumstances of our country are such as to demand a compound instead of a simple, a confederate instead of a sole, government, the essential point which will remain to be adjusted will be to discriminate the OBJECTS, as far as it can be done, which shall appertain to the different provinces or departments of power; allowing to each the most ample authority for fulfilling the objects committed to its charge. Shall the Union be constituted the guardian of the common safety? Are fleets and armies the guardian of the common safety? Are fleets and armies and revenues necessary to this purpose? The government of the Union must be empowered to pass all laws, and to make all regulations which have relation to them. The same must be the case in respect to commerce, and to every other matter to which its jurisdiction is permitted to extend. Is the administration of justice between the citizens of the same State the proper department of the local governments? These must possess all the authorities which are connected with this object, and with every other that may be allotted to their particular cognizance and direction. Not to confer in each case a degree of power commensurate to the end, would be to violate the most obvious rules of prudence and propriety, and improvidently to trust the great interests of the nation to hands which are disabled from managing them with vigor and success.

Who so likely to make suitable provisions for the public defence, as that body to which the guardianship of the public safety is confided; which, as the centre of information, will best understand the extent and urgency of the dangers that threaten; as the representative of the WHOLE, will feel itself most deeply interested in the preservation of every part; which, from the responsibility implied in the duty assigned to it, will be most sensibly impressed with the necessity of proper exertions; and which, by the extension of its authority throughout the States, can alone establish uniformity and concert in the plans and measures by which the common safety is to be secured? Is there not a manifest inconsistency in devolving upon the federal government the care of the general defense, and leaving in the State governments the *effective* powers by which it is to be provided for? Is not a want of cooperation the infallible consequence of such a system? And will not weakness, disorder, and undue distribution of the burdens and calamities of war, an unnecessary and intolerable increase of expense, be its natural and inevitable concomitants? Have we not had unequivocal experience of its effects in the course of the revolution which we have just accomplished?

Every view we may take of the subject, as candid inquirers after truth, will serve to convince us, that it is both unwise and dangerous to deny the federal government an unconfined authority, as to all those objects which are intrusted to its management. It will indeed deserve the most vigilant and careful attention of the people, to see that it be modelled in such a manner as to admit of its being safely vested with the requisite powers. If any plan which has been, or may be, offered to our consideration, should not, upon a dispassionate inspection, be found to answer this description, it ought to be rejected. A government, the constitution of which renders it unfit to be trusted with all the powers which a free people *ought to delegate to any government,* would be an unsafe and improper depositary of the NATIONAL INTERESTS. Wherever THESE can with propriety be confided, the coincident powers may safely accompany them. This is the true result of all just reasoning upon the subject. And the adversaries of the plan promulgated by the convention ought to have confined themselves to showing, that the internal structure of the proposed government was such as to render it unworthy of the confidence of the people. They ought not to have wandered into inflamatory declamations and unmeaning cavils about the extent of the powers. The POWERS are not too extensive for the OBJECTS of federal administration, or, in other words, for the management of our NATIONAL INTERESTS; nor can any satisfactory argument be framed to show that they are chargeable with such an excess. If it be true, as has been insinuated by some of the writers on the other side, that the difficulty arises from the nature of the thing, and that the extent of the country will not permit us to form a government in which such ample powers can safely be reposed, it would prove that we ought to contract our views, and resort to the expedient of separate confederacies, which will move within more practicable spheres. For the absurdity must continually stare us in the face of confiding to a government the direction of the most essential national interests, without daring to trust it to the authorities which are indispensable to their proper and efficient management. Let us not attempt to reconcile contradictions, but firmly embrace a rational alternative.

I trust, however, that the impracticability of one general system cannot be shown. I am greatly mistaken, if anything of weight has yet been advanced of this tendency; and I flatter myself that the observations which have been made in the course of these papers have served to place the reverse of that position in as clear a light as any matter still in the womb of time and experience can be susceptible of. This, at all events, must be evident, that the very difficulty itself, drawn from the extent of the country, is the strongest argument in favor of an energetic government; for any other can certainly never preserve the Union of so large an empire. If we embrace the tenets of those who oppose the adoption of the proposed Constitution, as the standard of our political creed, we cannot fail to verify the gloomy doctrines which predict the impracticability of a national system pervading entire limits of the present Confederacy.

JAMES MADISON

Federalist 39: The Conformity of the Plan to Republican Principles: An Objection in Respect to the Powers of the Convention Examined

Since Americans would never accept anything but a republican government, it was imperative that the Federalists demonstrate the consistency

of the Constitution with republican principles. In this essay Madison ex-
plained that the proposed system created a republic because all political
power would derive from the people, even though it would be exercised
indirectly through their representatives. To allay lingering fears that the
Constitution would abolish the states, Madison demonstrated that the
new government would be partly federal and partly national.

The last paper having concluded the observations which were meant to introduce a candid survey of the plan of government reported by the convention, we now proceed to the execution of that part of our undertaking.

The first question that offers itself is, whether the general form and aspect of the government be strictly republican. It is evident that no other form would be reconcilable with the genius of the people of America; with the fundamental principles of the Revolution; or with that honorable determination which animates every votary of freedom, to rest all our political experiments on the capacity of mankind for self-government. If the plan of the convention, therefore, be found to depart from the republican character, its advocates must abandon it as no longer defensible.

What, then, are the distinctive characters of the republican form? Were an answer to this question to be sought, not by recurring to principles, but in the application of the term by political writers, to the constitutions of different States, no satisfactory one would ever be found. Holland, in which no particle of the supreme authority is derived from the people, has passed almost universally under the denomination of a republic. The same title has been bestowed on Venice, where absolute power over the great body of the people is exercised, in the most absolute manner, by a small body of hereditary nobles. Poland, which is a mixture of aristocracy and of monarchy in their worst forms, has been dignified with the same appellation. The government of England, which has one republican branch only, combined with an hereditary aristocracy and monarchy, has, with equal impropriety, been frequently placed on the list of republics. These examples, which are nearly as dissimilar to each other as to a genuine republic, show the extreme inaccuracy with which the term has been used in political disquisitions.

If we resort for a criterion to the different principles on which different forms of government are established, we may define a republic to be, or at least may bestow that name on, a government which derives all its powers directly or indirectly from the great body of the people, and is administered by persons holding their offices during pleasure, for a limited period, or during good behavior. It is *essential* to such a government that it be derived from the great body of the society, not from an inconsiderable proportion, or a favored class of it; otherwise a handful of tyrannical nobles, exercising their oppressions by a delegation of their powers, might aspire to the rank of republicans, and claim for their government the honorable title of republic. It is *sufficient* for such a government that the persons administering it be appointed, either directly or indirectly, by the people, and that they hold their appointments by either of the tenures just specified; otherwise every government in the United States, as well as every other popular government that has been or can be well organized or well executed, would be degraded from the republican character. According to the constitution of every State in the Union, some or other of the officers of government are appointed indirectly only by the people. According to most of them, the chief magistrate himself is so appointed. And according to one, this mode of appointment is extended to one of the coordinate branches of the legislature. According to all the constitutions, also, the tenure of the highest offices is extended to a definite period, and in many instances, both within the legislative and executive departments, to a period of years. According to the provisions of most of the constitutions, again, as well as according to the most respectable and received opinions on the subject, the members of the judiciary department are to retain their offices by the firm tenure of good behavior.

On comparing the Constitution planned by the convention with the standard here fixed, we perceive at once that it is, in the most rigid sense, conformable to it. The House of Representatives, like that of one branch at least of all the State legislatures, is elected immediately by the great body of the people. The Senate, like the present Congress, and the Senate of Maryland, derives its appointment indirectly from the people. The President's is indirectly derived from the choice of the people, according to the example in most of the States. Even the judges with all other of the Union, will, as in the several States, be the choice, though a remote choice, of the people themselves. The duration of the appointments is equally conformable to the republican standard, and to the model of State constitutions. The House of Representatives is periodically elective, as in all the States; and for the period of two years, as in the State of South Carolina. The Senate is elective, for the period of six years; which is but one year more than the period of the Senate of Maryland, and but two more than that of the Senates of New York and Virginia. The President is to continue in office for the period of four years; as in New York and Delaware the chief magistrate is elected for three years, and in South Carolina for two years. In the other States the election is annual. In several of the States, however, no constitutional provision is made for the impeachment of the chief magistrate. And in Delaware and Virginia he is not impeachable till out of office. The President of the United States is impeachable at any time during his continuance in office. The tenure by which the judges are to hold their places, is, as it unquestionably ought to be, that of good behavior. The tenure of the ministerial offices generally, will be a subject of legal regulation, conformably to the reason of the case and the example of the State constitutions.

Could any further proof be required of the republican complexion of this system, the most decisive one might be found in its absolute prohibition of titles of nobility, both under the federal and the State governments; and in its express guaranty of the republican form to each of the latter.

"But it was not sufficient," say the adversaries of the proposed Constitution, "for the convention to adhere to the republican form. They ought, with equal care, to have preserved the *federal* form, which regards the Union as a *Confederacy* of sovereign states; instead of which, they have framed a *national* government, which regards the Union as a *consolidation* of the States." And it is asked by what authority this bold and radical innovation was undertaken? The handle which has been made of this objection requires that it should be examined with some precision.

Without inquiring into the accuracy of the distinction on which the objection is founded, it will be necessary to a just estimate of its force, first, to ascertain the real character of the government in question; secondly, to inquire how far the convention were authorized to propose such a government; and thirdly, how far the duty they owed to their country could supply any defect of regular authority.

First—In order to ascertain the real character of the government, it may be considered in relation to the foundation on which it is to be established; to the sources from which its ordinary powers are to be drawn; to the operation of those powers; to the extent of them; and to the authority by which future changes in the government are to be introduced.

On examining the first relation, it appears, on one hand, that the Constitution is to be founded on the assent and ratification of the people of America, given by deputies elected for the special purpose; but, on the other, that this assent and ratification is to be given by the people, not as individuals composing one entire nation, but as composing the distinct and independent States to which they respectively belong. It is to be the assent and ratification of the several States, derived from the supreme authority in each State,—the authority of the people themselves. The act, therefore, establishing the Constitution, will not be a *national,* but a *federal* act.

That it will be a federal and not a national act, as these terms are understood by the objectors; the act of the people, as forming so many independent States, not as forming one aggregate nation, is obvious from this single consideration, that it is to result neither from the decision of the *majority* of the people of the Union, nor from that of *majority* of the

States, It must result from the *unanimous* assent of the several States that are parties to it, differing no otherwise from their ordinary assent than in its being expressed, not by the legislative authority, but by that of the people themselves. Were the people regarded in this transaction as forming one nation, the will of the majority of the whole people of the United States would bind the minority, in the same manner as the majority in each State must bind the minority; and the will of the majority must be determined either by a comparison of the individual votes, or by considering the will of the majority, of the States as evidence of the will of a majority of the people of the United States. Neither of these rules has been adopted. Each State, in ratifying the Constitution, is considered as a sovereign body, independent of all others, and only to be bound by its own voluntary act. In this relation, then, the new Constitution will, if established, be a *federal,* and not a *national* constitution.

The next relation is, to the sources from which the ordinary powers of government are to be derived. The House of Representatives will derive its powers from the people of America; and the people will be represented in the same proportion, and on the same principle, as they are in the legislature of a particular State. So far the government is *national,* not *federal.* The Senate, on the other hand, will derive its powers from the States, as political and coequal societies; and these will be represented on the principle of equality in the Senate, as they now are in the existing Congress. So far the government is *federal,* not *national.* The executive power will be derived from a very compound source. The immediate election of the President is to be made by the States in their political characters. The votes allotted to them are in a compound ratio, which considers them partly as unequal members of the same society. The eventual election, again, is to be made by that branch of the legislature which consists of the national representatives; but in this particular act they are to be thrown into the form of individual delegations, from so many distinct and coequal bodies politic. From this aspect of the government, it appears to be of a mixed character, presenting at least as many *federal* as *national* features.

The difference between a federal and national government, as it relates to the *operation* of the *government,* is supposed to consist in this, that in the former the powers operate on the political bodies composing the Confederacy, in their political capacities; in the latter, on the individual citizens composing the nation, in their individual capacities. On trying the Constitution by this criterion, it falls under the *national,* not the *federal* character; though perhaps not so completely as has been understood. In several cases, and particularly in the trial of controversies to which States may be parties, they must be viewed and proceeded against in their collective and political capacities only. So far the national countenance of the government on this side seems to be disfigured by a few federal features. But this blemish is perhaps unavoidable in any plan; and the operation of the government on the people, in their individual capacities, in its ordinary and most essential proceedings, may, on the whole, designate it, in this relation, a *national* government.

But if the government be national with regard to the *operation* of its powers, it changes its aspect again when we contemplate it in relation to the extent of its powers. The idea of a national government involves in it, not only an authority over the individual citizens, but an indefinite supremacy over all persons and things, so far as they are objects of lawful government. Among a people consolidated into one nation, this supremacy is completely vested in the national legislature. Among communities united for particular purposes, it is vested partly in the general and partly in the municipal legislatures. In the former case, the local authorities are subordinate to the supreme; and may be controlled, directed, or abolished by it at pleasure. In the latter, the local or municipal authorities form distinct and independent portions of the supremacy, no more subject, within their respective spheres, to the general authority, than the general authority is subject to them, within its own sphere. In this relation, then, the proposed government cannot be deemed a *national* one; since its jurisdiction extends to certain enumerated objects only, and leaves to the several States a residuary and inviolable sovereignty over all other objects. It is true that in controversies relating to the boundary between the two jurisdictions, the tribunal which is ultimately to decide, is to be established under the general government. But this does not change the principle of the case. The decision is to be impartially made, according to the rules of the Constitution; and all the usual and most effectual precautions are taken to secure this impartiality. Some such tribunal is clearly essential to prevent an appeal to the sword and a dissolution of the compact; and that it ought to be established under the general rather than under the local governments, or to speak more properly, that it could be safely established under the first alone, is a position not likely to be combated.

If we try the Constitution by its last relation to the authority by which amendments are to be made, we find it neither wholly *national* nor wholly *federal*. Were it wholly national, the supreme and ultimate authority would reside in the *majority* of the people of the Union; and this authority would be competent at all times, like that of a majority of every national society, to alter or abolish its established government. Were it wholly federal, on the other hand, the concurrence of each State in the Union would be essential to every alteration that would be binding on all. The mode provided by the plan of the convention is not founded on either of these principles. In requiring more than a majority, and particularly in computing the proportion by *States*, not by *citizens*, it departs

from the *national* and advances towards the *federal* character; in rendering the concurrence of less than the whole number of States sufficient,
it loses again the *federal* and partakes of the *national* character.

The proposed Constitution, therefore, is, in strictness, neither a national
nor a federal Constitution, but a composition of both. In its foundation it is
federal, not national; in the sources from which the ordinary powers of the
government are drawn, it is partly federal and partly national; in the operation of these powers, it is national, not federal; in the extent of them, again,
it is federal, not national; and, finally, in the authoritative mode of introducing amendments, it is neither wholly federal nor wholly national.

JAMES MADISON

Federalist 48: The Same Subject [the Separation of Powers] Continued with a View to the Means of Giving Efficacy in Practice to That Maxim

*Many state constitutions contained explicit provisions guaranteeing a
separation of powers, but the proposed Constitution blended legislative,
executive, and judicial powers in a way that seemed to threaten liberty.
Madison responded to Anti-Federalist criticisms with a reminder that
the different departments of government must be able to check one another, especially the legislature, which, in a republic, tends to draw "all
power into its impetuous vortex."*

It was shown in the last paper that the political apothegm there examined does not require that the legislative, executive, and judiciary departments should be wholly unconnected with each other. I shall
undertake, in the next place, to show that unless these departments
be so far connected and blended as to give to each a constitutional control over the others, the degree of separation which the maximum
requires, as essential to a free government, can never in practice be duly
maintained.

It is agreed on all sides, that the powers properly belonging to one of
the departments ought not to be directly and completely administered
by either of the other departments. It is equally evident, that none of
them ought to possess, directly or indirectly, an overruling influence
over the others, in the administration of their respective powers. It will
not be denied, that power is of an encroaching nature, and that it ought
to be effectually restrained from passing the limits assigned to it. After
discriminating, therefore, in theory, the several classes of power, as they

may in their nature be legislative, executive, or judiciary, the next and most difficult task is to provide some practical security for each, against the invasion of the others. What this security ought to be, is the great problem to be solved.

Will it be sufficient to mark, with precision, the boundaries of these departments in the constitution of the government, and to trust to these parchment barriers against the encroaching spirit of power? This is the security which appears to have been principally relied on by the compilers of most of the American constitutions. But experience assures us, that the efficacy of the provision has been greatly overrated; and that some more adequate defence is indispensably necessary for the more feeble, against the more powerful, members of the government. The legislative department is everywhere extending the sphere of its activity, and drawing all power into its impetuous vortex.

The founders of our republics have so much merit for the wisdom which they have displayed, that no task can be less pleasing than that of pointing out the errors into which they have fallen. A respect for truth, however, obliges us to remark, that they seem never for a moment to have turned their eyes from the danger to liberty from the overgrown and all-grasping prerogative of an hereditary magistrate, supported and fortified by an hereditary branch of the legislative authority. They seem never to have recollected the danger from legislative usurpations, which, by assembling all power in the same hands, must lead to the same tyranny as is threatened by executive usurpations.

In a government where numerous and extensive prerogatives are placed in the hands of an hereditary monarch, the executive department is very justly regarded as the source of danger, and watched with all the jealousy which a zeal for liberty ought to inspire. In a democracy, where a multitude of people exercise in person the legislative functions, and are continually exposed, by their incapacity for regular deliberation and concerted measures, to the ambitious intrigues of their executive magistrates, tyranny may well be apprehended, on some favorable emergency, to start up in the same quarter. But in a representative republic, where the executive magistracy is carefully limited, both in the extent and the duration of its power; and where the legislative power is exercised by an assembly, which is inspired, by a supposed influence over the people, with an intrepid confidence in its own strength; which is sufficiently numerous to feel all the passions which actuate a multitude, yet not so numerous as to be incapable of pursuing the objects of its passions, by means which reason prescribes; it is against the enterprising ambition of this department that the people ought to indulge all their jealousy and exhaust all their precautions.

The legislative department derives a superiority in our governments from other circumstances. Its constitutional powers being at once more extensive, and less susceptible of precise limits, it can, with the greater facility, mask, under complicated and indirect measures, the encroachments which it makes on the coordinate departments. It is not unfrequently a question of real nicety in legislative bodies, whether the operation of a particular measure will, or will not, extend beyond the legislative sphere. On the other side, the executive power being restrained within a narrower compass, and being more simple in its nature, and the judiciary being described by landmarks still less uncertain, projects of usurpation by either of these departments would immediately betray and defeat themselves. Nor is this all: as the legislative department alone has access to the pockets of the people, and has in some constitutions full discretion, and in all a prevailing influence, over the pecuniary rewards of those who fill the other departments, a dependence is thus created in the latter, which gives still greater facility to encroachments of the former.

I have appealed to our own experience for the truth of what I advance on this subject. Were it necessary to verify this experience by particular proofs, they might be multiplied without end. I might find a witness in every citizen who has shared in, or been attentive to, the course of public administrations. I might collect vouchers in abundance from the records and archives of every State in the Union. But as a more concise, and at the same time equally satisfactory, evidence, I will refer to the example of two States, attested by two unexceptionable authorities.

The first example is that of Virginia, a State which, as we have seen, has expressly declared in its constitution, that the three great departments ought not to be intermixed. The authority in support of it is Mr. Jefferson, who, besides his other advantages for remarking the operation of the government, was himself the chief magistrate of it. In order to convey fully the ideas with which his experience had impressed him on this subject, it will be necessary to quote a passage of some length from his very interesting "Notes on the State of Virginia," p. 195.

All the powers of government, legislative, executive, and judiciary, result to the legislative body. The concentrating these in the same hands, is precisely the definition of despotic government. It will be no alleviation, that these powers will be exercised by a plurality of hands, and not by a single one. One hundred and seventy-three despots would surely be as oppressive as one. Let those who doubt it, turn their eyes on the republic of Venice. As little will it avail us, that they are chosen by ourselves. An *elective despotism* was not the government we fought for; but one which should not only be founded on free principles, but in which the powers of government should be so divided and balanced among several bodies of magistracy, as that no one could transcend their legal limits, without being effectively checked and restrained by the others. For this reason, that convention which passed the ordnance of government, laid its foundation on this basis, that the legislative, executive, and judiciary departments should be separate and distinct, so that no person should exercise the powers of more than one of them at the same time. *But no barrier was provided between these several powers.* The judiciary and the executive members were left dependent on the legislative for their subsistence in office, and some of them for their continuance in it. If, therefore, the legislature assumes executive and judiciary powers, no opposition is likely to be made; nor, if made, can be effectual; because in that case they may put their proceedings into the form of acts of Assembly, which will render them obligatory on the other branches. They have accordingly, *in many instances, decided rights* which should have been left to *judiciary controversy,* and *the direction of the executive, during the whole time of their session, is becoming habitual and familiar.*

The other State which I shall take for an example is Pennsylvania; and the other authority, the Council of Censors, which assembled in the years 1783 and 1784. A part of the duty of this body, as marked out by the constitution, was "to inquire whether the constitution had been preserved inviolate in every part; and whether the legislative and executive branches of government had performed their duty as guardians of the people, or assumed to themselves, or exercised, other or greater powers than they are entitled to by the constitution." In the execution of this trust, the council were necessarily led to a comparison of both the legislative and executive proceedings, with the constitutional powers of these departments; and from the facts enumerated, and to the truth of most of which both sides in the council subscribed, it appears that the constitution had been flagrantly violated, by the legislature in a variety of important instances.

A great number of laws had been passed, violating, without any apparent necessity, the rule requiring that all bills of a public nature shall be previously printed for the consideration of the people; although this is one of the precautions chiefly relied on by the constitution against improper acts of the legislature.

The constitutional trial by jury had been violated, and powers assumed which had not been delegated by the constitution.

Executive powers had been usurped.

The salaries of the judges, which the constitution expressly requires to be fixed, had been occasionally varied; and cases belonging to the judiciary department frequently drawn within legislative cognizance and determination.

Those who wish to see the several particulars falling under each of these heads, may consult the journals of the council, which are in print. Some of them, it will be found, may be imputable to peculiar circumstances connected with the war; but the greater part of them may be considered as the spontaneous shoots of an ill-constituted government.

It appears, also, that the executive department had not been innocent of frequent breaches of the constitution. There are three observations, however, which ought to be made on this head: *first,* a great proportion of the instances were either immediately produced by the necessities of the war, or recommended by Congress or the commander-in-chief; *secondly,* in most of the other instances, they conformed either to the declared or the known sentiments of the legislative department; *thirdly,* the executive department of Pennsylvania is distinguished from that of the other States by the number of members composing it. In this respect, it has as much affinity to a legislative assembly as to an executive council. And being at once exempt from the restraint of an individual responsibility for the acts of the body, and deriving confidence from mutual example and joint influence, unauthorized measures would, of course, be more freely hazarded, than where the executive department is administered by a single hand, or by a few hands.

JAMES MADISON

Federalist 51: The Same Subject [the Separation of Powers] Continued with the Same View and Concluded

Second in importance only to Federalist 10, this essay laid out the theory of checks and balances behind the Constitution's institutional arrangements as well as the reasons for bicameralism. Full of lyrical expressions and memorable phrases, Madison's essay continued the argument that some deviation from a strict separation of powers is necessary to prevent dangerous concentrations of power. The Virginian argued that "ambition must be made to counteract ambition" if government is to control itself.

To what expedient, then, shall we finally resort, for maintaining in practice the necessary partition of power among the several departments as laid down in the Constitution? The only answer that can be given is that as all these exterior provisions are found to be inadequate the defect must be supplied, by so contriving the interior structure of the government as that its several constituent parts may, by their mutual relations, be the means of keeping each other in their proper places. Without presuming to undertake a full development of this important idea I will hazard a few general observations which may perhaps place it in a clearer light, and enable us to form a more correct judgment of the principles and structure of the government planned by the convention.

In order to lay a due foundation for that separate and distinct exercise of the different powers of government, which to a certain extent is admitted on all hands to be essential to the preservation of liberty, it is evident that each department should have a will of its own; and consequently should be so constituted that the members of each should have as little agency as possible in the appointment of the members of the others. Were this principle rigorously adhered to, it would require that all the appointments for the supreme executive, legislative, and judiciary magistracies should be drawn from the same fountain of authority, the people, through channels having no communication whatever with one another. Perhaps such a plan of constructing the several departments would be less difficult in practice than it may in contemplation appear. Some difficulties, however, and some additional expense would attend the execution of it. Some deviations, therefore, from the principle must be admitted. In the constitution of the judiciary department in particular, it might be inexpedient to insist rigorously on the principle: first, because peculiar qualifications being essential in the members, the primary consideration ought to be to select that mode of choice which best secures these qualifications; second, because the permanent tenure by which the appointments are held in that department must soon destroy all sense of dependence on the authority conferring them.

It is equally evident that the members of each department should be as little dependent as possible on those of the others for the emoluments annexed to their offices. Were the executive magistrate, or the judges, not independent of the legislature in this particular, their independence in every other would be merely nominal.

But the great security against a gradual concentration of the several powers in the same department consists in giving to those who administer each department the necessary constitutional means and personal motives to resist encroachments of the others. The provision for defense must in this, as in all other cases, be made commensurate to the danger of attack. Ambition must be made to counteract ambition. The interest of the man must be connected with the constitutional rights of the place. It may be a reflection on human nature that such devices should be necessary to control the abuses of government. But what is government itself but the greatest of all reflections on human nature? If men were angels, no government would be necessary. If angels were to govern men, neither external nor internal controls on government would be necessary. In framing a government which is to be administered by men over men, the great difficulty lies in this: you must first enable the government to control the governed; and in the next place oblige it to control itself. A dependence on the people is, no doubt, the primary control on the government; but experience has taught mankind the necessity of auxiliary precautions.

This policy of supplying, by opposite and rival interests, the defect of better motives, might be traced through the whole system of human affairs, private as well as public. We see it particularly displayed in all the subordinate distributions of power, where the constant aim is to divide and arrange the several offices in such a manner as that each may be a check on the other—that the private interest of every individual may be a sentinel over the public rights. These inventions of prudence cannot be less requisite in the distribution of the supreme powers of the State.

But it is not possible to give to each department an equal power of self-defense. In republican government, the legislative authority necessarily predominates. The remedy for this inconveniency is to divide the legislature into different branches; and to render them, by different modes of election and different principles of action, as little connected with each other as the nature of their common functions and their common dependence on the society will admit. It may even be necessary to guard against dangerous encroachments by still further precautions. As the weight of the legislative authority requires that it should be thus divided, the weakness of the executive may require, on the other hand, that it should be fortified. An absolute negative on the legislature appears, at first view, to be the natural defense with which the executive magistrate should be armed. But perhaps it would be neither altogether safe nor alone sufficient. On ordinary occasions it might not be exerted with the requisite firmness, and on extraordinary occasions it might be perfidiously abused. May not this defect of an absolute negative be supplied by some qualified connection between this weaker department and the weaker branch of the stronger department, by which the latter may be led to support the constitutional rights of the former, without being too much detached from the rights of its own department?

If the principles on which these observations are founded be just, as I persuade myself they are, and they be applied as a criterion to the several State constitutions, and to the federal Constitution, it will be found that if the latter does not perfectly correspond with them, the former are infinitely less able to bear such a test.

There are, moreover, two considerations particularly applicable to the federal system of America, which place that system in a very interesting point of view.

First. In a single republic, all the power surrendered by the people is submitted to the administration of a single government; and the usurpations are guarded against by a division of the government into distinct and separate departments. In the compound republic of America, the power surrendered by the people is first divided between two distinct governments, and then the portion allotted to each subdivided among distinct and separate departments. Hence a double security arises to the rights of the people. The different governments will control each other, at the same time that each will be controlled by itself.

Second. It is of great importance in a republic not only to guard the society against the oppression of its rulers, but to guard one part of the society against the injustice of the other part. Different interests necessarily exist in different classes of citizens. If a majority be united by a common interest, the rights of the minority will be insecure. There are but two methods of providing against this evil: the one by creating a will in the community independent of the majority—that is, of the society itself; the other, by comprehending in the society so many separate descriptions of citizens as will render an unjust combination of a majority of the whole very improbable, if not impracticable. The first method prevails in all governments possessing an hereditary or self-appointed authority. This, at best, is but a precarious security; because a power independent of the society may as well espouse the unjust views of the major as the rightful interests of the minor party, and may possibly be turned against both parties. The second method will be exemplified in the federal republic of the United States. Whilst all authority in it will be derived from and dependent on the society, the society itself will be broken into so many parts, interests and classes of citizens, that the rights of individuals, or of the minority, will be in little danger from interested combinations of the majority. In a free government the security for civil rights must be the same as that for religious rights. It consists in the one case in the multiplicity of interests, and in the other in the multiplicity of sects. The degree of security in both cases will depend on the number of interests and sects; and this may be presumed to depend on the extent of country and number of people comprehended under the same government. This view of the subject must particularly recommend a proper federal system to all the sincere and considerate friends of republican government, since it shows that in exact proportion as the territory of the Union may be formed into more circumscribed Confederacies, or States, oppressive combinations of a majority will be facilitated; the best security, under the republican forms, for the rights of every class of citizen, will be diminished; and consequently the stability and independence of some member of the government, the only other security, must be proportionally increased. Justice is the end of government. It is the end of civil society. It ever has been and ever will be pursued until it be obtained, or until liberty be lost in the pursuit. In a society under the forms of which the stronger faction can readily unite and oppress the weaker, anarchy may as truly be said to reign as in a state of nature, where the weaker individual is not secured against the violence of the stronger; and as, in the latter state, even the stronger individuals are prompted, by the uncertainty of their condition, to submit to a government which may protect the weak as well as themselves; so, in the former state, will the more powerful factions or parties be gradually induced, by a like motive, to wish for a government which will protect all parties, the weaker as well as the more powerful. It can be little doubted that if the State of Rhode Island was separated from the Confederacy and left to itself, the insecurity of rights under the popular form of government within such narrow limits would be displayed by such reiterated oppressions of factious majorities that some power altogether independent of the people would soon be called for by the voice of the very factions whose misrule had proved the necessity of it. In the extended republic of the United States, and among the great variety of interests, parties, and sects which it embraces, a coalition of a majority of the whole society could seldom take place on any other principles than those of justice and the general good; whilst there being thus less danger to a minor from the will of a major party, there must be less pretext, also, to provide for the security of the former, by introducing into the government a will not dependent on the latter, or, in other words, a will independent of the society itself. It is no less certain than it is important, notwithstanding the contrary opinions which have been entertained, that the larger the society, provided it lie within a practicable sphere, the more duly capable it will be of self-government. And happily for the *republican cause,* the practicable sphere may be carried to a very great extent by a judicious modification and mixture of the *federal principle.*

ALEXANDER HAMILTON

Federalist 70: The Same Subject [the Real Ch⟨ar⟩cter of the Executive] Continued in Relation to the Unit⟨y of⟩ he Executive, with an Examination of the Project of an ⟨Execu⟩tive Council

The presidency was one of the most contr⟨oversial⟩ features of the proposed Constitution because of its reser⟨vance⟩ to monarchy, which Americans had thoroughly repudiate⟨d⟩ ⟨in th⟩e—which the Articles of plained that a single and independen⟨t⟩ paper, Hamilton ex-

Confederation lacked—was absolutely necessary for "responsible," "energetic," and effective government.

There is an idea, which is not without its advocates, that a vigorous executive is inconsistent with the genius of republican government. The enlightened well-wishers to this species of government must at least hope that the supposition is destitute of foundation; since they can never admit its truth, without at the same time admitting the condemnation of their own principles. Energy in the executive is a leading character in the definition of good government. It is essential to the protection of the community against foreign attacks; it is not less essential to the steady administration of the laws; to the protection of property against those irregular and high-handed combinations which sometimes interrupt the ordinary course of justice; to the security of liberty against the enterprises and assaults of ambition, of faction, and of anarchy. Every man the least conversant in Roman history knows how often that republic was obliged to take refuge in the absolute power of a single man, under the formidable title of dictator, as well against the intrigues of ambitious individuals who aspired to the tyranny, and the seditions of whole classes of the community whose conduct threatened the existence of all government, as against the invasions of external enemies who menaced the conquest and destruction of Rome.

There can be no need, however, to multiply arguments or examples on this head. A feeble executive implies a feeble execution of the government. A feeble execution is but another phrase for a bad execution; and a government ill executed, whatever it may be in theory, must be, in practice, a bad government.

Taking it for granted, therefore, that all men of sense will agree in the necessity of an energetic executive, it will only remain to inquire, what are the ingredients which constitute this energy? How far can they be combined with those other ingredients which constitute safety in the republican sense? And how far does this combination characterize the plan which has been reported by the convention?

The ingredients which constitute energy in the executive are unity; duration; an adequate provision for its support; and competent powers.

The ingredients which constitute safety in the republican sense are a due dependence on the people, and a due responsibility.

Those politicians and statesmen who have been the most celebrated for the soundness of their principles and for the justness of their views have declared in favor of a single executive and a numerous legislature. They have, with great propriety, considered energy as the most necessary qualification of the former, and have regarded this as most applicable to power in a single hand; while they have, with equal propriety, considered the latter as best adapted to deliberation and wisdom, and best calculated to conciliate the confidence of the people and to secure their privileges and interests.

That unity is conducive to energy will not be disputed. Decision, activity, secrecy, and dispatch will generally characterize the proceedings of one man in a much more eminent degree than the proceedings of any greater number; and in proportion as the number is increased, these qualities will be diminished.

This unity may be destroyed in two ways: either by vesting the power in two or more magistrates of equal dignity and authority, or by vesting it ostensibly in one man, subject in whole or in part to the control and co-operation of others, in the capacity of counselors to him. Of the first, the two consuls of Rome may serve as an example; of the last, we shall find examples in the constitutions of several of the States. New York and New Jersey, if I recollect right, are the only States which have intrusted the executive authority wholly to single men. Both these methods of destroying the unity of the executive have their partisans; but the votaries of an executive council are the most numerous. They are both liable, if not to equal, to similar objections, and may in most lights be examined in conjunction.

The experience of other nations will afford little instruction on this head. As far, however, as it teaches anything, it teaches us not to be enamored of plurality in the executive. We have seen that the Achaeans, on an experiment of two Praetors, were induced to abolish one. The Roman history records many instances of mischiefs to the republic from the dissensions between the consuls, and between the military tribunes, who were at times substituted for the consuls. But it gives us no specimens of any peculiar advantages derived to the state from the circumstance of the plurality of those magistrates. That the dissensions between them were not more frequent or more fatal is matter of astonishment, until we advert to the singular position in which the republic was almost continually placed, and to the prudent policy pointed out by the circumstances of the state, and pursued by the consuls, of making a division of the government between them. The patricians engaged in a perpetual struggle with the plebeians for the preservation of their ancient authorities and dignities; the consuls, who were generally chosen out of the former body, were commonly united by the personal interest they had in the defense of the privileges of their order. In addition to this motive of union, after the arms of the republic had considerably expanded the bounds of its empire, it became an established custom with the consuls to divide the administration between themselves by lot—one of them remaining at Rome to govern the city and its environs, the other taking command in the more distant provinces. This expedient must no doubt have had great influence in preventing those collisions and rivalships which might otherwise have embroiled the peace of the republic.

But quitting the dim light of historical research, and attaching ourselves purely to the dictates of reason and good sense, we shall discover much greater cause to reject than to approve the idea of plurality in the executive, under any modification whatever.

Whenever two or more persons are engaged in any common enterprise or pursuit, there is always danger of difference of opinion. If it be a public trust or office in which they are clothed with equal dignity and authority; there is peculiar danger of personal emulation and even animosity. From either, and especially from all these causes, the most bitter dissensions are apt to spring. Whenever these happen, they lessen the respectability, weaken the authority, and distract the plans and operations of those whom they divide. If they should unfortunately assail the supreme executive magistracy of a country, consisting of a plurality of persons, they might impede or frustrate the most important measures of the government in the most critical emergencies of the state. And what is still worse, they might split the community into the most violent and irreconcilable factions, adhering differently to the different individuals who composed the magistracy.

Men often oppose a thing merely because they have had no agency in planning it, or because it may have been planned by those whom they dislike. But if they have been consulted, and have happened to disapprove, opposition then becomes, in their estimation, an indispensable duty of self-love. They seem to think themselves bound in honor, and by all the motives of personal infallibility, to defeat the success of what has been resolved upon contrary to their sentiments. Men of upright, benevolent tempers have too many opportunities of remarking, with horror, to what desperate lengths this disposition is sometimes carried, and how often the great interests of society are sacrificed to the vanity, to the conceit, and to the obstinacy of individuals, who have credit enough to make their passions and their caprices interesting to mankind. Perhaps the question now before the public may, in its consequences, afford melancholy proofs of the effects of this despicable frailty, or rather detestable vice, in the human character.

Upon the principles of a free government, inconveniences from the source just mentioned must necessarily be submitted to in the formation of the legislature; but it is unnecessary, and therefore unwise, to introduce them into the constitution of the executive. It is here too that they may be most pernicious. In the legislature, promptitude of decision is oftener an evil than a benefit. The differences of opinion, and the jarring of parties in that department of the government, though they may sometimes obstruct salutary plans, yet often promote deliberation and circumspection, and serve to check excesses in the majority. When a resolution too is once taken, the opposition must be at an end. That resolution is a law, and resistance to it punishable. But no favorable circumstances palliate or atone for the disadvantages of dissension in the executive department. Here they are pure and unmixed. There is no point at which they cease to operate. They serve to embarrass and weaken the execution of the plan or measure to which they relate, from the first step to the final conclusion of it. They constantly counteract those qualities in the executive which are the most necessary ingredients in its composition—vigor and expedition, and this without any counterbalancing good. In the conduct of war, in which the energy of the executive is the bulwark of the national security, everything would be to be apprehended from its plurality.

It must be confessed that these observations apply with principal weight to the first case supposed—that is, to a plurality of magistrates of equal dignity and authority, a scheme, the advocates for which are not likely to form a numerous sect; but they apply, though not with equal yet with considerable weight, to the project of a council, whose concurrence is made constitutionally necessary to the operations of the ostensible executive. An artful cabal in that council would be able to distract and to enervate the whole system of administration. If no such cabal should exist, the mere diversity of views and opinions would alone be sufficient to tincture the exercise of the executive authority with a spirit of habitual feebleness and dilatoriness.

But one of the weightiest objections to a plurality in the executive, and which lies as much against the last as the first plan is that it tends to conceal faults and destroy responsibility. Responsibility is of two kinds—to censure and to punishment. The first is the more important of the two, especially in an elective office. Men in public trust will much oftener act in such a manner as to render them unworthy of being any longer trusted, than in such a manner as to make them obnoxious to legal punishment. But the multiplication of the executive adds to the difficulty of detection in either case. It often becomes impossible, amidst mutual accusations, to determine on whom the blame or the punishment of a pernicious measure, or series of pernicious measures, ought really to fall. It is shifted from one to another with so much dexterity, and under such plausible appearances, that the public opinion is left in suspense about the real author. The circumstances which may have led to any national miscarriage or misfortune are sometimes so complicated that where there are a number of actors who may have had different degrees and kinds of agency, though we may clearly see upon the whole that there has been mismanagement, yet it may be impracticable to pronounce to whose account the evil which may have been incurred is truly chargeable.

"I was overruled by my council." "The council were so divided in their opinions that it was impossible to obtain any better resolution on the point." These and similar pretexts are constantly at hand, whether true or false. And who is there that will either take the trouble or incur the odium of a strict scrutiny into the secret springs of the transaction? Should there be found a citizen zealous enough to undertake the unpromising task, if there happened to be a collusion between the parties concerned, how easy it is to clothe the circumstances with so much ambiguity as to render it uncertain what was the precise conduct of any of those parties.

In the single instance in which the governor of this State is coupled with a council—that is, in the appointment to offices, we have seen the mischiefs of it in the view now under consideration. Scandalous appointments to important offices have been made. Some cases, indeed, have been so flagrant that ALL PARTIES have agreed in the impropriety of the thing. When inquiry has been made, the blame has been laid by the governor on the members of the council, who, on their part, have charged it upon his nomination; while the people remain altogether at a loss to determine by whose influence their interests have been committed to hands so unqualified and so manifestly improper. In tenderness to individuals, I forbear to descend to particulars.

It is evident from these considerations that the plurality of the executive tends to deprive the people of the two greatest securities they can have for the faithful exercise of any delegated power, *first*, the restraints of public opinion, which lose their efficacy, as well on account of the division of the censure attendant on bad measures among a number as on account of the uncertainty on whom it ought to fall; and, *second*, the opportunity of discovering with facility and clearness the misconduct of the persons they trust, in order either to their removal from office or to their actual punishment in cases which admit of it.

In England, the king is a perpetual magistrate; and it is a maxim which has obtained for the sake of the public peace that he is unaccountable for his administration, and his person sacred. Nothing, therefore, can be wiser in that kingdom than to annex to the king a constitutional council, who may be responsible to the nation for the advice they give. Without this, there would be no responsibility whatever in the executive department—an idea inadmissible in a free government. But even there the king is not bound by the resolutions of his council, though they are answerable for the advice they give. He is the absolute master of his own conduct in the exercise of his office and may observe or disregard the counsel given to him at his sole discretion.

But in a republic where every magistrate ought to be personally responsible for his behavior in office, the reason which in the British Constitution dictates the propriety of a council not only ceases to apply, but turns against the institution. In the monarchy of Great Britain, it furnishes a substitute for the prohibited responsibility of the Chief Magistrate, which serves in some degree as a hostage to the national justice for his good behavior. In the American republic, it would serve to destroy, or would greatly diminish, the intended and necessary responsibility of the Chief Magistrate himself.

The idea of a council to the executive, which has so generally obtained in the State constitutions, has been derived from that maxim of republican jealousy which considers power as safer in the hands of a number of men than of a single man. If the maxim should be admitted to be applicable to the case, I should contend that the advantage on that side would not counterbalance the numerous disadvantages on the opposite side. But I do not think the rule at all applicable to the executive power. I clearly concur in opinion, in this particular, with a writer whom the celebrated junius pronounces to be "deep, solid, and ingenious," that "the executive power is more easily confined when it is one"; that it is far more safe there should be a single object for the jealousy and watchfulness of the people; and, in a word, that all multiplication of the executive is rather dangerous than friendly to liberty.

A little consideration will satisfy us that the species of security sought for in the multiplication of the executive is unattainable. Numbers must be so great as to render combination difficult, or they are rather a source of danger than of security. The united credit and influence of several individuals must be more formidable to liberty than the credit and influence of either of them separately. When power, therefore, is placed in the hands of so small a number of men as to admit of their interests and views being easily combined in a common enterprise, by an artful leader, it becomes more liable to abuse, and more dangerous when abused, than if it be lodged in the hands of one man, who, from the very circumstance of his being alone, will be more narrowly watched and more readily suspected, and who cannot unite so great a mass of influence as when he is associated with others. The decemvirs of Rome, whose name denotes their number, were more to be dreaded in their usurpation than any ONE of them would have been. No person would think of proposing an executive much more numerous than that body; from six to a dozen have been suggested for the number of the council. The extreme of these numbers is not too great for an easy combination; and from such a combination America would have more to fear than from the ambition of any single individual. A council to a magistrate, who is himself responsible for what he does, are generally nothing better than a clog upon his good intentions, are often the instruments and accomplices of his bad, and are almost always a cloak to his faults.

I forbear to dwell upon the subject of expense; though it be evident that if the council should be numerous enough to answer the principal end aimed at by the institution, the salaries of the members, who must be drawn from their homes to reside at the seat of government, would form an item in the catalogue of public expenditures too serious to be incurred for an object of equivocal utility.

I will only add that, prior to the appearance of the Constitution, I rarely met with an intelligent man from any of the States who did not admit, as the result of experience, that the UNITY of the executive of this State was one of the best of the distinguishing features of our Constitution.

ALEXANDER HAMILTON

Federalist 78: A View of the Constitution of the Judicial Department in Relation to the Tenure of Good Behavior

Even though Hamilton argued in this essay that the judiciary would be the "least dangerous" branch of government since it would "have neither FORCE nor WILL but merely judgment," he defended the doctrine of judicial review as an essential component of a limited constitution. This doctrine laid the groundwork for a powerful judiciary that would period- ically rival the other two branches in their impact on the lives of Americans.

We proceed now to an examination of the judiciary department of the proposed government.

In unfolding the defects of the existing Confederation, the utility and necessity of a federal judicature have been clearly pointed out. It is the less necessary to recapitulate the considerations there urged, as the pro- priety of the institution in the abstract is not disputed; the only questions which have been raised being relative to the manner of constituting it, and to its extent. To these points, therefore, our observations shall be confined.

The manner of constituting it seems to embrace these several objects: First, the mode of appointing the judges. Second, the tenure by which they are to hold their places. Third, the partition of the judiciary author- ity between different courts, and their relations to each other.

First. As to the mode of appointing the judges; this is the same with that of appointing the officers of the Union in general, and has been so fully discussed in the two last numbers, that nothing can be said here which would not be useless repetition.

Second. As to the tenure by which the judges are to hold their places; this chiefly concerns their duration in office; the provisions for their support; the precautions for their responsibility.

According to the plan of the convention, all judges who may be appointed by the United States are to hold their offices *during good behavior*; which is conformable to the most approved of the State constitutions, and among the rest, to that of this State. Its propriety having been drawn into question by the adversaries of that plan, is no light symptom of the rage for objection, which disorders their imaginations and judgments. The standard of good behavior for the continuance in office of the judicial magistracy, is certainly one of the most valuable of the modern improvements in the practice of government. In a monarchy it is an excellent barrier to the despotism of the prince; in a republic it is no less excellent barrier to the encroachments and oppressions of the representative body. And it is the best expedient which can be devised in any government, to secure a steady, upright, and impartial administration of the laws.

Whoever attentively considers the different departments of power must perceive, that, in a government in which they are separated from each other, the judiciary, from the nature of its functions, will always be the least dangerous to the political rights of the Constitution; because it will be least in a capacity to annoy or injure them. The Executive not only dispenses the honors, but holds the sword of the community. The legislature not only commands the purse, but prescribes the rules by which the duties and rights of every citizen are to be regulated. The judiciary, on the contrary, has no influence over either the sword or the purse; no direction either of the strength or of the wealth of the society; and can take no active resolution whatever. It may truly be said to have neither FORCE nor WILL, but merely judgment, and must ultimately depend upon the aid of the executive arm even for the efficacy of its judgments.

This simple view of the matter suggests several important consequences. It proves incontestably, that the judiciary is beyond comparison the weakest of the three departments of power; that it can never attack with success either of the other two; and that all possible care is requisite to enable it to defend itself against their attacks. It equally proves, that though individual oppression may now and then proceed from the courts of justice, the general liberty of the people can never be endangered from that quarter; I mean so long as the judiciary remains truly distinct from both the legislature and the Executive. For I agree, that "there is no liberty, if the power of judging be not separated from the legislative and executive powers." And it proves, in the last place, that as liberty can have nothing to fear from the judiciary alone, but would have every thing to fear from its union with either of the other departments; that as all the effects of such a union must ensue from a dependence of the former on the latter, notwithstanding a nominal and apparent separation; that as, from the natural feebleness of the judiciary, it is in continual jeopardy of being overpowered, awed, or influenced by its coordinate branches; and that as nothing can contribute so much to its firmness and independence as permanency in office, this quality may therefore be justly regarded as an indispensable ingredient in its constitution, and, in a great measure, as the citadel of the public justice and the public security.

The complete independence of the courts of justice is peculiarly essential in a limited Constitution. By a limited Constitution, I understand one which contains certain specified exceptions to the legislative authority; such, for instance, as that it shall pass no bills of attainder, no *ex-post-facto* laws, and the like. Limitations of this kind can be preserved in practice no other way than through the medium of courts of justice, whose duty it must be to declare all acts contrary to the manifest tenor of the Constitution void. Without this, all the reservations of particular rights or privileges would amount to nothing.

Some perplexity respecting the rights of the courts to pronounce legislative acts void, because contrary to the constitution, has arisen from an imagination that the doctrine would imply a superiority of the judiciary to the legislative power. It is urged that the authority which can declare the acts of another void, must necessarily be superior to the one whose acts may be declared void. As this doctrine is of great importance in all the American constitutions, a brief discussion of the ground on which it rests cannot be unacceptable.

There is no position which depends on clearer principles, than that every act of a delegated authority, contrary to the tenor of the commission under which it is exercised, is void. No legislative act, therefore, contrary to the Constitution, can be valid. To deny this, would be to affirm, that the deputy is greater than his principal; that the servant is above his master; that the representatives of the people are superior to the people themselves; that men acting by virtue of powers, may do not only what their powers do not authorize, but what they forbid.

If it be said that the legislative body are themselves the constitutional judges of their own powers, and that the construction they put upon them is conclusive upon the other departments, it may be answered, that this cannot be the natural presumption, where it is not to be collected from any particular provisions in the Constitution. It is not otherwise to be supposed, that the Constitution could intend to enable the representatives of the people to substitute their *will* to that of their constituents. It is far more rational to suppose, that the courts were designed to be an intermediate body between the people and the legislature, in order, among other things, to keep the latter within the limits assigned to their authority. The interpretation of the laws is the proper and peculiar province of the courts. A constitution is, in fact, and must be regarded by the judges, as a fundamental law. It therefore belongs to them to ascertain its meaning, as well as the meaning of any particular act proceeding from the legislative body. If there should happen to be an irreconcilable variance between the two, that which has the superior obligation and validity ought, of course, to be preferred; or, in other words, the Constitution ought to be preferred to the statute, the intention of the people to the intention of their agents.

Nor does this conclusion by any means suppose a superiority of the judicial to the legislative power. It only supposes that the power of the people is superior to both; and that where the will of the legislature, declared in its statues, stands in opposition to that of the people, declared in the Constitution, the judges ought to be governed by the latter rather than the former. They ought to regulate their decisions by the fundamental laws, rather than by those which are not fundamental.

This exercise of judicial discretion, in determining between two contradictory laws, is exemplified in a familiar instance. It not uncommonly happens, that there are two statutes existing at one time, clashing in whole or in part with each other, and neither of them containing any repealing clause or expression. In such a case, it is the province of the courts to liquidate and fix their meaning and operation. So far as they can, by any fair construction, be reconciled to each other, reason and law conspire to dictate that this should be done; where this is impracticable, it becomes a matter of necessity to give effect to one, in exclusion of the other. The rule which has obtained in the courts for determining their relative validity is, that the last in order of time shall be preferred to the first. But this is a mere rule of construction, not derived from any positive law, but from the nature and reason of the thing. It is a rule not enjoined upon the courts by legislative provision, but adopted by themselves, as consonant to truth and propriety, for the direction of their conduct as interpreters of the law. They thought it reasonable, that between the interfering acts of an *equal* authority, that which was the last indication of its will should have the preference.

But in regard to the interfering acts of a superior and subordinate authority, of an original and derivative power, the nature and reason of the thing indicate the converse of that rule as proper to be followed. They teach us that the prior act of a superior ought to be preferred to the subsequent act of an inferior and subordinate authority; and that accordingly, whenever a particular statute contravenes the Constitution, it will be the duty of the judicial tribunals to adhere to the latter and disregard the former.

It can be of no weight to say that the courts, on the pretence of a repugnancy, may substitute their own pleasure to the constitutional intentions of the legislature. This might as well happen in the case of two contradictory statutes; or it might as well happen in every adjudication upon any single statute. The courts must declare the sense of the law; and if they should be disposed to exercise WILL instead of JUDGMENT, the consequence would equally be the substitution of their pleasure to that of the legislative body. The observation, if it prove any thing, would prove that there ought to be no judges distinct from that body.

If, then, the courts of justice are to be considered as the bulwarks of a limited Constitution against legislative encroachments, this consideration will afford a strong argument for the permanent tenure of judicial offices, since nothing will contribute so much as this to that independent spirit in the judges which must be essential to the faithful performance of so arduous a duty.

This independence of the judges is equally requisite to guard the Constitution and the rights of individuals from the effects of those ill humors, which the arts of designing men or the influence of particular conjectures, sometimes disseminate among the people themselves, and which, though they speedily give place to better information, and more deliberate reflection, have a tendency, in the meantime, to occasion dangerous innovations in the government, and serious oppressions of the minor party in the community. Though I trust the friends of the proposed Constitution will never concur with its enemies, in questioning that fundamental principle of republican government, which admits the rights of the people to alter or abolish the established Constitution, whenever they find it inconsistent with their happiness, yet it is not to be inferred from this principle, that the representatives of the people, whenever a momentary inclination happens to lay hold of a majority of their constituents, incompatible with the provisions in the existing Constitution, would, on that account, be justifiable, in a violation of those provisions; or that the courts would be under a greater obligation to connive at infractions in this shape, than when they had proceeded wholly from the cabals of the representative body. Until the people have, by some solemn and authoritative act, annulled or changed the established form, it is binding upon themselves collectively, as well as individually; and no presumption or, even knowledge, of their sentiments, can warrant their representatives in a departure from it, prior to such an act. But it is easy to see, that it would require an uncommon portion of fortitude in the judges to do their duty as faithful guardians of the Constitution, where legislative invasions of it had been instigated by the major voice of the community.

But it is not with a view to infractions of the Constitution only, that the independence of the judges may be an essential safeguard against the effects of occasional ill humors in the society. These sometimes extend no farther than to the injury of the private rights of particular classes of citizens, by unjust and partial laws. Here also the firmness of the judicial magistracy is of vast importance in mitigating the severity and confining the operation of such laws. It not only serves to moderate the immediate mischiefs of those which may have been passed but it operates as a check upon the legislative body in passing them; who, perceiving that obstacles to the success of iniquitious intention are to be expected from the scruples of the courts, are in a manner compelled by the very motives of the injustices they mediate, to qualify their attempts. This is a circumstance calculated to have more influence upon the character of our governments, than but few may be aware of. The benefits of the integrity and moderation of the judiciary have already been felt in more States than one; and though they may have displeased those whose sinister expectations they may have disappointed, they must have commanded the esteem and applause of all the virtuous and disinterested. Considerate men, of every description, ought to prize whatever will tend to beget or fortify that temper in the courts; as no man can be sure that he may not be tomorrow the victim of a spirit of injustice, by which he may be a gainer today. And every man must now feel, that the inevitable tendency of such a spirit is to sap the foundations of public and private confidence, and to introduce in its stead universal distrust and distress.

That inflexible and uniform adherence to the rights of the Constitution, and of individuals, which we perceive to be indispensable in the courts of justice, can certainly not be expected from judges who hold their offices by a temporary commission. Periodical appointments, however regulated, or by whomsoever made, would, in some way or other, be fatal to their necessary independence. If the power of making them was committed either to the Executive or legislature, there would be danger of an improper complaisance to the branch which possessed it; if to both, there would be an unwillingness to hazard the displeasure of either; if to the people, or to persons chosen by them for the special purpose, there would be too great a disposition to consult popularity, to justify a reliance that nothing would be consulted but the Constitution and the laws.

There is yet a further and a weightier reason for the permanency of the judicial offices, which is deducible from the nature of the qualifications they require. It has been frequently remarked, with great propriety, that a voluminous code of laws is one of the inconveniences necessarily connected with the advantages of a free government. To avoid an arbitrary discretion in the courts, it is indispensable that they should be bound down by strict rules and precedents, which serve to define and point out their duty in every particular case that comes before them; and it will readily be conceived from the variety of controversies which grow out of the folly and wickedness of mankind, that the records of those precedents must unavoidably swell to a very considerable bulk, and must demand long and laborious study to acquire a competent knowledge of them. Hence, it is, that there can be but few men in the society who will have sufficient skill in the laws to qualify them for the stations of judges. And making the proper deductions for the ordinary depravity of human nature, the number must be still smaller of those who unite the requisite integrity with the requisite knowledge. These considerations apprise us, that the government can have no great option between fit character; and that a temporary duration in office, which would naturally discourage such characters from quitting a lucrative line of practice to accept a seat on the bench, would have a tendency to throw the administration of justice into hands less able, and less well qualified, to conduct it with utility and dignity. In the present circumstances of this country, and in those in which it is likely to be for a long time to come, the disadvantages on this score would be greater than they may at first sight appear; but it must be confessed, that they are far inferior to those which present themselves under the other aspects of the subject.

Upon the whole, there can be no room to doubt that the convention acted wisely in copying from the models of those constitutions which have established *good behavior* as the tenure of their judicial offices, in point of duration; and that so far from being blameable on this account, their plan would have been inexcusably defective, if it had wanted this important feature of good government. The experience of Great Britain affords an illustrious comment on the excellence of the institution.

ALEXANDER HAMILTON

Federalist 84: Concerning Several Miscellaneous Objections

In the penultimate paper of the Federalist, *Hamilton turned to the most serious objection to the Constitution: the absence of a bill of rights. He responded with several arguments, but his most important one involved the claim that a bill of rights was both unnecessary and dangerous in a popular government because it would make exceptions to powers that were never granted.*

In the course of the foregoing review of the Constitution, I have taken notice of, and endeavoured to answer, most of the objections which have appeared against it. There however remain a few which either did not fall naturally under any particular head or were forgotten in their proper places. These shall now be discussed; but as the subject has been drawn into great length, I shall so far consult brevity as to comprise all my observations on these miscellaneous points in a single paper.

The most considerable of these remaining objections is that the plan of the convention contains no bill of rights. Among other answers given to this, it has been upon different occasions remarked that the constitutions of several of the States are in a similar predicament. I add that New York is of this number. And yet the opposers of the new system in this State, who profess an unlimited admiration for its constitution, are among the most intemperate partisans of a bill of rights. To justify their zeal in this matter they allege two things: one is that, though the constitution of New York has no bill of rights prefixed to it, yet it contains, in the body of it, various provisions in favor of particular privileges and rights which, in sub-stance, amount to the same thing; the other is that the Constitution adopts, in their full extent, the common and statute laws of Great Britain, by which many other rights not expressed in it are equally secured.

To the first I answer that the Constitution proposed by the convention contains, as well as the constitution of this State, a number of such pro-visions.

Independent of those which relate to the structure of the government, we find the following: Article 1, section 3, clause 7—"Judgment in cases of impeachment shall not extend further than to removal from office and disqualification to hold and enjoy any office of honor, trust, or profit un-der the United States; but the party convicted shall, nevertheless, be liable and subject to indictment, trial, judgment, and punishment accord-ing to law." Section 9, of the same article, clause 2—"The privilege of the writ of *habeas corpus* shall not be suspended, unless when in cases of re-bellion or invasion the public safety may require it." Clause 3—"No bill of attainder or *ex post facto* law shall be passed." Clause 7—"No title of nobility shall be granted by the United States; and no person holding any office of profit or trust under them shall, without the consent of the Con-gress, accept of any present emolument, office, or title of any kind what-ever, from any king, prince, or foreign State." Article 3, section 2, clause 3—"The trial of all crimes, except in cases of impeachment, shall be by jury; and such trial shall be held in the State where the said crimes shall have been committed; but when not committed within any State, the trial shall be at such place or places as the Congress may by law have di-rected." Section 3, of the same article—"Treason against the United States shall consist only in levying war against them, or in adhering to their enemies, giving them aid and comfort. No person shall be convicted of treason, unless on the testimony of two witnesses to the same overt act, or on confession in open court." And clause 3, of the same section—"The Congress shall have the power to declare the punishment of treason but no attainder of treason shall work corruption of blood, or forfeiture except during the life of the person attainted."

It may well be a question whether these are not, upon the whole, of equal importance with any which are to be found in the constitution of this State. The establishment of the writ of *habeas corpus*, the prohibition of *ex post facto* laws, and of TITLES OF NOBILITY, *to which we have no corresponding provision in our Constitution*, are perhaps greater securities to liberty and republicanism than any it contains. The creation of crimes after the commission of the fact, or in other words, the subjecting of men to punishment for things which, when they were done, were breaches of no law, and the practice of arbitrary imprisonments, have been, in all ages, the favorite and most formidable instruments of tyranny. The observations of the judicious Blackstone, in reference to the latter, are well worthy of recital: "To bereave a man of life [says he] or by violence to confiscate his estate, without accusation or trial, would be so gross and notorious an act of despotism as must at once convey the alarm of tyranny throughout the whole nation; but confinement of the person, by secretly hurrying him to jail, where his sufferings are unknown or forgotten, is a less public, a less striking, and therefore a *more dangerous engine* of arbitrary government." And as a remedy for this fatal evil he is everywhere peculiarly emphatical in his encomiums on the *habeas corpus* act, which in one place he calls "the BULWARK of the British Constitution."

Nothing need be said to illustrate the importance of the prohibition of titles of nobility. This may truly be denominated the cornerstone of republican government; for so long as they are excluded there can never be serious danger that the government will be any other than that of the people.

To the second, that is, to the pretended establishment of the common and statute law by the Constitution, I answer that they are expressly made subject "to such alterations and provisions as the legislature shall from time to time make concerning the same." They are therefore at any moment liable to repeal by the ordinary legislative power, and of course have no constitutional sanction. The only use of the declaration was to recognize the ancient law and to remove doubts which might have been occasioned by the Revolution. This consequently can be considered as no part of a declaration of rights, which under our constitutions must be intended as limitations of the power of the government itself.

It has been several times truly remarked that bills of rights are, in their origin, stipulations between kings and their subjects, abridgments of prerogative in favour of privilege, reservations of rights not surrendered to the prince. Such was MAGNA CARTA, obtained by the barons, sword in hand, from King John. Such were the subsequent confirmations of that charter by subsequent princes. Such was the *Petition of Right* assented to by Charles the First in the beginning of his reign. Such, also, was the Declaration of Right presented by the Lords and Commons to the Prince of Orange in 1688, and afterwards thrown into the form of an act of Parliament called the Bill of Rights. It is evident, therefore, that, according to their primitive signification, they have no application to constitutions, professedly founded upon the power of the people and executed by their immediate representatives and servants. Here, in strictness, the people surrender nothing; and as they retain everything they have no need of particular reservations, "WE, THE PEOPLE of the United States, to secure the blessings of liberty to ourselves and our posterity, do *ordain* and *establish* this Constitution for the United States of America." Here is a better recognition of popular rights than volumes of those aphorisms which make the principal figure in several of our State bills of rights and which would sound much better in a treatise of ethics than in a constitution of government.

But a minute detail of particular rights is certainly far less applicable to a Constitution like that under consideration, which is merely intended to regulate the general political interests of the nation, than to a constitution which has the regulation of every species of personal and private concerns. If, therefore, the loud clamors against the plan of the convention, on this score, are well founded, no epithets of reprobation will be too strong for the constitution of this State. But the truth is that both of them contain all which, in relation to their objects, is reasonably to be desired.

I go further and affirm that bills of rights, in the sense and to the extent in which they are contended for, are not only unnecessary in the proposed Constitution but would even be dangerous. They would contain various exceptions to powers which are not granted; and, on this very account, would afford a colorable pretext to claim more than were granted. For why declare that things shall not be done which there is no power to do? Why, for instance, should it be said that the liberty of the press shall not be restrained, when no power is given by which restrictions may be imposed? I will not contend that such a provision would confer a regulating power; but it is evident that it would furnish, to men disposed to usurp, a plausible pretense for claiming that power. They might urge with a semblance of reason that the Constitution ought not to be charged with the absurdity of providing against the abuse of an authority which was not given, and that the provision against restraining the liberty of the press afforded a clear implication that a power to prescribe proper regulations concerning it was intended to be vested in the national government. This may serve as a specimen of the numerous handles which would be given to the doctrine of constructive powers, by the indulgence of an injudicious zeal for bills of rights.

On the subject of the liberty of the press, as much as has been said, I cannot forbear adding a remark or two: in the first place, I observe that there is not a syllable concerning it in the constitution of this State; in the next, I contend that whatever has been said about it in that of any other State amounts to nothing. What signifies a declaration that "the liberty of the press shall be inviolably preserved"? What is the liberty of the press? Who can give it any definition which would not leave the utmost latitude for evasion? I hold it to be impracticable; and from this I infer that its security, whatever fine declarations may be inserted in any constitution respecting it, must altogether depend on public opinion, and on the general spirit of the people and of the government. And here, after all, as is intimated upon another occasion, must we seek for the only solid basis of all our rights.

There remains but one other view of this matter to conclude the point. The truth is, after all the declamations we have heard, that the Constitution is itself, in every rational sense, and to every useful purpose, A BILL OF RIGHTS. The several bills of rights in Great Britain form its Constitution, and conversely the constitution of each State is its bill of rights. And the proposed Constitution, if adopted, will be the bill of rights of the Union. Is it one object of a bill of rights to declare and specify the political privileges of the citizens in the structure and administration of the government? This is done in the most ample and precise manner in the plan of the convention; comprehending various precautions for the public security which are not to be found in any of the State constitutions. Is another object of a bill of rights to define certain immunities and modes of proceeding, which are relative to personal and private concerns? This we have seen has also been attended to in a variety of cases in the same plan. Adverting therefore to the substantial meaning of a bill of rights, it is absurd to allege that it is not to be found in the work of the convention. It may be said that it does not go far enough though it will not be easy to make this appear; but it can with no propriety be contended that there is no such thing. It certainly must be immaterial what mode is observed as to the order of declaring the rights of the citizens if they are to be found in any part of the instrument which establishes the government. And hence it must be apparent that much of what has been said on this subject rests merely on verbal and nominal distinctions, entirely foreign from the substance of the thing.

Another objection which has been made, and which, from the frequency of its repetition, it is to be presumed is relied on, is of this nature: "It is improper [say the objectors] to confer such large powers as are proposed upon the national government, because the seat of that government must of necessity be too remote from many of the States to admit of a proper knowledge on the part of the constituent of the conduct of the representative body." This argument, if it proves anything, proves that there ought to be no general government whatever. For the powers which, it seems to be agreed on all hands, ought to be vested in the Union, cannot be safely intrusted to a body which is not under every requisite control. But there are satisfactory reasons to show that the objection is in reality not well founded. There is in most of the arguments which relate to distance a palpable illusion of the imagination. What are the sources of information by which the people in Montgomery County must regulate their judgment of the conduct of their representatives in the State legislature? Of personal observation they can have no benefit. This is confined to the citizens on the spot. They must therefore depend on the information of intelligent men, in whom they confide; and how must these men obtain their information? Evidently from the complexion of public measures, from the public prints, from the correspondences with their representatives, and with other persons who reside at the place of their deliberations. This does not apply to Montgomery County only, but to all the counties at any considerable distance from the seat of government.

It is equally evident that the same sources of information would be open to the people in relation to the conduct of their representatives in the general government and the impediments to a prompt communication which distance may be supposed to create will be overbalanced by the effects of the vigilance of the State governments. The executive and legislative bodies of each State will be so many sentinels over the persons employed in every department of the national administration; and as it will be in their power to adopt and pursue a regular and effectual system of intelligence, they can never be at a loss to know the behavior of those who represent their constituents in the national councils, and can readily communicate the same knowledge to the people. Their disposition to apprise the community of whatever may prejudice its interests from another quarter may be relied upon, if it were only from the rivalship of power. And we may conclude with the fullest assurance that the people, through that channel, will be better informed of the conduct of their national representatives than they can be by any means they now possess, of that of their State representatives.

It ought also to be remembered that the citizens who inhabit the country at and near the seat of government will, in all questions that affect the general liberty and prosperity, have the same interest with those who are at a distance, and that they will stand ready to sound the alarm when necessary, and to point out the actors in any pernicious project. The public papers will be expeditious messengers of intelligence to the most remote inhabitants of the Union.

Among the many extraordinary objections which have appeared against the proposed Constitution, the most extraordinary and the least colorable one is derived from the want of some provision respecting the debts due *to* the United States. This has been represented as a tacit relinquishment of those debts, and as a wicked contrivance to screen public defaulters. The newspapers have teemed with the most inflammatory railings on this head; and yet there is nothing clearer than that the suggestion is entirely void of foundation, and is the offspring of extreme ignorance or extreme dishonesty. In addition to the remarks I have made upon the subject in another place. I shall only observe that as it is a plain dictate of common sense, so it is also an established doctrine of political law, that *"States neither lose any of their rights, nor are discharged from any of their obligations, by a change in the form of their civil government."*

The last objection of any consequence, which I at present recollect, turns upon the article of expense. If it were even true that the adoption of the proposed government would occasion a considerable increase of expense, it would be an objection that ought to have no weight against the plan.

The great bulk of the citizens of America are with reason convinced that Union is the basis of their political happiness. Men of sense of all parties now with few exceptions agree that it cannot be preserved under the present system, nor without radical alterations; that new and extensive powers ought to be granted to the national head, and that these require a different organization of the federal government—a single body being an unsafe depositary of such ample authorities. In conceding all this, the question of expense must be given up; for it is impossible, with any degree of safety, to narrow the foundation upon which the system is to stand. The two branches of the legislature are, in the first instance, to consist of only sixty-five persons, which is the same number of which Congress, under the existing Confederation, may be composed. It is true that this number is intended to be increased; but this is to keep pace with the increase of the population and resources of the country. It is evident that a less number would, even in the first instance, have been unsafe, and that a continuance of the present number would, in a more advanced stage of population, be a very inadequate representation of the people.

Whence is the dreaded augmentation of expense to spring? One source pointed out is the multiplication of offices under the new government. Let us examine this a little.

It is evident that the principal departments of the administration under the present government are the same which will be required under the new. There are now a Secretary at War, a Secretary for Foreign Affairs, a Secretary for Domestic Affairs, a Board of Treasury, consisting of three persons, a treasurer, assistants, clerks, etc. These offices are indispensable under any system and will suffice under the new as well as under the old. As to ambassadors and other ministers and agents in foreign countries, the proposed Constitution can make no other difference than to render their characters, where they reside, more respectable, and their services more useful. As to persons to be employed in the collection of the revenues, it is unquestionably true that these will form a very considerable addition to the number of federal officers; but it will not follow that this will occasion an increase of public expense. It will be in most cases nothing more than an exchange of State officers for national officers. In the collection of all duties, for instance, the persons employed will be wholly of the latter description. The States individually will stand in no need of any for this purpose. What difference can it make in point of expense to pay officers of the customs appointed by the State or those appointed by the United States? There is no good reason to suppose that either the number or the salaries of the latter will be greater than those of the former.

Where then are we to seek for those additional articles of expense which are to swell the account to the enormous size that has been represented to us? The chief item which occurs to me respects the support of the judges of the United States. I do not add the President, because there is now a president of Congress, whose expenses may not be far, if anything, short of those which will be incurred on account of the President of the United States. The support of the judges will clearly be an extra expense, but to what extent will depend on the particular plan which may be adopted in practice in regard to this matter. But it can upon no reasonable plan amount to a sum which will be an object of material consequence.

Let us now see what there is to counterbalance any extra expense that may attend the establishment of the proposed government. The first thing that presents itself is that a great part of the business which now keeps Congress sitting through the year will be transacted by the President. Even the management of foreign negotiations will naturally devolve upon him, according to general principles concerted with the Senate, and subject to their final concurrence. Hence it is evident that a portion of the year will suffice for the session of both the Senate and the House of Representatives; we may suppose about a fourth for the latter and a third, or perhaps a half, for the former. The extra business of treaties and appointments may give this extra occupation to the Senate. From this circumstance we may infer that, until the House of Representatives shall be increased greatly beyond its present number, there will be a considerable saving of expense from the difference between the constant session of the present and the temporary session of the future Congress.

But there is another circumstance of great importance in the view of economy. The business of the United States has hitherto occupied the State legislatures, as well as Congress. The latter has made requisitions which the former have had to provide for. Hence it has happened that the sessions of the State legislatures have been protracted greatly beyond what was necessary for the execution of the mere local business of the States. More than half their time has been frequently employed in matters which related to the United States. Now the members who compose

the legislatures of the several States amount to two thousand and upwards, which number has hitherto performed what under the new system
will be done in the first instance by sixty-five persons, and probably at no
future period by above a fourth or a fifth of that number. The Congress
under the proposed government will do all the business of the United
States themselves, without the intervention of the State legislatures, who
thenceforth will have only to attend to the affairs of their particular
States, and will not have to sit in any proportion as long as they have
heretofore done. This difference in the time of the sessions of the State
legislatures will be all clear gain, and will alone form an article of saving,
which may be regarded as an equivalent for any additional objects of expense that may be occasioned by the adoption of the new system.

The result from these observations is that the sources of additional expense from the establishment of the proposed Constitution are much
fewer than may have been imagined; that they are counterbalanced by
considerable objects of saving; and that while it is questionable on which
side the scale will preponderate, it is certain that a government less expensive would be incompetent to the purpose of the Union.

THOMAS JEFFERSON

Letters on the Constitution (1787, 1789)

*Jefferson was still in France when the battle over ratification got under-
way, but he followed events in America very closely. Jefferson supported
ratification of the Constitution, but he had reservations about some of
its features and strongly recommended the inclusion of a bill of rights to
help preserve the republican character of government. He feared the
proposed government might be too "energetic" because the framers had
overreacted to Shays's Rebellion and underestimated the virtue of the
people.*

To James Madison (1787)

I like much the general idea of framing a government, which should go
on of itself, peaceably, without needing continual recurrence to the
State legislatures. I like the organization of the government into legisla-

tive, judiciary, and executive. I like the power given the legislature to levy taxes, and for that reason solely, I approve of the greater House being chosen by the people directly. For though I think a House, so chosen, will be very far inferior to the present Congress, will be very illy qualified to legislate for the Union, for foreign nations, etc.; yet this evil does not weigh against the good of preserving inviolate the fundamental principle, that the people are not to be taxed but by representatives chosen immediately by themselves. I am captivated by the compromise of the opposite claims of the great and little States, of the latter to equal, and the former to proportional influence. I am much pleased, too, with the substitution of the method of voting by persons, instead of that of voting by States: and I like the negative given to the Executive, conjointly with a third of either House; though I should have liked it better, had the judiciary been associated for that purpose, or invested separately with a similar power. There are other good things of less moment.

I will now tell you what I do not like. First, the omission of a bill of rights, providing clearly, and without the aid of sophism, for freedom of religion, freedom of the press, protection against standing armies, restriction of monopolies, the eternal and unremitting force of the *habeas corpus* laws, and trials by jury in all matters of fact triable by the laws of the land, and not by the laws of nations. To say, as Mr. [James] Wilson does, that a bill of rights was not necessary, because all is reserved in the case of the general government which is not given, while in the particular ones, all is given which is not reserved, might do for the audience to which it was addressed: but it is surely a *gratis dictum*, the reverse of which might just as well be said; and it is opposed by strong inferences from the body of the instrument, as well as from the omission of the clause of our present Confederation, which had made the reservation in express terms. It was hard to conclude, because there has been a want of uniformity among the States as to the cases triable by jury, because some have been so incautious as to dispense with this mode of trial in certain cases, therefore the more prudent States shall be reduced to the same level of calamity. It would have been much more just and wise to have concluded the other way, that as most of the States had preserved with jealousy this sacred palladium of liberty, those who had wandered, should be brought back to it: and to have established general right rather than general wrong. For I consider all the ill as established, which may be established. I have a right to nothing, which another has a right to take away; and Congress will have a right to take away trials by jury in all civil cases. Let me add, that a bill of rights is what the people are entitled to against every government on earth, general or particular, and what no just government should refuse, or rest on inference.

The second feature I dislike, and strongly dislike, is the abandon-ment, in every instance, of the principle of rotation in office, and most particularly in the case of the President. Reason and experience tell us, that the first magistrate will always be re-elected if he may be re-elected. He is then an officer for life. This once observed, it becomes of so much consequence to certain nations to have a friend or a foe at the head of our affairs, that they will interfere with money and with arms. A Galloman, or an Angloman, will be supported by the nation he be-friends. If once elected, and at a second or third election outvoted by one or two votes, he will pretend false votes, foul play, hold possession of the reins of government, be supported by the States voting for him, especially if they be the central ones, lying in a compact body them-selves, and separating their opponents; and they will be aided by one nation in Europe while the majority are aided by another. The election of a President of America, some years hence, will be much more inter-esting to certain nations of Europe, than ever the election of a King of Poland was. Reflect on all the instances in history, ancient and modern, of elective monarchies, and say, if they do not give foundation for my fears. * * * It may be said, that if elections are to be attended with these disorders, the less frequently they are repeated the better. But experi-ence says, that to free them from disorder, they must be rendered less interesting by a necessity of change. No foreign power, nor domestic party, will waste their blood and money to elect a person, who must go out at the end of a short period. The power of removing every fourth year by the vote of the people, is a power which they will not exercise, and if they were disposed to exercise it, they would not be permitted. The King of Poland is removable every day by the diet. But they never remove him. Nor would Russia, the Emperor, etc. permit them to do it. Smaller objections are, the appeals on matters of fact as well as law; and the binding all persons, legislative, executive, and judiciary, by oath, to maintain that constitution. * * *

I have thus told you freely what I like, and what I dislike, merely as a matter of curiosity; for I know it is not in my power to offer matter of in-formation to your judgment, which has been formed after hearing and weighing every thing which the wisdom of man can offer on these sub-jects. I own, I am not a friend to a very energetic government. It is always oppressive. It places the governors indeed more at their ease, at the ex-pense of the people. * * * Nor will any degree of power in the hands of government prevent insurrections. In England, where the hand of power is heavier than with us, there are seldom half a dozen years without an in-surrection. * * * And say, finally, whether peace is best preserved by giving energy to the government, or information to the people. This last is the most certain and the most legitimate engine of government. Educate and inform the whole mass of the people. Enable them to see that it is their interest to preserve peace and order, and they will preserve them. And it requires no very high degree of education to convince them of this. They are the only sure reliance for the preservation of our liberty. After all, it is my principle that the will of the majority should prevail. If they approve the proposed constitution in all its parts, I shall concur in it cheerfully, in hopes they will amend it, whenever they shall find it works wrong. This reliance cannot deceive us, as long as we remain virtuous; and I think we shall be so, as long as agriculture is our principal object, which will be the case, while there remain vacant lands in any part of America. When we get piled upon one another in large cities, as in Europe, we shall become corrupt as in Europe, and go to eating one another as they do there.

To David Humphreys (1789)

The operations which have taken place in America lately fill me with pleasure. In the first place, they realize the confidence I had, that, whenever our affairs go obviously wrong, the good sense of the people will interpose, and set them to rights. The example of changing a constitution, by assembling the wise men of the State, instead of assembling armies, will be worth as much to the world as the former examples we had given them. The constitution, too, which was the result of our deliberations, is unquestionably the wisest ever yet presented to men, and some of the accommodations of interest which it has adopted are greatly pleasing to me, who have before had occasions of seeing how difficult those interests were to accommodate. A general concurrence of opinion seems to authorize us to say it has some defects. I am one of those who think it a defect, that the important rights, not placed in security by the frame of the constitution itself, were not explicitly secured by a supplementary declaration. There are rights which it is useless to surrender to the government, and which governments have yet always been found to invade. These are the rights of thinking, and publishing our thoughts by speaking or writing; the right of free commerce; the right of personal freedom. There are instruments for administering the government so peculiarly trust-worthy, that we should never leave the legislature at liberty to change them. The new constitution has secured these in the executive and legislative departments; but not in the judiciary. It should have established trials by the people themselves, that is to say, by jury. There are instruments so dangerous to the rights of the nation, and which place them so totally at the mercy of their governors, that those governors, whether legislative or executive, should be restrained from keeping such instruments on foot, but in well defined cases. Such an instrument is a standing army. We are now allowed to say, such a declaration of rights, as a supplement to the constitution, where this is silent, is wanting, to secure us in these points. The general voice has legitimated this objection. It has not, however, authorized me to consider as a real defect, what I thought, and still think one, the perpetual re-eligibility of the President. But three States out of eleven, having declared against this, we must suppose we are wrong, according to the fundamental law of every society, the *lex majoris partis*, to which we are bound to submit. And should the majority change their opinion, and become sensible that this trait in their constitution is wrong, I would wish it to remain uncorrected, as long as we can avail ourselves of the services of our great leader, whose talents and whose weight of character, I consider as peculiarly necessary to get the government so under way, as that it may afterwards be carried on by subordinate characters.

RICHARD HENRY LEE (?)

Letters from the Federal Farmer (1787)

There is much uncertainty about the authorship of these highly popular letters critical of the Constitution. Speculation has long focused on Richard Henry Lee (1733–1794). A signer of the Declaration of Independence, the Virginian Lee had served as president of the Continental Congress, where he allied himself with the radical Samuel Adams. The author expresses serious reservations about a centralized national government in a set of widely reprinted essays that set out many of the Anti-Federalist objections to the Constitution.

LETTER I

October 8th, 1787

My uniform federal attachments, and the interest I have in the protection of property, and a steady execution of the laws, will convince you, that, if I am under any bias at all, it is in favor of any general system which shall promise those advantages. The instability of our laws increases my wishes for firm and steady government; but then, I can consent to no government, which, in my opinion, is not calculated equally to preserve the rights of all orders of men in the community. * * * I am not disposed to unreasonably contend about forms. I know our situation is critical, and it behooves us to make the best of it. A federal government of some sort is necessary. We have suffered the present to languish; and whether the confederation was capable or not originally of answering any valuable purposes, it is now but of little importance. * * * A constitution is now presented which we may reject, or which we may accept with or without amendments, and to which point we ought to direct our exertions is the question. To determine this question with propriety; we must attentively examine the system itself, and the probable consequences of either step. * * *

The first principal question that occurs is, Whether, considering our situation, we ought to precipitate the adoption of the proposed constitution? If we remain cool and temperate, we are in no immediate danger of any commotions; we are in a state of perfect peace, and in no danger of invasions; the state governments are in the full exercise of their powers; and our governments answer all present exigencies, except the regulation of trade, securing credit, in some cases, and providing for the interest, in some instances, of the public debts; and whether we adopt a change three or nine months hence, can make but little odds with the private circumstances of individuals; their happiness and prosperity, after all, depend principally upon their own exertions. We are hardly recovered from a long and distressing war: The farmers, fishmen, etc. have not fully repaired the waste made by it. Industry and frugality are again assuming their proper station. Private debts are lessened, and public debts incurred by the war have been, by various ways, diminished; and the public lands have now become a productive source for diminishing them much more. I know uneasy men, who with very much to precipitate, do not admit all these facts; but they are facts well known to all men who are thoroughly informed in the affairs of this country. It must, however, be admitted, that our federal system is defective, and that some of the state governments are not well administered; but, then, we impute to the defects in our governments many evils and embarrassments which are most clearly the result of the late war. * * *

It is natural for men, who wish to hasten the adoption of a measure, to tell us, now is the crisis—now is the critical moment which must be seized or all will be lost; and to shut the door against free enquiry, whenever conscious the thing presented has defects in it, which time and investigation will probably discover. This has been the custom of tyrants, and their dependents in all ages. If it is true, what has been so often said, that the people of this country cannot change their condition for the worse, I presume it still behooves them to endeavour deliberately to change it for the better. The fickle and ardent, in any community are the proper tools for establishing despotic government. But it is deliberate and thinking men, who must establish and secure governments on free principles. * * *

Our object has been all along, to reform our federal system, and to strengthen our governments—to establish peace, order and justice in the community—but a new object now presents. The plan of government now proposed is evidently calculated totally to change, in time, our condition as a people. Instead of being thirteen republics, under a federal head, it is clearly designed to make us one consolidated government. * * * This consolidation of the states has been the object of several men in this country for some time past. Whether such a change can ever be effected, in any manner; whether it can be effected without convulsions and civil wars; whether such a change will not totally destroy the liberties of this country—time only can determine.

To have a just idea of the government before us, and to show that a consolidated one is the object in view, it is necessary not only to examine the plan, but also its history, and the politics of its particular friends.

The confederation was formed when great confidence was placed in the voluntary exertions of individuals, and of the respective states; and the framers of it, to guard against usurpation, so limited, and checked the powers, that, in many respects, they are inadequate to the exigencies of the union. We find, therefore, members of congress urging alterations in the federal system almost as soon as it was adopted. It was early proposed to vest congress with powers to levy an impost, to regulate trade, etc. but such was known to be the caution of the states in parting with power, that the vestment even of these, was proposed to be under several checks and limitations. During the war, the general confusion, and the introduction of paper money, infused in the minds of people vague ideas respecting government and credit. We expected too much from the return of peace, and of course we have been disappointed. Our governments have been new and unsettled; and several legislatures, by making tender, suspension, and paper money laws, have given just cause of uneasiness to creditors. By these and other causes, several orders of men in the community have been prepared, by degrees, for a change of government; and this very abuse of power in the legislatures, which in some cases has been charged upon the democratic part of the community, has furnished aristocratical men with those very weapons, and those very means, with which, in great measure, they are rapidly effecting their favourite object. And should an oppressive government be the consequence of the proposed change, posterity may reproach not only a few overbearing, unprincipled men, but those parties in the states which have misused their powers.

The conduct of several legislatures, touching paper money, and tender laws, has prepared many honest men for changes in government, which otherwise they would not have thought of—when by the evils, on the one hand, and by the secret instigations of artful men, on the other, the minds of men were become sufficiently uneasy, a bold step was taken, which is usually followed by a revolution, or a civil war. * * *

The first interesting question, therefore suggested, is, how far the states can be consolidated into one entire government on free principles. In considering this question extensive objects are to be taken into view, and important changes in the forms of government to be carefully attended to in all their consequences. The happiness of the people at large must be the great object with every honest statesman, and he will direct every movement to this point. If we are so situated as a people, as not to be able to enjoy equal happiness and advantages under one government, the consolidation of the states cannot be admitted.

LETTER II

October 9, 1787

There are certain unalienable and fundamental rights, which in forming the social compact, ought to be explicitly ascertained and fixed—a free and enlightened people, in forming this compact, will not resign all their rights to those who govern, and they will fix limits to their legislators and rulers, which will soon be plainly seen by those who are governed, as well as by those who govern: and the latter will know they cannot be passed unperceived by the former, and without giving a general alarm—These rights should be made the basis of every constitution; and if a people be so situated, or have such different opinions that they cannot agree in ascertaining and fixing them, it is a very strong argument against their attempting to form one entire society, to live under one system of laws only.

LETTER III

October 10th, 1787

The great object of a free people must be so to form their government and laws, and so to administer them, as to create a confidence in, and respect for the laws; and thereby induce the sensible and virtuous part of the community to declare in favor of the laws, and to support them without an expensive military force. * * * I am fully convinced that we must organize the national government on different principles, and make the parts of it more efficient, and secure in it more effectually the different interests in the community. ＊ ＊ ＊ It is not my object to multiply objections, or to contend about inconsiderable powers or amendments. I wish the system adopted with a few alterations; but those, in my mind, are essential ones. ＊ ＊ ＊

First. As to the organization—the House of Representatives, the democrative branch, as it is called, is to consist of 65 members: that is, about one representative for fifty thousand inhabitants, to be chosen biennially—the federal legislature may increase this number to one for each thirty thousand inhabitants, abating fractional numbers in each state.—Thirty-three representatives will make a quorum for doing business, and a majority of those present determine the sense of the house.—I have no idea that the interests, feelings, and opinions of three or four millions of people, especially touching internal taxation, can be collected in such a house.—In the nature of things, nine times in ten, men of the elevated classes in the community only can be chosen.—Connecticut, for instance, will have five representatives—not one man in a hundred of those who form the democrative branch in the state legislature, will, on a fair computation, be one of the five.—The people of this country in one sense, may all be democratic; but if we make the proper distinction between the few men of wealth and abilities, and consider them, as we ought, as the natural aristocracy of the country, and the great body of the people, the middle and lower classes, as the democracy, this federal representative branch will have but very little democracy in it, even this small representation is not secured on proper principles. ＊ ＊ ＊

In the second place it is necessary ＊ ＊ ＊ to examine the extent, and the probable operations of some of those extensive powers proposed to be vested in this government. These powers, legislative, executive, and judicial, respect internal as well as external objects. Those respecting external objects, as all foreign concerns, commerce, imposts, all causes arising on the seas, peace and war, and Indian affairs can be lodged no where else, with any propriety, but in this government. Many powers that respect internal objects ought clearly to be lodged in it; as those to regulate trade between the states, weights and measures, the coin or current monies, post-offices, naturalization, etc. These powers may be exercised without essentially effecting the internal police of the respective states: But powers to lay and collect internal taxes, to form the militia, to make bankrupt laws, and to decide on appeals, questions arising on the internal laws of the respective states, are of a very serious nature, and carry with them almost all other powers. These taken in connection with the others, and powers to raise armies and build navies, proposed to be lodged in this government, appear to me to comprehend all the essential powers in this community, and those which will be left to the states will be of no great importance. ＊ ＊ ＊

LETTER IV

October 12th, 1787

Third, there appears to me to be not only a premature deposit of some important powers in the general government—but many of those deposited there are undefined, and may be used to good or bad purposes as honest or designing men shall prevail. * * *

4th. There are certain rights which we have always held sacred in the United States, and recognized in all our constitutions, and which, by the adoption of the new constitution in its present form, will be left unsecured. By article 6, the proposed constitution, and the laws of the United States, which shall be made in pursuance thereof; and all treaties made, or which shall be made under the authority of the United States, shall be the supreme law of the land; and the judges in every state shall be bound thereby; anything in the constitution or laws of any state to the contrary notwithstanding. * * *

It is proper the national laws should be supreme, and superior to state or district laws; but then the national laws ought to yield to unalienable or fundamental rights—and national laws, made by a few men, should extend only to a few national objects. This will not be the case with the laws of congress: To have any proper idea of their extent, we must carefully examine the legislative, executive and judicial powers proposed to be lodged in the general government, and consider them in connection with a general clause in art. I, sect. 8, in these words (after enumerating a number of powers) 'To make all laws which shall be necessary and proper for carrying into execution the foregoing powers, and all other powers vested by this constitution in the government of the United States, or in any department or officer thereof.'—The powers of this government as has been observed, extend to internal as well as external objects, and to those objects to which all others are subordinate; it is almost impossible to have a just conception of their powers, or of the extent and number of the laws which may be deemed necessary and proper to carry them into effect, till we shall come to exercise those powers and make the laws. * * *

It may also be worthy our examination, how far the provision for amending this plan, when it shall be adopted, is of any importance. No measures can be taken towards amendments, unless two-thirds of the congress, or two-thirds of the legislature of the several states shall agree.—While power is in the hands of the people, or democratic part of the community, more especially as at present, it is easy, according to the general course of human affairs, for the few influential men in the community, to obtain conventions, alterations in government, and to persuade the common people that they may change for the better, and to get from them a part of the power: But when power is once transferred from the many to the few, all changes become extremely difficult; the government, in this case, being beneficial to the few, they will be exceedingly artful and adroit in preventing any measures which may lead to a change; and nothing will produce it, but great exertions and severe struggles on the part of the common people. Every man of reflection must see, that the change now proposed, is a transfer of power from the many to the few, and the probability is, the artful and ever active aristocracy, will prevent all peaceful measures for changes, unless when they shall discover some favorable moment to increase their own influence.

LETTER V

October 15th, 1787

Thus I have examined the federal constitution as far as a few days leisure would permit. It opens to my mind a new scene; instead of seeing powers cautiously lodged in the hands of numerous legislators, and many magistrates, we see all important powers collecting in one centre, where a few men will possess them almost at discretion. And instead of checks in the formation of the government, to secure the rights of the people against the usurpations of those they appoint to govern, we are to understand the equal division of lands among our people, and the strong arm furnished them by nature and situation, are to secure them against those usurpations. If there are advantages in the equal division of our lands, and the strong and manly habits of our people, we ought to establish governments calculated to give duration to them, and not governments which never can work naturally, till that equality of property, and those free and manly habits shall be destroyed; these evidently are not the natural basis of the proposed constitution. * * *

There are, however, in my opinion, many good things in the proposed system. It is founded on elective principles, and the deposits of powers in different hands, is essentially right. The guards against those evils we have experienced in some states in legislation are valuable indeed; but the value of every feature in this system is vastly lessened for the want of that one important feature in a free government, a representation of the people. Because we have sometimes abused democracy, I am not among those men who think a democratic branch a nuisance; which branch shall be sufficiently numerous to admit some of the best informed men of each order in the community into the administration of government. * * *

I have admitted that we want a federal system—that we have a system presented, which, with several alterations may be made a tolerable good one—I have admitted there is a well founded uneasiness among creditors and mercantile men. In this situation of things, you ask me what I think ought to be done? My opinion in this case is only the opinion of an individual, and so far only as it corresponds with the opinions of the honest and substantial part of the community, is it entitled to consideration. Though I am fully satisfied that the state conventions ought most seriously to direct their exertions to altering and amending the system proposed before they shall adopt it—yet I have not sufficiently examined the subject, or formed an opinion, how far it will be practicable for those conventions to carry their amendments. As to the idea, that it will be in vain for those conventions to attempt amendments, it cannot be admitted. * * * It is true there may be danger in delay; but there is danger in adopting the system in its present form; and I see the danger in either case will arise principally from the conduct and views of two very unprincipled parties in the United States—two fires, between which the honest and substantial people have long found themselves situated. One party is composed of little insurgents, men in debt, who want no law, and who want a share of the property of others; these are called levellers, Shayites, etc. The other party is composed of a few, but more dangerous men, with their servile dependents; these avariciously grasp at all power and property; you may discover in all the actions of these men, an evident dislike to free and equal government, and they will go systematically to work to change, essentially, the forms of government in this country. * * * Between these two parties is the weight of the community; the men of middling property, men not in debt on the one hand, and men, on the other, content with republican governments, and not aiming at immense fortunes, offices and power. In 1786, the little insurgents, the levellers, came forth, invaded the rights of others, and attempted to establish governments according to their wills. Their movements evidently gave encouragement to the other party, which, in 1787, has taken the political field, and with its fashionable dependants, and the tongue and the pen, is endeavoring to establish in a great haste, a politer kind of government. These two parties, which will probably be opposed or united as it may suit their interests and views, are really insignificant, compared with the solid, free, and independent part of the community. * * * The sensible and judicious part of the community will carefully weigh all these circumstances; they will view the late convention as a respectable body of men—America probably never will see an assembly of men, of a like number, more respectable. But the members of the convention met without knowing the sentiments of one man in ten thousand in these states respecting the new ground taken. Their doings are but the first attempts in the most important scene ever opened. Though each individual in the state conventions will not, probably, be so respectable as each individual in the federal convention, yet as the state conventions will probably consist of fifteen hundred or two thousand men of abilities, and versed in the science of government, collected from all parts of the community and from all orders of men, it must be acknowledged that the weight of respectability will be in them—In them will be collected the solid sense and the real political character of the country. Being revisers of the subject, they will possess peculiar advantages. To say that these conventions ought not to attempt, coolly and deliberately, the revision of the system, or that they cannot amend it, is very foolish and very assuming. * * * Men who wish the people of this country to determine for themselves, and deliberately to fit the government to their situation, must feel some degree of indignation at those attempts to hurry the adoption of a system, and to shut the door against examination. The very attempts to create suspicions, that those who make them have secret views, or see some defects in the system, which, in the hurry of affairs, they expect will escape the eye of a free people.

ROBERT YATES (?)

Essays of Brutus (1787–1788)

The Essays of Brutus, *like the* Letters from the Federal Farmer, *have no definitive author, although for many years it was assumed they were written by Robert Yates (1738/9–1801), an important figure in New York state politics since the Revolution. "Brutus's" essays, which were reprinted in Philadelphia and Boston, first appeared in the* New York Journal *and helped elect Anti-Federalists to the state ratifying convention. Like many other Anti-Federalists, Brutus feared a consolidated system of government stretching over an extensive territory, but he also wrote of the dangers of an independent judiciary.*

To the Citizens of the State of New-York.

When the public is called to investigate and decide upon a question in which not only the present members of the community are deeply interested, but upon which the happiness and misery of generations yet unborn is in great measure suspended, the benevolent mind cannot help feeling itself peculiarly interested in the result. * * *

Perhaps this country never saw so critical a period in their political concerns. We have felt the feebleness of the ties by which these United States are held together, and the want of sufficient energy in our present confederation, to manage, in some instances, our general concerns. Various expedients have been proposed to remedy these evils, but none have succeeded. At length a Convention of the states has been assembled, they have formed a constitution which will now, probably, be submitted to the people to ratify or reject, who are the fountain of all power, to whom alone it of right belongs to make or unmake constitutions, or forms of government, at their pleasure. The most important question that was ever proposed to your decision, or to the decision of any people under heaven, is before you, and you are to decide upon it by men of your own election, chosen specially for this purpose. If the constitution, offered to your acceptance, be a wise one, calculated to preserve the invaluable blessings of liberty, to secure the inestimable rights of mankind, and promote human happiness, then, if you accept it, you will lay a lasting foundation of happiness for millions yet unborn; generations to come will rise up and call you blessed. * * * But if, on the other hand, this form of government contains principles that will lead to the subversion of liberty—if it tends to establish a despotism, or, what is worse, a tyrannic aristocracy; then, if you adopt it, this only remaining assylum for liberty will be shut up, and posterity will execrate your memory. * * *

With these few introductory remarks, I shall proceed to a consideration of this constitution:

The first question that presents itself on the subject is, whether a confederated government be the best for the United States or not? * * * Or in other words, whether the thirteen United States should be reduced to one great republic, governed by one legislature, and under the direction of one executive and judicial; or whether they should continue thirteen confederated republics, under the direction and controul of a supreme federal head for certain defined national purposes only?

This enquiry is important, because, although the government reported by the convention does not go to a perfect and entire consolidation, yet it approaches so near to it, that it must, if executed, certainly and infallibly terminate in it.

This government is to possess absolute and uncontroulable power, legislative, executive and judicial, with respect to every object to which it extends, for by the last clause of section 8th, article 1st, it is declared "that the Congress shall have power to make all laws which shall be necessary and proper for carrying into execution the foregoing powers, and all other powers vested by this constitution, in the government of the United States; or in any department or office thereof." And by the 6th article, it is declared "that this constitution, and the laws of the United States, which shall be made in pursuance thereof, and the treaties made, or which shall be made, under the authority of the United States, shall be the supreme law of the land; and the judges in every state shall be bound thereby, any thing in the constitution, or law of any state to the contrary notwithstanding." It appears from these articles that there is no need of any intervention of the state governments, between the Congress and the people, to execute any one power vested in the general government, and that the constitution and laws of every state are nullified and declared void, so far as they are or shall be inconsistent with this constitution, or the laws made in pursuance of it, or with treaties made under the authority of the United States.—The government then, so far as it extends, is a complete one, and not a confederation. * * * The powers of the general legislature extend to every case that is of the least importance—there is nothing valuable to human nature, nothing dear to freemen, but what is within its power. It has authority to make laws which will affect the lives, the liberty, and property of every man in the United States; nor can the constitution or laws of any state, in any way prevent or impede the full and complete execution of every power given. The legislative power is competent to lay taxes, duties, imposts, and excises; * * * —there is no limitation to this power, unless it be said that the clause which directs the use to which those taxes, and duties shall be applied, may be said to be a limitation: but this is no restriction of the power at all, for by this clause they are to be applied to pay the debts and provide for the common defence and general welfare of the United States; but the legislature have authority to contract debts at their discretion; they are the sole judges of what is necessary to provide for the common defence, and they only are to determine what is for the general welfare; this power therefore is neither more nor less, than a power to lay and collect taxes, imposts, and excises, at their pleasure; not only [is] the power to lay taxes unlimited, as to the amount they may require, but it is perfect and absolute to raise them in any mode they please. No state legislature, or any power in the state governments, have any more to do in carrying this into effect, than the authority of one state has to do with that of another. In the business therefore of laying and collecting taxes, the idea of confederation is totally lost, and that of one entire republic is embraced. It is proper here to remark, that the authority to lay and collect taxes is the most important of any power that can be granted; it connects with it almost all other powers, or at least will in process of time draw all other after it; it is the great mean of protection, security, and defence, in a good government, and the great engine of oppression and tyranny in a bad one. * * * Every one who has thought on the subject, must be convinced that but small sums of money can be collected in any country, by direct taxe[s], when the federal government begins to exercise the right of taxation in all its parts, the legislatures of the several states will find it impossible to raise monies to support their governments. Without money they cannot be supported, and they must dwindle away, and, as before observed, their powers absorbed in that of the general government. * * *

The judicial power of the United States is to be vested in a supreme court, and in such inferior courts as Congress may from time to time ordain and establish. * * * The powers of these courts are very extensive; their jurisdiction comprehends all civil causes, except such as arise between citizens of the same state; and it extends to all cases in law and equity arising under the constitution. One inferior court must be established, I presume, in each state, at least, with the necessary executive officers appendant thereto. It is easy to see, that in the common course of things, these courts will eclipse the dignity, and take away from the respectability, of the state courts. These courts will be, in themselves, totally independent of the states, deriving their authority from the United States, and receiving from them fixed salaries; and in the course of human events it is to be expected, that they will swallow up all the powers of the courts in the respective states.

How far the clause in the 8th section of the 1st article may operate to do away all idea of confederated states, and to effect an entire consolidation of the whole into one general government, it is impossible to say. The powers given by this article are very general and comprehensive, and it may receive a construction to justify the passing almost any law. A power to make all laws, which shall be *necessary* and *proper,* for carrying into execution, all powers vested by the constitution in the government of the United States, or any department or officer thereof, is a power very comprehensive and definite [indefinite?], and may, for ought I know, be exercised in a such manner as entirely to abolish the state legislatures. * * *

Let us now proceed to enquire, as I at first proposed, whether it be best the thirteen United States should be reduced to one great republic, or not? It is here taken for granted, that all agree in this, that whatever government we adopt, it ought to be a free one; that it should be so framed as to secure the liberty of the citizens of America, and such a one as to admit of a full, fair, and equal representation of the people. The question then will be, whether a government thus constituted, and founded on such principles, is practicable, and can be exercised over the whole United States, reduced into one state?

History furnishes no example of a free republic, any thing like the extent of the United States. The Grecian republics were of small extent; so also was that of the Romans. Both of these, it is true, in process of time, extended their conquests over large territories of country; and the consequence was, that their governments were changed from that of free governments to those of the most tyrannical that ever existed in the world.

Not only the opinion of the greatest men, and the experience of mankind are against the idea of an extensive republic, but a variety of reasons may be drawn from the reason and nature of things, against it. In every government, the will of the sovereign is the law. In despotic governments, the supreme authority being lodged in one, his will is law, and can be as easily expressed to a large extensive territory as to a small one. In a pure democracy the people are the sovereign, and their will is declared by themselves; for this purpose they must all come together to deliberate, and decide. This kind of government cannot be exercised, therefore, over a country of any considerable extent; it must be confined to a single city, or at least limited to such bounds as that the people can conveniently assemble, be able to debate, understand the subject submitted to them, and declare their opinion concerning it.

In a free republic, although all laws are derived from the consent of the people, yet the people do not declare their consent by themselves in person, but by representatives, chosen by them, who are supposed to know the minds of their constituents, and to be possessed of integrity to declare this mind. * * *

In every free government, the people must give their assent to the laws by which they are governed. This is the true criterion between a free government and an arbitrary one. The former are ruled by the will of the whole, expressed in any manner they may agree upon; the latter by the will of one, or a few. If the people are to give their assent to the laws, by persons chosen and appointed by them, the manner of the choice and the number chosen, must be such, as to possess, be disposed, and consequently qualified to declare the sentiments of the people; for if they do not know, or are not disposed to speak the sentiments of the people, the people do not govern, but the sovereignty is in a few. Now, in a large extended country, it is impossible to have a representation, possessing the sentiments, and of integrity, to declare the minds of the people, without having it so numerous and unwieldly, as to be subject in great measure to the inconveniency of a democratic government.

The territory of the United States is of vast extent; it now contains near three millions of souls, and is capable of containing much more than ten times that number. Is it practicable for a country, so large and so numerous as they will soon become, to elect a representation, that will speak their sentiments, without their becoming so numerous as to be incapable of transacting public business? It certainly is not. * * *

In a republic, the manners, sentiments, and interests of the people should be similar. If this be not the case, there will be a constant clashing of opinions; and the representatives of one part will be continually striving against those of the other. * * * This will retard the operations of government, and prevent such conclusions as will promote the public good. If we apply this remark to the condition of the United States, we shall be convinced that it forbids that we should be one government. The United States includes a variety of climates. The productions of the different parts of the union are very variant, and their interests, of consequence, diverse. Their manners and habits differ as much as their climates and productions; and their sentiments are by no means coincident. The laws and customs of the several states are, in many respects, very diverse, and in some opposite; each would be in favor of its own interests and customs, and, of consequence, a legislature, formed of representatives from the respective parts, would not only be too numerous to act with any care or decision, but would be composed of such heterogeneous and discordant principles, as would constantly be contending with each other.

In a republic of such vast extent as the United States, the legislature cannot attend to the various concerns and wants of its different parts. It cannot be sufficiently numerous to be acquainted with the local condition and wants of the different districts, and if it could, it is impossible it should have sufficient time to attend to and provide for all the variety of cases of this nature, that would be continually arising.

In so extensive a republic, the great officers of government would soon become above the controul of the people, and abuse their power to the purpose of aggrandizing themselves, and oppressing them. The trust committed to the executive offices, in a country of the extent of the United States, must be various and of magnitude. The command of all the troops and navy of the republic, the appointment of officers, the power of pardoning offences, the collecting of all the public revenues, and the power of expending them, with a number of other powers, must be lodged and exercised in every state, in the hands of a few. When these are attended with great honor and emolument, as they always will be in large states, so as greatly to interest men to pursue them, and to be proper objects for ambitious and designing men, such men will be ever restless in their pursuit after them. They will use the power, when they have acquired it, to the purposes of gratifying their own interest and ambition, and it is scarcely possible, in a very large republic, to call them to account for their misconduct, or to prevent their abuse of power. * * *

These are some of the reasons by which it appears, that a free republic cannot long subsist over a country of the great extent of these states. If then this new constitution is calculated to consolidate the thirteen states into one, as it evidently is, it ought not to be adopted. * * *

To the Citizens of the State of New-York.

I flatter myself that my last address established this position, that to reduce the Thirteen States into one government, would prove the destruction of your liberties.

But lest this truth should be doubted by some, I will now proceed to consider its merits.

Though it should be admitted, that the argument[s] against reducing all the states into one consolidated government, are not sufficient fully to establish this point; yet they will, at least, justify this conclusion, that in forming a constitution for such a country, great care should be taken to limit and definite its powers, adjust its parts, and guard against an abuse of authority. How far attention has been paid to these objects, shall be the subject of future enquiry. When a building is to be erected which is intended to stand for ages, the foundation should be firmly laid. The constitution proposed to your acceptance, is designed not for yourselves alone, but for generations yet unborn. The principles, therefore, upon which the social compact is founded, ought to have been clearly and precisely stated, and the most express and full declaration of rights to have been made—But on this subject there is almost an entire silence.

If we may collect the sentiments of the people of America, from their own most solemn declarations, they hold this truth as self evident, that all men are by nature free. No one man, therefore, or any class of men, have a right, by the law of nature, or of God, to assume or exercise authority over their fellows. The origin of society then is to be sought, not in any natural right which one man has to exercise authority over another, but in the united consent of those who associate. The mutual wants of men, at first dictated the propriety of forming societies; and when they were established, protection and defence pointed out the necessity of instituting government. * * * The common good, therefore, is the end of civil government, and common consent, the foundation on which it is established. To effect this end, it was necessary that a certain portion of natural liberty should be surrendered, in order, that what remained should be preserved: how great a proportion of natural freedom is necessary to be yielded by individuals, when they submit to government, I shall not now enquire. So much, however, must be given up, as will be sufficient to enable those, to whom the administration of the government is committed, to establish laws for the promoting the happiness of the community, and to carry those laws into effect. But it is not necessary, for this purpose, that individuals should relinquish all their natural rights. Some are of such a nature that they cannot be surrendered. Of this kind are the rights of conscience, the right of enjoying and defending life, etc. Others are not necessary to be resigned, in order to attain the end for which government is instituted, these therefore ought not to be given up. To surrender them, would counteract the very end of government, to wit, the common good. * * * From these observations it appears, that in forming a government on its true principles, the foundation should be laid in the manner I before stated, by expressly reserving to the people such of their essential natural rights, as are not necessary to be parted with. * * * But rulers have the same propensities as other men; they are as likely to use the power with which they are vested for private purposes, and to the injury and oppression of those over whom they are placed, as individuals in a state of nature are to injure and oppress one another. It is therefore as proper that bounds should be set to their authority, as that government should have at first been instituted to restrain private injuries. * * *

This principle, which seems so evidently founded in the reason and nature of things, is confirmed by universal experience. Those who have governed, have been found in all ages ever active to enlarge their powers and abridge the public liberty. This has induced the people in all countries, where any sense of freedom remained, to fix barriers against the encroachments of their rulers. * * * I presume, to an American, then, that this principle is a fundamental one, in all the constitutions of our own states; there is not one of them but what is either founded on a declaration or bill of rights, or has certain express reservation of rights interwoven in the body of them. From this it appears, that at a time when the pulse of liberty beat high and when an appeal was made to the people to form constitutions for the government of themselves, it was their universal sense, that such declarations should make a part of their frames of government. It is therefore the more astonishing, that this grand security, to the rights of the people, is not to be found in this constitution.

It has been said, in answer to this objection, that such declaration[s] of rights, however requisite they might be in the constitutions of the states, are not necessary in the general constitution, because, "in the former case, every thing which is not reserved is given, but in the latter the reverse of the proposition prevails, and every thing which is not given is reserved." * * * It requires but little attention to discover, that this mode of reasoning is rather specious than solid. The powers, rights, and authority, granted to the general government by this constitution, are as complete, with respect to every object to which they extend, as that of any state government—It reaches to every thing which concerns human happiness— Life, liberty, and property, are under its controul. There is the same reason, therefore, that the exercise of power, in this case, should be restrained within proper limits, as in that of the state governments. To set this matter in a clear light, permit me to instance some of the articles of the bills of rights of the individual states, and apply them to the case in question.

For the security of life, in criminal prosecutions, the bills of rights of most of the states have declared, that no man shall be held to answer for a crime until he is made fully acquainted with the charge brought against him; he shall not be compelled to accuse, or furnish evidence against himself—The witnesses against him shall be brought face to face, and he shall be fully heard by himself or counsel. That it is essential to the security of life and liberty, that trial of facts be in the vicinity where they happen. Are not provisions of this kind as necessary in the general government, as in that of a particular state? The powers vested in the new Congress extend in many cases to life; they are authorised to provide for the punishment of a variety of capital crimes, and no restraint is laid upon them in its exercise, save only, that "the trial of all crimes, except in cases of impeachment, shall be by jury: and such trial shall be in the state where the said crimes shall have been committed." * * *

For the security of liberty it has been declared, "that excessive bail should not be required, nor excessive fines imposed, nor cruel or unusual punishments inflicted—That all warrants, without oath or affirmation, to search suspected places, or seize any person, his papers or property, are grievous and oppressive." * * *

These provisions are as necessary under the general government as under that of the individual states; for the power of the former is as complete to the purpose of requiring bail, imposing fines, inflicting punishments, granting search warrants, and seizing persons, papers, or property, in certain cases, as the other.

For the purpose of securing the property of the citizens, it is declared by all the states, "that in all controversies at law, respecting property, the ancient mode of trial by jury is one of the best securities of the rights of the people, and ought to remain sacred and inviolable." * * *

Does not the same necessity exist of reserving this right, under this national compact, as in that of these states? Yet nothing is said respecting it. In the bills of rights of the states it is declared, that a well regulated militia is the proper and natural defence of a free government—That as standing armies in time of peace are dangerous, they are not to be kept up, and that the military should be kept under strict subordination to, and controuled by the civil power. * * *

The same security is as necessary in this constitution, and much more so; for the general government will have the sole power to raise and to pay armies, and are under no controul in the exercise of it; yet nothing of this is to be found in this new system.

I might proceed to instance a number of other rights, which were as necessary to be reserved, such as, that elections should be free, that the liberty of the press should be held sacred; but the instances adduced, are sufficient to prove, that this argument is without foundation.—Besides, it is evident, that the reason here assigned was not the true one, why the framers of this constitution omitted a bill of rights; if it had been, they would not have made certain reservations, while they totally omitted others of more importance. We find they have, in the 9th section of the 1st article, declared, that the writ of habeas corpus shall not be suspended, unless in cases of rebellion—that no bill of attainder, or expost facto law, shall be passed—that no title of nobility shall be granted by the United States, &c. If every thing which is not given is reserved, what propriety is there in these exceptions? * * * Does this constitution any where grant the power of suspending the habeas corpus, to make expost facto laws, pass bills of attainder, or grant titles of nobility? It certainly does not in express terms. The only answer that can be given is, that these are implied in the general powers granted. With equal truth it may be said, that all the powers, which the bills of right, guard against the abuse of, are contained or implied in the general ones granted by this constitution.

So far it is from being true, that a bill of rights is less necessary in the general constitution than in those of the states, the contrary is evidently the fact.—This system, if it is possible for the people of America to accede to it, will be an original compact; and being the last, will, in the nature of things, vacate every former agreement inconsistent with it. For it being a plan of government received and ratified by the whole people, all other forms, which are in existence at the time of its adoption, must yield to it. This is expressed in positive and unequivocal terms, in the 6th article, "That this constitution and the laws of the United States, which shall be made in pursuance thereof, and all treaties made, or which shall be made, under the authority of the United States, shall be the supreme law of the land; and the judges in every state shall be bound thereby, any thing in the *constitution* or laws of any state, *to the contrary* notwithstanding.

"The senators and representatives before-mentioned, and the members of the several state legislatures, and all executive and judicial of officers, both of the United States, and of the several states, shall be bound, by oath or affirmation, to support this constitution."

It is therefore not only necessarily implied thereby, but positively expressed, that the different state constitutions are repealed and entirely done away, so far as they are inconsistent with this, with the laws which shall be made in pursuance thereof, or with treaties made, or which shall be made under the authority of the United States; of what avail will the constitutions of the respective states be to preserve the rights of its citizens? Should they be plead, the answer would be, the constitution of the United States, and the laws made in pursuance thereof, is the supreme law, and all legislatures and judicial officers, whether of the general or state governments, are bound by oath to support it. No priviledge, reserved by the bills of rights, or secured by the state government, can limit the power granted by this, or restrain any laws made in pursuance of it. It stands therefore on its own bottom, and must receive a construction by itself without any reference to any other. ∗ ∗ ∗ —And hence it was of the highest importance, that the most precise and express declarations and reservations of rights should have been made. ∗ ∗ ∗

So clear a point is this, that I cannot help suspecting, that persons who attempt to persuade people, that such reservations were less necessary under this constitution than under those of the states, are wilfully endeavouring to deceive, and to lead you into an absolute state of vassalage.

PATRICK HENRY

Debate in the Virginia Ratifying Convention (1788)

The Revolutionary hero who famously cried, "Give me liberty or give me death," Patrick Henry (1736–1799), served five terms as governor of Virginia before leading the Anti-Federalist assault against the Constitution with his fiery oratory in the Virginia ratification convention. The outcome of the struggle in this crucial state was critical to the success of the Constitution, and perhaps to the fate of the Union itself. In this selection from his stirring opening speech in the Virginia convention, Henry warned that the Constitution would establish a consolidated government, which would not only violate the American spirit but would also threaten the liberty of the people. Although Virginia eventually ratified the Constitution by the margin of 89 to 79, Anti-Federalists such as Henry succeeded in convincing fellow Virginian James Madison to seek a bill of rights during the first Congress.

I rose yesterday to ask a question which arose in my own mind. When I asked that question, I thought the meaning of interrogation was obvious. The fate of this question and of America may depend on this. Have they said, We, the states? Have they made a proposal of a compact between states? If they had, this would be a confederation. It is otherwise most clearly a consolidated government. The question turns, sir, on that poor little thing—the expression, We, the *people*, instead of the *states*, of America. I need not take much pains to show that the principles of this system are extremely pernicious, impolitic, and dangerous. Is this a monarchy, like England—a compact between prince and people, with checks on the former to secure the liberty of the latter? Is this a confederacy, like Holland—an association of a number of independent states, each of which retains its individual sovereignty? It is not a democracy, wherein the people retain all their rights securely. Had these principles been adhered to, we should not have been brought to this alarming transition, from a confederacy to a consolidated government. We have no detail of these great considerations, which, in my opinion, ought to have abounded before we should recur to a government of this kind. Here is a resolution as radical as that which separated us from Great Britain. It is radical in this transition; our rights and privileges are endangered, and the sovereignty of the states will be relinquished: and cannot we plainly see that this is actually the case? The rights of conscience, trial by jury, liberty of the press, all your immunities and franchises, all pretensions to human rights and privileges, are rendered insecure, if not lost, by this change, so loudly talked of by some, and inconsiderately by others. Is this tame relinquishment of rights worthy of freemen? Is it worthy of that manly fortitude that ought to characterize republicans? It is said eight states have adopted this plan. I declare that if twelve states and a half had adopted it, I would, with manly firmness, and in spite of an erring world, reject it. You are not to inquire how your trade may be increased, nor how you are to become a great and powerful people, but how your liberties can be secured; for liberty ought to be the direct end of your government.

* * *

Is it necessary for your liberty that you should abandon those great rights by the adoption of this system? Is the relinquishment of the trial by jury and the liberty of the press necessary for your liberty? Will the abandonment of your most sacred rights tend to the security of your liberty? Liberty, the greatest of all earthly blessings—give us that precious jewel, and you may take everything else! But I am fearful I have lived long enough to become an old-fashioned fellow. Perhaps an invincible attachment to the dearest rights of man may, in these refined, enlightened days, be deemed old-fashioned; if so, I am contented to be so. I say, the time has been when every pulse of my heart beat for American liberty, and which, I believe, had a counterpart in the breast of every true American; but suspicions have gone forth—suspicions of my integrity—publicly reported that my professions are not real. Twenty-three years ago was I supposed a traitor to my country? I was then said to be the bane of sedition, because I supported the rights of my country. I may be thought suspicious when I say our privileges and rights are in danger. But, sir, a number of the people of this country are weak enough to think these things are too true. I am happy to find that the gentleman on the other side declares they are groundless. But, sir, suspicion, is a virtue as long as its object is the preservation of the public good, and as long as it stays within proper bounds: should it fall on me, I am contented: conscious rectitude is a powerful consolation. I trust there are many who think my professions for the public good to be real. Let your suspicion look to both sides. There are many on the other side, who possibly may have been persuaded to the necessity of these measures, which I conceive to be dangerous to your liberty. Guard with jealous attention the public liberty. Suspect every one who approaches that jewel. Unfortunately, nothing will preserve it but downright force. Whenever you give up that force, you are inevitably ruined. I am answered by gentlemen, that, though I might speak of terrors, yet the fact was, that we were surrounded by none of the dangers I apprehended. I conceive this new government to be one of those dangers: it has produced those horrors which distress many of our best citizens. We are come hither to preserve the poor commonwealth of Virginia, if it can be possibly done: something must be done to preserve your liberty and mine. The Confederation, this same despised government, merits, in my opinion, the highest encomium: it carried us through a long and dangerous war; it rendered us victorious in that bloody conflict with a powerful nation; it has secured us a territory greater than any European monarch possesses: and shall a government which has been thus strong and vigorous, be accused of imbecility, and abandoned for want of energy? Consider what you are about to do before you part with the government. Take longer time in reckoning things; revolutions like this have happened in almost every country in Europe; similar examples are to be found in ancient Greece and ancient Rome—instances of the people losing their liberty by their own carelessness and the ambition of a few. We are cautioned by the honorable gentleman, who presides, against faction and turbulence. I acknowledge that licentiousness is dangerous, and that it ought to be provided against: I acknowledge, also, the new form of government may effectually prevent it: yet there is another thing it will as effectually do—it will oppress and ruin the people.

There are sufficient guards placed against sedition and licentiousness; for, when power is give to this government to suppress these, or for any other purpose, the language it assumes is clear, express, and unequivocal; but when this Constitution speaks of privileges, there is an ambiguity, sir, a fatal ambiguity—an ambiguity which is very astonishing. In the clause under consideration, there is the strangest language that I can conceive. I mean, when it says that there shall not be more representatives than one for every thirty thousand. Now, sir, how easy is it to evade this privilege! "The number shall not exceed one for every thirty thousand." This may be satisfied by one representative from each state. Let our numbers be ever so great, this immense continent may, by this artful expression, be reduced to have but thirteen representatives. I confess this construction is not natural; but the ambiguity of the expression lays a good ground for a quarrel. Why was it not clearly and unequivocally expressed, that they should be entitled to have one for every thirty thousand? This would have obviated all disputes; and was this difficult to be done? What is the inference? When population increases, and a state shall send representatives in this proportion, Congress *may* remand them, because the right of having one for every thirty thousand is not clearly expressed. This possibility of reducing the number to one for each state approximates to probability by that other expression—"but each state shall at least have one representative." Now, is it not clear that, from the first expression, the number might be reduced so much that some states should have no representatives at all, were it not for the insertion of this last expression? And as this is the only restriction upon them, we may fairly conclude that they *may* restrain the number to one from each state. Perhaps the same horrors may hang over my mind again. I shall be told I am continually afraid: but, sir, I have strong cause of apprehension. In some parts of the plan before you, the great rights of freemen are endangered; in other parts, absolutely taken away. How does your trial by jury stand? In civil cases gone—not sufficiently secured in criminal—this best privilege is gone. But we are told that we need not fear; because those in power, being our representatives, will not abuse the powers we put in their hands. I am not well versed in history, but I will submit to your recollection, whether liberty has been destroyed most often by the licentiousness of the people, or by the tyranny of rulers. I imagine, sir, you will find the balance on the side of tyranny. Happy will you be if you miss the fate of those nations, who, omitting to resist their oppressors, or negligently suffering their liberty to be wrested from them, have groaned under intolerable despotism! Most of the human race are now in this deplorable condition; and those nations who have gone in search of grandeur, power, and splendor, have also fallen a sacrifice, and been the victims of their own folly. While they acquired those visionary blessings, they lost their freedom. My great objection to this government is, that it does not leave us the means of defending our rights, or of waging war against tyrants. It is urged by some gentlemen, that this new plan will bring us an acquisition of strength—an army and the militia of the states. This is an idea extremely ridiculous; the gentlemen cannot be earnest. This acquisition will trample on our fallen liberty. Let my beloved Americans guard against that fatal lethargy that has pervaded the universe. Have we the means of resisting disciplined armies, when our only defence, the militia, is put into the hands of Congress? The honorable gentleman said that great danger would ensue if the Convention rose without adopting this system. I ask, Where is that danger? I see none. Other gentlemen have told us, within these walls, that the union is gone, or that the union will be gone. Is not this trifling with the judgment of their fellow-citizens? Till they tell us the grounds of their fears. I will consider them as imaginary. I rose to make inquiry where those dangers were; they could make no answer: I believe I never shall have that answer. Is there a disposition in the people of this country to revolt against the dominion of laws? Has there been a single tumult in Virginia? Have not the people of Virginia, when laboring under the severest pressure of accumulated distresses, manifested the most cordial acquiescence in the execution of the laws? What could be more awful than their unanimous acquiescence under general distresses? Is there any revolution in Virginia? Whither is the spirit of America gone? Whither is the genius of America fled? It was but yesterday, when our enemies marched in triumph through our country. Yet the people of this country could not be appalled by their pompous armaments: they stopped their career, and victoriously captured them. Where is the peril, now, compared to that? Some minds are agitated by foreign alarms. Happily for us, there is no real danger from Europe; that country is engaged in more arduous business: from that quarter there is no cause of fear: you may sleep in safety forever for them.

Where is the danger? If, sir, there was any, I would recur to the American spirit to defend us; that spirit which has enabled us to surmount the greatest difficulties: to that illustrious spirit I address my most fervent prayer to prevent our adopting a system destructive to liberty.

* * *

A standing army we shall have, also, to execute the execrable commands of tyranny; and how are you to punish them? will you order them to be punished? Who shall obey these orders? Will your mace-bearer be a match for a disciplined regiment? In what situation are we to be? The clause before you gives a power of direct taxation, unbounded and unlimited, exclusive power of legislation, in all cases whatsoever, for ten miles square, and over all places purchased for the erection of forts, magazines, arsenals, dockyards, &c. What resistance could be made? The attempt would be madness. You will find all the strength of this country in the hands of your enemies; their garrisons will naturally be the strongest places in the country. Your militia is given up to Congress, also, in another part of this plan: they will therefore act as they think proper: all power will be in their own possession. You cannot force them to receive their punishment: of what service would militia be to you, when, most probably, you will not have a single musket in the state? for, as arms are to be provided by Congress, they may or may not furnish them.

Let me here call your attention to that part which gives the Congress power "to provide for organizing, arming, and disciplining the militia, and for governing such part of them as may be employed in the service of the United States—reserving to the states, respectively, the appointment of the officers, and the authority of training the militia according to the discipline prescribed by Congress." By this, sir, you see that their control over our last and best defence is unlimited. If they neglect or refuse to discipline or arm our militia, they will be useless: the states can do neither—this power being exclusively given to Congress. The power of appointing officers over men not disciplined or armed is ridiculous; so that this pretended little remains of power left to the states may, at the pleasure of Congress, be rendered nugatory. Our situation will be deplorable indeed: nor can we ever expect to get this government amended, since I have already shown that a very small minority may prevent it, and that small minority interested in the continuance of the oppression. Will the oppressor let go the oppressed? Was there ever an instance? Can the annals of mankind exhibit one single example where rulers overcharged with power willingly let go the oppressed, though solicited and requested most earnestly? The application for amendments will therefore be fruitless. Sometimes, the oppressed have got loose by one of those bloody struggles that desolate a country; but a willing relinquishment of power is one of those things which human nature never was, nor ever will be, capable of.

The honorable gentleman's observations, respecting the people's right of being the agents in the formation of this government, are not accurate, in my humble conception. The distinction between a national government and a confederacy is not sufficiently discerned. Had the delegates, who were sent to Philadelphia, a power to propose a consolidated government instead of a confederacy? Were they not deputed by states, and not by the people? The assent of the people, in their collective capacity, is not necessary to the formation of a federal government. The people have no right to enter into leagues, alliances, or confederations, they are not the proper agents for this purpose. States and foreign powers are the only proper agents for this kind of government. Show me an instance where the people have exercised this business. Has it not always gone through the legislatures? I refer you to the treaties with France, Holland, and other nations. How were they made? Were they not made by the states? Are the people, therefore, in their aggregate capacity, the proper persons to form a confederacy? This, therefore, ought to depend on the consent of the legislatures, the people having never sent delegates to make any proposition for changing the government. Yet I must say, at the same time, that it was made on grounds the most pure; and perhaps I might have been brought to consent to it so far as to the change of government. But there is one thing in it which I never would acquiesce in. I mean, the changing it into a consolidated government, which is so abhorrent to my mind. [The honorable gentleman then went on to the figure we make with foreign nations; the contemptible one we make in France and Holland; which, according to the substance of the notes, he attributes to the present feeble government.] An opinion has gone forth, we find, that we are contemptible people: the time has been when we were thought otherwise. Under the same despised government, we commanded the respect of all Europe: wherefore are we now reckoned otherwise? The American spirit has fled from hence: it has gone to regions where it has never been expected; it has gone to the people of France, in search of a splendid government—a strong, energetic government. Shall we imitate the example of those nations who have gone from a simple to a splendid government? Are those nations more worthy of our imitation? What can make an adequate satisfaction to them for the loss they have suffered in attaining such a government—for the loss of their liberty? If we admit this consolidated government, it will be because we like a great, splendid one. Some way or other we must be a great and mighty empire; we must have an army, and a navy, and a number of things. When the American spirit was in its youth, the language of America was different: liberty, sir, was then the primary object. We are descended from a people whose government was founded on liberty: our glorious forefathers of Great Britain made liberty the foundation of every thing. That country is become a great, mighty, and splendid nation; not because their government is strong and energetic, but, sir, because liberty is its direct end and foundation. We drew the spirit of liberty from our British ancestors: by that spirit we have triumphed over every difficulty. But now, sir, the American spirit, assisted by the ropes and chains of consolidation, is about to convert this country into a powerful and mighty empire. If you make the citizens of this country agree to become the subjects of one great consolidated empire of America, your government will not have sufficient energy to keep them together. Such a government is incompatible with the genius of republicanism. There will be no checks, no real balances, in this government. What can avail your specious, imaginary balances, your rope-dancing, chain-rattling, ridiculous ideal checks and contrivances? But, sir, we are not feared by foreigners; we do not make nations tremble. Would this constitute happiness, or secure liberty? I trust, sir, our political hemisphere will ever direct their operations to the security of those objectes.

*   *   *

This Constitution is said to have beautiful features; but when I come to examine these features, sir, they appear to me horribly frightful. Among other deformities, it has an awful squinting; it squints towards monarchy; and does not this raise indignation in the breast of every true American?

Your President may easily become king. Your Senate is so imperfectly constructed that your dearest rights may be sacrificed by what may be a small minority; and a very small minority may continue forever unchangeably this government, although horridly defective. Where are your checks in this government? Your strongholds will be in the hands of your enemies. It is on a supposition that your American governors shall be honest, that all the good qualities of this government are founded; but its defective and imperfect construction puts it in their power to perpetrate the worst of mischiefs, should they be bad men; and, sir, would not all the world, from the eastern to the western hemisphere, blame our distracted folly in resting our rights upon the contingency of our rulers being good or bad? Show me that age and country where the rights and liberties of the people were placed on the sole chance of their rulers being good men, without a consequent loss of liberty! I say that the loss of that dearest privilege has ever followed, with absolute certainty, every such mad attempt.

If your American chief be a man of ambition and abilities, how easy is it for him to render himself absolute! The army is in his hands, and if he be a man of address, it will be attached to him, and it will be the subject of long meditation with him to seize the first auspicious moment to accomplish his design; and, sir, will the American spirit solely relieve you when this happens? I would rather infinitely—and I am sure most of this Convention are of the same opinion—have a king, lords, and commons, than a government so replete with such insupportable evils. If we make a king, we may prescribe the rules by which he shall rule his people, and interpose such checks as shall prevent him from infringing them; but the President, in the field, at the head of his army, can prescribe the terms on which he shall reign master, so far that it will puzzle any American ever to get his neck from under the galling yoke. I cannot with patience think of this idea. If ever he violates the laws, one of two things will happen: he will come at the head of his army, to carry every thing before him; or he will give bail, or do what Mr. Chief Justice will order him. If he be guilty, will not the recollection of his crimes teach him to make one bold push for the American throne? will not the immense difference between being master of every thing, and being ignominiously tried and punished, powerfully excite him to make this bold push? But, sir, where is the existing force to punish him? Can he not, at the head of his army, beat down every opposition? Away with your President! we shall have a king: the army will salute him monarch: your militia will leave you, and assist in making him king, and fight against you: and what have you to oppose this force? What will then become of you and your rights? Will not absolute despotism ensue?

JAMES MADISON

Address to the House of Representatives on Amending the Constitution (1789)

During the ratification struggle in Virginia, Madison promised that he would promote changes to the Constitution. As a member of the first Congress, he fulfilled that promise by introducing a series of amendments addressing Anti-Federalist concerns about threats to individual liberty and state sovereignty. In a speech designed to conciliate the Constitution's opponents—many of whom were elected to Congress—Madison explained why it was necessary and proper to guard against abuses of power.

I t cannot be a secret to the gentlemen in this House, that, notwithstanding the ratification of this system of Government by eleven of the thirteen United States, in some cases unanimously, in others by large majorities; yet still there is a great number of our constituents who are dissatisfied with it; among whom are many respectable for their talents and patriotism, and respectable for the jealousy they have for their liberty, which, though mistaken in its object, is laudable in its motive. There is a great body of the people falling under this description, who at present feel much inclined to join their support to the cause of Federalism, if they were satisfied on this one point. We ought not to disregard their inclination, but, on principles of amity and moderation, conform to their wishes, and expressly declare the great rights of mankind secured under this constitution. The acquiescence which our fellow-citizens show under the Government, calls upon us for a like return of moderation. But perhaps there is a stronger motive than this for our going into a consideration of the subject. It is to provide those securities for liberty which are required by part of the community; I allude in a particular manner to those two States that have not thought fit to throw themselves into the bosom of the Confederacy. It is a desirable thing, on our part as well as theirs, that a re-union should take place as soon as possible. I have no doubt, if we proceed to take those steps which would be prudent and requisite at this juncture, that in a short time we should see that disposition prevailing in those States which have not come in, that we have seen prevailing in those States which have embraced the constitution.

But I will candidly acknowledge, that, over and above all these considerations, I do conceive that the constitution may be amended; that is to say, if all power is subject to abuse, that then it is possible the abuse of the powers of the General Government may be guarded against in a more secure manner than is now done, while no one advantage arising from the exercise of that power shall be damaged or endangered by it. We have in this way something to gain, and, if we proceed with caution, nothing to lose. And in this case it is necessary to proceed with caution; for while we feel all these inducements to go into a revisal of the constitution, we must feel for the constitution itself, and make that revisal a moderate one. I should be unwilling to see a door opened for a reconsideration of the whole structure of the Government—for a reconsideration of the principles and the substance of the powers given; because I doubt, if such a door were opened, we should be very likely to stop at that point which would be safe to the Government itself. But I do wish to see a door opened to consider, so far as to incorporate those provisions for the security of rights, against which I believe no serious objection has been made by any class of our constituents; such as would be likely to meet with the concurrence of two-thirds of both Houses, and the approbation of three-fourths of the State Legislatures. I will not propose a single alteration which I do not wish to see take place, as intrinsically proper in itself, or proper because it is wished for by a respectable number of my fellow-citizens; and therefore I shall not propose a single alteration but is likely to meet the concurrence required by the constitution. There have been objections of various kinds made against the constitution. Some were levelled against its structure because the President was without a council; because the Senate, which is a legislative body, had judicial powers in trials on impeachments; and because the powers of that body were compounded in other respects, in a manner that did not correspond with a particular theory; because it grants more power than is supposed to be necessary for every good purpose, and controls the ordinary powers of the State Governments. I know some respectable characters who oppose this Government on these grounds; but I believe that the great mass of the people who opposed it, disliked it because it did not contain effectual provisions against encroachments on particular rights, and those safeguards which they have been long accustomed to have interposed between them and the magistrate who exercises the sovereign power; nor ought we to consider them safe, while a great number of our fellow-citizens think these securities necessary.

It is a fortunate thing that the objection to the Government has been made on the ground I stated; because it will be practicable, on that ground, to obviate the objection, so far as to satisfy the public mind that their liberties will be perpetual, and this without endangering any part of the constitution, which is considered as essential to the existence of the Government by those who promoted its adoption.

The amendments which have occurred to me, proper to be recommended by Congress to the State Legislatures, are these:

First. That there be prefixed to the constitution a declaration, that all power is originally vested in, and consequently derived from, the people.

That Government is instituted and ought to be exercised for the benefit of the people; which consists in the enjoyment of life and liberty, with the right of acquiring and using property, and generally of pursuing and obtaining happiness and safety.

That the people have an indubitable, unalienable, and indefeasible right to reform or change their Government, whenever it be found adverse or inadequate to the purposes of its institution.

Secondly. That in article 1st, section 2, clause 3, these words be struck out, to-wit: "The number of Representatives shall not exceed one for every thirty thousand, but each State shall have at least one Representative, and until such enumeration shall be made;" and that in place thereof be inserted these words, to-wit: "After the first actual enumeration, there shall be one Representative for every thirty thousand, until the number amounts to _____, after which the proportion shall be so regulated by Congress, that the number shall never be less than _____, nor more than _____, but each State shall, after the first enumeration, have at least two Representatives; and prior thereto."

Thirdly. That in article 1st, section 6, clause 1, there be added to the end of the first sentence, these words, to-wit: "But no law varying the compensation last ascertained shall operate before the next ensuing election of Representatives."

Fourthly. That in article 1st, section 9, between clauses 3 and 4, be inserted these clauses, to-wit: The Civil rights of none shall be abridged on account of religious belief or worship, nor shall any national religion be established, nor shall the full and equal rights of conscience be in any manner or on any pretext, infringed.

The people shall not be deprived or abridged of their right to speak, to write, or to publish their sentiments; and the freedom of the press, as one of the great bulwarks of liberty, shall be inviolable.

The people shall not be restrained from peaceably assembling and consulting for their common good; nor from applying to the Legislature by petitions, or remonstrances, for redress of their grievances.

The right of the people to keep and bear arms shall not be infringed; a well armed and well regulated militia being the best security of a free country: but no person religiously scrupulous of bearing arms shall be compelled to render military service in person.

No soldier shall in time of peace be quartered in any house without the consent of the owner; nor at any time, but in a manner warranted by law.

No person shall be subject, except in cases of impeachment, to more than one punishment or one trial for the same offense; nor shall be compelled to be a witness against himself; nor be deprived of life, liberty, or property, without due process of law; nor be obliged to relinquish his property, where it may be necessary for public use, without a just compensation.

Excessive bail shall not be required, nor excessive fines imposed, nor cruel and unusual punishments inflicted.

The rights of the people to be secured in their persons; their houses, their papers, and their other property, from all unreasonable searches and seizures, shall not be violated by warrants issued without probable cause, supported by oath or affirmation, or not particularly describing the places to be searched, or the persons or things to be seized.

In all criminal prosecutions, the accused shall enjoy the right to a speedy and public trial, to be informed of the cause and nature of the accusation, to be confronted with his accusers, and the witnesses against him; to have a compulsory process for obtaining witnesses in his favor; and to have the assistance of counsel for his defense.

The exceptions here or elsewhere in the constitution, made in favor of particular rights, shall not be so construed as to diminish the just importance of other rights retained by the people, or as to enlarge the powers delegated by the constitution; but either as actual limitations of such powers, or as inserted merely for greater caution.

Fifthly. That in article 1st, section 10, between clauses 1 and 2, be inserted this clause, to-wit:

No State shall violate the equal rights of conscience, or the freedom of the press, or the trial by jury in criminal cases.

Sixthly. That, in article 3d, section 2, be annexed to the end of clause 2d, these words, to-wit:

But no appeal to such court shall be allowed where the value in controversy shall not amount to _____ dollars; nor shall any fact triable by jury, according to the course of common law, be otherwise re-examinable than may consist with the principles of common law.

Seventhly. That in article 3d, section 2, the third clause be struck out, and in its place be inserted the clauses following, to-wit:

The trial of all crimes (except in cases of impeachments, and cases arising in the land or naval forces, or the militia when on actual service, in time of war or public danger) shall be by an impartial jury of freeholders of the vicinage, with the requisite of unanimity for conviction, of the right of challenge, and other accustomed requisites; and in all crimes punishable with loss of life or member, presentment or indictment by a grand jury shall be an essential preliminary, provided that in cases of crimes committed within any county which may be in possession of an enemy, or in which a general insurrection many prevail, the trial may by law be authorized in some other county of the same State, as near as may be to the seat of the offence.

In cases of crimes committed not within any county, the trial may by law be in such county as the laws shall have prescribed. In suits at common law, between man and man, the trial by jury, as one of the best securities to the rights of the people, ought to remain inviolate.

Eighthly. That immediately after article 6th, be inserted, as article 7th, the clauses following, to-wit:

The powers delegated by this constitution are appropriated to the departments to which they are respectively distributed: so that the legislative department shall never exercise the powers vested in the executive or judicial nor the executive exercise the powers vested in the legislative or judicial, nor the judicial exercise the power vested in the legislative or executive departments.

The powers not delegated by this constitution, nor prohibited by it to the States, are reserved to the States respectively.

Ninthly. That article 7th be numbered as article 8th.

The first of these amendments relates to what may be called a bill of rights. I will own that I never considered this provision so essential to the federal constitution, as to make it improper to ratify it, until such an amendment was added; at the same time, I always conceived, that in a certain form, and to a certain extent, such a provision was neither improper nor altogether useless. I am aware, that a great number of the most respectable friends to the Government, and champions for republican liberty, have thought such a provision, not only unnecessary, but even improper; nay, I believe some have gone so far as to think it even dangerous. Some policy has been made use of, perhaps, by gentlemen on both sides of the question: I acknowledge the ingenuity of those arguments which were drawn against the constitution, by a comparison with the policy of Great Britain, in establishing a declaration of rights; but there is too great a difference in the case to warrant the comparison: therefore, the arguments drawn from that source were in a great measure inapplicable. In the declaration of rights which that country has established, the truth is, they have gone no farther than to raise a barrier against the power of the Crown; the power of the Legislature is left altogether indefinite. Although I know whenever the great rights, the trial by jury, freedom of the press, or liberty of conscience, come in question in that body, the invasion of them is resisted by able advocates, yet their Magna Charta does not contain any one provision for the security of those rights, respecting which the people of America are most alarmed. The freedom of the press and rights of conscience, those choicest privileges of the people, are unguarded in the British constitution.

But although the case may be widely different, and it may not be thought necessary to provide limits for the legislative power in that country, yet a different opinion prevails in the United States. The people of many States have thought it necessary to raise barriers against power in all forms and departments of Government, and I am inclined to believe, if once bills of rights are established in all the States, as well as the federal constitution, we shall find that although some of them are rather unimportant, yet, upon the whole they will have a salutary tendency.

It may be said, in some instances, they do no more than state the perfect equality of mankind. This, to be sure, is an absolute truth, yet it is not absolutely necessary to be inserted at the head of a constitution.

In some instances they assert those rights which are exercised by the peoples in forming and establishing a plan of Government. In other instances, they specify those rights which are retained when particular powers are given up to be exercised by the Legislature. In other instances, they specify positive rights, which may seem to result from the nature of the compact. Trial by jury cannot be considered as a natural right, but a right resulting from a social compact which regulates the action of the community, but is as essential to secure the liberty of the people as any one of the pre-existent rights of nature. In other instances, they lay down dogmatic maxims with respect to the construction of the Government; declaring that the legislative, executive, and judicial branches shall be kept separate and distinct. Perhaps the best way of securing this in practice is, to provide such checks as will prevent the encroachment of the one upon the other.

But whatever may be the form which the several States have adopted in making declarations in favor of particular rights, the great object in view is to limit and qualify the powers of Government, by excepting out of the grant of power those cases in which the Government ought not to act, or to act only in a particular mode. They point these exceptions sometimes against the abuse of the executive power, sometimes against the legislative, and, in some cases, against the community itself; or, in other words, against the majority in favor of the minority.

In our Government it is, perhaps, less necessary to guard against the abuse in the executive department than any other; because it is not the stronger branch of the system, but the weaker. It therefore must be levelled against the legislative, for it is the most powerful, and most likely to be abused, because it is under the least control. Hence, so far as a declaration of rights can tend to prevent the exercise of undue power, it cannot be doubted but such declaration is proper. But I confess that I do conceive, that in a Government modified like this of the United States, the great danger lies rather in the abuse of the community than in the legislative body. The prescriptions in favor of liberty ought to be levelled against that quarter where the greatest danger lies, namely, that which possesses the highest prerogative of power. But this is not found in either the executive or legislative departments of Government, but in the body of the people, operating by the majority against the minority.

It may be thought that all paper barriers against the power of the community are too weak to be worthy of attention. I am sensible they are not so strong as to satisfy gentlemen of every description who have seen and examined thoroughly the texture of such a defence; yet, as they have a tendency to impress some degree of respect for them, to establish the public opinion in their favor, and rouse the attention of the whole community, it may be one means to control the majority from those acts to which they might be otherwise inclined.

The Bill of Rights (1791)

Madison preferred to integrate amendments directly into the body of the existing Constitution, but the House decided to attach them at the end instead. Congress condensed Madison's proposals into twelve amendments, ten of which were eventually ratified by the states as the Bill of Rights. The two that failed ratification would have restricted pay raises for Congress members and increased the number of representatives. The Bill of Rights guarantees many of those individual rights and liberties that have come to define American freedom.

AMENDMENT I

Congress shall make no law respecting an establishment of religion, or prohibiting the free exercise thereof; or abridging the freedom of speech, or of the press; or the right of the people peaceably to assemble, and to petition the Government for a redress of grievances.

AMENDMENT II

A well regulated Militia, being necessary to the security of a free State, the right of the people to keep and bear Arms, shall not be infringed.

AMENDMENT III

No Soldier shall, in time of peace be quartered in any house, without the consent of the Owner, nor in time of war, but in a manner to be prescribed by law.

AMENDMENT IV

The right of the people to be secure in their persons, houses, papers, and effects, against unreasonable searches and seizures, shall not be violated, and no Warrants shall issue, but upon probable cause, supported by Oath or affirmation, and particularly describing the place to be searched, and the persons or things to be seized.

AMENDMENT V

No person shall be held to answer for a capital, or otherwise infamous crime, unless on a presentment or indictment of a Grand Jury, except in cases arising in the land or naval forces, or in the Militia, when an actual service in time of War or public danger; nor shall any person be subject for the same offence to be twice put in jeopardy of life or limb; nor shall be compelled in any criminal case to be a witness against himself, nor be deprived of life, liberty, or property, without due process of law; nor shall private property be taken for public use, without just compensation.

AMENDMENT VI

In all criminal prosecutions, the accused shall enjoy the right to a speedy and public trial, by an impartial Jury of the State and district wherein the crime shall have been committed, which district shall have been previously ascertained by law, and to be informed of the nature and cause of the accusation; to be confronted with the witness against him; to have compulsory process for obtaining witness in his favor, and to have the Assistance of Counsel for his defence.

AMENDMENT VII

In Suits at common law, where the value in controversy shall exceed twenty dollars, the right of trial by jury shall be preserved, and no fact tried by a jury, shall be otherwise re-examined in any Court of the United States, than according to the rules of the common law.

Amendment VIII

Excessive bail shall not be required, nor excessive fines imposed, nor cruel and unusual punishments inflicted.

Amendment IX

The enumeration in the Constitution, of certain rights, shall not be construed to deny or disparage others retained by the people.

Amendment X

The powers not delegated to the United States by the Constitution, nor prohibited by it to the States, are reserved to the States respectively, or to the people.

PART III

DEMOCRACY

AND UNION

1791–1865

The election of Thomas Jefferson in 1800 was the beginning of the end of the epoch of state building, with the activist Marshall Court soon to give definitive shape to the Constitution and the state. It also marked the routinization of ordinary politics, which had emerged for the first time in the second Washington administration, almost overwhelming it with divisive partisan warfare. The new American state would have a less than heroic politics of parties and partisanship. It was a rollicking politics, with undertones of mass democracy. It was an epoch during which new kinds of leaders searched for alternatives to a republican system of ideals and virtues led by self-anointed leaders from Virginia and Massachusetts. New leadership drove steadily toward universal male, non-slave suffrage in an increasingly mobile, fluid civil society. This new system adulterated the old eastern establishment by bringing in outsiders from the South and the West. The domination of the presidency by Virginia and Massachusetts state builders gave way to more of what Woodrow Wilson would call "congressional government," which was itself possible only with a party system.

This new arrangement persisted for about a century—from the 1830s to the 1930s. The Founders abjured political parties; Washington devoted a considerable part of his 1797 Farewell Address to the "baneful effects" of party. Yet, despite their protestations, party was essential to their vision. By 1797, Hamilton, Adams, Madison—almost everyone but Washington—had turned Federalism, an ideology, and the Federalists into a political party, thus ensuring that some kind of "anti-Federalism" would form in opposition. By 1800, over 90 percent of the members of the House of Representatives were regular, party-voting Federalists or Republicans.

Meanwhile, the theory of federalism was being realized in practice, as we have already suggested. Congress was consistently concerned with promoting commerce to foster a national common market by means beyond the jurisdiction of the individual states. With equal consistency, Congress left to the state legislatures the regulation of moral and social life. The national government became a patronage state, and the state governments became, collectively, a regulatory state. To the lower governments devolved the most divisive decisions that governments make.

Republics are inherently fragile. (The average life of a French republic—until the Fifth Republic in 1959—was roughly thirteen years.) The American republic endured in its original form for nearly two-thirds of its history. All the while, however, union and democracy, as well as liberalism and democracy, were on a collision course with the dark side of the American national character— slavery. Our signature characters in this period, Andrew Jackson and Abraham Lincoln, would have preferred to keep slavery off the national agenda. Among those pushing them the other way, providing a subtext, were Frederick Douglass, Harriet Beecher Stowe, and John C. Calhoun.

Andrew Jackson: The Presidency and Democracy

Andrew Jackson was one part rough-hewn western frontiersman and one part pragmatic aristocrat. He was a self-made American who benefited from a modest legacy left him by family remaining in Ireland. He was a lawyer with no legal training and little command of jurisprudence, but he was resourceful enough to make a good income representing creditors against those subsistence farmers and workers who were to become a major constituency for his Democratic party. Jackson came to national fame because of his role at the battle of New Orleans, with little ideological or larger vision. He showed none of the promise of young Abraham Lincoln. The historian Wilfred Binkley put it this way: "Social forces created the Jacksonian movement, and previous to his election to the presidency Jackson had not contributed one idea to it." In effect, Jackson was also self-made as president—the rich legacy he left was based on "on-the-job training."

Jackson was, instinctively, a democrat, especially by early nineteenth century standards. He broke the domination of the elites of the eastern seaboard by nationalizing American politics. Jackson replaced the nomination of presidential candidates by party caucuses in Congress ("King Caucus") with nomination in national party conventions. And (with the help of Martin Van Buren) Jackson restored the bottoms-up party organization that Jefferson had begun to develop but that had been set aside in the post-1812 "Era of Good Feeling." All this President Jackson did in direct contradiction of the antiparty position the popular General Jackson had taken in a letter to President-Elect Monroe in 1816, when he had written, "Now is the time to exterminate the monster called party spirit . . . [by] selecting characters . . . *without any regard to party*" (emphasis added).

Jackson's was the first truly modern party, built through a coalition of many competing parts—from the lower urban and rural classes to tidewater planters desperate for lower tariffs, to petty non-slave-owning planters, to Westerners oriented toward a rapid parceling out of public lands. The Democratic coalition was held together by Jackson's own larger-than-life, heroic personality, along with government patronage. In addition to public lands, patronage was in tariffs, various subsidies, and the placing of federal treasury deposits in "pet banks." There was also patronage in jobs, called the "spoils system" by the opposition and "rotation in office" by Jackson himself.

In fact, Jackson's defense of rotation in office may have been his major contribution to American democratic political thought. The basic premise of rotation in office became the slogan of his party: "One man is as good as another." His argument was not merely a rationalization of his goal of purging government of long-serving oligarchs and replacing them with cronies. His was genuinely a democrat's solution to a democrat's problem, which deserves quotation from his First Annual Message to Congress at some length:

> There are perhaps few men who can for any great length of time enjoy office and power without being more or less under the influence of feelings unfavorable to the faithful discharge of their public duties. . . . Office [comes to be] considered as a species of property, and government rather as a means of promoting individual interest. . . . The duties of all public officers are, or at least admit of being made, so plain and simple that men of intelligence may readily qualify themselves for their performance. . . . [M]ore is lost by the long continuance of men in office than is generally to be gained by their experience. . . . [N]o one man has any more intrinsic right to official station than another. . . . No individual wrong is, therefore, done by removal . . . and although individual stress may be sometimes produced, it would, by promoting *that rotation which constitutes a leading principle in the republican creed, give healthful action to the system.*

Equally important was Jackson's critique of aspects of emerging American capitalism. Although the term *capitalism* was not in use until 1848, Jackson was convinced that corporate forms of business were a threat to democracy, first because of their size and second because the corporate status given to them by government usually constituted privileged monopolies. This is why Jackson took on the Bank of the United States—the largest of all American corporations except for the U.S. government. The monopoly status of corporations was weakened by John Marshall's Supreme Court in *Dartmouth College v. Woodward* in 1819 and further weakened by the thoroughly Jacksonian Court under Chief Justice Taney in 1837, but Jackson and adherents of Jacksonianism still considered corporations a threat because they were artificial, legal fictions that had a life above and beyond their human participants. Political scientist Anne Norton best captures the Jacksonian case:

> Democrats, particularly agrarian democrats, were reluctant to accept the notion of the fictive personality [i.e., the legal fiction that corporations were "persons"] and the possession of rights by corporations. Men who adhered to a philosophy of natural rights were particularly incensed at the notion that fictive persons might have contractual rights equal (and, as it happened, ultimately superior) to those of persons by nature.

This Jacksonian fear would be confirmed by the Supreme Court in 1886 with its historic holding that a corporation was a person under the Fourteenth Amendment and was thus entitled to the due process and equal protection rights of that amendment. (See *Santa Clara County v. Southern Pacific Railroad* [1886].) Jacksonians feared the aristocratic nature of any titles, statuses, ranks, hierarchy, and other artificial distinctions. And they feared, as Norton notes, "the creation of an artificial system of valuation which superceded the natural rights, and natural equality, of all men." For Jacksonians, money had to be "hard money," that is, a metallic currency. Paper money, stocks, and bonds were not to be trusted. Neither were banks. Local banks were acceptable but not the corporate banks (namely, the Bank of the United States), which had the power to create money, to alter its value, and to speculate against changes in its value. For Jackson, a new economics should produce "material product," not just paper, which banks "spewed forth."

This application of home-grown economic ideology, which led to the destruction of the Second Bank of the United States, was more than mere southern, postfeudal, precapitalist hubris. It was also the application of an evolving political theory: a democracy of real people exercising the power of their presence in the executive branch, in legislatures and voting booths versus corporate structures, those fictitious persons exercising their power in remote, impersonal markets. The power of those markets meant that democracy was losing its grip just as it was coming into its own. Jackson had a primitive sense of the serious threat the new economy posed to the new democracy.

Slavery and States' Rights

Andrew Jackson was thus a great democrat, who as president contributed to the theory as well as the practice of democratic government. But there was another side to the Jacksonian character. A slaveholder, Jackson showed none of Jefferson's sense of guilt in the peculiar institution; and, as a general and as president, he took the lead in emptying the South of its Indian tribes.

Jackson was also a confirmed nationalist who favored western expansion. With equal intensity, Jackson opposed nullification—the idea that individual states could repudiate congressional action—even going so far as to issue a presidential proclamation that "the object of nullification is disunion and disunion by armed force is treason." This contributed to the intense competition mounted by the South to fill out the continent with new states, expanding slavery to a sufficient number of those new southern states to prevent the northern free states from gaining enough votes in Congress to abolish slavery by constitutional amendment.

These two issues, nullification and continental expansion, produced one of America's few genuine political theorists, John C. Calhoun. Calhoun, a South Carolinian, started out as a man of action, a political figure with qualities of character and ambition that made him presidential timber. He had been a thoroughgoing economic nationalist, the personal selection of John Quincy Adams to serve as vice president (1825–1829), and a supporter of Jackson in 1828, with every prospect of being Jackson's successor. But states' rights got in the way. National protective tariff policies had discriminated against South Carolina and other southern planter states, and the Tariff of 1828, the so-called Tariff of Abominations, was the last straw. Calhoun's theory of nullification in opposition to the tariff argued that a state could exercise its sovereign right to repeal a federal law insofar as it applied to that particular state. Considerably short of a theory of the sovereign right of secession, Calhoun's position made the strongest possible case for states' rights.

The Supreme Court provided a more practical way of blunting the threat to national unity posed by slavery. Issued in 1833, *Barron v. Baltimore* was the most important legal interpretation of the meaning of federalism since the Tenth Amendment was adopted in 1791.

One could almost say that the Civil War was fought to reverse *Barron* and that the Fourteenth Amendment contained the terms of the surrender of the Confederacy. John Barron owned a commercial wharf on the bay in Baltimore. The city dumped its excess excavation in the water, making the bay too shallow for cargo vessels. Barron sued the city, citing the Fifth Amendment: "private property [shall not be] taken for public use, without just compensation." When the case reached the Supreme Court, Chief Justice Marshall wrote an opinion that probably startled no educated person in 1833:

> The Constitution was ordained and established by the people of the United States, for their own government and not for the government of individual states. Each state established a constitution for itself. . . . If these propositions be correct, *the Fifth Amendment must be understood as restraining the powers of the General Government, not as applicable to the States.*

Barron informed Americans that the Constitution made state governments sovereign in matters of control over persons residing within their respective borders. And the Fugitive Slave Act of 1850, coupled with *Dred Scott v. Sandford* in 1857, dashed all hope that slavery would disappear spontaneously because it was incompatible with the national moral character and a modern capitalist economy.

Nor could the Union be preserved by the Jacksonian system of democratic politics. Abraham Lincoln was a product of that system but would be the link to the American future through the second American revolution, the Civil War. Yet the authors of that revolution were neither Lincoln nor any other professional politicians.

An intellectual, Harriet Beecher Stowe was the spark that lit the prairie fire. Stowe's *Uncle Tom's Cabin* was an antislavery novel, one of protest and prophecy. It was not written as a manifesto for a social movement, yet it is said to have earned from Lincoln the pronouncement that Stowe was "the little lady who made this big war." The novel sold over 300,000 copies in 1852, the year of its publication, and well over a million by the end of the Civil War—in a country of scarcely 25 million people. It was also dramatized in theater productions throughout the North.

Meanwhile, the great authors of the American Renaissance— Emerson, Thoreau, Hawthorne, and Melville—were not preoccupied with politics. Emerson and Thoreau did join Theodore Parker and the younger Thomas Wentworth Higginson in praising John Brown's antislavery martyrdom in particular and denouncing slavery in general as immoral, but they left their mark on individual emancipation in general rather than emancipation of slaves in particular. Thus, although the transcendentalists earned a place in intellectual history by articulating a strong individualist philosophy, they did not make a comparable contribution to the history of political thought because they did not pay sufficient attention to the place of the individual (white or black, slave or free) within the institutional and constitutional structures of the United States. Thoreau may have come closest to genuine political thought in "Resistance to Civil Government." He provides the closest connection between the transcendental covenant for the individual and democracy, abstractly, and the problem of the individual, democracy, and government, concretely:

> Those who, while they disapprove of the character and measures of a government, yield to it their allegiance and support are undoubtedly its most conscientious supporters, and so frequently the most serious obstacle to reform.

Abraham Lincoln: Law and the Constitution

Young Abraham Lincoln bore witness to the horrors of the slave system. Yet, though the story he told was heartfelt, he used it as part of an appeal to put aside the spirit of radical individualism, and civil disobedience, urging obedience to government and all its laws:

> Let every American . . . swear by the blood of the Revolution never to violate in the least particular the laws of the country. . . . [L]et me not be understood as saying there are no bad laws. . . . I mean to say that, although bad laws, if they exist, should be repealed as soon as possible, still while they continue in force . . . they should be religiously observed.

Lincoln was not ready in 1838 when he made that speech, nor was he ready in 1860, to confront the abolition of slavery head on. Although he was adamantly against compromising with the South, his was a pro-Union stand, which meant that he was also uncompromisingly against those who proposed voluntary or "peaceable dissolution." It was this staunch pro-Union stand that made his election to the presidency the last straw for the South.

Lincoln's pro-Union approach to the crisis may have appeared then as well as now to be the soft-pedaling or evasiveness of a presidential candidate in an election in which the critical issue of slavery was above and beyond compromise. Yet the sacred indissolubility of the Union was the principle that would elevate his arguments to a realm of political thought attained by few prominent authors of his day. This is why Lincoln provides our text (and Calhoun only the subtext) of this era of crisis and war over the fate of the "peculiar institution" of slavery and, through that, the fate of America's other, less peculiar institutions. And this is also why the political theorist Judith Shklar would describe Emerson as "the American philosopher . . . [who] tried to grasp and represent the entire world," whereas Lincoln and Calhoun could be studied for their contribution to *American* political thought.

Lincoln was capable of compromise. As late as 1845, he wrote, "I hold it to be a paramount duty of us in the free states, due to the Union of the States, and perhaps to liberty itself (paradox though it may seem) to let the slavery of the other states alone." Yet, he never wavered in his view that slavery was immoral. The concordance between these two contradictory positions was Madisonian and constitutionalist, a form of state-building or state-maintenance theory. If, thanks to the Fugitive Slave Act of 1850 and the Dred Scott decision of 1857, the Constitution as interpreted by the Supreme Court did not permit a state to exclude slavery, then Lincoln feared "we shall awake to the reality . . . that the Supreme Court has made [every free state] a slave State." Lincoln, the historian Richard Hofstadter claims, "took the slavery question out of the realm of moral and legal dispute [first] by dramatizing it in terms of free labor's self-interest . . . [and second by] emphasizing that slavery would become a nation-wide American institution if its geographical spread were not severely restricted at once." In another speech, Lincoln proclaimed that "preventing slavery from becoming a nation-wide institution is *the purpose* of [the Republican party]" (emphasis added). Lincoln was never apologetic in his racist view that Africans were an inferior race, though he did hold the then courageous view that blacks were equal to whites in having a right to enjoy the fruits of their labor.

Lincoln and Calhoun could hardly have been further apart on the morality of slavery and the right of slave states to remain slave states within the Constitution. But they were not far apart in their approaches to a solution to the problem of disunion. Calhoun, like

Lincoln, looked back to the political thought of the great American state builders. This is why he—although like Lincoln a man of action with a career in politics—is ranked by Hofstadter even above Lincoln as "a brilliant if narrow dialectician, probably the last American statesman to do any primary political thinking." We can apply the same characterization to Lincoln, who, following Madison, was also a "narrow dialectician" trying valiantly to find a structural or institutional solution to substantive moral problems.

Calhoun's basic premise was the same as Madison's, the rights of minorities and their protection against the "tyranny of the majority." His first issue, as alluded to earlier, was the tariff that would, he argued, convert the southern planter states into "the serfs of the system" unless states had the right to declare an obnoxious national law null and void. The failure of nullification pushed Calhoun to a higher level of generality, toward genuine political theory in *A Disquisition on Government*, published in 1848, the same year as Marx and Engel's *Communist Manifesto*. The coincidence goes even deeper, inasmuch as both Calhoun and Marx, without any awareness of each other, relied heavily on John Locke's labor theory of value. Calhoun was not alone in praising slavery as superior to "free labor" in its allegedly more humane treatment of workers. For example, he was joined by the more radical and at the time more widely read George Fitzhugh, whose 1854 book, *Sociology for the South*, carried the proslavery argument, as he put it, "to its logical conclusion": slavery for the North. Lincoln read it and was disgusted by it. But Calhoun was unique in proposing a new American constitution without need of a new revolution. His theory of "concurrent majorities" posited that each state (especially each slave state) comprised "organic communities" whose "concurrent voice" would work like Rousseau's "general will." They represented the true voice of each state in acquiescing to or vetoing an executive action or a law passed by Congress. To top off Calhoun's constitutional system, there would be two presidents—one for each of the two recognized sections—free and slave—each having power to veto acts of Congress in response to the will of the respective states. This is confederation with a vengeance! It was an institutional, structural solution, as Judith Shklar notes, adding to the "checks and balances" already embedded in the Constitution "an intricate system of vetoes" to protect minorities and to "stem the tide of political decay."

But this vital subtext to the debate over slavery and union ultimately did not provide a viable route to a new American synthesis.

Enter Lincoln, the constitutional conservative, who as a young politician had counseled obedience to law and faith in the Constitution. Like Calhoun, Lincoln adhered to the Founders' preference for institutions and procedures rather than confronting policy differences head on. After all, this was the approach taken in 1787 with the infamous Three-fifths Compromise to determine representation in the House of Representatives in Article I, Section 2: "Representatives . . . shall be apportioned among the several States . . . according to their respective Numbers, which shall be determined by adding to the Whole Number of free Persons . . . *three-fifths of all other Persons*" (emphasis added). In return, the South agreed that Congress would have power to prohibit the importation of slaves (a far cry from actually abolishing slavery), but only after 1808. These provisions were eliminated in 1868 by the Fourteenth Amendment.

Lincoln had been conspicuously silent about slavery during the months preceding the 1860 election. William H. Seward, the leading candidate for the Republican presidential nomination, probably lost his chance because he appeared too extreme not only to moderates but to men as radical on slavery as he was. The most widely shared second choice for president, Lincoln "waged one of the most laconic campaigns in history," according to the historian David Potter. This "unusual silence" arose out of "Lincoln's firm conviction that sectional antagonism fed upon discussion of sectional issues." Lincoln's "policy of silence" continued through the election and through President Buchanan's "lame duck" administration while waiting for his inauguration, which took place on March 4, 1861. Yet Lincoln's reticence did not lessen southern resolve to secede.

Lincoln broke his silence in his first inaugural address, delivered to a Congress from which seven southern states had already seceded. In that speech, Lincoln revealed his radicalism. He was adamant on two things. The institution of slavery—where it stood in 1860—would *not* be interfered with; and the Constitution would *not* be altered to accommodate that institution. Calhoun's Constitution had served his conservatism. Lincoln's conservatism had served his Constitution.

In 1865, the bloodiest and costliest war in American history was won and the Union was saved. But was this second American revolution complete? With compensated emancipation that would end slavery without destroying the capital of slaveholders, Lincoln at first sought to save the Union by betraying that revolution. He announced the plan in his second State of the Union message in February 1862, combining it with an ill-defined proposal for repatriation of the freed slaves. Since the Emancipation Proclamation had an immediate effect on very few slaves, the real victory of the Union came three years after the war with the Fourteenth Amendment, which in effect, reversed *Barron v. Baltimore* in a single sentence: "All persons born and naturalized in the United States, and subject to the jurisdiction thereof, are citizens of the United States *and of the state wherein they reside*." When rights were nationalized, the Union would be, at last, "one nation, indivisible."

BIBLIOGRAPHY

Binkley, Wilfred. *American Political Parties: Their Natural History.* New York: Knopf, 1962.

Hofstadter, Richard. *The American Political Tradition.* New York: Knopf, 1948.

Lincoln, Abraham. "The Perpetuation of Our Political Institutions." Address before the Young Men's Lyceum of Springfield, Illinois, January 27, 1838. In *Collected Works of Abraham Lincoln*, vol.1, pp.108–15. Ann Arbor: University of Michigan Digital Library Production Services, 2001. http://name.umdl.umich.edu/lincoln1.

Norton, Anne. *Alternative Americas: A Reading of Antebellum Political Culture.* Chicago: University of Chicago Press, 1986.

Potter, David. *Lincoln and His Party in the Secession Crisis.* Baton Rouge: Louisiana State University Press, 1995.

Shklar, Judith N. *Redeeming American Political Thought.* Chicago: University of Chicago Press, 1998.

The Federalist and Jeffersonian Visions

ALEXANDER HAMILTON

First Report on the Public Credit (1790)

The various states and the national government had accumulated an enormous public debt as a result of the Revolutionary War. In response to a request by Congress for information on the state of the debt, Secretary of the Treasury Hamilton proposed a plan that would fund the debt, repay current holders of government securities instead of original buyers, and have the national government assume the debts of the states. Even though his recommendations drew strong criticism, Hamilton's scheme was adopted and helped restore the nation's credit. Hamilton hoped that his plan to pay interest to holders of the public debt would lead wealthy Americans to identify their own financial interests with the strength of the national government.

The Secretary of the Treasury ＊ ＊ ＊ has felt, in no small degree, the anxieties which naturally flow ＊ ＊ ＊ from a deep and solemn conviction of the momentous nature of the truth contained in the resolution under which his investigations have been conducted,—'That an adequate provision for the support of the public credit is a matter of high importance to the honor and prosperity of the United States.' ＊ ＊ ＊

In the opinion of the Secretary, the wisdom of the House, in giving their explicit sanction to the proposition which has been stated, cannot but be applauded by all who will seriously consider and trace, through their obvious consequences, these plain and undeniable truths:

That exigencies are to be expected to occur, in the affairs of nations, in which there will be a necessity for borrowing.

That loans in time of public danger, especially from foreign war, are found an indispensable resource, even to the wealthiest of them.

And that, in a country which, like this, is possessed of little active wealth, or, in other words, little moneyed capital, the necessity for that resource must, in such emergencies, be proportionably urgent.

And as, on the one hand, the necessity for borrowing in particular emergencies cannot be doubted, so, on the other, it is equally evident that, to be able to borrow upon good terms, it is essential that the credit of a nation should be well established. * * *

To attempt to enumerate the complicated variety of mischiefs, in the whole system of the social economy, which proceed from a neglect of the maxims that uphold public credit, and justify the solicitude manifested by the House on this point, would be an improper intrusion on their time and patience.

In so strong a light, nevertheless, do they appear to the Secretary, that, on their due observance, at the present critical juncture, materially depends, in his judgment, the individual and aggregate prosperity of the citizens of the United States; their relief from the embarrassments they now experience; their character as a people; the cause of good government.

If the maintenance of public credit, then, be truly so important, the next inquiry which suggests itself is: By what means is it to be effected? The ready answer to which question is, by good faith; by a punctual performance of contracts. States, like individuals, who observe their engagements are respected and trusted, while the reverse is the fate of those who pursue an opposite conduct.

Every breach of the public engagements, whether from choice or necessity, is, in different degrees, hurtful to public credit. When such a necessity does truly exist, the evils of it are only to be palliated by a scrupulous attention, on the part of the Government, to carry the violation no further than the necessity absolutely requires, and to manifest, if the nature of the case admit of it, a sincere disposition to make reparation whenever circumstances shall permit. But, with every possible mitigation, credit must suffer, and numerous mischiefs ensue. It is, therefore, highly important, when an appearance of necessity seems to press upon the public councils, that they should examine well its reality, and be perfectly assured that there is no method of escaping from it, before they yield to its suggestions. For, though it cannot safely be affirmed that occasions have never existed, or may not exist, in which violations of the public faith, in this respect, are inevitable; yet there is great reason to believe that they exist far less frequently than precedents indicate, and are oftenest either pretended, through levity or want of firmness; or supposed, through want of knowledge. Expedients often have been devised to effect, consistently with good faith, what has been done in contravention of it. Those who are most commonly creditors of a nation, are generally speaking, enlightened men; and there are signal examples to warrant a conclusion that, when a candid and fair appeal is made to them they will understand their true interest too well to refuse their concurrence in such modifications of their claims as any real necessity may demand.

While the observance of that good faith, which is the basis of public credit, is recommended by the strongest inducements of political expediency, it is enforced by considerations of still greater authority. These are arguments for it which rest on the immutable principles of moral obligation. And in proportion as the mind is disposed to contemplate, in the order of Providence, an intimate connection between public virtue and public happiness, will be its repugnancy to a violation of those principles.

This reflection derives additional strength from the nature of the debt of the United States. It was the price of liberty. The faith of America has been repeatedly pledged for it, and with solemnities that give peculiar force to the obligation. There is, indeed, reason to regret that it has not hitherto been kept; that the necessities of the war, conspiring with inexperience in the subjects of finance, produced direct infractions; and that the subsequent period has been a continued scene of negative violation or non-compliance. But a diminution of this regret arises from the reflection, that the last seven years have exhibited an earnest and uniform effort, on the part of the Government of the Union, to retrieve the national credit, by doing justice to the creditors of the nation; and that the embarrassments of a defective Constitution, which defeated this laudable effort, have ceased.

From this evidence of a favorable disposition given by the former Government, the institution of a new one, clothed with powers competent to calling forth the resources of the community, has excited correspondent expectations. A general belief accordingly prevails, that the credit of the United States will quickly be established on the firm foundation of an effectual provision for the existing debt. The influence which this has had at home is witnessed by the rapid increase that has taken place in the market value of the public securities. From January to November, they rose thirty-three and a third per cent.; and, from that period to this time, they have risen fifty per cent. more; and the intelligence from abroad announces effects proportionably favorable to our national credit and consequence.

It cannot but merit particular attention, that, among ourselves, the most enlightened friends of good government are those whose expectations are the highest.

To justify and preserve their confidence; to promote the increasing respectability of the American name; to answer the calls of justice; to restore landed property to its due value; to furnish new resources, both to agriculture and commerce; to cement more closely the union of the

States; to add to their security against foreign attack; to establish public order on the basis of an upright and liberal policy;—these are the great and invaluable ends to be secured by a proper and adequate provision, at the present period, for the support of public credit.

To this provision we are invited, not only by the general considerations which have been noticed, but by others of a more particular nature. It will procure, to every class of the community, some important advantages, and remove some no less important disadvantages.

The advantage to the public creditors, from the increased value of that part of their property which constitutes the public debt, needs no explanation.

But there is a consequence of this, less obvious, though not less true, in which every other citizen is interested. It is a well-known fact, that, in countries in which the national debt is properly funded, and an object of established confidence, it answers most of the purposes of money. Transfers of stock or public debt are there equivalent to payments in species; or, in other words, stock in the principal transactions of business, passes current as specie. The same thing would, in all probability, happen here under the like circumstances.

The benefits of this are various and obvious:

First.—Trade is extended by it, because there is a larger capital to carry it on, and the merchant can, at the same time, afford to trade for smaller profits; as his stock, which, when unemployed, brings him an interest from the Government, serves him also as money when he has a call for it in his commercial operations.

Secondly.—Agriculture and manufactures are also promoted by it, for the like reason, that more capital can be commanded to be employed in both; and because the merchant, whose enterprise in foreign trade gives to them activity and extension, has greater means for enterprise.

Thirdly.—The interest of money will be lowered by it; for this is always in a ratio to the quantity of money, and to the quickness of circulation. This circumstance will enable both the public and individuals to borrow on easier and cheaper terms.

And from the combination of these effects, additional aids will be furnished to labor, to industry, and to arts of every kind. * * *

Having now taken a concise view of the inducements to a proper provision for the public debt, the next enquiry which presents itself is, what ought to be the nature of such a provision? This requires some preliminary discussions.

It is agreed on all hands, that the part of the debt which has been contracted abroad, and is denominated the foreign debt, ought to be provided for, according to the precise terms of the contracts relating to it.

The discussions, which can arise, therefore, will have reference essentially to the domestic part of it, or to that which has been contracted at home. It is to be regretted, that there is not the same unanimity of sentiment on this part as on the other.

The Secretary has too much deference for the opinions of every part of the community, not to have observed one, which has, more than once, made its appearance in the public prints, and which is occasionally to be met with in conversation. It involves this question, whether a discrimination ought not be made between original holders of the public securities, and present possessors, by purchase. Those who advocate a discrimination are for making a full provision for the securities of the former, at their nominal value; but contend, that the latter ought to receive no more than the cost to them, and the interest: And the idea is sometimes suggested of making good the difference to the primitive possessor.

In favor of this scheme, it is alledged, that it would be unreasonable to pay twenty shillings in the pound, to one who had not given more for it than three or four. And it is added, that it would be hard to aggravate the misfortune of the first owner, who, probably through necessity, parted with his property at so great a loss, by obliging him to contribute to the profit of the person, who had speculated on his distresses.

The Secretary, after the most mature reflection on the force of this argument, is induced to reject the doctrine it contains, as equally unjust and impolitic, as highly injurious, even to the original holders of public securities; as ruinous to public credit.

It is inconsistent with justice, because in the first place, it is a breach of contract; in violation of the rights of a fair purchaser.

The nature of the contract in its origin, is, that the public will pay the sum expressed in the security, to the first holder, or his *assignee*. The *intent*, in making the security assignable, is, that the proprietor may be able to make use of his property, by selling it for as much as it *may be worth in the market*, and that the buyer may be *safe* in the purchase.

Every buyer therefore stands exactly in the place of the seller, has the same rights with him to the identical sum expressed in the security, and having acquired that right, by fair purchase, and in conformity to the original *agreement* and *intention* of the government, his claim cannot be disputed, without manifest injustice.

That he is to be considered as a fair purchaser, results from this: Whatever necessity the seller may have been under, was occasioned by the government, in not making a proper provision for its debts. The buyer had no agency in it, and therefore ought not to suffer. He is not even chargeable with having taken an undue advantage. He paid what the commodity was worth in the market, and took the risks of reimbursement upon himself. He, of course, gave a fair equivalent, and ought to reap the benefit of his hazard; a hazard which was far from inconsiderable, and which, perhaps, turned on little less than a revolution in government.

That the case of those, who parted with their securities from necessity, is a hard one, cannot be denied. But whatever complaint of injury, or claim of redress, they may have, respects the government solely. They have not only nothing to object to the persons who relieved their necessities, by giving them the current price of their property, but they are even under an implied condition to contribute to the reimbursement of those persons. They knew, that by the terms of the contract with themselves, the public were bound to pay to those, to whom they should convey their title, the sums stipulated to be paid to them; and, that as citizens of the United States, they were to bear their proportion of the contribution for that purpose.

* * *

But though many of the original holders sold from necessity, it does not follow, that this was the case with all of them. It may well be supposed, that some of them did it either through want of confidence in an eventual provision, or from the allurements of some profitable speculation. How shall it be ascertained, in any case, that the money, which the original holder obtained for his security, was not more beneficial to him, than if he had held it to the present time, to avail himself of the provision which shall be made? How shall it be known, whether if the purchaser had employed his money in some other way, he would not be in a better situation, than by having applied it in the purchase of securities, though he should now receive their full amount? And if neither of these things can be known, how shall it be determined whether a discrimination, independent of the breach of contract, would not do a real injury to purchasers; and if it included a compensation to the primitive proprietors, would not give them an advantage, to which they had no equitable pretension.

It may well be imagined, also, that there are not wanting instances, in which individuals, urged by a present necessity, parted with the securities received by them from the public, and shortly after replaced them with others, as an indemnity for their first loss. Shall they be deprived of the indemnity which they have endeavoured to secure by so provident an arrangement?

Questions of this sort, on a close inspection, multiply themselves without end, and demonstrate the injustices of a discrimination, even on the most subtile calculations of equity, abstracted from the obligation of contract.

The difficulties too of regulating the details of a plan for that purpose, which would have even the semblance of equity, would be found immense.

It may well be doubted whether they would not be insurmountable, and replete with such absurd, as well as inequitable consequences, as to disgust even the proposers of the measure. * * *

But there is still a point in view in which it will appear perhaps even more exceptionable, than in either of the former. It would be repugnant to an express provision of the Constitution of the United States. This provision is, that "all debts contracted and engagements entered into before the adoption of that Constitution shall be as valid against the United States under it, as under the confederation," which amounts to a constitutional ratification of the contracts respecting the debt, in the state in which they existed under the confederation. And resorting to that standard, there can be no doubt, that the rights of assignees and original holders, must be considered as equal. * * *

The Secretary concluding, that a discrimination, between the different classes of creditors of the United States, cannot with propriety be *made,* proceeds to examine whether a difference ought to be permitted to *remain* between them, and another description of public creditors—those of the states individually.

The Secretary, after mature reflection on this point, entertains a full conviction, that an assumption of the debts of the particular states by the union, and a like provision for them, as for those of the union, will be a measure of sound policy and substantial justice.

It would, in the opinion of the Secretary, contribute, in an eminent degree, to an orderly stable and satisfactory arrangement of the national finances.

Admitting, as ought to be the case, that a provision must be made in some way or other, for the entire debt; it will follow, that no greater revenues will be required, whether that provision be made wholly by the United States, or partly by them, and partly by the states separately.

The principal question then must be, whether such a provision cannot be more conveniently and effectually made, by one general plan issuing from one authority, than by different plans or originating in different authorities. * * *

If all the public creditors receive their dues from one source, distributed with an equal hand, their interest will be the same. And having the same interests, they will unite in the support of the fiscal arrangements of the government: As these, too, can be made with more convenience, where there is no competition: These circumstances combined will insure to the revenue laws a more ready and more satisfactory execution.

If on the contrary there are distinct provisions, there will be distinct interests, drawing different ways. That union and concert of views, among the creditors, which in every government is of great importance to their security, and to that of public credit, will not only not exist, but will be likely to give place to mutual jealousy and opposition. And from this cause, the operation of the systems which may be adopted, both by the particular states, and by the union, with relation to their respective debts, will be in danger of being counteracted.

There are several reasons, which render it probable, that the situation of the state creditors would be worse, than that of the creditors of the union, if there be not a national assumption of the state debts. Of these it will be sufficient to mention two; one, that a principal branch of revenue is exclusively vested in the union; the other, that a state must always be checked in the imposition of taxes on articles of consumption, from the want of power to extend the same regulation to the other states, and from the tendency of partial duties to injure its industry and commerce. Should the state creditors stand upon a less eligible footing than the others, it is unnatural to expect they would see with pleasure a provision for them. The influence which their dissatisfaction might have, could not but operate injuriously, both for the creditors, and the credit, of the United States.

* * *

Deeply impressed, as the Secretary is, with a full and deliberate conviction, that the establishment of public credit, upon the basis of a satisfactory provision, for the public debt is, under the present circumstances of this country, the true desideratum towards relief from individual and national embarrassments will be likely to press still more severely upon the community—He cannot but indulge an anxious wish, that an effectual plan for that purpose may, during the present session, be the result of the united wisdom of the legislature.

ALEXANDER HAMILTON

Opinion on the Constitutionality of the Bank (1791)

Hamilton's proposal to charter a national bank with the power to issue bank notes resulted in one of the first great debates over the meaning of the Constitution. Written in response to Washington's request for advice on the bank question, Hamilton's argument that the creation of a bank was "necessary and proper" established the tradition of "loose constructionism." According to Hamilton's theory of constitutional interpretation,

the implied powers of government are just as valid and important as its
expressed powers. His view prevailed.

I n entering upon the argument it ought to be premised that the objections of the Secretary of State and the Attorney-General are founded on a general denial of the authority of the United States to erect corporations. The latter, indeed, expressly admits, that if there be anything in the bill which is not warranted by the Constitution, it is the clause of incorporation.

Now it appears to the Secretary of the Treasury that this *general principle* is *inherent* in the very *definition* of government, and *essential* to every step of the progress to be made by that of the United States, namely: That every power vested in a government is in its nature *sovereign*, and includes, by *force* of the *term*, a right to employ all the *means* requisite and fairly applicable to the attainment of the *ends* of such power, and which are not precluded by restrictions and exceptions specified in the Constitution, or not immoral, or not contrary to the *essential ends* of political society.

If it would be necessary to bring proof to a proposition so clear, as that which affirms that the powers of the federal government, as to *its objects*, were sovereign, there is a clause of its Constitution which would be decisive. It is that which declares that the Constitution, and the laws of the United States made in pursuance of it, * * * shall be the *supreme law of the land*. The power which can create the *supreme law of the land*, in any case, is doubtless *sovereign* as to such case.

This general and indisputable principle puts at once an end to the *abstract* question, whether the United States have power to erect a corporation; that is to say, to give a *legal* or *artificial capacity* to one or more persons, distinct from the *natural*. For it is unquestionably incident to *sovereign power* to erect corporations, and consequently to *that* of the United States, in *relation* to the *objects* intrusted to the management of the government. The difference is this: where the authority of the government is general, it can create corporations in *all cases*; where it is confined to certain branches of legislation, it can create corporations *only* in those cases.

It is not denied that there are *implied* as well as *expressed powers*, and that the *former* are as effectually delegated as the *latter*. And for the sake of accuracy it shall be mentioned, that there is another class of powers, which may be properly denominated *resulting powers*. It will not be doubted, that if the United States should make a conquest of any of the territories of its neighbours, they would possess sovereign jurisdiction over the conquered territory. This would be rather a result from the whole mass of the powers of the government, and from the nature of political society, than a consequence of either of the powers specially enumerated. * * *

It is conceded that *implied powers* are to be considered as delegated equally with *expressed ones*. Then it follows, that as a power of erecting a corporation may as well be *implied* as any other thing, it may as well be employed as an *instrument* or *means* of carrying into execution any of the specified powers, as any other *instrument* or *means* whatever. The only question must be, in this, as in every other case, whether the means to be employed, or, in this instance, the corporation to be erected, has a natural relation to any of the acknowledged objects or lawful ends of the government. Thus a corporation may not be erected by Congress for superintending the police of the city of Philadelphia, because they are not authorized to *regulate* the *police* of that city. But one may be erected in relation to the collection of taxes, or to the trade with foreign countries, or to the trade between the States, or with the Indian tribes; because it is the province of the federal government to *regulate* those objects, and because it is incident to a general *sovereign* or *legislative* power to *regulate* a thing, to employ all the means which relate to its regulation to the best and greatest advantage.

Through this mode of reasoning respecting the right of employing all the means requisite to the execution of the specified powers of the government, it is to be objected, that none but necessary and proper means are to be employed; and the Secretary of State maintains, that no means are to be considered *necessary* but those without which the grant of the power would be *nugatory*. * * *

It is essential to the being of the national government, that so erroneous a conception of the meaning of the word *necessary* should be exploded.

It is certain, that neither the grammatical nor popular sense of the term requires that construction. According to both, *necessary* often means no more than *needful, requisite, incidental, useful,* or *conducive to*. * * * And it is the true one in which it is to be understood as used in the Constitution. The whole turn of the clause containing it indicates, that it was the intent of the Convention, by that clause, to give a liberal latitude to the exercise of the specified powers. The expressions have peculiar comprehensiveness. They are, "to make all *laws* necessary and proper for *carrying into execution* the *foregoing powers,* and all *other powers,* vested by the Constitution in the *government* of the United States, or in any *department* or *officer* thereof."

To understand the word as the Secretary of State does, would be to depart from its obvious and popular sense, and to give it a restrictive operation, an idea never before entertained. It would be to give it the same force as if the word *absolutely* or *indispensably* had been prefixed to it. * * *

The *degree* in which a measure is necessary, can never be a *test* of the legal right to adopt it; that must be a matter of opinion, and can only be a *test* of expediency. The *relation* between the *measure* and the *end*; between the *nature* of the *means* employed towards the execution of a power, and the object of that power, must be the criterion of constitutionality, not the more or less of *necessity* or *utility*. ＊ ＊ ＊

This restrictive interpretation of the word *necessary* is also contrary to this sound maxim of construction; namely, that the powers contained in a constitution of government, especially those which concern the general administration of the affairs of a country, its finances, trade, defence &c., ought to be construed liberally in advancement of the public good. ＊ ＊ ＊ The means by which national exigencies are to be provided for, national inconveniences obviated, national prosperity promoted, are of such infinite variety, extent, and complexity, that there must of necessity be great latitude of discretion in the selection and application of those means. Hence, consequently, the necessity and propriety of exercising the authorities intrusted to a government on principles of liberal construction. ＊ ＊ ＊

But the doctrine which is contended for is not chargeable with the consequences imputed to it. It does not affirm that the National Government is sovereign in all respects, but that it is sovereign to a certain extent; that it is, to the extent of the objects of its specified powers.

It leaves, therefore, a criterion of what is constitutional, and of what is not so. This criterion is the *end*, to which the measure relates as a *means*. If the *end* be clearly comprehended within any of the specified powers, and if the measure have an obvious relation to that *end*, and is not forbidden by any particular provision of the Constitution, it may safely be deemed to come within the compass of the national authority. There is also this further criterion, which may materially assist the decision; Does the proposed measure abridge a pre-existing right of any State or of any individual? If it does not, there is a strong presumption in favor of its constitutionality, and slighter relations to any declared object of the Constitution may be permitted to turn the scale. ＊ ＊ ＊

It is presumed to have been satisfactorily shown in the course of the preceding observations:

1. That the power of the government, as to the objects intrusted to its management, is, in its nature, sovereign.
2. That the right of erecting corporations is one inherent in, and inseparable from, the idea of sovereign power.
3. That the position, that the government of the United States can exercise no power but such as is delegated to it by its Constitution, does not militate against this principle.
4. That the word *necessary*, in the general clause, can have no *restrictive*

operation derogating from the force of this principle; indeed, that the degree in which a measure is or is not *necessary*, cannot be a *test* of *constitutional right*, but of *expediency only*.

5. That the power to erect corporations is not to be considered as an *independent* or *substantive* power, but as an *incidental* and *auxiliary* one, and was therefore more properly left to implication than expressly granted.

6. That the principle in question does not extend the power of the government beyond the prescribed limits, because it only affirms a power to *incorporate* for purposes *within the sphere* of the *specified powers*.

And lastly, that the right to exercise such a power in certain cases is unequivocally granted in the most *positive* and *comprehensive* terms. * * *

To all which it only remains to be added that such a power has actually been exercised in two very imminent instances: namely in the erection of two governments one, northwest of the river Ohio, and the other southwest—the *last, independent of any antecedent compact*. And there results a full and complete demonstration, that the Secretary of State and Attorney General are mistaken, when they deny generally the power of the National government to erect corporations.

It shall now be endeavoured to be shewn that there is a power to erect one of the kind proposed by the bill. This will be done, by tracing a natural and obvious relation between the institution of a bank, and the objects of several of the enumerated powers of the government; and by shewing that, *politically* speaking, it is necessary to the effectual execution of one or more of those powers. In the course of this investigation, various instances will be stated, by way of illustration of a right to erect corporation under those powers. * * *

A Bank relates to the collection of taxes in two ways; *indirectly*, by increasing the quantity of circulating medium and quickening circulation, which facilitates the means of paying—*directly*, by creating a *convenient species* of *medium* in which they are to be paid. * * *

A Bank has a direct relation to the power of borrowing money, because it is an usual and in sudden emergencies an essential instrument in the obtaining of loans to government.

A nation is threatened with war. Large sums are wanted, on a sudden, to make the requisite preparations. Taxes are laid for the purpose, but it requires time to obtain the benefit of them. Anticipation is indispensable. If there be a bank, the supply can, at once be had; if there be none loans from Individuals must be sought. The progress of these is often too slow for the exigency; in some situations they are not practicable at all. Frequently when they are, it is of great consequence to be able to anticipate the product of them by advances from a bank.

The essentiality of such an institution as an instrument of loans is exemplified at this very moment. An Indian expedition is to be prosecuted. The only fund out of which the money can arise consistently with the public engagements, is a tax which will only begin to be collected in July next. The preparations, however, are instantly to be made. The money must therefore be borrowed. And of whom could it be borrowed, if there were no public banks? * * *

The institution of a bank has also a natural relation to the regulation of trade between the States: in so far as it is conducive to the creation of a convenient medium of *exchange* between them, and to the keeping up a full circulation by preventing the frequent displacement of the metals in reciprocal remittances. Money is the very hinge on which commerce turns. And this does not mean merely gold and silver, many other things have served the purpose with different degrees of utility. Paper has been extensively employed. * * *

The very general power of laying and collecting taxes and appropriating their proceeds—that of borrowing money indefinitely—that of coining money and regulating foreign coins—that of making all needful rules and regulations respecting the property of the United States—these powers combined, as well as the reason and nature of the thing speak strongly this language: That it is the manifest design and scope of the constitution to vest in Congress all the powers requisite to the effectual administration of the finances of the United States. As far as concerns this object, there appears to be no parsimony of power.

ALEXANDER HAMILTON

Report on Manufactures (1791)

Early in 1790, the House asked Hamilton to develop a strategy that would make the United States less dependent on imports of foreign manufactures, especially military supplies. In the final report detailing his vision of economic nationalism, the treasury secretary enthusiastically endorsed the use of government power to promote the development of domestic manufacturing as part of a well-balanced economy. The report reveals Hamilton's foresight in welcoming

America's anticipated transition from a modest, agrarian economy to a powerful, industrial one.

The expediency of encouraging manufactures in the United States, which was not long since deemed very questionable, appears at this time to be pretty generally admitted. The embarrassments which have obstructed the progress of our external trade, have led to serious reflections on the necessity of enlarging the sphere of our domestic commerce. The restrictive regulations, which, in foreign markets, abridge the vent of the increasing surplus of our agricultural produce, serve to beget an earnest desire that a more extensive demand for that surplus may be created at home; and the complete success which has rewarded manufacturing enterprise in some valuable branches, conspiring with the promising symptoms which attend some less mature essays in others, justify a hope that the obstacles to the growth of this species of industry are less formidable than they were apprehended to be, and that it is not difficult to find, in its further extension, a full indemnification for any external disadvantages, which are or may be experienced, as well as an accession of resources, favorable to national independence and safety.

There are still, nevertheless, respectable patrons of opinions unfriendly to the encouragement of manufactures. The following are, substantially, the arguments by which these opinions are defended:

"In every country (say those who entertain them) agriculture is the most beneficial and productive object of human industry. This position, generally if not universally true, applies with peculiar emphasis to the United States, on account of their immense tracts of fertile territory, uninhabited and unimproved. Nothing can afford so advantageous an employment for capital and labor, as the conversion of this extensive wilderness into cultivated farms. Nothing, equally with this, can contribute to the population, strength, and real riches of the country.

"To endeavor, by the extraordinary patronage of government, to accelerate the growth of manufactures, is, in fact, to endeavor, by force and art, to transfer the natural current of industry from a more to a less beneficial channel. Whatever has such a tendency, must necessarily be unwise; indeed, it can hardly ever be wise in a government to attempt to give a direction to the industry of its citizens. This, under the quick-sighted guidance of private interests, will, if left to itself, infallibly find its own way to the most profitable employment; and it is by such employment, that the public prosperity will be most effectually promoted. To leave industry to itself, therefore, is, in almost every case, the soundest as well as the simplest policy.

"This policy is not only recommended to the United States, by considcrations which affect all nations; it is, in manner, dictated to them by the imperious force of a very peculiar situation. The smallness of their population compared with their territory; the constant allurements to emigration from the settled to the unsettled parts of the country; the facility with which the less independent condition of an artisan can be exchanged for the more independent condition of a farmer;—these, and similar causes, conspire to produce, and, for a length of time, must continue to occasion, a scarcity of hands for manufacturing occupation, and dearness of labor generally. To these disadvantages for the prosecution of manufactures, a deficiency of pecuniary capital being added, the prospect of a successful competition with the manufactures of Europe, must be regarded as little less than desperate. Extensive manufactures can only be the offspring of a redundant, at least of a full, population. Till the latter shall characterize the situation of this country, 't is vain to hope for the former.

"If, contrary to the natural course of things, an unseasonable and premature spring can be given to certain fabrics, by heavy duties, prohibitions, bounties, or by other forced expedients, this will only be to sacrifice the interests of the community to those of particular classes. Besides the misdirection of labor, a virtual monopoly, will be given to the persons employed on such fabrics; and an enhancement of price, the inevitable consequence of every monopoly, must be defrayed at the expense of the other parts of society. It is far preferable, that those persons should be engaged in the cultivation of the earth, and that we should procure, in exchange for its productions, the commodities with which foreigners are able to supply us in greater perfection and upon better terms."

This mode of reasoning is founded upon facts and principles which have certainly respectable pretensions. If it had governed the conduct of nations more generally than it has done, there is room to suppose that it might have carried them faster to prosperity and greatness than they have attained by the pursuit of maxims too widely opposite. Most general theories, however, admit of numerous exceptions, and there are few, if any, of the political kind, which do not blend a considerable portion of error with the truths they inculcate.

* * * In order to [reach] an accurate judgment how far that which has been just stated ought to be deemed liable to a similar imputation, it is necessary to advert carefully to the considerations which plead in favor of manufactures, and which appear to recommend the special and positive encouragement of them in certain cases and under certain reasonable limitations.

It ought readily be conceded that the cultivation of the earth, as the primary and most certain source of national supply, as the immediate and chief source of subsistence to a man, as the principal source of those materials which constitute the nutriment of other kinds of labor, as including a state most favorable to the freedom and independence of the human mind—one, perhaps, most conducive to the multiplication of the human species, has intrinsically a strong claim to pre-eminence over every other kind of industry.

But, that it has a title to any thing like an exclusive predilection, in any country, ought to be admitted with great caution; that it is even more productive than every other branch of industry, requires more evidence than has yet been given in support of the position. That its real interests, precious and important as, without the help of exaggeration, they truly are, will be advanced, rather than injured, by the due encouragement of manufactures, may, it is believed, be satisfactorily demonstrated. And it is also believed that the expediency of such encouragement, in a general view, may be shown to be recommended by the most cogent and persuasive motives of national policy. * * *

It is now proper to proceed a step further, and to enumerate the principal circumstances from which it may be inferred that manufacturing establishments not only occasion a positive augmentation of the produce and revenue of the society, but that they contribute essentially to rendering them greater than they could possibly be without such establishments. These circumstances are:

1. The division of labor.
2. An extension of the use of machinery.
3. Additional employment to classes of the community not ordinarily engaged in the business.
4. The promoting of emigration from foreign countries.
5. The furnishing greater scope for the diversity of talents and dispositions, which discriminate men from each other.
6. The affording a more ample and various field for enterprise.
7. The creating, in some instances, a new, and securing, in all, a more certain and steady demand for the surplus produce of the soil.

Each of these circumstances has a considerable influence upon the total mass of industrious effort in a community; together, they add to it a degree of energy and effect which is not easily conceived. Some comments upon each of them, in the order in which they have been stated, may serve to explain their importance.

1. As to the division of labor.

It has justly been observed, that there is scarcely any thing of greater moment in the economy of a nation than the proper division of labor. The separation of occupations causes each to be carried to a much greater perfection than it could possibly acquire if they were blended. This arises principally from three circumstances:

1st. The greater skill and dexterity naturally resulting from a constant and undivided application to a single object. * * *

2d. The economy of time, by avoiding the loss of it, incident to a frequent transition from one operation to another of a different nature. * * *

3d. An extension of the use of machinery. A man occupied on a single object will have it more in his power, and will be more naturally led to exert his imagination, in devising methods to facilitate and abridge labor, than if he were perplexed by a variety of independent and dissimilar operations. Besides this the fabrication of machines, in numerous instances, becoming itself a distinct trade, the artist who follows it has all the advantages which have been enumerated, for improvement in his particular art; and, in both ways, the invention and application of machinery are extended.

And from these causes united, the mere separation of the occupation of the cultivator from that of the artificer, has the effect of augmenting the productive powers of labor, and with them, the total mass of the produce or revenue of a country. * * *

2. As to an extension of the use of machinery, a point which, though partly anticipated, requires to be placed in one or two additional lights.

The employment of machinery forms an item of great importance in the general mass of national industry. It is an artificial force brought in aid of the natural force of man; and, to all the purposes of labor, is an increase of hands, an accession of strength, unencumbered too by the expense of maintaining the laborer. * * *

3. As to the additional employment of classes of the community not originally engaged in the particular business.

This is not among the least valuable of the means by which manufacturing institutions contribute to augment the general stock of industry and production. In places where those institutions prevail, besides the persons regularly engaged in them, they afford occasional and extra employment to industrious individuals and families, who are willing to devote the leisure resulting from the intermissions of their ordinary pursuits to collateral labors, as a resource for multiplying their acquisitions or their enjoyments. The husbandman himself experiences a new source of profit and support from the increased industry of his wife and daughters, invited and stimulated by the demands of the neighboring manufactories.

Besides this advantage of occasional employment to classes having different occupations, there is another, of a nature allied to it, and of a similar tendency. This is the employment of persons who would otherwise be idle, and in many cases a burthen on the community, either from the bias of temper, habit, infirmity of body, or some other cause, indisposing or disqualifying them for the toils of the country. It is worthy of particular remark that, in general, women and children are rendered more useful, and the latter more early useful, by manufacturing establishments, than they would otherwise be. Of the number of persons employed in the cotton manufactories of Great Britain, it is computed that four sevenths, nearly, are women and children, of whom the greatest proportion are children, and many of them of a tender age.

And thus it appears to be one of the attributes of manufactures, and one of no small consequence, to give occasion to the exertion of a greater quantity of industry, even by the same number of persons, where they happen to prevail, than would exist if there were no such establishments.

4. As to the promoting of emigration from foreign countries.

* * * Manufacturers who, listening to the powerful invitations of a better price for their fabrics or their labor, of greater cheapness of provisions and raw materials, of an exemption from the chief part of the taxes, burthens, and restraints which they endure in the Old World, of greater personal independence and consequence, under the operation of a more equal government, and of what is far more precious than mere religious toleration, a perfect equality of religious privileges, would probably flock from Europe to the United States, to pursue their own trades or professions, if they were once made sensible of the advantages they would enjoy, and were inspired with an assurance of encouragement and employment, will, with difficulty, be induced to transplant themselves, with a view to becoming cultivators of land.

5. AS TO THE FURNISHING GREATER SCOPE FOR THE DIVERSITY OF TALENTS AND DISPOSITIONS, WHICH DISCRIMINATE MEN FROM EACH OTHER.

This is a much more powerful means of augmenting the fund of national industry, than may at first sight appear. It is a just observation, that minds of the strongest and most active powers for their proper objects, fall below mediocrity, and labor without effect, if confined to uncongenial pursuits. And it is thence to be inferred, that the results of human exertion may be immensely increased by diversifying its objects. When all the different kinds of industry obtain in a community, each individual can find his proper element, and can call into activity the whole vigor of his nature. And the community is benefited by the services of its respective members, in the manner in which each can serve it with most effect. * * *

6. AS TO THE AFFORDING A MORE AMPLE AND VARIOUS FIELD FOR ENTERPRISE.

* * * To cherish and stimulate the activity of the human mind, by multiplying the objects of enterprise, is not among the least considerable of the expedients by which the wealth of a nation may be promoted. Even things in themselves not positively advantageous sometimes become so, by their tendency to provoke exertion. Every new scene which is opened to the busy nature of man to rouse and exert itself, is the addition of a new energy to the general stock of effort.

The spirit of enterprise, useful and prolific as it is, must necessarily be contracted or expanded, in proportion to the simplicity or variety of the occupations and productions which are to be found in a society. It must be less in a nation of mere cultivators, than in a nation of cultivators and merchants; less in a nation of cultivators and merchants, than in a nation of cultivators, artificers, and merchants.

7. AS TO THE CREATING, IN SOME INSTANCES, A NEW, AND SECURING, IN ALL, A MORE CERTAIN AND STEADY DEMAND FOR THE SURPLUS PRODUCE OF THE SOIL.

This is among the most important of the circumstances which have been indicated. It is a principal means by which the establishment of manufactures contributes to an augmentation of the produce or revenue of a country, and has an immediate and direct relation to the prosperity of agriculture.

It is evident that the exertions of the husbandman will be steady or fluctuating, vigorous or feeble, in proportion to the steadiness or fluctuation, adequateness or inadequateness, of the markets on which he must depend for the vent of the surplus which may be produced by this labor; and that such surplus, in the ordinary course of things, will be greater or less in the same proportion.

For the purpose of this vent, a domestic market is greatly to be preferred to a foreign one; because it is, in the nature of things, far more to be relied upon.

It is a primary object of the policy of nations, to be able to supply themselves with subsistence from their own soils; and manufacturing nations, as far as circumstances permit, endeavor to procure from the same source the raw materials necessary for their own fabrics. * * *

To secure such a market there is no other expedient than to promote manufacturing establishments. Manufacturers, who constitute the most numerous class, after the cultivators of land, are for that reason the principal consumers of the surplus of their labor. * * *

It merits particular observation, that the multiplication of manufactories not only furnishes a market for those articles which have been accustomed to be produced in abundance in a country, but it likewise creates a demand for such as were either unknown or produced in inconsiderable quantities. * * *

In order to [form] a better judgment of the Means proper to be restored to by the United States, it will be of use to Advert to those which have been employed with success in other Countries. The principal of these are—

1. Protecting duties—or duties on those foreign articles which are the rivals of the domestic ones intended to be encouraged. * * *

II. Prohibitions of rival articles, or duties equivalent to prohibitions. * * *

III. Prohibitions of the exportation of the materials and manufactures. * * *

IV. Pecuniary bounties.

[The last of these] has been one of the most efficacious means of encouraging manufactures, and, is in some views, the best. Though it has not yet been practiced upon by the Government of the United States (unless the allowance on the exportation of dried and pickled Fish and salted meat could be considered a bounty), and though it is less favored by Public Opinion than some other modes. Its advantages are these—

1. It is a species of encouragement more positive and direct than any other, and for that very reason, has a more immediate tendency to

stimulate and uphold new enterprises, increasing the chances of profit, and diminishing the risks of loss, in the first attempts.

2. It avoids the inconvenience of a temporary augmentation of price, which is incident to some other modes, or it produces it to a less degree, either by making no addition to the charges on the rival foreign article, as in the Case of protecting duties, or by making a smaller addition. * * *

3. Bounties have not, like high protecting duties, a tendency to produce scarcity. * * *

4. Bounties are sometimes not only the best, but the only proper expedient for uniting the encouragement of a new object of agriculture, with that of a new object of manufacture. It is the Interest of the farmer to have the production of the raw material promoted, by counteracting the interference of the foreign material of the same kind. It is the Interest of the manufacturer to have the material abundant and cheap. If prior to the domestic production of the Material, in sufficient quantity, to supply the manufacturer on good terms, a duty be laid upon the importation of it from abroad, with a view to promote the raising of it at home, the Interests both of the Farmer and Manufacturer will be disserved. By either destroying the requisite supply, or raising the price of the article beyond what can be afforded to be given for it, by the Conductor of an infant manufacture, it is abandoned or fails; and there being no domestic manufactories to create a demand for the raw material, which is raised by the farmer, it is in vain, that the Competition of the like foreign article may have been destroyed.

It cannot escape notice, that the duty upon the importation of an article can no otherwise aid the domestic production of it, than by giving the latter greater advantages in the home market. It can have no influence upon the advantageous sale of the article produced in foreign markets; no tendency, therefore, to promote its exportation.

The true way to conciliate these two interests is to lay a duty on foreign *manufactures* of the materiel, the growth of which is desired to be encouraged, and to apply the produce of that duty, by way of bounty, either upon the production of the material itself or upon its manufacture at home, or upon both. In this disposition of the thing, the Manufacturer commences his enterprise under every advantage which is attainable, as to quantity or price of the raw material: And the Farmer, if the bounty be immediately to him, is enabled by it to enter into a successful competition with the foreign material; if the bounty be to the manufacturer on so much of the domestic material as he consumes, the operation is nearly the same; he has a motive of interest to prefer the domestic Commodity, if of equal quality, even at a higher price than the foreign, so long as the difference of prices is any thing short of the bounty which is allowed upon the article.

A Question has been made concerning the Constitutional right of the Government of the United States to apply this species of encouragement, but there is certainly no good foundation for such a question. The National Legislature has express authority "To lay and Collect taxes, duties, imposts, and excises, to pay the Debts, and provide for the *Common defence* and *general welfare*" with no other qualifications that that "all duties, imposts, and excises shall be *uniform* throughout the United States, and that no capitation or other direct tax shall be laid unless in proportion to numbers ascertained by a census or enumeration taken on the principles prescribed in the Constitution," and that "no tax or duty shall be laid on articles exported from any States."

These three qualifications expected the power to *raise money* is plenary and *indefinite,* and the objects to which it may be *appropriated* are no less comprehensive than the payment of the Public debts, and the providing for the common defence and *general Welfare*. The terms *"general Welfare"* were doubtless intended to signify more than was expressed or imported in those which Preceded; otherwise, numerous exigencies incident to the affairs of a nation would have been left without a provision. The phrase is as comprehensive as any that could have been used; because it was not fit that the constitutional authority of the Union to appropriate its revenues should have been restricted within narrower limits than the "General Welfare" and because this necessarily embraces a vast variety of particulars, which are susceptible neither of specification or of definition.

It is therefore of necessity left to the discretion of the National Legislature, to pronounce upon the objects, which concern the general Welfare, and for which under that description, an appropriation of money is requisite and proper. And there seems to be no room for a doubt that whatever concerns the general interests of *Learning,* of *Agriculture,* of *Manufactures,* and of *Commerce,* are within the sphere of the national Councils, *as far as regards an application of money*.

The only qualification of the generality of the Phrase in question, which seems to be admissible, is this—That the object to which an appropriation of money is to be made be *General,* and not *local;* its operation extending in fact, or by possibility, throughout the Union, and not being confined to a particular spot.

No objection ought to arise to this construction from a supposition that it would imply a power to do what ever else should appear to Congress conducive to the General Welfare. A power to appropriate money with this lattitude which is granted too *in express terms* would not carry a power to do any other thing not authorized in the constitution, either expressly or by fair implication.

In countries where there is great private wealth, much may be effected by the voluntary contributions of patriotic individuals; but in a community situated like that of the United States, the public purse must supply the deficiency of private resource. In what can it be so useful, as in prompting and improving the efforts of industry?

All which is humbly submitted.

Alexander Hamilton,
Secy of the Treasury

GEORGE WASHINGTON

Farewell Address (1796)

One of the most famous leave-takings in American history, George Washington's "Farewell Address" was actually never delivered as a speech, but was published in newspapers on September 17, 1796. Its purpose was to make clear that Washington would not consider a third term, but it has endured because of his warnings against sectional and party strife, as well as for his advice that America beware of overly involving itself in foreign entanglements. Following Washington's instructions, Alexander Hamilton drafted the text of the address.

While, then, every part of our country thus feels an immediate and particular interest in union, all the parts combined can not fail to find in the united mass of means and efforts greater strength, greater resource, proportionably greater security from external danger, a less frequent interruption of their peace by foreign nations, and what is of inestimable value, they must derive from union an exemption from those broils and wars between themselves which so frequently afflict neighboring countries not tied together by the same governments, which their own rivalships alone would be sufficient to produce, but which opposite foreign alliances, attachments, and intrigues would stimulate and imbitter. Hence, likewise, they will avoid the necessity of those overgrown military establishments which, under any form of government, are inauspicious to liberty, and which are to be regarded as particularly hostile to republican liberty. In this sense it is that your union ought to be considered as a main prop of your liberty, and that the love of the one ought to endear to you the preservation of the other. * * *

In contemplating the causes which may disturb our union it occurs as matter of serious concern that any ground should have been furnished for characterizing parties by *geographical* discriminations—*Northern* and *Southern, Atlantic* and *Western*—whence designing men may endeavor to excite a belief that there is a real difference of local interests and views. One of the expedients of party to acquire influence within particular districts is to misrepresent the opinions and aims of other districts. You can not shield yourselves too much against the jealousies and heart-burnings which spring from these misrepresentations; they tend to render alien to each other those who ought to be bound together by fraternal affection. * * *

To the efficacy and permanency of your union a government for the whole is indispensable. * * * This Government, the offspring of our own choice, uninfluenced and unawed, adopted upon full investigation and mature deliberation, completely free in its principles, in the distribution of its powers, uniting security with energy, and containing within itself a provision for its own amendment, has a just claim to your confidence and your support. Respect for its authority, compliance with its laws, acquiescence in its measures, are duties enjoined by the fundamental maxims of true liberty. The basis of our political systems is the right of the people to make and to alter their constitutions of government. But the constitution which at any time exists till changed by an explicit and authentic act of the whole people is sacredly obligatory upon all. The very idea of the power and the right of the people to establish government presupposes the duty of every individual to obey the established government.

I have already intimated to you the danger of parties in the State, with particular reference to the founding of them on geographical discriminations. Let me now take a more comprehensive view, and warn you in the most solemn manner against the baneful effects of the spirit of party generally.

This spirit, unfortunately, is inseparable from our nature, having its root in the strongest passions of the human mind. It exists under different shapes in all governments, more or less stifled, controlled, or repressed; but in those of the popular form it is seen in its greatest rankness and is truly their worst enemy. * * *

It serves always to distract the public councils and enfeeble the public administration. It agitates the community with ill-founded jealousies and false alarms; kindles the animosity of one part against another; foments occasionally riot and insurrection. It opens the door to foreign influence and corruption, which find a facilitated access to the government itself through the channels of party passion. Thus the policy and the will of one country are subjected to the policy and will of another.

There is an opinion that parties in free countries are useful checks upon the administration of the government, and serve to keep alive the spirit of liberty. This within certain limits is probably true; and in governments of a monarchical cast patriotism may look with indulgence, if not with favor, upon the spirit of party. But in those of the popular character, in governments purely elective, it is a spirit not to be encouraged. From their natural tendency it is certain there will always be enough of that spirit for every salutary purpose; and there being constant danger of excess, the effort ought to be by force of public opinion to mitigate and assuage it. A fire not to be quenched, it demands a uniform vigilance to prevent its bursting into a flame, lest, instead of warming, it should consume. * * *

Observe good faith and justice toward all nations. Cultivate peace and harmony with all. Religion and morality enjoin this conduct. And can it be that good policy does not equally enjoin it? It will be worthy of a free, enlightened, and at no distant period a great nation to give to mankind the magnanimous and too novel example of a people always guided by an exalted justice and benevolence. Who can doubt that in the course of time and things the fruits of such a plan would richly repay any temporary advantages which might be lost by a steady adherence to it? Can it be that Providence has not connected the permanent felicity of a nation with its virtue? The experiment, at least, is recommended by every sentiment which ennobles human nature. Alas! is it rendered impossible by its vices?

In the execution of such a plan nothing is more essential than that permanent, inveterate antipathies against particular nations and passionate attachments for others should be excluded, and that in place of them just and amicable feelings toward all should be cultivated. The nation which indulges toward another an habitual hatred or an habitual fondness is in some degree a slave. It is a have to its animosity or to its affection, either of which is sufficient to lead it astray from its duty and its interest. Antipathy in one nation against another disposes each more readily to offer insult and injury, to lay hold of slight causes of umbrage, and to be haughty and intractable when accidental or trifling occasions of dispute occur. * * *

So, likewise, a passionate attachment of one nation for another produces a variety of evils. Sympathy for the favorite nation, facilitating the illusion of an imaginary common interest in cases where no real common interest exists, and infusing into one the enmities of the other, betrays the former into a participation in the quarrels and wars of the latter without adequate inducement or justification. It leads also to concessions to the favorite nation of privileges denied to others, which is apt doubly to injure the nation making the concessions by unnecessarily parting with what ought to have been retained, and by exciting jealousy, ill will, and a disposition to retaliate in the parties from whom equal privileges are withheld; and it gives to ambitious, corrupted, or deluded citizens (who devote themselves to the favorite nation) facility to betray or sacrifice the interests of their own country without odium, sometimes even with popularity, gilding with the appearances of a virtuous sense of obligation, a commendable deference for public opinion, or a laudable zeal for public good the base or foolish compliances of ambition, corruption, or infatuation. * * *

Against the insidious wiles of foreign influence (I conjure you to believe me, fellow-citizens) the jealousy of a free people ought to be *constantly* awake, since history and experience prove that foreign influence is one of the most baneful foes of republican government. But that jealousy, to be useful, must be impartial, else it becomes the instrument of the very influence to be avoided, instead of a defense against it. Excessive partiality for one foreign nation and excessive dislike of another cause those whom they actuate to see danger only on one side, and serve to veil and even second the arts of influence on the other. Real patriots who may resist the intrigues of the favorite are liable to become suspected and odious, while its tools and dupes usurp the applause and confidence of the people to surrender their interests.

The great rule of conduct for us in regard to foreign nations is, in extending our commercial relations to have with them as little *political* connection as possible. So far as we have already formed engagements let them be fulfilled with perfect good faith. Here let us stop.

Europe has a set of primary interests which to us have none or a very remote relation. Hence she must be engaged in frequent controversies, the causes of which are essentially foreign to our concerns. Hence, therefore, it must be unwise in us to implicate ourselves by artificial ties in the ordinary vicissitudes of her politics or the ordinary combinations and collisions of her friendships or enmities.

Our detached and distant situation invites and enables us to pursue a different course. If we remain one people, under an efficient government, the period is not far off when we may defy material injury from external annoyance; when we may take such an attitude as will cause the neutrality we may at any time resolve upon to be scrupulously respected; when belligerent nations, under the impossibility of making acquisitions upon us, will not lightly hazard the giving us provocation; when we may choose peace or war, as our interest, guided by justice, shall counsel.

Why forego the advantages of so peculiar a situation? Why quit our own to stand upon foreign ground? Why, by interweaving our destiny with that of any part of Europe, entangle our peace and prosperity in the toils of European ambition, rivalship, interest, humor, or caprice?

It is our true policy to steer clear of permanent alliances with any portion of the foreign world, so far, I mean, as we are now at liberty to do it; for let me not be understood as capable of patronizing infidelity to existing engagements. I hold the maxim no less applicable to public than to private affairs that honesty is always the best policy. I repeat, therefore, let those engagements be observed in their genuine sense. But in my opinion it is unnecessary and would be unwise to extend them.

Taking care always to keep ourselves by suitable establishments on a respectable defensive posture, we may safely trust to temporary alliances for extraordinary emergencies.

Harmony, liberal intercourse with all nations are recommended by policy, humanity, and interest. But even our commercial policy should hold an equal and impartial hand, neither seeking nor granting exclusive favors or preferences; consulting the natural course of things; diffusing and diversifying by gentle means the streams of commerce, but forcing nothing; establishing with powers so disposed, in order to give trade a stable course, to define the rights of our merchants, and to enable the Government to support them, conventional rules of intercourse, the best that present circumstances and mutual opinion will permit, but temporary and liable to be from time to time abandoned or varied as experience and circumstances shall dictate; constantly keeping in view that it is folly in one nation to look for disinterested favors from another; that it must pay with a portion of its independence for whatever it may accept under that character; that by such acceptance it may place itself in the condition of having given equivalents for nominal favors, and yet of being reproached with ingratitude for not giving more. There can be no greater error than to expect or calculate upon real favors from nation to nation. It is an illusion which experience must cure, which a just pride ought to discard.

JOHN MARSHALL

Marbury v. Madison (1803)

The Virginia Federalist John Marshall (1755–1835) was appointed as the fourth chief justice of the Supreme Court by John Adams after serving as a member of Congress and as secretary of state under President Adams. In perhaps the most important case in the Court's history,

Marshall established the Court's authority to review—and nullify—acts by the coordinate branches of government. Marshall had to decide whether the Court could compel Secretary of State James Madison to deliver a commission to William Marbury, who had been appointed to a judicial office by President Adams just before he left office following his bitter defeat in the 1800 presidential election. In a brilliant decision designed to assert the Court's authority without forcing a confrontation with President Jefferson, the Marshall Court ruled that it had the power to review the case and that Marbury was entitled to his commission, but it decided that it did not actually have the power to issue a writ of mandamus ordering Madison to deliver the commission.

The authority, therefore, given to the Supreme Court by the act establishing the judicial courts of the United States to issue writs of *mandamus* to public officers appears not to be warranted by the Constitution; and it becomes necessary to inquire whether a jurisdiction so conferred can be exercised.

The question whether an act repugnant to the Constitution can become the law of the land is a question deeply interesting to the United States; but, happily, not of an intricacy proportioned to its interest. It seems only necessary to recognize certain principles supposed to have been long and well established to decide it.

That the people have an original right to establish for their future government such principles as in their opinion shall most conduce to their own happiness is the basis on which the whole American fabric has been erected. The exercise of this original right is a very great exertion, nor can it, nor ought it to be frequently repeated. The principles, therefore, so established are deemed fundamental. And as the authority from which they proceed is supreme and can seldom act, they are designed to be permanent.

This original and supreme will organizes the government, and assigns to different departments their respective powers. It may either stop here or establish certain limits not to be transcended by those departments.

The government of the United States is of the latter description. The powers of the Legislature are defined and limited; and that those limits may not be mistaken or forgotten the Constitution is written. To what purpose are powers limited and to what purpose is that limitation committed to writing, if these limits may at any time be passed by those intended to be restrained? The distinction between a government with limited and unlimited powers is abolished if those limits do not confine the persons on whom they are imposed and if acts prohibited and acts allowed are of equal obligation. It is a proposition too plain to be contested, that the Constitution controls any legislative act repugnant to it; or that the Legislature may alter the Constitution by an ordinary act.

Between these alternatives there is no middle ground. The Constitution is either a superior, paramount law, unchangeable by ordinary means, or it is on a level with ordinary legislative acts, and like other acts is alterable when the Legislature shall please to alter it.

If the former part of the alternative be true, then a legislative act contrary to the Constitution is not law; if the latter part be true, then written Constitutions are absurd attempts on the part of the people to limit a power in its own nature illimitable.

Certainly all those who have framed written Constitutions contemplate them as forming the fundamental and paramount law of the nation, and consequently the theory of every such government must be that an act of the Legislature repugnant to the Constitution is void.

This theory is essentially attached to a written Constitution, and is consequently to be considered by this court as one of the fundamental principles of our society. It is not, therefore, to be lost sight of in the further consideration of this subject.

If an act of the Legislature repugnant to the Constitution is void, does it, notwithstanding its invalidity, bind the courts and oblige them to give it effect? Or, in other words, though it be not law, does it constitute a rule as operative as if it was a law? This would be to overthrow in fact what was established in theory, and would seem, at first view, an absurdity too gross to be insisted on. It shall, however, receive a more attentive consideration.

It is emphatically the province and duty of the judicial department to say what the law is. Those who apply the rule to particular cases must of necessity expound and interpret that rule. If two laws conflict with each other the courts must decide on the operation of each.

So, if a law be in opposition to the Constitution; if both the law and the Constitution apply to a particular case, so that the court must either decide that case conformably to the law, disregarding the Constitution, or conformably to the Constitution, disregarding the law, the court must determine which of these conflicting rules governs the case. This is of the very essence of judicial duty.

If, then, the courts are to regard the Constitution, and the Constitution is superior to any ordinary act of the Legislature, the Constitution, and not such ordinary act, must govern the case to which they both apply.

Those, then, who controvert the principle that the Constitution is to be considered in court as a paramount law are reduced to the necessity of maintaining that courts must close their eyes on the Constitution and see only the law.

This doctrine would subvert the very foundation of all written Constitutions. It would declare that an act which, according to the principles and theory of our government, is entirely void, is yet, in practice, completely obligatory. It would declare that, if the Legislature shall do what is expressly forbidden, such act, notwithstanding the express prohibition, is in reality effectual. It would be giving to the Legislature a practical and real omnipotence with the same breath which professes to restrict their powers within narrow limits. It is prescribing limits and declaring that those limits may be passed at pleasure.

That it thus reduces to nothing what we have deemed the greatest improvement on political institutions, a written Constitution, would of itself be sufficient in America, where written Constitutions have been viewed with so much reverence, for rejecting the construction. But the peculiar expressions of the Constitution of the United States furnish additional arguments in favor of its rejection.

The judicial power of the United States is extended to all cases arising under the Constitution.

Could it be the intention of those who gave this power to say that in using it the Constitution should not be looked into? That a case arising under the Constitution should be decided without examining the instrument under which it arises?

This is too extravagant to be maintained.

In some cases, then, the Constitution must be looked into by the judges, and if they can open it at all, what part of it are they forbidden to read or to obey?

There are many other parts of the Constitution which serve to illustrate this subject.

It is declared that "no tax or duty shall be laid on articles exported from any State." Suppose a duty on the export of cotton, of tobacco, or of flour, and a suit instituted to recover it, ought judgment to be rendered in such a case? Ought the judges to close their eyes on the Constitution and only see the law?

The Constitution declares "that no bill of attainder or *ex post facto* law shall be passed."

If, however, such a bill should be passed, and a person should be prosecuted under it, must the court condemn to death those victims whom the Constitution endeavors to preserve?

"No person," says the Constitution, "shall be convicted of treason, unless on the testimony of two witnesses to the same overt act, or on confession in open court."

Here the language of the Constitution is addressed especially to the courts. It prescribes directly for them a rule of evidence not to be departed from. If the Legislature should change that rule, and declare *one* witness, or a confession *out* of court, sufficient for conviction, must the constitutional principle yield to the legislative act?

From these and many other selections which might be made, it is apparent that the framers of the Constitution contemplated that instrument as a rule for the government of *courts*, as well as of the Legislature.

Why otherwise does it direct the judges to take an oath to support it? This oath certainly applies in an especial manner to their conduct in their official character. How immoral to impose it on them if they were to be used as the instruments, and the knowing instruments, for violating what they swear to support!

The oath of office, too, imposed by the Legislature, is completely demonstrative of the legislative opinion on this subject. It is in these words: "I do solemnly swear that I will administer justice without respect to persons and do equal right to the poor and to the rich; and that, I will faithfully and impartially discharge all the duties incumbent on me as ————, according to the best of my abilities and understanding, agreeably to the *Constitution* and laws of the United States."

Why does a judge swear to discharge his duties agreeably to the Constitution of the United States, if that Constitution forms no rule for his government? if it is closed upon him, and cannot be inspected by him?

If such be the real state of things, this is worse than solemn mockery. To prescribe, or to take this oath, becomes equally a crime.

It is also not entirely unworthy of observation, that, in declaring what shall be the *supreme* law of the land, the *Constitution* itself is first mentioned, and not the laws of the United States generally, but those only which shall be made in *pursuance* of the Constitution, have that rank.

Thus the particular phraseology of the Constitution of the United States confirms and strengthens the principle supposed to be essential to all written Constitutions that a law repugnant to the Constitution is void, and that *courts*, as well as other departments, are bound by that instrument.

JOHN MARSHALL

McCulloch v. Maryland (1819)

A staunch nationalist, Marshall often relied on Hamiltonian principles of constitutional interpretation to justify broad powers for the federal government. In a landmark decision that reinforced the supremacy of the national government over the states, Marshall's Court upheld the constitutionality of the Second Bank of the United States and ruled that the states did not have the power to tax an instrumentality of the national government. Even though many former opponents of the bank now accepted its legitimacy, Republicans recoiled at Marshall's expansive reading of the powers of the national government and disapproved of the Court's imperious tone.

I n the case now to be determined, the defendant, a sovereign state, denies the obligation of a law enacted by the legislature of the Union, and the plaintiff, on his part, contests the validity of an act which has been passed by the legislature of that state. The constitution of our country, in its most interesting and vital parts, is to be considered; the conflicting powers of the government of the Union and of its members, as marked in that constitution, are to be discussed; and an opinion given, which may essentially influence the great operations of the government. No tribunal can approach such a question without a deep sense of its importance, and of the awful responsibility involved in its decision. But it must be decided peacefully, or remain a source of hostile legislation, perhaps of hostility of a still more serious nature; and if it is to be so decided, by this tribunal alone can the decision be made. On the Supreme Court of the United States has the constitution of our country devolved this important duty.

The first question made in the cause is, has Congress power to incorporate a bank? * * *

In discussing this question, the counsel for the state of Maryland have deemed it of some importance, in the construction of the constitution, to consider that instrument not as emanating from the people, but as the act of sovereign and independent states. The powers of the general government, it has been said, are delegated by the states, who alone are truly sovereign; and must be exercised in subordination to the states, who alone possess supreme dominion.

It would be difficult to sustain this proposition. The convention which framed the constitution was indeed elected by the state legislatures. But the instrument, when it came from their hands, was a mere proposal, without obligation, or pretensions to it. It was reported to the then existing Congress of the United States, with a request that it might 'be submitted to a convention of delegates, chosen in each state by the people thereof, under the recommendation of its legislature, for their assent and ratification.' This mode of proceeding was adopted; and by the convention, by Congress, and by the state legislatures, the instrument was submitted to the people. They acted upon it in the only manner in which they can act safely, effectively, and wisely, on such a subject, by assembling in convention. It is true, they assembled in their several states—and where else should they have assembled? No political dreamer was ever wild enough to think of breaking down the lines which separate the states, and of compounding the American people into one common mass. Of consequence, when they act, they act in their states. But the measures they adopt do not, on that account, cease to be the measures of the people themselves, or become the measures of the state governments.

From these conventions the constitution derives its whole authority. The government proceeds directly from the people; is 'ordained and established' in the name of the people; and is declared to be ordained, 'in order to form a more perfect union, establish justice, insure domestic tranquillity, and secure the blessings of liberty to themselves and to their posterity.' The assent of the states, in their sovereign capacity, is implied in calling a convention, and thus submitting that instrument to the people. But the people were at perfect liberty to accept or reject it; and their act was final. It required not the affirmance, and could not be negatived, by the state governments. The constitution, when thus adopted, was of complete obligation, and bound the state sovereignties! * * *

The government of the Union, then (whatever may be the influence of this fact on the case), is, emphatically, and truly, a government of the people. In form and in substance it emanates from them. Its powers are granted by them, and are to be exercised directly on them, and for their benefit.

This government is acknowledged by all to be one of enumerated powers. The principle, that it can exercise only the powers granted to it, would seem too apparent to have required to be enforced by all those arguments which its enlightened friends, while it was pending before the people, found it necessary to urge. That principle is now universally admitted. * * *

If any one proposition could command the universal assent of mankind, we might expect it would be this—that the government of the Union, though limited in its powers, is supreme within its sphere of action. This would seem to result necessarily from its nature. It is the government of all; its powers are delegated by all; it represents all, and acts for all. Though any one state may be willing to control its operations, no state is willing to allow others to control them. The nation, on those subjects on which it can act, must necessarily bind its component parts. But this question is not left to mere reason; the people have, in express terms, decided it by saying, 'this constitution, and the laws of the United States, which shall be made in pursuance thereof,' 'shall be the supreme law of the land,' and by requiring that the members of the state legislatures, and the officers of the executive and judicial departments of the states shall take the oath of fidelity to it. * * *

Among the enumerated powers, we do not find that of establishing a bank or creating a corporation. But there is no phrase in the instrument which, like the articles of confederation, excludes incidental or implied powers; and which requires that everything granted shall be expressly and minutely described. Even the 10th amendment, which was framed for the purpose of quieting the excessive jealousies which had been excited, omits the word 'expressly,' and declares only that the powers 'not delegated to the United States, nor prohibited to the states, are reserved to the states or to the people'; thus leaving the question, whether the particular power which may become the subject of contest has been delegated to the one government, or prohibited to the other, to depend on a fair construction of the whole instrument. The men who drew and adopted this amendment had experienced the embarrassments resulting from the insertion of this word in the articles of confederation, and probably omitted it to avoid those embarrassments. A constitution, to contain an accurate detail of all the subdivisions of which its great powers will admit, and of all the means by which they may be carried into execution, would partake of a prolixity of a legal code, and could scarcely be embraced by the human mind. It would probably never be understood by the public. Its nature, therefore, requires that only its great outlines should be marked, its important objects designated, and the minor ingredients which compose those objects be deduced from the nature of the objects themselves. * * * In considering this question, then, we must never forget that it is a constitution we are expounding.

Although, among the enumerated powers of government, we do not find the word 'bank' or 'incorporation,' we find the great powers to lay and collect taxes; to borrow money; to regulate commerce; to declare and conduct a war; and to raise and support armies and navies. The sword and the purse, all the external relations, and no inconsiderable portion of the industry of the nation, are entrusted to its government. It can never be pretended that these vast powers draw after them others of inferior importance, merely because they are inferior. Such an idea can never be advanced. But it may with great reason be contended, that a government, entrusted with such ample powers, on the due execution of which the happiness and prosperity of the nation so vitally depends, must also be entrusted with ample means for their execution. The power being given, it is the interest of the nation to facilitate its execution. It can never be their interest, and cannot be presumed to have been their intention, to clog and embarrass its execution by withholding the most appropriate means. * * * Can we adopt that construction (unless the words imperiously require it) which would impute to the framers of that instrument, when granting these powers for the public good, the intention of impeding their exercise by withholding a choice of means? If, indeed, such be the mandate of the constitution, we have only to obey; but that instrument does not profess to enumerate the means by which the powers it confers may be executed; nor does it prohibit the creation of a corporation, if the existence of such a being be essential to the beneficial exercise of those powers. It is, then, the subject of fair inquiry, how far such means may be employed. It is not denied that the powers given to the government imply the ordinary means of execution. * * * But it is denied that the government has its choice of means; or, that it may employ the most convenient means, if, to employ them, it be necessary to erect a corporation. * * *

The creation of a corporation, it is said, appertains to sovereignty. This is admitted. But to what portion of sovereignty does it appertain? Does it belong to one more than to another? In America, the powers of sovereignty are divided between the government of the Union, and those of the States. They are each sovereign, with respect to the objects committed to it, and neither sovereign with respect to the objects committed to the other. * * * The power of creating a corporation, though appertaining to sovereignty, is not, like the power of making war, or levying taxes, or of regulating commerce, a great substantive and independent power, which cannot be implied as incidental to other powers, or used as a means of executing them. It is never the end for which other powers are exercised, but a means by which other objects are accomplished. No contributions are made to charity for the sake of an incorporation, but a corporation is created to administer the charity; no seminary of learning is instituted in order to be incorporated, but the corporate character is conferred to subserve the purposes of education. No city was ever built with the sole object of being incorporated, but is incorporated as affording the best means of being well governed. The power of creating a corporation is never used for its own sake, but for the purpose of effecting something else. No sufficient reason is, therefore, perceived, why it may not pass as incidental to those powers which are expressly given, if it be a direct mode of executing them.

But the constitution of the United States has not left the right of Congress to employ the necessary means for the execution of the powers conferred on the government to general reasoning. To its enumeration of powers is added that of making 'all laws which shall be necessary and proper, for carrying into execution the foregoing powers, and all other powers vested by this constitution, in the government of the United States, or in any department thereof.'

The counsel for the State of Maryland have urged various arguments, to prove that this clause, though in terms a grant of power, is not so in effect; but is really restrictive of the general right, which might otherwise be implied, of selecting means for executing the enumerated powers.

In support of this proposition, they have found it necessary to contend, that this clause was inserted for the purpose of conferring on Congress the power of making laws. ∗ ∗ ∗

But could this be the object for which it was inserted? ∗ ∗ ∗ Could it be necessary to say that a legislature should exercise legislative powers in the shape of legislation? ∗ ∗ ∗ That a legislature, endowed with legislative powers, can legislate, is a proposition too self-evident to have been questioned.

But the argument on which most reliance is placed, is drawn from the peculiar language of this clause. Congress is not empowered by it to make all laws, which may have relation to the powers conferred on the government, but such only as may be 'necessary and proper' for carrying them into execution. The word 'necessary' is considered as controlling the whole sentence, and as limiting the right to pass laws for the execution of the granted powers, to such as are indispensable, and without which the power would be nugatory. That it excludes the choice of means, and leaves to Congress, in each case, that only which is most direct and simple.

Is it true that this is the sense in which the word 'necessary' is always used? Does it always import an absolute physical necessity, so strong that one thing, to which another may be termed necessary, cannot exist without that other? We think it does not. ∗ ∗ ∗ Such is the character of human language, that no word conveys to the mind, in all situations, one single definite idea; and nothing is more common than to use words in a figurative sense. Almost all compositions contain words, which, taken in their rigorous sense, would convey a meaning different from that which is obviously intended. ∗ ∗ ∗ The word 'necessary' is of this description. It has not a fixed character peculiar to itself. It admits of all degrees of comparison; and is often connected with other words, which increase or diminish the impression the mind receives of the urgency it imports. A thing may be necessary, very necessary, absolutely or indispensably necessary. To no mind would the same idea be conveyed to these several phrases. ∗ ∗ ∗ This word, then, like others, is used in various senses; and, in its construction, the subject, the context, the intention of the person using them, are all to be taken into view.

Let this be done in the case under consideration. The subject is the execution of those great powers on which the welfare of a nation essentially depends. It must have been the intention of those who gave these powers, to insure, as far as human prudence could insure, their beneficial execution. This could not be done by confiding the choice of means of such narrow limits as not to leave it in the power of Congress to adopt any which might be appropriate, and which were conducive to

the end. This provision is made in a constitution intended to endure for
ages to come, and, consequently, to be adapted to the various crises of
human affairs. To have prescribed the means by which government
should, in all future time, execute its powers, would have been to
change, entirely, the character of the instrument, and give it the properties of a legal code. It would have been an unwise attempt to provide,
by immutable rules, for exigencies which, if foreseen at all, must have
been seen dimly, and which can be best provided for as they occur. To
have declared that the best means shall not be used, but those alone
without which the power given would be nugatory, would have been to
deprive the legislature of the capacity to avail itself of experience, to exercise its reason, and to accommodate its legislation to circumstances.
If we apply this principle of construction to any of the powers of the
government, we shall find it so pernicious in its operation that we shall
be compelled to discard it. * * *

If this limited construction of the word 'necessary' must be abandoned in order to punish, whence is derived the rule which would re-
instate it, when the government would carry its powers into execution by
means not vindictive in their nature? If the word 'necessary' means
'needful,' 'requisite,' 'essential,' 'conducive to,' in order to let in the
power of punishment for the infraction of law; why is it not equally comprehensive when required to authorize the use of means which facilitate
the execution of the powers of government without the infliction of
punishment? * * *

But the argument which most conclusively demonstrates the error of
the construction contended for by the counsel for the state of Maryland,
is founded on the intention of the convention, as manifested in the whole
clause. To waste time and argument in proving that without it Congress
might carry its powers into execution, would be not much less idle than
to hold a lighted taper to the sun. As little can it be required to prove, that
in the absence of this clause, Congress would have some choice of means.
* * * This clause, as construed by the state of Maryland, would abridge,
and almost annihilate this useful and necessary right of the legislature to
select its means. That this could not be intended, is, we should think, had
it not been already controverted, too apparent for controversy. We think
so for the following reasons:

1st. The clause is placed among the powers of Congress, not among
the limitations on those powers.

2d. Its terms purport to enlarge, not to diminish the powers vested in
the government. It purports to be an additional power, not a restriction
on those already granted. * * *

The result of the most careful and attentive consideration bestowed upon this clause is, that if it does not enlarge, it cannot be construed to restrain the powers of Congress, or to impair the right of the legislature to exercise its best judgment in the selection of measures to carry into execution the constitutional powers of the government. If no other motive for its insertion can be suggested, a sufficient one is found in the desire to remove all doubts respecting the right to legislate on that vast mass of incidental powers which must be involved in the constitution, if that instrument be not a splendid bauble.

We admit, as all must admit, that the powers of the government are limited, and that its limits are not to be transcended. But we think the sound construction of the constitution must allow to the national legislature that discretion, with respect to the means by which the powers it confers are to be carried into execution, which will enable that body to perform the high duties assigned to it, in the manner most beneficial to the people. Let the end be legitimate, let it be within the scope of the constitution, and all means which are appropriate, which are plainly adapted to that end, which are not prohibited, but consist with the letter and spirit of the constitution, are constitutional. * * *

If a corporation may be employed indiscriminately with other means to carry into execution the powers of the government, no particular reason can be assigned for excluding the use of a bank, if required for its fiscal operations. To use one, must be within the discretion of Congress, if it be an appropriate mode of executing the powers of government. That it is a convenient, a useful, and essential instrument in the prosecution of its fiscal operations, is not now a subject of controversy. * * *

It being the opinion of the court that the act incorporating the bank is constitutional, and that the power of establishing a branch in the state of Maryland might be properly exercised by the bank itself, we proceed to inquire:

2. Whether the state of Maryland may, without violating the constitution, tax that branch?

That the power of taxation is one of vital importance; that it is retained by the states; that it is not abridged by the grant of a similar power to the government of the Union; that it is to be concurrently exercised by the two governments: are truths which have never been denied. But, such is the paramount character of the constitution that its capacity to withdraw any subject from the action of even this power, is admitted. * * *

On this ground the counsel for the bank place its claim to be exempted from the power of a state to tax its operations. There is no express provision for the case, but the claim has been sustained on a principle which so entirely pervades the constitution, is so intermixed with the materials which compose it, so interwoven with its web, so blended with its texture, as to be incapable of being separated from it without rending it into shreds.

This great principle is, that the constitution and the laws made in pursuance thereof are supreme; that they control the constitution and laws of the respective states, and cannot be controlled by them. From this, which may be almost termed an axiom, other propositions are deduced as corollaries, on the truth or error of which, and on their application to this case, the cause has been supposed to depend. These are 1st. that a power to create implies a power to preserve. 2d. That a power to destroy, if wielded by a different hand, is hostile to, and incompatible with these powers to create and to preserve. 3d. That where this repugnancy exists, that authority which is supreme must control, not yield to that over which it is supreme. * * *

That the power of taxing it by the states may be exercised so as to destroy it, is too obvious to be denied. But taxation is said to be an absolute power, which acknowledges no other limits than those expressly prescribed in the constitution, and like sovereign power of every other description, is trusted to the discretion of those who use it. But the very terms of this argument admit that the sovereignty of the state, in the article of taxation itself, is subordinate to, and may be controlled by the constitution of the United States. How far it has been controlled by that instrument must be a question of construction. * * *

The sovereignty of a state extends to everything which exists by its own authority, or is introduced by its permission; but does it extend to those means which are employed by Congress to carry into execution powers conferred on that body by the people of the United States? We think it demonstrable that it does not. Those powers are not given by the people of a single state. They are given by the people of the United States, to a government whose laws, made in pursuance of the constitution, are declared to be supreme. Consequently, the people of a single state cannot confer a sovereignty which will extend over them. * * *

We find, then, on just theory, a total failure of this original right to tax the means employed by the government of the Union, for the execution of its powers. The right never existed, and the question whether it has been surrendered, cannot arise.

But, waiving this theory for the present, let us resume the inquiry, whether this power can be exercised by the respective states, consistently with a fair construction of the constitution.

That the power to tax involves the power to destroy; that the power to destroy may defeat and render useless the power to create; that there is a plain repugnance, in conferring on one government a power to control the constitutional measures of another, which other, with re-spect to those very measures, is declared to be supreme over that which exerts the control, are propositions not to be denied. But all inconsis-tencies are to be reconciled by the magic of the word CONFIDENCE. Taxation, it is said, does not necessarily and unavoidably destroy. To carry it to the excess of destruction would be an abuse, to presume which, would banish that confidence which is essential to all govern-ment.

But is this a case of confidence? Would the people of any one state trust those of another with a power to control the most insignificant op-erations of their state government? We know they would not. Why, then, should we suppose that the people of any one state should be willing to trust those of another with a power to control the operations of a govern-ment to which they have confided the most important and most valuable interests? In the legislature of the Union alone, are all represented. The legislature of the Union alone, therefore, can be trusted by the people with the power of controlling measures which concern all, in the confi-dence that it will not be abused. This, then, is not a case of confidence, and we must consider it as it really is.

If we apply the principle for which the state of Maryland contends, to the constitution generally, we shall find it capable of changing totally the character of that instrument. We shall find it capable of arresting all the measures of the government, and of prostrating it at the foot of the states. The American people have declared their constitution, and the laws made in pursuance thereof, to be supreme; but this principle would transfer the supremacy, in fact, to the states.

If the states may tax one instrument, employed by the government in the execution of its powers, they may tax any and every other instrument. They may tax the mail; they may tax the mint; they may tax patent-rights; they may tax the papers of the custom-house; they may tax judicial pro-cess; they may tax all the means employed by the government, to an ex-cess which would defeat all the ends of government. * * *

This is not all. If the controlling power of the states be established; if their supremacy as to taxation be acknowledged; what is to restrain their exercising this control in any shape they may please to give it? Their sov-ereignty is not confined to taxation. That is not the only mode in which it might be displayed. The question is, in truth, a question of supremacy; and if the right of the states to tax the means employed by the general government be conceded, the declaration that the constitution, and the laws made in pursuance thereof, shall be the supreme law of the land, is empty and unmeaning declamation.

THOMAS JEFFERSON

A Bill for Establishing Religious Freedom (1777)

Though written prior to 1791, several of our selections, like this one, involve ideals he would hold throughout his public career. Firmly committed to religious toleration and the separation of church and state, Jefferson drafted in 1777 a bill to establish religious liberty that the Virginia General Assembly finally passed, with minor changes, in 1786. Jefferson was so proud of this achievement that he chose to have mention of it inscribed on his tombstone along with two other major accomplishments: the writing of the Declaration of Independence and the founding of the University of Virginia.

SECTION I

Well aware that the opinions and belief of men depend not on their own will, but follow involuntarily the evidence proposed to their minds; that Almighty God hath created the mind free, and manifested his supreme will that free it shall remain by making it altogether insusceptible of restraint; that all attempts to influence it by temporal punishments, or burthens, or by civil incapacitations, tend only to beget habits of hypocrisy and meanness, and are a departure from the plan of the holy author of our religion, who being lord both of body and mind, yet chose not to propagate it by coercions on either, as was in his Almighty power to do, but to extend it by its influence on reason alone; that the impious presumption of legislators and rulers, civil as well as ecclesiastical, who, being themselves but fallible and uninspired men, have assumed dominion over the faith of others, setting up their own opinions and modes of thinking as the only true and infallible, and as such endeavoring to impose them on others, hath established and maintained false religions over the greatest part of the world and through all time: That to compel a man to furnish contributions of money for the propagation of opinions which he disbelieves and abhors, is sinful and tyrannical; that even the forcing him to support this or that teacher of his own religious persuasion, is depriving him of the comfortable liberty of giving his contributions to the particular pastor whose morals he would make his pattern, and whose powers he feels most persuasive to righteousness; and is withdrawing from the ministry those temporary rewards, which proceeding from an approbation of their personal conduct, are an additional incitement to earnest and unremitting labours for the instruction of mankind; that our civil rights have no dependance on our religious opinions, any more than our opinions in physics or geometry; that therefore the proscribing any citizen as unworthy the public confidence by laying upon him an incapacity of being called to offices of trust and emolument, unless he profess or renounce this or that religious opinion, is depriving him injuriously of those privileges and advantages to which, in common with his fellow citizens, he has a natural right; that it tends also to corrupt the principles of that very religion it is meant to encourage, by bribing, with a monopoly of worldly honours and emoluments, those who will externally profess and conform to it; that though indeed these are criminal who do not withstand such temptation, yet neither are those innocent who lay the bait in their way; that the opinions of men are not the object of civil government, nor under its jurisdiction; that to suffer the civil magistrate to intrude his powers into the field of opinion and to restrain the profession or propagation of principles on supposition of their ill tendency is a dangerous falacy, which at once destroys all religious liberty, because he being of course judge of that tendency will make his opinions the rule of judgment, and approve or condemn the sentiments of others only as they shall square with or differ from his own; that it is time enough for rightful purposes of civil government for its officers to interfere when principles break out into overt acts against peace and good order; and finally, that truth is great and will prevail if left to herself; that she is the proper and sufficient antagonist to error, and has nothing to fear from the conflict unless by human interposition disarmed of her natural weapons, free argument and debate; errors ceasing to be dangerous when it is permitted freely to contradict them.

SECT. II.

We the General Assembly of Virginia do enact that no man shall be compelled to frequent or support any religious worship, place, or ministry whatsoever, nor shall be enforced, restrained, molested, or burthened in his body or goods, nor shall otherwise suffer, on account of his religious opinions or belief; but that all men shall be free to profess, and by argument to maintain, their opinions in matters of religion, and that the same shall in no wise diminish, enlarge, or affect their civil capacities.

SECT. III.

And though we well know that this Assembly, elected by the people for the ordinary purposes of legislation only, have no power to restrain the acts of succeeding Assemblies, constituted with powers equal to our own, and that therefore to declare this act irrevocable would be of no effect in law; yet we are free to declare, and do declare, that the rights hereby asserted are of the natural rights of mankind, and that if any act shall be hereafter passed to repeal the present or to narrow its operation, such act will be an infringement of natural right.

THOMAS JEFFERSON

Notes on the State of Virgina (1784)

Jefferson wrote his only book in response to a questionnaire about Virginia from François de Marbois, the secretary of the French legation in America. Written in 1781–82 and first published in Paris in 1784, this successful book is a veritable catalogue of Jeffersonian views. He uncharacteristically muses on the despotic potential of legislatures in Query XIII. The discussion of laws (Query XIV) has Jefferson's vision of free public education. His memorable depiction of governmental uninvolvement in religion is found in Query XVII, and his discussion of manufacture (Query XIX) contains his famous agrarian ideal of American farmers as "the chosen people of God."

QUERY XIII: CONSTITUTION

This constitution [the Virginia constitution of 1776] was formed when we were new and unexperienced in the science of government. It was the first, too, which was formed in the whole United States. No wonder then that time and trial have discovered very capital defects in it.

1. The majority of the men in the state, who pay and fight for its support, are unrepresented in the legislature, the roll of freeholders entitled to vote not including generally the half of those on the roll of the militia, or of the tax-gatherers.

2. Among those who share the representation, the shares are very unequal. Thus the county of Warwick, with only one hundred fighting men, has an equal representation with the county of Loudon, which has 1746. * * *

* * * It will appear at once that nineteen thousand men, living below the falls of the rivers, possess half of the senate, and want four members only of possessing a majority of the house of delegates; a want more than supplied by the vicinity of their situation to the seat of government, and of course the greater degree of convenience and punctuality with which their members may and will attend in the legislature. These nineteen thousand, therefore, living in one part of the country, give law to upwards of thirty thousand living in another, and appoint all their chief officers executive and judiciary. From the difference of their situation and circumstances, their interests will often be very different.

3. The senate is, by its constitution, too homogenous with the house of delegates. Being chosen by the same electors, at the same time, and out of the same subjects, the choice falls of course on men of the same description. The purpose of establishing different houses of legislation is to introduce the influence of different interests or different principles. Thus in Great Britain it is said their constitution relies on the house of commons for honesty, and the lords for wisdom; which would be a rational reliance, if honesty were to be bought with money, and if wisdom were hereditary. In some of the American States, the delegates and senators are so chosen, as that the first represent the persons, and the second the property of the State. But with us, wealth and wisdom have equal chance for admission into both houses. We do not, therefore, derive from the separation of our legislature into two houses, those benefits which a proper complication of principles is capable of producing, and those which alone can compensate the evils which may be produced by their dissensions.

4. All the powers of government, legislative, executive, and judiciary, result to the legislative body. The concentrating these in the same hands is precisely the definition of despotic government. It will be no alleviation that these powers will be exercised by a plurality of hands, and not by a single one. 173 despots would surely be as oppressive as one. * * * An *elective despotism* was not the government we fought for, but one which should not only be founded on free principles, but in which the powers of government should be so divided and balanced

among several bodies of magistracy, as that no one could transcend their legal limits, without being effectually checked and restrained by the others. For this reason that convention, which passed the ordinance of government, laid its foundation on this basis, that the legislative, executive and judiciary departments should be separate and distinct, so that no person should exercise the powers of more than one of them at the same time. But no barrier was provided between these several powers. The judiciary and executive members were left dependent on the legislative, for their subsistence in office, and some of them for their continuance in it. If therefore the legislature assumes executive and judiciary powers, no opposition is likely to be made; nor, if made, can it be effectual; because in that case they may put their proceedings into the form of an act of assembly, which will render them obligatory on the other branches. They have accordingly in many instances, decided rights which should have been left to judiciary controversy: and the direction of the executive, during the whole time of their session, is becoming habitual and familiar. And this is done with no ill intention. The views of the present members are perfectly upright. When they are led out of their regular province, it is by art in others, and inadvertence in themselves. And this will probably be the case for some time to come. But it will not be a very long time. Mankind soon learn to make interested uses of every right and power which they possess, or may assume. The public money and public liberty, intended to have been deposited with three branches of magistracy, but found inadvertently to be in the hands of one only, will soon be discovered to be sources of wealth and dominion to those who hold them; distinguished, too, by this tempting circumstance, that they are the instrument, as well as the object, of acquisition. With money we will get men, said Caesar, and with men we will get money. Nor should our assembly be deluded by the integrity of their own purposes, and conclude that these unlimited powers will never be abused, because themselves are not disposed to abuse them. They should look forward to a time, and that not a distant one, when a corruption in this, as in the country from which we derive our origin, will have seized the heads of government, and be spread by them through the body of the people; when they will purchase the voices of the people, and make them pay the price. Human nature is the same on every side of the Atlantic, and will be alike influenced by the same causes. The time to guard against corruption and tyranny, is before they shall have gotten hold of us. It is better to keep the wolf out of the fold, than to trust to drawing his teeth and talons after he shall have entered.

* * *

QUERY XIV: LAWS

* * *

Another object of the revisal is, to diffuse knowledge more generally through the mass of the people. This bill proposes to lay off every county into small districts of five or six miles square, called hundreds, and in each of them to establish a school for teaching reading, writing, and arithmetic. The tutor to be supported by the hundred, and every person in it entitled to send their children three years gratis, and as much longer as they please, paying for it. These schools to be under a visitor, who is annually to chuse the boy, of best genius in the school, of those whose parents are too poor to give them further education, and to send him forward to one of the grammar schools, of which twenty are proposed to be erected in different parts of the country, for teaching Greek, Latin, geography, and the higher branches of numerical arithmetic. Of the boys thus sent in any one year, trial is to be made at the grammar schools one or two years, and the best genius of the whole selected, and continued six years, and the residue dismissed. By this means twenty of the best geniusses will be raked from the rubbish annually, and be instructed, at the public expence, so far as the grammar schools go. At the end of six years instruction, one half are to be discontinued (from among whom the grammar schools will probably be supplied with future masters); and the other half, who are to be chosen for the superiority of their parts and disposition, are to be sent and continued three years in the study of such sciences as they shall chuse, at William and Mary college, the plan of which is proposed to be enlarged, as will be hereafter explained, and extended to all the useful sciences. The ultimate result of the whole scheme of education would be the teaching all the children of the state reading, writing, and common arithmetic: turning out ten annually of superior genius, well taught in Greek, Latin, geography, and the higher branches of arithmetic: turning out ten others annually, of still superior parts, who, to those branches of learning, shall have added such of the sciences as their genius shall have led them to: the furnishing to the wealthier part of the people convenient schools, at which their children may be educated, at their own expence.—The general objects of this law are to provide an education adapted to the years, to the capacity, and the condition of every one, and directed to their freedom and happiness. Specific details were not proper for the law. These must be the business of the visitors entrusted with its execution. The first stage of this education being the schools of the hundreds, wherein the great mass of the people will receive their instruction, the principal foundations of future order will be laid here. Instead therefore of putting the

Bible and Testament into the hands of the children, at an age when their judgments are not sufficiently matured for religious inquiries, their memories may here be stored with the most useful facts from Grecian, Roman, European and American history. The first elements of morality too may be instilled into their minds; such as, when further developed as their judgments advance in strength, may teach them how to work out their own greatest happiness, by shewing them that it does not depend on the condition of life in which chance has placed them, but is always the result of a good conscience, good health, occupation, and freedom in all just pursuits.—Those whom either the wealth of their parents or the adoption of the state shall destine to higher degrees of learning, will go on to the grammar schools, which constitute the next stage, there to be instructed in the languages. The learning Greek and Latin, I am told, is going into disuse in Europe. I know not what their manners and occupations may call for: but it would be very ill-judged in us to follow their example in this instance. There is a certain period of life, say from eight to fifteen or sixteen years of age, when the mind, like the body, is not yet firm enough for laborious and close operations. If applied to such, it falls an early victim to premature exertion; exhibiting indeed at first, in these young and tender subjects, the flattering appearance of their being men while they are yet children, but ending in reducing them to be children when they should be men. The memory is then most susceptible and tenacious of impressions; and the learning of languages being chiefly a work of memory, it seems precisely fitted to the powers of this period, which is long enough too for acquiring the most useful languages ancient and modern. I do not pretend that language is science. It is only an instrument for the attainment of science. But that time is not lost which is employed in providing tools for future operation: more especially as in this case the books put into the hands of the youth for this purpose may be such as will at the same time impress their minds with useful facts and good principles. If this period be suffered to pass in idleness, the mind becomes lethargic and impotent, as would the body it inhabits if unexercised during the same time. The sympathy between body and mind during their rise, progress and decline, is too strict and obvious to endanger our being misled while we reason from the one to the other.— As soon as they are of sufficient age, it is supposed they will be sent on from the grammar schools to the university, which constitutes our third and last stage, there to study those sciences which may be adapted to their views.—By that part of our plan which prescribes the selection of the youths of genius from among the classes of the poor, we hope to avail the state of those talents which nature has sown as liberally among the poor as the rich, but which perish without use, if not sought for and

we have submitted to them. The rights of conscience we never submitted, we could not submit. We are answerable for them to our God. The legitimate powers of government extend to such acts only as are injurious to others. But it does me no injury for my neighbor to say there are twenty gods, or no god. It neither picks my pocket nor breaks my leg. If it be said his testimony in a court of justice cannot be relied on, reject it then, and be the stigma on him. Constraint may make him worse by making him a hypocrite, but it will never make him a truer man. It may fix him obstinately in his errors, but will not cure them. Reason and free inquiry are the only effectual agents against error. Give a loose to them, they will support the true religion by bringing every false one to their tribunal, to the test of their investigation. They are the natural enemies of error, and of error only. Had not the Roman government permitted free inquiry, christianity could never have been introduced. Had not free inquiry been indulged, at the aera of the reformation, the corruptions of christianity could not have been purged away. If it be restrained now, the present corruptions will be protected, and new ones encouraged. Was the government to prescribe to us our medicine and diet, our bodies would be in such keeping as our souls are now. Thus in France the emetic was once forbidden as a medicine, and the potatoe as an article of food. Government is just as infallible, too, when it fixes systems in physics. Galileo was sent to the inquisition for affirming that the earth was a sphere; the government had declared it to be as flat as a trencher, and Galileo was obliged to abjure his error. This error however at length prevailed, the earth became a globe, and Descartes declared it was whirled round its axis by a vortex. The government in which he lived was wise enough to see that this was no question of civil jurisdiction, or we should all have been involved by authority in vortices. In fact the vortices have been exploded, and the Newtonian principle of gravitation is now more firmly established, on the basis of reason, than it would be were the government to step in and to make it an article of necessary faith. Reason and experiment have been indulged, and error has fled before them. It is error alone which needs the support of government. Truth can stand by itself. Subject opinion to coercion: whom will you make your inquisitors? Fallible men; men governed by bad passions, by private as well as public reasons. And why subject it to coercion? To produce uniformity. But is uniformity of opinion desireable? No more than of face and stature. Introduce the bed of Procrustes then, and as there is danger that the large men may beat the small, make us all of a size, by lopping the former and stretching the latter. Difference of opinion is advantageous in religion. The several sects perform the office of a Censor morum over each other. Is uniformity attainable? Millions of innocent men, women and children, since the introduction of Christianity, have been burnt, tortured, fined, imprisoned: yet we have not advanced one inch towards uniformity. What has been the effect of coercion? To make one half the world fools, and the other half hypocrites. To support roguery and error all over the earth. Let us reflect that it is inhabited by a thousand millions of people. That these profess probably a thousand different systems of religion. That ours is but one of that thousand. That if there be but one right, and ours that one, we should wish to see the 999 wandering sects gathered into the fold of truth. But against such a majority we cannot effect this by force. Reason and persuasion are the only practicable instruments. To make way for these, free inquiry must be indulged; and how can we wish others to indulge it while we refuse it ourselves. But every state, says an inquisitor, has established some religion. "No two, say I, have established the same." Is this a proof of the infallibility of establishments? Our sister states of Pennsylvania and New York, however, have long subsisted without any establishment at all. The experiment was new and doubtful when they made it. It has answered beyond conception. They flourish infinitely. Religion is well supported; of various kinds indeed, but all good enough; all sufficient to preserve peace and order: or if a sect arises whose tenets would subvert morals, good sense has fair play, and reasons and laughs it out of doors, without suffering the state to be troubled with it. They do not hang more malefactors than we do. They are not more disturbed with religious dissentions. On the contrary, their harmony is unparalleled, and can be ascribed to nothing but their unbounded tolerance, because there is no other circumstance in which they differ from every nation on earth. They have made the happy discovery, that the way to silence religious disputes, is to take no notice of them. Let us too give this experiment fair play, and get rid, while we may, of those tyrannical laws. It is true we are as yet secured against them by the spirit of the times. I doubt whether the people of this country would suffer an execution for heresy, or a three years imprisonment for not comprehending the mysteries of the trinity. But is the spirit of the people an infallible, a permanent reliance? Is it government? Is this the kind of protection we receive in return for the rights we give up? Besides, the spirit of the times may alter, will alter. Our rulers will become corrupt, our people careless. A single zealot may commence persecuter, and better men be his victims. It can never be too often repeated, that the time for fixing every essential right on a legal basis is while our rulers are honest, and ourselves united. From the conclusion of this war we shall be going down hill. It will not then be necessary to resort every moment to the people for support. They will be forgotten therefore, and their rights disregarded. They will forget themselves, but in the sole faculty of making money, and will never think of uniting to effect a due respect for their rights. The shackles, therefore, which shall not be knocked off at the conclusion of this war, will remain on us long, will be made heavier and heavier, till our rights shall revive or expire in a convulsion.

QUERY XIX: MANUFACTURES

We never had an interior trade of any importance. Our exterior commerce has suffered very much from the beginning of the present contest. During this time we have manufactured within our families the most necessary articles of cloathing. Those of cotton will bear some comparison with the same kinds of manufacture in Europe; but those of wool, flax and hemp are very coarse, unsightly, and unpleasant: and such is our attachment to agriculture, and such our preference for foreign manufactures, that be it wise or unwise, our people will certainly return as soon as they can, to the raising raw materials, and exchanging them for finer manufactures than they are able to execute themselves.

The political oeconomists of Europe have established it as a principle, that every State should endeavour to manufacture for itself; and this principle, like many others, we transfer to America, without calculating the difference of circumstance which should often produce a difference of result. In Europe the lands are either cultivated, or locked up against the cultivator. Manufacture must therefore be resorted to, of necessity, not of choice, to support the surplus of their people. But we have an immensity of land courting the industry of the husbandman. Is it best then that all our citizens should be employed in its improvement, or that one half should be called off from that to exercise manufactures and handicraft arts for the other? Those who labour in the earth are the chosen people of God, if ever he had a chosen people, whose breasts he has made his peculiar deposit for substantial and genuine virtue. It is the focus in which he keeps alive that sacred fire, which otherwise might escape from the face of the earth. Corruption of morals in the mass of cultivators is a phaenomenon of which no age nor nation has furnished an example. It is the mark set on those, who not looking up to heaven, to their own soil and industry, as does the husbandman, for their subsistence, depend for it on casualties and caprice of customers. Dependance begets subservience and venality, suffocates the germ of virtue, and prepares fit tools for the designs of ambition. This, the natural progress and consequence of the arts, has sometimes perhaps been retarded by accidental circumstances: but, generally speaking the proportion which the aggregate of the other classes of citizens bears in any state to that of its husbandmen, is the proportion of its unsound to its healthy parts, and is a good enough barometer whereby to measure its degree of corruption. While we have land to labour then, let us never wish to see our citizens occupied at a work-bench, or twirling a distaff. Carpenters, masons, smiths, are wanting in husbandry: but, for the general operations of manufacture, let our work-shops remain in Europe. It is better to carry provisions and materials to workmen there, than bring them to the provisions and materials, and with them their manners and principles. The loss by the transportation of commodities across the Atlantic will be made up in happiness and permanence of government. The mobs of great cities add just so much to the support of pure government, as sores do to the strength of the human body. It is the manners and spirit of a people which preserve a republic in vigour. A degeneracy in these is a canker which soon eats to the heart of its laws and constitution.

THOMAS JEFFERSON

Opinion on the Constitutionality of the Bank (1791)

In response to President Washington's request for opinions on the constitutionality of Hamilton's proposed bank, Secretary of State Jefferson argued that the incorporation of a national bank would violate both the Constitution and a number of state laws. According to Jefferson's doctrine of strict construction, the federal government is narrowly limited to those "powers specially enumerated" in the Constitution.

The bill for establishing a national bank, in 1791, undertakes, among other things:

1. To form the subscribers into a corporation.
2. To enable them in their corporate capacities to receive grants of lands; and so far is against the laws of *mortmain*.
3. To make *alien* subscribers capable of holding lands; and so far is against the laws of *alienage*.

4. To transmit these lands, on the death of a proprietor, to a certain line of successors; and so far changes the course of *descents*.

5. To put the lands out of the reach of forfeiture or escheat; and so far is against the laws of *forfeiture* and *escheat*.

6. To transmit personal chattels to successors in a certain line; and so far is against the laws of *distribution*.

7. To give them the sole and exclusive right of banking under the national authority; and so far is against the laws of *monopoly*.

8. To communicate to them a power to make laws paramount to the laws of the states; for so they must be construed to protect the institution from the control of the state legislatures; and so, probably, they will be construed.

I consider the foundation of the Constitution as laid on this ground that *all powers not delegated to the United States, by the Constitution, nor prohibited by it to the states, are reserved to the states, or to the people* (10th amend.). To take a single step beyond the boundaries thus specially drawn around the powers of Congress, is to take possession of a boundless field of power, no longer susceptible of any definition.

The incorporation of a bank, and the powers assumed by this bill, have not, in my opinion, been delegated to the United States by the Constitution.

I. *They are not among the powers specially enumerated.* For these are,—

1. A power to *lay taxes* for the purpose of paying the debts of the United States. But no debt is paid by this bill, nor any tax laid. Were it a bill to raise money, its origination in the Senate would condemn it by the Constitution.

2. "To borrow money." But this bill neither borrows money nor insures the borrowing it. The proprietors of the bank will be just as free as any other money-holders to lend or not to lend their money to the public. The operation proposed in the bill, first to lend them two millions, and then to borrow them back again, cannot change the nature of the latter act, which will still be a payment, and not a loan, call it by what name you please.

3. "To regulate commerce with foreign nations, and among the states, and with the Indian tribes." To erect a bank, and to regulate commerce, are very different acts. He who erects a bank creates a subject of commerce in its bills; so does he who makes a bushel of wheat, or digs a dollar out of the mines; yet neither of these persons regulates commerce thereby. To make a thing which may be bought and sold, is not to prescribe

regulations for buying and selling. Besides, if this were an exercise of the power of regulating commerce, it would be void, as extending as much to the internal commerce of every state, as to its external. For the power given to Congress by the Constitution does not extend to the internal regulation of the commerce of a state * * * which remain exclusively with its own legislature; but to its external commerce only, that is to say, its commerce with another state, or with foreign nations, or with the Indian tribes. Accordingly the bill does not propose the measure as a "regulation of trade," but as "productive of considerable advantages to trade." Still less are these powers covered by any other of the special enumerations.

II. Nor are they within either of the general phrases, which are the two following:—

1. "To lay taxes to provide for the general welfare of the United States;" that is to say, "to lay taxes *for the purpose* of providing for the general welfare;" for the laying of taxes is the *power*, and the general welfare the *purpose* for which the power is to be exercised. Congress are not to lay taxes *ad libitum for any purpose they please*; but only *to pay the debts or provide for the welfare of the Union*. In like manner, they are not *to do anything they please* to provide for the general welfare, but only *to lay taxes* for that purpose. To consider the latter phrase, not as describing the purpose of the first, but as giving a distinct and independent power to do any act they please which might be for the good of the Union, would render all the preceding and subsequent enumerations of power completely useless. It would reduce the whole instrument to a single phrase—that of instituting a Congress with power to do whatever would be for the good of the United States; and, as they would be the sole judges of the good or evil, it would be also a power to do whatever evil they pleased.

It is an established rule of construction, where a phrase will bear either of two meanings, to give it that which will allow some meaning to the other parts of the instrument, and not that which will render all the others useless. Certainly no such universal power was meant to be given them. It was intended to lace them up straitly within the enumerated powers, and those without which, as means, these powers could not be carried into effect. It is known that the very power now proposed *as a means*, was rejected *as an end* by the Convention which formed the Constitution. A proposition was made to them to authorize Congress to open canals, and an amendatory one to empower them to incorporate. But the whole was rejected and one of the reasons of objection urged in debate was that they then would have a power to erect a bank, which would render great cities, where there were prejudices and jealousies on that subject, adverse to the reception of the Constitution.

2. The second general phrase is, "to make all laws *necessary* and proper for carrying into execution the enumerated powers." But they can all be carried into execution without a bank. A bank therefore, is *not necessary*, and consequently not authorized by this phrase.

It has been urged that a bank will give great facility or convenience in the collection of taxes. Suppose this were true; yet the Constitution allows only the means which are "necessary," not those which are merely "convenient," for effecting the enumerated powers. If such a latitude of construction be allowed to this phrase as to give any non-enumerated power, it will go to every one; for there is no one which ingenuity may not torture into a *convenience in some way or other, to some one* of so long a list of enumerated powers. It would swallow up all the delegated powers, and reduce the whole to one power, as before observed. Therefore it was that the Constitution restrained them to the *necessary* means; that is to say, to those means without which the grant of the power would be nugatory. * * *

Perhaps, indeed, bank bills may be a more *convenient* vehicle than treasury orders. But a little *difference* in the degree of convenience cannot constitute the necessity which the Constitution makes the ground for assuming any non-enumerated power. * * *

Can it be thought that the Constitution intended that for a shade or two of *convenience*, more or less, Congress should be authorized to break down the most ancient and fundamental laws of the several states, such as those against mortmain, the laws of alienage, the rules of descent, the acts of distribution, the laws of escheat and forfeiture, and the laws of monopoly?

Nothing but a necessity invincible by other means, can justify such a prostitution of laws, which constitute the pillars of our whole system of jurisprudence. Will Congress be too strait-laced to carry the Constitution into honest effect, unless they may pass over the foundation—laws of the state governments, for the slightest convenience of theirs?

The negative of the President is the shield provided by the Constitution to protect against the invasions of the legislature; 1. *The rights of the executive*; 2. *Of the judiciary*; 3. *Of the states and state legislatures*. The present is the case of a right remaining exclusively with the states, and is, consequently, one of those intended by the Constitution to be placed under his protection.

It must be added, however, that, unless the President's mind, on a view of everything which is urged for and against this bill, is tolerably clear that it is unauthorized by the Constitution; if the *pro* and the *con* hang so evenly as to balance his judgment, a just respect for the wisdom of the legislature would naturally decide the balance in favor of their opinion. It is chiefly for cases where they are clearly misled by error, ambition, or interest, that the Constitution has placed a check in the negative of the President.

THOMAS JEFFERSON

First Inaugural Address (1801)

Jefferson's first inaugural address was a conciliatory speech that sought to ease the tensions between Federalists and Republicans, but it also affirmed the "sacred principle" that the will of a "reasonable" majority should prevail in government. The new president also asserted his belief that the general government should be small and "frugal" in order to allow the state governments and individual citizens to pursue their own activities without interference.

Friends and Fellow-Citizens:

Called upon to undertake the duties of the first executive office of our country, I avail myself of the presence of that portion of my fellow-citizens which is here assembled to express my grateful thanks for the favor with which they have been pleased to look toward me, to declare a sincere consciousness that the task is above my talents, and that I approach it with those anxious and awful presentiments which the greatness of the charge and the weakness of my powers so justly inspire. A rising nation, spread over a wide and fruitful land, traversing all the seas with the rich productions of their industry, engaged in commerce with nations who feel power and forget right, advancing rapidly to destinies beyond the reach of mortal eye—when I contemplate these transcendent objects, and see the honor, the happiness, and the hopes of this beloved country committed to the issue and the auspices of this day, I shrink from the contemplation, and humble myself before the magnitude of the undertaking. Utterly, indeed, should I despair did not the presence of many whom I here see remind me that in the other high authorities provided by our Constitution I shall find resources of wisdom, of virtue, and of zeal on which to rely under all difficulties. To you, then, gentlemen, who are charged with the sovereign functions of legislation, and to those associated with you, I look with encouragement for that guidance and support which may enable us to steer with safety the vessel in which we are all embarked amidst the conflicting elements of a troubled world.

During the contest of opinion through which we have passed the animation of discussions and of exertions has sometimes worn an aspect which might impose on strangers unused to think freely and to speak and to write what they think; but this being now decided by the voice of the nation, announced according to the rules of the Constitution, all will, of course, arrange themselves under the will of the law, and unite in common efforts for the common good. All, too, will bear in mind this sacred principle, that though the will of the majority is in all cases to prevail, that will to be rightful must be reasonable; that the minority possess their equal rights, which equal law must protect, and to violate would be oppression. Let us, then, fellow-citizens, unite with one heart and one mind. Let us restore to social intercourse that harmony and affection without which liberty and even life itself are but dreary things. And let us reflect that, having banished from our land that religious intolerance under which mankind so long bled and suffered, we have yet gained little if we countenance a political intolerance as despotic, as wicked, and capable of as bitter and bloody persecutions. During the throes and convulsions of the ancient world, during the agonizing spasms of infuriated man, seeking through blood and slaughter his long-lost liberty, it was not wonderful that the agitation of the billows should reach even this distant and peaceful shore; that this should be more felt and feared by some and less by others, and should divide opinions as to measures of safety. But every difference of opinion is not a difference of principle. We have called by different names brethren of the same principle. We are all Republicans, we are all Federalists. If there be any among us who would wish to dissolve this Union or to change its republican form, let them stand undisturbed as monuments of the safety with which error of opinion may be tolerated where reason is left free to combat it. I know, indeed, that some honest men fear that a republican government can not be strong, that this Government is not strong enough; but would the honest patriot, in the full tide of successful experiment, abandon a government which has so far kept us free and firm on the theoretic and visionary fear that this Government, the world's best hope, may by possibility want energy to preserve itself? I trust not. I believe this, on the contrary, the strongest Government on earth. I believe it the only one where every man, at the call of the law, would fly to the standard of the law, and would meet invasions of the public order as his own personal concern. Sometimes it is said that man can not be trusted with the government of himself. Can he, then, be trusted with the government of others? Or have we found angels in the forms of kings to govern him? Let history answer this question.

Let us, then, with courage and confidence pursue our own Federal and Republican principles, our attachment to union and representative government. Kindly separated by nature and a wide ocean from the exterminating havoc of one quarter of the globe; too high-minded to endure the degradations of the others; possessing a chosen country, with room enough for our descendants to the thousandth and thousandth generation; entertaining a due sense of our equal right to the use of our own faculties, to the acquisitions of our own industry, to honor and confidence from our fellow-citizens, resulting not from birth, but from our actions and their sense of them; enlightened by a benign religion, professed, indeed, and practiced in various forms, yet all of them inculcating honesty, truth, temperance, gratitude, and the love of man; acknowledging and adoring an overruling Providence, which by all its dispensations proves that it delights in the happiness of man here and his greater happiness hereafter—with all these blessings, what more is necessary to make us a happy and a prosperous people? Still one thing more, fellow-citizens—a wise and frugal Government, which shall restrain men from injuring one another, shall leave them otherwise free to regulate their own pursuits of industry and improvement, and shall not take from the mouth of labor the bread it has earned. This is the sum of good government, and this is necessary to close the circle of our felicities.

About to enter, fellow-citizens, on the exercise of duties which comprehend everything dear and valuable to you, it is proper you should understand what I deem the essential principles of our Government, and consequently those which ought to shape its Administration. I will compress them within the narrowest compass they will bear, stating the general principle, but not all its limitations. Equal and exact justice to all men, of whatever state or persuasion, religious or political; peace, commerce, and honest friendship with all nations, entangling alliances with none; the support of the State governments in all their rights, as the most competent administrations for our domestic concerns and the surest bulwarks against antirepublican tendencies; the preservation of the General Government in its whole constitutional vigor, as the sheet anchor of our peace at home and safety abroad; a jealous care of the right of election by the people—a mild and safe corrective of abuses which are lopped by the sword of revolution where peaceable remedies are unprovided; absolute acquiescence in the decisions of the majority, the vital principle of republics, from which is no appeal but to force, the vital principle and immediate parent of despotism; a well-disciplined militia, our best reliance in peace and for the first moments of war, till regulars may relieve them; the supremacy of the civil over the military authority; economy in the public expense, that labor may be lightly burthened; the honest payment of our debts and sacred preservation of the public faith; encouragement of agriculture, and of commerce as its handmaid; the diffusion of information and arraignment of all abuses at the bar of the public reason; freedom of religion; freedom of the press, and freedom of person under the protection of the habeas corpus, and trial by juries impartially selected. These principles form the bright constellation which has gone before us and guided our steps through an age of revolution and reformation. The wisdom of our sages and blood of our heroes have been devoted to their attainment. They should be the creed of our political faith, the text of civic instruction, the touchstone by which to try the services of those we trust; and should we wander from them in moments of error or of alarm, let us hasten to retrace our steps and to regain the road which alone leads to peace, liberty, and safety.

I repair, then, fellow-citizens, to the post you have assigned me. With experience enough in subordinate offices to have seen the difficulties of this the greatest of all, I have learnt to expect that it will rarely fall to the lot of imperfect man to retire from this station with the reputation and the favor which bring him into it. Without pretensions to that high confidence you reposed in our first and greatest revolutionary character, whose preëminent services had entitled him to the first place in his country's love and destined for him the fairest page in the volume of faithful history, I ask so much confidence only as may give firmness and effect to the legal administration of your affairs. I shall often go wrong through defect of judgment. When right, I shall often be thought wrong by those whose positions will not command a view of the whole ground. I ask your indulgence for my own errors, which will never be intentional, and your support against the errors of others, who may condemn what they would not if seen in all its parts. The approbation implied by your suffrage *is* a great consolation to me for the past, and my future solicitude will be to retain the good opinion of those who have bestowed it in advance, to conciliate that of others by doing them all the good in my power, and to be instrumental to the happiness and freedom of all.

Relying, then, on the patronage of your good will, I advance with obedience to the work, ready to retire from it whenever you become sensible how much better choice it is in your power to make. And may that Infinite Power which rules the destinies of the universe lead our councils to what is best, and give them a favorable issue for your peace and prosperity.

THOMAS JEFFERSON

Second Inaugural Address (1805)

In his second inaugural address, Jefferson reiterated some of the ideas he expressed in his first inaugural speech but focused more heavily on the topic of frugality in government. Especially interesting are his comments about America's "aboriginal inhabitants."

On taking this station on a former occasion, I declared the principles on which I believed it my duty to administer the affairs of our commonwealth. My conscience tells me that I have, on every occasion, acted up to that declaration, according to its obvious import, and to the understanding of every candid mind.

In the transaction of your foreign affairs, we have endeavored to cultivate the friendship of all nations, and especially of those with which we have the most important relations. We have done them justice on all occasions, favored where favor was lawful, and cherished mutual interests and intercourse on fair and equal terms. We are firmly convinced, and we act on that conviction, that with nations, as with individuals, our interests soundly calculated, will ever be found inseparable from our moral duties; and history bears witness to the fact, that a just nation is taken on its word, when recourse is had to armaments and wars to bridle others.

At home, fellow citizens, you best know whether we have done well or ill. The suppression of unnecessary offices, of useless establishments and expenses, enabled us to discontinue our internal taxes. These covering our land with officers, and opening our doors to their intrusions, had already begun that process of domiciliary vexation which, once entered, is scarcely to be restrained from reaching successively every article of produce and property. If among these taxes some minor ones fell which had not been inconvenient, it was because their amount would not have paid the officers who collected them, and because, if they had any merit, the state authorities might adopt them, instead of others less approved.

The remaining revenue on the consumption of foreign articles, is paid cheerfully by those who can afford to add foreign luxuries to domestic comforts, being collected on our seaboards and frontiers only, and incorporated with the transactions of our mercantile citizens, it may be the pleasure and pride of an American to ask, what farmer, what mechanic, what laborer, ever sees a taxgatherer of the United States? These contributions enable us to support the current expenses of the government, to fulfill contracts with foreign nations, to extinguish the native right of soil within our limits, to extend those limits, and to apply such a surplus to our public debts, as places at a short day their final redemption, and that redemption once affected, the revenue thereby liberated may, by a just repartition among the states, and a corresponding amendment of the constitution, be applied, *in time of peace,* to rivers, canals, roads, arts, manufactures, education, and other great objects within each state. *In time of war,* if injustice, by ourselves or others, must sometimes produce war, increased as the same revenue will be increased by population and consumption, and aided by other resources reserved for that crisis, it may meet within the year all the expenses of the year, without encroaching on the rights of future generations, by burdening them with the debts of the past. War will then be but a suspension of useful works, and a return to a state of peace, a return to the progress of improvement.

I have said, fellow citizens, that the income reserved had enabled us to extend our limits; but that extension may possibly pay for itself before we are called on, and in the meantime, may keep down the accruing interest; in all events, it will repay the advances we have made. I know that the acquisition of Louisiana has been disapproved by some, from a candid apprehension that the enlargement of our territory would endanger its union. But who can limit the extent to which the federative principle may operate effectively? The larger our association, the less will it be shaken by local passions; and in any view, is it not better that the opposite bank of the Mississippi should be settled by our own brethren and children, than by strangers of another family? With which shall we be most likely to live in harmony and friendly intercourse?

In matters of religion, I have considered that its free exercise is placed by the constitution independent of the powers of the general government. I have therefore undertaken, on no occasion, to prescribe the religious exercises suited to it; but have left them, as the constitution found them, under the direction and discipline of state or church authorities acknowledged by the several religious societies.

The aboriginal inhabitants of these countries I have regarded with the commiseration their history inspires. Endowed with the faculties and the rights of men, breathing an ardent love of liberty and independence, and occupying a country which left them no desire but to be undisturbed, the stream of overflowing population from other regions directed itself on these shores; without power to divert, or habits to contend against, they have been overwhelmed by the current, or driven before it; now reduced within limits too narrow for the hunter's state, humanity enjoins us to teach them agriculture and the domestic arts; to encourage them to that industry which alone can enable them to maintain their place in existence, and to prepare them in time for that state of society, which to bodily comforts adds the improvement of the mind and morals. We have therefore liberally furnished them with the implements of husbandry and household use; we have placed among them instructors in the arts of first necessity; and they are covered with the aegis of the law against aggressors from among ourselves.

But the endeavors to enlighten them on the fate which awaits their present course of life, to induce them to exercise their reason, follow its dictates, and change their pursuits with the change of circumstances, have powerful obstacles to encounter; they are combated by the habits of their bodies, prejudice of their minds, ignorance, pride, and the influence of interested and crafty individuals among them, who feel themselves something in the present order of things, and fear to become nothing in any other. These persons inculcate a sanctimonious reverence for the customs of their ancestors; that whatever they did must be done through all time; that reason is a false guide, and to advance under its counsel, in their physical, moral, or political condition, is perilous innovation; that their duty is to remain as their Creator made them, ignorance being safety, and knowledge full of danger; in short, my friends, among them is seen the action and counteraction of good sense and bigotry; they, too, have their anti-philosophers, who find an interest in keeping things in their present state, who dread reformation, and exert all their faculties to maintain the ascendency of habit over the duty of improving our reason, and obeying its mandates.

THOMAS JEFFERSON

Selected Letters

To Reverend James Madison (1785)

In this letter to a cousin of his protégé James Madison, Jefferson proposed a progressive tax and more equitable divisions of land as remedies for the wretched poverty that he witnessed in France. Implicit in the letter is a creative and almost revolutionary reading of John Locke's theory of property, one that Thomas Paine would later articulate in his Agrarian Justice.

The property of this country is absolutely concentrated in a very few hands, having revenues of from half a million of guineas a year downwards. These employ the flower of the country as servants, some of them having as many as 200 domestics, not labouring. They employ also a great number of manufacturers, & tradesmen, & lastly the class of labouring husbandmen. But after all there comes the most numerous of all the classes, that is, the poor who cannot find work. I asked myself what could be the reason that so many should be permitted to beg who are willing to work, in a country where there is a very considerable proportion of uncultivated lands? These lands are undisturbed only for the sake of game. It should seem then that it must be because of the enormous wealth of the proprietors which places them above attention to the encrease of their revenues by permitting these lands to be laboured. I am conscious that an equal division of property is impracticable. But the consequences of this enormous inequality producing so much misery to the bulk of mankind, legislators cannot invent too many devices for subdividing property, only taking care to let their subdivisions go hand in hand with the natural affections of the human mind. The descent of property of every kind therefore to all the children, or to all the brothers & sisters, or other relations in equal degree is a politic measure, and a practicable one. Another means of silently lessening the inequality of property is to exempt all from taxation below a certain point, & to tax the higher portions of property in geometrical progression as they rise. Whenever there is in any country, uncultivated lands and unemployed poor, it is clear that the laws of property have been so far extended as to violate natural right. The earth is given as a common stock for man to labour & live on. If for the encouragement of industry we allow it to be appropriated, we must take care that other employment be provided to those excluded from the appropriation. If we do not the fundamental right to labour the earth returns to the unemployed. It is too soon yet in our country to say that every man who cannot find employment but who can find uncultivated land shall be at liberty to cultivate it, paying a moderate rent. But it is not too soon to provide by every possible means that as few as possible shall be without a little portion of land. The small land holders are the most precious part of a state.

To Colonel Edward Carrington (1787)

Jefferson, unlike many of the Founders, consistently supported the right and ability of the people to govern themselves directly. In support of this idea, the Virginian stressed the importance of a free press and the general diffusion of knowledge to enlighten the people.

T he tumults in America I expected would have produced in Europe an unfavorable opinion of our political state. But it has not. On the contrary, the small effect of these tumults seems to have given more confidence in the firmness of our governments. The interposition of the people themselves on the side of government has had a great effect on the opinion here. I am persuaded myself that the good sense of the people will always be found to be the best army. They may be led astray for a moment, but will soon correct themselves. The people are the only censors of their governors; and even their errors will tend to keep these to the true principles of their institution. To punish these errors too severely would be to suppress the only safeguard of the public liberty. The way to prevent these irregular interpositions of the people, is to give them full information of their affairs through the channel of the public papers, and to contrive that those papers should penetrate the whole mass of the people. The basis of our governments being the opinion of the people, the very first object should be to keep that right; and were it left to me to decide whether we should have a government without newspapers, or newspapers without a government, I should not hesitate a moment to prefer the latter. But I should mean that every man should receive those papers, and be capable of reading them. I am convinced that those societies (as the Indians) which live without government, enjoy in their general mass an infinitely greater degree of happiness than those who live under the European governments. Among the former, public opinion is in the place of law, and restrains morals as powerfully as laws ever did anywhere. Among the latter, under pretence of governing, they have divided their nations into two classes, wolves and sheep. I do not exaggerate. This is a true picture of Europe. Cherish, therefore, the spirit of our people, and keep alive their attention. Do not be too severe upon their errors, but reclaim them by enlightening them. If once they become inattentive to the public affairs, you and I, and Congress and Assemblies, Judges and Governors, shall all become wolves. It seems to be the law of our general nature, in spite of individual exceptions; and experience declares that man is the only animal which devours his own kind; for I can apply no milder term to the governments of Europe, and to the general prey of the rich on the poor.

To William S. Smith (1787)

A firm believer that the vigilance of the people is the best defense against tyranny, Jefferson wrote that occasional rebellions can be valuable exercises in popular sovereignty and serious warnings to rulers.

God forbid we should ever be twenty years without such a rebellion [Shays's Rebellion]. The people cannot be all, and always, well-informed. The part which is wrong will be discontented in proportion to the importance of the facts they misconceive. If they remain quiet under such misconceptions, it is a lethargy, the forerunner of death to the public liberty. We have had thirteen States independent for eleven years. There has been one rebellion. That comes to one rebellion in a century and a half for each State. What country before ever existed a century and a half without a rebellion? And what country can preserve its liberties if its rulers are not warned from time to time that this people preserve the spirit of resistance? Let them take arms. The remedy is to set them right as to facts, pardon and pacify them. What signify a few lives lost in a century or two? The tree of liberty must be refreshed from time to time with the blood of patriots and tyrants. It is its natural manure. Our convention has been too much impressed by the insurrection of Massachusetts, and on the spur of the moment they are setting up a kite to keep the hen yard in order.

To James Madison (1789)

In this letter Jefferson articulated a position he held throughout his life: "The earth belongs always to the living generation," which has no obligations to the past and no right to bind future generations.

The question Whether one generation of men has a right to bind another, seems never to have been started either on this or our side of the water. Yet it is a question of such consequences as not only to merit decision, but place also, among the fundamental principles of every government. The course of reflection in which we are immersed here on the elementary principles of society has presented this question to my mind; and that no such obligation can be transmitted I think very capable of proof. I set out on this ground which I suppose to be self evident, "that the earth belongs in usufruct to the living;" that the dead have neither powers nor rights over it. The portion occupied by any individual ceases to be his when himself ceases to be, and reverts to the society. If the society has formed no rules for the appropriation of its lands in severalty, it will be taken by the first occupants. These will generally be the wife and children of the decedent. If they have formed rules of appropriation, those rules may give it to the wife and children, or to some one of them, or to the legatee of the deceased. So they may give it to his creditor. But the child, the legatee or creditor takes it, not by any natural right, but by a law of the society of which they are members, and to which they are subject. Then no man can by natural right oblige the lands he occupied, or the persons who succeed him in that occupation, to the paiment of debts contracted by him. For if he could, he might during his own life, eat up the usufruct of the lands for several generations to come, and then the lands would belong to the dead, and not to the living, which would be reverse of our principle.

What is true of every member of the society individually, is true of them all collectively, since the rights of the whole can be no more than the sum of the rights of individuals. To keep our ideas clear when applying them to a multitude, let us suppose a whole generation of men to be born on the same day, to attain mature age on the same day, and to die the same day, leaving a succeeding generation in the moment of attaining their mature age all together. Let the ripe age be supposed of 21. years, and their period of life 34. years more, that being the average term given by the bills of mortality to persons who have already attained 21. years of age. Each successive generation would, in this way, come on and go off the stage at a fixed moment, as individuals do now. Then I say the earth belongs to each of these generations during it's course, fully, and in their own right. The 2d. generation receives it clear of the debts and incumbrances of the 1st., the 3d. of the 2d. and so on. For if the 1st. could charge it with a debt, then the earth would belong to the dead and not the living generation. Then no generation can contract debts greater than may be paid during the course of it's own existence. At 21. years of age they may bind themselves and their lands for 34. years to come: at 22. for 33: at 23 for 32. and at 54 for one year only; because these are the terms of life which remain to them at the respective epochs. But a material difference must be noted between the succession of an individual and that of a whole generation. Individuals are parts only of a society, subject to the laws of a whole. These laws may appropriate the portion of land occupied by a decedent to his creditor rather than to any other, or to his child, on condition he satisfies his creditor. But when a whole generation, that is, the whole society dies, as in the case we have supposed, and another generation or society succeeds, this forms a whole, and there is no superior who can give their territory to a third society, who may have lent money to their predecessors beyond their faculty of paying.

What is true of a generation all arriving to self-government on the same day, and dying all on the same day, is true of those on a constant course of decay and renewal, with this only difference. A generation coming in and going out entire, as in the first case, would have a right in the 1st year of their self dominion to contract a debt for 33. years, in the 10th. for 24. in the 20th. for 14. in the 30th. for 4. whereas generations changing daily, by daily deaths and births, have one constant term beginning at the date of their contract, and ending when a majority of those of full age at that date shall be dead. The length of that term may be estimated from the tables of mortality, corrected by the circumstances of climate, occupation &c. peculiar to the country of the contractors. Take, for instance, the table of M. de Buffon wherein he states that 23,994 deaths, and the ages at which they happened. Suppose a society in which 23,994 persons are born every year and live to the ages stated in this table. The conditions of that society will be as follows. 1st. it will consist constantly of 617,703 persons of all ages. 2dly. of those living at any one instant of time, one half will be dead in 24. years 8. months. 3dly. 10,675 will arrive every year at the age of 21. years complete. 4thly. it will constantly have 348,417 persons of all ages above 21. years. 5ly. and the half of those of 21. years and upwards living at any one instant of time will be dead in 18. years 8. months, or say 19. years as the nearest integral number. Then 19. years is the term beyond which neither the representatives of a nation, nor even the whole nation itself assembled, can validly extend a debt. * * *

* * * I suppose that the received opinion, that the public debts of one generation devolve on the next, has been suggested by our seeing habitually in private life that he who succeeds to lands is required to pay the debts of his ancestor or testator, without considering that this requisition is municipal only, not moral, flowing from the will of the society which has found it convenient to appropriate the lands become vacant by the death of their occupant on the condition of a paiment of his debts; but that between society and society, or generation and generation there is no municipal obligation, no umpire but the law of nature. We seem not to have perceived that, by the law of nature, one generation is to another as one independant nation to another. * * *

* * * On similar ground it may be proved that no society can make a perpetual constitution, or even a perpetual law. The earth belongs always to the living generation. They may manage it then, and what proceeds from it, as they please, during their usufruct. They are masters too of their own persons, and consequently may govern them as they please. But persons and property make the sum of the objects of government. The constitution and the laws of their predecessors extinguished them, in their natural course, with those whose will gave them being. This could preserve that being till it ceased to be itself, and no longer. Every constitution,

then, and every law, naturally expires at the end of 19. years. If it be enforced longer, it is an act of force and not of right.

To Elbridge Gerry (1799)

This letter is perhaps Jefferson's most concise summary of his republican political principles, offered here in response to what he discerns to be the monarchical ideals of the Federalist administration.

I shall make to you a profession of my political faith; in confidence that you will consider every future imputation on me of a contrary complexion, as bearing on its front the mark of falsehood and calumny.

I do then, with sincere zeal, wish an inviolable preservation of our present federal constitution, according to the true sense in which it was adopted by the States, that in which it was advocated by its friends, and not that which its enemies apprehended, who therefore became its enemies; and I am opposed to the monarchising its features by the forms of its administration, with a view to conciliate a first transition to a President and Senate for life, and from that to a hereditary tenure of these offices, and thus to worm out the elective principle. I am for preserving to the States the powers not yielded by them to the union, and to the legislature of the Union its constitutional share in the division of powers; and I am not for transferring all the powers of the States to the general government, and all those of that government to the Executive branch. I am for a government rigorously frugal and simple, applying all the possible savings of the public revenue to the discharge of the national debt and not for a multiplication of officers and salaries merely to make partisans and for increasing, by every device, the public debt, on the principle of its being a public blessing. I am for relying, for internal defence, on our militia solely, till actual invasion, and for such a naval force only as may protect our coasts and harbors from such depredations as we have experienced; and not for a standing army in time of peace, which may overawe the public sentiment; nor for a navy, which, by its own expenses and the eternal wars in which it will implicate us, will grind us with public burdens, and sink us under them. I am for free commerce with all nations; political connection with none; and little or no diplomatic establishment. And I am not for linking ourselves by new treaties with the quarrels of Europe; entering that field of slaughter to preserve their balance, or joining in the confederacy of kings to war against the principles of liberty. I am for freedom of religion, and against all maneuvres to bring about a legal ascendancy of one sect over another; for freedom of the press, and against all violations of the constitution to silence by force and not by reason the complaints or criticisms, just or unjust, of our citizens against the conduct of their agents. And I am for encouraging the progress of science in all its branches; and not for raising a hue and cry against the sacred name of philosophy; for awing the human mind by stories of raw head and bloody bones to a distrust of its own vision, and to repose implicitly on that of others; to go backwards instead of forwards to look for improvements; to believe that government, religion, morality, and every other science were in the highest perfection in ages of the darkest ignorance, and that nothing can ever be devised more perfect than what was established by our forefathers. To these I will add, that I was a sincere well-wisher to the success of the French revolution, and still wish it may end in the establishment of a free and well-ordered republic; but I have not been insensible under the atrocious depredations they have committed on our commerce. The first object of my heart is my own country. In that is embarked my family, my fortune, and my own existence. I have not one farthing of interest, nor one fibre of attachment out of it, nor a single motive of preference of any one nation to another, but in proportion as they are more or less friendly to us. But though deeply feeling the injuries of France, I did not think war the surest means of redressing them. I did believe, that a mission sincerely disposed to preserve peace, would obtain for us a peaceable and honorable settlement and retribution; and I appeal to you to say, whether this might not have been obtained, if either of your colleagues had been of the same sentiment with yourself.

To a Committee of the Danbury Baptist Association (1802)

The Baptists were staunch defenders of religious liberty. In response to a letter congratulating him on his election to the presidency, Jefferson replies with a letter that contains his ideas of a "wall of separation between Church and State."

GENTLEMEN:—The affectionate sentiments of esteem and approbation which you are so good as to express towards me, on behalf of the Danbury Baptist Association, give me the highest satisfaction. My duties dictate a faithful and zealous pursuit of the interests of my constituents, and in proportion as they are persuaded of my fidelity to those duties, the discharge of them becomes more and more pleasing.

Believing with you that religion is a matter which lies solely between man and his God, that he owes account to none other for his faith or his worship, that the legislative powers of government reach actions only, and not opinions, I contemplate with sovereign reverence that act of the whole American people which declared that their legislature should "make no law respecting an establishment of religion, or prohibiting the free exercise thereof," thus building a wall of separation between Church and State. Adhering to this expression of the supreme will of the nation in behalf of the rights of conscience, I shall see with sincere satisfaction the progress of those sentiments which tend to restore to man all his natural rights, convinced he has no natural right in opposition to his social duties.

I reciprocate your kind prayers for the protection and blessing of the common Father and Creator of man, and tender you for yourselves and your religious association, assurances of my high respect and esteem.

To John Adams (1813)

After a long period of estrangement following the bitter presidential election of 1800, Jefferson and John Adams resumed a friendship and steady correspondence that had begun during the Revolutionary War. In response to a question on aristocracy that Adams raised, the Virginian explained that the best government is one that elevates the "natural aristocracy" of "virtue and wisdom" over the "artificial aristocracy" of wealth and birth. In this letter Jefferson also reiterated his belief in the importance of wards, those "little republics" that educate the people in self-government.

For I agree with you that there is a natural aristocracy among men. The grounds of this are virtue and talents. Formerly, bodily powers gave place among the aristoi. But since the invention of gunpowder has armed the weak as well as the strong with missile death, bodily strength, like beauty, good humor, politeness and other accomplishments, has become but an auxiliary ground of distinction. There is also an artificial aristocracy, founded on wealth and birth, without either virtue or talents; for with these it would belong to the first class. The natural aristocracy I consider as the most precious gift of nature, for the instruction, the trusts, and government of society. And indeed, it would have been inconsistent in creation to have formed man for the social state, and not to have provided virtue and wisdom enough to manage the concerns of the society. May we not even say, that that form of government is the best, which provides the most effectually for a pure selection of these natural aristoi into the offices of government? The artificial aristocracy is a mischievous ingredient in government, and provision should be made to prevent its ascendency. On the question, what is the best provision, you and I differ; but we differ as rational friends, using the free exercise of our own reason, and mutually indulging its errors. You think it best to put the pseudo-aristoi into a separate chamber of legislation, where they may be hindered from doing mischief by their co-ordinate branches, and where, also, they may be a protection to wealth against the Agrarian and plundering enterprises of the majority of the people. I think that to give them power in order to prevent them from doing mischief, is arming them for it, and increasing instead of remedying the evil. For if the co-ordinate branches can arrest their action, so may they that of the co-ordinates. Mischief may be done negatively as well as positively. Of this, a cabal in the Senate of the United States has furnished many proofs. Nor do I believe them necessary to protect the wealthy; because enough of these will find their way into every branch of the legislation, to protect themselves. From fifteen to twenty legislatures of our own, in action for thirty years past, have proved that no fears of an equalization of property are to be apprehended from them. I think the best remedy is exactly that provided by all our constitutions, to leave to the citizens the free election and separation of the aristoi from the pseudo-aristoi, of the wheat from the chaff. In general they will elect the really good and wise. In some instances, wealth may corrupt, and birth blind them; but not in sufficient degree to endanger the society.

It is probable that our difference of opinion may, in some measure, be produced by a difference of character in those among whom we live. From what I have seen of Massachusetts and Connecticut myself, and still more from what I have heard, and the character given of the former by yourself, who know them so much better, there seems to be in those two States a traditionary reverence for certain families, which has rendered the offices of the government nearly hereditary in those families. I presume that from an early period of your history, members of those families happening to possess virtue and talents, have honestly exercised them for the good of the people, and by their services have endeared their names to them. In coupling Connecticut with you, I mean it politically only, not morally. For having made the Bible the common law of their land, they seem to have modeled their morality on the story of Jacob and Laban. But although this hereditary succession to office with you, may, in some degree, be founded in real family merit, yet in a much higher degree, it has proceeded from your strict alliance of Church and State. These families are canonised in the eyes of the people on common principles, "you tickle me, and I will tickle you." In Virginia we have nothing of this. Our clergy, before the revolution, having been secured against rivalship by fixed salaries, did not give themselves the trouble of acquiring influence over the people. Of wealth, there were great accumulations in particular families, handed down from generation to generation, under the English law of entails. But the only object of ambition for the wealthy was a seat in the King's Council. All their court then was paid to the crown and its creatures; and they Philipised in all collisions between the King and the people. Hence they were unpopular; and that unpopularity continues attached to their names. A Randolph, a Carter, or a Burwell must have great personal superiority over a common competitor to be elected by the people even at this day. At the first session of our legislature after the Declaration of Independence, we passed a law abolishing entails. And this was followed by one abolishing the privilege of primogeniture, and dividing the lands of intestates equally among all their children, or other representatives. These laws, drawn by myself, laid the axe to the foot of pseudo-aristocracy. And had another which I prepared been adopted by the legislature, our work would have been complete. It was a bill for the more general diffusion of learning. This proposed to divide every county into wards of five or six miles square, like your townships; to establish in each ward a free school for reading, writing and common arithmetic; to provide for the annual selection of the best subjects from these schools, who might receive at the public expense a higher degree of education at a district school; and from these district schools to select a certain number of the most promising subjects, to be completed at an University, where all the useful sciences should be taught. Worth and genius would thus have been sought out from every condition of life, and completely prepared by education for defeating the competition of wealth and birth for public trusts. My proposition had, for a further object, to impart to these wards those portions of self-government for which they are best qualified, by confiding to them the care of their poor, their roads, police, elections, the nomination of jurors, administration of justice in small cases, elementary exercises of militia; in short, to have made them little republics, with a warden at the head of each, for all those concerns which, being under their eye, they would better manage than the larger republics of the county or State. A general call of ward meetings by their wardens on the same day through the State, would at any time produce the genuine sense of the people on any required point, and would enable the State to act in mass, as your people have so often done, and with so much effect by their town meetings. The law for religious freedom, which made a part of this system, having put down the aristocracy of the clergy, and restored to the citizen the freedom of the mind, and those of entails and descents nurturing an equality of condition among them, this on education would have raised the mass of the people to the high ground of moral respectability necessary to their own safety, and to orderly government; and would have completed the great object of qualifying them to select the veritable aristoi, for the trusts of government, to the exclusion of the pseudalists. * * * Although this law has not yet been acted on but in a small and inefficient degree, it is still considered as before the legislature, with other bills of the revised code, not yet taken up, and I have great hope that some patriotic spirit will, at a favorable moment, call it up, and make it the key-stone of the arch of our government.

With respect to aristocracy, we should further consider, that before the establishment of the American States, nothing was known to history but the man of the old world, crowded within limits either small or overcharged, and steeped in the vices which that situation generates. A government adapted to such men would be one thing; but a very different one, that for the man of these States. Here every one may have land to labor for himself, if he chooses; or, preferring the exercise of any other industry, may exact for it such compensation as not only to afford a comfortable subsistence, but wherewith to provide for a cessation from labor in old age. Every one, by his property, or by his satisfactory situation, is interested in the support of law and order. And such men may safely and advantageously reserve to themselves a wholesome control over their public affairs, and a degree of freedom, which, in the hands of the *canaille* of the cities of Europe, would be instantly perverted to the demolition and destruction of everything public and private. The history of the last twenty-five years of France, and of the last forty years in America, nay of its last two hundred years, proves the truth of both parts of this observation.

But even in Europe a change has sensibly taken place in the mind of man. Science had liberated the ideas of those who read and reflect, and the American example had kindled feelings of right in the people. An insurrection has consequently begun, of science, talents, and courage, against rank and birth, which have fallen into contempt. It has failed in its first effort, because the mobs of the cities, the instrument used for its accomplishment, debased by ignorance, poverty, and vice, could not be restrained to rational action. But the world will recover from the panic of this first catastrophe. Science is progressive, and talents and enterprise on the alert. Resort may be had to the people of the country, a more governable power from their principles and subordination; and rank, and birth, and tinsel-aristocracy will finally shrink into insignificance, even there. This, however, we have no right to meddle with. It suffices for us, if the moral and physical condition of our own citizens qualifies them to select the able and good for the direction of their government, with a recurrance of elections at such short periods as will enable them to displace an unfaithful servant, before the mischief he meditates may be irremediable.

I have thus stated my opinion on a point on which we differ, not with a view to controversy, for we are both too old to change opinions which are the result of a long life of inquiry and reflection; but on the suggestions of a former letter of yours, that we ought not to die before we have explained ourselves to each other. We acted in perfect harmony, through a long and perilous contest for our liberty and independence. A constitution has been acquired, which, though neither of us thinks perfect, yet both consider as competent to render our fellow citizens the happiest and the securest on whom the sun has ever shone. If we do not think exactly alike as to its imperfections, it matters little to our country, which, after devoting to it long lives of disinterested labor, we have delivered over to our successors in life, who will be able to take care of it and of themselves.

To Pierre Samuel Dupont de Nemours (1816)

This letter is perhaps the most succinct statement of Jefferson's views on the basic goodness and sociability of human nature in general and the democratic character of the American people in particular.

I received, my dear friend, your letter covering the constitution for your Equinoctial republics. * * * I suppose it well-formed for those for whom it was intended, and the excellence of every government is its adaptation to the state of those to be governed by it. For us it would not do. Distinguishing between the structure of the government and the moral principles on which you prescribe its administration, with the latter we concur cordially, with the former we should not. We of the United States, you know, are constitutionally and conscientiously democrats. We consider society as one of the natural wants with which man has been created; that he has been endowed with faculties and qualities to effect its satisfaction by concurrence of others having the same want; that when, by the exercise of these faculties, he has procured a state of society, it is one of his acquisitions which he has a right to regulate and control, jointly indeed with all those who have concurred in the procurement, whom he cannot exclude from its use or direction more than they him. We think experience has proved it safer, for the mass of individuals composing the society, to reserve to themselves personally the exercise of all rightful powers to which they are competent, and to delegate those to which they are not competent to deputies named, and removable for unfaithful conduct by themselves immediately. Hence, with us, the people (by which is meant the mass of individuals composing the society) being competent to judge of the facts occurring in ordinary life, they have retained the functions of judges of facts under the name of jurors; but being unqualified for the management of affairs requiring intelligence above the common level, yet competent judges of human character, they chose, for their management, representatives, some by themselves immediately, others by electors chosen by themselves. * * *

But when we come to the moral principles on which the government is to be administered, we come to what is proper for all conditions of society. I meet you there in all the benevolence and rectitude of your native character, and I love myself always most where I concur most with you. Liberty, truth, probity, honor are declared to be the four cardinal principles of your society. I believe with you that morality, compassion, generosity are innate elements of the human constitution; that there exists a right independent of force; that a right to property is founded in our natural wants, in the means with which we are endowed to satisfy these wants, and the right to what we acquire by those means without violating the similar rights of other sensible beings; that no one has a right to obstruct another exercising his faculties innocently for the relief of sensibilities made a part of his nature; that justice is the fundamental law of society; that the majority, oppressing an individual, is guilty of a crime, abuses its strength, and by acting on the law of the strongest breaks up the foundations of society; that action by the citizens in person, in affairs within their reach and competence, and in all others by representatives, chosen immediately and removable by themselves, constitutes the essence of a republic; that all governments are more or less republican in proportion as this principle enters more or less into their composition; and that a government by representation is capable of extension over a greater surface of country than one of any other form. These, my friend, are the essentials in which you and I agree; however, in our zeal for their maintenance we may be perplexed and divaricate as to the structure of society most likely to secure them.

In the constitution of Spain, as proposed by the late Cortes, there was a principle entirely new to me and not noticed in yours, that no person born after that day should ever acquire the rights of citizenship until he could read and write. It is impossible sufficiently to estimate the wisdom of this provision. Of all those which have been thought of for securing fidelity in the administration of the government, constant ralliance to the principles of the constitution, and progressive amendments with the progressive advances of the human mind or changes in human affairs, it is the most effectual. Enlighten the people generally, and tyranny and oppressions of body and mind will vanish like evil spirits at the dawn of day.

Although I do not with some enthusiasts believe that the human condition will ever advance to such a state of perfection as that there shall no longer be pain or vice in the world, yet I believe it susceptible of much improvement, and most of all in matters of government and religion, and that the diffusion of knowledge among the people is to be the instrument by which it is to be effected.

To Samuel Kercheval (1816)

In a lengthy response to a question on representation, Jefferson warned against undue worship of the Constitution as an impediment to progress and argued that a ward system modeled after the New England townships was the best way for the people to preserve and exercise self-government.

Some men look at constitutions with sanctimonious reverence, and deem them like the arc of the covenant, too sacred to be touched. They ascribe to the men of the preceding age a wisdom more than human, and suppose what they did to be beyond amendment. I knew that age well; I belonged to it, and labored with it. It deserved well of its country. It was very like the present, but without the experience of the present; and forty years of experience in government is worth a century of book-reading; and this they would say themselves, were they to rise from the dead. I am certainly not an advocate for frequent and untried changes in laws and constitutions. I think moderate imperfections had better be borne with; because, when once known, we accommodate ourselves to them, and find practical means of correcting their ill effects. But I know also, that laws and institutions must go hand in hand with the progress of the human mind. As that becomes more developed, more enlightened, as new discoveries are made, new truths disclosed, and manners and opinions change with the change of circumstances, institutions must advance also, and keep pace with the times. We might as well require a man to wear still the coat which fitted him when a boy, as civilized society to remain ever under the regimen of their barbarous ancestors. It is this preposterous idea which has lately deluged Europe in blood. Their monarchs, instead of wisely yielding to the gradual change of circumstances, of favoring progressive accommodation to progressive improvement, have clung to old abuses, entrenched themselves behind steady habits, and obliged their subjects to seek through blood and violence rash and ruinous innovations, which, had they been referred to the peaceful deliberations and collected wisdom of the nation, would have been put into acceptable and salutary forms. Let us follow no such examples, nor weakly believe that one generation is not as capable as another of taking care of itself, and of ordering its own affairs. Let us, as our sister States have done, avail ourselves of our reason and experience, to correct the crude essays of our first and unexperienced, although wise, virtuous, and well-meaning councils. And lastly, let us provide in our constitution for its revision at stated periods. What these periods should be, nature herself indicates. By the European tables of mortality, of the adults living at any one moment of time, a majority will be dead in about nineteen years. At the end of that period, then, a new majority is come into place; or, in other words, a new generation. Each generation is as independent as the one preceding, as that was of all which had gone before. It has then, like them, a right to choose for itself the form of government it believes most promotive of its own happiness; consequently, to accommodate to the circumstances in which it finds itself, that received from its predecessors; and it is for the peace and good of mankind that a solemn opportunity of doing this every nineteen or twenty years, should be provided by the constitution; so that it may be handed on, with periodical repairs, from generation to generation, to the end of time, if anything human can so long endure. It is now forty years since the constitution of Virginia was formed. The same tables inform us, that, within that period, two-thirds of the adults then living are now dead. Have then the remaining third, even if they had the wish, the right to hold in obedience to their will, and to laws heretofore made by them, the other two-thirds, who, with themselves compose the present mass of adults? If they have not, who has? The dead? But the dead have no rights. They are nothing; and nothing cannot own something. Where there is no substance, there can be no accident. This corporeal globe, and everything upon it, belong to its present corporeal inhabitants, during their generation. They alone have a right to direct what is the concern of themselves, alone and to declare the law of that direction; and this declaration can only be made by their majority. That majority, then, has a right to depute representatives to a convention, and to make the constitution what they think will be the best for themselves. But how collect their voice? This is the real difficulty. If invited by private authority, or county or district meetings, these divisions are so large that few will attend; and their voice will be imperfectly, or falsely pronounced. Here then, would be one of the advantages of the ward divisions I have proposed. The mayor of every ward, on a question like the present, would call his ward together, take the simple yea or nay of its members, convey these to the county court, who would hand on those of all its wards to the proper general authority; and the voice of the whole people would be thus fairly, fully, and peaceably expressed, discussed, and decided by the common reason of the society. If this avenue be shut to the call of suffrance, it will make itself heard through that of force, and we shall go on, as other nations are doing, in the endless circle of oppression, rebellion, reformation; and oppression, rebellion, reformation, again; and so on forever.

To Judge Spencer Roane (1819)

Jefferson feared the unlimited power Marshall's decisions gave the Supreme Court. In a letter to a fellow Virginian, written shortly after McCulloch v. Maryland, he claimed that each branch of government should have equal power to decide on constitutionality.

The revolution of 1800 * * * was as real a revolution in the principles of our government as that of 1776 was in its form; not effected indeed by the sword, as that, but by the rational and peaceable instrument of reform, the suffrage of the people. The nation declared its will by dismissing functionaries of one principle, and electing those of another, in the two branches, executive and legislative, submitted to their election. Over the judiciary department, the Constitution had deprived them of their control. That, therefore, has continued the reprobated system, and * * * after twenty years' confirmation of the federated system by the voice of the nation, declared through the medium of elections, we find the judiciary on every occasion, still driving us into consolidation.

In denying the right they usurp of exclusively explaining the Constitution, I go further than you do, if I understand rightly your quotation from *The Federalist*, of an opinion that "the judiciary is the last resort in relation *to the other departments* of the government, but not in relation to the rights of the parties to the compact under which the Judiciary is derived." If this opinion be sound, then indeed is our Constitution a complete *felo de se*. For intending to establish three departments, coordinate and independent, that they might check and balance one another, it has given, according to this opinion, to one of them alone, the right to prescribe rules for the government of the others, and to that one too, which is unelected by, and independent of the nation. For experience has already shown that the impeachment it has provided is not even a scarecrow. * * * The Constitution, on this hypothesis, is a mere thing of wax in the hands of the judiciary, which they may twist and shape into any form they please. It should be remembered, as an axiom of eternal truth in politics, that whatever power in any government is independent, is absolute also; in theory only, at first, while the spirit of the people is up, but in practice, as fast as that relaxes. Independence can be trusted nowhere but with the people in mass. They are inherently independent of all but moral law. My construction of the Constitution is * * * that each department is truly independent of the others, and has an equal right to decide for itself what is the meaning of the Constitution in the cases submitted to its action; and especially, where it is to act ultimately and without appeal.

JAMES MADISON AND THOMAS JEFFERSON

Virginia and Kentucky Resolutions (1798)

In response to the Alien and Sedition Acts of 1798, which were passed by Federalists to suppress criticism of the Adams administration, Jefferson, who was vice president, and Madison, who was then out of office, drafted the Kentucky Resolutions and the Virginia Resolutions, respectively. In addition to protesting the despotic and unconstitutional nature of the acts, these Republicans asserted the right of the states to interpret the constitutionality of congressional acts and to "interpose," or resist, those acts when they violate the Constitution. The resolutions, which Federalists denounced as treasonable, contain a classic defense of states' rights and express the theory that the powers of the federal government derive from a compact among the states rather than from the people as a whole.

Kentucky Resolutions

I Resolved, that the several States composing the United States of America, are not united on the principle of unlimited submission to their general government; but that by compact under the style and title of a Constitution for the United States and of amendments thereto, they constituted a general government for special purposes, delegated to that government certain definite powers, reserving each State to itself, the residuary mass of right to their own self-government; and that whensoever the general government assumes undelegated powers, its acts are unauthoritative, void, and of no force: That to this compact each State acceded as a State, and is an integral party, its co-States forming, as to itself, the other party: That the government created by this compact was not made the exclusive or final judge of the extent of the powers delegated to itself; since that would have made its discretion, and not the Constitution, the measure of its powers; but that as in all other cases of compact among parties having no common Judge, each party has an equal right to judge for itself, as well of infractions as of the mode and measure of redress. * * *

III. *Resolved,* that it is true as a general principle, and is also expressly declared by one of the amendments to the Constitution that "the powers not delegated to the United States by the Constitution, nor prohibited by it to the States, are reserved to the States respectively, or to the people;" and that no power over the freedom of religion, freedom of speech, or freedom of the press being delegated to the United States by the Constitution, nor prohibited by it to the States, all lawful powers respecting the same did of right remain, and were reserved to the States, or to the people: That thus was manifested their determination to retain to themselves the right of judging how far the licentiousness of speech and of the press may be abridged without lessening their useful freedom, and how far those abuses which cannot be separated from their use should be tolerated rather than the use be destroyed; and thus also they guarded against all abridgment by the United States of the freedom of religious opinions and exercises, and retained to themselves the right of protecting the same, as this State, by a law passed on the general demand of its citizens, had already protected them from all human restraint or interference: And that in addition to this general principle and express declaration, another and more special provision has been made by one of the amendments to the Constitution which expressly declares, that "Congress shall make no law respecting an establishment of religion, or prohibiting the free exercise thereof, or abridging the freedom of speech, or of the press," thereby guarding in the same sentence, and under the same words the freedom of religion, of speech, and of the press in so much, that whatever violates either, throws down the sanctuary which covers the others, and that libels, falsehoods, defamation equally with heresy and false religion are withheld from the cognizance of Federal tribunals. That therefore [the Sedition Act], which does abridge the freedom of the press, is not law, but is altogether void and of no effect.

IV. *Resolved,* that alien friends are under the jurisdiction and protection of the laws of the State wherein they are; that no power over them has been delegated to the United States, nor prohibited to the individual States distinct from their power over citizens; and it being true as a general principle [Alien Act of June 22, 1798], which assumes power over

alien friends not delegated by the Constitution, is not law, but is altogether void and of no force. * * *

VI. *Resolved,* that the imprisonment of a person under the protection
of the laws of this Commonwealth on his failure to obey the simple order
of the President to depart out of the United States, as is undertaken by
the said act entitled "An act concerning aliens," is contrary to the Constitution, one amendment to which has provided, that "no person shall be
deprived of liberty without due process of law," and that another having
provided "that in all criminal prosecutions, the accused shall enjoy the
right to a public trial by an impartial jury, to be informed of the nature
and cause of the accusation, to be confronted with the witnesses against
him, to have compulsory process for obtaining witnesses in his favour,
and to have the assistance of counsel for his defense," the same act undertaking to authorize the President to remove a person out of the United
States, who is under the protection of the law, on his own suspicion,
without accusation, without jury, without public trial, without confrontation of the witnesses against him, without having witnesses in his favour,
without defense, without counsel, is contrary to these provisions also of
the Constitution, is therefore not law, but utterly void, and of no force.
That transferring the power of judging any person, who is under the protection of the laws, from the courts to the President of the United States,
as is undertaken by the same act concerning aliens, is against the article
of the Constitution which provides, that "the judicial power of the United
States shall be vested in courts, the judges of which shall hold their offices during good behavior," and that the said act is void for that reason
also and it is further to be noted, that this transfer of judiciary power is
to that magistrate of the general government who already possesses all
the executive, and a qualified negative in all the legislative powers.

VII. *Resolved,* that the construction applied by the general government
(as is evinced by sundry of their proceedings) to those parts of the Constitution of the United States which delegate to Congress a power to lay
and collect taxes, duties, imposts, and excises: to pay the debts, and provide for the common defense, and general welfare of the United States,
and to make all laws which shall be necessary and proper for carrying
into execution the powers vested by the Constitution in the government
of the United States, or any department thereof, goes to the destruction
of all the limits prescribed to their power by the Constitution: That words
meant by that instrument to be subsidiary only to the execution of the
limited powers ought not to be so construed as themselves to give unlimited powers, nor a part so to be taken as to destroy the whole residue of
the instrument: That the proceedings of the general government under
color of these articles will be a fit and necessary subject for revisal and

correction at a time of greater tranquillity, while those specified in the preceding resolutions call for immediate redress. * * *

IX. *Resolved,* lastly, that the Governor of this Commonwealth be, and is hereby authorized and requested to communicate the preceding Resolutions to the Legislatures of the several States, to assure them that this Commonwealth considers Union for specified National purposes, and particularly for those specified in their late Federal Compact, to be friendly to the peace, happiness, and prosperity of all the States: that faithful to that compact according to the plain intent and meaning in which it was understood and acceded to by the several parties, it is sincerely anxious for its preservation: that it does also believe, that to take from the States all the powers of self-government, and transfer them to a general and consolidated government, without regard to the special delegations and reservations solemnly agreed to in that compact, is not for the peace, happiness, or prosperity of these States: And that, therefore, this Commonwealth is determined, as it doubts not its co-States are, tamely to submit to undelegated and consequently unlimited powers in no man or body of men on earth. * * * That the friendless alien has indeed been selected as the safest subject of a first experiment, but the citizen will soon follow, or rather has already followed: for, already has a sedition act marked him as its prey: that these and successive acts of the same character, unless arrested on the threshold, may tend to drive these States into revolution and blood, and will furnish new calumnies against Republican governments, and new pretexts for those who wish it to be believed, that man cannot be governed but by a rod of iron: that it would be a dangerous delusion were a confidence in the men of our choice to silence our fears for the safety of our rights: that confidence is everywhere the parent of despotism: free government is founded in jealousy and not in confidence; it is jealousy and not confidence which prescribes limited Constitutions to bind down those whom we are obliged to trust with power: that our Constitution has accordingly fixed the limits to which and no further our confidence may go; and let the honest advocate of confidence read the alien and sedition acts, and say if the Constitution has not been wise in fixing limits to the government it created, and whether we should be wise in destroying those limits; let him say what the government is if it be not a tyranny, which the men of our choice have conferred on the President, and the President of our choice has assented to and accepted over the friendly strangers, to whom the mild spirit of our country and its laws had pledged hospitality and protection: that the men of our choice have more respected the bare suspicions of the President than the solid rights of innocence, the claims of justification, the sacred force of truth, and the forms and substance of law and justice. In questions of power then let no more be heard of confidence in man, but bind him down from mischief by the claims of the Constitution. That this Commonwealth does therefore call on its co-States for an expression of their sentiments on the acts concerning aliens, and for the punishment of certain crimes herein before specified, plainly declaring whether these acts are or are not authorized by the Federal Compact. And it doubts not that their sense will be so announced as to prove their attachment unaltered to limited government, whether general or particular, and that the rights and liberties of their co-States will be exposed to no dangers by remaining embarked on a common bottom with their own, that they will concur with this commonwealth in considering the said acts so palpably against the Constitution as to amount to an undisguised declaration, that the compact is not meant to be the measure of the powers of the general government, but that it will proceed in the exercise over these States of all powers whatsoever: That they will view this as seizing the rights of the States and consolidating them in the hands of the general government with a power assumed to bind the States (not merely in cases made Federal) but in all cases whatsoever, by laws made, not with their consent, but by others against their consent: That this would be to surrender the form of gov ernment we have chosen, and to live under one deriving its powers from its own will, and not from our authority; and that the co-States, recurring to their natural right in cases not made Federal, will concur in declaring these acts void and of no force, and will each unite with this Commonwealth in requesting their repeal at the next session of Congress.

Virginia Resolutions

R esolved, That the General Assembly of Virginia doth unequivocally express a firm resolution to maintain and defend the Constitution of the United States, and the Constitution of this state, against every aggression either foreign or domestic; and that they will support the Government of the United States in all measures warranted by the former.

That this Assembly most solemnly declares a warm attachment to the union of the states, to maintain which it pledges all its powers; and that, for this end, it is their duty to watch over and oppose every infraction of those principles which constitute the only basis of that union, because a faithful observance of them can alone secure its existence and the public happiness.

That this Assembly doth explicitly and peremptorily declare, that it views the powers of the Federal Government as resulting from the compact to which the states are parties, as limited by the plain sense and intention of the instrument constituting that compact, as no further valid than they are authorized by the grants enumerated in that compact; and that, in case of a deliberate, palpable, and dangerous exercise of other powers, not granted by the said compact, the states, who are parties thereto, have the right, and are in duty bound, to interpose, for arresting the progress of the evil, and for maintaining, within their respective limits, the authorities, rights, and liberties, appertaining to them.

That the General Assembly doth also express its deep regret, that a spirit has, in sundry instances, been manifested by the Federal Government to enlarge its powers by forced constructions of the constitutional charter which defines them; and that indications have appeared of a design to expound certain general phrases (which, having been copied from the very limited grant of powers in the former Articles of Confederation, were the less liable to be misconstrued) so as to destroy the meaning and effect of the particular enumeration which necessarily explains and limits the general phrases, and so as to consolidate the states, by degrees, into one sovereignty, the obvious tendency and inevitable consequence of which would be, to transform the present republican system of the United States into an absolute, or, at best, a mixed monarchy.

That the General Assembly doth particularly PROTEST against the palpable and alarming infractions of the Constitution, in the two late cases of the "Alien and Sedition Acts," passed at the last session of Congress; the first of which exercises a power nowhere delegated to the Federal Government, and which, by uniting legislative and judicial powers to those of [the] executive, subverts the general principles of free government, as well as the particular organization and positive provisions of the Federal Constitution; and the other of which acts exercises, in like manner, a power not delegated by the Constitution, but, on the contrary, expressly and positively forbidden by one of the amendments thereto,—a power which, more than any other, ought to produce universal alarm, because it is levelled against the right of freely examining public characters and measures, and of free communication among the people thereon, which has ever been justly deemed the only effectual guardian of every other right.

That this state having, by its Convention which ratified the Federal Constitution, expressly declared that, among other essential rights, "the liberty of conscience and of the press cannot be cancelled, abridged, restrained, or modified, by any authority of the United States," and from its extreme anxiety to guard these rights from every possible attack of sophistry and ambition, having, with other states, recommended an amendment for that purpose, which amendment was, in due time, annexed to the Constitution,—it would mark a reproachful inconsistency, and criminal degeneracy, if an indifference were now shown to the palpable violation of one of the rights thus declared and secured, and to the establishment of a precedent which may be fatal to the other.

That the good people of this commonwealth, having ever felt and continuing to feel the most sincere affection for their brethren of the other states; the truest anxiety for establishing and perpetuating the union of all; and the most scrupulous fidelity to that Constitution, which is the pledge of mutual friendship, and the instrument of mutual happiness, the General Assembly doth solemnly appeal to the like dispositions in the other states, in confidence that they will concur with this Commonwealth in declaring, as it docs hereby declare, that the acts aforesaid are unconstitutional; and that the necessary and proper measures will be taken *by each* for cooperating with this state, in maintaining unimpaired the authorities, rights, and liberties, reserved to the states respectively, or to the people.

JAMES MADISON

Report to the Virginia General Assembly (1800)

In a report on the Alien and Sedition Acts delivered to the Virginia legislature, Madison elaborated his views on the constitutional limits on the federal government and the right of the states to "interpose for arresting the progress of evil." Although Madison's report is a direct response to the political controversy at hand, it is also one of the most sophisticated defenses of the rights to free speech and a free press in an elective system of government. Madison argued that the very idea of free government implies the right of the people to examine and criticize public officials.

The resolution declares, *first*, that "it views the powers of the Federal Government, as resulting from the compact to which the states are parties," in other words, that the federal powers are derived from the Constitution, and that the Constitution is a compact to which the states are parties.

Clear as the position must seem, that the federal powers are derived from the Constitution, and from that alone, the committee are not unapprized of a late doctrine which opens another source of federal powers, not less extensive and important, than it is new and unexpected. The examination of this doctrine will be most conveniently connected with a review of a succeeding resolution. The committee satisfy themselves here with briefly remarking, that in all the co-temporary discussions and comments, which the Constitution underwent, it was constantly justified and recommended on the ground, that the powers not given to the government, were withheld from it; and that if any doubt could have existed on this subject, under the original text of the Constitution, it is removed as far as words could remove it, by the 12th amendment, now a part of the Constitution, which expressly declares, "that the powers not delegated to the United States, by the Constitution, nor prohibited by it to the states, are reserved to the states respectively, or to the people."* * *

The next position is, that the General Assembly views the powers of the Federal Government, "as limited by the plain sense and intention of the instrument constituting that compact," and "as no farther valid than they are authorized by the grants therein enumerated." It does not seem possible that any just objection can lie against either of these clauses. The first amounts merely to a declaration that the compact ought to have the interpretation, plainly intended by the parties to it; the other, to a declaration, that it ought to have the execution and effect intended by them. If the powers granted, be valid, it is solely because they are granted; and if the granted powers are valid, because granted, all other powers not granted, must not be valid.

The resolution having taken this view of the federal compact, proceeds to infer, "that in case of a deliberate, palpable, and dangerous exercise of other powers not granted by the said compact, the states who are parties thereto, have the right, and are in duty bound to interpose for arresting the progress of the evil, and for maintaining within their respective limits, the authorities, rights and liberties appertaining to them."

It appears to your committee to be a plain principle, founded in common sense, illustrated by common practice, and essential to the nature of compacts; that where resort can be had to no tribunal superior to the authority of the parties, the parties themselves must be the rightful judges in the last resort, whether the bargain made, has been pursued or violated. The constitution of the United States was formed by the sanction of the states, given by each in its sovereign capacity. It adds to the stability and dignity, as well as to the authority of the constitution, that it rests on this legitimate and solid foundation. The states then being the parties to the constitutional compact, and in their sovereign capacity, it follows of necessity, that there can be no tribunal above their authority, to decide in the last resort, whether the compact made by them be violated; and consequently that as the parties to it, they must themselves decide in the last resort, such questions as may be of sufficient magnitude to require their interposition. * * *

The resolution has accordingly guarded against any misapprehension of its object, by expressly requiring for such an interposition "the case of a *deliberate, palpable* and *dangerous* breach of the constitution, by the exercise of *powers not granted* by it." It must be a case, not of a light and transient nature, but of a nature *dangerous* to the great purposes for which the constitution was established. It must be a case moreover not obscure or doubtful in its construction, but plain and *palpable*. Lastly, it must be a case not resulting from a partial consideration, or hasty determination; but a case stampt with a final consideration and *deliberate* adherence. It is not necessary because the resolution does not require, that the question should be discussed, how far the exercise of any particular power, ungranted by the constitution, would justify the interposition of the parties to it. As cases might easily be stated, which none would contend, ought to fall within that description: Cases, on the other hand, might, with equal ease, be stated, so flagrant and so fatal as to unite every opinion in placing them within the description. * * *

But it is objected that the judicial authority is to be regarded as the sole expositor of the constitution, in the last resort; and it may be asked for what reason, the declaration by the General Assembly, supposing it to be theoretically true, could be required at the present day and in so solemn a manner.

On this objection it might be observed *first*, that there may be instances of usurped power, which the forms of the constitution would never draw within the controul of the judicial department: secondly, that if the decision of the judiciary be raised above the authority of the sovereign parties to the constitution, the decisions of the other departments, not carried by the forms of the constitution before the judiciary, must be equally authoritative and final with the decisions of that department. But the proper answer to the objection is, that the resolution of the General Assembly relates to those great and extraordinary cases, in which all the forms of the constitution may prove ineffectual against infractions dangerous to the essential rights of the parties to it. The resolution supposes that dangerous powers not delegated, may not only be usurped and executed by the other departments, but that the Judicial Department also may exercise or sanction dangerous powers beyond the grant of the constitution; and consequently that the ultimate right of the parties to the constitution, to judge whether the compact has been dangerously violated, must extend to violations by one delegated authority, as well as by another; by the judiciary, as well as by the executive, or the legislature. * * *

The part of the constitution which seems most to be recurred to, in defence of the "Sedition Act," is the last clause of the above section, empowering Congress "to make all laws which shall be necessary and proper for carrying into execution the foregoing powers, and all other powers vested by this constitution in the government of the United States, or in any department or officer thereof."

The plain import of this clause is, that Congress shall have all the incidental or instrumental powers, necessary and proper for carrying into execution all the express powers; whether they be vested in the government of the United States, more collectively, or in the several departments, or officers thereof. It is not a grant of new powers to Congress, but merely a declaration, for the removal of all uncertainty, that the means of carrying into execution, those otherwise granted, are included in the grant.

Whenever, therefore a question arises concerning the constitutionality of a particular power; the first question is, whether the power be expressed in the constitution. If it be, the question is decided. If it be not expressed; the next enquiry must be, whether it is properly an incident to an express power, and necessary to its execution. If it be, it may be exercised by Congress. If it be not; Congress cannot exercise it.

Let the question be asked, then, whether the power over the press exercised in the "sedition act," be found among the powers expressly vested in the Congress? This is not pretended. * * *

It must be recollected by many, and could be shewn to the satisfaction of all, that the construction here put on the terms 'necessary and proper' is precisely the construction which prevailed during the discussions and ratifications of the constitution. It may be added, and cannot too often be repeated, that it is a construction absolutely necessary to maintain their consistency with the peculiar character of the government, as possessed of particular and defined powers only; not of the general and indefinite powers vested in ordinary governments. For if the power to *suppress insurrections*, includes a power to *punish libels*, or if the power to *punish*, includes a power to *prevent*, by all the means that may have that *tendency*; such is the relation and influence among the most remote subjects of legislation, that a power over a very few, would carry with it a power over all. And it must be wholly immaterial, whether unlimited powers be exercised under the name of unlimited powers, or be exercised under the name of unlimited means of carrying into execution, limited powers. * * *

It is deemed to be a sound opinion, that the sedition act, in its definition of some of the crimes created, is an abridgment of the freedom of publication, recognized by principles of the common law in England.

The freedom of the press under the common law, is, in the defences of the sedition act, made to consist in an exemption from all *previous* restraint on printed publications, by persons authorized to inspect and prohibit them. It appears to the committee, that this idea of the freedom of the press, can never be admitted to be the American idea of it: since a law inflicting penalties on printed publications, would have a similar effect with a law authorizing a previous restraint on them. It would seem a mockery to say, that no law should be passed, preventing publications from being made, but that laws might be passed for punishing them in case they should be made.

The essential difference between the British government, and the American constitutions, will place this subject in the clearest light.

In the British government, the danger of encroachments on the rights of the people, is understood to be confined to the executive magistrate. The representatives of the people in the legislature, are not only exempt themselves, from distrust, but are considered as sufficient guardians of the rights of their constituents against the danger from the executive. Hence it is a principle, that the parliament is unlimited in its power; or in their own language, is omnipotent. Hence too, all the ramparts for protecting the rights of the people, such as their magna charta, their bill of rights, &c. are not reared against the parliament, but against the royal prerogative. They are merely legislative precautions, against executive usurpations. Under such a government as this, an exemption of the press from previous restraint by licenses appointed by the king, is all the freedom that can be secured to it.

In the United States, the case is altogether different. The people, not the government, possess the absolute sovereignty. The legislature, no less than the executive, is under limitations of power. Encroachments are regarded as possible from the one, as well as from the other. Hence in the United States, the great and essential rights of the people are secured against legislative, as well as against executive ambition. They are secured, not by laws paramount to prerogative; but by constitutions paramount to laws. This security of the freedom of the press, requires that it should be exempt, not only from previous restraint by the executive, as in Great Britain; but from legislative restraint also; and this exemption, to be effectual, must be an exemption, not only from the previous inspection of licensers, but from the subsequent penalty of laws.

The state of the press, therefore, under the common law, can not in this point of view, be the standard of its freedom, in the United States. * * *

The nature of governments elective, limited and responsible, in all their branches, may well be supposed to require a greater freedom of animadversion, than might be tolerated by the genius of such a government as that of Great Britain. In the latter, it is a maxim, that the king, an hereditary, not a responsible magistrate, can do no wrong; and that the legislature, which in two thirds of its composition, is also hereditary, not responsible, can do what it pleases. In the United States, the executive magistrates are not held to be infallible, nor the legislatures to be omnipotent; and both being elective, are both responsible. Is it not natural and necessary, under such different circumstances, that a different degree of freedom, in the use of the press, should be contemplated? * * *

The practice in America must be entitled to much more respect. In every state, probably, in the union, the press has exerted a freedom in canvassing the merits and measures of public men, of every description, which has not been confined to the strict limits of the common law. On this footing, the freedom of the press has stood; on this footing it yet stands. And it will not be a breach, either of truth or of candour, to say, that no persons or presses are in the habit of more unrestrained animadversions on the proceedings and functionaries of the state governments, than the persons and presses most zealous, in vindicating the act of Congress for punishing similar animadversions on the government of the United States.

The last remark will not be understood, as claiming for the state governments an immunity greater than they have heretofore enjoyed. Some degree of abuse is inseparable from the proper use of every thing; and in no instance is this more true, than in that of the press. It has accordingly been decided by the practice of the states, that it is better to leave a few of its noxious branches, to their luxuriant growth, than by pruning them away, to injure the vigor of those yielding the proper fruits. And can the wisdom of this policy be doubted by any who reflect, that to the press alone, chequered as it is with abuses, the world is indebted for all the triumphs which have been gained by reason and humanity, over error and oppression; who reflect that to the same beneficent source, the United States owe much of the lights which conducted them to the rank of a free and independent nation; and which have improved their political system, into a shape so auspicious to their happiness. Had "Sedition acts," forbidding every publication that might bring the constituted agents into contempt or disrepute, or that might excite the hatred of the people against the authors of unjust or pernicious measures, been uniformly enforced against the press; might not the United States have been languishing at this day, under the infirmities of a sickly confederation? Might they not possibly be miserable colonies, groaning under a foreign yoke? * * *

In the first place, where simple and naked facts alone are in question, there is sufficient difficulty in some cases, and sufficient trouble and vexation in all, of meeting a prosecution from the government, with the full and formal proof, necessary in a court of law.

But in the next place, it must be obvious to the plainest minds, that opinions, and inferences, and conjectural observations, are not only in many cases inseparable from the facts, but may often be more the objects of the prosecution than the facts themselves; or may even be altogether abstracted from particular facts; and that opinions and inferences, and conjectural observations, cannot be subjects of that kind of proof which appertains to facts, before a court of law.

Again, it is no less obvious, that the *intent* to defame or bring into contempt or disrepute, or hatred, which is made a condition of the offence created by the act; cannot prevent its pernicious influence, on the freedom of the press. For omitting the enquiry, how far the malice of the intent is an inference of the law from the mere publication; it is manifestly impossible to punish the intent to bring those who administer the government into disrepute or contempt, without striking at the right of freely discussing public characters and measures: because those who engage in such discussions, must expect and *intend* to excite these unfavorable sentiments, so far as they may be thought to be deserved. To prohibit therefore the intent to excite those unfavorable sentiments against those who administer the government, is equivalent to a prohibition of the actual excitement of them; and to prohibit the actual excitement of them, is equivalent to a prohibition of discussions having that tendency and effect; which, again, is equivalent to a protection of those who administer the government, if they should at any time deserve the contempt or hatred of the people, against being exposed to it, by free animadversions on their characters and conduct. Nor can there be a doubt, if those in public trust be shielded by penal laws from such strictures of the press, as may expose them to contempt or disrepute, or hatred, where they may deserve it, that in exact proportion as they may deserve to be exposed, will be the certainty and criminality of the intent to expose them, and the vigilance of prosecuting and punishing it; nor a doubt, that a government thus intrenched in penal statutes, against the just and natural effects of a culpable administration, will easily evade the responsibility, which is essential to a faithful discharge of its duty.

Let it be recollected, lastly, that the right of electing the members of the government, constitutes more particularly the essence of a free and responsible government. The value and efficacy of this right, depends on the knowledge of the comparative merits and demerits of the candidates for public trust; and on the equal freedom, consequently, of examining and discussing these merits and demerits of the candidates respectively. It has been seen that a number of important elections will take place whilst the act is in force; although it should not be continued beyond the term to which it is limited. Should there happen, then, as is extremely probable in relation to some or other of the branches of the government, to be competitions between those who are, and those who are not, members of the government; what will be the situations of the competitors? Not equal; because the characters of the former will be covered by the "sedition act" from animadversions exposing them to disrepute among the people; whilst the latter may be exposed to the contempt and hatred of the people, without a violation of the act. What will be the situation of the people? Not free; because they will be compelled to make their election between competitors, whose pretensions they are not permitted by the act, equally to examine, to discuss, and to ascertain. And from both these situations, will not those in power derive an undue advantage for continuing themselves in it; which by impairing the right of election, endangers the blessings of the government founded on it.

It is with justice, therefore, that the General Assembly hath affirmed in the resolution, as well that the right of freely examining public characters and measures, and of free communication thereon, is the only effectual guardian of every other right; as that this particular right is leveled at, by the power exercised in the "sedition act."

Jacksonian Democracy

HENRY CLAY

Speech on the Tariff (1824)

Henry Clay (1777–1852) was nicknamed the "Great Compromiser" for his role in promoting the Missouri Compromise of 1820, the Compromise Tariff of 1833, and the Compromise of 1850. He was a successful lawyer in Kentucky before becoming a member of Congress, where he served as Speaker of the House and then as a senator. Clay began his political career as a Jeffersonian Republican but became a leader of the Whig Party and twice ran as the party's nominee for president. A self-proclaimed nationalist, Clay argued that a protective tariff was necessary for the creation of a "home market" that would encourage the growth of domestic manufactures. Jacksonians repudiated this almost Hamiltonian belief in governmental intervention in economic life.

In casting our eyes around us, the most prominent circumstance which fixes our attention, and challenges our deepest regret, is the general distress which pervades the whole country. * * * This distress pervades every part of the Union, every class of society; all feel it, though it may be felt, at different places, in different degrees. It is like the atmosphere which surrounds us—all must inhale it, and none can escape it. * * *

What, * * * I would ask, is the cause of the unhappy condition of our country, which I have faintly depicted? It is to be found in the fact that, during almost the whole existence of this Government, we have shaped our industry, our navigation, and our commerce, in reference to an extraordinary war in Europe, and to foreign markets, which no longer exist; in the fact that we have depended too much upon foreign sources of supply, and excited too little the native; in the fact that, whilst we have cultivated, with assiduous care, our foreign resources, we have suffered those at home to wither, in a state of neglect and abandonment. * * *

The greatest want of civilized society is a market for the sale and exchange of the surplus of the produce of the labor of its members. This market may exist at home or abroad, or both, but it must exist somewhere, if society prospers, and wherever it does exist, it should be competent to the absorption of the entire surplus of production. It is most desirable that there should be both a home and a foreign market. But, with respect to their relative superiority, I cannot entertain a doubt. The home market is first in order, and paramount in importance. The object of the bill under consideration is to create this home market, and to lay the foundations of a genuine American policy. * * *

* * * The policy of all Europe is adverse to the reception of our agricultural produce, so far as it comes into collision with its own; and, under that limitation, we are absolutely forbid to enter their ports, except under circumstances which deprive them of all value as a steady market. * * *

Our agricultural is our greatest interest. It ought ever to be predominant. All others should bend to it. And, in considering what is for its advantage, we should contemplate it in all its varieties, of planting, farming, and grazing. Can we do nothing to invigorate it? * * * We must then change somewhat our course. We must give a new direction to some portion of our industry. We must speedily adopt a genuine American policy. Still cherishing a foreign market, let us create also a home market, to give further scope to the consumption of the produce of American industry. Let us counteract the policy of foreigners, and withdraw the support which we now give to their industry, and stimulate that of our own country. It should be a prominent object with wise legislators, to multiply the vocations and extend the business of society, as far as it can be done by the protection of our interests at home, against the injurious effects of foreign legislation. * * *

The creation of a home market is not only necessary to procure for our agriculture a just reward of its labors, but it is indispensable to obtain a supply of our necessary wants. If we cannot sell, we cannot buy. That portion of our population (and we have seen that it is not less than four-fifths) which makes comparatively nothing that foreigners will buy, has nothing to make purchases with from foreigners.

* * *

* * * The superiority of the home market results, 1st, from its steadiness and comparative certainty at all times; 2d, from the creation of reciprocal interest; 3d, from its greater security; and, lastly, from an ultimate and not distant augmentation of consumption, and, consequently, of

comfort from increased quantity and reduced prices. But this home market, highly desirable as it is, can only be created and cherished by the PROTECTION of our own legislation against the inevitable prostration of our industry, which must ensue from the action of foreign policy and legislation. * * *

This is only to be accomplished by the establishment of a tariff, to the consideration of which I am now brought.

And what is this tariff? It seems to have been regarded as a sort of monster, huge and deformed; a wild beast, endowed with tremendous powers of destruction, about to be let loose among our people, if not to devour them, at least to consume their substance. But let us calm our passions, and deliberately survey this alarming, this terrific being. The sole object of the tariff is to tax the produce of foreign industry, with the view of promoting American industry. The tax is exclusively levelled at foreign industry. That is the avowed and the direct purpose of the tariff. If it subjects any part of American industry to burdens, that is an effect not intended, but is altogether incidental, and perfectly voluntary.

It had been treated as an imposition of burdens upon one part of the community by design for the benefit of another; as if, in fact, money were taken from the pockets of one portion of the people and put into the pockets of another. But, is that a fair representation of it? No man pays the duty assessed on the foreign article by compulsion, but voluntarily; and this voluntary duty, if paid, goes into the common exchequer, for the common benefit of all. * * *

We perceive that the proposed measure, instead of sacrificing the South to the other parts of the Union, seeks only to preserve them from being absolutely sacrificed under the operation of the tacit compact which I have described. Supposing the South to be actually incompetent, or disinclined to embark at all in the business of manufacturing, is not its interest, nevertheless, likely to be promoted by creating a new and an American source of supply for its consumption? Now foreign Powers, and Great Britain principally, have the monopoly of the supply of Southern consumption. If this bill should pass, an American competitor in the supply of the South would be raised up, and ultimately, I cannot doubt, that it will be supplied more cheaply and better. * * *

The second objection to the proposed bill is, that it will diminish the amount of our exports. It can have no effect upon our exports, except those which are sent to Europe. Except tobacco and rice, we send there nothing but the raw materials. The argument is, that Europe will not buy of us if we do not buy of her. The first objection to it is, that it calls upon us to look to the question, and to take care of European ability in legislating for American interests. Now, if, in legislating for their interests, they would

consider and provide for our ability, the principle of reciprocity would enjoin us so to regulate our intercourse with them, as to leave their ability
unimpaired. But I have shown that, in the adoption of their own policy,
their inquiry is strictly limited to a consideration of their peculiar interests,
without any regard to that of ours.

JOHN QUINCY ADAMS

First Annual Message to Congress (1825)

*The son of John and Abigail Adams, John Quincy Adams (1767–1848)
held public office as a diplomat, Massachusetts state senator, United
States senator, secretary of state under James Monroe, president of the
United States, and member of the House of Representatives after serving as president. Adams shared the Whig ideal of federal sponsorship of
national projects, which the Jacksonians opposed. Adams proposed federal spending on extensive internal improvements, a national university,
the first astronomical observatory, and other significant projects.*

In inviting the attention of Congress to the subject of internal improvements upon a view thus enlarged it is not my design to recommend the equipment of an expedition for circumnavigating the globe for
purposes of scientific research and inquiry. We have objects of useful
investigation nearer home, and to which our cares may be more beneficially applied. The interior of our own territories has yet been very imperfectly explored. Our coasts along many degrees of latitude upon the
shores of the Pacific Ocean, though much frequented by our spirited
commercial navigators, have been barely visited by our public ships. The
River of the West, first fully discovered and navigated by a countryman of
our own, still bears the name of the ship in which he ascended its waters,
and claims the protection of our armed national flag at its mouth. With
the establishment of a military post there or at some other point of that
coast, recommended by my predecessor and already matured in the deliberations of the last Congress, I would suggest the expediency of connecting the equipment of a public ship for the exploration of the whole
northwest coast of this continent.

The establishment of an uniform standard of weights and measures
was one of the specific objects contemplated in the formation of our

Constitution, and to fix that standard was one of the powers delegated by express terms in that instrument to Congress. The Governments of Great Britain and France have scarcely ceased to be occupied with inquiries and speculations on the same subject since the existence of our Constitution, and with them it has expanded into profound, laborious, and expensive researches into the figure of the earth and the comparative length of the pendulum vibrating seconds in various latitudes from the equator to the pole. These researches have resulted in the composition and publication of several works highly interesting to the cause of science. The experiments are yet in the process of performance. Some of them have recently been made on our own shores, within the walls of one of our own colleges, and partly by one of our own fellow-citizens. It would be honorable to our country if the sequel of the same experiments should be countenanced by the patronage of our Government, as they have hitherto been by those of France and Britain.

Connected with the establishment of an university, or separate from it, might be undertaken the erection of an astronomical observatory, with provision for the support of an astronomer, to be in constant attendance of observation upon the phenomena of the heavens, and for the periodical publication of his observations. It is with no feeling of pride as an American that the remark may be made that on the comparatively small territorial surface of Europe there are existing upward of 130 of these light-houses of the skies, while throughout the whole American hemisphere there is not one. If we reflect a moment upon the discoveries which in the last four centuries have been made in the physical constitution of the universe by the means of these buildings and of observers stationed in them, shall we doubt of their usefulness to every nation? And while scarcely a year passes over our heads without bringing some new astronomical discovery to light, which we must fain receive at second hand from Europe, are we not cutting ourselves off from the means of returning light for light while we have neither observatory nor observer upon our half of the globe and the earth revolves in perpetual darkness to our unsearching eyes? * * *

The Constitution under which you are assembled is a charter of limited powers. After full and solemn deliberation upon all or any of the objects which, urged by an irresistible sense of my own duty, I have recommended to your attention should you come to the conclusion that, however desirable in themselves, the enactment of laws for effecting them would transcend the powers committed to you by that venerable instrument which we are all bound to support, let no consideration induce you to assume the exercise of powers not granted to you by the people. But if the power to exercise exclusive legislation in all cases whatsoever over the District of Columbia; if the power to lay and collect taxes, duties, imposts, and excises, to pay the debts and provide for the common defense and general welfare of the United States; if the power to regulate commerce with foreign nations and among the several States and with the Indian tribes, to fix the standard of weights and measures, to establish post-offices and post-roads, to declare war, to raise and support armies, to provide and maintain a navy, to dispose of and make all needful rules and regulations respecting the territory or other property belonging to the United States, and to make all laws which shall be necessary and proper for carrying these powers into execution—if these powers and others enumerated in the Constitution may be effectually brought into action by laws promoting the improvement of agriculture, commerce, and manufactures, the cultivation and encouragement of the mechanic and of the elegant arts, the advancement of literature, and the progress of the sciences, ornamental and profound, to refrain from exercising them for the benefit of the people themselves would be to hide in the earth the talent committed to our charge—would be treachery to the most sacred of trusts.

The spirit of improvement is abroad upon the earth. It stimulates the hearts and sharpens the faculties not of our fellow-citizens alone, but of the nations of Europe and of their rulers. While dwelling with pleasing satisfaction upon the superior excellence of our political institutions, let us not be unmindful that liberty is power; that the nation blessed with the largest portion of liberty must in proportion to its numbers be the most powerful nation upon earth, and that the tenure of power by man is, in the moral purposes of his Creator, upon condition that it shall be exercised to ends of beneficence, to improve the condition of himself and his fellow-men. While foreign nations less blessed with that freedom which is power than ourselves are advancing with gigantic strides in the career of public improvement, were we to slumber in indolence or fold up our arms and proclaim to the world that we are palsied by the will of our constituents, would it not be to cast away the bounties of Providence and doom ourselves to perpetual inferiority? In the course of the year now drawing to its close we have beheld, under the auspices and at the expense of one State of this Union, a new university unfolding its portals to the sons of science and holding up the torch of human improvement to eyes that seek the light. We have seen under persevering and enlightened enterprise of another State the waters of our Western lakes [Erie Canal] mingle with those of the ocean. If undertakings like these have been accomplished in the compass of a few years by the authority of single members of our Confederation, can we, the representative authorities of the whole Union, fall behind our fellow-servants in the exercise of the trust committed to us for the benefit of our common sovereign by the accomplishment of works important to the whole and to which neither the authority nor the resources of any one State can be adequate?

JOHN R. COOKE AND ABEL P. UPSHUR

Debate in the Virginia Constitutional Convention (1829-1830)

Jacksonians sought to increase democratic participation in American politics, a subject debated at length in various efforts to rewrite the state constitutions. In 1829 and 1830, Virginia held a constitutional convention at which delegates debated extending the right of suffrage beyond landholders. John R. Cooke, a radical democrat, defended the proposal in terms of natural law and the inherent goodness and sociability of human nature. Abel P. Upshur, a judge and career politician, made the argument that government originates in a social contract to protect property, which is the only thing that gives individuals a genuine stake in society. Why not give the vote to women? he asks dismissively of those who argue from the law of nature.

John R. Cooke

Sir, the fathers of the Revolution did but reiterate those great and sacred truths which had been illustrated by the genius of Locke, and Sydney, and Milton: truths for which Hampden, and a host of his compatriots, had poured out their blood in vain.

Driven from Europe, by Kings, and Priests, and Nobles, those simple truths were received, with favour, by the sturdy yeomanry who dwelt on the western shores of the Atlantic. The love of liberty, aye, Sir, and of equality too, grew with the growth, and strengthened with the strength, of the Colonies. It declared war, at last, not only against the power of the King, but against the privilege of the Noble, and laid the deep foundations of our Republic on the sovereignty of the people and the equality of men.

The sacred instrument, for sacred I will dare to call it, notwithstanding the sneers which its very name excites in this assembly of Republicans, the sacred instrument in which those great principles were declared, was ushered into existence under circumstances the most impressive and solemn. The 'Declaration of the Rights of the people of Virginia,' was made by an assembly of sages and patriots, who had just involved their country in all the horrors of war, in all the dangers of an unequal contest with the most powerful nation on earth, for the sake of the noble and elevated principles which that instrument announces and declares. For the sake of those principles, they had imperilled their lives, their fortunes, their wives, their children, their country; and, in one word, all that is dear to man. For the sake of those principles, they had spread havoc and desolation over their native land, and consigned to ruin and poverty a whole generation of the people of Virginia.

And for what did they make these mighty sacrifices! For wild 'abstractions, and metaphysical subleties!' No, Sir. For principles of eternal truth; as practical, in character, as they are vital, in importance; for principles deep-seated in the nature of man, by whose development, alone, he can attain the happiness which is the great object of his being. Those principles are,

'That all power is vested in, and consequently derived from, *the people.*'

'That all men are, by nature, *equally* free.' And

'That a *majority of the community* possesses, by the law of nature and necessity, a right to control its concerns. * * *

I say, then, Sir, with a confidence inspired by a deep conviction of the truth of what I advance, that the principles of the *sovereignty of the people*, the *equality of men*, and the *right of the majority*, set forth in the 'Declaration of the Rights of the people of Virginia,' so far from being 'wild and visionary,' so far from being 'abstractions and metaphysical subleties,' are the very principles which alone give a *distinctive* character to our institutions, are the principles which have had the *practical* effect in Virginia, of abolishing *kingly power*, and *aristocratic privilege*, substituting for them an elective magistracy, deriving their power *from* the people, and responsible to the people.

But it has been said that the authors of the Declaration of Rights themselves, admitted, in effect, the abstract and *unpractical* character of the principles which it contains, by establishing a Government whose practical regulations are wholly inconsistent with those theoretical principles. That while, in the Declaration of Rights, they asserted that all power is vested in *the people*, and should be exercised by a *majority* of the people, they established a Government in which *unequal counties*, expressing their sense by the representatives of a *selected few* in those counties, to wit, the *freeholders*, were the real political *units*, or essential *elements* of political power. * * *

Sir, the argument would be a good one if the premises which support it were correct. But it is *not true* that the authors of the Declaration of Rights *established* the anomalous Government under which we have lived these fifty years and more. There can be no grosser error than to suppose that the Constitution of Virginia was *formed* in 1776. Its two great distinctive features, the *sectional* and the *aristocratic* had been given to it a century before. * * *

What then, was the situation in which the framers of the Constitution were placed?—While they framed that instrument they were almost within hearing of the thunder of hostile cannon. * * * It would have been the very height of folly, at such a crisis, to create disaffection in the minds of the *freeholders*, by stripping them of their exclusive powers, and to exasperate the smaller *counties* by degrading them from the rank which they had held under the royal Government. In leaving the *freeholders* and the *counties* as they found them, the framers of the Constitution bowed to the supreme law of necessity, and acted like wise and *practical* statesmen.

No, Sir, it was not reserved for *us* to discover the inconsistency between their theoretical principles, and their practical regulations. They saw it themselves, and deplored it. In the very heat of the war which was waged for these 'abstractions'—in the hurly burly of the conflict, one statesman, at least, was found, to point out those inconsistencies, and to urge home on the people of Virginia the 'new and unheard of' principle, that in the apportionment of representation, regard should be had to the white population only. As early as 1781, Mr. Jefferson exhorted the people of Virginia, in the most earnest and impressive language, to reduce the principle to practice, 'so soon as leisure should be afforded them, for intrenching, within good forms, the rights for which they had bled.'

From that time to this, the spirit of reform has never slept. From that time to this, the friends of liberty have continually lifted up their voices against the inequality and injustice of our system of Government. Incessantly baffled and defeated, they have not abandoned their purpose; and after a struggle for fifty years, the purpose seems at length on the eve of accomplishment. The Representatives of the people of Virginia have at length assembled in Convention to revise the Constitution of the State. A special committee of this Convention has recommended, among other measures of reform, the adoption of a resolution,

'That in the apportionment of representation, in the House of Delegates, regard should be had to white population exclusively.' * * *

It is alleged, then, Sir, that * * * there is a great *practical* principle, wholly overlooked in the resolution of the Select Committee, of vital and *paramount* importance. The principle in question, and the argument by which it is sustained, when broadly and fairly developed, amount to this:

1. That the security of property is one of the most essential elements of the prosperity and happiness of a community, and should be sedulously provided for by its institutions.

2. That men naturally love property, and the comforts and advantages it will purchase.

3. That this love of wealth is so strong, that the *poor* are the natural enemies of the *rich*, and feel a strong and habitual inclination to strip them of their wealth, or, at least, to throw on them alone all the burthens of society.

4. That the *poor*, being more numerous in every community than all the classes above them, would have the *power*, as well as the *inclination*, thus to oppress the rich, if admitted to an equal participation with them in political power; and

5. That it is therefore necessary to restrain, limit and diminish the power of this natural majority; of this many-headed and hungry monster, *the many*, by some artificial regulation in *the Constitution, or fundamental law*, of every community. And if this be not done, either directly, by limitations on the right of suffrage, or indirectly, by some artificial distribution of political power, in the apportionment of representation, like that contained in the amendment, property will be invaded, all the multiplied evils of anarchy will ensue, till the society, groaning under the yoke of unbridled democracy, will be driven to prefer to its stormy sway, the despotic Government of a single master. And this is said to be the natural death of the Government of *numbers*.

Sir, if this statement of the argument be a little over-coloured by imputing to those who advance it epithets which they are too prudent to use, it is nevertheless, like all good caricatures, a striking likeness.

To this argument I answer that, like most unsound arguments, it is founded on a bold assumption of false premises. It is founded on the assumption that men are, by nature, *robbers*, and are restrained from incessant invasions of the rights of each other, only by fear or coercion. But, is this a just picture of that compound creature *man*? Sir, I conceive it to be a libel on the race, disproved by every page of its history. If you will look there you will find that man, though sometimes driven by stormy passions to the commission of atrocious crimes, is by nature and habit neither a wolf nor a tiger. That he is an *affectionate*, a *social*, a *patriotic*, a *conscientious* and a *religious* creature. In him, alone, of all animals, has nature implanted the feeling of *affection for his kindred*, after the attainment of maturity. This alone is a restraint on the excess of his natural desire for property as extensive as the ties of blood that bind him to his fellow man.

Designing, moreover, that man shall live in *communities*, where alone he can exist, nature has given to him the *social feeling*; the feeling of attachment to those around him. Intending that for the most perfect development of his high faculties, and for the attainment of the greatest degree of comfort and happiness of which he is susceptible, man should associate in *nations*, she implanted in him a feeling, the glorious displays of which had shed lustre around so many pages of his history. I mean *the love of country or patriotism*. Designing that he should attain to happiness through the practice of virtue, and in that way only, she erected in each man's bosom the tribunal of *conscience*, which passes in review all the actions of the individual, and pronounces sentence of condemnation on every manifest deviation from moral rectitude. To add sanctions to the decisions of conscience, the also implanted in his bosom an intuitive belief in the existence of an intelligence governing the world, who would reward virtue and punish vice in a future state of being. Man is therefore, by nature a *religious* creature, whose conduct is more or less regulated by the love or fear of the unknown governor of the Universe. Above all, the light of revealed religion has shone for ages on the world, and that Divine system of morals which commands us 'to do unto others as we would have them do unto us,' has shed its benign influence on the hearts of countless thousands, of the high and the low, the wise and the foolish, the *rich* and the *poor*. But we are asked to believe that all these natural feelings, all these social affections, all these monitions of conscience, all these religious impressions, all these Christian charities, all these hopes of future rewards and fears of future punishments, are dead, and silent, and inoperative in the bosom of man. The love of property is the great engrossing passion which swallows up all other passions, and feelings, and principles; and this not in particular cases only, but in all men. The poor man is fatally and inevitably the enemy of the rich, and will wage a war of rapine against him, if once let loose from the restraints of the fundamental law. A doctrine monstrous, hateful and incredible!

But, Sir, if I were even to admit, for a moment, the truth of the revolting proposition that the desire for property swallows up all the other feelings of man, does it follow that the aspirants after the enjoyments that property confers, will seek to attain their object in the manner which the argument in question supposes? If it be contended that man is a greedy and avaricious, it will, still, not be denied, that he is a reasoning and calculating, animal. When he desires to *attain* property, it is in order that he may *possess and enjoy it*. But if he join in establishing the rule that the right of the strongest is the best right, what security has he that he, in his turn, will not soon be deprived of his property by some one stronger than himself? Sir, the *very* desire for property implies the desire to possess it *securely*. And he who has a strong desire to possess it, and a high relish, in anticipation, of the pleasure of enjoying it securely, will be a firm supporter of the laws which secure that possession, and a decided enemy to every systematic invasion of the rule of *meum* and *tuum*. In other words, man is sagacious enough to know that as a general and public rule of action, the maxim that honesty is the best policy, is the safest and best maxim. And when he deviates from that rule he always hopes that the violation will go undiscovered, or otherwise escape punishment. So true is this, that I am persuaded that if a nation could be found consisting exclusively of rogues and swindlers, there would not be found in the legislative code of that nation a systematic invasion of the right of property, such as the argument for the proposed amendment apprehends and seeks to provide against.

Communities of men are sagacious enough to know and follow their real interest. And, Sir, I do not, and cannot believe that it is, or ever was the real interest of any class in the community, or of any community to commit gross and flagrant abuses of power, to disregard the monitions of conscience to break down the barriers and obliterate the distinctions between right and wrong, and thus to involve society in all the horrors of anarchy. The principles of justice are the foundation of the social fabric, and rash and foolish is he and blind to his true interest, who undermines the foundation and tumbles the fabric in ruins.

Thus far I have reasoned *a priori*. But what are the lessons which history and experience teach us, in pursuing this enquiry?—We need not go far for examples. Let us look at the experience of our good old Commonwealth of Virginia. From the foundation of the Commonwealth the slave-holding population of Virginia has held the supreme power in the State. From the foundation of the Commonwealth there has existed and there still exists, a numerous population of our western frontier, who are comparatively destitute of slave-property, and whose wealth has ever consisted in cattle more than in any other description of property. Now if the argument of those who support the proposed amendment be a sound one, it would follow that as it is and always has been the interest (according to *their* views of interest) of the slave-holding population to shift from themselves, and to lay on others, the burthens of Government, they would impose heavy taxes on the cattle, the property of the helpless minority, and oppress them by this and every other species of fiscal exaction. And yet the very reverse is the fact. For the slave-holders, invested with supreme power, and urged to its exercise by their 'interest,' have not only not overtaxed the cattle of their western brethren, but have, in fact, imposed on them, except at one period of danger and distress from foreign war, no tax at all, and when the pressure ceased the law imposing the tax was instantly repealed. And why?—Because they were governed by the principles of justice, and the feelings of honour. Because they thought, and justly, that the people of the frontier, burthened as they were with 'the first expenses of society,' and engaged in laying the very foundations of the social fabric, could ill endure the additional burthen of a tax on their flocks and herds. Because the non-slave holders of the west were at their mercy, and every feeling of honour and magnanimity forbade them to oppress the weak. I say, then, Sir, that the slave-holders of Virginia have shewn by their conduct in this particular case, the incorrectness of the theory which supposes man to be habitually governed by a blind and reckless cupidity; by the sordid feelings alone of his nature, to the exclusion of the nobler.

Abel P. Upshur

It is contended by our opponents, that the proper basis of representation in the General Assembly, is white population alone, because this principle results necessarily from the right which the majority possess, to rule the minority. I have been forcibly struck with the fact, that in all the arguments upon this subject here and elsewhere, this right in a majority is assumed as a postulate. It has not yet been proved, nor have I even heard an attempt to prove it. * * *

There are two kinds of majority. There is a majority in interest, as well as a majority in number. If the first be within the contemplation of gentlemen, there is an end of all discussion. It is precisely the principle for which we contend, and we shall be happy to unite with them in so regulating this matter, that those who have the greatest stake in the Government, shall have the greatest share of power in the administration of it. But this is not what gentlemen mean. They mean, for they distinctly say so, that a majority in number only, without regard to property, shall give the rule. It is the propriety of this rule, which I now propose to examine.

If there be, as our opponents assume, an original, *a priori*, inherent and indestructible right in a majority to control a minority, from what source permit me to inquire, is that right derived? If it exist at all, it must I apprehend, be found either in some positive compact or agreement conferring it, or else in some order of our nature, independent of all compact, and consequently prior to all Government. If gentlemen claim the right here as springing from positive compact, from *what compact* does it spring? Not certainly from that Constitution of Government which we are now revising; for the chief purpose for which we have been brought together, is to correct a supposed defect in the Constitution, in this very particular. Not certainly from any other Constitution or form of Government, for to none other are we at liberty to look, for any grant of power, or any principle which can bind us. The right then, is not conventional. Its source must be found beyond all civil society, prior to all social compact, and independent of its sanctions. We must look for it in the law of nature; we have indeed been distinctly told, that it exists in "necessity and nature;" and upon that ground only, has it hitherto been claimed. I propose now to inquire whether the law of nature does indeed, confer this right or not.

Let me not be misunderstood, Sir. I am not inquiring whether, according to the form and nature of our institutions, a majority ought or ought not to rule. That inquiry will be made hereafter. At present, I propose only to prove that there is *no original a priori* principle in the law of nature, which gives to a majority a right to control a minority; and of course, that we are not bound by any obligation *prior to society*, to adopt that principle in our civil institutions.

If there be any thing in the law of nature which confers the right now contended for, in what part of her code, I would ask, is it to be found? For my own part, I incline strongly to think, that, closely examined, the law of nature will be found to confer no other right than this: the right in every creature to use the powers derived from nature, in such mode as will best promote its own happiness. If this be not the law of nature, she is certainly but little obeyed in any of the living departments of her *empire*. Throughout her boundless domain, the law of force gives the only rule of right. The lion devours the ox; the ox drives the lamb from the green pasture; the lamb exerts the same law of power over the animal that is weaker and more timid than itself; and thus the rule runs, throughout all the gradations of life, until at last, the worm devours us all. But, if there be another law independent of force, which gives to a greater number a right to control a smaller number, to what consequence does it lead? Gentlemen must themselves admit, that all men are by nature *equal*, for this is the very foundation of their claim of right in a majority. If this be so, each individual has his rights, which are precisely equal to the rights of his fellow. But the right of a majority to rule necessarily implies a right to impose restraints, in some form or other; either upon the freedom of opinion or the freedom of action. And what follows? * * * That majority has a right to restrain, to abridge, and consequently, to destroy all the rights of the lesser number. That is to say, while all are by nature equal, and all derive from nature the same rights in every respect, there shall yet be a number, only one less than a majority of the whole, who may not by the law of nature possess any rights at all! * * *

To such absurdities are we inevitably driven when we attempt to apply principles deduced from a state of nature, to a state of society; a state which pre-supposes that nature with all her rights and all her laws, has been shaken off! Indeed, Sir, the whole reasoning is fallacious, because it is founded on a state of things which in all probability, never had existence at all. It goes back to a state prior to all history, and about which we know nothing beyond mere conjecture. The first accounts which we have of man, are of man, in a social state. Wherever he has been found, and however rude his condition, he has been bound to his fellows by some form of association, in advance of a state of nature. If we may indulge any conjecture upon such a subject, the probability is that he was first urged into society, by a strong *feeling of property* implanted in his nature; by a feeling that he had, or at least, that he ought to have, a better title than another, to whatever his own labour had appropriated. The necessity of securing this right and protecting him in the enjoyment of it, in all probability, first suggested the idea of the social compact. Although property therefore, is strictly speaking the creature of society, yet a *feeling* of property was probably its creator. The result would be, that at the very moment that two human beings first came together, the social compact was formed. * * *

The subject, Mr. Chairman, is scarcely worth the examination it has received. I will pursue it no farther, since I have no intention to give you a treatise on natural law, instead of an argument upon the practical subject of Government. I have thought it necessary to go thus far into an examination of the subject, because gentlemen have founded themselves upon what they are pleased to consider an axiom, that there is in a majority, an *a priori*, *inherent* and *indestructible* right to rule a minority, under all circumstances, and in every conceivable condition of things. And one of them at least has been understood by me, as referring this right to the law of nature; a law which he supposes, society cannot repeal, and which therefore, is of original and universal authority. Surely this is a very great mistake. Nay, Sir, there is proof enough before us that gentlemen themselves, who claim this right, and who seek to give it solemnity by referring it to the very law of our being, do not venture to carry it into the details of their own system. If there be a right in a majority of persons or of *white* persons, to rule a minority, upon what principle is it that the right of suffrage is restricted? *All* are counted, in making up the majority; and each one of the majority ought of consequence, to possess a share in its rights. Why then do you not admit women to the polls? Nature has stamped no such inferiority upon that sex, as to disqualify it under all circumstances, for a safe and judicious exercise of the right of suffrage. And why exclude minors? Infants who have not acquired language, or whose intellects are not sufficiently unfolded to enable them to understand their own actions, may be excluded from the necessity of the case. But at what time, in the ordinary course of nature, do these disabilities cease? Gentlemen say, at the age of twenty-one years. And why so? Not certainly because nature declares it; for the faculties attain maturity at different periods, in different latitudes of the earth. In one latitude we are ripe at sixteen; in another, not until 30; and even among ourselves, we see many, under the age of twenty-one who possess more wisdom and more power of general usefulness, than can be found in others of fifty; far more than in those who have approached their second childhood. What is there then, which indicates the precise period of twenty-one years, as the earliest at which these members of the ruling majority, may exercise the rights which belong to them? This, and this only: that the rule which is furnished by nature, is unfit for a state of society, and we are compelled, in our own defence, to adopt an arbitrary rule of our own, which is better suited to our actual condition. There is no one among us so wild and visionary, as to desire universal suffrage, and yet it is perfectly certain that, at the moment when you limit that right, in however small a degree, you depart from the *principle* that a majority shall rule. If you establish any disqualification whatever, there is no *natural necessity*, nor even a *moral certainty*, that a majority in any given community, will not come within the exception. * * *

In truth, Mr. Chairman, *there are no original principles of Government at all*. Novel and strange as the idea may appear, it is nevertheless, strictly true, in the sense in which I announce it. There are no original principles, existing in the nature of things and independent of agreement, to which Government must of necessity conform, in order to be either legitimate or philosophical. The principles of Government, are those principles only, which the people who form the Government, choose to *adopt and apply to themselves*. Principles do not precede, but spring out of Government. If this should be considered a dangerous novelty in this age of improvement, when all old fashioned things are rejected as worthless; let us test the doctrine by reference to examples. In Turkey, the Government is centered in one man; in England, it resides in King, Lords, and Commons, and in the Republics of the United States, we profess to repose it in the people alone. The principles of all these Governments are essentially different; and yet will it be said that the Governments of Turkey and England are no Governments at all, or not legitimate Governments, because in them, the will of a majority does not give the rules? Or, will it be said, that our own Governments are not legitimate, because they do not conform to the despotic principles of Turkey, nor recognise the aristocracy of England? If there be these original principles at all, we must presume that they are uniform in themselves, and universal in their application. It will not do to say that there is one principle for one place, and another principle for another place. The conclusion resulting from the reasoning of gentlemen will be, that there is one Government in the world which is *really* a Government, rightful and legitimate; and all other forms of social compact, however long, or however firmly established, are no Governments at all. Every Government is legitimate which springs directly from the will of the people, or to which the people have consented to give allegiance. And I am not going too far, in asserting that Governments are free or otherwise, only in proportion as the people have been consulted in forming them, and as their rulers are directly responsible to them for the execution of their will. It matters not what form they assume, nor who are the immediate depositories of political power. It may suit the purposes of the people, as it once suited those of Rome, to invest all authority in a Dictator; and if the people choose this form of Government; if their interest and safety require that they shall submit to it, what original principle is there which renders it illegitimate? If the majority possesses all power, they possess the power to *surrender* their power. And if it be just and wise that they should do so, it is still their own Government, and no one can impugn its legitimacy.

I have thus, Mr. Chairman, endeavored to prove, that there is not in nature, nor even in sound political science, any fundamental principle applicable to this subject, which is mandatory upon us. We are at perfect liberty to choose our own principle; * * *

I admit, as a general proposition, that in free Governments, power ought to be given to the majority; and why? The rule is founded in the idea that there is an identity, though not an equality of interests, in the several members of the body politic: in which case the presumption naturally arises, that the greater number possess the greater interest. But the rule no longer applies, when the reason of it fails. * * * If the interests of the several parts of the Commonwealth were identical, it would be, we admit, safe and proper that a majority of *persons only* should give the rule of political power. But our interests are not identical, and the difference between us arises from property alone. We therefore contend that property ought to be considered, in fixing the basis of representation.

What, Sir, are the constituent elements of society? Persons and *property*. What are the subjects of Legislation? Persons *and property*. Was there ever a society seen on earth, which consisted only of men, women and children? The very idea of society, carries with it the idea of property, as its necessary and inseparable attendant. History cannot show any form of the social compact, at any time, or in any place, into which property did not enter as a constituent element, nor one in which that element did not enjoy protection in a greater or less degree. Nor was there ever a society in which the protection once extended to property, was afterwards withdrawn, which did not fall an easy prey to violence and disorder. Society cannot exist without property; it constitutes the full half of its being. Take away all protection from property, and our next business is to cut each other's throats. All experience proves this. The safety of men depends on the safety of property; the rights of persons must mingle in the ruin of the rights of property. And shall it not then be protected? Sir, your Government cannot move an inch without property. * * * And what are the subjects upon which the law-making power is called to act? Persons *and property*. To these two subjects, and not to one of them alone, is the business of legislation confined. * * * If then, Sir, property is thus necessary to the very being of society; thus indispensable to every movement of Government; if it be that subject upon which Government chiefly acts; is it not, I would ask, entitled to such protection as shall be above all suspicion, and free from every hazard? It appears to me that I need only announce the proposition, to secure the assent of every gentleman present.

Sir, the obligations of man in his social state are two-fold; to bear arms, and to pay taxes for the support of Government. The obligation to bear arms, results from the duty which society owes him, to protect his rights of person. The society which protects me, I am bound to protect in return. The obligation to pay taxes, results from the protection extended to property. Not a protection against foreign enemies; not a protection by swords and bayonets merely; but a protection derived from a prompt and correct administration of justice; a protection against the violence, the fraud, or the injustice of my neighbor. In this protection, the owner of property is alone interested. Here, then, is the plain agreement between Government on the one hand, and the tax-paying citizen on the other. It is an agreement which results, of necessity, from the social compact; and when the consideration is fairly paid, how can you honestly withhold the equivalent? * * *

If men enter into the social compact upon unequal terms; if one man brings into the partnership, his rights of person alone, and another brings into it, equal rights of person and all the rights of property beside, can they be said to have an equal interest in the common stock? Shall not he who has most at stake; who has, not only a greater interest, but a *peculiar* interest in society, possess an authority proportioned to that interest, and adequate to its protection? * * *

I must remind the gentlemen, that they have admitted the principle, that property must be protected, and protected in the very form now proposed; they are obliged to admit it. It would be a wild and impracticable scheme of Government, which did not admit it. Among all the various and numerous propositions, lying upon your table, is there one which goes the length of proposing *universal suffrage?* There is none. Yet this subject is in direct connexion with that. Why do you not admit a pauper to vote? He is a person: he counts one in your numerical majority. In rights strictly personal, he has as much interest in the Government as any other citizen. He is liable to commit the same offences, and to become exposed to the same punishments as the rich man. Why, then, shall he not vote? Because, thereby, he would receive an influence over property; and all who own it, feel it to be unsafe, to put the power of controlling it, into the hands of those who are not the owners. If you go on population one, as the basis of representation, you will be obliged to go the length of giving the elective franchise to every human being over twenty-one years; yes, and under twenty-one years, on whom your penal laws take effect; an experiment, which has met with nothing but utter and disastrous failure, wherever it has been tried. No, Mr. Chairman: Let us be consistent. Let us openly acknowledge the truth; let us boldly take the bull by the horns, and incorporate this influence of property as a leading principle in our Constitution.

FRANCES WRIGHT

Of Existing Evils, and Their Remedy (1829)

The Jacksonian movement involved diverse demands for reform. The Scottish-born social reformer Frances Wright (1795–1852) lectured and wrote on behalf of women's rights, education, labor, and birth control as the editor of the New Harmony Gazette *and the publisher of the* Free Enquirer. *In 1825 the social activist established Nashoba, a socialist community in western Tennessee, where she emancipated and educated slaves she purchased. In this selection, taken from a lecture she delivered in Philadelphia, Wright proposed a system of national education as the best remedy for ignorance and poverty. Universal education, she argued in candid, class-laden language, would provide the only secure foundation for equality and liberty.*

I shall now present a few observations on the necessity of commencing, and gradually perfecting, a radical reform in your existing outlays of time and money—on and in churches, theological colleges, privileged and exclusive seminaries of all descriptions, religious Sabbath schools, and all their aids and adjuncts of Bibles, tracts, missionaries, priests, and preachers, multiplied and multiplying throughout the land, until they promise to absorb more capital than did the temple of Solomon, and to devour more of the first fruits of industry than did the tribe of Levi in the plenitude of its power;—on the necessity, I say of substituting for your present cumbrous, expensive, useless, or rather pernicious, system of partial, opinionative, and dogmatical instruction, one at once national, rational, and republican; one which shall take for its study, our own world and our own nature; for its object, the improvement of man; and for its means, the practical development of truth, the removal of temptations to evil, and the gradual equalization of human condition, human duties, and human enjoyments, by the equal diffusion of knowledge without distinction of class or sect—both of which distinctions are inconsistent with republican institutions as they are with reason and with common sense, with virtue and with happiness.

Time is it in this land to commence this reform. Time is it to check the ambition of an organized clergy, the demoralizing effects of a false system of law; to heal the strife fomented by sectarian religion and legal disputes; to bring down the pride of ideal wealth, and to raise honest industry to honour. Time is it to search out the misery in the land, and to heal it at the source. Time is it to remember the poor and the afflicted, ay! and the vicious and the depraved. Time is it to perceive that every sorrow which corrodes the human heart, every vice which diseases the body and the mind, every crime which startles the ear and sends back the blood affrighted to the heart—is the product of one evil, the foul growth from one root, the distorted progeny of one corrupt parent—IGNORANCE.

Time is it to perceive this truth; to proclaim it on the housetop, in the market place, in city and forest, throughout the land; to acknowledge it in the depths of our hearts, and to apply all our energies to the adoption of those salutary measures which this salutary truth spontaneously suggests. Time is it, I say, to turn our churches into halls of science, our schools of faith into schools of knowledge, our privileged colleges into state institutions for all the youth of the land. Time is it to arrest our speculations respecting unseen worlds and inconceivable mysteries, and to address our inquiries to the improvement of our human condition, and our efforts to the practical illustration of those beautiful principles of liberty and equality enshrined in the political institutions, and, first and chief, in the national declaration of independence.

And by whom and how, are these changes to be effected? By whom! And do a free people ask the question! By themselves. By themselves—*the people*.

I am addressing the people of Philadelphia—the people of a city where Jefferson penned the glorious declaration which awoke this nation and the world—the city, where the larum so astounding to tyranny, so fraught with hope, and joy, and exulting triumph to humankind, was first sounded in the ears of Americans. I speak to the descendants of those men who heard from the steps of their old state house the principles of liberty and equality first proclaimed to man. I speak to the inhabitants of a city founded by the most peaceful, the most humane, and the most practical of all Christian sects. I speak to mechanics who are uniting for the discovery of their interests and the protection of their rights. I speak to a public whose benevolence has been long harrowed by increasing pauperism, and whose social order and social happiness are threatened by increasing vice. I speak to sectarians who are weary of sectarianism. I speak to honest men who tremble for their honesty. I speak to the *dishonest* whose integrity has fallen before the discouragements waiting upon industry; and who, by slow degrees, or in moments of desperation, have forsaken honest labour, because without a reward, for fraudulent speculation, because it promised one chance of success to a thousand chances of ruin. I speak to parents anxious for their offspring—to husbands who, while shortening their exis tence by excess of labour, foresee, at their death, not sorrow alone, but un-requited industry and hopeless penury, involving shame, and perhaps infamy, for their oppressed widows and unprotected children. I speak to human beings surrounded by human suffering—to fellow citizens pledged to fellow feeling—to republicans pledged to equal rights and, as a consequent, to equal condition and equal enjoyments; and I call them—oh, would that my voice were loud to reach every ear, and persuasive to reach every heart!—I call them to UNITE; and to unite for the consideration of the evils around us—for the discovery and application of their remedy.

Dreadful has been the distress exhibited during the past year, not in this city only, but in every city throughout the whole extent of this vast republic. Long had the mass of evil been accumulated, ere it attracted attention; and, would we understand how far the plague is to spread, or what is to be its termination, we must look to Europe.

We are fast traveling in the footsteps of Europe, my friends; for her principles of action are ours. We have in all our habits and usages, the same vices, and, with these same vices, we must have, as we see we have, the same evils.

The great principles stamped in America's declaration of independence, are true, are great, are sublime, and are *all her own*. But her usages, her law, her religion, her education, are false, narrow, prejudiced, ignorant, and are the relic of dark ages—the gift and bequeathment of king-governed, priest-ridden nations, whose supremacy, indeed, the people of America have challenged and overthrown, but whose example they are still following.

A foreigner, I have looked round on this land unblinded by local prejudices or national predilections; a friend to human-kind, zealous for human improvement, enamoured to enthusiasm, if you will, of human liberty, I first sought this country to see in operation those principles consecrated in her national institutions, and whose simple grandeur had fired the enthusiasm and cheered the heart of my childhood, disgusted as it was with the idle parade and pride of unjust power inherent in European aristocracy. Delighted with the sound of political liberty, the absence of bayonets and constrained taxation, I spake and published, as I felt, in praise of American institutions; and called, and, I believe, first generally awakened, the attention of the European public to their study and appreciation.

The result of my observation has been the conviction, that the reform commenced at the revolution of '76 has been but little improved through the term of years which have succeeded; that the national policy of the country was then indeed changed, but that its social economy has remained such as it was in the days of its European vassalage.

In confirmation of this, I will request you to observe, that your religion is the same as that of monarchial England—taught from the same books, and promulgated and sustained by similar means, viz. a salaried priesthood, set apart from the people; sectarian churches, in whose property the people have no share, and over whose use and occupancy the people have no control; expensive missions, treasury funds, associations, and above all, a compulsory power, compounded at once of accumulated wealth, established custom, extensive correspondence, and a system of education imbued with its spirit and all pervaded by its influence.

Again, in proof of the similarity between your internal policy and that of monarchial England, I will request you to observe that *her law is your law*. Every part and parcel of that absurd, cruel, ignorant, inconsistent, incomprehensible jumble, styled the common law of England—every part and parcel of it, I say, not abrogated or altered expressly by legislative statutes, which has been very rarely done, is at this hour the law of revolutionized America.

Farther, in proof of the identity of your fabric of civil polity with that of aristocratical England, I will request you to observe that the system of education pursued in both countries is, with little variation, one and the same. There you have endowed universities, privileged by custom, enriched by ancient royal favour, protected by parliamentary statutes, and devoted to the upholding, perpetuating, and strengthening the power and privilege to which they owe their origin. There, too, you have parish schools under the control of the parish priest, and a press every where coerced by law, swayed, bribed, or silenced by ascendant parties or tyrannous authority. And *here* have we not colleges with endowments still held by the royal charters which first bestowed them, and colleges with lands and money granted by American legislatures—not for the advantage of the American people, but for that of their rulers; for the children of privileged professions upon whom is thus entailed the privilege of their fathers, and that as certainly as the son of a duke is born to a dukedom in England. *Here* have we not also schools controlled by the clergy; nay, have we not all our public institutions, scientific, literary, judicial, or humane, ridden by the spirit of orthodoxy, and invaded, perverted, vitiated, and tormented by opinionative distinctions? And *here* have we not a press paralyzed by fear, disgraced by party, and ruled by loud-tongued fanaticism, or aspiring and threatening sectarian ambition? And more, my friends, see we not, in this nation of confederated freemen, as many distinctions of class as afflict the aristocracies of Britain, or the despotism of the Russias; and more distinctions of sect than ever cursed all the nations of Europe together, from the preaching of Peter the hermit, to the trances of Madame Krudner, or the miracles of Prince Hohenlohe?

Surely all these are singular anomalies in a republic. Sparta, when she conceived her democracy, commenced with educational equality; when she aimed at national union, she cemented that union in childhood—at the public board, in the gymnasium, in the temple, in the common habits, common feelings, common duties, and common condition. And so, notwithstanding all the errors with which her institutions were fraught, and all the vices which arose out of those errors did she [not] present for ages a wondrous sample of democratic union, and consequently of national prosperity?

What then, is wanted here? What Sparta had—a *national education*. And what Sparta, in many respects, had not—a *rational education*. Hitherto, my friends, in government as in every branch of morals, we have but too much mistaken words for truths, and forms for principles. To render men free, it sufficeth not to proclaim their liberty; to make them equal, it sufficeth not to call them so. True, the 4th of July, '76, commenced a new era for our race. True, the sun of promise then rose upon the world. But let us not mistake for the fulness of light what was but its harbinger. Let us not conceive that man in signing the declaration of his rights secured their possession; that having framed the theory, he had not, and hath not still, the practice to seek.

Your fathers, indeed, on the day from which dates your existence as a nation, opened the gates of the temple of human liberty. But think not they entered, nor that you have entered the sanctuary. They passed not, nor have you passed, even the threshold.

Who speaks of liberty while the human mind is in chains? Who of equality while the thousands are in squalid wretchedness, the millions harassed with health-destroying labour, the few afflicted with health-destroying idleness, and all tormented by health-destroying solicitude? Look abroad on the misery which is gaining on the land! Mark the strife, and the discord, and the jealousies, the shock of interests and opinions, the hatreds of sect, the estrangements of class, the pride of wealth, the debasement of poverty, the helplessness of youth unprotected, of age uncomforted, of industry unrewarded, of ignorance unenlightened, of vice unreclaimed, of misery unpitied, of sickness, hunger, and nakedness unsatisfied, unalleviated, and unheeded. Go! mark all the wrongs and the wretchedness with which the eye and the ear and the heart are familiar, and then echo in triumph and celebrate in jubilee the insulting declaration—*all men are free and equal!*

That evils exist, none that have eyes, ears, and hearts can dispute. That these evils are on the increase, none who have watched the fluctuations of trade, the sinking price of labour, the growth of pauperism, and the increase of crime, will dispute. Little need be said here to the people of Philadelphia. The researches made by the public spirited among their own citizens, have but too well substantiated the suffering condition of a large mass of their population. In Boston, in New-York, in Baltimore, the voice of distress hath, in like manner, burst the barriers raised, and so long sustained, by the pride of honest industry, unused to ask from charity what it hath been wont to earn by the sweat of the brow. In each and every city necessity has constrained inquiry; and in each and every city inquiry has elicited the same appalling facts: that the hardest labour is often without a reward adequate to the sustenance of the labourer; that when, by over exertion and all the diseases, and often vices, which excess of exertion induces, the labourer, whose patient sedulous industry supplies the community with all its comforts, and the rich with all their luxuries—when he, I say, is brought to an untimely grave by those exertions which, while sustaining the life of others, cut short his own—when he is mowed down by that labour whose products form the boasted wealth of the state, he leaves a family, to whom the strength of his manhood had barely furnished bread, to lean upon the weakness of a soul-stricken mother, and hurry her to the grave of her father. * * *

Such is the information gleaned from the report of the committee lately appointed by the town meeting of the city and county of Philadelphia, and as verbatim reiterated in every populous city throughout the land. And what are the remedies suggested by our corporations, our newspaper editors, our religious societies, our tracts, and our sermons? Some have ordained fasts, multiplied prayers, and recommended pious submission to a Providence who should have instituted all this calamity for the purpose of fulfilling the words of a Jewish prophet, "the poor shall never cease from the land." Some, less spiritual-minded, have called for larger jails and more poor houses; some, for increased poor rates and additional benevolent societies; others, for compulsory laws protective of labour, and fixing a minimum, below which it shall be penal to reduce it; while others, and those not the least able to appreciate all the difficulties of the question, have sought the last resource of suffering poverty and oppressed industry in the humanity and sense of justice of the wealthier classes of society.

This last is the forlorn hope presented in the touching document signed by Matthew Carey and his fellow labourers.

It were easy to observe, in reply to each and all of the palliatives variously suggested for evils, which none profess to remedy, that to punish crime when committed is not to prevent its commission; to force the work of the poor in poor houses is only farther to glut an already unproductive market; to multiply charities is only to increase pauperism; that to fix by statute the monied price of labour would be impossible in itself, and, if possible, mischievous no less to the labourer than to the employer; and that, under the existing state of things, for human beings to lean upon the compassion and justice of their fellow creatures, is to lean upon a rotten reed.

I believe no individual, possessed of common sense and common feeling, can have studied the report of the committee to which I have referred, or the multitude of similar documents furnished elsewhere, without acknowledging that reform, and that not slight nor partial, but radical and universal, is called for. All must admit that no such reform—that is, that no remedy commensurate with the evil, has been suggested, and would we but reflect, we should perceive that no efficient remedy *can* be suggested, or if suggested, applied, until the people are generally engaged in its discovery and its application for themselves.

In this nation, any more than in any other nation, the mass has never reflected for the mass; the people, as a body, have never addressed themselves to the study of their own condition, and to the just and fair interpretation of their common interests. And, as it was with their national independence, so shall it be with their national happiness—it shall be found only when the mass shall seek it. No people have ever received liberty *in gift*. Given, it were not appreciated; it were not understood. Won without exertion, it were lost as readily. Let the people of America recall the ten years of war and tribulation by which they purchased their national independence. Let efforts as strenuous be now made, not with the sword of steel, indeed, but with the sword of the spirit, and their farther enfranchisement from poverty, starvation, and dependence, must be equally successful.

Great reforms are not wrought in a day. Evils which are the accumulated results of accumulated errors, are not to be struck down at a blow by the rod of a magician. A free people may boast that all power is in their hands; but no effectual power can be in their hands until knowledge be in their minds.

But how may knowledge be imparted to their minds? Such effective knowledge as shall render apparent to all the interests of all, and demonstrate the simple truths—that a nation to be strong, must be united; to be united, must be equal in condition; to be equal in condition, must be similar in habits and in feeling; to be similar in habits and in feeling, *must be raised in national institutions, as the children of a common family, and citizens of a common country.*

Before entering on the development of the means I have here suggested for paving our way to the reform of those evils which now press upon humanity, and which, carried, perhaps, to their acme in some of the nations of Europe, are gaining ground in these United States with a rapidity alarming to all who know how to read the present, or to calculate the future—I must observe, that I am fully aware of the difficulty of convincing all minds of the urgency of these evils, and of the impossibility of engaging all classes in the application of their remedy.

In the first place, the popular suffering, great as it is, weighs not with a sufficiently equal pressure on all parts of the country; and, in the second, affects not equally all classes of the population, so as to excite to that union of exertion, which once made, the reform is effected and the nation redeemed.

While the evil day is only in prospect, or while it visits our neighbour but spares ourselves, such is the selfishness generated by existing habits, and such the supineness generated by that selfishness, that we are but too prone to shrink from every effort not absolutely and immediately necessary for the supply of our own wants or the increase of our own luxuries.

* * *

I know how difficult it is—reared as we all are in the distinctions of class, to say nothing of sect, to conceive of our interests as associated with those of the whole community. The man possessed of a dollar, feels himself to be not merely one hundred cents richer, but also one hundred cents *better,* then the man who is pennyless; so on through all the gradations of earthly possessions—the estimate of our own moral and political importance swelling always in a ratio exactly proportionate to the growth of our purse. The rich man who can leave a clear independence to his children, is given to estimate them as he estimates himself, and to imagine something in their nature distinct from that of the less privileged heirs of hard labour and harder fare.

* * *

But it is first to the rich, I would speak. Can the man of opulence feel tranquil under the prospect of leaving to such guardianship as existing law or individual integrity may supply, the minds, bodies, morals, or even the fortune of their children? I myself was an orphan: and I know that the very law which was my protector, sucked away a portion of my little inheritance, while that law, insufficient and avaricious as it was, alone shielded me from spoliation by my guardian. I know, too, that my youth was one of tribulation, albeit passed in the envied luxuries of aristocracy. I know that the orphan's bread may be watered with tears, even when the worst evil be not there—*dependence*.

Can, then, the rich be without solicitude, when they leave to the mercy of a heartless world the beings of their creation? Who shall cherish their young sensibilities? Who shall stand between them and oppression? Who shall whisper peace in the hour of affliction? Who shall supply principle in the hour of temptation? Who shall lead the tender mind to distinguish between the good and the evil? Who shall fortify it against the corruption of wealth, or prepare it for the day of adversity? Such, looking upon life as it is must be the anxious thoughts even of the wealthy. What must be the thoughts of the poor man, it needs not that we should picture.

But, my friends, however differing in degree may be the anxiety of the rich and the poor, still, in its nature, is it the same. Doubt, uncertainty, apprehension, are before all. We hear of deathbed affliction.

* * *

We have here, then, found an evil common to all classes, and one that is entailed from generation to generation. The measure I am about to suggest, whenever adopted, will blot this now universal affliction from existence; it will also, in the outset, alleviate those popular distresses whose poignancy and happy increase weigh on the heart of philanthropy, and crush the best hopes of enlightened patriotism. It must further, when carried into full effect, work the radical cure of every disease which now afflicts the body politic, and build up for this nation a sound constitution, embracing at once, public prosperity, individual integrity, and universal happiness.

This measure, my friends, has been long present to my mind, as befitting the adoption of the American people; as alone calculated to form an enlightened, a virtuous, and a happy community; as alone capable of supplying a remedy to the evils under which we groan; as alone commensurate with the interests of the human family, and consistent with the political institutions of this great confederated republic.

I had occasion formerly to observe, in allusion to the efforts already made, and yet making, in the cause of popular instruction, more or less throughout the Union, that, as yet, the true principle has not been hit, and that until it be hit, all reform must be slow and inefficient.

The noble example of New-England has been imitated by other states, until all not possessed of common schools blush for the popular remissness. But, after all, how can *common schools,* under their best form, and in fullest supply, effect even the purpose which they have in view?

The object proposed by common schools (if I rightly understand it) is to impart to the whole population those means for the acquirement of knowledge which are in common use: reading and writing. To these are added arithmetic, and occasionally, perhaps, some imperfect lessons in the simpler sciences. But I would ask, supposing these institutions should even be made to embrace all the branches of intellectual knowledge, and, thus, science offered gratis to all the children of the land, how are the children of the very class, for whom we suppose the schools instituted to be supplied with food and raiment, or instructed in the trade necessary to their future subsistence, while they are following these studies? How are they, I ask, to be fed and clothed, when, as all facts show, the labour of the parents is often insufficient for their own sustenance, and, almost universally, inadequate to the provision of the family without the united efforts of all its members? In your manufacturing districts you have children worked for twelve hours a day; and in the rapid and certain progress of the existing system, you will soon have them, as in England, *worked to death,* and yet unable, through the period of their miserable existence, to earn a pittance sufficient to satisfy the cravings of hunger. At this present time, what leisure or what spirit, think you, have the children of the miserable widows of Philadelphia, realizing, according to the most favourable estimate of your city and county committee, sixteen dollars per annum, for food and clothing? what leisure or what spirit may their children find for visiting a school, although the same should be open to them from sunrise to sunset? Or what leisure have usually the children of your most thriving mechanics, after their strength is sufficiently developed to spin, sew, weave, or wield a tool? It seems to me, my friends, that to build school houses now-a-days is something like building churches. When you have them, you need some measure to ensure their being occupied.

But, as our time is short, and myself somewhat fatigued by continued exertions, I must hasten to the rapid development of the system of instruction and protection which has occurred to me as capable, and alone capable, of opening the door to universal reform.

In lieu of all common schools, high schools, colleges, seminaries, houses of refuge, or any other juvenile institution, instructional or protective, I would suggest that the state legislatures be directed (after laying off the whole in townships or hundreds) to organize, at suitable distances, and in convenient and healthy situations, establishments for the general reception of all the children resident within the said school district. These establishments to be devoted, severally, to children between a certain age. Say, the first, infants between two and four, or two and six, according to the density of the population, and such other local circumstances as might render a greater or less number of establishments necessary or practicable. The next to receive children from four to eight, or six to twelve years. The next from twelve to sixteen, or to an older age if found desirable. Each establishment to be furnished with instructors in every branch of knowledge, intellectual and operative, with all the apparatus, land, and conveniences necessary for the best development of all knowledge; the same, whether operative or intellectual, being always calculated to the age and strength of the pupils.

To obviate, in the commencement, every evil result possible from the first mixture of a young population, so variously raised in error or neglect, a due separation should be made in each establishment; by which means those entering with bad habits would be kept apart from the others until corrected. How rapidly reform may be effected on the plastic disposition of childhood, has been sufficiently proved in your houses of refuge, more especially when such establishments have been under *liberal* superintendence, as was formerly the case in New-York. Under their orthodox directors, those asylums of youth have been converted into jails.

It will be understood that, in the proposed establishments, the children would pass from one to the other in regular succession, and that the parents who would necessarily be resident in their close neighbourhood, could visit the children at suitable hours, but, in no case, interfere with or interrupt the rules of the institution.

In the older establishments, the well directed and well protected labour of the pupil would, in time, suffice for, and then exceed their own support; when the surplus might be devoted to the maintenance of the infant establishments.

In the beginning, and until all debt was cleared off, and so long as the same should be found favourable to the promotion of these best palladiums of a nation's happiness, a double tax might be at once expedient and politic.

First, a moderate tax per head for every child, to be laid upon its parents conjointly, or divided between them, due attention being always paid to the varying strength of the two sexes, and to the undue depreciation which now rests on female labour. The more effectually to correct the latter injustice, as well as to consult the convenience of the industrious classes generally, this parental tax might be rendered payable either in money, or in labour, produce, or domestic manufactures, and should be continued for each child until the age when juvenile labour should be found, on the average, equivalent to the educational expenses, which, I have reason to believe, would be at twelve years.

This first tax on parents to embrace equally the whole population; as, however moderate it would inculcate a certain forethought in all the human family; more especially where it is most wanted—in young persons, who before they assumed the responsibility of parents, would estimate their fitness to meet it.

The second tax to be on property, increasing in per centage with the wealth of the individual. In this manner I conceive the rich would contribute, according to their riches, to the relief of the poor, and to the support of the state by raising up its best bulwark—an enlightened and united generation.

Preparatory to, or connected with, such measures, a registry should be opened by the state, with offices through all the townships, where on the birth of every child, or within a certain time appointed, the same should be entered together with the names of its parents. When two years old, the parental tax should be payable, and the juvenile institution open for the child's reception; from which time forward it would be under the protective care and guardianship of the state, while it need never be removed from the daily, weekly, or frequent inspection of the parents.

Orphans, of course, would find here an open asylum. If possessed of property, a contribution would be paid for its revenue to the common educational fund; if unprovided, they would be sustained out of the same.

In these nurseries of a free nation, no inequality must be allowed to enter. Fed at a common board; clothed in a common garb, uniting neatness with simplicity and convenience; raised in the exercise of common duties, in the acquirement of the same knowledge and practice of the same industry, varied only according to individual taste and capabilities; in the exercise of the same virtues, in the enjoyment of the same pleasures; in the study of the same nature; in pursuit of the same object—their own and each other's happiness—say! would not such a race, when arrived at manhood and womanhood, work out the reform of society—perfect the free institutions of America.

I have drawn but a sketch, nor could I presume to draw the picture of that which the mind's eye hath seen alone, and which it is for the people of this land to realize.

In this sketch, my friends, there is nothing but what is practical and practicable: nothing but what you yourselves may contribute to effect.

Let the popular suffrage be exercised with a view to the popular good. Let the industrious classes, and all honest men of all classes, unite for the sending to the legislatures those who will represent the real interests of the many, not the imagined interests of the few—of the people at large, not of any profession or class.

To develope farther my views on this all important subject at the present time, would be to fatigue your attention, and exhaust my own strength. I shall prosecute this subject in the periodical of which I am editor, which, in common with my public discourses, have been, and will ever be, devoted to the common cause of human improvement, and addressed to humankind without distinction of nation, class, or sect. May you, my fellow beings, unite in the same cause, in the same spirit! May you learn to seek truth without fear! May you farther learn to advocate truth as you distinguish it; to be valiant in its defence, and peaceful while valiant; to meet all things, and bear all things, and dare all things for the correction of abuses, and the effecting, in private and in public, in your own minds, through the minds of your children, friends, and companions, and, above all, *through your legislatures*, a radical reform in all your measures, whether as citizens, or as men!

ANDREW JACKSON

First Annual Message to Congress (1829)

The son of Irish immigrants, Andrew Jackson (1767–1845) distinguished himself as a military hero during the War of 1812 and had a brief career in Congress before becoming the seventh president and the first elected from an area west of the Appalachians. He appeared to many to be the embodiment of democratic and egalitarian ideals at a time when all property qualifications for white male voters were being eliminated. In his first address to Congress, Jackson expressed his commitment to majority rule, rotation in office, direct election of public officials, and other principles associated with political democracy in this period.

I consider it one of the most urgent of my duties to bring to your attention the propriety of amending that part of our Constitution which relates to the election of President and Vice-President. Our system of government was by its framers deemed an experiment, and they therefore consistently provided a mode of remedying its defects.

To the people belongs the right of electing their Chief Magistrate; it was never designed that their choice should in any case be defeated, either by the intervention of electoral colleges or by the agency confided, under certain contingencies, to the House of Representatives. Experience proves that in proportion as agents to execute the will of the people are multiplied there is danger of their wishes being frustrated. Some may be unfaithful; all are liable to err. So far, therefore, as the people can with convenience speak, it is safer for them to express their own will. * * *

One may err from ignorance of the wishes of his constituents; another from a conviction that it is his duty to be governed by his own judgment of the fitness of the candidates; finally, although all were inflexibly honest, all accurately informed of the wishes of their constituents, yet under the present mode of election a minority may often elect a President, and when this happens it may reasonably be expected that efforts will be made on the part of the majority to rectify this injurious operation of their institutions. But although no evil of this character should result from such a perversion of the first principle of our system—*that the majority is to govern*—it must be very certain that a President elected by a minority cannot enjoy the confidence necessary to the successful discharge of his duties.

In this as in all other matters of public concern policy requires that as few impediments as possible should exist to the free operation of the public will. Let us, then, endeavor so to amend our system that the office of Chief Magistrate may not be conferred upon any citizen but in pursuance of a fair expression of the will of the majority.

I would therefore recommend such an amendment of the Constitution as may remove all intermediate agency in the election of the President and Vice-President. The mode may be so regulated as to preserve to each State its present relative weight in the election, and a failure in the first attempt may be provided for by confining the second to a choice between the two highest candidates. In connection with such an amendment it would seem advisable to limit the service of the chief magistrate to a single term of either four or six years. If, however, it should not be adopted, it is worthy of consideration whether a provision disqualifying for office the Representatives in Congress on whom such an election may have devolved would not be proper.

While members of Congress can be constitutionally appointed to offices of trust and profit it will be the practice, even under the most conscientious adherence to duty, to select them for such stations as they are believed to be better qualified to fill than other citizens; but the purity of our Government would doubtless be promoted by their exclusion from all appointments in the gift of the President, in whose election they may have been officially concerned. The nature of the judicial office and the necessity of securing in the Cabinet and in diplomatic stations of the highest rank the best talents and political experience should, perhaps, except these from the exclusion.

There are, perhaps, few men who can for any great length of time enjoy office and power without being more or less under the influence of feelings unfavorable to the faithful discharge of their public duties. Their integrity may be proof against improper considerations immediately addressed to themselves, but they are apt to acquire a habit of looking with indifference upon the public interests and of tolerating conduct from which an unpracticed man would revolt. Office is considered as a species of property, and government rather as a means of promoting individual interests than as an instrument created solely for the service of the people. Corruption in some and in others a perversion of correct feelings and principles divert government from its legitimate ends and make it an engine for the support of the few at the expense of the many. The duties of all public officers are, or at least admit of being made, so plain and simple that men of intelligence may readily qualify themselves for their performance; and I can not but believe that more is lost by the long continuance of men in office than is generally to be gained by their experience. I submit, therefore, to your consideration whether the efficiency of the Government would not be promoted and official industry and integrity better secured by a general extension of the law which limits appointments to four years.

In a country where offices are created solely for the benefit of the people no one man has any more intrinsic right to official station than another. Offices were not established to give support to particular men at the public expense. No individual wrong is, therefore, done by removal, since neither appointment to nor continuance in office is matter of right. The incumbent became an officer with a view to public benefits, and when these require his removal they are not to be sacrificed to private interests. It is the people, and they alone, who have a right to complain when a bad officer is substituted for a good one. He who is removed has the same means of obtaining a living that are enjoyed by the millions who never held office. The proposed limitation would destroy the idea of property now so generally connected with official station, and although individual distress may be sometimes produced, it would, by promoting that rotation which constitutes a leading principle in the republican creed, give healthful action to the system.

No very considerable change has occurred during the recess of Congress in the condition of either our agriculture, commerce, or manufactures. The operation of the tariff has not proved so injurious to the two former or as beneficial to the latter as was anticipated. Importations of foreign goods have not been sensibly diminished, while domestic competition, under an illusive excitement, has increased the production much beyond the demand for home consumption. The consequences have been low prices, temporary embarrassment, and partial loss. That such of our manufacturing establishments as are based upon capital and are prudently managed will survive the shock and be ultimately profitable there is no good reason to doubt.

To regulate its conduct so as to promote equally the prosperity of these three cardinal interests is one of the most difficult tasks of Government; and it may be regretted that the complicated restrictions which now embarrass the intercourse of nations could not by common consent be abolished, and commerce allowed to flow in those channels to which individual enterprise, always its surest guide, might direct it. But we must ever expect selfish legislation in other nations, and are therefore compelled to adapt our own to their regulations in the manner best calculated to avoid serious injury and to harmonize the conflicting interests of our agriculture, our commerce, and our manufactures. Under these impressions I invite your attention to the existing tariff, believing that some of its provisions require modification.

The general rule to be applied in graduating the duties upon articles of foreign growth or manufacture is that which will place our own in fair competition with those of other countries; and the inducements to advance even a step beyond this point are controlling in regard to those articles which are of primary necessity in time of war. When we reflect upon the difficulty and delicacy of this operation, it is important that it should never be attempted but with the utmost caution. Frequent legislation in regard to any branch of industry, affecting its value, and by which its capital may be transferred to new channels, must always be productive of hazardous speculation and loss.

In deliberating, therefore, on these interesting subjects local feelings and prejudices should be merged in the patriotic determination to promote the great interests of the whole. All attempts to connect them with the party conflicts of the day are necessarily injurious, and should be discountenanced. Our action upon them should be under the control of higher and purer motives. Legislation subjected to such influences can never be just, and will not long retain the sanction of a people whose active patriotism is not bound by sectional limits nor insensible to that spirit of concession and forbearance which gave life to our political ascendency, the North, the South, the East, and the West should unite in diminishing any burthen of which either may justly complain.

The agricultural interest of our country is so essentially connected with every other and so superior in importance to them all that it is scarcely necessary to invite to it your particular attention. It is principally as manufactures and commerce tend to increase the value of agricultural productions and to extend their application to the wants and comforts of society that they deserve the fostering care of Government. * * *

This state of the finances exhibits the resources of the nation in an aspect highly flattering to its industry and auspicious of the ability of Government in a very short time to extinguish the public debt. When this shall be done our population will be relieved from a considerable portion of its present burthens, and will find not only new motives to patriotic affection, but additional means for the display of individual enterprise. The fiscal power of the States will also be increased, and may be more extensively exerted in favor of education and other public objects, while ample means will remain in the Federal Government to promote the general weal in all the modes permitted to this authority.

After the extinction of the public debt it is not probable that any adjustment of the tariff upon principles satisfactory to the people of the Union will until a remote period, if ever, leave the Government without a considerable surplus in the Treasury beyond what may be required for its current service. As, then, the period approaches when the application of the revenue to the payment of debt will cease, the disposition of the surplus will present a subject for the serious deliberation of Congress; and it may be fortunate for the country that it is yet to be decided. Considered in connection with the difficulties which have heretofore attended appropriations for purposes of internal improvement, and with those which this experience tells us will certainly arise whenever power over such subjects may be exercised by the General Government, it is hoped that it may lead to the adoption of some plan which will reconcile the diversified interests of the States and strengthen the bonds which unite them. Every member of the Union, in peace and in war, will be benefited by the improvement of inland navigation and the construction of highways in the several States. Let us, then, endeavor to attain this benefit in a mode which will be satisfactory to all. That hitherto adopted has by many of our fellow-citizens been deprecated as an infraction of the Constitution, while by others it has been viewed as inexpedient. All feel that it has been employed at the expense of harmony in the legislative councils.

To avoid these evils it appears to me that the most safe, just, and federal disposition which could be made of the surplus revenue would be its apportionment among the several States according to their ratio of representation, and should this measure not be found warranted by the Constitution that it would be expedient to propose to the States an amendment authorizing it. I regard an appeal to the source of power in cases of real doubt, and where its exercise is deemed indispensable to the general welfare, as among the most sacred of all our obligations. Upon this country more than any other has, in the providence of God, been cast the special guardianship of the great principle of adherence to written constitutions. If it fail here, all hope in regard to it will be extinguished. That this was intended to be a government of limited and specific, and not general, powers must be admitted by all, and it is our duty to preserve for it the character intended by its framers. If experience points out the necessity for an enlargement of these powers, let us apply for it to those for whose benefit it is to be exercised, and not undermine the whole system by a resort to overstrained constructions. The scheme has worked well. It has exceeded the hopes of those who devised it, and become an object of admiration to the world. We are responsible to our country and to the glorious cause of self-government for the preservation of so great a good. The great mass of legislation relating to our internal affairs was intended to be left where the Federal Convention found it—in the State governments. Nothing is clearer, in my view, than that we are chiefly indebted for the success of the Constitution under which we are now acting to the watchful and auxiliary operation of the State authorities. This is not the reflection of a day, but belongs to the most deeply rooted convictions of my mind. I can not, therefore, too strongly or too earnestly, for my own sense of its importance, warn you against all encroachments upon the legitimate sphere of State sovereignty. Sustained by its healthful and invigorating influence the federal system can never fall.

ANDREW JACKSON

Veto of Maysville Road Bill (1830)

Proponents of internal improvements contended that the federal government had a responsibility to harmonize the conflicting sectional interests of the country into a coherent "American System." Heavily influenced by Vice President Martin Van Buren, Jackson's veto of the

Maysville Road Bill represented a major setback for internal improve-
ments. The larger significance of the veto message is that it exemplifies
Jackson's views on federalism, state sovereignty, and the necessity of
constitutional amendments in extending the powers of the national
government.

Gentlemen: I have maturely considered the bill proposing to authorize "a subscription of stock in the Maysville, Washington, Paris,
and Lexington Turnpike Road Company," and now return the same to the
House of Representatives, in which it originated, with my objections to
its passage. * * *

The constitutional power of the Federal Government to construct or
promote works of internal improvement presents itself in two points of
view—the first as bearing upon the sovereignty of the States within
whose limits their execution is contemplated, if jurisdiction of the territory which they may occupy be claimed as necessary to their preservation
and use; the second as asserting the simple right to appropriate money
from the National Treasury in aid of such works when undertaken by
State authority, surrendering the claim of jurisdiction. In the first view
the question of power is an open one, and can be decided without the
embarrassments attending the other, arising from the practice of the
Government. Although frequently and strenuously attempted, the power
to this extent has never been exercised by the Government in a single
instance. It does not, in my opinion, possess it; and no bill, therefore,
which admits it can receive my official sanction.

But in the other view of the power the question is differently situated.
The ground taken at an early period of the Government was "that whenever
money has been raised by the general authority and is to be applied to a
particular measure, a question arises whether the particular measure be
within the enumerated authorities vested in Congress. If it be, the money
requisite for it may be applied to it; if not, no such application can be
made."

The bill before me does not call for a more definite opinion upon the
particular circumstances which will warrant appropriations of money by
Congress to aid works of internal improvement, for although the extension of the power to apply money beyond that of carrying into effect the
object for which it is appropriated has * * * been long claimed and exercised by the Federal Government, yet such grants have always been professedly under the control of the general principle that the works which
might be thus aided should be "of a general, not local, national, not
State," character. A disregard of this distinction would of necessity lead to
the subversion of the federal system. That even this is an unsafe one,

arbitrary in its nature, and liable, consequently, to great abuses, is too obvious to require the confirmation of experience. It is, however, sufficiently definite and imperative to my mind to forbid my approbation of any bill having the character of the one under consideration. I have given to its provisions all the reflection demanded by a just regard for the interests of those of our fellow-citizens who have desired its passage, and by the respect which is due to a coördinate branch of the Government, but I am not able to view it in any other light than as a measure of purely local character; or, if it can be considered national, that no further distinction between the appropriate duties of the General and State Governments need be attempted, for there can be no local interest that may not with equal propriety be denominated national. It has no connection with any established system of improvements; is exclusively within the limits of a State, starting at a point on the Ohio River and running out 60 miles to an interior town, and even as far as the State is interested conferring partial instead of general advantages.

Considering the magnitude and importance of the power, and the embarrassments to which, from the very nature of the thing, its exercise must necessarily be subjected, the real friends of internal improvement ought not to be willing to confide it to accident and chance. * * *

In the other view of the subject, and the only remaining one which it is my intention to present at this time, is involved the expediency of embarking in a system of internal improvement without a previous amendment of the Constitution explaining and defining the precise powers of the Federal Government over it. Assuming the right to appropriate money to aid in the construction of national works to be warranted by the contemporaneous and continued exposition of the Constitution, its insufficiency for the successful prosecution of them must be admitted by all candid minds. If we look to usage to define the extent of the right, that will be found so variant and embracing so much that has been overruled as to involve the whole subject in great uncertainty and to render the execution of our respective duties in relation to it replete with difficulty and embarrassment. It is in regard to such works and the acquisition of additional territory that the practice obtained its first footing. In most, if not all, other disputed questions of appropriation the construction of the Constitution may be regarded as unsettled if the right to apply money in the enumerated cases is placed on the ground of usage. * * *

If it be the wish of the people that the construction of roads and canals should be conducted by the Federal Government, it is not only highly expedient, but indispensably necessary, that a previous amendment of the Constitution, delegating the necessary power and defining and restricting its exercise with reference to the sovereignty of the States, should be made. Without it nothing extensively useful can be effected.

ANDREW JACKSON

Bank Veto Message (1832)

The charter of the Second National Bank was due to expire in 1836, but Jackson's opponents rushed a recharter bill through Congress to embarrass the president by forcing him to choose between alienating supporters and appearing hostile to sound banking. Even though members of his cabinet were divided over the bank issue, they agreed that a veto was necessary for political reasons. Jackson's controversial veto message expressed his animosity toward concentrations of power in economics and politics as well as his fears that equal opportunity was threatened in America by government policies that made "the rich richer and the potent more powerful" at the expense of "the farmers, mechanics, and laborers."

The present corporate body, denominated the president, directors, and company of the Bank of the United States, will have existed at the time this act is intended to take effect twenty years. It enjoys an exclusive privilege of banking under the authority of the General Government, a monopoly of its favor and support, and, as a necessary consequence, almost a monopoly of the foreign and domestic exchange. The powers, privileges, and favors bestowed upon it in the original charter, by increasing the value of the stock far above its par value, operated as a gratuity of many millions to the stockholders. * * *

The act before me proposes another gratuity to the holders of the same stock, and in many cases to the same men, of at least seven millions more. * * * It is not our own citizens only who are to receive the bounty of our Government. More than eight millions of the stock of this bank are held by foreigners. By this act the American Republic proposes virtually to make them a present of some millions of dollars. For these gratuities to foreigners and to some of our own opulent citizens the act secures no equivalent whatever. They are the certain gains of the present stockholders under the operation of this act, after making full allowance for the payment of the bonus.

Every monopoly and all exclusive privileges are granted at the expense of the public, which ought to receive a fair equivalent. The many millions which this act proposes to bestow on the stockholders of the existing bank must come directly or indirectly out of the earnings of the American people. * * *

It is not conceivable how the present stockholders can have any claim to the special favor of the Government. The present corporation has enjoyed its monopoly during the period stipulated in the original contract. If we must have such a corporation, why should not the Government sell out the whole stock and thus secure to the people the full market value of the privileges granted? Why should not Congress create and sell twenty-eight millions of stock, incorporating the purchasers with all the powers and privileges secured in this act and putting the premium upon the sales into the Treasury?

But this act does not permit competition in the purchase of this monopoly. It seems to be predicated on the erroneous idea that the present stockholders have a prescriptive right not only to the favor but to the bounty of Government. It appears that more than a fourth part of the stock is held by foreigners and the residue is held by a few hundred of our own citizens, chiefly of the richest class. For their benefit does this act exclude the whole American people from competition in the purchase of this monopoly and dispose of it for many millions less than it is worth. This seems the less excusable because some of our citizens not now stockholders petitioned that the door of competition might be opened, and offered to take a charter on terms much more favorable to the Government and country.

But this proposition, although made by men whose aggregate wealth is believed to be equal to all the private stock in the existing bank, has been set aside, and the bounty of our Government is proposed to be again bestowed on the few who have been fortunate enough to secure the stock and at this moment wield the power of the existing institution. I can not perceive the justice or policy of this course. If our Government must sell monopolies, it would seem to be its duty to take nothing less than their full value, and if gratuities must be made once in fifteen or twenty years let them not be bestowed on the subjects of a foreign government nor upon a designated and favored class of men in our own country. It is but justice and good policy, as far as the nature of the case will admit, to confine our favors to our own fellow-citizens, and let each in his turn enjoy an opportunity to profit by our bounty. In the bearings of the act before me upon these points I find ample reasons why it should not become a law. * * *

Is there no danger to our liberty and independence in a bank that in its nature has so little to bind it to our country? The president of the bank has told us that most of the State banks exist by its forbearance. Should its influence become concentered, as it may under the operation of such an act as this, in the hands of a self-elected directory whose interests are identified with those of the foreign stockholders, will there not be cause to tremble for the purity of our elections in peace and for the independence of our country in war? Their power would be great whenever they might choose to exert it; but if this monopoly were regularly renewed every fifteen or twenty years on terms proposed by themselves, they might seldom in peace put forth their strength to influence elections or control the affairs of the nation. But if any private citizen or public functionary should interpose to curtail its powers or prevent a renewal of its privileges, it can not be doubted that he would be made to feel its influence.

Should the stock of the bank principally pass into the hands of the subjects of a foreign country, and we should unfortunately become involved in a war with that country, what would be our condition? Of the course which would be pursued by a bank almost wholly owned by the subjects of a foreign power, and managed by those whose interests, if not affections, would run in the same direction there can be no doubt. All its operations within would be in aid of the hostile fleets and armies without. Controlling our currency, receiving our public moneys, and holding thousands of our citizens in dependence, it would be more formidable and dangerous than the naval and military power of the enemy.

If we must have a bank with private stockholders, every consideration of sound policy and every impulse of American feeling admonishes that it should be *purely American*. Its stockholders should be composed exclusively of our own citizens, who at least ought to be friendly to our Government and willing to support it in times of difficulty and danger. * * *

The bank is professedly established as an agent of the executive branch of the Government, and its constitutionality is maintained on that ground. Neither upon the propriety of present action nor upon the provisions of this act was the Executive consulted. It has had no opportunity to say that it neither needs nor wants an agent clothed with such powers and favored by such exemptions. There is nothing in its legitimate functions which makes it necessary or proper. Whatever interest or influence, whether public or private, has given birth to this act, it can not be found either in the wishes or necessities of the executive department, by which present action is deemed premature, and the powers conferred upon its agent not only unnecessary, but dangerous to the Government and country.

It is to be regretted that the rich and powerful too often bend the acts of government to their selfish purposes. Distinctions in society will always exist under every just government. Equality of talents, of education, or of wealth can not be produced by human institutions. In the full enjoyment of the gifts of Heaven and the fruits of superior industry, economy, and virtue, every man is equally entitled to protection by law; but when the laws undertake to add to these natural and just advantages artificial distinctions, to grant titles, gratuities, and exclusive privileges, to make the rich richer and the potent more powerful, the humble members of society—the farmers, mechanics, and laborers—who have neither the time nor the means of securing like favors to themselves, have a right to complain of the injustice of their Government. There are no necessary evils in government. Its evils exist only in its abuses. If it would confine itself to equal protection, and, as Heaven does its rains, shower its favors alike on the high and the low, the rich and the poor, it would be an unqualified blessing. In the act before me there seems to be a wide and unnecessary departure from these just principles.

Nor is our Government to be maintained or our Union preserved by invasions of the rights and powers of the several States. In thus attempting to make our General Government strong we make it weak. Its true strength consists in leaving individuals and States as much as possible to themselves—in making itself felt, not in its power, but in its beneficence; not in its control, but in its protection; not in binding the States more closely to the center, but leaving each to move unobstructed in its proper orbit.

Experience should teach us wisdom. Most of the difficulties our Government now encounters and most of the dangers which impend over our Union have sprung from an abandonment of the legitimate objects of Government by our national legislation, and the adoption of such principles as are embodied in this act. Many of our rich men have not been content with equal protection and equal benefits, but have besought us to make them richer by act of Congress. By attempting to gratify their desires we have in the results of our legislation arrayed section against section, interest against interest, and man against man, in a fearful commotion which threatens to shake the foundations of our Union. It is time to pause in our career to review our principles, and if possible revive that devoted patriotism and spirit of compromise which distinguished the sages of the Revolution and the fathers of our Union. If we can not at once, in justice to interests vested under improvident legislation, make our Government what it ought to be, we can at least take a stand against all new grants of monopolies and exclusive privileges, against any prostitution of our Government to the advancement of the few at the expense of the many, and in favor of compromise and gradual reform in our code of laws and system of political economy. ✳ ✳ ✳

ANDREW JACKSON

Farewell Address (1837)

*Modeled on Washington's farewell remarks to the nation, Jackson's
farewell address is a provocative summary of his views on the dangers of
moneyed interests and sectionalism to popular democracy and to the
Union. He praises the producer classes, whose success depends upon
their own steady "industry and economy" rather than on sudden and un-
deserved market windfalls. Equally interesting are his comments on
America's "Indian tribes."*

We have now lived almost fifty years under the Constitution
framed by the sages and patriots of the Revolution. * * *

Our Constitution is no longer a doubtful experiment, and at the end of
nearly half a century we find that it has preserved unimpaired the liberties of the people, secured the rights of property, and that our country has
improved and is flourishing beyond any former example in the history of
nations.

In our domestic concerns there is everything to encourage us, and if you
are true to yourselves nothing can impede your march to the highest point
of national prosperity. The States which had so long been retarded in their
improvement by the Indian tribes residing in the midst of them are at
length relieved from the evil, and this unhappy race—the original dwellers
in our land—are now placed in a situation where we may well hope that
they will share in the blessings of civilization and be saved from that degradation and destruction to which they were rapidly hastening while they remained in the States; and while the safety and comfort of our own citizens
have been greatly promoted by their removal, the philanthropist will rejoice
that the remnant of that ill-fated race has been at length placed beyond the
reach of injury or oppression, and that the paternal care of the General
Government will hereafter watch over them and protect them. * * *

The necessity of watching with jealous anxiety for the preservation of
the Union was earnestly pressed upon his fellow-citizens by the Father of
his Country in his Farewell Address. He has there told us that "while experience shall not have demonstrated its impracticability, there will

always be reason to distrust the patriotism of those who in any quarter may endeavor to weaken its bands;" and he has cautioned us in the strongest terms against the formation of parties on geographical discriminations, as one of the means which might disturb our Union and to which designing men would be likely to resort. * * *

The Federal Constitution was then regarded by him as an experiment— and he so speaks of it in his Address—but an experiment upon the success of which the best hopes of his country depended; and we all know that he was prepared to lay down his life, if necessary, to secure to it a full and a fair trial. The trial has been made. It has succeeded beyond the proudest hopes of those who framed it. Every quarter of this widely extended nation has felt its blessings and shared in the general prosperity produced by its adoption. But amid this general prosperity and splendid success the dangers of which he warned us are becoming every day more evident, and the signs of evil are sufficiently apparent to awaken the deepest anxiety in the bosom of the patriot. We behold systematic efforts publicly made to sow the seeds of discord between different parts of the United States and to place party divisions directly upon geographical distinctions; to excite the *South* against the *North* and the *North* against the *South,* and to force into the controversy the most delicate and exciting topics—topics upon which it is impossible that a large portion of the Union can ever speak without strong emotion. Appeals, too, are constantly made to sectional interests in order to influence the election of the Chief Magistrate, as if it were desired that he should favor a particular quarter of the country instead of fulfilling the duties of his station with impartial justice to all; and the possible dissolution of the Union has at length become an ordinary and familiar subject of discussion. * * *

The honorable feeling of State pride and local attachments finds a place in the bosoms of the most enlightened and pure. But while such men are conscious of their own integrity and honesty of purpose, they ought never to forget that the citizens of other States are their political brethren, and that however mistaken they may be in their views, the great body of them are equally honest and upright with themselves. Mutual suspicions and reproaches may in time create mutual hostility, and artful and designing men will always be found who are ready to foment these fatal divisions and to inflame the natural jealousies of different sections of the country. * * *

What have you to gain by division and dissension? Delude not yourselves with the belief that a breach once made may be afterwards repaired. If the Union is once severed, the line of separation will grow wider and wider, and the controversies which are now debated and settled in the halls of legislation will then be tried in fields of battle and determined by the sword. Neither should you deceive yourselves with the hope that the first line of separation would be the permanent one, and that nothing but harmony and concord would be found in the new associations formed upon the dissolution of this Union. Local interests would still be found there, and unchastened ambition. And if the recollection of common dangers, in which the people of these United States stood side by side against the common foe, the memory of victories won by their united valor, the prosperity and happiness they have enjoyed under the present Constitution, the proud name they bear as citizens of this great Republic—if all these recollections and proofs of common interest are not strong enough to bind us together as one people, what tie will hold united the new divisions of empire when these bonds have been broken and this Union dissevered? The first line of separation would not last for a single generation; new fragments would be torn off, new leaders would spring up, and this great and glorious Republic would soon be broken into a multitude of petty States, without commerce, without credit, jealous of one another, armed for mutual aggression, loaded with taxes to pay armies and leaders, seeking aid against each other from foreign powers, insulted and trampled upon by the nations of Europe, until, harassed with conflicts and humbled and debased in spirit, they would be ready to submit to the absolute dominion of any military adventurer and to surrender their liberty for the sake of repose. * * *

There is too much at stake to allow pride or passion to influence your decision. Never for a moment believe that the great body of the citizens of any State or States can deliberately intend to do wrong. They may, under the influence of temporary excitement or misguided opinions, commit mistakes; they may be misled for a time by the suggestions of self-interest; but in a community so enlightened and patriotic as the people of the United States argument will soon make them sensible of their errors, and when convinced they will be ready to repair them. If they have no higher, or better motives to govern them, they will at least perceive that their own interest requires them to be just to others, as they hope to receive justice at their hands.

But in order to maintain the Union unimpaired it is absolutely necessary that the laws passed by the constituted authorities should be faithfully executed in every part of the country, and that every good citizen should at all times stand ready to put down, with the combined force of the nation, every attempt at unlawful resistance, under whatever pretext it may be made or whatever shape it may assume. Unconstitutional or oppressive laws may no doubt be passed by Congress, either from erroneous views or the want of due consideration; if they are within the reach of judicial authority, the remedy is easy and peaceful; and if, from the character of the law, it is an abuse of power not within the control of the judiciary, then free discussion and calm appeals to reason and to the justice of the people will not fail to redress the wrong. But until the law shall be declared void by the courts or repealed by Congress no individual or combination of individuals can be justified in forcibly resisting its execution. It is impossible that any government can continue to exist upon any other principles. It would cease to be a government and be unworthy of the name if it had not the power to enforce the execution of its own laws within its own sphere of action. * * *

But the Constitution can not be maintained nor the Union preserved, in opposition to public feeling, by the mere exertion of the coercive powers confided to the General Government. The foundations must be laid in the affections of the people, in the security it gives to life, liberty, character, and property in every quarter of the country, and in the fraternal attachment which the citizens of the several States bear to one another as members of one political family, mutually contributing to promote the happiness of each other. Hence the citizens of every State should studiously avoid everything calculated to wound the sensibility or offend the just pride of the people of other States, and they should frown upon any proceedings within their own borders likely to disturb the tranquillity of their political brethren in other portions of the Union. In a country so extensive as the United States, and with pursuits so varied, the internal regulations of the several States must frequently differ from one another in important particulars, and this difference is unavoidably increased by the varying principles upon which the American Colonies were originally planted—principles which had taken deep root in their social relations before the Revolution, and therefore of necessity influencing their policy since they became free and independent States. But each State has the unquestionable right to regulate its own internal concerns according to its own pleasure. * * *

[A]ll efforts on the part of people of other States to cast odium upon their institutions, and all measures calculated to disturb their rights of property or to put in jeopardy their peace and internal tranquillity, are in direct opposition to the spirit in which the Union was formed, and must endanger its safety. Motives of philanthropy may be assigned for this unwarrantable interference, and weak men may persuade themselves for a moment that they are laboring in the cause of humanity and asserting the rights of the human race; but everyone, upon sober reflection, will see that nothing but mischief can come from these improper assaults upon the feelings and rights of others. Rest assured that the men found busy in this work of discord are not worthy of your confidence, and deserve your strongest reprobation.

In the legislation of Congress also, and in every measure of the General Government, justice to every portion of the United States should be faithfully observed. No free government can stand without virtue in the people and a lofty spirit of patriotism, and if the sordid feelings of mere selfishness shall usurp the place which ought to be filled by public spirit, the legislation of Congress will soon be converted into a scramble for personal and sectional advantages. Under our free institutions the citizens of every quarter of our country are capable of attaining a high degree of prosperity and happiness without seeking to profit themselves at the expense of others; and every such attempt must in the end fail to succeed, for the people in every part of the United States are too enlightened not to understand their own rights and interests and to detect and defeat every effort to gain undue advantages over them; and when such designs are discovered it naturally provokes resentments which can not always be easily allayed. Justice—full and ample justice—to every portion of the United States should be the ruling principle of every freeman, and should guide the deliberations of every public body, whether it be State or national.

It is well known that there have always been those amongst us who wish to enlarge the powers of the General Government, and experience would seem to indicate that there is a tendency on the part of this Government to overstep the boundaries marked out for it by the Constitution. Its legitimate authority is abundantly sufficient for all the purposes for which it was created, and its powers being expressly enumerated, there can be no justification for claiming anything beyond them. Every attempt to exercise power beyond these limits should be promptly and firmly opposed, for one evil example will lead to other measures still more mischievous; and if the principle of constructive powers or supposed advantages or temporary circumstances shall ever be permitted to justify the assumption of a power not given by the Constitution, the General Government will before long absorb all the powers of legislation, and you will have in effect but one consolidated government. From the extent of our country, its diversified interests, different pursuits, and different habits, it is too obvious for argument that a single consolidated government would be wholly inadequate to watch over and protect its interests; and every friend of our free institutions should be always prepared to maintain unimpaired and in full vigor the rights and sovereignty of the States and to confine the action of the General Government strictly to the sphere of its appropriate duties.

There is, perhaps, no one of the powers conferred on the Federal Government so liable to abuse as the taxing power. The most productive and convenient sources of revenue were necessarily given to it, that it might be able to perform the important duties imposed upon it; and the taxes which it lays upon commerce being concealed from the real payer in the price of the article, they do not so readily attract the attention of the people as smaller sums demanded from them directly by the taxgatherer. But the tax imposed on goods enhances by so much the price of the commodity to the consumer, and as many of these duties are imposed on articles of necessity which are daily used by the great body of the people, the money raised by these imposts is drawn from their pockets. Congress has no right under the Constitution to take money from the people unless it is required to execute some one of the specific powers intrusted to the Government; and if they raise more than is necessary for such purposes, it is an abuse of the power of taxation, and unjust and oppressive. It may indeed happen that the revenue will sometimes exceed the amount anticipated when the taxes were laid. When, however, this ascertained, it is easy to reduce them, and in such a case it is unquestionably the duty of the Government to reduce them, for no circumstances can justify it in assuming a power not given to it by the Constitution nor in taking away the money of the people when it is not needed for the legitimate wants of the Government.

Plain as these principles appear to be, you will yet find there is a constant effort to induce the General Government to go beyond the limits of its taxing power and to impose unnecessary burdens upon the people. Many powerful interests are continually at work to procure heavy duties on commerce and to swell the revenue beyond the real necessities of the public service, and the country has already felt the injurious effects of their combined influence. They succeeded in obtaining a tariff of duties bearing most oppressively on the agricultural and laboring classes of society and producing a revenue that could not be usefully employed within the range of the powers conferred upon Congress, and in order to fasten upon the people this unjust and unequal system of taxation extravagant schemes of internal improvement were got up in various quarters to squander the money and to purchase support. Thus one unconstitutional measure was intended to be upheld by another, and the abuse of the power of taxation was to be maintained by usurping the power of expending the money in internal improvements. You can not have forgotten the severe and doubtful struggle through which we passed when the executive department of the Government by its veto endeavored to arrest this prodigal scheme of injustice and to bring back the legislation of Congress to the boundaries prescribed by the Constitution. The good sense and practical judgment of the people when the subject was brought before them sustained the course of the Executive, and this plan of unconstitutional expenditures for the purposes of corrupt influence is, I trust, finally overthrown.

The result of this decision has been felt in the rapid extinguishment of the public debt and the large accumulation of a surplus in the Treasury, notwithstanding the tariff was reduced and is now very far below the amount originally contemplated by its advocates. But, rely upon it, the design to collect an extravagant revenue and to burden you with taxes beyond the economical wants of the Government is not yet abandoned. The various interests which have combined together to impose a heavy tariff and to produce an overflowing Treasury are too strong and have too much at stake to surrender the contest. The corporations and wealthy individuals who are engaged in large manufacturing establishments desire a high tariff to increase their gains. Designing politicians will support it to conciliate their favor and to obtain the means of profuse expenditure for the purpose of purchasing influence in other quarters; and since the people have decided that the Federal Government can not be permitted to employ its income in internal improvements, efforts will be made to seduce and mislead the citizens of the several States by holding out to them the deceitful prospect of benefits to be derived from a surplus revenue collected by the General Government and annually divided among the States; and if, encouraged by these fallacious hopes, the States should disregard the principles of economy which ought to characterize every republican government, and should indulge in lavish expenditures exceeding their resources, they will before long find themselves oppressed with debts which they are unable to pay, and the temptation will become irresistible to support a high tariff in order to obtain a surplus for distribution. Do not allow yourselves, my fellow-citizens, to be misled on this subject. The Federal Government can not collect a surplus for such purposes without violating the principles of the Constitution and assuming powers which have not been granted. It is, moreover, a system of injustice, and if persisted in will inevitably lead to corruption, and must end in ruin. The surplus revenue will be drawn from the pockets of the people— from the farmer, the mechanic, and the laboring classes of society; but who will receive it when distributed among the States, where it is to be disposed of by leading State politicians, who have friends to favor and political partisans to gratify? It will certainly not be returned to those who paid it and who have most need of it and are honestly entitled to it. There is but one safe rule, and that is to confine the General Government rigidly within the sphere of its appropriate duties. It has no power to raise a revenue or impose taxes except for the purposes enumerated in the Constitution, and if its income is found to exceed these wants it should be forthwith reduced and the burden of the people so far lightened.

In reviewing the conflicts which have taken place between different interests in the United States and the policy pursued since the adoption of our present form of Government, we find nothing that has produced such deep-seated evil as the course of legislation in relation to the currency. The Constitution of the United States unquestionably intended to secure to the people a circulating medium of gold and silver. But the establishment of a national bank by Congress, with the privilege of issuing paper money receivable in the payment of the public dues, and the unfortunate course of legislation in the several States upon the same subject, drove from general circulation the constitutional currency and substituted one of paper in its place. * * *

The paper system being founded on public confidence and having of itself no intrinsic value, it is liable to great and sudden fluctuations, thereby rendering property insecure and the wages of labor unsteady and uncertain. The corporations which create the paper money can not be relied upon to keep the circulating medium uniform in amount. In times of prosperity, when confidence is high, they are tempted by the prospect of gain or by the influence of those who hope to profit by it to extend their issues of paper beyond the bounds of discretion and the reasonable demands of business; and when these issues have been pushed on from day to day, until public confidence is at length shaken, then a reaction takes place, and they immediately withdraw the credits they have given, suddenly curtail their issues, and produce an unexpected and ruinous contraction of the circulating medium, which is felt by the whole community. The banks by this means save themselves, and the mischievous consequences of their imprudence or cupidity are visited upon the public. Nor does the evil stop here. These ebbs and flows in the currency and these indiscreet extensions of credit naturally engender a spirit of speculation injurious to the habits and character of the people. We have already seen its effects in the wild spirit of speculation in the public lands and various kinds of stock which within the last year or two seized upon such a multitude of our citizens and threatened to pervade all classes of society and to withdraw their attention from the sober pursuits of honest industry. It is not by encouraging this spirit that we shall best preserve public virtue and promote the true interests of our country; but if your currency continues as exclusively paper as it now is, it will foster this eager desire to amass wealth without labor; it will multiply the number of dependents on bank accommodations and bank favors; the temptation to obtain money at any sacrifice will become stronger and stronger, and inevitably lead to corruption, which will find its way into your public councils and destroy at no distant day the purity of your Government. Some of the evils which arise from this system of paper press with peculiar hardship upon the class of society least able to bear it. A portion of this currency frequently becomes depreciated or worthless, and all of it is easily counterfeited in such a manner as to require peculiar skill and much experience to distinguish the counterfeit from the genuine note. These frauds are most generally perpetrated in the smaller notes, which are used in the daily transactions of ordinary business, and the losses occasioned by them are commonly thrown upon the laboring classes of society, whose situation and pursuits put it out of their power to guard themselves from these impositions, and whose daily wages are necessary for their subsistence. It is the duty of every government so to regulate its currency as to protect this numerous class, as far as practicable, from the impositions of avarice and fraud. It is more especially the duty of the United States, where the Government is emphatically the Government of the people, and where this respectable portion of our citizens are so proudly distinguished from the laboring classes of all other nations by their independent spirit, their love of liberty, their intelligence, and their high tone of moral character. Their industry in peace is the source of our wealth and their bravery in war has covered us with glory; and the Government of the United States will but ill discharge its duties if it leaves them a prey to such dishonest impositions. Yet it is evident that their interests can not be effectually protected unless silver and gold are restored to circulation.

These views alone of the paper currency are sufficient to call for immediate reform; but there is another consideration which should still more strongly press it upon your attention.

Recent events have proved that the paper-money system of this country may be used as an engine to undermine your free institutions, and that those who desire to engross all power in the hands of the few and to govern by corruption or force are aware of its power and prepared to employ it. Your banks now furnish your only circulating medium, and money is plenty or scarce according to the quantity of notes issued by them. While they have capitals not greatly disproportioned to each other, they are competitors in business, and no one of them can exercise dominion over the rest; and although in the present state of the currency these banks may and do operate injuriously upon the habits of business, the pecuniary concerns, and the moral tone of society, yet, from their number and dispersed situation, they can not combine for the purposes of political influence, and whatever may be the dispositions of some of them their power of mischief must necessarily be confined to a narrow space and felt only in their immediate neighborhoods.

But when the charter for the Bank of the United States was obtained from Congress it perfected the schemes of the paper system and gave to its advocates the position they have struggled to obtain from the commencement of the Federal Government to the present hour. The immense capital and peculiar privileges bestowed upon it enabled it to exercise despotic sway over the other banks in every part of the country. From its superior strength it could seriously injure, if not destroy, the business of any one of them which might incur its resentment; and it openly claimed for itself the power of regulating the currency throughout the United States. In other words, it asserted (and it undoubtedly possessed) the power to make money plenty or scarce at its pleasure, at any time and in any quarter of the Union, by controlling the issues of other banks and permitting an expansion or compelling a general contraction of the circulating medium, according to its own will. The other banking institutions were sensible of its strength, and they soon generally became its obedient instruments, ready at all times to execute its mandates; and with the banks necessarily went also that numerous class of persons in our commercial cities who depend altogether on bank credits for their solvency and means of business, and who are therefore obliged, for their own safety, to propitiate the favor of the money power by distinguished zeal and devotion in its service. The result of the ill-advised legislation which established this great monopoly was to concentrate the whole moneyed power of the Union, with its boundless means of corruption and its numerous dependents, under the direction and command of one acknowledged head, thus organizing this particular interest as one body and securing to it unity and concert of action throughout the United States, and enabling it to bring forward upon any occasion its entire and undivided strength to support or defeat any measure of the Government. In the hands of this formidable power, thus perfectly organized, was also placed unlimited dominion over the amount of the circulating medium, giving it the power to regulate the value of property and the fruits of labor in every quarter of the Union, and to bestow prosperity or bring ruin upon any city or section of the country as might best comport with its own interest or policy.

We are not left to conjecture how the moneyed power, thus organized and with such a weapon in its hands, would be likely to use it. The distress and alarm which pervaded and agitated the whole country when the Bank of the United States waged war upon the people in order to compel them to submit to its demands can not yet be forgotten. The ruthless and unsparing temper with which whole cities and communities were oppressed, individuals impoverished and ruined, and a scene of cheerful prosperity suddenly changed into one of gloom and despondency ought to be indelibly impressed on the memory of the people of the United States. If such was its power in a time of peace, what would it not have been in a season of war, with an enemy at your doors? No nation but the freemen of the United States could have come out victorious from such a contest; yet, if you had not conquered, the Government would have passed from the hands of the many to the hands of the few, and this organized money power from its secret conclave would have dictated the choice of your highest officers and compelled you to make peace or war, as best suited their own wishes. The forms of your Government might for a time have remained, but its living spirit would have departed from it.

The distress and sufferings inflicted on the people by the bank are some of the fruits of that system of policy which is continually striving to enlarge the authority of the Federal Government beyond the limits fixed by the Constitution. The powers enumerated in that instrument do not confer on Congress the right to establish such a corporation as the Bank of the United States, and the evil consequences which followed may warn us of the danger of departing from the true rule of construction and of permitting temporary circumstances or the hope of better promoting the public welfare to influence in any degree our decisions upon the extent of the authority of the General Government. Let us abide by the Constitution as it is written, or amend it in the constitutional mode if it is found to be defective.

The severe lessons of experience will, I doubt not, be sufficient to prevent Congress from again chartering such a monopoly, even if the Consti tution did not present an insuperable objection to it. But you must remember, my fellow-citizens, that eternal vigilance by the people is the price of liberty, and that you must pay the price if you wish to secure the blessing. It behooves you, therefore, to be watchful in your States as well as in the Federal Government. The power which the moneyed interest can exercise, when concentrated under a single head and with our present system of currency, was sufficiently demonstrated in the struggle made by the Bank of the United States. Defeated in the General Government, the same class of intriguers and politicians will now resort to the States and endeavor to obtain there the same organization which they failed to perpetuate in the Union; and with specious and deceitful plans of public advantages and State interests and State pride they will endeavor to establish in the different States one moneyed institution with overgrown capital and exclusive privileges sufficient to enable it to control the operations of the other banks. Such an institution will be pregnant with the same evils produced by the Bank of the United States, although its sphere of action is more confined, and in the State in which it is chartered the money power will be able to embody its whole strength and to move together with undivided force to accomplish any object it may wish to attain. You have already had abundant evidence of its power to inflict injury upon the agricultural, mechanical, and laboring classes of society, and over those whose engagements in trade or speculation render them dependent on bank facilities the dominion of the State monopoly will be absolute and their obedience unlimited. With such a bank and a paper currency the money power would in a few years govern the State and control its measures, and if a sufficient number of States can be induced to create such establishments the time will soon come when it will again take the field against the United States and succeed in perfecting and perpetuating its organization by a charter from Congress.

It is one of the serious evils of our present system of banking that it enables one class of society—and that by no means a numerous one—by its control over the currency, to act injuriously upon the interests of all the others and to exercise more than its just proportion of influence in political affairs. The agricultural, the mechanical, and the laboring classes have little or no share in the direction of the great moneyed corporations, and from their habits and the nature of their pursuits they are incapable of forming extensive combinations to act together with united force. Such concert of action may sometimes be produced in a single city or in a small district of country by means of personal communications with each other, but they have no regular or active correspondence with those who are engaged in similar pursuits in distant places; they have but little patronage to give to the press, and exercise but a small share of influence over it; they have no crowd of dependents about them who hope to grow rich without labor by their countenance and favor, and who are therefore always ready to execute their wishes. The planter, the farmer, the mechanic, and the laborer all know that their success depends upon their own industry and economy, and that they must not expect to become suddenly rich by the fruits of their toil. Yet these classes of society form the great body of the people of the United States; they are the bone and sinew of the country—men who love liberty and desire nothing but equal rights and equal laws, and who, moreover, hold the great mass of our national wealth, although it is distributed in moderate amounts among the millions of freemen who posses it. But with overwhelming numbers and wealth on their side they are in constant danger of losing their fair influence in the Government, and with difficulty maintain their just rights against the incessant efforts daily made to encroach upon them. The mischief springs from the power which the moneyed interest derives from a paper currency which they are able to control, from the multitude of corporations with exclusive privileges which they have succeeded in obtaining in the different States, and which are employed altogether for their benefit; and unless you become more watchful in your States and check this spirit of monopoly and thirst for exclusive privileges you will in the end find that the most important powers of Government have been given or bartered away, and the control over your dearest interests has passed into the hands of these corporations.

The paper-money system and its natural associations—monopoly and exclusive privileges—have already struck their roots too deep in the soil, and it will require all your efforts to check its further growth and to eradicate the evil. The men who profit by the abuses and desire to perpetuate them will continue to besiege the halls of legislation in the General Government as well as in the States, and will seek by every artifice to mislead and deceive the public servants. It is to yourselves that you must look for safety and the means of guarding and perpetuating your free institutions. In your hands is rightfully placed the sovereignty of the country, and to you everyone placed in authority is ultimately responsible. It is always in your power to see that the wishes of the people are carried into faithful execution, and their will, when once made known, must sooner or later be obeyed; and while the people remain, as I trust they ever will, uncorrupted and incorruptible, and continue watchful and jealous of their rights, the Government is safe, and the cause of freedom will continue to triumph over all its enemies.

But it will require steady and persevering exertions on your part to rid yourselves of the iniquities and mischiefs of the paper system and to check the spirit of monopoly and other abuses which have sprung up with it, and of which it is the main support. So many interests are united to resist all reform on this subject that you must not hope the conflict will be a short one nor success easy. My humble efforts have not been spared during my administration of the Government to restore the constitutional currency of gold and silver, and something, I trust, has been done toward the accomplishment of this most desirable object; but enough yet remains to require all your energy and perseverance. The power, however, is in your hands, and the remedy must and will be applied if you determine upon it.

DANIEL WEBSTER

Speech on Jackson's Veto of the United States Bank Bill (1832)

As one of the leaders of the Whig Party and a chief spokesman for eastern business interests, the Massachusetts senator Daniel Webster headed the opposition against Jackson and the Democrats during the Bank War. Webster, who was widely regarded as America's greatest orator at the time, delivered his speech on the bank only a day after Jackson sent his veto message to Congress. In responding to Jackson's objections, Webster accused the president of demagoguery for instigating class conflict and defended the private management of the bank as the best way to promote the public interest.

Mr. President, I will not conceal my opinion that the affairs of the country are approaching an important and dangerous crisis. At the very moment of almost unparalleled general prosperity, there appears an unaccountable disposition to destroy the most useful and most approved institutions of the government. Indeed, it seems to be in the midst of all this national happiness that some are found openly to question the advantages of the Constitution itself; and many more ready to embarrass the exercise of its just power, weaken its authority, and undermine its foundations. How far these notions may be carried it is impossible yet to say. We have before us the practical result of one of them. The bank has fallen, or is to fall. * * *

Before proceeding to the constitutional question, there are some other topics, treated in the message, which ought to be noticed. It commences by an inflamed statement of what it calls the "favor" bestowed upon the original bank by the government, or, indeed, as it is phrased, the "monopoly of its favor and support"; and through the whole message all possible changes are rung on the "gratuity," the "exclusive privileges," and "monopoly," of the bank charter. Now, Sir, the truth is, that the powers conferred on the bank are such, and no others, as are usually conferred on similar institutions. They constitute no monopoly, although some of them are of necessity, and with propriety, exclusive privileges. "The original act," says the message, "operated as a gratuity of many millions to the stockholders." What fair foundation is there for this remark? The stockholders received their charter, not gratuitously, but for a valuable consideration in money, prescribed by Congress, and actually paid.

* * *

* * * The message proceeds to declare, that the present act proposes another donation, another gratuity, to the same men, of at least seven millions more. It seems to me that this is an extraordinary statement, and an extraordinary style of argument, for such a subject and on such an occasion. In the first place, the facts are all assumed; they are taken for true without evidence. There are no proofs that any benefit to that amount will accrue to the stockholders, nor any experience to justify the expectation of it. It rests on random estimates, or mere conjecture. But suppose the continuance of the charter should prove beneficial to the stockholders; do they not pay for it? They give twice as much for a charter of fifteen years, as was given before for one of twenty. And if the proposed *bonus,* or premium, be not, in the President's judgment, large enough, would he, nevertheless, on such a mere matter of opinion as that, negative the whole bill? May not Congress be trusted to decide even on such a subject as the amount of the money premium to be received by government for a charter of this kind?

But, Sir, there is a larger and a much more just view of this subject. The bill was not passed for the purpose of benefiting the present stockholders. Their benefit, if any, is incidental and collateral. Nor was it passed on any idea that they had a right to a renewed charter, although the message argues against such right, as if it had been somewhere set up and asserted. No such right has been asserted by any body. Congress passed the bill, not as a bounty or a favor to the present stockholders, nor to comply with any demand of right on their part; but to promote great public interests, for great public objects. Every bank must have some stockholders, unless it be such a bank as the President has recommended, and in regard to which he seems not likely to find much concurrence of other men's opinions; and if the stockholders, whoever they may be, conduct the affairs of the bank prudently, the expectation is always, of course, that they will make it profitable to themselves, as well as useful to the public. If a bank charter is not to be granted, because, to some extent, it may be profitable to the stockholders, no charter can be granted. The objection lies against all banks.

Sir, the object aimed at by such institutions is to connect the public safety and convenience with private interests. It has been found by experience, that banks are safest under private management, and that government banks are among the most dangerous of all inventions. Now, Sir, the whole drift of the message is to reverse the settled judgment of all the civilized world, and to set up government banks, independent of private interest or private control. For this purpose the message labors, even beyond the measure of all its other labors, to create jealousies and prejudices, on the ground of the alleged benefit which individuals will derive from the renewal of this charter. Much less effort is made to show that government, or the public, will be injured by the bill, than that individuals will profit by it. Following up the impulses of the same spirit, the message goes on gravely to allege, that the act, as passed by Congress, proposes to make a *present* of some millions of dollars to foreigners, because a portion of the stock is held by foreigners. Sir, how would this sort of argument apply to other cases? The President has shown himself not only willing, but anxious, to pay off the three per cent stock of the United States at *par,* notwithstanding that it is notorious that foreigners are owners of the greater part of it. Why should he not call that a donation to foreigners of many millions? * * *

From the commencement of the government, it has been thought desirable to invite, rather than to repel, the introduction of foreign capital. Our stocks have all been open to foreign subscriptions; and the State banks, in like manner, are free to foreign ownership. Whatever State has created a debt has been willing that foreigners should become purchasers, and desirous of it.

* * *

* * * It is easy to say that there is danger to liberty, danger to independence, in a bank open to foreign stockholders, because it is easy to say any thing. But neither reason nor experience proves any such danger. The foreign stockholder cannot be a director. He has no voice even in the choice of directors. His money is placed entirely in the management of the directors appointed by the President and Senate and by the American stockholders. So far as there is dependence or influence either way, it is to the disadvantage of the foreign stockholder. He has parted with the control over his own property, instead of exercising control over the property or over the actions of others. * * *

In order to justify its alarm for the security of our independence, the message supposes a case. It supposes that the bank should pass principally into the hands of the subjects of a foreign country, and that we should be involved in war with that country, and then it exclaims, "What would be our condition?" Why, Sir, it is plain that all the advantages would be on our side. The bank would still be our institution, subject to our own laws, and all its directors elected by ourselves; and our means would be enhanced, not by the confiscation and plunder, but by the proper use, of the foreign capital in our hands. And, Sir, it is singular enough, that this very state of war, from which this argument against a bank is drawn, is the very thing which, more than all others, convinced the country and the government of the necessity of a national bank. So much was the want of such an institution felt in the late war, that the subject engaged the attention of Congress, constantly, from the declaration of that war down to the time when the existing bank was actually established; so that in this respect, as well as in others, the argument of the message is directly opposed to the whole experience of the government, and to the general and long-settled convictions of the country. * * *

Mr. President, we have arrived at a new epoch. We are entering on experiments, with the government and the Constitution of the country, hitherto untried, and of fearful and appalling aspect. This message calls us to the contemplation of a future which little resembles the past. Its principles are at war with all that public opinion has sustained, and all which the experience of the government has sanctioned. It denies first principles; it contradicts truths, heretofore received as indisputable. It denies to the judiciary the interpretation of law, and claims to divide with Congress the power of originating statutes. It extends the grasp of executive pretension over every power of the government. But this is not all. It presents the chief magistrate of the Union in the attitude of arguing away the powers of that government over which he has been chosen to preside; and adopting for this purpose modes of reasoning which, even under the influence of all proper feeling towards high official station, it is difficult to regard as respectable. It appeals to every prejudice which may betray men into a mistaken view of their own interests, and to every passion which may lead them to disobey the impulses of their understanding. It urges all the specious topics of State rights and national encroachment against that which a great majority of the States have affirmed to be rightful, and in which all of them have acquiesced. It sows, in an unsparing manner, the seeds of jealousy and ill-will against that government of which its author is the official head. It raises a cry, that liberty is in danger, at the very moment when it puts forth claims to powers heretofore unknown and unheard of. It effects alarm for the public freedom, when nothing endangers that freedom so much as its own unparalleled pretences. This, even, is not all. It manifestly seeks to inflame the poor against the rich; it wantonly attacks whole classes of the people, for the purpose of turning against them the prejudices and the resentments of other classes. It is a state paper which finds no topic too exciting for its use, no passion too inflammable for it address and its solicitation.

Such is this message. It remains now for the people of the United States to choose between the principles here avowed and their government. These cannot subsist together. The one or the other must be rejected. If the sentiments of the message shall receive general approbation, the Constitution will have perished even earlier than the moment which its enemies originally allowed for the termination of its existence. It will not have survived to its fiftieth year.

ROGER B. TANEY

Charles River Bridge v. Warren Bridge (1837)

A leading figure in the fight against the national bank, Roger Brooke Taney (1777–1864) became the fifth chief justice of the Supreme Court after serving as Andrew Jackson's attorney general. On the Court, Taney often ruled against exclusive privileges and other interests antithetical to Jacksonian democracy. The Charles River Bridge Company, which received a charter in 1785 to operate a toll bridge, brought suit against the Warren Bridge Company after Massachusetts issued the latter company a charter to build another bridge near the sight of the first due to increased traffic over the river. In his opinion for the Court, Taney decided that it is unreasonable to conclude that a state would limit its ability to serve the common good by granting exclusive rights in the absence of an explicit grant. Taney denied that property rights of private parties should automatically prevail since "the community also have rights."

Borrowing, as we have done, our system of jurisprudence from the English law * * * it would present a singular spectacle, if, while the courts in England are restraining, within the strictest limits, the spirit of monopoly, and exclusive privileges in nature of monopolies, and confining corporations to the privileges plainly given to them in their charter, the courts of this country should be found enlarging these privileges by implication; and construing a statute more unfavorably to the public, and to the rights of the community, than would be done in a like case in an English court of justice. * * *

The case now before the court is, in principle, precisely the same [as that of *Providence Bank* v. *Billings* (1830)]. It is a charter from a state; the act of incorporation is silent in relation to the contested power. The argument in favor of the proprietors of the Charles River bridge, is the same, almost in words, with that used by the Providence Bank; that is, that the power claimed by the state, if it exists, may be so used as to destroy the value of the franchise they have granted to the corporation. The argument must receive the same answer; and the fact that the power has been already exercised, so as to destroy the value of the franchise, cannot in any degree affect the principle. The existence of the power does not, and cannot, depend upon the circumstance of its having been exercised or not.

It may, perhaps, be said, that in the case of the Providence Bank, this court were speaking of the taxing power; which is of vital importance to the very existence of every government. But the object and end of all government is to promote the happiness and prosperity of the community by which it is established; and it can never be assumed, that the government intended to diminish its power of accomplishing the end for which it was created. And in a country like ours, free, active and enterprising, continually advancing in numbers and wealth, new channels of communication are daily found necessary, both for travel and trade, and are essential to the comfort, convenience and prosperity of the people. A state ought never to be presumed to surrender this power, because, like the taxing power, the whole community have an interest in preserving it undiminished. And when a corporation alleges, that a state has surrendered, for seventy years, its power of improvement and public accommodation, in a great and important line of travel, along which a vast number of its citizens must daily pass, the community have a right to insist, in the language of this court, above quoted, "that its abandonment ought not to be presumed, in a case, in which the deliberate purpose of the state to abandon it does not appear." The continued existence of a government would be of no great value, if, by implications and presumptions, it was disarmed of the powers necessary to accomplish the ends of its creation, and the functions it was designed to perform, transferred to the hands of privileged corporations. The rule of construction announced by the court, was not confined to the taxing power, nor is it so limited, in the opinion delivered. On the contrary, it was distinctly placed on the ground, that the interests of the community were concerned in preserving, undiminished, the power then in question; and whenever any power of the state is said to be surrendered or diminished, whether it be the taxing power, or any other affecting the public interest, the same principle applies, and the rule of construction must be the same. No one will question, that the interests of the great body of the people of the state, would, in this instance, be affected by the surrender of this great line of travel to a single corporation, with the right to exact toll, and exclude competition, for seventy years. While the rights of private property are sacredly guarded, we must not forget, that the community also have rights, and that the happiness and well-being of every citizen depends on their faithful preservation.

Adopting the rule of construction above stated as the settled one, we proceed to apply it to the charter of 1785 to the proprietors of the Charles River bridge. This act of incorporation is in the usual form, and the privileges such as are commonly given to corporations of that kind. It confers on them the ordinary faculties of a corporation, for the purpose of building the bridge; and establishes certain rates of toll, which the company are authorized to take. This is the whole grant. There is no exclusive privilege given to them over the waters of Charles river, above or below their bridge; no right to erect another bridge themselves, nor to prevent other persons from erecting one, no engagement from the State, that another shall not be erected; and no undertaking not to sanction competition, nor to make improvements that may diminish the amount of its income. Upon all these subjects the charter is silent; and nothing is said in it about a line of travel, so much insisted on in the argument, in which they are to have exclusive privileges. No words are used from which an intention to grant any of these rights can be inferred. If the plaintiff is entitled to them, it must be implied, simply from the nature of the grant, and cannot be inferred from the words by which the grant is made. * * *

The inquiry then is, does the charter contain such a contract on the part of the State? Is there any such stipulation to be found in that instrument? It must be admitted on all hands, that there is none—no words that even relate to another bridge, or to the diminution of their tolls, or to the line of travel. If a contract on that subject can be gathered from the charter, it must be by implication, and cannot be found in the words used. Can such an agreement be implied? The rule of construction before stated is an answer to the question. In charters of this description, no rights are taken from the public, or given to the corporation, beyond those which the words of the charter, by their natural and proper construction, purport to convey. There are no words which import such a contract as the plaintiffs in error contend for, and none can be implied. * * * The whole community are interested in this inquiry, and they have a right to require that the power of promoting their comfort and convenience, and of advancing the public prosperity, by providing safe, convenient, and cheap ways for the transportation of produce and the purposes of travel, shall not be construed to have been surrendered or diminished by the State, unless it shall appear by plain words that it was intended to be done. * * *

Indeed, the practice and usage of almost every State in the Union old enough to have commenced the work of internal improvement, is opposed to the doctrine contended for on the part of the plaintiffs in error. Turnpike roads have been made in succession, on the same line of travel; the later ones interfering materially with the profits of the first. These corporations have, in some instances, been utterly ruined by the introduction of newer and better modes of transportation and travelling. In some cases, railroads have rendered the turnpike roads on the same line of travel so entirely useless, that the franchise of the turnpike corporation is not worth preserving. Yet in none of these cases have the corporations supposed that their privileges were invaded, or any contract violated on the part of the State. * * *

And what would be the fruits of this doctrine of implied contracts on the part of the States, and of property in a line of travel by a corporation, if it should now be sanctioned by this court? To what results would it lead us? If it is to be found in the charter to this bridge, the same process of reasoning must discover it, in the various acts which have been passed, within the last forty years, for turnpike companies. * * * If this court should establish the principles now contended for, what is to become of the numerous railroads established on the same line of travel with turnpike companies, and which have rendered the franchises of the turnpike corporations of no value? Let it once be understood that such charters carry with them these implied contracts, and give this unknown and undefined property in a line of travelling, and you will soon find the old turnpike corporations awakening from their sleep and calling upon this court to put down the improvements which have taken their place. The millions of property which have been invested in railroads and canals upon lines of travel which had been before occupied by turnpike corporations will be put in jeopardy. We shall be thrown back to the improvements of the last century, and obliged to stand still until the claims of the old turnpike corporations shall be satisfied, and they shall consent to permit these States to avail themselves of the lights of modern science, and to partake of the benefit of those improvements which are now adding to the wealth and prosperity, and the convenience and comfort, of every other part of the civilized world. Nor is this all. This court will find itself impelled to fix, by some arbitrary rule, the width of this new kind of property in a line of travel. * * * This court are not prepared to sanction the principles which must lead to such results.

GEORGE BANCROFT

The Office of the People in Art, Government, and Religion (1835)

Until his switch to the Republican party over the slavery issue in the 1850s, the great American historian George Bancroft (1800–1891) was a firm Democrat in the Whig-dominated state of Massachusetts. In addition to pursuing an academic and literary career, Bancroft held a number of patronage posts after Democrats noticed a very pro-Jackson article he wrote for the North American Review *in 1831. In this selection from an oration he delivered at Williams College, an almost lyrical hymn to the American people, the historian expressed a confidence in the popular masses typical of Jacksonian Democrats.*

The best government rests on the people and not on the few, on persons and not on property, on the free development of public opinion and not on authority; because the munificent Author of our being has conferred the gifts of mind upon every member of the human race without distinction of outward circumstances. Whatever of other possessions may be engrossed, mind asserts its own independence. Lands, estates, the produce of mines, the prolific abundance of the seas, may be usurped by a privileged class. Avarice, assuming the form of ambitious power, may grasp realm after realm, subdue continents, compass the earth in its schemes of aggrandizement, and sigh after other worlds; but mind eludes the power of appropriation; it exists only in its own individuality; it is a property which cannot be confiscated and cannot be torn away; it laughs at chains; it bursts from imprisonment; it defies monopoly. A government of equal rights must, therefore, rest upon mind; not wealth, not brute force, the sum of the moral intelligence of the community should rule the State. Prescription can no more assume to be a valid plea for political injustice; society studies to eradicate established abuses, and to bring social institutions and laws into harmony with moral right; not dismayed by the natural and necessary imperfections of all human effort, and not giving way to despair, because every hope does not at once ripen into fruit.

The public happiness is the true object of legislation, and can be secured only by the masses of mankind themselves awakening to the knowledge and the care of their own interests. Our free institutions have reversed the false and ignoble distinctions between men; and refusing to gratify the pride of caste, have acknowledged the common mind to be the true material for a commonwealth. Every thing has hitherto been done for the happy few. It is not possible to endow an aristocracy with greater benefits than they have already enjoyed; there is no room to hope that individuals will be more highly gifted or more fully developed than the greatest sages of past times. The world can advance only through the culture of the moral and intellectual powers of the people. To accomplish this end by means of the people themselves, is the highest purpose of government. If it be the duty of the individual to strive after a perfection like the perfection of God, how much more ought a nation to be the image of Deity. The common mind is the true Parian marble, fit to be wrought into likeness to a God. The duty of America is to secure the culture and the happiness of the masses by their reliance on themselves.

The absence of the prejudices of the old world leaves us here the opportunity of consulting independent truth; and man is left to apply the instinct of freedom to every social relation and public interest. We have approached so near to nature, that we can hear her gentlest whispers; we have made Humanity our lawgiver and our oracle; and, therefore, the nation receives, vivifies and applies principles, which in Europe the wisest accept with distrust. Freedom of mind and of conscience, freedom of the seas, freedom of industry, equality of franchises, each great truth is firmly grasped, comprehended and enforced; for the multitude is neither rash nor fickle. In truth, it is less fickle than these who profess to be its guides. Its natural dialectics surpass the logic of the schools. Political action has never been so consistent and so unwavering, as when it results from a feeling or a principle, diffused through society. The people is firm and tranquil in its movements, and necessarily acts with moderation, because it becomes but slowly impregnated with new ideas; and effects no changes, except in harmony with the knowledge which it has acquired. Besides, where it is permanently possessed of power, there exists neither the occasion nor the desire for frequent change. It is not the parent of tumult; sedition is bred in the lap of luxury, and its chosen emissaries are the beggared spendthrift and the impoverished libertine. The government by the people is in very truth the strongest government in the world. Discarding the implements of terror, it dares to rule by moral force, and has its citadel in the heart.

Such is the political system which rests on reason, reflection, and the free expression of deliberate choice. There may be those who scoff at the suggestion, that the decision of the whole is to be preferred to the judgment of the enlightened few. They say in their hearts that the masses are ignorant; that farmers know nothing of legislation; that mechanics should not quit their workshops to join in forming public opinion. But true political science does indeed venerate the masses. It maintains, not as has been perversely asserted, that "the people can make right," but that the people can DISCERN right. Individuals are but shadows, too often engrossed by the pursuit of shadows; the race is immortal: individuals are of limited sagacity; the common mind is infinite in its experience: individuals are languid and blind; the many are ever wakeful: individuals are corrupt; the race has been redeemed: individuals are time-serving; the masses are fearless: individuals may be false, the masses are ingenuous and sincere: individuals claim the divine sanction of truth for the deceitful conceptions of their own fancies; the Spirit of God breathes through the combined intelligence of the people. Truth is not to be ascertained by the impulses of an individual; it emerges from the contradictions of personal opinions; it raises itself in majestic serenity above the strifes of parties and the conflict of sects; it acknowledges neither the solitary mind, nor the separate faction as its oracle; but owns as its only faithful interpreter the dictates of pure reason itself, proclaimed by the general voice of mankind. The decrees of the universal conscience are the nearest approach to the presence of God in the soul of man.

Thus the opinion which we respect is, indeed, not the opinion of one or of a few, but the sagacity of the many. It is hard for the pride of cultivated philosophy to put its ear to the ground, and listen reverently to the voice of lowly humanity; yet the people collectively are wiser than the most gifted individual, for all his wisdom constitutes but a part of theirs.

* * *

The organ of truth is the invisible decision of the unbiased world; she pleads before no tribunal but public opinion; she owns no safe interpreter but the common mind; she knows no court of appeals but the soul of humanity. It is when the multitude give counsel, that right purposes find safety; theirs is the fixedness that cannot be shaken; theirs is the understanding which exceeds in wisdom; theirs is the heart, of which the largeness is as the sand on the sea-shore.

It is not by vast armies, by immense natural resources, by accumulations of treasure, that the greatest results in modern civilization have been accomplished. The traces of the career of conquest pass away, hardly leaving a scar on the national intelligence. The famous battle grounds of victory are, most of them, comparatively indifferent to the human race; barren fields of blood, the scourges of their times, but affecting the social condition as little as the raging of a pestilence. Not one benevolent institution, not one ameliorating principle in the Roman state, was a voluntary concession of the aristocracy; each useful element was borrowed from the Democracies of Greece, or was a reluctant concession to the demands of the people. The same is true in modern political life. It is the confession of an enemy to Democracy, that "ALL THE GREAT AND NOBLE INSTITUTIONS OF THE WORLD HAVE COME FROM POPULAR EFFORTS."

It is the uniform tendency of the popular element to elevate and bless Humanity. The exact measure of the progress of civilization is the degree in which the intelligence of the common mind has prevailed over wealth and brute force; in other words, the measure of the progress of civilization is the progress of the people. Every great object, connected with the benevolent exertions of the day, has reference to the culture of those powers which are alone the common inheritance.

* * *

The right to universal education being thus acknowledged by our conscience, not less than by our laws, it follows, that the people is the true recipient of truth. Do not seek to conciliate individuals; do not dread the frowns of a sect; do not yield to the proscriptions of a party; but pour out truth into the common mind. Let the waters of intelligence, like the rains of heaven, descend on the whole earth. And be not discouraged by the dread of encountering ignorance. *The prejudices of ignorance are more easily removed than the prejudices of interest; the first are blindly adopted; the second wilfully preferred.* Intelligence must be diffused among the whole people; truth must be scattered among those who have no interest to suppress its growth. The seeds that fall on the exchange, or in the hum of business, may be choked by the thorns that spring up in the hotbed of avarice; the seeds that are let fall in the saloon, may be like those dropped by the wayside, which take no root. Let the young aspirant after glory scatter the seeds of truth broadcast on the wide bosom of Humanity; in the deep, fertile soil of the public mind. There it will strike deep root and spring up, and bear an hundred-fold, and bloom for ages, and ripen fruit through remote generations.

* * *

Yes, reforms in society are only effected through the masses of the people, and through them have continually taken place. New truths have been successively developed, and, becoming the common property of the human family, have improved its condition. This progress is advanced by every sect, precisely because each sect, to obtain vitality, does of necessity embody a truth; by every political party, for the conflicts of party are the war of ideas; by every nationality, for a nation cannot exist as such, till humanity makes it a special trustee of some part of its wealth for the ultimate benefit of all. The irresistible tendency of the human race is therefore to advancement, for absolute power has never succeeded, and can never succeed, in suppressing a single truth. An idea once revealed may find its admission into every living breast and live there. Like God it becomes immortal and omnipresent. The movement of the species is upward, irresistibly upward. The individual is often lost; Providence never disowns the race. No principle once promulgated, has ever been forgotten. No "timely tramp" of a despot's foot ever trod out one idea. The world cannot retrograde; the dark ages cannot return. Dynasties perish; cities are buried; nations have been victims to error, or martyrs for right; Humanity has always been on the advance; gaining maturity, universality, and power.

Yes, truth is immortal; it cannot be destroyed; it is invincible, it cannot long be resisted. Not every great principle has yet been generated; but when once proclaimed and diffused, it lives without end, in the safe custody of the race. States may pass away; every just principle of legislation which has been once established will endure. Philosophy has sometimes forgotten God; a great people never did. The skepticism of the last century could not uproot Christianity, because it lived in the hearts of the millions. Do you think that infidelity is spreading? Christianity never lived in the hearts of so many millions as at this moment. The forms under which it is professed may decay, for they, like all that is the work of man's hands, are subject to the changes and chances of mortal being; but the spirit of truth is incorruptible; it may be developed, illustrated, and applied; it never can die; it never can decline.

No truth can perish; no truth can pass away. The flame is undying, though generations disappear. Wherever moral truth has started into being, Humanity claims and guards the bequest. Each generation gathers together the imperishable children of the past, and increases them by new sons of light, alike radiant with immortality.

ORESTES BROWNSON

The Laboring Classes (1840)

Before his conversion to Roman Catholicism in 1844, self-educated Orestes Augustus Brownson (1803–1876) was a Universalist minister, a Unitarian minister, and the pastor of his own Society for Christian Progress and Union. An early advocate of Owenite social and labor reform, Brownson opposed the abolition of slavery because he believed it was more humane than the capitalist system of wage labor. In this excerpt from an issue of the Boston Quarterly Review *(later called Brownson's Quarterly Review), a personal-opinion journal he published for more than three decades, Brownson recommended a series of religious, social, and political reforms "to emancipate the proletaries" from the poverty and oppression of so-called free labor.*

What we would ask is, throughout the Christian world, the actual condition of the laboring classes, viewed simply and exclusively in their capacity of laborers? They constitute at least a moiety of the human race. We exclude the nobility, we exclude also the middle class, and include only actual laborers, who are laborers and not proprietors, owners of none of the funds of production, neither houses, shops, nor lands, nor implements of labor, being therefore solely dependent on their hands. We have no means of ascertaining their precise proportion to the whole number of the race; but we think we may estimate them at one half. In any contest they will be as two to one, because the large class of proprietors who are not employers, but laborers on their own lands or in their own shops, will make common cause with them.

Now we will not so belie our acquaintance with political economy, as to allege that these alone perform all that is necessary to the production of wealth. We are not ignorant of the fact, that the merchant, who is literally the common carrier and exchange dealer, performs a useful service, and is therefore entitled to a portion of the proceeds of labor. But make all necessary deductions on his account, and then ask what portion of the remainder is retained, either in kind or in its equivalent, in the hands of the original producer, the workingman? All over the world this fact stares us in the face, the workingman is poor and depressed, while a large portion of the nonworkingmen, in the sense we now use the term, are wealthy. It may be laid down as a general rule, with but few exceptions, that men are rewarded in an inverse ratio to the amount of actual service they perform. Under every government on earth the largest salaries are annexed to those offices, which demand of their incumbents the least amount of actual labor either mental or manual. And this is in perfect harmony with the whole system of repartition of the fruits of industry, which obtains in every department of society. Now here is the system which prevails, and here is its result. The whole class of simple laborers are poor, and in general unable to procure anything beyond the bare necessaries of life.

In regard to labor two systems obtain; one that of slave labor, the other that of free labor. Of the two, the first is, in our judgment, except so far as the feelings are concerned, decidedly the least oppressive. If the slave has never been a free man, we think, as a general rule, his sufferings are less than those of the free laborer at wages. As to actual freedom one has just about as much as the other. The laborer at wages has all the disadvantages of freedom and none of its blessings, while the slave, if denied the blessings, is freed from the disadvantages. We are no advocates of slavery, we are as heartily opposed to it as any modern abolitionist can be; but we say frankly that, if there must always be a laboring population distinct from proprietors and employers, we regard the slave system as decidedly preferable to the system at wages. It is no pleasant thing to go days without food, to lie idle for weeks, seeking work and finding none, to rise in the morning with a wife and children you love, and know not where to procure them a breakfast, and to see constantly before you no brighter prospect than the almshouse. Yet these are no unfrequent incidents in the lives of our laboring population. Even in seasons of general prosperity, when there was only the ordinary cry of "hard times," we have seen hundreds of people in a not very populous village, in a wealthy portion of our common country, suffering for the want of the necessaries of life, willing to work, and yet finding no work to do. Many and many is the application of a poor man for work, merely for his food, we have seen rejected. These things are little thought of, for the applicants are poor; they fill no conspicuous place in society, and they have no biographers. But their wrongs are chronicled in heaven. It is said there is no want in this country. There may be less than in some other countries. But death by actual starvation in this country is, we apprehend, no uncommon occurrence. The sufferings of a quiet, unassuming but useful class of females in our cities, in general sempstresses, too proud to beg or to apply to the alms-house, are not easily told. They are industrious; they do all that they can find to do; but yet the little there is for them to do; and the miserable pittance they receive for it, is hardly sufficient to keep soul and body together. And yet there is a man who employs them to make shirts, trousers, &c., and grows rich on their labors. He is one of our respectable citizens, perhaps is praised in the newspapers for his liberal donations to some charitable institution. He passes among us as a pattern of morality, and is honored as a worthy Christian. And why should he not be, since our *Christian* community is made up of such as he, and since our clergy would not dare question his piety, lest they should incur the reproach of infidelity, and lose their standing, and their salaries? Nay, since our clergy are raised up, educated, fashioned, and sustained by such as he? Not a few of our churches rest on Mammon for their foundation. The basement is a trader's shop.

We pass through our manufacturing villages, most of them appear neat and flourishing. The operatives are well dressed, and we are told, well paid. They are said to be healthy, contented, and happy. This is the fair side of the picture; the side exhibited to distinguished visitors. There is a dark side, moral as well as physical. Of the common operatives, few, if any, by their wages, acquire a competence. A few of what Carlyle terms not inaptly the *body-servants* are well paid, and now and then an agent or an overseer rides in his coach. But the great mass wear out their health, spirits, and morals, without becoming one whit better off than when they commenced labor. The bills of mortality in these factory villages are not striking, we admit, for the poor girls when they can toil no longer go home to die. The average life, working life we mean, of the girls that come to Lowell, for instance, from Maine, New Hampshire, and Vermont, we have been assured, is only about three years. What becomes of them then? Few of them ever marry; fewer still ever return to their native places with reputations unimpaired. "She has worked in a Factory," is almost enough to damn to infamy the most worthy and virtuous girl. We know no sadder sight on earth than one of our factory villages presents, when the bell at break of day, or at the hour of breakfast, or dinner, calls out its hundreds or thousands of operatives. We stand and look at these hard working men and women hurrying in all directions, and ask ourselves, where go the proceeds of their labors? The man who employs them, and for whom they are toiling as so many slaves, is one of our city nabobs, revelling in luxury; or he is a member of our legislature, enacting laws to put money in his own pocket; or he is a member of Congress, contending for a high Tariff to tax the poor for the benefit of the rich; or in these times he is shedding crocodile tears over the deplorable condition of the poor laborer, while he docks his wages twenty-five percent; building miniature log cabins, shouting Harrison and "hard cider." And this man too would fain pass for a Christian and a republican. He shouts for liberty, stickles for equality, and is horrified at a Southern planter who keeps slaves.

One thing is certain; that of the amount actually produced by the operative, he retains a less proportion than it costs the master to feed, clothe, and lodge his slave. Wages is a cunning device of the devil, for the benefit of tender consciences, who would retain all the advantages of the slave system, without the expense, trouble, and odium of being slave-holders. * * *

Now the great work for this age and the coming, is to raise up the laborer, and to realize in our own social arrangements and in the actual condition of all men, that equality between man and man, which God has established between the rights of one and those of another. In other words, our business is to emancipate the proletaries, as the past has emancipated the slaves. This is our work. There must be no class of our fellow men doomed to toil through life as mere workmen at wages. If wages are tolerated it must be, in the case of the individual operative, only under such conditions that by the time he is of a proper age to settle in life, he shall have accumulated enough to be an independent laborer on his own capital,—on his own farm or in his own shop. Here is our work. How is it to be done?

Reformers in general answer this question, or what they deem its equivalent, in a manner which we cannot but regard as very unsatisfactory. They would have all men wise, good, and happy; but in order to make them so, they tell us that we want not external changes, but internal, and therefore instead of declaiming against society and seeking to disturb existing social arrangements, we should confine ourselves to the individual reason and conscience; seek merely to lead the individual to repentance, and to reformation of life; make the individual a practical, a truly religious man, and all evils will either disappear, or be sanctified to the spiritual growth of the soul. * * *

This theory, however, is exposed to one slight objection, that of being condemned by something like six thousand years' experience. For six thousand years its beauty has been extolled, its praises sung, and its blessings sought, under every advantage which learning, fashion, wealth, and power can secure; and yet under its practical operations, we are assured, that mankind, though totally depraved at first, have been growing worse and worse ever since.

For our part, we yield to none in our reverence for science and religion; but we confess that we look not for the regeneration of the race from priests and pedagogues. They have had a fair trial. They cannot construct the temple of God. They cannot conceive its plan, and they know not how to build. They daub with untempered mortar, and the walls they erect tumble down if so much as a fox attempt to go up thereon. In a word they always league with the people's masters, and seek to reform without disturbing the social arrangements which render reform necessary. They would change the consequents without changing the antecedents, secure to men the rewards of holiness, while they continue their allegiance to the devil. We have no faith in priests and pedagogues. They merely cry peace, peace, and that too when there is no peace, and can be none. * * *

* * * Make all your rich men good Christians, and you have lessened not the evils of existing inequality in wealth. The mischievous effects of this inequality do not result from the personal characters of either rich or poor, but from itself, and they will continue, just so long as there are rich men and poor men in the same community. You must abolish the system or accept its consequences. No man can serve both God and Mammon. If you will serve the devil, you must look to the devil for your wages; we know no other way. * * *

The evil we have pointed out, we have said, is not of individual creation, and it is not to be removed by individual effort, saving so far as individual effort induces the combined effort of the mass. But whence has this evil originated? How comes it that all over the world the working classes are depressed, are the low and vulgar, and virtually the slaves of the nonworking classes? This is an inquiry which has not yet received the attention it deserves. * * *

The cause of the inequality, we speak of, must be sought in history, and be regarded as having its root in Providence, or in human nature, only in that sense in which all historical facts have their origin in these. * * *

We may offend in what we say, but we cannot help that. We insist upon it, that the complete and final destruction of the priestly order, in every practical sense of the word priest, is the first step to be taken towards elevating the laboring classes. Priests are, in their capacity of priests, necessarily enemies to freedom and equality. All reasoning demonstrates this, and all history proves it. There must be no class of men set apart and authorized, either by law or fashion, to speak to us in the name of God, or to be the interpreters of the word of God. * * *

The next step in this work of elevating the working classes will be to resuscitate the Christianity of Christ. The Christianity of the Church has done its work. We have had enough of that Christianity. It is powerless for good, but by no means powerless for evil. It now unmans us and hinders the growth of God's kingdom. The moral energy which is awakened it misdirects, and makes its deluded disciples believe that they have done their duty to God when they have joined the church, offered a prayer, sung a psalm, and contributed of their means to send out a missionary to preach unintelligible dogmas to the poor heathen, who, God knows, have unintelligible dogmas enough already, and more than enough. All this must be abandoned, and Christianity, as it came from Christ, be taken up, and preached, and preached in simplicity and in power.

According to the Christianity of Christ, no man can enter the kingdom of God who does not labor with all zeal and diligence to establish the kingdom of God on the earth—who does not labor to bring down the high and bring up the low; to break the fetters of the bound and set the captive free; to destroy all oppression, establish the reign of justice, which is the reign of equality, between man and man; to introduce new heavens and a new earth, wherein dwelleth righteousness, wherein all shall be as brothers, loving one another, and no one possessing what another lacketh. No man can be a Christian who does not labor to reform society, to mold it according to the will of God and the nature of man, so that free scope shall be given to every man to unfold himself in all beauty and power, and to grow up into the stature of a perfect man in Christ Jesus. No man can be a Christian who does not refrain from all practices by which the rich grow richer and the poor poorer, and who does not do all in his power to elevate the laboring classes, so that one man shall not be doomed to toil while another enjoys the fruits; so that each man shall be free and independent, sitting under "his own vine and fig tree with none to molest or to make afraid." We grant the power of Christianity in working out the reform we demand; we agree that one of the most efficient means of elevating the workingmen is to Christianize the community. But you must Christianize it. It is the gospel of Jesus you must preach, and not the gospel of the priests. Preach the gospel of Jesus, and that will turn every man's attention to the crying evil we have designated, and will arm every Christian with power to effect those changes in social arrangements which shall secure to all men the equality of position and condition which it is already acknowledged they possess in relation to their rights. But let it be the genuine gospel that you preach, and not that pseudo-gospel which lulls the conscience asleep and permits men to feel that they may be servants of God while they are slaves to the world, the flesh, and the devil, and while they ride roughshod over the hearts of their prostrate brethren. We must preach no gospel that permits men to feel that they are honorable men and good Christians, although rich and with eyes standing out with fatness, while the great mass of their brethren are suffering from iniquitous laws, from mischievous social arrangements, and pining away for the want of the refinements and even the necessaries of life.

We cannot proceed a single step with the least safety, in the great work of elevating the laboring classes, without the exaltation of sentiment, the generous sympathy and the moral courage which Christianity alone is fitted to produce or quicken. But it is lamentable to see how, by means of the mistakes of the Church, the moral courage, the generous sympathy, the exaltation of sentiment Christianity does actually produce or quicken is perverted, and made efficient only in producing evil or hindering the growth of good. Here is wherefore it is necessary on the one hand to condemn in the most pointed terms the Christianity of the Church, and to bring out on the other hand in all its clearness, brilliancy, and glory the Christianity of Christ.

We speak strongly and pointedly on this subject, because we are desirous of arresting attention. We would draw the public attention to the striking contrast which actually exists between the Christianity of Christ, and the Christianity of the Church. That moral and intellectual energy which exists in our country, indeed throughout Christendom, and which would, if rightly directed, transform this wilderness world into a blooming paradise of God, is now by the pseudo-gospel, which is preached, rendered wholly inefficient, by being wasted on that which, even if effected, would leave all the crying evils of the times untouched. Under the influence of the Church, our efforts are not directed to the reorganization of society, to the introduction of equality between man and man, to the removal of the corruptions of the rich, and the wretchedness of the poor. * * *

Having, by breaking down the power of the priesthood and the Christianity of the priests, obtained an open field and freedom for our operations, and by preaching the true Gospel of Jesus, directed all minds to the great social reform needed, and quickened in all souls the moral power to live for it or to die for it; our next resort must be to government, to legislative enactments. Government is instituted to be the agent of society, or more properly the organ through which society may perform its legitimate functions. It is not the master of society; its business is not to control society, but to be the organ through which society effects its will. Society has never to petition government; government is its servant, and subject to its commands.

Now the evils of which we have complained are of a social nature. That is, they have their root in the constitution of society as it is, and they have attained to their present growth by means of social influences, the action of government, or laws, and of systems and institutions upheld by society, and of which individuals are the slaves. This being the case, it is evident that they are to be removed only by the action of society, that is, by government, for the action of society is government.

But what shall government do? Its first doing must be an undoing. There has been thus far quite too much government, as well as government of the wrong kind. The first act of government we want, is a still further limitation of itself. It must begin by circumscribing within narrower limits its powers. And then it must proceed to repeal all laws which bear against the laboring classes, and then to enact such laws as are necessary to enable them to maintain their equality. We have no faith in those systems of elevating the working classes, which propose to elevate them without calling in the aid of the government. We must have government, and legislation expressly directed to this end.

But again what legislation do we want so far as this country is concerned? We want first the legislation which shall free the government, whether State or Federal, from the control of the Banks. The Banks represent the interest of the employer, and therefore of necessity interests adverse to those of the employed; that is, they represent the interests of the business community in opposition to the laboring community. So long as the government remains under the control of the Banks, so long it must be in the hands of the natural enemies of the laboring classes, and may be made, nay, will be made, an instrument of depressing them yet lower. It is obvious then that, if our object be the elevation of the laboring classes, we must destroy the power of the Banks over the government, and place the government in the hands of the laboring classes themselves, or in the hands of those, if such there be, who have an identity of interest with them. But this cannot be done so long as the Banks exist. Such is the subtle influence of credit, and such the power of capital, that a banking system like ours, if sustained, necessarily and inevitably becomes the real and efficient government of the country. We have been struggling for ten years in this country against the power of the banks, struggling to free merely the Federal government from their grasp, but with humiliating success. At this moment, the contest is almost doubtful,—not indeed in our mind, but in the minds of a no small portion of our countrymen. The partizans of the Banks count on certain victory. The Banks discount freely to build "log cabins," to purchase "hard cider," and to defray the expense of manufacturing enthusiasm for a cause which is at war with the interests of the people. That they will succeed, we do not for one moment believe; but that they could maintain the struggle so long, and be as strong as they now are, at the end of ten years' constant hostility, proves but all too well the power of the Banks, and their fatal influence on the political action of the community. The present character, standing, and resources of the Bank party, prove to a demonstration that the Banks must be destroyed, or the laborer not elevated. Uncompromising hostility to the whole banking system should therefore be the motto of every working man, and of every friend of Humanity. The system must be destroyed. On this point [there] must be no misgiving, no subterfuge, no palliation. The system is at war with the rights and interest of labor, and it must go. Every friend of the system must be marked as an enemy to his race, to his country, and especially to the laborer. No matter who he is, in what party he is found, or what name he bears, he is, in our judgment, no true democrat, as he can be no true Christian.

Following the distraction of the Banks, must come that of all monopolies, of all *privilege*. There are many of these. We cannot specify them all; we therefore select only one, the greatest of them all, the privilege which some have of being born rich while others are born poor. It will be seen at once that we allude to the hereditary descent of property, an anomaly in our American system, which must be removed, or the system itself will be destroyed. We cannot now go into a discussion of this subject, but we promise to resume it at our earliest opportunity. We only say now, that as we have abolished hereditary monarchy and hereditary nobility, we must complete the work by abolishing hereditary property. A man shall have all he honestly acquires, so long as he himself belongs to the world in which he acquires it. But his power over his property must cease with his life, and his property must then become the property of the state, to be disposed of by some equitable law for the use of the generation which takes his place. Here is the principle without any of its details, and this is the grand legislative measure to which we look forward. We see no means of elevating the laboring classes which can be effectual without this. And is this a measure to be easily carried? Not at all. It will cost infinitely more than it cost to abolish either hereditary monarchy or hereditary nobility. It is a great measure, and a startling [one]. The rich, the business community, will never voluntarily consent to it, and we think we know too much of human nature to believe that it will ever be effected peaceably. It will be effected only by the strong arm of physical force. It will come, if it ever come at all, only at the conclusion of war, the like of which the world as yet has never witnessed, and from which, however inevitable it may seem to the eye of philosophy, the heart of Humanity recoils with horror.

We are not ready for this measure yet. There is much previous work to be done, and we should be the last to bring it before the legislature. The time, however, has come for its free and full discussion. It must be canvassed in the public mind, and society prepared for acting on it. No doubt they who broach it, and especially they who support it, will experience a due share of contumely and abuse. They will be regarded by the part of the community they oppose, or may be thought to oppose, as "graceless varlets," against whom every man of substance should set his face. But this is not, after all, a thing to disturb a wise man, not to deter a true man from telling, his whole thought. He who is worthy of the name of man, speaks what he honestly believes the interests of his race demand, and seldom disquiets himself about what may be the consequences to himself. Men have, for what they believed the cause of God or man, endured the dungeon, the scaffold, the stake, the cross, and they can do it again, if need be. This subject must be freely, boldly, and fully discussed, whatever may be the fate of those who discuss it.

Individualism and Democracy

JAMES FENIMORE COOPER

The American Democrat (1838)

*The well-educated son of a wealthy Federalist, James Fenimore Cooper
(1789–1851) wrote more than two dozen novels, including several stories of frontier adventure such as The Last of the Mohicans (1826) and
The Deerslayer (1841), which were known as the Leatherstocking
Tales. Cooper championed political democracy and supported Jackson,
but he never felt comfortable with the social egalitarianism of American life after his return from a seven-year sojourn in Europe. Even
though America's first great novelist supported such "American principles" as political liberty and limited government, he rejected the proposition that "one man is as good as another." He did support equal
opportunity because it rewards merit. This selection is from the chapter
"On Station" in his lengthy 1838 essay on American politics, The American Democrat, originally intended to be a textbook for older school
students.*

Political, or publick station, is that which is derived from office, and,
in a democracy, must embrace men of very different degrees of
leisure, refinement, habits and knowledge. This is characteristick of the
institutions, which, under a popular government, confer on political station more power than rank, since the latter is expressly avoided in this
system.

Social station is that which one possesses in the ordinary associations,
and is dependent on birth, education, personal qualities, property, tastes,
habits, and, in some instances, on caprice, or fashion. Although the latter
undeniably is sometimes admitted to control social station, it generally
depends, however, on the other considerations named.

Social station, in the main, is a consequence of property. So long as there is civilization there must be the rights of property, and so long as there are the rights of property, their obvious consequences must follow. All that democracies legitimately attempt is to prevent the advantages which accompany social station from accumulating rights that do not properly belong to the condition, which is effected by pronouncing that it shall have no factitious political aids.

They who have reasoned ignorantly, or who have aimed at effecting their personal ends by flattering the popular feeling, have boldly affirmed that "one man is as good as another"; a maxim that is true in neither nature, revealed morals, nor political theory.

That one man is not as good as another in natural qualities, is proved on the testimony of our sense. One man is stronger than another; he is handsomer, taller, swifter, wiser, or braver, than all his fellows. In short, the physical and moral qualities are unequally distributed, and, as a necessary consequence, in none of them, can one man be justly said to be as good as another. Perhaps no two human beings can be found so precisely equal in every thing, that one shall not be pronounced the superior of the other; which, of course, establishes the fact that there is no natural equality.

The advocates of exclusive political privileges reason on this circumstance by assuming, that as nature has made differences between men, those institutions which create political orders, are no more than carrying out the great designs of providence. The error of their argument is in supposing it a confirmation of the designs of nature to attempt to supplant her, for, while the latter has rendered men unequal, it is not from male to male, according to the order of primogeniture, as is usually established by human ordinances. In order not to interfere with the inequality of nature, her laws must be left to their own operations, which is just what is done in democracies, after a proper attention has been paid to the peace of society, by protecting the weak against the strong.

That one man is not deemed as good as another in the grand moral system of providence, is revealed to us in Holy Writ, by the scheme of future rewards and punishments, as well as by the whole history of those whom God has favored in this world, for their piety, or punished for their rebellion. As compared with perfect holiness, all men are frail; but, as compared with each other, we are throughout the whole of sacred history made to see, that, in a moral sense, one man is not as good as another. The evil doer is punished, while they who are distinguished for their qualities and acts, are intended to be preferred.

The absolute moral and physical equality that are inferred by the maxim, that "one man is as good as another," would at once do away with the elections, since a lottery would be both simpler, easier and cheaper than the present mode of selecting representatives. Men, in such a case, would draw lots for office, as they are now drawn for juries. Choice supposes a preference, and preference inequality of merit, or of fitness.

We are then to discard all visionary theories on this head, and look at things as they are. All that the most popular institutions attempt, is to prohibit that one *race* of men shall be made better than another by law, from father to son, which would be defeating the intentions of providence, creating a superiority that exists in neither physical nor moral nature, and substituting a political scheme for the will of God and the force of things.

As a principle, one man is as good as another in rights. Such is the extent of the most liberal institutions of this country, and this provision is not general. The slave is not as good as his owner, even in rights. But in those states where slavery does not exist, all men have essentially the same rights, an equality, which, so far from establishing that "one man is as good as another," in a social sense, is the very means of producing the inequality of condition that actually exists. By possessing the same rights to exercise their respective faculties, the active and frugal become more wealthy than the idle and dissolute; the wise and gifted more trusted than the silly and ignorant; the polished and refined more respected and sought, than the rude and vulgar.

In most countries, birth is a principal source of social distinction, society being divided into castes, the noble having an hereditary claim to be the superior of the plebian. This is an unwise and an arbitrary distinction that has led to most of the social diseases of the old world, and from which America is happily exempt. But great care must be had in construing the principles which have led to this great change, for America is the first important country of modern times, in which such positive distinctions have been destroyed.

Still some legal differences, and more social advantages, are produced by birth, even in America. The child inherits the property, and a portion of the consideration of the parent. Without the first of these privileges, men would not exert themselves to acquire more property than would suffice for their own personal necessities, parental affection being one of the most powerful incentives to industry. Without such an inducement, then, it would follow that civilization would become stationary, or, it would recede; the incentives of individuality and of the affections, being absolutely necessary to impel men to endure the labor and privations that alone can advance it.

The hereditary consideration of the child, so long as it is kept within due bounds, by being confined to a natural sentiment, is also productive of good, since no more active inducement to great and glorious deeds can offer, than the deeply seated interest that man takes in his posterity. All that reason and justice require is effected, by setting bounds to such advantages, in denying hereditary claims to trusts and power; but evil would be the day, and ominous the symptom, when a people shall deny that any portion of the consideration of the ancestor is due to the descendant.

It is as vain to think of altogether setting aside sentiment and the affections, in regulating human affairs, as to imagine it possible to raise a nature, known to be erring and weak, to the level of perfection. * * *

It is a natural consequence of the rights of property and of the sentiment named, that birth should produce some advantages, in a social sense, even in the most democratical of the American communities. The son imbibes a portion of the intelligence, refinement and habits of the father, and he shares in his associations. These must be enumerated as the legitimate advantages of birth, and without invading the private arrangements of families and individuals, and establishing a perfect community of education, they are unavoidable. Men of the same habits, the same degree of cultivation and refinement, the same opinions, naturally associate together, in every class of life. The day laborer will not mingle with the slave; the skilful mechanic feels his superiority over the mere laborer, claims higher wages and has a pride in his craft; the man in trade justly fancies that his habits elevate him above the mechanic, so far as social position is concerned, and the man of refinement, with his education, tastes and sentiments, is superior to all. Idle declamation on these points, does not impair the force of things, and life is a series of facts. These inequalities of condition, of manners, of mental cultivation must exist, unless it be intended to reduce all to a common level of ignorance and vulgarity, which would be virtually to return to a condition of barbarism.

The result of these undeniable facts, is the inequalities of social station, in America, as elsewhere, though it is an inequality that exists without any more arbitrary distinctions than are indispensably connected with the maintenance of civilization. In a social sense, there are orders here, as in all other countries, but the classes run into each other more easily, the lines of separation are less strongly drawn, and their shadows are more intimately blended.

This social inequality of America is an unavoidable result of the institutions, though nowhere proclaimed in them, the different constitutions maintaining a profound silence on the subject, they who framed them probably knowing that it is as much a consequence of civilized society, as breathing is a vital function of animal life.

We live in an age when the words aristocrat and democrat are much used, without regard to the real significations. An aristocrat is one of a few who possess the political power of a country; a democrat, one of the many. The words are also properly applied to those who entertain notions favorable to aristocratical or democratical forms of government. Such persons are not necessarily either aristocrats or democrats in fact, but merely so in opinion. Thus a member of a democratical government may have an aristocratical bias, and vice versa.

To call a man who has the habits and opinions of a gentleman, an aristocrat from that fact alone, is an abuse of terms and betrays ignorance of the true principles of government, as well as of the world. It must be an equivocal freedom under which every one is not the master of his own innocent acts and associations; and he is a sneaking democrat indeed who will submit to be dictated to, in those habits over which neither law nor morality assumes a right of control.

Some men fancy that a democrat can only be one who seeks the level, social, mental and moral, of the majority, a rule that would at once exclude all men of refinement, education, and taste from the class. These persons are enemies of democracy, as they at once render it impracticable. They are usually great sticklers for their own associations and habits, too, though unable to comprehend any of a nature that are superior. They are, in truth, aristocrats in principle, though assuming a contrary pretension, the groundwork of all their feelings and arguments being self. Such is not the intention of liberty, whose aim is to leave every man to be the master of his own acts; denying hereditary honors, it is true, as unjust and unnecessary, but not denying the inevitable consequences of civilization.

The law of God is the only rule of conduct in this, as in other matters. Each man should do as he would be done by. Were the question put to the greatest advocate of indiscriminate association, whether he would submit to have his company and habits dictated to him, he would be one of the first to resist the tyranny; for they who are the most rigid in maintaining their own claims in such matters, are usually the loudest in decrying those whom they fancy to be better off than themselves. Indeed, it may be taken as a rule in social intercourse, that he who is the most apt to question the pretensions of others is the most conscious of the doubtful position he himself occupies; thus establishing the very claims he affects to deny, by letting his jealousy of it be seen. Manners, education, and refinement, are positive things, and they bring with them innocent tastes which are productive of high enjoyments; and it is as unjust to deny their possessors their indulgence as it would be to insist on the less fortunate's passing the time they would rather devote to athletic amusements, in listening to operas for which they have no relish, sung in a language they do not understand.

All that democracy means, is as equal a participation in rights as is practicable; and to pretend that social equality is a condition of popular institutions is to assume that the latter are destructive of civilization, for, as nothing is more self-evident than the impossibility of raising all men to the highest standard of tastes and refinement, the alternative would be to reduce the entire community to the lowest. The whole embarrassment on this point exists in the difficulty of making men comprehend qualities they do not themselves possess. We can all perceive the difference between ourselves and our inferiors, but when it comes to a question of the difference between us and our superiors, we fail to appreciate merits of which we have no proper conceptions. In face of this obvious difficulty, there is the safe and just governing rule, already mentioned, or that of permitting every one to be the undisturbed judge of his own habits and associations, so long as they are innocent and do not impair the rights of others to be equally judges for themselves. It follows, that social intercourse must regulate itself, independently of institutions, with the exception that the latter, while they withhold no natural, bestow no factitious advantages beyond those which are inseparable from the rights of property, and general civilization.

In a democracy, men are just as free to aim at the highest attainable places in society, as to attain the largest fortunes; and it would be clearly unworthy of all noble sentiment to say that the grovelling competition for money shall alone be free, while that which enlists all the liberal acquirements and elevated sentiments of the race, is denied the democrat. Such an avowal would be at once a declaration of the inferiority of the system, since nothing but ignorance and vulgarity could be its fruits.

The democratic gentleman must differ in many essential particulars from the aristocratical gentleman, though in their ordinary habits and tastes they are virtually identical. Their principles vary; and, to a slight degree, their deportment accordingly. The democrat, recognizing the right of all to participate in power, will be more liberal in his general sentiments, a quality of superiority in itself; but in conceding this much to his fellow man, he will proudly maintain his own independence of vulgar domination as indispensable to his personal habits. The same principles and manliness that would induce him to depose a royal despot would induce him to resist a vulgar tyrant.

There is no more capital, though more common error, than to suppose him an aristocrat who maintains his independence of habits; for democracy asserts the control of the majority only in matters of law, and not in matters of custom. The very object of the institution is the utmost practicable personal liberty, and to affirm the contrary would be sacrificing the end to the means.

An aristocrat, therefore, is merely one who fortifies his exclusive privileges by positive institutions, and a democrat, one who is willing to admit of a free competition in all things. To say, however, that the last supposes this competition will lead to nothing is an assumption that means are employed without any reference to an end. He is the purest democrat who best maintains his rights, and no rights can be dearer to a man of cultivation than exemptions from unseasonable invasions on his time by the coarse minded and ignorant.

RALPH WALDO EMERSON

Self-Reliance (1840)

The New England poet and philosophical essayist Ralph Waldo Emerson (1803–1882) was the leading exponent of transcendentalism, a philosophical movement that stressed the individual's relation to nature. Like other members of this school of thought, Emerson advocated the intellectual and moral self-sufficiency of the individual against the effects of social conformity and the crowd mentality. A classic tribute to the sanctity of individual spontaneity and authenticity, the following essay calls on the individual to "be doctrine, society, law, to himself," even to be inconsistent, for "a foolish consistency is the hobgoblin of small minds."

Society everywhere is in conspiracy against the manhood of every one of its members. Society is a joint-stock company, in which the members agree, for the better securing of his bread to each shareholder, to surrender the liberty and culture of the eater. The virtue in most request is conformity. Self-reliance is its aversion. It loves not realities and creators, but names and customs.

Whoso would be a man, must be a nonconformist. He who would gather immortal palms must not be hindered by the name of goodness, but must explore if it be goodness. Nothing is at last sacred but the integrity of your own mind. Absolve you to yourself, and you shall have the suffrage of the world. I remember an answer which when quite young I was prompted to make to a valued adviser who was wont to importune me with the dear old doctrines of the church. On my saying, "What have I to do with the sacredness of traditions, if I live wholly from within?"

my friend suggested,—"But these impulses may be from below not from above." I replied, "They do not seem to me to be such; but if I am the Devil's child, I will live then from the Devil." No law can be sacred to me but that of my nature. Good and bad are but names very readily transferable to that or this; the only right is what is after my constitution; the only wrong what is against it. A man is to carry himself in the presence of all opposition as if every thing were titular and ephemeral but he. I am ashamed to think how easily we capitulate to badges and names, to large societies and dead institutions. Every decent and well-spoken individual affects and sways me more than is right. I ought to go upright and vital, and speak the rude truth in all ways. If malice and vanity wear the coat of philanthropy, shall that pass? If an angry bigot assumes this bountiful cause of Abolition, and comes to me with his last news from Barbadoes, why should I not say to him, "Go love thy infant; love thy wood-chopper; be good-natured and modest; have that grace; and never varnish your hard, uncharitable ambition with this incredible tenderness for black folk a thousand miles off. Thy love afar is spite at home." Rough and graceless would be such greeting, but truth is handsomer than the affectation of love. Your goodness must have some edge to it,—else it is none. The doctrine of hatred must be preached, as the counteraction of the doctrine of love, when that pules and whines. I shun father and mother and wife and brother when my genius calls me. I would write on the lintels of the door-post, *Whim.* I hope it is somewhat better than whim at last, but we cannot spend the day in explanation. Expect me not to show cause why I seek or why I exclude company. Then again, do not tell me, as a good man did to-day, of my obligation to put all poor men in good situations. Are they *my* poor? I tell thee, thou foolish philanthropist, that I grudge the dollar, the dime, the cent I give to such men as do not belong to me and to whom I do not belong. There is a class of persons to whom by all spiritual affinity I am bought and sold; for them I will go to prison if need be; but your miscellaneous popular charities; the education at college of fools; the building of meeting-houses to the vain end to which many now stand; aims to sots, and the thousand-fold Relief Societies;—though I confess with shame I sometimes succumb and give the dollar, it is a wicked dollar, which by and by I shall have the manhood to withhold. * * *

What I must do is all that concerns me, not what the people think. This rule, equally arduous in actual and in intellectual life, may serve for the whole distinction between greatness and meanness. It is the harder because you will always find those who think they know what is your duty better than you know it. It is easy in the world to live after the world's opinion; it is easy in solitude to live after our own; but the great man is he who in the midst of the crowd keeps with perfect sweetness the independence of solitude. * * *

The other terror that scares us from self-trust is our consistency; a reverence for our past act or word because the eyes of others have no other data for computing our orbit than our past acts, and we are loth to disappoint them.

But why should you keep your head over your shoulder? Why drag about this corpse of your memory, lest you contradict somewhat you have stated in this or that public place? Suppose you should contradict yourself; what then? It seems to be a rule of wisdom never to rely on your memory alone, scarcely even in acts of pure memory, but to bring the past for judgment into the thousand-eyed present, and live ever in a new day. In your metaphysics you have denied personality to the Deity, yet when the devout motions of the soul come, yield to them heart and life, though they should clothe God with shape and color. Leave your theory, as Joseph his coat in the hand of the harlot, and flee.

A foolish consistency is the hobgoblin of little minds, adored by little statesmen and philosophers and divines. With consistency a great soul has simply nothing to do. He may as well concern himself with his shadow on the wall. Speak what you think now in hard words and to-morrow speak what to-morrow thinks in hard words again, though it contradict every thing you said to-day.—"Ah, so you shall be sure to be misunderstood." —Is it so bad then to be misunderstood? Pythagoras was misunderstood, and Socrates, and Jesus, and Luther, and Copernicus, and Galileo, and Newton, and every pure and wise spirit that ever took flesh. To be great is to be misunderstood. * * *

I hope in these days we have heard the last of conformity and consistency. Let the words be gazetted and ridiculous henceforward. Instead of the gong for dinner, let us hear a whistle from the Spartan file. Let us never bow and apologize more. A great man is coming to eat at my house. I do not wish to please him; I wish that he should wish to please me. I will stand here for humanity, and though I would make it kind, I would make it true. Let us affront and reprimand the smooth mediocrity and squalid contentment of the times, and hurl in the face of custom and trade and office, the fact which is the upshot of all history, that there is a great responsible Thinker and Actor working wherever a man works; that a true man belongs to no other time or place, but is the center of things. Where he is, there is nature. He measures you and all men and all events. Ordinarily, every body in society reminds us of somewhat else, or of some other person. Character, reality, reminds you of nothing else; it takes place of the whole creation. The man must be so much that he must make all circumstances indifferent. Every true man is a cause, a country, and an age; requires infinite spaces and numbers and time fully to accomplish his design;—and posterity seem to follow his steps as a train of clients. A man Cæsar is born, and for ages after we have a Roman Empire. Christ is born, and millions of minds so grow and cleave to his genius that he is confounded with virtue and the possible of man. An institution is the lengthened shadow of one man; as, Monachism, of the Hermit Antony; the Reformation, of Luther; Quakerism, of Fox; Methodism, of Wesley; Abolition, of Clarkson. Scipio, Milton called "the height of Rome;" and all history resolves itself very easily into the biography of a few stout and earnest persons.

Let a man then know his worth, and keep things under his feet. Let him not peep or steal, or skulk up and down with the air of a charity-boy, a bastard, or an interloper in the world which exists for him. But the man in the street, finding no worth in himself which corresponds to the force which built a tower or sculptured a marble god, feels poor when he looks on these. To him a palace, a statue, or a costly book have an alien and forbidding air, much like a gay equipage, and seem to say like that, "Who are you, Sir?" Yet they all are his, suitors for his notice, petitioners to his faculties that they will come out and take possession. The picture waits for my verdict; it is not to command me, but I am to settle its claims to praise. That popular fable of the sot who was picked up dead-drunk in the street, carried to the duke's house, washed and dressed and laid in the duke's bed, and, on his waking, treated with all obsequious ceremony like the duke, and assured that he had been insane, owes its popularity to the fact that it symbolizes so well the state of man, who is in the world a sort of sot, but now and then wakes up, exercises his reason and finds himself a true prince. * * *

The populace think that your rejection of popular standards is a rejection of all standard, and mere antinomianism; and the bold sensualist will use the name of philosophy to gild his crimes. But the law of consciousness abides. There are two confessionals, in one or the other of which we must be shriven. You may fulfil your round of duties by clearing yourself in the *direct,* or in the *reflex* way. Consider whether you have satisfied your relations to father, mother, cousin, neighbor, town, cat, and dog—whether any of these can upbraid you. But I may also neglect this reflex standard and absolve me to myself. I have my own stern claims and perfect circle. It denies the name of duty to many offices that are called duties. But if I can discharge its debts it enables me to dispense with the popular code. If any one imagines that this law is lax, let him keep its commandment one day.

And truly it demands something godlike in him who has cast off the common motives of humanity and has ventured to trust himself for a taskmaster. High be his heart, faithful his will, clear his sight, that he may in good earnest be doctrine, society, law, to himself, that a simple purpose may be to him as strong as iron necessity is to others!

If any man consider the present aspects of what is called by distinction *society*, he will see the need of these ethics. The sinew and heart of man seem to be drawn out, and we are become timorous, desponding whimperers. We are afraid of truth, afraid of fortune, afraid of death, and afraid of each other. Our age yields no great and perfect persons. We want men and women who shall renovate life and our social state, but we see that most natures are insolvent, cannot satisfy their own wants, have an ambition out of all proportion to their practical force and do lean and beg day and night continually. Our housekeeping is mendicant, our arts, our occupations, our marriages, our religion we have not chosen, but society has chosen for us. We are parlor soldiers. We shun the rugged battle of fate, where strength is born. * * *

It is easy to see that a greater self-reliance must work a revolution in all the offices and relations of men; in their religion; in their education; in their pursuits; their modes of living; their association; in their property; in their speculative views. * * *

Insist on yourself; never imitate. Your own gift you can present every moment with the cumulative force of a whole life's cultivation; but of the adopted talent of another you have only an extemporaneous half possession. That which each can do best, none but his Maker can teach him. No man yet knows what it is, nor can, till that person has exhibited it. Where is the master who could have taught Shakspeare? Where is the master who could have instructed Franklin, or Washington, or Bacon, or Newton? Every great man is a unique. * * *

And so the reliance on Property, including the reliance on governments which protect it, is the want of self-reliance. Men have looked away from themselves and at things so long that they have come to esteem the religious, learned and civil institutions as guards of property, and they deprecate assaults on these, because they feel them to be assaults on property. They measure their esteem of each other by what each has, and not by what each is. But a cultivated man becomes ashamed of his property, out of new respect for his nature. Especially he hates what he has if he see that it is accidental,—came to him by inheritance, or gift, or crime; then he feels that it is not having; it does not belong to him, has no root in him and merely lies there because no revolution or no robber takes it away. But that which a man is, does always by necessity acquire; and what the man acquires, is living property, which does not wait the beck of rulers, or mobs or revolutions, or fire, or storm, or bankruptcies, but perpetually renews itself wherever the man breathes. "Thy lot or portion of life," said the Caliph Ali, "is seeking after thee; therefore be at rest from seeking after it." Our dependence on these foreign goods leads us to our slavish respect for numbers. The political parties meet in numerous conventions; the greater the concourse and with each new uproar of announcement, The delegation from Essex! The Democrats from New Hampshire! The Whigs of Maine! the young patriot feels himself stronger than before by a new thousand of eyes and arms. In like manner the reformers summon conventions and vote and resolve in multitude. Not so, O friends! will the God deign to enter and inhabit you, but by a method precisely the reverse. It is only as a man puts off all foreign support and stands alone that I see him to be strong and to prevail. He is weaker by every recruit to his banner. Is not a man better than a town? Ask nothing of men, and, in the endless mutation, thou only firm column must presently appear the upholder of all that surrounds thee. He who knows that power is inborn, that he is weak because he has looked for good out of him and elsewhere, and, so perceiving, throws himself unhesitatingly on his thought, instantly rights himself, stands in the erect position, commands his limbs, works miracles; just as a man who stands on his feet is stronger than a man who stands on his head. * * *

RALPH WALDO EMERSON

Politics (1849)

Like other transcendentalists, Emerson was an abolitionist who deplored the current state of politics because the government neglected the growth of the individual and failed to secure equal rights for all individuals, including women, wage laborers, and slaves. As a consequence, Emerson argued that "the less government we have the better." In this essay, he suggested that government should cultivate the kind of independent, self-reliant character appropriate for a democracy.

In dealing with the State we ought to remember that its institutions are not aboriginal, though they existed before we were born; that they are not superior to the citizen; that every one of them was once the act of a single man; every law and usage was a man's expedient to meet a particular case; that they all are imitable, all alterable; we may make as good, we may make better. Society is an illusion to the young citizen. It lies before him in rigid repose, with certain names, men and institutions rooted like oak-trees to the centre, round which all arrange themselves the best they can. But the old statesman knows that society is fluid; there are no such roots and centres, but any particle may suddenly become the centre of the movement and compel the system to gyrate round it; as every man of strong will, like Pisistratus or Cromwell, does for a time, and every man of truth, like Plato or Paul, does forever. But politics rest on necessary foundations, and cannot be treated with levity. Republics abound in young civilians who believe that the laws make the city, that grave modifications of the policy and modes of living and employments of the population, that commerce, education and religion may be voted in or out; and that any measure, though it were absurd, may be imposed on a people if only you can get sufficient voices to make it a law. But the wise know that foolish legislation is a rope of sand which perishes in the twisting; that the State must follow and not lead the character and progress of the citizen; the strongest usurper is quickly got rid of; and they only who build on Ideas, build for eternity; and that the form of government which prevails is the expression of what cultivation exists in the population which permits it. The law is only a memorandum. ⋆ ⋆ ⋆

The history of the State sketches in coarse outline the progress of thought, and follows at a distance the delicacy of culture and of aspiration.

The theory of politics which has possessed the mind of men, and which they have expressed the best they could in their laws and in their revolutions, considers persons and property as the two objects for whose protection government exists. Of persons, all have equal rights, in virtue of being identical in nature. This interest of course with its whole power demands a democracy. Whilst the rights of all as persons are equal, in virtue of their access to reason, their rights in property are very unequal. One man owns his clothes, and another owns a county. This accident, depending primarily on the skill and virtue of the parties, of which there is every degree, and secondarily on patrimony, falls unequally, and its rights of course are unequal. Personal rights, universally the same, demand a government framed on the ratio of the census; property demands a government framed on the ratio of owners and of owning. Laban, who has flocks and herds, wishes them looked after by an officer on the frontiers, lest the Midianites shall drive them off; and pays a tax to that end. Jacob has no flocks or herds and no fear of the Midianites, and pays no tax to the officer. It seemed fit that Laban and Jacob should have equal rights to elect the officer who is to defend their persons, but that Laban and not Jacob should elect the officer who is to guard the sheep and cattle. And if question arise whether additional officers or watch-towers should be provided, must not Laban and Isaac, and those who must sell part of their herds to buy protection for the rest, judge better of this, and with more right, than Jacob, who, because he is a youth and a traveller, eats their bread and not his own?

In the earliest society the proprietors made their own wealth, and so long as it comes to the owners in the direct way, no other opinion would arise in any equitable community than that property should make the law for property, and persons the law for persons.

But property passes through donation or inheritance to those who do not create it. Gift, in one case, makes it as really the new owner's, as labor made it the first owner's: in the other case, of patrimony, the law makes an ownership which will be valid in each man's view according to the estimate which he sets on the public tranquillity.

It was not, however, found easy to embody the readily admitted principle that property should make law for property, and persons for persons; since persons and property mixed themselves in every transaction. At last it seemed settled that the rightful distinction was that the proprietors should have more elective franchise than non-proprietors, on the Spartan principle of "calling that which is just, equal; not that which is equal, just."

That principle no longer looks so self-evident as it appeared in former times, partly because doubts have arisen whether too much weight had not been allowed in the laws to property, and such a structure given to our usages as allowed the rich to encroach on the poor, and to keep them poor; but mainly because there is an instinctive sense, however obscure and yet inarticulate, that the whole constitution of property, on its present tenures, is injurious, and its influence on persons deteriorating and degrading; that truly the only interest for the consideration of the State is persons; that property will always follow persons; that the highest end of government is the culture of men; and that if men can be educated, the institutions will share their improvement and the moral sentiment will write the law of the land.

If it be not easy to settle the equity of this question, the peril is less when we take note of our natural defences. We are kept by better guards than the vigilance of such magistrates as we commonly elect. Society always consists in greatest part of young and foolish persons. The old, who have seen through the hypocrisy of courts and statesmen, die and leave no wisdom to their sons. They believe their own newspaper, as their fathers did at their age. With such an ignorant and deceivable majority, States would soon run to ruin, but that there are limitations beyond which the folly and ambition of governors cannot go. Things have their laws, as well as men; and things refuse to be trifled with. Property will be protected. Corn will not grow unless it is planted and manured; but the farmer will not plant or hoe it unless the chances are a hundred to one that he will cut and harvest it. Under any forms, persons and property must and will have their just sway. They exert their power, as steadily as matter its attraction. * * *

The boundaries of personal influence it is impossible to fix, as persons are organs of moral or supernatural force. Under the dominion of an idea which possesses the minds of multitudes, as civil freedom, or the religious sentiment, the powers of persons are no longer subjects of calculation. A nation of men unanimously bent on freedom or conquest can easily confound the arithmetic of statists, and achieve extravagant actions, out of all proportion to their means; as the Greeks, the Saracens, the Swiss, the Americans, and the French have done. * * *

The same necessity which secures the rights of person and property against the malignity or folly of the magistrate, determines the form and methods of governing, which are proper to each nation and to its habit of thought, and nowise transferable to other states of society. In this country we are very vain of our political institutions, which are singular in this, that they sprung, within the memory of living men, from the character and condition of the people, which they still express with sufficient fidelity,—and we ostentatiously prefer them to any other in history. They are not better, but only fitter for us. We may be wise in asserting the advantage in modern times of the democratic form, but to other states of society, in which religion consecrated the monarchical, that and not this was expedient. Democracy is better for us, because the religious sentiment of the present time accords better with it. Born democrats, we are nowise qualified to judge of monarchy, which, to our fathers living in the monarchical idea, was also relatively right. But our institutions, though in coincidence with the spirit of the age, have not any exemption from the practical defects which have discredited other forms. Every actual State is corrupt. Good men must not obey the laws too well. What satire on government can equal the severity of censure conveyed in the word *politic*, which now for ages has signified *cunning*, intimating that the State is a trick?

The same benign necessity and the same practical abuse appear in the parties, into which each State divides itself, of opponents and defenders of the administration of the government. Parties are also founded on instincts, and have better guides to their own humble aims than the sagacity of their leaders. They have nothing perverse in their origin, but rudely mark some real and lasting relation. We might as wisely reprove the east wind or the frost, as a political party, whose members, for the most part, could give no account of their position, but stand for the defence of those interests in which they find themselves. Our quarrel with them begins when they quit this deep natural ground at the bidding of some leader,

and obeying personal considerations, throw themselves into the maintenance and defence of points nowise belonging to their system. A party is
perpetually corrupted by personality. Whilst we absolve the association
from dishonesty, we cannot extend the same charity to their leaders. They
reap the rewards of the docility and zeal of the masses which they direct.
Ordinarily our parties are parties of circumstance, and not of principle; as
the planting interest in conflict with the commercial; the party of capitalists and that of operatives: parties which are identical in their moral character, and which can easily change ground with each other in the support
of many of their measures. Parties of principle, as, religious sects, or the
party of free-trade, of universal suffrage, of abolition of slavery, of abolition of capital punishment,—degenerate into personalities, or would inspire enthusiasm. The vice of our leading parties in this country (which
may be cited as a fair specimen of these societies of opinion) is that they
do not plant themselves on the deep and necessary grounds to which they
are respectively entitled, but lash themselves to fury in the carrying of
some local and momentary measure, nowise useful to the commonwealth. Of the two great parties which at this hour almost share the nation between them, I should say that one has the best cause, and the
other contains the best men. The philosopher, the poet, or the religious
man, will of course wish to cast his vote with the democrat, for free-
trade, for wide suffrage, for the abolition of legal cruelties in the penal
code, and for facilitating in every manner the access of the young and the
poor to the sources of wealth and power. But he can rarely accept the
persons whom the so-called popular party propose to him as representatives of these liberalities. They have not at heart the ends which give to
the name of democracy what hope and virtue are in it. The spirit of our
American radicalism is destructive and aimless: it is not loving; it has no
ulterior and divine ends, but is destructive only out of hatred and selfishness. On the other side, the conservative party, composed of the most
moderate, able and cultivated part of the population, is timid, and merely
defensive of property. It vindicates no right, it aspires to no real good, it
brands no crime, it proposes no generous policy; it does not build, nor
write, nor cherish the arts, nor foster religion, nor establish schools, nor
encourage science, nor emancipate the slave, nor befriend the poor, or
the Indian, or the immigrant. From neither party, when in power, has the
world any benefit to expect in science, art, or humanity, at all commensurate with the resources of the nation.

I do not for these defects despair of our republic. We are not at the
mercy of any waves of chance. In the strife of ferocious parties, human
nature always finds itself cherished; as the children of the convicts at
Botany Bay are found to have as healthy a moral sentiment as other chil-

dren. Citizens of feudal states are alarmed at our democratic institutions lapsing into anarchy, and the older and more cautious among ourselves are learning from Europeans to look with some terror at our turbulent freedom. It is said that in our license of construing the Constitution, and in the despotism of public opinion, we have no anchor; and one foreign observer thinks he has found the safeguard in the sanctity of Marriage among us; and another thinks he has found it in our Calvinism. Fisher Ames expressed the popular security more wisely, when he compared a monarchy and a republic, saying that a monarchy is a merchantman, which sails well, but will sometimes strike on a rock and go to the bottom; whilst a republic is a raft, which would never sink, but then your feet are always in water. No forms can have any dangerous importance whilst we are befriended by the laws of things. * * *

The fact of two poles, of two forces, centripetal and centrifugal, is universal, and each force by its own activity develops the other. Wild liberty develops iron conscience. Want of liberty, by strengthening law and decorum, stupefies conscience. 'Lynch-law' prevails only where there is greater hardihood and self-subsistency in the leaders. A mob cannot be a permanency; everybody's interest requires that it should not exist, and only justice satisfies all.

We must trust infinitely to the beneficent necessity which shines through all laws. Human nature expresses itself in them as characteristically as in statues, or songs, or railroads; and an abstract of the codes of nations would be a transcript of the common conscience. Governments have their origin in the moral identity of men. Reason for one is seen to be reason for another, and for every other. There is a middle measure which satisfies all parties, be they never so many or so resolute for their own. Every man finds a sanction for his simplest claims and deeds, in decisions of his own mind, which he calls Truth and Holiness. In these decisions all the citizens find a perfect agreement, and only in these; not in what is good to eat, good to wear, good use of time, or what amount of land or of public aid each is entitled to claim. This truth and justice men presently endeavor to make application of to the measuring of land, the apportionment of service, the protection of life and property. Their first endeavors, no doubt, are very awkward. Yet absolute right is the first governor; or, every government is an impure theocracy. The idea after which each community is aiming to make and mend its law, is the will of the wise man. The wise man it cannot find in nature, and it makes awkward but earnest efforts to secure his government by contrivance; as by causing the entire people to give their voices on every measure; or by a double choice to get the representation of the whole; or by a selection of the best citizens; or to secure the advantages of efficiency and internal peace by confiding the government to one, who may himself select his agents. All forms of government symbolize an immortal government, common to all dynasties and independent of numbers, perfect where two men exist, perfect where there is only one man. * * *

I can see well enough a great difference between my setting myself down to a self-control, and my going to make somebody else act after my views; but when a quarter of the human race assume to tell me what I must do, I may be too much disturbed by the circumstances to see so clearly the absurdity of their command. Therefore all public ends look vague and quixotic beside private ones. For any laws but those which men make for themselves are laughable. If I put myself in the place of my child, and we stand in one thought and see that things are thus or thus, that perception is law for him and me. We are both there, both act. But if, without carrying him into the thought, I look over into his plot, and, guessing how it is with him, ordain this or that, he will never obey me. This is the history of governments,—one man does something which is to bind another. A man who cannot be acquainted with me, taxes me; looking from afar at me ordains that a part of my labor shall go to this or that whimsical end,— not as I, but as he happens to fancy. Behold the consequence. Of all debts men are least willing to pay the taxes. What a satire is this on government! Everywhere they think they get their money's worth, except for these.

Hence the less government we have the better,—the fewer laws, and the less confided power. The antidote to this abuse of formal government is the influence of private character, the growth of the Individual; the appearance of the principal to supersede the proxy; the appearance of the wise man; of whom the existing government is, it must be owned, but a shabby imitation. That which all things tend to educe; which freedom, cultivation, intercourse, revolutions, go to form and deliver, is character; that is the end of Nature, to reach unto this coronation of her king. To educate the wise man the State exists, and with the appearance of the wise man the State expires. The appearance of character makes the State unnecessary. The wise man is the State. He needs no army, fort, or navy,—he loves men too well; no bribe, or feast, or palace, to draw friends to him; no vantage ground, no favorable circumstance. He needs no library, for he has not done thinking; no church, for he is a prophet; no statute-book, for he has the lawgiver; no money, for he is value; no road, for he is at home where he is; no experience, for the life of the creator shoots through him, and looks from his eyes. He has no personal friends, for he who has the spell to draw the prayer and piety of all men unto him needs not husband and educate a few to share with him a select and poetic life. His relation to men is angelic; his memory is myrrh to them; his presence, frankincense and flowers.

We think our civilization near its meridian, but we are yet only at the cock-crowing and the morning star. In our barbarous society the influence of character is in its infancy. As a political power, as the rightful lord who is to tumble all rulers from their chairs, its presence is hardly yet suspected. * * *

The tendencies of the times favor the idea of self-government, and leave the individual, for all code, to the rewards and penalties of his own constitution; which work with more energy than we believe whilst we depend on artificial restraints. The movement in this direction has been very marked in modern history. Much has been blind and discreditable, but the nature of the revolution is not affected by the vices of the revolters; for this is a purely moral force. It was never adopted by any party in history, neither can be. It separates the individual from all party, and unites him at the same time to the race. It promises a recognition of higher rights than those of personal freedom, or the security of property. A man has a right to be employed, to be trusted, to be loved, to be revered. The power of love, as the basis of a State, has never been tried. We must not imagine that all things are lapsing into confusion if every tender protestant be not compelled to bear his part in certain social conventions; nor doubt that roads can be built, letters carried, and the fruit of labor secured, when the government of force is at an end. Are our methods now so excellent that all competition is hopeless? could not a nation of friends even devise better ways? On the other hand, let not the most conservative and timid fear anything from a premature surrender of the bayonet and the system of force. For, according to the order of nature, which is quite superior to our will, it stands thus; there will always be a government of force where men are selfish; and when they are pure enough to abjure the code of force they will be wise enough to see how these public ends of the post-office, of the highway, of commerce and the exchange of property, of museums and libraries, of institutions of art and science can be answered.

We live in a very low state of the world, and pay unwilling tribute to governments founded on force. There is not, among the most religious and instructed men of the most religious and civil nations, a reliance on the moral sentiment and a sufficient belief in the unity of things, to persuade them that society can be maintained without artificial restraints, as well as the solar system; or that the private citizen might be reasonable and a good neighbor, without the hint of a jail or a confiscation. What is strange too, there never was in any man sufficient faith in the power of rectitude to inspire him with the broad design of renovating the State on the principle of right and love. All those who have pretended this design have been partial reformers, and have admitted in some manner the supremacy of the bad State. I do not call to mind a single human being who has steadily denied the authority of the laws, on the simple ground of his own moral nature. Such designs, full of genius and full of faith as they are, are not entertained except avowedly as air-pictures. If the individual who exhibits them dare to think them practicable, he disgusts scholars and churchmen; and men of talent and women of superior sentiments cannot hide their contempt. Not the less does nature continue to fill the heart of youth with suggestions of this enthusiasm, and there are now men,—if indeed I can speak in the plural number,—more exactly, I will say, I have just been conversing with one man, to whom no weight of adverse experience will make it for a moment appear impossible that thousands of human beings might exercise towards each other the grandest and simplest sentiments, as well as a knot of friends, or a pair of lovers.

HENRY DAVID THOREAU

Resistance to Civil Government (1849)

A close friend of Emerson, the transcendentalist philosopher, essayist, and poet Henry David Thoreau (1817–1862) is best known as the author of Walden, *a reflection on humanity's relation to the natural environment that was based on Thoreau's own two-year seclusion at Walden Pond in Concord, Massachusetts. Thoreau spent a night in jail for refusing to pay his poll tax to a government that he believed was waging an unjust, imperialist war in Mexico and that condoned slavery. Thoreau explained the principles that motivated his act of conscientious objection in "Resistance to Civil Government," often referred to as "Civil Disobedience," a lecture to the Concord Lyceum that was printed in May 1849. Although it received little attention at the time, Thoreau's essay on the relation between the individual and the state has since become a classic defense of individual conscience against unjust laws.*

I heartily accept the motto, "That government is best which governs least;" and I should like to see it acted up to more rapidly and systematically. Carried out, it finally amounts to this, which also I believe,—"That government is best which governs not at all;" and when men are prepared for it, that will be the kind of government which they will have. Government is at best but an expedient; but most governments are usually, and all governments are sometimes, inexpedient. The objections which have been brought against a standing army, and they are many and weighty, and deserve to prevail, may also at last be brought against a standing government. The standing army is only an arm of the standing government. The government itself, which is only the mode which the people have chosen to execute their will, is equally liable to be abused and perverted before the people can act through it. Witness the present Mexican war, the work of comparatively a few individuals using the standing government as their tool; for, in the outset, the people would not have consented to this measure.

This American government,—what is it but a tradition, though a recent one, endeavoring to transmit itself unimpaired to posterity, but each instant losing some of its integrity? It has not the vitality and force of a single living man; for a single man can bend it to his will. It is a sort of wooden gun to the people themselves. But it is not the less necessary for this; for the people must have some complicated machinery or other, and hear its din, to satisfy that idea of government which they have. Governments show thus how successfully men can be imposed on, even impose on themselves, for their own advantage. It is excellent, we must all allow. Yet this government never of itself furthered any enterprise, but by the alacrity with which it got out of its way. *It* does not keep the country free. *It* does not settle the West. *It* does not educate. The character inherent in the American people has done all that has been accomplished; and it would have done somewhat more, if the government had not sometimes got in its way. For government is an expedient by which men would fain succeed in letting one another alone; and, as has been said, when it is most expedient, the governed are most let alone by it. Trade and commerce, if they were not made of india-rubber, would never manage to bounce over the obstacles which legislators are continually putting in their way; and, if one were to judge these men wholly by the effects of their actions and not partly by their intentions, they would deserve to be classed and punished with those mischievous persons who put obstructions on the railroads.

But, to speak practically and as a citizen, unlike those who call themselves no-government men, I ask for, not *at once* no government, but at once a better government. Let every man make known what kind of government would command his respect, and that will be one step toward obtaining it.

After all, the practical reason why, when the power is once in the hands of the people, a majority are permitted, and for a long period continue, to rule is not because they are most likely to be in the right, nor because this seems fairest to the minority, but because they are physically the strongest. But a government in which the majority rule in all cases cannot be based on justice, even as far as men understand it. Can there not be a government in which majorities do not virtually decide right and wrong, but conscience?—in which majorities decide only those questions to which the rule of expediency is applicable? Must the citizen ever for a moment, or in the least degree, resign his conscience to the legislator? Why has every man a conscience, then? I think that we should be men first, and subjects afterward. It is not desirable to cultivate a respect for the law, so much as for the right. The only obligation which I have a right to assume is to do at any time what I think right. It is truly enough said that a corporation has no conscience; but a corporation of conscientious men is a corporation with a conscience. Law never made men a whit more just; and, by means of their respect for it, even the well-disposed are daily made the agents of injustice. A common and natural result of an undue respect for law is, that you may see a file of soldiers, colonel, captain, corporal, privates, powder-monkeys, and all, marching in admirable order over hill and dale to the wars, against their wills, ay, against their common sense and consciences, which makes it very steep marching indeed, and produces a palpitation of the heart. They have no doubt that it is a damnable business in which they are concerned; they are all peaceably inclined. Now, what are they? Men at all? or small movable forts and magazines, at the service of some unscrupulous man in power? * * *

The mass of men serve the state thus, not as men mainly, but as machines, with their bodies. They are the standing army, and the militia, jailers, constables, posse comitatus, etc. In most cases there is no free exercise whatever of the judgment or of the moral sense; but they put themselves on a level with wood and earth and stones; and wooden men can perhaps be manufactured that will serve the purpose as well. Such command no more respect than men of straw or a lump of dirt. They have the same sort of worth only as horses and dogs. Yet such as these even are commonly esteemed good citizens. Others—as most legislators, politicians, lawyers, ministers, and office-holders—serve the state chiefly with their heads; and, as they rarely make any moral distinctions, they are as likely to serve the devil, without *intending* it, as God. A very few—as heroes, patriots, martyrs, reformers in the great sense, and *men*—serve the state with their consciences also, and so necessarily resist it for the most part; and they are commonly treated as enemies by it. * * *

How does it become a man to behave toward this American government to-day? I answer, that he cannot without disgrace be associated with it. I cannot for an instant recognize that political organization as *my* government which is the *slave's* government also.

All men recognize the right of revolution; that is, the right to refuse allegiance to, and to resist, the government, when its tyranny or its inefficiency are great and unendurable. But almost all say that such is not the case now. But such was the case, they think, in the Revolution of '75. If one were to tell me that this was a bad government because it taxed certain foreign commodities brought to its ports, it is most probable that I should not make an ado about it, for I can do without them. All machines have their friction; and possibly this does enough good to counterbalance the evil. At any rate, it is a great evil to make a stir about it. But when the friction comes to have its machine, and oppression and robbery are organized, I say, let us not have such a machine any longer. In other words, when a sixth of the population of a nation which has undertaken to be the refuge of liberty are slaves, and a whole country is unjustly overrun and conquered by a foreign army, and subjected to military law, I think that it is not too soon for honest men to rebel and revolutionize. What makes this duty the more urgent is the fact that the country so overrun is not our own, but ours is the invading army. * * *

Unjust laws exist: shall we be content to obey them, or shall we endeavor to amend them, and obey them until we have succeeded, or shall we transgress them at once? Men generally, under such a government as this, think that they ought to wait until they have persuaded the majority to alter them. They think that, if they should resist, the remedy would be worse than the evil. But it is the fault of the government itself that the remedy *is* worse than the evil. *It* makes it worse. Why is it not more apt to anticipate and provide for reform? Why does it not cherish its wise minority? Why does it cry and resist before it is hurt? Why does it not encourage its citizens to be on the alert to point out its faults, and *do* better than it would have them? Why does it always crucify Christ, and excommunicate Copernicus and Luther, and pronounce Washington and Franklin rebels? * * *

I do not hesitate to say, that those who call themselves Abolitionists should at once effectually withdraw their support, both in person and property, from the government of Massachusetts, and not wait till they constitute a majority of one, before they suffer the right to prevail through them. I think that it is enough if they have God on their side, without waiting for that other one. Moreover, any man more right than his neighbors constitutes a majority of one already.

I meet this American government, or its representative, the State government, directly, and face to face, once a year—no more—in the person of its tax-gatherer; this is the only mode in which a man situated as I am necessarily meets it; and it then says distinctly, Recognize me; and the simplest, the most effectual, and, in the present posture of affairs, the indispensablest mode of treating with it on this head, of expressing your little satisfaction with and love for it, is to deny it then. My civil neighbor, the tax-gatherer, is the very man I have to deal with,—for it is, after all, with men and not with parchment that I quarrel,—and he has voluntarily chosen to be an agent of the government. How shall he ever know well what he is and does as an officer of the government, or as a man, until he is obliged to consider whether he shall treat me, his neighbor, for whom he has respect, as a neighbor and well-disposed man, or as a maniac and disturber of the peace, and see if he can get over this obstruction to his neighborliness without a ruder and more impetuous thought or speech corresponding with his action. I know this well, that if one thousand, if one hundred, if ten men whom I could name,—if then *honest* men only,—ay, if *one* HONEST man, in this State of Massachusetts, *ceasing to hold slaves*, were actually to withdraw from this copartnership, and be locked up in the county jail therefor, it would be the abolition of slavery in America. For it matters not how small the beginning may seem to be: what is once well done is done forever. * * *

Under a government which imprisons any unjustly, the true place for a just man is also a prison. The proper place to-day, the only place which Massachusetts has provided for her freer and less desponding spirits, is in her prisons, to be put out and locked out of the State by her own act, as they have already put themselves out by their principles. It is there that the fugitive slave, and the Mexican prisoner on parole, and the Indian come to plead the wrongs of his race should find them; on that separate, but more free and honorable, ground, where the State places those who are not *with* her, but *against* her,—the only house in a slave State in which a free man can abide with honor. If any think that their influence would be lost there, and their voices no longer afflict the ear of the State, that they would not be as an enemy within its walls, they do not know by how much truth is stronger than error, nor how much more eloquently and effectively he can combat injustice who has experienced a little in his own person. Cast your whole vote, not a strip of paper merely, but your whole influence. A minority is powerless while it conforms to the majority; it is not even a minority then; but it is irresistible when it clogs by its whole weight. If the alternative is to keep all just men in prison, or give up war and slavery, the State will not hesitate which to choose. If a thousand men were not to pay their tax-bills this year, that would not be a violent and bloody measure, as it would be to pay them, and enable the State to commit violence and shed innocent blood. This is, in fact, the definition of a peaceable revolution, if any such is possible. If the tax-gatherer, or any other public officer, asks me, as one has done, "But what shall I do?" my answer is, "If you really wish to do anything, resign your office." When the subject has refused allegiance, and the officer has resigned his office, then the revolution is accomplished. But even suppose blood should flow. Is there not a sort of blood shed when the conscience is wounded? Through this wound a man's real manhood and immortality flow out, and he bleeds to an everlasting death. I see this blood flowing now. * * *

I have paid no poll-tax for six years. I was put into a jail once on this account, for one night; and, as I stood considering the walls of solid stone, two or three feet thick, the door of wood and iron, a foot thick, and the iron grating which strained the light, I could not help being struck with the foolishness of that institution which treated me as if I were mere flesh and blood and bones, to be locked up. I wondered that it should have concluded at length that this was the best use it could put me to, and had never thought to avail itself of my services in some way. I saw that, if there was a wall of stone between me and my townsmen, there was a still more difficult one to climb or break through before they could get to be as free as I was. I did not for a moment feel confined, and the walls seemed a great waste of stone and mortar. I felt as if I alone of all my townsmen had paid my tax. They plainly did not know how to treat me, but behaved like persons who are underbred. In every threat and in every compliment there was a blunder; for they thought that my chief desire was to stand the other side of that stone wall. I could not but smile to see how industriously they locked the door on my meditations, which followed them out again without let or hindrance, and *they* were really all that was dangerous. As they could not reach me, they had resolved to punish my body; just as boys, if they cannot come at some person against whom they have a spite, will abuse his dog. I saw that the State was half-witted, that it was timid as a lone woman with her silver spoons, and that it did not know its friends from its foes, and I lost all my remaining respect for it, and pitied it.

Thus the State never intentionally confronts a man's sense, intellectual or moral, but only his body, his senses. It is not armed with superior wit or honesty, but with superior physical strength. I was not born to be forced. I will breathe after my own fashion. Let us see who is the strongest. What force has a multitude? They only can force me who obey a higher law than I. They force me to become like themselves. I do not hear of *men* being *forced* to live this way or that by masses of men. What sort of life were that to live? When I meet a government which says to me, "Your money or your life," why should I be in haste to give it my money? It may be in a great strait, and not know what to do: I cannot help that. It must help itself; do as I do. It is not worth the while to snivel about it. I am not responsible for the successful working of the machinery of society. I am not the son of the engineer. I perceive that, when an acorn and a chestnut fall side by side, the one does not remain inert to make way for the other, but both obey their own laws, and spring and grow and flourish as best they can, till one, perchance, overshadows and destroys the other. If a plant cannot live according to its nature, it dies; and so a man. * * *

I know that most men think differently from myself; but those whose lives are by profession devoted to the study of these or kindred subjects content me as little as any. Statesmen and legislators, standing so completely within the institution, never distinctly and nakedly behold it. They speak of moving society, but have no resting-place without it. They may be men of a certain experience and discrimination, and have no doubt invented ingenious and even useful systems, for which we sincerely thank them; but all their wit and usefulness lie within certain not very wide limits. They are wont to forget that the world is not governed by policy and expediency. Webster never goes behind government, and so cannot speak with authority about it. His words are wisdom to those legislators who contemplate no essential reform in the existing government; but for thinkers, and those who legislate for all time, he never once glances at the subject. I know of those whose serene and wise speculations on this theme would soon reveal the limits of his mind's range and hospitality. Yet, compared with the cheap professions of most reformers, and the still cheaper wisdom and eloquence of politicians in general, his are almost the only sensible and valuable words, and we thank Heaven for him. Comparatively, he is always strong, original, and, above all, practical. Still, his quality is not wisdom, but prudence. The lawyer's truth is not Truth, but consistency or a consistent expediency. Truth is always in harmony with herself, and is not concerned chiefly to reveal the justice that may consist with wrong-doing. He well deserves to be called, as he has been called, the Defender of the Constitution. There are really no blows to be given by him but defensive ones. He is not a leader, but a follower. His leaders are the men of '87. "I have never made an effort," he says, "and never propose to make an effort; I have never countenanced an effort, and never mean to countenance an effort, to disturb the arrangement as originally made, by which the various States came into the Union." Still thinking of the sanction which the Constitution gives to slavery, he says, "Because it was a part of the original compact,—let it stand." Notwithstanding his special acuteness and ability, he is unable to take a fact out of its merely political relations, and behold it as it lies absolutely to be disposed of by the intellect,—what, for instance, it behooves a man to do here in America to-day with regard to slavery. * * *

The authority of government, even such as I am willing to submit to,— for I will cheerfully obey those who know and can do better than I, and in many things even those who neither know nor can do so well,—is still an impure one: to be strictly just, it must have the sanction and consent of the governed. It can have no pure right over my person and property but what I concede to it. The progress from an absolute to a limited monarchy, from a limited monarchy to a democracy, is a progress toward a true respect for the individual. Even the Chinese philosopher was wise enough to regard the individual as the basis of the empire. Is a democracy, such as we know it, the last improvement possible in government? Is it not possible to take a step further towards recognizing and organizing the rights of man? There will never be a really free and enlightened State until the State comes to recognize the individual as a higher and independent power, from which all its own power and authority are derived, and treats him accordingly. I please myself with imagining a State at last which can afford to be just to all men, and to treat the individual with respect as a neighbor; which even would not think it inconsistent with its own repose if a few were to live aloof from it, not meddling with it, nor embraced by it, who fulfilled all the duties of neighbors and fellow-men. A State which bore this kind of fruit, and suffered it to drop off as fast as it ripened, would prepare the way for a still more perfect and glorious State, which also I have imagined, but not yet anywhere seen.

HENRY DAVID THOREAU

Life Without Principle (1863)

Related to Thoreau's commitment to the moral and intellectual development of individual character was his deep aversion to the vulgarity of politics and the hustle and bustle of modern life. In this essay, published posthumously in the Atlantic Monthly, *the naturalist criticized the drudgery of work that is done merely for money because it dehumanizes and stifles the development of the mind.*

Let us consider the way in which we spend our lives.

This world is a place of business. What an infinite bustle! I am awaked almost every night by the panting of the locomotive. It interrupts my dreams. There is no sabbath. It would be glorious to see mankind at leisure for once. It is nothing but work, work, work. I cannot easily buy a blank-book to write thoughts in; they are commonly ruled for dollars and cents. An Irishman, seeing me making a minute in the fields, took it for granted that I was calculating my wages. If a man was tossed out of a window when an infant, and so made a cripple for life, or scared out of

his wits by the Indians, it is regretted chiefly because he was thus incapacitated for—business! I think that there is nothing, not even crime,
more opposed to poetry, to philosophy, ay, to life itself, than this incessant
business.

There is a coarse and boisterous money-making fellow in the outskirts
of our town, who is going to build a bank-wall under the hill along the
edge of his meadow. The powers have put this into his head to keep him
out of mischief, and he wishes me to spend three weeks digging there
with him. The result will be that he will perhaps get some more money
to hoard, and leave for his heirs to spend foolishly. If I do this, most will
commend me as an industrious and hard-working man; but if I choose to
devote myself to certain labors which yield more real profit, though but
little money, they may be inclined to look on me as an idler. Nevertheless,
as I do not need the police of meaningless labor to regulate me, and do
not see anything absolutely praiseworthy in this fellow's undertaking any
more than in many an enterprise of our own or foreign governments,
however amusing it may be to him or them, I prefer to finish my education at a different school.

If a man walk in the woods for love of them half of each day, he is in
danger of being regarded as a loafer; but if he spends his whole day as a
speculator, shearing off those woods and making earth bald before her
time, he is esteemed an industrious and enterprising citizen. As if a town
had no interest in its forests but to cut them down!

Most men would feel insulted if it were proposed to employ them in
throwing stones over a wall, and then in throwing them back, merely that
they might earn their wages. But many are no more worthily employed
now. * * *

The ways by which you may get money almost without exception lead
downward. To have done anything by which you earned money *merely* is to
have been truly idle or worse. If the laborer gets no more than the wages
which his employer pays him, he is cheated, he cheats himself. If you
would get money as a writer or lecturer, you must be popular, which is to go
down perpendicularly. Those services which the community will most readily pay for, it is most disagreeable to render. You are paid for being something less than a man. The state does not commonly reward a genius any
more wisely. Even the poet laureate would rather not have to celebrate the
accidents of royalty. He must be bribed with a pipe of wine; and perhaps
another poet is called away from his muse to gauge that very pipe. * * *

The aim of the laborer should be, not to get his living, to get "a good
job," but to perform well a certain work; and, even in a pecuniary sense,
it would be economy for a town to pay its laborers so well that they would
not feel that they were working for low ends, as for a livelihood merely,

but for scientific, or even moral ends. Do not hire a man who does your work for money, but him who does it for love of it.

It is remarkable that there are few men so well employed, so much to their minds, but that a little money or fame would commonly buy them off from their present pursuit. I see advertisements for *active* young men, as if activity were the whole of a young man's capital. Yet I have been surprised when one has with confidence proposed to me, a grown man, to embark in some enterprise of his, as if I had absolutely nothing to do, my life having been a complete failure hitherto. What a doubtful compliment this to pay me! * * *

The community has no bribe that will tempt a wise man. You may raise money enough to tunnel a mountain, but you cannot raise money enough to hire a man who is minding *his own* business. An efficient and valuable man does what he can, whether the community pay him for it or not. The inefficient offer their inefficiency to the highest bidder, and are forever expecting to be put into office. One would suppose that they were rarely disappointed.

Perhaps I am more than usually jealous with respect to my freedom. I feel that my connection with and obligation to society are still very slight and transient. Those slight labors which afford me a livelihood, and by which it is allowed that I am to some extent serviceable to my contemporaries, are as yet commonly a pleasure to me, and I am not often reminded that they are a necessity. So far I am successful. But I foresee that if my wants should be much increased, the labor required to supply them would become a drudgery. If I should sell both my forenoons and afternoons to society, as most appear to do, I am sure that for me there would be nothing left worth living for. I trust that I shall never thus sell my birthright for a mess of pottage. I wish to suggest that a man may be very industrious, and yet not spend his time well. There is no more fatal blunderer than he who consumes the greater part of his life getting his living. All great enterprises are self-supporting. The poet, for instance, must sustain his body by his poetry, as a steam planing-mill feeds its boilers with the shavings it makes. You must get your living by loving. But as it is said of the merchants that ninety-seven in a hundred fail, so the life of men generally, tried by this standard, is a failure, and bankruptcy may be surely prophesied.

Merely to come into the world the heir of a fortune is not to be born, but to be still-born, rather. To be supported by the charity of friends, or a government pension,—provided you continue to breathe,—by whatever fine synonyms you describe these relations, is to go into the almshouse. * * *

It is remarkable that there is little or nothing to be remembered written on the subject of getting a living; how to make getting a living not merely honest and honorable, but altogether inviting and glorious; for if *getting* a living is not so, then living is not. One would think, from looking at literature, that this question had never disturbed a solitary individual's musings. Is it that men are too much disgusted with their experience to speak of it? * * * Cold and hunger seem more friendly to my nature than those methods which men have adopted and advise to ward them off.

The title *wise* is, for the most part, falsely applied. How can one be a wise man, if he does not know any better how to live than other men?—if he is only more cunning and intellectually subtle? Does Wisdom work in a tread-mill? or does she teach how to succeed *by her example?* Is there any such thing as wisdom not applied to life? Is she merely the miller who grinds the finest logic? It is pertinent to ask if Plato got his *living* in a better way or more successfully than his contemporaries,—or did he succumb to the difficulties of life like other men? Did he seem to prevail over some of them merely by indifference, or by assuming grand airs? or find it easier to live, because his aunt remembered him in her will? The ways in which most men get their living, that is, live, are mere makeshifts, and a shirking of the real business of life,—chiefly because they do not know, but partly because they do not mean, any better.

The rush to California, for instance, and the attitude, not merely of merchants, but of philosophers and prophets, so called, in relation to it, reflect the greatest disgrace on mankind. That so many are ready to live by luck, and so get the means of commanding the labor of others less lucky, without contributing any value to society! And that is called enterprise! I know of no more startling development of the immorality of trade, and all the common modes of getting a living. The philosophy and poetry and religion of such a mankind are not worth the dust of a puffball. The hog that gets his living by rooting, stirring up the soil so, would be ashamed of such company. * * *

To speak impartially, the best men that I know are not serene, a world in themselves. For the most part, they dwell in forms, and flatter and study effect only more finely than the rest. We select granite for the underpinning of our houses and barns; we build fences of stone; but we do not ourselves rest on an underpinning of granitic truth, the lowest primitive rock. Our sills are rotten. What stuff is the man made of who is not coexistent in our thought with the purest and subtilest truth? I often accuse my finest acquaintances of an immense frivolity; for, while there are manners and compliments we do not meet, we do not teach one another the lessons of honesty and sincerity that the brutes do, or of steadiness and solidity that the rocks do. The fault is commonly mutual, however; for we do not habitually demand any more of each other. * * *

Just so hollow and ineffectual, for the most part, is our ordinary conversation. Surface meets surface. When our life ceases to be inward and private, conversation degenerates into mere gossip. We rarely meet a man who can tell us any news which he has not read in a newspaper, or been told by his neighbor; and, for the most part, the only difference between us and our fellow is that he has seen the newspaper, or been out to tea, and we have not. In proportion as our inward life fails, we go more constantly and desperately to the post-office. You may depend on it, that the poor fellow who walks away with the greatest number of letters, proud of his extensive correspondence, has not heard from himself this long while. * * *

If we have thus desecrated ourselves,—as who has not?—the remedy will be by wariness and devotion to reconsecrate ourselves, and make once more a fane of the mind. We should treat our minds, that is, ourselves, as innocent and ingenuous children, whose guardians we are, and be careful what objects and what subjects we thrust on their attention. Read not the Times. Read the Eternities. Conventionalities are at length as bad as impurities. Even the facts of science may dust the mind by their dryness, unless they are in a sense effaced each morning, or rather rendered fertile by the dews of fresh and living truth. Knowledge does not come to us by details, but in flashes of light from heaven. Yes, every thought that passes through the mind helps to wear and tear it, and to deepen the ruts, which, as in the streets of Pompeii, evince how much it has been used. How many things there are concerning which we might well deliberate whether we had better know them,—had better let their peddling-carts be driven, even at the slowest trot or walk, over that bridge of glorious span by which we trust to pass at last from the farthest brink of time to the nearest shore of eternity! Have we no culture, no refinement,—but skill only to live coarsely and serve the Devil?—to acquire a little worldly wealth, or fame, or liberty, and make a false show with it, as if we were all husk and shell, with no tender and living kernel to us? Shall our institutions be like those chestnut burs which contain abortive nuts, perfect only to prick the fingers?

America is said to be the arena on which the battle of freedom is to be fought; but surely it cannot be freedom in a merely political sense that is meant. Even if we grant that the American has freed himself from a political tyrant, he is still the slave of an economical and moral tyrant. Now that the republic—the *res-publica*—has been settled, it is time to look after the *res-privata*,—the private state,—to see, as the Roman senate charged its consuls, "*ne quid res-*PRIVATA *detrimenti caperet*," that the *private* state receive no detriment.

Do we call this the land of the free? What is it to be free from King George and continue the slaves of King Prejudice? What is it to be born free and not to live free? What is the value of any political freedom, but as a means to moral freedom? Is it a freedom to be slaves, or a freedom to be free, of which we boast? We are a nation of politicians, concerned about the outmost defenses only of freedom. It is our children's children who may perchance be really free. We tax ourselves unjustly. There is a part of us which is not represented. It is taxation without representation. We quarter troops, we quarter fools and cattle of all sorts upon ourselves. We quarter our gross bodies on our poor souls, till the former eat up all the latter's substance.

With respect to a true culture and manhood, we are essentially provincial still, not metropolitan,—mere Jonathans. We are provincial, because we do not find at home our standards; because we do not worship truth, but the reflection of truth; because we are warped and narrowed by an exclusive devotion to trade and commerce and manufactures and agriculture and the like, which are but means, and not the end. * * *

The chief want, in every State that I have been into, was a high and earnest purpose in its inhabitants. This alone draws out "the great resources" of Nature, and at last taxes her beyond her resources; for man naturally dies out of her. When we want culture more than potatoes, and illumination more than sugar-plums, then the great resources of a world are taxed and drawn out, and the result, or staple production, is, not slaves, nor operatives, but men,—those rare fruits called heroes, saints, poets, philosophers, and redeemers. * * *

What is called politics is comparatively something so superficial and inhuman, that practically I have never fairly recognized that it concerns me at all. The newspapers, I perceive, devote some of their columns specially to politics or government without charge; and this, one would say, is all that saves it; but as I love literature and to some extent the truth also, I never read those columns at any rate. I do not wish to blunt my sense of right so much. I have not got to answer for having read a single President's Message. A strange age of the world this, when empires, kingdoms, and republics come a-begging to a private man's door, and utter their complaints at his elbow! I cannot take up a newspaper but I find that some wretched government or other, hard pushed and on its last legs, is interceding with me, the reader, to vote for it. * * *

Those things which now most engage the attention of men, as politics and the daily routine, are, it is true, vital functions of human society, but should be unconsciously performed, like the corresponding functions of the physical body. They are *infra*-human, a kind of vegetation. I sometimes awake to a half-consciousness of them going on about me, as a man may become conscious of some of the processes of digestion in a morbid state, and so have the dyspepsia, as it is called. It is as if a thinker submitted himself to be rasped by the great gizzard of creation. Politics is, as it were, the gizzard of society, full of grit and gravel, and the two political parties are its two opposite halves,—sometimes split into quarters, it may be, which grind on each other. Not only individuals, but states, have thus a confirmed dyspepsia, which expresses itself, you can imagine by what sort of eloquence. Thus our life is not altogether a forgetting, but also, alas! to a great extent, a remembering, of that which we should never have been conscious of, certainly not in our waking hours. Why should we not meet, not always as dyspeptics, to tell our bad dreams, but sometimes as *eu*peptics, to congratulate each other on the ever-glorious morning? I do not make an exorbitant demand, surely.

WALT WHITMAN

Democratic Vistas (1871)

Walt Whitman (1819–1892), the poet laureate of American democracy, remained firmly committed to political democracy throughout his life, but he became increasingly ambivalent about American society, which he believed was becoming crude and drab. In Democratic Vistas, a collection of essays, Whitman eulogized democracy as "life's gymnasium" even as he noted its tendency toward vulgarity and homogeneity. In this selection, Whitman argued that the purpose of government is to cultivate the latent creativity and independence of the individual and to train the individual to "become a law, and series of laws, unto himself."

I will not gloss over the appalling dangers of universal suffrage in the United States. In fact, it is to admit and face these dangers I am writing. To him or her within whose thought rages the battle, advancing, retreating, between Democracy's convictions, aspirations, and the People's crudeness, vice, caprices, I mainly write this book.

I shall use the words America and Democracy as convertible terms. * * * The United States are destined either to surmount the gorgeous history of feudalism, or else prove the most tremendous failure of time. Not the least doubtful am I on any prospects of their material success. The triumphant future of their business, geographic, and productive departments, on larger scales and in more varieties than ever, is certain. In those respects the Republic must soon (if she does not already) outstrip all examples hitherto afforded, and dominate the world.

Admitting all this, with the priceless value of our political institutions, general suffrage (and cheerfully acknowledging the latest, widest opening of the doors,) I say that, far deeper than these, what finally and only is to make of our Western World a Nationality superior to any hitherto known, and out-topping the past, must be vigorous, yet unsuspected Literatures, perfect personalities and sociologies, original, transcendental, and expressing (what, in highest sense, are not yet expressed at all,) Democracy and the Modern. With these, and out of these, I promulge new races of Teachers, and of perfect Women, indispensable to endow the birth-stock of a New World. * * *

I say that Democracy can never prove itself beyond cavil, until it founds and luxuriantly grows its own forms of arts, poems, schools, theology, displacing all that exists, or that has been produced anywhere in the past, under opposite influences.

It is curious to me that while so many voices, pens, minds, in the press, lecture-rooms, in our Congress, etc., are discussing intellectual topics, pecuniary dangers, legislative problems, the suffrage, tariff and labor questions, and the various business and benevolent needs of America, with propositions, remedies, often worth deep attention, there is one need, a hiatus, and the profoundest, that no eye seems to perceive, no voice to state. Our fundamental want to-day in the United States, with closest, amplest reference to present conditions, and to the future, is of a class, and the clear idea of a class, of native Authors, Literatures, far different, far higher in grade than any yet known, sacerdotal, modern, fit to cope with our occasions, lands, permeating the whole mass of American mentality, taste, belief, breathing into it a new breath of life, giving it decision, affecting politics far more than the popular superficial suffrage, with results inside and underneath the elections of Presidents or Congresses, radiating, begetting appropriate teachers and schools, manners, costumes, and, as its grandest result, accomplishing, (what neither the schools nor the churches and their clergy have hitherto accomplished, and without which this nation will no more stand, permanently, soundly, than a house will stand without a substratum,) a religious and moral character beneath the political and productive and intellectual bases of The States. * * *

First, let us see what we can make out of a brief, general, sentimental cosideration of political Democracy, and whence it has arisen, with regard to some of its current features, as an aggregate, and as the basic structure of our future literature and authorship. We shall, it is true, quickly and continually find the origin-idea of the singleness of man, individualism, asserting itself, and cropping forth, even from the opposite ideas. But the mass, or lump character, for imperative reasons, is to be ever carefully weighed, borne in mind, and provided for. Only from it, and from its proper regulation and potency, comes the other, comes the chance of Individualism. The two are contradictory, but our task is to reconcile them.

The political history of the past may be summed up as having grown out of what underlies the words Order, Safety, Caste, and especially out of the need of some prompt deciding Authority, and of Cohesion, at all cost. * * *

For after the rest is said—after the many time-honored and really true things for subordination, experience, rights of property, etc., have been listened to and acquiesced in—after the valuable and well-settled statement of our duties and relations in society is thoroughly conned over and exhausted—it remains to bring forward and modify everything else with the idea of that Something a man is, (last precious consolation of the drudging poor,) standing apart from all else, divine in his own right, and a woman in hers, sole and untouchable by any canons of authority, or any rule derived from precedent, state-safety, the acts of legislatures, or even from what is called religion, modesty, or art.

The radiation of this truth is the key of the most significant doings of our immediately preceding three centuries, and has been the political genesis and life of America. Advancing visibly, it still more advances invisibly. Underneath the fluctuations of the expressions of society, as well as the movements of the politics of the leading nations of the world, we see steadily pressing ahead, and strengthening itself, even in the midst of immense tendencies toward aggregation, this image of completeness in separatism, of individual personal dignity, of a single person, either male or female, characterized in the main, not from extrinsic acquirements or position, but in the pride of himself or herself alone; and, as an eventful conclusion and summing up, (or else the entire scheme of things is aimless, a cheat, a crash,) the simple idea that the last, best dependence is to be upon Humanity itself, and its own inherent, normal, full-grown qualities, without any superstitious support whatever. This idea of perfect individualism it is indeed that deepest tinges and gives character to the idea of the Aggregate. For it is mainly or altogether to serve independent separatism that we favor a strong generalization, consolidation. As it is to give the best vitality and freedom to the rights of the States, (every bit as important as the right of Nationality, the union,) that we insist on the identity of the Union at all hazards.

The purpose of Democracy—supplanting old belief in the necessary absoluteness of established dynastic rulership, temporal, ecclesiastical, and scholastic, as furnishing the only security against chaos, crime, and ignorance—is, through many transmigrations, and amid endless ridicules,

arguments, and ostensible failures, to illustrate, at all hazards, this doctrine or theory that man, properly trained in sanest, highest freedom, may
and must become a law, and series of laws, unto himself, surrounding and
providing for, not only his own personal control, but all his relations to
other individuals, and to the State; and that, while other theories, as in
the past histories of nations, have proved wise enough, and indispensable
perhaps for their conditions, *this,* as matters now stand in our civilized
world, is the only Scheme worth working for, as warranting results like
those of Nature's laws, reliable, when once established, to carry on themselves. * * *

As to the political section of Democracy, which introduces and breaks
ground for further and vaster sections, few probably are the minds, even
in These Republican States, that fully comprehend the aptness of that
phrase, 'THE GOVERNMENT OF THE PEOPLE, BY THE PEOPLE, FOR THE PEO-
PLE,' which we inherit from the lips of Abraham Lincoln; a formula whose
verbal shape is homely wit, but whose scope includes both the totality and
all minutiae of the lesson.

The People! Like our huge earth itself, which, to ordinary scansion, is
full of vulgar contradictions and offence, Man, viewed in the lump, dis-
pleases, and is a constant puzzle and affront to the merely educated
classes. The rare, cosmical, artist-mind, lit with the Infinite, alone confronts his manifold and oceanic qualities, but taste, intelligence and culture, (so-called,) have been against the masses, and remain so. There is
plenty of glamour about the most damnable crimes and hoggish mean-
nesses, special and general, of the Feudal and dynastic world over there,
with its *personnel* of lords and queens and courts, so well-dressed and so
handsome. But the People are ungrammatical, untidy, and their sins
gaunt and ill-bred. * * *

I know nothing more rare, even in this country, than a fit scientific estimate and reverent appreciation of the People—of their measureless
wealth of latent power and capacity, their vast, artistic contrasts of lights
and shades—with, in America, their entire reliability in emergencies, and
a certain breadth of historic grandeur, of peace or war, far surpassing all
the vaunted samples of book-heroes, or any *haut ton* coteries, in all the
records of the world.

The movements of the late Secession war, and their results, to any sense
that studies well and comprehends them, show that Popular Democracy,
whatever its faults and dangers, practically justifies itself beyond the
proudest claims and wildest hopes of its enthusiasts. Probably no future
age can know, but I well know, how the gist of this fiercest and most resolute of the world's warlike contentions resided exclusively in the un-
named, unknown rank and file; and how the brunt of its labor of death was,

to all essential purposes, Volunteered. The People, of their own choice, fighting, dying for their own idea, insolently attacked by the Secession-Slave-Power, and its very existence imperiled. Descending to detail, entering any of the armies, and mixing with the private soldiers, we see and have seen august spectacles. We have seen the alacrity with which the American-born populace, the peaceablest and most good-natured race in the world, and the most personally independent and intelligent, and the least fitted to submit to the irksomeness and exasperation of regimental discipline, sprang, at the first tap of the drum, to arms—not for gain, nor even glory, nor to repel invasion—but for an emblem, a mere abstraction— for the life, *the safety of the Flag.* We have seen the unequaled docility and obedience of these soldiers. We have seen them tried long and long by hopelessness, mismanagement, and by defeat; have seen the incredible slaughter toward or through which the armies (as at first Fredericksburg, and afterward at the Wilderness,) still unhesitatingly obeyed orders to advance. We have seen them in trench, or crouching behind breastwork, or tramping in deep mud, or amid pouring rain or thick-falling snow, or under forced marches in hottest summer (as on the road to get to Gettysburg)— vast suffocating swarms, divisions, corps, with every single man so grimed and black with sweat and dust, his own mother would not have known him—his clothes all dirty, stained and torn, with sour, accumulated sweat for perfume—many a comrade, perhaps a brother, sun-struck, staggering out, dying, by the roadside, of exhaustion—yet the great bulk bearing steadily on, cheery enough, hollow-bellied from hunger, but sinewy with unconquerable resolution. * * *

What have we here, if not, towering above all talk and argument, the plentifully-supplied, last-needed proof of Democracy, in its personalities? Curiously enough, too, the proof on this point comes, I should say, every bit as much from the South, as from the North. Although I have spoken only of the latter, yet I deliberately include all. Grand, common stock! to me the accomplished and convincing growth, prophetic of the future; proof undeniable to sharpest sense, of perfect beauty, tenderness and pluck, that never Feudal Lord, nor Greek, nor Roman breed, yet rivaled. * * *

I, as Democrat, see clearly enough, (as already illustrated,) the crude, defective streaks in all the strata of the common people; the specimens and vast collections of the ignorant, the credulous, the unfit and uncouth, the incapable, and the very low and poor. The eminent person just mentioned, sneeringly asks whether we expect to elevate and improve a Nation's politics by absorbing such morbid collections and qualities therein. The point is a formidable one, and there will doubtless always be numbers of solid and reflective citizens who will never get over it. Our answer is general, and is involved in the scope and letter of this essay. We believe the ulterior object of political and all other government, (having, of course, provided for the police, the safety of life, property, and for the basic statute and common law, and their administration, always first in order,) to be, among the rest, not merely to rule, to repress disorder, etc., but to develop, to open up to cultivation, to encourage the possibilities of all beneficent and manly outcroppage, and of that aspiration for independence, and the pride and self-respect latent in all characters. (Or, if there be exceptions, we cannot, fixing our eyes on them alone, make theirs the rule for all.)

I say the mission of government, henceforth, in civilized lands, is not repression alone, and not authority alone, not even of law, nor by that favorite standard of the eminent writer, the rule of the best men, the born heroes and captains of the race, (as if such ever, or one time out of a hundred, got into the big places, elective or dynastic!)—but, higher than the highest arbitrary rule, to train comunities through all their grades, beginning with individuals and ending there again, to rule themselves. * * *

To be a voter with the rest is not so much; and this, like every institute, will have its imperfections. But to become an enfranchised man, and now, impediments removed, to stand and start without humiliation, and equal with the rest; to commence, or have the road cleared to commence, the grand experiment of development, whose end, (perhaps requiring several generations,) may be the forming of a full-grown man or woman— that is something. To ballast the State is also secured, and in our times is to be secured, in no other way.

We do not, (at any rate I do not,) put it either on the ground that the People, the masses, even the best of them, are, in their latent or exhibited qualities, essentially sensible and good—nor on the ground of their rights; but that, good or bad, rights or no rights, the Democratic formula is the only safe and preservative one for coming times. We endow the masses with the suffrage for their own sake, no doubt; then, perhaps still more, from another point of view, for community's sake. * * *

I say of all dangers to a Nation, as things exist in our day, there can be no greater one than having certain portions of the people set off from the rest by a line drawn—they not privileged as others, but degraded, humiliated, made of no account. Much quackery teems, of course, even on Democracy's side, yet does not really affect the orbic quality of the matter. To work in, if we may so term it, and justify God, his divine aggregate, the People, (or, the veritable horned and sharp-tailed Devil, *his* aggregate, if there be who convulsively insist upon it,)—this, I say, is what Democracy is for; and this is what our America means, and is doing—may I not say, has done? * * *

And, truly, whatever may be said in the way of abstract argument, for or against the theory of a wider democratizing of institutions in any civilized country, much trouble might well be saved to all European lands by recognizing this palpable fact, (for a palpable fact it is,) that some form of such democratizing is about the only resource now left. * * *

The eager and often inconsiderate appeals of reformers and revolutionists are indispensable to counter-balance the inertness and fossilism making so large a part of human institutions. The latter will always take care of themselves—the danger being that they rapidly tend to ossify us. The former is to be treated with indulgence, and even respect. As circulation to air, so is agitation and a plentiful degree of speculative license to political and moral sanity. Indirectly, but surely, goodness, virtue, law, (of the very best,) follow Freedom. These, to Democracy, are what the keel is to the ship, or saltness to the ocean.

The true gravitation-hold of Liberalism in the United States will be a more universal ownership of property, general homesteads, general comfort—a vast, intertwining reticulation of wealth. As the human frame, or, indeed, any object in this manifold Universe, is best kept together by the simple miracle of its own cohesion, and the necessity, exercise and profit thereof, so a great and varied Nationality, occupying millions of square miles, were firmest held and knit by the principle of the safety and endurance of the aggregate of its middling property owners.

So that, from another point of view, ungracious as it may sound, and a paradox after what we have been saying, Democracy looks with suspicious, ill-satisfied eye upon the very poor, the ignorant, and on those out of business. She asks for men and women with occupations, well-off, owners of houses and acres, and with cash in the bank—and with some cravings for literature, too; and must have them, and hastens to make them. Luckily, the seed is already well-sown, and has taken ineradicable root. * * *

Political Democracy, as it exists and practically works in America, with all its threatening evils, supplies a training-school for making grand young men. It is life's gymnasium, not of good only, but of all. We try often, though we fall back often. A grave delight, fit for freedom's athletes, fills these arenas, and fully satisfies, out of the action in them, irrespective of success. Whatever we do not attain, we at any rate attain the experiences of the fight, the hardening of the strong campaign, and throb with currents of attempt at least. Time is ample. Let the victors come after us. Not for nothing does evil play its part among men. Judging from the main portions of the history of the world, so far, justice is always in jeopardy, peace walks amid hourly pitfalls, and of slavery, misery, meanness, the craft of tyrants and the credulity of the populace, in some of their protean forms, no voice can at any time say, They are not. The clouds break a little, and the sun shines out—but soon and certain the lowering darkness falls again, as if to last forever. Yet is there an immortal courage and prophecy in every sane soul that cannot, must not, under any circumstances, capitulate. *Vive,* the attack—the perennial assault! *Vive,* the unpopular cause—the spirit that audaciously aims—the never-abandoned efforts, pursued the same amid opposing proofs and precedents. * * *

The average man of a land at last only is important. He, in These States, remains immortal owner and boss, deriving good uses, somehow, out of any sort of servant in office, even the basest; because, (certain universal requisites, and their settled regularity and protection, being first secured,) a Nation like ours, in a sort of geological formation state, trying continually new experiments, choosing new delegations, is not served by the best men only, but sometimes more by those that provoke it—by the combats they arouse. Thus national rage, fury, discussion, etc., better than content. Thus, also, the warning signals, invaluable for after times.

What is more dramatic than the spectacle we have seen repeated, and doubtless long shall see—the popular judgment taking the successful candidates on trial in the offices—standing off, as it were, and observing them and their doings for a while, and always giving, finally, the fit, exactly due reward?

I think, after all, the sublimest part of political history, and its culmination, is currently issuing from the American people. I know nothing grander, better exercise, better digestion, more positive proof of the past, the triumphant result of faith in humankind, than a well-contested American national election. * * *

As I perceive, the tendencies of our day, in The States, (and I entirely respect them,) are toward those vast and sweeping movements, influences, moral and physical, of humanity, now and always current over the planet, on the scale of the impulses of the elements. Then it is also good to reduce the whole matter to the consideration of a single self, a man, a woman, on permanent grounds. Even for the treatment of the universal, in politics, metaphysics, or anything, sooner or later we come down to one single, solitary Soul.

There is, in sanest hours, a consciousness, a thought that rises, independent, lifted out from all else, calm, like the stars, shining eternal. This is the thought of Identity—yours for you, whoever you are, as mine for me. Miracle of miracles, beyond statement, most spiritual and vaguest of earth's dreams, yet hardest basic fact, and only entrance to all facts. In such devout hours, in the midst of the significant wonders of heaven and earth, (significant only because of the Me in the centre,) creeds, conventions, fall away and become of no account before this simple idea. Under the luminousness of real vision, it alone takes possession, takes value. Like the shadowy dwarf in the fable, once liberated and looked upon, it expands over the whole earth, and spreads to the roof of heaven.

The quality of BEING, in the object's self, according to its own central idea and purpose, and of growing therefrom and thereto—not criticism by other standards, and adjustments thereto—is the lesson of Nature. True, the full man wisely gathers, culls, absorbs; but if, engaged disproportionately in that, he slights or overlays the precious idiocrasy and special nativity and intention that he is, the man's self, the main thing, is a failure, however wide his general cultivation. Thus, in our times, refinement and delicatesse are not only attended to sufficiently, but threaten to eat us up, like a cancer. Already, the Democratic genius watches, illpleased, these tendencies. Provision for a little healthy rudeness, savage virtue, justification of what one has in one's self, whatever it is, is demanded. Negative qualities, even deficiencies, would be a relief. Singleness and normal simplicity, and separation, amid this more and more complex, more and more artificialized, state of society—how pensively we yearn for them! how we would welcome their return!

Women in the Early Republic

ABIGAIL ADAMS

Letter to John Adams (1776)

Even in the earliest years of the republic, some women drew attention to the injustice of male authority. The wife of John Adams, Abigail Smith Adams (1744–1818) was a prolific letter writer, who maintained correspondences with many leading Revolutionary figures. A strong supporter of colonial independence and a firm opponent of slavery, Adams was also one of the earliest advocates of women's rights in America. In a letter to her husband composed at the height of the movement for independence, Adams adopted the language of the revolution in formulating her critique of male tyranny over women.

I have sometimes been ready to think that the passion for Liberty cannot be Equally Strong in the Breasts of those who have been accustomed to deprive their fellow Creatures of theirs. Of this I am certain that it is not founded upon that generous and christian principal of doing unto others as we would that others should do unto us.

I long to hear that you have declared an independency—and by the way in the new Code of Laws which I suppose it will be necessary for you to make I desire you would Remember the Ladies, and be more generous and favourable to them than your ancestors. Do not put such unlimited power into the hands of the Husbands. Remember all Men would be tyrants if they could. If particular care and attention is not paid to the Ladies we are determined to foment a Rebellion, and will not hold ourselves bound by any Laws in which we have no voice, or Representation.

That your Sex are Naturally Tyrannical is a Truth so thoroughly established as to admit of no dispute, but such of you as wish to be happy willingly give up the harsh title of Master for the more tender and endearing one of Friend. Why then, not put it out of the power of the vicious and the Lawless to use us with cruelty and indignity with impunity. Men of Sense in all Ages abhor those customs which treat us only as the vassals of your Sex. Regard us then as Beings placed by providence under your protection and in imitation of the Supreme Being make use of that power only for our happiness.

JUDITH SARGENT STEVENS MURRAY
(CONSTANTIA)

On the Equality of the Sexes (1790)

"Constantia" was the pen name used by the Massachusetts essayist and poet Judith Sargent Stevens Murray (1751–1820), a patriotic supporter of the Revolutionary War who established the first Universalist congregation in Boston with her husband, John Murray. An early advocate of economic reforms that would make women more self-sufficient, Murray believed that social practices reinforced harmful stereotypes and perpetuated inequality between the sexes. In this selection from an essay that appeared in the Massachusetts Magazine, Murray proposed—much as did Mary Wollstonecraft, her English contemporary—that any observable intellectual differences between men and women were the result of unequal educational opportunities that stunted the intellectual growth of women.

May not the intellectual powers be ranged under these four heads— imagination, reason, memory, and judgment. The province of imagination hath long since been surrendered up to us, and we have been crowned undoubted sovereigns of the regions of fancy. Invention is perhaps the most arduous effort of the mind; this branch of imagination hath been particularly ceded to us, and we have been time out of mind invested with that creative faculty. Observe the variety of fashions (here I bar the contemptuous smile) which distinguish and adorn the female world; how continually they are changing, insomuch that they almost render the wise man's assertion problematical, and we are ready to say, *there is something new under the sun.* Now what a playfulness, what an exuberance of fancy, what strength of inventive imagination, doth this continual variation discover? Again, it hath been observed, that if the turpitude of the conduct of our sex, hath been ever so enormous, so extremely ready are we, that the very first thought presents with an apology, so plausible, as to produce our actions even in an amiable light. Another instance of our creative powers, is our talent for slander; how ingenious are we at inventive scandal? what a formidable story can we in a moment fabricate merely from the force of a prolifick imagination? how many reputations, in the fertile brain of a female, have been utterly despoiled? how industrious are we at improving a hint? suspicion how easily do we convert into conviction, and conviction, embellished by the power of eloquence, stalks abroad to the surprise and confusion of unsuspecting innocence. Perhaps it will be asked if I furnish these facts as instances of excellency in our sex. Certainly not; but as proofs of a creative faculty, of a lively imagination. Assuredly great activity of mind is thereby discovered, and was this activity properly directed, what beneficial effects would follow. Is the needle and kitchen sufficient to employ the operations of a soul thus organized? I should conceive not. Nay, it is a truth that those very departments leave the intelligent principle vacant, and at liberty for speculation. Are we deficient in reason? we can only reason from what we know, and if an opportunity of acquiring knowledge hath been denied us, the inferiority of our sex cannot fairly be deduced from thence. Memory, I believe, will be allowed us in common, since every one's experience must testify, that a loquacious old woman is as frequently met with, as a communicative old man; their subjects are alike drawn from the fund of other times, and the transactions of their youth, or of maturer life, entertain, or perhaps fatigue you, in the evening of their lives. "But our judgment is not so strong—we do not distinguish so well."—Yet it may be questioned, from what doth this superiority, in this determining faculty of the soul, proceed. May we not trace its source in the difference of education, and continued advantages? Will it be said that the judgment of a male of two years old, is more sage than that of a female of the same age? I believe the reverse is generally observed to be true. But from that period what partiality! how is the one exalted, and the other depressed, by the contrary modes of education which are adopted! the one is taught to aspire, and the other is early confined and limited. As their years increase, the sister must be wholly domesticated, while the brother is led by the hand through all the flowery paths of science. Grant that their minds are by nature equal, yet who shall wonder at the *apparent* superiority, if indeed custom becomes *second nature*; nay if it taketh the place of nature, and that it doth the experience of each day will evince. At length arrived at womanhood, the uncultivated fair one feels a void, which the employments allotted her are by no means capable of filling. What can she do? to books she may not apply; or if she doth, *to those only of the novel kind*, lest she merit the appellation of a *learned lady*; and what ideas have been affixed to this term, the observation of many can testify. Fashion, scandal, and sometimes what is still more reprehensible, are then called in to her relief; and who can say to what lengths the liberties she takes may proceed. Meantime she herself is most un happy; she feels the want of a cultivated mind. Is she single, she in vain seeks to fill up time from sexual employments or amusements. Is she united to a person whose soul nature made equal to her own, education hath set him so far above her, that in those entertainments which are productive of such rational felicity, she is not qualified to accompany him. She experiences a mortifying consciousness of inferiority, which embitters every enjoyment. Doth the person to whom her adverse fate hath consigned her, possess a mind incapable of improvement, she is equally wretched, in being so closely connected with an individual whom she cannot but despise. Now, was she permitted the same instructors as her brother (with an eye however to their particular departments) for the employment of a rational mind an ample field would be opened. * * *

Will it be urged that those acquirements would supersede our domestick duties. I answer that every requisite in female economy is easily attained; and, with truth I can add, that when once attained, they require no further *mental attention*. Nay, while we are pursuing the needle, or the superintendency of the family, I repeat, that our minds are at full liberty for reflection; that imagination may exert itself in full vigor; and that if a just foundation is early laid, our ideas will then be worthy of rational beings. If we were industrious we might easily find time to arrange them upon paper, or should avocations press too hard for such an indulgence, the hours allotted for conversation would at least become more refined and rational. Should it still be vociferated, "Your domestick employments are sufficient"—I would calmly ask, is it reasonable, that a candidate for immortality, for the joys of heaven, an intelligent being, who is to spend an eternity in contemplating the works of Deity, should at present be so degraded, as to be allowed no other ideas, than those which are suggested by the mechanism of a pudding, or the sewing the seams of a garment? Pity that all such censurers of female improvement do not go one step further, and deny their future existence; to be consistent they surely ought.

Yes, ye lordly, ye haughty sex, our souls are by nature *equal* to yours; the same breath of God animates, enlivens, and invigorates us; and that we are not fallen lower than yourselves, let those witness who have greatly towered above the various discouragements by which they have been so heavily oppressed; and though I am unacquainted with the list of celebrated characters on either side, yet from the observations I have made in the contracted circle in which I have moved, I dare confidently believe, that from the commencement of time to the present day, there hath been as many females, as males, who, by the *mere force of natural powers*, have merited the crown of applause; who, *thus unassisted*, have seized the wreath of fame.

ANGELINA GRIMKÉ

Letter to Catharine E. Beecher (1837)

Angelina (Emily) Grimké (1805–1879) was a white abolitionist from South Carolina who crusaded against slavery after joining the Quakers and moving to the North in her twenties. Along with her sister Sarah, Angelina became involved in the women's rights movement after a letter from the General Association of Congregational Ministers of Massachusetts criticized her for "unwomanly" behavior in lecturing against slavery before mixed audiences. In her Letters to Catharine Beecher, a series first published in The Liberator and in The Emancipator, Angelina Grimké linked the abolitionist and women's rights causes as part of a larger struggle for human rights in which all persons are treated as "moral beings."

LETTER XII

The investigation of the rights of the slave has led me to a better understanding of my own. I have found the Anti-Slavery cause to be the high school of morals in our land—the school in which *human rights* are more fully investigated, and better understood and taught, than in any other. Here a great fundamental principle is uplifted and illuminated, and from this central light, rays innumerable stream all around. Human beings have *rights*, because they are *moral* beings: the rights of *all* men grow out of their moral nature; and as all men have the same moral nature, they have essentially the same rights. These rights may be wrested from the slave, but they cannot be alienated: his title to himself is as perfect *now*, as is that of Lyman Beecher: it is stamped on his moral being, and is, like it, imperishable. Now if rights are founded in the nature of our moral being, then the *mere circumstance of sex* does not give to man higher rights and responsibilities, than to woman. To suppose that it does, would be to deny the self-evident truth, that the "physical constitution is the mere instrument of the moral nature." To suppose that it does, would be to break up utterly the relations, of the two natures, and to reverse their functions, exalting the animal nature into a monarch, and humbling the moral into a slave; making the former a proprietor, and the latter its property. When human beings are regarded as *moral* beings, *sex*, instead of being enthroned upon the summit, administering upon rights and responsibilities, sinks into insignificance and nothingness. My doctrine then is, that whatever it is morally right for man to do, it is morally right for woman to do. Our duties originate, not from difference of sex, but from the diversity of our relations in life, the various gifts and talents committed to our care, and the different eras in which we live.

This regulation of duty by the mere circumstance of sex, rather than by the fundamental principle of moral being, has led to all that multifarious train of evils flowing out of the anti-christian doctrine of masculine and feminine virtues. By this doctrine, man has been converted into the warrior, and clothed with sternness, and those other kindred qualities, which in common estimation belong to his character as a *man*; whilst woman has been taught to lean upon an arm of flesh, to sit as a doll arrayed in "gold, and pearls, and costly array," to be admired for her personal charms, and caressed and humored like a spoiled child, or converted into a mere drudge to suit the convenience of her lord and master. * * * This principle has given to man a charter for the exercise of tyranny and self-ishness, pride and arrogance, lust and brutal violence. It has robbed woman of essential rights, the right to think and speak and act; the right to share their responsibilities, perils, and toils; the right to fulfil the great end of her being, as a moral, intellectual and immortal creature, and of glorifying God in her body and her spirit which are His. Hitherto, instead of being a helpmeet to man, as a companion, a co-worker, an equal; she has been a mere appendage of his being, an instrument of his convenience and pleasure, the pretty toy with which he w[h]iled away his leisure moments, or the pet animal whom he humored into playfulness and submission. Woman, instead of being regarded as the equal of man, has uniformly been looked down upon as his inferior, a mere gift to fill up the measure of his happiness. In the poetry of romantic gallantry," it is true, she has been called "the last *best* gift of God to man;" but I believe I speak forth the words of truth and soberness when I affirm, that woman never was given to man. She was created, like him, in the image of God, and crowned with glory and honor; created only a little lower than the angels,—not, as is almost universally assumed, a little lower than man; on her brow, as well as on his, was placed the "diadem of beauty," and in her hand the sceptre of universal dominion. Gen: i. 27, 28. "The last *best* *gift* of God to Man!" Where is the scripture warrant for this "rhetorical flourish, this splendid absurdity?" Let us examine the account of her creation. "And the rib which the Lord God had taken from man, made he a woman, and brought her unto the man." Not as a gift—for Adam immediately recognized her *as a part of himself*—("this is now bone of my bone, and flesh of my flesh")—a companion and equal, not one hair's breadth beneath him in the majesty and glory of her moral being; not placed under his authority as a *subject*, but by his side, on the same platform of human rights, under the government of God only. This idea of woman's being "the last best gift of God to man," however pretty it may sound to the ears of those who love to discourse upon "the poetry of romantic chivalry," has nevertheless been the means of sinking her from an *end* into a mere *means*—of turning her into an *appendage* to man, instead of recognizing her as *a part of man*—of destroying her individuality, and rights, and responsibilities, and merging her moral being in that of man. Instead of *Jehovah* being *her* king, *her* lawgiver, and *her* judge, she has been taken out of the exalted scale of existence in which He placed her, and subjected to the despotic control of man.

I have often been amused at the vain efforts made to define the rights and responsibilities of immortal beings as *men* and *women*. No one has yet found out just where the line of separation between them should be drawn, and for this simple reason, that no one knows just how far below man woman is, whether she be a head shorter in her moral responsibilities, or head and shoulders, or the full length of his noble stature, below him, i.e. under his feet. Confusion, uncertainty, and great inconsistencies, must exist on this point, so long as woman is regarded in the least degree inferior to man; but place her where her Maker placed her, on the same high level of human rights with man, side by side with him, and difficulties vanish, the mountains of perplexity flow down at the presence of this grand equalizing principle. Measure her rights and duties by the unerring standard of *moral being*, not by the false weights and measures of a mere circumstance of her human existence, and then the truth will be self-evident, that whatever it is *morally* right for a man to do, it is *morally* right for a woman to do. I recognize no rights but *human* rights—I know nothing of men's rights and women's rights; for in Christ Jesus, there is neither male nor female. It is my solemn conviction, that, until this principle of equality is recognised and embodied in practice, the Church can do nothing effectual for the permanent reformation of the world. Woman was the first transgressor, and the first victim of power. In all heathen nations, she has been the slave of man, and Christian nations have never acknowledged her rights. Nay more, no Christian denomination or Society has ever acknowledged them on the broad basis of humanity. I know that in some denominations, she is permitted to preach the gospel; not from the conviction of her rights, nor upon the ground of her equality as a *human being*, but of her equality in spiritual gifts—for we find that woman, even in these Societies, is allowed no voice in framing the Discipline by which she is to be governed. Now, I believe it is woman's right to have a voice in all the laws and regulations by which she is to be *governed*, whether in Church or State; and that the present arrangements of society, on these points, are *a violation of human rights, a rank usurpation of power*, a violent seizure and confiscation of what is sacredly and inalienably hers— thus inflicting upon woman outrageous wrongs, working mischief incalculable in the social circle, and in its influence on the world producing only evil, and that continually. *If* Ecclesiastical and Civil governments are ordained of God, *then* I contend that woman has just as much right to sit in solemn counsel in Conventions, Conferences, Associations and General Assemblies, as man—just as much right to sit upon the throne of England, or in the Presidential chair of the United States.

Dost thou ask me, if I would wish to see woman engaged in the contention and strife of sectarian controversy, or in the intrigues of political partizans? I say no! never—never. I rejoice that she does not stand on the same platform which man now occupies in these respects; but I mourn, also, that he should thus prostitute his higher nature, and vilely cast away his birthright. I prize the purity of *his* character as highly as I do that of hers. As a moral being, *whatever it is morally wrong for her to do, it is morally wrong for him to do.* The fallacious doctrine of male and female virtues has well nigh ruined all that is morally great and lovely in his character: he has been quite as deep a sufferer by it as woman, though mostly in different respects and by other processes. * * *

Thou sayest, "an ignorant, a narrow-minded, or a stupid woman, cannot feel nor understand the rationality, the propriety, of the beauty of this relation"—i.e. subordination to man. Now, verily, it does appear to me, that nothing but a narrow-minded view of the subject of human rights and responsibilities can induce any one to believe in *this subordination to a fallible* being. Sure I am, that the signs of the times clearly indicate a vast and rapid change in public sentiment, on this subject. Sure I am that she is not to be, as she has been, "*a mere second-hand agent*" in the regeneration of a fallen world. Not that "she will carry her measures by tormenting when she cannot please, or by petulant complaints or obtrusive interference, in matters which are out of her sphere, and which she cannot comprehend." But just in proportion as her moral and intellectual capacities become enlarged, she will rise higher and higher in the scale of creation, until she reaches that elevation prepared for her by her Maker, and upon whose summit she was originally stationed, only "a little lower than the angels." Then will it be seen that nothing which concerns the well-being of mankind is either beyond her sphere, or above her comprehension: *Then* will it be seen "that America will be distinguished above all other nations for well educated women, and for the influence they will exert on the general interests of society."

SARAH M. GRIMKÉ

Letters on the Equality of the Sexes and the Condition of Woman (1837)

Like her sister Angelina, Sarah (Moore) Grimké (1792–1873) became a Quaker abolitionist who helped pioneer the women's rights movement during the nineteenth century. Sarah and her sister lectured against slavery as the first female agents of the American Anti-Slavery Society. In her abolitionist writings, Sarah encouraged Southern women to use moral suasion to help abolish slavery. In a series of letters written to Mary S. Parker, the president of the Boston Female Anti-Slavery Society, Sarah explained her view that women are entitled to the same rights and privileges as men, since both were created in the image of God and are subject only to His divine law.

LETTER III

Haverhill, 7th Mo. 1837

D EAR FRIEND,—When I last addressed thee, I had not seen the Pastoral Letter of the General Association. It has since fallen into my hands, and I must digress from my intention of exhibiting the condition of women in different parts of the world, in order to make some remarks on this extraordinary document. I am persuaded that when the minds of men and women become emancipated from the thraldom of superstition and 'traditions of men,' the sentiments contained in the Pastoral Letter will be recurred to with as much astonishment as the opinions of Cotton Mather and other distinguished men of his day, on the subject of witchcraft; nor will it be deemed less wonderful, that a body of divines should gravely assemble and endeavor to prove that woman has no right to 'open her mouth for the dumb,' than it now is that judges should have sat on the trials of witches, and solemnly condemned nineteen persons and one dog to death for witchcraft.

But to the letter. It says, 'We invite your attention to the dangers which at present seem to threaten the FEMALE CHARACTER with widespread and permanent injury.' I rejoice that they have called the attention of my sex to this subject, because I believe if woman investigates it, she will soon discover that danger is impending, though from a totally different source from that which the Association apprehends,—danger from those who, having long held the reins of *usurped* authority, are unwilling to permit us to fill that sphere which God created us to move in, and who have entered into league to crush the immortal mind of woman. I rejoice, because I am persuaded that the rights of woman, like the rights of slaves, need only be examined to be understood and asserted, even by some of those, who are now endeavoring to smother the irrepressible desire for mental and spiritual freedom which glows in the breast of many, who hardly dare to speak their sentiments.

'The appropriate duties and influence of women are clearly stated in the New Testament. Those duties are unobtrusive and private, but the sources of *mighty power*. When the mild, *dependent*, softening influence of woman upon the sternness of man's opinions is fully exercised, society feels the effects of it in a thousand ways.' No one can desire more earnestly than I do, that woman may move exactly in the sphere which her Creator has assigned her; and I believe her having been displaced from that sphere has introduced confusion into the world. It is, therefore, of vast importance to herself and to all the rational creation, that she should ascertain what are her duties and her privileges as a responsible and immortal being. The New Testament has been referred to, and I am willing to abide by its decisions, but must enter my protest against the false translation of some passages by the MEN who did that work, and against the perverted interpretation by the MEN who undertook to write commentaries thereon. I am inclined to think, when we are admitted to the honor of studying Greek and Hebrew, we shall produce some various readings of the Bible a little different from those we now have.

The Lord Jesus defines the duties of his followers in his Sermon on the Mount. He lays down grand principles by which they should be governed, without any reference to sex or condition.—'Ye are the light of the world. A city that is set on a hill cannot be hid. Neither do men light a candle and put it under a bushel, but on a candlestick, and it giveth light unto all that are in the house. Let your light so shine before men, that they may see your good works, and glorify your Father which is in Heaven.' I follow him through all his precepts, and find him giving the same directions to women as to men, never even referring to the distinction now so strenuously insisted upon between masculine and feminine virtues: this is one of the anti-christian 'traditions of men' which are taught instead of the commandments of God. men and women were CREATED EQUAL; they are both moral and accountable beings, and whatever is *right* for man to do, is *right* for woman.

But the influence of woman, says the Association, is to be private and unobtrusive; her light is not to shine before man like that of her brethren; but she is passively to let the lords of the creation, as they call themselves, put the bushel over it, lest peradventure it might appear that the world has been benefitted by the rays of *her* candle. So that her quenched light, according to their judgment, will be of more use than if it were set on the candlestick. 'Her influence is the source of mighty power.' This has ever been the flattering language of man since he laid aside the whip as a means to keep woman in subjection. He spares her body; but the war he has waged against her mind, her heart, and her soul, has been no less destructive to her as a moral being. How monstrous, how anti-christian, is the doctrine that woman is to be dependent on man! Where, in all the sacred Scriptures, is this taught? Alas! she has too well learned the lesson, which MAN has labored to teach her. She has surrendered her dearest RIGHTS, and been satisfied with the privileges which man has assumed to grant her; she has been amused with the show of power, whilst man has absorbed all the reality into himself. He has adorned the creature whom God gave him as a companion, with baubles and gewgaws, turned her attention to personal attractions, offered incense to her vanity, and made her the instrument of his selfish gratification, a plaything to please his eye and amuse his hours of leisure. 'Rule by obedience and by submission sway,' or in other words, study to be a hypocrite, pretend to submit, but gain your point, has been the code of household morality which woman has been taught. The poet has sung, in sickly strains, the loveliness of woman's dependence upon man, and now we find it reechoed by those who profess to teach the religion of the Bible. God says, 'Cease ye from man whose breath is in his nostrils, for wherein is he to be accounted of?' Man says, depend upon me. God says, 'HE will teach us of his ways.' Man says, believe it not, I am to be your teacher. This doctrine of dependence upon man is utterly at variance with the doctrine of the Bible. In that book I find nothing like the softness of woman, nor the sternness of man: both are equally commanded to bring forth the fruits of the Spirit, love, meekness, gentleness, &c.

But we are told, 'the power of woman is in her dependence, flowing from a consciousness of that weakness which God has given her for her protection.' If physical weakness is alluded to, I cheerfully concede the superiority; if brute force is what my brethren are claiming, I am willing to let them have all the honor they desire; but if they mean to intimate, that mental or moral weakness belongs to woman, more than to man, I utterly disclaim the charge. Our powers of mind have been crushed, as far as man could do it, our sense of morality has been impaired by his interpretation of our duties; but no where does God say that he made any distinction between us, as moral and intelligent beings.

'We appreciate,' say the Association, 'the *unostentatious* prayers and efforts of woman in advancing the cause of religion at home and abroad, in leading religious inquirers to THE PASTOR for instruction.' Several points here demand attention. If public prayers and public efforts are necessarily ostentatious, then 'Anna the prophetess, (or preacher,) who departed not from the temple, but served God with fastings and prayers night and day,' 'and spake of Christ to all them that looked for redemption in Israel,' was ostentatious in her efforts. Then, the apostle Paul encourages women to be ostentatious in their efforts to spread the gospel, when he gives them directions how they should appear, when engaged in praying, or preaching in the public assemblies. Then, the whole association of Congregational ministers are ostentatious, in the efforts they are making in preaching and praying to convert souls.

But woman may be permitted to lead religious inquirers to the pastors for instruction. Now this is assuming that all pastors are better qualified to give instruction than woman. This I utterly deny. I have suffered too keenly from the teaching of man, to lead any one to him for instruction. The Lord Jesus says,—'Come unto me and learn of men.' He points his followers to no man; and when woman is made the favored instrument of rousing a sinner to his lost and helpless condition, she has no right to substitute any teacher for Christ; all she has to do is, to turn the contrite inquirer to the 'Lamb of God which taketh away the sins of the world.' More souls have probably been lost by going down to Egypt for help, and by trusting in man in the early stages of religious experience, than by any other error. Instead of the petition being offered to God,—'Lead me in thy truth, and TEACH me, for thou art the God of my salvation,'—instead of relying on the precious promises—'What man is he that feareth the Lord? him shall HE TEACH in the way that he shall choose'—'I will instruct thee and TEACH thee in the way which thou shalt go—I will guide thee with mine eye'—the young convert is directed to go to man, as if he were in the place of God, and his instructions essential to an advancement in the path of righteousness. That woman can have but a poor conception of the privilege of being taught of God, what he alone can teach, who would turn the 'religious inquirer aside' from the fountain of living waters, where he might slake his thirst for spiritual instruction, to those broken cisterns which can hold no water, and therefore cannot satisfy the panting spirit.

The business of men and women, who are ORDAINED OF GOD to preach the unsearchable riches of Christ to a lost and perishing world, is to lead souls to Christ, and not to Pastors for instruction.

The General Association say, that 'when woman assumes the place and tone of man as a public reformer, our care and protection of her seem unnecessary; we put ourselves in self-defence against her, and her character becomes unnatural.' Here again the unscriptural notion is held up, that there is a distinction between the duties of men and women as moral beings; that what is virtue in man, is vice in woman; and women who dare to obey the command of Jehovah, 'Cry aloud, spare not, lift up thy voice like a trumpet, and show my people their transgression,' are threatened with having the protection of the brethren withdrawn. If this is all they do, we shall not even know the time when our chastisement is inflicted; our trust is in the Lord Jehovah, and in him is everlasting strength. The motto of woman, when she is engaged in the great work of public reformation should be,— 'The Lord is my light and my salvation; whom shall I fear? The Lord is the strength of my life; of whom shall I be afraid?' She must feel, if she feels rightly, that she is fulfilling one of the important duties laid upon her as an accountable being, and that her character, instead of being 'unnatural,' is in exact accordance with the will of Him to whom, and to no other, she is responsible for the talents and the gifts confided to her. As to the pretty simile, introduced into the 'Pastoral Letter,' 'If the vine whose strength and beauty is to lean upon the trellis work, and half conceal its clusters, thinks to assume the independence and the overshadowing nature of the elm,' &c. I shall only remark that it might well suit the poet's fancy, who sings of sparkling eyes and coral lips, and knights in armor clad; but it seems to me utterly inconsistent with the dignity of a Christian body, to endeavor to draw such in antiscriptural distinction between men and women. Ah! how many of my sex feel in the domination thus unrighteously exercised over them, under the gentle appellation of *protection*, that what they have leaned upon has proved a broken reed at best, and oft a spear.

Thine in the bonds of womanhood,

SARAH M. GRIMKE.

LETTER VIII

Brookline, 1837.

During the early part of my life, my lot was cast among the butterflies of the *fashionable* world; and of this class of women, I am constrained to say, both from experience and observation, that their education is miserably deficient; that they are taught to regard marriage as the one thing needful, the only avenue to distinction: hence to attract the notice and win the attentions of men, by their external charms, is the chief business of fashionable girls. They seldom think that men will be allured by intellectual acquirements, because they find, that where any mental superiority exists a woman is generally shunned and regarded as stepping out of her 'appropriate sphere,' which, in their view, is to dress, to dance, to set out to the best possible advantage her person, to read the novels which inundate the press, and which do more to destroy her character as a rational creature, than any thing else. Fashionable women regard themselves, and are regarded by men, as pretty toys or as mere instruments of pleasure; and the vacuity of mind, the heartlessness, the frivolity which is the necessary result of this false and debasing estimate of women, can only be fully understood by those who have mingled in the folly and wickedness of fashionable life; and who have been called from such pursuits by the voice of the Lord Jesus, inviting their weary and heavy laden souls to come unto Him and learn of Him, that they may find something worthy of their immortal spirit, and their intellectual powers; that they may learn the high and holy purposes of their creation, and consecrate themselves unto the service of God; and not, as is now the case, to the pleasure of man.

There is another and much more numerous class in this country, who are withdrawn by education or circumstances from the circle of fashionable amusements, but who are brought up with the dangerous and absurd idea, that *marriage* is a kind of preferment; and that to be able to keep their husband's house, and render his situation comfortable, is the end of her being. Much that she does and says and thinks is done in reference to this situation; and to be married is too often held up to the view of girls as the sine qua non of human happiness and human existence. For this purpose more than for any other, I verily believe the majority of girls are trained. This is demonstrated by the imperfect education which is bestowed upon them, and the little pains taken to cultivate their minds, after they leave school, by the little time allowed them for reading, and by the idea being constantly inculcated, that although all household concerns should be attended to with scrupulous punctuality at particular seasons, the improvement of their intellectual capacities is only a secondary consideration, and may serve as an occupation to fill up the odds and ends of time. In most families, it is considered a matter of far more consequence to call a girl off from making a pie, or a pudding, than to interrupt her whilst engaged in her studies. This mode of training necessarily exalts, in their view, the animal above the intellectual and spiritual nature, and teaches women to regard themselves as a kind of machinery, necessary to keep the domestic engine in order, but of little value as the *intelligent* companions of men.

Let no one think, from these remarks, that I regard a knowledge of housewifery as beneath the acquisition of women. Far from it: I believe that a complete knowledge of household affairs is an indispensable requisite in a woman's education,—that by the mistress of a family, whether married or single, doing her duty thoroughly and *understandingly*, the happiness of the family is increased to an incalculable degree, as well as a vast amount of time and money saved. All I complain of is, that our education consists so almost exclusively in culinary and other manual operations. I do long to see the time, when it will no longer be necessary for women to expend so many precious hours in furnishing 'a well spread table,' but that their husbands will forego some of their accustomed indulgences in this way, and encourage their wives to devote some portion of their time to mental cultivation, even at the expense of having to dine sometimes on baked potatoes, or bread and butter. * * *

The influence of women over the minds and character of *children* of both sexes, is allowed to be far greater than that of men. This being the case by the very ordering of nature, women should be prepared by education for the performance of their sacred duties as mothers and as sisters. * * *

There is another way in which the general opinion, that women are inferior to men, is manifested, that bears with tremendous effect on the laboring class, and indeed on almost all who are obliged to earn a subsistence, whether it be by mental or physical exertion—I allude to the disproportionate value set on the time and labor of men and of women. A man who is engaged in teaching, can always, I believe, command a higher price for tuition than a woman—even when he teaches the same branches, and is not in any respect superior to the woman. This I know is the case in boarding and other schools with which I have been acquainted, and it is so in every occupation in which the sexes engage indiscriminately. As for example, in tailoring, a man has twice, or three times as much for making a waistcoat or pantaloons as a woman, although the work done by each may be equally good. In those employments which are peculiar to women, their time is estimated at only half the value of that of men. A woman who goes out to wash, works as hard in proportion as a wood sawyer, or a coal heaver, but she is not generally able to make more than half as much by a day's work. The low remuneration which women receive for their work, has claimed the attention of a few philanthropists, and I hope it will continue to do so until some remedy is applied for this enormous evil. I have known a widow, left with four or five children, to provide for, unable to leave home because her helpless babes demand her attention, compelled to earn a scanty subsistence, by making coarse shirts at 12 1-2 cents a piece, or by taking in washing, for which she was paid by some wealthy persons 12 1-2 cents per dozen. All these things evince the low estimation in which woman is held. There is yet another and more disastrous consequence arising from this unscriptural information—women being educated, from the earliest childhood, to regard themselves as inferior creatures, have not that self-respect which conscious equality would engender, and hence when their virtue is assailed, they yield to temptation with facility, under the idea that it rather exalts than debases them, to be connected with a superior being.

There is another class of women in this country, to whom I can not refer, without feelings of the deepest shame and sorrow. I allude to our female slaves. Our southern cities are whelmed beneath a tide of pollution; the virtue of female slaves is wholly at the mercy of irresponsible tyrants, and women are bought and sold in our slave markets, to gratify the brutal lust of those who bear the name of Christians. In our slave States, if amid all her degradation and ignorance, a woman desires to present virtue unsullied, she is either bribed or whipped into compliance or if she dares resist her seducer, her life by the laws of some of the slave States may be, and has actually been sacrificed to the fury of disappointed passion. Where such laws do not exist, the Power which is necessarily vested in the master over his property, leaves the defenceless slave entirely at his mercy, and the sufferings of some females on this account, both physical and mental, are intense. * * *

Nor does the colored woman suffer alone: the moral purity of the whole woman is deeply contaminated. In the daily habit of seeing the virtue of her enslaved sister sacrificed without hesitancy or remorse, she looks upon the crimes of seduction and illicit intercourse without horror, and although not personally involved in the guilt, she loses that value for innocence in her own, as well as the other sex, which is one of the strongest safeguards to virtue. She lives in habitual intercourse with men, whom she knows to be polluted by licentiousness, and often is she compelled to witness in her own domestic circle, those disgusting and heart-sickening jealousies and strifes which disgraced and distracted the family of Abraham. In addition to all this, the female slaves suffer every species of degradation and cruelty which the most wanton barbarity can inflict; they are indecently divested of their clothing, sometimes tied up and severely whipped, sometimes prostrated on the earth, while their naked bodies are torn by the scorpion lash.

> *'The whip on WOMAN's shrinking flesh!*
> *Our soil yet reddening with the stains*
> *Caught from her scourging warm and fresh*

Can any American woman look at these scenes of shocking licentiousness and cruelty, and fold her hands in apathy, and say, 'I have nothing to do with slavery'? *She cannot and be guiltless.*

I cannot close this letter, without saying a few words on the benefits to be derived by men, as well as women, from the opinions I advocate relative to the equality of the sexes. Many women are now supported, in idleness and extravagance, by the industry of their husbands, fathers, or brothers, who are compelled to toll out their existance at the counting house, or in the printing office, or some other laborious occupation while the wife and daughters and sisters take no part in the support of the family and appear to think that their sole business is to spend the hard bought earnings of their male friends. I deeply regret such a state of things, because I believe that we women felt their responsibility, for the support of themselves, or their families it would add strength and dignity to their characters, and teach them more true sympathy for their husbands, than is now generally manifested—a sympathy which would be exhibited by actions as well as words. Our brethren may reject my doctrine, because it runs counter to common opinions, and because it wounds their pride; but I believe they would be 'partakers of the benefit' resulting from the Equality of the Sexes, and would find that woman, as their equal, was unspeakably more valuable than woman as their inferior, both as a moral and an intellectual being.

Thine in the bonds of womanhood,

SARAH M. GRIMKE.

CATHARINE E. BEECHER

A Treatise on Domestic Economy (1841)

A sister of the novelist Harriet Beecher Stowe and of the famous preacher Henry Ward Beecher, Catharine Beecher (1800–1878) was an important writer on women's issues during the mid-nineteenth century. She is associated with the widely held ideal of "republican motherhood," which envisioned women's role in politics as developing in her family the moral and intellectual qualities of citizenship required for the functioning of democratic institutions.

There are some reasons, why American women should feel an interest in the support of the democratic institutions of their Country, which it is important that they should consider. The great maxim, which is the basis of all our civil and political institutions, is, that "all men are created equal," and that they are equally entitled to "life, liberty, and the pursuit of happiness."

But it can readily be seen, that this is only another mode of expressing the fundamental principle which the Great Ruler of the Universe has established, as the law of His eternal government. "Thou shalt love they neighbor as theyself;" and "Whatsoever ye would that men should do to you, do ye even so to them," are the Scripture forms, by which the Supreme Lawgiver requires that each individual of our race shall regard the happiness of others, as of the same value as his own; and which forbid any institution, in private or civil life, which secures advantages to one class, by sacrificing the interests of another.

The principles of democracy, then, are identical with the principles of Christianity.

But, in order that each individual may pursue and secure the highest degree of happiness within his reach, unimpeded by the selfish interests of others, a system of laws must be established, which sustain certain relations and dependencies in social and civil life. What these relations and their attending obligations shall be, are to be determined, not with reference to the wishes and interests of a few, but solely with reference to the general good of all; so that each individual shall have his own interest, as well as the public benefit, secured by them.

For this purpose, it is needful that certain relations be sustained, which involve the duties of subordination. There must be the magistrate and the subject, one of whom is the superior, and the other the inferior. There must be the relations of husband and wife, parent and child, teacher and pupil, employer and employed, each involving the relative duties of subordination. The superior, in certain particulars, is to direct, and the inferior is to yield obedience. Society could never go forward, harmoniously, nor could any craft or profession be successfully pursued, unless these superior and subordinate relations be instituted and sustained.

But who shall take the higher, and who the subordinate, stations in social and civil life? This matter, in the case of parents and children, is decided by the Creator. He has given children to the control of parents, as their superiors, and to them they remain subordinate, to a certain age, or so long as they are members of their household. And parents can delegate such a portion of their authority to teachers and employers, as the interests of their children require.

In most other cases, in a truly democratic state, each individual is allowed to choose for himself, who shall take the position of his superior. No woman is forced to obey any husband but the one she chooses for herself; nor is she obliged to take a husband, if she prefers to remain single. So every domestic, and every artisan or laborer, after passing from parental control, can choose the employer to whom he is to accord obedience, or, if he prefers to relinquish certain advantages, he can remain without taking a subordinate place to any employer.

Each subject, also, has equal power with every other, to decide who shall be his superior as a ruler. The weakest, the poorest, the most illiterate, has the same opportunity to determine this question, as the richest, the most learned, and the most exalted.

And the various privileges that wealth secures, are equally open to all classes. Every man may aim at riches, unimpeded by any law or institution which secures peculiar privileges to a favored class, at the expense of another. Every law, and every institution, is tested by examining whether it secures equal advantages to all; and, if the people become convinced that any regulation sacrifices the good of the majority to the interests of the smaller number, they have power to abolish it.

The institutions of monarchical and aristocratic nations are based on precisely opposite principles. They secure, to certain small and favored classes, advantages, which can be maintained, only by sacrificing the interests of the great mass of the people. Thus, the throne and aristocracy of England are supported by laws and customs, which burden the lower classes with taxes, so enormous, as to deprive them of all the luxuries, and of most of the comforts, of life. Poor dwellings, scanty food, unhealthy employments, excessive labor, and entire destitution of the means and time for education, are appointed for the lower classes, that a few may live in palaces, and riot in every indulgence.

The tendencies of democratic institutions, in reference to the rights and interests of the female sex, have been fully developed in the United States; and it is in this aspect, that the subject is one of peculiar interest to American women. In this Country, it is established, both by opinion and by practice, that woman has an equal interest in all social and civil concerns; and that no domestic, civil, or political, institution, is right, which sacrifices her interest to promote that of the other sex. But in order to secure her the more firmly in all these privileges, it is decided, that, in the domestic relation, she take a subordinate station, and that, in civil and political concerns, her interests be intrusted to the other sex, without her taking any part in voting, or in making and administering laws. The result of this order of things has been fairly tested, and is thus portrayed by M. De Tocqueville, a writer, who, for intelligence, fidelity, and ability, ranks second to none.

"There are people in Europe, who, confounding together the different characteristics of the sexes, would make of man and woman, beings not only equal, but alike. They would give to both the same functions, impose on both the same duties, and grant to both the same rights. They would mix them in all things—their business, their occupations, their pleasures. It may readily be conceived that, by thus attempting to make one sex equal to the other, both are degraded; and, from so preposterous a medley of the works of Nature, nothing could ever result, but weak men and disorderly women.

"It is not thus that the Americans understand the species of democratic equality, which may be established between the sexes. They admit, that, as Nature has appointed such wide differences between the physical and moral constitutions of man and woman, her manifest design was, to give a distinct employment to their various faculties; and they hold, that improvement does not consist in making beings so dissimilar do pretty nearly the same things, but in getting each of them to fulfil their respective tasks, in the best possible manner. The Americans have applied to the sexes the great principle of political economy, which governs the manufactories of our age, by carefully dividing the duties of man from those of woman, in order that the great work of society may be the better carried on. ᚹ ᚹ ᚹ

"Thus the Americans do not think that man and woman have either the duty, or the right, to perform the same offices, but they show an equal regard for both their respective parts; and, though their lot is different, they consider both of them, as beings of equal value. They do not give to the courage of woman the same form, or the same direction, as to that of man; but they never doubt her courage: and if they hold that man and his partner ought not always to exercise their intellect and understanding in the same manner, they at least believe the understanding of the one to be as sound as that of the other, and her intellect to be as clear. Thus, then, while they have allowed the social inferiority of woman to subsist, they have done all they could to raise her, morally and intellectually, to the level of man; and, in this respect, they appear to me to have excellently understood the true principle of democratic improvement.

"As for myself, I do not hesitate to avow, that, although the women of the United States are confined within the narrow circle of domestic life, and their situation is, in some respects, one of extreme dependence, I have nowhere seen women occupying a loftier position; and if I were asked, now I am drawing to the close of this work, in which I have spoken of so many important things done by the Americans, to what the singular prosperity and growing strength of that people ought mainly to be attributed, I should reply,—*to the superiority of their women.*"

This testimony of a foreigner, who has had abundant opportunities of making a comparison, is sanctioned by the assent of all candid and intelligent men, who have enjoyed similar opportunities.

It appears, then, that, it is in America, alone, that women are raised to an equality with the other sex; and that, both in theory and practice, their interests are regarded as of equal value. They are made subordinate in station, only where a regard to their best interests demands it, while, as if in compensation for this, by custom and courtesy, they are always treated as superiors. Universally, in this Country, through every class of society, precedence is given to woman, in all the comforts, conveniences, and courtesies, of life.

In civil and political affairs, American women take no interest or concern, except so far as they sympathize with their family and personal friends; but in all cases, in which they do feel a concern, their opinions and feelings have a consideration, equal, or even superior, to that of the other sex.

In matters pertaining to the education of their children, in the selection and support of a clergyman, in all benevolent enterprises, and in all questions relating to morals or manners, they have a superior influence. In such concerns, it would be impossible to carry a point, contrary to their judgment and feelings; while an enterprise, sustained by them, will seldom fail of success.

If those who are bewailing themselves over the fancied wrongs and injuries of women in this Nation, could only see things as they are, they would know, that, whatever remnants of a barbarous or aristocratic age may remain in our civil institutions, in reference to the interests of women, it is only because they are ignorant of them, or do not use their influence to have them rectified; for it is very certain that there is nothing reasonable, which American women would unite in asking, that would not readily be bestowed.

The preceding remarks, then, illustrate the position, that the democratic institutions of this Country are in reality no other than the principles of Christianity carried into operation, and that they tend to place woman in her true position in society, as having equal rights with the other sex; and that, in fact, they have secured to American women a lofty and fortunate position, which, as yet, has been attained by the women of no other nation.

There is another topic, presented in the work of the above author, which demands the profound attention of American women.

The following is taken from that part of the Introduction to the work, illustrating the position, that, for ages, there has been a constant progress, in all civilized nations, towards the democratic equality attained in this Country.

"The various occurrences of national existence have every where turned to the advantage of democracy; all men have aided it by their exertions; those who have intentionally labored in its cause, and those who have served it unwittingly; those who have fought for it, and those who have declared themselves its opponents, have all been driven along in the same track, have all labored to one end;" "all have been blind instruments in the hands of God."

"The gradual developement of the equality of conditions, is, therefore, a Providential fact; and it possesses all the characteristics of a Divine decree: it is universal, it is durable, it constantly eludes all human interference, and all events, as well as all men, contribute to its progress." * * *

It thus appears, that the sublime and elevating anticipations which have filled the mind and heart of the religious world, have become so far developed, that philosophers and statesmen are perceiving the signs, and are predicting the approach, of the same grand consummation. There is a day advancing, "by seers predicted, and by poets sung," when the curse of selfishness shall be removed; when "scenes surpassing fable, and yet true," shall be realized; when all nations shall rejoice and be made blessed, under those benevolent influences, which the Messiah came to establish on earth.

And this is the Country, which the Disposer of events designs shall go forth as the cynosure of nations, to guide them to the light and blessedness of that day. To us is committed the grand, the responsible privilege, of exhibiting to the world, the beneficient influences of Christianity, when carried into every social, civil, and political institution; and, though we have, as yet, made such imperfect advances, already the light is streaming into the dark prison-house of despotic lands, while startled kings and sages, philosophers and statesmen, are watching us with that interest, which a career so illustrious, and so involving their own destiny, is calculated to excite. They are studying our institutions, scrutinizing our experience, and watching for our mistakes, that they may learn whether "a social revolution, so irresistible, be advantageous or prejudicial to mankind."

There are persons, who regard these interesting truths merely as food for national vanity; but evey reflecting and Christian mind, must consider it as an occasion for solemn and anxious reflection. Are we, then, a spectacle to the world? Has the Eternal Lawgiver appointed us to work out a problem, involving the destiny of the whole earth? Are such momentous interests to be advanced or retarded, just in proportion as we are faithful to our high trust? "What manner of persons, then, ought we to be," in attempting to sustain so solemn, so glorious a responsibility?

But the part to be enacted by American women, in this great moral enterprise, is the point to which special attention should here be directed.

The success of democratic institutions, as is conceded by all, depends upon the intellectual and moral character of the mass of the people. If they are intelligent and virtuous, democracy is a blessing; but if they are ignorant and wicked, it is only a curse, and as much more dreadful than any other form of civil government, as a thousand tyrants are more to be dreaded than one. It is equally conceded, that the formation of the moral and intellectual character of the young is committed mainly to the female hand. The mother forms the character of the future man; the sister bends the fibres that are hereafter to be the forest tree; the wife sways the heart, whose energies may turn for good or for evil the destinies of a nation. Let the women of a country be made virtuous and intelligent, and the men will certainly be the same. The proper education of a man decides the welfare of an individual; but educate a woman, and the interests of a whole family are secured.

If this be so, as none will deny, then to American women, more than to any others on earth, is committed the exalted privilege of extending over the world those blessed influences, which are to renovate degraded man, and "clothe all climes with beauty."

No American woman, then, has any occasion for feeling that hers is an humble or insignificant lot. The value of what an individual accomplishes, is to be estimated by the importance of the enterprise achieved, and not by the particular position of the laborer. The drops of heaven which freshen the earth, are each of equal value, whether they fall in the lowland meadow, or the princely parterre. The builders of a temple are of equal importance, whether they labor on the foundations, or toil upon the dome.

Thus, also, with those labors which are to be made effectual in the regeneration of the Earth. And it is by forming a habit of regarding the apparently insignificant efforts of each isolated laborer, in a comprehensive manner, as indispensible portions of a grand result, that the minds of all, however humble their sphere of service, can be invigorated and cheered. The woman, who is rearing a family of children; the woman, who labors in the schoolroom; the woman, who, in her retired chamber, earns, with her needle, the mite, which contributes to the intellectual and moral elevation of her Country; even the humble domestic, whose example and influence may be moulding and forming young minds, while her faithful services sustain a prosperous domestic state;—each and all may be animated by the consciousness, that they are agents in accomplishing the greatest work that ever was committed to human responsibility. It is the building of a glorious temple, whose base shall be coextensive with the bounds of the earth, whose summit shall pierce the skies, whose splendor shall beam on all lands; and those who hew the lowliest stone, as much as those who carve the highest capital, will be equally honored, when its top-stone shall be laid, with new rejoicings of the morning stars, and shoutings of the sons of God.

ELIZABETH CADY STANTON

The Seneca Falls Declaration of Sentiments and Resolutions (1848)

The leading figure in the women's rights movement of the mid-nineteenth century, Elizabeth Cady Stanton (1815–1902) first became involved in politics through the abolitionist movement. In 1848 she led the fight to secure property rights for women in New York, and helped organize the first feminist convention in America, at Seneca Falls, New York. She was the primary author of the Seneca Falls Declaration of Sentiments and Resolutions, which was modeled after the Declaration of Independence. The document was a clarion call for equal rights, equal opportunity, and equal treatment for men and women in politics, religion, and work, but its most significant proposal was for women's suffrage, a cause that Stanton pursued throughout her life.

When, in the course of human events, it becomes necessary for one portion of the family of man to assume among the people of the earth a position different from that which they have hitherto occupied, but one to which the laws of nature and of nature's God entitle them, a decent respect to the opinions of mankind requires that they should declare the causes that impel them to such a course.

We hold these truths to be self-evident: that all men and women are created equal; that they are endowed by their Creator with certain inalienable rights; that among these are life, liberty, and the pursuit of happiness; that to secure these rights governments are instituted, deriving their just powers from the consent of the governed. Whenever any form of government becomes destructive of these ends, it is the right of those who suffer from it to refuse allegiance to it, and to insist upon the institution of a new government, laying its foundation on such principles, and organizing its powers in such form, as to them shall seem most likely to effect their safety and happiness. Prudence, indeed, will dictate that governments long established should not be changed for light and transient causes; and accordingly all experience hath shown that mankind are more disposed to suffer, while evils are sufferable, than to right themselves by abolishing the forms to which they were accustomed. But when a long train of abuses and usurpations, pursuing invariably the same object evinces a design to reduce them under absolute despotism, it is their duty to throw off such government, and to provide new guards for their future security. Such has been the patient sufferance of the women under this government, and such is now the necessity which constrains them to demand the equal station to which they are entitled.

The history of mankind is a history of repeated injuries and usurpations on the part of man toward woman, having in direct object the establishment of an absolute tyranny over her. To prove this, let facts be submitted to a candid world.

He has never permitted her to exercise her inalienable right to the elective franchise.

He has compelled her to submit to laws, in the formation of which she had no voice.

He has withheld from her rights which are given to the most ignorant and degraded men—both natives and foreigners.

Having deprived her of this first right of a citizen, the elective franchise, thereby leaving her without representation in the halls of legislation, he has oppressed her on all sides.

He has made her, if married, in the eye of the law, civilly dead.

He has taken from her all right in property, even to the wages she earns.

He has made her, morally, an irresponsible being, as she can commit many crimes with impunity, provided they be done in the presence of her husband. In the covenant of marriage, she is compelled to promise obedience to her husband, he becoming, to all intents and purposes, her master—the law giving him power to deprive her of her liberty, and to administer chastisement.

He has so framed the laws of divorce, as to what shall be the proper causes, and in case of separation, to whom the guardianship of the children shall be given, as to be wholly regardless of the happiness of women—the law, in all cases, going upon a false supposition of the supremacy of man, and giving all power into his hands.

After depriving her of all rights as a married woman, if single, and the owner of property, he has taxed her to support a government which recognizes her only when her property can be made profitable to it.

He has monopolized nearly all the profitable employments, and from those she is permitted to follow, she receives but a scanty remuneration. He closes against her all the avenues to wealth and distinction which he considers most honorable to himself. As a teacher of theology, medicine, or law, she is not known.

He has denied her the facilities for obtaining a thorough education, all colleges being closed against her.

He allows her in Church, as well as State, but a subordinate position, claiming Apostolic authority for her exclusion from the ministry, and, with some exceptions, from any public participation in the affairs of the Church.

He has created a false public sentiment by giving to the world a different code of morals for men and women, by which moral delinquencies which exclude women from society, are not only tolerated, but deemed of little account in man.

He has usurped the prerogative of Jehovah himself, claiming it as his right to assign for her a sphere of action, when that belongs to her conscience and to her God.

He has endeavored, in every way that he could, to destroy her confidence in her own powers, to lessen her self-respect, and to make her willing to lead a dependent and abject life.

Now, in view of this entire disfranchisement of one-half the people of this country, their social and religious degradation—in view of the unjust laws above mentioned, and because women do feel themselves aggrieved, oppressed, and fraudulently deprived of their most sacred rights, we insist that they have immediate admission to all the rights and privileges which belong to them as citizens of the United States.

In entering upon the great work before us, we anticipate no small amount of misconception, misrepresentation, and ridicule; but we shall use every instrumentality within our power to effect our object. We shall employ agents, circulate tracts, petition the State and National legislatures, and endeavor to enlist the pulpit and the press in our behalf. We hope this Convention will be followed by a series of Conventions embracing every part of the country.

RESOLUTIONS

WHEREAS, The great precept of nature is conceded to be, that "man shall pursue his own true, and substantial happiness." Blackstone in his Commentaries remarks, that this law of Nature being coeval with mankind, and dictated by God himself, is of course superior in obligation to any other. It is binding over all the globe, in all countries and at all times; no human laws are of any validity if contrary to this, and such of them as are valid, derive all their force, and all their validity, and all their authority, mediately and immediately, from this original; therefore,

Resolved, That such laws as conflict, in any way, with the true and substantial happiness of woman, are contrary to the great precept of nature and of no validity, for this is "superior in obligation to any other."

Resolved, That all laws which prevent woman from occupying such a station in society as her conscience shall dictate, or which place her in a position inferior to that of man, are contrary to the great precept of nature, and therefore of no force or authority.

Resolved, That woman is man's equal—was intended to be so by the Creator, and the highest good of the race demands that she should be recognized as such.

Resolved, That the women of this country ought to be enlightened in regard to the laws under which they live, that they may no longer publish their degradation by declaring themselves satisfied with their present position, nor their ignorance, by asserting that they have all the rights they want.

Resolved, That in as much as man, while claiming for himself intellectual superiority, does accord to woman moral superiority, it is preeminently his duty to encourage her to speak and teach, as she has an opportunity, in all religious assemblies.

Resolved, That the same amount of virtue, delicacy, and refinement of behavior that is required of woman in the social state, should also be required of man, and the same transgressions should be visited with equal severity on both man and woman.

Resolved, That the objection of indelicacy and impropriety, which is so often brought against woman when she addresses a public audience, comes with a very ill-grace from those who encourage, by their attendance, her appearance on the stage, in the concert, or in feats of the circus.

Resolved, That woman has too long rested satisfied in the circumscribed limits which corrupt customs and a perverted application of the Scriptures have marked out for her, and that it is time she should move in the enlarged sphere which her great Creator has assigned her.

Resolved, That it is the duty of the women of this country to secure to themselves their sacred right to the elective franchise.

Resolved, That the equality of human rights results necessarily from the fact of the identity of the race in capabilities and responsibilities.

Resolved, therefore, That, being invested by the Creator with the same capabilities, and the same consciousness of responsibility for their exercise, it is demonstrably the right and duty of woman, equally with man, to promote every righteous cause by every righteous means; and especially in regard to the great subjects of morals and religion, it is self-evidently her right to participate with her brother in teaching them, both in private and in public, by writing and by speaking, by any instrumentalities proper to be used, and in any assemblies proper to be held; and this being a self-evident truth growing out of the divinely implanted principles of human nature, any custom or authority adverse to it, whether modern or wearing the hoary sanction of antiquity, is to be regarded as a self-evident falsehood, and at war with mankind.

ELIZABETH CADY STANTON

Address to the New York State Legislature (1860)

In a speech she delivered to the New York State legislature, Stanton argued that free women suffer worse degradation and oppression than Southern slaves because "the prejudice against sex is more deeply rooted and more unreasonably maintained than that against color." Instead of calling for legislation to improve the plight of women, Stanton urged legislators to remove artificial barriers to independence and "self-support."

You who had read the history of nations, from Moses down to our last election, where have you ever seen one class looking after the interests of another? Any of you can readily see the defects in other governments, and pronounce sentence against those who have sacrificed the masses to themselves; but when we come to our own case, we are blinded by custom and self-interest. Some of you who have no capital can see the injustice which the laborer suffers; some of you who have no slaves, can see the cruelty of his oppression; but who of you appreciate the galling humiliation, the refinements of degradation, to which women (the mothers, wives, sisters, and daughters of freemen) are subject, in this the last half of the nineteenth century? How many of you have ever read even the laws concerning them that now disgrace your statute-books? In cruelty and tyranny, they are not surpassed by any slaveholding code in the Southern States; in fact they are worse, by just so far as woman, from her social position, refinement, and education, is on a more equal ground with the oppressor.

Allow me just here to call the attention of that party now so much interested in the slave of the Carolinas, to the similarity in his condition and that of the mothers, wives, and daughters of the Empire State. The negro has no name. He is Cuffy Douglas or Cuffy Brooks, just whose Cuffy he may chance to be. The woman has no name. She is Mrs. Richard Roe or

Mrs. John Doe, just whose Mrs. she may chance to be. Cuffy has no right to his earnings; he can not buy or sell, or lay up anything that he can call his own. Mrs. Roe has no right to her earnings; she can neither buy nor sell, make contracts, nor lay up anything that she can call her own. Cuffy has no right to his children; they can be sold from him at any time. Mrs. Roe has no right to her children; they may be bound out to cancel a father's debts of honor. The unborn child, even, by the last will of the father, may be placed under the guardianship of a stranger and a foreigner. Cuffy has no legal existence; he is subject to restraint and moderate chastisement. Mrs. Roe has no legal existence; she has not the best right to her own person. The husband has the power to restrain, and administer moderate chastisement.

Blackstone [author of *Commentaries on the Laws of England*] declares that the husband and wife are one, and learned commentators have decided that that one is the husband. In all civil codes, you will find them classified as one. Certain rights and immunities, such and such privileges are to be secured to white male citizens. What have women and negroes to do with rights? What know they of government, war, or glory?

The prejudice against color, of which we hear so much, is no stronger than that against sex. It is produced by the same cause, and manifested very much in the same way. The negro's skin and the woman's sex are both *prima facie* evidence that they were intended to be in subjection to the white Saxon man. The few social privileges which the man gives the woman, he makes up to the negro in civil rights. The woman may sit at the same table and eat with the white man; the free negro may hold property and vote. The woman may sit in the same pew with the white man in church; the free negro may enter the pulpit and preach. Now, with the black man's right to suffrage, the right unquestioned even by Paul, to minister at the altar, it is evident that the prejudice against sex is more deeply rooted and more unreasonably maintained than that against color.

Just imagine an inhabitant of another planet entertaining himself some pleasant evening in searching over our great national compact, our Declaration of Independence, our Constitutions, or some of our statute-books; what would he think of those "women and negroes" that must be so fenced in, so guarded against? Why, he would certainly suppose we were monsters, like those fabulous giants or Brobdingnagians of olden times, so dangerous to civilized man, from our size, ferocity, and power. Then let him take up our poets, from Pope down to Dana; let him listen to our Fourth of July toasts, and some of the sentimental adultations of social life, and no logic could convince him that this creature of the law, and this angel of the family altar, could be one and the same being. Man is in such a labyrinth of contradictions with his marital and property rights; he is so befogged on the whole question of maidens, wives, and mothers, that from pure benevolence we should relieve him from this troublesome branch of legislation. We should vote, and make laws for ourselves. Do not be alarmed, dear ladies! You need spend no time reading Grotius, Coke, Puffendorf, Blackstone, Bentham, Kent, and Story to find out what you need. We may safely trust the shrewd selfishness of the white man, and consent to live under the same broad code where he has so comfortably ensconced himself. Any legislation that will do for man, we may abide by most cheerfully. * * *

Now do not think, gentlemen, we wish you to do a great many troublesome things for us. We do not ask our legislators to spend a whole session in fixing up a code of laws to satisfy a class of most unreasonable women. We ask no more than the poor devils in the Scripture asked, "Let us alone." In mercy, let us take care of ourselves, our property, our children, and our homes. True, we are not so strong, so wise, so crafty as you are, but if any kind friend leaves us a little money, or we can by great industry earn fifty cents a day, we would rather buy bread and clothes for our children than cigars and champagne for our legal protectors. There has been a great deal written and said about protection. We, as a class, are tired of one kind of protection, that which leaves us everything to do, to dare, and to suffer, and strips us of all means for its accomplishment. We would not tax man to take care of us. No, the Great Father has endowed all his creatures with the necessary powers for self support, self defense, and protection. We do not ask man to represent us; it is hard enough in times like these for man to carry backbone enough to represent himself. So long as the mass of men spend most of their time on the fence, not knowing which way to jump, they are surely in no condition to tell us where we had better stand. In pity for man, we would no longer hang like a millstone round his neck. Undo what man did for us in the dark ages, and strike out all special legislation for us; strike the words "white male" from all your constitutions, and then, with fair sailing, let us sink or swim, live or die, survive or perish together.

Slavery and Free Labor

BENJAMIN RUSH

An Address . . . Upon Slave Keeping (1773)

The anomaly of American slavery was already a concern in the Revolutionary era. Our first three selections in this section bear witness to the complex attitudes of the Founders. The Philadelphia physician Benjamin Rush (1746–1813) was a leader of the American Revolution and a close friend of Thomas Jefferson. He served as a member of the Second Continental Congress and signed the Declaration of Independence. In addition to his humanitarian efforts on behalf of insane patients and his proposals for free public education for both boys and girls, Rush prescribed remedies for the social ills of tobacco, alcohol, capital punishment, and slavery. This Enlightenment reformer refuted racist justifications for slavery and attacked it as an outrage against Christianity, against the principles of justice, and even against the economic interests of masters.

Without entering into the history of the facts which relate to the slave-trade, I shall proceed immediately to combat the principal arguments which are used to support it.

And here I need hardly say any thing in favor of the Intellects of the Negroes, or of their capacities for virtue and happiness, although these have been supposed by some to be inferior to those of the inhabitants of Europe. The accounts which travellers give us of their ingenuity, humanity, and strong attachment to their parents, relations, friends and country, show us that they are equal to the Europeans, when we allow for the diversity of temper and genius which is occasioned by climate. We have many well attested anecdotes of as sublime and disinterested virtue among them as ever adorned a Roman or a Christian character. But we are to distinguish between an African in his own country, and an African in a state of slavery in America. Slavery is so foreign to the human mind, that the moral faculties, as well as those of the understanding are debased, and rendered torpid by it. All the vices which are charged upon the Negroes in the southern colonies and the West-Indies, such as Idleness, Treachery, Theft, and the like, are the genuine offspring of slavery, and serve as an argument to prove that they were not intended, by Providence for it.

Nor let it be said, in the present Age, that their black color (as it is commonly called), either subjects them to, or qualifies them for slavery. The vulgar notion of their being descended from Cain, who was supposed to have been marked with this color, is too absurd to need a refutation.— Without enquiring into the Cause of this blackness, I shall only add upon this subject, that so far from being a curse, it subjects the Negroes to no inconveniencies, but on the contrary qualifies them for that part of the Globe in which providence has placed them. The ravages of heat, diseases and time, appear less in their faces than in a white one; and when we exclude variety of color from our ideas of Beauty, they may be said to possess every thing necessary to constitute it in common with the white people.

It has been urged by the inhabitants of the Sugar Islands and South Carolina, that it would be impossible to carry on the manufactories of Sugar, Rice, and Indigo, without Negro slaves. No manufactory can ever be of consequence enough to society, to admit the least violation of the laws of justice or humanity. But I am far from thinking the arguments used in favor of employing Negroes for the cultivation of these articles, should have any weight ⋆ ⋆ ⋆

What advantage, then, has accrued to Europe, civilized as it is, and thoroughly versed in the laws of nature, and the rights of mankind, by legally authorizing in our colonies, the daily outrages against human nature, permitting them to debase man almost below the level of the beasts of the field? These slavish laws have proved as opposite to its interest, as they are to its honor, and to the laws of humanity. This remark I have often made.

Liberty and property form the basis of abundance, and good agriculture: I never observed it to flourish where those rights of mankind were not firmly established. The earth which multiplies her productions with a kind of profusion, under the hands of the free-born laborer seems to shrink into barrenness under the sweat of the slave. Such is the will of the great Author of our Nature, who has created man free, and assigned to him the earth, that he might cultivate his possession with the sweat of his brow; but still should enjoy his Liberty.

Now if the plantations in the islands and the southern colonies were more limited, and freemen only employed in working them, the general product would be greater, although the profits to individuals would be less,—a circumstance this, which by diminishing opulence in a few, would suppress luxury and vice, and promote that equal distribution of property, which appears best calculated to promote the welfare of society. * * *

Future ages, therefore, when they read the accounts of the Slave Trade (—if they do not regard them as fabulous)——will be at a loss which to condemn most, our folly or our guilt, in abetting this direct violation of the laws of nature and religion.

But there are some who have gone so far as to say that slavery is not repugnant to the genius of Christianity, and that it is not forbidden in any part of the Scriptures. Natural and revealed Religion always speak the same things, although the latter delivers its precepts with a louder, and more distinct voice than the former. If it could be proved that no testimony was to be found in the Bible against a practice so pregnant with evils of the most destructive tendency to society, it would be sufficient to overthrow its divine original. We read it is true of Abraham's having slaves born in his house; and we have reason to believe, that part of the riches of the patriarchs consisted in them: but we can no more infer the lawfulness of the practice, from the short account which the Jewish historian gives us of these facts, than we can vindicate telling a lie, because Rahab is not condemned for it in the account which is given of her deceiving the king of Jericho. We read that some of the same men indulged themselves in a plurality of wives, without any strictures being made upon their conduct for it; and yet no one will pretend to say, that this is not forbidden in many parts of the Old Testament. * * *

But with regard to their own countrymen, it is plain, perpetual slavery was not tolerated. Hence, at the end of seven years or in the year of the jubilee, all the Hebrew slaves were set at liberty, and it was held unlawful to detain them in servitude longer than that time, except by their own consent. But if, in the partial revelation which GOD made, of his will to the Jews, we find such testimonies against slavery, what may we not expect from the Gospel, the design of which was to abolish all distinctions of name and country. While the Jews thought they complied with the precepts of the law, in confining the love of their neighbour "to the children of their own people," Christ commands us to look upon all mankind even our enemies as our neighbours and brethren, and "in all things, to do unto them whatever we would wish they should do unto us." He tells us further that his "Kingdom is not of this World," and therefore constantly avoids saying any thing that might interfere directly with the Roman or Jewish governments: so that altho' he does not call upon masters to emancipate their slaves, or upon slaves to assert that liberty wherewith God and nature had made them free, yet there is scarcely a parable or a sermon in the whole history of his life, but what contains the strongest arguments against slavery. Every prohibition of covetousness—intemperance—

pride—uncleanness—theft—and murder, which he delivered,—every lesson of meekness, humility, forbearance, charity, self-denial, and brotherly-
love which he taught, are levelled against this evil;—for slavery, while it
includes all the former vices, necessarily excludes the practice of all the
latter virtues, both from the master and the slave.—Let such, therefore,
who vindicate the traffic of buying and selling souls, seek some modern
system of religion to support it, and not presume to sanctify their crimes
by attempting to reconcile it to the sublime and perfect Religion of the
Great Author of Christianity.

There are some amongst us who cannot help allowing the force of our
last argument, but plead as a motive for importing and keeping slaves,
that they become acquainted with the principles of the religion of our
country.—This is like justifying a highway robbery because part of the
money acquired in this manner was appropriated to some religious
use.—Christianity will never be propagated by any other methods than
those employed by Christ and his apostles. Slavery is an engine as little
fitted for that purpose as fire or the sword. A Christian slave is a contradiction in terms. But if we enquire into the methods employed for converting the Negroes to Christianity, we shall find the means suited to the
end proposed. In many places Sunday is appropriated to work for themselves. Reading and writing are discouraged among them. A belief is
even inculcated among some, that they have no souls. In a word,—Every
attempt to instruct or convert them, has been constantly opposed by
their masters. Nor has the example of their Christian masters any tendency to prejudice them in favor of our religion. How often do they betray, in their sudden transports of anger and resentment (against which
there is no restraint provided towards their Negroes) the most violent
degrees of passion and fury!— What luxury—what ingratitude to the
supreme being—what impiety in their ordinary conversation do some of
them discover in the presence of their slaves; I say nothing of the dissolution of marriage vows, or the entire abolition of matrimony, which the
frequent sale of them introduces, and which are directly contrary to the
law of nature and the principles of Christianity. Would to heaven I could
here conceal the shocking violations of chastity, which some of them are
obliged to undergo without daring to complain. Husbands have been
forced to prostitute their wives, and mothers their daughters, to gratify
the brutal lust of a master. This—all—this is practised—blush—ye impure and hardened monsters, while I repeat it——by men who call
themselves Christians!

But it will be asked here, What steps shall we take to remedy this evil,
and what shall we do with those slaves we have already in this country? This
is indeed a most difficult question. But let every man contrive to answer it

for himself. If you possessed an estate which was bequeathed to you by your ancestors, and were afterwards convinced that it was the just property of another man, would you think it right to continue in the possession of it? would you not give it up immediately to the lawful owner? The voice of all mankind would mark him for a villain who would refuse to comply with this demand of justice. And is not keeping a slave after you are convinced of the unlawfulness of it—a crime of the same nature? All the money you save, or acquire by their labor is stolen from them; and however plausible the excuse may be that you form to reconcile it to your consciences, yet be assured that your crime stands registered in the court of Heaven as a breach of the eighth commandment.

The first step to be taken to put a stop to slavery in this country, is to leave off importing slaves. For this purpose let our assemblies unite in petitioning the King and Parliament to dissolve the African Company. It is by this incorporated band of robbers that the trade has been chiefly carried on to America. * * *

Let such of our countrymen as engage in the slave trade, be shunned as the greatest enemies to our country, and, let the vessels which bring the slaves to us, be avoided as if they bore in them the seeds of that forbidden fruit, whose baneful taste destroyed both the natural and moral world.——As for the Negroes among us, who, from having acquired all the low vices of slavery, or who, from age or infirmities are unfit to be set at liberty, I would propose, for the good of society, that they should continue the property of those with whom they grew old, or from whom they contracted those vices and infirmities. But let the young Negroes be educated in the principles of virtue and religion—let them be taught to read and write——and afterwards instructed in some business, whereby they may be able to maintain themselves. Let laws be made to limit the time of their servitude, and to entitle them to all the privileges of free-born British subjects. At any rate let retribution be done to God and to society.

And now my countrymen, What shall I add more to rouse up your indignation against slave-keeping. Consider the many complicated crimes it involves in it. Think of the bloody wars which are fomented by it, among the African nations, or if these are too common to affect you, think of the pangs which attend the dissolution of the ties of nature in those who are stolen from their relations. Think of the many thousands who perish by sickness, melancholy and suicide, in their voyages to America. Pursue the poor devoted victims to one of the West India islands, and see them exposed there to public sale. Hear their cries, and see their looks of tenderness at each other upon being separated.—Mothers are torn from their daughters, and brothers from brothers, without the liberty of a parting embrace. Their master's name is now marked upon their breasts with a red hot iron. But let us pursue them into a sugar field, and behold a scene still more affecting than this————See! the poor wretches with what reluctance they take their instruments of labor into their hands.—Some of them, overcome with heat and sickness, seek to refresh themselves by a little rest,——But, behold an overseer approaches them.—In vain they sue for pity.——He lifts up his whip, while streams of blood follow every stroke. Neither age nor sex are spared.—Methinks one of them is a woman far advanced in her pregnancy.—At a little distance from these behold a man, who from his countenance and deportment appears as if he was descended from illustrious ancestors.——Yes.—He is the son of a prince, and was torn, by a stratagem, from an amiable wife and two young children—Mark his sullen looks!—now he bids defiance to the tyranny of his master, and in an instant plunges a knife into his heart.—But, let us return from this Scene, and see the various modes of arbitrary punishments inflicted upon them by their masters. Behold one covered with stripes, into which melted wax is poured—another tied down to a block or a stake—a third suspended in the air by his thumbs—a fourth obliged to set or stand upon red hot iron———a fifth,————I cannot relate it.————Where now is law or justice?——Let us fly to them to step in for their relief.——   Alas!——The one is silent, and the other denounces more terrible punishments upon them. Let us attend the place appointed for inflicting the penalties of the law. See here one without a limb, whose only crime was an attempt to regain his liberty—another led to a gallows for eating a morsel of bread, to which his labor gave him a better title than his master—a third famishing on a gibbet———a fourth, in a flame of fire!—his shrieks pierce the heavens.————O! God! Where is thy vengeance!——   O! humanity—justice—liberty—religion!——Where,—where are ye fled.————

Ye men of sense and virtue————Ye advocates for American liberty, rouse up and espouse the cause of humanity and general liberty. Bear a testimony against a vice which degrades human nature, and dissolves that universal tie of benevolence which should connect all the children of men together in one great family.——The plant of liberty is of so tender a nature, that it cannot thrive long in the neighbourhood of slavery. Remember the eyes of all Europe are fixed upon you, to preserve an asylum for freedom in this country, after the last pillars of it are fallen in every other quarter of the globe.

But chiefly——ye ministers of the gospel, whose dominion over the principles and actions of men is so universally acknowledged and felt,——Ye who estimate the worth of your fellow creatures by their immortality, and therefore must look upon all mankind as equal;—let your zeal keep pace with your opportunities to put a stop to slavery. While you inforce the duties of "tithe and cummin," neglect not the weightier laws of justice and humanity. Slavery is an Hydra sin, and includes in it every violation of the precepts of the Law and the Gospel. In vain will you command your flocks to offer up the incense of faith and charity, while they continue to mingle the sweat and blood of Negro slaves with their sacrifices. * * * Remember that national crimes require national punishments, and without declaring what punishment awaits this evil, you may venture to assure them, that it cannot pass with impunity, unless God shall cease to be just or merciful.

THOMAS PAINE

African Slavery in America (1775)

Almost immediately on his arrival in Philadelphia in 1774, Paine became involved in various reform activities, including membership in the first antislavery association in America. In an anonymous article signed "Justice and Humanity," Paine denounced slavery as a hypocritical violation of natural law that invites divine retribution.

To Americans: That some desperate wretches should be willing to steal and enslave men by violence and murder for gain, is rather lamentable than strange. But that many civilized, nay, Christianized people should approve, and be concerned in the savage practice, is surprising; and still persist, though it has been so often proved contrary to the light of nature, to every principle of justice and humanity, and even good policy, by a succession of eminent men, and several late publications.

Our traders in MEN (*an unnatural commodity!*) must know the wickedness of that SLAVE-TRADE, if they attend to reasoning, or the dictates of their own hearts; and such as shun and stiffle all these, wilfully sacrifice conscience, and the character of integrity to that golden idol.

The managers of that trade themselves, and others, testify, that many of these African nations inhabit fertile countries, are industrious farmers, enjoy plenty, and lived quietly, averse to war, before the Europeans debauched them with liquors, and bribing them against one another; and that these inoffensive people are brought into slavery, by stealing them, tempting kings to sell subjects, which they can have no right to do, and hiring one tribe to war against another, in order to catch prisoners. By such wicked and inhuman ways the English are said to enslave towards one hundred thousand yearly; of which thirty thousand are supposed to die by barbarous treatment in the first year; besides all that are slain in the unnatural wars excited to take them. So much innocent blood have the managers and supporters of this inhuman trade to answer for to the common Lord of all!

Many of these were not prisoners of war, and redeemed from savage conquerors, as some plead; and they who were such prisoners, the English, who promote the war for that very end, are the guilty authors of their being so; and if they were redeemed, as is alleged, they would owe nothing to the redeemer but what he paid for them.

They show as little reason as conscience who put the matter by with saying—'Men, in some cases, are lawfully made slaves, and why may not these?' So men, in some cases, are lawfully put to death, deprived of their goods, without their consent; may any man, therefore, be treated so, without any conviction of desert? Nor is this plea mended by adding— 'They are set forth to us as slaves, and we buy them without farther inquiry, let the sellers see to it.' Such men may as well join with a known band of robbers, buy their ill-got goods, and help on the trade; ignorance is no more pleadable in one case than the other; the sellers plainly own how they obtain them. But none can lawfully buy without evidence that they are not concurring with men-stealers; and as the true owner has a right to reclaim his goods that were stolen, and sold; so the slave, who is proper owner of his freedom, has a right to reclaim it, however often sold.

Most shocking of all is alleging the sacred scriptures to favour this wicked practice. One would have thought none but infidel cavillers would endeavour to make them appear contrary to the plain dictates of natural light, and conscience, in a matter of common justice and humanity; which they cannot be. Such worthy men, as referred to before, judged otherways; Mr Baxter declared, *the slave-traders should be called devils, rather than Christians; and that it is a heinous crime to buy them.* But some say, the practice was permitted to the Jews'. To which may be replied:

1. The example of the Jews, in many things, may not be imitated by us; they had not only orders to cut off several nations altogether, but if they were obliged to war with others, and conquered them, to cut off every male; they were suffered to use polygamy and divorces, and other things utterly unlawful to us under clearer light.

2. The plea is, in a great measure, false; they had no permission to catch and enslave people who never injured them.

3. Such arguments ill become us, *since the time of reformation came,* under gospel light. All distinctions of nations, and privileges of one above others, are ceased; Christians are taught to *account all men their neighbours; and love their neighbours as themselves; and do to all men as they*

would be done by; to do good to all men; and man-stealing is ranked with enormous trimes. Is the barbarous enslaving our inoffensive neighbours, and treating them like wild beasts subdued by force, reconcilable with all these *divine precepts?* Is this doing to them as we would desire they should do to us? If they could carry off and enslave some thousands of us, would we think it just?—One would almost wish they could for once; it might convince more than reason, or the Bible.

As much in vain, perhaps, will they search ancient history for examples of the modern slave-trade. Too many nations enslaved the prisoners they took in war. But to go to nations with whom there is no war, who have no way provoked, without farther design of conquest, purely to catch inoffensive people, like wild beasts, for slaves, is an height of outrage against humanity and justice, that seems left by heathen nations to be practised by pretended Christians. How shameful are all attempts to colour and excuse it!

As these people are not convicted of forfeiting freedom, they have still a natural perfect right to it; and the governments whenever they come should in justice set them free, and punish those who hold them in slavery.

So monstrous is the making and keeping them slaves at all, abstracted from the barbarous usage they suffer, and the many evils attending the practice; as selling husbands away from wives, children from parents, and from each other, in violation of sacred and natural ties; and opening the way for adulteries, incests, and many shocking consequences, for all of which the guilty masters must answer to the final Judge.

If the slavery of the parents be unjust, much more is their children's; if the parents were justly slaves, yet the children are born free; this is the natural, perfect right of all mankind; they are nothing but a just recompense to those who bring them up: And as much less is commonly spent on them than others, they have a right, in justice, to be proportionably sooner free.

Certainly one may, with as much reason and decency, plead for murder, robbery, lewdness, and barbarity, as for this practice. They are not more contrary to the natural dictates of conscience, and feelings of humanity; nay, they are all comprehended in it.

But the chief design of this paper is not to disprove it, which many have sufficiently done, but to entreat Americans to consider.

1. With that consistency, or decency they complain so loudly of attempts to enslave them, while they hold so many hundred thousands in slavery; and annually enslave many thousands more, without any pretence of authority, or claim upon them?

2. How just, how suitable to our crime is the punishment with which providence threatens us? We have enslaved multitudes, and shed much

innocent blood in doing it; and now are threatened with the same. And while others' evils are confessed, and bewailed, why not this especially, and publicly; than which no other vice, if all others, has brought so much guilt on the land?

3. Whether, then, all ought not immediately to discontinue and renounce it, with grief and abhorrence? Should not every society bear testimony against it, and account obstinate persisters in it bad men, enemies to their country, and exclude them from fellowship; as they often do for much lesser faults?

4. The great question may be—What should be done with those who are enslaved already? To turn the old and infirm free, would be injustice and cruelty; they who enjoyed the labours of their better days should keep, and treat them humanely. As to the rest, let prudent men, with the assistance of legislatures, determine what is practicable for masters, and best for them. Perhaps some could give them lands upon reasonable rent, some, employing them in their labour still, might give them some reasonable allowances for it; so as all may have some property, and fruits of their labours at their own disposal, and be encouraged to industry; the family may live together, and enjoy the natural satisfaction of exercising relative affections and duties, with civil protection, and other advantages, like fellow men. Perhaps they might sometime form useful barrier settlements on the frontiers. Thus they may become interested in the public welfare, and assist in promoting it; instead of being dangerous, as now they are, should any enemy promise them a better condition.

5. The past treatment of Africans must naturally fill them with abhorrence of Christians; lead them to think our religion would make them more inhuman savages, if they embraced it: thus the gain of that trade has been pursued in opposition to the Redeemer's cause, and the happiness of men. Are we not, therefore, bound in duty to him and to them to repair these injuries, as far as possible, by taking some proper measures to instruct, not only the slaves here, but the Africans in their own countries? Primitive Christians laboured always to spread their *divine religion*; and this is equally our duty while there is an heathen nation. But what singular obligations are we under to these injured people!

These are the sentiments of

JUSTICE AND HUMANITY.

THOMAS JEFFERSON

Notes on the State of Virginia (1784)

Even though Jefferson often called for the abolition of slavery in Virginia and cited the slave trade as one of the grievances against King George III in his original draft of the Declaration of Independence, he owned several hundred slaves, whom he did not free at his death, as other Southerners sometimes did. In spite of his abolitionist sentiments, Jefferson shared the racial prejudices of his day. In his book Notes on the State of Virginia, *he speculates on the character of American Indians and blacks, suggesting that racial mixing would "stain" whites.*

The Indian of North America being more within our reach, I can speak of him somewhat from my own knowledge, but more from the information of others better acquainted with him, and on whose truth and judgment I can rely. From these sources I am able to say, in contradiction to this representation, that he is neither more defective in ardor, nor more impotent with his female, than the white reduced to the same diet and exercise: that he is brave, when an enterprise depends on bravery, education with him making the point of honor consist in the destruction of an enemy by strategem, and in the preservation of his own person free from injury; or perhaps this is nature; while it is education which teaches us to honor force more than finesse; that he will defend himself against an host of enemies, always choosing to be killed, rather than to surrender, though it be to the whites, who he knows will treat him well: that in other situations also he meets death with more deliberation, and endures tortures with a firmness unknown almost to religious enthusiasm with us: that he is affectionate to his children, careful of them, and indulgent in the extreme: that his affections comprehend his other connections, weakening, as with us, from circle to circle, as they recede from the center: that his friendships are strong and faithful to the uttermost extremity: that his sensibility is keen, even the warriors weeping most bitterly on the loss of their children, though in general they endeavor to appear superior to human events: that his vivacity and activity of mind is equal to ours in the same situation; hence his eagerness for hunting, and for games of chance. The women are submitted to unjust drudgery. This I believe is the case with every barbarous people. With such, force is law. The stronger sex therefore imposes on the weaker. It is civilization alone which replaces women in the enjoyment of their natural equality. That first teaches us to subdue the selfish passions, and to respect those rights in others which we value in ourselves. Were we in equal barbarism, our females would be equal drudges. The man with them is less strong than with us, but their woman stronger than ours; and both for the same obvious reason; because our man and their woman is habituated to labor, and formed by it. With both races the sex which is indulged with ease is least athletic. An Indian man is small in the hand and wrist for the same reason for which a sailor is large and strong in the arms and shoulders, and a porter in the legs and thighs.—They raise fewer children than we do. The causes of this are to be found, not in a difference of nature, but of circumstance. The women very frequently attending the men in their parties of war and of hunting, child-bearing becomes extremely inconvenient to them. It is said, therefore, that they have learnt the practice of procuring abortion by the use of some vegetable; and that it even extends to prevent conception for a considerable time after. During these parties they are exposed to numerous hazards, to excessive exertions, to the greatest extremities of hunger. Even at their homes the nation depends for food, through a certain part of every year, on the gleanings of the forest: that is, they experience a famine once in every year. With all animals, if the female be badly fed, or not fed at all, her young perish: and if both male and female be reduced to like want, generation becomes less active, less productive. To the obstacles then of want and hazard, which nature has opposed to the multiplication of wild animals, for the purpose of restraining their numbers within certain bounds, those of labor and of voluntary abortion are added with the Indian. No wonder then if they multiply less than we do. Where food is regularly supplied, a single farm will shew more of cattle, than a whole country of forests can of buffaloes. The same Indian women, when married to white traders, who feed them and their children plentifully and regularly, who exempt them from excessive drudgery, who keep them stationary and unexposed to accident, produce and raise as many children as the white women. Instances are known, under these circumstances, of their rearing a dozen children. An inhuman practice once prevailed in this country of making slaves of the Indians. It is a fact well known with us, that the Indian women so enslaved produced and raised as numerous families as either the whites or blacks among whom they lived.—It has been said, that Indians have less hair than the whites, except on the head. But this is a fact of which fair proof can scarcely be had. With them it is disgraceful to be hairy on the body. They say it likens them to hogs. They therefore pluck the hair as fast as it appears. But the traders who marry their women, and prevail on them to discontinue this practice, say, that nature is the same with them as with the whites. Nor, if the fact be true, is the consequence necessary which has been drawn from it. Negroes have notoriously less hair than the whites; yet they are more ardent * * * The principles of their society forbidding all compulsion, they are to be led to duty and to enterprise by personal influence and persuasion. Hence eloquence in council, bravery and address in war, become the foundations of all consequence with them. To these acquirements all their faculties are directed. Of their bravery and address in war we have multiplied proofs, because we have been the subjects on which they were exercised. Of their eminence in or-atory we have fewer examples, because it is displayed chiefly in their own councils. Some, however, we have of very superior luster. I may challenge the whole orations of Demosthenes and Cicero, and of any more eminent orator, if Europe has furnished more eminent, to produce a single pas-sage, superior to the speech of Logan, a Mingo chief, to Lord Dunmore, when governor of this state. And, as a testimony of their talents in this line, I beg leave to introduce it, first stating the incidents necessary for understanding it. In the spring of the year 1774, a robbery and murder were committed on an inhabitant of the frontiers of Virginia, by two In-dians of the Shawanee tribe. The neighboring whites, according to their custom, undertook to punish this outrage in a summary way. Col. Cresap, a man infamous for the many murders he had committed on those much-injured people, collected a party, and proceeded down the Kanhaway in quest of vengeance. Unfortunately a canoe of women and children, with one man only, was seen coming from the opposite shore, unarmed and unsuspecting an hostile attack from the whites. Cresap and his party concealed themselves on the bank of the river, and the moment the canoe reached the shore, singled out their objects, and, at one fire, killed every person in it. This happened to be the family of Logan, who had long been distinguished as a friend of the whites. This unworthy return provoked his vengeance. He accordingly signalized himself in the war which en-sued. In the autumn of the same year a decisive battle was fought at the mouth of the Great Kanhaway, between the collected forces of the Shawanese, Mingoes, and Delawares, and a detachment of the Virginia militia. The Indians were defeated, and sued for peace. Logan, however, disdained to be seen among the suppliants. But, lest the sincerity of a treaty should be distrusted, from which so distinguished a chief absented himself, he sent by a messenger the following speech to be delivered to Lord Dunmore.

"I appeal to any white man to say, if ever he entered Logan's cabin hungry, and he gave him not meat; if ever he came cold and naked, and he clothed him not. During the course of the last long and bloody war, Logan remained idle in his cabin, an advocate for peace. Such was my love for the whites, that my countrymen pointed as they passed, and said, 'Logan is the friend of white men.' I had even thought to have lived with you, but for the injuries of one man. Col. Cresap, the last spring, in cold blood, and unprovoked, murdered all the relations of Logan, not sparing even my women and children. There runs not a drop of my blood in the veins of any living creature. This called on me for revenge. I have sought it: I have killed many: I have fully glutted my vengeance. For my country, I rejoice at the beams of peace. But do not harbor a thought that mine is the joy of fear. Logan never felt fear. He will not turn on his heel to save his life. Who is there to mourn for Logan?—Not one."

Before we condemn the Indians of this continent as wanting genius, we must consider that letters have not yet been introduced among them. Were we to compare them in their present state with the Europeans North of the Alps, when the Roman arms and arts first crossed those mountains, the comparison would be unequal, because, at that time those parts of Europe were swarming with numbers; because numbers produce emulation, and multiply the chances of improvement, and one improvement begets another. Yet I may safely ask, how many good poets, how many able mathematicians, how many great inventors in arts or sciences, had Europe North of the Alps then produced? And it was sixteen centuries after this before a Newton could be formed. I do not mean to deny, that there are varieties in the race of man, distinguished by their powers both of body and mind. I believe there are, as I see to be the case in the races of other animals. I only mean to suggest a doubt, whether the bulk and faculties of animals depend on the side of the Atlantic on which their food happens to grow, or which furnishes the elements of which they are compounded? Whether nature has enlisted herself as a Cis or Trans-Atlantic partisan? I am induced to suspect, there has been more eloquence than sound reasoning displayed in support of this theory; that it is one of those cases where the judgment has been seduced by a glowing pen: and whilst I render every tribute of honor and esteem to the celebrated zoologist, who has added, and is still adding so many precious things to the treasures of science, I must doubt whether in this instance he has not cherished error also, by lending her for a moment his vivid imagination and bewitching language. * * *

* * * [Ought we] to emancipate all slaves born after passing the act. The bill reported by the revisors does not itself contain this proposition; but an amendment containing it was prepared, to be offered to the legislature whenever the bill should be taken up, and further directing, that

they should continue with their parents to a certain age, then be brought up, at the public expense, to tillage, arts or sciences, according to their geniuses, till the females should be eighteen, and the males twenty-one years of age, when they should be colonized to such place as the circumstances of the time should render most proper, sending them out with arms, implements of household and of the handicraft arts, seeds, pairs of the useful domestic animals, &c. to declare them a free and independent people, and extend to them our alliance and protection, till they have acquired strength; and to send vessels at the same time to other parts of the world for an equal number of white inhabitants; to induce whom to migrate hither, proper encouragements were to be proposed. It will probably be asked, Why not retain and incorporate the blacks into the state, and thus save the expense of supplying, by importation of white settlers, the vacancies they will leave? Deep rooted prejudices entertained by the whites; ten thousand recollections, by the blacks, of the injuries they have sustained; new provocations; the real distinctions which nature has made; and many other circumstances, will divide us into parties, and produce convulsions which will probably never end but in the extermination of the one of the other race.—To these objections, which are political, may be added others, which are physical and moral. The first difference which strikes us is that of color.

Whether the black of the negro resides in the reticular membrane between the skin and scarf-skin, or in the scarf-skin itself; whether it proceeds from the color of the blood, the color of the bile, or from that of some other secretion, the difference is fixed in nature, and is as real as if its seat and cause were better known to us. And is this difference of no importance? Is it not the foundation of a greater or less share of beauty in the two races? Are not the fine mixtures of red and white, the expressions of every passion by greater or less suffusions of color in the one, preferable to that eternal monotony, which reigns in the countenances, that immovable veil of black which covers the emotions of the other race? Add to these, flowing hair, a more elegant symmetry of form, their own judgment in favor of the whites, declared by their preference of them, as uniformly as is the preference of the Oran-ûtan for the black woman over those of his own species. The circumstance of superior beauty, is thought worthy attention in the propagation of our horses, dogs, and other domestic animals; why not in that of man? Besides those of color, figure, and hair, there are other physical distinctions proving a difference of race. They have less hair on the face and body. They secrete less by the kidneys, and more by the glands of the skin, which gives them a very strong and disagreeable odor. This greater degree of transpiration, renders them more tolerant of heat, and less so of cold than the whites. Perhaps, too, a difference of structure in the pulmonary apparatus, which a late ingenious experimentalist has discovered to be the principal regulator of animal heat, may have disabled them from extricating, in the act of inspiration, so much of that fluid from the outer air, or obliged them in expiration, to part with more of it. They seem to require less sleep. A black after hard labor through the day, will be induced by the slightest amusements to sit up till midnight, or later, though knowing he must be out with the first dawn of the morning. They are at least as brave, and more adventuresome. But this may perhaps proceed from a want of forethought, which prevents their seeing a danger till it be present. When present, they do not go through it with more coolness or steadiness than the whites. They are more ardent after their female; but love seems with them to be more an eager desire, than a tender delicate mixture of sentiment and sensation. Their griefs are transient. Those numberless afflictions, which render it doubtful whether heaven has given life to us in mercy or in wrath, are less felt, and sooner forgotten with them. In general, their existence appears to participate more of sensation than reflection. To this must be ascribed their disposition to sleep when abstracted from their diversions, and unemployed in labor. An animal whose body is at rest, and who does not reflect must be disposed to sleep of course. Comparing them by their faculties of memory, reason, and imagination, it appears to me that in memory they are equal to the whites; in reason much inferior, as I think one could scarcely be found capable of tracing and comprehending the investigations of Euclid; and that in imagination they are dull, tasteless, and anomalous. It would be unfair to follow them to Africa for this investigation. We will consider them here, on the same stage with the whites, and where the facts are not apocryphal on which a judgment is to be formed. It will be right to make great allowances for the difference of condition, of education, of conversation, of the sphere in which they move. Many millions of them have been brought to, and born in America. Most of them, indeed, have been confined to tillage, to their own homes, and their own society; yet many have been so situated, that they might have availed themselves of the conversation of their masters; many have been brought up to the handicraft arts, and from that circumstance have always been associated with the whites. Some have been liberally educated, and all have lived in countries where the arts and sciences are cultivated to a considerable degree, and all have had before their eyes samples of the best works from abroad. * * *

But never yet could I find that a black had uttered a thought above the level of plain narration; never saw even an elementary trait of painting or sculpture. In music they are more generally gifted than the whites with accurate ears for tune and time, and they have been found capable of imagining a small catch. Whether they will be equal to the composition of a more extensive run of melody, or of complicated harmony, is yet to be proved. Misery is often the parent of the most affecting touches in poetry. Among the blacks is misery enough, God knows, but no poetry. Love is the peculiar œstrum of the poet. Their love is ardent, but it kindles the senses only, not the imagination. Religion, indeed, has produced a Phyllis Whately; but it could not produce a poet. The compositions published under her name are below the dignity of criticism. The heroes of the Dunciad are, to her, as Hercules to the author of that poem. Ignatius Sancho has approached nearer to merit in composition; yet his letters do more honor to the heart than the head. They breathe the purest effusions of friendship and general philanthropy, and show how great a degree of the latter may be compounded with strong religious zeal. He is often happy in the turn of his compliments, and his style is easy and familiar, except when he affects a Shandean fabrication of words. But his imagination is wild and extravagant, escapes incessantly from every restraint of reason and taste, and, in the course of its vagaries, leaves a tract of thought as incoherent and eccentric, as is the course of a meteor through the sky. His subjects should often have led him to a process of sober reasoning; yet we find him always substituting sentiment for demonstration. Upon the whole, though we admit him to the first place among those of his own color who have presented themselves to the public judgment, yet when we compare him with the writers of the race among whom he lived and particularly with the epistolary class in which he has taken his own stand, we are compelled to enrol him at the bottom of the column. This criticism supposes the letters published under his name to be genuine, and to have received amendment from no other hand; points which would not be of easy investigation. The improvement of the blacks in body and mind, in the first instance of their mixture with the whites, has been observed by every one, and proves that their inferiority is not the effect merely of their condition of life. We know that among the Romans, about the Augustan age especially, the condition of their slaves was much more deplorable than that of the blacks on the continent of America. The two sexes were confined in separate apartments, because to raise a child cost the master more than to buy one.

It is not their condition, then, but nature, which has produced the distinction. Whether further observation will or will not verify the conjecture, that nature has been less bountiful to them in the endowments of the head, I believe that in those of the heart she will be found to have done them justice. That disposition to theft with which they have been branded, must be ascribed to their situation, and not to any depravity of the moral sense. The man in whose favor no laws of property exist, probably feels himself less bound to respect those made in favor of others. When arguing for ourselves, we lay it down as a fundamental, that laws, to be just, must give a reciprocation of right; that, without this, they are mere arbitrary rules of conduct, founded in force, and not in conscience; and it is a problem which I give to the master to solve, whether the religious precepts against the violation of property were not framed for him as well as his slave? And whether the slave may not as justifiably take a little from one who has taken all from him, as he may slay one who would slay him? That a change in the relations in which a man is placed should change his ideas of moral right or wrong, is neither new, nor peculiar to the color of the blacks. Homer tells us it was so two thousand six hundred years ago.

> *Jove fix'd it certain, that whatever day*
> *Makes man a slave, takes half his worth away.*

But the slaves of which Homer speaks were whites. Notwithstanding these considerations which must weaken their respect for the laws of property, we find among them numerous instances of the most rigid integrity, and as many as among their better instructed masters, of benevolence, gratitude, and unshaken fidelity. The opinion that they are inferior in the faculties of reason and imagination, must be hazarded with great diffidence. To justify a general conclusion, requires many observations, even where the subject may be submitted to the anatomical knife, to optical glasses, to analysis by fire or by solvents. How much more then where it is a faculty, not a substance, we are examining; where it eludes the research of all the senses; where the conditions of its existence are various and variously combined; where the effects of those which are present or absent bid defiance to calculation; let me add too, as a circumstance of great tenderness, where our conclusion would degrade a whole race of men from the rank in the scale of beings which their Creator may perhaps have given them. To our reproach it must be said, that though for a century and a half we have had under our eyes the races of black and of red men, they have never yet been viewed by us as subjects of natural history. I advance it, therefore, as a suspicion only, that the blacks, whether originally a distinct race, or made distinct by time and circumstances, are inferior to the whites in the endowments both of body and mind. It is not against experience to suppose that different species of the same genus, or varieties of the same species, may possess different qualifications. Will not a lover of natural history then, one who views the gradations in all the races of animals with the eye of philosophy, excuse an effort to keep those in the department of man as distinct as nature has formed them? This unfortunate difference of color, and perhaps of faculty, is a powerful obstacle to the emancipation of these people. Many of their advocates, while they wish to vindicate the liberty of human nature, are anxious also to preserve its dignity and beauty. Some of these, embarrassed by the question, "What further is to be done with them?" join themselves in opposition with those who are actuated by sordid avarice only. Among the Romans emancipation required but one effort. The slave, when made free, might mix with, without staining the blood of his master. But with us a second is necessary, unknown to history. When freed, he is to be removed beyond the reach of mixture.

WILLIAM LLOYD GARRISON

The Liberator (1831)

Heavily influenced by the Quaker abolitionist Benjamin Lundy, the journalist William Lloyd Garrison (1805–1879) worked tirelessly for the immediate emancipation of all slaves. He often castigated both proponents and moderate opponents of slavery, resulting in a conviction for libeling a New England merchant involved in the slave trade and a bounty on his head in Georgia. This abolitionist even attacked the Constitution as "a covenant with death, an agreement with Hell." In 1844, the uncompromising Garrison formulated the principle of "No Union with Slaveholders" and began to agitate for Northern secession from the slaveholding states. Even though he was a pacifist, he supported Abraham Lincoln's efforts in the Civil War. In the first issue of The Liberator, a radical antislavery journal he founded in 1831, Garrison announced his refusal to compromise on or deal moderately with the issue of slavery. The second excerpt from The Liberator, written several years later, reveals the depths of Garrison's religious conviction that slavery was a grave national sin. Garrison revealed his plans to expand his moral crusade against southern slavery to the wider cause of "universal emancipation" and establishing the kingdom of God on earth. One of the distinctive features of this essay is Garrison's use of the Christian doctrine that God works through human governments to punish wickedness and sinfulness.

During my recent tour for the purpose of exciting the minds of the people by a series of discourses on the subject of slavery, every place that I visited gave fresh evidence of the fact, that a greater revolution in public sentiment was to be effected in the free states—*and particularly in New England*—than at the south. I found contempt more bitter, opposition more active, detraction more relentless, prejudice more stubborn, and apathy more frozen, than among slave owners themselves. Of course, there were individual exceptions to the contrary. This state of things afflicted, but did not dishearten me. I determined, at every hazard, to lift up the standard of emancipation in the eyes of the nation, *within sight of Bunker Hill and in the birth place of liberty.* That standard is now unfurled; and long may it float, unhurt by the spoliations of time or the missiles of a desperate foe—yea, till every chain be broken, and every bondman set free! Let southern oppressors tremble—let their secret abettors tremble—let their Northern apologists tremble—let all the enemies of the persecuted blacks tremble.

I deem the publication of my original Prospectus unnecessary, as it has obtained a wide circulation. The principles therein inculcated will be steadily pursued in this paper, excepting that I shall not array myself as the political partisan of any man. In defending the great cause of human rights, I wish to derive the assistance of all religions and of all parties.

Assenting to the "self-evident truth" maintained in the American Declaration of Independence, "that all men are created equal, and endowed by their Creator with certain inalienable rights—among which are life, liberty and the pursuit of happiness," I shall strenuously contend for the immediate enfranchisement of our slave population. In Park-street Church, on the Fourth of July, 1829, in an address on slavery, I unreflectingly assented to the popular but pernicious doctrine of *gradual* abolition. I seize this opportunity to make a full and unequivocal recantation, and thus publicly to ask pardon of my God, of my country, and of my brethren the poor slaves, for having uttered a sentiment so full of timidity, injustice and absurdity. A similar recantation, from my pen, was published in the *Genius of Universal Emancipation* at Baltimore, in September, 1829. My conscience is now satisfied.

I am aware, that many object to the severity of my language; but is there not cause for severity? I *will be* as harsh as truth, and as uncompromising as justice. On this subject, I do not wish to think, or speak, or write, with moderation. No! no! Tell a man whose house is on fire to give a moderate alarm; tell him to moderately rescue his wife from the hands of the ravisher; tell the mother to gradually extricate her babe from the fire into which it has fallen;—but urge me not to use moderation in a cause like the present. I am in earnest—I will not equivocate—I will not excuse—I will not retreat a single inch—AND I WILL BE HEARD. The apathy of the people is enough to make every statue leap from its pedestal, and to hasten the resurrection of the dead.

It is pretended, that I am retarding the cause of emancipation, by the coarseness of my invective, and the precipitancy of my measures. *The charge is not true.* On this question my influence,—humble as it is,—is felt at this moment to a considerable extent, and shall be felt in coming years—not perniciously, but beneficially—not as a curse, but as a blessing; and posterity will bear testimony that I was right. I desire to thank God, that he enables me to disregard "the fear of man which bringeth a snare" and to speak his truth in its simplicity and power. * * *

* * *

* * * In commencing this publication, we had but a single object in view—the total abolition of American slavery, and as a just consequence, the complete enfranchisement of our colored countrymen. * * *

In entering upon our eighth volume, the abolition of slavery will still be the grand object of our labors, though not, perhaps, so exclusively as heretofore. There are other topics, which, in our opinion, are intimately connected with the great doctrine of inalienable human rights; and which, while they conflict with no religious sect, or political party, as such, are pregnant with momentous consequences to the freedom, equality and happiness of mankind. These we shall discuss as time and opportunity may permit.

The motto upon our banner has been from the commencement of our moral warfare, 'OUR COUNTRY IS THE WORLD—OUR COUNTRYMEN ARE ALL MANKIND." We trust that it will be our only epitaph. Another motto we have chosen is, 'UNIVERSAL EMANCIPATION.' Up to this time, we have limited its application to those who are held in this country, by southern taskmasters, as marketable commodities, goods and chattels, and implements of husbandry. Henceforth, we shall use it in its widest latitude: the emancipation of our whole race from the dominion of man, from the thraldom of self, from the government of brute force, from the bondage of sin—and bringing them under the dominion of God, the control of an inward spirit, the government of the law of love, and into the obedience and liberty of Christ, who is '*the same*, yesterday, TO-DAY, and forever.' * * *

Next to the overthrow of slavery, the cause of PEACE will command our attention. The doctrine of non-resistance, as commonly received and practised by Friends, and certain members of other religious denominations, we conceive to be utterly indefensible in its application to national wars;—not that it 'goes too far,' but that it does not go far enough. If a nation may not redress its wrongs by physical force—if it may not repel or punish a foreign enemy who comes to plunder, enslave or murder its inhabitants—then it may not resort to arms to quell an insurrection, or send to prison or suspend upon a gibbet any transgressors upon its soil. If the slaves of the South have not an undoubted right to resist their masters in the last resort, then no man, or body of men, may appeal to the law of violence in self-defence—for none have suffered, or can suffer, more than they. If, when men are robbed of their earnings, their liberties, their personal ownership, their wives and children, they may not resist, in no case can physical resistance be allowable, either in an individual or collective capacity. Now, the doctrine we shall endeavor to inculcate is, that the kingdoms of this world are to become the kingdoms of our Lord and of his Christ; consequently, that they are all to be supplanted, whether they are called despotic, monarchical or republican, and he only who is King of kings, and Lord of lords, is to rule in righteousness. The kingdom of God is to be established IN ALL THE EARTH, and it shall never be destroyed, but it shall 'BREAK IN PIECES AND CONSUME ALL OTHERS:' its elements are righteousness and peace, and joy in the Holy Ghost: without are dogs, and sorcerers, and whoremongers and murderers, and idolators, and whatsoever loveth and maketh a lie. Its government is one of love, not of military coercion or physical restraint: its laws are not written upon parchment, but upon the hearts of its subjects—they are not conceived in the wisdom of man, but framed by the Spirit of God: its weapons are not carnal, but spiritual: its soldiers are clad in the whole armor of God. * * * Hence, when smitten on the one cheek, they turn the other also; being defamed, they entreat; being reviled, they bless; being persecuted, they suffer it; they take joyfully the spoiling of their goods; they rejoice, inasmuch as they are partakers of Christ's sufferings, they are sheep in the midst of wolves; in no extremity whatever, even if their enemies are determined to nail them to the cross with Jesus, and if they like him could summon legions of angels to their rescue, will they resort to the law of violence.

As to the governments of this world, whatever their titles or forms, we shall endeavor to prove, that, in their essential elements, and as at present administered, they are all Anti-Christ; that they can never, by human wisdom, be brought into conformity to the will of God; that they cannot be maintained, except by naval and military power; that all their penal enactments being a dead letter without an army to carry them into effect, are virtually written in human blood; and that the followers of Jesus should instinctively shun their stations of honor, power and emolument— at the same time 'submitting to every ordinance of man for the Lord's sake,' and offering no *physical* resistance to any of their mandates, however unjust or tyrannical. * * *

Human governments are to be viewed as judicial punishments. If a people turn the grace of God into lasciviousness, or make their liberty an occasion for anarchy,—or if they refuse to belong to the 'one fold and one Shepherd,'—they shall be scourged by the governments of their own choosing, and burdened with taxation, and subjected to physical control, and torn by factions, and made to eat the fruit of their evil doings, until they are prepared to receive the liberty and the rest which remain, on earth as well as in heaven, for THE PEOPLE OF GOD. * * *

So long as men condemn the perfect government of the Most High, and will not fill up the measure of Christ's sufferings in their own persons, just so long will they desire to usurp authority over each other—just so long will they pertinaciously cling to human governments, *fashioned in the likeness and administered in the spirit of their own disobedience.* Now, if the prayer of our Lord be not a mockery; if the kingdom of God is to come universally, and his will be done ON EARTH AS IT IS IN HEAVEN; and if, in that kingdom, no carnal weapon can be wielded, and swords are beaten into ploughshares, and spears into pruning hooks, and there is none to molest or make afraid, and no statute-book but the bible, and no judge but Christ; then why are not Christians obligated to come out NOW, and be separate from 'the kingdoms of this world,' which are all based upon THE PRINCIPLE OF VIOLENCE, and which require their officers and servants to govern and be governed by that principle? How, then, is the wickedness of men to be overcome? Not by lacerating their bodies, or incarcerating them in dungeons, or putting them upon tread-mills, or exiling them from their native country, or suspending them upon gibbets— O no!—but simply by returning good for evil, and blessing for cursing; by using those spiritual weapons which are 'mighty, through God, to the pulling down of strongholds'; by the power of that faith which overcomes the world; by ceasing to look to man for a redress of injuries, however grievous, but committing the soul in well-doing, as unto a faithful Creator, and leaving it with God to bestow recompense—'for it is written, Vengence is mine; I will repay, saith the Lord.'

These are among the views we shall offer in connection with the heaven-originated cause of PEACE,—views which any person is at liberty to controvert in our columns, and for which no man or body of men is responsible but ourselves. If any man shall affirm that the anti-slavery cause, as such, or any anti-slavery society, is answerable for our sentiments on this subject, to him may be justly applied the apostolic declaration, 'the truth is not in him.' We regret, indeed, that the principles of abolitionists seem to be quite unsettled upon a question of such vast importance, and so vitally connected with the bloodless overthrow of slavery. It is time for all our friends to know where they stand. If those, whose yokes they are endeavoring to break by the fire and hammer of God's word, would not, in their opinion, be justified in appealing to physical force, how can they justify others of a different complexion in doing the same thing? And if they conscientiously believe that the slaves would be guiltless in shedding the blood of their merciless oppressors, let them say so unequivocally—for there is no neutral ground in this matter, and the time is near at hand when they will be compelled to take sides. * * *

WILLIAM LLOYD GARRISON

Declaration of Sentiments of the American Anti-Slavery Society (1833)

A year after he spearheaded the formation of the New England Anti-Slavery Society in 1832, Garrison helped organize the American Anti-Slavery Society and served as its first corresponding secretary. The group splintered in 1840 largely because Garrison welcomed women in the abolitionist cause. He authored the national organization's Declaration of Sentiments, which combined a Lockean concern for natural rights with religious anxieties about the moral implications of slavery for the nation.

More than fifty-seven years have elapsed, since a band of patriots convened in this place, to devise measures for the deliverance of this country from a foreign yoke. The corner-stone upon which they founded the Temple of Freedom was broadly this—'That all men are created equal; that they are endowed by their Creator with certain inalienable rights; that among these are life, LIBERTY, and the pursuit of happiness.' At the sound of their trumpet-call, three millions of people rose up as from the sleep of death, and rushed to the strife of blood; deeming it more glorious to die instantly as freemen, than desirable to live one hour as slaves. They were few in number—poor in resources; but the honest conviction that Truth, Justice and Right were on their side, made them invincible.

We have met together for the achievement of an enterprise, without which that of our fathers is incomplete; and which, for its magnitude, solemnity, and probable results upon the destiny of the world, as far transcends theirs as moral truth does physical force.

In purity of motive, in earnestness of zeal, in decision of purpose, in intrepidity of action, in steadfastness of faith, in sincerity of spirit, we would not be inferior to them.

Their principles led them to wage war against their oppressors, and to spill human blood like water, in order to be free. Ours forbid the doing of evil that good may come, and lead us to reject, and to entreat the oppressed to reject, the use of all carnal weapons for deliverance from bondage; relying solely upon those which are spiritual, and mighty through God to the pulling down of strongholds.

Their measures were physical resistance—the marshalling in arms—the hostile array—the mortal encounter. Ours shall be such only as the opposition of moral purity to moral corruption—the destruction of error by the potency of truth—the overthrow of prejudice by the power of love—and the abolition of slavery by the spirit of repentance.

Their grievances, great as they were, were trifling in comparison with the wrongs and sufferings of those for whom we plead. Our fathers were never slaves—never bought and sold like cattle—never shut out from the light of knowledge and religion—never subjected to the lash of brutal task-masters.

But those, for whose emancipation we are striving—constituting at the present time at least one-sixth part of our countrymen—are recognized by law, and treated by their fellow-beings, as marketable commodities, as goods and chattels, as brute beasts; are plundered daily of the fruits of their toil without redress; really enjoy no constitutional nor legal protection from licentious and murderous outrages upon their persons; and are ruthlessly torn asunder—the tender babe from the arms of its frantic mother—the heart-broken wife from her weeping husband—at the caprice or pleasure of irresponsible tyrants. For the crime of having a dark complexion, they suffer the pangs of hunger, the infliction of stripes, the ignominy of brutal servitude. They are kept in heathenish darkness by laws expressly enacted to make their instruction a criminal offence.

These are the prominent circumstances in the condition of more than two millions of our people, the proof of which may be found in thousands of indisputable facts, and in the laws of the slaveholding States.

Hence we maintain—that, in view of the civil and religious privileges of this nation, the guilt of its oppression is unequalled by any other on the face of the earth; and, therefore, that it is bound to repent instantly, to undo the heavy burdens, and to let the oppressed go free.

We further maintain—that no man has a right to enslave or imbrute his brother—to hold or acknowledge him, for one moment, as a piece of merchandize—to keep back his hire by fraud—or to brutalize his mind, by denying him the means of intellectual, social and moral improvement.

The right to enjoy liberty is inalienable. To invade it is to usurp the prerogative of Jehovah. Every man has a right to his own body—to the products of his own labor—to the protection of law—and to the common advantages of society. It is piracy to buy or steal a native African, and subject him to servitude. Surely, the sin is as great to enslave an American as an African.

Therefore we believe and affirm—that there is no difference, in principle, between the African slave trade and American slavery:

That every American citizen, who detains a human being in involuntary bondage as his property, is, according to Scripture, (Ex. xxi. 16,) a man-stealer:

That the slaves ought instantly to be set free, and brought under the protection of law:

That if they had lived from the time of Pharaoh down to the present period, and had been entailed through successive generations, their right to be free could never have been alienated, but their claims would have constantly risen in solemnity:

That all those laws which are now in force, admitting the right of slavery, are therefore, before God, utterly null and void; being an audacious usurpation of the Divine prerogative, a daring infringement on the law of nature, a base overthrow of the very foundations of the social compact, a complete extinction of all the relations, endearments and obligations of mankind, and a presumptuous transgression of all the holy commandments; and that therefore they ought instantly to be abrogated.

We further believe and affirm—that all persons of color, who possess the qualifications which are demanded of others, ought to be admitted forthwith to the enjoyment of the same privileges, and the exercise of the same prerogatives, as others; and that the paths of preferment, of wealth, and of intelligence, should be opened as widely to them as to persons of a white complexion.

We maintain that no compensation should be given to the planters emancipating their slaves:

Because it would be a surrender of the great fundamental principle, that man cannot hold property in man:

Because slavery is a crime, and therefore is not an article to be sold:

Because the holders of slaves are not the just proprietors of what they claim; freeing the slaves is not depriving them of property, but restoring it to its rightful owner; it is not wronging the master, but righting the slave—restoring him to himself:

Because immediate and general emancipation would only destroy nominal, not real property; it would not amputate a limb or break a bone of the slaves, but by infusing motives into their breasts, would make them doubly valuable to the masters as free laborers; and

Because, if compensation is to be given at all, it should be given to the outraged and guiltless slaves, and not to those who have plundered and abused them.

We regard as delusive, cruel and dangerous, any scheme of expatriation which pretends to aid, either directly or indirectly, in the emancipation of the slaves, or to be a substitute for the immediate and total abolition of slavery.

We fully and unanimously recognize the sovereignty of each State, to legislate exclusively on the subject of the slavery which is tolerated within its limits; we concede that Congress, under the present national compact, has no right to interfere with any of the slave States, in relation to this momentous subject:

But we maintain that Congress has a right, and is solemnly bound, to suppress the domestic slave trade between the several States, and to abolish slavery in those portions of our territory which the Constitution has placed under its exclusive jurisdiction.

We also maintain that there are, at the present time, the highest obligations resting upon the people of the free States to remove slavery by moral and political action, as prescribed in the Constitution of the United States. They are now living under a pledge of their tremendous physical force, to fasten the galling fetters of tyranny upon the limbs of millions in the Southern States; they are liable to be called at any moment to suppress a general insurrection of the slaves; they authorize the slave owners to vote for three-fifths of his slaves as property, and thus enable him to perpetuate his oppression; they support a standing army at the South for its protection; and they seize the slave, who has escaped into their territories, and send him back to be tortured by an enraged master or a brutal driver. This relation to slavery is criminal, and full of danger: IT MUST BE BROKEN UP.

These are our views and principles—these our designs and measures. With entire confidence in the overruling justice of God, we plant ourselves upon the Declaration of our Independence and the truths of Divine Revelation, as upon the Everlasting Rock.

We shall organize Anti-Slavery Societies, if possible, in every city, town and village in our land.

We shall send forth agents to lift up the voice of remonstrance, of warning, of entreaty, and of rebuke.

We shall circulate, unsparingly and extensively, anti-slavery tracts and periodicals.

We shall enlist the pulpit and the press in the cause of the suffering and the dumb.

We shall aim at a purification of the churches from all participation in the guilt of slavery.

We shall encourage the labor of freemen rather than that of slaves, by giving a preference to their productions: and

We shall spare no exertions nor means to bring the whole nation to speedy repentance.

Our trust for victory is solely in God. We may be personally defeated, but our principles never! Truth, Justice, Reason, Humanity, must and will gloriously triumph. Already a host is coming up to the help of the Lord against the mighty, and the prospect before us is full of encouragement.

Submitting this Declaration to the candid examination of the people of this country, and of the friends of liberty throughout the world, we hereby affix our signatures to it; pledging ourselves that, under the guidance and by the help of Almighty God, we will do all that in us lies, consistently with this Declaration of our principles, to overthrow the most execrable system of slavery that has ever been witnessed upon earth; to deliver our land from its deadliest curse; to wipe out the foulest stain which rests upon our national escutcheon; and to secure to the colored population of the United States, all the rights and privileges which belong to them as men, and as Americans—come what may to our persons, our interests, or our reputation—whether we live to witness the triumph of Liberty, Justice and Humanity, or perish untimely as martyrs in this great, benevolent, and holy cause.

WILLIAM ELLERY CHANNING

Slavery (1835)

The Congregationalist minister and Unitarian William Ellery Channing (1780–1842) joined the abolitionist cause after a two-year residence as a tutor on a Virginia plantaton. A champion of national literature and intellectual freedom in America, Channing developed philosophical Lockean arguments against slavery as contrary to human rights and human nature. He repudiated slavery as a gross violation of the natural right to the fruits of one's own labor and a threat to the rights of everyone.

The slave-holder claims the slave as his Property. The very idea of a slave is, that he belongs to another, that he is bound to live and labor for another, to be another's instrument, and to make another's will his habitual law, however adverse to his own. Another owns him, and, of course, has a right to his time and strength, a right to the fruits of his labor, a right to task him without his consent, and to determine the kind and duration of his toil, a right to confine him to any bounds, a right to extort the required work by stripes, a right, in a word, to use him as a tool, without contract, against his will, and in denial of his right to dispose of himself, or to use his power for his own good. "A slave," says the Louisiana code, "is in the power of the master to whom he belongs. The master may sell him, dispose of his person, his industry, his labor; he can do nothing, possess nothing, nor acquire any thing, but which must belong to his master." "Slaves shall be deemed, taken, reputed, and adjudged," say the South-Carolina laws, "to be chattels personal in the hands of their masters, and possessions to all intents and purposes whatsoever." Such is slavery, a claim to man as property.

Now this claim of property in a human being is altogether false, groundless. No such right of man in man can exist. A human being cannot be justly owned. To hold and treat him as property is to inflict a great wrong, to incur the guilt of oppression.

This position there is a difficulty in maintaining, on account of its exceeding obviousness. It is too plain for proof. To defend it is like trying to confirm a self-evident truth. To find arguments is not easy, because an argument is something clearer than the proposition to be sustained. The man who, on hearing the claim to property in man, does not see and feel distinctly that it is a cruel usurpation, is hardly to be reached by reasoning, for it is hard to find any plainer principles than what he begins with denying. I will endeavour, however, to illustrate the truth which I have stated.

1. It is plain, that, if one man may be held as property, then every other man may be so held. If there be nothing in human nature, in our common nature, which excludes and forbids the conversion of him who possesses it into an article of property; if the right of the free to liberty is founded, not on their essential attributes as rational and moral beings, but on certain adventitious, accidental circumstances, into which they have been thrown; then every human being, by a change of circumstances, may justly be held and treated by another as property. If one man may be rightfully reduced to slavery, then there is not a human being on whom the same chain may not be imposed. Now let every reader ask himself this plain question: Could I, can I, be rightfully seized, and made an article of property; be made a passive instrument of another's will and pleasure; be subjected to another's irresponsible power; be subjected to stripes at another's will; be denied the control and use of my own limbs and faculties for my own good? Does any man, so questioned, doubt, waver, look about him for an answer? Is not the reply given immediately, intuitively, by his whole inward being? * * * This deep assurance, that we cannot be rightfully made another's property, does not rest on the hue of our skins, or the place of our birth, or our strength, or wealth. These things do not enter our thoughts. The consciousness of in-

destructible rights is a part of our moral being. The consciousness of our humanity involves the persuasion, that we cannot be owned as a tree or a brute. As men, we cannot justly be made slaves. Then no man can be rightfully enslaved. In casting the yoke from ourselves as an unspeakable wrong, we condemn ourselves as wrong-doers and oppressors in laying it on any who share our nature.—It is not necessary to inquire whether a man, by extreme guilt, may not forfeit the rights of his nature, and be justly punished with slavery. On this point crude notions prevail. But the discussion would be foreign to the present subject. We are now not speaking of criminals. We speak of innocent men, who have given us no hold on them by guilt; and our own consciousness is a proof that such cannot rightfully be seized as property by a fellow-creature.

2. A man cannot be seized and held as property, because he has Rights. What these rights are, whether few or many, or whether all men have the same, are questions for future discussion. All that is assumed now is, that every human being has *some* rights. This truth cannot be denied, but by denying to a portion of the race that moral nature which is the sure and only foundation of rights. This truth has never, I believe, been disputed. It is even recognized in the very codes of slave legislation, which, while they strip a man of liberty, affirm his right to life, and threaten his murderer with punishment. Now, I say, a being having rights cannot justly be made property; for this claim over him virtually annuls all his rights. It strips him of all power to assert them. It makes it a crime to assert them. The very essence of slavery is, to put a man defenceless into the hands of another. The right claimed by the master, to task, to force, to imprison, to whip, and to punish the slave, at discretion, and especially to prevent the least resistance to his will, is a virtual denial and subversion of all the rights of the victim of his power. The two cannot stand together. Can we doubt which of them ought to fall?

3. Another argument against property is to be found in the Essential Equality of men. I know that this doctrine, so venerable in the eyes of our fathers, has lately been denied. Verbal logicians, have told us that men are "born equal" only in the sense of being equally born. They have asked whether all are equally tall, strong, or beautiful; or whether nature, Procrustes-like, reduces all her children to one standard of intellect and virtue. By such arguments it is attempted to set aside the principle of equality, on which the soundest moralists have reared the structure of social duty; and in these ways the old foundations of despotic power, which our fathers in their simplicity thought they had subverted, are laid again by their sons.

It is freely granted, that there are innumerable diversities among men; but be it remembered, they are ordained to bind men together, and not to subdue one to the other; ordained to give means and occasions of mutual aid, and to carry forward each and all, so that the good of all is equally intended in this distribution of various gifts. Be it also remembered, that these diversities among men are as nothing in comparison with the attributes in which they agree; and it is this which constitutes their essential equality. All men have the same rational nature and the same power of conscience, and all are equally made for indefinite improvement of these divine faculties, and for the happiness to be found in their virtuous use. * * * Thus equal are men; and among these equals, who can substantiate his claim to make others his property, his tools, the mere instruments of his private interest and gratification? Let this claim begin, and where will it stop? If one may assert it, why not all? Among these partakers of the same rational and moral nature, who can make good a right over others, which others may not establish over himself? * * * The equality of nature makes slavery a wrong. Nature's seal is affixed to no instrument by which property in a single human being is conveyed.

4. That a human being cannot be justly held and used as property, is apparent from the very nature of property. Property is an exclusive right. It shuts out all claim but that of the possessor. What one man owns, cannot belong to another. What, then, is the consequence of holding a human being as property? Plainly this. He can have no right to himself. His limbs are, in truth, not morally his own. He has not a right to his own strength. It belongs to another. His will, intellect, and muscles, all the powers of body and mind which are exercised in labor, he is bound to regard as another's. Now, if there be property in any thing, it is that of a man in his own person, mind, and strength. All other rights are weak, unmeaning, compared with this, and, in denying this, all right is denied. It is true, that an individual may forfeit by crime his right to the use of his limbs, perhaps to his limbs, and even to life. But the very idea of forfeiture implies, that the right was originally possessed. It is true, that a man may by contract give to another a limited right to his strength. But he gives only because he possesses it, and gives it for considerations which he deems beneficial to himself; and the right conferred ceases at once on violation of the conditions on which it was bestowed. To deny the right of a human being to himself, to his own limbs and faculties, to his energy of body and mind, is an absurdity too gross to be confuted by any thing but a simple statement. Yet this absurdity is involved in the idea of his belonging to another.

5. We have a plain recognition of the principle now laid down, in the universal indignation excited towards a man who makes another his slave. Our laws know no higher crime than that of reducing a man to slavery. To steal or to buy an African on his own shores, is piracy. In this act the greatest wrong is inflicted, the most sacred right violated. But if a human being

cannot without infinite injustice be seized as property, then he cannot without equal wrong be held and used as such. The wrong in the first seizure lies in the destination of a human being to future bondage, to the criminal use of him as a chattel or brute. Can that very use, which makes the original seizure an enormous wrong, become gradually innocent? If the slave receive injury without measure at the first moment of the outrage, is he less injured by being held fast the second or the third? Does the duration of wrong, the increase of it by continuance, convert it into right? It is true, in many cases, that length of possession is considered as giving a right, where the goods were acquired by unlawful means. But in these cases, the goods were such as might justly be appropriated to individual use. They were intended by the Creator to be owned. They fulfill their purpose by passing into the hands of an exclusive possessor. It is essential to rightful property in a thing, that the thing from its nature may be rightfully appropriated. If it cannot originally be made one's own without crime, it certainly cannot be continued as such without guilt. Now the ground, on which the seizure of the African on his own shore is condemned, is, that he is a man, who has by his nature a right to be free. Ought not, then, the same condemnation to light on the continuance of his yoke? Still more. Whence is it, that length of possession is considered by the laws as conferring a right? I answer, from the difficulty of determining the original proprietor, and from the apprehension of unsettling all property by carrying back inquiry beyond a certain time. Suppose, however, an article of property to be of such a nature that it could bear the name of the true original owner stamped on it in bright and indelible characters. In this case, the whole ground, on which length of possession bars other claims, would fail. The proprietor would not be concealed, or rendered doubtful by the lapse of time. Would not he, who should receive such an article from a robber or a succession of robbers, be involved in their guilt? Now the true owner of a human being is made manifest to all. It is Himself. No brand on the slave was ever so conspicuous as the mark of property which God has set on him. God, in making him a rational and moral being, has put a glorious-stamp on him, which all the slave legislation and slave-markets of worlds cannot efface. Hence, no right accrues to the master from the length of the wrong which has been done to the slave.

6. Another argument against the right of property in man, may be drawn from a very obvious principle of moral science. It is a plain truth, universally received, that every right supposes or involves a corresponding obligation. If, then, a man has a right to another's person or powers, the latter is under obligation to give himself up as a chattel to the former. This is his duty. He is bound to be a slave; and bound not merely by the Christian law, which enjoins submission to injury, not merely by prudential

considerations, or by the claims of public order and peace; but bound because another has a right of ownership, has a moral claim to him, so that
he would be guilty of dishonesty, of robbery, in withdrawing himself from
this other's service. It is his duty to work for his master, though all compulsion were withdrawn; and in deserting him he would commit the
crime of taking away another man's property, as truly as if he were to
carry off his owner's purse. Now do we not instantly feel, can we help
feeling, that this is false? Is the slave thus morally bound? When the
African was first brought to these shores, would he have violated a
solemn obligation by slipping his chain, and flying back to his native
home? Would he not have been bound to seize the precious opportunity
of escape? Is the slave under a moral obligation to confine himself, his
wife, and children, to a spot where their union in a moment may be
forcibly dissolved? Ought he not, if he can, to place himself and his family under the guardianship of equal laws? Should we blame him for leaving his yoke? Do we not feel, that, in the same condition, a sense of duty
would quicken our flying steps? Where, then, is the obligation which
would necessarily be imposed, if the right existed which the master
claims? The absence of obligation proves the want of the right. The claim
is groundless. It is a cruel wrong.

7. I come now to what is to my own mind the great argument against
seizing and using a man as property. He cannot be property in the sight
of God and justice, because he is a Rational, Moral, Immortal Being; because created in God's image, and therefore in the highest sense his
child; because created to unfold godlike faculties, and to govern himself
by a Divine Law written on his heart, and republished in God's Word.
His whole nature forbids that he should be seized as property. From his
very nature it follows, that so to seize him is to offer an insult to his
Maker, and to inflict aggravated social wrong. Into every human being
God has breathed an immortal spirit, more precious than the whole outward creation. No earthly or celestial language can exaggerate the worth
of a human being. No matter how obscure his condition. Thought, Reason, Conscience, the capacity of Virtue, the capacity of Christian Love,
an immortal Destiny, an intimate moral connection with God,—here are
attributes of our common humanity which reduce to insignificance all
outward distinctions, and make every human being unspeakably dear to
his Maker. No matter how ignorant he may be. The capacity of Improvement allies him to the more instructed of his race, and places within his
reach the knowledge and happiness of higher worlds. Every human being has in him the germ of the greatest idea in the universe, the idea of
God; and to unfold this is the end of his existence. Every human being
has in his breast the elements of that Divine, Everlasting Law, which the

highest orders of the creation obey. He has the idea of Duty; and to unfold, revere, obey this, is the very purpose for which life was given. Every human being has the idea of what is meant by that word, Truth; that is, he sees, however dimly, the great object of Divine and created intelligence, and is capable of ever-enlarging perceptions of truth. Every human being has affections, which may be purified and expanded into a Sublime Love. He has, too, the idea of Happiness, and a thirst for it which cannot be appeased. Such is our nature. Wherever we see a man, we see the possessor of these great capacities. Did God make such a being to be owned as a tree or a brute? How plainly was he made to exercise, unfold, improve his highest powers, made for a moral, spiritual good! and how is he wronged, and his Creator opposed, when he is forced and broken into a tool to another's physical enjoyment!

Such a being was plainly made for an End in Himself. He is a Person, not a Thing. He is an End, not a mere Instrument or Means. He was made for his own virtue and happiness. Is this end reconcilable with his being held and used as a chattel? The sacrifice of such a being to another's will, to another's present, outward, ill-comprehended good, is the greatest violence which can be offered to any creature of God. It is to degrade him from his rank in the universe, to make him a means, not an end, to cast him out from God's spiritual family into the brutal herd. * * *

I now proceed to the second division of the subject. I am to show, that man has sacred Rights, the gifts of God, and inseparable from human nature, which are violated by slavery. Some important principles, which belong to this head, were necessarily anticipated under the preceding; but they need a fuller exposition. The whole subject of Rights needs to be reconsidered. Speculations and reasonings about it have lately been given to the public, not only false, but dangerous to freedom, and there is a strong tendency to injurious views. Rights are made to depend on circumstances, so that pretences may easily be made or created for violating them successively, till none shall remain. Human rights have been represented as so modified and circumscribed by men's entrance into the social state, that only the shadows of them are left. They have been spoken of as absorbed in the public good; so that a man may be innocently enslaved, if the public good shall so require. To meet fully all these errors, for such I hold them, a larger work than the present is required. The nature of man, his relations to the state, the limits of civil government, the elements of the public good, and the degree to which the individual must be surrendered to this good, these are topics which the present subject involves. I cannot enter into them particularly, but shall lay down what seem to me the great and true principles in regard to them. I shall show, that man has rights from his very nature, not the gifts of society, but of God; that they are not surrendered on entering the social state; that they must not be taken away under the plea of public good; that the Individual is never to be sacrificed to the Community; that the idea of Rights is to prevail above all the interests of the state.

Man has rights by nature. The disposition of some to deride abstract rights, as if all rights were uncertain, mutable, and conceded by society, shows a lamentable ignorance of human nature. Whoever understands this must see in it an immovable foundation of rights. These are gifts of the Creator, bound up indissolubly with our moral constitution. In the order of things, they precede society, lie at its foundation, constitute man's capacity for it, and are the great objects of social institutions. The consciousness of rights is not a creation of human art, a conventional sentiment, but essential to and inseparable from the human soul.

Man's rights belong to him as a Moral Being, as capable of perceiving moral distinctions, as a subject of moral obligation. As soon as he becomes conscious of Duty, a kindred consciousness springs up, that he has a Right to do what the sense of duty enjoins, and that no foreign will or power can obstruct his moral action without crime. He feels, that the sense of duty was given to him as a Law, that it makes him responsible for himself, that to exercise, unfold, and obey it is the end of his being, and that he has a right to exercise and obey it without hindrance or opposition. A consciousness of dignity, however obscure, belongs also to this divine principle; and, though he may want words to do justice to his thoughts, he feels that he has that within him which makes him essentially equal to all around him.

The sense of duty is the foundation of human rights. In other words, the same inward principle, which teaches the former, bears witness to the latter. Duties and Rights must stand or fall together. It has been too common to oppose them to one another; but they are indissolubly joined together. That same inward principle, which teaches a man what he is bound to do to others, teaches equally, and at the same instant, what others are bound to do to *him*. That same voice, which forbids him to injure a single fellow-creature, forbids every fellow-creature to do *him* harm. His conscience, in revealing the moral law, does not reveal a law for himself only, but speaks as a Universal Legislator. He has an intuitive conviction, that the obligations of this divine code press on others as truly as on himself. * * * Accordingly there is no deeper principle in human nature, than the consciousness of rights. So profound, so ineradicable is this sentiment, that the oppressions of ages have nowhere wholly stifled it.

Having shown the foundation of human rights in human nature, it may be asked what they are. Perhaps they do not admit very accurate definition, any more than human duties; for the Spiritual cannot be weighed and measured like the Material. * * * And yet, perhaps they may be comprehended in one sentence. They may all be comprised in the right, which belongs to every rational being, to exercise his powers for the promotion of his own and others' Happiness and Virtue. These are the great purposes of his existence. For these his powers were given, and to these he is bound to devote them. He is bound to make himself and others better and happier, according to his ability. His ability for this work is a sacred trust from God, the greatest of all trusts. He must answer for the waste or abuse of it. He consequently suffers an unspeakable wrong, when stripped of it by others, or forbidden to employ it for the ends for which it is given; when the powers, which God has given for such generous uses, are impaired or destroyed by others, or the means for their action and growth are forcibly withheld. As every human being is bound to employ his faculties for his own and others' good, there is an obligation on each to leave all free for the accomplishment of this end; and whoever respects this obligation, whoever uses his own, without invading others' powers, or obstructing others' duties, has a sacred, indefeasible right to be unassailed, unobstructed, unharmed by all with whom he may be connected. Here is the grand, all-comprehending right of human nature. Every man should revere it, should assert it for himself and for all, and should bear solemn testimony against every infraction of it, by whomsoever made or endured. * * *

Perhaps nothing has done more to impair the sense of the reality and sacredness of human rights, and to sanction oppression, than loose ideas as to the change made in man's natural rights by his entrance into civil society. It is commonly said, that men part with a portion of these by becoming a community, a body politic; that government consists of powers surrendered by the individual; and it is said, "If certain rights and powers may be surrendered, why not others? why not all? what limit is to be set? The good of the community, to which a part is given up, may demand the whole; and in this good, all private rights are merged." This is the logic of despotism. We are grieved that it finds its way into republics, and that it sets down the great principles of freedom as abstractions and metaphysical theories, good enough for the cloister, but too refined for practical and real life.

Human rights, however, are not to be so reasoned away. They belong, as we have seen, to man as a moral being, and nothing can divest him of them but the destruction of his nature. They are not to be given up to society as a prey. On the contrary, the great end of civil society is to secure them. The great end of government is to repress *all wrong*. Its highest function is to protect the weak against the powerful, so that the obscurest human being may enjoy his rights in peace. Strange that an institution, built on the idea of Rights, should be used to unsettle this idea, to confuse our moral perceptions, to sanctify wrongs as means of general good!

ANGELINA GRIMKÉ

Appeal to the Christian Women of the South (1836)

The Grimké sisters, who faced imprisonment in the South for their abolitionist activities in the North, often couched their arguments against slavery in religious terms. Relying heavily on scripture to refute defenders of slavery, Angelina also appealed to women's religious sentiments, urging them to become involved in abolitionist activities. In particular, she encouraged women to use the power of moral suasion to persuade men "that slavery is a crime against God and man."

I have thus, I think, clearly proved to you seven propositions, viz.: First, that slavery is contrary to the declaration of our independence. Second, that it is contrary to the first charter of human rights given to Adam, and renewed to Noah. Third, that the fact of slavery having been the subject of prophecy, furnishes *no* excuse whatever to slavedealers. Fourth, that no such system existed under the patriarchal dispensation. Fifth, that *slavery never* existed under the Jewish dispensation; but so far otherwise, that every servant was placed under the *protection of law,* and care taken not only to prevent all *involuntary* servitude, but all *voluntary perpetual* bondage. Sixth, that slavery in America reduces a *man* to a *thing,* a "chattel personal," *robs him* of *all* his rights as a *human being,* fetters both his mind and body, and protects the *master* in the most unnatural and unreasonable power, whilst it *throws him out* of the protection of law. Seventh, that slavery is contrary to the example and precepts of our holy and merciful Redeemer, and of his apostles.

But perhaps you will be ready to query, why appeal to *women* on this subject? *We* do not make the laws which perpetuate slavery. *No* legislative power is vested in *us; we* can do nothing to overthrow the system, even if we wished to do so. To this I reply, I know you do not make the laws, but I also know that *you are the wives and mothers, the sisters and daughters of those who do;* and if you really suppose *you* can do nothing to overthrow slavery, you are greatly mistaken. You can do much in every way: four things I will name. 1st. You can read on this subject. 2d. You can pray over this subject. 3d. You can speak on this subject. 4th. You can *act* on this subject. I have not placed reading before praying because I regard it more important, but because, in order to pray aright, we must understand what we are praying for; it is only then we can "pray with the understanding and the spirit also."

1. Read then on the subject of slavery. Search the Scriptures daily, whether the things I have told you are true. Other books and papers might be a great help to you in this investigation, but they are not necessary, and it is hardly probable that your Committees of Vigilance will allow you to have any other. The *Bible* then is the book I want you to read in the spirit of inquiry, and the spirit of prayer. Even the enemies of Abolitionists, acknowledge that their doctrines are drawn from it. In the great mob in Boston last autumn, when the books and papers of the Anti-Slavery Society were thrown out of the windows of their office, an individual laid hold of the Bible and was about tossing it out to the ground, when another reminded him that it was the Bible he had in his hand. "O! *'tis all one,*" he replied, and out went the sacred volume along with the rest. We thank him for the acknowledgment. Yes, "*it is all one,*" for our books and papers are mostly commentaries on the Bible, and the Declaration. Read the *Bible* then, it contains the words of Jesus, and they are spirit and life. Judge for yourselves whether *he sanctioned* such a system of oppression and crime.

2. Pray over this subject. When you have entered into your closets, and shut to the doors, then pray to your father, who seeth in secret, that he would open your eyes to see whether slavery is *sinful,* and if it is, that he would enable you to bear a faithful, open and unshrinking testimony against it, and to do whatsoever your hands find to do, leaving the consequences entirely to him, who still says to us whenever we try to reason away duty from the fear of consequences, "*What is that to thee, follow thou me.*" Pray also for that poor slave, that he may be kept patient and submissive under his hard lot, until God is pleased to open the door of freedom to him without violence or bloodshed. Pray too for the master that his heart may be softened, and he made willing to acknowledge, as Joseph's brethren did, "Verily we are guilty concerning our brother," before he will be compelled to add in consequence of Divine judgment, "therefore is all this evil come upon us." Pray also for all your brethren and sisters who are laboring in the righteous cause of Emancipation in the Northern States, England and the world. There is great encouragement for prayer in these words of our Lord. "Whatsoever ye shall ask the Father *in my name,* he *will give* it to you"— Pray then without ceasing, in the closet and the social circle.

3. Speak on this subject. It is through the tongue, the pen, and the press, that truth is principally propagated. Speak then to your relatives,

your friends, your acquaintances on the subject of slavery; be not afraid if you are conscientiously convinced it is *sinful,* to say so openly, but calmly, and to let your sentiments be known. If you are served by the slaves of others, try to ameliorate their condition as much as possible; never aggravate their faults, and thus add fuel to the fire of anger already kindled in a master and mistress's bosom; remember their extreme ignorance, and consider them as your Heavenly Father does the *less* culpable on this account, even when they do wrong things. Discountenance *all* cruelty to them, all starvation, all corporal chastisement; these may brutalize and *break* their spirits, but will never bond them to willing, cheerful obedience. If possible, see that they are comfortably and *seasonably* fed, whether in the house or the field; it is unreasonable and cruel to expect slaves to wait for their breakfast until eleven o'clock, when they rise at five or six. Do all you can, to induce their owners to clothe them well, and to allow them many little indulgences which would contribute to their comfort. Above all, try to persuade your husband, father, brothers and sons, that *slavery is a crime against God and man,* and that it is a great sin to keep *human beings* in such abject ignorance; to deny them the privilege of learning to read and write. The Catholics are universally condemned, for denying the Bible to the common people, but, *slaveholders must not* blame them, for *they* are doing the *very same thing,* and for the very same reason, neither of these systems can bear the light which bursts from the pages of that Holy Book. And lastly, endeavour to inculcate submission on the part of the slaves, but whilst doing this be faithful in pleading the cause of the oppressed.

> *Will* you *behold unheeding,*
> *Life's holiest feelings crushed.*
> *Where* woman's *heart is bleeding,*
> *Shall* woman's *heart be hushed?*

4. Act on this subject. Some of you *own* slaves yourselves. If you believe slavery is *Sinful,* set them at liberty, "undo the heavy burdens and let the oppressed go free." If they wish to remain with you, pay them wages, if not let them leave you. Should they remain teach them, and have them taught the common branches of an English education; they have minds and those minds, *ought to be improved.* So precious a talent as intellect, never was given to be wrapt in a napkin and buried in the earth. It is the *duty* of all, as far as they can, to improve their own mental faculties, because we are commanded to love God with *all our minds,* as well as with all our hearts, and we commit a great sin, if we *forbid or prevent* that cultivation of the mind in others, which would enable them to

perform this duty. Teach your servants then to read &c, and encourage them to believe it is their *duty* to learn, if it were only that they might read the Bible.

But some of you will say, we can neither free our slaves nor teach them to read, for the laws of our state forbid it. Be not surprised when I say such wicked laws *ought to be no barrier* in the way of your duty.

The *women of the South can overthrow* this horrible system of oppression and cruelty, licentiousness and wrong. Such appeals to your legislatures would be irresistible, for there is something in the heart of man which *will bend under moral suasion*. There is a swift witness for truth in his bosom, which *will respond to truth* when it is uttered with calmness and dignity. If you could obtain but six signatures to such a petition in only one state, I would say, send up that petition, and be not in the least discouraged by the scoffs and jeers of the heartless, or the resolution of the house to lay it on the table. It will be a great thing if the subject can be introduced into your legislatures in any way, even by *women,* and *they* will be the most likely to introduce it there in the best possible manner, as a matter of *morals* and *religion,* not of expediency or politics. You may petition, too, the different ecclesiastical bodies of the slave states. Slavery must be attacked with the whole power of truth and the sword of the spirit. You must take it up on *Christian* ground, and fight against it with Christian weapons, whilst your feet are shod with the preparation of the gospel of peace. And *you are now* loudly called upon by the cries of the widow and the orphan, to arise and gird yourselves for this great moral conflict, with the whole armour of righteousness upon the right hand and on the left.

The great fundamental principle of Abolitionists is, that man cannot rightfully hold his fellow man as property. Therefore, we affirm that *every slaveholder is a man-stealer.* We do so, for the following reasons: to steal a man is to rob him of himself. It matters not whether this be done in Guinea, or Carolina; a man is a *man,* and *as* as man he has *inalienable* rights, among which is the right to personal *liberty.* Now if every man has an *inalienable* right to personal liberty, it follows, that he cannot rightfully be reduced to slavery. But I find in these United States, 2,250,000 men, women and children, robbed of that to which they have an *inalienable* right. How comes this to pass? Where millions are plundered, are there no *plunderers?* If, then, the slaves have been robbed of their liberty, *who* has robbed them? Not the man who stole their forefathers from Africa, but he who now holds them in bondage; no matter *how* they came into his possession, whether he inherited them, or bought them, or seized them at their birth on his own plantation. The only difference I can see between the original man-stealer, who caught the African in his native country, and the American slaveholder, is, that the former committed *one* act of robbery, while the other perpetrates the same crime *continually*. Slaveholding is the perpetrating of acts, all of the same kind, in a *series*, the first of which is technically called man-stealing. The *first* act robbed the man of himself; and the same state of mind that prompted *that act, keeps up the series,* having *taken* his all from him: it *keeps* his all from him, not only *refusing* to *restore,* but still robbing him of all he gets, and as fast as he gets it. Slaveholding, then, is *the constant or habitual perpetration of the act of man-stealing. To make* a slave is *man-stealing*—the ACT *itself*—to *hold* him such is man-stealing—the *habit,* the *permanent* state, made up of *individual* acts. In other words—to *begin* to hold a slave is man-stealing—to *keep on* holding him is merely a *repetition* of the first act—a doing the same identical thing *all the time.* A series of the same acts continued for a length of time is a *habit*—*a permanent state.* And the *first* of this series of the *same* acts that make up this *habit* or state is just like all the rest.

* * *

These are Abolition sentiments on the subject of slaveholding; and although our principles are universally held by our opposers at the North, yet I am told on the 44th page of thy book, that "the word man-stealer has one peculiar signification, and is no more synonymous with slaveholder than it is with sheep-stealer." I must acknowledge, thou hast only confirmed my opinion of the difference which I had believed to exist between Abolitionists and their opponents. As well might Saul have declared, that he held similar views with Stephen, when he stood by and kept the raiment of those who slew him.

I know that a broad line of distinction is drawn between our principles and our measures, by those who are anxious to "avoid the appearance of evil"—very desirous of retaining the fair character of enemies to slavery. Now, our *measures* are simply the carrying out of our *principles;* and we find, that just in proportion as individuals embrace our principles, in spirit and in truth, they cease to cavil at our measures.

* * *

Real Abolitionists know full well, that the slave never has been, and never can be, a whit the better for mere abstractions, floating in the *head* of any man; and they also know, that *principles, fixed in the heart,* are things of another sort. The former have never done any good in the world, because they possess no vitality, and therefore cannot bring forth *the fruits* of holy, untiring effort; but the latter live in the lives of their possessors, and breathe in their words. And I am free to express my belief, that *all* who really and heartily approve our *principles,* will also approve our *measures;* and that, too, just as certainly as a good tree will bring forth good fruit.

But there is another peculiarity in the views of Abolitionists. We hold that the North is guilty of the crime of slaveholding—we assert that it is a *national* sin: on the contrary, in thy book, I find the following acknowledgement:—"*Most* persons in the non-slaveholding States, have considered the matter of southern slavery as one in which they were no more called to interfere, than in the abolition of the press-gang system in England, or the tithe-system in Ireland." Now I cannot see how the same principles can produce such entirely different opinions. "Can a good tree bring forth corrupt fruit?" This I deny, and cannot admit what thou art anxious to prove, viz. that "Public opinion may have been *wrong* on this point, and yet *right* on all those great *principles* of rectitude and justice relative to slavery." If Abolition principles are generally adopted at the North, how comes it to pass, that there is no abolition action here, except what is put forth by a few despised fanatics, as they are called? Is there any living faith without works? Can the sap circulate vigorously, and yet neither blossoms put forth nor fruit appear?

Again, I am told on the 7th page, that all Northern Christians believe it is a sin to hold a man in slavery for "*mere purposes of gain*"; as if this was the *whole* abolition principle on this subject. I can assure thee that Abolitionists do not stop here. Our principle is, that *no circumstances can ever justify* a man in holding his fellow man as *property*; it matters not what *motive* he may give for such a monstrous violation of the laws of God. The claim to him as *property* is an annhilation of his right to himself, which is the foundation upon which all his other rights are built. It is high-handed robbery of Jehovah; for He has declared, "All souls are *mine*." For myself, I believe there are hundreds of thousands at the South, who do *not* hold their slaves, by any means, as much "for the purposes of gain," as they do from *the lust of power*: this is the passion that reigns triumphant there, and those who do not know this, have much yet to learn. Where, then, is the similarity in our views?

THEODORE DWIGHT WELD

Slavery As It Is: Testimony of a Thousand Witnesses (1839)

The husband of Angelina Grimké, Theodore Dwight Weld (1803–1895) was an advocate of temperance and educational reform who became involved in the abolitionist movement through the religious revivals of the

1830s. After helping establish the American Anti-Slavery Society, Weld published the massive and well-researched antislavery book Slavery As It Is, *which contained evidence of terrible mistreatment taken from thousands of southern newspapers and firsthand accounts, including his wife's childhood recollections of life in Charleston, South Carolina. The book was immensely successful and influential: it sold over 100,000 copies in its first year and provided the basis for Harriet Beecher Stowe's* Uncle Tom's Cabin.

R eader, you are empannelled as a juror to try a plain case and bring in an honest verdict. The question at issue is not one of law, but of fact—"What is the actual condition of the slaves in the United States?" A plainer case never went to a jury. Look at it. TWENTY-SEVEN HUNDRED THOU-SAND PERSONS in this country, men, women, and children, are in SLAVERY. Is slavery, as a condition for human beings, good, bad, or indifferent? We submit the question without argument. You have common sense, and con-science, and a human heart;—pronounce upon it. You have a wife, or a husband, a child, a father, a mother, a brother or a sister—make the case your own, make it theirs, and bring in your verdict. The case of Human Rights against Slavery has been adjudicated in the court of conscience times innumerable. The same verdict has always been rendered—"guilty;" the same sentence has always been pronounced, "Let it be accursed;" * * *

There is not a man on earth who does not believe that slavery is a curse. Human beings may be inconsistent, but human *nature* is true to herself. She has uttered her testimony against slavery with a shriek ever since the monster was begotten; and till it perishes amidst the execrations of the universe, she will traverse the world on its track, dealing her bolts upon its head, and dashing against it her condemning brand. * * *

Two millions seven hundred thousand persons in these States are in this condition. They were made slaves and are held such by force, and by being put in fear, and this for no crime! Reader, what have you to say of such treatment? Is it right, just, benevolent? Suppose I should seize you, rob you of your liberty, drive you into the field, and make you work with-out pay as long as you live, would that be justice and kindness, or mon-strous injustice and cruelty? Now, every body knows that the slaveholders do these things to the slaves every day, and yet it is stoutly affirmed that they treat them well and kindly, and that their tender regard for their slaves restrains the masters from inflicting cruelties upon them. We shall go into no metaphysics to show the absurdity of this pretence. The man who *robs* you every day, is, forsooth, quite too tender-hearted ever to cuff or kick you! True, he can snatch your money, but he does it gently lest he should hurt you. He can empty your pockets without qualms, but if your *stomach* is empty, it cuts him to the quick. He can make you work a life time without pay, but loves you too well to let you go hungry. He fleeces you of your *rights* with a relish, but is shocked if you work bareheaded in summer, or in winter without warm stockings. He can make you go without your *liberty*, but never without a shirt. He can crush, in you, all hope of bettering your condition, by vowing that you shall die his slave, but though he can coolly torture your feelings, he is too compassionate to lacerate your back—he can break your heart, but he is very tender of your skin. He can strip you of all protection and thus expose you to all outrages, but if you are exposed to the *weather*, half clad and half sheltered, how yearn his tender bowels! What! slaveholders talk of treating men well, and yet not only rob them of all they get, and as fast as they get it, but rob them of *themselves*, also; their very hands and feet, all their muscles, and limbs, and senses, their bodies and minds, their time and liberty and earnings, their free speech and rights of conscience, their right to acquire knowledge, and property, and reputation;—and yet they, who plunder them of all these, would fain make us believe that their soft hearts ooze out so lovingly toward their slaves that they always keep them well housed and well clad, never push them too hard in the field, never make their dear backs smart, nor let their dear stomachs get empty.

But there is no end to these absurdities. Are slaveholders dunces, or do they take all the rest of the world to be, that they think to bandage our eyes with such thin gauzes? Protesting their kind regard for those whom they hourly plunder of all they have and all they get! What! when they have seized their victims, and annihilated all their *rights*, still claim to be the special guardians of their *happiness!* Plunderers of their liberty, yet the careful suppliers of their wants? Robbers of their earnings, yet watchful sentinels round their interests, and kind providers of their comforts? Filching all their time, yet granting generous donations for rest and sleep? Stealing the use of their muscles, yet thoughtful of their ease? Putting them under *drivers*, yet careful that they are not hard-pushed? Too humane forsooth to stint the stomachs of their slaves, yet force their *minds* to starve, and brandish over them pains and penalties, if they dare to reach forth for the smallest crumb of knowledge, even a letter of the alphabet!

It is no marvel that slaveholders are always talking of their *kind treatment* of their slaves. The only marvel is, that men of sense caw be gulled by such professions. Despots always insist that they are merciful. * * *

Slaveholders, the world over, have sung the praises of their tender mercies towards their slaves. Even the wretches that plied the African slave trade, tried to rebut Clarkson's proofs of their cruelties, by speeches, affidavits, and published pamphlets, setting forth the accommodations of the "middle passage," and their kind attentions to the comfort of those whom they had stolen from their homes, and kept stowed away under hatches, during a voyage of four thousand miles. * * *

As slaveholders and their apologists are volunteer witnesses in their own cause, and are flooding the world with testimony that their slaves are kindly treated; that they are well fed, well clothed, well housed, well lodged, moderately worked, and bountifully provided with all things needful for their comfort, we propose—first, to disprove their assertions by the testimony of a multitude of impartial witnesses, and then to put slaveholders themselves through a course of cross-questioning which shall draw their condemnation out of their own mouths, We will prove that the slaves in the United States are treated with barbarous inhumanity; that they are overworked, underfed, wretchedly clad and lodged, and have insufficient sleep; that they are often made to wear round their necks iron collars armed with prongs, to drag heavy chains and weights at their feet while working in the field, and to wear yokes, and bells, and iron horns; that they are often kept confined in the stocks day and night for weeks together, made to wear gags in their mouths for hours or days, have some of their front teeth torn out or broken off, that they may be easily detected when they run away; that they are frequently flogged with terrible severity, have red pepper rubbed into their lacerated flesh, and hot brine, spirits of turpentine, &c., poured over the gashes to increase the torture; that they are often stripped naked, their backs and limbs cut knives, bruised and mangled by scores and hundred of blows with the paddle, and terribly torn by claws of cats, drawn over them by their tormentors; that they are often hunted with bloodhounds and shot down like beasts, or torn in pieces by dogs; that they are often suspended by the arms and whipped and beaten till they faint, and when revived by restoratives, beaten again till they faint, and sometimes till they die; that their ears are often cut off, their eyes knocked out, their bones broken, their flesh branded with red hot irons; that they are maimed, mutilated and burned to death over slow fires. All these things, and more, and worse, we shall *prove*. Reader, we know whereof we affirm, we have weighed it well; *more and worse* WE WILL PROVE. Mark these words, and read on; we will establish all these facts by the testimony of scores and hundreds of eye witnesses, by the testimony of *slaveholders* in all parts of the slave states, by slaveholding members of Congress and of state legislatures, by ambassadors to foreign courts, by judges, by doctors of divinity, and clergymen of all denominations, by merchants, mechanics, lawyers and physicians, by presidents and professors in colleges and *professional* seminaries, by planters, overseers and drivers. We shall show, not merely that such deeds are committed, but that they are frequent; not done in corners, but before the sun; not in one of the slave states, but in ail of them; not perpetrated by brutal overseers and drivers merely, but by magistrates, by legislators, by professors of religion, by preachers of the gospel, by governors of states, by "gentlemen of property and standing," and by delicate females moving in the "highest circles of society."

DAVID WALKER

Appeal . . . to the Colored Citizens of the World . . . (1829)

David Walker (1785–1830) was a free black from North Carolina who wrote for Freedom's Journal, *the first black newspaper in America. In his* Appeal . . . to the Colored Citizens of the World . . . , *a radical pamphlet that went through multiple reprintings, Walker urged slaves to rebel and called on blacks everywhere to live up to the dignity befitting creatures made in God's image. He also drew particular attention to Jefferson's writings about Negroes. As a dealer in second-hand clothes, Walker concealed copies of his pamphlet in the garments he sold to seamen as a way to disseminate his antislavery ideas in the South. Partly as a result of the circulation of these smuggled pamphlets, southern states passed legislation prohibiting slaves from learning to read and write. Walker himself died in mysterious circumstances after receiving numerous death threats.*

I am fully aware, in making this appeal to my much afflicted and suffering brethren, that I shall not only be assailed by those whose greatest earthly desires are, to keep us in abject ignorance and wretchedness, and who are of the firm conviction that heaven has designed us and our children to be slaves and beasts of burden to them and their children * * * Can our condition be any worse? Can it be more mean and abject? If there are any changes, will they not be for the better, though they may appear for the worse at first? Can they get us any lower? Where can they get us? They are afraid to treat us worse, for they know well, the day they do it they are gone * * * I appeal to heaven for my motive in writing, who knows that my object is, if possible, to awaken in the breasts of my afflicted, degraded and slumbering brethren, a spirit of enquiry and investigation respecting our miseries and wretchedness in this *Republican Land of Liberty*!!!! * * * And as the inhuman system of slavery, is the source from which most of our miseries proceed, I shall begin with that curse to nations; which has spread terror and devastation through so many nations of antiquity, and which is raging to such a pitch at the present day in Spain and in Portugal * * * The fact is, the labor of slaves comes so cheap to the avaricious usurpers, and is, as they think, of such great utility to the country where it exists, that those who are actuated by sordid avarice only, overlook the evils, which will as sure as the Lord lives, follow after the good. In fact, they are so happy to keep in ignorance and degradation, and to receive the homage and the labor of the slaves, they forget that God rules in the armies of heaven and among the inhabitants of the earth, having his ears continually open to the cries, tears, and groans of his oppressed people; and being a just and holy Being will at one day appear fully in behalf of the oppressed, and arrest the progress of the avaricious oppressors; for although the destruction of the oppressors God may not effect by the oppressed, yet the Lord our God will bring other destructions upon them—for not infrequently will he cause them to rise up one against another, to be split and divided, and to oppress each other, and sometimes to open hostilities with sword in hand * * * Their destruction may indeed be procrastinated a while, but can it continue long while they are oppressing the Lord's people? Has He not the hearts of all men in His hand? Will he suffer one part of his creatures to go on oppressing another like brutes always, with impunity? And yet those avaricious wretches are calling for Peace!!! I declare it does appear to me, as though some nations think God is asleep, or that he made the Africans for nothing else but to dig their mines and work their farms, or they cannot believe history, sacred or profane. I ask every man who has a heart and is blessed with the privilege of believing—Is not God a God of justice to all his creatures? Do you say he is? Then if he gives peace and tranquility to tyrants, and permits them to keep our fathers, our mothers, ourselves, and our children in eternal ignorance, and wretchedness to support them and their families, would he be to us a God of Justice?? I ask, O ye Christians!! who hold us and our children, in the most abject ignorance and degradation, that ever a people were afflicted with since the world began—I say, if God gives you peace and tranquility, and suffers you thus to go on afflicting us and our children, who have never given you the least provocation, Would he be to us a God of Justice? If you will allow that we are men, who feel for each other, does not the blood of our fathers and of us their children, cry aloud to the Lord of Sabaoth against you, for the cruelties and murders with which you have, and do continue to afflict us * * *

I promised to demonstrate to the satisfaction of the most incredulous, that we, the colored people of these United States of America, are the most wretched, degraded, and abject set of beings that ever lived since the world began, and that the white Americans having reduced us to the wretched state of slavery, treat us in that condition more cruelly (they being an enlightened and christian people) than any heathen nation did any people whom it had reduced to our condition. * * * To prove farther that the condition of the Israelites was better under the Egyptians than ours is under the whites, I call upon the professing christians, I call upon the philanthropist, I call upon the very tyrant himself, to show me a page of history, either sacred or profane, on which a verse can be found, which maintains, that the Egyptians heaped the insupportable insult upon the children of Israel by telling them that they were not of the human family. Can the whites deny this charge? Have they not, after having reduced us to the deplorable condition of slaves under their feet, held us up as descending originally from the tribes of Monkeys and Orang-Outangs? O! my God! I appeal to every man of feeling—is not this unsupportable? Is it not heaping the most gross insult upon our miseries, because they have got us under their feet and we cannot help ourselves? * * * Has not Mr. Jefferson declared to the world, that we are inferior to the whites, both in the endowments of our bodies and of minds? It is indeed surprising, that a man of such great learning, combined with such excellent natural parts, should speak so of a set of men in chains. * * * Here, let me ask Mr. Jefferson (but he is gone, to answer at the bar of God, for the deeds done in his body while living), therefore I ask the whole American people, had I not rather die, or be put to death than to be a slave to any tyrant, who takes not only my own, but my wife and children's lives by inches? Yea, I would meet death with avidity far in preference to such servile submission to the murderous hands of tyrants. Mr. Jefferson's very severe remarks on us have been so extensively argued upon by men whose attainments in literature, I shall never be able to reach, that I would not have meddled with it, were it not to solicit each of my brethren, who has the spirit of a man, to buy a copy of Mr. Jefferson's "Notes on Virginia," and put it in the hand of his son. For let no one of us suppose that the refutations which have been written by our white friends are enough— they are *whites*—we are *blacks*. * * * The whites have always been an unjust, jealous, unmerciful, avaricious and blood thirsty set of beings, always seeking after power and authority. * * * In fact, take them as a body, they are ten times more cruel, avaricious and unmerciful than ever they were; for while they were heathens, they were bad enough it is true, but it is positively a fact that they were not quite so audacious as to go and take vessel loads of men, women, and children, and in cold blood and through devilishness, throw them into the sea and murder them in all kinds of ways. While they were heathens, they were too ignorant for such barbarity. But being christians, enlightened and sensible, they are now completely prepared for such hellish cruelties * * * The whites have had the essence of the gospel as it was preached by my master and his apostles—the Ethiopians have not * * * the Lord will give it to them to their satisfaction * * *

Ignorance, my brethren, is a mist, low down into the very dark and almost impenetrable abyss of which, our fathers for many centuries have been plunged. The christians, and enlightened of Europe, and some of Asia, seeing the ignorance and consequent degradation of our fathers, instead of trying to enlighten them, by teaching them that religion and light with which God had blessed them, they have plunged them into wretchedness ten thousand times more intolerable, than if they had left them entirely to the Lord, and to add to their miseries, deep down into which they have plunged them, tell them, that they are an inferior and distinct race of beings * * * The whites want slaves, and want us for their slaves, but some of them will curse the day they ever saw us. As true as the sun ever shone in its meridian splendor, my colour will root some of them out of the very face of the earth. They shall have enough of making slaves of, and butchering, and murdering us in the manner which they have. No doubt some may say that I write with a bad spirit, and that I being a black, wish these things to occur. Whether I write with a bad or good spirit, I say if these things do not occur in their proper time, it is because the world in which we live does not exist, and we are deceived with regard to its existence * * * I should like to see the whites repent peradventure God may have mercy on them, some however, have gone so far that their cup must be filled. Ignorance and treachery, one against the other—a servile and abject submission to the lash of tyrants, we see plainly, my brethren, are not the natural elements of the blacks, as the Americans try to make us believe; but these are misfortunes which God has suffered our fathers to be enveloped in for so many ages, no doubt in consequence of their disobedience to their Maker and which do, indeed, reign at this time among us, almost to the destruction of all other principles, for I must truly say, that ignorance, the mother of treachery and deceit, gnaws into our very vitals. Ignorance, as it now exists among us, produces a state of things, O my Lord! too horrible to present to the world. Any man who is curious to see the full force of ignorance developed among the colored people of the United States of America, has only to go into the southern and western states of this confederacy, where, if he is not a tyrant, but has the feelings of a human being, who can feel for a fellow creature, he may see enough to make his very heart bleed! He may see there, a son take his mother, who bore almost the pains of death to give him birth, and by the command of a tyrant, strip her as naked as she came into the world, and apply the cow-hide to her, until she falls a victim to death in the road! He may see a husband take his dear wife, not unfrequently in a pregnant state, and perhaps far advanced, and beat her for an unmerciful wretch, until his infant falls a lifeless lump at her feet! Can the Americans escape God Almighty? If they do, can he be to us a God of Justice? * * *

How can, Oh! how can those enemies but say that we and our children are not of the Human Family, but were made by our creator to be an inheritance to them and theirs forever? How can the slave-holders but say that they can bribe the best coloured person in the country, to sell his brethren for a trifling sum of money, and take that atrocity to confirm them in their avaricious opinion, that we were made to be the slaves of them and their children?

How could Mr. Jefferson but say, "I advance it therefore as a suspicion only, that the blacks, whether originally a distinct race, or made distinct by time and circumstances, are *inferior to the whites in the endowments both of body and mind?* It is not against experience to suppose that different species of the same genus, or varieties of the same species, may possess different qualifications. [Here, my brethren, listen to him.] Will not a love of natural history then, one who views the gradations in all the races of animals with the eye of philosophy, excuse any effort to keep those in the department of man as distinct as nature has formed them? * * * This unfortunate difference of colour, and perhaps of faculty, is a powerful obstacle to the emancipation of these people. Many of their advocates, while they wish to vindicate the liberty of human nature are anxious also to preserve its dignity and beauty. Some of these, embarrassed by the question, 'What further is to be done with them?' join themselves in opposition with those who are actuated by sordid avarice only." * * * For my part, I am glad that Mr. Jefferson has advanced his position for your sake; for you will either have to contradict or confirm him by your own actions and not by what our friends have said or done for us; for those things are other men's labors and do not satisfy the Americans who are waiting for us to prove to them ourselves that we are men before they will be willing to admit the fact * * *

Men of colour, who are also of sense, for you particularly is my appeal designed. Our more ignorant brethren are not liable to penetrate its value. I call upon you therefore to cast your eyes upon the wretchedness of your brethren and to do your utmost to enlighten them—*go to work and enlighten your brethren*—Let the Lord see you doing what you can to rescue them and yourselves from degradation * * * There is a great work for you to do, as trifling as some of you may think of it. You have to prove to the Americans and the world, that we are men, and not brutes as we have been represented, and by millions treated. Remember, to let the aim of your labours among your brethren, and particularly the youths, be the dissemination of education and religion. It is lamentable, that many of our children go to school, from four until they are eight or ten, and sometimes fifteen years of age, and leave school knowing but a little more about the grammar of their language than a horse does about handling a musket, and not a few of them are really so ignorant, that they are unable to answer a person correctly, general questions in geography, and to hear them read would only be to disgust a man who has a taste for reading * * * Some few of them, may make out to scribble tolerably well, over half a sheet of paper, which I believe has hitherto been a powerful obstacle in our way, to keep us from acquiring knowledge * * * The cause of this almost universal ignorance amongst us, I appeal to our school-masters to declare. Here is a fact, which I take from the mouth of a young coloured man, who has been in Massachusetts nearly nine years, and who knows grammar this day, nearly as well as he did the day he first entered the school-house, under a white master. This young man says—"my master would never allow me to study grammar." I asked him why? "The school committee forbid the colored children learning grammar, they would not allow any but the white children to study grammar." It is a notorious fact that the major part of the white Americans have, ever since we have been among them, tried to keep us ignorant and make us believe that God made us and our children to be the slaves to them and theirs. Oh! My God, have mercy on Christian Americans!

Religion, my brethren, is a substance of deep consideration among all nations of the earth * * * But pure, and undefiled religion, such as was preached by Jesus Christ and his apostles, is hard to be found in all the earth * * * Indeed, the way in which religion was and is conducted by the Europeans and their descendants, one might believe it was a plan fabricated by themselves and the devils to oppress us!

The wicked and ungodly, seeing their preachers treat us with so much cruelty, they say: our preachers, who must be right, if any body are, treat them like brutes, and why cannot we?—They think it is no harm to keep them in slavery and put the whip to them, and why cannot we do the same!—They being preachers of the gospel of Jesus Christ, if it were any harm, they would surely preach against their oppression and do their utmost to erase it from the country; not only in one or two cities, but one continual cry would be raised in all parts of this confederacy and would cease only with the complete overthrow of the system of slavery, in every part of the country. But how far the American preachers are from preaching against slavery and oppression, which have carried their country to the brink of a precipice; * * * Can the American preachers appeal unto God, the Maker and Searcher of hearts, and tell him, with the Bible in their hands, that they make no distinction on account of men's colour? Can they say, O God! thou knowest all things—thou knowest that we make no distinction between thy creatures to whom we have to preach thy Word? * * * I believe you cannot be so wicked as to tell him that his Gospel was that of *distinction* * * * What right, then, has one of us, to despise another and to treat him cruel, on account of his colour, which none but the God who made it can alter? Can there be a greater absurdity in nature, and particularly in a free republican country? But the Americans, having introduced slavery among them, their hearts having become almost seared, as with an hot iron, and God has nearly given them up to believe a lie in preference to the truth!!! and I am awfully afraid that this pride, prejudice, avarice and blood, will, before long, prove the final ruin of this happy republic, or land of liberty!!! Can anything be a greater mockery of religion than the way in which it is conducted by the Americans?

* * *

Man, in all ages, and all nations of the earth, is the same. Man is a peculiar creature—he is the image of his God, though he may be subjected to the most wretched condition upon earth, yet that spirit and feeling which constitute the creature man, can never be entirely erased from his breast, because the God who made him after his own image, planted it in his heart; he cannot get rid of it. The whites knowing this, they do not know what to do; they are afraid that we, being men, and not brutes, will retaliate, and woe will be to them; therefore, that dreadful fear, together with an avaricious spirit, and the natural love in them to be called masters, bring them to the resolve that they will keep us in ignorance and wretchedness, as long as they possibly can * * * Do the colonizationists think to send us off without first being reconciled to us? * * * Methinks colonizationists think they have a set of brutes to deal with, sure enough. Do they think to drive us from our country and homes, after having enriched it with our blood and tears, and keep back millions of our dear brethren, sunk in the most barbarous wretchedness, to dig up gold and silver for them and their children?

Now Americans, I ask you candidly, was your sufferings under Great Britain one hundredth part as cruel and tyrannical as you have rendered ours under you? Some of you, no doubt, believe that we will never throw off your murderous government, and "provide new guards for our future security." * * * Some of the whites are ignorant enough to tell us, that we ought to be submissive to them, that they may keep their feet on our throats. And if we do not submit to be beaten to death by them, we are bad creatures and of course must be damned. If any man wishes to hear this doctrine openly preached to us by the American preachers, let him go into the Southern and Western sections of this country. I do not speak from hearsay, what I have written, is what I have seen and heard myself. No man may think that my book is made up of conjecture, I have travelled and observed nearly the whole of those things myself, and what little I did not get by my own observation, I received from those among the whites and blacks, in whom the greatest confidence may be placed. The Americans may be as vigilant as they please, but they cannot be vigilant enough for the Lord, neither can they hide themselves, where he will not find and bring them out. * * *

Remember Americans, that we must and shall be free, and enlightened as you are, will you wait until we shall, under God, obtain our liberty by the crushing arm of power? Will it not be dreadful for you? I speak Americans for your good. We must and shall be free I say, in spite of you * * * Throw away your fears and prejudices then, and enlighten us and treat us like men, and we will like you more than we do now hate you, and tell us no more about colonization, for America is as much our country, as it is yours. Treat us like men, and there is no danger but we will all live in peace and happiness together. For we are not like you, hard hearted, unmerciful and unforgiving. What a happy country this will be, if the whites will listen. What nation under heaven, will be able to do anything with us, unless God gives us up into his hand? But Americans, I declare to you, while you keep us in bondage, and treat us like brutes, to make us support you and your families, we cannot be your friends. You do not look for it, do you? Treat us then like men, and we will be your friends.

FREDERICK DOUGLASS

What Are the Colored People Doing for Themselves? (1848)

The abolitionist and women's rights supporter Frederick Douglass (1817–1895) was born a slave in Maryland, but educated himself and eventually escaped. Douglass joined the abolitionist movement after accepting an invitation to describe his experiences as a slave at an anti-slavery convention in Massachusetts. After a two-year speaking tour in

Great Britain, Douglass returned to America with enough money to pur-
chase his freedom (which was necessary because of fears of recapture
after the publication of his autobiography) and to establish the North
Star, an antislavery newspaper whose name was later changed to Fred-
erick Douglass's Paper. During the Civil War he became an adviser to
President Lincoln. In the following selection, Douglass called on free
blacks to take a greater interest in the slavery question as well as in ad-
vancing their progress both as individuals and as a race.

The present is a time when every colored man in the land should bring this important question home to his own heart. It is not enough to know that white men and women are nobly devoting them-selves to our cause; we should know what is being done among ourselves. That our white friends have done, and are still doing, a great and good work for us, is a fact which ought to excite in us sentiments of the pro-foundest gratitude; but it must never be forgotten that when they have ex-erted all their energies, devised every scheme, and done all they can do in asserting our rights, proclaiming our wrongs, and rebuking our foes, their labor is lost—yea, worse than lost, unless we are found in the faithful discharge of our anti-slavery duties. If there be one evil spirit among us, for the casting out of which we pray more earnestly than another, it is that lazy, mean and cowardly spirit, that robs us of all manly self-reliance, and teaches us to depend upon others for the accomplishment of that which we should achieve with our own hands. Our white friends can and are rapidly removing the barriers to our improvement, which themselves have set up; but the main work must be commenced, carried on, and con-cluded by ourselves. While in no circumstances should we undervalue or fail to appreciate the self-sacrificing efforts of our friends, it should never be lost sight of, that our destiny, for good or for evil, for time and for eter-nity, is, by an all-wise God, committed to us; and that all the helps or hin-drances with which we may meet on earth, can never release us from this high and heaven-imposed responsibility. It is evident that we can be im-proved and elevated only just so fast and far as we shall improve and ele-vate ourselves. We must rise or fall, succeed or fail, by our own merits. If we are careless and unconcerned about our own rights and interests, it is not within the power of all the earth combined to raise us from our pres-ent degraded condition. * * *

We say the present is a time when every colored man should ask him-self the question, What am I doing to elevate and improve my condition, and that of my brethren at large? * * *

It is a doctrine held by many good men, in Europe as well as in Amer-ica, that every oppressed people will gain their rights just as soon as they prove themselves worthy of them; and although we may justly object to the extent to which this doctrine is carried, especially in reference to ourselves as a people, it must still be evident to all that there is a great truth in it.

One of the first things necessary to prove the colored man worthy of equal freedom, is an earnest and persevering effort on his part to gain it. We deserve no earthly or heavenly blessing, for which we are unwilling to labor. For our part, we despise a freedom and equality obtained for us by others, and for which we have been unwilling to labor. A man who will not labor to gain his rights, is a man who would not, if he had them, prize and defend them. What is the use of standing a man on his feet, if, when we let him go, his head is again brought to the pavement? Look out for ourselves as we will—beg and pray to our white friends for assistance as much as we will—and that assistance may come, and come at the needed time; but unless we, the colored people of America, shall set about the work of our own regeneration and improvement, we are doomed to drag on in our present miserable and degraded condition for ages. Would that we could speak to every colored man, woman and child in the land, and, with the help of Heaven, we would thunder into their ears their duties and responsibilities, until a spirit should be roused among them, never to be lulled till the last chain is broken. * * *

What we, the colored people, want, is *character*, and this nobody can give us. * * * We must get character for ourselves, as a people. A change in our political condition would do very little for us without this. Character is the important thing, and without it we must continue to be marked for degradation and stamped with the brand of inferiority. With character, we shall be powerful. Nothing can harm us when we get character. * * *

The fact that we are limited and circumscribed, ought rather to incite us to a more vigorous and persevering use of the elevating means within our reach, than to dishearten us. The means of education, though not so free and open to us as to white persons, are nevertheless at our command to such an extent as to make education possible; and these, thank God, are increasing. Let us educate our children; even though it should us subject to a coarser and scantier diet, and disrobe us of our few fine garments. "For the want of knowledge we are killed all the day." Get wisdom—get understanding, is a peculiarly valuable exhortation to us, and the compliance with it is our only hope in this land.—It is idle, a hollow mockery, for us to pray to God to break the oppressor's power, while we neglect the means of knowledge which will give us the ability to break this power.— God will help us when we help ourselves. Our oppressors have divested us of many valuable blessings and facilities for improvement and elevation; but, thank heaven, they have not yet been able to take from us the privilege of being honest, industrious, sober and intelligent. We may read and understand—we may speak and write—we may expose our wrongs—we may appeal to the sense of justice yet alive in the public mind, and by an honest, upright life, we may at last wring from a reluctant public the all-important confession, that we are men, worthy men, good citizens, good Christians, and ought to be treated as such.

FREDERICK DOUGLASS

Lectures on Slavery (1850)

In a series of lectures, Douglass movingly described the dehumanizing cruelty of slavery to both the body and the mind of the slave, who is de-prived of the most basic rights. Douglass did not limit his moral con-demnation to slave keepers, though. Because they allowed slavery to corrupt the most cherished American principles and institutions on both sides of the Mason-Dixon line, Douglass asserted, "the whole American people are responsible for slavery, and must share, in its guilt and shame, with the most obdurate man-stealers of the south."

A very slight acquaintance with the history of American slavery is suffi-cient to show that it is an evil of which it will be difficult to rid this country. It is not the creature of a moment, which to-day is, and to-morrow is not; it is not a pigmy, which a slight blow may demolish; it is no youthful upstart, whose impertinent pratings may be silenced by a dignified con-tempt. No: it is an evil of gigantic proportions, and of long standing.

Its origin in this country dates back to the landing of the pilgrims on Plymouth rock.—It was here more than two centuries ago. The first spot poisoned by its leprous presence, was a small plantation in Virginia. The slaves, at that time, numbered only twenty. They have now increased to the frightful number of three millions; and from that narrow plantation, they are now spread over by far the largest half of the American Union. Indeed, slavery forms an important part of the entire history of the Amer-ican people. Its presence may be seen in all American affairs. It has be-come interwoven with all American institutions, and has anchored itself in the very soil of the American Constitution. It has thrown its paralysing arm over freedom of speech, and the liberty of the press; and has created for itself morals and manners favorable to its own continuance. It has seduced the church, corrupted the pulpit, and brought the powers of both into degrading bondage; and now, in the pride of its power, it even threatens to bring down that grand political edifice, the American Union, unless every member of this republic shall so far disregard his conscience and his God as to yield to its infernal behests.

That must be a powerful influence which can truly be said to govern a nation; and that slavery governs the American people, is indisputably true. * * * Having said thus much upon the power and prevalence of slavery, allow me to speak of the nature of slavery itself; and here I can speak, in part, from experience—I can speak with the authority of positive knowledge. * * *

First of all, I will state, as well as I can, the legal and social relation of master and slave. A master is one (to speak in the vocabulary of the Southern States) who claims and exercises a right of property in the person of a fellow man. This he does with the force of the law and the sanction of Southern religion. The law gives the master absolute power over the slave. He may work him, flog him, hire him out, sell him, and, in certain contingencies, *kill* him, with perfect impunity. The slave is a human being, divested of all rights—reduced to the level of a brute—a mere "chattel" in the eye of the law—placed beyond the circle of human brotherhood—cut off from his kind—his name, which the "recording angel" may have enrolled in heaven, among the blest, is impiously inserted in a *master's ledger*, with horses, sheep and swine. In law, the slave has no wife, no children, no country, and no home. He can own nothing, possess nothing, acquire nothing, but what must belong to another. To eat the fruit of his own toil, to clothe his person with the work of his own hands, is considered stealing. He toils that another may reap the fruit; he is industrious that another may live in idleness; he eats unbolted meal, that another may eat the bread of fine flour; he labors in chains at home, under a burning sun and a biting lash, that another may ride in ease and splendor abroad; he lives in ignorance, that another may be educated; he is abused, that another may be exalted; he rests his toil-worn limbs on the cold, damp ground, that another may repose on the softest pillow; he is clad in coarse and tattered raiment, that another may be arrayed in purple and fine linen; he is sheltered only by the wretched hovel, that a master may dwell in a magnificent mansion; and to this condition he is bound down as by an arm of iron.

From this monstrous relation, there springs an unceasing stream of most revolting cruelties. The very accompaniments of the slave system, stamp it as the offspring of hell itself. To ensure good behavior, the slaveholder relies on *the whip*; to induce proper humility, he relies on *the whip*; to rebuke what he is pleased to term insolence, he relies on *the whip*; to supply the place of wages, as an incentive to toil, he relies on *the whip*; to bind down the spirit of the slave, to imbrute and to destroy his manhood, he relies on *the whip*, the chain, the gag, the thumb-screw, the pillory, the bowie-knife, the pistol, and the blood-hound. These are the necessary and unvarying accompaniments of the system. * * *

Nor is slavery more adverse to the conscience than it is to the mind.

This is shown by the fact that in every State of the American Union, where slavery exists, except the State of Kentucky, there are laws, *absolutely* prohibitory of education among the slaves. The crime of teaching a slave to read is punishable with severe fines and imprisonment, and, in some instances, with *death itself.* * * *

It is perfectly well understood at the South that to educate a slave is to make him discontented with slavery, and to invest him with a power which shall open to him the treasures of freedom; and since the object of the slaveholder is to maintain complete authority over his slave, his constant vigilance is exercised to prevent everything which militates against, or endangers the stability of his authority. Education being among the menacing influences, and, perhaps, the most dangerous, is, therefore, the most cautiously guarded against. * * *

We are sometimes told of the contentment of the slaves, and are entertained with vivid pictures of their happiness. We are told that they often dance and sing; that their masters frequently give them wherewith to make merry; in fine, that that they have little of which to complain. I admit that the slave *does* sometimes sing, dance, and appear to be merry. But what does this prove? It only proves to my mind, that though slavery is armed with a thousand stings, it is not able entirely to kill the elastic spirit of the bondman. That spirit will rise and walk abroad, despite of whips and chains, and extract from the cup of nature, occasional drops of joy and gladness. No thanks to the slaveholder, nor to slavery, that the vivacious captive may sometimes dance in his chains, his very mirth in such circumstances, stands before God, as an accusing angel against his enslaver. * * *

While this nation is guilty of the enslavement of three millions of innocent men and women, it is as idle to think of having a sound and lasting peace, as it is to think there is no God, to take cognizance of the affairs of men. There can be no peace to the wicked while slavery continues in the land, it will be condemned, and while it is condemned there will be agitation; Nature must cease to be nature; Men must become monsters; Humanity must be transformed; Christianity must be exterminated; all ideas of justice, and the laws of eternal goodness must be utterly blotted out from the human soul, ere a system so foul and infernal can escape condemnation, or this guilty Republic can have a sound and enduring Peace. * * *

This evening I shall aim to expose further the wickedness of the slave system—to show that its evils are not confined to the Southern States; but that they overshadow the whole country; and that every American citizen is responsible for its existence, and is solemnly required, by the highest convictions of duty and safety, to labor for its utter extirpation from the land.

* * *

The northern people have been long connected with slavery; they have been linked to a decaying corpse, which has destroyed the moral health. The union of the government; the union of the north and south, in the political parties; the union in the religious organizations of the land, have all served to deaden the moral sense of the northern people, and to impregnate them with sentiments and ideas forever in conflict with what as a nation we call *genius of American institutions*. Rightly viewed, this is an alarming fact, and ought to rally all that is pure, just, and holy in one determined effort to crush the monster of corruption, and to scatter "its guilty profits" to the winds. In a high moral sense, as well as in a national sense, the whole American people are responsible for slavery, and must share, in its guilt and shame, with the most obdurate men-stealers of the south.

FREDERICK DOUGLASS

What to the Slave Is the Fourth of July? (1852)

In an oration delivered in Rochester, New York, that was later published as a pamphlet, Douglass expressed a mix of guarded optimism and bitter recrimination about the issue of slavery. Even though he characterized the Fourth of July as a hypocritical sham from the point of view of the slave, Douglass expressed hope that the young nation could still live up to the ideals of the Declaration of Independence.

Fellow Citizens, I am not wanting in respect for the fathers of this republic. The signers of the Declaration of Independence were brave men. They were great men too—great enough to give fame to a great age. It does not often happen to a nation to raise, at one time, such a number of truly great men. The point from which I am compelled to view them is not, certainly, the most favorable; and yet I cannot contemplate their great deeds with less than admiration. They were statesmen, patriots and heroes, and for the good they did, and the principles they contended for, I will unite with you to honor their memory.

They loved their country better than their own private interests; and, though this is not the highest form of human excellence, all will concede that it is a rare virtue, and that when it is exhibited, it ought to command respect. He who will, intelligently, lay down his life for his country, is a man whom it is not in human nature to despise. Your fathers staked their lives, their fortunes, and their sacred honor, on the cause of their country. In their admiration of liberty, they lost sight of all other interests.

They were peace men; but they preferred revolution to peaceful submission to bondage. They were quiet men; but they did not shrink from agitating against oppression. They showed forbearance; but that they knew its limits. They believed in order; but not in the order of tyranny. With them, nothing, was *"settled"* that was not right. With them, justice, liberty and humanity were *"final;"* not slavery and oppression. You may well cherish the memory of such men. They were great in their day and generation. Their solid manhood stands out the more as we contrast it with these degenerate times. * * *

Fellow-citizens, pardon me, allow me to ask, why am I called upon to speak here to-day? What have I, or those I represent, to do with your national independence? Are the great principles of political freedom and of natural justice, embodied in that Declaration of Independence, extended to us? and am I, therefore, called upon to bring our humble offering to the national altar, and to confess the benefits and express devout gratitude for the blessings resulting from your independence to us?

Would to God, both for your sakes and ours, that an affirmative answer could be truthfully returned to these questions! Then would my task be light, and my burden easy and delightful.

But, such is not the state of the case. I say it with a sad sense of the disparity between us. I am not included within the pale of this glorious anniversary! Your high independence only reveals the immeasurable distance between us. The blessings in which you, this day, rejoice, are not enjoyed in common.—The rich inheritance of justice, liberty, prosperity and independence, bequeathed by your fathers, is shared by you, not by me. The sunlight that brought life and healing to you, has brought stripes and death to me. This Fourth [of] July is *yours*, not *mine*. *You* may rejoice, I must mourn. To drag a man in fetters into the grand illuminated temple of liberty, and call upon him to join you in joyous anthems, were inhuman mockery and sacrilegious irony. Do you mean, citizens, to mock me, by asking me to speak to-day? If so, there is a parallel to your conduct. And let me warn you that it is dangerous to copy the example of a nation whose crimes, towering up to heaven, were thrown down by the breath of the Almighty, burying that nation in irrecoverable ruin! I can to-day take up the plaintive lament of a peeled and woe-smitten people!

Fellow-citizens; above your national, tumultous joy, I hear the mournful wail of millions! whose chains, heavy and grievous yesterday, are, to-day, rendered more intolerable by the jubilee shouts that reach them. If I do forget, if I do not faithfully remember those bleeding children of sorrow this day, "may my right hand forget her cunning, and may my tongue cleave to the roof of my mouth!" To forget them, to pass lightly over their wrongs, and to chime in with the popular theme, would be treason most scandalous and shocking, and would make me a reproach before God and the world. My subject, then, fellow-citizens, is AMERICAN SLAVERY. I shall see, this day, and its popular characteristics, from the slave's point of view. Standing, there, identified with the American bondman, making his wrongs mine, I do not hesitate to declare, with all my soul, that the character and conduct of this nation never looked blacker to me than on this 4th of July! Whether we turn to the declarations of the past, or to the professions of the present, the conduct of the nation seems equally hideous and revolting. America is false to the past, false to the present, and solemnly binds herself to be false to the future. Standing with God and the crushed and bleeding slave on this occasion, I will, in the name of humanity which is outraged, in the name of liberty which is fettered, in the name of the constitution and the Bible, which are disregarded and trampled upon, dare to call in question and to denounce, with all the emphasis I can command, everything that serves to perpetuate slavery—the great sin and shame of America! "I will not equivocate; I will not excuse;" I will use the severest language I can command; and yet not one word shall escape me that any man, whose judgment is not blinded by prejudice, or who is not at heart a slaveholder, shall not confess to be right and just.

But I fancy I hear some one of my audience say, it is just in this circumstance that you and your brother abolitionists fail to make a favorable impression on the public mind. Would you argue more, and denounce less, would you persuade more, and rebuke less, your cause would be much more likely to succeed. But, I submit, where all is plain there is nothing to-be argued. What point in the anti-slavery creed would you have me argue? On what branch of the subject do the people of this country need light? Must I undertake to prove that the slave is a man? That point is conceded already. Nobody doubts it. The slaveholders themselves acknowledge it in the enactment of laws for their government. They acknowledge it when they punish disobedience on the part of the slave. There are seventy-two crimes in the State of Virginia, which, if committed by a black man, (no matter how ignorant he be,) subject him to the punishment of death; while only two of the same crimes will subject a white man to the like punishment.—What is this but the acknowledgement that the slave is a moral, intellectual and responsible being? The manhood of the slave is conceded. It is admitted in the fact that Southern statute books are covered with enactments forbidding, under severe fines and penalties, the teaching of the slave to read or to write.— When you can point to any such laws, in reference to the beasts of the field, then I may consent to argue the manhood of the slave. When the dogs in your streets, when the fowls of the air, when the cattle on your hills, when the fish of the sea, and the reptiles that crawl, shall be unable to distinguish the slave from a brute, *then* will I argue with you that the slave is a man!

For the present, it is enough to affirm the equal manhood of the negro race. Is it not astonishing that, while we are ploughing, planting and reaping, using all kinds of mechanical tools, erecting houses, constructing bridges, building ships, working in metals of brass, iron, copper, silver and gold; that, while we are reading, writing and cyphering, acting as clerks, merchants and secretaries, having among us lawyers, doctors, ministers, poets, authors, editors, orators and teachers; that, while we are engaged in all manner of enterprises common to other men, digging gold in California, capturing the whale in the Pacific, feeding sheep and cattle on the hill-side, living, moving, acting, thinking, planning, living in families as husbands, wives and children, and, above all, confessing and worshipping the Christian's God, and looking hopefully for life and immortality beyond the grave, we are called upon to prove that we are men!

Would you have me argue that man is entitled to liberty? that he is the rightful owner of his own body? You have already declared it. Must I argue the wrongfulness of slavery? Is that a question for Republicans? Is it to be settled by the rules of logic and argumentation, as a matter beset with great difficulty, involving a doubtful application of the principle of justice, hard to be understood? How should I look today, in the presence of Americans, dividing, and subdividing a discourse, to show that men have a natural right to freedom? speaking of it relatively, and positively, negatively, and affirmatively. To do so, would be to make myself ridiculous, and to offer an insult to your understanding.—There is not a man beneath the canopy of heaven, that does not know that slavery is wrong *for him*.

What, am I to argue that it is wrong to make men brutes, to rob them of their liberty, to work them without wages, to keep them ignorant of their relations to their fellow men, to beat them with sticks, to flay their flesh with the lash, to load their limbs with irons, to hunt them with dogs, to sell them at auction, to sunder their families, to knock out their teeth, to burn their flesh, to starve them into obedience and submission to their masters? Must I argue that a system thus marked with blood, and stained with pollution, is *wrong*? No! I will not. I have better employments for my time and strength, than such arguments would imply.

What, then, remains to be argued? Is it that slavery is not divine; that God did not establish it; that our doctors of divinity are mistaken? There is blasphemy in the thought. That which is inhuman, cannot be divine! *Who* can reason on such a proposition? They that can, may; I cannot. The time for such argument is past.

At a time like this, scorching irony, not convincing argument, is needed. O! had I the ability, and could I reach the nation's ear, I would, to-day, pour out a fiery stream of biting ridicule, blasting reproach, withering sarcasm, and stern rebuke. For it is not light that is needed, but fire; it is not the gentle shower, but thunder. We need the storm, the whirlwind, and the earthquake. The feeling of the nation must be quickened; the conscience of the nation must be roused; the propriety of the nation must be startled; the hypocrisy of the nation must be exposed; and its crimes against God and man must be proclaimed and denounced.

What, to the American slave, is your 4th of July? I answer, a day that reveals to him, more than all other days in the year, the gross injustice and cruelty to which he is the constant victim. To him, your celebration is a sham; your boasted liberty, an unholy license; your national greatness, swelling vanity; your sounds of rejoicing are empty and heartless; your denunciations of tyrants, brass fronted impudence; your shouts of liberty and equality, hollow mockery; your prayers and hymns, your sermons and thanksgivings, with all your religious parade, and solemnity, are, to him, mere bombast, fraud, deception, impiety, and hypocrisy—a thin veil to cover up crimes which would disgrace a nation of savages. There is not a nation on the earth guilty of practices, more shocking and bloody, than are the people of these United States, at this very hour.

HARRIET BEECHER STOWE

Uncle Tom's Cabin, or Life Among the Lowly (1852)

The Connecticut native Harriet Beecher Stowe (1811–1896) was a successful writer who became involved in the antislavery movement after moving to Cincinnati near a community of slaveholders. She wrote several novels, but none had the enormous impact of Uncle Tom's Cabin, *which was based largely on what she learned about life in the South from fugitive slaves she met in Cincinnati. The book, which was first published serially in the* National Era *and made into a successful play, generated widespread popular support for abolition because of its shockingly realistic depiction of the destructive effects of slavery on the individual slave and on family life among slaves. The book is still regarded by many as one of the causes of the Civil War. In the following selection, the title character finally defies his vicious master, Simon Legree.*

Slowly the weary, dispirited creatures wound their way into the room, and with crouching reluctance, presented their baskets to be weighed.

Legree noted on a slate, on the side of which was pasted a list of names, the amount.

Tom's basket was weighed and approved; and he looked, with an anxious glance, for the success of the woman he had befriended.

Tottering with weakness, she came forward, and delivered her basket. It was of full weight, as Legree well perceived; but, affecting anger, he said,

"What, you lazy beast! short again! stand aside, you'll catch it, pretty soon!"

The woman gave a groan of utter despair, and sat down on a board.

The person who had been called Misse Cassy now came forward, and, with a haughty, negligent air, delivered her basket. As she delivered it, Legree looked in her eyes with a sneering yet inquiring glance.

She fixed her black eyes steadily on him, her lips moved slightly, and she said something in French. What it was, no one knew; but Legree's face became perfectly demoniacal in its expression, as she spoke; he half raised his hand, as if to strike,—a gesture which she regarded with fierce disdain, as she turned and walked away.

"And now," said Legree, "come here, you Tom. You see, I told ye I didn't buy ye jest for the common work; I mean to promote ye, and make a driver of ye; and tonight ye may jest as well begin to get yer hand in. Now, ye jest take this yer gal and flog her; ye've seen enough on't to know how."

"I beg Mas'r's pardon," said Tom; "hopes Mas'r won't set me at that. It's what I an't used to,—never did,—and can't do, no way possible."

"Ye'll larn a pretty smart chance of things ye never did know, before I've done with ye!" said Legree, taking up a cow-hide, and striking Tom a heavy blow across the cheek, and following up the infliction by a shower of blows.

"There!" he said, as he stopped to rest; "now, will ye tell me ye can't do it?"

"Yes, Mas'r," said Tom, putting up his hand, to wipe the blood that trickled down his face. "I'm willin' to work night and day, and work while there's life and breath in me; but this yer thing I can't feel it right to do;—and, Mas'r, I *never* shall do it,—*never!*"

Tom had a remarkably smooth, soft voice, and a habitually respectful manner, that had given Legree an idea that he would be cowardly, and easily subdued. When he spoke these last words, a thrill of amazement went through every one; the poor woman clasped her hands, and said, "O Lord!" and every one involuntarily looked at each other and drew in their breath, as if to prepare for the storm that was about to burst.

Legree looked stupefied and confounded; but at last burst forth,—

"What! ye blasted black beast! tell *me* ye don't think it *right* to do what I tell ye! What have any of you cussed cattle to do with thinking what's right? I'll put a stop to it! Why, what do ye think ye are? May be ye think ye'r a gentleman, master Tom, to be a telling your master what's right, and what an't! So you pretend it's wrong to flog the gal!"

"I think so, Mas'r," said Tom; "the poor crittur's sick and feeble; 'twould be downright cruel, and it's what I never will do, nor begin to. Mas'r, if you mean to kill me, kill me; but, as to my raising my hand agin any one here, I never shall,—I'll die first!"

Tom spoke in a mild voice, but with a decision that could not be mistaken. Legree shook with anger; his greenish eyes glared fiercely, and his very whiskers seemed to curl with passion; but, like some ferocious beast, that plays with its victim before he devours it, he kept back his strong impulse to proceed to immediate violence, and broke out into bitter raillery.

"Well, here's a pious dog, at last, let down among us sinners!—a saint, a gentleman, and no less, to talk to us sinners about our sins! Powerful holy crittur, he must be! Here, you rascal, you make believe to be so pious,—didn't you never hear, out of yer Bible, "Servants, obey yer masters"? An't I yer master? Didn't I pay down twelve hundred dollars cash, for all there is inside yer old cussed black shell? An't yer mine, now, body and soul?" he said, giving Tom a violent kick with his heavy boot; "tell me!"

In the very depth of physical suffering, bowed by brutal oppression, this question shot a gleam of joy and triumph through Tom's soul. He suddenly stretched himself up, and, looking earnestly to heaven, while the tears and blood that flowed down his face mingled, he exclaimed,—

"No! no! no! my soul an't yours, Mas'r! You haven't bought it,—ye can't buy it! It's been bought and paid for, by one that is able to keep it;—no matter, no matter, you can't harm me!"

"I can't!" said Legree, with a sneer; "we'll see,—we'll see! Here, Sambo, Quimbo, give this dog such a breakin' in as he won't get over, this month!"

The two gigantic Negroes that now laid hold of Tom, with fiendish exultation in their faces, might have formed no unapt personification of the powers of darkness. The poor woman screamed with apprehension, and all rose, as by a general impulse, while they dragged him unresisting from the place.

JOHN C. CALHOUN

Speeches on Slavery (1837, 1838)

The South Carolinian John Caldwell Calhoun (1782–1850) entered national politics in 1811 as a congressman, became secretary of war under James Monroe, and served as vice president under both John Quincy Adams and Andrew Jackson. Although he was a prominent nationalist with a solid reputation for being, in the words of John Quincy Adams, "above all sectional and factious prejudices" early in his political career, Calhoun became a leading defender of southern slave interests when he joined the Senate in 1833. In the Senate, he tirelessly promoted states' rights and unapologetically defended slavery as a "positive good."

Speech on the Reception of Abolition Petitions (1837)

However sound the great body of the non-slaveholding States are at present, in the course of a few years they will be succeeded by those who will have been taught to hate the people and institutions of nearly one-half of this Union, with a hatred more deadly than one hostile nation ever entertained towards another. It is easy to see the end. By the necessary course of events, if left to themselves, we must become, finally, two people. It is impossible under the deadly hatred which must spring up between the two great sections, if the present causes are permitted to operate unchecked, that we should continue under the same political system. The conflicting elements would burst the Union asunder, powerful as are the links which hold it together. Abolition and the Union cannot co-exist. As the friend of the Union I openly proclaim it,—and the sooner it is known the better. The former may now be controlled, but in a short time it will be beyond the power of man to arrest the course of events. We of the South will not, cannot surrender our institutions. To maintain the existing relations between the two races, inhabiting that section of the Union, is indispensable to the peace and happiness of both. It cannot be subverted without drenching the country in blood, and extirpating one or the other of the races. Be it good or bad, it has grown up with our society and institutions, and is so interwoven with them, that to destroy it would be to destroy us as a people. But let me not be understood as admitting, even by implication, that the existing relations between the two races in the slaveholding States is an evil:—far otherwise; I hold it to be a good, as it has thus far proved itself to be to both, and will continue to prove so if not disturbed by the fell spirit of abolition. I appeal to facts. Never before has the black race of Central Africa, from the dawn of history to the present day, attained a condition so civilized and so improved, not only physically, but morally and intellectually. It came among us in a low, degraded, and savage condition, and in the course of a few generations it has grown up under the fostering care of our institutions, reviled as they have been, to its present comparatively civilized condition. This, with the rapid increase of numbers, is conclusive proof of the general happiness of the race, in spite of all the exaggerated tales to the contrary.

In the mean time, the white or European race has not degenerated. It has kept pace with its brethren in other sections of the Union where slavery does not exist. It is odious to make comparison: but I appeal to all sides whether the South is not equal in virtue, intelligence, patriotism, courage, disinterestedness, and all the high qualities which adorn our nature. I ask whether we have not contributed our full share of talents and political wisdom in forming and sustaining this political fabric; and whether we have not constantly inclined most strongly to the side of liberty, and been the first to see and first to resist the encroachments of power. In one thing only are we inferior—the arts of gain; we acknowledge that we are less wealthy than the Northern section of this Union, but I trace this mainly to the fiscal action of this Government, which has extracted much from, and spent little among us. Had it been the reverse,—if the exaction had been from the other section, and the expenditure with us, this point of superiority would not be against us now, as it was not at the formation of this Government.

But I take higher ground. I hold that in the present state of civilization, where two races of different origin, and distinguished by color, and other physical differences, as well as intellectual, are brought together, the relation now existing in the slaveholding States between the two, is, instead of an evil, a good—a positive good. I feel myself called upon to speak freely upon the subject where the honor and interests of those I represent are involved. I hold then, that there never has yet existed a wealthy and civilized society in which one portion of the community did not, in point of fact, live on the labor of the other. Broad and general as is this assertion, it is fully borne out by history. This is not the proper occasion, but if it were, it would not be difficult to trace the various devices by which the wealth of all civilized communities has been so unequally divided, and to show by what means so small a share has been allotted to those by whose labor it was produced, and so large a share given to the non-producing classes. The devices are almost innumerable, from the brute force and gross superstition of ancient times, to the subtle and artful fiscal contrivances of modern. I might well challenge a comparison between them and the more direct, simple, and patriarchal mode by which the labor of the African race is, among us, commanded by the European. I may say with truth, that in few countries so much is left to the share of the laborer, and so little exacted from him, or where there is more kind attention paid to him in sickness or infirmities of age. Compare his condition with the tenants of the poor houses in the more civilized portions of Europe—look at the sick, and the old and infirm slave, on one hand, in the midst of his family and friends, under the kind superintending care of his master and mistress, and compare it with the forlorn and wretched condition of the pauper in the poor house. But I will not dwell on this aspect of the question; I turn to the political; and here I fearlessly assert that the existing relation between the two races in the South, against which these blind fanatics are waging war, forms the most solid and durable foundation on which to rear free and stable political institutions. It is useless to disguise the fact. There is and always has been in an advanced stage of wealth and civilization, a conflict between labor and capital. The condition of society in the South exempts us from the disorders and dangers resulting from this conflict; and which explains why it is that the political condition of the slaveholding States has been so much more stable and quiet than that of the North. The advantages of the former, in this respect, will become more and more manifest if left undisturbed by interference from without, as the country advances in wealth and numbers. We have, in fact, but just entered that condition of society where the strength and durability of our political institutions are to be tested; and I venture nothing in predicting that the experience of the next generation will fully test how vastly more favorable our condition of society is to that of other sections for free and stable institutions, provided we are not disturbed by the interference of others, or shall have sufficient intelligence and spirit to resist promptly and successfully such interference. It rests with ourselves to meet and repel them. I look not for aid to this Government, or to the other States; not but there are kind feelings towards us on the part of the great body of the non-slaveholding States; but as kind as their feelings may be, we may rest assured that no political party in these States will risk their ascendency for our safety. If we do not defend ourselves none will defend us; if we yield we will be more and more pressed as we recede; and if we submit we will be trampled under foot.

Be assured that emancipation itself would not satisfy these fanatics:— that gained, the next step would be to raise the negroes to a social and political equality with the whites; and that being effected, we would soon find the present condition of the two races reversed. They and their northern allies would be the masters, and we the slaves; the condition of the white race in the British West India Islands, bad as it is, would be happiness to ours. There the mother country is interested in sustaining the supremacy of the European race. It is true that the authority of the former master is destroyed, but the African will there still be a slave, not to individuals but to the community,—forced to labor, not by the authority of the overseer, but by the bayonet of the soldiery and the rod of the civil magistrate.

Surrounded as the slaveholding States are with such imminent perils, I rejoice to think that our means of defence are ample, if we shall prove to have the intelligence and spirit to see and apply them before it is too late. All we want is concert, to lay aside all party differences, and unite with zeal and energy in repelling approaching dangers. Let there be concert of action, and we shall find ample means of security without resorting to secession or disunion. I speak with full knowledge and a thorough examination of the subject, and for one, see my way clearly. One thing alarms me—the eager pursuit of gain which overspreads the land, and which absorbs every faculty of the mind and every feeling of the heart. Of all passions avarice is the most blind and compromising—the last to see and the first to yield to danger. I dare not hope that any thing I can say will arouse the South to a due sense of danger; I fear it is beyond the power of mortal voice to awaken it in time from the fatal security into which it has fallen.

Speech on the Importance of Domestic Slavery (1838)

CALHOUN'S RESOLUTIONS:

*R*esolved, That in the adoption of the Federal Constitution, the States adopting the same acted severally, as free, independent, and sovereign States; and that each, for itself, by its own voluntary assent, entered the Union with the view to its increased security against all dangers, *domestic* as well as foreign, and the more perfect and secure enjoyment of its advantages, natural, political, and social.

Resolved, That in delegating a portion of their powers to be exercised by the Federal Government, the States retained, severally, the exclusive and sole right over their own domestic institutions and police, and are alone responsible for them, and that any intermeddling of any one or more States, or a combination of their citizens, with the domestic institutions and police of the others, on any ground, or under any pretext whatever, political, moral, or religious, with the view to their alteration, or subversion, is an assumption of superiority not warranted by the Constitution, insulting to the States interfered with, tending to endanger their domestic peace and tranquility, subversive of the objects for which the Constitution was formed, and, by necessary consequence, tending to weaken and destroy the Union itself.

Resolved, That this Government was instituted and adopted by the several States of this Union as a common agent, in order to carry into effect the powers which they had delegated by the Constitution for their mutual security and prosperity; and that, in fulfilment of this high and sacred trust, this Government is bound so to exercise its powers as to give, as far as may be practicable, increased stability and security to the domestic institutions of the States that compose the Union; and that it is the solemn duty of the Government to resist all attempts by one portion of the Union to use it as an instrument to attack the domestic institutions of another, or to weaken or destroy such institutions, instead of strengthening and upholding them, as it is in duty bound to do.

Resolved, That domestic slavery, as it exists in the Southern and Western States of this Union, composes an important part of their domestic institutions, inherited from their ancestors, and existing at the adoption of the Constitution, by which it is recognised as constituting an essential element in the distribution of its powers among the States; and that no change of opinion, or feeling, on the part of the other States of the Union in relation to it, can justify them or their citizens in open and systematic attacks thereon, with the view to its overthrow; and that all such attacks are in manifest violation of the mutual and solemn pledge to protect and defend each other, given by the States, respectively, on entering into the Constitutional compact, which formed the Union, and as such is a manifest breach of faith, and a violation of the most solemn obligations, moral and religious.

Resolved, That the intermeddling of any State or States, or their citizens, to abolish slavery in this District, or any of the Territories, on the ground, or under the pretext, that it is immoral or sinful; or the passage of any act or measure of Congress, with that view, would be a direct and dangerous attack on the institutions of all the slaveholding States.

Resolved, That the union of these States rests on an equality of rights and advantages among its members; and that whatever destroys that equality, tends to destroy the Union itself; and that it is the solemn duty of all, and more especially of this body, which represents the States in their corporate capacity, to resist all attempts to discriminate between the States in extending the benefits of the Government to the several portions of the Union; and that to refuse to extend to the Southern and Western States any advantage which would tend to strengthen, or render them more secure, or increase their limits or population by the annexation of new territory or States, on the assumption or under the pretext that the institution of slavery, as it exists among them, is immoral or sinful, or otherwise obnoxious, would be contrary to that equality of rights and advantages which the Constitution was intended to secure alike to all the members of the Union, and would, in effect, disfranchise the slaveholding States, withholding from them the advantages, while it subjected them to the burthens, of the Government.

He saw (said Mr. C.) in the question before us the fate of the South. It was a higher than the mere naked question of master and slave. It involved a great political institution, essential to the peace and existence of one-half of this Union. A mysterious Providence had brought together two races, from different portions of the globe, and placed them together in nearly equal numbers in the Southern portion of this Union. They were there inseparably united, beyond the possibility of separation. Experience had shown that the existing relation between them secured the peace and happiness of both. Each had improved; the inferior greatly; so much so, that it had attained a degree of civilization never before attained by the black race in any age or country. Under no other relation could they coexist together. To destroy it was to involve a whole region in slaughter, carnage, and desolation; and, come what will, we must defend and preserve it.

This agitation has produced one happy effect at least; it has compelled us to the South to look into the nature and character of this great institution, and to correct many false impressions that even we had entertained in relation to it. Many in the South once believed that it was a moral and political evil; that folly and delusion are gone; we see it now in its true light, and regard it as the most safe and stable basis for free institutions in the world. It is impossible with us that the conflict can take place between labor and capital, which make it so difficult to establish and maintain free institutions in all wealthy and highly civilized nations where such institutions as ours do not exist. The Southern States are an aggregate, in fact, of communities, not of individuals. Every plantation is a little community, with the master at its head, who concentrates in himself the united interests of capital and labor, of which he is the common representative. These small communities aggregated make the State in all, whose action, labor, and capital is equally represented and perfectly harmonized. Hence the harmony, the union, and stability of that section, which is rarely disturbed through the action of this Government. The blessing of this state of things extends beyond the limits of the South. It makes that section the balance of the system; the great conservative power, which prevents other portions, less fortunately constituted, from rushing into conflict. In this tendency to conflict in the North between labor and capital, which is constantly on the increase, the weight of the South has and will ever be found on the Conservative side; against the aggression of one or the other side, which ever may tend to disturb the equilibrium of our political system. This is our natural position, the salutary influence of which has thus far preserved, and will long continue to preserve, our free institutions, if we should be left undisturbed. Such are the institutions which these deluded madmen are stirring heaven and earth to destroy, and which we are called on to defend by the highest and most solemn obligations that can be imposed on us as men and patriots.

JOHN C. CALHOUN

A Disquisition on Government (1848)

Calhoun's defense of the rights of minorities in his posthumously published Disquisition on Government *was based on a very straightforward theory about the social nature of man and the inevitability of conflict in society. Borrowing much from Madison's Federalist 10, Calhoun's doctrine of the "concurrent majority" is one of the most original attempts in American political thought to reconcile the principle of majority rule with the protection of minority rights. Calhoun argued that the only way to protect sectional minorities, such as the southern states with their institution of slavery, was to give them a defensive veto over the national policies that directly affected their interests. In the course of his argument Calhoun cavalierly dismisses the Lockean liberal ideals on which so much of American political thought was hitherto based.*

In order to have a clear and just conception of the nature and object of government, it is indispensable to understand correctly what that constitution or law of our nature is, in which government originates; or, to express it more fully and accurately—that law, without which government would not, and with which, it must necessarily exist. Without this, it is as impossible to lay any solid foundation for the science of government, as it would be to lay one for that of astronomy, without a like understanding of that constitution or law of the material world, according to which the several bodies composing the solar system mutually act on each other, and by which they are kept in their respective spheres. The first question, accordingly, to be considered is—What is that constitution or law of our nature, without which government would not exist, and with which its existence is necessary?

In considering this, I assume, as an incontestable fact, that man is so constituted as to be a social being. His inclinations and wants, physical and moral, irresistibly impel him to associate with his kind; and he has, accordingly, never been found, in any age or country, in any state other than the social. In no other, indeed, could he exist; and in no other— were it possible for him to exist—could he attain to a full development of his moral and intellectual faculties, or raise himself, in the scale of being, much above the level of the brute creation.

I next assume, also, as a fact not less incontestable, that, while man is so constituted as to make the social state necessary to his existence and the full development of his faculties, this state itself cannot exist without government. The assumption rests on universal experience. In no age or country has any society or community ever been found, whether enlightened or savage, without government of some description.

Having assumed these, as unquestionable phenomena of our nature, I shall, without further remark, proceed to the investigation of the primary and important question—What is that constitution of our nature, which, while it impels man to associate with his kind, renders it impossible for society to exist without government?

The answer will be found in the fact (not less incontestable than either of the others) that, while man is created for the social state, and is accordingly so formed as to feel what affects others, as well as what affects himself, he is, at the same time, so constituted as to feel more intensely what affects him directly, than what affects him indirectly though others; or, to express it differently, he is so constituted, that his direct or individual affections are stronger than his sympathetic or social feelings. I intentionally avoid the expression, *selfish* feelings, as applicable to the former; because, as commonly used, it implies an unusual excess of the individual over the social feelings, in the person to whom it is applied; and, consequently, something depraved and vicious. My object is, to exclude such inference, and to restrict the inquiry exclusively to facts in their bearings on the subject under consideration, viewed as mere phenomena appertaining to our nature—constituted as it is; and which are as unquestionable as is that of gravitation, or any other phenomenon of the material world.

* * *

I might go farther, and assert this to be a phenomenon, not of our nature only, but of all animated existence, throughout its entire range, so far as our knowledge extends. It would, indeed, seem to be essentially connected with the great law of self-preservation which pervades all that feels, from man down to the lowest and most insignificant reptile or insect. In none is it stronger than in man. His social feelings may, indeed, in a state of safety and abundance, combined with high intellectual and moral culture, acquire great expansion and force; but not so great as to overpower this all-pervading and essential law of animated existence.

But that constitution of our nature which makes us feel more intensely what affects us directly than what affects us indirectly through others, necessarily leads to conflict between individuals. Each, in consequence, has a greater regard for his own safety or happiness, than for the safety or happiness of others; and, where these come in opposition, is ready to sacrifice the interests of others to his own. And hence, the tendency to a universal state of conflict, between individual and individual; accompanied by the connected passions of suspicion, jealousy, anger and revenge—followed by insolence, fraud and cruelty—and, if not prevented by some controlling power, ending in a state of universal discord and confusion, destructive of the social state and the ends for which it is ordained. This controlling power, wherever vested, or by whomsoever exercised, is GOVERNMENT.

It follows, then, that man is so constituted, that government is necessary to the existence of society, and society to his existence, and the perfection of his faculties. It follows, also, that government has its origin in this twofold constitution of his nature; the sympathetic or social feelings constituting the remote—and the individual or direct, the proximate cause.

* * *

But government, although intended to protect and preserve society, has itself a strong tendency to disorder and abuse of its powers, as all experience and almost every page of history testify. The cause is to be found in the same constitution of our nature which makes government indispensable. The powers which it is necessary for government to possess, in order to repress violence and preserve order, cannot execute themselves. They must be administered by men in whom, like others, the individual are stronger than the social feelings. And hence, the powers vested in them to prevent injustice and oppression on the part of others, will, if left unguarded, be by them converted into instruments to oppress the rest of the community. That, by which this is prevented, by whatever name called, is what is meant by CONSTITUTION, in its most comprehensive sense, when applied to GOVERNMENT.

Having its origin in the same principle of our nature, *constitution* stands to *government*, as *government* stands to *society*; and, as the end for which society is ordained, would be defeated without government, so that for which government is ordained would, in a great measure, be defeated without constitution. But they differ in this striking particular. There is no difficulty in forming government. It is not even a matter of choice, whether there shall be one or not. Like breathing, it is not permitted to depend on our volition. Necessity will force it on all communities in some one form or another. Very different is the case as to constitution. Instead of a matter of necessity, it is one of the most difficult tasks imposed on man to form a constitution worthy of the name; while, to form a perfect one—one that would completely counteract the tendency of government to oppression and abuse, and hold it strictly to the great ends for which it is ordained— has thus far exceeded human wisdom, and possibly ever will. From this, another striking difference results. Constitution is the contrivance of man, while government is of Divine ordination. Man is left to perfect what the wisdom of the Infinite ordained, as necessary to preserve the race.

With these remarks, I proceed to the consideration of the important and difficult question: How is this tendency of government to be counteracted? Or, to express it more fully—How can those who are invested with the powers of government be prevented from employing them, as the means of aggrandizing themselves, instead of using them to protect and preserve society? It cannot be done by instituting a higher power to control the government, and those who administer it. This would be but to change the seat of authority, and to make this bigger power, in reality, the government; with the same tendency, on the part of those who might control its powers, to pervert them into instruments of aggrandizement. Nor can it be done by limiting the powers of government, so as to make it too feeble to be made an instrument of abuse; for, passing by the difficulty of so limiting its powers, without creating a power higher than the government itself to enforce the observance of the limitations, it is a sufficient objection that it would, if practicable, defeat the end for which government is ordained, by making it too feeble to protect and preserve society. The powers necessary for this purpose will ever prove sufficient to aggrandize those who control it, at the expense of the rest of the community.

* * *

There is but one way in which this can possibly be done; and that is, by such an organism as will furnish the ruled with the means of resisting successfully this tendency on the part of the rulers to oppression and abuse. Power can only be resisted by power—and tendency by tendency.

Those who exercise power and those subject to its exercise—the rulers and the ruled—stand in antagonistic relations to each other. The same constitution of our nature which leads rulers to oppress the ruled—regardless of the object for which government is ordained—will, with equal strength, lead the ruled to resist, when possessed of the means of making peaceable and effective resistance. Such an organism, then, as will furnish the means by which resistance may be systematically and peaceably made on the part of the ruled to oppression and abuse of power on the part of the rulers, is the first and indispensable step towards *forming* a constitutional government. And as this can only be effected by or through the right of suffrage—(the right on the part of the ruled to choose their rulers at proper intervals, and to hold them thereby responsible for their conduct)—the responsibility of the rulers to the ruled, through the right of suffrage, is the indispensable and primary principle in the *foundation* of a constitutional government. When this right is properly guarded, and the people sufficiently enlightened to understand their own rights and the interests of the community, and duly to appreciate the motives and conduct of those appointed to make and execute the laws, it is all-sufficient to give to those who elect, effective control over those they have elected.

I call the right of suffrage the indispensable and primary principle; for it would be a great and dangerous mistake to suppose, as many do, that it is, of itself, sufficient to form constitutional governments. To this erroneous opinion may be traced one of the causes, why so few attempts to form constitutional governments have succeeded; and why, of the few which have, so small a number have had durable existence. It has led, not only to mistakes in the attempts to form such governments, but to their overthrow, when they have, by some good fortune, been correctly formed. So far from being, of itself, sufficient—however well guarded it might be, and however enlightened the people—it would, unaided by other provisions, leave the government as absolute, as it would be in the hands of irresponsible rulers; and with a tendency, at least as strong, towards oppression and abuse of its powers; as I shall next proceed to explain.

The right of suffrage, of itself, can do no more than give complete control to those who elect, over the conduct of those they have elected. In doing this, it accomplishes all it possibly can accomplish. This is its aim—and when this is attained, its end is fulfilled. It can do no more, however enlightened the people, or however widely extended or well guarded the right may be. The sum total, then, of its effects, when most successful, is, to make those elected, the true and faithful representatives of those who elected them—instead of irresponsible rulers—as they would be without it; and thus, by converting it into an agency, and the rulers into agents, to divest government of all claims to sovereignty, and to retain it unimpaired to the community. But it is manifest that the right of suffrage, in making these changes, transfers, in reality, the actual control over the government, from those who make and execute the laws, to the body of the community; and, thereby, places the powers of the government as fully in the mass of the community, as they would be if they, in fact, had assembled, made, and executed the laws themselves, without the intervention of representatives or agents. The more perfectly it does this, the more perfectly it accomplishes its ends; but in doing so, it only changes the seat of authority, without counteracting, in the least, the tendency of the government to oppression and abuse of its powers.

If the whole community had the same interests, so that the interests of each and every portion would be so affected by the action of the government, that the laws which oppressed or impoverished one portion, would necessarily oppress and impoverish all others—or the reverse—then the right of suffrage, of itself, would be all-sufficient to counteract the tendency of the government to oppression and abuse of its powers; and, of course, would form, of itself, a perfect constitutional government. The interest of all being the same, by supposition, as far as the action of the government was concerned, all would have like interests as to what laws should be made, and how they should be executed. All strife and struggle would cease as to who should be elected to make and execute them. The only question would be, who was most fit; who the wisest and most capable of understanding the common interest of the whole. This decided, the election would pass off quietly, and without party discord; as no one portion could advance its own peculiar interest without regard to the rest, by electing a favorite candidate.

But such is not the case. On the contrary, nothing is more difficult than to equalize the action of the government, in reference to the various and diversified interests of the community; and nothing more easy than to pervert its powers into instruments to aggrandize and enrich one or more interests by oppressing and impoverishing the others; and this too, under the operation of laws, couched in general terms—and which, on their face, appear fair and equal. Nor is this the case in some particular communities only. It is so in all; the small and the great—the poor and the rich—irrespective of pursuits, productions, or degrees of civilization—with, however, this difference, that the more extensive and populous the country, the more diversified the condition and pursuits of its population, and the richer, more luxurious, and dissimilar the people, the more difficult is it to equalize the action of the government—and the more easy for one portion of the community to pervert its powers to oppress, and plunder the other.

Such being the case, it necessarily results, that the right of suffrage, by placing the control of the government in the community must, from the same constitution of our nature which makes government necessary to preserve society, lead to conflict among its different interests—each striving to obtain possession of its powers, as the means of protecting itself against the others—or of advancing its respective interests, regardless of the interests of others. For this purpose, a struggle will take place between the various interests to obtain a majority, in order to control the government. If no one interest be strong enough, of itself, to obtain it, a combination will be formed between those whose interests are most alike—each conceding something to the others, until a sufficient number is obtained to make a majority. The process may be slow, and much time may be required before a compact, organized majority can be thus formed; but formed it will be in time, even without preconcert or design, by the sure workings of that principle or constitution of our nature in which government itself originates. When once formed, the community will be divided into two great parties—a major and minor—between which there will be incessant struggles on the one side to retain, and on the other to obtain the majority—and, thereby, the control of the government and the advantages it confers.

* * *

As, then, the right of suffrage, without some other provision, cannot counteract this tendency of government, the next question for consideration is—What is that other provision? This demands the most serious consideration; for of all the questions embraced in the science of government, it involves a principle, the most important, and the least understood; and when understood, the most difficult of application in practice. It is, indeed, emphatically, that principle which *makes* the constitution, in its strict and limited sense.

From what has been said, it is manifest, that this provision must be of a character calculated to prevent any one interest, or combination of interests, from using the powers of government to aggrandize itself at the expense of the others. Here lies the evil: and just in proportion as it shall prevent, or fail to prevent it, in the same degree it will effect, or fail to effect the end intended to be accomplished. There is but one certain mode in which this result can be secured; and that is, by the adoption of some restriction or limitation, which shall so effectually prevent any one interest, or combination of interests, from obtaining the exclusive control of the government, as to render hopeless all attempts directed to that end. There is, again, but one mode in which this can be effected; and that is, by taking the sense of each interest or portion of the community, which may be unequally and injuriously affected by the action of the government, separately, through its own majority, or in some other way by which its voice may be fairly expressed; and to require the consent of each interest, either to put or to keep the government in action. This, too, can be accomplished only in one way—and that is, by such an organism of the government—and, if necessary for the purpose, of the community also— as will, by dividing and distributing the powers of government, give to each division or interest, through its appropriate organ, either a concurrent voice in making and executing the laws, or a veto on their execution. It is only by such an organism, that the assent of each can be made necessary to put the government in motion; or the power made effectual to arrest its action, when put in motion—and it is only by the one or the other that the different interests, orders, classes, or portions, into which the community may be divided, can be protected, and all conflict and struggle between them prevented—by rendering it impossible to put or to keep it in action, without the concurrent consent of all.

Such an organism as this, combined with the right of suffrage, constitutes, in fact, the elements of constitutional government. The one, by rendering those who make and execute the laws responsible to those on whom they operate, prevents the rulers from oppressing the ruled; and the other, by making it impossible for any one interest or combination of interests or class, or order, or portion of the community, to obtain exclusive control, prevents any one of them from oppressing the other. It is clear, that oppression and abuse of power must come, if at all, from the one or the other quarter. From no other can they come. It follows, that the two, suffrage and proper organism combined, are sufficient to counteract the tendency of government to oppression and abuse of power; and to restrict it to the fulfilment of the great ends for which it is ordained. * * *

It may be readily inferred, from what has been stated, that the effect of organism is neither to supersede nor diminish the importance of the right of suffrage; but to aid and perfect it. The object of the latter is, to collect the sense of the community. The more fully and perfectly it accomplishes this, the more fully and perfectly it fulfils its end. But the most it can do, of itself, is to collect the sense of the greater number; that is, of the stronger interests, or combination of interests; and to assume this to be the sense of the community. It is only when aided by a proper organism that it can collect the sense of the entire community—of each and all its interests; of each, through its appropriate organ, and of the whole, through all of them united. This would truly be the sense of the entire community; for whatever diversity each interest might have within itself—as all would have the same interest in reference to the action of the government, the individuals composing each would be fully and truly represented by its own majority or appropriate organ, regarded in reference to the other interests. In brief, every individual of every interest might trust, with confidence, its majority or appropriate organ, against that of every other interest.

It results, from what has been said, that there are two different modes in which the sense of the community may be taken; one, simply by the right of suffrage, unaided; the other, by the right through a proper organism. Each collects the sense of the majority. But one regards numbers only, and considers the whole community as a unit, having but one common interest throughout; and collects the sense of the greater number of the whole, as that of the community. The other, on the contrary, regards interests as well as numbers—considering the community as made up of different and conflicting interests, as far as the action of the government is concerned; and takes the sense of each, through its majority or appropriate organ, and the united sense of all, as the sense of the entire community. The former of these I shall call the numerical, or absolute majority; and the latter, the concurrent, or constitutional majority. I call it the constitutional majority, because it is an essential element in every constitutional government—be its form what it may. So great is the difference, politically speaking, between the two majorities, that they cannot be confounded, without leading to great and fatal errors; and yet the distinction between them has been so entirely overlooked, that when the term *majority* is used in political discussions, it is applied exclusively to designate the numerical—as if there were no other. Until this distinction is recognized, and better understood, there will continue to be great liability to error in properly constructing constitutional governments, especially of the popular form, and of preserving them when properly constructed. Until then, the latter will have a strong tendency to slide, first, into the government of the numerical majority, and, finally, into absolute government of some other form. To show that such must be the case, and at the same time to mark more strongly the difference between the two, in order to guard against the danger of overlooking it, I propose to consider the subject more at length.

The first and leading error which naturally arises from overlooking the distinction referred to, is, to confound the numerical majority with the people; and this so completely as to regard them as identical. This is a consequence that necessarily results from considering the numerical as the only majority. All admit, that a popular government, or democracy, is the government of the people; for the terms imply this. A perfect government of the kind would be one which would embrace the consent of every citizen or member of the community; but as this is impracticable, in the opinion of those who regard the numerical as the only majority, and who can perceive no other way by which the sense of the people can be taken—they are compelled to adopt this as the only true basis of popular government, in contradistinction to governments of the aristocratical or monarchical form. Being thus constrained, they are, in the next place, forced to regard the numerical majority, as, in effect, the entire people; that is, the greater part as the whole; and the government of the greater part as the government of the whole. It is thus the two come to be confounded, and a part made identical with the whole. And it is thus, also that all the rights, powers, and immunities of the whole people come to be attributed to the numerical majority; and, among others, the supreme, sovereign authority of establishing and abolishing governments at pleasure.

This radical error, the consequence of confounding the two, and of regarding the numerical as the only majority, has contributed more than any other cause, to prevent the formation of popular constitutional governments—and to destroy them even when they have been formed. It leads to the conclusion that, in their formation and establishment nothing more is necessary than the right of suffrage—and the allotment to each division of the community a representation in the government, in proportion to numbers. If the numerical majority were really the people; and if, to take its sense truly, were to take the sense of the people truly, a government so constituted would be a true and perfect model of a popular constitutional government; and every departure from it would detract from its excellence. But, as such is not the case—as the numerical majority, instead of being the people, is only a portion of them—such a government, instead of being a true and perfect model of the people's government, that is, a people self-governed, is but the government of a part, over a part—the major over the minor portion.

But this misconception of the true elements of constitutional government does not stop here. It leads to others equally false and fatal, in reference to the best means of preserving and perpetuating them, when, from some fortunate combination of circumstances, they are correctly formed. For they who fall into these errors regard the restrictions which organism imposes on the will of the numerical majority as restrictions on the will of the people, and, therefore, as not only useless, but wrongful and mischievous. And hence they endeavor to destroy organism, under the delusive hope of making government more democratic.

* * *

The necessary consequence of taking the sense of the community by the concurrent majority is, as has been explained, to give to each interest or portion of the community a negative on the others. It is this mutual negative among its various conflicting interests, which invests each with the power of protecting itself—and places the rights and safety of each, where only they can be securely placed, under its own guardianship. Without this there can be no systematic, peaceful, or effective resistance to the natural tendency of each to come into conflict with the others: and without this there can be no constitution. It is this negative power—the power of preventing or arresting the action of the government—be it called by what term it may—veto, interposition, nullification, check, or balance of power—which, in fact, forms the constitution. They are all but different names for the negative power. In all its forms, and under all its names, it results from the concurrent majority. Without this there can be no negative; and, without a negative, no constitution. The assertion is true in reference to all constitutional governments, be their forms what they may. It is, indeed, the negative power which makes the constitution—and the positive which makes the government. The one is the power of acting—and the other the power of preventing or arresting action. The two, combined, make constitutional governments.

But, as there can be no constitution without the negative power, and no negative power without the concurrent majority—it follows, necessarily, that where the numerical majority has the sole control of the government, there can be no constitution; as constitution implies limitation or restriction—and, of course, is inconsistent with the idea of sole or exclusive power. And hence, the numerical, unmixed with the concurrent majority, necessarily forms, in all cases, absolute government.

* * *

From this there results another distinction, which, although secondary in its character, very strongly marks the difference between these forms of government. I refer to their respective conservative principle—that is, the principle by which they are upheld and preserved. This principle, in constitutional governments, is *compromise*—and in absolute governments, is *force*—as will be next explained.

It has been already shown, that the same constitution of man which leads those who govern to oppress the governed—if not prevented—will, with equal force and certainty, lead the latter to resist oppression, when possessed of the means of doing so peaceably and successfully. But absolute governments, of all forms, exclude all other means of resistance to their authority, than that of force; and, of course, leave no other alternative to the governed, but to acquiesce in oppression, however great it may be, or to resort to force to put down the government. But the dread of such a resort must necessarily lead the government to prepare to meet force in order to protect itself; and hence, of necessity, force becomes the conservative principle of all such governments.

On the contrary, the government of the concurrent majority, where the organism is perfect, excludes the possibility of oppression, by giving to each interest, or portion, or order—where there are established classes—the means of protecting itself, by its negative, against all measures calculated to advance the peculiar interests of others at its expense. Its effect, then, is, to cause the different interests, portions, or orders—as the case may be—to desist from attempting to adopt any measure calculated to promote the prosperity of one, or more, by sacrificing that of others; and thus to force them to unite in such measures only as would promote the prosperity of all, as the only means to prevent the suspension of the action of the government—and, thereby, to avoid anarchy, the greatest of all evils. It is by means of such authorized and effectual resistance, that oppression is prevented, and the necessity of resorting to force superseded, in governments of the concurrent majority—and, hence, compromise, instead of force, becomes their conservative principle.

* * *

In another particular, governments of the concurrent majority have greatly the advantage. I allude to the difference in their respective tendency, in reference to dividing or uniting the community. That of the concurrent, as has been shown, is to unite the community, let its interests be ever so diversified or opposed; while that of the numerical is to divide it into two conflicting portions, let its interests be, naturally, ever so united and identified.

That the numerical majority will divide the community, let it be ever so homogeneous, into two great parties, which will be engaged in perpetual struggles to obtain the control of the government, has already been established. The great importance of the object at stake, must necessarily form strong party attachments and party antipathies—attachments on the part of the members of each to their respective parties, through whose efforts they hope to accomplish an object dear to all; and antipathies to the opposite party, as presenting the only obstacle to success.

* * *

The concurrent majority, on the other hand, tends to unite the most opposite and conflicting interests, and to blend the whole in one common attachment to the country. By giving to each interest, or portion, the power of self-protection, all strife and struggle between them for ascendency, is prevented; and, thereby, not only every feeling calculated to weaken the attachment to the whole is suppressed, but the individual and the social feelings are made to unite in one common devotion to country. Each sees and feels that it can best promote its own prosperity by conciliating the goodwill, and promoting the prosperity of the others. And hence, there will be diffused throughout the whole community kind feelings between its different portions; and, instead of antipathy, a rivalry amongst them to promote the interests of each other, as far as this can be done consistently with the interest of all. Under the combined influence of these causes, the interests of each would be merged in the common interests of the whole; and thus, the community would become a unit, by becoming the common centre of attachment of all its parts. And hence, instead of faction, strife, and struggle for party ascendency, there would be patriotism, nationality, harmony, and a struggle only for supremacy in promoting the common good of the whole.

* * *

To perfect society, it is necessary to develop the faculties, intellectual and moral, with which man is endowed. But the main spring to their development, and, through this, to progress, improvement and civilization, with all their blessings, is the desire of individuals to better their condition. For, this purpose, liberty and security are indispensable. Liberty leaves each free to pursue the course he may deem best to promote his interest and happiness, as far as it may be compatible with the primary end for which government is ordained—while security gives assurance to each, that he shall not be deprived of the fruits of his exertions to better his condition. These combined, give to this desire the strongest impulse of which it is susceptible. For, to extend liberty beyond the limits assigned, would be to weaken the government and to render it incompetent to fulfil its primary end—the protection of society against dangers, internal and external. The effect of this would be, insecurity; and, of insecurity—to weaken the impulse of individuals to better their condition, and thereby retard progress and improvement. On the other hand, to extend the powers of the government, so as to contract the sphere assigned to liberty, would have the same effect, by disabling individuals in their efforts to better their condition.

Herein is to be found the principle which assigns to power and liberty their proper spheres, and reconciles each to the other under all circumstances. For, if power be necessary to secure to liberty the fruits of its exertions, liberty, in turn, repays power with interest, by increased population, wealth, and other advantages, which progress and improvement bestow on the community. By thus assigning to each its appropriate sphere, all conflicts between them cease; and each is made to co-operate with and assist the other, in fulfilling the great ends for which government is ordained.

But the principle, applied to different communities, will assign to them different limits. It will assign a larger sphere to power and a more contracted one to liberty, or the reverse, according to circumstances. To the former, there must ever be allotted, under all circumstances, a sphere sufficiently large to protect the community against danger from without and violence and anarchy within. The residuum belongs to liberty. More cannot be safely or rightly allotted to it.

* * *

The principle, in all communities, according to these numerous and various causes, assigns to power and liberty their proper spheres. To allow to liberty, in any case, a sphere of action more extended than this assigns, would lead to anarchy; and this, probably, in the end, to a contraction instead of an enlargement of its sphere. Liberty, then, when forced on a people unfit for it, would, instead of a blessing, be a curse; as it would, in its reaction, lead directly to anarchy—the greatest of all curses. No people, indeed, can long enjoy more liberty than that to which their situation and advanced intelligence and morals fairly entitle them. If more than this be allowed, they must soon fall into confusion and disorder—to be followed, if not by anarchy and despotism, by a change to a form of government more simple and absolute; and, therefore, better suited to their condition. And hence, although it may be true, that a people may not have as much liberty as they are fairly entitled to, and are capable of enjoying—yet the reverse is questionably true—that no people can long possess more than they are fairly entitled to.

Liberty, indeed, though among the greatest of blessings, is not so great as that of protection; inasmuch, as the end of the former is the progress and improvement of the race—while that of the latter is its preservation and perpetuation. And hence, when the two come into conflict, liberty must, and ever ought, to yield to protection; as the existence of the race is of greater moment than its improvement.

It follows, from what has been stated, that it is a great and dangerous error to suppose that all people are equally entitled to liberty. It is a reward to be earned, not a blessing to be gratuitously lavished on all alike—a reward reserved for the intelligent, the patriotic, the virtuous and deserving—and not a boon to be bestowed on a people too ignorant, degraded and vicious, to be capable either of appreciating or of enjoying it. Nor is it any disparagement to liberty, that such is, and ought to be the case. On the contrary, its greatest praise—its proudest distinction is, that an all-wise Providence has reserved it, as the noblest and highest reward for the development of our faculties, moral and intellectual. A reward more appropriate than liberty could not be conferred on the deserving—nor a punishment inflicted on the undeserving more just, than to be subject to lawless and despotic rule. This dispensation seems to be the result of some fixed law—and every effort to disturb or defeat it, by attempting to elevate a people in the scale of liberty, above the point to which they are entitled to rise, must ever prove abortive, and end in disappointment. The progress of a people rising from a lower to a higher point in the scale of liberty, is necessarily slow—and by attempting to precipitate, we either retard, or permanently defeat it.

There is another error, not less great and dangerous, usually associated with the one which has just been considered. I refer to the opinion, that liberty and equality are so intimately united, that liberty cannot be perfect without perfect equality.

That they are united to a certain extent—and that equality of citizens, in the eyes of the law, is essential to liberty in a popular government, is conceded. But to go further, and make equality of *condition* essential to liberty, would be to destroy both liberty and progress. The reason is, that inequality of condition, while it is a necessary consequence of liberty, is, at the same time, indispensable to progress. In order to understand why this is so, it is necessary to bear in mind, that the main spring to progress is, the desire of individuals to better their condition; and that the strongest impulse which can be given to it is, to leave individuals free to exert themselves in the manner they may deem best for that purpose, as far at least as it can be done consistently with the ends for which government is ordained—and to secure to all the fruits of their exertions. Now, as individuals differ greatly from each other, in intelligence, sagacity, energy, perseverance, skill, habit of industry and economy, physical power, position and opportunity—the necessary effect of leaving all free to exert themselves to better their condition, must be a corresponding inequality between those who may possess these qualities and advantages in a high degree, and those who may be deficient in them. The only means by which this result can be prevented are, either to impose such restrictions on the exertions of those who may possess them in a high degree, as will place them on a level with those who do not; or to deprive them of the fruits of their exertions. But to impose such restrictions on them would be destructive of liberty—while, to deprive them of the fruits of their exertions, would be to destroy the desire of bettering their condition. It is, indeed, this inequality of condition between the front and rear ranks, in the march of progress, which gives so strong an impulse to the former to maintain their position, and to the latter to press forward into their files. This gives to progress its greatest impulse. To force the front rank back to the rear, or attempt to push forward the rear into line with the front, by the interposition of the government, would put an end to the impulse, and effectually arrest the march of progress.

These great and dangerous errors have their origin in the prevalent opinion that all men are born free and equal—than which nothing can be more unfounded and false. It rests upon the assumption of a fact, which is contrary to universal observation, in whatever light it may be regarded. It is, indeed, difficult to explain how an opinion so destitute of all sound reason, ever could have been so extensively entertained, unless we regard it as being confounded with another, which has some semblance of truth—but which, when properly understood, is not less false and dangerous. I refer to the assertion, that all men are equal in the state of nature; meaning, by a state of nature, a state of individuality, supposed to have existed prior to the social and political state; and in which men lived apart and independent of each other. If such a state ever did exist, all men would have been, indeed, free and equal in it; that is, free to do as they pleased, and exempt from the authority or control of others—as, by supposition, it existed anterior to society and government. But such a state is purely hypothetical. It never did, nor can exist; as it is inconsistent with the preservation and perpetuation of the race. It is, therefore, a great misnomer to call it *the state of nature.* Instead of being the natural state of man, it is, of all conceivable states, the most opposed to his nature—most repugnant to his feelings, and most incompatible with his wants. His natural state is, the social and political—the one for which his Creator made him, and the only one in which he can preserve and perfect his race. As, then, there never was such a state as the, so called, state of nature, and never can be, it follows, that men, instead of being born in it, are born in the social and political state; and of course, instead of being born free and equal, are born subject, not only to parental authority, but to the laws and institutions of the country where born, and under whose protection they draw their first breath.

* * *

The concurrent majority, then, is better suited to enlarge and secure the bounds of liberty, because it is better suited to prevent government from passing beyond its proper limits, and to restrict it to its primary end—the protection of the community. But in doing this, it leaves, necessarily, all beyond it open and free to individual exertions; and thus enlarges and secures the sphere of liberty to the greatest extent which the condition of the community will admit, as has been explained. The tendency of government to pass beyond its proper limits is what exposes liberty to danger, and renders it insecure; and it is the strong counteraction of governments of the concurrent majority to this tendency which makes them so favorable to liberty. On the contrary, those of the numerical, instead of opposing and counteracting this tendency, add to it increased strength, in consequence of the violent party struggles incident to them, as has been fully explained. And hence their encroachments on liberty, and the danger to which it is exposed under such governments.

* * *

Such being the case, the interest of each individual may be safely confided to the majority, or voice of his portion, against that of all others, and, of course, the government itself. It is only through an organism which vests each with a negative, in some one form or another, that those who have like interests in preventing the government from passing beyond its proper sphere, and encroaching on the rights and liberty of individuals, can cooperate peaceably and effectually in resisting the encroachments of power, and thereby preserve their rights and liberty. Individual resistance is too feeble, and the difficulty of concert and co-operation too great, unaided by such an organism, to oppose, successfully, the organized power of government, with all the means of the community at its disposal; especially in populous countries of great extent, where concert and co-operation are almost impossible. Even when the oppression of the government comes to be too great to be borne, and force is resorted to in order to overthrow it, the result is rarely ever followed by the establishment of liberty. The force sufficient to overthrow an oppressive government is usually sufficient to establish one equally, or more, oppressive in its place. And hence, in no governments, except those that rest on the principle of the concurrent or constitutional majority, can the people guard their liberty against power; and hence, also, when lost, the great difficulty and uncertainty of regaining it by force.

* * *

But to form a juster estimate of the full force of this impulse to compromise, there must be added that, in governments of the concurrent majority, each portion, in order to advance its own peculiar interests, would have to conciliate all others, by showing a disposition to advance theirs; and, for this purpose, each would select those to represent it, whose wisdom, patriotism, and weight of character, would command the confidence of the others. Under its influence—and with representatives so well qualified to accomplish the object for which they were selected—the prevailing desire would be, to promote the common interests of the whole; and, hence, the competition would be, not which should yield the least to promote the common good, but which should yield the most. It is thus, that concession would cease to be considered a sacrifice—would become a free-will offering on the altar of the country, and lose the name of compromise. And herein is to be found the feature, which distinguishes governments of the concurrent majority so strikingly from those of the numerical. In the latter, each faction, in the struggle to obtain the control of the government, elevates to power the designing, the artful, and unscrupulous, who, in their devotion to party—instead of aiming at the good of the whole—aim exclusively at securing the ascendency of party.

GEORGE FITZHUGH

Sociology for the South; or, the Failure of Free Society (1854)

The Virginia planter and lawyer George Fitzhugh (1806–1881) was an unabashed proponent of the positive benefits of slavery. Throughout his books and articles in proslavery periodicals such as DeBow's Southern Review, Fitzhugh endorsed black slavery as a humane alternative to what he described as the exploitative "wage-slavery" of northern capitalism. In Sociology for the South, Fitzhugh offered a scathing critique of the irredeemable selfishness and ruthlessness of liberalism and individualism, in contrast to the worry-free paternalism of slavery. The Virginian likened Negroes to irresponsible children who must be governed and protected by their loving and rational guardians.

Liberty and equality are new things under the sun. The free states of antiquity abounded with slaves. The feudal system that supplanted Roman institutions changed the form of slavery, but brought with it neither liberty nor equality. France and the Northern States of our Union have alone fully and fairly tried the experiment of a social organization founded upon universal liberty and equality of rights. England has only approximated to this condition in her commercial and manufacturing cities. The examples of small communities in Europe are not fit exponents of the working of the system. In France and in our Northern States the experiment has already failed, if we are to form our opinions from the discontent of the masses, or to believe the evidence of the Socialists, Communists, Anti-Renters, and a thousand other agrarian sects that have arisen in these countries, and threaten to subvert the whole social fabric. The leaders of these sects, at least in France, comprise within their ranks the greater number of the most cultivated and profound minds in the nation, who have made government their study. Add to the evidence of these social philosophers, who, watching closely the working of the system, have proclaimed to the world its total failure, the condition of the working classes, and we have conclusive proof that liberty and equality have not conduced to enhance the comfort or the happiness of the people.

Crime and pauperism have increased. Riots, trade unions, strikes for higher wages, discontent breaking out into revolution, are things of daily occurrence, and show that the poor see and feel quite as clearly as the philosophers, that their condition is far worse under the new than under the old order of things. Radicalism and Chartism in England owe their birth to the free and equal institutions of her commercial and manufacturing districts, and are little heard of in the quiet farming districts, where remnants of feudalism still exist in the relation of landlord and tenant, and in the laws of entail and primogeniture.

So much for experiment. We will now endeavor to treat the subject theoretically, and to show that the system is on its face self-destructive and impracticable. When we look to the vegetable, animal and human kingdoms, we discover in them all a constant conflict, war, or race of competition, the result of which is, that the weaker or less healthy genera, species and individuals are continually displaced and exterminated by the stronger and more hardy. It is a means by which some contend Nature is perfecting her own work. We, however, witness the war, but do not see the improvement. Although from the earliest date of recorded history, one race of plants has been eating out and taking the place of another, the stronger or more cunning animals have been destroying the feebler, and man exterminating and supplanting his fellow, still the plants, the animals and the men of to-day seem not at all superior, even in those qualities of strength and hardihood to which they owe their continued existence, to those of thousands of years ago. To this propensity of the strong to oppress and destroy the weak, government owes its existence. So strong is this propensity, and so destructive to human existence, that man has never yet been found so savage as to be without government. Forgetful of this important fact, which is the origin of all governments, the political economists and the advocates of liberty and equality propose to enhance the well being of man by trammeling his conduct as little as possible, and encouraging what they call FREE COMPETITION. Now, free competition is but another name for liberty and equality, and we must acquire precise and accurate notions about it in order to ascertain how free institutions will work. It is, then, that war or conflict to which Nature impels her creatures, and which government was intended to restrict. It is true, it is that war somewhat modified and restricted, for the warmest friends of freedom would have some government. The question is, whether the proposed restrictions are sufficient to neutralize the self-destructive tendencies which nature impresses on society. We proceed to show that the war of the wits, of mind with mind, which free competition or liberty and equality beget and encourage, is quite as oppressive, cruel and exterminating, as the war of the sword, of theft, robbery, and murder, which it forbids. It is only substituting strength of mind for strength of body. Men are told it is their duty to compete, to endeavor to get ahead of and supplant their fellow men, by the exercise of all the intellectual and moral strength with which nature and education have endowed them. "Might makes right," is the order of creation, and this law of nature, so far as mental might is concerned, is restored by liberty to man. The struggle to better one's condition, to pull others down or supplant them, is the great organic law of free society. All men being equal, all aspire to the highest honors and the largest possessions. Good men and bad men teach their children one and the same lesson—"Go ahead, push your way in the world." In such society, virtue, if virtue there be, loses all her loveliness because of her selfish aims. None but the selfish virtues are encouraged, because none other aid a man in the race of free competition. Good men and bad men have the same end in view, are in pursuit of the same object—self-promotion, self-elevation. The good man is prudent, cautious, and cunning of fence; he knows well the arts (the virtues, if you please,) which will advance his fortunes and enable him to depress and supplant others; he bides his time, takes advantage of the follies; the improvidence, and vices of others, and makes his fortune out of the misfortunes of his fellow men. The bad man is rash, hasty, and unskillful. He is equally selfish, but not half so cunning. Selfishness is almost the only motive of human conduct with good and bad in free society, where every man is taught that he may change and better his condition. A vulgar adage, "Every man for himself, and devil take the hindmost," is the moral which liberty and free competition inculcate. Now, there are no more honors and wealth in proportion to numbers, in this generation, than in the one which preceded it; population fully keeps pace with the means of subsistence; hence, those who better their condition or rise to higher places in society, do so generally by pulling down others or pushing them from their places. Where men of strong minds, of strong wills, and of great self-control, come into free competition with the weak and improvident, the latter soon become the inmates of jails and penitentiaries.

The statistics of France, England and America show that pauperism and crime advance *pari passu* with liberty and equality. How can it be otherwise, when all society is combined to oppress the poor and weak minded? The rich man, however good he may be, employs the laborer who will work for the least wages. If he be a good man, his punctuality enables him to cheapen the wages of the poor man. The poor war with one another in the race of competition, in order to get employment, by underbidding; for laborers are more abundant than employers. Population increases faster than capital. * * *

We do not set children and women free because they are not capable of taking care of themselves, not equal to the constant struggle of society.

To set them free would be to give the lamb to the wolf to take care of. Society would quickly devour them. If the children of ten years of age were remitted to all the rights of person and property which men enjoy, all can perceive how soon ruin and penury would overtake them. But half of mankind are but grown-up children, and liberty is as fatal to them as it would be to children. * * *

One step more, and that the most difficult in this process of reasoning and illustration, and we have done with this part of our subject. Liberty and equality throw the whole weight of society on its weakest members; they combine all men in oppressing precisely that part of mankind who most need sympathy, aid and protection. The very astute and avaricious man, when left free to exercise his faculties, is injured by no one in the field of competition, but levies a tax on all with whom he deals. The sensible and prudent, but less astute man, is seldom worsted in competing with his fellow men, and generally benefited. The very simple and improvident man is the prey of every body. The simple man represents a class, the common day laborers. The employer cheapens their wages, and the retail dealer takes advantage of their ignorance, their inability to visit other markets, and their want of credit, to charge them enormous profits. They bear the whole weight of society on their shoulders; they are the producers and artificers of all the necessaries, the comforts, the luxuries, the pomp and splendor of the world; they create it all, and enjoy none of it; they are the muzzled ox that treadeth out the straw; they are at constant war with those above them, asking higher wages but getting lower; for they are also at war with each other, underbidding to get employment. This process of underbidding never ceases so long as employers want profits or laborers want employment. It ends when wages are reduced too low to afford subsistence, in filling poor-houses, and jails, and graves. It has reached that point already in France, England and Ireland. A half million died of hunger in one year in Ireland—they died because in the eye of the law they were the equals, and liberty had made them the enemies, of their landlords and employers. Had they been vassals or serfs, they would have been beloved, cherished and taken care of by those same landlords and employers. Slaves never die of hunger, scarcely ever feel want.

The bestowing upon men equality of rights, is but giving license to the strong to oppress the weak. It begets the grossest inequalities of condition. Menials and day laborers are and must be as numerous as in a land of slavery. And these menials and laborers are only taken care of while young, strong and healthy. If the laborer gets sick, his wages cease just as his demands are greatest. If two of the poor get married, who being young and healthy, are getting good wages, in a few years they may have four children. Their wants have increased, but the mother has enough to do to nurse the four children, and the wages of the husband must support six. There is no equality, except in theory, in such society, and there is no liberty. The men of property, those who own lands and money, are masters of the poor; masters, with none of the feelings, interests or sympathies of masters; they employ them when they please, and for what they please, and may leave them to die in the highway, for it is the only home to which the poor in free countries are entitled. They (the property holders) beheaded Charles Stuart and Louis Capet, because these kings asserted a divine right to govern wrong, and forgot that office was a trust to be exercised for the benefit of the governed; and yet they seem to think that property is of divine right, and that they may abuse its possession to the detriment of the rest of society, as much as they please. A pretty exchange the world would make, to get rid of kings who often love and protect the poor, and get in their place a million of pelting, petty officers in the garb of money-changers and land-owners, who think that as they own all the property, the rest of mankind have no right to a living, except on the conditions they may prescribe. " 'Tis better to fall before the lion than the wolf," and modern liberty has substituted a thousand wolves for a few lions. The vulgar landlords, capitalists and employers of to-day, have the liberties and lives of the people more completely in their hands, than had the kings, barons and gentlemen of former times; and they hate and oppress the people as cordially as the people despise them. But these vulgar parvenus, these psalm-singing regicides, these worshipers of Mammon, "have but taught bloody instructions, which being taught, return to plague the inventor." The king's office was a trust, so are your lands, houses and money. Society permits you to hold them, because private property well administered conduces to the good of all society. *This is your only title;* you lose your right to your property, as the king did to his crown, so soon as you cease faithfully to execute your trust; you can't make commons and forests of your lands and starve mankind; you must manage your lands to produce the most food and raiment for mankind, or you forfeit your title; you may not understand this philosophy, but you feel that it is true, and are trembling in your seats as you hear the murmurings and threats of the starving poor.

The moral effect of free society is to banish Christian virtue, that virtue which bids us love our neighbor as ourself, and to substitute the very equivocal virtues proceeding from mere selfishness. The intense struggle to better each one's pecuniary condition, the rivalries, the jealousies, the hostilities which it begets, leave neither time nor inclination to cultivate the heart or the head. Every finer feeling of our nature is chilled and benumbed by its selfish atmosphere; affection is under the ban, because affection makes us less regardful of mere self; hospitality is considered criminal waste, chivalry a stumbling-block, and the code of honor foolishness; taste, sentiment, imagination, are forbidden ground, because no money is to be made by them. Gorgeous pageantry and sensual luxury are the only pleasures indulged in, because they alone are understood and appreciated, and they are appreciated just for what they cost in dollars and cents. What makes money, and what costs money, are alone desired. Temperance, frugality, thrift, attention to business, industry, and skill in making bargains, are virtues in high repute, because they enable us to supplant others and increase our own wealth. The character of our Northern brethren, and of the Dutch, is proof enough of the justice of these reflections. The Puritan fathers had lived in Holland, and probably imported Norway rats and Dutch morality in the Mayflower.

Liberty and equality are not only destructive to the morals, but to the happiness of society. Foreigners have all remarked on the care-worn, thoughtful, unhappy countenances of our people, and the remark only applies to the North, for travellers see little of us at the South, who live far from highways and cities, in contentment on our farms.

The facility with which men may improve their condition would, indeed, be a consideration much in favor of free society, if it did not involve as a necessary consequence the equal facility and liability to lose grade and fortune. As many fall as rise. The wealth of society hardly keeps pace with its numbers. All cannot be rich. The rich and the poor change places oftener than where there are fixed hereditary distinctions; so often, that the sense of insecurity makes every one unhappy. * * *

* * * Those who rise, pull down a class as numerous, and often more worthy than themselves, to the abyss of misery and penury. Painful as it may be, the reader shall look with us at this dark side of the picture; he shall view the vanquished as well as the victors on this battle-ground of competition; he shall see those who were delicately reared, taught no tricks of trade, no shifts of thrifty avarice, spurned, insulted, downtrodden by the coarse and vulgar whose wits and whose appetites had been sharpened by necessity. If he can sympathize with fallen virtue or detest successful vice, he will see nothing in this picture to admire. * * *

In Boston, a city famed for its wealth and the prudence of its inhabitants, nine-tenths of the men in business fail. In the slaveholding South, except in new settlements, failures are extremely rare; small properties descend from generation to generation in the same family; there is as much stability and permanency of property as is compatible with energy and activity in society; fortunes are made rather by virtuous industry than by tricks, cunning and speculation.

We have thus attempted to prove from theory and from actual experiment, that a society of universal liberty and equality is absurd and impracticable. We have performed our task, we know, indifferently, but hope we have furnished suggestions that may be profitably used by those more accustomed to authorship.

We now come in the order of our subject to treat of the various new sects of philosophers that have appeared of late years in France and in our free States, who, disgusted with society as it exists, propose to re-organize it on entirely new principles. We have never heard of a convert to any of these theories in the slave States. If we are not all contented, still none see evils of such magnitude in society as to require its entire subversion and reconstruction. We shall group all these sects together, because they all concur in the great truth that Free Competition is the bane of free society; they all concur, too, in modifying or wholly destroying the institution of private property. Many of them, seeing that property enables its owners to exercise a more grinding oppression than kings ever did, would destroy its tenure altogether. In France, especially, these sects are headed by men of great ability, who saw the experiment of liberty and equality fairly tested in France after the revolution of 1792. They saw, as all the world did, that it failed to promote human happiness or well-being.

France found the Consulate and the Empire havens of bliss compared with the stormy ocean of liberty and equality on which she had been tossed. Wise, however, as these Socialists and Communists of France are, they cannot create a man, a tree, or a new system of society; these are God's works, which man may train, trim and modify, but cannot create. The attempt to establish government on purely theoretical abstract speculation, regardless of circumstance and experience, has always failed; never more signally than with the Socialists.

The frequent experience of the Abbé Sieyès' paper structures of government, which lasted so short a time, should have taught them caution; but they were bolder reformers than he; they had a fair field for their experiment after the expulsion of Louis Phillippe; they tried it, and their failure was complete and ridiculous. The Abbé's structures were adamant compared to theirs. The rule of the weak Louis Napoleon was welcomed as a fortunate escape from their schemes of universal benevolence, which issued in universal bankruptcy.

The sufferings of the Irish, and the complaints of the Radicals and Chartists, have given birth to a new party in England, called Young England. This party saw in the estrangement and hostility of classes, and the sufferings of the poor, the same evils of free competition that had given rise to Socialism in France; though less talented than the Socialists, they came much nearer discovering the remedy for these evils.

Young England belongs to the most conservative wing of the tory party; he inculcates strict subordination of rank; would have the employer kind, attentive and paternal, in his treatment of the operative. The operative, humble, affectionate and obedient to his employer. He is young, and sentimental, and would spread his doctrines in tracts, sonnets and novels; but society must be ruled by sterner stuff than sentiment. Self-interest makes the employer and free laborer enemies. The one prefers to pay low wages, the other needs high wages. War, constant war, is the result, in which the operative perishes, but is not vanquished; he is hydra-headed, and when he dies two take his place. But numbers diminish his strength. The competition among laborers to get employment begets an intestine war, more destructive than the war from above. There is but one remedy for this evil, so inherent in free society, and that is, to identify the interests of the weak and the strong, the poor and the rich. Domestic Slavery does this far better than any other institution. Feudalism only answered the purpose in so far as Feudalism retained the features of slavery. To it (slavery) Greece and Rome, Egypt and Judea, and all the other distinguished States of antiquity, were indebted for their great prosperity and high civilization. * * *

But this high civilization and domestic slavery did not merely co-exist, they were cause and effect. Every scholar whose mind is at all imbued with ancient history and literature, sees that Greece and Rome were indebted to this institution alone for the taste, the leisure and the means to cultivate their heads and their hearts; had they been tied down to Yankee notions of thrift, they might have produced a Franklin, with his "penny saved is a penny gained"; they might have had utilitarian philosophers and invented the spinning jenny, but they never would have produced a poet, an orator, a sculptor or an architect; they would never have uttered a lofty sentiment, achieved a glorious feat in war, or created a single work of art. * * *

And now Equality where are thy monuments? And Echo answers where! Echo deep, deep, from the bowels of the earth, where women and children drag out their lives in darkness, harnessed like horses to heavy cars loaded with ore. Or, perhaps, it is an echo from some grand, gloomy and monotonous factory, where pallid children work fourteen hours a day, and go home at night to sleep in damp cellars. It may be too, this cellar contains aged parents too old to work, and cast off by their employer to die. Great railroads and mighty steamships too, thou mayest boast, but still the operatives who construct them are beings destined to poverty and neglect. Not a vestige of art canst thou boast; not a ray of genius illumes thy handiwork. The sordid spirit of Mammon presides o'er all, and from all proceed the sighs and groans of the oppressed.

Domestic slavery in the Southern States has produced the same results in elevating the character of the master that it did in Greece and Rome. He is lofty and independent in his sentiments, generous, affectionate, brave and eloquent; he is superior to the Northerner in every thing but the arts of thrift. History proves this. * * * Scipio and Aristides, Calhoun and Washington, are the noble results of domestic slavery. Like Egyptian obelisks 'mid the waste of time—simple, severe, sublime,—they point ever heavenward, and lift the soul by their examples. * * *

But the chief and far most important enquiry is, how does slavery affect the condition of the slave? One of the wildest sects of Communists in France proposes not only to hold all property in common, but to divide the profits, not according to each man's input and labor, but according to each man's wants. Now this is precisely the system of domestic slavery with us. We provide for each slave, in old age and in infancy, in sickness and in health, not according to his labor, but according to his wants. The master's wants are more costly and refined, and he therefore gets a larger share of the profits. A Southern farm is the beau ideal of Communism; it is a joint concern, in which the slave consumes more than the master, of the coarse products, and is far happier, because although the concern may fail, he is always sure of a support; he is only transferred to another master to participate in the profits of another concern; he marries when he pleases, because he knows be will have to work no more with a family than without one, and whether he live or die, that family will be taken care of; he exhibits all the pride of ownership, despises a partner in a smaller concern, "a poor man's negro," boasts of "our crops, horses, fields and cattle;" and is as happy as a human being can be. And why should he not?—he enjoys as much of the fruits of the farm as he is capable of doing, and the wealthiest can do no more. Great wealth brings many additional cares, but few additional enjoyments. Our stomachs do not increase in capacity with our fortunes. We want no more clothing to keep us warm. We may create new wants, but we cannot create new pleasures. The intellectual enjoyments which wealth affords are probably balanced by the new cares it brings along with it.

There is no rivalry, no competition to get employment among slaves, as among free laborers. Nor is there a war between master and slave. The master's interest prevents his reducing the slave's allowance or wages in infancy or sickness, for he might lose the slave by so doing. His feeling for his slave never permits him to stint him in old age. The slaves are all well fed, well clad, have plenty of fuel, and are happy. They have no dread of the future—no fear of want. A state of dependence is the only condition in which reciprocal affection can exist among human beings—the only situation in which the war of competition ceases, and peace, amity and good will arise. A state of independence always begets more or less of jealous rivalry and hostility. A man loves his children because they are weak, helpless and dependent. He loves his wife for similar reasons. When his children grow up and assert their independence, he is apt to transfer his affection to his grandchildren. He ceases to love his wife when she becomes masculine or rebellious; but slaves are always dependent, never the rivals of their master. Hence, though men are often found at variance with wife or children, we never saw one who did not like his slaves, and rarely a slave who was not devoted to his master. "I am thy servant!" disarms me of the power of master. Every man feels the beauty, force and truth of this sentiment of Sterne. But he who acknowledges its truth, tacitly admits that dependence is a tie of affection, that the relation of master and slave is one of mutual good will. Volumes written on the subject would not prove as much as this single sentiment. It has found its way to the heart of every reader, and carried conviction along with it. The slaveholder is like other men; he will not tread on the worm nor break the bruised reed. The ready submission of the slave, nine times out of ten, disarms his wrath even when the slave has offended. The habit of command may make him imperious and fit him for rule; but he is only imperious when thwarted or crossed by his equals; he would scorn to put on airs of command among blacks, whether slaves or free; he always speaks to them in a kind and subdued tone. We go farther, and say the slaveholder is better than others—because he has greater occasion for the exercise of the affections. His whole life is spent in providing for the minutest wants of others, in taking care of them in sickness and in health. Hence he is the least selfish of men. Is not the old bachelor who retires to seclusion, always selfish? Is not the head of a large family almost always kind and benevolent? And is not the slaveholder the head of the largest family? Nature compels master and slave to be friends; nature makes employers and free laborers enemies.

The institution of slavery gives full development and full play to the affections. Free society chills, stints and eradicates them. In a homely way the farm will support all, and we are not in a hurry to send our children into the world, to push their way and make their fortunes, with a capital of knavish maxims. We are better husbands, better fathers, better friends, and better neighbors than our Northern brethren. The tie of kindred to the fifth degree is often a tie of affection with us. First cousins are scarcely acknowledged at the North, and even children are prematurely pushed off into the world. Love for others is the organic law of our society, as self-love is of theirs.

Every social structure must have its substratum. In free society this substratum, the weak, poor and ignorant, is borne down upon and oppressed with continually increasing weight by all above. We have solved the problem of relieving this substratum from the pressure from above. The slaves are the substratum, and the master's feelings and interests alike prevent him from bearing down upon and oppressing them. With us the pressure on society is like that of air or water, so equally diffused as not any where to be felt. With them it is the pressure of the enormous screw, never yielding, continually increasing. Free laborers are little better than trespassers on this earth given by God to all mankind. The birds of the air have nests, and the foxes have holes, but they have not where to lay their heads. They are driven to cities to dwell in damp and crowded cellars, and thousands are even forced to lie in the open air. This accounts for the rapid growth of Northern cities. The feudal Barons were more generous and hospitable and less tyrannical than the petty land-holders of modern times. Besides, each inhabitant of the barony was considered as having some right of residence, some claim to protection from the Lord of the Manor. A few of them escaped to the municipalities for purposes of trade, and to enjoy a larger liberty. Now penury and the want of a home drive thousands to towns. The slave always has a home, always an interest in the proceeds of the soil. * * *

In France, England, Scotland and Ireland, the genius of famine hovers o'er the land. Emigrants, like a flock of hungry pigeons or Egyptian locusts, are alighting on the North. Every green thing will soon be consumed. The hollow, bloated prosperity which she now enjoys is destined soon to pass away. Her wealth does not increase with her numbers; she is dependent for the very necessaries of life on the slaveholding States. If those States cut off commercial intercourse with her, as they certainly will do if she does not speedily cease interference with slavery, she will be without food or clothing for her overgrown population. She is already threatened with a social revolution. * * *

At the slaveholding South all is peace, quiet, plenty and contentment. We have no mobs, no trade unions, no strikes for higher wages, no armed resistance to the law, but little jealousy of the rich by the poor. We have but few in our jails, and fewer in our poor houses. We produce enough of the comforts and necessaries of life for a population three or four times as numerous as ours. We are wholly exempt from the torrent of pauperism, crime, agrarianism, and infidelity which Europe is pouring from her jails and alms houses on the already crowded North. Population increases slowly, wealth rapidly. * * * Wealth is more equally distributed than at the North, where a few millionaires own most of the property of the country. (These millionaires are men of cold hearts and weak minds; they know how to make money, but not how to use it, either for the benefit of themselves or of others.) High intellectual and moral attainments, refinement of head and heart, give standing to a man in the South, however poor he may be. Money is, with few exceptions, the only thing that ennobles at the

North. We have poor among us, but none who are over-worked and under-fed. We do not crowd cities because lands are abundant and their owners kind, merciful and hospitable. The poor are as hospitable as the rich, the negro as the white man. Nobody dreams of turning a friend, a relative, or a stranger from his door. The very negro who deems it no crime to steal, would scorn to sell his hospitality. We have no loafers, because the poor relative or friend who borrows our horse, or spends a week under our roof, is a welcome guest. The loose economy, the wasteful mode of living at the South, is a blessing when rightly considered; it keeps want, scarcity and famine at a distance, because it leaves room for retrenchment. The nice, accurate economy of France, England and New England, keeps society always on the verge of famine, because it leaves no room to retrench, that is to live on a part only of what they now consume. Our society exhibits no appearance of precocity, no symptoms of decay. A long course of continuing improvement is in prospect before us, with no limits which human foresight can descry. Actual liberty and equality with our white population has been approached much nearer than in the free States. Few of our whites ever work as day laborers, none as cooks, scullions, ostlers, body servants, or in other menial capacities. One free citizen does not lord it over another; hence that feeling of independence and equality that distinguishes us; hence that pride of character, that self-respect, that gives us ascendancy when we come in contact with Northerners. It is a distinction to be a Southerner, as it was once to be a Roman citizen.

* * * Until the last fifteen years, our great error was to imitate Northern habits, customs and institutions. Our circumstances are so opposite to theirs, that whatever suits them is almost sure not to suit us. Until that time, in truth, we distrusted our social system. We thought slavery morally wrong, we thought it would not last, we thought it unprofitable. The Abolitionists assailed us; we looked more closely into our circumstances; became satisfied that slavery was morally right, that it would continue ever to exist, that it was as profitable as it was humane. This begat self-confidence, self-reliance. Since then our improvement has been rapid. Now we may safely say, that we are the happiest, most contented and prosperous people on earth. The intermeddling of foreign pseudo-philanthopists in our affairs, though it has occasioned great irritation and indignation, has been of inestimable advantage in teaching us to form a right estimate of our condition. This intermeddling will soon cease; the poor at home in thunder tones demand their whole attention and all their charity. Self-preservation will compel them to listen to their demands. Moreover, light is breaking in upon us from abroad. All parties in England now agree that the attempt to put down the slave trade has greatly aggravated its horrors, without at all diminishing the trade itself. It is proposed to withdraw her fleet from the

African coast. France has already given notice that she will withdraw hers. America will follow the example. The emancipation of the slaves in the West Indies is admitted to have been a failure in all respects. The late masters have been ruined, the liberated slaves refuse to work, and are fast returning to the savage state, and England herself has sustained a severe blow in the present diminution and prospective annihilation of the once enormous imports from her West Indian colonies.

In conclusion, we will repeat the propositions, in somewhat different phraseology, with which we set out. First—That Liberty and Equality, with their concomitant Free Competition, beget a war in society that is as destructive to its weaker members as the custom of exposing the deformed and crippled children. Secondly—That slavery protects the weaker members of society just as do the relations of parent, guardian and husband, and is as necessary, as natural, and almost as universal as those relations. Is our demonstration imperfect? Does universal experience sustain our theory? Should the conclusions to which we have arrived appear strange and startling, let them therefore not be rejected without examination. The world has had but little opportunity to contrast the working of Liberty and Equality with the old order of things, which always partook more or less of the character of domestic slavery. The strong prepossession in the public mind in favor of the new system, makes it reluctant to attribute the evil phenomena which it exhibits, to defects inherent in the system itself. That these defects should not have been foreseen and pointed out by any process of *a priori* reasoning, is but another proof of the fallibility of human sagacity and foresight when attempting to foretell the operation of new institutions. It is as much as human reason can do, when examining the complex frame of society, to trace effects back to their causes—much more than it can do, to foresee what effects new causes will produce. We invite investigation.

GEORGE FITZHUGH

Cannibals All! or, Slaves Without Masters (1857)

Fitzhugh argued that the capitalist system of free labor amounted to a form of social cannibalism that established a war of all against all. In addition to attacking the individualistic system of northern wage labor as cruel and exploitative and the idea of government by consent as an anarchistic doctrine, Fitzhugh argued provocatively that "the negro slaves of the South are the happiest, and, in some sense, the freest people in the world" because they live without a care in the world.

We are all, North and South, engaged in the White Slave Trade, and he who succeeds best is esteemed most respectable. It is far more cruel than the Black Slave Trade, because it exacts more of its slaves, and neither protects nor governs them. We boast that it exacts more when we say, "that the *profits* made from employing free labor are greater than those from slave labor." The profits, made from free labor, are the amount of the products of such labor, which the employer, by means of the command which capital or skill gives him, takes away, exacts, or "exploitates" from the free laborer. The profits of slave labor are that portion of the products of such labor which the power of the master enables him to appropriate. These profits are less, because the master allows the slave to retain a larger share of the results of his own labor than do the employers of free labor. But we not only boast that the White Slave Trade is more exacting and fraudulent (in fact, though not in intention) than Black Slavery; but we also boast that it is more cruel, in leaving the laborer to take care of himself and family out of the pittance which skill or capital have allowed him to retain. When the day's labor is ended, he is free, but is overburdened with the cares of family and household, which make his freedom an empty and delusive mockery. But his employer is really free, and may enjoy the profits made by others' labor, without a care, or a trouble, as to their well-being. The negro slave is free, too, when the labors of the day are over, and free in mind as well as body; for the master provides food, raiment, house, fuel, and everything else necessary to the physical well-being of himself and family. The master's labors commence just when the slave's end. No wonder men should prefer white slavery to capital, to negro slavery, since it is more profitable, and is free from all the cares and labors of black slave-holding.

Now, reader, if you wish to know yourself—to "descant on your own deformity"—read on. But if you would cherish self-conceit, self-esteem, or self-appreciation, throw down our book; for we will dispel illusions which have promoted your happiness, and show you that what you have considered and practiced as virtue is little better than moral Cannibalism. But you will find yourself in numerous and respectable company; for all good and respectable people are "Cannibals all" who do not labor, or who are successfully trying to live without labor, on the unrequited labor of other people.

* * *

But, reader, we do not wish to fire into the flock. "Thou art the man!" You are a Cannibal! and if a successful one, pride yourself on the number of your victims quite as much as any Fiji chieftain, who breakfasts, dines, and sups on human flesh—and your conscience smites you, if you have failed to succeed, quite as much as his, when he returns from an unsuccessful foray.

Probably, you are a lawyer, or a merchant, or a doctor, who has made by your business fifty thousand dollars, and retired to live on your capital. But, mark! not to spend your capital. That would be vulgar, disreputable, criminal. That would be, to live by your own labor; for your capital is your amassed labor. That would be to do as common working men do; for they take the pittance which their employers leave them to live on. They live by labor; for they exchange the results of their own labor for the products of other people's labor. It is, no doubt, an honest, vulgar way of living, but not at all a respectable way. The respectable way of living is to make other people work for you, and to pay them nothing for so doing—and to have no concern about them after their work is done. Hence, white slave-holding is much more respectable than negro slavery—for the master works nearly as hard for the negro as he for the master. But you, my virtuous, respectable leader, exact three thousand dollars per annum from white labor (for your income is the product of white labor) and make not one cent of return in any form. You retain your capital, and never labor, and yet live in luxury on the labor of others. Capital commands labor, as the master does the slave. Neither pays for labor, but the master permits the slave to retain a larger allowance from the proceeds of his own labor, and hence "free labor is cheaper than slave labor." You, with the command over labor which your capital gives you, are a slave owner—a master, without the obligations of a master. They who work for you, who create your income, are slaves, without the rights of slaves. Slaves without a master! Whilst you were engaged in amassing your capital, in seeking to become independent, you were in the White Slave Trade. To become independent is to be able to make other people support you, without being obliged to labor for *them*. Now, what man in society is not seeking to attain this situation? He who attains it is a slave owner, in the worst sense. He who is in pursuit of it is engaged in the slave trade. You, reader, without property, in free society, are theoretically in a worse condition than slaves. Practically, their condition corresponds with this theory, as history and statistics everywhere demonstrate. The capitalists, in free society, live in ten times the luxury and show that Southern masters do, because the slaves to capital work harder and cost less than negro slaves.

The negro slaves of the South are the happiest, and, in some sense, the freest people in the world. The children and the aged and infirm work not at all, and yet have all the comforts and necessaries of life provided for them. They enjoy liberty, because they are oppressed neither by care nor labor. The women do little hard work, and are protected from the despotism of their husbands by their masters. The negro man and stout boys work, on the average, in good weather, not more than nine hours a day. The balance of their time is spent in perfect abandon. Besides, they have their Sabbaths and holidays. White men, with so much of license and liberty, would die of ennui; but negroes luxuriate in corporeal and mental repose. With their faces upturned to the sun, they can sleep at any hour; and quiet sleep is the greatest of human enjoyments.

* * * We do not know whether free laborers ever sleep. They are fools to do so; for, whilst they sleep, the wily and watchful capitalist is devising means to ensnare and exploitate them. The free laborer must work or starve. He is more of a slave than the negro, because he works longer and harder for less allowance than the slave, and has no holiday, because the cares of life with him begin when its labors end. He has no liberty, and not a single right.

* * *

Free laborers have not a thousandth part of the rights and liberties of negro slaves. Indeed, they have not a single liberty, unless it be the right or liberty to die. But the reader may think that he and other capitalists and employers are freer than negro slaves. Your capital would soon vanish, if you dared indulge in the liberty and abandon of negroes. You hold your wealth and position by the tenure of constant watchfulness, care, and circumspection. You never labor; but you are never free.

Where a few own the soil, they have unlimited power over the balance of society, until domestic slavery comes in to compel them to permit this balance of society to draw a sufficient and comfortable living from *terra mater*. Free society asserts the right of a few to the earth—slavery maintains that it belongs, in different degrees, to all.

But, reader, well may you follow the slave trade. It is the only trade worth following, and slaves the only property worth owning. All other is worthless * * * except in so far as it vests the owner with the power to command the labors of others—to enslave them. Give you a palace, ten thousand acres of land, sumptuous clothes, equipage, and every other luxury; and with your artificial wants you are poorer than Robinson Crusoe, or the lowest working man, if you have no slaves to capital, or domestic slaves. Your capital will not bring you an income of a cent, nor supply one of your wants, without labor. Labor is indispensable to give value to property, and if you owned every thing else, and did not own labor, you would be poor.

* * *

"Property in man" is what all are struggling to obtain. Why should they not be obliged to take care of man, their property, as they do of their horses and their hounds, their cattle and their sheep. Now, under the delusive name of liberty, you work him "from morn to dewy eve"—from infancy to old age—then turn him out to starve. You treat your horses and hounds better. Capital is a cruel master. The free slave trade, the commonest, yet the cruellest of trades. * * *

Slavery is an indispensable police institution—especially so to check the cruelty and tyranny of vicious and depraved husbands and parents. Husbands and parents have, in theory and practice, a power over their subjects more despotic than kings; and the ignorant and vicious exercise their power more oppressively than kings. Every man is not fit to be king, yet all must have wives and children. Put a master over them to check their power, and we need not resort to the unnatural remedies of woman's rights, limited marriages, voluntary divorces, and free love, as proposed by the abolitionists. * * *

We may be doing Mr. Jefferson injustice in assuming that his "fundamental principles" and Mr. Seward's "higher law" mean the same thing; but the injustice can be very little, as they both mean just nothing at all, unless it be a determination to inaugurate anarchy, and to do all sorts of mischief. We refer the reader to the chapter on the Declaration of Independence, &c., in our *Sociology* for a further dissertation on the fundamental powder-cask abstractions, on which our glorious institutions *affect* to repose. We say *affect*, because we are sure neither their repose nor their permanence would be disturbed by the removal of the counterfeit foundation.

The true greatness of Mr. Jefferson was his fitness for revolution. He was the genius of innovation, the architect of ruin, the inaugurator of anarchy. His mission was to pull down, not to build up. He thought everything false as well in the physical as in the moral world. He fed his horses on potatoes, and defended harbors with gunboats, because it was contrary to human experience with human opinion. He proposed to govern boys without the authority of masters or the control of religion, supplying their places with Laissez Faire philosophy, and morality from the pages of Lawrence Sterne. His character, like his philosophy, is exceptional—invaluable in urging on revolution, but useless, if not dangerous, in quiet times.

We would not restrict, control, or take away a single human right or liberty which experience showed was already sufficiently governed and restricted by public opinion. But we do believe that the slaveholding South is the only country on the globe that can safely tolerate the rights and liberties which we have discussed.

The annals of revolutionary Virginia were illustrated by three great and useful men. The mighty mind of Jefferson, fitted to pull down; the plastic hand of Madison to build up; and the powerful arm of Washington to defend, sustain, and conserve.

We are the friend of popular government, but only so long as conservatism is the interest of the governing class. At the South, the interests and feelings of many non-property holders, are identified with those of a comparatively few property holders. It is not necessary to the security of property, that a majority of voters should own property; but where the pauper majority becomes so large as to disconnect the mass of them in feeling and interest from the property holding class, revolution and agrarianism are inevitable. We will not undertake to say that events are tending this way at the North. The absence of laws of entail and primogeniture may prevent it; yet we fear the worst, for, despite the laws of equal inheritance and distribution, wealth is accumulating in few hands, and pauperism is increasing. We shall attempt hereafter to show that a system of very small entails might correct this tendency. * * *

All modern philosophy converges to a single point—the overthrow of all government, the substitution of the untrammelled "Sovereignty of the Individual" for the Sovereignty of Society, and the inauguration of anarchy. First domestic slavery, next religious institutions, then separate property, then political government, and, finally, family government and family relations, are to be swept away. This is the distinctly avowed programme of all able abolitionists and socialists; and towards this end the doctrines and the practices of the weakest and most timid among them tend.

We do not agree with the authors of the Declaration of Independence, that governments "derive their just powers from the consent of the governed." The women, the children, the negroes, and but few of the non-property holders were consulted, or consented to the Revolution, or the governments that ensued from its success. As to these, the new governments were self-elected despotisms, and the governing class self-elected despots. Those governments originated in force, and have been continued by force. All governments must originate in force, and be continued by force. The very term, government, implies that it is carried on against the consent of the governed. Fathers do not derive their authority, as heads of families, from the consent of wife and children, nor do they govern their families by their consent. They never take the vote of the family as to the labors to be performed, the moneys to be expended, or as to anything else. Masters dare not take the vote of slaves as to their government. If they did, constant holiday, dissipation, and extravagance would be the result. Captains of ships are not appointed by the consent of the crew, and never take their vote, even in "doubling Cape Horn." If they did, the crew would generally vote to get drunk, and the ship would never weather the cape. Not even in the most democratic countries are soldiers governed by their consent, nor is their vote taken on the eve of battle. They have some how lost (or never had) the "inalienable rights of life, liberty, and the pursuit of happiness", and, whether Americans or Russians, are forced into battle without and often against their consent. The ancient republics where governed by a small class of adult male citizens who assumed and exercised the government without the consent of the governed. The South is governed just as those ancient republics were. In the county in which we live, there are eighteen thousand souls, and only twelve hundred voters. But we twelve hundred, the governors, never asked and never intend to ask the consent of the sixteen thousand eight hundred whom we govern. Were we to do so, we should soon have an "organized anarchy." The governments of Europe could not exist a week without the positive force of standing armies.

They are all governments of force, not of consent. Even in our North, the women, children, and free negroes, constitute four-fifths of the population; and they are all governed without their consent. But they mean to correct this gross and glaring iniquity at the North. They hold that all men, women, and negroes, and smart children are equals, and entitled to equal rights. The widows and free negroes begin to vote in some of those States, and they will have to let all colors and sexes and ages vote soon, or give up the glorious principles of human equality and universal emancipation.

The experiment which they will make, we fear, is absurd in theory, and the symptoms of approaching anarchy and agrarianism among them leave no doubt that its practical operation will be no better than its theory. Anti-rentism, "vote-myself-a-farm-ism," and all the other Isms, are but the spattering drops that precede a social deluge.

Abolition ultimates in "Consent Government"; Consent Government in Anarchy, Free Love, Agrarianism, &c., &c., and "Self-elected Despotism" winds up the play.

If the interests of the governors, or governing class, be not conservative, they certainly will not conserve institutions injurious to their interests. There never was and never can be an old society, in which the immediate interests of a majority of human souls do not conflict with all established order, all right of property, and all existing institutions. Immediate interest is all the mass look to; and they would be sure to revolutionize government, as often as the situation of the majority was worse than that of the minority. Divide all property to-day, and a year hence the inequalities of property would provoke a re-division.

In the South, the interest of the governing class is eminently conservative, and the South is fast becoming the most conservative of nations.

Already, at the North, government vibrates and oscillates between Radicalism and Conservatism; at present, Radicalism or Black Republicanism is in the ascendant.

The number of paupers is rapidly increasing; radical and agrarian doctrines are spreading; the women and the children, and the negroes, will soon be let in to vote; and then they will try the experiment of "Consent Government and Constituted Anarchy."

* * *

Looking to theory, to the examples of the Ancient Republics, and to England under the Plantagenets, we shall find that Southern institutions are far the best now existing in the world.

We think speculations as to constructing governments are little worth; for all government is the gradual accretion of Nature, time and circumstances. Yet these theories have occurred to us, and, as they are conservative, we will suggest them. In slaveholding countries all freemen should vote and govern, because their interests are conservative. In free states, the government should be in the hands of the landowners, who are also conservative. * * *

A word, at parting, to Northern Conservatives. A like danger threatens North and South, proceeding from the same source. Abolitionism is maturing what Political Economy began. With inexorable sequence Let Alone is made to usher in No-Government. North and South our danger is the same, and our remedies, though differing in degree, must in character be the same. Let Alone must be repudiated, if we would have any Government. We must, in all sections, act upon the principle that the world is "too little governed." You of the North need not institute negro slavery, far less reduce white men to the state of negro slavery. But the masses require more of protection, and the masses and philosophers equally require more of control. * * *

The mass of mankind cannot be governed by Law. More of despotic discretion, and less of Law, is what the world wants. We take our leave by saying, "THERE IS TOO MUCH OF LAW AND TOO LITTLE OF GOVERNMENT IN THIS WORLD."

Physical force, not moral suasion, governs the world. The negro sees the driver's lash, becomes accustomed to obedient, cheerful industry, and is not aware that the lash is the force that impels him. The free citizen fulfills, "con amore," his round of social, political and domestic duties, and never dreams that the Law, with its fines and jails, penitentiaries and halters, or Public Opinion, with its ostracism, its mobs, and its tar and feathers, help to keep him revolving in his orbit. Yet, remove these physical forces, and how many good citizens would shoot, like fiery comets, from their spheres, and disturb society with their eccentricities and their crimes.

ROGER B. TANEY

Dred Scott v. Sandford (1857)

Dred Scott was a Missouri slave who was briefly taken by his master to the free state of Illinois and the free Wisconsin Territory. With the aid of antislavery sympathizers, Scott sued for his freedom in Missouri state courts on the grounds that his residence in free territory effectively made him free. A lower court ruled in Scott's favor, but both the upper court in Missouri and the U.S. Supreme Court held against Scott. The 7-to-2 decision of the Supreme Court infuriated abolitionists with its ruling that blacks, who had "no rights which any white man was bound to respect," could not be citizens and that slaves were no different from any other kind of property. Chief Justice Taney's opinion further fanned the flames of the sectional crisis by declaring that Congress did not have the authority to prohibit slavery in the territories, thus invalidating the Missouri Compromise of 1820. Instead of settling the controversy over slavery, the decision actually revitalized the Republican Party and northern sentiment against slavery.

And upon a full and careful consideration of the subject, the court is of opinion that, upon the facts stated in the plea in abatement, Dred Scott was not a citizen of Missouri within the meaning of the Constitution of the United States, and not entitled as such to sue in its courts; and, consequently, that the Circuit Court had no jurisdiction of the case, and that the judgment on the plea in abatement is erroneous. * * *

We proceed, therefore, to inquire whether the facts relied on by the plaintiff entitled him to his freedom. * * *

In considering this part of the controversy, two questions arise: 1st. Was he, together with his family, free in Missouri by reason of the stay in the territory of the United States hereinbefore mentioned? And 2d, If they were not, is Scott himself free by reason of his removal to Rock Island, in the State of Illinois, as stated in the above admissions?

We proceed to examine the first question.

The Act of Congress, upon which the plaintiff relies, [the Missouri compromise] declares that slavery and involuntary servitude, except as a punishment for crime, shall be forever prohibited in all that part of the territory ceded by France, under the name of Louisiana, which lies north of thirty-six degrees thirty minutes north latitude, and not included within the limits of Missouri. And the difficulty which meets us at the threshold of this part of the inquiry is, whether Congress was authorized to pass this law under any of the powers granted to it by the Constitution; for if the authority is not given by that instrument, it is the duty of this court to declare it void and inoperative, and incapable of conferring freedom upon any one who is held as a slave under the laws of any one of the States.

The counsel for the plaintiff has laid much stress upon that article in the Constitution which confers on Congress the power "to dispose of and make all needful rules and regulations respecting the territory or other property belonging to the United States;" but, in the judgment of the court, that provision has no bearing on the present controversy, and the power there given, whatever it may be, is confined, and was intended to be confined, to the territory which at that time belonged to, or was claimed by, the United States, and was within their boundaries as settled by the treaty with Great Britain, and can have no influence upon a territory afterwards acquired from a foreign Government. It was a special provision for a known and particular territory, and to meet a present emergency, and nothing more. * * *

But the power of Congress over the person or property of a citizen can never be a mere discretionary power under our Constitution and form of Government. The powers of the Government and the rights and privileges of the citizen are regulated and plainly defined by the Constitution itself. And when the Territory becomes a part of the United States, the Federal Government enters into possession in the character impressed upon it by those who created it. It enters upon it with its powers over the citizen strictly defined, and limited by the Constitution, from which it derives its own existence, and by virtue of which alone it continues to exist and act as a Government and sovereignty. It has no power of any kind beyond it; and it cannot, when it enters a Territory of the United States, put off its character, and assume discretionary or despotic powers which the Constitution has denied to it. It cannot create for itself a new character separated from the citizens of the United States, and the duties it owes them under the provisions of the Constitution. The Territory being a part of the United States, the Government and the citizen both enter it under the authority of the Constitution, with their respective rights defined and marked out; and the Federal Government can exercise no power over his person or property, beyond what that instrument confers, nor lawfully deny any right which it has reserved. * * *

The rights of private property have been guarded with equal care. Thus the rights of property are united with the rights of person, and placed on the same ground by the fifth amendment to the Constitution. * * * An Act of Congress which deprives a person of the United States of his liberty or property merely because he came himself or brought his property into a particular Territory of the United States, and who had committed no offense against the laws, could hardly be dignified with the name of due process of law. * * *

And this prohibition is not confined to the States, but the words are general, and extend to the whole territory over which the Constitution gives it power to legislate, including those portions of it remaining under territorial government, as well as that covered by States. It is a total absence of power everywhere within the dominion of the United States, and places the citizens of a territory, so far as these rights are concerned, on the same footing with citizens of the States, and guards them as firmly and plainly against any inroads which the general government might attempt, under the plea of implied or incidental powers. And if Congress itself cannot do this—if it is beyond the powers conferred on the Federal Government—it will be admitted, we presume, that it could not authorize a territorial government to exercise them. It could confer no power on any local government, established by its authority, to violate the provisions of the Constitution.

It seems, however, to be supposed, that there is a difference between property in a slave and other property, and that different rules may be applied to it in expounding the Constitution of the United States. And the laws and usages of nations, and the writings of eminent jurists upon the relation of master and slave and their mutual rights and duties, and the powers which governments may exercise over it, have been dwelt upon in the argument.

But * * * if the Constitution recognizes the right of property of the master in a slave, and makes no distinction between that description of property and other property owned by a citizen, no tribunal, acting under the authority of the United States, whether it be legislative, executive, or judicial, has a right to draw such a distinction, or deny to it the benefit of the provisions and guarantees which have been provided for the protection of private property against the encroachments of the Government.

Now * * * the right of property in a slave is distinctly and expressly affirmed in the Constitution. The right to traffic in it, like an ordinary article of merchandise and property, was guaranteed to the citizens of the United States, in every State that might desire it, for twenty years. And the Government in express terms is pledged to protect it in all future time, if the slave escapes from his owner. * * * And no word can be found in the Constitution which gives Congress a greater power over slave property, or which entitles property of that kind to less protection than property of any other description. The only power conferred is the power coupled with the duty of guarding and protecting the owner in his rights.

Upon these considerations, it is the opinion of the court that the Act of Congress [the Missouri compromise] which prohibited a citizen from holding and owning property of this kind in the territory of the United States north of the line therein mentioned, is not warranted by the Constitution, and is therefore void; and that neither Dred Scott himself, nor any of his family, were made free by being carried into this territory; even if they had been carried there by the owner, with the intention of becoming a permanent resident.

JAMES HENRY HAMMOND

"Mud Sill" Speech (1858)

A protégé of John C. Calhoun, the wealthy lawyer and editor James Henry Hammond (1807–1864) served as South Carolina's governor and as a member of both houses of Congress. His numerous writings helped develop the racist ideology that underpinned proslavery arguments in the 1850s. According to Hammond's notorious "mud sill" theory, which he articulated in a speech on the Senate floor, the enslavement of an inferior race incapable of freedom provides the necessary foundation for the civilization and progress of a superior race. In particular, Hammond argued that black slavery was a necessary precondition for the values of freedom, equality, and democracy cherished by whites.

But, sir, the greatest strength of the South arises from the harmony of her political and social institutions. This harmony gives her a frame of society, the best in the world, and an extent of political freedom, combined with entire security, such as no other people ever enjoyed upon the face of the earth. Society precedes government; creates it, and ought to control it; but as far as we can look back in historic times we find the case different; for government is no sooner created than it becomes too strong for society, and shapes and moulds, as well as controls it. In later centuries the progress of civilization and of intelligence has made the divergence so great as to produce civil wars and revolutions; and it is nothing now but the want of harmony between governments and societies which occasions all the uneasiness and trouble and terror that we see abroad. It was this that brought on the American Revolution. We threw off a Government not adapted to our social system, and made one for ourselves. The question is, how far have we succeeded? The South, so far as that is concerned, is satisfied, harmonious, and prosperous, but demands to be let alone.

In all social systems there must be a class to do the menial duties, to perform the drudgery of life. That is, a class requiring but a low order of intellect and but little skill. Its requisites are vigor, docility, fidelity. Such a class you must have, or you would not have that other class which leads progress, civilization, and refinement. It constitutes the very mud-sill of society and of political government; and you might as well attempt to build a house in the air, as to build either the one or the other, except on this mud-sill. Fortunately for the South, she found a race adapted to that purpose to her hand. A race inferior to her own, but eminently qualified in temper, in vigor, in docility, in capacity to stand the climate, to answer all her purposes. We use them for our purpose, and call them slaves. We found them slaves by the common "consent of mankind," which, according to Cicero, "*lex naturæ est.*" The highest proof of what is Nature's law. We are old-fashioned at the South yet; slave is a word discarded now by "ears polite;" I will not characterize that class at the North by that term; but you have it; it is there; it is everywhere; it is eternal.

The Senator from New York said yesterday that the whole world had abolished slavery. Aye, the *name*, but not the *thing*; all the powers of the earth cannot abolish that. God only can do it when he repeals the *fiat*, "the poor ye always have with you;" for the man who lives by daily labor, and scarcely lives at that, and who has to put out his labor in the market, and take the best he can get for it; in short, your whole hireling class of manual laborers and "operatives," as you call them, are essentially slaves. The difference between us is, that our slaves are hired for life and well compensated; there is no starvation, no begging, no want of employment among our people, and not too much employment either. Yours are hired by the day, not cared for, and scantily compensated, which may be proved in the most painful manner, at any hour in any street in any of your large towns. Why, you meet more beggars in one day, in any single street of the city of New York, than you would meet in a lifetime in the whole South. We do not think that whites should be slaves either by law or necessity. Our slaves are black, of another and inferior race. The *status* in which we have placed them is an elevation. They are elevated from the condition in which God first created them, by being made our slaves. None of that race on the whole face of the globe can be compared with the slaves of the South. They are happy, content, unaspiring, and utterly incapable, from intellectual weakness, ever to give us any trouble by their aspirations. Yours are white, of your own race; you are brothers of one blood. They are your equals in natural endowment of intellect, and they feel galled by their degradation. Our slaves do not vote. We give them no political power. Yours do vote, and, being the majority, they are the depositaries of all your political power. If they knew the tremendous secret, that the ballot-box is stronger than "an army with banners," and could combine, where would you be? Your society would be reconstructed, your government overthrown, your property divided, not as they have mistakenly attempted to initiate such proceedings by meeting in parks, with arms in their hands, but by the quiet process of the ballot-box.

ABRAHAM LINCOLN

Speech at Peoria, Illinois (1854)

The sixteenth president of the United States, Abraham Lincoln (1809–1865) was born in Kentucky. He eventually moved to Illinois, where he established a modest law practice and served as a state legislator. He was elected to Congress in 1846, but did not seek reelection. He achieved national prominence during his unsuccessful 1858 bid for the Senate as the nominee of the newly formed Republican Party. Four years earlier, he had attracted the attention of free-soil and free-labor advocates with a speech denouncing Democratic Senator Stephen A. Douglas's proposal to allow a majority of voters in territories seeking statehood to decide whether or not to permit slavery. Lincoln's speech at Peoria was not only a lively defense of "the SPIRIT of COMPROMISE" as embodied in the Missouri Compromise, it was also a thorough statement of Lincoln's moral and political convictions. Although he claimed to detest slavery as a flagrant violation of human rights and republican principles as formulated in the Declaration of Independence, Lincoln made it clear that his first priority was the preservation of the Union.

The repeal of the Missouri Compromise, and the propriety of its restoration, constitute the subject of what I am about to say. * * *

And as this subject is no other than part and parcel of the larger general question of domestic slavery, I wish to make and to keep the distinction between the existing institution and the extension of it, so broad and so clear that no honest man can misunderstand me, and no dishonest one successfully misrepresent me. * * *

During this long period of time Nebraska had remained, substantially an uninhabited country, but now emigration to, and settlement within it began to take place. It is about one third as large as the present United States, and its importance so long overlooked, begins to come into view. The restriction of slavery by the Missouri Compromise directly applies to it; in fact, was first made, and has since been maintained, expressly for it. In 1853, a bill to give it a territorial government passed the House of Representatives, and, in the hands of Judge Douglas, failed of passing the Senate only for want of time. This bill contained no repeal of the Missouri Compromise. Indeed, when it was assailed because it did not contain such repeal, Judge Douglas defended it in its existing form. On January 4th, 1854, Judge Douglas introduces a new bill to give Nebraska territorial government. He accompanies this bill with a report, in which last, he expressly recommends that the Missouri Compromise shall neither be affirmed nor repealed.

Before long the bill is so modified as to make two territories instead of one; calling the Southern one Kansas.

Also, about a month after the introduction of the bill, on the judge's own motion, it is so amended as to declare the Missouri Compromise inoperative and void; and, substantially, that the People who go and settle there may establish slavery, or exclude it, as they may see fit. In this shape the bill passed both branches of congress, and became a law.

This is the *repeal* of the Missouri Compromise. The foregoing history may not be precisely accurate in every particular; but I am sure it is sufficiently so, for all the uses I shall attempt to make of it, and in it, we have before us, the chief material enabling us to correctly judge whether the repeal of the Missouri Compromise is right or wrong.

I think, and shall try to show, that it is wrong; wrong in its direct effect, letting slavery into Kansas and Nebraska—and wrong in its prospective principle, allowing it to spread to every other part of the wide world, where men can be found inclined to take it.

This *declared* indifference, but as I must think, covert real *zeal* for the spread of slavery, I can not but hate. I hate it because of the monstrous injustice of slavery itself. I hate it because it deprives our republican example of its just influence in the world—enables the enemies of free institutions,

with plausibility, to taunt us as hypocrites—causes the real friends of freedom to doubt our sincerity, and especially because it forces so many really
good men amongst ourselves into an open war with the very fundamental
principles of civil liberty—criticising the Declaration of Independence, and
insisting that there is no right principle of action but *self-interest.*

Before proceeding, let me say I think I have no prejudice against the
Southern people. They are just what we would be in their situation. If
slavery did not now exist amongst them, they would not introduce it. If it
did now exist amongst us, we should not instantly give it up. This I believe
of the masses north and south. Doubtless there are individuals, on both
sides, who would not hold slaves under any circumstances; and others
who would gladly introduce slavery anew, if it were out of existence. We
know that some southern men do free their slaves, go north, and become
tip-top abolitionists; while some northern ones go south, and become
most cruel slave-masters.

When southern people tell us they are no more responsible for the origin of slavery, than we; I acknowledge the fact. When it is said that the
institution exists; and that it is very difficult to get rid of it, in any satisfactory way, I can understand and appreciate the saying. I surely will not
blame them for not doing what I should not know how to do myself. If all
earthly power were given me, I should not know what to do, as to the existing institution. My first impulse would be to free all the slaves, and
send them to Liberia,—to their own native land. But a moment's reflection would convince me, that whatever of high hope, (as I think there is)
there may be in this, in the long run, its sudden execution is impossible.
If they were all landed there in a day, they would all perish in the next ten
days; and there are not surplus shipping and surplus money enough in
the world to carry them there in many times ten days. What then? Free
them all, and keep them among us as underlings? Is it quite certain that
this betters their condition? I think I would not hold one in slavery, at any
rate; yet the point is not clear enough for me to denounce people upon.
What next? Free them, and make them politically and socially, our
equals? My own feelings will not admit of this; and if mine would, we
well know that those of the great mass of white people will not. Whether
this feeling accords with justice and sound judgment, is not the sole
question, if indeed, it is any part of it. A universal feeling, whether well or
ill-founded, can not be safely disregarded. We can not, then, make them
equals. It does seem to me that systems of gradual emancipation might
be adopted; but for their tardiness in this, I will not undertake to judge
our brethren of the south.

When they remind us of their constitutional rights, I acknowledge
them, not grudgingly, but fully, and fairly; and I would give them any

legislation for the reclaiming of their fugitives, which should not, in its stringency, be more likely to carry a free man into slavery, than our ordinary criminal laws are to hang an innocent one.

But all this; to my judgment, furnishes no more excuse for permitting slavery to go into our own free territory, than it would for reviving the African slave trade by law. The law which forbids the bringing of slaves *from* Africa; and that which has so long forbid the taking them *to* Nebraska, can hardly be distinguished on any moral principle; and the repeal of the former could find quite as plausible excuses as that of the latter. * * *

Equal justice to the South, it is said, requires us to consent to the extension of slavery to new countries. That is to say, inasmuch as you do not object to my taking my hog to Nebraska, therefore I must not object to you taking your slave. Now I admit that this is perfectly logical, if there is no difference between hogs and negroes. But while you thus require me to deny the humanity of the negro, I wish to ask whether you of the South, yourselves, have ever been willing to do as much? It is kindly provided that of all those who come into the world only a small percentage are natural tyrants. That percentage is no larger in the slave States than in the free. The great majority South, as well as North, have human sympathies, of which they can no more divest themselves than they can of their sensibility to physical pain. These sympathies in the bosoms of the Southern people manifest, in many ways, their sense of the wrong of slavery, and their consciousness that, after all, there is humanity in the Negro. * * *

* * * I trust I understand and truly estimate the right of self-government. My faith in the proposition that each man should do precisely as he pleases with all which is exclusively his own lies at the foundation of the sense of justice there is in me. I extend the principle to communities of men as well as to individuals. I so extend it because it is politically wise in saving us from broils about matters which do not concern us. Here, or at Washington, I would not trouble myself with the oyster laws of Virginia, or the cranberry laws of Indiana. The doctrine of self-government is right,—absolutely and eternally right,—but it has no just application as here attempted. Or perhaps I should rather say that whether it has such application depends upon whether a Negro is not or is a man. If he is not a man, in that case he who is a man may as a matter of self-government do just what he pleases with him. But if the Negro is a man, is it not to that extent a total destruction of self-government to say that he too shall not govern himself? When the white man governs himself, that is self-government; but when he governs himself and also governs another man, that is more than self-government—that is despotism.

If the Negro is a man, why then my ancient faith teaches me that 'all men are created equal,' and that there can be no moral right in connection with one man's making a slave of another.

Judge Douglas frequently, with bitter irony and sarcasm, paraphrases our argument by saying, 'The white people of Nebraska are good enough to govern themselves, but they are not good enough to govern a few miserable Negroes!'

Well! I doubt not that the people of Nebraska are and will continue to be as good as the average of people elsewhere. I do not say the contrary. What I do say is that no man is good enough to govern another man without that other's consent. I say this is the leading principle, the sheet-anchor of American republicanism. * * *

But Nebraska is urged as a great Union-saving measure. Well, I too go for saving the Union. Much as I hate slavery, I would consent to the extension of it rather than see the Union dissolved, just as I would consent to any great evil to avoid a greater one. But when I go to Union-saving, I must believe, at least, that the means I employ have some adaptation to the end. To my mind, Nebraska has no such adaptation. It hath no relish of salvation in it. It is an aggravation, rather, of the only one thing which ever endangers the Union. * * *

The Missouri Compromise ought to be restored. For the sake of the Union, it ought to be restored. We ought to elect a House of Representatives which will vote its restoration. If by any means, we omit to do this, what follows? Slavery may or may not be established in Nebraska. But whether it be or not, we shall have repudiated—discarded from the councils of the Nation—the SPIRIT of COMPROMISE; for who after this will ever trust in a national compromise? The spirit of mutual concession—that spirit which first gave us the constitution, and which has thrice saved the Union—we shall have strangled and cast from us forever. And what shall we have in lieu of it? The South flushed with triumph and tempted to excesses; the North, betrayed, as they believe, brooding on wrong and burning for revenge. One side will provoke; the other resent. The one will taunt, the other defy; one agrees [aggresses?], the other retaliates. Already a few in the North, defy all constitutional restraints, resist the execution of the fugitive slave law, and even menace the institution of slavery in the states where it exists.

* * *

Fellow countrymen—Americans south, as well as north, shall we make no effort to arrest this? Already the liberal party throughout the world, express the apprehension "that the one retrograde institution in America, is undermining the principles of progress, and fatally violating the noblest political system the world ever saw." This is not the taunt of enemies, but the warning of friends. Is it quite safe to disregard it—to despise it? Is there no danger to liberty itself, in discarding the earliest practice, and first precept of our ancient faith? In our greedy chase to make profit of the negro, let us beware, lest we "cancel and tear to pieces" even the white man's charter of freedom.

Our republican robe is soiled, and trailed in the dust. Let us repurify it. Let us turn and wash it white, in the spirit, if not the blood, of the Revolution. Let us turn slavery from its claims of "moral right," back upon its existing legal rights, and its arguments of "necessity." Let us return it to the position our fathers gave it; and there let it rest in peace. Let us re-adopt the Declaration of Independence, and with it, the practices, and policy, which harmonize with it. Let north and south—let all Americans—let all lovers of liberty everywhere—join in the great and good work. If we do this, we shall not only have saved the Union; but we shall have so saved it, as to make, and to keep it, forever worthy of the saving. We shall have so saved it, that the succeeding millions of free happy people, the world over, shall rise up, and call us blessed, to the latest generations.

ABRAHAM LINCOLN

Speech on the *Dred Scott* Decision in Springfield, Illinois (1857)

Lincoln often spoke eloquently about the Declaration of Independence as the touchstone of American values, but contemporary social attitudes did as much as the principles of the founding to shape his views on racial relations. In a speech criticizing the Dred Scott decision, Lincoln emphasized that the Declaration set a standard of universal equality for the benefit of future generations. Even though he asserted that all are equal in their rights, especially the right to enjoy the products of one's labor, he also stated that there were significant differences between blacks and whites that made them unequal in other respects. Moreover, Lincoln accepted the need to keep the two races separate and praised the free states for being more successful than the slave states in this regard.

nd now as to the Dred Scott decision. That decision declares two
propositions—first, that a Negro cannot sue in the United States
courts; and secondly, that Congress cannot prohibit slavery in the Territories. It was made by a divided court—dividing differently on the different points. Judge Douglas does not discuss the merits of the decision, and
in that respect I shall follow his example. * * *

He denounces all who question the correctness of that decision, as offering violent resistance to it. But who resists it? Who has, in spite of the
decision, declared Dred Scott free, and resisted the authority of his master over him?

Judicial decisions have two uses—first, to absolutely determine the
case decided; and secondly, to indicate to the public how other similar
cases will be decided when they arise. For the latter use, they are called
'precedents' and 'authorities.'

We believe as much as Judge Douglas (perhaps more) in obedience
to, and respect for, the judicial department of government. We think its
decisions on constitutional questions, when fully settled, should control not only the particular cases decided, but the general policy of the
country, subject to be disturbed only by amendments of the Constitution as provided in that instrument itself. More than this would be revolution. But we think the Dred Scott decision is erroneous. We know
the court that made it has often overruled its own decisions, and we
shall do what we can to have it to overrule this. We offer no resistance
to it. * * *

But Judge Douglas considers this view awful. Hear him:

> The courts are the tribunals prescribed by the Constitution and created
> by the authority of the people to determine, expound, and enforce the
> law. Hence, whoever resists the final decision of the highest judicial
> tribunal aims a deadly blow at our whole republican system of
> government—a blow which, if successful, would place all our rights and
> liberties at the mercy of passion, anarchy, and violence. I repeat, there-
> fore, that if resistance to the decisions of the Supreme Court of the
> United States, in a matter like the points decided in the Dred Scott case,
> clearly within their jurisdiction as defined by the Constitution, shall be
> forced upon the country as a political issue, it will become a distinct and
> naked issue between the friends and enemies of the Constitution—the
> friends and the enemies of the supremacy of the laws.

Again and again have I heard Judge Douglas denounce that bank decision and applaud General Jackson for disregarding it. It would be interesting for him to look over his recent speech, and see how exactly his

fierce philippics against us for resisting Supreme Court decisions fall upon his own head. It will call to mind a long and fierce political war in this country, upon an issue which, in his own language, and, of course, in his own changeless estimation, was 'a distinct issue between the friends and the enemies of the Constitution,' and in which war he fought in the ranks of the enemies of the Constitution.

* * *

* * * There is a natural disgust in the minds of nearly all white people, to the idea of an indiscriminate amalgamation of the white and black races; and Judge Douglas evidently is basing his chief hope, upon the chances of being able to appropriate the benefit of this disgust to himself. If he can, by much drumming and repeating, fasten the odium of that idea upon his adversaries, he thinks he can struggle through the storm. He therefore clings to this hope, as a drowning man to the last plank. He makes an occasion for lugging it in from the opposition to the Dred Scott decision. He finds the Republicans insisting that the Declaration of Independence includes *all* men, black as well as white; and forthwith he boldly denies that it includes negroes at all, and proceeds to argue gravely that all who contend it does, do so only because they want to vote, and eat, and sleep, and marry with negroes! He will have it that they cannot be consistent else. Now I protest against that counterfeit logic which concludes that, because I do not want a black woman for a *slave* I must necessarily want her for a *wife*. I need not have her for either, I can just leave her alone. In some respects she certainly is not my equal; but in her natural right to eat the bread she earns with her own hands without asking leave of any one else, she is my equal, and the equal of all others.

Chief Justice Taney, in his opinion in the Dred Scott case, admits that the language of the Declaration is broad enough to include the whole human family, but he and Judge Douglas argue that the authors of that instrument did not intend to include negroes, by the fact that they did not at once, actually place them on an equality with the whites. Now this grave argument comes to just nothing at all, by the other fact, that they did not at once, *or ever afterwards,* actually place all white people on an equality with one or another. And this is the staple argument of both the Chief Justice and the Senator, for doing this obvious violence to the plain unmistakable language of the Declaration. I think the authors of that notable instrument intended to include *all* men, but they did not intend to declare all men equal *in all respects.* They did not mean to say all were equal in color, size, intellect, moral developments, or social capacity. They defined with tolerable distinctness, in what respects they did consider all men created equal—equal in "certain inalienable rights, among which are life, liberty, and the pursuit of happiness." This they said, and this meant. They did not mean to assert the obvious untruth, that all were then actually enjoying that equality, nor yet, that they were about to confer it immediately upon them. In fact they had no power to confer such a boon. They meant simply to declare the *right,* so that the *enforcement* of it might follow as fast as circumstances should permit. They meant to set up a standard maxim for free society, which should be familiar to all, and revered by all; constantly looked to, constantly labored for, and even though never perfectly attained, constantly approximated, and thereby constantly spreading and deepening its influence, and augmenting the happiness and value of life to all people of all colors everywhere. The assertion that "all men are created equal" was of no practical use in effecting our separation from Great Britain; and it was placed in the Declaration, not for that, but for future use. Its authors meant it to be, thank God, it is now proving itself, a stumbling block to those who in after times might seek to turn a free people back into the hateful paths of despotism. They knew the proneness of prosperity to breed tyrants, and they meant when such should re-appear in this fair land and commence their vocation they should find left for them at least one hard nut to crack.

I have now briefly expressed my view of the *meaning* and *objects* of that part of the Declaration of Independence which declares that "all men are created equal."

Now let us hear Judge Douglas' view of the same subject, as I find it in the printed report of his late speech. Here it is:

No man can vindicate the character, motives and conduct of the signers of the Declaration of Independence, except upon the hypothesis that they referred to the white race alone, and not to the African, when they declared all men to have been created equal—that they were speaking of British subjects on this continent being equal to British subjects born and residing in Great Britain—that they were entitled to the same inalienable rights, and among them were enumerated life, liberty and the pursuit of happiness. The Declaration was adopted for the purpose of justifying the colonists in the eyes of the civilized world in withdrawing their allegiance from the British crown, and dissolving their connection with the mother country.

My good friends, read that carefully over some leisure hour, and ponder well upon it—see what a mere wreck—mangled ruin—it makes of our once glorious Declaration.

"They were speaking of British subjects on this continent being equal to British subjects born and residing in Great Britain!" Why, according to this, not only negroes but white people outside of Great Britain and

America are not spoken of in that instrument. The English, Irish and Scotch, along with white Americans, were included to be sure, but the French, Germans and other white people of the world are all gone to pot along with the Judge's inferior races.

I had thought the Declaration promised something better than the condition of British subjects; but no, it only meant that we should be *equal* to them in their own oppressed and *unequal* condition. According to that, it gave no promise that having kicked off the King and Lords of Great Britain, we should not at once be saddled with a King and Lords of our own.

I had thought the Declaration contemplated the progressive improvement in the condition of all men everywhere; but no, it merely "was adopted for the purpose of justifying the colonists in the eyes of the civilized world in withdrawing their allegiance from the British crown, and dissolving their connection with the mother country." Why, that object having been effected some eighty years ago, the Declaration is of no practical use now—mere rubbish—old wadding left to rot on the battlefield after the victory is won.

I understand you are preparing to celebrate the "Fourth," tomorrow week. What for? The doings of that day had no reference to the present; and quite half of you are not even descendants of those who were referred to at that day. But I suppose you will celebrate; and will even go so far as to read the Declaration. Suppose after you read it once in the old fashioned way, you read it once more with Justice Douglas' version. It will then run thus: "We hold these truths to be self-evident that all British subjects who were on this continent eighty-one years ago, were created equal to all British subjects born and *then* residing in Great Britain."

And now I appeal to all—to Democrats as well as others,—are you really willing that the Declaration shall be thus frittered away?—thus left no more at most, than an interesting memorial of the dead past? thus shorn of its vitality, and practical value; and left without the *germ* or even the *suggestion* of the individual rights of man in it?

But Judge Douglas is especially horrified at the thought of the mixing blood by the white and black races: agreed for once—a thousand times agreed. There are white men enough to marry all the white women, and black men enough to marry all the black women; and so let them be married. On this point we fully agree with the Judge; and when he shall show that his policy is better adapted to prevent amalgamation than ours we shall drops ours, and adopt his. Let us see. In 1850 there were in the United States, 405,751, mulattoes. Very few of these are the offspring of whites and *free* blacks; nearly all have sprung from black *slaves* and white masters. A separation of the races is the only perfect preventive of amalgamation but as an immediate separation is impossible the next best thing is to *keep* them apart *where* they are not already together. If white and black people never get together in Kansas, they will never mix blood in Kansas. That is at least one self-evident truth. A few free colored persons may get into the free States, in any event; but their number is too insignificant to amount to much in the way of mixing blood. In 1850 there were in the free states, 56,649 mulattoes; but for the most part they were not born there—they came from the slave States, ready made up. In the same year the slave States had 348,874 mulattoes all of home production. The proportion of free mulattoes to free blacks—the only colored classes in the free states—is much greater in the slave than in the free states. It is worthy of note too, that among the free states those which make the colored man the nearest to equal the white, have, proportionably the fewest mulattoes and the least of amalgamation. In New Hampshire, the State which goes farthest towards equality between the races, there are just 184 Mulattoes while there are in Virginia—how many do you think? 79,775, being 23,126 more than in all the free States together.

These statistics show that slavery is the greatest source of amalgamation; and next to it, not the elevation, but the degeneration of the free blacks. Yet Judge Douglas dreads the slightest restraints on the spread of slavery, and the slightest human recognition of the negro, as tending horribly to amalgamation.

This very Dred Scott case affords a strong test as to which party most favors amalgamation, the Republican or the dear Union saving Democracy. Dred Scott, his wife and two daughters were all involved in the suit. We desired the court to have held that they were citizens so far at least as to entitle them to a hearing as to whether they were free or not; and then, also, that they were in fact and in law really free. Could we have had our way, the chances of these black girls, ever mixing their blood with that of white people, would have been diminished at least to the extent that it could not have been without their consent. But Judge Douglas is delighted to have them decided to be slaves, and not human enough to have a hearing, even if they were free, and thus left subject to the forced concubinage of their masters, and liable to become the mothers of mulattoes in spite of themselves—the very state of case that produces nine tenths of all the mulattoes—all the mixing of blood in the nation.

Of course, I state this case as an illustration only, not meaning to say or intimate that the master of Dred Scott and his family, or any more than a per centage of masters generally, are inclined to exercise this particular power which they hold over their female slaves.

I have said that the separation of the races is the only perfect preventive of amalgamation. I have no right to say all the members of the Republican party are in favor of this, nor to say that as a party they are in favor of it. There is nothing in their platform directly on the subject. But I can say a very large proportion of its members are for it, and that the chief plank in their platform—opposition to the spread of slavery—is most favorable to that separation.

Such separation, if ever effected at all, must be effected by colonization; and no political party, as such, is now doing anything directly for colonization. Party operations at present only favor or retard colonization incidentally. The enterprise is a difficult one; but "when there is a will there is a way;" and what colonization needs most is a hearty will. Will springs from the two elements of moral sense and self-interest. Let us be brought to believe it is morally right, and, at the same time, favorable to, or, at least, not against, our interest, to transfer the African to his native clime, and we shall find a way to do it, however great the task may be. The children of Israel, to such numbers as to include four hundred thousand fighting men, went out of Egyptian bondage in a body.

How differently the respective courses of the Democratic and Republican parties incidentally bear on the question of forming a will—a public sentiment—for colonization, is easy to see. The Republicans inculcate, with whatever of ability they can, that the negro is a man; that his bondage is cruelly wrong, and that the field of his oppression ought not to be enlarged. The Democrats deny his manhood; deny, or dwarf to insignificance, the wrong of his bondage: so far as possible, crush all sympathy for him, and cultivate and excite hatred and disgust against him; compliment themselves as Union-savers for doing so; and call the indefinite outspreading of his bondage "a sacred right of self-government."

ABRAHAM LINCOLN

Letter to Boston Republicans (1859)

In a letter declining an invitation to attend a festival in Boston commemorating Thomas Jefferson's birthday, Lincoln noted the remarkable fact that the newly formed Republicans, rather than the descendants of Jefferson's party, more faithfully represented the third president's commitment to both personal and property rights.

G entlemen

Your kind note inviting me to attend a Festival in Boston, on the 13th. Inst. in honor of the birth-day of Thomas Jefferson, was duly received. My engagements are such that I can not attend.

Bearing in mind that about seventy years ago, two great political parties were first formed in this country, that Thomas Jefferson was the head of one of them, and Boston the headquarters of the other, it is both curious and interesting that those supposed to descend politically from the party opposed to Jefferson, should now be celebrating his birth-day in their own original seat of empire, while those claiming political descent from him have nearly ceased to breathe his name everywhere.

Remembering too, that the Jefferson party were formed upon their supposed superior devotion to the *personal* rights of men, holding the rights of *property* to be secondary only, and greatly inferior, and then assuming that the so-called democracy of to-day, are the Jefferson, and their opponents, the anti-Jefferson parties, it will be equally interesting to note how completely the two have changed hands as to the principle upon which they were originally supposed to be divided.

The democracy of to-day hold the *liberty* of one man to be absolutely nothing, when in conflict with another man's right of *property*. Republicans, on the contrary, are for both the *man* and the *dollar*; but in cases of conflict, the man *before* the dollar.

I remember once being much amused at seeing two partially intoxicated men engage in a fight with their great-coats on, which fight, after a long, and rather harmless contest, ended in each having fought himself *out* of his own coat, and *into* that of the other. If the two leading parties of this day are really identical with the two in the days of Jefferson and Adams, they have performed about the same feat as the two drunken men.

But soberly, it is now no child's play to save the principles of Jefferson from total overthrow in this nation.

One would start with great confidence that he could convince any sane child that the simpler propositions of Euclid are true; but, nevertheless, he would fail, utterly, with one who should deny the definitions and axioms. The principles of Jefferson are the definitions and axioms of free society. And yet they are denied, and evaded, with no small show of success. One dashingly calls them "glittering generalities"; another bluntly calls them "self evident lies"; and still others insidiously argue that they apply only to "superior races."

These expressions, differing in form, are identical in object and effect— the supplanting the principles of free government, and restoring those of classification, caste, and legitimacy. They would delight a convocation of crowned heads, plotting against the people. They are the vanguard—the miners, and sappers—of returning despotism. We must repulse them, or they will subjugate us.

This is a world of compensations; and he who would be no slave, must consent to *have* no slave. Those who deny freedom to others, deserve it not for themselves; and, under a just God, can not long retain it.

All honor to Jefferson—to the man who, in the concrete pressure of a struggle for national independence by a single people, had the coolness, forecast, and capacity to introduce into a merely revolutionary document, an abstract truth, applicable to all men and all times, and so to embalm it there, that to-day, and in all coming days, it shall be a rebuke and a stumbling-block to the very harbingers of re-appearing tyranny and oppression.

ABRAHAM LINCOLN

Address Before the Wisconsin State Agricultural Society (1859)

In a speech he delivered to the Wisconsin Agricultural Society, Lincoln articulated his social theory of labor. In response to critics who alleged that the wage earner, like the slave, "is fatally fixed in that condition for life," Lincoln argued that for most Americans, wage labor was merely a stepping stone on the path to economic independence and a means of bettering their condition. Eventually, Lincoln claimed, wage laborers who worked hard could accumulate enough capital to start their own businesses and hire other workers. In the course of the address Lincoln explicitly repudiates the "mud-sill" rationale for slave labor.

The world is agreed that labor is the source from which human wants are mainly supplied. There is no dispute upon this point. From this point, however, men immediately diverge. Much disputation is maintained as to the best way of applying and controlling the labor element. By some it is assumed that labor is available only in connection with capital—that nobody labors, unless somebody else owning capital, somehow, by the use of it, induces him to do it. Having assumed this, they proceed to consider whether it is best that capital shall hire laborers, and thus induce them to work by their own consent, or buy them, and drive them to it, without their consent. Having proceeded so far, they naturally conclude that all laborers are naturally either hired laborers or slaves. They further assume that whoever is once a hired laborer, is fatally fixed in that condition for life; and thence again, that his condition is as bad as, or worse than, that of a slave. This is the "mud-sill" theory. But another class of reasoners hold the opinion that there is no such relation between capital and labor as assumed; that there is no such thing as a free man being fatally fixed for life in the condition of a hired laborer; that both these assumptions are false, and all inferences from them groundless. They hold that labor is prior to, and independent of, capital; that, in fact, capital is the fruit of labor, and could never have existed if labor had not first existed; that labor can exist without capital, but that capital could never have existed without labor. Hence they hold that labor is the superior—greatly the superior—of capital.

They do not deny that there is, and probably always will be, a relation between labor and capital. The error, as they hold, is in assuming that the whole labor of the world exists within that relation. A few men own capital; and that few avoid labor themselves, and with their capital hire or buy another few to labor for them. A large majority belong to neither class—neither work for others, nor have others working for them. Even in all our slave States except South Carolina, a majority of the whole people of all colors are neither slaves nor masters. In these free States, a large majority are neither hirers nor hired. Men, with their families—wives, sons, and daughters—work for themselves, on their farms, in their houses, and in their shops, taking the whole product to themselves, and asking no favors of capital on the one hand, nor of hirelings or slaves on the other. It is not forgotten that a considerable number of persons mingle their own labor with capital—that is, labor with their own hands, and also buy slaves or hire free men to labor for them; but this is only a mixed, and not a distinct, class. No principle stated is disturbed by the existence of this mixed class. Again, as has already been said, the opponents of the "mud-sill" theory insist that there is not, of necessity, any such thing as the free hired laborer being fixed to that condition for life. There is demonstration for saying this. Many independent men in this assembly doubtless a few years ago were hired laborers. And their case is almost, if not quite, the general rule.

The prudent, penniless beginner in the world labors for wages awhile, saves a surplus with which to buy tools or land for himself, then labors on his own account another while, and at length hires another new beginner to help him. This, say its advocates, is free labor—the just, and generous, and prosperous system, which opens the way for all, gives hope to all, and energy, and progress, and improvement of condition to all. If any continue through life in the condition of the hired laborer, it is not the fault of the system, but because of either a dependent nature which prefers it, or improvidence, folly, or singular misfortune. I have said this much about the elements of labor generally, as introductory to the consideration of a new phase which that element is in process of assuming. The old general rule was that educated people did not perform manual labor. They managed to eat their bread, leaving the toil of producing it to the uneducated. This was not an insupportable evil to the working bees, so long as the class of drones remained very small. But now, especially in these free States, nearly all are educated—quite too nearly all to leave the labor of the uneducated in any wise adequate to the support of the whole. It follows from this that henceforth educated people must labor. Otherwise, education itself would become a positive and intolerable evil. No country can sustain in idleness more than a small percentage of its numbers. The great majority must labor at something productive. From these premises the problem springs, "How can labor and education be the most satisfactorily combined?"

By the "mud-sill" theory it is assumed that labor and education are incompatible, and any practical combination of them impossible. According to that theory, a blind horse upon a tread-mill is a perfect illustration of what a laborer should be—all the better for being blind, that he could not kick understandingly. According to that theory, the education of laborers is not only useless but pernicious and dangerous. In fact, it is, in some sort, deemed a misfortune that laborers should have heads at all. Those same heads are regarded as explosive materials, only to be safely kept in damp places, as far as possible from that peculiar sort of fire which ignites them. A Yankee who could invent a strong-handed man without a head would receive the everlasting gratitude of the "mud-sill" advocates.

But free labor says, "No." Free labor argues that as the Author of man makes every individual with one head and one pair of hands, it was probably intended that heads and hands should coöperate as friends, and that that particular head should direct and control that pair of hands. As each man has one mouth to be fed, and one pair of hands to furnish food, it was probably intended that that particular pair of hands should feed that particular mouth—that each head is the natural guardian, director, and protector of the hands and mouth inseparably connected with it; and that being so, every head should be cultivated and improved by whatever will add to its capacity for performing its charge. In one word, free labor insists on universal education.

I have so far stated the opposite theories of "mud-sill" and "free labor," without declaring any preference of my own between them. On an occasion like this, I ought not to declare any. I suppose, however, I shall not be mistaken in assuming as a fact that the people of Wisconsin prefer free labor, with its natural companion, education.

This leads to the further reflection that no other human occupation opens so wide a field for the profitable and agreeable combination of labor with cultivated thought, as agriculture. I know nothing so pleasant to the mind as the discovery of anything that is at once new and valuable—nothing that so lightens and sweetens toil as the hopeful pursuit of such discovery. And how vast and how varied a field is agriculture for such discovery! The mind, already trained to thought in the country school, or higher school, cannot fail to find there an exhaustless source of enjoyment. Every blade of grass is a study; and to produce two where there was but one is both a profit and a pleasure. And not grass alone, but soils, seeds, and seasons—hedges, ditches, and fences—draining, droughts, and irrigation—plowing, hoeing, and harrowing—reaping, mowing, and threshing—saving crops, pests of crops, diseases of crops, and what will prevent or cure them—implements, utensils, and machines, their relative merits, and how to improve them—hogs, horses, and cattle—sheep, goats, and poultry—trees, shrubs, fruits, plants, and flowers—the thousand things of which these are specimens—each a world of study within itself.

In all this, book-learning is available. A capacity and taste for reading gives access to whatever has already been discovered by others. It is the key, or one of the keys, to the already solved problems. And not only so: it gives a relish and facility for successfully pursuing the unsolved ones. The rudiments of science are available, and highly available. Some knowledge of botany assists in dealing with the vegetable world—with all growing crops. Chemistry assists in the analysis of soils, selection and application of manures, and in numerous other ways. The mechanical branches of natural philosophy are ready help in almost everything, but especially in reference to implements and machinery.

The thought recurs that education—cultivated thought—can best be combined with agricultural labor, or any labor, on the principle of thorough work; that careless, half-performed, slovenly work makes no place for such combination; and thorough work, again, renders sufficient the smallest quantity of ground to each man; and this, again, conforms to what must occur in a world less inclined to wars and more devoted to the arts of peace than heretofore. Population must increase rapidly, more rapidly than in former times, and erelong the most valuable of all arts will be the art of deriving a comfortable subsistence from the smallest area of soil. No community whose every member possesses this art, can ever be the victim of oppression in any of its forms. Such community will be alike independent of crowned kings, money kings, and land kings.

ABRAHAM LINCOLN

Cooper Union Address (1860)

Lincoln attracted considerable attention as a Republican candidate for the presidency with a speech he delivered at Cooper Union in New York City. After reviewing the history of slavery in the United States, the Republican politician labeled abolitionists as the true conservatives, since they were the ones who most faithfully represented the ideals of the Founders.

Some of you delight to flaunt in our faces the warning against sectional parties given by Washington in his Farewell Address. Less than eight years before Washington gave that warning, he had, as President of the United States, approved and signed an act of Congress, enforcing the prohibition of slavery in the Northwestern Territory, which act embodied the policy of the Government upon that subject up to and at the very moment he penned that warning; and about one year after he penned it, he wrote La Fayette that he considered that prohibition a wise measure, expressing in the same connection his hope that we should at some time have a confederacy of free States.

Bearing this in mind, and seeing that sectionalism has since arisen upon this same subject, is that warning a weapon in your hands against us, or in our hands against you? Could Washington himself speak, would he cast the blame of that sectionalism upon us, who sustain his policy, or upon you who repudiate it? We respect that warning of Washington, and we commend it to you, together with his example pointing to the right application of it.

But you say you are conservative—eminently conservative—while we are revolutionary, destructive, or something of the sort. What is conservatism? Is it not adherence to the old and tried, against the new and untried? We stick to, contend for, the identical old policy on the point in controversy which was adopted by "our fathers who framed the Government under which we live;" while you with one accord reject, and scout, and spit upon that old policy, and insist upon substituting something new. True, you disagree among yourselves as to what that substitute shall be. You are divided on new propositions and plans, but you are unanimous in rejecting and denouncing the old policy of the fathers. Some of you are for reviving the foreign slave trade; some for a Congressional Slave-Code for the Territories; some for Congress forbidding the Territories to prohibit Slavery within their limits; some for maintaining Slavery in the Territories through the judiciary; some for the "gur-reat pur-rinciple" that "if one man would enslave another, no third man should object," fantastically called "Popular Sovereignty;" but never a man among you in favor of federal prohibition of slavery in federal territories, according to the practice of "our fathers who framed the Government under which we live." Not one of all your various plans can show a precedent or an advocate in the century within which our Government originated. Consider, then, whether your claim of conservatism for yourselves, and your charge of destructiveness against us, are based on the most clear and stable foundations.

Again, you say we have made the slavery question more prominent than it formerly was. We deny it. We admit that it is more prominent, but we deny that we made it so. It was not we, but you, who discarded the old policy of the fathers. We resisted, we still resist, your innovation; and thence comes the greater prominence of the question. Would you have that question reduced to its former proportions? Go back to that old policy. What has been will be again, under the same conditions. If you would have the peace of the old times, readopt the precepts and policy of the old times.

ABRAHAM LINCOLN

New Haven Address (1860)

In a campaign speech he gave to an audience in New Haven, Connecticut, the Republican presidential candidate succinctly offered his philosophy of free labor. Everyone, black or white, humble or poor, should be free to "better his condition" in the "race of life."

nother specimen of this bushwhacking—that "shoe strike." Now be it understood that I do not pretend to know all about the matter. I am merely going to speculate a little about some of its phases, and at the outset. I am glad to see that a system of labor prevails in New England under which laborers can strike when they want to, where they are not obliged to work under all circumstances, and are not tied down and obliged to labor whether you pay them or not! I like the system which lets a man quit when he wants to, and wish it might prevail everywhere. One of the reasons why I am opposed to slavery is just here. What is the true condition of the laborer? I take it that it is best for all to leave each man free to acquire property as fast as he can. Some will get wealthy. I don't believe in a law to prevent a man from getting rich; it would do more harm than good. So while we do not propose any war upon capital, we do wish to allow the humblest man an equal chance to get rich with everybody else. When one starts poor, as most do in the race of life, free society is such that he knows he can better his condition; he knows that there is no fixed condition of labor for his whole life. I am not ashamed to confess that twenty-five years ago I was a hired laborer, mauling rails, at work on a flatboat—just what might happen to any poor man's son. I want every man to have a chance—and I believe a black man is entitled to it—in which he can better his condition—when he may look forward and hope to be a hired laborer this year and the next, work for himself afterward, and finally to hire men to work for him. This is the true system.

ABRAHAM LINCOLN

First Inaugural Address (1861)

In 1860, Lincoln won the bitterly divided four-way contest for the presidency with only 39 percent of the popular vote and without the support of a single southern state. When Lincoln delivered his first inaugural address to Congress, seven southern states had already seceded from the Union, and Confederate forces had laid siege to Fort Sumter in the harbor of Charleston, South Carolina. Although the Republican president tried to reassure the southern states that he would not "interfere with the institution of slavery in the States where it exists," he also reminded them of the perpetuity and inviolability of the Union in the context of a theory of government that flatly rejected the principles of secession and minority rule.

F ellow-citizens of the United States:
     In compliance with a custom as old as the government itself, I appear before you to address you briefly, and to take in your presence the oath prescribed by the Constitution of the United States to be taken by the President "before he enters on the execution of his office."

I do not consider it necessary at present for me to discuss those matters of administration about which there is no special anxiety or excitement.

Apprehension seems to exist among the people of the Southern States that by the accession of a Republican administration their property and their peace and personal security are to be endangered. There has never been any reasonable cause for such apprehension. Indeed, the most ample evidence to the contrary has all the while existed and been open to their inspection. It is found in nearly all the published speeches of him who now addresses you. I do but quote from one of those speeches when I declare that "I have no purpose, directly or indirectly, to interfere with the institution of slavery in the States where it exists. I believe I have no lawful right to do so, and I have no inclination to do so." Those who nominated and elected me did so with full knowledge that I had made this and many similar declarations, and had never recanted them. And, more than this, they placed in the platform for my acceptance, and as a law to themselves and to me, the clear and emphatic resolution which I now read:—

"*Resolved*, That the maintenance inviolate of the rights of the States, and especially the right of each State to order and control its own domestic institutions according to its own judgment exclusively, is essential to that balance of power on which the perfection and endurance of our political fabric depend, and we denounce the lawless invasion by armed force of the soil of any State or Territory, no matter under what pretext, as among the gravest of crimes." I now reiterate these sentiments; and, in doing so, I only press upon the public attention the most conclusive evidence of which the case is susceptible, that the property, peace, and security of no section are to be in any wise endangered by the now incoming administration. I add, too, that all the protection which, consistently with the Constitution and the laws, can be given, will be cheerfully given to all the States when lawfully demanded, for whatever cause—as cheerfully to one section as to another.

There is much controversy about the delivering up of fugitives from service or labor. The clause I now read is as plainly written in the Constitution as any other of its provisions:—

"No person held to service or labour in one State, under the laws thereof, escaping into another, shall in consequence of any law or regulation therein, be discharged from such service or labour, but shall be delivered up on claim of the party to whom such service or labour may be due."

It is scarcely questioned that this provision was intended by those who made it for the reclaiming of what we call fugitive slaves; and the intention of the lawgiver is the law. All members of Congress swear their support to the whole Constitution—to this provision as much as to any other. To the proposition, then, that slaves whose cases come within the terms of this clause "shall be delivered up," their oaths are unanimous. Now, if they would make the effort in good temper, could they not with nearly equal unanimity frame and pass a law by means of which to keep good that unanimous oath?

There is some difference of opinion whether this clause should be enforced by national or by State authority; but surely that difference is not a very material one. If the slave is to be surrendered, it can be of but little consequence to him or to others by which authority it is done. And should any one in any case be content that his oath shall go unkept on a merely unsubstantial controversy as to how it shall be kept?

Again, in any law upon this subject, ought not all the safeguards of liberty known in civilized and humane jurisprudence to be introduced, so that a free man be not, in any case, surrendered as a slave? And might it not be well at the same time to provide by law for the enforcement of that clause in the Constitution which guarantees that "the citizens of each State shall be entitled to all privileges and immunities of citizens in the several States"?

I take the official oath to-day with no mental reservations, and with no purpose to construe the Constitution or laws by any hypercritical rules. And while I do not choose now to specify particular acts of Congress as proper to be enforced, I do suggest that it will be much safer for all, both in official and private stations, to conform to and abide by all those acts which stand unrepealed, than to violate any of them, trusting to find impunity in having them held to be unconstitutional.

It is seventy-two years since the first inauguration of a President under our National Constitution. During that period fifteen different and greatly distinguished citizens have, in succession, administered the executive branch of the government. They have conducted it through many perils, and generally with great success. Yet, with all this scope of precedent, I now enter upon the same task for the brief constitutional term of four years under great and peculiar difficulty. A disruption of the Federal Union, heretofore only menaced, is now formidably attempted.

I hold that, in contemplation of universal law and of the Constitution, the Union of these States is perpetual. Perpetuity is implied, if not expressed, in the fundamental law of all national governments. It is safe to assert that no government proper ever had a provision in its organic law for its own termination. Continue to execute all the express provisions of our National Constitution, and the Union will endure forever—it being impossible to destroy it except by some action not provided for in the instrument itself.

Again, if the United States be not a government proper, but an association of States in the nature of contract merely, can it, as a contract, be peaceably unmade by less than all the parties who made it? One party to a contract may violate it—break it, so to speak; but does it not require all to lawfully rescind it?

Descending from these general principles, we find the proposition that in legal contemplation the Union is perpetual confirmed by the history of the Union itself. The Union is much older than the Constitution. It was formed, in fact, by the Articles of Association in 1774. It was matured and continued by the Declaration of Independence in 1776. It was further matured, and the faith of all the then thirteen States expressly plighted and engaged that it should be perpetual, by the Articles of Confederation in 1778. And, finally, in 1787, one of the declared objects for ordaining and establishing the Constitution was "to form a more perfect Union."

But if the destruction of the Union by one or by a part only of the States be lawfully possible, the Union is less perfect than before the Constitution, having lost the vital element of perpetuity.

It follows from these views that no State upon its own mere motion can lawfully get out of the Union: that resolves and ordinances to that effect are legally void; and that acts of violence, within any State or States, against the authority of the United States, are insurrectionary or revolutionary, according to circumstances.

I therefore consider that, in view of the Constitution and the laws, the Union is unbroken; and to the extent of my ability I shall take care, as the Constitution itself expressly enjoins upon me, that the laws of the Union be faithfully executed in all the States. Doing this I deem to be only a simple duty on my part; and I shall perform it so far as practicable, unless my rightful masters, the American people, shall withhold the requisite means, or in some authoritative manner direct the contrary. I trust this will not be regarded as a menace, but only as the declared purpose of the Union that it will constitutionally defend and maintain itself.

In doing this there needs to be no bloodshed or violence; and there shall be none, unless it be forced upon the national authority. The power confided to me will be used to hold, occupy, and possess the property and places belonging to the government, and to collect the duties and imposts; but beyond what may be necessary for these objects, there will be no invasion, no using of force against or among the people anywhere. Where hostility to the United States, in any interior locality, shall be so great and universal as to prevent competent resident citizens from holding the Federal offices, there will be no attempt to force obnoxious strangers among the people for that object. While the strict legal right may exist in the government to enforce the exercise of these officers, the attempt to do so would be so irritating, and so nearly impracticable withal, that I deem it better to forego for the time the uses of such officers.

The mails, unless repelled, will continue to be furnished in all parts of the Union. So far as possible, the people everywhere shall have that sense of perfect security which is most favorable to calm thought and reflection. The course here indicated will be followed unless current events and experience shall show a modification or change to be proper, and in every case and exigency my best discretion will be exercised according to circumstances actually existing, and with a view and a hope of a peaceful solution of the national troubles and the restoration of fraternal sympathies and affections.

That there are persons in one section or another who seek to destroy the Union at all events, and are glad of any pretext to do it, I will neither affirm nor deny; but if there be such, I need address no word to them. To those, however, who really love the Union may I not speak?

Before entering upon so great a matter as the destruction of our national fabric, with all its benefits, its memories, and its hopes, would it not be wise to ascertain precisely why we do it? Will you hazard so desperate a step while there is any possibility that any portion of the ills you fly from have no real existence? Will you, while the certain ills you fly to are greater than all the real ones you fly from—will you risk the commission of so fearful a mistake?

All profess to be content in the Union if all constitutional rights can be maintained. It is true, then, that any right, plainly written in the Constitution, has been denied? I think not. Happily the human mind is so constituted that no party can reach to the audacity of doing this. Think, if you can, of a single instance in which a plainly written provision of the Constitution has ever been denied. If by the mere force of numbers a majority should deprive a minority of any clearly written constitutional right, it might, in a moral point of view, justify revolution—certainly would if such a right were a vital one. But such is not our case. All the vital rights of minorities and of individuals are so plainly assured to them by affirmations and negations, guaranties and prohibitions, in the Constitution, that controversies never arise concerning them. But no organic law can ever be framed with a provision specifically applicable to every question which may occur in practical administration. No foresight can anticipate, nor any document of reasonable length contain, express provisions for all possible questions. Shall fugitives from labor be surrendered by national or by State authority? The Constitution does not expressly say. *May* Congress prohibit slavery in the Territories? The Constitution does not expressly say. *Must* Congress protect slavery in the Territories? The Constitution does not expressly say.

From questions of this class spring all our constitutional controversies, and we divide upon them into majorities and minorities. If the minority will not acquiesce, the majority must, or the government must cease. There is no other alternative; for continuing the government is acquiescence on one side or the other.

If a minority in such case will secede rather than acquiesce, they make a precedent which in turn will divide and ruin them; for a minority of their own will secede from them whenever a majority refuses to be controlled by such minority. For instance, why may not any portion of a new confederacy a year or two hence arbitrarily secede again, precisely as portions of the present Union now claim to secede from it? All who cherish disunion sentiments are now being educated to the exact temper of doing this.

Is there such a perfect identity of interest among the States to compose a new Union, as to produce harmony only, and prevent renewed secession?

Plainly, the central idea of secession is the essence of anarchy. A majority held in restraint by constitutional checks and limitations, and always changing easily with deliberate changes of popular opinions and sentiments, is the only true sovereign of a free people. Whoever rejects it does, of necessity, fly to anarchy or to despotism. Unanimity is impossible; the rule of a minority, as a permanent arrangement, is wholly inadmissible; so that, rejecting the majority principle, anarchy or despotism in some form is all that is left.

I do not forget the position, assumed by some, that constitutional questions are to be decided by the Supreme Court; nor do I deny that such decisions must be binding, in any case, upon the parties to a suit, as to the object of that suit, while they are also entitled to very high respect and consideration in all parallel cases by all other departments of the government. And while it is obviously possible that such decision may be erroneous in any given case, still the evil effect following it, being limited to that particular case, with the chance that it may be overruled and never become a precedent for other cases, can better be borne than could the evils of a different practice. At the same time, the candid citizen must confess that if the policy of the government, upon vital questions affecting the whole people, is to be irrevocably fixed by decisions of the

Supreme Court, the instant they are made, in ordinary litigation between parties in personal actions, the people will have ceased to be their own rulers, having to that extent practically resigned their government into the hands of that eminent tribunal. Nor is there in this view any assault upon the court or the judges. It is a duty from which they may not shrink to decide cases properly brought before them and it is no fault of theirs if others seek to turn their decisions to political purposes.

One section of our country believes slavery is right, and ought to be extended, while the other believes it is wrong, and ought not to be extended. This is the only substantial dispute. The fugitive-slave clause of the Constitution, and the law for the suppression of the foreign slave trade, are each as well enforced, perhaps, as any law can ever be in a community where the moral sense of the people imperfectly supports the law itself. The great body of the people abide by the dry legal obligation in both cases, and a few break over in each. This, I think, cannot be perfectly cured; and it would be worse in both cases after the separation of the sections than before. The foreign slave trade, now imperfectly suppressed, would be ultimately revived, without restriction, in one section, while fugitive slaves, now only partially surrendered, would not be surrendered at all by the other.

Physically speaking, we cannot separate. We cannot remove our respective sections from each other, nor build an impassable wall between them. A husband and wife may be divorced, and go out of the presence and beyond the reach of each other; but the different parts of our country cannot do this. They cannot but remain face to face, and intercourse, either amicable or hostile, must continue between them. Is it possible, then, to make that intercourse more advantageous or more satisfactory after separation than before? Can aliens make treaties easier than friends can make laws? Can treaties be more faithfully enforced between aliens than laws can among friends? Suppose you go to war, you cannot fight always; and when, after much loss on both sides, and no gain on either, you cease fighting, the identical old questions as to terms of intercourse are again upon you.

This country, with its institutions, belongs to the people who inhabit it. Whenever they shall grow weary of the existing government, they can exercise their constitutional right of amending it, or their revolutionary right to dismember or overthrow it. I cannot be ignorant of the fact that many worthy and patriotic citizens are desirous of having the National Constitution amended. While I make no recommendation of amendments, I full recognize the rightful authority of the people over the whole subject, to be exercised in either of the modes prescribed in the instrument itself; and I should, under existing circumstances, favor rather than oppose a fair opportunity being afforded the people to act upon it. I will venture to add that to me the convention mode seems preferable, in that it allows amendments to originate with the people themselves, instead of only permitting them to take or reject propositions originated by others not especially chosen for the purpose, and which might not be precisely such as they would wish to either accept or refuse. I understand a proposed amendment to the Constitution—which amendment, however, I have not seen—has passed Congress, to the effect that the Federal Government shall never interfere with the domestic institutions of the States, including that of persons held to service. To avoid misconstruction of what I have said, I depart from my purpose not to speak of particular amendments so far as to say that, holding such a provision to now be implied constitutional law, I have no objection to its being made express and irrevocable.

The chief magistrate derives all his authority from the people, and they have conferred none upon him to fix terms for the separation of the States. The people themselves can do this also if they choose; but the Executive, as such, has nothing to do with it. His duty is to administer the present government, as it came to his hands, and to transmit it, unimpaired by him, to his successor.

Why should there not be a patient confidence in the ultimate justice of the people? Is there any better or equal hope in the world? In our present differences, is either party without faith of being in the right? If the Almighty Ruler of Nations, with His eternal truth and justice, be on your side of the North, or on yours of the South, that truth and that justice will surely prevail by the judgment of this great tribunal of the American people.

By the frame of the government under which we live, this same people have wisely given their public servants but little power for mischief; and have, with equal wisdom, provided for the return of that little to their own hands at very short intervals. While the people retain their virtue and vigilance, no administration, by any extreme of wickedness or folly, can very seriously injure the government in the short space of four years.

My countrymen, one and all, think calmly and well upon this whole subject. Nothing valuable can be lost by taking time. If there be an object to hurry any of you in hot haste to a step which you would never take deliberately, that object will be frustrated by taking time; but no good object can be frustrated by it. Such of you as are now dissatisfied still have the old Constitution unimpaired, and, on the sensitive point, the laws of your own framing under it; while the new administration will have no immediate power, if it would, to change either. If it were admitted that you who are dissatisfied hold the right side in the dispute, there still is no single good reason for precipitate action. Intelligence, patriotism, Christianity, and a firm reliance on Him who has never yet forsaken this favored land, are still competent to adjust in the best way all our present difficulty.

In your hands, my dissatisfied fellow-countrymen, and not in mine, is the momentous issue of civil war. The government will not assail you. You can have no conflict without being yourselves the aggressors. You have no oath registered in heaven to destroy the government, while I shall have the most solemn one to "preserve, protect, and defend it."

I am loath to close. We are not enemies, but friends. We must not be enemies. Though passion may have strained, it must not break our bonds of affection. The mystic chords of memory, stretching from every battle-field and patriot grave to every living heart and hearthstone all over the broad land, will yet swell the chorus of the Union when again touched, as surely they will be, by the better angels of our nature.

ABRAHAM LINCOLN

Address to Congress (1861)

Lincoln had already responded to the secession of eleven southern states and the commencement of hostilities with a series of controversial war measures (including the suspension of the writ of habeas corpus, the declaration of martial law, and numerous arrests) when he convened a special session of Congress on July 4. Vehemently denying the doctrine of state sovereignty as inconsistent with the Constitution, the president defended his actions as commander in chief and the principles of the federal Union.

At the beginning of the present Presidential term, four months ago, the functions of the Federal Government were found to be generally suspended within the several States of South Carolina, Georgia, Alabama, Mississippi, Louisiana, and Florida, excepting only those of the Post-office Department. * * *

The purpose to sever the Federal Union was openly avowed. In accordance with this purpose, an ordinance had been adopted in each of these States, declaring the States respectively to be separated from the national Union. A formula for instituting a combined government of these States had been promulgated; and this illegal organization, in the character of confederate States, was already invoking recognition, aid, and intervention from foreign powers. * * *

And this issue embraces more than the fate of these United States. It presents to the whole family of man the question whether a constitutional republic or democracy—a government of the people by the same people—can or cannot maintain its territorial integrity against its own domestic foes. It presents the question whether discontented individuals, too few in number to control administration according to organic law in any case, can always, upon the pretenses made in this case, or on any other pretenses, or arbitrarily without any pretense, break up their government, and thus practically put an end to free government upon the earth. It forces us to ask: Is there in all republics this inherent and fatal weakness? Must a government, of necessity, be too *strong* for the liberties of its own people, or too *weak* to maintain its own existence?

So viewing the issue, no choice was left but to call out the war power of the government, and so to resist force employed for its destruction by force for its preservation. * * *

The forbearance of this government had been so extraordinary and so long continued as to lead some foreign nations to shape their action as if they supposed the early destruction of our national Union was probable. While this, on discovery, gave the executive some concern, he is now happy to say that the sovereignty and rights of the United States are now everywhere practically respected by foreign powers, and a general sympathy with the country is manifested throughout the world. * * *

It might seem, at first thought, to be of little difference whether the present movement at the South be called "secession" or "rebellion." The movers, however, well understand the difference. At the beginning they knew they could never raise their treason to any respectable magnitude by any name which implies *violation* of law. They knew their people possessed as much of moral sense, as much of devotion to law and order, and as much pride in and reverence for the history and government of their common country as any other civilized and patriotic people. They knew they could make no advancement directly in the teeth of these strong and noble sentiments. Accordingly, they commenced by an insidious debauching of the public mind. They invented an ingenious sophism which, if conceeded, was followed by perfectly logical steps, through all the incidents, to the complete destruction of the Union. The sophism itself is that any State of the Union may *consistently* with the national Constitution, and therefore lawfully and peacefully, withdraw from the Union without the consent of the Union or of any other State. * * *

This sophism derives much, perhaps the whole, of its currency from the assumption that there is some omnipotent and sacred supremacy pertaining to a State—to each State of our Federal Union. Our States have neither more nor less power than that reserved to them in the Union by the Constitution—no one of them ever having been a State out of the Union. The original ones passed into the Union even before they cast off their British colonial dependence; and the new ones each came into the Union directly from a condition of dependence, excepting Texas. And even Texas in its temporary independence was never designated a State. The new ones only took the designation of States on coming into the Union, while that name was first adopted for the old ones in and by the Declaration of Independence. * * * Having never been States either in substance or in name outside of the Union, whence this magical omnipotence of "State rights," asserting a claim of power to lawfully destroy the Union itself? Much is said about the "sovereignty" of the States; but the word even is not in the national Constitution, nor, as is believed, in any of the State constitutions. What is "sovereignty" in the political sense of the term? Would it be far wrong to define it as "a political community without a political superior"? Tested by this, no one of our States except Texas ever was a sovereignty. * * * The States have their status in the Union, and they have no other legal status. If they break from this, they can only do so against law and by revolution. The Union, and not themselves separately, procured their independence and their liberty. By conquest or purchase the Union gave each of them whatever of independence or liberty it has. The Union is older than any of the States, and, in fact, it created them as States. Originally some dependent colonies made the Union, and, in turn, the Union threw off their old dependence for them, and made them States, such as they are. Not one of them ever had a State constitution independent of the Union. Of course, it is not forgotten that all the new States framed their constitutions before they entered the Union—nevertheless, dependent upon and preparatory to coming into the Union. * * *

What is now combated is the position that secession is consistent with the Constitution—is lawful and peaceful. It is not contended that there is any express law for it; and nothing should ever be implied as law which leads to unjust or absurd consequences. * * *

The seceders insist that our Constitution admits of secession. They have assumed to make a national constitution of their own, in which of necessity they have either discarded or retained the right of secession as they insist it exists in ours. If they have discarded it, they thereby admit that on principle it ought not to be in ours. If they have retained it, by their own construction of ours, they show that to be consistent they must secede from one another whenever they shall find it the easiest way of settling their debts, or effecting any other selfish or unjust object. The principle itself is one of disintegration and upon which no government can possibly endure. * * *

It may well be questioned whether there is to-day a majority of the legally qualified voters of any State except perhaps South Carolina in favor of disunion. There is much reason to believe that the Union men are the majority in many, if not in every other one, of the so-called seceded States. * * *

This is essentially a people's contest. On the side of the Union it is a struggle for maintaining in the world that form and substance of government whose leading object is to elevate the condition of men—to lift artificial weights from all shoulders; to clear the paths of laudable pursuit for all; to afford all an unfettered start, and a fair chance in the race of life. Yielding to partial and temporary departures, from necessity, this is the leading object of the government for whose existence we contend. * * *

Our popular government has often been called an experiment. Two points in it our people have already settled—the successful establishing and the successful administering of it. One still remains—its successful maintenance against a formidable internal attempt to overthrow it. It is now for them to demonstrate to the world that those who can fairly carry an election can also suppress a rebellion; that ballots are the rightful and peaceful successors of bullets; and that when ballots have fairly and constitutionally decided, there can be no successful appeal back to bullets; that there can be no successful appeal, except to ballots themselves, at succeeding elections. Such will be a great lesson of peace: teaching men that what they cannot take by an election, neither can they take it by war; teaching all the folly of being the beginners of a war.

ABRAHAM LINCOLN

Second Annual Message to Congress (1862)

In his second annual message to Congress, Lincoln offered a set of com-
promises on slavery in the hopes of bringing the Civil War to a peaceful
conclusion. He proposed amendments to the Constitution that would
gradually emancipate slaves, compensate slaveholders, and colonize

*freed blacks outside the United States as the best way to spare "both
races from the evils of sudden derangement." Moreover, Lincoln argued,
emancipation would increase the demand for white labor and lead to an
increase in wages.*

I recommend the adoption of the following resolution and articles
amendatory to the Constitution of the United States:

*Resolved by the Senate and House of Representatives of the United
States of America in Congress assembled.* (two-thirds of both houses
concurring,) That the following articles be proposed to the legislatures
(or conventions) of the several States as amendments to the Constitution of the United States, all or any of which articles when ratified by
three-fourths of the said legislatures (or conventions) to be valid as part
or parts of the said Constitution, viz:

Article ——.

Every State, wherein slavery now exists, which shall abolish the same
therein, at any time, or times, before the first day of January, in the year
of our Lord one thousand and nine hundred, shall receive compensation from the United States as follows, to wit:

"The President of the United States shall deliver to every such State,
bonds of the United States, bearing interest at the rate of —— per cent,
per annum, to an amount equal to the aggregate sum of ——— for
each slave shown to have been therein, by the eig[h]th census of the
United States, said bonds to be delivered to such State by instalments,
or in one parcel, at the completion of the abolishment, accordingly as
the same shall have been gradual, or at one time, within such State;
and interest shall begin to run upon any such bond, only from the
proper time of its delivery as aforesaid. Any State having received bonds
as aforesaid, and afterwards reintroducing or tolerating slavery therein,
shall refund to the United States the bonds so received, or the value
thereof, and all interest paid thereon.

Article ——.

All slaves who shall have enjoyed actual freedom by the chances of the
war, at any time before the end of the rebellion, shall be forever free;
but all owners of such, who shall not have been disloyal, shall be compensated for them, at the same rates as is provided for States adopting
abolishment of slavery, but in such way, that no slave shall be twice accounted for.

Article ——.

Congress may appropriate money, and otherwise provide, for colonizing
free colored persons, with their own consent, at any place or places
without the United States.

I beg indulgence to discuss these proposed articles at some length. Without slavery the rebellion could never have existed; without slavery it could not continue.

Among the friends of the Union there is great diversity, of sentiment, and of policy, in regard to slavery, and the African race amongst us. Some would perpetuate slavery; some would abolish it suddenly, and without compensation; some would abolish it gradually, and with compensation; some would remove the freed people from us, and some would retain them with us; and there are yet other minor diversities. Because of these diversities, we waste much strength in struggles among ourselves. By mutual concession we should harmonize, and act together. This would be compromise; but it would be compromise among the friends, and not with the enemies of the Union. These articles are intended to embody a plan of such mutual concessions. If the plan shall be adopted, it is assumed that emancipation will follow, at least, in several of the States.

As to the first article, the main points are: first, the emancipation; secondly, the length of time for consummating it—thirty-seven years; and thirdly, the compensation.

The emancipation will be unsatisfactory to the advocates of perpetual slavery; but the length of time should greatly mitigate their dissatisfaction. The time spares both races from the evils of sudden derangement—in fact, from the necessity of any derangement—while most of those whose habitual course of thought will be disturbed by the measure will have passed away before its consummation. They will never see it. Another class will hail the prospect of emancipation, but will deprecate the length of time. They will feel that it gives too little to the now living slaves. But it really gives them much. It saves them from the vagrant destitution which must largely attend immediate emancipation in localities where their numbers are very great; and it gives the inspiring assurance that their posterity shall be free forever. The plan leaves to each State, choosing to act under it, to abolish slavery now, or at the end of the century, or at any intermediate time, or by degrees, extending over the whole or any part of the period; and it obliges no two states to proceed alike. It also provides for compensation, and generally the mode of making it. This, it would seem, must further mitigate the dissatisfaction of those who favor perpetual slavery, and especially of those who are to receive the compensation. Doubtless some of those who are to pay, and not to receive will object. Yet the measure is both just and economical. In a certain sense the liberation of slaves is the destruction of property—property acquired by descent, or by purchase, the same as any other property. It is no less true for having been often said, that the people of the south are not more responsible for the original introduction of this property, than are the people of the north; and when it is remembered how unhesitatingly we all use cotton and sugar, and share the profits of dealing in them, it may not be quite safe to say, that the south has been more responsible than the north for its continuance. If then, for a common object, this property is to be sacrificed is it not just that it be done at a common charge? * * *

As to the second article, I think it would be impracticable to return to bondage the class of persons therein contemplated. Some of them, doubtless, in the property sense, belong to loyal owners; and hence, provision is made in this article for compensating such.

The third article relates to the future of the freed people. It does not oblige, but merely authorizes, Congress to aid in colonizing such as may consent. This ought not to be regarded as objectionable, on the one hand, or on the other, in so much as it comes to nothing, unless by the mutual consent of the people to be deported, and the American voters, through their representatives in Congress.

I cannot make it better known than it already is, that I strongly favor colonization. And yet I wish to say there is an objection urged against free colored people remaining in the country, which is largely imaginary, if not sometimes malicious.

It is insisted that their presence would injure, and displace white labor and white laborers. If there ever could be a proper time for mere catch arguments, that time surely is not now. In times like the present, men should utter nothing for which they would not willingly be responsible through time and eternity. Is it true, then, that colored people can displace any more white labor, by being free, than by remaining slaves? If they stay in their old places, they jostle no white laborers; if they leave their old places, they leave them open to white laborers. Logially, there is neither more nor less of it. Emancipation, even without deportation, would probably enhance the wages of white labor, and, very surely, would not reduce them. Thus, the customary amount of labor would still have to be performed; the freed people would surely not do more than their old proportion of it, and very probably, for a time, would do less, leaving an increased part to white laborers, bringing their labor into greater demand, and, consequently, enhancing the wages of it. With deportation, even to a limited extent, enhanced wages to white labor is mathematically certain. Labor is like any other commodity in the market—increase the demand for it, and you increase the price of it. Reduce the supply of black labor, by colonizing the black laborer out of the country, and, by precisely so much, you increase the demand for, and wages of, white labor.

But it is dreaded that the freed people will swarm forth, and cover the whole land? Are they not already in the land? Will liberation make them any more numerous? Equally distributed among the whites of the whole country, and there would be but one colored to seven whites. Could the one, in any way, greatly disturb the seven? There are many communities now, having more than one free colored person, to seven whites; and this, without any apparent consciousness of evil from it.

ABRAHAM LINCOLN

Gettysburg Address (1863)

Lincoln delivered one of the most memorable speeches in the history of American political thought at the dedication of the national cemetery at Gettysburg, where the critical—and bloody—Civil War battle had been waged.

Fourscore and seven years ago our fathers brought forth on this continent a new nation, conceived in liberty, and dedicated to the proposition that all men are created equal.

Now we are engaged in a great civil war, testing whether that nation, or any nation so conceived and so dedicated, can long endure. We are met on a great battlefield of that war. We have come to dedicate a portion of that field as a final resting-place for those who here gave their lives that that nation might live. It is altogether fitting and proper that we should do this.

But, in a larger sense, we cannot dedicate—we cannot consecrate—we cannot hallow—this ground. The brave men, living and dead, who struggled here, have consecrated it far above our poor power to add or detract. The world will little note nor long remember what we say here, but it can never forget what they did here. It is for us, the living, rather, to be dedicated here to the unfinished work which they who fought here have thus far so nobly advanced. It is rather for us to be here dedicated to the great task remaining before us—that from these honored dead we take increased devotion to that cause for which they gave the last full measure of devotion; that we here highly resolve that these dead shall not have died in vain; that this nation, under God, shall have a new birth of freedom; and that government of the people, by the people, for the people, shall not perish from the earth.

ABRAHAM LINCOLN

Second Inaugural Address (1865)

Lincoln used the occasion of his second inaugural address to report on the favorable progress of the war and to prepare the way for peace with the South. In a conciliatory remark directed at the South as well as the North, the president admonished Americans to conclude the war "with malice toward none" and "with charity for all."

FELLOW-COUNTRYMEN:—At this second appearing to take the oath of the presidential office there is less occasion for an extended address than there was at the first. Then a statement somewhat in detail of a course to be pursued seemed fitting and proper. Now, at the expiration of four years, during which public declarations have been constantly called forth on every point and phase of the great contest which still absorbs the attention and engrosses the energies of the nation, little that is new could be presented. The progress of our arms, upon which all else chiefly depends, is as well known to the public as to myself, and it is, I trust, reasonably satisfactory and encouraging to all. With high hope for the future, no prediction in regard to it is ventured.

On the occasion corresponding to this four years ago all thoughts were anxiously directed to an impending civil war. All dreaded it, all sought to avert it. While the inaugural address was being delivered from this place, devoted altogether to *saving* the Union without war, insurgent agents were in the city seeking to *destroy* it without war—seeking to dissolve the Union and divide effects by negotiation. Both parties deprecated war, but one of them would *make* war rather than let the nation survive, and the other would *accept* war rather than let it perish, and the war came.

One eighth of the whole population was colored slaves, not distributed generally over the Union, but localized in the southern part of it. These slaves constituted a peculiar and powerful interest. All knew that this interest was somehow the cause of the war. To strengthen, perpetuate, and extend this interest was the object for which the insurgents would rend the Union even by war, while the Government claimed no right to do more than to restrict the territorial enlargement of it. Neither party expected for the war the magnitude or the duration which it has already attained. Neither anticipated that the *cause* of the conflict might cease with or even before the conflict itself should cease. Each looked for an easier triumph, and a result less fundamental and astounding. Both read the same Bible and pray to the same God, and each invokes His aid against the other. It may seem strange that any men should dare to ask a just God's assistance in wringing their bread from the sweat of other men's faces, but let us judge not, that we be not judged. The prayers of both could not be answered. That of neither has been answered fully. The Almighty has His own purposes. "Woe unto the world because of offenses; for it must needs be that offenses come, but woe to that man by whom the offense cometh." If we shall suppose that American slavery is one of those offenses which, in the providence of God, must needs come, but which, having continued through His appointed time, He now wills to remove, and that He gives to both North and South this terrible war as the woe due to those by whom the offense came, shall we discern therein any departure from those divine attributes which the believers in a living God always ascribe to Him? Fondly do we hope, fervently do we pray, that this mighty scourge of war may speedily pass away. Yet, if God wills that it continue until all the wealth piled by the bondman's two hundred and fifty years of unrequited toil shall be sunk, and until every drop of blood drawn with the lash shall be paid by another drawn with the sword, as was said three thousand years ago, so still it must be said, "The judgments of the Lord are true and righteous altogether."

With malice toward none, with charity for all, with firmness in the right as God gives us to see the right, let us strive on to finish the work we are in, to bind up the nation's wounds, to care for him who shall have borne the battle and for his widow and his orphan, to do all which may achieve and cherish a just and a lasting peace among ourselves and with all nations.

PART IV

CAPITALISM,

INDIVIDUALISM,

AND REFORM

1865–1932

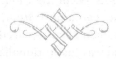

I f Rip Van Winkle had slept from 1850 to 1880, he might have awakened and resumed his life as an American citizen without realizing there had been a civil war. The government was largely the same as it had been. The three great amendments to the Constitution—the Thirteenth, Fourteenth, and Fifteenth—had been ratified; in fact they were essentially the terms of surrender and the conditions for admitting the Confederate states back into the Union on equal terms. And those amendments gave Congress the "power to enforce, by appropriate legislation, the provisions of [these articles]." But in the *Slaughterhouse* decision in 1873 the Supreme Court invalidated these new powers of Congress with the argument that "it was manifestly not the intent" of the Fourteenth Amendment to produce a revolution in federalism "by transfer[ring] the security and protection of all the civil rights . . . from the State to the federal government." Thus, for all practical purposes the "dual federalism" established by *Barron v. Baltimore*—a decision that decreed in 1833 that the freedoms guaranteed in the Bill of Rights did not restrict the state governments—kept the governmental structure where it had been in the *status quo ante bellum*. Blacks were no longer slaves, but the slave laws had been replaced by Jim Crow laws, and American-style apartheid was institutionalized.

Yet in virtually all other respects, Rip Van Winkle would not have recognized this as his country. At least four revolutions were well under way by the 1880s. First, agriculture was transformed from subsistence farming to cash-crop farming, exposing farmers to markets, the business cycle, monopolies—and politics. A second revolution turned surplus subsistence farmers plus millions of new European immigrants into a highly productive but highly regimented working class. Although the vast majority of these workers did not develop a proletarian consciousness with a socialist ideology, they did try to organize in unions to cope with market forces. The third revolution was marked by the mechanization of industry, rolling in on railroad tracks, electric wires, and conveyor belts. The fourth was the revolutionary advancement of capitalism, which brought the other three together in the greatest economic boom in world history.

Capitalism, which got its name from Marx's 1848 *Communist Manifesto*, was a new kind of economy. Thus, capitalism and its adversaries grew together. And regardless of the success of capitalism in practice, capitalism as theory was constantly on the defensive. Economic expansion coupled with the regimentation of labor and the vast inequality in the distribution of income spawned hosts of critics. Some prominent American writers drew their fire and inspiration from socialist sources. One of the most prominent of these was Jack London. Born and bred in the San Francisco slums, a vagrant, an ex-prisoner, railroad worker, and railway hobo, he was spectacularly self-taught and became a popular inspiration as an author. He was one of the few American leftists who was a Marxist as well as a socialist. London was a palpable influence on many other critics of capitalism, Upton Sinclair in particular. Other critics of a socialist but non-Marxist persuasion included Upton Sinclair, Mark Twain, Edward Bellamy, Theodore Dreiser, Lincoln Steffens, and even the American exile in Europe Henry James. Those committed to Marxist theory and its impulse toward direct, revolutionary action were lodged—and to that extent isolated—in the I.W.W., the Industrial Workers of the World, known as the Wobblies. But still, contrary to the implications of Engels's question "Why no socialism in America?" socialism itself was a widespread utopian dream; what Engels should have been asking is "why no *Marxism* in America?" W. E. B. Du Bois, one of the most prominent black critics, was a leading author and organizer of mobilization of blacks for social and economic advancement. Yet he remained adamantly mainstream and criticized the more radical black intellectuals as well as employers and the white-dominated unions that were contributing to the oppression of black laborers. Du Bois opposed Booker T. Washington on his right as well as Marcus Garvey on his left. It was only after seventy years of frustration that Du Bois, at the age of ninety-four, renounced his United States citizenship, joined the Communist Party, and moved to Ghana—just two years before the great 1963 March on Washington.

Of all the home-grown American antagonism toward capitalism from the 1880s to the 1930s, the one author whose writing came closest to genuine political theory was probably Henry George. Another self-made, self-educated, former manual laborer, George was certainly one of the great precursors of American progressivism. Without any grounding in the writings of the nineteenth-century luminaries in political economy, he discovered for himself the tendency—for him a universal law—that as wealth increases, so does poverty, at an equal or greater rate. But unlike Marx and most other critics of capitalism, George saw no inherent flaw in the system. The key to his thesis, the devil in his theory, was the economic concept of rent: George defined rent as an "unearned increment" accrued to the owners of land, the value of which was enhanced by the increased demand of a growing population. Thus, while the owners sat passively by, receiving all the benefit, the rest of the populace received nothing from the gains of their presence. His solution was one simple policy: a tax on that unearned increment, redistributed through better wages, better government, better public facilities. George's book became a bestseller, equaling the popularity of Adam Smith's work a century earlier. And his "single-tax" solution generated a national movement that nearly elected him mayor of New York City. George's theory of poverty increasing with progress was incomplete, as was his single-tax solution. His main contribution, however, was a larger message: contrary to the Social Darwinist argument, the economy was not an uncontrollable system like the climate or the cosmos, operating according to natural laws beyond human intervention. The economy was a human contrivance that could be changed whenever enough people got together in movements or unions or interest groups or parties and advanced a good enough argument.

Despite the vigorous popular criticism of capitalism and capitalists (who had earned the epithet "robber barons"), the dialectic between critics and apologists was overwhelmingly one sided in favor of the latter. The critics probably made their best contribution in the form of pressure sufficient to turn some industrialists into capitalist apologists, and a few of them even into part-time political theorists. This is why we have chosen Andrew Carnegie as the first signature figure of this epoch; other voices will be heard, but Carnegie set the terms of discourse.

Andrew Carnegie: Social Darwinism and the American Dream

Andrew Carnegie personified the heroic winner in the race of life. A child of a poor immigrant family from Scotland, a school dropout at age thirteen, Carnegie became a bobbin boy in a textile mill. Beginning from there, barefoot and suffering from malnutrition, Carnegie found work on the railroad. There he rose to clerk, telegrapher, secretary, middle manager, and then on to great fame and fortune—not for his talents as a manager or an inventor but as an entrepreneur. He made money trading in oil and in international trade in stocks and bonds. Then he risked all his accumulated wealth in a new way to make steel, the Bessemer converter.

Despite his meager formal education, Carnegie, more than any of the other "robber barons," thought and wrote about the ethical dimension of his work. He was also the first capitalist to dedicate his enormous fortune to good works. In fact, he virtually invented the modern foundation, a large, privately endowed corporation with a charter as a permanent institution devoted to philanthropy. Carnegie's "Gospel of Wealth"—an article that he expanded into a book—convinced the even wealthier John D. Rockefeller to turn to philanthropy as well.

The philanthropic impulse was no doubt genuine but was tinged with fear that the concentration of wealth might spawn class envy and, perhaps, socialism. Most capitalists believed that ultimately the interests of capital and labor—bourgeoisie and proletariat— were compatible; but some of them, led by Carnegie and Rockefeller, were ready to act to fulfill that prophecy.

Crucial for Andrew Carnegie was his conversion to "Mr. Herbert Spencer's *Social Statics*," as Justice Oliver Wendell Holmes put it derisively in his famous 1907 *Lochner v. New York* dissent. A British political economist who published a book with that title in 1854, Spencer virtually invented "Social Darwinism," a distillate of the classical economics of Adam Smith and David Ricardo combined with the evolutionary theory of Charles Darwin. The result was the doctrine that economic competition must be left ungoverned—as captured in the famous phrase *laissez-faire*— because free competition among autonomous individuals was a necessary condition for progress, for the advancement of the human race, through "survival of the fittest." Reading Spencer was life-transforming for Carnegie. It was, he wrote, as if "Light came in a flood, and all was clear." Carnegie reread Spencer through the works of Yale professor and Episcopal minister William Graham Sumner, who was Spencer's most important American intellectual disciple. Social Darwinism, from Spencer through Sumner and Carnegie's popularization, redefined "the race of life," thus providing the ultimate moral justification of radical individualism through a vulgarization of Darwin's theory of the origin of species. According to Sumner:

> Let it be understood that we cannot go outside of this alternative: liberty, inequality, survival of the fittest; not—liberty, equality, survival of the unfittest. The former carries society forward and

favors all its best members; the latter carries society downward and favors all its worst members.

To which his most apt pupil, the steel magnate Andrew Carnegie, responded, as though reciting catechism:

The law of competition . . . is here; we cannot evade it; no substitutes for it have been found; and while the law may be sometimes hard for the individual, it is best for the race . . . not only beneficial but essential for the future progress of the race.

As it turned out, the Supreme Court did indeed embody Herbert Spencer's *Social Statics* a good twenty years before Justice Holmes composed his dissent. *Santa Clara v. Southern Pacific Railroad* (1886), a holding of historic proportion, recognized corporations as "persons" under the Fourteenth Amendment, thus entitling them to all the privileges and immunities, and the equal protection of the law, afforded human beings:

The Court does not wish to hear argument on the question whether the provision in the Fourteenth Amendment to the Constitution, which forbids a State to deny to any person within its jurisdiction the equal protection of the laws, applies to these corporations. We are *all* of the opinion that it does. (emphasis added)

At the height of its lionization, however, Carnegie and Sumner's radical version of individualistic capitalism was sowing the seeds not of its own destruction but of its own transformation. All institutions, including free-market capitalism, are built on contradictions. That's what institutions are all about—to provide some stability over the competing needs and goals of individuals—and those contradictions are all the more dynamic and destabilizing when individualism and the race of life are dominant cultural values. Thus, as capitalism expanded, and as wealth took advantage of the efficiency of technology and the division of labor to become more concentrated, the radical individualism of Herbert Spencer, Andrew Carnegie, and William Graham Sumner was being slowly eroded.

Post–Civil War Capitalism and Radical Individualism

Thanks to the legions of critics of capitalism during the second half of the nineteenth century, it was already clear that although economics could drive, it could not steer. A mere sampling of signs of the coming sea change informs us that the epoch of classical, radical individualism was already on its way out well before the Great Depression. First was the transformation of the market toward "collective individualism." In the race of life, "time is money." But what is time? As firms and corporations grew larger, they altered the concept of time and the standard of rationality. As Alfred Chandler has put it in *The Visible Hand: The Managerial Revolution in American Business*, the managers of "modern business enterprises [preferred] policies that favored the long-term stability and growth of their enterprises to those that maximized current profits." Advantages of scale and specialization that came with growth permitted these enterprises "[to internalize] the activities of many business units," turning them over to "a group of managers . . . within a single enterprise . . . to carry out the functions formerly handled by price and market mechanisms." They thus reduced and replaced some of the very market mechanisms that were at the epicenter of the dynamic of classical competition between individuals and firms in a truly free market. This did not destroy the free market or render illegitimate any claims that its theory was made to "keep government out." But it did widen the gap between market theory and actual practices in the economy. And that opened the way for more critics, reformers, adapters, and revisionists.

Second was the socialization of ownership. The consolidation of business enterprise and the concentration of wealth during the latter half of the nineteenth century brought considerable benefits to the economy, but at a price. Thorstein Veblen, although generally a critic of capitalism, saw in these large corporations and coalitions of corporations a means of stabilizing wages and prices and, thus, the economy at large. But he was among many who were apprehensive about the expansion of the administrative component of these new business giants. Census figures indicate that in the seventy years following 1870, managerial employees grew by a factor in excess of ten and technicians by a factor of forty, all of which confirmed the prediction of the eminent German sociologist Max Weber that "industrial man" would occupy an "iron cage of bureaucracy." Beyond that, the most significant influence on society arising out of the rise of the management component was its effect on property as the main basis of business authority. Men with salaries would become as important actors in the marketplace as the owners of property. The influence of salaried managers was also enhanced by the "scientific management movement," which had emerged along with bureaucrats during the last two decades of the nineteenth century.

These developments were already having a profound influence, but they were not pulled together in a mature theory of capitalism and property until the publication in 1932 of *The Modern Corporation and Private Property*. The authors, Adolph Berle and Gardner Means, introduced their book with a generalization intended to shock:

> The translation of perhaps two-thirds of the industrial wealth of the country from individual ownership to ownership by the large, publicly financed corporations vitally changes the lives of property owners, the lives of workers, and the methods of property tenure. The *divorce of ownership from control* consequent on that process almost necessarily involves a new form of economic organization of society.

This separation of those who *own* (thousands of stockholders) from those few who *control* was popularly referred to as "the splitting of the property atom." Berle and Means characterized this as a "corporate system—as there was once a feudal system." Berle later referred to it as "collective capitalism," to emphasize the historic novelty of private property collectively owned. This was still private enterprise: the difference is the role of the individual in it. The gap between capitalist theory and practice had widened.

A third sign of the passing of classical radical individualism is seen in the development of American tort law. In French, *tort* means "wrong." In law, a tort is a "civil wrong," an injury inflicted without malice, in the innocent pursuit of some objective. A tort becomes a grievance of an injured party (the plaintiff) in a civil lawsuit against the alleged perpetrator (the defendant). The largest category of tort law in the nineteenth century was negligence—injuries resulting from conduct falling below some standard of due care, or failure to take reasonable steps to avoid inflicting harm. A good general rule for tort is "no liability without fault." Underlying torts is the mid-nineteenth-century theory of the obligation individuals owe to each other; thus, individual fault and responsibility must be found, in some form, for all injuries. Tort law (as a category of law) grew apace with the industrial revolution. Before 1840, few personal-injury cases reached American courts, but after 1840, there was an explosive growth of tort cases. Mechanization was the main cause, and the railroad led the way, with thousands of passengers and employees injured or dead.

A totally individualistic tort law approach to injury in a mechanized corporate world could not long stand. Consider this: the owners are thousands of stockholders not responsible for anything beyond the value of their shares; absentee employers and managers are far from the scene of the injuries; employees are all specialized to a task and are therefore dependent on each other to get their own work done; and labor-saving technologies add efficiency but also injury, rarely due to negligence. Thus, at the very high point of the development of free-market capitalism and the ethic of individualism, it became virtually impossible for courts, witnesses, juries, lawyers, and science to locate responsibility and fault. As Morton Horwitz has described in *The Transformation of American Law, 1870–1960*, state courts all over the country began temporizing by engaging in a balancing act between the rights of the individual and the requirements of the system. For example, principles of "contributory" and "proportionate" negligence were introduced by judges to produce bargains out of court between the injured individual plaintiff and the corporate defendants. Judicial balancing opened the way for statutory intervention by state legislatures, often on the side of the employee or customer.

This softening of the ethic of individual responsibility opened up opportunities for a new private industry, insurance—specifically, casualty or liability insurance. When first introduced in the 1820s, insurance was denounced as an immoral "contract to indemnify a man against the consequences of his own negligence." It took decades to develop a different conception of risk, based on the probability of occurrence rather than, as Horwitz put it, "who's to blame." The ultimate ethical leap to the socialization of blame came much later, with "no-fault" insurance. But "no-fault" was always implicit in insurance.

In this context, "socialization" has no particular relation to socialism. The non-Marxist critics who lambasted capitalism for its tendency to produce poverty along with progress were leaders in protecting and indemnifying individuals. And they were joined by another generation of non-Marxists and nonsocialists (as well as a few socialists such as Eugene V. Debs)—such leading lights as Lester Ward, Thorstein Veblen, Charles Beard, William James, and John Dewey. John P. Davis spoke for the whole new generation of critics in the introduction to his 1897 masterpiece, *Corporations*:

> So extensively have the people become organized in corporations for almost every social purpose that, it is feared, the integrity of the individual as the unit of society within the state has been seriously impaired.

Was the individual being collectivized, or just redefined?

And finally, nineteenth-century individualistic social thought received one of its strongest challenges from the germ theory of disease advanced by Louis Pasteur and Robert Koch. Germ theory had a normative effect on social thought comparable to the discovery of the New World and the confirmation of the theory that the world is round. The challenge is evident in the story of "Typhoid Mary." Mary Mallon had for years worked as a domestic servant and cook. While she was working for a prominent Long Island family in 1906, six of the eleven people in the house came down with typhoid. Mary soon left her employment in good health and went on to another job as a cook. Meanwhile, an inquisitive member of the afflicted family found that typhoid outbreaks had followed Mary from job to job. Mary refused to allow her blood and feces to be examined to determine if she was the carrier until the police took her forcefully to the hospital, where samples were taken and typhoid bacilli were found. Mary was confined without trial for two years and then released on condition that she never work again as a cook. But after a series of typhoid cases followed her, she was again jailed, this time for the remainder of her life.

The case of Typhoid Mary demonstrated that individuals bear no moral responsibility for communicable disease. We can all be carriers; we can all be victims. Public health professionals may have been the first to adopt this idea of a collective, interrelated social system; but it became part of American culture. Leaving aside the question of cause and effect, and adopting a Darwinian perspective, it becomes clear that the cultural environment of the late nineteenth century was hospitable to the idea of system: association, contingency and, above all, interdependence. The corporation is collective property. But so is personal property, with ownership collectivized through credit and debt and the installment plan. All of this is part of a revised economic system.

Thus, the socialized individual, as captured by the concept of interdependence, did not become the prevailing alternative to classical individualism until conditions were ripe. Its appearance in social thought seemed revolutionary when it was in fact evolutionary. From the perspective of 1927, John Dewey observed in *The Public and Its Problems*:

> [It] is no exaggeration to speak [as Woodrow Wilson did] of a "new age of human relations." . . . This invasion of the commu-

nity by the new and relatively impersonal and mechanical modes of combined human behavior is the outstanding fact of modern life.

By 1927, the "new age" was already a generation old. The social science associations founded between 1884 and 1905 all shared one fundamental tenet: "The assumption of interdependence." A founder of the American Economic Association, Richard Ely, deemed interdependence the "common denominator of the new economists who rejected laissez faire." Albion Small, one of the founders of the American Sociological Association, argued that the very justification of a new sociology rested on its sensitivity to what he called "vortex causation. . . . [We sociologists] are convinced that every social situation . . . is a resultant of causal factors which run in on that center [vortex] from every point of the compass." Woodrow Wilson, a political scientist, spoke the same language for the budding American Political Science Association in his 1913 book *The New Freedom*. The very formation of professional learned societies was a reflection as well as a cause of the interdependence their members employed as the scientific and theoretical lens on society and polity.

Well before the Great Depression, the newly emerging secular research university had already begun to reject most of the radical individualism of Andrew Carnegie and William Graham Sumner. Of equal importance in these years, women grew more vocal, as did many African Americans, and more often than not they, too, were messengers of bad news about laissez-faire capitalism. However moderate and reformist the content of their messages, they elicited the legendary urge to kill the messenger. They were bearers of bad news because grievances from the mouths or pens of members of castes were inherently radical. Women and blacks in this period were not simply separate classes. They were castes who for centuries were formally segregated by separate systems of law. Thus, their critiques were seen as radical because caste is a *system* of control, so that touching one component of the system has a ripple effect throughout all the components of that system. In a modernizing society, then, interdependence was a self-evident fact. The only way to deal with it was with some form of associationalism. The twentieth century needed a new prophet, a soothsaying successor to Andrew Carnegie and to the immensely popular novelist Horatio Alger, the prophets of classical individualism.

That successor was Dale Carnegie (no relation to the industrialist Carnegie).

The bestselling book bearing this message, *How to Win Friends and Influence People*, not published until 1936, presented a collection of Dale Carnegie's most famous addresses to packed audiences of corporate executives, sales managers, entrepreneurs and advertisers since 1912. The key to Carnegie's success is summed up in one simple observation that "about 15% of one's financial success is due to one's technical knowledge and about 85% is due to skill in human engineering—to personality and the ability to lead people." He reinforced this with a quote from one of his heroes, Herbert Spencer: "The great aim of education is not knowledge but action." One does not have to read the entire text to get the full message. Dale Carnegie provided neat summations of his philosophy in lists and tables, such as: "In a Nutshell: Fundamental Techniques in Handling People"; "Six Ways to Make People Like You"; "[How to] Be a Leader." When the race of life comes down to a matter of techniques of manipulation, Americans have made a great ethical leap from Andrew Carnegie to Dale Carnegie in one peaceful generation.

Woodrow Wilson: The Ambivalent Progressive

It is within this context that Woodrow Wilson comes forward as the period's second signature character, whose political thought closes the long post–Civil War epoch. Although Dale Carnegie was a sign of the times—part of the climate of opinion—the defining early twentieth-century political figure was Wilson. He is an especially good choice because he, like the era itself, was a mixture of contradictory elements.

The offspring of Presbyterian clergy on both sides of the family and a Southerner by upbringing, he was in many respects a throwback to America's Calvinist origins. Although he did not choose the clergy for himself, he had a clerical demeanor as a professor of political science at Johns Hopkins and Princeton and as president of Princeton, governor of New Jersey, and president of the United States. The historian George Tindall reports that when a friend insisted there are two sides to every question, Wilson shot back, "Yes, a right side and a wrong side." By inclination and education, he was more Tory than liberal; in Richard Hofstadter's view, "Wilson stood far closer to Edmund Burke than to Thomas Jefferson." It was no mere poetic license, then, for Hofstadter to give his brilliant biographical essay the title "Woodrow Wilson: The Conservative as Liberal."

There was indeed a streak of liberalism in Wilson, that is to say classic Manchester liberalism, with Smith's principle that pursuit of private interests was essential to the public good. But his liberalism was comfortable with Burkean conservatism because the capitalism of large corporations was committed more to long-term market stability than to maximum gain from cutthroat competition; and that required cooperative relations with the state as well as respect for established institutions. In fact, it was the organized corporate community—not its critics—that sought adoption of the Federal Trade Commission as a means of using government intervention to impose stabilizing rules of play.

Wilson's resolution of the philosophic struggle between the conservatism and the liberalism of the day was not a rejection of the former for the latter. Those who have carefully studied Wilson's ideas and writings would tend to place him with the Founders and Lincoln in the pantheon of American political thought. His admirers embrace Wilson's resolution as a synthesis of the framers' and martyred president's ideals. Those who accept him only as an outstanding politician with a good head on his shoulders see his resolution as only an amalgamation of those ideals. Either way, his writings and his performance as president were the bridge into the new American state.

Wilson's time as president in World War I and his passionate commitment to a postwar world "safe for democracy" made him a war president in American political memory, a tragic figure deprived of greatness and betrayed by Americans who rejected his plan of a League of Nations where countries would talk, not fight.

But Wilson's more lasting imprint is domestic. Following his student and academic days as a Burkean, with expressed admiration for Grover Cleveland, he turned away from these northeastern conservative attachments toward Theodore Roosevelt and the emergent progressivism that Roosevelt embodied. As Hofstadter put it, "both [Wilson and Roosevelt], within the limits of their respective party traditions, accepted conventional laissez-faire. . . . Both looked with disdain upon labor and Populist movements; both were suspicious of the trusts. . . . Both became late converts to the main body of progressive views."

Wilson's rise from university president to governor (1910) to president (1912) was probably the fastest ascent in presidential history. Although it was too fast to be planned, his positioning was perfect. Ex-president Teddy Roosevelt's return to the fray as the insurgent third candidate for 1912 put Wilson precisely in the middle, with President Taft on his right and Roosevelt on his left. And his victory, with Roosevelt's progressives coming in second and President Taft an unprecedented third, put Wilson in place to make the Democratic Party (still a southern party) ready to absorb most of the Progressive electorate as well as the increasingly popular Progressive program. This was the beginning of the end of southern conservative dominance of the Democratic Party—although that shift would take another twenty years before it was nearly complete.

Wilson's path from here is full confirmation of the old chestnut that "politics makes strange bedfellows." The first to realign from the Republican side to Wilson's were the larger business interests, who turned to Wilson "for relief." Although a decade earlier Wilson opposed government regulation of corporations and—with his advisor Louis Brandeis (who was soon to be a Wilson appointee to the Supreme Court)—embraced the right of workers to organize only for an "open shop," Wilson responded to the pressure of the times. In his private papers he rationalized his change of position as only a genuine intellectual could:

> The old time of individual competition is probably gone by. . . . We will do business henceforth . . . on a great and successful scale, by means of corporations.
>
> I am not afraid of any corporation, no matter how big. I am afraid of any corporation, however small, that is bad, . . . whose practices and actions are in restraint of trade . . . not reckoning size . . . but measuring and comprehending the exact damage done. (emphasis added)

The most instructive example among the several Wilsonian domestic policies is adoption of the Federal Trade Act, creating the Federal Trade Commission. It is well documented that organized business took the initiative for the FTC. In *The Triumph of Conservatism: A Reinterpretation of American History, 1900–1916*, the revisionist historian Gabriel Kolko writes "[T]here is no doubt that the National Chamber of Commerce [which supported it] . . . reflected the overwhelming opinion of virtually all types of business."

But why would the business sector, especially the corporate sector, favor the addition of another layer of national government regulation on top of the Interstate Commerce Act (1888, creating the Interstate Commerce Commission) and the Sherman Antitrust Act (1890)? As alluded to earlier, the "new [finance] capitalists" under Wilson's New Freedom were not like the earlier industrial capitalists. They seemed more concerned with stability than with unrestrained market competition.

This new attitude, embraced by trade associations, bankers associations, chambers of commerce, and so on, was genuine statism favoring a larger, stronger national state, just as strongly as such recognized statists as *The New Republic*'s Herbert Croly. They all sought a new independent regulatory commission armed with broad discretion to "act in the public interest" to advance *"fair trade."* This is a large leap from the Interstate Commerce Commission's and the Sherman Act's power to fight against *"unfair* trade."

This partnership of business and government—and government sponsorship of interest groups committed to a stable economy—goes by several names in the political economy literature. A name preferred by the more left-leaning critics is "political capitalism," most widely associated with Gabriel Kolko. He inspired several other younger scholars, who chose another name for the same phenomenon: "corporate liberalism." Wilson had almost the same thing in mind with his New Freedom and his understanding of progressivism.

At *The New Republic*, Croly was joined by his junior colleague and lapsed socialist Walter Lippmann in search of a national and corporate solution to "the promise of American life." Oliver Wendell Holmes, Jr., brought this New Nationalism to the Supreme Court. His most revealing corporatist statement was, as so often for Holmes, a dissenting opinion. He recognized the "ever-increasing right and scope of combination"; but workers had the same right of combination as their employers, with the "same liberty . . . to support their interest." As R. Jeffrey Lustig puts it in his book on corporate liberalism, "Holmes . . . was a group theorist with a vengeance." To whatever extent corporations and their combinations reduced competition, it would be (quoting Holmes) "for the purposes of industrial order." Finally, his most famous corporatist argument for the right of association was his *Lochner* dissent, in which he proclaimed that the Fourteenth Amendment did not enact Herbert Spencer's *Social Statics*.

This flow of progressivism, corporatism, political capitalism, and corporate liberalism was interrupted by the administrations of Harding and Coolidge, who were classical laissez-faire liberals in the tradition of Adam Smith and Herbert Spencer. Herbert Hoover, in turn, held out to the bitter end for the radical individualistic race of life. But the individual and competition had changed—to the voluntary associations of individuals, indeed with a little help from benevolent government sponsorship. Just how much sponsorship and just how benevolent it ultimately was were issues that would preoccupy American political thought after 1932.

BIBLIOGRAPHY

Berle, Adolph A., and Gardner C. Means. *The Modern Corporation and Private Property.* New York: Harcourt, 1932.

Carnegie, Dale. *How to Win Friends and Influence People.* New York: Simon & Schuster, 1936.

Chandler, Alfred D. *The Visible Hand: The Managerial Revolution in American Business.* Cambridge: Harvard University Press, 1977.

Davis, John P. *Corporations: A Study of the Origin and Development of Great Business Combinations and of Their Relation to the Authority of the State.* Washington, DC: BeardBooks, 2000.

Dewey, John. *The Public and Its Problems.* New York: Henry Holt & Company, 1927.

Forbath, William E. *Law and the Shaping of the American Labor Movement.* Cambridge: Harvard University Press, 1991.

Haskell, Thomas. *The Emergence of Professional Social Science.* Baltimore: Johns Hopkins University Press, 2000.

Hession, Charles H., and Hyman Sardy. *Ascent to Affluence: A History of American Economic Development.* Boston: Allyn & Bacon, 1971.

Hofstadter, Richard. *The American Political Tradition.* New York: Knopf, 1948.

Horwitz, Morton J. *The Transformation of American Law, 1870–1960.* New York: Oxford University Press, 1992.

Kolko, Gabriel. *The Triumph of Conservatism: A Reinterpretation of American History, 1900–1916.* Glencoe, IL: Free Press, 1963.

Lustig, R. Jeffrey. *Corporate Liberalism: The Origins of American Political Theory, 1890–1920.* Berkeley: University of California Press, 1982.

Tindall, George, and David Shi. *America: A Narrative History,* 7th ed. New York: Norton, 2007.

Weinstein, James. *The Corporate Ideal in the United States, 1900–1918.* Boston: Beacon Press, 1968.

Social Darwinism, the Intellectuals, and Populism

WILLIAM GRAHAM SUMNER

What Social Classes Owe to Each Other (1884)

Ordained as an Episcopal priest, the sociologist and economist William Graham Sumner (1840–1910) was a disciple of the English Social Darwinist philosopher Herbert Spencer. As chair of political and social science at Yale University he preached the Social Darwinist ideals of individual liberty and laissez faire and the middle-class Protestant values of hard work and traditional family life. But Sumner was not simply a defender of the status quo. He denounced paternalistic policies to aid the poor not only because he felt they prevented the "survival of the fittest," but also because he saw them as undermining civil liberty. In his principal book on politics, What Social Classes Owe to Each Other, *Sumner repudiated humanitarian state action on the grounds that it threatened the "Forgotten Man" and violated the primary "social duty" to mind one's own business and take care of one's "own self."*

We are told every day that great social problems stand before us and demand a solution, and we are assailed by oracles, threats, and warnings in reference to those problems. There is a school of writers who are playing quite a role as the heralds of the coming duty and the coming woe. They assume to speak for a large, but vague and undefined, constituency, who set the task, exact a fulfillment, and threaten punishment for default. The task or problem is not specifically defined. Part of the task which devolves on those who are subject to the duty is to define the problem. They are told only that something is the matter; that it behooves them to find out what it is, and how to correct it, and then to work out the cure. All this is more or less truculently set forth.

After reading and listening to a great deal of this sort of assertion I find that the question forms itself with more and more distinctness in my mind: Who are those who assume to put hard questions to other people and to demand a solution of them? How did they acquire the right to demand that others should solve their world-problems for them? Who are they who are held to consider and solve all questions, and how did they fall under this duty?

So far as I can find out what the classes are who are respectively endowed with the rights and duties of posing and solving social problems, they are as follows: Those who are bound to solve the problems are the rich, comfortable, prosperous, virtuous, respectable, educated, and healthy; those whose right it is to set the problems are those who have been less fortunate or less successful in the struggle for existence. The problem itself seems to be, How shall the latter be made as comfortable as the former? To solve this problem, and make us all equally well off, is assumed to be the duty of the former class; the penalty, if they fail of this, is to be bloodshed and destruction. If they cannot make everybody else as well off as themselves, they are to be brought down to the same misery as others.

During the last ten years I have read a great many books and articles, especially by German writers, in which an attempt has been made to set up "the State" as an entity having conscience, power, and will sublimated above human limitations, and as constituting a tutelary genius over us all. I have never been able to find in history or experience anything to fit this concept. I once lived in Germany for two years, but I certainly saw nothing of it there then. Whether the State which Bismarck is moulding will fit the notion is at best a matter of faith and hope. My notion of the State has dwindled with growing experience of life. As an abstraction, the State is to me only All-of-us. In practice—that is, when it exercises will or adopts a line of action—it is only a little group of men chosen in a very haphazard way by the majority of us to perform certain services for all of us. The majority do not go about their selection very rationally, and they are almost always disappointed by the results of their own operation. Hence "the State," instead of offering resources of wisdom, right reason, and pure moral sense beyond what the average of us possess, generally offers much less of all those things. Furthermore, it often turns out in practice that "the State" is not even the known and accredited servants of the State, but, as has been well said, is only some obscure clerk, hidden in the recesses of a Government bureau, into whose power the chance has fallen for the moment to pull one of the stops which control the Government machine. * * *

The little group of public servants who, as I have said, constitute the State, when the State determines on anything, could not do much for themselves or anybody else by their own force. If they do anything, they must dispose of men, as in an army, or of capital, as in a treasury. But the army, or police, or *posse comitatus,* is more or less All-of-us, and the capital in the treasury is the product of the labor and saving of All-of-us. Therefore, when the State means power-to-do it means All-of-us, as brute force or as industrial force.

If anybody is to benefit from the action of the State it must be Some-of-us. If, then, the question is raised, What ought the State to do for labor, for trade, for manufactures, for the poor, for the learned professions? etc., etc.—that is, for a class or an interest—it is really the question, What ought All-of-us to do for Some-of-us? But Some-of-us are included in All-of-us, and, so far as they get the benefit of their own efforts, it is the same as if they worked for themselves, and they may be cancelled out of All-of-us. Then the question which remains it, What ought Some-of-us to do for Others-of-us? or, What do social classes owe to each other?

I now propose to try to find out whether there is any class in society which lies under the duty and burden of fighting the battles of life for any other class, or of solving social problems for the satisfaction of any other class; also, whether there is any class which has the right to formulate demands on "society"—that is, on other classes; also, whether there is anything but a fallacy and a superstition in the notion that "the State" owes anything to anybody except peace, order, and the guarantees of rights. * * *

It is commonly asserted that there are in the United States no classes, and any allusion to classes is resented. On the other hand, we constantly read and hear discussions of social topics in which the existence of social classes is assumed as a simple fact. "The poor," "the weak," "the laborers," are expressions which are used as if they had exact and well-understood definition. Discussions are made to bear upon the assumed rights, wrongs, and misfortunes of certain social classes; and all public speaking and writing consists, in a large measure, of the discussion of general plans for meeting the wishes of classes of people who have not been able to satisfy their own desires. These classes are sometimes discontented, and sometimes not. Sometimes they are discontented and envious. They do not take their achievements as a fair measure of their rights. They do not blame themselves or their parents for their lot, as compared with that of other people. Sometimes they claim that they have a right to everything of which they feel the need for their happiness on earth. To make such a claim against God and Nature would, of course, be only to say that we claim a right to live on earth if we can. But God and Nature have ordained the chances and conditions of life on earth once for all. The case cannot be reopened. We cannot get a revision of the laws of human life. We are absolutely shut up to the need and duty, if we would learn how to live happily, of investigating the laws of Nature, and deducing the rules of right living in the world as it is. These are very wearisome and commonplace tasks. They consist in labor and self-denial repeated over and over again in learning and doing. When the people whose claims we are considering are told to apply themselves to these tasks they become irritated and feel almost insulted. They formulate their claims as rights against society—that is, against some other men. In their view they have a right, not only to *pursue* happiness, but to *get* it; and if they fail to get, they think they have a claim to the aid of other men—that is, to the labor and self-denial of other men—to get it for them. They find orators and poets who tell them that they have grievances, so long as they have unsatisfied desires. * * *

Certain ills belong to the hardships of human life. They are natural. They are part of the struggle with Nature for existence. We cannot blame our fellowmen for our share of these. My neighbor and I are both struggling to free ourselves from these ills. The fact that my neighbor has succeeded in this struggle better than I constitutes no grievance for me. Certain other ills are due to the malice of men, and to the imperfections or errors of civil institutions. These ills are an object of agitation, and a subject of discussion. The former class of ills is to be met only by manly effort and energy; the latter may be corrected by associated effort. The former class of ills is constantly grouped and generalized, and made the object of social schemes. We shall see, as we go on, what that means. The second class of ills may fall on certain social classes, and reform will take the form of interference by other classes in favor of that one. The last fact is, no doubt, the reason why people have been led, not noticing distinctions, to believe that the same method was applicable to the other class of ills. The distinction here made between the ills which belong to the struggle and those which are due to the faults of human institutions is of prime importance. * * *

The humanitarians, philanthropists, and reformers, looking at the facts of life as they present themselves, find enough which is sad and unpromising in the condition of many members of society. They see wealth and poverty side by side. They note great inequality of social position and social chances. They eagerly set about the attempt to account for what they see, and to devise schemes for remedying what they do not like. In their eagerness to recommend the less fortunate classes to pity and consideration they forget all about the rights of other classes; they gloss over all the faults of the classes in question, and they exaggerate their misfortunes and their virtues. They invent new theories of property, distorting rights and perpetuating injustice, as anyone is sure to do who sets about the readjustment of social relations with the interests of one group distinctly before his mind, and the interests of all other groups thrown into the background. When I have read certain of these discussions I have thought that it must be quite disreputable to be respectable, quite dishonest to own property, quite unjust to go one's own way and earn one's own living, and that the only really admirable person was the good-for-nothing. The man who by his own effort raises himself above poverty appears, in these discussions, to be of no account. The man who has done nothing to raise himself above poverty finds that the social doctors flock about him, bringing the capital which they have collected from the other class, and promising him the aid of the State to give him what the other had to work for. In all these schemes and projects the organized intervention of society through the State is either planned or hoped for, and the State is thus made to become the protector and guardian of certain classes. The agents who are to direct the State action are, of course, the reformers and philanthropists. Their schemes, therefore, may always be reduced to this type—that A and B decide what C shall do for D. It will be interesting to inquire, at a later period of our discussion, who C is, and what the effect is upon him of all these arrangements. In all the discussions attention is concentrated on A and B, the noble social reformers, and on D, the "poor man." I call C the Forgotten Man, because I have never seen that any notice was taken of him in any of the discussions. When we have disposed of A, B, and D we can better appreciate the case of C, and I think that we shall find that he deserves our attention, for the worth of his character and the magnitude of his unmerited burdens. Here it may suffice to observe that, on the theories of the social philosophers to whom I have referred, we should get a new maxim of judicious living: Poverty is the best policy. If you get wealth, you will have to support other people; if you do not get wealth, it will be the duty of other people to support you.

No doubt one chief reason for the unclear and contradictory theories of class relations lies in the fact that our society, largely controlled in all its organization by one set of doctrines, still contains survivals of old social theories which are totally inconsistent with the former. In the Middle Ages men were united by custom and prescription into associations, ranks, guilds, and communities of various kinds. These ties endured as long as life lasted. Consequently society was dependent, throughout all its details, on status, and the tie, or bond, was sentimental. In our modern state, and in the United States more than anywhere else, the social structure is based on contract, and status is of the least importance. Contract, however, is rational—even rationalistic. It is also realistic, cold, and matter-of-fact. A contract relation is based on a sufficient reason, not on custom or prescription. It is not permanent. It endures only so long as the reason for it endures. In a state based on contract sentiment is out of place in any public or common affairs. It is relegated to the sphere of private and personal relations, where it depends not at all on class types, but on personal acquaintance and personal estimates. The sentimentalists among us always seize upon the survivals of the old order. They want to save them and restore them. Much of the loose thinking also which troubles us in our social discussions arises from the fact that men do not distinguish the elements of status and of contract which may be found in our society.

Whether social philosophers think it desirable or not, it is out of the question to go back to status or to the sentimental relations which once united baron and retainer, master and servant, teacher and pupil, comrade and comrade. That we have lost some grace and elegance is undeniable. That life once held more poetry and romance is true enough. But it seems impossible that any one who has studied the matter should doubt that we have gained immeasurably, and that our farther gains lie in going forward, not in going backward. The feudal ties can never be restored. If they could be restored they would bring back personal caprice, favoritism, sycophancy, and intrigue. A society based on contract is a society of free and independent men, who form ties without favor or obligation, and co-operate without cringing or intrigue. A society based on contract, therefore, gives the utmost room and chance for individual development, and for all the self-reliance and dignity of a free man. That a society of free men, cooperating under contract, is by far the strongest society which has ever yet existed; that no such society has ever yet developed the full measure of strength of which it is capable; and that the only social improvements which are now conceivable lie in the direction of more complete realization of a society of free men united by contract, are points which cannot be controverted. It followed, however, that one man, in a free state, cannot claim help from and cannot be charged to give help to, another. * * *

The notion of civil liberty which we have inherited is that of *a status created for the individual by laws and institutions, the effect of which is that each man is guaranteed the use of all his own powers exclusively for his own welfare.* It is not at all a matter of elections, or universal suffrage, or democracy. All institutions are to be tested by the degree to which they guarantee liberty. It is not to be admitted for a moment that liberty is a means to social ends, and that it may be impaired for major considerations. Any one who so argues has lost the bearing and relation of all the facts and factors in a free state. A human being has a life to live, a career to run. He is a centre of powers to work, and of capacities to suffer. What his powers may be—whether they can carry him far or not; what his chances may be, whether wide or restricted; what his fortune may be, whether to suffer much or little—are questions of his personal destiny which he must work out and endure as he can; but for all that concerns the bearing of the society and its institutions upon that man, and upon the sum of happiness to which he can attain during his life on earth, the product of all history and all philosophy up to this time is summed up in the doctrine, that he should be left free to do the most for himself that he can, and should be guaranteed the exclusive enjoyment of all that he does. If the society—that is to say, in plain terms, if his fellow-men, either individually, by groups, or in a mass—impinge upon him otherwise than to surround him with neutral conditions of security, they must do so under the strictest responsibility to justify themselves. Jealousy and prejudice against all such interferences are high political virtues in a free man. It is not at all the function of the State to make men happy. They must make themselves happy in their own way, and at their own risk. The functions of the State lie entirely in the conditions or chances which can be affected by civil organization. Hence, liberty for labor and security for earnings are the ends for which civil institutions exist, not means which may be employed for ulterior ends. The free man who steps forward to claim his inheritance and endowment as a free and equal member of a great civil body must understand that his duties and responsibilities are measured to him by the same scale as his rights and his powers. He wants to be subject to no man. He wants to be equal to his fellows, as all sovereigns are equal. So be it; but he cannot escape the deduction that he can call no man to his aid. The other sovereigns will not respect his independence if he becomes dependent, and they cannot respect his equality if he sues for favors. The free man in a free democracy, [is free only] when he cut off all the ties by which he might have made others pull him up. He must take all the consequences of his new status. He is, in a certain sense, an isolated man. The family tie does not bring to him disgrace for the misdeeds of his relatives, as it once would have done, but neither does it furnish him with the support which it once would have given. The relations of men are open and free, but they are also loose. A free man in a free democracy derogates from his rank if he takes a favor for which he does not render an equivalent.

A free man in a free democracy has no duty whatever toward other men of the same rank and standing, except respect, courtesy, and goodwill. We cannot say that there are no classes, when we are speaking politically, and then say that there are classes, when we are telling A what it is his duty to do for B. In a free state every man is held and expected to take care of himself and his family, to make no trouble for his neighbor, and to contribute his full share to public interests and common necessities. If he fails in this he throws burdens on others. He does not thereby acquire rights against the others. On the contrary, he only accumulates obligations toward them; and if he is allowed to make his deficiencies a ground of new claims, he passes over into the position of a privileged or petted person—emancipated from duties, endowed with claims. This is the inevitable result of combining democratic political theories with humanitarian social theories. It would be aside from my present purpose to show, but it is worth noticing in passing, that one result of such inconsistency must surely be to undermine democracy, to increase the power of wealth in the democracy, and to hasten the subjection of democracy to plutocracy; for a man who accepts any share which he has not earned in another man's capital cannot be an independent citizen. * * *

The aggregation of large fortunes is not at all a thing to be regretted. On the contrary, it is a necessary condition of many forms of social advance. If we should set a limit to the accumulation of wealth, we should say to our most valuable producers, "We do not want you to do us the services which you best understand how to perform, beyond a certain point," it would be like killing off our generals in war. * * *

The maxim, or injunction, to which a study of capital leads us is, Get capital. In a community where the standard of living is high, and the conditions of production are favorable, there is a wide margin within which an individual may practise self-denial and win capital without suffering, if he has not the charge of a family. That it requires energy, courage, perseverance, and prudence is not to be denied. Any one who believes that any good thing on this earth can be got without those virtues may believe in the philosopher's stone or the fountain of youth. If there were any Utopia its inhabitants would certainly be very insipid and characterless. * * *

The history of the human race is one long story of attempts by certain persons and classes to obtain control of the power of the State, so as to win earthly gratifications at the expense of others. People constantly assume that there is something metaphysical and sentimental about government. At bottom there are two chief things with which government has to deal. They are, the property of men and the honor of women. These it has to defend against crime. The capital which, as we have seen, is the condition of all welfare on earth, the fortification of existence, and the means of growth, is an object of cupidity. Some want to get it without paying the price of industry and economy. In ancient times they made use of force. They organized bands of robbers. They plundered laborers and merchants. Chief of all, however, they found that means of robbery which consisted in gaining control of the civil organization—the State—and using its poetry and romance as a glamour under cover of which they made robbery lawful. They developed high-spun theories of nationality, patriotism, and loyalty. They took all the rank, glory, power, and prestige of the great civil organization, and they took all the rights. They threw on others the burdens and the duties. At one time, no doubt, feudalism was an organization which drew together again the fragments of a dissolved society; but when the lawyers had applied the Roman law to modern kings, and feudal nobles had been converted into an aristocracy of court nobles, the feudal nobility no longer served any purpose.

In modern times the great phenomenon has been the growth of the middle class out of the mediaeval cities, the accumulation of wealth, and the encroachment of wealth, as a social power, on the ground formerly occupied by rank and birth. The middle class has been obliged to fight for its rights against the feudal class, and it has, during three or four centuries, gradually invented and established institutions to guarantee personal and property rights against the arbitrary will of kings and nobles.

In its turn wealth is now becoming a power in three or four countries, gradually invented by the State, and, like every other power, it is liable to abuse unless restrained by checks and guarantees. There is an insolence of wealth, as there is an insolence of rank. A plutocracy might be even far worse than an aristocracy. Aristocrats have always had their class vices and their class virtues. They have always been, as a class, chargeable with licentiousness and gambling. They have, however, as a class, despised lying and stealing. They have always pretended to maintain a standard of honor, although the definition and the code of honor have suffered many changes and shocking deterioration. The middle class has always abhorred gambling and licentiousness, but it has not always been strict about truth and pecuniary fidelity. That there is a code and standard of mercantile honor which is quite as pure and grand as any military code, is beyond question, but it has never yet been established and defined by long usage and the concurrent support of a large and influential society. The feudal code has, through centuries, bred a high type of men, and constituted a caste. The mercantile code has not yet done so, but the wealthy class has attempted to merge itself in or to imitate the feudal class. * * *

The consequence is, that the wealth-power has been developed, while the moral and social sanctions by which that power ought to be controlled have not yet been developed. A plutocracy would be a civil organization in which the power resides in wealth, in which a man might have whatever he could buy, in which the rights, interests, and feelings of those who could not pay would be overridden. * * *

In the United States the opponent of plutocracy is democracy. Nowhere else in the world has the power of wealth come to be discussed in its political aspects as it is here. Nowhere else does the question arise as it does here. I have given some reasons for this in former chapters. Nowhere in the world is the danger of plutocracy as formidable as it is here. To it we appose the power of numbers as it is presented by democracy. Democracy itself, however, is new and experimental. It has not yet existed long enough to find its appropriate forms. It has no prestige from antiquity such as aristocracy possesses. It has, indeed, none of the surroundings which appeal to the imagination. On the other hand, democracy is rooted in the physical, economic, and social circumstances of the United States. This country cannot be other than democratic for an indefinite period in the future. Its political processes will also be republican. The affection of the people for democracy makes them blind and uncritical in regard to it, and they are as fond of the political fallacies to which democracy lends itself as they are of its sound and correct interpretation, or fonder. Can democracy develop itself and at the same time curb plutocracy? * * *

For now I come to the particular point which I desire to bring forward against all the denunciations and complainings about the power of chartered corporations and aggregated capital. If charters have been given which confer undue powers, who gave them? Our legislators did. Who elected these legislators? We did. If we are a free, self-governing people, we must understand that it costs vigilance and exertion to be self-governing. It costs far more vigilance and exertion to be so under the democratic form, where we have no aids from tradition or prestige, than under other forms. If we are a free, self-governing people, we can blame nobody but ourselves for our misfortunes. No one will come to help us out of them. It will do no good to heap law upon law, or to try by constitutional provisions simply to abstain from the use of powers which we find we always abuse. How can we get bad legislators to pass a law which shall hinder bad legislators from passing a bad law? That is what we are trying to do by many of our proposed remedies. The task before us, however, is one which calls for fresh reserves of moral force and political virtue from the very foundations of the social body. Surely it is not a new thing to us to learn that men are greedy and covetous, and that they will be selfish and tyrannical if they dare. The plutocrats are simply trying to do what the generals, nobles, and priests have done in the past—get the power of the State into their hands, so as to bend the rights of others to their own advantage; and what we need to do is to recognize the fact that we are face to face with the same old foes—the vices and passions of human nature. One of the oldest and most mischievous fallacies in this country has been the notion that we are better than other nations, and that Government has a smaller and easier task here than elsewhere. This fallacy has hindered us from recognizing our old foes as soon as we should have done. Then, again, these vices and passions take good care here to deck themselves out in the trappings of democratic watchwords and phrases, so that they are more often greeted with cheers than with opposition when they first appear. The plan of electing men to represent us who systematically surrender public to private interests, and then trying to cure the mischief by newspaper and platform declamation against capital and corporations, is an entire failure.

The new foes must be met, as the old ones were met—by institutions and guarantees. The problem of civil liberty is constantly renewed. Solved once, it re-appears in a new form. The old constitutional guarantees were all aimed against king and nobles. New ones must be invented to hold the power of wealth to that responsibility without which no power whatever is consistent with liberty. The judiciary has given the most satisfactory evidence that it is competent to the new duty which devolves upon it. The courts have proved, in every case in which they have been called upon, that there are remedies, that they are adequate, and that they can be brought to bear upon the cases. The chief need seems to be more power of voluntary combination and cooperation among those who are aggrieved. Such cooperation is a constant necessity under free self-government; and when, in any community, men lose the power of voluntary cooperation in furtherance or defense of their own interests, they deserve to suffer, with no other remedy than newspaper denunciations and platform declamations. Of course, in such a state of things, political mountebanks come forward and propose fierce measures which can be paraded for political effect. Such measures would be hostile to all our institutions, would destroy capital, overthrow credit, and impair the most essential interests of society. On the side of political machinery there is no ground for hope, but only for fear. On the side of constitutional guarantees and the independent action of self-governing freemen there is every ground for hope. * * *

Every man and woman in society has one big duty. That is, to take care of his or her own self. This is a social duty. For, fortunately, the matter stands so that the duty of making the best of one's self individually is not a separate thing from the duty of filling one's place in society, but the two are one, and the latter is accomplished when the former is done. The common notion, however, seems to be that one has a duty to society, as a special and separate thing, and that this duty consists in considering and deciding what other people ought to do. Now, the man who can do anything for or about anybody else than himself is fit to be head of a family; and when he becomes head of a family he has duties to his wife and his children, in addition to the former big duty. Then, again, any man who can take care of himself and his family is in a very exceptional position, and his family is in a very exceptional position, if he does not find in his immediate surroundings people who need his care and have some sort of a personal claim upon him. If, now, he is able to fulfill all this, and to take care of anybody outside his family and his dependents, he must have a surplus of energy, wisdom, and moral virtue beyond what he needs for his own business. No man has this; for a family is a charge which is capable of infinite development, and no man could suffice to the full measure of duty for which a family may draw upon him. Neither can a man give to society so advantageous an employment of his services, whatever they are, in any other way as by spending them on his family.

The danger of minding other people's business is twofold. First, there is the danger that a man may leave his own business unattended to; and, second, there is the danger of an impertinent interference with another's affairs. The "friends of humanity" almost always run into both dangers. I am one of humanity, and I do not want any volunteer friends. I regard friendship as mutual, and I want to have my say about it. I suppose that other components of humanity feel in the same way about it. If so, they must regard any one who assumes the *role* of a friend of humanity as impertinent. The reference to the friend of humanity back to his own business is obviously the next step. * * *

The amateur social doctors are like the amateur physicians—they always begin with the question of *remedies*, and they go at this without any diagnosis or any knowledge of the anatomy or physiology of society. They never have any doubt of the efficacy of their remedies. They never take account of any ulterior effects which may be apprehended from the remedy itself. It generally troubles them not a whit that their remedy implies a complete reconstruction of society or even a reconstitution of human nature. Against all such social quackery the obvious injunction to the quacks is, to mind their own business. * * *

The type and formula of most schemes of philanthropy or humanitarianism is this: A and B put their heads together to decide what C shall be made to do for D. The radical vice of all these schemes, from a sociological point of view, is that C is not allowed a voice in the matter, and his position, character, and interests, as well as the ultimate effects on society through C's interests, are entirely overlooked. I call C the Forgotten Man. For once let us look him up and consider his case, for the characteristic of all social doctors, is, that they fix their minds on some man or group of men whose case appeals to the sympathies and the imagination, and they plan remedies addressed to the particular trouble; they do not understand that all the parts of society hold together, and that forces which are set in action act and react throughout the whole organism, until an equilibrium is produced by a readjustment of all interests and rights. They therefore ignore entirely the source from which they must draw all the energy which they employ in their remedies, and they ignore all the effects on other members of society than the ones they have in view. They are always under the dominion of the superstition of government, and, forgetting that a government produces nothing at all, they leave out of sight the first fact to be remembered in all social discussion—that the State cannot get a cent for any man without taking it from some other man, and this latter must be a man who has produced and saved it. This latter is the Forgotten Man. * * *

There is a beautiful notion afloat in our literature and in the minds of our people that men are born to certain "natural rights." If that were true, there would be something on earth which was got for nothing, and this world would not be the place it is at all. The fact is, that there is no right whatever inherited by man which has not an equivalent and corresponding duty by the side of it, as the price of it. The rights, advantages, capital, knowledge, and all other goods which we inherit from past generations have been won by the struggles and sufferings of past generations; and the fact that the race lives, though men die, and that the race can by heredity accumulate within some cycle its victories over Nature, is one of the facts which make civilization possible. The struggles of the race as a whole produce the possessions of the race as a whole. Something for nothing is not to be found on earth.

If there were such things as natural rights, the question would arise, Against whom are they good? Who has the corresponding obligation to satisfy these rights? There can be no rights against Nature, except to get out of her what ever we can, which is only the fact of the struggle for existence stated over again. The common assertion is, that the rights are good against society; that is, that society is bound to obtain and secure them for the persons interested. Society, however, is only the persons interested plus some other persons; and as the persons interested have by the hypothesis failed to win the rights, we come to this, that natural rights are the claims which certain persons have by prerogative against some other persons. Such is the actual interpretation in practice of natural rights—claims which some people have by prerogative on other people.

This theory is a very far-reaching one, and of course it is adequate to furnish a foundation for a whole social philosophy. In its widest extension it comes to mean that if any man finds himself uncomfortable in this world, it must be somebody else's fault, and that somebody is bound to come and make him comfortable. Now, the people who are most uncomfortable in this world (for if we should tell all our troubles it would not be found to be a very comfortable world for anybody) are those who have neglected their duties, and consequently have failed to get their rights. The people who can be called upon to serve the uncomfortable must be those who have done their duty, as the world goes, tolerably well. Consequently the doctrine which we are discussing turns out to be in practice only a scheme for making injustice prevail in human society by reversing the distribution of rewards and punishments between those who have done their duty and those who have not. ✳ ✳ ✳

The greatest social evil with which we have to contend is jobbery. Whatever there is in legislative charters, watering stocks, etc., etc., which is objectionable, comes under the head of jobbery. Jobbery is any scheme which aims to gain, not by the legitimate fruits of industry and enterprise, but by extorting from somebody a part of his product under guise of some pretended industrial undertaking. Of course it is only a modification when the undertaking in question has some legitimate character, but the occasion is used to graft upon it devices for obtaining what has not been earned. Jobbery is the vice of plutocracy, and it is the especial form under which plutocracy corrupts a democratic and republican form of government. The United States is deeply afflicted with it, and the problem of civil liberty here is to conquer it. It affects everything which we really need to have done to such an extent that we have to do without public objects which we need through fear of jobbery. Our public buildings are jobs—not always, but often. They are not needed, or are costly beyond all necessity or even decent luxury. Internal improvements are jobs. They are not made because they are needed to meet needs which have been experienced. They are made to serve private ends, often incidentally the political interests of the persons who vote the appropriations. ✳ ✳ ✳

The greatest job of all is a protective tariff. It includes the biggest log-rolling and the widest corruption of economic and political ideas. It was said that there would be a rebellion if the taxes were not taken off whiskey and tobacco, which taxes were paid into the public Treasury. Just then the importations of Sumatra tobacco became important enough to affect the market. The Connecticut tobacco-growers at once called for an import duty on tobacco which would keep up the price of their product. So it appears that if the tax on tobacco is paid to the Federal Treasury there will be a rebellion, but if it is paid to the Connecticut tobacco-raisers there will be no rebellion at all. The farmers have long paid tribute to the manufacturers; now the manufacturing and other laborers are to pay tribute to the farmers. The system is made more comprehensive and complete, and we all are living on each other more than ever.

Now, the plan of plundering each other produces nothing. It only wastes. All the material over which the protected interests wrangle and grab must be got from somebody outside of their circle. The talk is all about the American laborer and American industry, but in every case in which there is not an actual production of wealth by industry there are two laborers and two industries to be considered—the one who gets and the one who gives. Every protected industry has to plead, as the major premise of its argument, that any industry which does not pay *ought* to be carried on at the expense of the consumers of the product, and, as its minor premise, that the industry in question does not pay; that is, that it cannot reproduce a capital equal in value to that which it consumes plus the current rate of profit. Hence every such industry must be a parasite on some other industry. What is the other industry? Who is the other man? This, the real question, is always overlooked.

In all jobbery the case is the same. There is a victim somewhere who is paying for it all. The doors of waste and extravagance stand open, and there seems to be a general agreement to squander and spend. It all belongs to somebody. There is somebody who had to contribute it, and who will have to find more. Nothing is ever said about him. Attention is all absorbed by the clamorous interests, the importunate petitioners, the plausible schemers, the pitiless bores. Now, who is the victim? He is the Forgotten Man. If we go to find him, we shall find him hard at work tilling the soil to get out of it the fund for all the jobbery, the object of all the plunder, the cost of all the economic quackery, and the pay of all the politicians and statesmen who have sacrificed his interests to his enemies. We shall find him an honest, sober, industrious citizen, unknown outside his little circle, paying his debts and his taxes, supporting the church and the school, reading his party newspaper, and cheering for his pet politician. * * *

It is the Forgotten Man who is threatened by every extension of the paternal theory of government. It is he who must work and pay. When, therefore, the statesmen and social philosophers sit down to think what the State can do or ought to do, they really mean to decide what the Forgotten Man shall do. What the Forgotten Man wants, therefore, is a fuller realization of constitutional liberty. He is suffering from the fact that there are yet mixed in our institutions mediaeval theories of protection, regulation, and authority, and modern theories of independence and individual liberty and responsibility. The consequence of this mixed state of things is, that those who are clever enough to get into control use the paternal theory by which to measure their own rights—that is, they assume privileges; and they use the theory of liberty to measure their own duties—that is, when it comes to the duties, they want to be "let alone." The Forgotten Man never gets into control. He has to pay both ways. His rights are measured to him by the theory of liberty—that is, he has only such as he can conquer; his duties are measured to him on the paternal theory—that is, he must discharge all which are laid upon him, as is the fortune of parents. In a paternal relation there are always two parties, a father and a child; and when we use the paternal relation metaphorically, it is of the first importance to know who is to be father and who is to be child. The *role* of parent falls always to the Forgotten Man. What he wants, therefore, is that ambiguities in our institutions be cleared up, and that liberty be more fully realized. * * *

We each owe it to the other to guarantee rights. Rights do not pertain to *results,* but only to *chances.* They pertain to the conditions of the struggle for existence, not to any of the results of it; to the *pursuit* of happiness, not to the possession of happiness. It cannot be said that each one has a right to have some property, because if one man had such a right some other man or men would be under a corresponding obligation to provide him with some property. Each has a right to acquire and possess property if he can. It is plain what fallacies are developed when we overlook this distinction. Those fallacies run through *all* socialistic schemes and theories. If we take rights to pertain to results, and then say that rights must be equal, we come to say that men have a right to be equally happy, and so on in all the details. Rights should be equal, because they pertain to chances, and all ought to have equal chances so far as chances are provided or limited by the action of society. This, however, will not produce equal results, but it is right just because it will produce unequal results—that is, results which shall be proportioned to the merits of individuals. We each owe it to the other to guarantee mutually the chance to earn, to possess, to learn, to marry, etc., etc., against any interference which would prevent the exercise to those rights by a person who wishes to prosecute and enjoy them in peace for the pursuit of happiness. If we generalize this, it means that All-of-us ought to guarantee rights to each of us. But our modern free, constitutional States are constructed entirely on the notion of rights, and we regard them as performing their functions more and more perfectly according as they guarantee rights in consonance with the constantly corrected and expanded notions of rights from one generation to another. Therefore, when we say that we owe it to each other to guarantee rights we only say that we ought to prosecute and improve our political science.

WILLIAM GRAHAM SUMNER

The Absurd Effort to Make the World Over (1894)

Sumner rejected schemes for large-scale social reform as unnatural and futile attempts to prevent inevitable developments in industrial organization. In this article, which appeared in Forum, the Social Darwinist challenged the assertion that democracy creates greater social benefits than industrial capitalism does.

It will not probably be denied that the burden of proof is on those who affirm that our social condition is utterly diseased and in need of radical regeneration. My task at present, therefore, is entirely negative and critical: to examine the allegations of fact and the doctrines which are put forward to prove the correctness of the diagnosis and to warrant the use of the remedies proposed. * * *

When anyone asserts that the class of skilled and unskilled manual laborers of the United States is worse off now in respect to diet, clothing, lodgings, furniture, fuel, and lights; in respect to the age at which they can marry; the number of children they can provide for; the start in life which they can give to their children, and their chances of accumulating capital, than they ever have been at any former time, he makes a reckless assertion for which no facts have been offered in proof. Upon an appeal to facts, the contrary of this assertion would be clearly established. It suffices, therefore, to challenge those who are responsible for the assertion to make it good. * * *

Nine-tenths of the socialistic and semi-socialistic, and sentimental or ethical, suggestions by which we are overwhelmed come from failure to understand the phenomena of the industrial organization and its expansion. It controls us all because we are all in it. It creates the conditions of our existence, sets the limits of our social activity, regulates the bonds of our social relations, determines our conceptions of good and evil, suggests our life-philosophy, molds our inherited political institutions, and reforms the oldest and toughest customs, like marriage and property. I repeat that the turmoil of heterogeneous and antagonistic social whims and speculations in which we live is due to the failure to understand what the industrial organization is and its all-pervading control over human life, while the traditions of our school of philosophy lead us always to approach the industrial organization, not from the side of objective study, but from that of philosophical doctrine. Hence it is that we find that the method of measuring what we see happening by what are called ethical standards, and of proposing to attack the phenomena by methods thence deduced, is so popular.

The advance of a new country from the very simplest social coordination up to the highest organization is a most interesting and instructive chance to study the development of the organization. It has of course been attended all the way along by stricter subordination and higher discipline. All organization implies restriction of liberty. The gain of power is won by narrowing individual range. The methods of business in colonial days were loose and slack to an inconceivable degree. The movement of industry has been all the time toward promptitude, punctuality, and reliability. It has been attended all the way by lamentations about the good old times; about the decline of small industries; about the lost spirit of comradeship between employer and employee; about the narrowing of the interests of the workman; about his conversion into a machine or into a "ware," and about industrial war. These lamentations have all had reference to unquestionable phenomena attendant on advancing organization.

* * * I must expect to be told here, according to the current fashions of thinking, that we ought to control the development of the organization. The first instinct of the modern man is to get a law passed to forbid or prevent what, in his wisdom, he disapproves. A thing which is inevitable, however, is one which we cannot control. We have to make up our minds to it, adjust ourselves to it, and sit down to live with it. Its inevitableness may be disputed, in which case we must reexamine it; but if our analysis is correct, when we reach what is inevitable we reach the end, and our regulations must apply to ourselves, not to the social facts.

Now the intensification of the social organization is what gives us greater social power. It is to it that we owe our increased comfort and abundance. We are none of us ready to sacrifice this. On the contrary, we want more of it. We would not return to the colonial simplicity and the colonial exiguity if we could. If not, then we must pay the price. Our life is bounded on every side by conditions. We can have this if we will agree to submit to that. In the case of industrial power and product the great condition is combination of force under discipline and strict coordination. Hence the wild language about wage-slavery and capitalistic tyranny. * * *

The movement of the industrial organization which has just been described has brought out a great demand for men capable of managing great enterprises. Such have been called "captains of industry." The analogy with military leaders suggested by this name is not misleading. The great leaders in the development of the industrial organization need those talents of executive and administrative skill, power to command, courage, and fortitude, which were formerly called for in military affairs and scarcely anywhere else. The industrial army is also as dependent on its captains as a military body is on its generals. One of the worst features of the existing system is that the employees have a constant risk in their employer. If he is not competent to manage the business with success, they suffer with him. Capital also is dependent on the skill of the captain of industry for the certainty and magnitude of its profits. Under these circumstances there has been a great demand for men having the requisite ability for this function. As the organization has advanced, with more impersonal bonds of coherence and wider scope of operations, the value of this functionary has rapidly increased. The possession of the requisite ability is a natural monopoly. Consequently, all the conditions have concurred to give to those who possessed this monopoly excessive and constantly advancing rates of remuneration.

Another social function of the first importance in an intense organization is the solution of those crises in the operation of it which are called the conjuncture of the market. It is through the market that the lines of relation run which preserve the system in harmonious and rhythmical operation. The conjuncture is the momentary sharper misadjustment of supply and demand which indicates that a redistribution of productive effort is called for. The industrial organization needs to be insured against these conjunctures, which, if neglected, produce a crisis and catastrophe; and it needs that they shall be anticipated and guarded against as far as skill and foresight can do it. The rewards of this function for the bankers and capitalists who perform it are very great. The captains of industry and the capitalists who operate on the conjuncture, therefore, if they are successful, win, in these days, great fortunes in a short time. There are no earnings which are more legitimate or for which greater services are rendered to the whole industrial body. The popular notions about this matter really assume that all the wealth accumulated by these classes of persons would be here just the same if they had not existed. They are supposed to have appropriated it out of the common stock. This is so far from being true that, on the contrary, their own wealth would not be but for themselves; and besides that, millions more of wealth, many-fold greater than their own, scattered in the hands of thousands, would not exist but for them. * * *

But it is repeated until it has become a commonplace which people are afraid to question, that there is some social danger in the possession of large amounts of wealth by individuals. I ask, Why? I heard a lecture two years ago by a man who holds perhaps the first chair of political economy in the world. He said, among other things, that there was great danger in our day from great accumulations; that this danger ought to be met by taxation, and he referred to the fortune of the Rothschilds and to the great fortunes made in America to prove his point. He omitted, however, to state in what the danger consisted or to specify what harm has ever been done by the Rothschild fortunes or by the great fortunes accumulated in America.

* * *

Great figures are set out as to the magnitude of certain fortunes and the proportionate amount of the national wealth held by a fraction of the population, and eloquent exclamation-points are set against them. If the figures were beyond criticism, what would they prove? Where is the rich man who is oppressing anybody? If there was one, the newspapers would ring with it. The facts about the accumulation of wealth do not constitute a plutocracy, as I will show below. Wealth, in itself considered, is only power, like steam, or electricity, or knowledge. The question of its good or ill turns on the question how it will be used. To prove any harm in aggregations of wealth it must be shown that great wealth is, as a rule, in the ordinary course of social affairs, put to a mischievous use. This cannot be shown beyond the very slightest degree, if at all. * * *

Although we cannot criticise democracy profitably, it may be said of it, with reference to our present subject, that up to this time democracy never has done anything, either in politics, social affairs, or industry, to prove its power to bless mankind. If we confine our attention to the United States, there are three difficulties with regard to its alleged achievements, and they all have the most serious bearing on the proposed democratization of industry.

1. The time during which democracy has been tried in the United States is too short to warrant any inferences. A century or two is a very short time in the life of political institutions, and if the circumstances change rapidly during the period the experiment is vitiated.

2. The greatest question of all about American democracy is whether it is a cause or a consequence. It is popularly assumed to be a cause, and we ascribe to its beneficent action all the political vitality, all the easiness of social relations, all the industrial activity and enterprise which we experience and which we value and enjoy. I submit, however, that, on a more thorough examination of the matter, we shall find that democracy is a consequence. There are economic and sociological causes for our political vitality and vigor, for the ease and elasticity of our social relations, and for

our industrial power and success. Those causes have also produced democracy, given it success, and have made its faults and errors innocuous. * * *

3. It is by no means certain that democracy in the United States has not, up to this time, been living on a capital inherited from aristocracy and industrialism. We have no pure democracy. Our democracy is limited at every turn by institutions which were developed in England in connection with industrialism and aristocracy, and these institutions are of the essence of our system. While our people are passionately democratic in temper and will not tolerate a doctrine that one man is not as good as another, they have common sense enough to know that he is not; and it seems that they love and cling to the conservative institutions quite as strongly as they do to the democratic philosophy. They are, therefore, ruled by men who talk philosophy and govern by the institutions. Now it is open to Mr. Bellamy to say that the reason why democracy in America seems to be open to the charge made in the last paragraph, of responsibility for all the ill which he now finds in our society, is because it has been infected with industrialism (capitalism); but in that case he must widen the scope of his proposition and undertake to purify democracy before turning industry over to it. The socialists generally seem to think that they make their undertakings easier when they widen their scope, and make them easiest when they propose to remake everything; but in truth social tasks increase in difficulty in an enormous ratio as they are widened in scope.

The question, therefore, arises, if it is proposed to reorganize the social system on the principles of American democracy, whether the institutions of industrialism are to be retained. If so, all the virus of capitalism will be retained. It is forgotten, in many schemes of social reformation in which it is proposed to mix what we like with what we do not like, in order to extirpate the latter, that each must undergo a reaction from the other, and that what we like may be extirpated by what we do not like. We may find that instead of democratizing capitalism we have capitalized democracy—that is, have brought in plutocracy. Plutocracy is a political system in which the ruling force is wealth. * * *

If this poor old world is as bad as they say, one more reflection may check the zeal of the headlong reformer. It is at any rate a tough old world. It has taken its trend and curvature and all its twists and tangles from a long course of formation. All its wry and crooked gnarls and knobs are therefore stiff and stubborn. If we puny men by our arts can do anything at all to straighten them, it will only be by modifying the tendencies of some of the forces at work, so that, after a sufficient time, their action may be changed a little and slowly the lines of movement may be modified. This effort, however, can at most be only slight, and it will take a long time. In the meantime spontaneous forces will be at work, compared with which our efforts are like those of a man trying to deflect a river, and these forces will have changed the whole problem before our interferences have time to make themselves felt. The great stream of time and earthly things will sweep on just the same in spite of us. It bears with it now all the errors and follies of the past, the wreckage of all the philosophies, the fragments of all the civilizations, the wisdom of all the abandoned ethical systems, the debris of all the institutions, and the penalties of all the mistakes. It is only in imagination that we stand by and look at and criticize it and plan to change it. Everyone of us is a child of his age and cannot get out of it. He is in the stream and is swept along with it. All his sciences and philosophy come to him out of it. Therefore the tide will not be changed by us. It will swallow up both us and our experiments. It will absorb the efforts at change and take them into itself as new but trivial components, and the great movement of tradition and work will go on unchanged by our fads and schemes. The things which will change it are the great discoveries and inventions, the new reactions inside the social organism, and the changes in the earth itself on account of changes in the cosmical forces. These causes will make of it just what, in fidelity to them, it ought to be. The men will be carried along with it and be made by it. The utmost they can do by their cleverness will be to note and record their course as they are carried along, which is what we do now, and is that which leads us to the vain fancy that we can make or guide the movement. That is why it is the greatest folly of which a man can be capable, to sit down with a slate and pencil to plan out a new social world.

WILLIAM GRAHAM SUMNER

The Challenge of Facts (1895)

Sumner often railed against socialism and what he labeled schools of sentimental philosophy for ignoring and violating what he considered the brute facts of nature: scarcity, competition, and the necessity of work. In this selection, Sumner argued that liberty under law, property rights, laissez-faire capitalism, and inequality were more natural responses to the harsh facts of nature than the utopian schemes of socialists, who promoted a dangerous combination of "not-liberty, equality, [and] survival of the unfittest."

ocialism is no new thing. In one form or another it is to be found throughout all history. It arises from an observation of certain harsh facts in the lot of man on earth, the concrete expression of which is poverty and misery. These facts challenge us. It is folly to try to shut our eyes to them. We have first to notice what they are, and then to face them squarely.

Man is born under the necessity of sustaining the existence he has received by an onerous struggle against nature, both to win what is essential to his life and to ward off what is prejudicial to it. He is born under a burden and a necessity. Nature holds what is essential to him, but she offers nothing gratuitously. He may win for his use what she holds, if he can. Only the most meager and inadequate supply for human needs can be obtained directly from nature. There are trees which may be used for fuel and for dwellings, but labor is required to fit them for this use. There are ores in the ground, but labor is necessary to get out the metals and make tools or weapons. For any real satisfaction, labor is necessary to fit the products of nature for human use. In this struggle every individual is under the pressure of the necessities for food, clothing, shelter, fuel, and every individual brings with him more or less energy for the conflict necessary to supply his needs. The relation, therefore, between each man's needs and each man's energy, or "individualism," is the first fact of human life.

* * *

Private property, also, which we have seen to be a feature of society organized in accordance with the natural conditions of the struggle for existence produces inequalities between men. The struggle for existence is aimed against nature. It is from her niggardly hand that we have to wrest the satisfactions for our needs, but our fellow-men are our competitors for the meager supply. Competition, therefore, is a law of nature. Nature is entirely neutral; she submits to him who most energetically and resolutely assails her. She grants her rewards to the fittest, therefore, without regard to other considerations of any kind. If, then, there be liberty, men get from her just in proportion to their works, and their having and enjoying are just in proportion to their being and their doing. Such is the system of nature. If we do not like it, and if we try to amend it, there is only one way in which we can do it. We can take from the better and give to the worse. We can deflect the penalties of those who have done ill and throw them on those who have done better. We can take the rewards from those who have done better and give them to those who have done worse. We shall thus lessen the inequalities. We shall favor the survival of the unfittest, and we shall accomplish this by destroying liberty. Let it be understood that we cannot go outside of this alternative: liberty, inequality, survival of the fittest; not-liberty, equality, survival of the unfittest. The former carries society forward and favors all its best members; the latter carries society downwards and favors all its worst members. * * *

What we mean by liberty is civil liberty, or liberty under law; and this means the guarantees of law that a man shall not be interfered with while using his own powers for his own welfare. It is, therefore, a civil and political status; and that nation has the freest institutions in which the guarantees of peace for the laborer and security for the capitalist are the highest. Liberty, therefore, does not by any means do away with the struggle for existence. We might as well try to do away with the need of eating, for that would, in effect, be the same thing. What civil liberty does is to turn the competition of man with man from violence and brute force into an industrial competition under which men vie with one another for the acquisition of material goods by industry, energy, skill, frugality, prudence, temperance, and other industrial virtues.

* * *

The origin of socialism, which is the extreme development of the sentimental philosophy, lies in the undisputed facts which I described at the outset. The socialist regards this misery as the fault of society. He thinks that we can organize society as we like and that an organization can be devised in which poverty and misery shall disappear. He goes further even than this. He assumes that men have artificially organized society as it now exists. Hence if anything is disagreeable or hard in the present state of society it follows, on that view, that the task of organizing society has been imperfectly and badly performed, and that it needs to be done over again. These are the assumptions with which the socialist starts, and many socialists seem also to believe that if they can destroy belief in an Almighty God who is supposed to have made the world such as it is, they will then have overthrown the belief that there is a fixed order in human nature and human life which man can scarcely alter at all, and, if at all, only infinitesimally.

The truth is that the social order is fixed by laws of nature precisely analogous to those of the physical order. The most that man can do is by ignorance and self-conceit to mar the operation of social laws. The evils of society are to a great extent the result of the dogmatism and self-interest of statesmen, philosophers, and ecclesiastics who in past time have done just what the socialists now want to do. Instead of studying the natural laws of the social order, they assumed that they could organize society as they chose, they made up their minds what kind of a society they wanted to make, and they planned their little measures for the ends they had resolved upon. It will take centuries of scientific study of the facts of nature to eliminate from human society the mischievous institutions and traditions which the said statesmen, philosophers, and ecclesiastics have introduced into it. Let us not, however, even then delude ourselves with any impossible hopes. The hardships of life would not be eliminated if the laws of nature acted directly and without interference. The task of right living forever changes its form, but let us not imagine that that task will ever reach a final solution or that any race of men on this earth can ever be emancipated from the necessity of industry, prudence, continence, and temperance if they are to pass their lives prosperously. If you believe the contrary you must suppose that some men can come to exist who shall know nothing of old age, disease, and death.

* * *

The sound student of sociology can hold out to mankind, as individuals or as a race, only one hope of better and happier living. That hope lies in an enhancement of the industrial virtues and of the moral forces which thence arise. Industry, self-denial, and temperance are the laws of prosperity for men and states; without them advance in the arts and in wealth means only corruption and decay through luxury and vice. With them progress in the arts and increasing wealth are the prime conditions of an advancing civilization which is sound enough to endure. The power of the human race to-day over the conditions of prosperous and happy living are sufficient to banish poverty and misery if it were not for folly and vice. The earth does not begin to be populated up to its power to support population on the present stage of the arts; if the United States were as densely populated as the British Islands, we should have 1,000,000,000 people here. If, therefore, men were willing to set to work with energy and courage to subdue the outlying parts of the earth, all might live in plenty and prosperity. But if they insist on remaining in the slums of great cities or on the borders of an old society, and on a comparatively exhausted soil, there is no device of economist or statesman which can prevent them from falling victims to poverty and misery or from succumbing in the competition of life to those who have greater command of capital. The socialist or philanthropist who nourishes them in their situation and saves them from the distress of it is only cultivating the distress which he pretends to cure.

WILLIAM GRAHAM SUMNER

Consolidation of Wealth: Economic Aspects (1902)

In an essay that first appeared in the Independent, *Sumner provided a classic articulation of the trickle-down theory of economics, which states that the financial success of those at the top inevitably benefits those at the bottom. This argument was part of a larger effort to prove that large concentrations of wealth are a necessary and beneficial part of the evolutionary process.*

It is a consequence of the principle just stated that at every point in the history of civilization it has always been necessary to concentrate capital in large amounts relatively to existing facts. * * * If we could get rid of some of our notions about liberty and equality, and could lay aside this eighteenth century philosophy, according to which human society is to be brought into a state of blessedness, we might get some insight into the might of the societal organization; what it does for us, and what it makes us do. Every day that passes brings us new phenomena of struggle and effort between parts of the societal organization. What do they all mean? They mean that all the individuals and groups are forced against each other in a ceaseless war of interests, by their selfish and mutual efforts to fulfill their career on earth, within the conditions set for them by the state of the arts, the facts of the societal organization, and the current dogmas of world philosophy. As each must win his living, or his fortune, or keep his fortune, under these conditions it is difficult to see what can be meant in the sphere of industrial or economic effort, by a "free man." It is no wonder that we so often hear angry outcries about being "a slave" from persons who have had a little experience of the contrast between the current notions and the actual facts. * * *

I am quite well aware that, in what I have said, I have not met the thoughts and feelings of people who are most troubled about the "concentration of wealth." I have tried to set forth the economic necessity for the concentration of wealth. I maintain that this is the controlling consideration. Those who care most about the concentration are indifferent to this consideration. What strikes them most is the fact that there are some rich men. I will, therefore, try to show that this fact also is only another economic justification of the concentration of wealth.

I often see statements published, in which the objectors lay stress upon the great inequalities of fortune, and, having set forth the contrast between rich and poor, they rest their case. What law of nature, religion, ethics, or the State is not violated by *inequalities* of fortune? The inequalities prove nothing. Others argue that great fortunes are won by privileges created by law and not by legitimate enterprise and ability. This statement is true, but it is entirely irrelevant. We have to discuss the concentration of wealth within the facts of the institutions, laws, usages and customs which our ancestors have bequeathed to us and which we allow to stand. If it is proposed to change any of these parts of the societal order, that is a proper subject of discussion, but it is aside from the concentration of wealth. So long as tariffs, patents, etc., are a part of the system in which we live, how can it be expected that people will not take advantage of them? What else are they for?

* * *

Hence the modern methods offer very great opportunities, and the rewards of those men who can "size up" a situation, and develop its controlling elements with sagacity and good judgment, are very great. It is well that they are so, because these rewards stimulate to the utmost all the ambitions and able men, and they will make it certain that great and useful inventions will not long remain unexploited as they did formerly. Here comes, then, a new reaction on the economic system. New energy is infused into it, with hope and confidence. We could not spare this stimulus and keep up our work of production. I may add that we could not spare it and keep up the air of contentment and enthusiastic cheerfulness which characterizes our society. No man can acquire a million without helping a million men to increase their little fortunes all the way down through all the social grades. In some points of view it is an error that we fix our attention so much upon the very rich and overlook the prosperous mass, but the compensating advantage is that the great successes stimulate emulation the most powerfully.

What matters it then that some millionaires are idle, or silly, or vulgar, that their ideas are sometimes futile, and their plans grotesque, when they turn aside from money-making? How do they differ in this from any other class? The millionaires are a product of natural selection, acting on the whole body of men, to pick out those who can meet the requirement of certain work to be done. In this respect they are just like the great statesmen, or scientific men, or military men. It is because they are thus selected that wealth aggregates under their hands—both their own and that intrusted to them. Let one of them make a mistake and see how quickly the concentration gives way to dispersion. They may fairly be regarded as the naturally selected agents of society for certain work. They get high wages and live in luxury, but the bargain is a good one for society. There is the intensest competition for their place and occupation. This assures us that all who are competent for this function will be employed in it, so that the cost of it will be reduced to the lowest terms, and furthermore that the competitors will study the proper conduct to be observed in their occupation. This will bring discipline and the correction of arrogance and masterfulness.

ANDREW CARNEGIE

The Gospel of Wealth (1889)

The Scottish-born steel industrialist Andrew Carnegie (1835–1919) epitomized the self-made man in the late nineteenth century. He made his way from telegraph messenger to steel magnate and founder of the United States Steel Company. He pursued a number of philanthropic projects, from public libraries to private universities. Carnegie firmly believed that with great individual wealth come social responsibilities. In "The Gospel of Wealth," an essay that first appeared in the North American Review, Carnegie defended the vast inequalities between rich and poor as an inevitable byproduct of "Individualism, Private Property, the Law of Accumulation of Wealth, and the Law of Competition." However, the steel tycoon also invoked the Protestant notion of stewardship to support his claim that the rich have an obligation to distribute the surplus of their wealth for the benefit of society.

The problem of our age is the proper administration of wealth, so that the ties of brotherhood may still bind together the rich and poor in harmonious relationship. The conditions of human life have not only been changed, but revolutionized, within the past few hundred years. * * * The contrast between the palace of the millionaire and the cottage of the laborer with us to-day measures the change which has come with civilization.

This change, however, is not to be deplored, but welcomed as highly beneficial. It is well, nay, essential for the progress of the race, that the houses of some should be homes for all that is highest and best in literature and the arts, and for all the refinements of civilization, rather than that none should be so. Much better this great irregularity than universal squalor. * * * But whether the change be for good or ill, it is upon us, beyond our power to alter, and therefore to be accepted and made the best of. It is a waste of time to criticize the inevitable.

It is easy to see how the change has come. One illustration will serve for almost every phase of the cause. In the manufacture of products we have the whole story. It applies to all combinations of human industry, as stimulated and enlarged by the inventions of this scientific age. Formerly articles were manufactured at the domestic hearth or in small shops which formed part of the household. The master and his apprentices worked side by side, the latter living with the master, and therefore subject to the same conditions. When these apprentices rose to be masters, there was little or no change in their mode of life, and they, in turn, educated in the same routine succeeding apprentices. There was, substantially, social equality, and even political equality, for those engaged in industrial pursuits had then little or no political voice in the State. * * *

Today [as a result of industrialization] the world obtains commodities of excellent quality at prices which even the generation preceding this would have deemed incredible. In the commercial world similar causes have produced similar results, and the race is benefited thereby. The poor enjoy what the rich could not before afford. What were the luxuries have become the necessaries of life. The laborer has now more comforts than the farmer had a few generations ago. The farmer has more luxuries than the landlord had, and is more richly clad and better housed. The landlord has books and pictures rarer, and appointments more artistic, than the King could then obtain.

The price we pay for this salutary change is, no doubt, great. We assemble thousands of operatives in the factory, in the mine, and in the counting-house, of whom the employer can know little or nothing, and to whom the employer is little better than a myth. All intercourse between them is at an end. Rigid Castes are formed, and, as usual, mutual ignorance breeds mutual distrust. Each Caste is without sympathy for the other, and ready to credit anything disparaging in regard to it. Under the law of competition, the employer of thousands is forced into the strictest economies, among which the rates paid to labor figure prominently, and often there is friction between the employer and the employed, between capital and labor, between rich and poor. Human society loses homogeneity.

The price which society pays for the law of competition, like the price it pays for cheap comforts and luxuries, is also great; but the advantages of this law are also greater still, for it is to this law that we owe our wonderful material development, which brings improved conditions in its train. But, whether the law be benign or not, we must say of it, as we say of the change in the conditions of men to which we have referred: It is here; we cannot evade it; no substitutes for it have been found; and while the law may be sometimes hard for the individual, it is best for the race, because it insures the survival of the fittest in every department. We accept and welcome, therefore, as conditions to which we must accommodate ourselves, great inequality of environment, the concentration of business, industrial and commercial, in the hands of a few, and the law of competition between these, as being not only beneficial, but essential for the future progress of the race. Having accepted these, it follows that there must be great scope for the exercise of special ability in the merchant and in the manufacturer who has to conduct affairs upon a great scale. That this talent for organization and management is rare among men is proved by the fact that it invariably secures for its possessor enormous rewards, no matter where or under what laws or conditions. The experienced in affairs always rate the MAN whose services can be obtained as a partner as not only the first consideration, but such as to render the question of his capital scarcely worth considering, for such men soon create capital; while, without the special talent required, capital soon takes wings. * * * It is a law, as certain as any of the others named, that men possessed of this peculiar talent for affairs, under the free play of economic forces, must, of necessity, soon be in receipt of more revenue than can be judiciously expended upon themselves; and this law is as beneficial for the race as the others.

Objections to the foundations upon which society is based are not in order, because the condition of the race is better with these than it has been with any others which have been tried. Of the effect of any new substitutes proposed we cannot be sure. The Socialist or Anarchist who seeks to overturn present conditions is to be regarded as attacking the foundation upon which civilization itself rests, for civilization took its start from the day that the capable, industrious workman said to his incompetent and lazy fellow, 'If thou dost not sow, thou shalt not reap,' and thus ended primitive Communism by separating the drones from the bees. One who studies this subject will soon be brought face to face with the conclusion that upon the sacredness of property civilization itself depends—the right of the laborer to his hundred dollars in the savings bank, and equally the legal right of the millionaire to his millions. To those who propose to substitute Communism for this intense Individualism the answer, therefore is: The race has tried that. All progress from that barbarous day to the present time has resulted from its displacement. Not evil, but good, has come to the race from the accumulation of wealth by those who have the ability and energy that produce it. But even if we admit for a moment that it might be better for the race to discard its present foundation, Individualism,—that it is a nobler ideal that man should labor, not for himself alone, but in and for a brotherhood of his fellows, and share with them all in common, realizing Swedenborg's idea of Heaven, where, as he says, the angels derive their happiness, not from laboring for self, but for each other,—even admit all this, and a sufficient answer is, This is not evolution, but revolution. * * * We might as well urge the destruction of the highest existing type of man because he failed to reach our ideal as to favor the destruction of Individualism, Private Property, the Law of Accumulation of Wealth, and the Law of Competition; for these are the highest results of human experience, the soil in which society so far has produced the best fruit. Unequally or unjustly, perhaps, as these laws sometimes operate, and imperfect as they appear to the Idealist, they are, nevertheless, like the highest type of man, the best and most valuable of all that humanity has yet accomplished.

We start, then, with a condition of affairs under which the best interests of the race are promoted, but which inevitably gives wealth to the few. Thus far, accepting conditions as they exist, the situation can be surveyed and pronounced good. The question then arises,—and, if the foregoing be correct, it is the only question with which we have to deal,—What is the proper mode of administering wealth after the laws upon which civilization is founded have thrown it into the hands of the few? And it is of this great question that I believe I offer the true solution. It will be understood that *fortunes* are here spoken of, not moderate sums saved by many years of effort, the returns from which are required for the comfortable maintenance and education of families. This is not *wealth*, but only *competence*, which it should be the aim of all to acquire.

* * *

There are but three modes in which surplus wealth can be disposed of. It can be left to the families of the decedents; or it can be bequeathed for public purposes; or finally, it can be administered during their lives by its possessors. Under the first and second modes most of the wealth of the world that has reached the few has hitherto been applied. Let us in turn consider each of these modes. The first is the most injudicious. In monarchical countries, the estates and the greatest portion of the wealth are left to the first son, that the vanity of the parent may be gratified by the thought that his name and title are to descend to succeeding generations unimpaired. The condition of this class in Europe today teaches the futility of such hopes or ambitions. The successors have become impoverished through their follies, or from the fall in the value of land. Even in

Great Britain the strict law of entail has been found inadequate to maintain the status of an hereditary class. Its soil is rapidly passing into the hands of the stranger. Under republican institutions the division of property among the children is much fairer, but the question which forces itself upon thoughtful men in all lands is: Why should men leave great fortunes to their children? If this is done from affection, is it not misguided affection? Observation teaches that, generally speaking, it is not well for the children that they should be so burdened. Neither is it well for the state. Beyond providing for the wife and daughters moderate sources of income, and very moderate allowances indeed, if any, for the sons, men may well hesitate, for it is no longer questionable that great sums bequeathed often work more for the injury than for the good of the recipients. Wise men will soon conclude that, for the best interests of the members of their families, and of the state, such bequests are an improper use of their means.

It is not suggested that men who have failed to educate their sons to earn a livelihood shall cast them adrift in poverty. If any man has seen fit to rear his sons with a view to their living idle lives, or, what is highly commendable, has instilled in them the sentiment that they are in a position to labor for public ends without reference to pecuniary considerations, then, of course, the duty of the parent is to see that such are provided for in *moderation*. There are instances of millionaires' sons unspoiled by wealth, who, being rich, still perform great services in the community. Such are the very salt of the earth, as valuable as, unfortunately, they are rare. It is not the exception, however, but the rule, that men must regard; and, looking at the usual result of enormous sums conferred upon legatees, the thoughtful man must shortly say, "I would as soon leave my son a curse as the almighty dollar," and admit to himself that it is not the welfare of the children, but family pride, which inspires these enormous legacies.

As to the second mode, that of leaving wealth at death for public uses, it may be said that this is only a means for the disposal of wealth, provided a man is content to wait until he is dead before he becomes of much good in the world. Knowledge of the results of legacies bequeathed is not calculated to inspire the brightest hopes of much posthumous good being accomplished. The cases are not few in which the real object sought by the testator is not attained, nor are they few in which his real wishes are thwarted. In many cases the bequests are so used as to become only monuments of his folly. It is well to remember that it requires the exercise of not less ability than that which acquired the wealth to use it so as to be really beneficial to the community. Besides this, it may fairly be said that no man is to be extolled for doing what he cannot help doing, nor is he to be thanked by the community to which he only leaves wealth at death. Men who leave vast sums in this way may fairly be thought men who would not have left it at all, had they been able to take it with them. The memories of such cannot be held in grateful remembrance, for there is no grace in their gifts. It is not to be wondered at that such bequests seem so generally to lack the blessing.

The growing disposition to tax more and more heavily large estates left at death is a cheering indication of the growth of a salutary change in public opinion. The State of Pennsylvania now takes—subject to some exceptions—one tenth of the property left by its citizens. The budget presented in the British Parliament the other day proposes to increase the death-duties; and, most significant of all, the new tax is to be a graduated one. Of all forms of taxation, this seems the wisest. Men who continue hoarding great sums all their lives, the proper use of which for public ends would work good to the community, should be made to feel that the community, in the form of the state, cannot thus be deprived of its proper share. By taxing estates heavily at death the state marks its condemnation of the selfish millionaire's unworthy life.

It is desirable that nations should go much further in this direction. Indeed, it is difficult to set bounds to the share of a rich man's estate which should go at his death to the public through the agency of the state, and by all means such taxes should be graduated, beginning at nothing upon moderate sums to dependents, and increasing rapidly as the amounts swell. * * * This policy would work powerfully to induce the rich man to attend to the administration of wealth during his life, which is the end that society should always have in view, as being by far the most fruitful for the people. Nor need it be feared that this policy would sap the root of enterprise and render men less anxious to accumulate, for, to the class whose ambition, it is to leave great fortunes and be talked about after their death, it will attract even more attention, and, indeed, be a somewhat nobler ambition to have enormous sums paid over to the state from their fortunes.

There remains, then, only one mode of using great fortunes; but in this we have the true antidote for the temporary unequal distribution of wealth, the reconciliation of the rich and the poor—a reign of harmony— another ideal, differing, indeed, from that of the Communist in requiring only the further evolution of existing conditions, not the total overthrow of our civilization. It is founded upon the present most intense individualism, and the race is prepared to put it in practice by degrees whenever it pleases. Under its sway we shall have an ideal state, in which the surplus wealth of the few will become, in the best sense, the property of the many, because administered for the common good; and this wealth, passing through the hands of the few, can be made a much more potent force for the elevation of our race than if it had been distributed in small sums to the people themselves. Even the poorest can be made to see this, and to agree that great sums gathered by some of their fellow-citizens and spent for public purposes, from which the masses reap the principal benefit, are more valuable to them than if scattered among them through the course of many years in trifling amounts.

* * *

Poor and restricted are our opportunities in this life; narrow our horizon; our best work most imperfect; but rich men should be thankful for one inestimable boon. They have it in their power during their lives to busy themselves in organizing benefactions from which the masses of their fellows will derive lasting advantage, and thus dignify their own lives. The highest life is probably reached, not by such imitation of the life of Christ as Count Tolstoi gives us, but, while animated by Christ's spirit, by recognizing the changed conditions of this age, and adopting modes of expressing this spirit suitable to the changed conditions under which we live; still laboring for the good of our fellows, which was the essence of his life and teaching, but laboring in a different manner.

This, then, is held to be the duty of the man of Wealth: First, to set an example of modest, unostentatious living, shunning display or extravagance; to provide moderately for the legitimate wants of those dependent upon him; and after doing so to consider all surplus revenues which come to him simply as trust funds, which he is called upon to administer, and strictly bound as a matter of duty to administer in the manner which, in his judgment, is best calculated to produce the most beneficial results for the community—the man of wealth thus becoming the mere agent and trustee for his poorer brethren, bringing to their service his superior wisdom, experience, and ability to administer, doing for them better than they would or could do for themselves. * * *

Thus is the problem of Rich and Poor to be solved. The laws of accumulation will be left free: the laws of distribution free. Individualism will continue, but the millionaire will be but a trustee for the poor; intrusted for a season with a great part of the increased wealth of the community, but administering it for the community far better than it could or would have done for itself. The best minds will thus have reached a stage in the development of the race in which it is clearly seen that there is no mode of disposing of surplus wealth creditable to thoughtful and earnest men whose hands it flows save by using it year by year for the general good. This day already dawns. But a little while, and although, without incurring the pity of their fellows, men may die sharers in great business enterprises from which their capital cannot be or has not been withdrawn, and is left chiefly at death for public uses, yet the man who dies leaving behind him millions of available wealth, which was his to administer during life, will pass away "unwept, unhonored, and unsung," no matter to what uses he leaves the dross which he cannot take with him. Of such as these the public verdict will then be: "The man who dies thus rich dies disgraced."

Such, in my opinion, is the true Gospel concerning Wealth, obedience to which is destined some day to solve the problem of the Rich and the Poor, and to bring "Peace on earth, among men Good-Will."

RUSSELL H. CONWELL

Acres of Diamonds (1891)

The lawyer and publisher Russell Herman Conwell (1843–1925) was a Baptist minister who founded Temple University. Conwell earned a sizeable fortune in lecture fees and royalties for "Acres of Diamonds," which he delivered thousands of times. He extolled the virtues of moneymaking and offered moral justifications for the acquisitive activities of wealthy industrialists. In his lectures, Conwell celebrated the United States as a land of opportunity in which "everyone can and should get rich and then use his money to promote the well-being of others." Those who failed to get rich, according to the Christian minister, were poor through their own fault and had failed in their Christian duty.

I often wish I could see the younger people, and would that the Academy had been filled to-night with our high-school scholars, and our grammar-school scholars, that I could have them to talk to. While I would have preferred such an audience as that, because they are most susceptible, as they have not grown up into their prejudices as we have, they have not gotten into any custom that they cannot break, they have not met with any failures as we have; and while I could perhaps do such an audience as that more good than I can do grown-up people, yet I will do the best I can with the material I have. I say to you that you have 'acres of diamonds' in Philadelphia right where you now live. 'Oh,' but you say, 'you cannot know much about your city if you think there are any "acres of diamonds" here.' * * *

I say * * * that the opportunity to get rich, to attain unto great wealth, is here in Philadelphia now, within the reach of almost every man and woman who hears me speak tonight, and I mean just what I say. I have not come to this platform even under these circumstances to recite something to you. I have come to tell you what in God's sight I believe to be the truth, and if the years of life have been of any value to me in the attainment of common sense, I know I am right; that the men and women sitting here, who found it difficult perhaps to buy a ticket to this lecture or gathering to-night, have within their reach 'acres of diamonds,' opportunities to get largely wealthy. There never was a place on earth more adapted than the city of Philadelphia to-day, and never in the history of the world did a poor man without capital have such an opportunity to get rich quickly and honestly as he has now in our city. * * *

I say that you ought to get rich, and it is your duty to get rich. How many of my pious brethren say to me, 'Do you, a Christian minister, spend your time going up and down the country advising young people to get rich, to get money?' 'Yes, of course I do.' They say, 'Isn't that awful! Why don't you preach the gospel instead of preaching about man's making money?' 'Because to make money honestly is to preach the gospel.' That is the reason. The men who get rich may be the most honest men you find in the community.

'Oh,' but says some young man here to-night, 'I have been told all my life that if a person has money he is very dishonest and dishonorable and mean and contemptible.' My friend, that is the reason why you have none, because you have that idea of people. The foundation of your faith is altogether false. Let me say here clearly, and say it briefly, though subject to discussion which I have not time for here, ninety-eight out of one hundred of the rich men of America are honest. That is why they are rich. That is why they are trusted with money. That is why they carry on great enterprises and find plenty of people to work with them. It is because they are honest men. * * *

For a man to have money, even in large sums, is not an inconsistent thing. We preach against covetousness, and you know we do, in the pulpit, and oftentimes preach against it so long and use the terms about 'filthy lucre' so extremely that Christians get the idea that when we stand in the pulpit we believe it is wicked for any man to have money—until the collection-basket goes around, and then we almost swear at the people because they don't give more money. Oh, the inconsistency of such doctrines as that!

Money is power, and you ought to be reasonably ambitious to have it. You ought because you can do more good with it than you could without it. Money printed your Bible, money builds your churches, money sends your missionaries, and money pays your preachers, and you would not have many of them, either, if you did not pay them. I am always willing that my church should raise my salary, because the church that pays the largest salary always raises it the easiest. You never knew an exception to it in your life. The man who gets the largest salary can do the most good with the power that is furnished to him. Of course he can if his spirit be right to use it for what it is given to him.

I say, then, you ought to have money. If you can honestly attain unto riches in Philadelphia, it is your Christian and godly duty to do so. It is an awful mistake of these pious people to think you must be awfully poor in order to be pious.

Some men say, 'Don't you sympathize with the poor people?' Of course I do, or else I would not have been lecturing these years. I won't give in but what I sympathize with the poor, but the number of poor who are to be sympathized with is very small. To sympathize with a man whom God has punished for his sins, thus to help him when God would still continue a just punishment, is to do wrong, no doubt about it, and we do that more than we help those who are deserving. While we should sympathize with God's poor—that is, those who cannot help themselves—let us remember there is not a poor person in the United States who was not made poor by his own shortcomings, or by the shortcomings of some one else. It is all wrong to be poor, anyhow. * * *

'Well, then, you can measure the good you have been to this city by what this city has paid you, because a man can judge very well what he is worth by what he receives; that is, in what he is to the world at this time. If you have not made over a thousand dollars in twenty years in Philadelphia, it would have been better for Philadelphia if they had kicked you out of the city nineteen years and nine months ago. A man has no right to keep a store in Philadelphia twenty years and not make at least five hundred thousand dollars, even though it be a corner grocery up-town.' You say, 'You cannot make five thousand dollars in a store now.' Oh, my friends, if you will just take only four blocks around you, and find out what the people want and what you ought to supply and set them down with your pencil, and figure up the profits you would make if you did supply them, you would very soon see it. There is wealth right within the sound of your voice. * * *

Arise, ye millions of Philadelphians, trust in God and man, and believe in the great opportunities that are right here—not over in New York or Boston, but here—for business, for everything that is worth living for on earth. There was never an opportunity greater. Let us talk up our own city. * * *

'When are you going to be great?' 'When I am elected to some political office.' Young man, won't you learn a lesson in the primer of politics that it is a *prima facie* evidence of littleness to hold office under our form of government? Great men get into office sometimes, but what this country needs is men that will do what we tell them to do. * * *

I know of a great many young women, now that woman's suffrage is coming, who say, 'I am going to be President of the United States some day.' * * * I want to say right here what I say to the young men, that if you only get the privilege of casting one vote, you don't get anything that is worth while. Unless you can control more than one vote, you will be unknown, and your influence so dissipated as practically not to be felt. This country is not run by votes. Do you think it is? It is governed by influence. It is governed by the ambitions and the enterprises which control votes. * * *

Greatness consists not in the holding of some future office, but really consists in doing great deeds with little means and the accomplishments of vast purposes from the private ranks of life. To be great at all one must be great here, now, in Philadelphia. He who can give to this city better streets and better sidewalks, better schools and more colleges, more happiness and more civilization, more of God, he will be great anywhere. Let every man or woman here, if you never hear me again, remember this, that if you wish to be great at all, you must begin where you are and what you are, in Philadelphia, now. He that can give to his city any blessing, he who can be a good citizen while he lives here, he that can make better homes, he that can be a blessing whether he works in the shop or sits behind the counter or keeps house, whatever be his life, he who would be great anywhere must first be great in his own Philadelphia.

HENRY GEORGE

Progress and Poverty (1879)

The social critic Henry George (1839–1897) was an economist and land reformer who favored the abolition of all taxes except for a tax on the unearned profit obtained from rising land values caused not by improvement but by increased demand through population growth. Noting the paradox that in a time of such great progress there was so much want, George attributed the poverty of most Americans to regressive land policies. In Progress and Poverty, which was widely read and translated into many languages, George argued that the govern-

*ment could use the huge revenues it would generate from a tax on di-
minishing supplies of idle land to fund a variety of socially beneficial
public works.*

The present century has been marked by a prodigious increase in
wealth-producing power. The utilization of steam and electricity, the
introduction of improved processes and labor-saving machinery, the
greater subdivision and grander scale of production, the wonderful facili-
tation of exchanges, have multiplied enormously the effectiveness of labor.

At the beginning of this marvelous era it was natural to expect, and it
was expected, that labor-saving inventions would lighten the toil and improve the condition of the laborer; that the enormous increase in the power
of producing wealth would make real poverty a thing of the past. * * *

Now, however, we are coming into collision with facts which there
can be no mistaking. From all parts of the civilized world come complaints of industrial depression; of labor condemned to involuntary idleness; of capital massed and wasting; of pecuniary distress among business
men; of want and suffering and anxiety among the working classes. All
the dull, deadening pain, all the keen, maddening anguish, that to great
masses of men are involved in the words 'hard times,' afflict the world
today. * * *

And, unpleasant as it may be to admit it, it is at last becoming evident
that the enormous increase in productive power which has marked the
present century is still going on with accelerating ratio, has no tendency
to extirpate poverty or to lighten the burdens of those compelled to
toil. * * * The march of invention has clothed mankind with powers of
which a century ago the boldest imagination could not have dreamed.
But in factories where labor-saving machinery has reached its most wonderful development, little children are at work; wherever the new forces
are anything like fully utilized, large classes are maintained by charity or
live on the verge of recourse to it; amid the greatest accumulations of
wealth, men die of starvation, and puny infants suckle dry breasts; while
everywhere the greed of gain, the worship of wealth, shows the force of
the fear of want. * * *

This association of poverty with progress is the great enigma of our
times. It is the central fact from which spring industrial, social, and political difficulties that perplex the world, and with which statesmanship
and philanthropy and education grapple in vain. * * *

I propose in the following pages to attempt to solve by the methods of
political economy the great problem I have outlined. I propose to seek the
law which associates poverty with progress, and increases want with advancing wealth; and I believe that in the explanation of this paradox we

shall find the explanation of those recurring seasons of industrial and commercial paralysis which, viewed independent of their relations to more general phenomena, seem so inexplicable. * * *

The term rent, in its economic sense—that is, when used, as I am using it, to distinguish that part of the produce which accrues to the owners of land or other natural capabilities by virtue of their ownership—differs in meaning from the word rent as commonly used. In some respects this economic meaning is narrower than the common meaning; in other respects it is wider.

It is narrower in this: In common speech, we apply the word rent to payments for the use of buildings, machinery, fixtures, etc., as well as to payments for the use of land or other natural capabilities; and in speaking of the rent of a house or the rent of a farm, we do not separate the price for the use of the improvements from the price for the use of the bare land. But in the economic meaning of rent, payments for the use of any of the products of human exertion are excluded, and of the lumped payments for the use of houses, farms, etc., only that part is rent which constitutes the consideration for the use of the land—that part paid for the use of buildings or other improvements being properly interest, as it is a consideration for the use of capital.

It is wider in this: In common speech we only speak of rent when owner and user are distinct persons. But in the economic sense there is also rent where the same person is both owner and user. Where owner and user are thus the same person, whatever part of his income he might obtain by letting the land to another is rent, while the return for his labor and capital are that part of his income which they would yield him did he hire instead of owning the land. Rent is also expressed in a selling price. When land is purchased, the payment which is made for the ownership, or right to perpetual use, is rent commuted or capitalized. If I buy land for a small price and hold it until I can sell it for a large price, I have become rich, not by wages for my labor or by interest upon my capital, but by the increase of rent. Rent, in short, is the share in the wealth produced which the exclusive right to the use of natural capabilities gives to the owner. Wherever land has an exchange value there is rent in the economic meaning of the term. Wherever land having a value is used, either by owner or hirer, there is rent actual; wherever it is not used, but still has a value, there is rent potential. It is this capacity of yielding rent which gives value to land. Until its ownership will confer some advantage, land has no value.

Thus rent or land value does not arise from the productiveness or utility of land. It in no wise represents any help or advantage given to production, but simply the power of securing a part of the results of production. No matter what are its capabilities, land can yield no rent and have no value until some one is willing to give labor or the results of labor for the privilege of using it; and what any one will thus give, depends not upon the capacity of the land, but upon its capacity as compared with that of land that can be had for nothing. I may have very rich land, but it will yield no rent and have no value so long as there is other land as good to be had without cost. But when this other land is appropriated, and the best land to be had for nothing is inferior, either in fertility, situation, or other quality, my land will begin to have a value and yield rent. And though the productiveness of my land may decrease, yet if the productiveness of the land to be had without charge decreases in greater proportion, the rent I can get, and consequently the value of my land, will steadily increase. Rent, in short, is the price of monopoly, arising from the reduction to individual ownership of natural elements which human exertion can neither produce nor increase. * * *

There is but one way to remove an evil—and that is, to remove its cause. Poverty deepens as wealth increases, and wages are forced down while productive power grows, because land, which is the source of all wealth and the field of all labor, is monopolized. To extirpate poverty, to make wages what justice commands they should be, the full earnings of the laborer, we must therefore substitute for the individual ownership of land a common ownership. Nothing else will go to the cause of the evil—in nothing else is there the slightest hope.

This, then, is the remedy for the unjust and unequal distribution of wealth apparent in modern civilization, and for all the evils which flow from it:

We must make land common property. * * *

If the remedy to which we have been led is the true one, it must be consistent with justice; it must be practicable of application; it must accord with the tendencies of social development, and must harmonize with other reforms. * * *

I thus propose to show that the laws of the universe do not deny the natural aspirations of the human heart; that the progress of society might be, and, if it is to continue, must be, toward equality, not toward inequality; and that the economic harmonies prove the truth perceived by the Stoic Emperor—

'We are made for co-operation—like feet, like hands, like eyelids, like the rows of the upper and lower teeth.'

* * *

When it is proposed to abolish private property in land the first question that will arise is that of justice. Though often warped by habit, superstititon, and selfishness into the most distorted forms, the sentiment of justice is yet fundamental to the human mind, and whatever dispute arouses the passions of men, the conflict is sure to rage, not so much as to the question 'Is it wise?' as to the question 'Is it right?' * * *

What constitutes the rightful basis of property? What is it that enables a man to justly say of a thing, 'It is mine!' From what springs the sentiment which acknowledges his exclusive right as against all the world? Is it not, primarily, the right of a man to himself, to the use of his own powers, to the enjoyment of the fruits of his own exertions? Is it not this individual right, which springs from and is testified to by the natural facts of individual organization—the fact that each particular pair of hands obey a particular brain and are related to a particular stomach; the fact that each man is definite, coherent, independent whole—which alone justifies individual ownership? As a man belongs to himself, so his labor when put in concrete form belongs to him.

And for this reason, that which a man makes or produces is his own, as against all the world—to enjoy or to destroy, to use, to exchange, or to give. No one else can rightfully claim it, and his exclusive right to it involves no wrong to any one else. Thus there is to everything produced by human exertion a clear and indisputable title to exclusive possession and enjoyment, which is perfectly consistent with justice, as it descends from the original producer, in whom it is vested by natural law. The pen with which I am writing is justly mine. No other human being can rightfully lay claim to it, for in me is the title of the producers who made it. It has become mine, because transferred to me by the stationer, to whom it was transferred by the importer, who obtained the exclusive right to it by transfer from the manufacturer, in whom, by the same process of purchase, vested the rights of those who dug the material from the ground and shaped it into a pen. Thus, my exclusive right of ownership in the pen springs from the natural right of the individual to the use of his own faculties. * * *

This right of ownership that springs from labor excludes the possibility of any other right of ownership. If a man be rightfully entitled to the produce of his labor, then no one can be rightfully entitled to the ownership of anything which is not the produce of his labor, or the labor of some one else from whom the right has passed to him. If production give to the producer the right to exclusive possession and enjoyment, there can rightfully be no exclusive possession and enjoyment of anything not the production of labor, and the recognition of private property in land is a wrong. For the right to produce of labor cannot be enjoyed without the right to the free use of the opportunities offered by nature, and to admit the right of property in these is to deny the right of property in the produce of labor. When non-producers can claim as rent a portion of the wealth created by producers, the right of the producers to the fruits of their labor is to that extent denied. * * *

The moment this distinction is realized, that moment is it seen that the sanction which natural justice gives to one species of property is denied to the other; that the rightfulness which attaches to individual property in the produce of labor implies the wrongfulness of individual property in land; that, whereas the recognition of the one places all men upon equal terms, securing to each the due reward of his labor, the recognition of the other is the denial of the equal rights of men, permitting those who do not labor to take the natural reward of those who do.

Whatever may be said for the institution of private property in land, it is therefore plain that it cannot be defended on the score of justice.

The equal right of all men to the use of land is as clear as their equal right to breathe the air—it is a right proclaimed by the fact of their existence. For we cannot suppose that some men have a right to be in this world and others no right. * * *

But a question of method remains. How shall we do it?

We should satisfy the law of justice, we should meet all economic requirements, by at one stroke abolishing all private titles, declaring all land public property, and letting it out to the highest bidders in lots to suit, under such conditions as would sacredly guard the private right to improvements.

Thus we should secure, in a more complex state of society, the same equality of rights that in a ruder state were secured by equal partitions of the soil, and by giving the use of the land to whoever could procure the most from it, we should secure the greatest production. * * *

But such a plan, though perfectly feasible, does not seem to me the best. Or rather I propose to accomplish the same thing in a simpler, easier, and quieter way, than that of formally confiscating all the land and formally letting it out to the highest bidders.

To do that would involve a needless shock to present customs and habits of thought—which is to be avoided.

To do that would involve a needless extension of governmental machinery—which is to be avoided.

I do not propose either to purchase or to confiscate private property in land. The first would be unjust; the second, needless. Let the individuals who now hold it still retain, if they want to, possession of what they are pleased to call *their* land. Let them continue to call it *their* land. Let them buy and sell, and bequeath and devise it. We may safely leave them the shell, if we take the kernel. *It is not necessary to confiscate land; it is only necessary to confiscate rent.* * * *

What I, therefore, propose, as the simple yet sovereign remedy, which will raise wages, increase the earnings of capital, extirpate pauperism, abolish poverty, give remunerative employment to whoever wishes it, afford free scope to human powers, lessen crime, elevate morals, and taste, and intelligence, purify government and carry civilization to yet nobler heights, is—*to appropriate rent by taxation.*

In this way, the State may become the universal landlord without calling herself so, and without assuming a single new function. In form, the ownership of land would remain just as now. No owner of land need be dispossessed, and no restriction need be placed upon the amount of land any one could hold. For, rent being taken by the State in taxes, land, no matter in whose name it stood, or in what parcels it was held, would be really common property, and every member of the community would participate in the advantages of its ownership.

Now, insomuch as the taxation of rent, or land values, must necessarily be increased just as we abolish other taxes, we may put the proposition into practical form by proposing—

To abolish all taxation save that upon land values. * * *

Experience has taught me (for I have been for some years endeavoring to popularize this proposition) that wherever the idea of concentrating all taxation upon land values finds lodgment sufficient to induce consideration, it invariably makes way, but that there are few of the classes most to be benefited by it, who at first, or even for a long time afterwards, see its full significance and power. It is difficult for workingmen to get over the idea that there is a real antagonism between capital and labor. It is difficult for small farmers and homestead owners to get over the idea that to put all taxes on the value of land would be to unduly tax them. It is difficult for both classes to get over the idea that to exempt capital from taxation would be to make the rich richer, and the poor poorer. These ideas spring from confused thought. But behind ignorance and prejudice there is a powerful interest, which has hitherto dominated literature, education, and opinion.

The reform I propose accords with all that is politically, socially, or morally desirable. It has the qualities of a true reform, for it will make all other reforms easier. What is it but the carrying out in letter and spirit of the truth enunciated in the Declaration of Independence—the 'self-evident' truth that is the heart and soul of the Declaration—'*That all men are created equal; that they are endowed by their Creator with certain inalienable rights; that among them are life, liberty, and the pursuit of happiness!*'

These rights are denied when the equal right to land—on which and by which men alone can live—is denied. Equality of political rights will not compensate for the denial of the equal right to the bounty of nature. Political liberty, when the equal right to land is denied, becomes, as population increases and invention goes on, merely the liberty to compete for employment at starvation wages. This is the truth that we have ignored. * * *

The fiat has gone forth! With steam and electricity, and the new powers born of progress, forces have entered the world that will either compel us to a higher plane or overwhelm us, as nation after nation, as civilization after civilization, have been overwhelmed before. It is the delusion which precedes destruction that sees in the popular unrest with which the civilized world is feverishly pulsing, only the passing effect of ephemeral causes. Between democratic ideas and the aristocratic adjustments of society there is an irreconcilable conflict. Here in the United States, as there in Europe, it may be seen arising. We cannot go on permitting men to vote and forcing them to tramp. We cannot go on educating boys and girls in our public schools and then refusing them the right to earn an honest living. We cannot go on prating of the inalienable rights of man and then denying the inalienable right to the bounty of the Creator. Even now, in old bottles the new wine begins to ferment, and elemental forces gather for the strife!

EDWARD BELLAMY

Looking Backward (1889)

The social critic Edward Bellamy (1850–1898) was an associate editor for the Springfield Union and an editorial writer for the New York Evening Post who advocated the nationalization of large industries and public services. His utopian novel Looking Backward was a popular and critical success, selling hundreds of thousands of copies in its first few years in print and inspiring the formation of over one hundred fifty "New Nationalist" clubs. In the novel, the protagonist Julian West reawakens in the year 2000 after falling asleep during the social strife of 1887. The two other main characters, Dr. Leete and his daughter Edith, tell him about America in 2000. It has a rational and egalitarian socialist system that provides for the needs of everyone and has replaced the ruthless competition of the Gilded Age with a spirit of solidarity and cooperation.

"I must know a little more about the sort of Boston I have come back to. You told me when we were upon the house-top that though a century only had elapsed since I fell asleep, it had been marked by greater changes in the conditions of humanity than many a previous millennium.

With the city before me I could well believe that, but I am very curious to know what some of the changes have been. To make a beginning somewhere, for the subject is doubtless a large one, what solution, if any, have you found for the labor question? It was the Sphinx's riddle of the nineteenth century, and when I dropped out the Sphinx was threatening to devour society, because the answer was not forthcoming. It is well worth sleeping a hundred years to learn what the right answer was, if, indeed, you have found it yet."

"As no such thing as the labor question is known nowadays," replied Dr. Leete, "and there is no way in which it could arise, I suppose we may claim to have solved it. Society would indeed have fully deserved being devoured if it had failed to answer a riddle so entirely simple. In fact, to speak by the book, it was not necessary for society to solve the riddle at all. It may be said to have solved itself. The solution came as the result of a process of industrial evolution which could not have terminated otherwise. All the society had to do was to recognize and cooperate with that evolution, when its tendency had become unmistakable."

"I can only say," I answered, "that at the time I fell asleep no such evolution had been recognized."

"It was in 1887 that you fell into this sleep, I think you said."

"Yes, May 30th, 1887."

* * *

"* * * The Bostonians of your day had the reputation of being great askers of questions, and I am going to show my descent by asking you one to begin with. What should you name as the most prominent feature of the labor troubles of your day?"

"Why, the strikes, of course," I replied.

"Exactly; but what made the strikes so formidable?"

"The great labor organizations."

"And what was the motive of these great organizations?"

"The workmen claimed they had to organize to get their rights from the big corporations," I replied.

"That is just it," said Dr. Leete; "the organization of labor and the strikes were an effect, merely, of the concentration of capital in greater masses than had ever been known before. Before this concentration began, while as yet commerce and industry were conducted by innumerable petty concerns with small capital, instead of a small number of great concerns with vast capital, the individual workman was relatively important and independent in his relations to the employer. Moreover, when a little capital or a new idea was enough to start a man in business for himself, workingmen were constantly becoming employers and there was no hard and fast line between the two classes. Labor unions were needless then, and general strikes out of the question. But when the era of small concerns with small capital was succeeded by that of the great aggregations of capital, all this was changed. The individual laborer, who had been relatively important to the small employer, was reduced to insignificance and powerlessness over against the great corporation, while at the same time the way upward to the grade of employer was closed to him. Self-defense drove him to union with his fellows.

"The records of the period show that the outcry against the concentration of capital was furious. Men believed that it threatened society with a form of tyranny more abhorrent than it had ever endured. They believed that the great corporations were preparing for them the yoke of a baser servitude than had ever been imposed on the race, servitude not to men but to soulless machines incapable of any motive but insatiable greed. Looking back, we cannot wonder at their desperation, for certainly humanity was never confronted with a fate more sordid and hideous than would have been the era of corporate tyranny which they anticipated.

"Meanwhile, without being in the smallest degree checked by the clamor against it, the absorption of business by ever larger monopolies continued. In the United States there was not, after the beginning of the last quarter of the century, any opportunity whatever for individual enterprise in any important field of industry, unless backed by a great capital. During the last decade of the century, such small businesses as still remained were fast-sailing survivals of a past epoch, or mere parasites on the great corporations, or else existed in fields too small to attract the great capitalists. Small businesses, as far as they still remained, were reduced to the condition of rats and mice, living in holes and corners, and counting on evading notice for the enjoyment of existence. The railroads had gone on combining till a few great syndicates controlled every rail in the land. In manufactories, every important staple was controlled by a syndicate. These syndicates, pools, trusts, or whatever their name, fixed prices and crushed all competition except when combinations as vast as themselves arose. Then a struggle, resulting in a still greater consolidation, ensued. The great city bazar crushed its country rivals with branch stores, and in the city itself absorbed its smaller rivals till the business of a whole quarter was concentrated under one roof, with a hundred former proprietors of shops serving as clerks. Having no business of his own to put his money in, the small capitalist, at the same time that he took service under the corporation, found no other investment for his money but its stocks and bonds, thus becoming doubly dependent upon it.

"The fact that the desperate popular opposition to the consolidation of business in a few powerful hands had no effect to check it proves that there must have been a strong economical reason for it. The small capitalists, with their innumerable petty concerns, had in fact yielded the field to the great aggregations of capital, because they belonged to a day of small things and were totally incompetent to the demands of an age of steam and telegraphs and the gigantic scale of its enterprises. To restore the former order of things, even if possible, would have involved returning to the day of stagecoaches. Oppressive and intolerable as was the regime of the great consolidations of capital, even its victims, while they cursed it, were forced to admit the prodigious increase of efficiency which had been imparted to the national industries, the vast economies effected by concentration of management and unity of organization, and to confess that since the new system had taken the place of the old the wealth of the world had increased at a rate before undreamed of. To be sure this vast increase had gone chiefly to make the rich richer, increasing the gap between them and the poor; but the fact remained that, as a means merely of producing wealth, capital had been proved efficient in proportion to its consolidation. The restoration of the old system with the subdivision of capital, if it were possible, might indeed bring back a greater equality of conditions, with more individual dignity and freedom, but it would be at the price of general poverty and the arrest of material progress.

"Was there, then, no way of commanding the services of the mighty wealth-producing principle of consolidated capital without bowing down to a plutocracy like that of Carthage? As soon as men began to ask themselves these questions, they found the answer ready for them. The movement toward the conduct of business by larger and larger aggregations of capital, the tendency toward monopolies, which had been so desperately and vainly resisted, was recognized at last, in its true significance, as a process which only needed to complete its logical evolution to open a golden future to humanity.

"Early in the last century the evolution was completed by the final consolidation of the entire capital of the nation. The industry and commerce of the country, ceasing to be conducted by a set of irresponsible corporations and syndicates of private persons at their caprice and for their profit, were intrusted to a single syndicate representing the people, to be conducted in the common interest for the common profit. The nation, that is to say, organized as the one great business corporation in which all other corporations were absorbed; it became the one capitalist in the place of all other capitalists, the sole employer, the final monopoly in which all previous and lesser monopolies were swallowed up, a monopoly in the profits and economies of which all citizens shared. The epoch of trusts had ended in The Great Trust. In a word, the people of the United States concluded to assume the conduct of their own business, just as one hundred odd years before they had assumed the conduct of their own government, organizing now for industrial purposes on precisely the same grounds that they had then organized for political purposes. At last, strangely late in the world's history, the obvious fact was perceived that no business is so essentially the public business as the industry and commerce on which the people's livelihood depends, and that to entrust it to private persons to be managed for private profit is a folly similar in kind, though vastly greater in magnitude, to that of surrendering the functions of political government to kings and nobles to be conducted for their personal glorification."

"Such a stupendous change as you describe," said I, "did not, of course, take place without great bloodshed and terrible convulsions."

"On the contrary," replied Dr. Leete, "there was absolutely no violence. The change had been long foreseen. Public opinion had become fully ripe for it, and the whole mass of the people was behind it. There was no more possibility of opposing it by force than by argument. On the other hand the popular sentiment toward the great corporations and those identified with them had ceased to be one of bitterness, as they came to realize their necessity as a link, a transition phase, in the evolution of the true industrial system. The most violent foes of the great private monopolies were now forced to recognize how invaluable and indispensable had been their office in educating the people up to the point of assuming control of their own business. Fifty years before, the consolidation of the industries of the country under national control would have seemed a very daring experiment to the most sanguine. But by a series of object lessons, seen and studied by all men, the great corporations had taught the people an entirely new set of ideas on this subject. They had seen for many years syndicates handling revenues greater than those of states, and directing the labors of hundreds of thousands of men with an efficiency and economy unattainable in smaller operations. It had come to be recognized as an axiom that the larger the business the simpler the principles that can be applied to it; that, as the machine is truer than the hand, so the system, which in a great concern does the work of the master's eye in a small business, turns out more accurate results. Thus it came about that, thanks to the corporations themselves, when it was proposed that the nation should assume their functions, the suggestion implied nothing which seemed impracticable even to the timid."

* * *

"Doctor," said I, in the course of our talk, "morally speaking, your social system is one which I should be insensate not to admire in comparison with any previously in vogue in the world, and especially with that of my own most unhappy century. If I were to fall into a mesmeric sleep to-night as lasting as that other, and meanwhile the course of time were to take a turn backward instead of forward, and I were to wake up again in the nineteenth century, when I had told my friends what I had seen, they would every one admit that your world was a paradise of order, equity, and felicity. But they were a very practical people, my contemporaries, and after expressing their admiration for the moral beauty and material splendor of the system, they would presently begin to cipher and ask how you got the money to make everybody so happy; for certainly, to support the whole nation at a rate of comfort, and even luxury, such as I see around me, must involve vastly greater wealth than the nation produced in my day. Now, while I could explain to them pretty nearly everything else of the main features of your system, I should quite fail to answer this question, and failing there, they would tell me, for they were very close cipherers, that I had been dreaming; nor would they ever believe anything else. In my day, I know that the total annual product of the nation, al-though it might have been divided with absolute equality, would not have come to more than three or four hundred dollars per head, not very much more than enough to supply the necessities of life with few or any of its comforts. How is it that you have so much more?"

"That is a very pertinent question, Mr. West," replied Dr. Leete, "and I should not blame your friends, in the case you supposed, if they declared your story all moonshine, failing a satisfactory reply to it. * * *

"Let us begin with a number of small items wherein we economize wealth as compared with you. We have no national, state, county, or mu-nicipal debts, or payments on their account. We have no sort of military or naval expenditures for men or materials, no army, navy, or militia. We have no revenue service, no swarm of tax assessors and collectors. As re-gards our judiciary, police, sheriffs, and jailors, the force which Massa-chusetts alone kept on foot in your day far more than suffices for the nation now. We have no criminal class preying upon the wealth of society as you had. The number of persons, more or less absolutely lost to the working force through physical disability, of the lame, sick, and debili-tated, which constituted such a burden on the able-bodied in your day, now that all live under conditions of health and comfort, has shrunk to scarcely perceptible proportions, and with every generation is becoming more completely eliminated.

"Another item wherein we save is the disuse of money and the thou-sand occupations connected with financial operations of all sorts, whereby an army of men was formerly taken away from useful employ-ments. Also consider that the waste of the very rich in your day on inor-dinate personal luxury has ceased, though, indeed, this item might easily be over-estimated. Again, consider that there are no idlers now, rich or poor,—no drones.

"A very important cause of former poverty was the vast waste of labor and materials which resulted from domestic washing and cooking, and the performing separately of innumerable other tasks to which we apply the cooperative plan.

"A larger economy than any of these—yes, of all together—is effected by the organization of our distributing system, by which the work done once by the merchants, traders, storekeepers, with their various grades of jobbers, wholesalers, retailers, agents, commercial travelers, and middle-men of all sorts, with an excessive waste of energy in needless transporta-tion and interminable handlings, is performed by one-tenth the number of hands and an unnecessary turn of not one wheel. Something of what our distributing system is like you know. Our statisticians calculate that one eightieth part of our workers suffices for all the processes of distribu-tion which in your day required one eighth of the population, so much being withdrawn from the force engaged in productive labor."

"I begin to see," I said, "where you get your greater wealth."

"The wastes which resulted from leaving the conduct of industry to ir-responsible individuals, wholly without mutual understanding or concert, were mainly four: first, the waste by mistaken undertakings; second, the waste from the competition and mutual hostility of those engaged in in-dustry; third, the waste by periodical gluts and crises, with the conse-quent interruptions of industry; fourth, the waste from idle capital and labor, at all times. Any one of these four great leaks, were all the others stopped, would suffice to make the difference between wealth and poverty on the part of a nation.

"Take the waste by mistaken undertakings, to begin with. In your day the production and distribution of commodities being without concert or organization, there was no means of knowing just what demand there was for any class of products, or what was the rate of supply. Therefore, any enterprise by a private capitalist was always a doubtful experiment. The projector having no general view of the field of industry and con-sumption, such as our government has, could never be sure either what the people wanted, or what arrangements other capitalists were making to supply them. In view of this, we are not surprised to learn that the chances were considered several to one in favor of the failure of any given business enterprise, and that it was common for persons who at last succeeded in making a hit to have failed repeatedly. If a shoemaker, for every pair of shoes he succeeded in completing, spoiled the leather of four or five pair, besides losing the time spent on them, he would stand about the same chance of getting rich as your contemporaries did with their system of private enterprise, and its average of four or five failures to one success.

"The next of the great wastes was that from competition. The field of industry was a battlefield as wide as the world, in which the workers wasted, in assailing one another, energies which, if expended in concerted effort, as today, would have enriched all. As for mercy or quarter in this warfare, there was absolutely no suggestion of it. To deliberately enter a field of business and destroy the enterprises of those who had occupied it previously, in order to plant one's own enterprise on their ruins, was an achievement which never failed to command popular admiration. Nor is there any stretch of fancy in comparing this sort of struggle with actual warfare, so far as concerns the mental agony and physical suffering which attended the struggle, and the misery which overwhelmed the defeated and those dependent on them. Now nothing about your age is, at first sight, more astounding to a man of modern times than the fact that men engaged in the same industry, instead of fraternizing as comrades and co-laborers to a common end, should have regarded each other as rivals and enemies to be throttled and overthrown. This certainly seems like sheer madness, a scene from bedlam. But more closely regarded, it is seen to be no such thing. Your contemporaries, with their mutual throat-cutting, knew very well what they were at. The producers of the nineteenth century were not, like ours, working together for the maintenance of the community, but each solely for his own maintenance at the expense of the community. If, in working to this end, he at the same time increased the aggregate wealth, that was merely incidental. It was just as feasible and as common to increase one's private hoard by practices injurious to the general welfare. One's worst enemies were necessarily those of his own trade, for, under your plan of making private profit the motive of production, a scarcity of the article he produced was what each particular producer desired. It was for his interest that no more of it should be produced than he himself could produce. To secure this consummation as far as circumstances permitted, by killing off and discouraging those engaged in his line of industry, was his constant effort. When he had killed off all he could, his policy was to combine with those he could not kill, and convert their mutual warfare into a warfare upon the public at large by cornering the market, as I believe you used to call it, and putting up prices to the highest point people would stand before going without the goods. The day dream of the nineteenth century producer was to gain absolute control of the supply of some necessity of life, so that he might keep the public at the verge of starvation, and always command famine prices for what he supplied. This, Mr. West, is what was called in the nineteenth century a system of production. I will leave it to you if it does not seem, in some of its aspects, a great deal more like a system for preventing production. Some time when we have plenty of leisure I am going to ask you to sit down with me and try to make me comprehend, as I never yet could, though I have studied the matter a great deal, how such shrewd fellows as your contemporaries appear to have been in many respects ever came to entrust the business of providing for the community to a class whose interest it was to starve it. I assure you that the wonder with us is, not that the world did not get rich under such a system, but that it did not perish outright from want. This wonder increases as we go on to consider some of the other prodigious wastes that characterized it.

"Apart from the waste of labor and capital by misdirected industry, and that from the constant bloodletting of your industrial warfare, your system was liable to periodical convulsions, overwhelming alike the wise and unwise, the successful cut-throat as well as his victim. I refer to the business crises at intervals of five to ten years, which wrecked the industries of the nation, prostrating all weak enterprises and crippling the strongest, and were followed by long periods, often of many years, of so-called dull times, during which the capitalists slowly regathered their dissipated strength while the laboring classes starved and rioted. Then would ensue another brief season of prosperity, followed in turn by another crisis and the ensuing years of exhaustion. As commerce developed, making the nations mutually dependent, these crises became world-wide, while the obstinacy of the ensuing state of collapse increased with the area affected by the convulsions, and the consequent lack of rallying centres. In proportion as the industries of the world multiplied and became complex, and the volume of capital involved was increased, these business cataclysms became more frequent, till, in the latter part of the nineteenth century, there were two years of bad times to one of good, and the system of industry, never before so extended or so imposing, seemed in danger of collapsing by its own weight. After endless discussions, your economists appear by that time to have settled down to the despairing conclusion that there was no more possibility of preventing or controlling these crises than if they had been drouths or hurricanes. It only remained to endure them as necessary evils, and when they had passed over to build up again the shattered structure of industry, as dwellers in an earthquake country keep on rebuilding their cities on the same site."

* * *

"In my day," I replied, "it was considered that the proper functions of government, strictly speaking, were limited to keeping the peace and defending the people against the public enemy, that is, to the military and police powers."

"And, in heaven's name, who are the public enemies?" exclaimed Dr. Leete. "Are they France, England, Germany, or hunger, cold, and nakedness? In your day governments were accustomed, on the slightest international misunderstanding, to seize upon the bodies of citizens and deliver them over by hundreds of thousands to death and mutilation, wasting their treasures the while like water; and all this oftenest for no imaginable profit to the victims. We have no wars now, and our governments no war powers, but in order to protect every citizen against hunger, cold, and nakedness, and provide for all his physical and mental needs, the function is assumed of directing his industry for a term of years. No, Mr. West, I am sure on reflection you will perceive that it was in your age, not in ours, that the extension of the functions of governments was extraordinary. Not even for the best ends would men now allow their governments such powers as were then used for the most maleficent."

"Leaving comparisons aside," I said, "the demagoguery and corruption of our public men would have been considered, in my day, insuperable objections to any assumption by government of the charge of the national industries. We should have thought that no arrangement could be worse than to entrust the politicians with control of the wealth-producing machinery of the country. Its material interests were quite too much the football of parties as it was."

"No doubt you were right," rejoined Dr. Leete, "but all that is changed now. We have no parties or politicians, and as for demagoguery and corruption, they are words having only an historical significance."

"Human nature itself must have changed very much," I said.

"Not at all," was Dr. Leete's reply, "but the conditions of human life have changed, and with them the motives of human action. The organization of society with you was such that officials were under a constant temptation to misuse their power for the private profit of themselves or others. Under such circumstances it seems almost strange that you dared entrust them with any of your affairs. Nowadays, on the contrary, society is so constituted that there is absolutely no way in which an official, however ill-disposed, could possibly make any profit for himself or any one else by a misuse of his power. Let him be as bad an official as you please, he cannot be a corrupt one. There is no motive to be. The social system no longer offers a premium on dishonesty. But these are matters which you can only understand as you come, with time, to know us better."

"But you have not yet told me how you have settled the labor problem. It is the problem of capital which we have been discussing," I said. "After the nation had assumed conduct of the mills, machinery, railroads, farms, mines, and capital in general of the country, the labor question still remained. In assuming the responsibilities of capital the nation had assumed the difficulties of the capitalist's position."

"The moment the nation assumed the responsibilities of capital those difficulties vanished," replied Dr. Leete. "The national organization of labor under one direction was the complete solution of what was, in your day and under your system, justly regarded as the insoluble labor problem. When the nation became the sole employer, all the citizens, by virtue of their citizenship, became employees, to be distributed according to the needs of industry."

"That is," I suggested, "you have simply applied the principle of universal military service, as it was understood in our day, to the labor question."

"Yes," said Dr. Leete, "that was something which followed as a matter of course as soon as the nation had become the sole capitalist. The people were already accustomed to the idea that the obligation of every citizen, not physically disabled, to contribute his military services to the defense of the nation was equal and absolute. That it was equally the duty of every citizen to contribute his quota of industrial or intellectual services to the maintenance of the nation was equally evident, though it was not until the nation became the employer of labor that citizens were able to render this sort of service with any pretense either of universality or equity. No organization of labor was possible when the employing power was divided among hundreds or thousands of individuals and corporations, between which concert of any kind was neither desired, nor indeed feasible. It constantly happened then that vast numbers who desired to labor could find no opportunity, and on the other hand, those who desired to evade a part or all of their debt could easily do so."

"Service, now, I suppose, is compulsory upon all," I suggested.

"It is rather a matter of course than of compulsion," replied Dr. Leete. "It is regarded as so absolutely natural and reasonable that the idea of its being compulsory has ceased to be thought of. He would be thought to be an incredibly contemptible person who should need compulsion in such a case. Nevertheless, to speak of service being compulsory would be a weak way to state its absolute inevitableness. Our entire social order is so wholly based upon and deduced from it that if it were conceivable that a man could escape it, he would be left with no possible way to provide for his existence. He would have excluded himself from the world, cut himself off from his kind, in a word, committed suicide."

"Is the term of service in this industrial army for life?"

"Oh, no; it both begins later and ends earlier than the average working period in your day. Your workshops were filled with children and old men, but we hold the period of youth sacred to education, and the period of maturity, when the physical forces begin to flag, equally sacred to ease and agreeable relaxation. The period of industrial service is twenty-four years, beginning at the close of the course of education at twenty-one and terminating at forty-five. After forty-five, while discharged from labor, the citizen still remains liable to special calls. In case of emergencies causing a sudden great increase in the demand for labor, till he reaches the age of fifty-five, but such calls are rarely, in fact almost never, made. The fifteenth day of October of every year is what we call Muster Day, because those who have reached the age of twenty-one are then mustered into the industrial service, and at the same time those who, after twenty-four years' service, have reached the age of forty-five, are honorably mustered out. It is the great day of the year with us, whence we reckon all other events, our Olympiad, save that it is annual. * * *

"You were surprised," [Dr. Leete] said, "at my saying that we got along without money or trade, but a moment's reflection will show that trade existed and money was needed in your day simply because the business of production was left in private hands, and that, consequently, they are superfluous now."

"I do not at once see how that follows," I replied.

"It is very simple," said Dr. Leete. "When innumerable different and independent persons produced the various things needful to life and comfort, endless exchanges between individuals were requisite in order that they might supply themselves with what they desired. These exchanges constituted trade, and money was essential as their medium. But as soon as the nation became the sole producer of all sorts of commodities, there was no need of exchanges between individuals that they might get what they required. Everything was procurable from one source, and nothing could be procured anywhere else. A system of direct distribution from the national storehouses took the place of trade, and for this money was unnecessary."

"How is this distribution managed?" I asked.

"On the simplest possible plan," replied Dr. Leete. "A credit corresponding to his share of the annual product of the nation is given to every citizen on the public books at the beginning of each year, and a credit card issued him with which he procures at the public storehouses, found in every community, whatever he desires whenever he desires it. This arrangement, you will see, totally obviates the necessity for business transactions of any sort between individuals and consumers. Perhaps you would like to see what our credit-cards are like.

"You observe," he pursued as I was curiously examining the piece of pasteboard he gave me, "that this card is issued for a certain number of dollars. We have kept the old word, but not the substance. The term, as we use it, answers to no real thing, but merely serves as an algebraical symbol for comparing the values of products with one another. For this purpose they are all priced in dollars and cents, just as in your day. The value of what I procure on this card is checked off by the clerk, who pricks out of these tiers of squares the price of what I order."

"If you wanted to buy something of your neighbor, could you transfer part of your credit to him as consideration?" I inquired.

"In the first place," replied Dr. Leete, "our neighbors have nothing to sell us, but in any event our credit would not be transferable, being strictly personal. Before the nation could even think of honoring any such transfer as you speak of, it would be bound to inquire into all the circumstances of the transaction, so as to be able to guarantee its absolute equity. It would have been reason enough, had there been no other, for abolishing money, that its possession was no indication of rightful title to it. In the hands of the man who had stolen it or murdered for it, it was as good as in those which had earned it by industry. People nowadays interchange gifts and favors out of friendship, but buying and selling is considered absolutely inconsistent with the mutual benevolence and disinterestedness which should prevail between citizens and the sense of community of interest which supports our social system. According to our ideas, buying and selling is essentially anti-social in all its tendencies. It is an education in self-seeking at the expense of others, and no society whose citizens are trained in such a school can possibly rise above a very low grade of civilization."

"What if you have to spend more than your card in any one year?" I asked.

"The provision is so ample that we are more likely not to spend it all," replied Dr. Leete. "But if extraordinary expenses should exhaust it, we can obtain a limited advance on the next year's credit, though this practice is not encouraged, and a heavy discount is charged to check it. Of course if a man showed himself a reckless spendthrift he would receive his allowance monthly or weekly instead of yearly, or if necessary not be permitted to handle it all."

"If you don't spend your allowance, I suppose it accumulates?"

"That is also permitted to a certain extent when a special outlay is anticipated. But unless notice to the contrary is given, it is presumed that the citizen who does not fully expend his credit did not have occasion to do so, and the balance is turned into the general surplus."

"Such a system does not encourage saving habits on the part of citizens," I said.

"It is not intended to," was the reply. "The nation is rich, and does not wish the people to deprive themselves of any good thing. In your day, men were bound to lay up goods and money against coming failure of the means of support and for their children. This necessity made parsimony a virtue. But now it would have no such laudable object, and, having lost its utility, it has ceased to be regarded as a virtue. No man any more has any care for the morrow, either for himself or his children, for the nation guarantees the nurture, education, and comfortble maintenance of every citizen from the cradle to the grave."

"That is a sweeping guarantee!" I said. "What certainty can there be that the value of a man's labor will recompense the nation for its outlay on him? On the whole, society may be able to support all its members, but some must earn less than enough for their support, and others more; and that brings us back once more to the wages question, on which you have hitherto said nothing. It was at just this point, if you remember, that our talk ended last evening; and I say again, as I did then, that here I should suppose a national industrial system like yours would find its main difficulty. How, I ask once more, can you adjust satisfactorily the comparative wages or renumeration of the multitude of avocations, so unlike and so incommensurable, which are necessary for the service of society? In our day the market rate determined the price of labor of all sorts, as well as of goods. The employer paid as little as he could, and the worker got as much. It was not a pretty system ethically, I admit; but it did, at least, furnish us a rough and ready formula for settling a question which must be settled ten thousand times a day if the world was ever going to get forward. There seemed to us no other practicable way of doing it."

"Yes," replied Dr. Leete, "it was the only practicable way under a system which made the interests of every individual antagonistic to those of every other; but it would have been a pity if humanity could never have devised a better plan, for yours was simply the application to the mutual relations of men of the devil's maxim, 'Your necessity is my opportunity.' The reward of any service depended not upon its difficulty, danger, or hardship, for throughout the world it seems that the most perilous, severe, and repulsive labor was done by the worst paid classes; but solely upon the strait of those who needed the service."

"All that is conceded," I said. "But, with all its defects, the plan of settling prices by the market rate was a practical plan; and I cannot conceive what satisfactory substitute you can have devised for it. The government being the only possible employer, there is of course no labor market or market rate. Wages of all sorts must be arbitrarily fixed by the government. I cannot imagine a more complex and delicate function than that must be, or one, however performed, more certain to breed universal dissatisfaction."

"I beg your pardon," replied Dr. Leete, "but I think you exaggerate the difficulty. Suppose a board of fairly sensible men were charged with settling the wages for all sorts of trades under a system which, like ours, guaranteed employment to all, while permitting the choice of avocations. Don't you see that, however unsatisfactory the first adjustment might be, the mistakes would soon correct themselves? The favored trades would have too many volunteers, and those discriminated against would lack them till the errors were set right. But this is aside from the purpose, for, though this plan would, I fancy, be practicable enough, it is no part of our system."

"How, then, do you regulate wages?" I once more asked.

Dr. Leete did not reply till after several moments of meditative silence. "I know, of course," he finally said, "enough of the old order of things to understand just what you mean by that question; and yet the present order is so utterly different at this point that I am a little at loss how to answer you best. You ask me how we regulate wages; I can only reply that there is no idea in the modern social economy which at all corresponds with what was meant by wages in your day."

"I suppose you mean that you have no money to pay wages in," said I. "But the credit given the worker at the government storehouse answers to his wages with us. How is the amount of the credit given respectively to the workers in different lines determined? By what title does the individual claim his particular share? What is the basis of allotment?"

"His title," replied Dr. Leete, "is his humanity. The basis of his claim is the fact that he is a man."

"The fact that he is a man!" I repeated, incredulously. "Do you possibly mean that all have the same share?"

"Most assuredly."

The readers of this book never having practically known any other arrangement, or perhaps very carefully considered the historical accounts of former epochs in which a very different system prevailed, cannot be expected to appreciate the stupor of amazement into which Dr. Leete's simple statement plunged me.

"You see," he said, smiling, "that it is not merely that we have no money to pay wages in, but, as I said, we have nothing at all answering to your idea of wages."

By this time I had pulled myself together sufficiently to voice some of the criticisms which, man of the nineteenth century as I was, came uppermost in my mind, upon this to me astounding arrangement. "Some men do twice the work of others!" I exclaimed. "Are the clever workmen content with a plan that ranks them with the indifferent?"

"We leave no possible ground for any complaint of injustice," replied Dr. Leete, "by requiring precisely the same measure of service from all."

"How can you do that, I should like to know, when no two men's powers are the same?"

"Nothing could be simpler," was Dr. Leete's reply. "We require of each that he shall make the same effort; that is, we demand of him the best service it is in his power to give."

"And supposing all do the best they can," I answered, "the amount of the product resulting is twice greater from one man than from another."

"Very true," replied Dr. Leete; "but the amount of the resulting product has nothing whatever to do with the question, which is one of desert. Desert is a moral question, and the amount of the product a material quantity. It would be an extraordinary sort of logic which should try to determine a moral question by a material standard. The amount of the effort alone is pertinent to the question of desert. All men who do their best, do the same. A man's endowments, however godlike, merely fix the measure of his duty. The man of great endowments who does not do all he might, though he may do more than a man of small endowments who does his best, is deemed a less deserving worker than the latter, and dies a debtor to his fellows. The Creator sets men's tasks for them by the faculties he gives them; we simply exact their fulfillment."

"No doubt that is very fine philosophy," I said; "nevertheless it seems hard that the man who produces twice as much as another, even if both do their best, should have only the same share."

"Does it, indeed, seem so to you?" responded Dr. Leete. "Now, do you know, that seems very curious to me? The way it strikes people nowadays is, that a man who can produce twice as much as another with the same effort, instead of being rewarded for doing so, ought to be punished if he does not do so. In the nineteenth century, when a horse pulled a heavier load than a goat, I suppose you rewarded him. Now, we should have whipped him soundly if he had not, on the ground that, being much stronger, he ought to. It is singular how ethical standards change." The doctor said this with such a twinkle in his eye that I was obliged to laugh.

"I suppose," I said, "that the real reason that we rewarded men for their endowments, while we considered those of horses and goats merely as fixing the service to be severally required of them, was that the animals, not being reasoning beings, naturally did the best they could, whereas men could only be induced to do so by rewarding them according to the amount of their product. That brings me to ask why, unless human nature has mightily changed in a hundred years, you are not under the same necessity."

"We are," replied Dr. Leete. "I don't think there has been any change in human nature in that respect since your duty. It is still so constituted that special incentives in the form of prizes, and advantages to be gained, are requisite to call out the best endeavors of the average man in any direction."

"But what inducement," I asked, "can a man have to put forth his best endeavors when, however much or little he accomplishes, his income remains the same? High characters may be moved by devotion to the common welfare under such a system, but does not the average man tend to rest back on his oar, reasoning that it is of no use to make a special effort, since the effort will not increase his income, nor its withholding diminish it?"

"Does it then really seem to you," answered my companion, "that human nature is insensible to any motives save fear of want and love of luxury, that you should expect security and equality of livelihood to leave them without possible incentives to effort? Your contemporaries did not really think so, though they might fancy they did. When it was a question of the grandest class of efforts, the most absolute self-devotion, they depended on quite other incentives. Not higher wages, but honor and the hope of men's gratitude, patriotism and the inspiration of duty, were the motives which they set before their soldiers when it was a question of dying for the nation, and never was there an age of the world when those motives did not call out what is best and noblest in men. And not only this, but when you come to analyze the love of money which was the general impulse to effort in your day, you find that the dread of want and desire of luxury was but one of several motives which the pursuit of money represented; the others, and with many the more influential, being desire of power, of social position, and reputation for ability and success. So you see that though we have abolished poverty and the fear of it, and inordinate luxury with the hope of it, we have not touched the greater part of the motives which underlay the love of money in former times, or any of those which prompted the supremer sorts of effort. The coarser motives, which no longer move us, have been replaced by higher motives wholly unknown to the mere wage earners of your age. Now that industry of whatever sort is no longer self-service, but service of the nation, patriotism, passion for humanity, impel the worker as in your day they did the soldier. The army of industry is an army, not alone by virtue of its perfect organization, but by reason also of the ardor of self-devotion which animates its members.

"But as you used to supplement the motives of patriotism with the love of glory, in order to stimulate the valor of your soldiers, so do we. Based as our industrial system is on the principle of requiring the same unit of effort from every man, that is, the best he can do, you will see that the means by which we spur the workers to do their best must be a very essential part of our scheme. With us, diligence in the national service is the sole and certain way to public repute, social distinction, and official power. The value of a man's services to society fixes his rank in it. Compared with the effect of our social arrangements in impelling men to be zealous in business, we deem the object-lessons of biting poverty and wanton luxury on which you depended a device as weak and uncertain as it was barbaric. The lust of honor even in your sordid day notoriously impelled men to more desperate effort than the love of money could."

HENRY DEMAREST LLOYD

Wealth Against Commonwealth (1894)

The socialist reformer Henry Demarest Lloyd (1847–1903) was a muckraking editor of the Chicago Tribune. *In his book-length indictment of the Standard Oil Company,* Wealth Against Commonwealth, *he describes the socially destructive effects of industrial monopolies. Rejecting the laissez-faire ideology of individual self-interest in favor of a political approach that acknowledges the interdependence of individuals, Lloyd warned of the "irrepressible conflict" between liberty and monopoly that confronted the nation.*

Nature is rich; but everywhere man, the heir of nature, is poor. Never in this happy country or elsewhere—except in the Land of Miracle, where "they did all eat and were filled"—has there been enough of anything for the people. Never since time began have all the sons and daughters of men been all warm, and all filled, and all shod and roofed. Never yet have all the virgins, wise or foolish, been able to fill their lamps with oil.

The world, enriched by thousands of generations of toilers and thinkers, has reached a fertility which can give every human being a plenty undreamed of even in the Utopias. But between this plenty ripening on the boughs of our civilization and the people hungering for it step the "cornerers," the syndicates, trusts, combinations, with the cry of "overproduction"—too much of everything. Holding back the riches of earth, sea, and sky from their fellows who famish and freeze in the dark, they declare to them that there is too much light and warmth and food. They assert the right, for their private profit, to regulate the consumption by the people of the necessaries of life, and to control production, not by the needs of humanity, but by the desires of a few for dividends. The coal syndicate thinks there is too much coal. There is too much iron, too much lumber, too much flour—for this or that syndicate.

The majority have never been able to buy enough of anything; but this minority have too much of everything to sell.

Liberty produces wealth, and wealth destroys liberty. "The splendid empire of Charles V," says Motley, "was erected upon the grave of liberty." Our bignesses—cities, factories, monopolies, fortunes, which are our empires, are the obesities of an age gluttonous beyond its powers of digestion. Mankind are crowding upon each other in the centers, and struggling to keep each other out of the feast set by the new sciences and the new fellowships. Our size has got beyond both our science and our conscience. The vision of the railroad stock-holder is not far-sighted enough to see into the office of the General Manager; the people cannot reach across even a ward of a city to rule their rulers; Captains of Industry "do not know" whether the men in the ranks are dying from lack of food and shelter; we cannot clean our cities nor our politics; the locomotive has more man-power than all the ballot-boxes, and mill-wheels wear out the hearts of workers unable to keep up beating time to their whirl. If mankind had gone on pursuing the ideals of the fighter, the time would necessarily have come when there would have been only a few, then only one, and then none left. This is what we are witnessing in the world of livelihoods. Our ideals of livelihood are ideals of mutual deglutition. We are rapidly reaching the stage where in each province only a few are left; that is the key to our times. Beyond the deep is another deep. This era is but a passing phase in the evolution of industrial Cæsars, and these Cæsars will be of a new type—corporate Cæsars.

For those who like the perpetual motion of a debate in which neither of the disputants is looking at the same side of the shield, there are infinite satisfactions in the current controversy as to whether there is any such thing as "monopoly." "There are none," says one side. "They are legion," says the other. "The idea that there can be such a thing is absurd," says one, who with half a dozen associates controls the source, the price, the quality, the quantity of nine-tenths of a great necessary of life. But "There will soon be a trust for every production, and a master to fix the price for every necessity of life," said the Senator who framed the United States Anti-Trust Law. This difference as to facts is due to a difference in the definitions through which the facts are regarded. Those who say "there are none" hold with the Attorney-General of the United States and the decision he quotes from the highest Federal court which had then passed on this question that no one has a monopoly unless there is a "disability" or "restriction" imposed by law on all who would compete. A syndicate that had succeeded in bottling for sale all the air of the earth would not have a monopoly in this view, unless there were on the statute-books a law forbidding every one else from selling air. No others could get air to sell; the people could not get air to breathe, but there would be no monopoly because there is no "legal restriction" on breathing or selling the atmosphere.

Excepting in the manufacture of postage-stamps, gold dollars, and a few other such cases of a "legal restriction," there are no monopolies according to this definition. It excludes the whole body of facts which the people include in their definition, and dismisses a great public question by a mere play on words. The other side of the shield was described by Judge Barrett, of the Supreme Court of New York. A monopoly he declared to be "any combination the tendency of which is to prevent competition in its broad and general sense, and to control and thus at will enhance prices to the detriment of the public. . . . Nor need it be permanent or complete. It is enough that it may be even temporarily and partially successful. The question in the end is, Does it inevitably tend to public injury?"

Those who insist that "there are none" are the fortunate ones who came up to the shield on its golden side. But common usage agrees with the language of Judge Barrett, because it exactly fits a fact which presses on common people heavily, and will grow heavier before it grows lighter.

The committee of Congress investigating trusts in 1889 did not report any list of these combinations to control markets, "for the reason that new ones are constantly forming, and that old ones are constantly extending their relations so as to cover new branches of the business and invade new territories."

It is true that such a list, like a dictionary, would begin to be wrong the moment it began to appear. But though only an instantaneous photograph of the whirlwind, it would give an idea, to be gained in no other way, of a movement shadowing two hemispheres. In an incredible number of the necessaries and luxuries of life, from meat to tombstones, some inner circle of the "fittest" has sought, and very often obtained, the sweet power which Judge Barrett found the sugar trust had. It "can close every refinery at will, close some and open others, limit the purchases of raw material (thus jeopardizing, and in a considerable degree controlling, its production), artificially limit the production of refined sugar, enhance the price to enrich themselves and their associates at the public expense, and depress the price when necessary to crush out and impoverish a foolhardy rival."

Corners are "acute" attacks of that which combinations exhibit as chronic. First a corner, then a pool, then a trust, has often been the genesis. The last stage, when the trust throws off the forms of combination and returns to the simpler dress of corporations, is already well along. Some of the "sympathetical co-operations" on record have no doubt ceased to exist. But that they should have been attempted is one of the signs of the time, and these attempts are repeated again and again until success is reached.

The line of development is from local to national, and from national to international. The amount of capital changes continually with the recrystallizations in progress. Not less than five hundred million dollars is in the coal combination, which our evidence shows to have flourished twenty-two years; that in oil has nearly if not quite two hundred millions; and the other combinations in which its members are leaders foot up hundreds of millions more. Hundreds of millions of dollars are united in the railroads and elevators of the Northwest against the wheat-growers. In cattle and meat there are not less than one hundred millions; in whiskey, thirty-five millions; and in beer a great deal more than that; in sugar, seventy-five millions; in leather, over a hundred millions; in gas, hundreds of millions. At this writing a union is being negotiated of all the piano-makers in the United States, to have a capital of fifty millions. Quite beyond ordinary comprehension is the magnitude of the syndicates, if there is more than one, which are going from city to city, consolidating all the gas works, electric-lighting companies, street-railways in each into single properties, and consolidating these into vast estates for central corporations of capitalists, controlling from metropolitan offices the transportation of the people of scores of cities. Such a syndicate negotiating in December, 1892, for the control of the street-railways of Brooklyn, was said by the New York *Times*, "on absolute authority, to have subscribed $23,000,000 towards that end, before a single move had been made or a price set on a single share of stock." It was in the same hands as those busy later in gathering together the coal-mines of Nova Scotia and putting them under American control. There are in round numbers ten thousand millions of dollars claiming dividends and interest in the railroads of the United States. Every year they are more closely pooled. The public saw them marshalled, as by one hand, in the maintenance of the high passenger rates to the World's Fair in the summer of 1893. Many rates are higher than thirty years ago.

Many thousands of millions of dollars are represented in these centralizations. It is a vast sum, and yet is but a minority of our wealth.

Laws against these combinations have been passed by Congress and by many of the States. There have been prosecutions under them by the State and Federal governments. The laws and the lawsuits have alike been futile.

In a few cases names and form of organization have been changed, in consequence of legal pursuit. The whiskey, sugar, and oil trusts had to hang out new signs. But the thing itself, the will and the power to control markets, livelihoods, and liberties, and the toleration of this by the public—this remains unimpaired; in truth, facilitated by the greater secrecy and compactness which have been the only results of the appeal to law.

The Attorney-General of the national government gives a large part of his annual report for 1893 to showing "what small basis there is for the popular impression" "that the aim and effect of this statute" (the Anti-Trust Law) "are to prohibit and prevent those aggregations of capital which are so common at the present day, and which sometimes are on so large a scale as to practically control all the branches of an extensive industry." This executive says of the action of the "co-ordinate" Legislature: "It would not be useful, even if it were possible, to ascertain the precise purposes of the framers of the statute." He is the officer charged with the duty of directing the prosecutions to enforce the law; but he declares that since, among other reasons, "all ownership of property is a monopoly, . . . any literal application of the provisions of the statute is out of the question." Nothing has been accomplished by all these appeals to the legislatures and the courts, except to prove that the evil lies deeper than any public sentiment or public intelligence yet existent, and is stronger than any public power yet at call.

What we call Monopoly is Business at the end of its journey. The concentration of wealth, the wiping out of the middle classes, are other names for it. To get it is, in the world of affairs, the chief end of man.

There are no solitary truths, Goethe says, and monopoly—as the greatest business fact of our civilization, which gives to business what other ages gave to war and religion—is our greatest social, political, and moral fact.

The men and women who do the work of the world have the right to the floor. Everywhere they are rising to "a point of information." They want to know how our labor and the gifts of nature are being ordered by those whom our ideals and consent have made Captains of Industry over us; how it is that we, who profess the religion of the Golden Rule and the political economy of service for service, come to divide our produce into incalculable power and pleasure for a few, and partial existence for the many who are the fountains of these powers and pleasures. This book is an attempt to help people answer these questions. It has been quarried out of official records, and it is a venture in realism in the world of realities. Decisions of courts and of special tribunals like the Interstate Commerce Commission, verdicts of juries in civil and criminal cases, reports of committees of the State Legislatures and of Congress, oath-sworn testimony given in legal proceedings and in official inquiries, corrected by rebutting testimony and by cross-examination—such are the sources of information.

* * *

We have given the prize of power to the strong, the cunning, the arithmetical, and we must expect nothing else but that they will use it cunningly and arithmetically. For what else can they suppose we gave it to them? If the power really flows from the people, and should be used for them; if its best administration can be got, as in government, only by the participation in it of men of all views and interests; if in the collision of all these, as in democracy, the better policy is progressively preponderant; if this is a policy which, with whatever defects, is better than that which can be evolved by narrower or more selfish or less multitudinous influences of persons or classes then this power should be taken up by the people. "The mere conflict of private interests will never produce a well-ordered commonwealth of labor," says the author of the article on political economy in the *Encyclopædia Britannica*. The failure of monarchy and feudalism and the visibly impending failure of our business system all reveal a law of nature. The harmony of things insists that that which is the source of power, wealth, and delight shall also be the ruler of it. That which is must also seem. It is the people from whom come the forces with which kings and millionaires ride the world, and until the people take their proper place in the seat of sovereignty, these pseudo owners—mere claimants and usurpers—will, by the very falsity and iniquity of their position, be pushed into deceit, tyranny, and cruelty, ending in downfall.

Thousands of years' experience has proved that government must begin where it ends—with the people; that the general welfare demands that they who exercise the powers and they upon whom these are exercised must be the same, and that higher political ideals can be realized only through higher political forms. Myriads of experiments to get the substance of liberty out of the forms of tyranny, to believe in princes, to trust good men to do good as kings, have taught the inexorable truth that, in the economy of nature, form and substance must move together, and are as inextricably interdependent as are, within our experience, what we call matter and spirit. Identical is the lesson we are learning with regard to industrial power and property. We are calling upon their owners, as mankind called upon kings in their day, to be good and kind, wise and sweet, and we are calling in vain. We are asking them not to be what we have made them to be. We put power into their hands and ask them not to use it as power. If this power is a trust for the people, the people betrayed it when they made private estates out of it for individuals. If the spirit of power is to change, institutions must change as much. Liberty recast the old forms of government into the Republic, and it must remould our institutions of wealth into the Commonwealth.

The question is not whether monopoly is to continue. The sun sets every night on a greater majority against it. We are face to face with the practical issue: Is it to go through ruin or reform? Can we forestall ruin by reform? If we wait to be forced by events we shall be astounded to find how much more radical they are than our utopias. Louis XVI waited until 1793, and gave his head and all his investitures to the people who in 1789 asked only to sit at his feet and speak their mind. Unless we reform of our own free will, nature will reform us by force, as nature does. Our evil courses have already gone too far in producing misery, plagues, hatreds, national enervation. Already the leader is unable to lead, and has begun to drive with judges armed with bayonets and Gatling guns. History is the serial obituary of the men who thought they could drive men.

Reform is the science and conscience with which mankind in its manhood overcomes temptations and escapes consequences by killing the germs. Ruin is already hard at work among us. Our libraries are full of the official inquiries and scientific interpretations which show how our master-motive is working decay in all our parts. The family crumbles into a competition between the father and the children whom he breeds to take his place in the factory, to unfit themselves to be fathers in their turn. A thorough, stalwart resimplification, a life governed by simple needs and loves, is the imperative want of the world. It will be accomplished: either self-conscious volition does it, or the slow wreck and decay of superfluous and unwholesome men and matters. The latter is the method of brutes and brute civilizations. The other is the method of man, so far as he is divine. Has not man, who has in personal reform risen above the brute method, come to the height at which he can achieve social reform in masses and by nations? We must learn; we can learn by reason. Why wait for the crueler teacher?

We have a people like which none has ever existed before. We have millions capable of conscious co-operation. The time must come in social evolution when the people can organize the free-will to choose salvation which the individual has been cultivating for 1900 years, and can adopt a policy more dignified and more effective than leaving themselves to be kicked along the path of reform by the recoil of their own vices. We must bring the size of our morality up to the size of our cities, corporations, and combinations, or these will be brought down to fit our half-grown virtue.

Industry and monopoly cannot live together. Our modern perfection of exchange and division of labor cannot last without equal perfection of morals and sympathy. Every one is living at the mercy of every one else in a way entirely peculiar to our times. Nothing is any longer made by a man; parts of things are made by parts of men, and become wholes by the luck of a good-humor which so far keeps men from flying asunder. It takes a whole company to make a match. A hundred men will easily produce a hundred million matches, but not one of them could make one match. No farm gets its plough from the cross-roads blacksmith, and no one in the chilled-steel factory knows the whole of the plough. The life of Boston hangs on a procession of reciprocities which must move, as steadily and sweetly as the roll of the planets, between its bakeries, the Falls of St. Anthony, and the valley of the Red River. Never was there a social machinery so delicate. Only on terms of love and justice can men endure contact so close.

The break-down of all other civilizations has been a slow decay. It took the Northerners hundreds of years to march to the Tiber. They grew their way through the old society as the tree planting itself on a grave is found to have sent its roots along every fibre and muscle of the dead. Our world is not the simple thing theirs was, of little groups sufficient to themselves, if need be. New York would begin to die to-morrow if it were not for Illinois and Dakota. We cannot afford a revulsion in the hearts by whose union locomotives run, mills grind, factories make. Practical men are speculating to-day on the possibility that our civilization may some afternoon be flashed away by the tick of a telegraph. All these co-operations can be scattered by a word of hate too many, and be left, with no one who knows how to make a plough or a match, a civilization cut off as by the Roman curse from food and fire. Less sensitive civilizations than ours have burst apart.

Liberty and monopoly cannot live together. What chance have we against the persistent coming and the easy coalescence of the confederated cliques, which aspire to say of all business, "This belongs to us," and whose members, though moving among us as brothers, are using against us, through the corporate forms we have given them, powers of invisibility, of entail and accumulation, unprecedented because impersonal and immortal, and, most peculiar of all, power to act as persons, as in the commission of crimes, with exemption from punishment as persons? Two classes study and practise politics and government: place hunters and privilege hunters. In a world of relativities like ours, size of area has a great deal to do with the truth of principles. America has grown so big— and the tickets to be voted, and the powers of government, and the duties of citizens, and the profits of personal use of public functions have all grown so big—that the average citizen has broken down. No man can half understand or half operate the fulness of this big citizenship, except by giving his whole time to it. This the place hunter can do, and the privilege hunter. Government, therefore—municipal, State, national—is passing into the hands of these two classes, specialized for the functions of power by their appetite for the fruits of power. The power of citizenship is relinquished by those who do not and cannot know how to exercise it to those who can and do—by those who have a livelihood to make to those who make politics their livelihood.

These specialists of the ward club, the primary, the campaign, the election, and office unite, by a law as irresistible as that of the sexes, with those who want all the goods of government—charters, contracts, rulings, permits. From this marriage it is easy to imagine that among some other people than ourselves, and in some other century than this, the offspring might be the most formidable, elusive, unrestrained, impersonal, and cruel tyranny the world has yet seen. There might come a time when the policeman and the railroad president would equally show that they cared nothing for the citizen, individually or collectively, because aware that they and not he were the government. Certainly such an attempt to corner "the dear people" and the earth and the fulness thereof will break down. It is for us to decide whether we will let it go on till it breaks down of itself, dragging down to die, as a savage dies of his vice, the civilization it has gripped with its hundred hands; or whether, while we are still young, still virtuous, we will break it down, self-consciously, as the civilized man, reforming, crushes down the evil. If we cannot find a remedy, all that we love in the word America must die. It will be an awful price to pay if this attempt at government of the people, by the people, for the people must perish from off the face of the earth to prove to mankind that political brotherhood cannot survive where industrial brotherhood is denied. But the demonstration is worth even that.

Aristotle's lost books of the Republics told the story of two hundred and fifty attempts at free government, and these were but some of the many that had to be melted down in the crucible of fate to teach Hamilton and Jefferson what they knew. Perhaps we must be melted by the same fierce flames to be a light to the feet of those who come after us. For as true as that a house divided against itself cannot stand, and that a nation half slave and half free cannot permanently endure, is it true that a people who are slaves to market-tyrants will surely come to be their slaves in all else, that all liberty begins to be lost when one liberty is lost, that a people half democratic and half plutocratic cannot permanently endure.

The secret of the history we are about to make is not that the world is poorer or worse. It is richer and better. Its new wealth is too great for the old forms. The success and beauties of our old mutualities have made us ready for new mutualities. The wonder of to-day is the modern multiplication of products by the union of forces; the marvel of to-morrow will be the greater product which will follow when that which is co-operatively produced is co-operatively enjoyed. It is the spectacle of its concentration in the private fortunes of our day which reveals this wealth to its real makers—the whole people—and summons them to extend the manners and institutions of civilization to this new tribal relation.

LESTER WARD

Sociocracy (1893)

The social scientist Lester Frank Ward (1841–1913) held a variety of posts in the federal government before becoming a professor of sociology at Brown University and the first president of the American Sociological Society in 1905. As a "reform Darwinist," Ward believed that the insights of sociology and education regarding "disinterested" and "strictly scientific" social laws would make it possible to plan a better society and promote social progress. "The individual has reigned long enough," he insisted. In response to proponents of individualistic, laissez-faire capitalism, Ward argued that the state could play a positive role as the protector of society to overcome social divisions. In his book Psychic Factors of Civilization, *he labeled this vision "sociocracy."*

Thus far attention has been chiefly confined to the science of society contemplated from the psychologic standpoint. But every applied science has its corresponding art. And although the social art is none other than this same government of which it has already been necessary to say so much, still, our social synthesis would be incomplete without some more special inquiry into the essential character of that art as a product of the combined consciousness, will, and intellect of society. Existing governments, it must be confessed, after all that can be said in their favor, realize this only to a very feeble extent. The social consciousness is as yet exceedingly faint, corresponding more nearly to that of a *cœnobium*, as in the *Flagellata* and *Ciliata*, than to any of the developed animal forms. The social will is, therefore, merely a mass of conflicting desires which largely neutralize one another and result in little advance movement in one settled direction. The social intellect proves a poor guide, not because it is not sufficiently vigorous, but because knowledge of those matters which principally concern society is so limited, while that which exists is chiefly lodged in the minds of those individuals who are allowed no voice in the affairs of state.

* * *

The general result is that the world, having passed through the stages of autocracy and aristocracy into the stage of democracy, has, by a natural reaction against personal power, so far minimized the governmental influence that the same spirit which formerly used government to advance self is now ushering in a fifth stage, viz., that of *plutocracy*, which thrives well in connection with a weak democracy or physiocracy, and aims to supersede it entirely. Its strongest hold is the widespread distrust of all government, and it leaves no stone unturned to fan the flame of misarchy. Instead of demanding more and stronger government it demands less and feebler. Shrewdly clamoring for individual liberty, it perpetually holds up the outrages committed by governments in their autocratic and aristocratic stages, and falsely insists that there is imminent danger of their reenactment. *Laissez faire* and the most extreme individualism, bordering on practical anarchy in all except the enforcement of existing proprietary rights, are loudly advocated, and the public mind is thus blinded to the real condition of things. The system of political economy that sprang up in France and England at the close of the aristocratic stage in those countries is still taught in the higher institutions of learning. It is highly favorable to the spread of plutocracy, and is pointed to by those who are to profit by that system of government as the invincible scientific foundation upon which it rests. Many honest political economists are still lured by the specious claims of this system and continue to uphold it, and at least one important treatise on social science, that of Herbert Spencer, defends it to the most extreme length. Thus firmly intrenched, it will require a titanic effort on the part of society to dislodge this baseless prejudice, and rescue itself once more from the rapacious jaws of human egoism under the crafty leadership of a developed and instructed rational faculty.

Under the system as it now exists the wealth of the world, however created, and irrespective of the claims of the producer, is made to flow toward certain centers of accumulation, to be enjoyed by those holding the keys to such situations. The world appears to be approaching a stage at which those who labor, no matter how skilled, how industrious, or how frugal, will receive, according to the "iron law" formulated by Ricardo, only so much for their services as will enable them "to subsist and to perpetuate their race." The rest finds its way into the hands of a comparatively few, usually non-producing, individuals, whom the usages and laws of all countries permit to claim that they own the very sources of all wealth and the right to allow or forbid its production.

These are great and serious evils, compared with which all the crimes, recognized as such, that would be committed if no government existed, would be as trifles. The underpaid labor, the prolonged and groveling drudgery, the wasted strength, the misery and squalor, the diseases resulting, and the premature deaths that would be prevented by a just distribution of the products of labor, would in a single year outweigh all the so-called crime of a century, for the prevention of which, it is said, government alone exists. This vast theater of woe is regarded as wholly outside the jurisdiction of government, while the most strenuous efforts are put forth to detect and punish the perpetrators of the least of the ordinary recognized crimes. This ignoring of great evils while so violently striking at small ones is the mark of an effete civilization, and warns us of the approaching dotage of the race.

Against the legitimate action of government in the protection of society from these worst of its evils, the instinctive hostility to government, or misarchy, above described, powerfully militates. In the face of it the government hesitates to take action, however clear the right or the method. But, as already remarked, this groundless over-caution against an impossible occurrence would not, in and of itself, have sufficed to prevent government from redressing such palpable wrongs. It has been nursed and kept alive for a specific purpose. It has formed the chief argument of those whose interests require the maintenance of the existing social order in relation to the distribution of wealth. Indeed, it is doubtful whether, without the incessant reiteration given to it by this class, it could have persisted to the present time. This inequitable economic system has itself been the product of centuries of astute management on the part of the shrewdest heads, with a view to securing by legal devices that undue share of the world's products which was formerly the reward of superior physical strength. It is clear to this class that their interests require a policy of strict non-interference on the part of government in what they call the natural laws of political economy, and they are quick to see that the old odium that still lingers among the people can be made a bulwark of strength for their position. They therefore never lose an opportunity to appeal to it in the most effective manner. Through the constant use of this *argumentum ad populum* the anti-government sentiment, which would naturally have smoldered and died out after its cause ceased to exist, is kept perpetually alive.

The great evils under which society now labors have grown up during the progress of intellectual supremacy. They have crept in stealthily during the gradual encroachment of organized cunning upon the domain of brute force. Over that vanishing domain, government retains its power, but it is still powerless in the expanding and now all-embracing field of psychic influence. No one ever claimed that in the trial of physical strength the booty should fall to the strongest. In all such cases the arm of government is stretched out and justice is enforced. But in those manifold, and far more unequal struggles now going on between mind and mind, or rather between the individual and an organized system, the product of ages of thought, it is customary to say that such matters must be left to regulate themselves, and that the fittest must be allowed to survive. Yet, to anyone who will candidly consider the matter, it must be clear that the first and principal acts of government openly and avowedly prevented, through forcible interference, the natural results of all trials of physical strength. These much-talked-of laws of nature are violated every time the highway robber is arrested and sent to jail.

Primitive government, when only brute force was employed, was strong enough to secure the just and equitable distribution of wealth. To-day, when mental force is everything, and physical force is nothing, it is powerless to accomplish this. This alone proves that government needs to be strengthened in its primary quality—the protection of society. There is no reasoning that applies to one kind of protection that does not apply equally to the other. It is utterly illogical to say that aggrandizement by physical force should be forbidden while aggrandizement by mental force or legal fiction should be permitted. It is absurd to claim that injustice committed by muscle should be regulated, while that committed by brain should be unrestrained.

While the modern plutocracy is not a form of government in the same sense that the other forms mentioned are, it is, nevertheless, easy to see that its power is as great as any government has ever wielded. The test of governmental power is usually the manner in which it taxes the people, and the strongest indictments ever drawn up against the worst forms of tyranny have been those which recited their oppressive methods of extorting tribute. But tithes are regarded as oppressive, and a fourth part of the yield of any industry would justify a revolt. Yet to-day there are many commodities for which the people pay two and three times as much as would cover the cost of production, transportation, and exchange at fair wages and fair profits. The monopolies in many lines actually tax the consumer from 25 to 75 per cent of the real value of the goods. Imagine an excise tax that should approach these figures! It was shown in Chap. XXXIII that under the operation of either monopoly or aggressive competition the price of everything is pushed up to the maximum limit that will be paid for the commodity in profitable quantities, and this wholly irrespective of the cost of production. No government in the world has now, or ever had, the power to enforce such an extortion as this. It is a governing power in the interest of favored individuals, which exceeds that of the most powerful monarch or despot that ever wielded a scepter.

What then is the remedy? How can society escape this last conquest of power by the egoistic intellect? It has overthrown the rule of brute force by the establishment of government. It has supplanted autocracy by aristocracy and this by democracy, and now it finds itself in the coils of plutocracy. Can it escape? Must it go back to autocracy for a power sufficient to cope with plutocracy? No autocrat ever had a tithe of that power. Shall it then let itself be crushed? It need not. There is one power and only one that is greater than that which now chiefly rules society. That power is society itself. There is one form of government that is stronger than autocracy or aristocracy or democracy, or even plutocracy, and that is *sociocracy*.

The individual has reigned long enough. The day has come for society to take its affairs into its own hands and shape its own destinies. The individual has acted as best he could. He has acted in the only way he could. With a consciousness, will, and intellect of his own he could do nothing else than pursue his natural ends. He should not be denounced nor called any names. He should not even be blamed. Nay, he should be praised, and even *imitated*. Society should learn its great lesson from him, should follow the path he has so clearly laid out that leads to success. It should imagine itself an individual, with all the interests of an individual, and becoming fully *conscious* of these interests it should pursue them with the same indomitable *will* with which the individual pursues his interests. Not only this, it must be guided, as he is guided, by the social *intellect*, armed with all the knowledge that all individuals combined, with so great labor, zeal, and talent have placed in its possession, constituting the social intelligence.

Sociocracy will differ from all other forms of government that have been devised, and yet that difference will not be so radical as to require a revolution. Just as absolute monarchy passed imperceptibly into limited monarchy, and this, in many states without even a change of name has passed into more or less pure democracy, so democracy is capable of passing as smoothly into sociocracy, and without taking on this unfamiliar name or changing that by which it is now known. For, though paradoxical, democracy, which is now the weakest of all forms of government, at least in the control of its own internal elements, is capable of becoming the strongest. Indeed, none of the other forms of government would be capable of passing directly into a government by society. Democracy is a phase through which they must first pass on any route that leads to the ultimate social stage which all governments must eventually attain if they persist.

How then, it may be asked, do democracy and sociocracy differ? How does society differ from the people? If the phrase "the people" really meant the people, the difference would be less. But that shibboleth of democratic states, where it means anything at all that can be described or defined, stands simply for the majority of qualified electors, no matter how small that majority may be. There is a sense in which the action of a majority may be looked upon as the action of society. At least, there is no denying the right of the majority to act for society, for to do this would involve either the denial of the right of government to act at all, or the admission of the right of a minority to act for society. But a majority acting for society is a different thing from society acting for itself, even though, as must always be the case, it acts through an agency chosen by its members. All democratic governments are largely party governments. The electors range themselves on one side or the other of some party line, the winning side considers itself the state as much as Louis the Fourteenth did. The losing party usually then regards the government as something alien to it and hostile, like an invader, and thinks of nothing but to gain strength enough to overthrow it at the next opportunity. While various issues are always brought forward and defended or attacked, it is obvious to the looker-on that the contestants care nothing for these, and merely use them to gain an advantage and win an election.

From the standpoint of society this is child's play. A very slight awakening of the social consciousness will banish it and substitute something more business-like. Once get rid of this puerile gaming spirit and have attention drawn to the real interests of society, and it will be seen that upon nearly all important questions all parties and all citizens are agreed, and that there is no need of this partisan strain upon the public energies. This is clearly shown at every change in the party complexion of the government. The victorious party which has been denouncing the government merely because it was in the hands of its political opponents boasts that it is going to revolutionize the country in the interest of good government, but the moment it comes into power and feels the weight of national responsibility it finds that it has little to do but carry out the laws in the same way that its predecessors had been doing.

There is a vast difference between all this outward show of partisanship and advocacy of so-called principles, and attention to the real interests and necessary business of the nation, which latter is what the government must do. It is a social duty. The pressure which is brought to enforce it is the power of the social will. But in the factitious excitement of partisan struggles where professional politicians and demagogues on the one hand, and the agents of plutocracy on the other, are shouting discordantly in the ears of the people, the real interests of society are, temporarily at least, lost sight of, clouded and obscured, and men lose their grasp on the real issues, forget even their own best interests, which, however selfish, would be a far safer guide, and the general result usually is that these are neglected and nations continue in the hands of mere politicians who are easily managed by the shrewd representatives of wealth.

LESTER WARD

Plutocracy and Paternalism (1895)

In a Forum article on what he considered the actual, as opposed to the popular or demagogic, meanings of plutocracy and paternalism, the sociologist Ward explained that the function of government is to protect the weak and prevent injustices. The problem in modern society, he said, was not too much government, as the proponents of laissez-faire capitalism claimed, but "undergovernment."

To judge from the tone of the popular press, the country would seem to be between the devil of state interference and the deep sea of gold. The two epithets, 'plutocracy' and 'paternalism,' so freely applied, are intended to characterize the worst tendencies of the times in these two opposite directions, and are calculated to engender the bitterest feelings in the public mind. If such a thing were possible, it would certainly be useful, standing aloof from the contest, to make a cool, unbiased analysis of the true meaning of these terms in their relation to the existing state of affairs. * * *

Justly or unjustly, society has made wealth a measure of worth. It is easy on general principles to prove that it is not such a measure. Every one is personally cognizant of numerous cases to the contrary. All will admit that, taken in the abstract, the principle is unsound, and yet all act upon it. Not rationally, not perhaps consciously, but still they do it. It is 'human nature' to respect those who have, and to care little for those who have not. There is a sort of feeling that if one is destitute there must be a reason for it. It is inevitably ascribed to some personal deficit. In a word, absence of means is, in one form or another, made to stand for absence of merit. Its cause is looked for in character. This is most clearly seen in the marked contrast between the indisposition to help the unsuccessful, and the willingness to help the successful. Aside from the prospect of a quid pro quo, no one wants to waste time, energy, or money on what is worthless,—and possession is the primary test of worth. * * *

Thus it comes about that wealth, in the existing state of society, is a tremendous power. It gives not only ease, plenty, luxury, but, what is infinitely more, the respect of all and the envy of the less favored. It gives, in a word, superiority; and the strongest craving of man's nature is, in one way or another, to be set over his fellows. When all this is considered, the futility of the proposal of certain reformers to eradicate the passion for proprietary acquisition becomes apparent. It may be assumed that this passion will continue for an indefinite period to be the ruling element of the industrial state. That it has done and is still doing incalculable service to society few will deny. That it may continue to be useful to the end of our present industrial era will probably be admitted by all but a small class. * * *

So much for plutocracy. Let us now turn to the other pole of public opinion and inquire into the meaning of 'paternalism.' Literally, of course, paternalism in government would be restricted to cases in which the governing power is vested in a single person, who may be regarded as well-disposed and seeking to rule his subjects for their own good, as a father governs his children. But a ruling family, or even a large ruling class, may be supposed to govern from similar motives. In either case the governed are not supposed to have any voice in the matter, but are cared for like children by the assumed wisdom of their rulers. How far from true paternalism is anything that exists in this or any other civilized country to-day may therefore be readily seen. No one will claim that there is any danger, in a representative government with universal suffrage, of any such state being brought about. This shows at the outset that the term is not used in its original and correct sense, but is merely borrowed and applied as a stigma to certain tendencies in republican governments which the users of it do not approve. What are these tendencies? In general it may be said that they are tendencies toward the assumption by the state of functions that are now entrusted to private enterprise.

On the one hand it is logically argued that the indefinite extension of such powers would eventuate in the most extreme socialistic system,— the conduct of all business by the state. On the other hand it is shown with equal logic that the entire relinquishment of the functions which the state has already assumed would be the abolition of government itself. The extremists of one party would land us in socialism; those of the other, in anarchy. But on one side it is said by the more moderate that the true function of government is the protection of society; to which it is replied by the other that such extension of governmental powers is in the interest of protection, viz., protection against the undue rapacity of private enterprise. Here, as almost everywhere else in the realm of politics, it is a question of quantity and not of quality. It is not a difference in principle, but in policy. It is the degree to which the fundamental principle of all government is to be carried out.

If we look for precedents and historical examples we find great diversity. If we take the question of government telegraphy we find that the United States is almost the only country in the civilized world that has not adopted it, while the reports from other countries are practically unanimous in its favor. That such a movement should be called paternalism is therefore quite gratuitous, and must spring from either pecuniary interest or unenlightened prejudice. From this on, up to the question of abolishing the private ownership of land, there is a multitude of problems presenting all shades of difference in the degree to which the principle of state action is to be applied in their solution. They need to be fearlessly investigated, coolly considered, and wisely decided in the true interests of the public. It was not the purpose of this article to discuss any of these questions, but simply to mention them in illustration of the popular use of the term 'paternalism.' It is clear that that term is employed solely to excite prejudice against the extension of the functions of the state, just as the term 'plutocracy' is used to arouse antagonism to the wealthy classes. The words have in these senses no natural meaning, and, with intelligent persons, should have no argumentative weight.

Are there, then, no dangerous or deleterious tendencies in modern society? There certainly are such, and they may be said to be in the direction of both plutocracy and paternalism, giving to these terms not a literal, but a real or scientific meaning, as denoting respectively the too great power of wealth, and the too great solicitude for and fostering of certain interests on the part of government.

The first law of economics is that every one may be depended upon at all times to seek his greatest gain. It is both natural and right that the individual should be ever seeking to acquire for himself and his; and this rather irrespective of the rest of the world. It was so in the olden time, when physical strength was almost the only force. It is so to-day, when business shrewdness is practically supreme. Government was instituted to protect the weak from the strong in this universal struggle to possess; or, what is the same thing, to protect society at large. Originally it was occupied solely with abuses caused by brute force. It is still, so far as this primary function of enforcing justice is concerned, practically limited to this class of abuses, relatively trifling as they are. Crime still means this, as it did in the days of King Arthur, and as it does to-day in barbaric countries. Any advantage gained by force is promptly met by the law; but advantage

gained by cunning, by superior knowledge,—if it be only of the technical-
ities of the law,—is not a crime, though its spirit be as bad as that of highway robbery and its consequences a thousand times worse.

From this point of view, then, modern society is suffering from the
very opposite of paternalism,—from undergovernment, from the failure
of government to keep pace with the change which civilization has
wrought in substituting intellectual for physical qualities as the workers
of injustice. Government to-day is powerless to perform its primary and
original function of protecting society. There was a time when brigandage
stalked abroad throughout Europe and no one was safe in life or property.
This was due to lack of adequate government. Man's nature has not
changed, but brigandage has succumbed to the strong arm of the law.
Human rapacity now works in subtler ways. Plutocracy is the modern
brigandage and can be dislodged only by the same power,—the power of
the state. All the evils of society are the result of the free flow of natural
propensities. The purpose of government is, as far as may be, to prevent
this from causing injustice. The physical passions of men are natural and
healthy, but they cannot be allowed to go unbridled. Government was established, not to lessen or even to alter them. Exactly the same is needed
to be done with the higher acquisitive faculty. It need not be condemned;
it cannot be suppressed: but it can and should be directed into harmless
ways and restricted to useful purposes. Properly viewed, too, this is to secure its maximum exercise and greatest freedom, for unrestrained license
soon leads to conflict, chokes its own free operation, and puts an end to
its activity. The true function of government is not to fetter but to liberate
the forces of society, not to diminish but to increase their effectiveness.
Unbridled competition destroys itself. The only competition that endures
is that which goes on under judicious regulations.

If, then, the danger of plutocracy is so largely due to insufficient government, where is the tendency to paternalism in the sense of too much
government? This opens up the last and most important aspect of the
subject. If there were no influences at work in society but those of unaided nature; if we had a pure physiocracy or government of nature, such
as prevails among wild animals, and the weak were thereby sacrificed that
the strong might survive to beget the strong, and thus elevate the race
along the lines of evolution,—however great the hardship, we might resign ourselves to it as part of the great cosmic scheme. But unfortunately
this is not the case. Without stopping to show that, from the standpoint
of a civilized society, the qualities which best fit men to gain advantage
over their fellows are the ones least useful to society at large, it will be
sufficient for the present purpose to point out that in the actual state of
society it is not even those who, from this biological point of view, are the

fittest, that become in fact the recipients of the greatest favors at the hands of society. This is due to the creation, by society itself, of artificial conditions that destroy the balance of forces and completely nullify all the beneficial effects that are secured by the operation of the natural law on the lower plane. Indeed, the effect is reversed, and instead of developing strength, either physical or mental, through activity incident to emulation, it tends to parasitic degeneracy through the pampered idleness of the favored classes.

What, in the last analysis, are these social conditions? They are at bottom integral parts of government. They are embodied in law. Largely they consist of statute law. Where this is wanting they rest on judicial decisions, often immemorial, and belonging to the *lex non scripta*. In a word, they constitute the great system of jurisprudence relating to property and business, gradually built up through the ages to make men secure in their possessions and safe in their business transactions, but which in our day, owing to entirely changed industrial conditions, has become the means of throwing unlimited opportunities in the way of some and of barring out the rest from all opportunities. This system of artificial props, bolsterings, and scaffoldings has grown so perfect as to make exertion needless for the protected class and hopeless for the neglected mass. * * *

And thus we have the remarkable fact, so persistently overlooked in all the discussions of current question, that government, which fails to protect the weak, is devoting all its energies to protecting the strong. It legalizes and promotes trusts and combinations; subsidizes corporations, and then absolves them from their obligations; sustains stockwatering schemes and all forms of speculation; grants without compensation the most valuable franchises, often in perpetuity; and in innumerable ways creates, defends, and protects a vast array of purely parasitic enterprises, calculated directly to foster the worst forms of municipal corruption. The proofs of each one of these counts lie about us on every hand. Only those who are blinded by interest or prejudice can fail to see them.

There is no greater danger to civilization than the threatened absorption by a few individuals of all the natural resources of the earth, so that they can literally extort tribute from the rest of mankind. If half a dozen persons could get possession of all the breadstuffs of a country, it would justify a revolution. Fortunately, from the nature of this product, this is impossible, although long strides in that direction have from time to time been taken. But it is otherwise with some other products which, if less indispensable, are still among the modern necessaries of life. All the petroleum of this country is owned by a single trust. If men could not live without it there is no telling how high the price would be raised. Nothing limits it but the question of how much the public will pay rather than do without. That indispensable product, coal, has well-nigh reached the same stage through the several railroad combinations that now control it. That which costs sixty cents to mine, and as much more to transport, cannot be obtained by the consumer for less than five or six dollars. Does it speak well for the common sense of a great people that they should continue to submit to such things? There seems to be no remedy except in the power of the nation. * * *

The very possession of wealth is only made possible by government. The safe conduct of all business depends upon the certain protection of law. The most powerful business combinations take place under legal forms. Even dishonest and swindling schemes, so long as they violate no penal statute, are protected by law. Speculation in the necessaries of life is legitimate business, and is upheld by the officers of the law though it result in famine; and even then bread riots are put down by the armed force of the state. Thus has society become the victim of its own system, against the natural effects of which it is powerless to protect itself. It has devised the best possible scheme for satisfying the rapacity of human nature.

And now, mark: The charge of paternalism is chiefly made by the class that enjoys the largest share of government protection. Those who denounce state interference are the ones who most frequently and successfully invoke it. The cry of laisscz-faire mainly goes up from the ones who, if really 'let alone,' would instantly lose their wealth-absorbing power. * * *

Nothing is more obvious to-day than the signal inability of capital and private enterprise to take care of themselves unaided by the state; and while they are incessantly denouncing 'paternalism,'—by which they mean the claim of the defenceless laborer and artisan to a share in this lavish state protection,—they are all the while besieging legislatures for relief from their own incompetency, and 'pleading the baby act' through a trained body of lawyers and lobbyists. The dispensing of national pap to this class should rather be called 'maternalism,' to which a square, open, and dignified paternalism would be infinitely preferable.

Still all these things must be regarded as perfectly natural, that is, inherent in the nature of man, and not as peculiar to any class. Therefore personalities and vituperation are entirely out of place. It is simply a question of whether they are going to be permitted to go on. The fault is altogether with the system. Nor should any one object to state protection of business interests. Even monopoly may be defended against aggressive competition on the ground of economy. The protection of the strong may not be too great, but there should be at the same time protection of the weak against the protected strong. It is not the purpose of this article to point out remedies, but tendencies, and it seems clear that right here are to be located the two greatest dangers to modern society. Here lies the only plutocracy, and here the only paternalism. The two are really one, and are embodied in the joint fact of state-protected monopoly.

IGNATIUS DONNELLY

Caesar's Column: A Story of the Twentieth Century (1891)

The novelist and social reformer Ignatius Donnelly (1831–1901) was a Republican congressman and the lieutenant governor of Minnesota before he became involved in political parties that promoted the interests of farmers and laborers. A sharp critic of bankers and financiers, Donnelly helped establish the Populist Party in 1892. In Caesar's Column, a utopian novel set in 1988, Donnelly depicted America as an oligarchical society with a large, impoverished working class. This futuristic novel offers government intervention organized on the principles of Christian socialism as a remedy for the dangerous concentrations of wealth and poverty that afflicted nineteenth-century America. As in much of Populist rhetoric, anti-Semitism and racism are readily at hand.

"Each generation found the condition of things more desperate and hopeless; every year multiplied the calamities of the world. The fools could not see that a great cause must continue to operate until checked by some higher power. And here there was no higher power that desired to check it. As the domination and arrogance of the ruling class increased, the capacity of the lower classes to resist, within the limits of law and constitution, decreased. Every avenue, in fact, was blocked by corruption. Juries, courts, legislatures, congresses, they were as if they were not. The people were walled in by impassable barriers. Nothing was left them but the primal, brute instincts of the animal man, and upon these they fell back, and the Brotherhood of Destruction arose. But no words can tell the sufferings that have been endured by the good men, here and there, who, during the past century, tried to save mankind. Some were simply ostracized from social intercourse with their caste; others were deprived of their means of living and forced down into the ranks of the wretched; and still others"—and here, I observed, his face grew ashy pale, and the muscles about his mouth twitched nervously— "still others had their liberty sworn away by purchased perjury, and were consigned to prisons, where they still languish, dressed in the hideous garb of ignominy, and performing the vile tasks of felons." After a pause, for I saw he was strangely disturbed, I said to him:

"How comes it that the people have so long submitted to these great wrongs? Did they not resist?"

"They did," he replied; "but the fruit of the tree of evil was not yet ripe. At the close of the nineteenth century, in all the great cities of America, there was a terrible outbreak of the workingmen; they destroyed much property and many lives, and held possession of the cities for several days. But the national government called for volunteers, and hundreds of thousands of warlike young men, sons of farmers, sprang to arms; and, after several terrible battles, they suppressed the revolution, with the slaughter of tens of thousands of those who took part in it; while afterwards the revengeful Oligarchy sent thousands of others to the gallows. And since then, in Europe and America, there have been other outbreaks, but all of them terminated in the same way. The condition of the world has, however, steadily grown worse and worse; the laboring classes have become more and more desperate. The farmers' sons could, for generations, be counted upon to fight the workmen; but the fruit has been steadily ripening. Now the yeomanry have lost possession of their lands; their farms have been sold under their feet; cunning laws transferred the fruit of their industry into the pockets of great combinations, who loaned it back to them again, secured by mortgages; and, as the pressure of the same robbery still continued, they at last lost their homes by means of the very wealth they had themselves produced. Now a single nabob owns a whole county; and a state is divided between a few great loan associations; and the men who once tilled the fields, as their owners, are driven to the cities to swell the cohorts of the miserable, or remain on the land a wretched peasantry, to contend for the means of life with vile hordes of Mongolian coolies. And all this in sight of the ruins of the handsome homes their ancestors once occupied! Hence the materials for armies have disappeared. Human greed has eaten away the very foundations on which it stood. And of the farmers who still remain nearly all are now members of our Brotherhood. When the Great Day comes, and the nation sends forth its call for volunteers, as in the past, that cry will echo in desolate places; or it will ring through the triumphant hearts of savage and desperate men who are hastening to the banquet of blood and destruction. And the wretched, yellow, under-fed coolies, with women's garments over their effeminate limbs, will not have the courage or the desire or the capacity to make soldiers and defend their oppressors."

"But have not the Oligarchy standing armies?" I asked.

"Yes. In Europe, however, they have been constrained, by inability to wring more taxes from the impoverished people, to gradually diminish their numbers. There, you know, the real government is now a coterie of bankers, mostly Israelites; and the kings and queens, and so-called presidents, are mere toys and puppets in their hands. All idea of national glory, all chivalry, all pride, all battles for territory or supremacy have long since ceased. Europe is a banking association conducted exclusively for the benefit of the bankers. Bonds take the place of national aspirations. To squeeze the wretched is the great end of government; to toil and submit, the destiny of the peoples.

"The task which Hannibal attempted, so disastrously, to subject the Latin and mixed-Gothic races of Europe to the domination of the Semitic blood, as represented in the merchant-city of Carthage, has been successfully accomplished in these latter days by the cousins of the Phœnicians, the Israelites. The nomadic children of Abraham have fought and schemed their way, through infinite depths of persecution, from their tents on the plains of Palestine, to a power higher than the thrones of Europe. The world is today Semitized. The children of Japheth lie prostrate slaves at the feet of the children of Shem; and the sons of Ham bow humbly before their august dominion.

"The standing armies of Europe are now simply armed police; for, as all the nations are owned by one power—the money power—there is no longer any danger of their assaulting each other. But in the greed of the sordid commercial spirit which dominates the continent they have reduced, not only the numbers, but the pay of the soldiers, until it is little better than the compensation earned by the wretched peasantry and the mechanics; while years of peace and plunder have made the rulers careless and secure. Hence our powerful association has spread among these people like wild-fire: the very armies are honeycombed with our ideas, and many of the soldiers belong to the Brotherhood.

"Here, in America, they have been wise enough to pay the soldiers of their standing army better salaries; and hence they do not so readily sympathize with our purposes. But we outnumber them ten to one, and do not fear them. * * *

"You are right," I replied; "there is nothing that will insure permanent peace but universal justice; that is the only soil that grows no poisons. Universal justice means equal opportunities for all men and a repression by law of those gigantic abnormal selfishnesses which ruin millions for the benefit of thousands. In the old days selfishness took the form of conquest, and the people were reduced to serfs. Then, in a later age, it assumed the shape of individual robbery and murder. Laws were made against these crimes. Then it broke forth in the shape of subtle combinations, 'rings,' or 'trusts,' as they called them, corporations, and all the other cunning devices of the day, some of which scarcely manifested themselves on the surface, but which transferred the substance of one man into the pockets of another, and reduced the people to slavery as completely and inevitably as ever the robber barons of old did the original owners of the soil of Europe."

* * *

"* * * In your Utopia, what would you do next?"

"I would set to work to make a list of all the laws, or parts of laws, or customs, or conditions which, either by commission or omission, gave any man an advantage over any other man; or which tended to concentrate the wealth of the community in the hands of a few. And having found out just what these wrongs or advantages were, I would abolish them *instanter*."

"Well, let us suppose," said Maximilian, "that you were not immediately murdered by the men whose privileges you had destroyed—even as the Gracchi were of old—what would you do next? Men differ in every detail. Some have more industry, or more strength, or more cunning, or more foresight, or more acquisitiveness than others. How are you to prevent these men from becoming richer than the rest?"

"I should not try to," I said. "These differences in men are fundamental, and not to be abolished by legislation; neither are the instincts you speak of in themselves injurious. Civilization, in fact, rests upon them. It is only in their excess that they become destructive. It is right and wise and proper for men to accumulate sufficient wealth to maintain their age in peace, dignity and plenty, and to be able to start their children into the arena of life sufficiently equipped. A thousand men in a community worth $10,000 or $50,000, or even $100,000 each, may be a benefit, perhaps a blessing; but one man worth fifty or one hundred millions, or, as we have them now-a-days, one thousand millions, is a threat against the safety and happiness of every man in the world. I should establish a maximum beyond which no man could own property. I should not stop his accumulations when he had reached that point, for with many men accumulation is an instinct; but I should require him to invest the surplus, under the direction of a governmental board of management, in great works for the benefit of the laboring classes. He should establish schools, colleges, orphan asylums, hospitals, model residences, gardens, parks, libraries, baths, places of amusement, music-halls, sea-side excursions in hot weather, fuel societies in cold weather, etc., etc. I should permit him to secure immortality by affixing his name to his benevolent works; and I should honor him still further by placing his statue in a great

national gallery set apart to perpetuate forever the memory of the benefactors of the race."

"But," said Maximilian, with a smile, "it would not take long for your
rich men, with their surplus wealth, to establish all those works you speak
of. What would you do with the accumulations of the rest?"

"Well," said I, "we should find plenty to do. We would put their money,
for instance, into a great fund and build national railroads, that would
bring the productions of the farmers to the workmen, and those of the
workmen to the farmers, at the least cost of transportation, and free from
the exactions of speculators and middlemen. Thus both farmers and
workmen would live better, at less expense and with less toil."

"All very pretty," said he; "but your middlemen would starve."

"Not at all," I replied; "the cunning never starve. There would be such
a splendid era of universal prosperity that they would simply turn their
skill and shrewdness into some new channels, in which, however, they
would have to give something of benefit, as an equivalent for the benefits
they received. Now they take the cream, and butter, and beef, while some
one else has to raise, feed and milk the cow."

"But," said he, "all this would not help our farmers in their present
condition—they are blotted off the land."

"True," I replied; "but just as I limited a man's possible wealth, so
should I limit the amount of land he could own. I would fix a maximum
of, say, 100 or 500 acres, or whatever amount might be deemed just and
reasonable. I should abolish all corporations, or turn them back into individual partnerships. Abraham Lincoln, in the great civil war of the last
century, gave the Southern insurgents so many days in which to lay
down their arms or lose their slaves. In the same way I should grant one
or two years' time, in which the great owners of land should sell their
estates, in small tracts, to actual occupants, to be paid for in install-
ments, on long time, without interest. And if they did not do so, then, at
the end of the period prescribed, I should confiscate the lands and sell
them, as the government in the old time sold the public lands, for so
much per acre, to actual settlers, and turn the proceeds over to the former owners."

"But, as you had abolished interest on money, there could be no mortgages, and the poor men would starve to death before they could raise a
crop."

"Then," I replied, "I should invoke the power of the nation, as was
done in that great civil war of 1861, and issue paper money, receivable
for all taxes, and secured by the guarantee of the faith and power of five
hundred million people; and make advances to carry these ruined peasants beyond the first years of distress—that money to be a loan to them,

without interest, and to be repaid as a tax on their land. Government is only a machine to insure justice and help the people, and we have not yet developed half its powers. And we are under no more necessity to limit ourselves to the governmental precedents of our ancestors than we are to confine ourselves to the narrow boundaries of their knowledge, or their inventive skill, or their theological beliefs. The trouble is that so many seem to regard government as a divine something which has fallen down upon us out of heaven, and therefore not to be improved upon or even criticised; while the truth is, it is simply a human device to secure human happiness, and in itself has no more sacredness than a wheelbarrow or a cooking-pot. The end of everything earthly is the good of man; and there is nothing sacred on earth but man, because he alone shares the Divine conscience."

* * *

"Government," I replied; "government—national, state and municipal— is the key to the future of the human race.

"There was a time when the town simply represented cowering peasants, clustered under the shadow of the baron's castle for protection. It advanced slowly and reluctantly along the road of civic development, scourged forward by the whip of necessity. We have but to expand the powers of government to solve the enigma of the world. Man separated is man savage; man gregarious is man civilized. A higher development in society requires that this instrumentality of co-operation shall be heightened in its powers. There was a time when every man provided, at great cost, for the carriage of his own letters. Now the government, for an infinitely small charge, takes the business off his hands. There was a time when each house had to provide itself with water. Now the municipality furnishes water to all. The same is true of light. At one time each family had to educate its own children; now the state educates them. Once every man went armed to protect himself. Now the city protects him by its armed police. These hints must be followed out. The city of the future must furnish doctors for all; lawyers for all; entertainments for all; business guidance for all. It will see to it that no man is plundered, and no man starved, who is willing to work.

* * *

"* * * Men are valued, not for themselves, but for their bank account. In the meantime these vast concentrations of capital are made at the expense of mankind. If, in a community of a thousand persons, there are one hundred millions of wealth, and it is equally divided between them, all are comfortable and happy. If, now, ten men, by cunning devices, grasp three-fourths of all this wealth, and put it in their pockets, there is but one-fourth left to divide among the nine hundred and ninety, and they are therefore poor and miserable. Within certain limits accumulation in one place represents denudation elsewhere.

"And thus, under the stimulus of shallow vanity," I continued, "a rivalry of barouches and bonnets—an emulation of waste and extravagance—all the powers of the minds of men are turned—not to lift up the world, but to degrade it. A crowd of little creatures—men and women—are displayed upon a high platform, in the face of mankind, parading and strutting about, with their noses in the air, as tickled as a monkey with a string of beads, and covered with a glory which is not their own, but which they have been able to purchase; crying aloud: 'Behold what I *have got!*' not, 'Behold what I *am!*'

"And then the inexpressible servility of those below them! The fools would not recognize Socrates if they fell over him in the street; but they can perceive Crœsus a mile off; they can smell him a block away; and they will dislocate their vertebræ abasing themselves before him. It reminds one of the time of Louis XIV. in France, when millions of people were in the extremest misery even unto starvation; while great grandees thought it the acme of earthly bliss and honor to help put the king to bed, or take off his dirty socks. And if a common man, by any chance, caught a glimpse of royalty changing its shirt, he felt as if he had looked into heaven and beheld Divinity creating worlds. Oh, it is enough to make a man loathe his species."

"Come, come," said Maximilian, "you grow bitter. Let us go to dinner before you abolish all the evils of the world, or I shall be disposed to quit New York and buy a corner lot in Utopia."

JAMES BAIRD WEAVER

A Call to Action (1892)

The lawyer and three-term member of the House of Representatives James Baird Weaver (1833–1912) was an agrarian radical and the presidential candidate of the Greenback party in 1880 and the Populist Party in 1892. A Call to Action, Weaver's campaign book in the presidential election of 1892, is a populist critique of trusts and monopolies and a demand that the American people resist the "vast and splendidly equipped army of extortionists, usurers, and oppressors."

If the master builders of our civilization one hundred years ago had been told that at the end of a single century, American society would present such melancholy contrasts of wealth and poverty, of individual happiness and widespread infelicity as are to be found to-day throughout the Republic, the person making the unwelcome prediction would have been looked upon as a misanthropist, and his loyalty to Democratic institutions would have been seriously called in question. Our federal machine, with its delicate inter-lace work of National, State and municipal supervision, each intended to secure perfect individual equality, was expected to captivate the world by its operation and insure domestic contentment and personal security to a degree never before realized by mankind.

But there is a vast difference between the generation which made the heroic struggle for Self-government in colonial days, and the third generation which is now engaged in a mad rush for wealth. The first took its stand upon the inalienable rights of man and made a fight which shook the world. But the leading spirits of the latter are entrenched behind class laws and revel in special privileges. It will require another revolution to overthrow them. That revolution is upon us even now.

* * * The millionaire and the pauper cannot, in this country, long dwell together in peace, and it is idle to attempt to patch up a truce between them. Enlightened self respect and a quickened sense of justice are impelling the multitude to demand an interpretation of the anomalous spectacle, constantly presented before their eyes, of a world filled with plenty and yet multitudes of people suffering for all that goes to make life desirable. They are calling to know why idleness should dwell in luxury and those who toil in want; and they are inquiring why one-half of God's children should be deprived of homes upon a planet which is large enough for all. The world will find a solution for these insufferable afflictions in the glorious era but just ahead. Even now the twilight discloses the outlines of a generous inheritance for all and we hear the chirping of sweet birds making ready to welcome with melody and gladness the advent of the full orbed day.

* * *

It is clear that trusts are contrary to public policy and hence in conflict with the Common law. They are monopolies organized to destroy competition and restrain trade. Enlightened public policy favors competition in the present condition of organized society. * * *

It is contended by those interested in Trusts that they tend to cheapen production and diminish the price of the article to the consumer. It is conceded that these results may follow temporarily and even permanently in some instances. But it is not the rule. When such effects ensue they are merely incidental to the controlling object of the association. Trusts are speculative in their purposes and formed to make money. Once they secure control of a given line of business they are masters of the situation and can dictate to the two great classes with which they deal—the producer of the raw material and the consumer of the finished product. They limit the price of the raw material so as to impoverish the producer, drive him to a single market, reduce the price of every class of labor connected with the trade, throw out of employ-ment large numbers of persons who had before been engaged in a mer-itorious calling and finally, prompted by insatiable avarice, they increase the price to the consumer and thus complete the circle of their depre-dations. Diminished prices is the bribe which they throw into the mar-ket to propitiate the public. They will take it back when it suits them to do so.

The Trust is organized commerce with the Golden Rule excluded and the trustees exempted from the restraints of conscience.

They argue that competition means war and is therefore destructive. The Trust is eminently docile and hence seeks to destroy competition in order that we may have peace. But the peace which they give us is like that which exists after the leopard has devoured the kid. This professed desire for peace is a false pretense. They dread the war of competition be-cause the people share in the spoils. When rid of that they always turn their guns upon the masses and depredate without limit or mercy. The main weapons of the trust are threats, intimidation, bribery, fraud, wreck and pillage. Take one well authenticated instance in the history of the Oat Meal Trust as an example. In 1887 this Trust decided that part of their mills should stand idle. They were accordingly closed. This resulted in the discharge of a large number of laborers who had to suffer in con-sequence. The mills which were continued in operation would produce seven million barrels of meal during the year. Shortly after shutting down the Trust advanced the price of meal one dollar per barrel and the public was forced to stand the assessment. The mills were more profitable when idle than when in operation.

The Sugar Trust has it within its power to levy a tribute of $30,000,000 upon the people of the United States by simply advancing the price of sugar one cent per pound for one year.

If popular tumult breaks out and legislation in restraint of these depre-dations is threatened, they can advance prices, extort campaign expenses and corruption funds from the people and force the disgruntled multi-tude to furnish the sinews of war for their own destruction. They not only have the power to do these things, but it is their known mode of warfare and they actually practice it from year to year.

The most distressing feature of this war of the Trusts is the fact that they control the articles which the plain people consume in their daily life. It cuts off their accumulations and deprives them of the staff upon which they fain would lean in their old age. * * *

* * * For nearly three hundred years the Anglo-Saxon race has been trying to arrest the encroachments of monopoly and yet the evil has flourished and gained in strength from age to age. The courts have come to the aid of enlightened sentiment, pronounced all such combinations contrary to public policy, illegal and their contracts void; and still they have continued to thrive. Thus far repressive and prohibitory legislation have proved unavailing. Experience has shown that when men, for the sake of gain, will openly violate the moral law and infringe upon the plain rights of their neighbors, they will not be restrained by ordinary prohibitory measures. It is the application of force to the situation and force must be met with force. The States should pass stringent penal statutes which will visit personal responsibility upon all agents and representatives of the trust who aid or assist in the transaction of its business within the State. The General Government, through its power to lay and collect taxes, should place an excise or internal revenue tax of from 25 to 40 per cent on all manufacturing plants, goods, wares or merchandise of whatever kind and wherever found when owned by or controlled in the interest of such combines or associations, and this tax should be a first lien upon such property until the tax is paid. The details of such a bill would not be difficult to frame. Such a law would destroy the Trust root and branch. Whenever the American people really try to overthrow these institutions they will be able to do so and to further postpone action is a crime. * * * One of the main charges against Charles the First, was that he had fostered and created monopolies. His head went to the block. * * * Nearly every great struggle of the English race has been caused by the unjust exactions of tribute— against the extortions of greed. Our own war for Independence was a war against taxes. Our late internal struggle was for the freedom of labor and the right of the laborer to possess and enjoy his own. That struggle is still on and it is now thundering at our gates with renewed energy. It will not down, though the Trust heap Ossa upon Pelion. The people will rise and overturn the despoilers though they shake the earth by the displacement.

These vast struggles are great teachers and the world is learning rapidly. We are coming to know that great combinations reduce the cost of production and soon the world will grasp the idea that the people can combine and protect themselves. In this combine, in this co-operation of all, there will be no discrimination and the bounties of Heaven will be open alike to the weak and the powerful. We welcome the conflict. There is no time to lose nor can the battle begin too soon. * * *

* * * The American people have entered upon the mightiest civic, struggle known to their history. Many of the giant wrongs which they are seeking to overthrow are as old as the race of man and are rock-rooted in the ignorant prejudices and controlling customs of every nation in christendom. We must expect to be confronted by a vast and splendidly equipped army of extortionists, usurers and oppressors marshalled from every nation under heaven. Every instrumentality known to man,—the state with its civic authority, learning with its lighted torch, armies with their commissions to take life, instruments of commerce essential to commercial intercourse, and the very soil upon which we live, move and have our being—all these things and more, are being perverted and used to enslave and impoverish the people. The Golden Rule is rejected by the heads of all the great departments of trade, and the law of Cain, which repudiates the obligations that we are mutually under to one another, is fostered and made the rule of action throughout the world. Corporate feudality has taken the place of chattel slavery and vaunts its power in every state.

The light of past civilization is shining full upon us all, and knowing that cause and effect follow closely upon each other, we believe that we fairly discern the outlines of the main events which the near future has in store for the American people. We do not claim to see clearly all the concomitant phenomena destined to follow the social earthquake just at hand. Such prevision is not accorded to man. But of this much we are certain: In their flight from their task masters the people have about reached the Red Sea. We can not retreat. Either the floods will be parted for us and close, as of old, upon our pursurers, or a life and death struggle will ensue between oppressors and oppressed—between those who would destroy and enslave and those who are seeking to enter into the inheritance prepared for them by a beneficent Father. Our danger lurks in the alternative stated. It behooves every man who desires a peaceful solution of our ever increasing complications to do all in his power to make the deliverance peaceful and humane. To further postpone the controversy is to invite chaos and challenge the arbitrament of the sword. Our past experience should be sufficient to warn us to steer clear of this abyss of peril and the hell of war.

All the Nations of antiquity were scourged exactly as our people are now being scourged. They were afflicted, they complained, rebelled and perished—oppressors and oppressed together. Their innate sense of justice enabled them to discern clearly between right and wrong, but their passion for revenge and thirst for blood made it impossible for the people to retain power even when the fortunes of war had placed it in their hands.

But thanks to the all-conquering strength of Christian enlightenment we are at the dawn of the golden age of popular power. We have
unshaken faith in the integrity and final triumph of the people. But
their march to power will not be unobstructed. The universal uprising
of the industrial forces will result in unifying the monopolistic and
plutocratic elements also, and through the business and social influences of these potential and awakened forces, thousands of well-meaning
professional and business men of all classes will be induced, for a time,
to make common cause against us. This makes it necessary for the
friends of reform to put forth herculean efforts to disabuse the minds of
well-meaning people concerning the underlying objects of the movement, and this calls for systematic, energetic, and constant educational
work, covering the whole range of the reforms proposed. It is also the
surest method of overcoming the obstacle of indifference among the
people.

THOMAS E. WATSON

The Negro Question in the South (1892)

*The Georgia Populist Thomas E. Watson (1856–1922) was a member of
the U.S. House of Representatives, the Senate, the vice-presidential
nominee of the Populist Party in 1896, and the publisher of the anti-
Catholic and anti-Semitic Tom Watson's Magazine. Although this agrarian rebel later supported a constitutional amendment that would
disenfranchise blacks, Watson worked to form a political alliance between black and white farmers early in his political career. In an article
published in the October 1892 issue of the* Arena, *Watson analyzed the
causes of the racial divide that prevented the two groups from recognizing their common economic aims and forming an alliance that would
transcend traditional party lines.*

And the problem is, can these two races, distinct in color, distinct in
social life, and distinct as political powers, dwell together in peace
and prosperity?

Upon a question so difficult and delicate no man should dogmatize—
nor dodge. The issue is here; grows more urgent every day, and must be
met.

It is safe to say that the present status of hostility between the races can only be sustained at the most imminent risk to both. It is leading by logical necessity to results which the imagination shrinks from contemplating. And the horrors of such a future can only be averted by honest attempts at a solution of the question which will be just to both races and beneficial to both.

Having given this subject much anxious thought, my opinion is that the future happiness of the two races will never be assured until the political motives which drive them asunder, into two distinct and hostile factions, can be removed. There must be a new policy inaugurated, whose purpose is to allay the passions and prejudices of race conflict, and which makes its appeal to the sober sense and honest judgment of the citizen regardless of his color.

To the success of this policy two things are indispensable—a common necessity acting upon both races, and a common benefit assured to both—without injury or humiliation to either.

Then, again, outsiders must let us alone. We must work out our own salvation. In no other way can it be done. Suggestions of Federal interference with our elections postpone the settlement and render our task the more difficult. Like all free people, we love home rule, and resent foreign compulsion of any sort. The Northern leader who really desires to see a better state of things in the South, puts his finger on the hands of the clock and forces them backward every time he intermeddles with the question. This is the literal truth; and the sooner it is well understood, the sooner we can accomplish our purpose.

What is that purpose? To outline a policy which compels the support of a great body of both races, from those motives which imperiously control human action, and which will thus obliterate forever the sharp and unreasoning political divisions of to-day.

The white people of the South will never support the Republican Party. This much is certain. The black people of the South will never support the Democratic Party. This is equally certain.

Hence, at the very beginning, we are met by the necessity of new political alliances. As long as the whites remain solidly Democratic, the blacks will remain solidly Republican.

As long as there was no choice, except as between the Democrats and the Republicans, the situation of the two races was bound to be one of antagonism. The Republican Party represented everything which was hateful to the whites; the Democratic Party, everything which was hateful to the blacks.

Therefore a new party was absolutely necessary. It has come, and it is doing its work with marvellous rapidity.

Why does a Southern Democrat leave his party and come to ours?

Because his industrial condition is pitiably bad; because he struggles against a system of laws which have almost filled him with despair; because he is told that he is without clothing because he produces too much cotton, and without food because corn is too plentiful; because he sees everybody growing rich off the products of labor except the laborer; because the millionnaires who manage the Democratic Party have contemptuously ignored his plea for a redress of grievances and have nothing to say to him beyond the cheerful advice to "work harder and live closer."

Why has this man joined the PEOPLE'S PARTY? Because the same grievances have been presented to the Republicans by the farmer of the West, and the millionnaires who control that party have replied to the petition with the soothing counsel that the Republican farmer of the West should "work more and talk less."

Therefore, if he were confined to a choice between the two old parties, the question would merely be (on these issues) whether the pot were larger than the kettle—the color of both being precisely the same. * * *

The key to the new political movement called the People's Party has been that the Democratic farmer was as ready to leave the Democratic ranks as the Republican farmer was to leave the Republican ranks. In exact proportion as the West received the assurance that the South was ready for a new party, it has moved. In exact proportion to the proof we could bring that the West had broken Republican ties, the South has moved. *Without* a decided break in both sections, neither would move. *With* that decided break, both moved.

The very same principle governs the race question in the South. The two races can never act together permanently, harmoniously, beneficially, till each race demonstrates to the other a readiness to leave old party affiliations and to form new ones, based upon the profound conviction that, in acting together, both races are seeking new laws which will benefit both. On no other basis under heaven can the "Negro Question" be solved. * * *

The People's Party will settle the race question. First, by enacting the Australian ballot system. Second, by offering to white and black a rallying point which is free from the odium of former discords and strifes. Third, by presenting a platform immensely beneficial to both races and injurious to neither. Fourth, by making it to the *interest* of both races to act together for the success of the platform. Fifth, by making it to the *interest* of the colored man to have the same patriotic zeal for the welfare of the South that the whites possess.

Now to illustrate. Take two planks of the People's Party platform: that pledging a free ballot under the Australian system and that which demands a distribution of currency to the people upon pledges of land, cotton, etc.

The guaranty as to the vote will suit the black man better than the Republican platform, because the latter contemplates Federal interference, which will lead to collisions and bloodshed. The Democratic platform contains no comfort to the Negro, because, while it denounces the Republican programme, as usual, it promises nothing which can be specified. It is a generality which does not even possess the virtue of being "glittering."

The People's Party, however, not only condemns Federal interference with elections, but also distinctly commits itself to the method by which every citizen shall have his constitutional right to the free exercise of his electoral choice. We pledge ourselves to isolate the voter from all coercive influences and give him the free and fair exercise of his franchise under state laws.

Now couple this with the financial plank which promises equality in the distribution of the national currency, at low rates of interest.

The white tenant lives adjoining the colored tenant. Their houses are almost equally destitute of comforts. Their living is confined to bare necessities. They are equally burdened with heavy taxes. They pay the same high rent for gullied and impoverished land.

They pay the same enormous prices for farm supplies. Christmas finds them both without any satisfactory return for a year's toil. Dull and heavy and unhappy, they both start the plows again when "New Year's" passes.

Now the People's Party says to these two men, "You are kept apart that you may be separately fleeced of your earnings. You are made to hate each other because upon that hatred is rested the keystone of the arch of financial despotism which enslaves you both. You are deceived and blinded that you may not see how this race antagonism perpetuates a monetary system which beggars both."

This is so obviously true it is no wonder both these unhappy laborers stop to listen. No wonder they begin to realize that no change of law can benefit the white tenant which does not benefit the black one likewise; that no system which now does injustice to one of them can fail to injure both. Their every material interest is identical. The moment this becomes a conviction, mere selfishness, the mere desire to better their conditions, escape onerous taxes, avoid usurious charges, lighten their rents, or change their precarious tenements into smiling, happy homes, will drive these two men together, just as their mutually inflamed prejudices now drive them apart.

Suppose these two men now to have become fully imbued with the idea that their material welfare depends upon the reforms we demand.

Then they act together to secure them. Every white reformer finds it to the vital interest of his home, his family, his fortune, to see to it that the vote of the colored reformer is freely cast and fairly counted.

Then what? Every colored voter will be thereafter a subject of industrial education and political teaching.

Concede that in the final event, a colored man will vote where his material interests dictate that he should vote; concede that in the South the accident of color can make no possible difference in the interests of farmers, croppers, and laborers; concede that under full and fair discussion the people can be depended upon to ascertain where their interests lie—and we reach the conclusion that the Southern race question can be solved by the People's Party on the simple proposition that each race will be led by self-interest to support that which benefits it, when so presented that neither is hindered by the bitter party antagonisms of the past.

Let the colored laborer realize that our platform gives him a better guaranty for political independence; for a fair return for his work; a better chance to buy a home and keep it; a better chance to educate his children and see them profitably employed; a better chance to have public life freed from race collisions: a better chance for every citizen to be considered as a *citizen* regardless of color in the making and enforcing of laws,—let all this be fully realized, and the race question at the South will have settled itself through the evolution of a political movement in which both whites and blacks recognize their surest way out of wretchedness into comfort and independence.

The illustration could be made quite as clearly from other planks in the People's Party platform. On questions of land, transportation and finance, especially, the welfare of the two races so clearly depends upon that which benefits either, that intelligent discussion would necessarily lead to just conclusions.

Why should the colored man always be taught that the white man of his neighborhood hates him, while a Northern man, who taxes every rag on his back, loves him? Why should not my tenant come to regard me as his friend rather than the manufacturer who plunders us both? Why should we perpetuate a policy which drives the black man into the arms of the Northern politician?

Why should we always allow Northern and Eastern Democrats to enslave us forever by threats of the Force Bill?

Let us draw the supposed teeth of this fabled dragon by founding our new policy upon justice—upon the simple but profound truth that, if the voice of passion can be hushed, the self-interest of both races will drive them to act in concert. There never was a day during the last twenty years when the South could not have flung the money power into the dust by patiently teaching the Negro that we could not be wretched under any system which would not afflict him likewise; that we could not prosper under any law which would not also bring its blessings to him.

To the emasculated individual who cries "Negro supremacy!" there is little to be said. His cowardice shows him to be a degeneration from the race which has never yet feared any other race. Existing under such conditions as they now do in this country, there is no earthly chance for Negro domination, unless we are ready to admit that the colored man is our superior in will power, courage, and intellect.

Not being prepared to make any such admission in favor of any race the sun ever shone on, I have no words which can portray my contempt for the white men, Anglo-Saxons, who can knock their knees together, and through their chattering teeth and pale lips admit that they are afraid the Negroes will "dominate us."

The question of social equality does not enter into the calculation at all. That is a thing each citizen decides for himself. No statute ever yet drew the latch of the humblest home—or ever will. Each citizen regulates his own visiting list—and always will.

The conclusion, then, seems to me to be this: the crushing burdens which now oppress both races in the South will cause each to make an effort to cast them off. They will see a similarity of cause and a similarity of remedy. They will recognize that each should help the other in the work of repealing bad laws and enacting good ones. They will become political allies, and neither can injure the other without weakening both. It will be to the interest of both that each should have justice. And on these broad lines of mutual interest, mutual forbearance, and mutual support the present will be made the stepping-stone to future peace and prosperity.

National People's Party Platform (1892)

Ignatius Donnelly wrote the preamble to the platform adopted by the Populist Party at its first national convention, held in Omaha, Nebraska, on July 4, 1892. The platform called on government to nationalize certain industries, coin silver, and enact other reforms to restore power to the "plain people" of America.

Assembled upon the one hundred and sixteenth anniversary of the Declaration of Independence, the People's Party of America, in their first national convention, invoking upon their action the blessing of Almighty God, put forth in the name and on behalf of the people of this country, the following preamble and declaration of principles:

The conditions which surround us best justify our co-operation; we meet in the midst of a nation brought to the verge of moral, political, and material ruin. Corruption dominates the ballot-box, the Legislatures, the Congress, and touches even the ermine of the bench. The people are demoralized; most of the States have been compelled to isolate the voters at the polling places to prevent universal intimidation or bribery. The newspapers are largely subsidized or muzzled, public opinion silenced, business prostrated, homes covered with mortgages, labor impoverished, and the land concentrating in the hands of capitalists. The urban workmen are denied the right of organization for self-protection, imported pauperized labor beats down their wages, a hireling standing army, unrecognized by our laws, is established to shoot them down, and they are rapidly degenerating into European conditions. The fruits of the toil of millions are boldly stolen to build up colossal fortunes for a few, unprecedented in the history of mankind; and the possessors of these, in turn, despise the Republic and endanger liberty. From the same prolific womb of governmental injustice we breed the two great classes—tramps and millionaires.

The national power to create money is appropriated to enrich bondholders; a vast public debt payable in legal-tender currency has been funded into gold-bearing bonds, thereby adding millions to the burdens of the people.

Silver, which has been accepted as coin since the dawn of history, has been demonetized to add to the purchasing power of gold by decreasing the value of all forms of property as well as human labor, and the supply of currency is purposely abridged to fatten usurers, bankrupt enterprise, and enslave industry. A vast conspiracy against mankind has been organized on two continents, and it is rapidly taking possession of the world. If not met and overthrown at once it forebodes terrible social convulsions, the destruction of civilization, or the establishment of an absolute despotism.

We have witnessed for more than a quarter of a century the struggles of the two great political parties for power and plunder, while grievous wrongs have been inflicted upon the suffering people. We charge that the controlling influences dominating both these parties have permitted the existing dreadful conditions to develop without serious effort to prevent or restrain them. Neither do they now promise us any substantial reform. They have agreed together to ignore, in the coming campaign, every issue but one. They propose to drown the outcries of a plundered people with the uproar of a sham battle over the tariff, so that capitalists, corporations, national banks, rings, trusts, watered stock, the demonetization of silver and the oppressions of the usurers may all be lost sight of. They propose to sacrifice our homes, lives, and children on the altar of mammon; to destroy the multitude in order to secure corruption funds from the millionaires.

Assembled on the anniversary of the birthday of the nation, and filled with the spirit of the grand general and chieftain who established our independence, we seek to restore the government of the Republic to the hands of the "plain people," with which class it originated. We assert our purposes to be identical with the purposes of the National Constitution; to form a more perfect union and establish justice, insure domestic tranquillity, provide for the common defence, promote the general welfare, and secure the blessings of liberty for ourselves and our posterity.

We declare that this Republic can only endure as a free government while built upon the love of the people for each other and for the nation; that it cannot be pinned together by bayonets; that the Civil War is over, and that every passion and resentment which grew out of it must die with it, and that we must be in fact, as we are in name, one united brotherhood of free [men].

Our country finds itself confronted by conditions for which there is no precedent in the history of the world; our annual agricultural productions amount to billions of dollars in value, which must, within a few weeks or months, be exchanged for billions of dollars' worth of commodities consumed in their production; the existing currency supply is wholly inadequate to make this exchange; the results are falling prices, the formation of combines and rings, the impoverishment of the producing class. We pledge ourselves that if given power we will labor to correct these evils by wise and reasonable legislation, in accordance with the terms of our platform.

We believe that the powers of government—in other words, of the people—should be expanded (as in the case of the postal service) as rapidly and as far as the good sense of an intelligent people and the teachings of experience shall justify, to the end that oppression, injustice, and poverty shall eventually cease in the land.

While our sympathies as a party of reform are naturally upon the side of every proposition which will tend to make men intelligent, virtuous, and temperate, we nevertheless regard these questions, important as they are, as secondary to the great issues now pressing for solution, and upon which not only our individual prosperity but the very existence of free institutions depend; and we ask all men to first help us to determine whether we are to have a republic to administer before we differ as to the conditions upon which it is to be administered, believing that the forces of reform this day organized will never cease to move forward until every wrong is righted and equal rights and equal privileges securely established for all the men and women of this country. We declare, therefore—

First.—That the union of the labor forces of the United States this day consummated shall be permanent and perpetual; may its spirit enter into all hearts for the salvation of the Republic and the uplifting of mankind.

Second.—Wealth belongs to him who creates it, and every dollar taken from industry without an equivalent is robbery. "If any will not work, neither shall he eat." The interests of rural and civil labor are the same; their enemies are identical.

Third.—We believe that the time has come when the railroad corporations will either own the people or the people must own the railroads; and should the government enter upon the work of owning and managing all railroads, we should favor an amendment to the constitution by which all persons engaged in the government service shall be placed under a civil-service regulation of the most rigid character, so as to prevent the increase of the power of the national administration by the use of such additional government employes.

FINANCE.—We demand a national currency, safe, sound, and flexible issued by the general government only, a full legal tender for all debts, public and private, and that without the use of banking corporations; a just, equitable, and efficient means of distribution direct to the people, at a tax not to exceed 2 per cent, per annum, to be provided as set forth in the sub-treasury plan of the Farmers' Alliance, or a better system; also by payments in discharge of its obligations for public improvements.

1. We demand free and unlimited coinage of silver and gold at the present legal ratio of 16 to 1.
2. We demand that the amount of circulating medium be speedily increased to not less than $50 per capita.
3. We demand a graduated income tax.
4. We believe that the money of the country should be kept as much as possible in the hands of the people, and hence we demand that all State and national revenues shall be limited to the necessary expenses of the government, economically and honestly administered.
5. We demand that postal savings banks be established by the government for the safe deposit of the earnings of the people and to facilitate exchange.

TRANSPORTATION.—Transportation being a means of exchange and a public necessity, the government should own and operate the railroads in the interest of the people. The telegraph and telephone, like the post-office system, being a necessity for the transmission of news, should be owned and operated by the government in the interest of the people.

LAND.—The land, including all the natural sources of wealth, is the heritage of the people, and should not be monopolized for speculative purposes, and alien ownership of land should be prohibited. All land now held by railroads and other corporations in excess of their actual needs, and all lands now owned, by aliens should be reclaimed by the government and held for actual settlers only.

SUPPLEMENTARY RESOLUTIONS
FROM PLATFORM COMMITTEE

Whereas, Other questions have been presented for our consideration, we hereby submit the following, not as a part of the Platform of the People's Party, but as resolutions expressive of the sentiment of this Convention.

1. RESOLVED, That we demand a free ballot and a fair count in all elections, and pledge ourselves to secure it to every legal voter without Federal intervention, through the adoption by the States of the unperverted Australian or secret ballot system.
2. RESOLVED, That the revenue derived from a graduated income tax should be applied to the reduction of the burden of taxation now levied upon the domestic industries of this country.
3. RESOLVED, That we pledge our support to fair and liberal pensions to ex-Union soldiers and sailors.
4. RESOLVED, That we condemn the fallacy of protecting American labor under the present system, which opens our ports to the pauper and criminal classes of the world and crowds out our wage-earners; and we denounce the present ineffective laws against contract labor, and demand the further restriction of undesirable immigration.
5. RESOLVED, That we cordially sympathize with the efforts of organized workingmen to shorten the hours of labor, and demand a rigid enforcement of the existing eight-hour law on Government work, and ask that a penalty clause be added to the said law.
6. RESOLVED, That we regard the maintenance of a large standing army of mercenaries, known as the Pinkerton system, as a menace to our liberties, and we demand its abolition; and we condemn the recent invasion of the Territory of Wyoming by the hired assassins of plutocracy, assisted by Federal officials.
7. RESOLVED, That we commend to the favorable consideration of the people and to the reform press the legislative system known as the initiative and referendum.

8. RESOLVED, That we favor a constitutional provision limiting the office of President and Vice-President to one term, and providing for the election of Senators of the United States by a direct vote of the people.

9. RESOLVED, That we oppose any subsidy or national aid to any private corporation for any purpose.

10. RESOLVED, That this convention sympathizes with the Knights of Labor and their righteous contest with the tyrannical combine of clothing manufacturers of Rochester, and declare it to be the duty of all who hate tyranny and oppression to refuse to purchase the goods made by the said manufacturers, or to patronize any merchants who sell such goods.

LORENZO DOW LEWELLING

Speech at Huron Place (1894)

The farmer and newspaper publisher Lorenzo Dow Lewelling (1846–1900) served as a Populist county chairman before becoming governor of Kansas in 1893. In a speech he delivered as governor at a Populist meeting in Kansas City, Lewelling compared the condition of farmers and workers in the present economy to the plight of slaves in the ante-bellum South. He explained that both were denied equal rights and both needed government to protect them from exploitation.

What is government to me if it does not make it possible for me to live? and provide for my family! The trouble has been, we have so much regard for the rights of property that we have forgotten the liberties of the individual. We have had some illustration of that in the great strike at Chicago and a number of other illustrations. I claim it is the business of the Government to make it possible for me to live and sustain the life of my family. If the Government don't do that, what better is the Government to me than a state of barbarism and everywhere we slay, and the slayer in turn is slain and so on the great theatre of life is one vast conspiracy all creatures from the worm to the man in turn rob their fellows. That my fellow citizens is the law of natural selection the survival of the fittest—not the survival of the fittest, but the survival of the strongest. It is time that man should rise above it.

* * * I have been asked why I was a Populist. I want to say to you, friends, that the same principles that made me a Republican in the early days, have today made me a populist, and I'll tell you what they are. I remember when I was a little boy my parents were the old line abolition kind of people that believed in equal rights to all and special privileges to none. God bless them for the sentiment, and don't you say so? Well, I remember in those days of the abolition question that we took a little paper called Uncle Lucas' Childs paper, and one side of the paper bore a motto about the size of a coin in the centre of a picture—a picture of an African slave with his hands uplifted and in chains, and around the rim of the coin a motto "Am I not a man and Brother?" That made a wonderful impression on my mind. I was taught thus in my infancy to stand for the man and woman who was down in the scale of life, and life's conflict. To stand for the weak against the strong, for God knows the strong can take care of themselves, and the weak are those that should be protected and provided for. And I say now, it is the duty of government to protect the weak, because the strong are able to protect themselves.

I say these are the reasons that made me a populist, and today my heart goes out to the working men and women of this nation as it went out to the black slave. I believe, and I say it freely, that the working men and women of this country, many of them, are simply today in the shackels of industrial slavery.

What kind of condition is it in which we live anyhow? You people of Kansas City are pretty well to-do and so are the people of Kansas generally, but they are not all over the country and there is some suffering here, we believe—we are so foolish as to believe that conditions might be improved by the government interfering and making it possible for the improvement of these conditions.

* * *

* * * I ask you now, what can the poor man do today that comes to you and says, I have hands to work with, I have bodily strength, I am willing to give all those for a morsel of bread—but you say, "I have no work to give you." What is he to do then? Can he go and lie down on the street for rest? No, because there [are] laws against vagabondage. Can he go and crawl into a box car and take a nap there? No. Because he is trespassing upon the rights and privileges of others. Can he go to the door and ask for something to eat? No, because there [are] laws against begging. Can he go out into the fields and cultivate the fields? No, because the field belongs to

somebody else. Can he draw a drink of water out of the spring or well in the field? No, because the spring or well belongs to the man who owns the field. What in the name of goodness is he to do? Answer me that question in the light of our present civilization and government. Don't you have some sympathy for the men in this position? Senator Ingalls told us some two years ago, there are over a million men in the United States who are in that condition, and today the number is swelled to three million. Oh, is it any wonder there are common wealers? Is it then a wonder there are anarchists? There is no greater crime breeder in the world than poverty. Poverty is the mother of it all; and I came here this evening asking you to join with me in the organization of a great anti-poverty society. Will you do it?

* * *

* * * The great throbbing centers of civilization seem to me to be dead to the instincts of humanity and alike dead to the teachings of the man of Bethlehem. The night of despair seems to me to be upon us. Call me calamity howler if you will. I wish I had the voice and pen and reputation of Jeremiah that I might howl Calamity until the people all over this broad land should hear me. It seems to me that the night of despair is really at hand. And I ask you who is to be responsible for our civil government, if you please, by which we are turned into beasts by conditions that the government might and should prevent? The golden age of the 19th century! * * *

* * * The People's party has stepped into the breach between the classes to demand justice for the poor as well as to the rich and for every man. The machinery of government has been arrayed against us. It seems to me that the Courts and Judges of this country have become the mere tools and vassals and jumping-jacks of the great corporations that pull the string while the courts and judges dance. That is the way it seems to me. So, these great corporations are forces against which we are to contend but I am willing, if you are willing, to place truth against the world. Truth is mighty and it will prevail.

We have come here today pleading for truth against error. Not for the individual. Men are nothing in a great contest of the people like this. It matters not who is the leader so that all the people stand together united for the great principles of humanity.

Now, my fellow citizens, I am about to close. I want to say to you in conclusion that I am with this people's party because I believe and have believed that it is feeling its way toward the sunlight of freedom for the toiling masses of this country and of other lands. I am with the people's party because it is feeling its way along the high walls of prejudice which shut out the sunlight of freedom, shut out relief from the outstretched hand of poverty. I am with the people's party because it aims at the defense and rescue of ten thousand children who die every year in this country from lack of food. I am with the people's party because it pleads for the 57,000 homeless children in the United States. I am with the People's party because it takes the side of 3,000,000 men who are out of employment at this very time and who in consequence are driven to desperation and crime. These, mark my friends, are only a few of the many reasons why the peoples' side in this great battle is the right side; and I believe that if there is a God in heaven, as I do believe, that he will hear the cry of his suffering children and the giant Despair will yet be slain by the great uprising of this nation. With these great principles of our common cause, we are going forth. We will be fearless as we go forth and we will be able to conquer. We will be able to subdue kingdoms and in time will stop the mouths of liars, out of weakness we will be made strong. We shall wax valiant in fight, and when November comes will put to flight the armies of the aliens. I thank you.

WILLIAM JENNINGS BRYAN

The "Cross of Gold" Speech (1896)

Elected to Congress in 1890, the three-time presidential candidate and populist reformer William Jennings Bryan (1860–1925) was a lifelong champion of democracy and "the plain people," which earned him the nickname "the Commoner." Although he is now best remembered for his controversial role in the infamous Scopes "monkey trial" of 1925, Bryan was a formidable political figure from the end of the nineteenth century until the second decade of the twentieth, when he served as secretary of state under Wilson. In this Chicago speech, perhaps the most famous Democratic National Convention speech ever, Bryan delivered an electrifying Populist attack on the gold standard as an oppressive tool of moneyed interests.

I would be presumptuous, indeed, to present myself against the distinguished gentlemen to whom you have listened if this were a mere measuring of abilities; but this is not a contest between persons. The humblest citizen in all the land, when clad in the armor of a righteous cause, is stronger than all the hosts of error. I come to speak to you in defense of a cause as holy as the cause of liberty—the cause of humanity.

When this debate is concluded, a motion will be made to lay upon the table the resolution offered in commendation of the Administration, and also, the resolution offered in condemnation of the Administration. We object to bringing this question down to the level of persons. The individual is but an atom; he is born, he acts, he dies; but principles are eternal; and this has been a contest over a principle.

Never before in the history of this country has there been witnessed such a contest as that through which we have just passed. Never before in the history of American politics has a great issue been fought out as this issue has been, by the voters of a great party. On the fourth of March 1895, a few Democrats, most of them members of Congress, issued an address to the Democrats of the nation, asserting that the money question was the paramount issue of the hour; declaring that a majority of the Democratic party had the right to control the action of the party on this paramount issue; and concluding with the request that the believers in the free coinage of silver in the Democratic party should organize, take charge of, and control the policy of the Democratic party. Three months later, at Memphis, an organization was perfected, and the silver Democrats went forth openly and courageously proclaiming their belief, and declaring that, if successful, they would crystallize into a platform the declaration which they had made. Then began the struggle. With a zeal approaching the zeal which inspired the Crusaders who followed Peter the Hermit, our silver Democrats went forth from victory unto victory until they are now assembled, not to discuss, not to debate, but to enter up the judgement already rendered by the plain people of this country. In this contest brother has been arrayed against brother, father against son. The warmest ties of love, acquaintance, and association have been disregarded; old leaders have been cast aside when they have refused to give expression to the sentiments of those whom they would lead, and new leaders have sprung up to give direction to this cause of truth. Thus has the contest been waged, and we have assembled here under as binding and solemn instructions as were ever imposed upon representatives of the people.

We do not come as individuals. As individuals we might have been glad to compliment the gentleman from New York [Senator Hill], but we know that the people for whom we speak would never be willing to put him in a position where he could thwart the will of the Democratic party. I say it was not a question of persons; it was a question of principle, and it is not with gladness, my friends, that we find ourselves brought into conflict with those who are now arrayed on the other side. * * *

When you [turning to the gold delegates] come before us and tell us that we are about to disturb your business interests, we reply that you have disturbed our business interests by your course.

We say to you that you have made the definition of a business man too limited in its application. The man who is employed for wages is as much a business man as his employer; the attorney in a country town is as much a business man as the corporation counsel in a great metropolis; the merchant at the cross-roads store is as much a business man as the merchant of New York; the farmer who goes forth in the morning and toils all day, who begins in the spring and toils all summer, and who by the application of brain and muscle to the natural resources of the country creates wealth, is as much a business man as the man who goes upon the Board of Trade and bets upon the price of grain; the miners who go down a thousand feet into the earth, or climb two thousand feet upon the cliffs, and bring forth from their hiding places the precious metals to be poured into the channels of trade are as much business men as the few financial magnates who, in a back room, corner the money of the world. We come to speak of this broader class of business men.

Ah, my friends, we say not one word against those who live upon the Atlantic Coast, but the hardy pioneers who have braved all the dangers of the wilderness, who have made the desert to blossom as the rose—the pioneers away out there [pointing to the West] who rear their children near to Nature's heart, where they can mingle their voices with the voices of the birds—out there where they have erected schoolhouses for the education of their young, churches where they praise their Creator, and cemeteries where rest the ashes of their dead—these people, we say, are as deserving of the consideration of our party as any people in this country. It is for these that we speak. We do not come as aggressors. Our war is not a war of conquest; we are fighting in the defense of our homes, our families, and posterity. We have petitioned, and our petitions have been scorned; we have entreated, and our entreaties have been disregarded; we have begged, and they have mocked when our calamity came. We beg no longer; we entreat no more; we petition no more. We defy them!

The gentleman from Wisconsin [Vilas] has said that he fears a Robespierre. My friends, in this land of the free you need not fear that a tyrant will spring up from among the people. What we need is an Andrew Jackson to stand, as Jackson stood, against the encroachments of organized wealth.

They tell us that this platform was made to catch votes. We reply to them that changing conditions make new issues; that the principles upon which Democracy rests are as everlasting as the hills, but that they must be applied to new conditions as they arise. Conditions have arisen, and we are here to meet those conditions. They tell us that the income tax ought not to be brought in here; that it is a new idea. They criticize us for our criticism of the Supreme Court of the United States. My friends, we have not criticized; we have simply called attention to what you already know. If you want criticisms read the dissenting opinions of the court. There you will find criticisms. They say that we passed an unconstitutional law; we deny it. The income tax was not unconstitutional when it was passed; it was not unconstitutional when it went before the Supreme Court for the first time; it did not become unconstitutional until one of the judges changed his mind, and we cannot be expected to know when a judge will change his mind. The income tax is just. It simply intends to put the burdens of government justly upon the backs of the people. I am in favor of an income tax. When I find a man who is not willing to bear his share of the burdens of the government which protects him, I find a man who is unworthy to enjoy the blessings of a government like ours.

They say that we are opposing national bank currency; it is true. If you will read what Thomas Benton said, you will find he said that, in searching history, he could find but one parallel to Andrew Jackson; that was Cicero, who destroyed the conspiracy of Cataline and saved Rome. Benton said that Cicero only did for Rome what Jackson did for us when he destroyed the bank conspiracy and saved America. We say in our platform we believe that the right to coin and issue money is a function of government. We believe it. We believe that it is a part of sovereignty, and can no more with safety be delegated to private individuals than we could afford to delegate to private individuals the power to make penal statutes or levy taxes. Mr. Jefferson, who was once regarded as good Democratic authority, seems to have differed in opinion from the gentleman who has addressed us on the part of the minority. Those who are opposed to this proposition tell us that the issue of paper money is a function of the bank, and that the government ought to go out of the banking business. I stand with Jefferson rather than with them, and tell them, as he did, that the issue of money is a function of government, and that the banks ought to go out of the governing business.

They complain about the plank which declares against life tenure in office. They have tried to strain it to mean that which it does not mean. What we oppose by that plank is the life tenure which is being built up in Washington, and which excludes from participation in official benefits the humbler members of society. * * *

And now, my friends, let me come to the paramount issue. If they ask us why it is that we say more on the money question than we say upon the tariff question, I reply that, if protection has slain its thousands, the gold standard has slain its tens of thousands. If they ask us why we do not embody in our platform all the things that we believe in, we reply that when we have restored the money of the Constitution, all other necessary reform will be possible; but that until this is done, there is no other reform that can be accomplished.

Why is it that within three months such a change has come over the country? Three months ago when it was confidently asserted that those who believed in the gold standard would frame our platform and nominate our candidates, even the advocates of the gold standard did not think that we could elect a President. And they had good reason for their doubt, because there is scarcely a State here today asking for the gold standard which is not in the absolute control of the Republican Party. But note the change. Mr. McKinley was nominated at St. Louis upon a platform which declared for the maintenance of the gold standard until it can be changed into bimetallism by international agreement. Mr. McKinley was the most popular man among the Republicans, and three months ago everybody in the Republican Party prophesied his election. How is it today? Why, the man who was once pleased to think that he looked like Napoleon—that man shudders today when he remembers that he was nominated on the anniversary of the battle of Waterloo.

Not only that, but as he listens, he can hear with ever-increasing distinctness the sound of the waves as they beat upon the lonely shores at St Helena.

Why this change? Ah, my friends, is not the reason for the change evident to any one who will look at the matter? No private character, however pure, no personal popularity, however great, can protect from the avenging wrath of an indignant people a man who will declare that he is in favor of fastening the gold standard upon this country, or who is willing to surrender the right of self-government and place the legislative control of our affairs in the hands of foreign potentates and powers.

We go forth confident that we shall win. Why? Because upon the paramount issue of this campaign there is not a spot of ground upon which the enemy will dare to challenge battle. If they tell us that the gold standard is a good thing, we shall point to their platform and tell them that their platform pledges the party to get rid of the gold standard and substitute bimetallism. If the gold standard is a good thing why try to get rid of it? I call your attention to the fact that some of the very people who are in this Convention today and who tell us that we ought to declare in favor of international bimetallism—thereby declaring that the gold standard is wrong and that the principle of bimetallism is better—these very people four months ago were open and avowed advocates of the gold standard, and were then telling us that we could not legislate two metals together, even with the aid of all the world. If the gold standard is a good thing, we ought to declare in favor of its retention and not in favor of abandoning it; and if the gold standard is a bad thing why should we wait until other nations are willing to help us to let go? Here is the line of battle, and we care not upon which issue they force the fight; we are prepared to meet them on either issue or on both. If they tell us that the gold standard is the standard of civilization, we reply to them that this, the most enlightened of all the nations of the earth, has never declared for a gold standard and that both the great parties this year are declaring against it. If the gold standard is the standard of civilization, why, my friends, should we not have it? If they come to meet us on that issue we can present the history of our nation. More than that; we can tell them that they will search the pages of history in vain to find a single instance where the common people of any land have ever declared themselves in favor of the gold standard. They can find where the holders of fixed investments have declared for a gold standard, but not where the masses have. Mr. Carlisle said in 1878 that this was a struggle between the "idle holders of idle capital" and "the struggling masses, who produce the wealth and pay the taxes of the country," and, my friends, the question we are to decide is: Upon which side will the Democratic party fight; upon the side of "the idle holders of idle capital" or upon the side of "the struggling masses"? That is the question which the party must answer first, and then it must be answered by each individual hereafter. The sympathies of the Democratic party, as shown by the platform, are on the side of the struggling masses who have ever been the foundation of the Democratic party. There are two ideas of government. There are those who believe that if you will only legislate to make the well-to-do prosperous, their prosperity will leak through on those below. The Democratic idea, however, has been that if you legislate to make the masses prosperous, their prosperity will find its way up through every class which rests upon them.

You come to us and tell us that the great cities are in favor of the gold standard; we reply that the great cities rest upon our broad and fertile prairies. Burn down your cities and leave our farms, and your cities will spring up again as if by magic; but destroy our farms and the grass will grow in the streets of every city in the country.

My friends, we declare that this nation is able to legislate for its own people on every question, without waiting for the aid or consent of any other nation on earth; and upon that issue we expect to carry every state in the Union. I shall not slander the inhabitants of the fair state of Massachusetts nor the inhabitants of the state of New York by saying that, when they are confronted with the proposition, they will declare that this nation is not able to attend to its own business. It is the issue of 1776 over again. Our ancestors, when but three millions in number, had the courage to declare their political independence of every other nation; shall we, their descendants, when we have grown to seventy millions, declare that we are less independent than our forefathers?

No, my friends, that will never be the verdict of our people. Therefore, we care not upon what lines the battle is fought. If they say bimetallism is good, but that we cannot have it until other nations help us, we reply, that instead of having a gold standard because England has, we will restore bimetallism, and then let England have bimetallism because the United States has it. If they dare to come out in the open field and defend the gold standard as a good thing, we will fight them to the uttermost. Having behind us the producing masses of this nation and the world, supported by the commercial interests, the laboring interests and the toilers everywhere, we will answer their demand for a gold standard by saying to them: You shall not press down upon the brow of labor this crown of thorns, you shall not crucify mankind upon a cross of gold.

Voices of Dissent

BENJAMIN TUCKER

Liberty (1881)

The individualist anarchist Benjamin Tucker (1854–1939) operated the Unique Book Shop in New York City and edited the prominent anarchist newspaper Liberty. *Tucker, who rejected the use of violence, helped translate and publish the works of European and American radical thinkers. In the Declaration of Purpose for the first issue of* Liberty, *Tucker expressed his belief that the greatest threat to liberty was the authority of the state and the church.*

Liberty enters the field of journalism to speak for herself because she finds no one willing to speak for her. She hears no voice that always champions her; she knows no pen that always writes in her defence; she sees no hand that is always lifted to avenge her wrongs or vindicate her rights. Many claim to speak in her name, but few really understand her. Still fewer have the courage and the opportunity to consistently fight for her. Her battle, then, is her own, to wage and win. She accepts it fearlessly and with a determined spirit.

Her foe, Authority, takes many shapes, but, broadly speaking, her enemies divide themselves into three classes: first, those who abhor her both as a means and as an end of progress, opposing her openly, avowedly, sincerely, consistently, universally; second, those who profess to believe in her as a means of progress, but who accept her only so far as they think she will subserve their own selfish interests, denying her and her blessings to the rest of the world; third, those who distrust her as a means of progress, believing in her only as an end to be obtained by first trampling upon, violating, and outraging her. These three phases of opposition to Liberty are met in almost every sphere of thought and human activity. Good representatives of the first are seen in the Catholic Church, and the Russian autocracy; of the second, in the Protestant

Church and the Manchester school of politics and political economy; of the third, in the atheism of Gambetta and the socialism of Karl Marx.

Through these forms of authority another line of demarcation runs transversely, separating the divine from the human; or better still, the religious from the secular. Liberty's victory over the former is well-nigh achieved. Last century Voltaire brought the authority of the supernatural into disrepute. The Church has been declining ever since. Her teeth are drawn, and though she still seems to show here and there vigorous signs of life, she does so in the violence of the death-agony upon her, and soon her power will be felt no more. It is human authority that hereafter is to be dreaded, and the State, its organ, that in the future is to be feared. Those who have lost their faith in gods only to put it in governments; those who have ceased to be Church-worshippers only to become State-worshippers; those who have abandoned pope for king or czar, and priest for president or parliament,—have indeed changed their battle-ground, but none the less are foes of Liberty still. The Church has become an object of derision; the State must be made equally so. The State is said by some to be a "necessary evil"; it must be made unnecessary. This century's battle, then, is with the State: the State, that debases man; the State, that prostitutes woman; the State, that corrupts children; the State, that trammels love; the State, that stifles thought; the State, that monopolizes land; the State, that limits credit; the State, that restricts exchange; the State, that gives idle capital the power of increase, and, through interest, rent, profit, and taxes, robs industrious labor of its products. * * *

Monopoly and privilege must be destroyed, opportunity afforded, and competition encouraged. This is Liberty's work, and "Down with Authority" her war-cry.

EMMA GOLDMAN

Anarchism: What It Really Stands For (1907)

*The revolutionary anarchist and feminist activist Emma Goldman
(1869–1940) emigrated to the United States from Russia in 1885 and
became involved in "direct action" following the trial of anarchists involved in the Chicago Haymarket Square Riot in 1886. "Red Emma,"
as she was known, participated in a variety of anarchist activities in
the United States from 1890 to 1917, when she was deported to Russia. The following selection, originally published in the anarchist journal Mother Earth, which Goldman edited for several years, exemplifies
her commitment to "the freest possible expression of all the latent
powers of the individual" against the tyranny of religion, property, and
government.*

The history of human growth and development is at the same time
the history of the terrible struggle of every new idea heralding the
approach of a brighter dawn. In its tenacious hold on tradition, the Old
has never hesitated to make use of the foulest and cruelest means to stay
the advent of the New, in whatever form or period the latter may have asserted itself. Nor need we retrace our steps into the distant past to realize
the enormity of opposition, difficulties, and hardships placed in the path
of every progressive idea. The rack, the thumbscrew, and the knout are
still with us; so are the convict's garb and the social wrath, all conspiring
against the spirit that is serenely marching on.

Anarchism could not hope to escape the fate of all other ideas of innovation. Indeed, as the most revolutionary and uncompromising innovator,
Anarchism must needs meet with the combined ignorance and venom of
the world it aims to reconstruct.

To deal even remotely with all that is being said and done against Anarchism would necessitate the writing of a whole volume. I shall therefore
meet only two of the principal objections. In so doing, I shall attempt to
elucidate what Anarchism really stands for.

The strange phenomenon of the opposition to Anarchism is that it
brings to light the relation between so-called intelligence and ignorance.
And yet this is not so very strange when we consider the relativity of all

things. The ignorant mass has in its favor that it makes no pretense of knowledge or tolerance. Acting, as it always does, by mere impulse, its reasons are like those of a child. "Why?" "Because." Yet the opposition of the uneducated to Anarchism deserves the same consideration as that of the intelligent man.

What, then, are the objections? First, Anarchism is impractical, though a beautiful ideal. Second, Anarchism stands for violence and destruction, hence it must be repudiated as vile and dangerous. Both the intelligent man and the ignorant mass judge not from a thorough knowledge of the subject, but either from hearsay or false interpretation.

A practical scheme, says Oscar Wilde, is either one already in existence, or a scheme that could be carried out under the existing conditions; but it is exactly the existing conditions that one objects to, and any scheme that could accept these conditions is wrong and foolish. The true criterion of the practical, therefore, is not whether the latter can keep intact the wrong or foolish; rather is it whether the scheme has vitality enough to leave the stagnant waters of the old, and build, as well as sustain, new life. In the light of this conception, Anarchism is indeed practical. More than any other idea, it is helping to do away with the wrong and foolish; more than any other idea, it is building and sustaining new life.

The emotions of the ignorant man are continuously kept at a pitch by the most blood-curdling stories about Anarchism. Not a thing too outrageous to be employed against this philosophy and its exponents. Therefore Anarchism represents to the unthinking what the proverbial bad man does to the child,—a black monster bent on swallowing everything; in short, destruction and violence.

Destruction and violence! How is the ordinary man to know that the most violent element in society is ignorance; that its power of destruction is the very thing Anarchism is combating? Nor is he aware that Anarchism, whose roots, as it were, are part of nature's forces, destroys, not healthful tissue, but parasitic growths that feed on the life's essence of society. It is merely clearing the soil from weeds and sagebrush, that it may eventually bear healthy fruit.

* * *

Anarchism urges man to think, to investigate, to analyze every proposition; but that the brain capacity of the average reader be not taxed too much, I also shall begin with a definition, and then elaborate on the latter.

ANARCHISM:—The philosophy of a new social order based on liberty unrestricted by man-made law; the theory that all forms of government

rest on violence, and are therefore wrong and harmful, as well as unnecessary.

The new social order rests, of course, on the materialistic basis of life;
but while all Anarchists agree that the main evil today is an economic
one, they maintain that the solution of that evil can be brought about
only through the consideration of *every phase* of life,—individual; as well
as the collective; the internal, as well as the external phases.

A thorough perusal of the history of human development will disclose
two elements in bitter conflict with each other; elements that are only
now beginning to be understood, not as foreign to each other, but as
closely related and truly harmonious, if only placed in proper environment: the individual and social instincts. The individual and society have
waged a relentless and bloody battle for ages, each striving for supremacy,
because each was blind to the value and importance of the other. The individual and social instincts,—the one a most potent factor for individual
endeavor, for growth, aspiration, self-realization; the other an equally potent factor for mutual helpfulness and social well-being.

* * *

Anarchism is the only philosophy which brings to man the consciousness of himself; which maintains that God, the State, and society are nonexistent, that their promises are null and void, since they can be fulfilled
only through man's subordination. Anarchism is therefore the teacher of
the unity of life; not merely in nature, but in man. There is no conflict between the individual and the social instincts, any more than there is between the heart and the lungs: the one the receptacle of a precious life
essence, the other the repository of the element that keeps the essence
pure and strong. The individual is the heart of society, conserving the
essence of social life; society is the lungs which are distributing the element to keep the life essence—that is, the individual—pure and strong.

"The one thing of value in the world," says Emerson, "is the active
soul; this every man contains within him. The soul active sees absolute
truth and utters truth and creates." In other words, the individual instinct
is the thing of value in the world. It is the true soul that sees and creates
the truth alive, out of which is to come a still greater truth, the re-born
social soul.

Anarchism is the great liberator of man from the phantoms that have
held him captive; it is the arbiter and pacifier of the two forces for individual and social harmony. To accomplish that unity, Anarchism has declared war on the pernicious influences which have so far prevented the
harmonious blending of individual and social instincts, the individual
and society.

Religion, the dominion of the human mind; Property, the dominion of human needs; and Government, the dominion of human conduct, represent the stronghold of man's enslavement and all the horrors it entails. Religion! How it dominates man's mind, how it humiliates and degrades his soul. God is everything, man is nothing, says religion. But out of that nothing God has created a kingdom so despotic, so tyrannical, so cruel, so terribly exacting that naught but gloom and tears and blood have ruled the world since gods began. Anarchism rouses man to rebellion against this black monster. Break your mental fetters, says Anarchism to man, for not until you think and judge for yourself will you get rid of the dominion of darkness, the greatest obstacle to all progress.

Property, the dominion of man's needs, the denial of the right to satisfy his needs. Time was when property claimed a divine right, when it came to man with the same refrain, even as religion, "Sacrifice! Abnegate! Submit!" The spirit of Anarchism has lifted man from his prostrate position. He now stands erect, with his face toward the light. He has learned to see the insatiable, devouring, devastating nature of property, and he is preparing to strike the monster dead.

"Property is robbery," said the great French Anarchist Proudhon. Yes, but without risk and danger to the robber. Monopolizing the accumulated efforts of man, property has robbed him of his birthright, and has turned him loose a pauper and an outcast. Property has not even the time-worn excuse that man does not create enough to satisfy all needs. The ABC student of economics knows that the productivity of labor within the last few decades far exceeds normal demand. But what are normal demands to an abnormal institution? The only demand that property recognizes is its own gluttonous appetite for greater wealth, because wealth means power; the power to subdue, to crush, to exploit, the power to enslave, to outrage, to degrade. America is particularly boastful of her great power, her enormous national wealth. Poor America, of what avail is all her wealth, if the individuals comprising the nation are wretchedly poor? If they live in squalor, in filth, in crime, with hope and joy gone, a homeless, soilless army of human prey.

* * *

Real wealth consists in things of utility and beauty, in things that help to create strong, beautiful bodies and surroundings inspiring to live in. But if man is doomed to wind cotton around a spool, or dig coal, or build roads for thirty years of his life, there can be no talk of wealth. What he gives to the world is only gray and hideous things, reflecting a dull and hideous existence,—too weak to live, too cowardly to die. Strange to say, there are people who extol this deadening method of centralized production as the proudest achievement of our age. They fail utterly to realize that if we are to continue in machine subserviency, our slavery is more complete than was our bondage to the King. They do not want to know that centralization is not only the death-knell of liberty, but also of health and beauty, of art and science, all these being impossible in a clock-like, mechanical atmosphere.

Anarchism cannot but repudiate such a method of production: its goal is the freest possible expression of all the latent powers of the individual. Oscar Wilde defines a perfect personality as "one who develops under perfect conditions, who is not wounded, maimed, or in danger." A perfect personality, then, is only possible in a state of society where man is free to choose the mode of work, the conditions of work, and the freedom to work. One to whom the making of a table, the building of a house, or the tilling of the soil, is what the painting is to the artist and the discovery to the scientist,—the result of inspiration, of intense longing, and deep interest in work as a creative force. That being the ideal of Anarchism, its economic arrangements must consist of voluntary productive and distributive associations, gradually developing into free communism, as the best means of producing with the least waste of human energy. Anarchism, however, also recognizes the right of the individual, or numbers of individuals, to arrange at all times for other forms of work, in harmony with their tastes and desires.

Such free display of human energy being possible only under complete individual and social freedom, Anarchism directs its forces against the third and greatest foe of all social equality; namely, the State, organized authority, or statutory law,—the dominion of human conduct.

Just as religion has fettered the human mind, and as property, or the monopoly of things, has subdued and stifled man's needs, so has the State enslaved his spirit, dictating every phase of conduct. "All government in essence," says Emerson, "is tyranny." It matters not whether it is government by divine right or majority rule. In every instance its aim is the absolute subordination of the individual.

Referring to the American government, the greatest American Anarchist, David Thoreau, said: "Government, what is it but a tradition, though a recent one, endeavoring to transmit itself unimpaired to posterity, but each instance losing its integrity; it has not the vitality and force of a single living man. Law never made man a whit more just; and by means of their respect for it, even the well disposed are daily made agents of injustice."

Indeed, the keynote of government is injustice. With the arrogance and self-sufficiency of the King who could do no wrong, governments ordain, judge, condemn, and punish the most insignificant offenses, while maintaining themselves by the greatest of all offenses, the annihilation of individual liberty. Thus Ouida is right when she maintains that "the State only aims at instilling those qualities in its public by which its demands are obeyed, and its exchequer is filled. Its highest attainment is the reduction of mankind to clockwork. In its atmosphere all those finer and more delicate liberties, which require treatment and spacious expansion, inevitably dry up and perish. The State requires a taxpaying machine in which there is no hitch, an exchequer in which there is never a deficit, and a public, monotonous, obedient, colorless, spiritless, moving humbly like a flock of sheep along a straight high road between two walls."

Yet even a flock of sheep would resist the chicanery of the State, if it were not for the corruptive, tyrannical, and oppressive methods it employs to serve its purposes. Therefore Bakunin repudiates the State as synonymous with the surrender of the liberty of the individual or small minorities,—the destruction of social relationship, the curtailment, or complete denial even, of life itself, for its own aggrandizement. The State is the altar of political freedom and, like the religious altar, it is maintained for the purpose of human sacrifice.

In fact, there is hardly a modern thinker who does not agree that government, organized authority, or the State, is necessary *only* to maintain or protect property and monopoly. It has proven efficient in that function only.

Even George Bernard Shaw, who hopes for the miraculous from the State under Fabianism, nevertheless admits that "it is at present a huge machine for robbing and slave-driving of the poor by brute force." This being the case, it is hard to see why the clever prefacer wishes to uphold the State after poverty shall have ceased to exist.

Unfortunately there are still a number of people who continue in the fatal belief that government rests on natural laws, that it maintains social order and harmony, that it diminishes crime, and that it prevents the lazy man from fleecing his fellows. I shall therefore examine these contentions.

A natural law is that factor in man which asserts itself freely and spontaneously without any external force, in harmony with the requirements of nature. For instance, the demand for nutrition, for sex gratification, for light, air, and exercise, is a natural law. But its expression needs not the machinery of government, needs not the club, the gun, the handcuff, or the prison. To obey such laws, if we may call it obedience, requires only spontaneity and free opportunity. That governments do not maintain themselves through such harmonious factors is proven by the terrible array of violence, force, and coercion all governments use in order to live. Thus Blackstone is right when he says, "Human laws are invalid, because they are contrary to the laws of nature."

Unless it be the order of Warsaw after the slaughter of thousands of people, it is difficult to ascribe to governments any capacity for order or social harmony. Order derived through submission and maintained by terror is not much of a safe guaranty; yet that is the only "order" that governments have ever maintained. True social harmony grows naturally out of solidarity of interests. In a society where those who always work never have anything, while those who never work enjoy everything, solidarity of interests is nonexistent; hence social harmony is but a myth. The only way organized authority meets this grave situation is by extending still greater privileges to those who have already monopolized the earth, and by still further enslaving the disinherited masses. Thus the entire arsenal of government—laws, police, soldiers, the courts, legislatures, prisons,— is strenuously engaged in "harmonizing" the most antagonistic elements in society.

The most absurd apology for authority and law is that they serve to diminish crime. Aside from the fact that the State is itself the greatest criminal, breaking every written and natural law, stealing in the form of taxes, killing in the form of war and capital punishment, it has come to an absolute standstill in coping with crime. It has failed utterly to destroy or even minimize the horrible scourge of its own creation.

Crime is naught but misdirected energy. So long as every institution of today, economic, political, social, and moral, conspires to misdirect human energy into wrong channels; so long as most people are out of place doing the things they hate to do, living a life they loathe to live, crime will be inevitable, and all the laws on the statutes can only increase, but never do away with, crime. What does society, as it exists today, know of the process of despair, the poverty, the horrors, the fearful struggle the human soul must pass on its way to crime and degradation.

The deterrent influence of law on the lazy man is too absurd to merit consideration. If society were only relieved of the waste and expense of keeping a lazy class, and the equally great expense of the paraphernalia of protection this lazy class requires, the social tables would contain an abundance for all, including even the occasional lazy individual. Besides, it is well to consider that laziness results either from special privileges, or physical and mental abnormalities. Our present insane system of production fosters both, and the most astounding phenomenon is that people should want to work at all now. Anarchism aims to strip labor of its deadening, dulling aspect, of its gloom and compulsion. It aims to make work an instrument of joy, of strength, of color, of real harmony, so that the poorest sort of a man should find in work both recreation and hope.

To achieve such an arrangement of life, government, with its unjust, arbitrary, repressive measures, must be done away with. At best it has but imposed one single mode of life upon all, without regard to individual and social variations and needs. In destroying government and statutory laws, Anarchism proposes to rescue the self-respect and independence of the individual from all restraint and invasion by authority. Only in freedom can man grow to his full stature. Only in freedom will he learn to think and move, and give the very best in him. Only in freedom will he realize the true force of the social bonds which knit men together, and which are the true foundation of a normal social life.

But what about human nature? Can it be changed? And if not, will it endure under Anarchism?

Poor human nature, what horrible crimes have been committed in thy name! Every fool, from king to policeman, from the flatheaded parson to the visionless dabbler in science, presumes to speak authoritatively of human nature. The greater the mental charlatan, the more definite his insistence on the wickedness and weaknesses of human nature. Yet, how can any one speak of it today, with every soul in a prison, with every heart fettered, wounded, and maimed?

John Burroughs has stated that experimental study of animals in captivity is absolutely useless. Their character, their habits, their appetites undergo a complete transformation when torn from their soil in field and forest. With human nature caged in a narrow space, whipped daily into submission, how can we speak of its potentialities?

Freedom, expansion, opportunity, and, above all, peace and repose, alone can teach us the real dominant factors of human nature and all its wonderful possibilities.

Anarchism, then, really stands for the liberation of the human mind from the dominion of religion; the liberation of the human body from the dominion of property; liberation from the shackles and restraint of government. Anarchism stands for a social order based on the free grouping of individuals for the purpose of producing real social wealth; an order that will guarantee to every human being free access to the earth and full enjoyment of the necessities of life, according to individual desires, tastes, and inclinations.

* * *

As to methods. Anarchism is not, as some may suppose, a theory of the future to be realized through divine inspiration. It is a living force in the affairs of our life, constantly creating new conditions. The methods of Anarchism therefore do not comprise an iron-clad program to be carried out under all circumstances. Methods must grow out of the economic needs of each place and clime, and of the intellectual and temperamental requirements of the individual. The serene, calm character of a Tolstoy will wish different methods for social reconstruction than the intense, overflowing personality of a Michael Bakunin or a Peter Kropotkin. Equally so it must be apparent that the economic and political needs of Russia will dictate more drastic measures than would England or America. Anarchism does not stand for military drill and uniformity; it does, however, stand for the spirit of revolt, in whatever form, against everything that hinders human growth. All Anarchists agree in that, as they also agree in their opposition to the political machinery as a means of bringing about the great social change.

"All voting," says Thoreau, "is a sort of gaming, like checkers, or backgammon, a playing with right and wrong; its obligation never exceeds that of expediency. Even voting for the right thing is doing nothing for it. A wise man will not leave the right to the mercy of chance, nor wish it to prevail through the power of the majority." A close examination of the machinery of politics and its achievements will bear out the logic of Thoreau.

What does the history of parliamentarism show? Nothing but failure and defeat, not even a single reform to ameliorate the economic and social stress of the people. Laws have been passed and enactments made for the improvement and protection of labor. Thus it was proven only last year that Illinois, with the most rigid laws for mine protection, had the greatest mine disasters. In States where child labor laws prevail, child exploitation is at its highest, and though with us the workers enjoy full political opportunities, capitalism has reached the most brazen zenith.

Even were the workers able to have their own representatives, for which our good Socialist politicians are clamoring, what chances are there for their honesty and good faith? One has but to bear in mind the process of politics to realize that its path of good intentions is full of pitfalls: wire-pulling, intriguing, flattering, lying, cheating; in fact, chicanery of every description, whereby the political aspirant can achieve success. Added to that is a complete demoralization of character and conviction, until nothing is left that would make one hope for anything from such a human derelict. Time and time again, the people were foolish enough to trust, believe, and support with their last farthing aspiring politicians, only to find themselves betrayed and cheated.

It may be claimed that men of integrity would not become corrupt in the political grinding mill. Perhaps not; but such men would be absolutely helpless to exert the slightest influence in behalf of labor, as indeed has been shown in numerous instances. The State is the economic master of its servants. Good men, if such there be, would either remain true to their political faith and lose their economic support, or they would cling to their economic master and be utterly unable to do the slightest good. The political arena leaves one no alternative, one must either be a dunce or a rogue.

The political superstition is still holding sway over the hearts and minds of the masses, but the true lovers of liberty will have no more to do with it. Instead, they believe with Stirner that man has as much liberty as he is willing to take. Anarchism therefore stands for direct action, the open defiance of, and resistance to, all laws and restrictions, economic, social, and moral. But defiance and resistance are illegal. Therein lies the salvation of man. Everything illegal necessitates integrity, self-reliance, and courage. In short, it calls for free, independent spirits, for "men who are men, and who have a bone in their backs which you cannot pass your hand through."

Universal suffrage itself owes its existence to direct action. If not for the spirit of rebellion, of the defiance on the part of the American revolutionary fathers, their posterity would still wear the King's coat. If not for the direct action of a John Brown and his comrades, America would still trade in the flesh of the black man. True, the trade in white flesh is still going on; but that, too, will have to be abolished by direct action. Trade-unionism, the economic arena of the modern gladiator, owes its existence to direct action. It is but recently that law and government have attempted to crush the trade-union movement, and condemned the exponents of man's right to organize to prison as conspirators. Had they sought to assert their cause through begging, pleading, and compromise, trade-unionism would today be a negligible quantity. In France, in Spain, in Italy, in Russia, nay even in England (witness the growing rebellion of English labor unions), direct, revolutionary, economic action has become so strong a force in the battle for industrial liberty as to make the world realize the tremendous importance of labor's power. The General Strike, the supreme expression of the economic consciousness of the workers, was ridiculed in America but a short time ago. Today every great strike, in order to win, must realize the importance of the solidaric general protest.

Direct action, having proven effective along economic lines, is equally potent in the environment of the individual. There a hundred forces encroach upon his being, and only persistent resistance to them will finally set him free. Direct action against the authority in the shop, direct action against the authority of the law, direct action against the invasive, meddlesome authority of our moral code, is the logical, consistent method of Anarchism.

Will it not lead to a revolution? Indeed, it will. No real social change has ever come about without a revolution. People are either not familiar with their history, or they have not yet learned that revolution is but thought carried into action.

Anarchism, the great leaven of thought, is today permeating every phase of human endeavor. Science, art, literature, the drama, the effort for economic betterment, in fact every individual and social opposition to the existing disorder of things, is illumined by the spiritual light of Anarchism. It is the philosophy of the sovereignty of the individual. It is the theory of social harmony. It is the great, surging, living truth that is reconstructing the world, and that will usher in the Dawn.

DANIEL DE LEON

Reform or Revolution (1896)

Born in the Dutch West Indies, the radical socialist Daniel De Leon (1852–1914) joined the Socialist Labor Party in 1890 and became an editor for its newspaper, The People. Dissatisfied with existing labor unions as insufficiently radical, De Leon established the Socialist Trade and Labor Alliance in 1895 and helped found the Industrial Workers of the World in 1905. As he demonstrates in his 1896 talk, "Reform or Revolution," De Leon strongly preferred aggressive revolutionary action to the reformist strategies favored by other labor leaders.

What, then, with an eye single upon the difference between RE-FORM and REVOLUTION, does Socialism mean? To point out that, I shall take up two or three of what I may style the principal centres of the movement.

One of these principal nerve centres is the question of "Government" or the question of "State."

Not until we reach the great works of the American Morgan, of Marx and Engels, and of other Socialist philosophers, is the matter handled with that scientific lucidity that proceeds from facts, leads to sound conclusions, and breaks the way to practical work. Not until you know and understand the history of the "State" and of "Government" will you understand one of the cardinal principles upon which Socialist Organization rests and will you be in a condition to organize successfully.

We are told that "Government" has always been as it is to-day, and always will be. This is the first fundamental error of what Karl Marx justly calls capitalistic vulgarity of thought.

When man started on his career, after having got beyond the state of the savage, he realized that co-operation was a necessity to him. He understood that together with others he could face his enemies in a better way than alone; he could hunt, fish, fight more successfully.

* * *

The Indian lived in the community condition. The Indian lived under a system of common property. As Franklin described it, in a sketch of the history and alleged sacredness of private property, there was no such thing as private property among the Indians. They co-operated, worked together, and they had a Central Directing Authority among them. In the Indian communities we find that Central Directing Authority consisting of the "Sachems." It makes no difference how that Central Directing Authority was elected, there it was. But note this: its function was to direct the co-operative or collective efforts of the communities, and, in so doing, it shared actively in the productive work of the communities. Without its work, the work of the communities would not have been done.

When, in the further development of society, the tools of production grew and developed—grew and developed beyond the point reached by the Indian; when the art of smelting iron ore was discovered; when thereby that leading social cataclysm, wrapped in the mists of ages, yet discernible, took place that rent former communal society in twain along the line of sex, the males being able, the females unable, to wield the tool of production—then society was cast into a new mold; the former community, with its democratic equality of rights and duties, vanished, and a new social system turns up, divided into two sections, the one able, the other unable, to work at production. The line that separated these two sections, being at first the line of sex, could, in the very nature of things, not yet be sharp or deep. Yet, notwithstanding, in the very shaping of these two sections—one able, the other unable, to feed itself—we have the first premonition of the CLASSES, of class distinctions, of the division of society into the INDEPENDENT and the DEPENDENT, into MASTER and SLAVES, RULER and RULED.

Simultaneously with this revolution, we find the first changes in the nature of the Central Directing Authority, of that body whose original function was to share in, by directing, production. Just as soon as economic equality is destroyed, and the economic classes crop up in society, the functions of the Central Directing Authority gradually begin to change, until finally, when, after a long range of years, moving slowly at first, and then with the present hurricane velocity under capitalism proper, the tool has developed further, and further, and still further, and has reached its present fabulous perfection and magnitude; when, through its private revolution by dividing society, no longer along the line of sex, but strictly along the line of ownership or non-ownership of the land on and the tool with which to work; when the privately owned, mammoth tool of to-day has reduced more than fifty-two per cent. of our population to the state of being utterly unable to feed without first selling themselves into wage-slavery, while it, at the same time, saps the ground from under about thirty-nine per cent. of our people, the middle class, whose puny tools, small capital, render them certain victims of competition with the large capitalists, and makes them desperate; when the economic law that asserts itself under the system of private ownership of the tool has concentrated these private owners into about eight per cent. of the nation's inhabitants, has thereby enabled this small capitalist class to live without toil, and to compel the majority, the class of the proletariat, to toil without living; when, finally, it has come to the pass in which our country now finds itself, that, as was stated in Congress, ninety-four per cent. of the taxes are spent in "protecting property"—the property of the trivially small capitalist class—and not in protecting life; when, in short, the privately owned tool has wrought this work, and the classes—the idle rich and the working poor—are in full bloom—then the Central Directing Authority of old stands transformed; its pristine functions of aiding in, by directing, production have been supplanted by the functions of holding down the dependent, the slave, the ruled, i.e., the WORKING CLASS. Then, and not before, lo, the State, the modern State, the CAPITALIST STATE! Then, lo, the Government, the modern Government, the CAPITALIST GOVERNMENT—equipped mainly, if not solely, with the means of suppression, of oppression, of tyranny!

In sight of these manifestations of the modern State, the Anarchist—the rose-water and the dirty-water variety alike—shouts: "Away with all central directing authority; see what it does; it can only do mischief; it always did mischief!" But Socialism is not Anarchy. Socialism does not, like the chicken in the fable, just out of the shell, start with the knowledge of that day. Socialism rejects the premises and the conclusions of Anarchy upon the State and upon Government. What Socialism says is: "Away with the economic system that alters the beneficent functions of the Central Directing Authority from an aid to production into a means of oppression." And it proceeds to show that, when the instruments of production shall be owned, no longer by the minority, but shall be restored to the Commonwealth; that when, as the result of this, no longer the minority or any portion of the people shall be in poverty, and classes, class distinctions and class rule shall, as they necessarily must, have vanished, that then the Central Directing Authority will lose all its repressive functions, and is bound to reassume the functions it had in the old communities of our ancestors, become again a necessary aid, and assist in production.

The Socialist, in the brilliant simile of Karl Marx, sees that a lone fiddler in his room needs no director; he can rap himself to order, with his fiddle to his shoulder, and start his dancing tune, and stop whenever he likes. But just as soon as you have an orchestra, you must also have an orchestra director—a central directing authority. If you don't, you may have a Salvation Army pow-wow, you may have a Louisiana negro breakdown; you may have an orthodox Jewish synagogue, where every man sings in whatever key he likes, but you won't have harmony—impossible.

It needs this central directing authority of the orchestra master to rap all the players to order at a given moment; to point out when they shall begin; when to have these play louder, when to have those play softer; when to put in this instrument, when to silence that; to regulate the time of all and preserve the accord. The orchestra director is not an oppressor, or his baton an insignia of tyranny; he is not there to bully anybody; he is as necessary or important as any or all of the members of the orchestra.

Our system of production is in the nature of an orchestra. No one man, no one town, no one State, can be said any longer to be independent of the other; the whole people of the United States, every individual therein, is dependent and interdependent upon all the others. The nature of the machinery of production; the subdivision of labor, which aids co-operation, and which co-operation fosters, and which is necessary to the plentifulness of production that civilization requires, compel a harmonious working together of all departments of labor, and thence compel the establishment of a Central Directing Authority, of an Orchestral Director, so to speak, of the orchestra of the Co-operative Commonwealth.

Such is the State or Government that the Socialist revolution carries in its womb. To-day, production is left to Anarchy, and only Tyranny, the twin sister of Anarchy, is organized.

Socialism, accordingly, implies organization; organization implies directing authority; and the one and the other are strict reflections of the revolutions undergone by the tool of production. Reform, on the other hand, skims the surface, and with "Referendums" and similar devices limits itself to external tinkerings.

The second nerve centre of Socialism that will serve to illustrate the difference between reform and revolution is its materialistic groundwork.

Take, for instance, the history of slavery. All of our ancestors—this may shock some of you, but it is a fact all the same—all of our ancestors were cannibals at one time. The human race, in its necessity to seek for food, often found it easier to make a raid and take from others the food they had gathered. In those olden, olden days of the barbarism of our ancestors, when they conquered a people and took away its property, they had no further use for the conquered; they killed them, spitted them over a good fire, roasted and ate them up. It was a simple and the only profitable way known of disposing of prisoners of war. They did with their captives very much what bees do yet; when they have raided and conquered a hive, they ruthlessly kill every single denizen of the captured hive.

Our ancestors continued cannibals until their social system had developed sufficiently to enable them to keep their prisoners under control. From that moment they found it was more profitable to keep their prisoners of war alive, and turn them into slaves to work for them, than it was to kill them off and eat them up. With that stage of material development, cannibalism was dropped. From the higher material plane on which our ancestors then stood, their moral vision enlarged and they presently realized that it was immoral to eat up a human being.

Cannibalism disappears to make room for chattel slavery. And what do we see? Watch the process of "moral development" in this country—the classic ground in many ways to study history in, for the reason that the whole development of mankind can be seen here, portrayed in a few years, so to speak. You know how, to-day, the Northern people put on airs of morality on the score of having "abolished chattel slavery," the "traffic in human flesh," "gone down South and fought, and bled, to free the negro," etc., etc. Yet we know that just as soon as manufacturing was introduced in the North, the North found that it was too expensive to own the negro and take care of him; that it was much cheaper not to own the worker; and, consequently, that they "religiously," "humanly" and "morally" sold their slaves to the South, while they transformed the white people of the North who had no means of production in their own hands, into wage slaves, and mercilessly ground them down. In the North, chattel slavery disappeared just as soon as the development of machinery rendered the institution unprofitable. The immorality of chattel slavery became clear to the North just as soon as, standing upon that higher plane that its higher material development raised it to, it acquired a better vision. The benighted South, on the contrary, that had no machinery, remained with eyes shut, and she stuck to slavery till the slave was knocked out of her fists.

Guided by the light of this and many similar lessons of history, Socialism builds upon the principle that the "moral sentiment," as illustrated by the fate of the slave, is not the cause, but a powerful aid to revolutions. The moral sentiment is to a movement as important as the sails are to a ship. Nevertheless, important though sails are, unless a ship is well laden, unless she is soundly, properly and scientifically constructed, the more sails you pile on and spread out, the surer she is to capsize. So with the organizations that are to carry out a revolution. Unless your Socialist organizations are as sound as a bell; unless they are as intolerant as science;

unless they will plant themselves squarely on the principle that two and two make four, and under no circumstances allow that they make five, the more feeling you put into them, the surer they are to capsize and go down. On the contrary, load your revolutionary ship with the proper lading of science; hold her strictly to the load-star; try no monkeyshines and no dillyings and dallyings with anything that is not strictly scientific, or with any man who does not stand on our uncompromisingly scientific platform; do that, and then unfurl freely the sails of morality; then the more your sails, the better off your ship; but not unless you do that, will you be safe, or can you prevail.

Socialism knows that revolutionary upheavals and transformations proceed from the rock-bed of material needs. With a full appreciation of and veneration for moral impulses that are balanced with scientific knowledge, it eschews, looks with just suspicion upon and gives a wide berth to balloon morality, or be it those malarial fevers that reformers love to dignify with the name of "moral feelings."

A third nerve centre of Socialism by which to distinguish reform from revolution is its manly, aggressive posture.

The laws that rule sociology run upon lines parallel with and are the exact counterparts of those that natural science has established prevail in biology.

In the first place, the central figure in biology is the species, not the individual specimen. Consequently, that is the central figure on the field of sociology that corresponds to and represents the species on the field of biology. In sociology, the economic classes take the place of the species in biology.

In the second place, struggle, and not piping peace; assimilation by the ruthless process of the expulsion of all elements that are not fit for assimilation, and not external coalition—such are the laws of growth in biology, and such they are and needs must be the laws of growth in sociology.

Hence, Socialism recognizes in modern society the existence of a struggle of classes, and the line that divides the combatants to be the economic line that separates the interests of the property-holding capitalist class from the interests of the propertyless class of the proletariat. As a final result of this, Socialism, with the Nazarene, spurns as futile, if not wicked, the method of cajolery and seduction, or the crying of "Peace, peace where there is no peace," and cuts a clean swath, while reform is eternally entangled in its course of charming, luring, decoying.

EUGENE V. DEBS

Unionism and Socialism (1904)

*The socialist labor organizer Eugene Victor Debs (1855–1926)
gained national prominence when he led the successful American
Railway Union strike against the Great Northern Railroad in 1894.
Four years later he founded what became known as the Socialist
Party of America. He was the party's candidate for president from
1900 to 1912 and again in 1920, when he was serving a prison term
for criticizing the government's enforcement of the 1917 Espionage
Act. His 1904 pamphlet "Unionism and Socialism" explained that
the labor movement consists of a political side and a trade-unionist
side that should draw on the latent power of workers and develop a
sense of class consciousness in the struggle to overthrow the capitalist system.*

The labor question, as it is called, has come to be recognized as the
foremost of our time. In some form it thrusts itself into every human
relation, and directly or indirectly has a part in every controversy. * * *

There has always been a labor question since man first exploited man
in the struggle for existence, but not until its true meaning was revealed
in the development of modern industry did it command serious thought
or intelligent consideration, and only then came any adequate conception
of its importance to the race. * * *

A century ago a boy served his apprenticeship and became the master
of his trade. The few simple tools with which work was then done were
generally owned by the man who used them; he could provide himself with
the small quantity of raw material he required, and freely follow his chosen pursuit and enjoy the fruit of his labor. But as everything had to be
produced by the work of his hands, production was a slow process, meagre
of results, and the worker found it necessary to devote from twelve to fifteen hours to his daily task to earn a sufficient amount to support himself
and family.

It required most of the time and energy of the average worker to produce enough to satisfy the physical wants of himself and those dependent
upon his labor.

There was little leisure for mental improvement, for recreation or so-cial intercourse. The best that can be said for the workingman of this pe-riod is that he enjoyed political freedom, controlled in large measure his own employment, by virtue of his owning the tools of his trade, appropri-ated to his own use the product of his labor and lived his quiet, uneventful round to the end of his days.

This was a new country, with boundless stretches of virgin soil. There was ample room and opportunity, air and sunlight, for all.

There was no millionaire in the United States; nor was there a tramp. These types are the products of the same system. The former is produced at the expense of the latter, and both at the expense of the working class. They appeared at the same time in the industrial development and they will disappear together with the abolition of the system that brought them into existence.

The application of machinery to productive industry was followed by tremendous and far-reaching changes in the whole structure of society. First among these was the change in the status of the worker, who, from an independent mechanic or small producer, was reduced to the level of a dependent wage worker. The machine had leaped, as it were, into the arena of industrial activity, and had left little or no room for the applica-tion of the worker's skill or the use of his individual tools.

The economic dependence of the working class became more and more rigidly fixed—and at the same time a new era dawned for the human race.

The more or less isolated individual artisans were converted into groups of associated workers and marshalled for the impending social revolution. * * *

The swift and vast concentration of capital and the unprecedented in-dustrial activity which marked the close of the nineteenth century were followed by the most extraordinary growth in the number and variety of trades-unions in the history of the movement; yet this expansion, re-markable as it was, has not only been equalled, but excelled, in the first years of the new century, the tide of unionism sweeping over the whole country, and rising steadily higher, notwithstanding the efforts put forth from a hundred sources controlled by the ruling class to restrain its march, impair its utility or stamp it out of existence. * * *

The enemies of unionism, while differing in method, are united solidly upon one point, and that is in the effort to misrepresent and discredit the men who, scorning and defying the capitalist exploiters and their min-ions, point steadily the straight and uncompromising course the move-ment must take if it is to accomplish its allotted task and safely reach its destined port.

These men, though frequently regarded as the enemies, are the true friends of trades-unionism and in good time are certain to be vindicated.

The more or less open enemies have inaugurated some interesting innovations during the past few years. The private armies the corporations used some years ago, such as Pinkerton mercenaries, coal and iron police, deputy marshals, etc., have been relegated to second place as out of date, or they are wholly out of commission. It has been found after repeated experiments that the courts are far more deadly to trades-unions, and that they operate noiselessly and with unerring precision.

The rapid fire injunction is a great improvement on the gatling gun. Nothing can get beyond its range and it never misses fire.

The capitalists are in entire control of the injunction artillery, and all the judicial gunner has to do is to touch it off at their command.

Step by step the writ of injunction has invaded the domain of trades-unionism, limiting its jurisdiction, curtailing its powers, sapping its strength and undermining its foundations, and this has been done by the courts in the name of the institutions they were designed to safeguard, but have shamelessly betrayed at the behest of the barons of capitalism.

Injunctions have been issued restraining the trades-unions and their members from striking, from boycotting, from voting funds to strikes, from levying assessments to support their members, from walking on the public highway, from asking non-union men not to take their places, from meeting to oppose wage reductions, from expelling a spy from membership, from holding conversation with those who had taken or were about to take their jobs, from congregating in public places, from holding meetings, from doing anything and everything, directly, indirectly or any other way, to interfere with the employing class in their unalienable right to operate their plants as their own interests may dictate, and to run things generally to suit themselves.

The courts have found it in line with judicial procedure to strike every weapon from labor's economic hand and leave it defenseless at the mercy of its exploiter: and now that the courts have gone to the last extremity in this nefarious plot of subjugation, labor, at last, is waking up to the fact that it has not been using its political arm in the struggle at all; that the ballot which it can wield is strong enough not only to disarm the enemy, but to drive that enemy entirely from the field.

The courts, so notoriously in control of capital, and so shamelessly perverted to its base and sordid purpose are, therefore, exercising a wholesome effect upon trades-unionism by compelling the members to note the class character of our capitalist government and driving them to the inevitable conclusion that the labor question is also a political question and that the working class must organize their political power that they may wrest the government from capitalist control and put an end to class rule forever.

Trades unionists for the most part learn slowly, but they learn surely, and fresh object lessons are prepared for them every day. * * *

They have seen the supreme court of the nation turn labor out without a hearing, while the corporation lawyers, who compose this august body, and who hold their commissions in virtue of the 'well done' of their capitalist retainers, solemnly descant upon the immaculate purity of our judicial institutions.

They have seen state legislatures, both Republican and Democratic, with never an exception, controlled bodily by the capitalist class and turn the committees of labor unions empty-handed from their doors.

They have seen state supreme courts declare as unconstitutional the last vestige of law upon the statute books that could by any possibility be construed as affording any shelter or relief to the labor union or its members.

They have seen these and many other things and will doubtless see many more before their eyes are opened as a class; but we are thankful for them all, painful though they be to us in having to bear witness to the suffering of our benighted brethren.

In this way only can they be made to see, to think, to act, and every wrong they suffer brings them nearer to their liberation.

The 'pure and simple' trade-union of the past does not answer the requirements of today, and they who insist that it does are blind to the changes going on about them, and out of harmony with the progressive forces of the age. * * *

The members of a trade-union should be taught the true import, the whole object of the labor movement and understand its entire program.

They should know that the labor movement means more, infinitely more, than a paltry increase in wages and the strike necessary to secure it; that while it engages to do all that possibly can be done to better the working conditions of its members its higher object is to overthrow the capitalist system of private ownership of the tools of labor, abolish wage-slavery and achieve the freedom of the whole working class and, in fact, of all mankind. * * *

The trades-union is an economic organization with distinct economic functions and as such is a part, a necessary part, but a part only of the Labor Movement; it has its own sphere of activity, its own program and is its own master within its economic limitations.

But the labor movement has also its political side and the trades-unionist must be educated to realize its importance and to understand that the political side of the movement must be *unionized* as well as the economic side; and that he is not in fact a union man at all who, although a member of the union on the economic side, is a non-unionist on the political side; and while striking for, votes against the working class.

The trades-union expresses the economic power and the Socialist party expresses the political power of the Labor movement.

The fully developed labor-unionist uses both his economic and political power in the interest of his class. He understands that the struggle between labor and capital is a class struggle; that the working class are in a great majority, but divided, some in trade-unions and some out of them, some in one political party and some in another; that because they are divided they are helpless and must submit to being robbed of what their labor produces, and treated with contempt; that they must unite their class in the trades-union on the one hand and in the Socialist party on the other hand; that industrially and politically they must act together as a class against the capitalist class and that this struggle is a class struggle, and that any workingman who deserts his union in a strike and goes to the other side is a scab, and any workingman who deserts his party on election day and goes over to the enemy is a betrayer of his class and an enemy of his fellowman.

Both sides are organized in this class struggle, the capitalists, however, far more thoroughly than the workers. In the first place the capitalists are, comparatively, few in number, while the workers number many millions. Next, the capitalists are men of financial means and resources, and can buy the best brains and command the highest order of ability the market affords. Then again, they own the earth, and the mills and mines and locomotives and ships and stores and the jobs that are attached to them, and this not only gives them tremendous advantage in the struggle, but makes them for the time the absolute masters of the situation.

The workers, on the other hand, are poor as a rule, and ignorant as a class, *but they are in an overwhelming majority.* In a word, they have the power, but are not conscious of it. This then is the supreme demand; to make them conscious of the power of their class, or class-conscious workingmen.

The working class alone does the world's work, has created its capital, produced its wealth, constructed its mills and factories, dug its canals, made its roadbeds, laid its rails and operates its trains, spanned the rivers with bridges and tunnelled the mountains, delved for the precious stones that glitter upon the bosom of vulgar idleness and reared the majestic palaces that shelter insolent parasites.

The working class alone—and by the working class I mean all useful workers, all who by the labor of their hands or the effort of their brains, or both in alliance, as they ought universally to be, increase the knowledge and add to the wealth of society—the working class alone is essential to society and therefore the only class that can survive in the world-wide struggle for freedom.

We have said that both classes, the capitalist class and the working class are organized for the class struggle, but the organization, especially that of the workers, is far from complete; indeed, it would be nearer exact to say that it has but just fairly begun. * * *

In the class struggle the workers must unite and fight together as one on both economic and political fields.

The Socialist party is to the workingman politically what the trades-union is to him industrially; the former is the party of his class, while the latter is the union of his trade.

The difference between them is that while the trades-union is confined to the trade, the Socialist party embraces the entire working class, and while the union is limited to bettering conditions under the wage system, the party is organized to conquer the political power of the nation, wipe out the wage system and make the workers themselves the masters of the earth. * * *

It is of vital importance to the trades-union that its members be class-conscious, that they understand the class struggle and their duty as union men on the political field, so that in every move that is made they will have the goal in view, and while taking advantage of every opportunity to secure concessions and enlarge their economic advantage, they will at the same time unite at the ballot box, not only to back up the economic struggle of the trades-union, but to finally wrest the government from capitalist control and establish the working class republic. * * *

Socialism also means a coming phase of civilization, next in order to the present one, in which the collective people will own and operate the sources and means of wealth production, in which all will have equal right to work and all will cooperate together in producing wealth and all will enjoy all the fruit of their collective labor. * * *

The capitalist system has had its day and, like other systems that have gone before, it must pass away when it has fulfilled its mission and made room for another system more in harmony with the forces of progress and with the onward march of civilization.

The centralization of capital, the concentration of industry and the co-operation of workingmen mark the beginning of the end. Competition is no longer 'the life of trade.' Only they are clamoring for 'competition' who have been worsted in the struggle and would like to have another deal.

The small class who won out in the game of competition and own the trusts want no more of it. They know what it is, and have had enough. * * *

No successful capitalist wants competition—for himself—he only wants it for the working class, so that he can buy his labor power at the lowest competitive price in the labor market. * * *

The day of individual effort, of small tools, free competition, hand labor, long hours and meagre results is gone never to return. The civilization reared upon this old foundation is crumbling.

The economic basis of society is being transformed.

The working class are being knit together in the bonds of cooperation, they are becoming conscious of their interests as a class, and marshalling the workers for the class struggle and collective ownership.

With the triumph of the workers the mode of production and distribution will be completely revolutionized.

Private ownership and production for profit will be supplanted by social ownership and production for use.

The economic interests of the workers will be mutual. They will work together in harmony instead of being arrayed against each other in competitive warfare.

The collective workers will own the machinery of production, and there will be work for all and all will receive their socially due share of the product of their cooperative labor.

It is for this great work that the workers and their sympathizers must organize and educate and agitate.

EUGENE V. DEBS

Speech to the Jury (1918)

An outspoken critic of the federal government during World War I, Debs was arrested in 1918 for a bitter antiwar speech he delivered in Canton, Ohio, in violation of the Espionage Act. In his closing statements to the jury, Debs delivered a stirring attack on militarism and capitalism as he defended the principles of socialism, free speech, and democracy. Debs spent two years of a ten-year sentence in prison for the antiwar speech.

I wish to admit the truth of all that has been testified to in this proceeding. I have no disposition to deny anything that is true. I would not, if I could, escape the results of an adverse verdict. I would not retract a word that I have uttered that I believe to be true to save myself from going to the penitentiary for the rest of my days.

I am charged in the indictment, first, that I did willfully cause and attempt to cause or incite, insubordination, mutiny, disloyalty and refusal of duty within the military forces of the United States; that I did obstruct and attempt to obstruct the recruiting and enlistment service of the United States. I am charged also with uttering words intended to bring into contempt and disrepute the form of government of the United States, the Constitution of the United States, the military forces of the United States, the flag of the United States, and the uniform of the army and navy.

* * *

I am accused further of uttering words intended to procure and incite resistance to the United States and to promote the cause of the Imperial German Government.

Gentlemen, you have heard the report of my speech at Canton on June 16, and I submit that there is not a word in that speech to warrant these charges. I admit having delivered the speech. I admit the accuracy of the speech in all of its main features as reported in this proceeding. There were two distinct reports. They vary somewhat, but they are agreed upon all the material statements embodied in that speech.

In what I had to say there my purpose was to educate the people to understand something about the social system in which we live and to prepare them to change this system by perfectly peaceable and orderly means into what I, as a Socialist, conceive to be a real democracy.

From what you heard in the address of counsel for the prosecution, you might naturally infer that I am an advocate of force and violence. It is not true. I have never advocated violence in any form. I always believed in education, in intelligence, in enlightenment, and I have always made my appeal to the reason and to the conscience of the people.

I admit being opposed to the present form of government. I admit being opposed to the present social system. I am doing what little I can, and have been for many years, to bring about a change that shall do away with the rule of the great body of the people by a relatively small class and establish in this country an industrial and social democracy.

* * * I have not a word to retract—not one. I uttered the truth. I made no statement in that speech that I am not prepared to prove. If there is a single falsehood in it, it has not been exposed. If there is a single statement in it that will not bear the light of truth, I will retract it. I will make all of the reparation in my power. But if what I said is true, and I believe it is, then whatever fate or fortune may have in store for me I shall preserve inviolate the integrity of my soul and stand by it to the end.

* * *

I have been accused of expressing sympathy for the Bolsheviki of Russia. I plead guilty to the charge. I have read a great deal about the Bolsheviki of Russia that is not true. I happen to know of my knowledge that they have been grossly misrepresented by the press of this country. Who are these much-maligned revolutionists of Russia? For years they had been the victims of a brutal Czar. They and their antecedents were sent to Siberia, lashed with a knout, if they even dreamed of freedom. At last the hour struck for a great change. The revolution came. The Czar was overthrown and his infamous regime ended. What followed? The common people of Russia came into power—the peasants, the toilers, the soldiers—and they proceeded as best they could to establish a government of the people.

* * * It may be that the much-despised Bolsheviki may fail at last, but let me say to you that they have written a chapter of glorious history. It will stand to their eternal credit. The leaders are now denounced as criminals and outlaws. Let me remind you that there was a time when George Washington, who is now revered as the father of his country, was denounced as a disloyalist; when Sam Adams, who is known to us as the father of the American Revolution, was condemned as an incendiary, and Patrick Henry, who delivered that inspired and inspiring oration, that aroused the Colonists, was condemned as a traitor. They were misunderstood at the time. They stood true to themselves, and they won an immortality of gratitude and glory.

When great changes occur in history, when great principles are involved, as a rule the majority are wrong. The minority are right. In every age there have been a few heroic souls who have been in advance of their time who have been misunderstood, maligned, persecuted, sometimes put to death. Long after their martyrdom monuments were erected to them and garlands were woven for their graves.

I have been accused of having obstructed the war. I admit it. Gentlemen, I abhor war. I would oppose the war if I stood alone. When I think of a cold, glittering steel bayonet being plunged in the white, quivering flesh of a human being, I recoil with horror. I have often wondered if I could take the life of my fellow man even to save my own.

Men talk about holy wars. There are none. Let me remind you that it was Benjamin Franklin who said, "There never was a good war or a bad peace."

* * *

I have read some history. I know that it is ruling classes that make war upon one another, and not the people. In all the history of this world the people have never yet declared a war. Not one. I do not believe that really civilized nations would murder one another. I would refuse to kill a human being on my own account. Why should I at the command of any one else, or at the command of any power on earth?

Twenty centuries ago there was one appeared upon earth we know as the Prince of Peace. He issued a command in which I believe. He said, "Love one another." He did not say, "Kill one another," but "love one another." * * * It was not long before he aroused the ill will and hatred of the usurers, the money changers, the profiteers, the high priests, the lawyers, the judges, the merchants, the bankers—in a word, the ruling class. They said of him just what the ruling class says of the Socialist today. "He is preaching dangerous doctrine. He is inciting the common rabble. He is a menace to peace and order." And they had him arraigned, tried, convicted, condemned, and they had his quivering body spiked to the gates of Jerusalem.

This has been the tragic history of the race. In the ancient world Socrates sought to teach some new truths to the people, and they made him drink the fatal hemlock. It has been true all along the track of the ages. The men and women who have been in advance, who have had new ideas, new ideals, who have had the courage to attack the established order of things, have all had to pay the same penalty.

A century and a half ago, when the American colonists were still foreign subjects, and when there were a few men who had faith in the common people and believed that they could rule themselves without a king, in that day to speak against the king was treason. If you read Bancroft or any other standard historian, you will find that a great majority of the colonists believed in the king and actually believed that he had a divine right to rule over them. They had been taught to believe that to say a word against the king, to question his so-called divine right, was sinful. There were ministers who opened their Bibles to prove that it was the patriotic duty of the people to loyally serve and support the king. But there were a few men in that day who said, "We don't need a king. We can govern ourselves." And they began an agitation that has been immortalized in history.

Washington, Adams, Paine—these were the rebels of their day. At first they were opposed by the people and denounced by the press. You can remember that it was Franklin who said to his compeers, "We have now to hang together or we'll hang separately by and by." And if the Revolution had failed, the revolutionary fathers would have been executed as felons. But it did not fail. Revolutions have a habit of succeeding when the time comes for them. The revolutionary forefathers were opposed to the form of government in their day. They were opposed to the social system of their time. They were denounced, they were condemned. But they had the moral courage to stand erect and defy all the storms of detraction; and that is why they are in history, and that is why the great respectable majority of their day sleep in forgotten graves. The world does not know they ever lived.

At a later time there began another mighty agitation in this country. It was against an institution that was deemed a very respectable one in its time, the institution of chattel slavery, that became all-powerful, that controlled the President, both branches of Congress, the Supreme Court, the press, to a very large extent the pulpit. All of the organized forces of society all the powers of government, upheld chattel slavery in that day. And again there were a few lovers of liberty who appeared. One of them was Elijah Lovejoy. Elijah Lovejoy was as much despised in his day as are the leaders of the I.W.W. in our day. Elijah Lovejoy was murdered in cold blood in Alton, Illinois, in 1837 simply because he was opposed to chattel slavery—just as I am opposed to wage slavery.

Chattel slavery disappeared. We are not yet free. We are engaged in another mighty agitation to-day. It is as wide as the world. It is the rise of the toiling and producing masses who are gradually becoming conscious of their interest, their power, as a class, who are organizing industrially and politically, who are slowly but surely developing the economic and political power that is to set them free. They are still in the minority, but they have learned how to wait, and to bide their time.

It is because I happen to be in this minority that I stand in your presence today, charged with crime. It is because I believe, as the revolutionary fathers believed in their day, that a change was due in the interests of the people, that the time had come for a better form of government, an improved system, a higher social order, a nobler humanity and a grander civilization. This minority that is so much misunderstood and so bitterly maligned is in alliance with the forces of evolution, and as certain as I stand before you this afternoon, it is but a question of time until this minority will become the conquering majority and inaugurate the greatest change in all of the history of the world. You may hasten the change; you may retard it; you can no more prevent it than you can prevent the coming of the sunrise on the morrow.

My friend, the assistant prosecutor, doesn't like what I had to say in my speech about internationalism. What is there objectionable to internationalism? If we had internationalism there would be no war. I believe in patriotism. I have never uttered a word against the flag. I love the flag as a symbol of freedom. I object only when that flag is prostituted to base purposes, to sordid ends, by those who, in the name of patriotism, would keep the people in subjection.

I believe, however, in a wider patriotism. Thomas Paine said, "My country is the world. To do good is my religion." Garrison said, "My country is the world and all mankind are my countrymen." That is the essence

of internationalism. I believe in it with all of my heart. I believe that nations have been pitted against nations long enough in hatred, in strife, in
warfare. I believe there ought to be a bond of unity between all of these
nations. I believe that the human race consists of one great family. I love
the people of this country, but I don't hate the people of any country on
earth—not even the Germans. I refuse to hate a human being because he
happens to be born in some other country. Why should I? To me it does
not make any difference where he was born or what the color of his skin
may be. Like myself, he is the image of his creator. He is a human being
endowed with the same faculties, he has the same aspirations, he is entitled to the same rights, and I would infinitely rather serve him and love
him than to hate him and kill him.

    * * * If I have criticized, if I ever condemned, it is because I have be-
lieved myself justified in doing so under the laws of the land. I have had
precedents for my attitude. This country has been engaged in a number
of wars, and every one of them has been opposed, every one of them has
been condemned by some of the most eminent men in the country. The
war of the Revolution was opposed. The Tory press denounced its leaders
as criminals and outlaws. And that was when they were under the "divine
right" of a king to rule men.

    The War of 1812 was opposed and condemned; the Mexican war was
bitterly condemned by Abraham Lincoln, by Charles Sumner, by Daniel
Webster and by Henry Clay. That war took place under the Polk administration. These men denounced the President; they condemned his administration; and they said that the war was a crime against humanity.
They were not indicted; they were not tried for crime. They are honored
to-day by all of their countrymen. The War of the Rebellion was opposed
and condemned. In 1864 the Democratic Party met in convention at
Chicago and passed a resolution condemning the war as a failure. What
would you say if the Socialist Party were to meet in convention to-day and
condemn the present war as a failure? You charge us with being disloyalists and traitors. Were the Democrats of 1864 disloyalists and traitors because they condemned the war as a failure?

    I believe in the Constitution of the United States. Isn't it strange that
we Socialists stand almost alone to-day in defending the Constitution of
the United States? The revolutionary fathers who had been oppressed
under king rule understood that free speech and free press and the right
of free assemblage by the people were the fundamental principles of
democratic government. The very first amendment to the Constitution
reads: "Congress shall make no law respecting an establishment of religion, or prohibiting the free exercise thereof; or abridging the freedom of
speech, or of the press; or the right of the people peaceably to assemble,

and to petition the government for a redress of grievances." That is perfectly plain English. It can be understood by a child. I believe that the revolutionary fathers meant just what is here stated—that Congress shall make no law abridging the freedom of speech or of the press, or of the right of the people to peaceably assemble, and to petition the government for a redress of grievances.

That is the right that I exercised at Canton on the 16th day of last June; and for the exercise of that right I now have to answer to this indictment. I believe in the right of free speech in war as well as in peace. I would not, under any circumstances, gag the lips of my biggest enemy. I would under no circumstances suppress free speech. It is far more dangerous to attempt to gag the people than to allow them to speak freely of what is in their hearts. I do not go as far as Wendell Phillips did. Wendell Phillips said that the glory of free men is that they trample unjust laws under their feet. That is how they repealed them. If a human being submits to having his lips sealed, to be in silence reduced to vassalage, he may have all else, but he is still lacking in all that dignifies and glorifies real manhood.

Now, notwithstanding this fundamental provision in the national law, Socialists' meetings have been broken up all over this country. Socialist speakers have been arrested by hundreds and flung into jail, where many of them are lying now. In some cases not even a charge was lodged against them, guilty of absolutely no crime except the crime of attempting to exercise the right guaranteed to them by the Constitution of the United States.

I have told you that I am no lawyer, but it seems to me that I know enough to know that if Congress enacts any law that conflicts with this provision in the Constitution, that law is void. If the Espionage Law finally stands, then the Constitution of the United States is dead. If that law is not the negation of every fundamental principle established by the Constitution, then certainly I am unable to read or to understand the English language.

* * *

The thing that the Kaiser incarnates and embodies, called militarism, I would, if I could, wipe from the face of the earth,—not only the militarism of Germany, but the militarism of the whole world. I am quite well aware of the fact that the war now deluging the world with blood was precipitated there. Not by the German people, but by the class that rules, oppresses, robs and degrades the German people. President Wilson has repeatedly said that we were not making war on the German people, and yet in war it is the people who are slain, and not the rulers who are responsible for the war.

With every drop in my veins I despise kaiserism, and all that kaiserism expresses and implies. I have sympathy with the suffering, struggling people everywhere. It does not make any difference under what flag they were born, or where they live, I have sympathy with them all. I would, if I could, establish a social system that would embrace them all. It is precisely at this point that we come to realize that there is a reason why the peoples of the various nations are pitted against each other in brutal warfare instead of being united in one all-embracing brotherhood.

War does not come by chance. War is not the result of accident. There is a definite cause for war, especially a modern war. The war that began in Europe can readily be accounted for. For the last forty years, under this international capitalist system, this exploiting system, these various nations of Europe have been preparing for the inevitable. And why? In all these nations the great industries are owned by a relatively small class. They are operated for the profit of that class. And great abundance is produced by the workers; but their wages will only buy back a small part of their product. What is the result? They have a vast surplus on hand; they have got to export it; they have got to find a foreign market for it. As a result of this these nations are pitted against each other. They are industrial rivals—competitors. They begin to arm themselves to open, to maintain the market and quickly dispose of their surplus. There is but the one market. All these nations are competitors for it, and sooner or later every war of trade becomes a war of blood.

Now, where there is exploitation there must be some form of militarism to support it. Wherever you find exploitation you find some form of military force. In a smaller way you find it in this country. It was there long before war was declared. For instance, when the miners out in Colorado entered upon a strike about four years ago, the state militia, that is under the control of the Standard Oil Company, marched upon a camp, where the miners and their wives and children were in tents,—and, by the way, a report of this strike was issued by the United States Commission on Industrial Relations. When the soldiers approached the camp at Ludlow, where these miners, with their wives and children, were, the miners, to prove that they were patriotic, placed flags above their tents, and when the state militia, that is paid by Rockefeller and controlled by Rockefeller, swooped down upon that camp, the first thing they did was to shoot these United States flags into tatters. Not one of them was indicted or tried because he was a traitor to his country. Pregnant women were killed, and a number of innocent children slain. This in the United States of America,—the fruit of exploitation. The miners wanted a little more of what they had been producing. But the Standard Oil Company wasn't rich enough. It insisted that all they were entitled to was just enough to keep them in working order. There is slavery for you. And when at last they protested, when they were tormented by hunger, when they saw their children in tatters, they were shot down as if they had been so many vagabond dogs.

* * * Men *are* fit for something better than slavery and cannon fodder; and the time will come, though I shall not live to see it, when slavery will be wiped from the earth, and when men will marvel that there ever was a time when men who called themselves civilized rushed upon each other like wild beasts and murdered one another, by methods so cruel and barbarous that they defy the power of man to describe. I can hear the shrieks of the soldiers of Europe in my dreams. I have imagination enough to see a battlefield. I can see it strewn with the legs of human beings, who but yesterday were in the flush and glory of their young manhood. I can see them at eventide, scattered about in remnants, their limbs torn from their bodies, their eyes gouged out. Yes, I can see them, and I can hear them. I have looked above and beyond this frightful scene. I think of the mothers who are bowed in the shadow of their last great grief—whose hearts are breaking. And I say to myself, "I am going to do the little that lies in my power to wipe from this earth that terrible scourge of war."

If I believed in war I could not be kept out of the first line trenches. I would not be patriotic at long range. I would be honest enough, if I believed in bloodshed, to shed my own. But I do not believe that the shedding of blood bears any actual testimony to patriotism, to lead a country to civilization. On the contrary, I believe that warfare, in all of its forms, is an impeachment of our social order, and a rebuke to our much vaunted Christian civilization.

SAMUEL GOMPERS

The American Labor Movement (1914)

The British-born labor leader Samuel Gompers (1850–1924) co-founded the American Federation of Labor, an umbrella organization for skilled craft workers that he led as president for every year except 1895 from 1886 to 1924. In statements to the U.S. Commission on Industrial Relations at hearings in New York City in 1914 that were later

published as a pamphlet, Gompers explained that the aims of the
American Federation of Labor were practical, not ideological. The
union, Gompers insisted, was more interested in "improvements here
and now" than in any "fixed program" or "species of speculative philos-
ophy." Gompers challenged the inhumanity of prevailing working con-
ditions, but not the system of capitalism itself.

The workers of the United States do not receive the full product of their labor. It is impossible for any one to say definitely what proportion the workers receive in payment for their labor, but due to the organized labor movement they have received and are receiving a larger share of the product of their labor than ever before in the history of modern industry. One of the functions of organized labor is to increase the share of the workers in the product of their labor. Organized labor makes constantly increasing demands upon society for rewards for the services which the workers give to society and without which civilized life would be impossible. The process of increasing the share is not always gradual, but it is continual. The organized labor movement has generally succeeded in forcing an increase in the proportion the workers receive of the general product.

The working people—and I prefer to say working people and to speak of them as really human beings—are prompted by the same desires, the same hopes of a better life as are all other people. They are not willing to wait for a better life until after they have shuffled off this mortal coil but they want improvements here and now. They want to make conditions better for their children so that they may be prepared to meet other and new problems of their time. The working people are pressing forward, making their demands and presenting their claims with whatever power they can exercise in a natural, normal manner to secure a larger and constantly increasing share of what they produce. They are working toward the highest and the best ideals of social justice.

The intelligent, common-sense workingmen prefer to deal with the problems of to-day, with which they must contend if they want to make advancements, rather than to deal with a picture and a dream which have never had, and, I am sure, will never have, any reality in the affairs of humanity, and which threaten, if they could be introduced, the most pernicious system for circumscribing effort and activity that has ever been invented.

The workers will never stop in any effort, nor will they stop at any point in an effort to secure greater improvements in conditions or for a better life in all its phases. Where these efforts may lead, what that better life may be, I do not care to predict. I decline to permit my mind or my activities to be labeled or limited by any particularism because of adherence to a theory or a dream. The A.F. of L. is neither governed in its activities by a so-called 'Social Philosophy,' nor does it work 'blindly from day to day.' Its work is well planned to be continually of the greatest benefit to the working people to protect and promote their rights and interest in every field of human activity.

The A.F. of L. is guided by the history of the past. It draws lessons from history in order to interpret conditions which confront working people so that it may work along the lines of least resistance to accomplish the best results in improving the conditions of the working men, women, and children, today, tomorrow, and tomorrow's morrow, making each day a better day than the one which went before. That is the guiding principle, philosophy, and aim of the labor movement.

In improving conditions from day to day the organized labor movement has no 'fixed program' for human progress. If you start out with a program everything must conform to it. With theorists, if facts do not conform to their theories, then so much the worse for the facts. Their declarations of theories and actions refuse to be hampered by facts. We do not set any particular standard, but work for the best possible conditions immediately obtainable for the workers. When they are obtained then we strive for better.

It does not require any elaborate social philosophy or great discernment to know that a wage of $3 a day and a workday of eight hours in sanitary workshops are better than $2.50 a day and a workday of twelve hours under perilous conditions. The working people will not stop when any particular point is reached; they will never stop in their efforts to obtain a better life for themselves, for their wives, for their children, and for all humanity. The object is to attain complete social justice.

The Socialist party has for its purpose the abolition of the present system of wages. Many employers agree with that purpose—the abolition of wages. But the A.F. of L. goes beyond the system which those dreamers have conceived.

The movement of the working people, whether under the A.F. of L. or not, will simply follow the human impulse for improvement in conditions wherever that may lead, and wherever that may lead they will go without aiming at any theoretical goal. Human impulse for self-betterment will lead constantly to the material, physical, social, and moral betterment of the people. We decline to commit our labor movement to any species of speculative philosophy.

The full value of production does not go to the actual working men today. A portion goes to investment, superintendence, agencies for the creation of wants among people, and many other things. Some of these are legitimate factors in industry entitled to reward, but many of them should be eliminated. The legitimate factors are superintendency, the creation of wants, administration, returns for investment in so far as it is honest investment and does not include watered stock of inflated holdings. * * *

The efforts of the American labor movement to secure a larger share of the income are directed against all who illegitimately stand between the workers and the attainment of a better life. This class includes all who have not made honest investment in honest enterprise. Employers, capitalists, stockholders, bondholders—the capitalist class generally—oppose the efforts of the workers in the A.F. of L. and in other organizations to obtain a larger share of the product. Very much of the opposition to the efforts of the working people to secure improved conditions has come from those who obtain what may be called an unearned share in the distribution. The beneficiaries of the present system of distribution desire to retain as much as possible of their present share or to increase that proportion. But an additional reason that leads to opposition is that there are employers who live in the twentieth century, yet who have the mental outlook of the sixteenth century in their attitude toward the working people, and who still imagine that they are 'masters of all they survey.' These employers think that any attempt upon the part of the working people to secure improvements in their condition is a spirit of rebellion that must be frowned down. But we organized workers have found that after we have had some contests with employers, whether we have won the battle or lost it, if we but maintain our organization there is less difficulty thereafter in reaching a joint agreement or a collective bargain involving improved conditions of the workers.

The stronger the organization of the workers the greater the likelihood of their securing concessions. These concessions are not altogether because of the strength shown by the employes, but result in part from the changed attitude of the employer.

An employer changes his policy when he is convinced that the working-men have demonstrated that they have a right to a voice in determining questions affecting the relations between themselves and their employers.

* * *

Because employers as a class are interested in maintaining or increasing their share of the general product and because workers are determined to demand a greater and ever greater share of this same general product the economic interests between these two are not harmonious. Upon this point I have been repeatedly misrepresented by socialist writers and orators whose frequent repetitions of that misrepresentation have finally convinced them of the truth of their assertion. No amount of emphatic repudiation of that statement, no matter how often that repudiation and denial have been expressed, has secured a change in the assertion that my position was contrary to the one I have just stated.

From my earliest understanding of the conditions that prevail in the industrial world I have been convinced and I have asserted that the economic interests of the employing class and those of the working class are not harmonious. That has been my position ever since—never changed in the slightest. There are times when, for temporary purposes, interests are reconcilable; but they are temporary only.

When a fair and reasonable opportunity presents itself for continued improvement in the conditions of the workers, the movement of the workers must necessarily go on and will go on. It will not be dominated by the so-called intellectuals or butters-in. The working class movement to be most effective must be conducted by the workers themselves. It is conducted by the working people in the interests of the working people. It is conducted against those who stand in the way, hostile to the advancement of conditions for the working people. It is conducted against those employers whoever they may be—the employers who refuse to understand modern industrial conditions and the constant need for the advancement of the working people and who refuse to accede to the demands of the workers. * * *

In the initial stages of the altered relations between workers and employers improvements are forced upon employers by collective bargains, strikes and boycotts. Later there is a realization upon the part of the employers that it is more costly to enter into long strikes and lockouts than to concede conditions without interrupting the industry. As the vision and the understanding of the employer change, his attitude toward his workmen and the relation between employer and workers also change, so that the sentiments and views of employers are often in entire accord with those of the organizations of working people.

However the gains made by the organized labor movement in this country have generally been wrung from the employing classes. What workingmen of America have obtained in improved conditions, higher wages, shorter hours of labor, was not handed to them on a silver platter. They have had to organize, they have had to show their teeth, they have had to strike, they have had to go hungry, and to make sacrifices in order to impress upon the employers their determination to be larger sharers in the products of labor. * * *

On the whole, the A.F. of L. recognizes that the struggle for improvement in the conditions of the workers is the struggle of the workers themselves. The unions affiliated to the A.F. of L. and the A.F. of L. in dealing with directly affiliated locals do not permit employers to become members of the unions. I know of no means by which the interests of the employers and of the workers can be harmonized in the full, broad sense of that term.

The labor representatives most useful to the organization and to the movement must devote their time and their thought to the interests of the labor organization and to the working people. It is the duty of the men usually designated as labor leaders to carry the work, preach the doctrine, to carry the message, the gospel of Labor, of justice to Labor, to any place on earth, to every people on earth, to defend that doctrine, to promote a better understanding among any and all. It is the duty of every labor leader to make his cause best known wherever any opportunity may be afforded.

It is not the practice of large employers of labor to carry the gospel of their interests wherever they can, particularly into the camp of organized labor. While the National Association of Manufacturers is absolutely hostile to the labor unions and everything they represent, yet it is not an association in which a labor leader is either accepted or tolerated. He therefore cannot take the doctrine and message of Labor there. The avowed purpose of the National Association of Manufacturers is an active organization for warfare against organized labor. It has a severer purpose, which is to prevent organizations of working people from protecting themselves or their interests. As a matter of fact, the president of that organization only a few days ago declared that he was going to form a 'new union' over our heads. It is on a par with pretended friends of labor, but with them it is simply treason to the interests of labor.

Employers in their relation to employes and to the labor movement are generally guided by their own economic interests, and the greater number of employers are not members of the N.A.M. and are not in accord with that association. In addition, I know that there are a number of employers who belong to the N.A.M. because of trade advantages which are secured through other activities of that association. Those of the employing class who have organized for the promotion of their own economic interests which are opposed to those of the working classes are against the organized labor movement. * * *

The A.F. of L. has an independent policy, an independent political policy—a policy so independent politically that it is independent of the Socialist party too. It is concerned more about achievements than it is about the instrumentality for achievement. We have achieved through the American labor movement more real betterment for the working people than has been accomplished by any other labor movement in the world.

The entire trade union movement of America is absolutely without any parties and without political affiliation. The large national organizations not affiliated to the A.F. of L. are also absolutely independent politically. * * *

There has been for many years an insistent effort to establish for these men some tribunal that would fix by legislation the wages, conditions of service, and hours of labor. Insistence for the enactment of legislation placing in a governmental board such power is always traceable to the larger interests that employ men. There is an underground process constantly at work to devise ways and means ostensibly and superficially wellsounding, but which contain a process and a method by which the status of the workmen can be fixed. The purpose is to tie them to their tasks, that the right of freedom of action shall be first impaired and then denied. Our friends, the members and leaders of the Socialist party, would gladly establish that in the wholesale. They do not understand the real struggle for freedom. * * *

The labor movement in this country has already become political as well as economic. I am not prepared to say what the next or the future generations may develop; but to the A.F. of L., and I suppose to the American working people, it is of less consequence what instrumentality is employed in the accomplishment of the purpose than the accomplishment of the purpose itself. We have in the United States secured legislation of the most substantial character without the use or the necessity of a so-called independent labor party. * * *

There is no necessity, in the United States at least, for dealing with these problems. Our problems are primarily industrial. I have my day dreams, and build my castles in the air, and sometimes allow my mind to run riot; but when I want to be of some service to my fellow workers now and hereafter I am going to get down to terra firma and help them in their present struggle.

ORESTES BROWNSON

The Woman Question (1869)

The former radical Orestes Brownson (1803–1876) became increasingly conservative after he converted to Catholicism in 1844. In an 1869 article written for the Catholic World, *Brownson criticized calls for women's suffrage as unnecessary and dangerous threats to the health and sanctity of the family. Brownson's article is a classic formulation of the traditional view that the appropriate role for a woman in politics is that of a wife and mother who educates her children in the values essential to republican governments.*

The Woman Question, though not yet an all-engrossing question in our own or in any other country, is exciting so much attention, and is so vigorously agitated, that no periodical can very well refuse to consider it. As yet, though entering into politics, it has not become a party question, and we think we may discuss it without overstepping the line we have marked out for ourselves—that of studiously avoiding all party politics; not because we have not the courage to discuss them, but because we have aims and purposes which appeal to all parties alike, and which can best be effected by letting party politics alone.

We say frankly in the outset that we are decidedly opposed to female suffrage and eligibility. The woman's rights women demand them both as a right, and complain that men, in refusing to concede them, withhold a natural right, and violate the equal rights on which the American republic professes to be based. We deny that women have a natural right to suffrage and eligibility; for neither is a natural right at all for either men or women. Either is a trust from civil society, not a natural and indefeasible right; and civil society confers either on whom it judges trustworthy, and on such conditions as it deems it expedient to annex. As the trust has never been conferred by civil society with us on women, they are deprived of no right by not being enfranchised.

* * * We ask not if women are equal, inferior, or superior to men; for the two sexes are different, and between things different in kind there is no relation of equality or of inequality. Of course, we hold that the woman was made for the man, not the man for the woman, and that the husband is the head of the wife, even as Christ is the head of the church; not the wife of the husband; but it suffices here to say that we do not object to the political enfranchisement of women on the ground of their feebleness, either of intellect or of body, or of any real incompetency to vote or to hold office. We are Catholics, and the church has always held in high honor chaste, modest, and worthy women as matrons, widows, or virgins. Her calendar has a full proportion of female saints, whose names she proposes to the honor and veneration of all the faithful. She bids the wife obey her husband in the Lord; but asserts her moral independence of him, leaves her conscience free, and holds her accountable for her own deeds.

* * *

Nor do we object to the political enfranchisement of women in the special interest of the male sex. Men and women have no separate interests. What elevates the one elevates the other; what degrades the one degrades the other. Men can not depress women, place them in a false position, make them toys or drudges, without doing an equal injury to themselves; and one ground of our dislike to the so-called woman's rights movement is, that it proceeds on the supposition that there is no inter-dependence between men and women, and seeks to render them mutually independent of each other, with entirely distinct and separate interests. * * *

* * * Each, in this world, is the complement of the other, and the more closely identified are their interests, the better is it for both. We, in opposing the political enfranchisement of women, seek the interest of men no more than we do the interest of women themselves.

Women, no doubt, undergo many wrongs, and are obliged to suffer many hardships, but seldom they alone. It is a world of trial, a world in which there are wrongs of all sorts, and sufferings of all kinds. We have lost paradise, and cannot regain it in this world. We must go through the valley of the shadow of death before reentering it. You cannot make earth heaven, and there is no use in trying; and least of all can you do it by political means. It is hard for the poor wife to have to maintain a lazy, idle, drunken vagabond of a husband, and three or four children into the bargain; it is hard for the wife delicately reared, accomplished, fitted to adorn the most intellectual, graceful, and polished society, accustomed to every luxury that wealth can procure, to find herself a widow reduced to poverty, and a family of young children to support, and unable to obtain any employment for which she is fitted as the means of supporting them. But men suffer too. It is no less hard for the poor, industrious, hard-working man to find what he earns wasted by an idle, extravagant, incompetent, and heedless wife, who prefers gadding and gossiping to taking care of her household. And how much easier is it for the man who is reduced from affluence to poverty, a widower with three or four motherless children to provide for? The reduction from affluence to poverty is sometimes the fault of the wife as well as of the husband. It is usually their joint fault. Women have wrongs, so have men; but a woman has as much power to make a man miserable as a man has to make a woman miserable; and she tyrannizes over him as often as he does over her. If he has more power of attack, nature has given her more power of defence. Her tongue is as formidable a weapon as his fists, and she knows well how, by her seeming meekness, gentleness, and apparent martyrdom, to work on his feelings, to enlist the sympathy of the neighborhood on her side and against him. Women are neither so wronged nor so helpless as *The Revolution* pretends. Men can be brutal, and women can tease and provoke.

But let the evils be as great as they may, and women as greatly wronged as is pretended, what can female suffrage and eligibility do by way of relieving them? All modern methods of reform are very much like dram-drinking. The dram needs to be constantly increased in frequency and quantity, while the prostration grows greater and greater, till the drinker gets the *delirium tremens*, becomes comatose, and dies. The extension of suffrage in modern times has cured or lessened no social or moral evil; and under it, as under any other political system, the rich grow richer and the poor poorer. Double the dram, enfranchise the women, give them the political right to vote and be voted for; what single moral or social evil will it prevent or cure? Will it make the drunken husband temperate, the lazy and idle industrious and diligent? Will it prevent the ups and downs of life, the fall from affluence to poverty, keep death out of the house, and prevent widowhood and orphanage? These things are beyond the reach of politics. You cannot legislate men or women into virtue, into sobriety, industry, providence. The doubled dram would only introduce a double poison into the system, a new element of discord into the family, and through the family into society, and hasten the moment of dissolution. When a false principle of reform is adopted, the evil sought to be cured is only aggravated.

* * *

The conclusive objection to the political enfranchisement of women is, that it would weaken and finally break up and destroy the Christian family. The social unit is the family, not the individual; and the greatest danger to American society is, that we are rapidly becoming a nation of isolated individuals, without family ties or affections. The family has already been much weakened, and is fast disappearing. We have broken away from the old homestead, have lost the restraining and purifying associations that gathered round it, and live away from home in hotels and boarding-houses. We are daily losing the faith, the virtues, the habits, and the manners without which the family cannot be sustained; and when the family goes, the nation goes too, or ceases to be worth preserving. God made the family the type and basis of society; "male and female made he them." A large and influential class of women not only neglect but disdain the retired and simple domestic virtues, and scorn to be tied down to the modest but essential duties—the drudgery, they call it—of wives and mothers. This, coupled with the separate pecuniary interests of husband and wife secured, and the facility of divorce *a vinculo matrimonii* allowed by the laws of most of the states of the Union, make the family, to a fearful extent, the mere shadow of what it was and of what it should be.

Extend now to women suffrage and eligibility; give them the political right to vote and to be voted for; render it feasible for them to enter the arena of political strife, to become canvassers in elections and candidates for office, and what remains of family union will soon be dissolved. The wife may espouse one political party, and the husband another, and it may well happen that the husband and wife may be rival candidates for the same office, and one or the other doomed to the mortification of defeat. Will the husband like to see his wife enter the lists against him, and triumph over him? Will the wife, fired with political ambition for place or power, be pleased to see her own husband enter the lists against her, and succeed at her expense? Will political rivalry and the passions it never fails to engender increase the mutual affection of husband and wife for each other, and promote domestic union and peace, or will it not carry into the bosom of the family all the strife, discord, anger, and division of the political canvass?

Then, when the wife and mother is engrossed in the political canvass, or in discharging her duties as a representative or senator in congress, a member of the cabinet, or a major-general in the field, what is to become of the children? The mother will have little leisure, perhaps less inclination, to attend to them. A stranger, or even the father, cannot supply her place. Children need a mother's care; her tender nursing, her sleepless vigilance, and her mild and loving but unfailing discipline. This she cannot devolve on the father, or turn over to strangers. Nobody can supply the place of a mother. Children, then, must be neglected; nay, they will be in the way, and be looked upon as an encumbrance. Mothers will repress their maternal instincts; and the horrible crime of infanticide before birth, now becoming so fearfully prevalent, and actually causing a decrease in the native population of several of the states of the Union as well as in more than one European country, will become more prevalent still, and the human race be threatened with extinction. Women in easy circumstances, and placing pleasure before duty, grow weary of the cares of maternity, and they would only become more weary still if the political arena were open to their ambition.

Woman was created to be a wife and a mother; that is her destiny. To that destiny all her instincts point, and for it nature has specially qualified her. Her proper sphere is home, and her proper function is the care of the household, to manage a family, to take care of children, and attend to their early training. For this she is endowed with patience, endurance, passive courage, quick sensibilities, a sympathetic nature, and great executive and administrative ability. She was born to be a queen in her own household, and to make home cheerful, bright, and happy. Surely those women who are wives and mothers should stay at home and discharge its duties; and the woman's rights party, by seeking to draw her away from the domestic sphere, where she is really great, noble, almost divine, and to throw her into the turmoil of political life, would rob her of her true dignity and worth, and place her in a position where all her special qualifications and peculiar excellences would count for nothing. She cannot be spared from home for that.

It is pretended that woman's generous sympathies, her nice sense of justice, and her indomitable perseverance in what she conceives to be right are needed to elevate our politics above the low, grovelling and sordid tastes of men; but while we admit that women will make almost any sacrifice to obtain their own will, and make less than men do of obstacles or consequences, we are not aware that they have a nicer or a truer sense of justice, or are more disinterested in their aims than men. All history proves that the corruptest epochs in a nation's life are precisely those in which women have mingled most in political affairs, and have had the most influence in their management. If they go into the political world, they will, if the distinction of sex is lost sight of, have no special advantage over men, nor be more influential for good or for evil. If they go as women, using all the blandishments, seductions, arts, and intrigues of their sex, their influence will tend more to corrupt and debase than to purify and elevate. Women usually will stick at nothing to carry their points; and when unable to carry them by appeals to the strength of the other sex, they will appeal to its weakness. When once they have thrown off their native modesty, and entered a public arena with men, they will go to lengths that men will not.

* * *

Women are not needed as men; they are needed as women, to do, not what men can do as well as they, but what men cannot do. There is nothing which more grieves the wise and good, or makes them tremble for the future of the country, than the growing neglect or laxity of family discipline; than the insubordination, the lawlessness, and precocious depravity of Young America. There is, with the children of this generation, almost a total lack of filial reverence and obedience. And whose fault is it? It is chiefly the fault of the mothers, who fail to govern their households, and to bring up their children in a Christian manner. Exceptions there happily are; but the number of children that grow up without any proper training or discipline at home is fearfully large, and their evil example corrupts not a few of those who are well brought up. The country is no better than the town. Wives forget what they owe to their husbands, are capricious and vain, often light and frivolous, extravagant and foolish, bent on having their own way, though ruinous to the family, and generally contriving, by coaxings, blandishments, or poutings, to get it. They set an ill example to their children, who soon lose all respect for the authority of the mother, who, as a wife, forgets to honor and obey her

husband, and who, seeing her have her own way with him, insist on having their own way with her, and usually succeed. As a rule, children are
no longer subjected to a steady and firm, but mild and judicious discipline, or trained to habits of filial obedience. Hence, our daughters,
when they become wives and mothers, have none of the habits or character necessary to govern their household and to train their children.
Those habits and that character are acquired only in a school of obedience, made pleasant and cheerful by a mother's playful smile and a
mother's love.

* * *

The duty we insist upon is especially necessary in a country like ours,
where there is so little respect for authority, and government is but the
echo of public opinion. Wives and mothers, by neglecting their domestic
duties and the proper family discipline, fail to offer the necessary resistance to growing lawlessness and crime, aggravated, if not generated, by
the false notions of freedom and equality so widely entertained. It is only
by home discipline, and the early habits of reverence and obedience to
which our children are trained, that the license the government tolerates,
and the courts hardly dare attempt to restrain, can be counteracted, and
the community made a law-loving and a law-abiding community. The very
bases of society have been sapped, and the conditions of good government despised, or denounced under the name of despotism. Social and
political life is poisoned in its source, and the blood of the nation corrupted, and chiefly because wives and mothers have failed in their domestic duties, and the discipline of their families. How, then, can the
community, the nation itself, subsist, if we call them away from home,
and render its duties still more irksome to them, instead of laboring to fit
them for a more faithful discharge of their duties?

VICTORIA WOODHULL

On Constitutional Equality (1871)

*The first woman ever to run for the American presidency, the social
reformer Victoria Woodhull (1838–1927) advocated free love, women's
suffrage, and socialism. After moving to New York City, Woodhull became the first female American stockbroker when she and her sister
Tennessee Claflin established a successful stock-brokerage firm. They*

also started publishing Woodhull and Claflin's Weekly, *where they printed the first English translation of* The Communist Manifesto *and championed equal rights for women. In 1870, Woodhull began lobbying Congress for women's suffrage. In her January 1871 testimony to the House Judiciary Committee, she asked Congress to pass legislation that would recognize the right of women to vote as implicit in the Fifteenth Amendment. She described her testimony and her argument in a lecture at Lincoln Hall in Washington, D.C., in February 1871.*

It was an honest zeal which first influenced me to appear before the public as a champion of a cause which receives alike the jeers of the common multitude and the railery of the select few. It is an honest zeal in the same, that inspires me with confidence to continue before it as its advocate, when but too conscious that I am of that portion of the people who are denied the privileges of freedom; who are not permitted the rights of citizens; and who are without voice, in the pursuit of justice, as one of that sovereignty to whom this government owes its existence, and to whom it will be held accountable, as it holds all accountable who set themselves against Human Rights.

* * *

I come before you, to declare that my sex are entitled to the inalienable right to life, liberty and the pursuit of happiness. The first two I cannot be deprived of except for cause and by due process of law; but upon the last, a right is usurped to place restrictions so general as to include the whole of my sex, and for which no reasons of public good can be assigned. I ask the right to pursue happiness by having a voice in that government to which I am accountable. I have not forfeited that right, still I am denied. Was assumed arbitrary authority ever more arbitrarily exercised? In practice, then, our laws are false to the principles which we profess. I have the right to life, to liberty, unless I forfeit it by an infringement upon others' rights, in which case the State becomes the arbiter and deprives me of them for the public good. I also have the right to pursue happiness, unless I forfeit it in the same way, and am denied it accordingly. It cannot be said, with any justice, that my pursuit of happiness in voting for any man for office, would be an infringement of one of his rights as a citizen or as an individual. I hold, then, that in denying me this right without my having forfeited it, that departure is made from the principles of the Constitution, and also from the true principles of government, for I am denied a right born with me, and which is inalienable. Nor can it be objected that women had no part in organizing this government. They were not denied. To-day we seek a voice in government and *are* denied.

There are *thousands* of male citizens in the country who seldom or never vote. They are not denied: they pursue happiness by not voting. Could it be assumed, because this body of citizens do not choose to exercise the right to vote, that they could be *permanently* denied the exercise thereof? *If* not, *neither* should it be assumed to deny women, who wish to vote, the right to do so.

And were it true that a majority of women do not wish to vote, it would be *no* reason why those who do, should be denied. If a right exist, and only *one in a million* desires to exercise it, *no* government should deny its enjoyment to that one. If the thousands of men who do not choose to vote should send their petitions to Congress, asking them to prevent others who do vote from so doing, would they listen to them? I went before Congress, to ask for myself and others of my sex, who wish to pursue our happiness by participating in government, protection in such pursuit, and I was told that Congress has not the necessary power.

If there are women who do not desire to have a voice in the laws to which they are accountable, and which they must contribute to support, let them speak for themselves; but they should not assume to speak for me, or for those whom I represent.

* * *

If freedom consists in having an *actual share* in appointing those who frame the laws, are not the women of this country in absolute *bondage*, and can government, in the face of the XV. Amendment, assume to deny them the right to vote, being in this "condition of servitude?" According to Franklin we are absolutely enslaved, for there *are* "governors set over us by other men," and we are "subject to the laws" they make. Is *not* Franklin good authority in matters of freedom? Again, rehearsing the arguments that have emanated from Congress and applying them to the present case, we learn that "It is idle to show that, in certain instances, the fathers failed to apply the sublime principles which they declared. Their failure can be *no* apology for those on whom the duty is now cast." Shall it be an apology *now*? Shall the omission of others to do justice keep the government from measuring it to those who now cry out for it? I went before Congress like Richelieu to his king asking for justice. Will they deny it as he did until the exigencies of the case compel them?

I *am* subject to tyranny! I am taxed in every conceivable way. For publishing a paper I must pay—for engaging in the banking and brokerage business I must pay—of what it is my fortune to acquire each year I must turn over a certain per cent.—I must pay high prices for tea, coffee and sugar: to *all* these must I submit, that *men's* government may be maintained, a government in the administration of which I am denied a voice, and from its edicts there is no appeal. I must submit to a heavy advance upon the first cost of *nearly everything I wear* in order that industries in which I have no interest may exist at my expense. I am compelled to pay extravagant rates of fare wherever I travel, because the franchises, extended to gigantic corporations, enable them to *sap* the vitality of the country, to make their *managers money kings*, by means of which they boast of being able to control not only legislators but even a State judiciary.

To be compelled to submit to *these* extortions that *such* ends may be gained, upon *any* pretext or under *any* circumstances, is bad enough; but to be compelled to submit to them, and also denied the right to cast my vote *against* them, is a tyranny *more* odious than that which, being rebelled against, gave this country independence.

* * *

Therefore it is, that instead of growing in republican liberty, we are departing from it. From an unassuming, acquiescent part of society, woman has gradually passed to an individualized human being, and as she has advanced, one after another evident right of the common people has been accorded to her. She has now become so *much* individualized as to demand the full and unrestrained exercise of *all* the rights which can be predicated of a people constructing a government based on individual sovereignty. She asks it, and shall Congress deny her? * * *

I now come to the previous condition of servitude, and there is much *more* in this than is at first apparent. We had become so accustomed to regard African slavery as servitude that we forgot there were other conditions of servitude besides. Slavery or a condition of servitude is, plainly speaking, subjection to the will of others. The negroes were subject to the will of their masters, were in a condition of servitude and had no power or authority as citizens over themselves.

I make the plain and broad assertion, that the women of this country are as *much* subject to men as the slaves were to their masters. The extent of the subjection may be less and its severity milder, but it is a complete subjection nevertheless. What can women do that men deny them? What could not the slave have done if not denied?

It is not the women who are happily situated, whose husbands hold positions of honor and trust, who are blessed by the bestowal of wealth, comforts and ease that I plead for. These do not feel their condition of servitude any more than the happy, well-treated slave felt her condition. Had slavery been of this kind it is at least questionable if it would not still have been in existence; but it was not all of this kind. Its barbarities, horrors and inhumanities roused the blood of some who were free, and by their efforts the male portion of a race were elevated by Congress to the exercise of the rights of citizenship. Thus would I have Congress regard woman, and shape their action, *not* from the condition of those who are so well cared for as not to wish a change to enlarge their sphere of action, but for the *toiling female millions*, who have human rights which should be respected.

It may be affirmed that the exercise of suffrage will not ameliorate their conditions. I affirm that it will, and for authority will refer to the improved condition of our fathers and also to the improved condition of the negroes since they acquired the rights of citizenship; since they were enfranchised: *and how enfranchised?* The XV. Amendment does not grant them the right to vote. Neither does it to me; *but it forbids* that a right already possessed shall be denied. If the male negroes, as citizens, possessed the right to vote, shall it be assumed that women citizens do not possess the same right? * * *

There is but one construction the language of this Amendment is susceptible of, and this becomes apparent if the section is properly rendered. It simply means that the right to vote shall not be denied on account of race to ANYBODY. By the interpolation of this word the sense of this Amendment is complete and unmistakable. From the simple negative it changes it to an all-powerful command, by which the sovereign people declare that the right to vote shall not be denied by the United States nor by any State to any person of any race.

We are now prepared to dispose of the sex argument. If the right to vote shall not be denied to any person of any race, how shall it be denied to the female part of all races? Even if it could be denied on account of sex, I ask, what warrant men have to presume that it is the *female* sex to whom such denial can be made instead of the *male* sex? Men, you are wrong, and you stand convicted before the world of denying me, a woman, the right to vote, not by any right of law, but simply because you have usurped the power so to do, just as all other tyrants in all ages have, to rule their subjects. The extent of the tyranny in either case being limited only by the power to enforce it.

* * *

Slavery will ever be regarded by all our descendants as a foul blotch upon the escutcheon of this country's honor, which ages alone can wash away. Congress know this, but they do not yet know how much *more* foul will this greater wrong be regarded by future ages. It should be the task of the next Congress to remove this damning thing. That Congress which recognized negroes as citizens is already reverenced for its mighty work. So, too, will that Congress which shall recognize women as citizens of equal rights with the negro be regarded with reverence in proportion to the magnitude of the result of its labors.

I assume then—

1st. That the rights, privileges and immunities of all citizens are equal.

2d. That no citizens as a class can be denied the right to vote, except they first forfeit it as a class.

3d. That the qualifications which a State may require of electors must be such as can be acquired by all persons by the same means.

4th. That the State may make regulations but cannot enforce prohibitions.

5th. That anything that may be required which is impossible of one-half of the people or any considerable class, possessing all the other qualifications required for electors, is not a qualification, but disfranchisement.

6th. That a State which disfranchises any part of its citizens on account of any natural quality is not possessed of a Republican form of government.

7th. That if a State has not a Republican form of government it is the solemn duty of Congress, under its Constitutional obligations, to guarantee it to its citizens resident therein.

Thus have I endeavored, as briefly as possible, to place before you my reasons for claiming the right to vote for myself and others of my sex who desire it. Neither upon general principles nor by special provision of the Constitution can I perceive that men have any right to deny it to us. So long as we did not *claim* it, it was not denied, but I do now claim that I am, *equally* with men, possessed of the right to vote, and if *no others* of my sex claim it, I will stand alone and reiterate my claim, and if the right is possessed, men have *no power* other than an usurped one to deny me.

The first official duty of every Congressman is to take a solemn oath to support and give vitality to the Constitution of the United States, not as they would, or might wish it to be, but as it is. That Constitution declares that women are citizens, and that citizens shall not be denied the right to vote. In the face of these facts, how can they, with that oath recorded, deliberately set at naught these plain declarations?

I went before Congress to demand a right, and memorialized them, setting forth my grievances, and frankly and fully to the extent of my ability I endeavored to make my claim clear. This is a vital matter, fraught with more momentous events than have ever yet dawned upon the world. Through it civilization will make a giant stride from barbarism toward perfection—a stride which will land the human race near the haven where every person living will become a law unto himself, where there shall be no need of Constitutions, Houses of Congress and Executives, such as are necessary now.

VICTORIA WOODHULL

The Principles of Social Freedom (1871)

An outspoken advocate of women's social freedom, Woodhull proudly accepted her critics' dismissal of her as an advocate of "free love." In November 1871, Woodhull announced to an audience of over three thousand people in Steinway Hall in New York City that she had the right "to change that love every day if I please."

It can now be asked: What is the legitimate sequence of Social Freedom? To which I unhesitatingly reply: Free Love, or freedom of the affections. "And are you a Free Lover?" is the almost incredulous query.

I repeat a frequent reply: "I am; and I can honestly, in the fullness of my soul, raise my voice to my Maker, and thank Him that *I am*, and that I have had the strength and the devotion to truth to stand before this traducing and vilifying community in a manner representative of that which shall come with healing on its wings for the bruised hearts and crushed affections of humanity."

And to those who denounce me for this I reply: "Yes, I am a Free Lover. I have an *inalienable, constitutional* and *natural* right to love whom I may, to love as *long* or as *short* a period as I can; to *change* that love *every day* if I please, and with *that* right neither *you* nor any *law* you can frame have *any* right to interfere. And I have the *further* right to demand a free and unrestricted exercise of that right, and it is *your duty* not only to *accord* it, but, as a community, to see that I am protected in it. I trust that I am fully understood, for I mean *just* that, and nothing less!"

To speak thus plainly and pointedly is a *duty I owe* to myself. The press have stigmatized me to the world as an advocate, theoretically and practically, of the doctrine of Free Love, upon which they have placed their stamp of moral deformity; the vulgar and inconsequent definition which they hold makes the theory an abomination. And though this conclusion is a no more legitimate and reasonable one than that would be which should call the Golden Rule a general license to all sorts of debauch, since Free Love bears the *same* relations to the moral deformities of which it stands accused as does the Golden Rule to the Law of the Despot, yet it obtains among many intelligent people. But they claim, in the language of one of these exponents, that "Words belong to the people; they are the common property of the mob. Now the common use, among the mob, of the term Free Love, is a synonym for promiscuity." Against this absurd proposition I oppose the assertion that words *do not* belong to the mob, but to that which they represent. Words are the exponents and interpretations of ideas. If I use a word which exactly interprets and represents what I would be understood to mean, shall I go to the *mob* and *ask* of *them* what interpretation *they* choose to place upon it? If lexicographers, when they prepare their dictionaries, were to go to the mob for the rendition of words, what kind of language would we have?

I claim that freedom means *to be free*, let the mob claim to the contrary as strenuously as they may. And I claim that love means an exhibition of the affections, let the mob claim what they may. And therefore, in compounding these words into Free Love, I claim that united they mean, and should be used to convey, their united definitions, the mob to the contrary notwithstanding. And when the term Free Love finds a place in dictionaries, it will prove my claim to have been correct, and that the mob have not received the attention of the lexicographers, since it will not be set down to signify sexual debauchery, and that only, or in any governing sense.

It is not only usual but also just, when people adopt a new theory, or promulgate a new doctrine, that they give it a name significant of its character. There are, however, exceptional cases to be found in all ages. The Jews coined the name of Christians, and, with withering contempt, hurled it upon the early followers of Christ. It was the most opprobrious epithet they could invent to express their detestation of those humble but honest and brave people. That name has now come to be considered as a synonym of all that is good, true and beautiful in the highest departments of our natures, and is revered in all civilized nations.

In precisely the same manner the Pharisees of to-day, who hold themselves to be representative of all there is that is good and pure, as did the Pharisees of old, have coined the word Free-Love, and flung it upon all who believe not alone in Religious and Political Freedom, but in that larger Freedom, which includes both these, Social Freedom.

For my part, I am extremely obliged to our thoughtful Pharisaical neighbors for the kindness shown us in the invention of so appropriate a name. If there is a more beautiful word in the English language than *love*, that word is *freedom*, and that *these two* words, which, with us, attach or belong to *everything* that is pure and good, should have been *joined* by our enemies, and *handed* over to us *already* coined, is certainly a high consideration, for which we should never cease to be thankful. And when we shall be accused of all sorts of wickedness and vileness by our enemies, who in this have been so just, may I not hope that, remembering how much they have done for us, we may be able to say, "Father, forgive them, for they know not what they do," and to forgive them ourselves with our whole hearts.

Of the love that says: "Bless *me*, darling;" of the love so called, which is nothing but selfishness, the appropriation of another soul as the means of one's own happiness merely, there is abundance in the world; and the still more animal, the mere desire for temporary gratification, with little worthy the name of love, also abounds. Even these are best left free, since as evils they will thus be best cured; but of that celestial love which says: "Bless *you*, darling," and which strives continually to confer blessings; of that genuine love whose office it is to bless others or another, there cannot be too much in the world, and when it shall be fully understood that this is the love which we mean and commend there will be no objection to the term Free Love, and none to the thing signified.

We not only *accept* our name, but we contend that *none* other could so well signify the *real* character of that which it designates—to be free and to love. But our enemies must be reminded that the fact of the existence and advocacy of such a doctrine cannot immediately elevate to high condition the great number who have been kept in degradation and misery by previous false systems. They must *not expect* at this early day of the new doctrine, that all debauchery has been cleansed out of men and women. In the haunts where it retreats, the benign influence of its magic presence has not yet penetrated. They must *not expect* that brutish men and debased women have as yet been touched by its wand of hope, and that they have already obeyed the bidding to come up higher. They must *not expect* that ignorance and fleshly lust have already been lifted to the region of intellect and moral purity. They must *not expect* that Free Love, before it is more than barely announced to the world, can perform what Christianity in eighteen hundred years has failed to do.

They must *not expect any* of these things have already been accomplished, but I will *tell* you what they *may* expect. They may expect *more* good to result from the perfect freedom which we advocate in *one century* than has resulted in a hundred centuries from all other causes, since the results will be in exact proportion to the extended application of the freedom. We have a legitimate right to predicate such results, since *all* freedom that has been practiced in all ages of the world has been beneficial *just* in proportion to the extent of human nature it covered.

Will any of you dare to stand up and assert that Religious Freedom ever produced a *single bad* result? or that Political Freedom *ever* injured a *single* soul who embraced and practiced it? If you can do so, then you may legitimately assert that Social Freedom *may* also produce *equally* bad results, but you cannot do otherwise, and be either conscientious or honest.

It is *too late* in the age for intelligent people to cry out *thief*, unless they have first been robbed, and it is equally late for them to succeed in crying down *anything* as of the devil to which a name attaches that angels love. It may be very proper and legitimate, and withal perfectly consistent, for philosophers of the *Tribune* school to bundle all the murderers, robbers and rascals together, and hand them over to our camp, labeled as Free Lovers. We will only object that they ought to hand the whole of humanity over, good, bad and indifferent, and not assort its worst representatives.

My friends, you see this thing we call Freedom is a large word, implying a deal more than people have ever yet been able to recognize. It reaches out its all-embracing arms, and while encircling our good friends and neighbors, does not neglect to also include their less worthy brothers and sisters, every one of whom is just as much entitled to the use of his freedom as is either one of us.

SUSAN B. ANTHONY

Speech About Her Indictment (1873)

An abolitionist and a lifelong supporter of the economic and political rights of women, Susan B. Anthony (1820–1906) pioneered the movement for women's suffrage and helped found the National Women's Suffrage Association in 1869. Although she successfully lobbied the New York State Legislature to pass the Married Women's Property Act in 1854, Anthony was unable to convince Congress to include women in the protections afforded by the Fourteenth and Fifteenth Amendments. Nevertheless, she defied the law and cast a vote in the presidential election of 1872. In the closing statements of her trial for illegal voting, Anthony asserted that women who were denied the right to vote were treated as mere subjects, not citizens.

The Court: The prisoner will stand up. Has the prisoner anything to say why sentence shall not be pronounced?

Miss Anthony: Yes, your honor, I have many things to say; for in your ordered verdict of guilty, you have trampled underfoot every vital principle of our government. My natural rights, my civil rights, my political rights, are all alike ignored. Robbed of the fundamental privilege of citizenship, I am degraded from the status of a citizen to that of a subject; and not only myself individually, but all of my sex, are, by your honor's verdict, doomed to political subjection under this so-called Republican government.

Judge Hunt: The Court can not listen to a rehearsal of arguments the prisoner's counsel has already consumed three hours in presenting.

Miss Anthony: May it please your honor, I am not arguing the question, but simply stating the reasons why sentence can not, in justice, be pronounced against me. Your denial of my citizen's right to vote is the denial of my right of consent as one of the governed, the denial of my right of representation as one of the taxed, the denial of my right to a trial by a jury of my peers as an offender against law, therefore, the denial of my sacred rights to life, liberty, property, and—

Judge Hunt: The Court can not allow the prisoner to go on.

Miss Anthony: But your honor will not deny me this one and only poor privilege of protest against this high-handed outrage upon my citizen's rights. May it please the Court to remember that since the day of my arrest last November, this is the first time that either myself or any person of my disfranchised class has been allowed a word of defense before judge or jury—

Judge Hunt: The prisoner must sit down; the Court can not allow it.

Miss Anthony: All my prosecutors, from the 8th Ward corner grocery politician, who entered the complaint, to the United States Marshal, Commissioner, District Attorney, District Judge, your honor on the bench, not one is my peer, but each and all are my political sovereigns; and had your honor submitted my case to the jury, as was clearly your duty, even when I should have had just cause of protest, for not one of those men was my peer; but, native or foreign, white or black, rich or poor, educated or ignorant, awake or asleep, sober or drunk, each and every man of them was my political superior; hence, in no sense, my peer. Even, under such circumstances, a commoner of England, tried before a jury of lords, would have far less cause to complain than should I, a woman, tried before a jury of men. Even my counsel, the Hon. Henry R. Selden, who has argued my cause so ably, so earnestly, so unanswerably before your honor, is my political sovereign. Precisely as no disfranchised person is entitled to sit upon a jury, and no woman is entitled to the franchise, so, none but a regularly admitted lawyer is allowed to practice in the courts, and no woman can gain admission to the bar—hence, jury, judge, counsel, must all be of the superior class.

Judge Hunt: The Court must insist—the prisoner has been tried according to the established forms of law.

Miss Anthony: Yes, your honor, but by forms of law all made by men, interpreted by men, administered by men, in favor of men, and against women; and hence, your honor's ordered verdict of guilty, against a United States citizen for the exercise of "that citizen's right to vote," simply because that citizen was a woman and not a man. But, yesterday, the same man-made forms of law declared it a crime punishable with $1,000 fine and six months' imprisonment, for you, or me, or any of us, to give a cup of cold water, a crust of bread, or a night's shelter to a panting fugitive as he was tracking his way to Canada. And every man or woman in whose veins coursed a drop of human sympathy violated that wicked law, reckless of consequences, and was justified in so doing. As then the slaves who got their freedom must take it over, or under, or through the unjust forms of law, precisely so now must women, to get their right to a voice in this Government, take it; and I have taken mine, and mean to take it at every possible opportunity.

Judge Hunt: The Court orders the prisoner to sit down. It will not allow another word.

Miss Anthony: When I was brought before your honor for trial, I hoped for a broad and liberal interpretation of the Constitution and its recent amendments, that should declare all United States citizens under its protecting aegis—that should declare equality of rights the national guarantee to all persons born or naturalized in the United States. But failing to get this justice—failing, even, to get a trial by a jury *not* of my peers—I ask not leniency at your hands—but rather the full rigors of the law.

Judge Hunt: The Court must insist—(Here the prisoner sat down.) *Judge Hunt:* The prisoner will stand up. (Here Miss Anthony arose again.) The sentence of the Court is that you pay a fine of one hundred dollars and the costs of the prosecution.

Miss Anthony: May it please your honor, I shall never pay a dollar of your unjust penalty. All the stock in trade I possess is a $10,000 debt, incurred by publishing my paper—*The Revolution*—four years ago, the sole object of which was to educate all women to do precisely as I have done, rebel against your man-made, unjust, unconstitutional forms of law, that tax, fine, imprison, and hang women, while they deny them the right of representation in the Government; and I shall work on with might and main to pay every dollar of that honest debt, but not a penny shall go to this unjust claim. And I shall earnestly and persistently continue to urge all women to the practical recognition of the old revolutionary maxim, that "Resistance to tyranny is obedience to God."

Judge Hunt: Madam, the Court will not order you committed until the fine is paid.

CHARLOTTE PERKINS GILMAN

Women and Economics (1898)

*The feminist writer and lecturer Charlotte Anna Perkins Gilman
(1860–1935) was the founder and editor of* Forerunner *and a founder of
the Woman's Peace Party. Gilman believed that the sexual division of labor and uncompensated domestic labor reinforced the subordinate social status of women while contributing to the productivity of men in the
marketplace. In* Women and Economics, *which was widely read and
translated into several languages, Gilman analyzed the domestic causes
of women's economically dependent status. Her radical proposals for
centralized kitchens, expert housekeeping, and other changes in household labor were intended for the betterment of women and society in
general.*

It is not motherhood that keeps the housewife on her feet from dawn
till dark; it is house service, not child service. Women work longer and
harder than most men, and not solely in maternal duties. The savage
mother carries the burdens, and does all menial service for the tribe. The
peasant mother toils in the fields, and the workingman's wife in the
home. Many mothers, even now, are wage-earners for the family, as well
as bearers and rearers of it. And the women who are not so occupied, the
women who belong to rich men,—here perhaps is the exhaustive devotion to maternity which is supposed to justify an admitted economic dependence. But we do not find it even among these. Women of ease and
wealth provide for their children better care than the poor woman can;
but they do not spend more time upon it themselves, nor more care and
effort. They have other occupation.

In spite of her supposed segregation to maternal duties, the human female, the world over, works at extra-maternal duties for hours enough to
provide her with an independent living, and then is denied independence
on the ground that motherhood prevents her working!

* * *

The working power of the mother has always been a prominent factor
in human life. She is the worker *par excellence*, but her work is not such
as to affect her economic status. Her living, all that she gets,—food,

clothing, ornaments, amusements, luxuries,—these bear no relation to her power to produce wealth, to her services in the house, or to her motherhood. These things bear relation only to the man she marries, the man she depends on,—to how much he has and how much he is willing to give her. The women whose splendid extravagance dazzles the world, whose economic goods are the greatest, are often neither houseworkers nor mothers, but simply the women who hold most power over the men who have the most money. The female of genus homo is economically dependent on the male. He is her food supply. * * *

As a natural consequence of our division of labor on sex-lines, giving to woman the home and to man the world in which to work, we have come to have a dense prejudice in favor of the essential womanliness of the home duties, as opposed to the essential manliness of every other kind of work. We have assumed that the preparation and serving of food and the removal of dirt, the nutritive and excretive processes of the family, are feminine functions; and we have also assumed that these processes must go on in what we call the home, which is the external expression of the family. In the home the human individual is fed, cleaned, warmed, and generally cared for, while not engaged in working in the world.

Human nutrition is a long process. There's many a ship 'twixt the cup and the lip, to paraphrase an old proverb. Food is produced by the human race collectively,—not by individuals for their own consumption, but by interrelated groups of individuals, all over the world, for the world's consumption. This collectively produced food circulates over the earth's surface through elaborate processes of transportation, exchange, and preparation, before it reaches the mouths of the consumers; and the final processes of selection and preparation are in the hands of woman. She is the final purchaser: she is the final handler in that process of human nutrition known as cooking, which is a sort of extra-organic digestion proven advantageous to our species. This department of human digestion has become a sex-function, supposed to pertain to women by nature.

Is it not time that the way to a man's heart through his stomach should be relinquished for some higher avenue? The stomach should be left to its natural uses, not made a thoroughfare for stranger passions and purposes; and the heart should be approached through higher channels. We need a new picture of our overworked blind god,—fat, greasy, pampered with sweetmeats by the poor worshippers long forced to pay their devotion through such degraded means.

No, the human race is not well nourished by making the process of feeding it a sex-function. The selection and preparation of food should be in the hands of trained experts. And woman should stand beside man as the comrade of his soul, not the servant of his body.

This will require large changes in our method of living. To feed the world by expert service, bringing to that great function the skill and experience of the trained specialist, the power of science, and the beauty of art, is impossible in the sexuo-economic relation. While we treat cooking as a sex-function common to all women and eating as a family function not otherwise rightly accomplished, we can develop no farther. We are spending much earnest study and hard labor to-day on the problem of teaching and training women in the art of cooking, both the wife and the servant; for, with our usual habit of considering voluntary individual conduct as the cause of conditions, we seek to modify conditions by changing individual conduct.

* * *

There was a time when kings and lords retained their private poets to praise and entertain them; but the poet is not truly great until he sings for the world. So the art of cooking can never be lifted to its true place as a human need and a social function by private service. Such an arrangement of our lives and of our houses as will allow cooking to become a profession is the only way in which to free this great art from its present limitations. It should be a reputable, well-paid profession, wherein those women or those men who were adapted to this form of labor could become cooks, as they would become composers or carpenters. Natural distinctions would be developed between the mere craftsman and the artist; and we should have large, new avenues of lucrative and honorable industry, and a new basis for human health and happiness.

This does not involve what is known as "co-operation." Co-operation, in the usual sense, is the union of families for the better performance of their supposed functions. The process fails because the principle is wrong. Cooking and cleaning are not family functions. We do not have a family mouth, a family stomach, a family face to be washed. Individuals require to be fed and cleaned from birth to death, quite irrespective of their family relations. The orphan, the bachelor, the childless widower, have as much need of these nutritive and excretive processes as any patriarchal parent. Eating is an individual function. Cooking is a social function. Neither is in the faintest degree a family function. That we have found it convenient in early stages of civilization to do our cooking at home proves no more than the allied fact that we have also found it convenient in such stages to do our weaving and spinning at home, our soap and candle making, our butchering and pickling, our baking and washing.

As society develops, its functions specialize; and the reason why this great race-function of cooking has been so retarded in its natural growth is that the economic dependence of women has kept them back from their share in human progress. When women stand free as economic agents, they will lift and free their arrested functions, to the much better fulfilment of their duties as wives and mothers and to the vast improvement in health and happiness of the human race.

Co-operation is not what is required for this, but trained professional service and such arrangement of our methods of living as shall allow us to benefit by such service. When numbers of people patronize the same tailor or baker or confectioner, they do not co-operate. Neither would they co-operate in patronizing the same cook. The change must come from the side of the cook, not from the side of the family. It must come through natural functional development in society, and it is so coming. Woman, recognizing that her duty as feeder and cleaner is a social duty, not a sexual one, must face the requirements of the situation, and prepare herself to meet them. A hundred years ago this could not have been done. Now it is being done, because the time is ripe for it.

If there should be built and opened in any of our large cities to-day a commodious and well-served apartment house for professional women with families, it would be filled at once. The apartments would be without kitchens; but there would be a kitchen belonging to the house from which meals could be served to the families in their rooms or in a common dining-room, as preferred. It would be a home where the cleaning was done by efficient workers, not hired separately by the families, but engaged by the manager of the establishment; and a roof-garden, day nursery, and kindergarten, under well-trained professional nurses and teachers, would insure proper care of the children. The demand for such provision is increasing daily, and must soon be met, not by a boarding-house or a lodging-house, a hotel, a restaurant, or any makeshift patching together of these; but by a permanent provision for the needs of women and children, of family privacy with collective advantage. This must be offered on a business basis to prove a substantial business success; and it will so prove, for it is a growing social need.

There are hundreds of thousands of women in New York City alone who are wage-earners, and who also have families; and the number increases. This is true not only among the poor and unskilled, but more and more among business women, professional women, scientific, artistic, literary women. Our school-teachers, who form a numerous class, are not entirely without relatives. To board does not satisfy the needs of a human soul. These women want homes, but they do not want the clumsy tangle of rudimentary industries that are supposed to accompany the home. The strain under which such women labor is no longer necessary. The privacy of the home could be as well maintained in such a building as described as in any house in a block, any room, flat, or apartment, under present methods. The food would be better, and would cost less; and this would be true of the service and of all common necessities.

In suburban homes this purpose could be accomplished much better by a grouping of adjacent houses, each distinct and having its own yard, but all kitchenless, and connected by covered ways with the eating-house. No detailed prophecy can be made of the precise forms which would ultimately prove most useful and pleasant; but the growing social need is for the specializing of the industries practised in the home and for the proper mechanical provision for them.

The cleaning required in each house would be much reduced by the removal of the two chief elements of household dirt—grease and ashes.

Meals could of course be served in the house as long as desired; but, when people become accustomed to pure, clean homes, where no steaming industry is carried on, they will gradually prefer to go to their food instead of having it brought to them. It is a perfectly natural process, and a healthful one, to go to one's food. And, after all, the changes between living in one room, and so having the cooking most absolutely convenient; going as far as the limits of a large house permit, to one's own dining-room; and going a little further to a dining-room not in one's own house, but near by,—these differ but in degree. Families could go to eat together, just as they can go to bathe together or to listen to music together; but, if it fell out that different individuals presumed to develope an appetite at different hours, they could meet it without interfering with other people's comfort or sacrificing their own. Any housewife knows the difficulty of always getting a family together at meals. Why try? Then arises sentiment, and asserts that family affection, family unity, the very existence of the family, depend on their being together at meals. A family unity which is only bound together with a table-cloth is of questionable value.

There are several professions involved in our clumsy method of housekeeping. A good cook is not necessarily a good manager, nor a good manager an accurate and thorough cleaner, nor a good cleaner a wise purchaser. Under the free development of these branches a woman could choose her position, train for it, and become a most valuable functionary in her special branch, all the while living in her own home; that is, she would live in it as a man lives in his home, spending certain hours of the day at work and others at home.

This division of the labor of housekeeping would require the service of fewer women for fewer hours a day. Where now twenty women in twenty homes work all the time, and insufficiently accomplish their varied duties, the same work in the hands of specialists could be done in less time by fewer people; and the others would be left free to do other work for which they were better fitted, thus increasing the productive power of the world. Attempts at co-operation so far have endeavored to lessen the existing labors of women without recognizing their need for other occupation, and this is one reason for their repeated failure. * * *

The organization of household industries will simplify and centralize its cleaning processes, allowing of many mechanical conveniences and the application of scientific skill and thoroughness. We shall be cleaner than we ever were before. There will be less work to do, and far better means of doing it. The daily needs of a well-plumbed house could be met easily by each individual in his or her own room or by one who liked to do such work; and the labor less frequently required would be furnished by an expert, who would clean one home after another with the swift skill of training and experience. The home would cease to be to us a workshop or a museum, and would become far more the personal expression of its occupants—the place of peace and rest, of love and privacy—than it can be in its present condition of arrested industrial development. And woman will fill her place in those industries with far better results than are now provided by her ceaseless struggles, her conscientious devotion, her pathetic ignorance and inefficiency.

JANE ADDAMS

If Men Were Seeking the Franchise (1913)

A founder of Hull House in Chicago, one of the most important settlement houses created to serve the poor in America's great cities, Jane Addams (1860–1935) was a tireless social reformer active in countless arenas of public life. She helped run Teddy Roosevelt's 1912 Progressive Party presidential campaign, was the first president of the Women's International League for Peace and Freedom, and a cowinner of the Nobel Peace Prize. She was also an ardent suffragist. In this piece, which appeared in a 1913 issue of the Ladies Home Journal, *she turned the tables and wrote of men demanding the vote.*

Let us imagine throughout this article, if we can sustain an absurd hypothesis so long, the result upon society if the matriarchal period had held its own; if the development of the State had closely followed that of the Family until the chief care of the former, as that of the latter, had come to be the nurture and education of children and the protection of the weak, sick and aged. In short let us imagine a hypothetical society organized upon the belief that "there is no wealth but life." With this Ruskinian foundation let us assume that the political machinery of such a society, the franchise and the rest of it, were in the hands of women because they had always best exercised those functions. Let us further imagine a given moment when these women, who in this hypothetical society had possessed political power from the very beginnings of the State, were being appealed to by the voteless men that men might be associated with women in the responsibilities of citizenship.

Plagiarizing somewhat upon recent suffrage speeches let us consider various replies which these citizen women might reasonably make to the men who were seeking the franchise; the men insisting that only through the use of the ballot could they share the duties of the State.

First, could not the women say: "Our most valid objection to extending the franchise to you is that you are so fond of fighting—you always have been since you were little boys. You'd very likely forget that the real object of the State is to nurture and protect life, and out of sheer vainglory you would be voting away huge sums of money for battleships, not one of which could last more than a few years, and yet each would cost ten million dollars; more money than all the buildings of Harvard University represent, although it is the richest educational institution in America. Every time a gun is fired in a battleship it expends, or rather explodes, seventeen hundred dollars, as much as a college education costs many a country boy, and yet you would be firing off these guns as mere salutes, with no enemy within three thousand miles, simply because you so enjoy the sound of shooting.

"Our educational needs are too great and serious to run any such risk. Democratic government itself is perilous unless the electorate is educated; our industries are suffering for lack of skilled workmen; more than half a million immigrants a year must be taught the underlying principles of republican government. Can we, the responsible voters, take the risk of wasting our taxes by extending the vote to those who have always been so ready to lose their heads over mere military display?"

Second, would not the hypothetical women, who would have been responsible for the advance of industry during these later centuries, as women actually were during the earlier centuries when they dragged home the game and transformed the pelts into shelter and clothing, say further to these disenfranchised men: "We have carefully built up a code of factory legislation for the protection of the workers in modern industry; we know that you men have always been careless about the house, perfectly indifferent to the necessity for sweeping and cleaning; if you were made responsible for factory legislation it is quite probable that you would let the workers in the textile mills contract tuberculosis through needlessly breathing the fluff, or the workers in machine shops through inhaling metal filings, both of which are now carried off by an excellent suction system which we women have insisted upon, but which it is almost impossible to have installed in a man-made State because the men think so little of dust and its evil effects. In many Nations in which political power is confined to men, and this is notably true in the United States of America, there is no protection even for the workers in white lead, although hundreds of them are yearly incapacitated from lead poisoning, and others actually die.

"We have also heard that in certain States, in order to save the paltry price of a guard which would protect a dangerous machine, men legislators allow careless boys and girls to lose their fingers and sometimes their hands, thereby crippling their entire futures. These male legislators do not make guarded machinery obligatory, although they know that when the heads of families are injured at these unprotected machines the State must care for them in hospitals, and when they are killed, that if necessary the State must provide for their widows and children in poorhouses."

These wise women, governing the State with the same care they had always put into the management of their families, would further place against these men seeking the franchise the charge that men do not really know how tender and delicate children are, and might therefore put them to work in factories, as indeed they have done in man-made States during the entire period of factory production. We can imagine these women saying: "We have been told that in certain States children are taken from their beds in the early morning before it is light and carried into cotton mills, where they are made to run back and forth tending the spinning frames until their immature little bodies are so bent and strained that they never regain their normal shapes; that little children are allowed to work in canneries for fifteen and seventeen hours until, utterly exhausted, they fall asleep among the debris of shells and husks."

Would not these responsible women voters gravely shake their heads and say that as long as men exalt business profit above human life it would be sheer folly to give them the franchise; that, of course, they would be slow to make such matters the subject of legislation?

Would not the enfranchised women furthermore say to these voteless men: "You have always been so eager to make money; what assurance have we that in your desire to get the largest amount of coal out of the ground in the shortest possible time you would not permit the mine supports to decay and mine damp to accumulate, until the percentage of accidents among miners would be simply heartbreaking? Then you are so reckless. Business seems to you a mere game with big prizes, and we have heard that in America, where the women have no vote, the loss of life in the huge steel mills is appalling; and that the number of young brake-men, fine young fellows, every one of them the pride of some mother, killed every year is beyond belief; that the average loss of life among the structural-iron workers who erect the huge office buildings and bridges is as disastrous in percentages as was the loss of life in the Battle of Bull Run. When the returns of this battle were reported to President Lincoln he burst into tears of sorrow and chagrin; but we have never heard of any President, Governor or Mayor weeping over the reports of this daily loss of life, although such reports have been presented to them by Govern-mental investigators; and this loss of life might easily be reduced by pro-tective legislation."

Having thus worked themselves into a fine state of irritation, analo-gous to that ever-recurrent uneasiness of men in the presence of insur-gent women who would interfere in the management of the State, would not these voting women add: "The trouble is that men have no imagina-tion, or rather what they have is so prone to run in the historic direction of the glory of the battlefield, that you cannot trust them with industrial affairs. Because a crew in a battle-ship was once lost under circum-stances which suggested perfidy the male representatives of two great Nations voted to go to war; yet in any day of the year in one of these Na-tions alone—the United States of America—as many men are killed through industrial accidents as this crew contained. These accidents oc-cur under circumstances which, if not perfidious, are at least so crimi-nally indifferent to human life as to merit Kipling's characterization that the situation is impious."

Certainly these irritated women would designate such indifference to human life as unpatriotic and unjustifiable, only to be accounted for be-cause men have not yet learned to connect patriotism with industrial af-fairs.

These conscientious women responsible for the State in which life was considered of more value than wealth would furthermore say: "Then, too, you men exhibit such curious survivals of the mere savage instinct of pun-ishment and revenge. The United States alone spends every year five hundred million dollars more on its policemen, courts and prisons than upon all its works of religion, charity and education. The price of one trial expended on a criminal early in life might save the State thousands of dollars and the man untold horrors. And yet with all this vast expendi-ture little is done to reduce crime. Men are kept in jails and peniten-tiaries where there is not even the semblance of education or reformatory measure; young men are returned over and over again to the same institution until they have grown old and gray, and in all of that time they have not once been taught a trade, nor have they been in any wise prepared to withstand the temptations of life.

"A homeless young girl looking for a lodging may be arrested for soliciting on the streets, and sent to prison for six months, although there is no proof against her save the impression of the policeman. A young girl under such suspicion may be obliged to answer the most harassing questions put to her by the city attorney, with no woman near to protect her from insult; she may be subjected to the most trying examination conducted by a physician in the presence of a policeman, and no matron to whom to appeal. At least these things happen constantly in the United States—in Chicago, for instance—but possibly not in the Scandinavian countries where juries of women sit upon such cases, women whose patience has been many times tested by wayward girls and who know the untold moral harm which may result from such a physical and psychic shock."

Then these same women would go further, and, because they had lived in a real world and had administered large affairs and were therefore not prudish and affected, would say: "Worse than anything which we have mentioned is the fact that in every man-ruled city the world over a great army of women are so set aside as outcasts that it is considered a shame to speak the mere name which designates them. Because their very existence is illegal they may be arrested whenever any police captain chooses; they may be brought before a magistrate, fined and imprisoned. The men whose money sustains their houses, supplies their tawdry clothing and provides them with intoxicating drinks and drugs, are never arrested, nor indeed are they even considered lawbreakers."

Would not these fearless women, whose concern for the morals of the family had always been able to express itself through State laws, have meted out equal punishment to men as well as to women, when they had equally transgressed the statute law?

Did the enfranchised women evoked by our imagination speak thus to the disenfranchised men, the latter would at least respect their scruples and their hesitation in regard to an extension of the obligation of citizenship. But what would be the temper of the masculine mind if the voting women representing the existing State should present to them only the following half-dozen objections, which are unhappily so familiar to many of us: If the women should say, first, that men would find politics corrupting; second, that they would doubtless vote as their wives and mothers did; third, that men's suffrage would only double the vote without changing results; fourth, that men's suffrage would diminish the respect for men; fifth, that most men do not want to vote; sixth, that the best men would not vote?

I do no believe that women broadened by life and its manifold experiences would actually present these six objections to men as real reasons for withholding the franchise from them, unless indeed they had long formed the habit of regarding men not as comrades and fellow-citizens, but as a class by themselves, in essential matters really inferior although always held sentimentally very much above them.

Certainly no such talk would be indulged in between men and women who had together embodied in political institutions the old affairs of life which had normally and historically belonged to both of them. If woman had adjusted herself to the changing demands of the State as she did to the historic mutations of her own house-hold she might naturally and without challenge have held the place in the State which she now holds in the family.

When Plato once related his dream of an ideal Republic he begged his fellow-citizens not to ridicule him because he considered the cooperation of women necessary for its fulfillment. He contended that so far as the guardianship of the State is concerned there is no distinction between the powers of men and women save those which custom has made.

BROOKS ADAMS

The American Democratic Ideal (1916)

A chorus of aristocratic dissent emerged in the early twentieth century against industrialism, secularism, progress, even democracy. In a 1916 speech to the august American Academy of Arts and Letters, Brooks Adams (1848–1921)—the brother of Charles Francis, Jr., and Henry, and author of The Law of Civilization and Decay *(1895)—bitterly indicted America's "democratic ideal" for valuing individualism and selfishness over duty and self-sacrifice.*

I know not how it may be with others, but I am aware of a growing reluctance to express my views in public, which of late has approached absolute repugnance. Perhaps this feeling may be due to the sombreness of age, but I rather incline to ascribe it to an apprehension of the future which dawned on me long ago, but which of late has deepened with a constantly augmenting acceleration. If I thought that anything that I could do would affect the final issue, I might be more inclined to effort;

but I perceive myself to be so far sundered from most of my countrymen that I shrink exceedingly from thrusting on them opinions which will give offense or, more likely still, excite derision. For when I look about me I see the American people as a whole quite satisfied that they have solved the riddle of the universe, and firmly convinced that by means of plenty of money, popular education, cheap transportation, universal suffrage, unlimited amusements, the moral uplift, and the "democratic ideal," they have only one more step to take to land them in perfection.

I cannot altogether share this optimism, and particularly I have doubts touching the American "democratic ideal." It is of these doubts that I intend to speak to-day, as I consider this apotheosis of the "democratic ideal" the profoundest and most far-reaching phenomenon of our age. Yet I so much dislike assuming the critical attitude that I should have declined the flattering invitation you have given me to address you had I deemed it quite becoming for a member of an association like this to refuse to participate in your proceedings when requested to do so by your officers. I have only this one claim to urge to your indulgence: at least I have not sought to vex you by obtruding my speculations on you.

I start with this proposition, which to me is self-evident, and which I therefore assume as axiomatic: that no organized social system, such as we commonly call a national civilization, can cohere against those enemies which must certainly beset it, if it fail to recognize as its primary standard of duty the obligation of the individual man and woman to sacrifice themselves for the whole community in time of need. And, furthermore, that this standard may be effective and not theoretical, it must be granted that the power to determine when the moment of need has arisen lies not with the individual, but with society in its corporate capacity. This last crucial attribute can never be admitted to inhere in private judgment.

I shall ask you to consider with me first the nature of the American "democratic ideal," and subsequently to test it by this standard. For my part, for the last twelve months this subject has been constantly in my thoughts, fixed there by the war now raging.

Last August I chanced to be in Paris when hostilities began, and I came home filled with the solemn impression of the French sense of duty made on me by seeing the whole manhood of France march to the frontier without a murmur and without a quaver. I knew that the same thing was going on in Germany. I thought that men could do no more. Now, the rights and wrongs of this war are, for my present purpose, immaterial; all that concerns me is the national standard it illustrates of self-sacrifice and of duty. And on both sides of the Rhine I found that standard good. It seemed to me also to be the true standard of pure democracy. For what can be more democratic than that prince and peasant, plutocrat and pauper, shall serve their country together side by side, marching in the same regiment, wearing the same uniform, submitting to the same discipline, enduring the same hardships, and dying the same death? In mass universal service is absolute equality. Some men, it is true, serve as officers, but these men are officers only because, by lives devoted to obedience, to self-denial, and to study, they have made themselves fit for command, and when the hour of danger is at hand this fitness for command is recognized by their countrymen who have chosen more lucrative or easier walks in life.

I had supposed that in our democracy these great facts would be appreciated and honored by all, even though it might possibly be argued that in America the necessity for such self-abnegation had not yet arisen. I never fell into greater error. Familiar as I am with American idiosyncrasies, I was astonished, on landing in New York, to find the German military system bitterly assailed as conflicting with the American "democratic ideal," and I asked myself why this should be. It is true that the German system of universal military service had been the first to be thoroughly organized, but that could not impeach its principle or make it conflict with a sound "democratic ideal."

I beg you to grant me an instant in which to explain myself. I wish to make it clear that I have never admired Germany as a whole, although I have known her rather intimately. A generation ago, when it was the fashion here almost to worship the Germans, even to their art, their literature, their language, and their manners, when eminent gentlemen who have no good word for Germany now used to insist to me at college that nothing but a Germanized education could suffice for the student, I rebelled. I protested that Germany had made no such contribution to our civilization, in comparison, for instance, with France, as to justify in us any such servile attitude, and that I could not admit her claims.

* * * In later years I have distrusted her ambitions, I have detested her manners, I have abhorred her language and her art, I have feared her competition, and I have been jealous of her navy, but I have never questioned in my heart that her military system of universal service is truly democratic, and I have wished that it might be adopted here. It never occurred to me that it could be denounced as undemocratic, or reviled as a tool of the Junker class, used by them for their own aggrandizement and for the oppression of the German people. Such an accusation would have seemed to me too shallow to be noticed. I could not comprehend how any sober-minded man who knew the history of the Seven Years War and of Jena could fail to perceive that the German military system was an effect of a struggle of a people for existence, and that the German people and

the German army are one. Their vices and their virtues are the same. To imagine that a handful of Prussian squires, most of whom are far from rich, could coerce millions of their countrymen from all ranks in life, who equally with the Junkers are trained and armed soldiers, into doing something which they thought harmful, and waging wars which they hated as ruinous or wrong, was and is to me a proposition too absurd to deserve serious refutation. What, then, I asked myself, could be the secret of the hostility of Americans to German universal military service, a hostility which Americans disguised under the phrase of faith in "democratic ideals"? And as I watched this phenomenon and meditated upon what I saw and heard, the suspicion which had long lain half-consciously in my mind ripened into the conviction that the real tyranny against which my countrymen revolted was the tyranny of universal self-sacrifice, and that they hated German universal military service because it rigorously demanded a sacrifice from every man from which they personally shrank; for, enforced in America, as it might be were Germany to prevail in this war, they would perhaps be constrained to give one year of their lives to their country.

If this inference were sound, it occurred to me that not improbably our "democratic ideal" consisted in the principle that men or women should not be obliged to conform to any standard of duty against their will, or, in short, in the principle of universal selfishness. Then I turned to our women for enlightenment, as the female sex is supposed to set ours an example in unselfishness. To instruct myself I read the modern feminist literature and followed a little the feminist debate, and very shortly I found my question answered.

Since civilization first dawned on earth the family has been the social unit on which all authority, all order, and all obedience has reposed. Therefore the family has been the cement of society, and the chief element in cohesion. To preserve the family, and thus to make society stable, the woman has always sacrificed herself for it, as the man has sacrificed himself for her upon the field of battle. The obligations and the sacrifices have been correlative. But I beheld our modern women shrilly repudiating such a standard of duty and such a theory of self-sacrifice. On the contrary, they denied that as individual units they owed society any duty as mothers or as wives, and maintained that their first duty was to themselves. If they found the bonds of the family irksome, they might renounce them and wander whither they would through the world in order to obtain a fuller life for themselves. This phase of individualism would appear to be an ultimate form of selfishness, and the final resolution of society into atoms, but none the less it would also appear to be the feminine interpretation of the American "democratic ideal."

Proceeding a little further, I come to the capitalistic class—a class which I take to be a far more powerful class with us than are the Prussian Junkers in Germany. Nothing, therefore, can be more important to our present purpose than to appreciate the standard recognized by them. I shall take but one test of many I applied, because time is pressing.

The railways are to a modern country what the arteries are to the human body. The national life-blood flows through them. They are a prime factor in our prosperity and contentment in time of peace, and our first means of defense in time of war. Though they are vital to our corporate life, our Government confides their administration to capitalists as trustees, who are supposed to collect for their work as trustees a reasonable compensation, which they levy on the public by a tax on transportation which we call rates. Very clearly no injustice could be more flagrant and no injury deeper than that such taxes should be unequal or excessive. I ask in what spirit this most sacred of trusts has been performed? The legislation that cumbers our statute-books, the cases that cram our law reports, and the wrecks upon the stock-market tell the tale better than could any words of mine. It is hardly a tale of self-abnegation to meet a standard of public duty, though it may well be an exemplification of the American "democratic ideal."

Next in order would naturally come labor. The spectacle in democratic England of hundreds of thousands of coal miners utilizing the extremity of their country's agony as a means of extorting from society a selfish pecuniary advantage for themselves brings before us vividly enough the workman's understanding of the "democratic ideal."

Supposing, for our own edification, we contemplate *ourselves*, we who are artists and literary men, and ask ourselves what our interpretation is of our "democratic ideal." At this suggestion there rises before my mind a vision of long ago. I was one evening conversing in a club with a well-known painter about some decorations which were attracting attention and were very costly, but which offended my taste as being frankly plutocratic. I observed that though they brought high prices, I questioned whether they conformed to any true canon of art. Like a flash he turned on me and said:

"And who are you to talk of artistic standards? In our world there is but one standard, and that the standard of price. That which sells is good art, that which does not sell is bad art. There can be no appeal from price."

I made no answer, for I saw that he was right. Art is a form of expression, and art can, therefore, express only the society which environs it, and our standard is money, or, in other words, the means of self-indulgence. I had been unconsciously thinking of the civilization which produced the old tower of Chartres and the Virgin's Portal at Paris, when monks, safe in their convents, could concentrate their souls on expressing the aspirations and the self-devotion of their age. I wondered whether we as literary men have in mind, when we do our work, an ideal which is our standard, as religion was their standard or as the verdict at Olympia was the standard of the Greeks; or do we worry little over the form or the substance of our labor, and think mostly of the artifices which may attract the public, and charm the publisher by stimulating sales. If we do the latter, we exemplify the American "democratic ideal," which denies any standard save the standard of self-interest which is incarnated in price.

I had reached this point in my reflections when it occurred to me to test my inferences by applying them to our collective public thought. After some hesitation I have concluded that, as a unified organism, we Americans are nearly incapable of continuous collective thought except at long intervals under the severest tension. For instance, during the Civil war one-half of our country sustained what might be called a train of partly digested collective thought through some four years, but on the return to the Union of the Southern States our thought became more disorderly than ever. Ordinarily we cannot think except individually or locally. Hence the particular interest must, as a rule, dominate the collective interest, so that scientific legislation is impossible, and no fixed policy can be long maintained. Thus we can formulate no scientific tariff, since our tariffs are made by combinations of private and local interests, with little or no relation to collective advantage. We can organize no effective army, because the money and the effort needed to construct an effective army must be frittered away to gratify localities; nor can we have a well-adjusted navy, because we can persist in no plan developed by a central intelligence. We call our appropriation bill for public works our pork-barrel, probably with only too good reason. But the point to be marked is that in our national legislature the instinct of unity, continuity, and order seldom prevails over individualism or disorder, with the result that our collective administration of public affairs may not unreasonably be termed chaotic.

Descending from the Union to the State, the same rule holds. This year a constitution was submitted to the voters of New York, the object of which was to check in some small measure the chaos of individualism in state affairs. It was defeated by an enormous majority because the "democratic ideal" does not tolerate the notion of unity or order at the cost of private self-interest.

But after all the most perfect exemplification of the American "democratic ideal," or the principle of selfishness in public affairs, occurs in our cities. In America there is one city administered on the principle of unity and self-restraint. It is Washington, but I suppose that no other municipality in the land would endure such a yoke, and the reason is plain. In Washington private interests are subordinated to public interests, but our "democratic ideal" contemplates a municipal system which yields an opposite result. Self-interest requires that our municipalities should be so organized that every rich man may buy such franchises as he needs to enrich himself, while every poor man may obtain his job at the public cost. This is the complete subordination of the principle of unity to that of diversity, of order to chaos, of the community to the individual, of self-sacrifice to selfishness. It is in fine the pure American "democratic ideal."

I submit most humbly that untold ages of human experience have proved to us that nature is inexorable and demands of us self-sacrifice if we would have our civilization, our country, our families, our art, or our literature survive. Unselfishness is what the words patriotism and maternal love mean. Those words mean that we cannot survive and live for ourselves alone. We cannot be individualistic, or selfish to an extreme, we cannot hope for salvation through our "democratic ideal." For, if we accept that, we accept the conclusion that our country can never exert her strength in the hour of peril, because we leave to private judgment the sacrifice which every citizen shall make her.

* * * We renounce a standard of duty. But surely sooner or later that mortal peril must arise which none can hope to escape, either from within or from without, and when we least expect it. "But of that day and hour knoweth no man, for ye know not what hour our Lord may come."

If it be true, as I do apprehend, that our "democratic ideal" is only a phrase to express our renunciation as a nation of all standards of duty, and the substitution therefor of a reference to private judgment; if we men are to leave to ourselves as individual units the decision as to how and when our country may exact from us our lives; if each woman may dissolve the family bond at pleasure; if, in fine, we are to have no standard of duty, of obedience, or, in substance, of right and wrong save selfish caprice; if we are to resolve our society from a firmly cohesive mass, unified by a common standard of duty and self-sacrifice, into a swarm of atoms selfishly fighting one another for money, as beggars scramble for coin, then I much fear that the hour cannot be far distant when some superior, because more cohesive and intelligent organism, such as nature has decreed shall always lie in wait for its victim, shall spring upon us and rend us as the strong have always rent those wretched, because feeble, creatures who are cursed with an aborted development.

TWELVE SOUTHERNERS

I'll Take My Stand (1930)

A group of twelve Southern writers and poets, centered at Vanderbilt University in Nashville, Tennessee, which included Robert Penn Warren, Allan Tate, John Crowe Ransom, and Donald Davidson, proudly stood their ground against industrialization and modernity. Their 1930 book I'll Take My Stand: The South and the Agrarian Tradition, *begins with their common rejection of industry and secularism.*

Nobody now proposes for the South, or for any other community in this country, an independent political destiny. That idea is thought to have been finished in 1865. But how far shall the South surrender its moral, social, and economic autonomy to the victorious principle of Union? That question remains open. The South is a minority section that has hitherto been jealous of its minority right to live its own kind of life. The South scarcely hopes to determine the other sections, but it does propose to determine itself, within the utmost limits of legal action. Of late, however, there is the melancholy fact that the South itself has wavered a little and shown signs of wanting to join up behind the common or American industrial ideal. It is against that tendency that this book is written. The younger Southerners, who are being converted frequently to the industrial gospel, must come back to the support of the Southern tradition. They must be persuaded to look very critically at the advantages of becoming a "new South" which will be only an undistinguished replica of the usual industrial community.

But there are many other minority communities opposed to industrialism, and wanting a much simpler economy to live by. The communities and private persons sharing the agrarian tastes are to be found widely within the Union. Proper living is a matter of the intelligence and the will, does not depend on the local climate or geography, and is capable of a definition which is general and not Southern at all. Southerners have a filial duty to discharge to their own section. But their cause is precarious and they must seek alliances with sympathetic communities everywhere. The members of the present group would be happy to be counted as members of a national agrarian movement.

Industrialism is the economic organization of the collective American society. It means the decision of society to invest its economic resources in the applied sciences. But the word science has acquired a certain sanctitude. It is out of order to quarrel with science in the abstract, or even with the applied sciences when their applications are made subject to criticism and intelligence. The capitalization of the applied sciences has now become extravagant and uncritical; it has enslaved our human energies to a degree now clearly felt to be burdensome. The apologists of industrialism do not like to meet this charge directly; so they often take refuge in saying that they are devoted simply to science! They are really devoted to the applied sciences and to practical production. Therefore it is necessary to employ a certain skepticism even at the expense of the Cult of Science, and to say, It is an Americanism, which looks innocent and disinterested, but really is not either.

* * *

Religion can hardly expect to flourish in an industrial society. Religion is our submission to the general intention of a nature that is fairly inscrutable; it is the sense of our rôle as creatures within it. But nature industrialized, transformed into cities and artificial habitations, manufactured into commodities, is no longer nature but a highly simplified picture of nature. We receive the illusion of having power over nature, and lose the sense of nature as something mysterious and contingent. The God of nature under these conditions is merely an amiable expression, a superfluity, and the philosophical understanding ordinarily carried in the religious experience is not there for us to have.

Nor do the arts have a proper life under industrialism, with the general decay of sensibility which attends it. Art depends, in general, like religion, on a right attitude to nature; and in particular on a free and disinterested observation of nature that occurs only in leisure. Neither the creation nor the understanding of works of art is possible in an industrial age except by some local and unlikely suspension of the industrial drive.

The amenities of life also suffer under the curse of a strictly-business or industrial civilization. They consist in such practices as manners, conversation, hospitality, sympathy, family life, romantic love—in the social exchanges which reveal and develop sensibility in human affairs. If religion and the arts are founded on right relations of man-to-nature, these are founded on right relations of man-to-man.

* * *

The "Humanists" are too abstract. Humanism, properly speaking, is not an abstract system, but a culture, the whole way in which we live, act, think, and feel. It is a kind of imaginatively balanced life lived out in a definite social tradition. And, in the concrete, we believe that this, the genuine humanism, was rooted in the agrarian life of the older South and of other parts of the country that shared in such a tradition. It was not an abstract moral "check" derived from the classics—it was not soft material poured in from the top. It was deeply founded in the way of life itself—in its tables, chairs, portraits, festivals, laws, marriage customs. We cannot recover our native humanism by adopting some standard of taste that is critical enough to question the contemporary arts but not critical enough to question the social and economic life which is their ground.

* * *

Opposed to the industrial society is the agrarian, which does not stand in particular need of definition. An agrarian society is hardly one that has no use at all for industries, for professional vocations, for scholars and artists, and for the life of cities. Technically, perhaps, an agrarian society is one in which agriculture is the leading vocation, whether for wealth, for pleasure, or for prestige—a form of labor that is pursued with intelligence and leisure, and that becomes the model to which the other forms approach as well as they may. But an agrarian regime will be secured readily enough where the superfluous industries are not allowed to rise against it. The theory of agrarianism is that the culture of the soil is the best and most sensitive of vocations, and that therefore it should have the economic preference and enlist the maximum number of workers.

These principles do not intend to be very specific in proposing any practical measures. How may the little agrarian community resist the Chamber of Commerce of its county seat, which is always trying to import some foreign industry that cannot be assimilated to the life-pattern of the community? Just what must the Southern leaders do to defend the traditional Southern life? How may the Southern and the Western agrarians unite for effective action? Should the agrarian forces try to capture the Democratic party, which historically is so closely affiliated with the defense of individualism, the small community, the state, the South? Or must the agrarians—even the Southern ones—abandon the Democratic party to its fate and try a new one? What legislation could most profitably be championed by the powerful agrarians in the Senate of the United States? What anti-industrial measures might promise to stop the advances of industrialism, or even undo some of them, with the least harm to those concerned? What policy should be pursued by the educators who have a tradition at heart? These and many other questions are of the greatest importance, but they cannot be answered here.

For, in conclusion, this much is clear: If a community, or a section, or a race, or an age, is groaning under industrialism, and well aware that it is an evil dispensation, it must find the way to throw it off. To think that this cannot be done is pusillanimous. And if the whole community, section, race, or age thinks it cannot be done, then it has simply lost its political genius and doomed itself to impotence.

Empire and Race

JAMES HARVEY SLATER AND JAMES ZACHARIAH GEORGE

Speeches on Chinese Immigration (1882)

Starting in the 1840s, the United States experienced its first great influx of immigrants. Although many immigrants from Europe experienced bigotry and discrimination, the small but growing number of Chinese workers who came to the American West to work in mining, agriculture, and the railroads were the first to face federal legal restrictions. The unprecedented Chinese Exclusion Act of 1882, which was supported by labor unions and many European immigrants, severely limited the number of Chinese who could come to the United States. As the speeches of senators James Harvey Slater (1826–1899) and James Zachariah George (1826–1897) indicate, many supporters of the legislation argued that restrictions on Chinese immigration were necessary to protect the dignity of labor and the cultural purity of the United States from "these hordes of heathens."

Mr. SLATER. Again, sir, we are told that in this legislation we are treading backward and forsaking the principles and traditions upon which our fathers one hundred years ago laid the foundations of government, and the Declaration of Independence is invoked as a sufficient argument and showing of this statement. The right to the pursuit of happiness is asserted as conclusive of the whole question. No one will deny the axiomatic and self-evident truths of the Declaration of Independence respecting human rights, but that they apply in this case may well be denied. The pursuit of happiness is certainly the inalienable right of every human being, but that pursuit must be regulated by human society and by human laws. It might be a great source of happiness to the highwayman to meet the honorable Senator from Massachusetts [Mr. HOAR] upon the highway and forcibly take from his possession his purse. Necessitous hunger and privation might impel to such an act, and the gold or currency that purse might be expected to contain would bring numberless benefits and blessings, not only to the highwayman, but also to those who might be dependent upon him; but the law of society steps in to protect the citizen in his right to go unmolested about his pursuits, and pronounces such acts criminal and affixes severe penalties to their commission.

So it is daily demonstrated in a thousand ways that the pursuit of happiness is circumscribed and limited by the laws and necessities of organized society. What is true of the individual members of a community in this respect is equally true of nations and peoples, and also true of individuals leaving their native land in search of happiness and to better their own condition among another people in another country. They have no right in the pursuit of their own happiness to inflict injury upon the people of other communities. To assert the right of aliens to impose themselves upon or into communities to which they are alien without their consent and to their detriment, is to assert a principle, when carried to its logical consequences, subversive of all human government. Such a principle leads inevitably to anarchy. The law of life and self-preservation is as important and necessary to communities as to individuals, and is as inalienable and inherent in the one case as in the other; and no principle is more firmly imbedded in the ethics of international law than that it is both the right and the duty of the paramount authority in every state, in whatever form that authority may be vested, and however it may be exercised, to protect the state and the people of the state from all and every evil that may threaten its safety or menace the interests, prosperity, or happiness of its people, be they few or many, and herein alone can be found justification for a resort to the arbitrament of war.

Disguise it as we may we cannot longer fail to recognize the fact that western civilization has met the eastern upon the shores of the Pacific. The westward march of the Caucasian has there met the same teeming hordes that generations ago gave a westward direction to his tireless energy by imposing on his east a living wall of Asiatics, impossible to pass or overcome. The Pacific Ocean until recently had proved an impassable barrier and no Mongolian had ever passed to its eastward shore. But recent developments in steamships and the establishment of lines of steam communication between San Francisco and the open ports of China and Japan have practically connected the two continents and bridged the intervening sea. So that for a few dollars a Chinese immigrant can come from any of the ports of China to San Francisco. At first but few came, some returned, and a larger number followed, and in that way the tide of immigrants swelled to considerable proportions. Almost from the first their coming was objected to, and as its effects became more and more apparent this opposition became more and more pronounced, until within the last seven or eight years it has been greatly intensified, and by its universality as well as intensity has served to hold in check and to keep down and diminish the number of Chinese coming to the United States.

From 1850 to 1880 more than 200,000 Chinese landed on the Pacific coast. The census of 1880 shows that there were in that year 105,000 remaining in this country; but persons well informed in the customs and manners of the Chinese affirm that this is far below the correct figures. The smallness of their present numbers as compared to the total population of the country has been strongly contrasted and urged as a reason for discrediting the earnest statements of the people of the Pacific States and Territories that this Chinese population is a menace to good order and good government and the best interest of the people there. But the fact is overlooked that even according to the census there are 75,000 in the State of California, and some ten thousand in the State of Oregon, while the appeal of the Trades Assembly of California, quoted by the honorable Senator from Delaware [Mr. BAYARD] on last Friday, estimates, after investigation, the Chinese population of California at 150,000, or 20 per cent. greater than the male whites capable of bearing arms. From this it would seem that the adult Chinese male laboring element in California was very nearly equal to the adult white laboring element. If, however, the census report be taken, then they constitute something like one-half of the male laboring element in that State.

But we are told by the honorable Senator from Massachusetts that the Chinese are the most easily governed race in the world; that every Chinaman in America has four hundred and ninety-nine Americans to control him. But the honorable Senator omitted to state that of the four hundred and ninety-nine Americans four hundred and eighty-seven of them were from one thousand to three thousand miles away from where the evils of Chinese emigration are being felt. Why, sir, in the Pacific States and Territories beyond Utah there are, according to the census reports, one Chinaman to every twelve of the white population, and I have no doubt that if the exact numbers of the Chinese population could be ascertained that the ratio would be one to every eight or ten of the white population. Carry this ratio throughout the United States and there would be a Chinese population of adult male laborers of near 5,000,000 to compete with white labor, to depress and demoralize it by underbidding and bringing it down to starvation prices. Let me bring it a little closer, Mr. President. Massachusetts has a population of 1,758,000. Now let the Senators of that State add to that population 175,000 adult Chinese laborers to compete with and underbid the working classes and they may be able to form some just conceptions of the condition of the poor laboring classes in the Pacific States and Territories. My impression is that there would be a small-sized bedlam in Massachusetts under such a state of facts. Pennsylvania has 4,282,000 population. I ask her Senators what effect it would have upon the laboring population of the great State to send into it 400,000 able-bodied laboring Chinese to depress the labor market in the struggle and competition that would ensue. The State of New York has a population of over 5,000,000; let the Senators of that State reflect what would be the effect of letting in 500,000 Chinese laborers to compete with their laboring population. If Senators will but reflect upon these facts they can readily comprehend how it is that there is such a wonderful unanimity in sentiment in every locality where the blight of this immigration has been felt; they will no longer be surprised at the steady and growing opposition to that class of immigrants, an opposition so universal that in a secret vote by concealed ballots no more than 800 votes were given favoring this immigration to 150,000 against it.

Mr. President, the honorable Senator from Massachusetts [Mr. HOAR] asked "What argument can be urged against the Chinese which was not heard against the negro within living memories!" I do not suppose that I can satisfy the honorable Senator of the fallacy of his reasoning, but I may call attention to the utter want of any parallelism between the relations of the negro to the people of the United States and that of the Chinese, who desire to come among us as immigrants. The negro was native to the soil, born and bred within our jurisdiction, speaking our language, having, in a large degree, our civilization, and adhering to our religion. He was with us, if not of us; his ancestors were brought here against their will, and the generation with which we had to deal had no land, clime, or country to call their own except the land in which they were born, and no ties with any people or race except those with whom they had been reared. From necessity they were to remain with and of us; the only question, was what should be the relation.

The Chinese are aliens, born in a foreign land, speak a foreign tongue, owe allegiance to a foreign government, are idolaters in religion, have a different civilization from ours, do not and will not assimilate with our people, come only to get money, and return; and they are inimical to our laws, evade them whenever and wherever they can. So numerous are they at home in their own country that existence among the lower orders of their people is, and has been for centuries, a struggle for existence, and through this ceaseless struggle they have developed into a race of people of such character and physical qualities as to be able to exist and thrive where and under conditions the white man would perish and die out. They bring their customs with them, and persistently adhere to and retain them. Having the protection of our laws they systematically evade and violate them. They persistently and secretly maintain a code of laws and a form of government of their own, which they enforce with seeming certainty and effectiveness. Those who come as immigrants are of the lowest orders of the Chinese population, largely criminal. They bring with them their filth and frightful and nameless diseases and contagions. They bring no families as a general rule, but numbers of their country women are brought for purposes of prostitution, and are bought and sold among themselves as slaves, and our laws and courts are powerless to prevent it. They enhance the cost of government, and increase the burdens of taxation, while they contribute practically nothing in the way of taxes. Their labor is essentially servile, and is demoralizing to every class of white labor with which it comes in competition.

These, sir, are the people for whom the honorable Senator would open wide the door of admission, or, being open, would refuse to close it, but rather invites these hordes of heathens that swarm like rats in a cellar and live in filth and degradation along the sea-coast of China to come and compete with and degrade American labor, and compares them to the colored people born and reared in America. The negro is thoroughly American, if he is not Caucasian; the Chinese are neither Caucasian nor American, but are alien to our race, customs, religion, and civilization. The bill is not directed against those already here, but against the hordes that threaten to come. The terms of the treaty place those here beyond the reach of legislative enactment, and effort is now being made to bring in a large number of Chinese laborers before legislation can be had. Last year's immigration was over 20,000. This fact sufficiently demonstrates their purpose to come. * * *

I believe that unless Congress adopts stringent restrictive legislation that multitudes of Chinese laborers—cooly laborers—will immigrate to our Pacific States. I have seen this morning a telegram from Portland, Oregon, stating that the Six Companies are now hurrying ten thousand laborers into Oregon, who are to be employed in constructing the Northern Pacific Railway.

I am one of those who believe that either the Anglo-Saxon race will possess the Pacific slope or the Mongolian race will possess it.

By adopting restrictive legislation it is believed we can preserve the great States and Territories of the Pacific slope for our own race. We have a right, under our treaty with China, and according to the laws of nations, to enact the legislation proposed. I am satisfied it is for our interest to enact it. Having the legal right to enact it, and it being for our interest to enact it, I favor and shall vote for this bill.

Mr. GEORGE. Mr. President, I have many reasons which impel me to give my most hearty support to this bill,

If it were true (which I deny) that this bill is in conflict with the logic of the political theories in regard to the rights of mankind, which have heretofore prevailed in this country, that is no insuperable objection to its passage. I do not deny that every measure should be weighed and considered in the light of accepted and recognized principles, but I do deny that every measure, however necessary to the welfare and the happiness of the people of the United States, however accordant to the teachings of experience and history, should be condemned because it conflicts with the theories of a speculative and Utopian scheme for the administration of the affairs of this world.

Our Government has attained its present astonishing grandeur and vigor because it is the result of the growth and development of Anglo Saxon ideas, put into practical operation by Anglo-Saxon common sense. It has not grown according to a rule prescribed by an inexorable logic, reasoning from premises which assumed an ideal perfection in human nature and attainable in human institutions. Our Constitution is the work of men, intended for the government of men, not of angels or demi-gods. It recognizes human frailties and human passions, and seeks no unattainable perfection. It was made by the American people for themselves and their posterity, not for the human race. It was ordained by the American people for their own happiness and their own welfare and the welfare of such others as they should choose of their own free will to admit to American citizenship. That our institutions are stable; that they attain the ends of good government—security to life, liberty, and property, the progress and happiness of the American people; that they can stand any strain, however great, occasioned by unlooked-for and calamitous emergencies, is because they were evolved and were modified as circumstances demanded, and were not the result of the *a priori* reasonings of political theorists.

The foundations were not laid according to any scientific rule, but according to the exigencies and needs of the people. The superstructure may be patch-work, but the different pieces are so dovetailed into each other, so skillfully joined, that the weakness of one part has up to this time been counterbalanced by the united strength of the whole. In short, sir, I may well say that the excellence, the strength, and durability of Anglo-Saxon political institutions result from the fact that they are both illogical and inconsistent. It is, therefore, no good reason why we should not relieve the people of the Pacific States of the great evil of Chinese immigration, so ably and fully presented by their Senators here; no reason why we should not adopt the amendment of the Senator from California prohibiting the naturalization of natives of the Chinese Empire, that we do tolerate the presence of another inferior race, and have conferred on them the privileges of American citizenship and imposed on them the discharge of its high duties. I prefer, sir, to expose myself to the charge of inconsistency rather than to disregard the known wishes of the white people of the Pacific States and to incur the hazards and dangers to which they are exposed.

I will not discount their judgment, formed from hard experience, in favor of the speculations of a humanitarian philosophy. Besides, sir, it is not so clear that our Constitution, with all its great strength and vigor, after embracing the African, can take in with safety even the more enlightened countrymen of Confucius.

Second. I give to this bill and the proposed amendments my hearty support for another reason. It will really and truly protect American labor. It furnishes no sham protection in the shape of a tax levied on all the labor of the country for the benefit of the capitalist, in the hope (often if not always a vain one) that he will divide it and give some small part to that inconsiderable number of laborers whom he employs.

This bill protects the American laborer directly and clearly, and not in a round-about and second-hand way. It gives this protection by its own force, and the vigor of its own beneficent provisions, independent of either the magnanimity or the charity of another, and that other too directly interested in withholding the protection.

As so well shown in the very able and exhaustive discussion of this subject by the Senator from California, [Mr. MILLER,] the Chinese laborer has an advantage over the American laborer. This is an undue advantage. It does not arise from superior industry, larger intelligence, or greater skill. It comes from the simple fact that the one is an American citizen, with the hopes and aspirations of an American citizen, and charged with the performance of the high duties to his country and his family incident to American citizenship; the other has none of these. For ages he has from necessity been inured to that hard and scanty sort of living, joined to incessant toil, which barely supports life. To compete with him the American laborer must be reduced to the same standard of living, condemned to the same ceaseless toil.

Are we prepared, sir, to invite the American laborer to this competition—to yoke him with this fellow to plow the fields, delve in the mine, or work in the shops of capital seeking the cheapest labor! Sir, we want no such laborers, either foreign or native. We want no class that can or will accept the bare necessaries of life only as the price of its labor. We want no class to whose vision is forever closed all prospect of advancement, comfort, independence, and progress. If there be such now anywhere in this broad land, it would be our first and highest duty, so far as we had constitutional power, to lift the dark veil of despair which shuts out the prospect of elevation and advancement. It is our duty to dignify and ennoble labor, not to debase and degrade it. The American laborer so far has been the grandest product of our free institutions. He has converted a continent from a wilderness into cultivated fields. He has built our towns and cities, our railroads and canals, our ships and our warehouses, the mansions of the rich, and the humble cottages of the poor. He has patiently sown, where in many instances others have reaped; he has built what others have enjoyed. Yet in the main he has been rewarded for his skill and toil. At the same time, sir, he has discharged with fidelity, and in the main with sound judgment, the duties, public and private, of American citizenship. In peace he has created all our great wealth and advanced the country to an unparalleled prosperity. In war he has carried, as a private, the musket and the knapsack, and braved the horrors and carnage of battle without the stimulus of personal ambition or the hope of personal renown. It is, sir, in my judgment, our duty to pass this bill. To reject it is to invite to our shores millions of an inferior and degraded race to drag down to their own level the American laborer.

And now, Mr. President, before I take my seat I wish to congratulate the Senators from the Pacific States on the skill and moderation with which they have discussed the relations of the American people with this inferior race. For once, sir, this subject has been discussed in a calm and philosophical spirit without exciting sectional animosities or rekindling the passions engendered by past contests and dissensions. The time may come—it is not here now—when the relations of another race to American citizenship must be, as all other questions ought to be, discussed in the like spirit. In the mean time, while discharging our duty freely in educating that race into a proper discharge of their duties as American citizens, advancing them to their full capacity, it will also be our duty to observe with care and impartiality the experiment of African citizenship. No man shall strive harder than I will to make the experiment successful, and no man will be more rejoiced if in the end it shall be all that those who initiated it shall desire. All that I ask for the white people of the South on this subject is what I am willing to grant, and I believe a majority of this body is willing to grant to the white people of the Pacific States, that their testimony, their experience, and their judgment shall not be discredited in a matter so deeply affecting their welfare.

The Constitution was ordained and established by white men, as they themselves declared in its preamble, "to secure the blessings of liberty to themselves (ourselves) and their (our) posterity," and I cannot doubt that this great pledge thus solemnly given will be as fully redeemed in favor of the white people of the South, should occasion for action arise, as I intend on my part and on their behalf to redeem it this day in favor of the white people of the Pacific States, by my vote to protect them against a degrading and destructive association with the inferior race now threatening to overrun them.

JOSIAH STRONG

Our Country (1885)

The Congregationalist minister Josiah Strong (1847–1916) was an ardent supporter of imperialist expansion and tight restrictions on immigration. In his popular book Our Country, *Strong insisted on the special role of the United States in spreading Western values throughout the world. A firm believer in the missionary role of the Anglo-Saxon race, which for him embodied the ideas of liberty and Christianity, Strong argued that God had prepared the way for North Americans to achieve the "highest civilization" that the world has ever known in the Darwinian "final competition of races."*

I t is not necessary to argue to those for whom I write that the two great needs of mankind, that all men may be lifted up into the light of the highest Christian civilization, are, first, a pure, spiritual Christianity, and, second, civil liberty. Without controversy, these are the forces which, in the past, have contributed most to the elevation of the human race, and they must continue to be, in the future, the most efficient ministers to its progress. It follows, then, that the Anglo-Saxon, as the great representative of these two ideas, the depositary of these two greatest blessings, sustains peculiar relations to the world's future, is divinely commissioned to be, in a peculiar sense, his brother's keeper. Add to this the fact of his rapidly increasing strength in modern times, and we have well nigh a demonstration of his destiny. * * *

There can be no reasonable doubt that North America is to be the great home of the Anglo-Saxon, the principal seat of his power, the center of his life and influence. Not only does it constitute seven-elevenths of his possessions, but his empire is unsevered, while the remaining four-elevenths are fragmentary and scattered over the earth. * * *

But we are to have not only the larger portion of the Anglo-Saxon race for generations to come, we may reasonably expect to develop the highest type of Anglo-Saxon civilization. If human progress follows a law of development, if

"Time's noblest offspring is the last,"

our civilization should be the noblest; for we are

"The heirs of all the ages in the foremost files of time,"

and not only do we occupy the latitude of power, but *our land is the last to be occupied in that latitude.* There is no other virgin soil in the North Temperate Zone. If the consummation of human progress is not to be looked for here, if there is yet to flower a higher civilization, where is the soil that is to produce it? * * *

Mr. Darwin is not only disposed to see, in the superior vigor of our people, an illustration of his favorite theory of natural selection, but even intimates that the world's history thus far has been simply preparatory for our future, and tributary to it. He says: "There is apparently much truth in the belief that the wonderful progress of the United States, as well as the character of the people, are the results of natural selection; for the more energetic, restless and courageous men from all parts of Europe have emigrated during the last ten or twelve generations to that great country, and have there succeeded best. Looking at the distant future, I do not think that the Rev. Mr. Zincke takes an exaggerated view when he says: 'All other series of events—as that which resulted in the culture of mind in Greece, and that which resulted in the Empire of Rome—only appear to have purpose and value when viewed in connection with, or rather as subsidiary to, the great stream of Anglo-Saxon emigration to the West.'"

There is abundant reason to believe that the Anglo-Saxon race is to be, is, indeed, already becoming, more effective here than in the mother country. * * *

It may be easily shown, and is of no small significance, that the two great ideas of which the Anglo-Saxon is the exponent are having a fuller development in the United States than in Great Britain. There the union of Church and State tends strongly to paralyze some of the members of the body of Christ. Here there is no such influence to destroy spiritual life and power. Here, also, has been evolved the form of government consistent with the largest possible civil liberty. Furthermore, it is significant that the marked characteristics of this race are being here emphasized most. Among the most striking features of the Anglo-Saxon is his money-making power—a power of increasing importance in the widening commerce of the world's future. We have seen, in a preceding chapter, that, although England is by far the richest nation of Europe, we have already outstripped her in the race after wealth, and we have only begun the development of our vast resources.

Again, another marked characteristic of the Anglo-Saxon is what may be called an instinct or genius for colonizing. His unequaled energy, his indomitable perseverance, and his personal independence, made him a pioneer. He excels all others in pushing his way into new countries. It was those in whom this tendency was strongest that came to America, and this inherited tendency has been further developed by the westward sweep of successive generations across the continent. So noticeable has this characteristic become that English visitors remark it. Charles Dickens once said that the typical American would hesitate to enter heaven unless assured that he could go further west.

Again, nothing more manifestly distinguishes the Anglo-Saxon than his intense and persistent energy; and he is developing in the United States an energy which, in eager activity and effectiveness, is peculiarly American. This is due partly to the fact that Americans are much better fed than Europeans, and partly to the undeveloped resources of a new country, but more largely to our climate, which acts as a constant stimulus.

* * * Moreover, our social institutions are stimulating. In Europe the various ranks of society are, like the strata of the earth, fixed and fossilized. There can be no great change without a terrible upheaval, a social earthquake. Here society is like the waters of the sea, mobile; as General Garfield said, and so signally illustrated in his own experience, that which is at the bottom today may one day flash on the crest of the highest wave. Every one is free to become whatever he can make of himself; free to transform himself from a rail-splitter or a tanner or a canal-boy, into the nation's President. Our aristocracy, unlike that of Europe, is open to all comers. Wealth, position, influence, are prizes offered for energy; and every farmer's boy, every apprentice and clerk, every friendless and penniless immigrant, is free to enter the lists. Thus many causes co-operate to produce here the most forceful and tremenduous energy in the world.

What is the significance of such facts? These tendencies infold the future; they are the mighty alphabet with which God writes his prophecies. May we not, by a careful laying together of the letters, spell out something of his meaning? It seems to me that God, with infinite wisdom and skill, is training the Anglo-Saxon race for an hour sure to come in the world's future. Heretofore there has always been in the history of the world a comparatively unoccupied land westward, into which the crowded countries of the East have poured their surplus populations. But the widening waves of migration, which millenniums ago rolled east and west from the valley of the Euphrates, meet today on our Pacific coast. There are no more new worlds. The unoccupied arable lands of the earth are limited, and will soon be taken. The time is coming when the pressure of population on the means of subsistence will be felt here as it is now felt in Europe and Asia. Then will the world enter upon a new stage of its history—*the final competition of races, for which the Anglo-Saxon is being schooled.* Long before the thousand millions are here, the mighty *centrifugal* tendency, inherent in this stock and strengthened in the United States, will assert itself. Then this race of unequaled energy, with all the majesty of numbers and the might of wealth behind it—the representative, let us hope, of the largest liberty, the purest Christianity, the highest civilization—having developed peculiarly aggressive traits calculated to impress its institutions upon mankind, will spread itself over the earth. If I read not amiss, this powerful race will move down upon Mexico, down upon Central and South America, out upon the islands of the sea, over upon Africa and beyond. And can any one doubt that the result of this competition of races will be the "survival of the fittest"?

"* * * Nothing can save the inferior race but a ready and pliant assimilation. Whether the feebler and more abject races are going to be regenerated and raised up, is already very much of a question. What if it should be God's plan to people the world with better and finer material? Certain it is, whatever expectations we may indulge, that there is a tremendous overbearing surge of power in the Christian nations, which, if the others are not speedily raised to some vastly higher capacity, will inevitably submerge and bury them forever. These great populations of Christendom— what are they doing, but throwing out their colonies on every side, and populating themselves, if I may so speak, into the possession of all countries and climes?" To this result no war of extermination is needful; the contest is not one of arms but of vitality and of civilization. "At the present day," says Mr. Darwin, "civilized nations are everywhere supplanting barbarous nations, excepting where the climate opposes a deadly barrier; and they succeed mainly, though not exclusively, through their arts, which are the products of the intellect." Thus the Finns were supplanted by the Aryan races in Europe and Asia, the Tartars by the Russians, and thus the aborigines of North America, Australia and New Zealand are now disappearing before the all-conquering Anglo-Saxons. It would seem as if these inferior tribes were only precursors of a superior race, voices in the wilderness crying: "Prepare ye the way of the Lord!" The savage is a hunter; by the incoming of civilization the game is driven away and disappears before the hunter becomes a herder or an agriculturist. The savage is ignorant of many diseases of civilization which, when he is exposed to them, attack him before he learns how to treat them. Civilization also has its vices, of which the uninitiated savage is innocent. He proves an apt learner of vice, but dull enough in the school of morals. Every civilization has its destructive and preservative elements. The Anglo-Saxon race would speedily decay but for the salt of Christianity. Bring savages into contact with our civilization, and its destructive forces become operative at once, while years are necessary to render effective the saving influence of Christian instruction. Moreover, the pioneer wave of our civilization carries with it more scum than salt. Where there is one missionary, there are hundreds of miners or traders or adventurers ready to debauch the native. Whether the extinction of inferior races before the advancing Anglo-Saxon seems to the reader sad or otherwise, it certainly appears probable. I know of nothing except climatic conditions to prevent this race from populating Africa as it has peopled North America. And those portions of Africa which are unfavorable to Anglo-Saxon life are less extensive than was once supposed. The Dutch Boers, after two centuries of life there, are as hardy as any race on earth. The Anglo-Saxon has established himself in climates totally diverse—Canada, South Africa, and India—and, through several generations, has preserved his essential race characteristics. He is not, of course, superior to climatic influences; but, even in warm climates, he is likely to retain his aggressive vigor long enough to supplant races already enfeebled. Thus, in what Dr. Bushnell calls "the out-populating power of the Christian stock," may be found God's final and complete solution of the dark problem of heathenism among many inferior peoples.

Some of the stronger races, doubtless, may be able to preserve their integrity; but, in order to compete with the Anglo-Saxon, they will probably be forced to adopt his methods and instruments, his civilization and his religion. Significant movements are now in progress among them. While the Christian religion was never more vital, or its hold upon the Anglo-Saxon mind stronger, there is taking place among the nations a wide-spread intellectual revolt against traditional beliefs. "In every corner of the world," said Mr. Froude, "there is the same phenomenon of the decay of established religions. . . . Among Mohammedans, Jews, Buddhists, Brahmins, traditionary creeds are losing their hold. An intellectual revolution is sweeping over the world, breaking down established opinions, dissolving foundations on which historical faiths have been built up." The contact of Christian with heathen nations is awaking the latter to new life. Old superstitions are loosening their grasp. The dead crust of fossil faiths is being shattered by the movements of life underneath. In Catholic countries, Catholicism is losing its influence over educated minds, and in some cases the masses have already lost all faith in it. Thus, while on this continent God is training the Anglo-Saxon race for its mission, a complemental work has been in progress in the great world beyond. God has two hands. Not only is he preparing in our civilization the die with which to stamp the nations, but, by what Southey called the "timing of Providence," he is preparing mankind to receive our impress.

Is there room for reasonable doubt that this race, unless devitalized by alcohol and tobacco, is destined to dispossess many weaker races, assimilate others and mold the remainder, until, in a very true and important sense, it has Anglo-Saxonized mankind? Already "the English language, saturated with Christian ideas, gathering up into itself the best thought of all the ages, is the great agent of Christian civilization throughout the world; at this moment affecting the destinies and molding the character of half the human race." Jacob Grimm, the German philologist, said of this language: "It seems chosen, like its people, to rule in future times in a still greater degree in all the comers of the earth." He predicted, indeed, that the language of Shakespeare would eventually become the language of mankind. Is not Tennyson's noble prophecy to find its fulfillment in Anglo-Saxondom's extending its dominion and influence—

"Till the war-drum throbs no longer, and the battle flags are furl'd
In the Parliament of man, the Federation of the world."

In my own mind, there is no doubt that the Anglo-Saxon is to exercise the commanding influence in the world's future; but the exact nature of that influence is, as yet, undetermined. How far his civilization will be materialistic and atheistic, and how long it will take thoroughly to Christianize and sweeten it, how rapidly he will hasten the coming of the kingdom wherein dwelleth righteousness, or how many ages he may retard it, is still uncertain; but *it is now being swiftly determined*. Let us weld together in a chain the various links of our logic which we have endeavored to forge. Is it manifest that the Anglo-Saxon holds in his hands the destinies of mankind for ages to come? Is it evident that the United States is to be the home of this race, the principal seat of his power, the great center of his influence? Is it true that the great West is to dominate the nation's future? Has it been shown that this generation is to determine the character, and hence the destiny, of the West? Then may God open the eyes of this generation! When Napoleon drew up his troops before the Mamelukes, under the shadow of the Pyramids, pointing to the latter, he said to his soldiers: "Remember that from yonder heights forty centuries look down on you." Men of this generation, from the pyramid top of opportunity on which God has set us, *we look down on forty centuries!* We stretch our hand into the future with power to mold the destinies of unborn millions.

> *"We are living, we are dwelling,*
> *In a grand and awful time,*
> *In an age on ages telling—*
> *To be living is sublime!"*

Notwithstanding the great perils which threaten it, I cannot think our civilization will perish; but I believe it is fully in the hands of the Christians of the United States, during the next fifteen or twenty years to hasten or retard the coming of Christ's kingdom in the world by hundreds, and perhaps thousands, of years. We of this generation and nation occupy the Gibraltar of the ages which commands the world's future.

THEODORE ROOSEVELT

The Winning of the West (1889–1896)

Theodore Roosevelt (1858–1919) entered public life at the age of twenty-three and served as a member of the New York State Assembly, a member of the U.S. Civil Service Commission, president of the New York City Board of Police Commissioners, and assistant secretary of the navy before becoming the twenty-sixth president of the United States on the assassination of William McKinley in 1901. As assistant secretary of the navy and as the leader of the Rough Riders in Cuba during the Spanish-American War, the vigorous adventurer pursued the expansionist vision that he outlined in The Winning of the West. Like many other works produced during this period, Roosevelt's four-volume history of the "spread of the English-speaking peoples" accepted the notion that different races have distinct historical destinies. This selection exemplifies Roosevelt's belief that the conquest of Indian territories was "for the benefit of civilization and in the interests of mankind."

Nor was there any alternative to these Indian wars. It is idle folly to speak of them as being the fault of the United States Government and it is even more idle to say that they could have been averted by treaty. Here and there, under exceptional circumstances or when a given tribe was feeble and unwarlike, the whites might gain the ground by a treaty entered into of their own free will by the Indians, without the least duress; but this was not possible with warlike and powerful tribes when once they realized that they were threatened with serious encroachment on their hunting-grounds. Moreover, looked at from the standpoint of the ultimate result, there was little real difference to the Indian whether the land was taken by treaty or by war. In the end the Delaware fared no better at the hands of the Quaker than the Wampanoag at the hands of the Puritan; the methods were far more humane in the one case than in the other, but the outcome was the same in both. No treaty could be satisfactory to the whites, no treaty served the needs of humanity and civilization, unless it gave the land to the Americans as unreservedly as any successful war.

As a matter of fact, the lands we have won from the Indians have been won as much by treaty as by war; but it was almost always war, or else the menace and possibility of war, that secured the treaty. In these treaties we have been more than just to the Indians; we have been abundantly generous, for we have paid them many times what they were entitled to; many times what we would have paid any civilized people whose claim was as vague and shadowy as theirs. By war or threat of war, or purchase, we have won from great civilized nations, from France, Spain, Russia, and Mexico, immense tracts of country already peopled by many tens of thousands of families; we have paid many millions of dollars to these nations for the land we took; but for every dollar thus paid to these great and powerful civilized commonwealths, we have paid ten, for lands less valuable, to the chiefs and warriors of the red tribes. No other conquering and colonizing nation has ever treated the original savage owners of the soil with such generosity as has the United States. Nor is the charge that the treaties with the Indians have been broken of weight itself; it depends always on the individual case. Many of the treaties were kept by the whites and broken by the Indians; others were broken by the whites themselves; and sometimes they did right. No treaties, whether between civilized nations or not, can ever be regarded as binding in perpetuity; with changing conditions, circumstances may arise which render it not only expedient, but imperative and honorable, to abrogate them.

Whether the whites won the land by treaty, by armed conquest, or, as was actually the case, by a mixture of both, mattered comparatively little so long as the land was won. It was all-important that it should be won, for the benefit of civilization and in the interests of mankind. It is, indeed, a warped, perverse, and silly morality which would forbid a course of conquest that has turned whole continents into the seats of mighty and flourishing civilized nations. All men of sane and wholesome thought must dismiss with impatient contempt the plea that these continents should be reserved for the use of scattered savage tribes, whose life was but a few degrees less meaningless, squalid, and ferocious than that of the wild beasts with whom they held joint ownership. It is as idle to apply to savages the rules of international morality which obtain between stable and cultured communities, as it would be to judge the fifth-century English conquest of Britain by the standards of to-day. Most fortunately, the hard, energetic, practical men who do the rough pioneer work of civilization in barbarous lands are not prone to false sentimentality. The people who are, are the people who stay at home. Often these stay-at-homes are too selfish and indolent, too lacking in imagination, to understand the race-importance of the work which is done by their pioneer brethren in wild and distant lands; and they judge them by standards which would only be applicable to quarrels in their own townships and parishes. Moreover, as each new land grows old, it misjudges the yet newer lands, as once it was itself misjudged. The home-staying Englishman of Britain grudges to the Africander [*sic*] his conquest of Matabeleland; and so the home-staying American of the Atlantic States dislikes to see the Western miners and cattlemen win for the use of their people the Sioux hunting-grounds. Nevertheless, it is the men actually on the borders of the longed-for ground, the men actually in contact with the savages, who in the end shape their own destinies.

The most ultimately righteous of all wars is a war with savages, though it is apt to be also the most terrible and inhuman. The rude, fierce settler who drives the savage from the land lays all civilized mankind under a debt to him. American and Indian, Boer and Zulu, Cossack and Tartar, New Zealander and Maori—in each case the victor, horrible though many of his deeds are, has laid deep the foundations for the future greatness of a mighty people. The consequences of struggles for territory between civilized nations seem small by comparison. Looked at from the standpoint of the ages, it is of little moment whether Lorraine is part of Germany or of France, whether the northern Adriatic cities pay homage to Austrian Kaiser or Italian King; but it is of incalculable importance that America, Australia, and Siberia should pass out of the hands of their red, black, and yellow aboriginal owners, and become the heritage of the dominant world races.

HENRY CABOT LODGE

Speech on a Literacy Test for Immigrants (1896)

In the 1896 Senate debate on literacy tests for immigrants, the Mass-
achusetts senator Henry Cabot Lodge (1850–1924) sought to pre-
serve what he considered the intellectual and moral quality of
American citizenship, which he believed was threatened by recent im-
migration from southern and eastern European nations. The senator,
who would later be the principal opponent of America's entering the
League of Nations, explained that the immigrants most likely to be
excluded by the literacy test were members of races "who are most
alien to the great body of the people of the United States" in moral
and intellectual character.

Mr. President, this bill is intended to amend the existing law so as to restrict still further immigration to the United States. Paupers, diseased persons, convicts, and contract laborers are now excluded. By this bill it is proposed to make a new class of excluded immigrants and add to those which have just been named the totally ignorant. The bill is of the simplest kind. The first section excludes from the country all immigrants who can not read and write either their own or some other language. The second section merely provides a simple test for determining whether the immigrant can read or write, and is added to the bill so as to define the duties of the immigrant inspectors, and to assure to all immigrants alike perfect justice and a fair test of their knowledge.

Two questions arise in connection with this bill. The first is as to the merits of this particular form of restriction; the second as to the general policy of restricting immigration at all. I desire to discuss briefly these two questions in the order in which I have stated them. The smaller question as to the merits of this particular bill comes first. The existing laws of the United States now exclude, as I have said, certain classes of immigrants who, it is universally agreed, would be most undesirable additions to our population. These exclusions have been enforced and the results have been beneficial, but the excluded classes are extremely limited and do not by any means cover all or even any considerable part of the immigrants whose presence here is undesirable or injurious, nor do they have any adequate effect in properly reducing the great body of immigration to this country. There can be no doubt that there is a very earnest desire on the part of the American people to restrict further and much more extensively than has yet been done foreign immigration to the United States. The question before the committee was how this could best be done; that is, by what method the largest number of undesirable immigrants and the smallest possible number of desirable immigrants could be shut out. * * *

It is not necessary for me here to do more than summarize the results of the committee's investigation, which have been set forth fully in their report. It is found, in the first place, that the illiteracy test will bear most heavily upon the Italians, Russians, Poles, Hungarians, Greeks, and Asiatics, and very lightly, or not at all, upon English-speaking emigrants or Germans, Scandinavians, and French. In other words, the races most affected by the illiteracy test are those whose emigration to this country has begun within the last twenty years and swelled rapidly to enormous proportions, races with which the English-speaking people have never hitherto assimilated, and who are most alien to the great body of the people of the United States. On the other hand, immigrants from the United Kingdom and of those races which are most closely related to the English-speaking people, and who with the English-speaking people themselves founded the American colonies and built up the United States, are affected but little by the proposed test. These races would not be prevented by this law from coming to this country in practically undiminished numbers. These kindred races also are those who alone go to the Western and Southern States, where immigrants are desired, and take up our unoccupied lands. The races which would suffer most seriously by exclusion under the proposed bill furnish the immigrants who do not go to the West or South, where immigration is needed, but who remain on the Atlantic Seaboard, where immigration is not needed and where their presence is most injurious and undesirable.

The statistics prepared by the committee show further that the immigrants excluded by the illiteracy test are those who remain for the most part in congested masses in our great cities. They furnish, as other tables show, a large proportion of the population of the slums. The committee's report proves that illiteracy runs parallel with the slum population, with criminals, paupers, and juvenile delinquents of foreign birth or parentage, whose percentage is out of all proportion to their share of the total population when compared with the percentage of the same classes among the native born. It also appears from investigations which have been made that the immigrants who would be shut out by the illiteracy test are those who bring least money to the country and come most quickly upon private or public charity for support. The replies of the governors of twenty-six States to the Immigration Restriction League show that in only two cases are immigrants of the classes affected by the illiteracy test desired, and those are of a single race. All the other immigrants mentioned by the governors as desirable belong to the races which are but slightly affected by the provisions of this bill. It is also proved that the classes now excluded by law, the criminals, the diseased, the paupers, and the contract laborers, are furnished chiefly by the same races as those most affected by the test of illiteracy. The same is true as to those immigrants who come to this country for a brief season and return to their native land, taking with them the money they have earned in the United States. There is no more hurtful and undesirable class of immigrants from every point of view than these "birds of passage," and the tables show that the races furnishing the largest number of "birds of passage" have also the greatest proportion of illiterates.

These facts prove to demonstrate that the exclusion of immigrants unable to read or write, as proposed by this bill, will operate against the most undesirable and harmful part of our present immigration and shut out elements which no thoughtful or patriotic man can wish to see multiplied among the people of the United States. The report of the committee also proves that this bill meets the great requirement of all legislation of this character in excluding the greatest proportion possible of thoroughly undesirable and dangerous immigrants and the smallest proportion of immigrants who are unobjectionable.

I have said enough to show what the effects of this bill would be, and that if enacted into law it would be fair in its operation and highly beneficial in its results. It now remains for me to discuss the second and larger question, as to the advisability of restricting immigration at all. This is a subject of the greatest magnitude and the most far-reaching importance. It has two sides, the economic and the social. As to the former, but few words are necessary. There is no one thing which does so much to bring about a reduction of wages and to injure the American wage earner as the unlimited introduction of cheap foreign labor through unrestricted immigration. Statistics show that the change in the race character of our immigration has been accompanied by a corresponding decline in its quality. The number of skilled mechanics and of persons trained to some occupation or pursuit has fallen off, while the number of those without occupation or training, that is, who are totally unskilled, has risen in our recent immigration to enormous proportions. This low, unskilled labor is the most deadly enemy of the American wage earner, and does more than anything else toward lowering his wages and forcing down his standard of living. * * *

It is not necessary to enter further into a discussion of the economic side of the general policy of restricting immigration. In this direction the argument is unanswerable. If we have any regard for the welfare, the wages, or the standard of life of American workingmen, we should take immediate steps to restrict foreign immigration. There is no danger, at present at all events, to our workingmen from the coming of skilled mechanics or of trained and educated men with a settled occupation or pursuit, for immigrants of this class will never seek to lower the American standard of life and wages. On the contrary, they desire the same standard for themselves. But there is an appalling danger to the American wage earner from the flood of low, unskilled, ignorant, foreign labor which has poured into the country for some years past, and which not only takes lower wages, but accepts a standard of life and living so low that the American workingman can not compete with it.

I now come to the aspect of this question which is graver and more serious than any other. The injury of unrestricted immigration to American wages and American standards of living is sufficiently plain and is bad enough, but the danger which this immigration threatens to the quality of our citizenship is far worse. That which it concerns us to know and that which is more vital to us as a people than all possible questions of tariff or currency is whether the quality of our citizenship is endangered by the present course and character of immigration to the United States. To determine this question intelligently we must look into the history of our race.

* * * It will be observed that with the exception of the Huguenot French, who formed but a small percentage of the total population, the people of the thirteen colonies were all of the same original race stocks. The Dutch, the Swedes, and the Germans simply blended again with the English-speaking people, who like them were descended from the Germanic tribes whom Cæsar fought and Tacitus described.

During the present century, down to 1875, there have been three large migrations to this country in addition to the always steady stream from Great Britain; one came from Ireland about the middle of the century, and somewhat later one from Germany and one from Scandinavia, in which is included Sweden, Denmark, and Norway. The Irish, although of a different race stock originally, have been closely associated with the English-speaking people for nearly a thousand years. They speak the same language, and during that long period the two races have lived side by side, and to some extent intermarried. The Germans and Scandinavians are again people of the same race stock as the English who founded and built up the colonies. During this century, down to 1875, then, as in the two which preceded it, there had been scarcely any immigration to this

country, except from kindred or allied races, and no other, which was sufficiently numerous to have produced any effect on the national characteristics, or to be taken into account here. Since 1875, however, there has
been a great change. While the people who for two hundred and fifty
years have been migrating to America have continued to furnish large
numbers of immigrants to the United States, other races of totally different race origin, with whom the English-speaking people have never hitherto been assimilated or brought in contact, have suddenly begun to
immigrate to the United States in large numbers. Russians, Hungarians,
Poles, Bohemians, Italians, Greeks, and even Asiatics, whose immigration to America was almost unknown twenty years ago, have during the
last twenty years poured in in steadily increasing numbers, until now they
nearly equal the immigration of those races kindred in blood or speech,
or both, by whom the United States has hitherto been built up and the
American people formed.

This momentous fact is the one which confronts us to-day, and if continued, it carries with it future consequences far deeper than any other
event of our times. It involves, in a word, nothing less than the possibility
of a great and perilous change in the very fabric of our race. * * *

Mr. President, more precious even than forms of government are the
mental and moral qualities which make what we call our race. While
those stand unimpaired all is safe. When those decline all is imperiled.
They are exposed to but a single danger, and that is by changing the quality of our race and citizenship through the wholesale infusion of races
whose traditions and inheritances, whose thoughts and whose beliefs are
wholly alien to ours and with whom we have never assimilated or even
been associated in the past. The danger has begun. It is small as yet,
comparatively speaking, but it is large enough to warn us to act while
there is yet time and while it can be done easily and efficiently. There lies
the peril at the portals of our land; there is pressing in the tide of unrestricted immigration. The time has certainly come, if not to stop, at least
to check, to sift, and to restrict those immigrants. In careless strength,
with generous hand, we have kept our gates wide open to all the world. If
we do not close them, we should at least place sentinels beside them to
challenge those who would pass through. The gates which admit men to
the United States and to citizenship in the great Republic should no
longer be left unguarded.

ALBERT J. BEVERIDGE

The March of the Flag (1898)

From 1899 to 1911, the great orator and historian Albert Jeremiah Beveridge (1862–1927) represented Indiana in the U.S. Senate, where he sponsored Progressive legislation to deal with unsanitary manufacturing conditions, child labor, and big business. Beveridge achieved national prominence during the Spanish-American War as an outspoken champion of American imperialism. Although he favored generous treatment of colonized peoples, Beveridge did not believe they were capable of self-government. In this speech, the senator explained that continued prosperity for "God's chosen people" required rejecting the arguments of imperialism's critics.

ELLOW-CITIZENS—It is a noble land that God has given us; a land that can feed and clothe the world: a land whose coast lines would inclose half the countries of Europe; a land set like a sentinel between the two imperial oceans of the globe; a greater England with a nobler destiny. It is a mighty people that He has planted on this soil; a people sprung from the most masterful blood of history; a people perpetually revitalized by the virile workingfolk of all the earth; a people imperial by virtue of their power, by right of their institutions, by authority of their heaven-directed purposes, the propagandists and not the misers of liberty. It is a glorious history our God has bestowed upon His chosen people; a history whose keynote was struck by Liberty Bell; a history heroic with faith in our mission and our future; a history of statesmen, who flung the boundaries of the Republic out into unexplored lands and savage wildernesses; a history of soldiers, who carried the flag across blazing deserts and through the ranks of hostile mountains, even to the gates of sunset: a history of a multiplying people, who overran a continent in half a century; a history divinely logical, in the process of whose tremendous reasoning we find ourselves to-day.

Therefore, in this campaign the question is larger than a party question. It is an American question. It is a world question. Shall the American people continue their resistless march toward the commercial supremacy of the world? Shall free institutions broaden their blessed reign as the children of liberty wax in strength until the empire of our principles is established over the hearts of all mankind? Have we no mission to perform—no duty to discharge to our fellow-man? Has the Almighty Father endowed us with gifts beyond our deserts, and marked us as the people of His peculiar favor, merely to rot in our own selfishness, as men and nations must who take cowardice for their companion and self for their deity—as China has, as India has, as Egypt has? Shall we be as the man who had one talent and hid it, or as he who had ten talents and used them until they grew to riches?

And shall we reap the reward that waits on the discharge of our high duty as the sovereign power of earth; shall we occupy new markets for what our farmers raise, new markets for what our factories make, new markets for what our merchants sell,—aye, and please God, new markets for what our ships shall carry? Shall we avail ourselves of new sources of supply of what we do not raise or make, so that what are luxuries to-day shall be necessities to-morrow? Shall we conduct the mightiest commerce of history with the best money known to man or shall we use the pauper money of Mexico, China and the Chicago platform? Shall we be worthy of our mighty past of progress, brushing aside, as we have always done, the spider webs of technicality, and march ever onward upon the highway of development, to the doing of real deeds, the achievement of real things, and the winning of real victories?

In a sentence, shall the American people endorse at the polls the American administration of William McKinley, which, under the guidance of Divine Providence, has started the Republic on its noblest career of prosperity, duty and glory; or shall the American people rebuke that administration, reverse the wheels of history, halt the career of the flag and turn to that purposeless horde of criticism and carping that is assailing the government at Washington? Shall it be McKinley, sound money and a world-conquering commerce, or Bryan, Bailey, Bland and Blackburn, a bastard currency and a policy of commercial retreat? In the only foreign war that this Nation has had in two generations, will you, the voters of this Republic and the guardians of its good repute, give the other nations of the world to understand that the American people do not approve and indorse the administration that conducted it? These are the questions that you must answer at the polls, and I well know how you will answer them. The thunder of American guns at Santiago and Manila will find its answer in the approval of the voters of the Republic. For the administration of William McKinley, in both peace and war, will receive the mightiest endorsement of a grateful people ever registered. In both peace and war, for we rely on the new birth of national prosperity as well as on the new birth of national glory. Think of both! Think of our country two years ago, and think of it to-day!

For William McKinley is continuing the policy that Jefferson began, Monroe continued, Seward advanced, Grant promoted, Harrison championed. Hawaii is ours; Porto Rico is to be ours; at the prayer of its people Cuba will finally be ours; in the islands of the East, even to the gates of Asia, coaling stations are to be ours; at the very least the flag of a liberal government is to float over the Philippines, and it will be the stars and stripes of glory. And the burning question of this campaign is whether the American people will accept the gifts of events; whether they will rise, as lifts their soaring destiny; whether they will proceed along the lines of national development surveyed by the statesmen of our past, or whether, for the first time, the American people doubt their mission, question their fate, prove apostate to the spirit of their race, and halt the ceaseless march of free institutions?

The opposition tells us that we ought not to govern a people without their consent. I answer, the rule of liberty that all just government derives its authority from the consent of the governed, applies only to those who are capable of self-government. We govern the Indians without their consent; we govern our Territories without their consent; we govern our children without their consent. I answer, would not the natives of the Philippines prefer the just, humane, civilizing government of this Republic to the savage, bloody rule of pillage and extortion from which we have rescued them? Do not the blazing fires of joy and the ringing bells of gladness in Porto Rico prove the welcome of our flag? And regardless of this formula of words made only for enlightened, self-governing peoples, do we owe no duty to the world? Shall we turn these peoples back to the reeking hands from which we have taken them? Shall we save them from those nations, to give them to a self-rule of tragedy? It would be like giving a razor to a babe and telling it to shave itself. It would be like giving a typewriter to an Esquimau and telling him to publish one of the great dailies of the world.

* * * There was not one reason for the land lust of our statesmen from Jefferson to Harrison other than the prophet and the Saxon within them. But today, we are raising more than we can consume. Today, we are making more than we can use. Therefore, we must find new markets for our produce, new occupation for our capital, new work for our labor. And so, while we did not need the territory taken during the past century at the time it was acquired, we do need what we have taken in 1898, and we need it now. Think of the thousands of Americans who will pour into Hawaii and Porto Rico when the Republic's laws cover those islands with justice and safety. Think of the tens of thousands of

Americans who will invade the Philippines when a liberal government shall establish order and equity there. Think of the hundreds of thousands of Americans who will build a soap-and-water, common school civilization of energy and industry in Cuba, when a government of law replaces the double reign of anarchy and tyranny. Think of the prosperous millions that empress of islands will support when, obedient to the law of political gravitation, her people ask for the highest honor liberty can bestow—the sacred order of the stars and stripes, the citizenship of the great Republic!

What does all this mean for every one of us? First of all, it means opportunity for all the glorious young manhood of the Republic. It means that the resources and the commerce of those immensely rich dominions will be increased as much as American energy is greater than Spanish sloth; for Americans, henceforth, will monopolize those resources and that commerce. In Cuba, alone, there are 15,000,000 acres of forest unacquainted with the ax. There are exhaustless mines of iron. There are priceless deposits of manganese. There are millions of acres yet unexplored. The resources of Porto Rico have only been trifled with. The resources of the Philippines have hardly been touched by the finger tips of modern methods. And they produce what we cannot, and they consume what we produce—the very predestination of reciprocity.

And William McKinley intends that their trade shall be ours. It means an opportunity for the rich man to do something with his money, besides hoarding it or lending it. It means occupation for every workingman in the country at wages which the development of new resources, the launching of new enterprises, the monopoly of new markets always brings. Cuba is as large as Pennsylvania, and is the richest spot on all the globe. Hawaii is as large as New Jersey; Porto Rico half as large as Hawaii; the Philippines larger than all New England, New York, New Jersey and Delaware. The trade of these islands, developed as we will develop it, will set every reaper in the Republic singing, every furnace spouting the flames of industry. * * *

* * * There are so many real things to be done—canals to be dug, railways to be laid, forests to be felled, cities to be builded, unviolated fields to be tilled, priceless markets to be won, ships to be launched, peoples to be saved, civilization to be proclaimed and the flag of liberty flung to the eager air of every sea. Is this an hour to waste upon triflers with Nature's laws? Is this a season to give our destiny over [to] word mongers and prosperity wreckers? No! It is an hour to remember your duty to the home. It is a moment to realize the opportunities Fate has opened to this favored people and to you. It is a time to bethink you of your Nation and its sovereignty of the seas. It is a time to remember that the God of our fa-

thers is our God and that the gifts and the duties He gave to them, enriched and multiplied, He renews to us, their children. It is a time to sustain that devoted man, servant of the people and of the most high God, who is guiding the Republic out into the ocean of infinite possibilities. It is a time to cheer the beloved President of God's chosen people, till the whole world is vocal with American loyalty to the American government and William McKinley, its head and chief.

Fellow-Americans, we are God's chosen people. Yonder at Bunker Hill and Yorktown His providence was above us. At New Orleans and on ensanguined seas His hand sustained us. Abraham Lincoln was His minister, and His was the altar of freedom the boys in blue set up on a hundred smoking battlefields. His power directed Dewey in the east, and He delivered the Spanish fleet into our hands on Liberty's natal day as He delivered the elder Armada into the hands of our English sires two centuries ago. His great purposes are revealed in the progress of the flag, which surpasses the intentions of Congresses and Cabinets, and leads us, like a holier pillar of cloud by day and pillar of fire by night, into situations unforeseen by finite wisdom and duties unexpected by the unprophetic heart of selfishness. The American people cannot use a dishonest medium of exchange; it is ours to set the world its example of right and honor. We cannot fly from our world duties; it is ours to execute the purposes of a fate that has driven us to be greater than our small intentions.

We cannot retreat from any soil where Providence has unfurled our banner; it is ours to save that soil for liberty and civilization. For liberty and civilization and God's promises fulfilled, the flag must henceforth be the symbol and the sign to all mankind.

Platform of the American Anti-Imperialist League (1899)

The American Anti-Imperialist League was founded in 1899 to oppose American annexation of the Philippines. The league, which was made up of various anti-imperialist leagues throughout the country but mostly in New England and the South, never gained a strong foothold in either major political party and found it difficult to get past charges of treason as the conflict in the Philippines dragged on. Nevertheless, the league's platform attacked imperialism as an un-American assault on the principles of liberty and government by consent.

W e hold that the policy known as imperialism is hostile to liberty and tends toward militarism, an evil from which it has been our glory to be free. We regret that it has become necessary in the land of Washington and Lincoln to reaffirm that all men, of whatever race or color, are entitled to life, liberty, and the pursuit of happiness. We maintain that governments derive their just powers from the consent of the governed. We insist that the subjugation of any people is "criminal aggression" and open disloyalty to the distinctive principles of our government.

We earnestly condemn the policy of the present national administration in the Philippines. It seeks to extinguish the spirit of 1776 in those islands. We deplore the sacrifice of our soldiers and sailors, whose bravery deserves admiration even in an unjust war. We denounce the slaughter of the Filipinos as a needless horror. We protest against the extension of American sovereignty by Spanish methods.

We demand the immediate cessation of the war against liberty, begun by Spain and continued by us. We urge that Congress be promptly convened to announce to the Filipinos our purpose to concede to them the independence for which they have so long fought and which of right is theirs.

The United States have always protested against the doctrine of international law which permits the subjugation of the weak by the strong. A self-governing state cannot accept sovereignty over an unwilling people. The United States cannot act upon the ancient heresy that might makes right.

Imperialists assume that with the destruction of self-government in the Philippines by American hands, all opposition here will cease. This is a grievous error. Much as we abhor the war of "criminal aggression" in the Philippines, greatly as we regret that the blood of the Filipinos is on American hands, we more deeply resent the betrayal of American institutions at home. The real firing line is not in the suburbs of Manila. The foe is of our own household. The attempt of 1861 was to divide the country. That of 1899 is to destroy its fundamental principles and noblest ideals.

Whether the ruthless slaughter of the Filipinos shall end next month or next year is but an incident in a contest that must go on until the declaration of independence and the constitution of the United States are rescued from the hands of their betrayers. Those who dispute about standards of value while the republic is undermined will be listened to as little as those who would wrangle about the small economies of the household while the house is on fire. The training of a great people for a century, the aspiration for liberty of a vast immigration are forces that will hurl aside those who in the delirium of conquest seek to destroy the character of our institutions.

We deny that the obligation of all citizens to support their government in times of grave national peril applies to the present situation. If an administration may with impunity ignore the issues upon which it was chosen, deliberately create a condition of war anywhere on the face of the globe, debauch the civil service for spoils to promote the adventure, organize a truth-suppressing censorship, and demand of all citizens a suspension of judgment and their unanimous support while it chooses to continue the fighting, representative government itself is imperiled.

We propose to contribute to the defeat of any person or party that stands for the forcible subjugation of any people. We shall oppose for re-election all who in the white house or in congress betray American liberty in pursuit of un-American ends. We still hope that both of our great political parties will support and defend the declaration of independence in the closing campaign of the century.

We hold with Abraham Lincoln, that "no man is good enough to govern another man without that other's consent. When the white man governs himself, that is self-government, but when he governs himself and also governs another man, that is more than self-government—that is despotism." "Our reliance is in the love of liberty which God has planted in us. Our defense is in the spirit which prizes liberty as the heritage of all men in all lands. Those who deny freedom to others deserve it not for themselves, and under a just God cannot long retain it."

We cordially invite the co-operation of all men and women who remain loyal to the declaration of independence and the constitution of the United States.

WILLIAM GRAHAM SUMNER

The Conquest of the United States by Spain (1899)

A jingoist press and a series of stunning American victories in the naval battle of Manila Bay and in the battle of San Juan Hill whipped up wide public support for American expansionism during the Spanish-American War. However, many anti-imperialists denounced American policy during the war as undermining the republican values of self-government and liberty that the nation was supposed to represent. In a passionate address that was later reprinted in the Yale Law Journal, *the Social Darwinist thinker William Graham Sumner warned that American imperialism imperiled the principles of liberty and equality on which the nation was founded.*

During the last year the public has been familiarized with descriptions of Spain and of Spanish methods of doing things until the name of Spain has become a symbol for a certain well-defined set of notions and policies. On the other hand, the name of the United States has always been, for all of us, a symbol for a state of things, a set of ideas and traditions, a group of views about social and political affairs. Spain was the first, for a long time the greatest, of the modern imperialistic states. The United States, by its historical origin, its traditions, and its principles, is the chief representative of the revolt and reaction against that kind of a state. I intend to show that, by the line of action now proposed to us, which we call expansion and imperialism, we are throwing away some of the most important elements of the American symbol and are adopting some of the most important elements of the Spanish symbol. We have beaten Spain in a military conflict, but we are submitting to be conquered by her on the field of ideas and policies. Expansionism and imperialism are nothing but the old philosophies of national prosperity which have brought Spain to where she now is. Those philosophies appeal to national vanity and national cupidity. They are seductive, especially upon the first view and the most superficial judgment, and therefore it cannot be denied that they are very strong for popular effect. They are delusions, and they will lead us to ruin unless we are hardheaded enough to resist them. * * *

* * * We boast that we are a self-governing people, and in this respect, particularly, we compare ourselves with pride with older nations. What is the difference after all? The Russians, whom we always think of as standing at the opposite pole of political institutions, have self-government, if you mean by it acquiescence in what a little group of people at the head of the government agree to do. The war with Spain was precipitated upon us headlong, without reflection or deliberation, and without any due formulation of public opinion. Whenever a voice was raised in behalf of deliberation and the recognized maxims of statesmanship, it was howled down in a storm of vituperation and cant. Everything was done to make us throw away sobriety of thought and calmness of judgment and to inflate all expressions with sensational epithets and turgid phrases. It cannot be denied that everything in regard to the war has been treated in an exalted strain of sentiment and rhetoric very unfavorable to the truth. At present the whole periodical press of the country seems to be occupied in tickling the national vanity to the utmost by representations about the war which are extravagant and fantastic. There will be a penalty to be

paid for all this. Nervous and sensational newspapers are just as corrupting, especially to young people, as nervous and sensational novels. The habit of expecting that all mental pabulum shall be highly spiced, and the corresponding loathing for whatever is soberly truthful, undermines character as much as any other vice. Patriotism is being prostituted into a nervous intoxication which is fatal to an apprehension of truth. It builds around us a fool's paradise, and it will lead us into errors about our position and relations just like those which we have been ridiculing in the case of Spain.

* * * Yet within a year it has become almost a doctrine with us that patriotism requires that we should hold our tongues while our interests, our institutions, our most sacred traditions, and our best established maxims have been trampled underfoot. There is no doubt that moral courage is the virtue which is more needed than any other in the modern democratic state, and that truckling to popularity is the worst political vice. The press, the platform, and the pulpit have all fallen under this vice, and there is evidence that the university also, which ought to be the last citadel of truth, is succumbing to it likewise. I have no doubt that the conservative classes of this country will yet look back with great regret to their acquiescence in the events of 1898 and the doctrines and precedents which have been silently established. Let us be well assured that self-government is not a matter of flags and Fourth of July orations, nor yet of strife to get offices. Eternal vigilance is the price of that as of every other political good. The perpetuity of self-government depends on the sound political sense of the people, and sound political sense is a matter of habit and practice. We can give it up and we can take instead pomp and glory. * * * If we Americans believe in self-government, why do we let it slip away from us? Why do we barter it away for military glory as Spain did?

There is not a civilized nation which does not talk about its civilizing mission just as grandly as we do. * * *

* * * We assume that what we like and practice, and what we think better, must come as a welcome blessing to Spanish-Americans and Filipinos. This is grossly and obviously untrue. They hate our ways. They are hostile to our ideas. Our religion, language, institutions, and manners offend them. They like their own ways, and if we appear amongst them as rulers, there will be social discord in all the great departments of social interest. The most important thing which we shall inherit from the Spaniards will be the task of suppressing rebellions. If the United States takes out of the hands of Spain her mission, on the ground that Spain is not executing it well, and if this nation in its turn attempts to be schoolmistress to others, it will shrivel up into the same vanity and self-conceit of which Spain now presents an example. To read our current literature

one would think that we were already well on the way to it. Now, the great reason why all these enterprises which begin by saying to somebody else, We know what is good for you better than you know yourself and we are going to make you do it, are false and wrong is that they violate liberty; or, to turn the same statement into other words, the reason why liberty, of which we Americans talk so much, is a good thing is that it means leaving people to live out their own lives in their own way, while we do the same. If we believe in liberty, as an American principle, why do we not stand by it? Why are we going to throw it away to enter upon a Spanish policy of dominion and regulation?

The Americans have been committed from the outset to the doctrine that all men are equal. We have elevated it into an absolute doctrine as a part of the theory of our social and political fabric. It has always been a domestic dogma in spite of its absolute form, and as a domestic dogma it has always stood in glaring contradiction to the facts about Indians and negroes and to our legislation about Chinamen. In its absolute form it must, of course, apply to Kanakas, Malays, Tagals, and Chinese just as much as to Yankees, Germans, and Irish. It is an astonishing event that we have lived to see American arms carry this domestic dogma out where it must be tested in its application to uncivilized and half-civilized peoples. At the first touch of the test we throw the doctrine away and adopt the Spanish doctrine. We are told by all the imperialists that these people are not fit for liberty and self-government; that it is rebellion for them to resist our beneficence; that we must send fleets and armies to kill them if they do it; that we must devise a government for them and administer it ourselves; that we may buy them or sell them as we please, and dispose of their "trade" for our own advantage. What is that but the policy of Spain to her dependencies? What can we expect as a consequence of it? Nothing but that it will bring us where Spain is now. * * *

Now what will hasten the day when our present advantages will wear out and when we shall come down to the conditions of the older and densely populated nations? The answer is: war, debt, taxation, diplomacy, a grand governmental system, pomp, glory, a big army and navy, lavish expenditures, political jobbery—in a word, imperialism.

In the old days the democratic masses of this country, who knew little about our modern doctrines of social philosophy, had a sound instinct on these matters, and it is no small ground of political disquietude to see it decline. They resisted every appeal to their vanity in the way of pomp and glory which they knew must be paid for. They dreaded a public debt and a standing army. They were narrow-minded and went too far with these notions, but they were, at least, right, if they wanted to strengthen democracy.

The great foe of democracy now and in the near future is plutocracy. Every year that passes brings out this antagonism more distinctly. It is to be the social war of the twentieth century. In that war militarism, expansion and imperialism will all favor plutocracy. In the first place, war and expansion will favor jobbery, both in the dependencies and at home. In the second place, they will take away the attention of the people from what the plutocrats are doing. In the third place, they will cause large expenditures of the people's money, the return for which will not go into the treasury, but into the hands of a few schemers. In the fourth place, they will call for a large public debt and taxes, and these things especially tend to make men unequal, because any social burdens bear more heavily on the weak than on the strong, and so make the weak weaker and the strong stronger. Therefore expansion and imperialism are a grand onslaught on democracy.

The point which I have tried to make in this lecture is that expansion and imperialism are at war with the best traditions, principles, and interests of the American people, and that they will plunge us into a network of difficult problems and political perils, which we might have avoided, while they offer us no corresponding advantage in return. * * *

* * * Our fathers would have an economical government, even if grand people called it a parsimonious one, and taxes should be no greater than were absolutely necessary to pay for such a government. The citizen was to keep all the rest of his earnings and use them as he thought best for the happiness of himself and his family; he was, above all, to be insured peace and quiet while he pursued his honest industry and obeyed the laws. No adventurous policies of conquest or ambition, such as, in the belief of our fathers, kings and nobles had forced, for their own advantage, on European states, would ever be undertaken by a free democratic republic. Therefore the citizen here would never be forced to leave his family or to give his sons to shed blood for glory and to leave widows and orphans in misery for nothing. Justice and law were to reign in the midst of simplicity, and a government which had little to do was to offer little field for ambition. In a society where industry, frugality, and prudence were honored, it was believed that the vices of wealth would never flourish.

We know that these beliefs, hopes, and intentions have been only partially fulfilled. We know that, as time has gone on and we have grown numerous and rich, some of these things have proved impossible ideals, incompatible with a large and flourishing society, but it is by virtue of this conception of a commonwealth that the United States has stood for something unique and grand in the history of mankind and that its people have been happy. It is by virtue of these ideals that we have been "isolated,"

isolated in a position which the other nations of the earth have observed in silent envy; and yet there are people who are boasting of their patriotism, because they say that we have taken our place now amongst the nations of the earth by virtue of this war.

My patriotism is of the kind which is outraged by the notion that the United States never was a great nation until in a petty three months' campaign it knocked to pieces a poor, decrepit, bankrupt old state like Spain. To hold such an opinion as that is to abandon all American standards, to put shame and scorn on all that our ancestors tried to build up here, and to go over to the standards of which Spain is a representative.

Thirteenth, Fourteenth, and Fifteenth Amendments (1865, 1868, 1870)

The Reconstruction amendments were sponsored by radical Republicans in Congress in an effort to guarantee national citizenship and the protection of fundamental rights to the newly freed slaves. Because Abraham Lincoln's Emancipation Proclamation of January 1, 1863, applied only to states in rebellion against the United States, slavery did not officially come to an end until the passage of the Thirteenth Amendment. The Fourteenth and Fifteenth Amendments were enacted in an effort to fulfill the promise of full citizenship to freedmen. Although the Supreme Court, well into the twentieth century, interpreted the Fourteenth Amendment very narrowly to promote economic liberty and freedom of contract, the amendment's equal-protection clause has since become the Constitution's most important guarantee of racial and gender equality.

Amendment XIII (1865)

*S*ection 1. Neither slavery nor involuntary servitude, except as a punishment for crime whereof the party shall have been duly convicted, shall exist within the United States, or any place subject to their jurisdiction.

Section 2. Congress shall have power to enforce this article by appropriate legislation.

Amendment XIV (1868)

ection 1. All persons born or naturalized in the United States and subject to the jurisdiction thereof, are citizens of the United States and of the State wherein they reside. No State shall make or enforce any law which shall abridge the privileges or immunities of citizens of the United States; nor shall any State deprive any person of life, liberty, or property, without the due process of law; nor deny to any person within its jurisdiction the equal protection of the laws.

Section 2. Representatives shall be apportioned among the several States according to their respective numbers, counting the whole number of persons in each State, excluding Indians not taxed. But when the right to vote at any election for the choice of electors for President and Vice-President of the United States, Representatives in Congress, the Executive and Judicial Officers of a State, or the members of the Legislature thereof, is denied to any of the male inhabitants of such State, being twenty-one years of age, and citizens of the United States, or in any way abridged, except for participation in rebellion, or other crime, the basis of representation therein shall be reduced in the proportion which the number of such male citizens shall bear to the whole number of male citizens twenty-one years of age in such State.

Section 3. No person shall be a Senator or Representative in Congress, or elector of President and Vice-President, or hold any office, civil or military, under the United States, or under any State, who, having previously taken an oath, as a member of Congress, or as an officer of the United States, or as a member of any State legislature, or as an executive or judicial officer of any State, to support the Constitution of the United States, shall have engaged in insurrection or rebellion against the same, or given aid or comfort to the enemies thereof. But Congress may by a vote of two-thirds of each House, remove such disability.

Section 4. The validity of the public debt of the United States, authorized by law, including debts incurred for payment of pensions and bounties for services in suppressing insurrection or rebellion, shall not be questioned. But neither the United States nor any State shall assume or pay any debt or obligation incurred in aid of insurrection or rebellion against the United States, or any claim for the loss or emancipation of any slave; but all such debts, obligations and claims shall be held illegal and void.

Section 5. The Congress shall have power to enforce, by appropriate legislation, the provisions of this article.

Amendment XV (1870)

Section 1. The right of citizens of the United States to vote shall not be denied or abridged by the United States or by any State on account of race, color, or previous condition of servitude.

Section 2. The Congress shall have power to enforce this article by appropriate legislation.

CHIEF JOSEPH

An Indian's View of Indian Affairs (1879)

Chief Joseph (1840?–1904), whose Indian name in English means Thunder Traveling over the Mountains, led the Nez Perce Indians during years of resistance to a policy of forced resettlement on confined reservations. After their capture in the Bear Paw Mountains, Chief Joseph signified the defeat of the Nez Perce with the pledge that he "would fight no more forever." In a moving account of his encounters with white policy makers and the U.S. Army published in the North American Review of April 1879, Chief Joseph captures the passing of his people's way of life.

My friends, I have been asked to show you my heart. I am glad to have a chance to do so. I want the white people to understand my people. Some of you think an Indian is like a wild animal. This is a great mistake. I will tell you all about our people, and then you can judge whether an Indian is a man or not. I believe much trouble and blood would be saved if we opened our hearts more. I will tell you in my way how the Indian sees things. The white man has more words to tell you how they look to him, but it does not require many words to speak the truth. What I have to say will come from my heart, and I will speak with a straight tongue. Ah-cum-kin-i-ma-me-hut (the Great Spirit) is looking at me, and will hear me.

My name is In-mut-too-yah-lat-lat (Thunder traveling over the Mountains). I am chief of the Wal-lam-wat-kin band of Chute-pa-lu, or Nez Percés (nose-pierced Indians). I was born in eastern Oregon, thirty-eight winters ago. My father was chief before me. When a young man, he was called Joseph by Mr. Spaulding, a missionary. He died a few years ago.

There was no stain on his hands of the blood of a white man. He left a good name on the earth. He advised me well for my people.

Our fathers gave us many laws, which they had learned from their fathers. These laws were good. They told us to treat all men as they treated us; that we should never be the first to break a bargain; that it was a disgrace to tell a lie; that we should speak only the truth; that it was a shame for one man to take from another his wife, or his property without paying for it. We were taught to believe that the Great Spirit sees and hears everything, and that he never forgets; that hereafter he will give every man a spirit-home according to his deserts: if he has been a good man, he will have a good home; if he has been a bad man, he will have a bad home. This I believe, and all my people believe the same.

We did not know there were other people besides the Indian until about one hundred winters ago, when some men with white faces came to our country. They brought many things with them to trade for furs and skins. They brought *tobacco,* which was new to us. They brought guns with flint stones on them, which frightened our women and children. Our people could not talk with these white-faced men, but they used signs which all people understand. These men were Frenchmen, and they called our people "Nez Percés," because they wore rings in their noses for ornaments. Although very few of our people wear them now, we are still called by the same name. These French trappers said a great many things to our fathers, which have been planted in our hearts. Some were good for us, but some were bad. Our people were divided in opinion about these men. Some thought they taught more bad than good. An Indian respects a brave man, but he despises a coward. He loves a straight tongue, but he hates a forked tongue. The French trappers told us some truths and some lies.

The first white men of your people who came to our country were named Lewis and Clarke. They also brought many things that our people had never seen. They talked straight, and our people gave them a great feast, as a proof that their hearts were friendly. These men were very kind. They made presents to our chiefs and our people made presents to them. We had a great many horses, of which we gave them what they needed, and they gave us guns and tobacco in return. All the Nez Percés made friends with Lewis and Clarke, and agreed to let them pass through their country, and never to make war on white men. This promise the Nez Percés have never broken. No white man can accuse them of bad faith, and speak with a straight tongue. It has always been the pride of the Nez Percés that they were the friends of the white men. When my father was a young man there came to our country a white man (Rev. Mr. Spaulding) who talked spirit law. He won the affections of our people because he spoke good things to them. At first he did not say anything about white men wanting to settle on our lands. Nothing was said about that until about twenty winters ago, when a number of white people came into our country and built houses and made farms. At first our people made no complaint. They thought there was room enough for all to live in peace, and they were learning many things from the white men that seemed to be good. But we soon found that the white men were growing rich very fast, and were greedy to possess everything the Indian had. My father was the first to see through the schemes of the white men, and he warned his tribe to be careful about trading with them. He had suspicion of men who seemed so anxious to make money. I was a boy then, but I remember well my father's caution. He had sharper eyes than the rest of our people.

Next there came a white officer (Governor Stevens), who invited all the Nez Percés to a treaty council. After the council was opened he made known his heart. He said there were a great many white people in the country, and many more would come; that he wanted the land marked out so that the Indians and white men could be separated. If they were to live in peace it was necessary, he said, that the Indians should have a country set apart for them, and in that country they must stay. My father, who represented his band, refused to have anything to do with the council, because he wished to be a free man. He claimed that no man owned any part of the earth, and a man could not sell what he did not own.

Mr. Spaulding took hold of my father's arm and said, "Come and sign the treaty." My father pushed him away, and said: "Why do you ask me to sign away my country? It is your business to talk to us about spirit matters, and not to talk to us about parting with our land." Governor Stevens urged my father to sign his treaty, but he refused. "I will not sign your paper," he said; "you go where you please, so do I; you are not a child, I am no child; I can think for myself. No man can think for me. I have no other home than this. I will not give it up to any man. My people would have no home. Take away your paper. I will not touch it with my hand."

My father left the council. Some of the chiefs of the other bands of the Nez Percés signed the treaty, and then Governor Stevens gave them presents of blankets. My father cautioned his people to take no presents, for "after a while," he said, "they will claim that you have accepted pay for your country." Since that time four bands of the Nez Percés have received annuities from the United States. My father was invited to many councils, and they tried hard to make him sign the treaty, but he was firm as the rock, and would not sign away his home. His refusal caused a difference among the Nez Percés.

Eight years later (1863) was the next treaty council. A chief called Lawyer, because he was a great talker, took the lead in this council, and sold nearly all the Nez Percés country. My father was not there. He said to me: "When you go into council with the white man, always remember your country. Do not give it away. The white man will cheat you out of your home. I have taken no pay from the United States. I have never sold our land." In this treaty Lawyer acted without authority from our band. He had no right to sell the Wallowa (*winding water*) country. That had always belonged to my father's own people, and the other bands had never disputed our right to it. No other Indians ever claimed Wallowa.

In order to have all people understand how much land we owned, my father planted poles around it and said:

"Inside is the home of my people—the white man may take the land outside. Inside this boundary all our people were born. It circles around the graves of our fathers, and we will never give up these graves to any man."

The United States claimed they had bought all the Nez Percés country outside of Lapwai Reservation, from Lawyer and other chiefs, but we continued to live on this land in peace until eight years ago, when white men began to come inside the bounds my father had set. We warned them against this great wrong, but they would not leave our land, and some bad blood was raised. The white men represented that we were going upon the war-path. They reported many things that were false.

The United States Government again asked for a treaty council. My father had become blind and feeble. He could no longer speak for his people. It was then that I took my father's place as chief. In this council I made my first speech to white men. I said to the agent who held the council:

"I did not want to come to this council, but I came hoping that we could save blood. The white man has no right to come here and take our country. We have never accepted any presents from the Government. Neither Lawyer nor any other chief had authority to sell this land. It has always belonged to my people. It came unclouded to them from our fathers, and we will defend this land as long as a drop of Indian blood warms the hearts of our men."

The agent said he had orders, from the Great White Chief at Washington, for us to go upon the Lapwai Reservation, and that if we obeyed he would help us in many ways. "You *must* move to the agency," he said. I answered him: "I will not. I do not need your help; we have plenty, and we are contented and happy if the white man will let us alone. The reservation is too small for so many people with all their stock. You can keep your presents; we can go to your towns and pay for all we need; we have plenty of horses and cattle to sell, and we won't have any help from you; we are free now; we can go where we please. Our fathers were born here.

Here they lived, here they died, here are their graves. We will never leave them." The agent went away, and we had peace for a little while.

Soon after this my father sent for me. I saw he was dying. I took his hand in mine. He said: "My son, my body is returning to my mother earth, and my spirit is going very soon to see the Great Spirit Chief. When I am gone, think of your country. You are the chief of these people. They look to you to guide them. Always remember that your father never sold his country. You must stop your ears whenever you are asked to sign a treaty selling your home. A few years more, and white men will be all around you. They have their eyes on this land. My son, never forget my dying words. This country holds your father's body. Never sell the bones of your father and your mother." I pressed my father's hand and told him I would protect his grave with my life. My father smiled and passed away to the spirit-land.

I buried him in that beautiful valley of winding waters. I love that land more than all the rest of the world. A man who would not love his father's grave is worse than a wild animal.

For a short time we lived quietly. But this could not last. * * *

Year after year we have been threatened, but no war was made upon my people until General Howard came to our country two years ago and told us that he was the white war-chief of all that country. He said: "I have a great many soldiers at my back. I am going to bring them up here, and then I will talk to you again. I will not let white men laugh at me the next time I come. The country belongs to the Government, and I intend to make you go upon the reservation." * * *

Then one of my chiefs—Too-hool-hool-suit—rose in the council and said to General Howard: "The Great Spirit Chief made the world as it is, and as he wanted it, and he made a part of it for us to live upon. I do not see where you get authority to say that we shall not live where he placed us."

General Howard lost his temper and said: "Shut up! I don't want to hear any more of such talk. The law says you shall go upon the reservation to live, and I want you to do so, but you persist in disobeying the law" (meaning the treaty). "If you do not move, I will take the matter into my own hand, and make you suffer for your disobedience."

Too-hool-hool-suit answered: "Who are you, that you ask us to talk, and then tell me I sha'n't talk? Are you the Great Spirit? Did you make the world? Did you make the sun? Did you make the rivers to run for us to drink? Did you make the grass to grow? Did you make all these things, that you talk to us as though we were boys? If you did, then you have the right to talk as you do." * * *

The council broke up for that day. On the next morning General Howard came to my lodge, and invited me to go with him and White-Bird and Looking-Glass, to look for land for my people. As we rode along we came to some good land that was already occupied by Indians and white people. General Howard, pointing to this land, said: "If you will come on to the reservation, I will give you these lands and move these people off."

I replied: "No. It would be wrong to disturb these people. I have no right to take their homes. I have never taken what did not belong to me. I will not now."

We rode all day upon the reservation, and found no good land unoccupied. I have been informed by men who do not lie that General Howard sent a letter that night, telling the soldiers at Walla Walla to go to Wallowa Valley, and drive us out upon our return home.

In the council, next day, General Howard informed me, in a haughty spirit, that he would give my people *thirty days* to go back home, collect all their stock, and move on to the reservation, saying, "If you are not here in that time, I shall consider that you want to fight, and will send my soldiers to drive you on."

* * *

Again I counseled peace, and I thought the danger was past. We had not complied with General Howard's order because we could not, but we intended to do so as soon as possible. I was leaving the council to kill beef for my family, when news came that [a] young man whose father had been killed had gone out with several other hot-blooded young braves and killed four white men. He rode up to the council and shouted: "Why do you sit here like women? The war has begun already." I was deeply grieved. All the lodges were moved except my brother's and my own. I saw clearly that the war was upon us when I learned that my young men had been secretly buying ammunition. I heard then that Too-hool-hool-suit, who had been imprisoned by General Howard, had succeeded in organizing a war-party. I knew that their acts would involve all my people. I saw that the war could not then be prevented. The time had passed. I counseled peace from the beginning. I knew that we were too weak to fight the United States. We had many grievances, but I knew that war would bring more. We had good white friends, who advised us against taking the warpath. My friend and brother, Mr. Chapman, who has been with us since the surrender, told us just how the war would end. Mr. Chapman took sides against us, and helped General Howard. I do not blame him for doing so. He tried hard to prevent bloodshed. We hoped the white settlers would not join the soldiers. Before the war commenced we had discussed this matter all over, and many of my people were in favor of warning them that if they took no part against us they should not be molested in the event of war being begun by General Howard. This plan was voted down in the war-council.

There were bad men among my people who had quarreled with white men, and they talked of their wrongs until they roused all the bad hearts in the council. Still I could not believe that they would begin the war. I know that my young men did a great wrong, but I ask, Who was first to blame? They had been insulted a thousand times; their fathers and brothers had been killed; their mothers and wives had been disgraced; they had been driven to madness by whisky sold to them by white men; they had been told by General Howard that all their horses and cattle which they had been unable to drive out of Wallowa were to fall into the hands of white men; and, added to all this, they were homeless and desperate.

I would have given my own life if I could have undone the killing of white men by my people. I blame my young men and I blame the white men. I blame General Howard for not giving my people time to get their stock away from Wallowa. I do not acknowledge that he had the right to order me to leave Wallowa at any time. I deny that either my father or myself ever sold that land. It is still our land. It may never again be our home, but my father sleeps there, and I love it as I love my mother. I left there, hoping to avoid bloodshed.

If General Howard had given me plenty of time to gather up my stock, and treated Too-hool-hool-suit as a man should be treated, there *would have been no war.*

My friends among white men have blamed me for the war. I am not to blame. When my young men began the killing, my heart was hurt. Although I did not justify them, I remembered all the insults I had endured, and my blood was on fire. Still I would have taken my people to the buffalo country without fighting, if possible.

I could see no other way to avoid a war. We moved over to White Bird Creek, sixteen miles away, and there encamped, intending to collect our stock before leaving; but the soldiers attacked us, and the first battle was fought. We numbered in that battle sixty men, and the soldiers a hundred. The fight lasted but a few minutes, when the soldiers retreated before us for twelve miles. They lost thirty-three killed, and had seven wounded. When an Indian fights, he only shoots to kill; but soldiers shoot at random. None of the soldiers were scalped. We do not believe in scalping, nor in killing wounded men. Soldiers do not kill many Indians unless they are wounded and left upon the battle-field. Then they kill Indians.

Seven days after the first battle, General Howard arrived in the Nez Percés country, bringing seven hundred more soldiers. It was now war in earnest. We crossed over Salmon River, hoping General Howard would follow. We were not disappointed. He did follow us, and we got back between him and his supplies, and cut him off for three days. He sent out two companies to open the way. We attacked them, killing one officer, two guides, and ten men.

We withdrew, hoping the soldiers would follow, but they had got fighting enough for that day. They intrenched themselves, and next day we attacked them again. The battle lasted all day, and was renewed next morning. We killed four and wounded seven or eight.

About this time General Howard found out that we were in his rear. Five days later he attacked us with three hundred and fifty soldiers and settlers. We had two hundred and fifty warriors. The fight lasted twenty-seven hours. We lost four killed and several wounded. General Howard's loss was twenty-nine men killed and sixty wounded.

The following day the soldiers charged upon us, and we retreated with our families and stock a few miles, leaving eighty lodges to fall into General Howard's hands.

Finding that we were outnumbered, we retreated to Bitter Root Valley. Here another body of soldiers came upon us and demanded our surrender. We refused. They said, "You can not get by us." We answered, "We are going by you without fighting if you will let us, but we are going by you anyhow." We then made a treaty with these soldiers. We agreed not to molest any one, and they agreed that we might pass through the Bitter Root country in peace. We bought provisions and traded stock with white men there.

We understood that there was to be no more war. We intended to go peaceably to the buffalo country, and leave the question of returning to our country to be settled afterward.

With this understanding we traveled on for four days, and, thinking that the trouble was all over, we stopped and prepared tent-poles to take with us. We started again, and at the end of two days we saw three white men passing our camp. Thinking that peace had been made, we did not molest them. We could have killed or taken them prisoners, but we did not suspect them of being spies, which they were.

That night the soldiers surrounded our camp. About daybreak one of my men went out to look after his horses. The soldiers saw him and shot him down like a coyote. I have since learned that these soldiers were not those we had left behind. They had come upon us from another direction. The new white war-chief's name was Gibbon. He charged upon us while some of my people were still asleep. We had a hard fight. Some of my men crept around and attacked the soldiers from the rear. In this battle we lost nearly all our lodges, but we finally drove General Gibbon back.

Finding that he was not able to capture us, he sent to his camp a few miles away for his big guns (cannons), but my men had captured them and all the ammunition. We damaged the big guns all we could, and carried away the powder and lead. In the fight with General Gibbon we lost fifty women and children and thirty fighting men. We remained long enough to bury our dead. The Nez Percés never make war on women and children; we could have killed a great many women and children while the war lasted, but we would feel ashamed to do so cowardly an act.

We never scalp our enemies, but when General Howard came up and joined General Gibbon, their Indian scouts dug up our dead and scalped them. I have been told that General Howard did not order this great shame to be done.

We retreated as rapidly as we could toward the buffalo country. After six days General Howard came close to us, and we went out and attacked him, and captured nearly all his horses and mules (about two hundred and fifty head). We then marched on to the Yellowstone Basin.

On the way we captured one white man and two white women. We released them at the end of three days. They were treated kindly. The women were not insulted. Can the white soldiers tell me of one time when Indian women were taken prisoners, and held three days and then released without being insulted? Were the Nez Percés women who fell into the hands of General Howard's soldiers treated with as much respect? I deny that a Nez Percé was ever guilty of such a crime.

A few days later we captured two more white men. One of them stole a horse and escaped. We gave the other a poor horse and told him he was free.

Nine days' march brought us to the mouth of Clarke's Fork of the Yellowstone. We did not know what had become of General Howard, but we supposed that he had sent for more horses and mules. He did not come up, but another new war-chief (General Sturgis) attacked us. We held him in check while we moved all our women and children and stock out of danger, leaving a few men to cover our retreat.

Several days passed, and we heard nothing of General Howard, or Gibbon, or Sturgis. We had repulsed each in turn, and began to feel secure, when another army, under General Miles, struck us. This was the fourth army, each of which outnumbered our fighting force, that we had encountered within sixty days.

We had no knowledge of General Miles's army until a short time before he made a charge upon us, cutting our camp in two, and capturing nearly all of our horses. About seventy men, myself among them, were cut off. My little daughter, twelve years of age, was with me. I gave her a rope, and told her to catch a horse and join the others who were cut off from the camp. I have not seen her since, but I have learned that she is alive and well.

I thought of my wife and children, who were now surrounded by soldiers, and I resolved to go to them or die. With a prayer in my mouth to the Great Spirit Chief who rules above, I dashed unarmed through the line of soldiers. It seemed to me that there were guns on every side, before and behind me. My clothes were cut to pieces and my horse was wounded, but I was not hurt. As I reached the door of my lodge, my wife handed me my rifle, saying: "Here's your gun. Fight!"

The soldiers kept up a continuous fire. Six of my men were killed in one spot near me. Ten or twelve soldiers charged into our camp and got possession of two lodges, killing three Nez Percés and losing three of their men, who fell inside our lines. I called my men to drive them back. We fought at close range, not more than twenty steps apart, and drove the soldiers back upon their main line, leaving their dead in our hands. We secured their arms and ammunition. We lost, the first day and night, eighteen men and three women. General Miles lost twenty-six killed and forty wounded. The following day General Miles sent a messenger into my camp under protection of a white flag. I sent my friend Yellow Bull to meet him.

Yellow Bull understood the messenger to say that General Miles wished me to consider the situation; that he did not want to kill my people unnecessarily. Yellow Bull understood this to be a demand for me to surrender and save blood. Upon reporting this message to me, Yellow Bull said he wondered whether General Miles was in earnest. I sent him back with my answer, that I had not made up my mind, but would think about it and send word soon. A little later he sent some Cheyenne scouts with another message. I went out to meet them. They said they believed that General Miles was sincere and really wanted peace. I walked on to General Miles's tent. He met me and we shook hands. He said, "Come, let us sit down by the fire and talk this matter over." I remained with him all night; next morning Yellow Bull came over to see if I was alive, and why I did not return.

General Miles would not let me leave the tent to see my friend alone.

Yellow Bull said to me: "They have got you in their power, and I am afraid they will never let you go again. I have an officer in our camp, and I will hold him until they let you go free."

I said: "I do not know what they mean to do with me, but if they kill me you must not kill the officer. It will do no good to avenge my death by killing him."

Yellow Bull returned to my camp. I did not make any agreement that day with General Miles. The battle was renewed while I was with him. I was very anxious about my people. I knew that we were near Sitting Bull's camp in King George's land, and I thought maybe the Nez Percés who had escaped would return with assistance. No great damage was done to either party during the night.

On the following morning I returned to my camp by agreement, meeting the officer who had been held a prisoner in my camp at the flag of truce. My people were divided about surrendering. We could have escaped from Bear Paw Mountain if we had left our wounded, old women, and children behind. We were unwilling to do this. We had never heard of a wounded Indian recovering while in the hands of white men.

On the evening of the fourth day General Howard came in with a small escort, together with my friend Chapman. We could not talk understandingly. General Miles said to me in plain voice, "If you will come out and give up your arms, I will spare your living and send you to your reservation." I do not know what passed between General Miles and General Howard.

I could not bear to see my wounded men and women suffer any longer; we had lost enough already. General Miles had proposed that we might return to our own country with what stock we had left. I thought we could start again. I believed General Miles, or *I never would have surrendered.* I have heard that he has been censured for making the promise to return us to Lapwai. He could not have made any other terms with me at that time. I would have held him in check until my friends came to my assistance, and then neither of the generals nor their soldiers would have ever left Bear Paw Mountain alive.

On the fifth day I went to General Miles and gave up my gun, and said, "From where the sun now stands I will fight no more." My people needed rest—we wanted peace.

I was told we could go with General Miles to Tongue River and stay there until spring, when we would be sent back to our country. Finally it was decided that we were to be taken to Tongue River. We had nothing to say about it. After our arrival at Tongue River, General Miles received orders to take us to Bismarck. The reason given was, that subsistence would be cheaper there. * * *

During the hot days (July, 1878) we received notice that we were to be moved farther away from our own country. We were not asked if we were willing to go. We were ordered to get into the railroad-cars. Three of my people died on the way to Baxter Springs. It was worse to die there than to die fighting in the mountains.

We were moved from Baxter Springs (Kansas) to the Indian Territory, and set down without our lodges. We had but little medicine, and we were nearly all sick. Seventy of my people have died since we moved there. * * *

Then the Inspector Chief (General McNiel) came to my camp and we had a long talk. He said I ought to have a home in the mountain country north, and that he would write a letter to the Great Chief at Washington.

Again the hope of seeing the mountains of Idaho and Oregon grew up in my heart.

At last I was granted permission to come to Washington and bring my friend Yellow Bull and our interpreter with me. I am glad we came. I have shaken hands with a great many friends, but there are some things I want to know which no one seems able to explain. I can not understand how the Government sends a man out to fight us, as it did General Miles, and then breaks his word. Such a Government has something wrong about it. I can not understand why so many chiefs are allowed to talk so many different ways, and promise so many different things. I have seen the Great Father Chief (the President), the next Great Chief (Secretary of the Interior), the Commissioner Chief (Hayt), the Law Chief (General Butler), and many other law chiefs (Congressmen), and they all say they are my friends, and that I shall have justice, but while their mouths all talk right I do not understand why nothing is done for my people. I have heard talk and talk, but nothing is done. Good words do not last long unless they amount to something. Words do not pay for my dead people. They do not pay for my country, now overrun by white men. They do not protect my father's grave. They do not pay for all my horses and cattle. Good words will not give me back my children. Good words will not make good the promise of your War Chief General Miles. Good words will not give my people good health and stop them from dying. Good words will not get my people a home where they can live in peace and take care of themselves. I am tired of talk that comes to nothing. It makes my heart sick when I remember all the good words and all the broken promises. There has been too much talking by men who had no right to talk. Too many misrepresentations have been made, too many misunderstandings have come up between the white men about the Indians. If the white man wants to live in peace with the Indian he can live in peace. There need be no trouble. Treat all men alike. Give them all the same law. Give them all an even chance to live and grow. All men were made by the same Great Spirit Chief. They are all brothers. The earth is the mother of all people, and all people should have equal rights upon it. You might as well expect the rivers to run backward as that any man who was born a free man should be contented when penned up and denied liberty to go where he pleases. If you tie a horse to a stake, do you expect he will grow fat? If you pen an Indian up on a small spot of earth, and compel him to stay there, he will not be contented, nor will he grow and prosper. I have asked some of the great white chiefs where they get their authority to say to the Indian that he shall stay in one place, while he sees white men going where they please. They can not tell me.

I only ask of the Government to be treated as all other men are treated. If I can not go to my own home, let me have a home in some country where my people will not die so fast. I would like to go to Bitter Root Valley. There my people would be healthy; where they are now they are dying. Three have died since I left my camp to come to Washington.

When I think of our condition my heart is heavy. I see men of my race treated as outlaws and driven from country to country, or shot down like animals.

I know that my race must change. We can not hold our own with the white men as we are. We only ask an even chance to live as other men live. We ask to be recognized as men. We ask that the same law shall work alike on all men. If the Indian breaks the law, punish him by the law. If the white man breaks the law, punish him also.

Let me be a free man—free to travel, free to stop, free to work, free to trade where I choose, free to choose my own teachers, free to follow the religion of my fathers, free to think and talk and act for myself—and I will obey every law, or submit to the penalty.

Whenever the white man treats the Indian as they treat each other, then we will have no more wars. We shall all be alike—brothers of one father and one mother, with one sky above us and one country around us, and one government for all. Then the Great Spirit Chief who rules above will smile upon this land, and send rain to wash out the bloody spots made by brothers' hands from the face of the earth. For this time the Indian race are waiting and praying. I hope that no more groans of wounded men and women will ever go to the ear of the Great Spirit Chief above, and that all people may be one people.

In-mut-too-yah-lat-lat has spoken for his people.

CHIEF JOSEPH, CRAZY HORSE, AND SMOHALLA

On Work and Property

Native American values and belief systems were often at odds with the liberal ideals of property and work held by settlers and policy makers in Washington. The more communal, less individualistic tribal perspective is evoked in these excerpts from undated speeches by three fabled nineteenth-century native leaders: Chief Joseph (1840?–1904);

the legendary Sioux warrior Crazy Horse (1849–1877); and the Wana-
pum medicine man Smohalla (1815–1907).

Chief Joseph

The earth was created by the assistance of the sun, and it should be left
as it was. * * * The country was made without lines of demarcation,
and it is no man's business to divide it. * * * I see the whites all over the
country gaining wealth, and see their desire to give us lands which are
worthless. * * * The earth and myself are of one mind. * * * I never said
the land was mine to do with it as I chose. The one who has the right to dispose of it is the one who has created it.

Crazy Horse

We did not ask you white men to come here. The Great Spirit gave
us this country as a home. You had yours. We did not interfere
with you. The Great Spirit gave us plenty of land to live on, and buffalo,
deer, antelope and other game. But you have come here; you are taking
my land from me; you are killing off our game, so it is hard for us to live.
Now, you tell us to work for a living, but the Great Spirit did not make us
to work, but to live by hunting. You white men can work if you want to.
We do not interfere with you, and again you say, why do you not become
civilized? We do not want your civilization! We would live as our fathers
did, and their fathers before them.

Smohalla

My young men shall never work. Men who work cannot dream; and
wisdom comes to us in dreams.

You ask me to plow the ground. Shall I take a knife and tear my
mother's breast? Then when I die she will not take me to her bosom to
rest.

You ask me to dig for stone. Shall I dig under her skin for her bones?
Then when I die I cannot enter her body and be born again.

You ask me to cut grass and make hay and sell it and be rich like white
men. But how dare I cut off my mother's hair?

HENRY BROWN AND
JOHN MARSHALL HARLAN

Plessy v. Ferguson (1896)

In Plessy v. Ferguson, the Supreme Court upheld as constitutional the segregation statutes ("Jim Crow" legislation) that all southern states had in place by the 1890s. Justice Henry Brown's (1836–1913) finding for the Court that "separate but equal" accommodations did not violate the Fourteenth Amendment would provide the legal sources for segregation until 1954, when the Court overturned Plessy. Justice John Marshall Harlan's vigorous dissent anticipated the argument the Court would itself invoke fifty-eight years later.

This case turns upon the constitutionality of an act of the general assembly of the state of Louisiana, passed in 1890, providing for separate railway carriages for the white and colored races. Acts 1890, No. 111, p. 152.

The first section of the statute enacts "that all railway companies carrying passengers in their coaches in this state, shall provide equal but separate accommodations for the white, and colored races, by providing two or more passenger coaches for each passenger train, or by dividing the passenger coaches by a partition so as to secure separate accommodations: provided, that this section shall not be construed to apply to street railroads. No person or persons shall be permitted to occupy seats in coaches, other than the ones assigned to them, on account of the race they belong to."

By the second section it was enacted "that, the officers of such passenger trains shall have power and are hereby required to assign each passenger to the coach or compartment used for the race to which such passenger belongs; any passenger insisting on going into a coach or compartment to which by race he does not belong, shall be liable to a fine of twenty-five dollars, or in lieu thereof to imprisonment for a period of not more than twenty days in the parish prison, and any officer of any railroad insisting on assigning a passenger to a coach or compartment other than the one set aside for the race to which said passenger belongs, shall be liable to a fine of twenty-five dollars, or in lieu thereof to imprisonment for a period of not more than twenty days in the parish prison; and should any passenger refuse to occupy the coach or compartment to which he or she is assigned by the officer of such railway, said officer shall have power to refuse to carry such passenger on his train, and for such refusal neither he nor the railway company which he represents shall be liable for damages in any of the courts of this state."

The third section provides penalties for the refusal or neglect of the officers, directors, conductors, and employes of railway companies to comply with the act, with a proviso that "nothing in the act shall be construed as applying to nurses attending children of the other race." The fourth section is immaterial.

The information filed in the criminal district court charged, in substance, that Plessy, being a passenger between two stations within the state of Louisiana, was assigned by officers of the company to the coach used for the race to which he belonged, but he insisted upon going into a coach used by the race to which he did not belong. Neither in the information nor plea was his particular race or color averred.

The petition for the writ of prohibition averred that petitioner was seven-eighths Caucasian and one-eighth African blood; that the mixture of colored blood was not discernible in him; and that he was entitled to every right, privilege, and immunity secured to citizens of the United States of the white race; and that, upon such theory, he took possession of a vacant seat in a coach where passengers of the white race were accommodated, and was ordered by the conductor to vacate said coach, and take a seat in another, assigned to persons of the colored race, and, having refused to comply with such demand, he was forcibly ejected, with the aid of a police officer, and imprisoned in the parish jail to answer a charge of having violated the above act.

The constitutionality of this act is attacked upon the ground that it conflicts both with the thirteenth amendment of the constitution, abolishing slavery, and the fourteenth amendment, which prohibits certain restrictive legislation on the part of the states.

1. That it does not conflict with the thirteenth amendment, which abolished slavery and involuntary servitude, except as a punishment for crime, is too clear for argument. * * *

2. By the fourteenth amendment, all persons born or naturalized in the United States, and subject to the jurisdiction thereof, are made citizens of the United States and of the state wherein they reside; and the states are forbidden from making or enforcing any law which shall abridge the privileges or immunities of citizens of the United States, or shall deprive any person of life, liberty, or property without due process of law, or deny to any person within their jurisdiction the equal protection of the laws. * * *

The object of the amendment was undoubtedly to enforce the absolute equality of the two races before the law, but, in the nature of things, it could not have been intended to abolish distinctions based upon color, or to enforce social, as distinguished from political, equality, or a commingling of the two races upon terms unsatisfactory to either. Laws permitting, and even requiring, their separation, in places where they are liable to be brought into contact, do not necessarily imply the inferiority of either race to the other, and have been generally, if not universally, recognized as within the competency of the state legislatures in the exercise of their police power. The most common instance of this is connected with the establishment of separate schools for white and colored children, which have been held to be a valid exercise of the legislative power even by courts of states where the political rights of the colored race have been longest and most earnestly enforced. * * *

So far, then, as a conflict with the fourteenth amendment is concerned, the case reduces itself to the question whether the statute of Louisiana is a reasonable regulation, and with respect to this there must necessarily be a large discretion on the part of the legislature. In determining the question of reasonableness, it is at liberty to act with reference to the established usages, customs, and traditions of the people, and with a view to the promotion of their comfort, and the preservation of the public peace and good order. Gauged by this standard, we cannot say that a law which authorizes or even requires the separation of the two races in public conveyances is unreasonable, or more obnoxious to the fourteenth amendment than the acts of congress requiring separate schools for colored children in the District of Columbia, the constitutionality of which does not seem to have been questioned, or the corresponding acts of state legislatures.

We consider the underlying fallacy of the plaintiff's argument to consist in the assumption that the enforced separation of the two races stamps the colored race with a badge of inferiority. If this be so, it is not by reason of anything found in the act, but solely because the colored race chooses to put that construction upon it. The argument necessarily assumes that if, as has been more than once the case, and is not unlikely to be so again, the colored race should become the dominant power in the state legislature, and should enact a law in precisely similar terms, it would thereby relegate the white race to an inferior position. We imagine that the white race, at least, would not acquiesce in this assumption. The argument also assumes that social prejudices may be overcome by legislation, and that equal rights cannot be secured to the negro except by an enforced commingling of the two races. We cannot accept this proposition. If the two races are to meet upon terms of social equality, it must be the result of natural affinities, a mutual appreciation of each other's merits and a voluntary consent of individuals. * * * Legislation is powerless to eradicate racial instincts or to abolish distinctions based upon physical differences, and the attempt to do so can only result in accentuating the difficulties of the present situation. If the civil and political rights of both races be equal one cannot be inferior to the other civilly or politically. If one race be inferior to the other socially, the Constitution of the United States cannot put them upon the same plane.

MR. JUSTICE HARLAN DISSENTING

* * * In respect of civil rights, common to all citizens, the Constitution of the United States does not, I think, permit any public authority to know the race of those entitled to be protected in the enjoyment of such rights. Every true man has pride of race, and under appropriate circumstances when the rights of others, his equals before the law, are not to be affected, it is his privilege to express such pride and to take such action based upon it as to him seems proper. But I deny that any legislative body or judicial tribunal may have regard to the race of citizens when the civil rights of those citizens are involved. Indeed, such legislation, as that here in question, is inconsistent not only with that equality of rights which pertains to citizenship, National and State, but with the personal liberty enjoyed by every one within the United States. * * *

The white race deems itself to be the dominant race in this country. And so it is, in prestige, in achievements, in education, in wealth and in power. So, I doubt not, it will continue to be for all time, if it remains true to its great heritage and holds fast to the principles of constitutional liberty. But in view of the Constitution, in the eye of the law, there is in this country no superior, dominant, ruling class of citizens. There is no caste here. Our Constitution is color-blind, and neither knows nor tolerates classes among citizens. In respect of civil rights, all citizens are equal before the law. The humblest is the peer of the most powerful. The law regards man as man, and takes no account of his surroundings or of his color when his civil rights as guaranteed by the supreme law of the land are involved. It is, therefore, to be regretted that this high tribunal, the final expositor of the fundamental law of the land, has reached the conclusion that it is competent for a State to regulate the enjoyment by citizens of their civil rights solely upon the basis of race. * * *

The arbitrary separation of citizens, on the basis of race, while they are on a public highway, is a badge of servitude wholly inconsistent with the civil freedom and the equality before the law established by the Constitution. It cannot be justified upon any legal grounds.

If evils will result from the commingling of the two races upon public highways established for the benefit of all, they will be infinitely less than those that will surely come from state legislation regulating the enjoyment of civil rights upon the basis of race. We boast of the freedom enjoyed by our people above all other peoples. But it is difficult to reconcile that boast with a state of the law which, practically, puts the brand of servitude and degradation upon a large class of our fellow-citizens, our equals before the law. The thin disguise of "equal" accommodations for passengers in railroad coaches will not mislead any one, nor atone for the wrong this day done.

BOOKER T. WASHINGTON

Atlanta Exposition Address (1895)

The prominent black educator Booker T. Washington (1856–1915) founded Tuskegee Normal and Industrial Institute in 1881 as a school for former slaves. As a moderate leader of the black community, Washington often mediated between white entrepreneurs and former slaves to establish a more important role for black labor in the postwar southern economy. Washington's address at the Atlanta Exposition in 1895, which he reprinted and defended in his autobiography Up from Slavery *(1901), reassured whites that blacks would not agitate for political and social equality, but would instead make loyal and law-abiding workers.*

One-third of the population of the South is of the Negro race. No enterprise seeking the material, civil, or moral welfare of this section can disregard this element of our population and reach the highest success. I but convey to you, Mr. President and Directors, the sentiment of the masses of my race when I say that in no way have the value and manhood of the American Negro been more fittingly and generously recognized than by the managers of this magnificent Exposition at every stage of its progress. It is a recognition that will do more to cement the friendship of the two races than any occurrence since the dawn of our freedom.

Not only this, but the opportunity here afforded will awaken among us a new era of industrial progress. Ignorant and inexperienced, it is not strange that in the first years of our new life we began at the top instead of at the bottom; that a seat in Congress or the state legislature was more sought than real estate or industrial skill; that the political convention or stump speaking had more attractions than starting a dairy farm or truck garden.

A ship lost at sea for many days suddenly sighted a friendly vessel. From the mast of the unfortunate vessel was seen a signal, "Water, water; we die of thirst!" The answer from the friendly vessel at once came back, "Cast down your bucket where you are." And a third and fourth signal for water was answered, "Cast down your bucket where you are." The captain of the distressed vessel, at last heeding the injunction, cast down his bucket, and it came up full of fresh, sparkling water from the mouth of the Amazon River. To those of my race who depend on bettering their condition in a foreign land or who underestimate the importance of cultivating friendly relations with the Southern white man, who is their next-door neighbour, I would say: "Cast down your bucket where you are"—cast it down in making friends in every manly way of the people of all races by whom we are surrounded.

Cast it down in agriculture, mechanics, in commerce, in domestic service, and in the professions. And in this connection it is well to bear in mind that whatever other sins the South may be called to bear, when it comes to business, pure and simple, it is in the South that the Negro is given a man's chance in the commercial world, and in nothing is this Exposition more eloquent than in emphasizing this chance. Our greatest danger is that in the great leap from slavery to freedom we may overlook the fact that the masses of us are to live by the productions of our hands, and fail to keep in mind that we shall prosper in proportion as we learn to dignify and glorify common labour and put brains and skill into the common occupations of life; shall prosper in proportion as we learn to draw the line between the superficial and the substantial, the ornamental gewgaws of life and the useful. No race can prosper till it learns that there is as much dignity in tilling a field as in writing a poem. It is at the bottom of life we must begin, and not at the top. Nor should we permit our grievances to overshadow our opportunities.

To those of the white race who look to the incoming of those of foreign birth and strange tongue and habits for the prosperity of the South, were I permitted I would repeat what I say to my own race, "Cast down your bucket where you are." Cast it down among the eight millions of Negroes whose habits you know, whose fidelity and love you have tested in days when to have proved treacherous meant the ruin of your firesides. Cast down your bucket among these people who have, without strikes and labour wars, tilled your fields, cleared your forests, builded your railroads and cities, and brought forth treasures from the bowels of the earth, and helped make possible this magnificent representation of the progress of the South. Casting down your bucket among my people, helping and encouraging them as you are doing on these grounds, and to education of head, hand, and heart, you will find that they will buy your surplus land, make blossom the waste places in your fields, and run your factories. While doing this, you can be sure in the future, as in the past, that you and your families will be surrounded by the most patient, faithful, law-abiding, and unresentful people that the world has seen. As we have proved our loyalty to you in the past, in nursing your children, watching by the sick-bed of your mothers and fathers, and often following them with tear-dimmed eyes to their graves, so in the future, in our humble way, we shall stand by you with a devotion that no foreigner can approach, ready to lay down our lives, if need be, in defence of yours, interlacing our industrial, commercial, civil, and religious life with yours in a way that shall make the interests of both races one. In all things that are purely social we can be as separate as the fingers, yet one as the hand in all things essential to mutual progress.

There is no defence or security for any of us except in the highest intelligence and development of all. If anywhere there are efforts tending to curtail the fullest growth of the Negro, let these efforts be turned into stimulating, encouraging, and making him the most useful and intelligent citizen. Effort or means so invested will pay a thousand per cent interest. These efforts will be twice blessed—"blessing him that gives and him that takes." * * *

The wisest among my race understand that the agitation of questions of social equality is the extremest folly, and that progress in the enjoyment of all the privileges that will come to us must be the result of severe and constant struggle rather than of artificial forcing. No race that has anything to contribute to the markets of the world is long in any degree ostracized. It is important and right that all privileges of the law be ours, but it is vastly more important that we be prepared for the exercises of these privileges. The opportunity to earn a dollar in a factory just now is worth infinitely more than the opportunity to spend a dollar in an opera-house.

In conclusion, may I repeat that nothing in thirty years has given us more hope and encouragement, and drawn us so near to you of the white race, as this opportunity offered by the Exposition; and here bending, as it were, over the altar that represents the results of the struggles of your race and mine, both starting practically empty-handed three decades ago, I pledge that in your effort to work out the great and intricate problem which God has laid at the doors of the South, you shall have at all times the patient, sympathetic help of my race; only let this be constantly in mind, that, while from representations in these buildings of the product of field, of forest, of mine, of factory, letters, and art, much good will come, yet far above and beyond material benefits will be that higher good, that, let us pray God, will come, in a blotting out of sectional differences and racial animosities and suspicions, in a determination to administer absolute justice, in a willing obedience among all classes to the mandates of law. This, this, coupled with our material prosperity, will bring into our beloved South a new heaven and a new earth. * * *

I am often asked to express myself more freely than I do upon the political condition and the political future of my race. These recollections of my experience in Atlanta give me the opportunity to do so briefly. My own belief is, although I have never before said so in so many words, that the time will come when the Negro in the South will be accorded all the political rights which his ability, character, and material possessions entitle him to. I think, though, that the opportunity to freely exercise such political rights will not come in any large degree through outside or artificial forcing, but will be accorded to the Negro by the Southern white people themselves, and that they will protect him in the exercise of those rights. Just as soon as the South gets over the old feeling that it is being forced by "foreigners," or "aliens," to do something which it does not want to do, I believe that the change in the direction that I have indicated is going to begin. In fact, there are indications that it is already beginning in a slight degree.

Let me illustrate my meaning. Suppose that some months before the opening of the Atlanta Exposition there had been a general demand from the press and public platform outside the South that a Negro be given a place on the opening programme, and that a Negro be placed upon the board of jurors of award. Would any such recognition of the race have taken place? I do not think so. The Atlanta officials went as far as they did because they felt it to be a pleasure, as well as a duty, to reward what they considered merit in the Negro race. Say what we will, there is something in human nature which we cannot blot out, which makes one man, in the end, recognize and reward merit in another, regardless of colour or race.

I believe it is the duty of the Negro—as the greater part of the race is already doing—to deport himself modestly in regard to political claims, depending upon the slow but sure influences that proceed from the possession of property, intelligence, and high character for the full recognition of his political rights. I think that the according of the full exercise of political rights is going to be a matter of natural, slow growth, not an over-night, gourd-vine affair. I do not believe that the Negro should cease voting, for a man cannot learn the exercise of self-government by ceasing to vote any more than a boy can learn to swim by keeping out of the water, but I do believe that in his voting he should more and more be influenced by those of intelligence and character who are his next-door neighbours.

I know coloured men who, through the encouragement, help, and advice of Southern white people, have accumulated thousands of dollars' worth of property, but who, at the same time, would never think of going to those same persons for advice concerning the casting of their ballots. This, it seems to me, is unwise and unreasonable, and should cease. In saying this I do not mean that the Negro should truckle, or not vote from principle, for the instant he ceases to vote from principle he loses the confidence and respect of the Southern white man even.

I do not believe that any state should make a law that permits an ignorant and poverty-stricken white man to vote, and prevents a black man in the same condition from voting. Such a law is not only unjust, but it will react, as all unjust laws do, in time; for the effect of such a law is to encourage the Negro to secure education and property, and at the same time it encourages the white man to remain in ignorance and poverty. I believe that in time, through the operation of intelligence and friendly race relations, all cheating at the ballot box in the South will cease. It will become apparent that the white man who begins by cheating a Negro out of his ballot soon learns to cheat a white man out of his, and that the man who does this ends his career of dishonesty by the theft of property or by some equally serious crime. In my opinion, the time will come when the South will encourage all of its citizens to vote. It will see that it pays better, from every standpoint, to have healthy, vigorous life than to have that political stagnation which always results when one-half of the population has no share and no interest in the government.

As a rule, I believe in universal, free suffrage, but I believe that in the South we are confronted with peculiar conditions that justify the protection of the ballot in many of the states, for a while at least, either by an educational test, a property test, or by both combined; but whatever tests are required, they should be made to apply with equal and exact justice to both races.

W. E. B. DU BOIS

The Souls of Black Folk (1903)

The black intellectual and civil rights activist William Edward Burghardt Du Bois (1868–1963) was a professor at Atlanta University, a founder of the Niagara Movement and the National Association for the Advancement of Colored People (NAACP), and the editor of the NAACP's journal The Crisis. In an important collection of his essays published in 1903 as The Souls of Black Folk, Du Bois captured the attention of intellectual America. The first essay, based on an Atlantic Monthly article that appeared under the title "Of Our Spiritual Strivings," described the double consciousness of blacks in America who strive to maintain their dual identities in a nation that robs them of their freedom. A vigorous and militant supporter of social and political equality for blacks, Du Bois strenuously opposed the accommodationist approach of Booker T. Washington. In one of the collection's essays, Du Bois criticized Washington for minimizing the pernicious effects of racism and preaching accommodation to blacks.

OF OUR SPIRITUAL STRIVINGS

Between me and the other world there is ever an unasked question: unasked by some through feelings of delicacy; by others through the difficulty of rightly framing it. All, nevertheless, flutter round it. They approach me in a half-hesitant sort of way, eye me curiously or compassionately, and then, instead of saying directly, How does it feel to be a problem? they say, I know an excellent colored man in my town; or, I fought at Mechanicsville; or, Do not these Southern outrages make your blood boil? At these I smile, or am interested, or reduce the boiling to a simmer, as the occasion may require. To the real question, How does it feel to be a problem? I answer seldom a word.

And yet, being a problem is a strange experience,—peculiar even for one who has never been anything else, save perhaps in babyhood and in Europe. It is in the early days of rollicking boyhood that the revelation first bursts upon one, all in a day, as it were. I remember well when the shadow swept across me. I was a little thing, away up in the hills of New England, where the dark Housatonic winds between Hoosac and Taghkanic to the sea. In a wee wooden schoolhouse, something put it into the boys' and girls' heads to buy gorgeous visiting-cards—ten cents a package—and exchange. The exchange was merry, till one girl, a tall newcomer, refused my card,—refused it peremptorily, with a glance. Then it dawned upon me with a certain suddenness that I was different from the others; or like, mayhap, in heart and life and longing, but shut out from their world by a vast veil. I had thereafter no desire to tear down that veil, to creep through; I held all beyond it in common contempt, and lived above it in a region of blue sky and great wandering shadows. That sky was bluest when I could beat my mates at examination-time, or beat them at a foot-race, or even beat their stringy heads. Alas, with the years all this fine contempt began to fade; for the words I longed for, and all their dazzling opportunities, were theirs, not mine. But they should not keep these prizes, I said; some, all, I would wrest from them. Just how I would do it I could never decide: by reading law, by healing the sick, by telling the wonderful tales that swam in my head,—some way. With other black boys the strife was not so fiercely sunny: their youth shrunk into tasteless syco-phancy, or into silent hatred of the pale world about them and mocking distrust of everything white; or wasted itself in a bitter cry, Why did God make me an outcast and a stranger in mine own house?

* * *

The shades of the prison-house closed round about us all: walls strait and stubborn to the whitest, but relentlessly narrow, tall, and unscalable to sons of night who must plod darkly on in resignation, or beat unavail-ing palms against the stone, or steadily, half hopelessly, watch the streak of blue above.

After the Egyptian and Indian, the Greek and Roman, the Teuton and Mongolian, the Negro is a sort of seventh son, born with a veil, and gifted with second-sight in this American world,—a world which yields him no true self-consciousness, but only lets him see himself through the revelation of the other world. It is a peculiar sensation, this double-consciousness, this sense of always looking at one's self through the eyes of others, of measuring one's soul by the tape of a world that looks on in amused contempt and pity. One ever feels his twoness,—an American, a Negro; two souls, two thoughts, two unreconciled strivings; two warring ideals in one dark body, whose dogged strength alone keeps it from being torn asunder.

The history of the American Negro is the history of this strife,—this longing to attain self-conscious manhood, to merge his double self into a better and truer self. In this merging he wishes neither of the older selves to be lost. He would not Africanize America, for America has too much to teach the world and Africa. He would not bleach his Negro soul in a flood of white Americanism, for he knows that Negro blood has a message for the world. He simply wishes to make it possible for a man to be both a Negro and an American, without being cursed and spit upon by his fel-lows, without having the doors of Opportunity closed roughly in his face.

This, then, is the end of his striving: to be a co-worker in the kingdom of culture, to escape both death and isolation, to husband and use his best powers and his latent genius. These powers of body and mind have in the past been strangely wasted, dispersed, or forgotten. The shadow of a mighty Negro past flits through the tale of Ethiopia the Shadowy and of Egypt the Sphinx. Through history, the powers of single black men flash here and there like falling stars, and die sometimes before the world has rightly gauged their brightness. Here in America, in the few days since Emancipation, the black man's turning hither and thither in hesitant and doubtful striving has often made his very strength to lose effectiveness, to seem like absence of power, like weakness. And yet it is not weakness,—it is the contradiction of double aims. The double-aimed struggle of the black artisan—on the one hand to escape white contempt for a nation of mere hewers of wood and drawers of water, and on the other hand to plough and nail and dig for a poverty-stricken horde—could only result in making him a poor craftsman, for he had but half a heart in either cause.

* * * By the poverty and ignorance of his people, the Negro minister or doctor was tempted toward quackery and demagogy; and by the criticism of the other world, toward ideals that made him ashamed of his lowly tasks. The would-be black *savant* was confronted by the paradox that the knowledge his people needed was a twice-told tale to his white neighbors, while the knowledge which would teach the white world was Greek to his own flesh and blood. The innate love of harmony and beauty that set the ruder souls of his people a-dancing and a-singing raised but confusion and doubt in the soul of the black artist; for the beauty revealed to him was the soul-beauty of a race which his larger audience despised, and he could not articulate the message of another people. This waste of double aims, this seeking to satisfy two unreconciled ideals, has wrought sad havoc with the courage and faith and deeds of ten thousand thousand people,—has sent them often wooing false gods and invoking false means of salvation, and at times has even seemed about to make them ashamed of themselves.

Away back in the days of bondage they thought to see in one divine event the end of all doubt and disappointment; few men ever worshipped Freedom with half such unquestioning faith as did the American Negro for two centuries. To him, so far as he thought and dreamed, slavery was indeed the sum of all villainies, the cause of all sorrow, the root of all prejudice; Emancipation was the key to a promised land of sweeter beauty than ever stretched before the eyes of wearied Israelites. In song and exhortation swelled one refrain—Liberty; in his tears and curses the God he implored had Freedom in his right hand. At last it came,—suddenly, fearfully, like a dream. With one wild carnival of blood and passion came the message in his own plaintive cadences:—

> "*Shout, O children!*
> *Shout, you're free!*
> *For God has bought your liberty!*"

Years have passed away since then,—ten, twenty, forty; forty years of national life, forty years of renewal and development, and yet the swarthy spectre sits in its accustomed seat at the Nation's feast. In vain do we cry to this our vastest social problem:—

> *"Take any shape but that, and my firm nerves*
> *Shall never tremble!"*

The Nation has not yet found peace from its sins; the freedman has not yet found in freedom his promised land. Whatever of good may have come in these years of change, the shadow of a deep disappointment rests upon the Negro people,—a disappointment all the more bitter because the unattained ideal was unbounded save by the simple ignorance of a lowly people.

The first decade was merely a prolongation of the vain search for freedom, the boon that seemed ever barely to elude their grasp,—like a tantalizing will-o'-the-wisp, maddening and misleading the headless host. The holocaust of war, the terrors of the Ku Klux Klan, the lies of carpetbaggers, the disorganization of industry, and the contradictory advice of friends and foes, left the bewildered serf with no new watchword beyond the old cry for freedom. As the time flew, however, he began to grasp a new idea. The ideal of liberty demanded for its attainment powerful means, and these the Fifteenth Amendment gave him. The ballot, which before he had looked upon as a visible sign of freedom, he now regarded as the chief means of gaining and perfecting the liberty with which war had partially endowed him. And why not? Had not votes made war and emancipated millions? Had not votes enfranchised the freedmen? Was anything impossible to a power that had done all this? A million black men started with renewed zeal to vote themselves into the kingdom. So the decade flew away, the revolution of 1876 came, and left the half-free serf weary, wondering, but still inspired. Slowly but steadily, in the following years, a new vision began gradually to replace the dream of political power,—a powerful movement, the rise of another ideal to guide the unguided, another pillar of fire by night after a clouded day. It was the ideal of "book-learning"; the curiosity, born of compulsory ignorance, to know and test the power of the cabalistic letters of the white man, the longing to know. Here at last seemed to have been discovered the mountain path to Canaan; longer than the highway of Emancipation and law, steep and rugged, but straight, leading to heights high enough to overlook life.

Up the new path the advance guard toiled, slowly, heavily, doggedly; only those who have watched and guided the faltering feet, the misty minds, the dull understandings, of the dark pupils of these schools know how faithfully, how piteously, this people strove to learn. It was weary work. The cold statistician wrote down the inches of progress here and there, noted also where here and there a foot had slipped or some one had fallen. To the tired climbers, the horizon was ever dark, the mists were often cold, the Canaan was always dim and far away. If, however, the

vistas disclosed as yet no goal, no resting-place, little but flattery and criticism, the journey at least gave leisure for reflection and self-examination;
it changed the child of Emancipation to the youth with dawning self-
consciousness, self-realization, self-respect. In those sombre forests of
his striving his own soul rose before him, and he saw himself,—darkly as
through a veil; and yet he saw in himself some faint revelation of his
power, of his mission.

He began to have a dim feeling that, to attain his place in the world, he
must be himself, and not another. For the first time he sought to analyze
the burden he bore upon his back, that dead-weight of social degradation
partially masked behind a half-named Negro problem. He felt his
poverty; without a cent, without a home, without land, tools, or savings,
he had entered into competition with rich, landed, skilled neighbors. To
be a poor man is hard, but to be a poor race in a land of dollars is the very
bottom of hardships. He felt the weight of his ignorance,—not simply of
letters, but of life, of business, of the humanities; the accumulated sloth
and shirking and awkwardness of decades and centuries shackled his
hands and feet. Nor was his burden all poverty and ignorance. The red
stain of bastardy, which two centuries of systematic legal defilement of
Negro women had stamped upon his race, meant not only the loss of ancient African chastity, but also the hereditary weight of a mass of corruption from white adulterers, threatening almost the obliteration of the
Negro home.

A people thus handicapped ought not to be asked to race with the
world, but rather allowed to give all its time and thought to its own social
problems. But alas! while sociologists gleefully count his bastards and his
prostitutes, the very soul of the toiling, sweating black man is darkened
by the shadow of a vast despair. Men call the shadow prejudice, and
learnedly explain it as the natural defence of culture against barbarism,
learning against ignorance, purity against crime, the "higher" against the
"lower" races. To which the Negro cries Amen! and swears that to so
much of this strange prejudice as is founded on just homage to civilization, culture, righteousness, and progress, he humbly bows and meekly
does obeisance. But before that nameless prejudice that leaps beyond all
this he stands helpless, dismayed, and well-nigh speechless; before that
personal disrespect and mockery, the ridicule and systematic humiliation,
the distortion of fact and wanton license of fancy, the cynical ignoring of
the better and the boisterous welcoming of the worse, the all-pervading
desire to inculcate disdain for everything black, from Toussaint to the
devil,—before this there rises a sickening despair that would disarm and
discourage any nation save that black host to whom "discouragement" is
an unwritten word.

But the facing of so vast a prejudice could not but bring the inevitable self-questioning, self-disparagement, and lowering of ideals which ever accompany repression and breed in an atmosphere of contempt and hate. Whisperings and portents came borne upon the four winds: Lo! we are diseased and dying, cried the dark hosts; we cannot write, our voting is vain; what need of education, since we must always cook and serve?

And the Nation echoed and enforced this self-criticism, saying: Be content to be servants, and nothing more; what need of higher culture for half-men? Away with the black man's ballot, by force or fraud,—and behold the suicide of a race! Nevertheless, out of the evil came something of good,—the more careful adjustment of education to real life, the clearer perception of the Negroes' social responsibilities, and the sobering realization of the meaning of progress.

So dawned the time of *Sturm und Drang:* storm and stress to-day rocks our little boat on the mad waters of the world-sea; there is within and without the sound of conflict, the burning of body and rending of soul; inspiration strives with doubt, and faith with vain questionings. The bright ideals of the past,—physical freedom, political power, the training of brains and the training of hands,—all these in turn have waxed and waned, until even the last grows dim and overcast. Are they all wrong,— all false? No, not that, but each alone was over-simple and incomplete,— the dreams of a credulous race-childhood, or the fond imaginings of the other world which does not know and does not want to know our power. To be really true, all these ideals must be melted and welded into one. The training of the schools we need to-day more than ever;—the training of deft hands, quick eyes and ears, and above all the broader, deeper, higher culture of gifted minds and pure hearts. The power of the ballot we need in sheer self-defence,—else what shall save us from a second slavery? Freedom, too, the long-sought, we still seek,—the freedom of life and limb, the freedom to work and think, the freedom to love and aspire. Work, culture, liberty,—all these we need, not singly but together, not successively but together, each growing and aiding each, and all striving toward that vaster ideal that swims before the Negro people, the ideal of human brotherhood, gained through the unifying ideal of Race; the ideal of fostering and developing the traits and talents of the Negro, not in opposition to or contempt for other races, but rather in large conformity to the greater ideals of the American Republic, in order that some day on American soil two world-races may give each to each those characteristics both so sadly lack. We the darker ones come even now not altogether empty-handed: there are to-day no truer exponents of the pure human spirit of the Declaration of Independence than the American Negroes; there is no true American music but the wild sweet melodies of the Negro slave; the American fairy tales and folklore are Indian and African; and, all in all, we black men seem the sole oasis of simple faith and reverence in a dusty desert of dollars and smartness.

Will America be poorer if she replace her brutal dyspeptic blundering with light-hearted but determined Negro humility? or her coarse and cruel wit with loving jovial good-humor? or her vulgar music with the soul of the Sorrow Songs?

Merely a concrete test of the underlying principles of the great republic is the Negro Problem, and the spiritual striving of the freedmen's sons is the travail of souls whose burden is almost beyond the measure of their strength, but who bear it in the name of an historic race, in the name of this the land of their fathers' fathers, and in the name of human opportunity. * * *

Of Mr. Booker T. Washington and Others

Easily the most striking thing in the history of the American Negro since 1876 is the ascendancy of Mr. Booker T. Washington. It began at the time when war memories and ideals were rapidly passing; a day of astonishing commercial development was dawning; a sense of doubt and hesitation overtook the freedmen's sons,—then it was that his leading began. Mr. Washington came, with a single definite programme, at the psychological moment when the nation was a little ashamed of having bestowed so much sentiment on Negroes, and was concentrating its energies on Dollars. His programme of industrial education, conciliation of the South, and submission and silence as to civil and political rights, was not wholly original; the Free Negroes from 1830 up to war-time had striven to build industrial schools, and the American Missionary Association had from the first taught various trades; and Price and others had sought a way of honorable alliance with the best of the Southerners. But Mr. Washington first indissolubly linked these things; he put enthusiasm, unlimited energy, and perfect faith into his programme, and changed it from a by-path into a veritable Way of Life. And the tale of the methods by which he did this is a fascinating study of human life.

It startled the nation to hear a Negro advocating such a programme after many decades of bitter complaint; it startled and won the applause of the South, it interested and won the admiration of the North; and after a confused murmur of protest, it silenced if it did not convert the Negroes themselves.

To gain the sympathy and coöperation of the various elements comprising the white South was Mr. Washington's first task; and this, at the time Tuskegee was founded, seemed, for a black man, well-nigh impossible. And yet ten years later it was done in the word spoken at Atlanta: "In all things purely social we can be as separate as the five fingers, and yet one as the hand in all things essential to mutual progress." This "Atlanta Compromise" is by all odds the most notable thing in Mr. Washington's career. The South interpreted it in different ways: the radicals received it as a complete surrender of the demand for civil and political equality; the conservatives, as a generously conceived working basis for mutual understanding. So both approved it, and to-day its author is certainly the most distinguished Southerner since Jefferson Davis, and the one with the largest personal following.

Next to this achievement comes Mr. Washington's work in gaining place and consideration in the North. Others less shrewd and tactful had formerly essayed to sit on these two stools and had fallen between them; but as Mr. Washington knew the heart of the South from birth and training, so by singular insight he intuitively grasped the spirit of the age which was dominating the North. And so thoroughly did he learn the speech and thought of triumphant commercialism, and the ideals of material prosperity, that the picture of a lone black boy poring over a French grammar amid the weeds and dirt of a neglected home soon seemed to him the acme of absurdities. One wonders what Socrates and St. Francis of Assisi would say to this.

And yet this very singleness of vision and thorough oneness with his age is a mark of the successful man. It is as though Nature must needs make men narrow in order to give them force. So Mr. Washington's cult has gained unquestioning followers, his work has wonderfully prospered, his friends are legion, and his enemies are confounded. To-day he stands as the one recognized spokesman of his ten million fellows, and one of the most notable figures in a nation of seventy millions. One hesitates, therefore, to criticise a life which, beginning with so little, has done so much. And yet the time is come when one may speak in all sincerity and utter courtesy of the mistakes and shortcomings of Mr. Washington's career, as well as of his triumphs, without being thought captious or envious, and without forgetting that it is easier to do ill than well in the world. ＊ ＊ ＊

Among his own people, however, Mr. Washington has encountered the strongest and most lasting opposition, amounting at times to bitterness, and even to-day continuing strong and insistent even though largely silenced in outward expression by the public opinion of the nation. Some of this opposition is, of course, mere envy; the disappointment of displaced demagogues and the spite of narrow minds. But aside from this, there is among educated and thoughtful colored men in all parts of the land a feeling of deep regret, sorrow, and apprehension at the wide currency and ascendancy which some of Mr. Washington's theories have gained. These same men admire his sincerity of purpose, and are willing to forgive much to honest endeavor which is doing something worth the doing. They coöperate with Mr. Washington as far as they conscientiously can; and, indeed, it is no ordinary tribute to this man's tact and power that, steering as he must between so many diverse interests and opinions, he so largely retains the respect of all.

But the hushing of the criticism of honest opponents is a dangerous thing. It leads some of the best of the critics to unfortunate silence and paralysis of effort, and others to burst into speech so passionately and intemperately as to lose listeners. Honest and earnest criticism from those whose interests are most nearly touched,—criticism of writers by readers, of government by those governed, of leaders by those led,—this is the soul of democracy and the safeguard of modern society. If the best of the American Negroes receive by outer pressure a leader whom they had not recognized before, manifestly there is here a certain palpable gain. Yet there is also irreparable loss,—a loss of that peculiarly valuable education which a group receives when by search and criticism it finds and commissions its own leaders.

But Booker T. Washington arose as essentially the leader not of one race but of two,—a compromiser between the South, the North, and the Negro. Naturally the Negroes resented, at first bitterly, signs of compromise which surrendered their civil and political rights, even though this was to be exchanged for larger chances of economic development. The rich and dominating North, however, was not only weary of the race problem, but was investing largely in Southern enterprise, and welcomed any method of peaceful coöperation. Thus, by national opinion, the Negroes began to recognize Mr. Washington's leadership; and the voice of criticism was hushed.

Mr. Washington represents in Negro thought the old attitude of adjustment and submission; but adjustment at such a peculiar time as to make his programme unique. This is an age of unusual economic development, and Mr. Washington's programme naturally takes an economic cast, becoming a gospel of Work and Money to such an extent as apparently almost completely to overshadow the higher aims of life.

Moreover, this is an age when the more advanced races are coming in closer contact with the less developed races, and the race-feeling is therefore intensified; and Mr. Washington's programme practically accepts the alleged inferiority of the Negro races. Again, in our own land, the reaction from the sentiment of war time has given impetus to race-prejudice against Negroes, and Mr. Washington withdraws many of the high demands of Negroes as men and American citizens. In other periods of intensified prejudice all the Negro's tendency to self-assertion has been called forth; at this period a policy of submission is advocated. In the history of nearly all other races and peoples the doctrine preached at such crises has been that manly self-respect is worth more than lands and houses, and that a people who voluntarily surrender such respect, or cease striving for it, are not worth civilizing.

In answer to this, it has been claimed that the Negro can survive only through submission. Mr. Washington distinctly asks that black people give up, at least for the present, three things,—

First, political power,
Second, insistence on civil rights,
Third, higher education of Negro youth,—

and concentrate all their energies on industrial education, and accumulation of wealth, and the conciliation of the South. This policy has been courageously and insistently advocated for over fifteen years, and has been triumphant for perhaps ten years. As a result of this tender of the palm-branch, what has been the return? In these years there have occurred:

1. The disfranchisement of the Negro.
2. The legal creation of a distinct status of civil inferiority for the Negro.
3. The steady withdrawal of aid from institutions for the higher training of the Negro.

These movements are not, to be sure, direct results of Mr. Washington's teachings; but his propaganda has, without a shadow of doubt, helped their speedier accomplishment. The question then comes: Is it possible, and probable, that nine millions of men can make effective progress in economic lines if they are deprived of political rights, made a servile caste, and allowed only the most meagre chance for developing their exceptional men? If history and reason give any distinct answer to these questions, it is an emphatic *No*. And Mr. Washington thus faces the triple paradox of his career:

1. He is striving nobly to make Negro artisans business men and property-owners; but it is utterly impossible, under modern competitive methods, for workingmen and property-owners to defend their rights and exist without the right of suffrage.
2. He insists on thrift and self-respect, but at the same time counsels a silent submission to civic inferiority such as is bound to sap the manhood of any race in the long run.

3. He advocates common-school and industrial training, and depreciates institutions of higher learning; but neither the Negro common-schools, nor Tuskegee itself, could remain open a day were it not for teachers trained in Negro colleges, or trained by their graduates.

This triple paradox in Mr. Washington's position is the object of criticism by two classes of colored Americans. One class is spiritually descended from Toussaint the Savior, through Gabriel, Vesey, and Turner, and they represent the attitude of revolt and revenge; they hate the white South blindly and distrust the white race generally, and so far as they agree on definite action, think that the Negro's only hope lies in emigration beyond the borders of the United States. And yet, by the irony of fate, nothing has more effectually made this programme seem hopeless than the recent course of the United States toward weaker and darker peoples in the West Indies, Hawaii, and the Philippines,—for where in the world may we go and be safe from lying and brute force?

The other class of Negroes who cannot agree with Mr. Washington has hitherto said little aloud. They deprecate the sight of scattered counsels, of internal disagreement; and especially they dislike making their just criticism of a useful and earnest man an excuse for a general discharge of venom from small-minded opponents. Nevertheless, the questions involved are so fundamental and serious that it is difficult to see how men like the Grimkes, Kelly Miller, J. W. E. Bowen, and other representatives of this group, can much longer be silent. Such men feel in conscience bound to ask of this nation three things:

1. The right to vote.
2. Civic equality.
3. The education of youth according to ability.

They acknowledge Mr. Washington's invaluable service in counselling patience and courtesy in such demands; they do not ask that ignorant black men vote when ignorant whites are debarred, or that any reasonable restrictions in the suffrage should not be applied; they know that the low social level of the mass of the race is responsible for much discrimination against it, but they also know, and the nation knows, that relentless color-prejudice is more often a cause than a result of the Negro's degradation; they seek the abatement of this relic of barbarism, and not its systematic encouragement and pampering by all agencies of social power from the Associated Press to the Church of Christ. They advocate, with Mr. Washington, a broad system of Negro common schools supplemented by thorough industrial training; but they are surprised that a man of Mr. Washington's insight cannot see that no such educational system ever has rested or can rest on any other basis than that of the well-equipped college and university, and they insist that there is a demand for a few such institutions throughout the South to train the best of the Negro youth as teachers, professional men, and leaders.

This group of men honor Mr. Washington for his attitude of conciliation toward the white South; they accept the "Atlanta Compromise" in its broadest interpretation; they recognize, with him, many signs of promise, many men of high purpose and fair judgment, in this section; they know that no easy task has been laid upon a region already tottering under heavy burdens. But, nevertheless, they insist that the way to truth and right lies in straightforward honesty, not in indiscriminate flattery; in praising those of the South who do well and criticising uncompromisingly those who do ill; in taking advantage of the opportunities at hand and urging their fellows to do the same, but at the same time in remembering that only a firm adherence to their higher ideals and aspirations will ever keep those ideals within the realm of possibility. They do not expect that the free right to vote, to enjoy civic rights, and to be educated, will come in a moment; they do not expect to see the bias and prejudices of years disappear at the blast of a trumpet; but they are absolutely certain that the way for a people to gain their reasonable rights is not by voluntarily throwing them away and insisting that they do not want them; that the way for a people to gain respect is not by continually belittling and ridiculing themselves; that, on the contrary, Negroes must insist continually, in season and out of season, that voting is necessary to modern manhood, that color discrimination is barbarism, and that black boys need education as well as white boys. * * *

It would be unjust to Mr. Washington not to acknowledge that in several instances he has opposed movements in the South which were unjust to the Negro; he sent memorials to the Louisiana and Alabama constitutional conventions, he has spoken against lynching, and in other ways has openly or silently set his influence against sinister schemes and unfortunate happenings. Notwithstanding this, it is equally true to assert that on the whole the distinct impression left by Mr. Washington's propaganda is, first, that the South is justified in its present attitude toward the Negro because of the Negro's degradation; secondly, that the prime cause of the Negro's failure to rise more quickly is his wrong education in the past; and, thirdly, that his future rise depends primarily on his own efforts. Each of these propositions is a dangerous half-truth. The supplementary truths must never be lost sight of: first, slavery and race-prejudice are potent if not sufficient causes of the Negro's position;

second, industrial and common-school training were necessarily slow in planting because they had to await the black teachers trained by higher institutions,—it being extremely doubtful if any essentially different development was possible, and certainly a Tuskegee was unthinkable before 1880; and, third, while it is a great truth to say that the Negro must strive and strive mightily to help himself, it is equally true that unless his striving be not simply seconded, but rather aroused and encouraged, by the initiative of the richer and wiser environing group, he cannot hope for great success.

In his failure to realize and impress this last point, Mr. Washington is especially to be criticised. His doctrine has tended to make the whites, North and South, shift the burden of the Negro problem to the Negro's shoulders and stand aside as critical and rather pessimistic spectators; when in fact the burden belongs to the nation, and the hands of none of us are clean if we bend not our energies to righting these great wrongs. * * *

The black men of America have a duty to perform, a duty stern and delicate,—a forward movement to oppose a part of the work of their greatest leader. So far as Mr. Washington preaches Thrift, Patience, and Industrial Training for the masses, we must hold up his hands and strive with him, rejoicing in his honors and glorying in the strength of this Joshua called of God and of man to lead the headless host. But so far as Mr. Washington apologizes for injustice, North or South, does not rightly value the privilege and duty of voting, belittles the emasculating effects of caste distinctions, and opposes the higher training and ambition of our brighter minds,—so far as he, the South, or the Nation, does this,—we must unceasingly and firmly oppose them.

By every civilized and peaceful method we must strive for the rights which the world accords to men, clinging unwaveringly to those great words which the sons of the Fathers would fain forget: "We hold these truths to be self-evident: That all men are created equal; that they are endowed by their Creator with certain unalienable rights; that among these are life, liberty, and the pursuit of happiness."

W. E. B. DU BOIS

The Talented Tenth (1903)

Du Bois saw Negro progress arising from exceptional men, a college-educated elite, not from an economic base of successful farmers, crafts-men, and businessmen. He made this case in an influential article written for a 1903 volume, The Negro Problem: A Series of Articles by Representative Negroes of Today, *which also contained a piece by Booker T. Washington, making the opposite case.*

The Negro race, like all races, is going to be saved by its exceptional men. The problem of education, then, among Negroes must first of all deal with the Talented Tenth; it is the problem of developing the Best of this race that they may guide the Mass away from the contamination and death of the Worst, in their own and other races. Now the training of men is a difficult and intricate task. Its technique is a matter for educational experts, but its object is for the vision of seers. If we make money the object of man-training, we shall develop money-makers but not necessarily men; if we make technical skill the object of education, we may possess artisans but not, in nature, men. Men we shall have only as we make manhood the object of the work of the schools—intelligence, broad sympathy, knowledge of the world that was and is, and of the relation of men to it—this is the curriculum of that Higher Education which must underlie true life. On this foundation we may build bread winning, skill of hand and quickness of brain, with never a fear lest the child and man mistake the means of living for the object of life. * * *

If this be true—and who can deny it—three tasks lay [sic] before me; first to show from the past that the Talented Tenth as they have risen among American Negroes have been worthy of leadership; secondly, to show how these men may be educated and developed; and thirdly, to show their relation to the Negro problem. * * *

From the very first it has been the educated and intelligent of the Negro people that have led and elevated the mass, and the sole obstacles that nullified and retarded their efforts were slavery and race prejudice; * * *

And so we come to the present—a day of cowardice and vacillation, of strident wide-voiced wrong and faint hearted compromise; of double-faced dallying with Truth and Right. Who are to-day guiding the work of the Negro people? The "exceptions" of course. And yet so sure as this Talented Tenth is pointed out, the blind worshippers of the Average cry out in alarm: "These are exceptions, look here at death, disease and crime—these are the happy rule." Of course they are the rule, because a silly nation made them the rule: Because for three long centuries this people lynched Negroes who dared to be brave, raped black women who dared to be virtuous, crushed dark-hued youth who dared to be ambitious, and encouraged and made to flourish servility and lewdness and apathy. But not even this was able to crush all manhood and chastity and aspiration from black folk. A saving remnant continually survives and persists, continually aspires, continually shows itself in thrift and ability and character. Exceptional it is to be sure, but this is its chiefest promise; it shows the capability of Negro blood, the promise of black men. * * * Is it fair, is it decent, is it Christian to ignore these facts of the Negro problem, to belittle such aspiration, to nullify such leadership and seek to crush these people back into the mass out of which by toil and travail, they and their fathers have raised themselves?

Can the masses of the Negro people be in any possible way more quickly raised than by the effort and example of this aristocracy of talent and character? Was there ever a nation on God's fair earth civilized from the bottom upward? Never; it is, ever was and ever will be from the top downward that culture filters. The Talented Tenth rises and pulls all that are worth the saving up to their vantage ground. This is the history of human progress. * * *

How then shall the leaders of a struggling people be trained and the hands of the risen few strengthened? There can be but one answer: The best and most capable of their youth must be schooled in the colleges and universities of the land. * * *

All men cannot go to college but some men must; every isolated group or nation must have its yeast, must have for the talented few centers of training where men are not so mystified and befuddled by the hard and necessary toil of earning a living, as to have no aims higher than their bellies, and no God greater than Gold. This is true training, and thus in the beginning were the favored sons of the freedmen trained. Out of the colleges of the North came, after the blood of war, Ware, Cravath, Chase, Andrews, Bumstead and Spence to build the foundations of knowledge and civilization in the black South. Where ought they to have begun to build? At the bottom, of course, quibbles the mole with his eyes in the earth. Aye! truly at the bottom, at the very bottom; at the bottom of knowledge, down in the very depths of knowledge there where the roots of justice strike into the lowest soil of Truth. And so they did begin; they founded colleges, and up from the colleges shot normal schools, and out from the normal schools went teachers, and around the normal teachers clustered other teachers to teach the public schools; the college trained in Greek and Latin and mathematics, 2,000 men; and these men trained full 50,000 others in morals and manners, and they in turn taught thrift and the alphabet to nine millions of men, who to-day hold $300,000,000 of property. It was a miracle—the most wonderful peace-battle of the 19th century, and yet to-day men smile at it, and in fine superiority tell us that it was all a strange mistake; that a proper way to found a system of education is first to gather the children and buy them spelling books and hoes; afterward men may look about for teachers, if haply they may find them; or again they would teach men Work, but as for Life—why, what has Work to do with Life, they ask vacantly. * * *

These figures illustrate vividly the function of the college-bred Negro. He is, as he ought to be, the group leader, the man who sets the ideals of the community where he lives, directs its thoughts and heads its social movements. It need hardly be argued that the Negro people need social leadership more than most groups; that they have no traditions to fall back upon, no long established customs, no strong family ties, no well de-fined social classes. All these things must be slowly and painfully evolved. The preacher was, even before the war, the group leader of the Negroes, and the church their greatest social institution. Naturally this preacher was ignorant and often immoral, and the problem of replacing the older type by better educated men has been a difficult one. Both by direct work and by direct influence on other preachers, and on congregations, the college-bred preacher has an opportunity for reformatory work and moral inspiration, the value of which cannot be overestimated.

It has, however, been in the furnishing of teachers that the Negro col-lege has found its peculiar function. Few persons realize how vast a work, how mighty a revolution has been thus accomplished. To furnish five mil-lions and more of ignorant people with teachers of their own race and blood, in one generation, was not only a very difficult undertaking, but a very important one, in that, it placed before the eyes of almost every Ne-gro child an attainable ideal. It brought the masses of the blacks in con-tact with modern civilization, made black men the leaders of their communities and trainers of the new generation. In this work college-bred Negroes were first teachers, and then teachers of teachers. And here it is that the broad culture of college work has been of peculiar value. Knowledge of life and its wider meaning, has been the point of the Ne-gro's deepest ignorance, and the sending out of teachers whose training has not been simply for bread winning, but also for human culture, has been of inestimable value in the training of these men. * * *

The main question, so far as the Southern Negro is concerned, is: What under the present circumstance, must a system of education do in order to raise the Negro as quickly as possible in the scale of civilization? The answer to this question seems to me clear: It must strengthen the Negro's character, increase his knowledge and teach him to earn a living. Now it goes without saying, that it is hard to do all these things simultaneously or suddenly, and that at the same time it will not do to give all the attention to one and neglect the others; we could give black boys trades, but that alone will not civilize a race of ex-slaves; we might simply increase their knowledge of the world, but this would not necessarily make them wish to use this knowledge honestly; we might seek to strengthen character and purpose, but to what end if this people have nothing to eat or to wear? * * * If then we start out to train an ignorant and unskilled people with a heritage of bad habits, our system of training must set before itself two great aims—the one dealing with knowledge and character, the other part seeking to give the child the technical knowledge necessary for him to earn a living under the present circumstances. These objects are accomplished in part by the opening of the common schools on the one, and of the industrial schools on the other. But only in part, for there must also be trained those who are to teach these schools—men and women of knowledge and culture and technical skill who understand modern civilization, and have the training and aptitude to impart it to the children under them. There must be teachers, and teachers of teachers, and to attempt to establish any sort of a system of common and industrial school training, without *first* (and I say *first* advisedly) without *first* providing for the higher training of the very best teachers, is simply throwing your money to the winds. * * * Nothing, in these latter days, has so dampened the faith of thinking Negroes in recent educational movements, as the fact that such movements have been accompanied by ridicule and denouncement and decrying of those very institutions of higher training which made the Negro public school possible, and make Negro industrial schools thinkable. * * *

I would not deny, or for a moment seem to deny, the paramount necessity of teaching the Negro to work, and to work steadily and skillfully; or seem to depreciate in the slightest degree the important part industrial schools must play in the accomplishment of these ends, but I *do* say, and insist upon it, that it is industrialism drunk with its vision of success, to imagine that its own work can be accomplished without providing for the training of broadly cultured men and women to teach its own teachers, and to teach the teachers of the public schools.

But I have already said that human education is not simply a matter of schools; it is much more a matter of family and group life—the training of one's home, of one's daily companions, of one's social class. Now the black boy of the South moves in a black world—a world with its own leaders, its own thoughts, its own ideals. In this world he gets by far the larger part of his life training, and through the eyes of this dark world he peers into the veiled world beyond. Who guides and determines the education which he receives in his world? His teachers here are the group-leaders of the Negro people—the physicians and clergymen, the trained fathers and mothers, the influential and forceful men about him of all kinds; here it is, if at all, that the culture of the surrounding world trickles through and is handed on by the graduates of the higher schools. Can such culture training of group leaders be neglected? Can we afford to ignore it? * * * You have no choice; either you must help furnish this race from within its own ranks with thoughtful men of trained leadership, or you must suffer the evil consequences of a headless misguided rabble.

I am an earnest advocate of manual training and trade teaching for black boys, and for white boys, too. I believe that next to the founding of Negro colleges the most valuable addition to Negro education since the war, has been industrial training for black boys. Nevertheless, I insist that the object of all true education is not to make men carpenters, it is to make carpenters men; there are two means of making the carpenter a man, each equally important: the first is to give the group and community in which he works, liberally trained teachers and leaders to teach him and his family what life means; the second is to give him sufficient intelligence and technical skill to make him an efficient workman; the first object demands the Negro college and college-bred men—not a quantity of such colleges, but a few of excellent quality; not too many college-bred men, but enough to leaven the lump, to inspire the masses, to raise the Talented Tenth to leadership; the second object demands a good system of common schools, well-taught, conveniently located and properly equipped. * * *

Further than this, after being provided with group leaders of civilization, and a foundation of intelligence in the public schools, the carpenter, in order to be a man, needs technical skill. This calls for trade schools. * * *

Even at this point, however, the difficulties were not surmounted. In the first place modern industry has taken great strides since the war, and the teaching of trades is no longer a simple matter. Machinery and long processes of work have greatly changed the work of the carpenter, the ironworker and the shoemaker. A really efficient workman must be to-day an intelligent man who has had good technical training in addition to thorough common school, and perhaps even higher training. * * *

Thus, again, in the manning of trade schools and manual training schools we are thrown back upon the higher training as its source and chief support. There was a time when any aged and wornout carpenter could teach in a trade school. But not so to-day. Indeed the demand for college-bred men by a school like Tuskegee, ought to make Mr. Booker T. Washington the firmest friend of higher training. Here he has as helpers the son of a Negro senator, trained in Greek and the humanities, and graduated at Harvard; the son of a Negro congressman and lawyer, trained in Latin and mathematics, and graduated at Oberlin; he has as his wife, a woman who read Virgil and Homer in the same class room with me; he has as college chaplain, a classical graduate of Atlanta University; as teacher of science, a graduate of Fisk; as teacher of history, a graduate of Smith,—indeed some thirty of his chief teachers are college graduates, and instead of studying French grammars in the midst of weeds, or buying pianos for dirty cabins, they are at Mr. Washington's right hand helping him in a noble work. And yet one of the effects of Mr. Washington's propaganda has been to throw doubt upon the expediency of such training for Negroes, as these persons have had.

Men of America, the problem is plain before you. Here is a race transplanted through the criminal foolishness of your fathers. Whether you like it or not the millions are here, and here they will remain. If you do not lift them up, they will pull you down. Education and work are the levers to uplift a people. Work alone will not do it unless inspired by the right ideals and guided by intelligence. Education must not simply teach work—it must teach Life. The Talented Tenth of the Negro race must be made leaders of thought and missionaries of culture among their people. No others can do this work and Negro colleges must train men for it. The Negro race, like all other races, is going to be saved by its exceptional men.

W. E. B. DU BOIS

The Immediate Program of the American Negro (1915)

W. E. B. Du Bois was closely connected to the NAACP after its founding in 1910, serving as its director of research and editor of its magazine, The Crisis. *Nevertheless, he had his own independent vision of Negro progress that went beyond the association's principal quest to protect Negroes' constitutional rights. He described this ideal in a 1915 piece in* The Crisis.

The immediate program of the American Negro means nothing unless it is mediate to his great ideal and the ultimate ends of his development. We need not waste time by seeking to deceive our enemies into thinking that we are going to be content with a half loaf, or by being willing to lull our friends into a false sense of our indifference and present satisfaction.

The American Negro demands equality—political equality, industrial equality and social equality; and he is never going to rest satisfied with anything less. He demands this in no spirit of braggadocio and with no obsequious envy of others, but as an absolute measure of self-defense and the only one that will assure to the darker races their ultimate survival on earth.

Only in a demand and a persistent demand for essential equality in the modern realm of human culture can any people show a real pride of race and a decent self-respect. For any group, nation or race to admit for a moment the present monstrous demand of the white race to be the inheritors of the earth, the arbiters of mankind and the sole owners of a heritage of culture which they did not create, nor even improve to any greater extent than the other great division of men—to admit such pretense for a moment is for the race to write itself down immediately as indisputably inferior in judgment, knowledge and common sense.

The equality in political, industrial and social life which modern men must have in order to live, is not to be confounded with sameness. On the contrary, in our case, it is rather insistence upon the right of diversity;—upon the right of a human being to be a man even if he does not wear the same cut of vest, the same curl of hair or the same color of skin. Human equality does not even entail, as is sometimes said, absolute equality of opportunity; for certainly the natural inequalities of inherent genius and varying gift make this a dubious phase [*phrase*]. But there is a more and more clearly recognized minimum of opportunity and maximum of freedom to be, to move and to think, which the modern world denies to no being which it recognizes as a real man.

These involve both negative and positive sides. They call for freedom on the one hand and power on the other. The Negro must have political freedom; taxation without representation is tyranny. American Negroes of today are ruled by tyrants who take what they please in taxes and give what they please in law and administration, in justice and in injustice; and the great mass of black people must stand helpless and voiceless before a condition which has time and time again caused other peoples to fight and die.

The Negro must have industrial freedom. Between the peonage of the rural South, the oppression of shrewd capitalists and the jealousy of certain trade unions, the Negro laborer is the most exploited class in the country, giving more hard toil for less money than any other American, and * * * [has] less voice in the conditions of his labor.

In social intercourse every effort is being made to-day from the President of the United States and the so-called Church of Christ down to saloons and boot-blacks to segregate, strangle and spiritually starve Negroes so as to give them the least possible chance to know and share civilization.

These shackles must go. But that is but the beginning. The Negro must have power; the power of men, the right to do, to know, to feel and to express that knowledge, action and spiritual gift. He must not simply be free from the political tyranny of white folk, he must have the right to vote and to rule over the citizens, white and black, to the extent of his proven foresight and ability. He must have a voice in the new industrial democracy which is building and the power to see to it that his children are not in the next generation trained to be the mudsills of society. He must have the right to social intercourse with his fellows. There was a time in the atomic individualistic group when "social intercourse" meant merely calls and tea-parties; to-day social intercourse means theatres, lectures, organizations, churches, clubs, excursions, travel, hotels,—it means in short Life; to bar a group from such methods of thinking, living and doing is to bar them from the world and bid them create a new world;—a task to which no single group is today equal; it is to crucify them and taunt them with not being able to live.

What now are the practical steps which must be taken to accomplish these ends?

First of all before taking steps the wise man knows the object and end of his journey. There are those who would advise the black man to pay little or no attention to where he is going so long as he keeps moving. They assume that God or his vice-regent the White Man will attend to the steering. This is arrant nonsense. The feet of those that aimlessly wander land as often in hell as in heaven. Conscious self-realizaion and self-direction is the watchword of modern man, and the first article in the program of any group that will survive must be the great aim, equality and power among men.

The practical steps to this are clear. First we must fight obstructions; by continual and increasing effort we must first make American courts either build up a body of decisions which will protect the plain legal rights of American citizens or else make them tear down the civil and political rights of all citizens in order to oppress a few. Either result will bring justice in the end. It is lots of fun and most ingenious just now for courts to twist law so as to say I shall not live here or vote there, or marry the woman who

wishes to marry me. But when to-morrow these decisions throttle all freedom and overthrow the foundation of democracy and decency, there is going to be some judicial house cleaning.

We must *secondly* seek in legislature and congress remedial legislation;
national aid to public school education, the removal of all legal discriminations based simply on race and color, and [of] those marriage laws
passed to make the seduction of black girls easy and without legal
penalty.

Third the human contact of human beings must be increased; the policy which brings into sympathetic touch and understanding, men and
women, rich and poor, capitalist and laborer, Asiatic and European, must
bring into closer contact and mutual knowledge the white and black people of this land. It is the most frightful indictment of a country which
dares to call itself civilized that it has allowed itself to drift into a state of
ignorance where ten million people are coming to believe that all white
people are liars and thieves, and the whites in turn to believe that the
chief industry of Negroes is raping white women.

Fourth only the publication of the truth repeatedly and incisively and
uncompromisingly can secure that change in public opinion which will
correct these awful lies. THE CRISIS, our record of the darker races, must
have a circulation not of 35,000 chiefly among colored folk but of at least
250,000 among all men who believe in men. It must not be a namby-
pamby box of salve, but a voice that thunders fact and is more anxious to
be true than pleasing. There should be a campaign of tract distribution—
short well written facts and arguments—rained over this land by millions
of copies, particularly in the South, where the white people know less
about the Negro than in any other part of the civilized world. The press
should be utilized—the 400 Negro weeklies, the great dailies and eventually the magazines, when we get magazine editors who will lead public
opinion instead of following afar with resonant brays. Lectures, lantern-
slides and moving pictures, co-operating with a bureau of information
and eventually becoming a Negro encyclopedia, all these are efforts along
the line of making human beings realize that Negroes are human.

Such is the program of work against obstructions. Let us now turn to
constructive effort. This may be summed up under (1) economic co-
operation (2) a revival of art and literature (3) political action (4) education and (5) organization.

Under economic co-operation we must strive to spread the idea among
colored people that the accumulation of wealth is for social rather than
individual ends. We must avoid, in the advancement of the Negro race,
the mistakes of ruthless exploitation which have marked modern economic history. To this end we must seek not simply home ownership,

small landholding and saving accounts, but also all forms of co-operation, both in production and distribution, profit sharing, building and loan associations, systematic charity for definite, practical ends, systematic migration from mob rule and robbery, to freedom and enfranchisement, the emancipation of women and the abolition of child labor.

In art and literature we should try to loose the tremendous emotional wealth of the Negro and the dramatic strength of his problems through writing, the stage, pageantry and other forms of art. We should resurrect forgotten ancient Negro art and history, and we should set the black man before the world as both a creative artist and a strong subject for artistic treatment.

In political action we should organize the votes of Negroes in such congressional districts as have any number of Negro voters. We should systematically interrogate candidates on matters vital to Negro freedom and uplift. We should train colored voters to reject the bribe of office and to accept only decent legal enactments both for their own uplift and for the uplift of laboring classes of all races and both sexes.

In education we must seek to give colored children free public school training. We must watch with grave suspicion the attempt of those who, under the guise of vocational training, would fasten ignorance and menial service on the Negro for another generation. Our children must not in large numbers, be forced into the servant class; for menial service is still, in the main, little more than an antiquated survival of impossible conditions. It has always been as statistics show, a main cause of bastardy and prostitution and despite its many marvelous exceptions it will never come to the light of decency and honor until the house servant becomes the Servant in the House. It is our duty then, not drastically but persistently, to seek out colored children of ability and genius, to open up to them broader, industrial opportunity and above all, to find that Talented Tenth and encourage it by the best and most exhaustive training in order to supply the Negro race and the world with leaders, thinkers and artists.

For the accomplishment of all these ends we must organize. Organization among us already has gone far but it must go much further and higher. Organization is sacrifice. It is sacrifice of opinions, of time, of work and of money, but it is, after all, the cheapest way of buying the most priceless of gifts—freedom and efficiency. I thank God that most of the money that supports the National Association for the Advancement of Colored People comes from black hands; a still larger proportion must so come, and we must not only support but control this and similar organizations and hold them unwaveringly to our objects, our aims and our ideals.

MARCUS GARVEY

The True Solution of the Negro Problem (1922)

Marcus Garvey (1887–1940) was the father of twentieth-century black nationalism, which, in his writings and speeches, he often expressed in terms of a separatist rejection of integrationist strategy and ideals. A West Indian who came to the United States in 1916, Garvey exalted blackness, repudiating American cultural ideals that privileged whiteness. His message of pride and economic separatism appealed to urban blacks, of whom more than half a million in over thirty cities joined his Universal Negro Improvement Association. Many of his followers were particularly drawn to his "Back to Africa" plans. The selections here come from Garvey's writings of the early 1920s.

As far as Negroes are concerned, in America we have the problem of lynching, peonage and dis-franchisement.

In the West Indies, South and Central America we have the problem of peonage, serfdom, industrial and political governmental inequality.

In Africa we have, not only peonage and serfdom, but outright slavery, racial exploitation and alien political monopoly.

We cannot allow a continuation of these crimes against our race. As four hundred million men, women and children, worthy of the existence given us by the Divine Creator, we are determined to solve our own problem, by redeeming our Motherland Africa from the hands of alien exploiters and found there a government, a nation of our own, strong enough to lend protection to the members of our race scattered all over the world, and to compel the respect of the nations and races of the earth.

Do they lynch Englishmen, Frenchmen, Germans or Japanese? No. And Why? Because these people are represented by great governments, mighty nations and empires, strongly organized. Yes, and ever ready to shed the last drop of blood and spend the last penny in the national treasury to protect the honor and integrity of a citizen outraged anywhere.

Until the Negro reaches this point of national independence, all he does as a race will count for naught, because the prejudice that will stand out against him even with his ballot in his hand, with his industrial progress to

show, will be of such an overwhelming nature as to perpetuate mob violence and mob rule, from which he will suffer, and which he will not be
able to stop with his industrial wealth and with his ballot.

You may argue that he can use his industrial wealth and his ballot to
force the government to recognize him, but he must understand that the
government is the people. That the majority of the people dictate the policy of governments, and if the majority are against a measure, a thing, or
a race, then the government is impotent to protect that measure, thing or
race.

If the Negro were to live in this Western Hemisphere for another five
hundred years he would still be outnumbered by other races who are prejudiced against him. He cannot resort to the government for protection for
government will be in the hands of the majority of the people who are
prejudiced against him, hence for the Negro to depend on the ballot and
his industrial progress alone, will be hopeless as it does not help him
when he is lynched, burned, jim-crowed and segregated. The future of
the Negro therefore, outside of Africa, spells ruin and disaster. * * *

Generally the public is kept misinformed of the truth surrounding
new movements of reform. Very seldom, if ever, reformers get the truth
told about them and their movements. Because of this natural attitude,
the Universal Negro Improvement Association has been greatly handicapped in its work, causing thereby one of the most liberal and helpful
human movements of the twentieth century to be held up to ridicule by
those who take pride in poking fun at anything not already successfully
established.

The white man of America has become the natural leader of the world.
He, because of his exalted position, is called upon to help in all human
efforts. From nations to individuals the appeal is made to him for aid in
all things affecting humanity, so, naturally, there can be no great mass
movement or change without first acquainting the leader on whose sympathy and advice the world moves.

It is because of this, and more so because of a desire to be Christian
friends with the white race, why I explain the aims and objects of the
Universal Negro Improvement Association.

The Universal Negro Improvement Association is an organization
among Negroes that is seeking to improve the condition of the race, with
the view of establishing a nation in Africa where Negroes will be given
the opportunity to develop by themselves, without creating the hatred
and animosity that now exist in countries of the white race through Negroes rivaling them for the highest and best positions in government, politics, society and industry. The organization believes in the rights of all
men, yellow, white and black. To us, the white race has a right to the

peaceful possession and occupation of countries of its own and in like manner the yellow and black races have their rights. It is only by an honest and liberal consideration of such rights can the world be blessed with the peace that is sought by Christian teachers and leaders. * * *

The following preamble to the constitution of the organization speaks for itself:

> "The Universal Negro Improvement Association and African Communities' League is a social, friendly, humanitarian, charitable, educational, institutional, constructive, and expansive society, and is founded by persons, desiring to the utmost to work for the general uplift of the Negro peoples of the world. And the members pledge themselves to do all in their power to conserve the rights of their noble race and to respect the rights of all mankind, believing always in the Brotherhood of Man and the Fatherhood of God. The motto of the organization is: One God! One Aim! One Destiny! Therefore, let justice be done to all mankind, realizing that if the strong oppresses the weak confusion and discontent will ever mark the path of man, but with love, faith and charity toward all the reign of peace and plenty will be heralded into the world and the generation of men shall be called Blessed."

The declared objects of the association are:

> "To establish a Universal Confraternity among the race; to promote the spirit of pride and love; to reclaim the fallen; to administer to and assist the needy; to assist in civilizing the backward tribes of Africa; to assist in the development of Independent Negro Nations and Communities; to establish a central nation for the race; to establish Commissaries or Agencies in the principal countries and cities of the world for the representation of all Negroes; to promote a conscientious Spiritual worship among the native tribes of Africa; to establish Universities, Colleges, Academies and Schools for the racial education and culture of the people; to work for better conditions among Negroes everywhere."

The organization of the Universal Negro Improvement Association has supplied among Negroes a long-felt want. Hitherto the other Negro movements in America, with the exception of the Tuskegee effort of Booker T. Washington, sought to teach the Negro to aspire to social equality with the whites, meaning thereby the right to intermarry and fraternize in every social way. This has been the source of much trouble and still some Negro organizations continue to preach this dangerous "race destroying doctrine" added to a program of political agitation and aggression. The Universal Negro Improvement Association on the other hand believes in and teaches the pride and purity of race. We believe that the white race should uphold its racial pride and perpetuate itself, and that the black race should do likewise. We believe that there is room enough in the world for the various race groups to grow and develop by themselves without seeking to destroy the Creator's plan by the constant introduction of mongrel types.

The unfortunate condition of slavery as imposed upon the Negro, and which caused the mongrelization of the race, should not be legalized and continued now to the harm and detriment of both races.

The time has really come to give the Negro a chance to develop himself to a moral-standard-man, and it is for such an opportunity that the Universal Negro Improvement Association seeks in the creation of an African nation for Negroes, where the greatest latitude would be given to work out this racial ideal.

There are hundreds of thousands of colored people in America who desire race amalgamation and miscegenation as a solution of the race problem. These people are, therefore, opposed to the race pride ideas of black and white; but the thoughtful of both races will naturally ignore the ravings of such persons and honestly work for the solution of a problem that has been forced upon us.

Liberal white America and race loving Negroes are bound to think at this time and thus evolve a program or plan by which there can be a fair and amicable settlement of the question.

We cannot put off the consideration of the matter, for time is pressing on our hands. The educated Negro is making rightful constitutional demands. The great white majority will never grant them, and thus we march on to danger if we do not now stop and adjust the matter.

The time is opportune to regulate the relationship between both races. Let the Negro have a country of his own. Help him to return to his original home, Africa, and there give him the opportunity to climb from the lowest to the highest positions in a state of his own. If not, then the nation will have to hearken to the demand of the aggressive, "social equality" organization, known as the National Association for the Advancement of Colored People, of which W. E. B. Du Bois is leader, which declares vehemently for social and political equality, viz.: Negroes and whites in the same hotels, homes, residential districts, public and private places, a Negro as president, members of the Cabinet, Governors of States, Mayors of cities, and leaders of society in the United States. In this agitation, DuBois is ably supported by the "Chicago Defender," a colored newspaper published in Chicago. This paper advocates Negroes in the Cabinet and Senate. All these, as everybody knows, are the Negroes' constitutional rights, but reason dictates that the masses of the white race will never stand by the ascendency of an opposite minority group to the favored positions in a government, society and industry that exist by the will of the majority, hence the demand of the Du Bois group of colored leaders will only lead, ultimately, to further disturbances in riots, lynching and mob rule. The only logical solution therefore, is to supply the Negro with opportunities and environments of his own, and there[by] point him to the fullness of his ambition. * * *

The Negro who seeks the White House in America could find ample play for his ambition in Africa. The Negro who seeks the office of Secretary of State in America would have a fair chance of demonstrating his diplomacy in Africa. The Negro who seeks a seat in the Senate or of being governor of a State in America, would be provided with a glorious chance for statesmanship in Africa.

The Negro has a claim on American white sympathy that cannot be denied. The Negro has labored for 300 years in contributing to America's greatness. White America will not be unmindful, therefore, of this consideration, but will treat him kindly. Yet it is realized that all human beings have a limit to their humanity. The humanity of white America, we realize, will seek self-protection and self-preservation, and that is why the thoughtful and reasonable Negro sees no hope in America for satisfying the aggressive program of the National Association for the Advancement of Colored People, but advances the reasonable plan of the Universal Negro Improvement Association, that of creating in Africa a nation and government for the Negro race.

This plan when properly undertaken and prosecuted will solve the race problem in America in fifty years. Africa affords a wonderful opportunity at the present time for colonization by the Negroes of the Western world. There is Liberia, already established as an independent Negro government. Let white America assist Afro-Americans to go there and help develop the country. Then, there are the late German colonies; let white sentiment force England and France to turn them over to the American and West Indian Negroes who fought for the Allies in the World's War. Then, France, England and Belgium owe America billions of dollars which they claim they cannot afford to repay immediately. Let them compromise by turning over Sierra Leone and the Ivory Coast on the West Coast of Africa and add them to Liberia and help make Liberia a state worthy of her history.

The Negroes of Africa and America are one in blood. They have sprung from the same common stock. They can work and live together and thus make their own racial contribution to the world.

Will deep thinking and liberal white America help? It is a considerate duty.

It is true that a large number of self-seeking colored agitators and so-called political leaders, who hanker after social equality and fight for the impossible in politics and governments, will rave, but remember that the slave-holder raved, but the North said, "Let the slaves go free"; the British Parliament raved when the Colonists said, "We want a free and American nation"; the Monarchists of France raved when the people declared for a more liberal form of government.

The masses of Negroes think differently from the self-appointed leaders of the race. The majority of Negro leaders are selfish, self-appointed and not elected by the people. The people desire freedom in a land of their own, while the colored politician desires office and social equality for himself in America, and that is why we are asking white America to help the masses to realize their objective. * * *

Surely the time has come for the Negro to look homeward. He has won civilization and Christianity at the price of slavery. The Negro who is thoughtful and serviceable, feels that God intended him to give to his brothers still in darkness, the light of his civilization. The very light element of Negroes do not want to go back to Africa. They believe that in time, through miscegenation, the American race will be of their type. This is a fallacy and in that respect the agitation of the mulatto leader, Dr. W. E. B. DuBois and the National Association for the Advancement of Colored People is dangerous to both races.

The off-colored people, being children of the Negro race, should combine to re-establish the purity of their own race, rather than seek to perpetuate the abuse of both races. That is to say, all elements of the Negro race should be encouraged to get together and form themselves into a healthy whole, rather than seeking to lose their identities through miscegenation and social intercourse with the white race. These statements are made because we desire an honest solution of the problem and no flattery or deception will bring that about.

Let the white and Negro people settle down in all seriousness and in true sympathy and solve the problem. When that is done, a new day of peace and good will will be ushered in.

The natural opponents among Negroes to a program of this kind are that lazy element who believe always in following the line of least resistance, being of themselves void of initiative and the pioneering spirit to do for themselves. The professional Negro leader and the class who are agitating for social equality feel that it is too much work for them to settle down and build up a civilization of their own. They feel it is easier to seize on to the civilization of the white man and under the guise of constitutional rights fight for those things that the white man has created. Natural reason suggests that the white man will not yield them, hence such leaders are but fools for their pains. Teach the Negro to do for himself, help him the best way possible in that direction; but to encourage him into the belief that he is going to possess himself of the things that others have fought and died for, is to build up in his mind false hopes never to be realized. As for instance, Dr. W. E. B. DuBois, who has been educated by white charity, is a brilliant scholar, but he is not a hard worker. He prefers to use his higher intellectual abilities to fight for a place among white men in society, industry and in politics, rather than use that ability to work and create for his own race that which the race could be able to take credit for. He would not think of repeating for his race the work of the Pilgrim Fathers or the Colonists who laid the foundation of America, but he prefers to fight and agitate for the privilege of dancing with a white lady at a ball at the Biltmore or at the Astoria hotels in New York. That kind of leadership will destroy the Negro in America and against which the Universal Negro Improvement Association is fighting.

The Universal Negro Improvement Association is composed of all shades of Negroes—blacks, mulattoes and yellows, who are all working honestly for the purification of their race, and for a sympathetic adjustment of the race problem.

HIRAM W. EVANS

The Klan's Fight for Americanism (1926)

Hiram W. Evans (1881–1966), from Alabama and Texas, was a former dentist who was the Imperial Wizard of the Ku Klux Klan from 1922 to 1939. The racist Klan leader believed that America was under attack by liberal intellectuals and foreign immigrants. In this selection, published originally as an article in The North American Review, *Evans claimed that the Klan represented a populist "protest movement" against the distressing political, economic, and cultural changes that had displaced "Nordic Americans" from the positions they once occupied.*

The Klan * * * has now come to speak for the great mass of Americans of the old pioneer stock. We believe that it does fairly and faithfully represent them, and our proof lies in their support. To understand the Klan, then, it is necessary to understand the character and present mind of the mass of old-stock Americans. The mass, it must be remembered, as distinguished from the intellectually mongrelized "Liberals".

These are, in the first place, a blend of various peoples of the so-called Nordic race, the race which, with all its faults, has given the world almost the whole of modern civilization. The Klan does not try to represent any people but these.

There is no need to recount the virtues of the American pioneers; but it is too often forgotten that in the pioneer period a selective process of intense rigor went on. From the first only hardy, adventurous and strong men and women dared the pioneer dangers; from among these all but the best died swiftly, so that the new Nordic blend which became the American race was bred up to a point probably the highest in history. This remarkable race character, along with the new-won continent and the new-created nation, made the inheritance of the old-stock Americans the richest ever given to a generation of men.

In spite of it, however, these Nordic Americans for the last generation have found themselves increasingly uncomfortable, and finally deeply distressed. There appeared first confusion in thought and opinion, a groping and hesitancy about national affairs and private life alike, in sharp contrast to the clear, straightforward purposes of our earlier years. There was futility in religion, too, which was in many ways even more distressing. Presently we began to find that we were dealing with strange ideas; policies that always sounded well, but somehow always made us still more uncomfortable.

Finally came the moral breakdown that has been going on for two decades. One by one all our traditional moral standards went by the boards, or were so disregarded that they ceased to be binding. The sacredness of our Sabbath, of our homes, of chastity, and finally even of our right to teach our own children in our own schools fundamental facts and truths were torn away from us. Those who maintained the old standards did so only in the face of constant ridicule.

Along with this went economic distress. The assurance for the future of our children dwindled. We found our great cities and the control of much of our industry and commerce taken over by strangers, who stacked the cards of success and prosperity against us. Shortly they came to dominate our government. The *bloc* system by which this was done is now familiar to all. Every kind of inhabitant except the Americans gathered in groups which operated as units in politics, under orders of corrupt, self-seeking and un-American leaders, who both by purchase and threat enforced their demands on politicians. Thus it came about that the interests of Americans were always the last to be considered by either national or city governments, and that the native Americans were constantly discriminated against, in business, in legislation and in administrative government.

So the Nordic American today is a stranger in large parts of the land his fathers gave him. Moreover, he is a most unwelcome stranger, one much spit upon, and one to whom even the right to have his own opinions and to work for his own interests is now denied with jeers and revilings. "We must Americanize the Americans," a distinguished immigrant said recently. Can anything more clearly show the state to which the real American has fallen in this country which was once his own?

* * *

All this has been true for years, but it was the World War that gave us our first hint of the real cause of our troubles, and began to crystallize our ideas. The war revealed that millions whom we had allowed to share our heritage and prosperity, and whom we had assumed had become part of us, were in fact not wholly so. They had other loyalties: each was willing—anxious!—to sacrifice the interests of the country that had given him shelter to the interests of the one he was supposed to have cast off; each in fact did use the freedom and political power we had given him against ourselves whenever he could see any profit for his older loyalty.

This, of course, was chiefly in international affairs, and the excitement caused by the discovery of disloyalty subsided rapidly after the war ended. But it was not forgotten by the Nordic Americans. They had been awakened and alarmed; they began to suspect that the hyphenism which had been shown was only a part of what existed; their quiet was not that of renewed sleep, but of strong men waiting very watchfully. And presently they began to form decisions about all those aliens who were Americans for profit only.

They decided that even the crossing of salt water did not dim a single spot on a leopard; that an alien usually remains an alien no matter what is done to him, what veneer of education he gets, what oaths he takes, nor what public attitudes he adopts. They decided that the melting pot was a ghastly failure, and remembered that the very name was coined by a member of one of the races—the Jews—which most determinedly refuses to melt. They decided that in every way, as well as in politics, the alien in the vast majority of cases is unalterably fixed in his instincts, character, thought and interests by centuries of racial selection and development, that he thinks first for his own people, works only with and for them, cares entirely for their interests, considers himself always one of them, and never an American. They decided that in character, instincts, thought, and purposes—in his whole soul—an alien remains fixedly alien to America and all it means.

They saw, too, that the alien was tearing down the American standard of living, especially in the lower walks. It became clear that while the American can out-work the alien, the alien can so far under-live the American as to force him out of all competetive labor. So they came to realize that the Nordic can easily survive and rule and increase if he holds for himself the advantages won by strength and daring of his ancestors in times of stress and peril, but that if he surrenders those advantages to the peoples who could not share the stress, he will soon be driven below the level at which he can exist by their low standards, low living and fast breeding. And they saw that the low standard aliens of Eastern and Southern Europe were doing just that thing to us.

They learned, though more slowly, that alien ideas are just as dangerous to us as the aliens themselves, no matter how plausible such ideas may sound. With most of the plain people this conclusion is based simply on the fact that the alien ideas do not work well for them. Others went deeper and came to understand that the differences in racial background, in breeding, instinct, character and emotional point of view are more important than logic. So ideas which may be perfectly healthy for an alien may also be poisonous for Americans.

Finally they learned the great secret of the propagandists; that success in corrupting public opinion depends on putting out the subversive ideas without revealing their source. They came to suspect that "prejudice" against foreign ideas is really a protective device of nature against mental food that may be indigestible. They saw, finally, that the alien leaders in America act on this theory, and that there is a steady flood of alien ideas being spread over the country, always carefully disguised as American.

As they learned all this the Nordic Americans have been gradually arousing themselves to defend their homes and their own kind of civilization. They have not known just how to go about it; the idealist philanthropy and good-natured generosity which led to the philosophy of the melting pot have died hard. Resistance to the peaceful invasion of the immigrant is no such simple matter as snatching up weapons and defending frontiers, nor has it much spectacular emotionalism to draw men to the colors.

The old-stock Americans are learning, however. They have begun to arm themselves for this new type of warfare. Most important, they have broken away from the fetters of the false ideals and philanthropy which put aliens ahead of their own children and their own race.

To do this they have had to reject completely—and perhaps for the moment the rejection is a bit too complete—the whole body of "Liberal" ideas which they had followed with such simple, unquestioning faith. The first and immediate cause of the break with Liberalism was that it had provided no defense against the alien invasion, but instead had excused it—even defended it against Americanism. Liberalism is today charged in the mind of most Americans with nothing less than national, racial and spiritual treason.

* * *

We are a movement of the plain people, very weak in the matter of culture, intellectual support, and trained leadership. We are demanding, and we expect to win, a return of power into the hands of the everyday, not highly cultured, not overly intellectualized, but entirely unspoiled and not de-Americanized, average citizen of the old stock. Our members and leaders are all of this class—the opposition of the intellectuals and liberals who held the leadership, betrayed Americanism, and from whom we expect to wrest control, is almost automatic.

This is undoubtedly a weakness. It lays us open to the charge of being "hicks" and "rubes" and "drivers of second hand Fords". We admit it. Far worse, it makes it hard for us to state our case and advocate our crusade in the most effective way, for most of us lack skill in language. Worst of all, the need of trained leaders constantly hampers our progress and leads to serious blunders and internal troubles. If the Klan ever should fail it would be from this cause. All this we on the inside know far better than our critics, and regret more. Our leadership is improving, but for many years the Klan will be seeking better leaders, and the leaders praying for greater wisdom.

Serious as this is, and strange though our attitude may seem to the intellectuals, it does not worry us greatly. Every popular movement has suffered from just this handicap, yet the popular movements have been the mainsprings of progress, and have usually had to win against the "best people" of their time. Moreover, we can depend on getting this intellectual backing shortly. It is notable that when the plain people begin to win with one of their movements, such as the Klan, the very intellectuals who have scoffed and fought most bitterly presently begin to dig up sound—at least well-sounding!—logic in support of the success. The movement, so far as can be judged, is neither hurt nor helped by this process.

* * *

Our critics have accused us of being merely a "protest movement", of being frightened; they say we fear alien competition, are in a panic because we cannot hold our own against the foreigners. That is partly true. We are a protest movement—protesting against being robbed. We are afraid of competition with peoples who would destroy our standard of living. We are suffering in many ways, we have been betrayed by our trusted leaders, we are half beaten already. But we are not frightened nor in a panic. We have merely awakened to the fact that we must fight for our own. We are going to fight—and win!

The Klan does not believe that the fact that it is emotional and instinctive, rather than coldly intellectual, is a weakness. All action comes from
emotion, rather than from ratiocination. Our emotions and the instincts
on which they are based have been bred into us for thousands of years; far
longer than reason has had a place in the human brain. They are the many-
times distilled product of experience; they still operate much more surely
and promptly than reason can. For centuries those who obeyed them have
lived and carried on the race; those in whom they were weak, or who failed
to obey, have died. They are the foundations of our American civilization,
even more than our great historic documents; they can be trusted where
the fine-haired reasoning of the denatured intellectuals cannot.

LANGSTON HUGHES

Let America Be America Again (1938)

*One of the most important black writers of the twentieth century,
Langston Hughes (1902–1967) was a poet, playwright, and essayist. He
was a central figure in New York City's Harlem Rennaissance, the black
literary and cultural explosion of the 1920s and the 1930s. In this, perhaps his most famous poem, originally published in Esquire magazine
and in the International Workers Order pamphlet A New Song, Hughes
writes of the freedom and equality about which America boasts, but
which it never realizes. This recurring theme resonates from Frederick
Douglass to Martin Luther King, Jr., and Malcolm X.*

> Let America be America again.
> Let it be the dream it used to be.
> Let it be the pioneer on the plain
> Seeking a home where he himself is free.
>
> (America never was America to me.)
>
> Let America be the dream the dreamers dreamed—
> Let it be that great strong land of love
> Where never kings connive nor tyrants scheme
> That any man be crushed by one above.
>
> (It never was America to me.)

O, let my land be a land where Liberty
Is crowned with no false patriotic wreath,
But opportunity is real, and life is free,
Equality is in the air we breathe.

(There's never been equality for me,
Nor freedom in this "homeland of the free.")

Say, who are you that mumbles in the dark?
And who are you that draws your veil across the stars?

I am the poor white, fooled and pushed apart,
I am the Negro bearing slavery's scars.
I am the red man driven from the land,
I am the immigrant clutching the hope I seek—
And finding only the same old stupid plan
Of dog eat dog, of mighty crush the weak.

I am the young man, full of strength and hope,
Tangled in that ancient endless chain
Of profit, power, gain, of grab the land!
Of grab the gold! Of grab the ways of satisfying need!
Of work the men! Of take the pay!
Of owning everything for one's own greed!

I am the farmer, bondsman to the soil.
I am the worker sold to the machine.
I am the Negro, servant to you all.
I am the people, humble, hungry, mean—
Hungry yet today despite the dream.
Beaten yet today—O, Pioneers!
I am the man who never got ahead,
The poorest worker bartered through the years.

Yet I'm the one who dreamt our basic dream
In the Old World while still a serf of kings,
Who dreamt a dream so strong, so brave, so true,
That even yet its mighty daring sings
In every brick and stone, in every furrow turned
That's made America the land it has become.
O, I'm the man who sailed those early seas
In search of what I meant to be my home—
For I'm the one who left dark Ireland's shore,
And Poland's plain, and England's grassy lea,
And torn from Black Africa's strand I came

To build a "homeland of the free."

The free?

Who said the free? Not me?
Surely not me? The millions on relief today?
The millions shot down when we strike?
The millions who have nothing for our pay?
For all the dreams we've dreamed
And all the songs we've sung
And all the hopes we've held
And all the flags we've hung,
The millions who have nothing for our pay—
Except the dream that's almost dead today.

O, let America be America again—
The land that never has been yet—
And yet must be—the land where *every* man is free.
The land that's mine—the poor man's, Indian's, Negro's, ME—
Who made America,
Whose sweat and blood, whose faith and pain,
Whose hand at the foundry, whose plow in the rain,
Must bring back our mighty dream again.

Sure, call me any ugly name you choose—
The steel of freedom does not stain.
From those who live like leeches on the people's lives,
We must take back our land again,
America!

O, yes,
I say it plain,
America never was America to me,
And yet I swear this oath—
America will be!

Out of the rack and ruin of our gangster death,
The rape and rot of graft, and stealth, and lies,
We, the people, must redeem
The land, the mines, the plants, the rivers.
The mountains and the endless plain—
All, all the stretch of these great green states—
And make America again!

The Progressive Era

LINCOLN STEFFENS

The Shame of the Cities (1904)

The muckraking journalist Lincoln Joseph Steffens (1866–1936) was a reporter for the New York Evening Post, *an editor for the* Commercial Advertiser, *and the managing editor of* McClure's Magazine. *Steffens's influential* McClure's *articles on municipal corruption, which were later published as* The Shame of the Cities, *were based on his extensive travels to cities throughout the United States. In his introduction to the book he argued that "politics is business" and that until the demand for good government increased, businessmen would continue to see politics as a way to promote their self-interest at the expense of the public good.*

This is not a book. It is a collection of articles reprinted from *McClure's Magazine*. Done as journalism, they are journalism still, and no further pretensions are set up for them in their new dress. * * * They were written with a purpose, they were published serially with a purpose, and they are reprinted now together to further that same purpose, which was and is—to sound for the civic pride of an apparently shameless citizenship.

There must be such a thing, we reasoned. All our big boasting could not be empty vanity, nor our pious pretensions hollow sham. American achievements in science, art, and business mean sound abilities at bottom, and our hypocrisy a race sense of fundamental ethics. Even in government we have given proofs of potential greatness, and our political failures are not complete; they are simply ridiculous. But they are ours. Not alone the triumphs and the statesmen, the defeats and the grafters also represent us, and just as truly. Why not see it so and say it?

Because, I heard, the American people won't "stand for" it. You may blame the politicians, or, indeed, any one class, but not all classes, not the people. Or you may put it on the ignorant foreign immigrant, or any one nationality, but not on all nationalities, not on the American people. But no one class is at fault, nor any one breed, nor any particular interest or group of interests. The misgovernment of the American people is misgovernment by the American people.

When I set out on my travels, an honest New Yorker told me honestly that I would find that the Irish, the Catholic Irish, were at the bottom of it all everywhere. The first city I went to was St. Louis, a German city. The next was Minneapolis, a Scandinavian city, with a leadership of New Englanders. Then came Pittsburg, Scotch Presbyterian, and that was what my New York friend was. "Ah, but they are all foreign populations," I heard. The next city was Philadelphia, the purest American community of all, and the most hopeless. And after that came Chicago and New York, both mongrel-bred, but the one a triumph of reform, the other the best example of good government that I had seen. The "foreign element" excuse is one of the hypocritical lies that save us from the clear sight of ourselves.

Another such conceit of our egotism is that which deplores our politics and lauds our business. This is the wail of the typical American citizen. Now, the typical American citizen is the business man. The typical business man is a bad citizen; he is busy. If he is a "big business man" and very busy, he does not neglect, he is busy with politics, oh, very busy and very businesslike. I found him buying boodlers in St. Louis, defending grafters in Minneapolis, originating corruption in Pittsburg, sharing with bosses in Philadelphia, deploring reform in Chicago, and beating good government with corruption funds in New York. He is a self-righteous fraud, this big business man. He is the chief source of corruption, and it were a boon if he would neglect politics. But he is not the business man that neglects politics; that worthy is the good citizen, the typical business man. He too is busy, he is the one that has no use and therefore no time for politics. When his neglect has permitted bad government to go so far that he can be stirred to action, he is unhappy, and he looks around for a cure that shall be quick, so that he may hurry back to the shop. Naturally, too, when he talks politics, he talks shop. His patent remedy is quack; it is business.

"Give us a business man," he says ("like me," he means). "Let him introduce business methods into politics and government; then I shall be left alone to attend to my business."

There is hardly an office from United States Senator down to Alderman in any part of the country to which the business man has not been elected; yet politics remains corrupt, government pretty bad, and the selfish citizen has to hold himself in readiness like the old volunteer firemen to rush forth at any hour, in any weather, to prevent the fire; and he goes out sometimes and he puts out the fire (after the damage is done) and he goes back to the shop sighing for the business man in politics. The business man has failed in politics as he has in citizenship. Why?

Because politics is business. That's what's the matter with it. That's what's the matter with everything,—art, literature, religion, journalism, law, medicine,—they're all business, and all—as you see them. Make politics a sport, as they do in England, or a profession, as they do in Germany, and we'll have—well, something else than we have now,—if we want it, which is another question. But don't try to reform politics with the banker, the lawyer, and the dry-goods merchant, for these are business men and there are two great hindrances to their achievement of reform: one is that they are different from, but no better than, the politicians; the other is that politics is not "their line." There are exceptions both ways. Many politicians have gone out into business and done well (Tammany ex-mayors, and nearly all the old bosses of Philadelphia are prominent financiers in their cities), and business men have gone into politics and done well (Mark Hanna, for example). They haven't reformed their adopted trades, however, though they have sometimes sharpened them most pointedly. The politician is a business man with a specialty. When a business man of some other line learns the business of politics, he is a politician, and there is not much reform left in him. Consider the United States Senate, and believe me.

The commercial spirit is the spirit of profit, not patriotism; of credit, not honor; of individual gain, not national prosperity; of trade and dickering, not principle. "My business is sacred," says the business man in his heart. "Whatever prospers my business, is good; it must be. Whatever hinders it, is wrong; it must be. A bribe is bad, that is, it is a bad thing to take; but it is not so bad to give one, not if it is necessary to my business." "Business is business" is not a political sentiment, but our politician has caught it. He takes essentially the same view of the bribe, only he saves his self-respect by piling all his contempt upon the bribe-giver, and he has the great advantage of candor. "It is wrong, maybe," he says, "but if a rich merchant can afford to do business with me for the sake of a convenience or to increase his already great wealth, I can afford, for the sake of a living, to meet him half way. I make no pretensions to virtue, not even on Sunday."

And as for giving bad government or good, how about the merchant who gives bad goods or good goods, according to the demand?

But there is hope, not alone despair, in the commercialism of our politics. If our political leaders are to be always a lot of political merchants, they will supply any demand we may create. All we have to do is to establish a steady demand for good government. The boss has us split up into parties. To him parties are nothing but means to his corrupt ends. He "bolts" his party, but we must not; the bribe-giver changes his party, from one election to another, from one county to another, from one city to another, but the honest voter must not. Why? Because if the honest voter cared no more for his party than the politician and the grafter, then the honest vote would govern, and that would be bad—for graft. It is idiotic, this devotion to a machine that is used to take our sovereignty from us. If we would leave parties to the politicians, and would vote not for the party, not even for men, but for the city, and the State, and the nation, we should rule parties, and cities, and States, and nation. If we would vote in mass on the more promising ticket, or, if the two are equally bad, would throw out the party that is in, and wait till the next election and then throw out the other party that is in—then, I say, the commercial politician would feel a demand for good government and he would supply it. That process would take a generation or more to complete, for the politicians now really do not know what good government is. But it has taken as long to develop bad government, and the politicians know what that is. If it would not "go," they would offer something else, and, if the demand were steady, they, being so commercial, would "deliver the goods."

But do the people want good government? Tammany says they don't. Are the people honest? Are the people better than Tammany? Are they better than the merchant and the politician? Isn't our corrupt government, after all, representative?

President Roosevelt has been sneered at for going about the country preaching, as a cure for our American evils, good conduct in the individual, simple honesty, courage, and efficiency. "Platitudes!" the sophisticated say. Platitudes? If my observations have been true, the literal adoption of Mr. Roosevelt's reform scheme would result in a revolution, more radical and terrible to existing institutions, from the Congress to the Church, from the bank to the ward organization, than socialism or even than anarchy. Why, that would change all of us—not alone our neighbors, not alone the grafters, but you and me.

No, the contemned methods of our despised politics are the master methods of our braggart business, and the corruption that shocks us in public affairs we practice ourselves in our private concerns. There is no essential difference between the pull that gets your wife into society or a favorable review for your book, and that which gets a heeler into office, a thief out of jail, and a rich man's son on the board of directors of a corporation; none between the corruption of a labor union, a bank, and a political machine; none between a dummy director of a trust and the caucus-bound member of a legislature; none between a labor boss like Sam Parks, a boss of banks like John D. Rockefeller, a boss of railroads like J. P. Morgan, and a political boss like Matthew S. Quay. The boss is not a political, he is an American institution, the product of a freed people that have not the spirit to be free.

And it's all a moral weakness; a weakness right where we think we are strongest. Oh, we are good—on Sunday, and we are "fearfully patriotic" on the Fourth of July. But the bribe we pay to the janitor to prefer our interests to the landlord's, is the little brother of the bribe passed to the alderman to sell a city street, and the father of the air-brake stock assigned to the president of a railroad to have this life-saving invention adopted on his road. And as for graft, railroad passes, saloon and bawdy-house blackmail, and watered stock, all these belong to the same family. We are pathetically proud of our democratic institutions and our republican form of government, of our grand Constitution and our just laws. We are a free and sovereign people, we govern ourselves and the government is ours. But that is the point. We are responsible, not our leaders, since we follow them. We *let* them divert our loyalty from the United States to some "party"; we *let* them boss the party and turn our municipal democracies into autocracies and our republican nation into a plutocracy. We cheat our govenment and we let our leaders loot it, and we let them wheedle and bribe our sovereignty from us. True, they pass for us strict laws, but we are content to let them pass also bad laws, giving away public property in exchange; and our good, and often impossible, laws we allow to be used for oppression and blackmail. And what can we say? We break our own laws and rob our own government, the lady at the custom-house, the lyncher with his rope, and the captain of industry with his bribe and his rebate. The spirit of graft and of lawlessness is the American spirit. * * *

We Americans may have failed. We may be mercenary and selfish. Democracy with us may be impossible and corruption inevitable, but these articles, if they have proved nothing else, have demonstrated beyond doubt that we can stand the truth; that there is pride in the character of American citizenship; and that this pride may be a power in the land. So this little volume, a record of shame and yet of self-respect, a disgraceful confession, yet a declaration of honor, is dedicated, in all good faith, to the accused—to all the citizens of all the cities in the United States.

UPTON SINCLAIR

The Jungle (1906)

The social reformer Upton Beall Sinclair, Jr. (1878–1968), was a prolific writer of novels, essays, and nonfiction books such as the "Dead Hand" series, which exposed what he saw as the noxious effects of capitalism and political corruption. Sinclair, who made an unsuccessful run for the governorship of California in 1934, is best known for his dramatic exposé of the meat-packing industry in Chicago. His novel The Jungle *dramatized the squalor and dangers of working conditions in the "Beef Trust." Told through the story of the Lithuanian immigrant Jurgis Rudkus, it contributed to the passage of the first Pure Food Act.*

There was scarcely a thing needed in the business that Durham and Company did not make for themselves. There was a great steam-power plant and an electricity plant. There was a barrel factory, and a boiler-repair shop. There was a building to which the grease was piped, and made into soap and lard; and then there was a factory for making lard cans, and another for making soap boxes. There was a building in which the bristles were cleaned and dried, for the making of hair cushions and such things; there was a building where the skins were dried and tanned, there was another where heads and feet were made into glue, and another where bones were made into fertilizer. No tiniest particle of organic matter was wasted in Durham's. Out of the horns of the cattle they made combs, buttons, hair-pins, and imitation ivory; out of the shin bones and other big bones they cut knife and tooth-brush handles, and mouth-pieces for pipes; out of the hoofs they cut hair-pins and buttons, before they had made the rest into glue. From such things as feet, knuckles, hide clippings, and sinews came such strange and unlikely products as gelatin, isinglass, and phosphorus, bone-black, shoe-blacking, and bone-oil. They had curled-hair works for the cattle-tails, and a "wool-pullery" for the sheep skins; they made pepsin from the stomachs of the pigs, and albumen from the blood, and violin strings from the ill-smelling entrails. When there was nothing else to be done with a thing, they first put it into a tank and got out of it all the tallow and grease, and then they made it into fertilizer. All these industries were gathered into buildings near by, connected by galleries and railroads with the main establishment; and it was estimated that they had handled nearly a quarter of a billion of animals since the founding of the plant by the elder Durham a generation or more ago. If you counted with it the other big plants—and they were now really all one—it was, so Jokubas informed them, the greatest aggregation of labor and capital ever gathered in one place. It employed thirty thousand men; it supported directly two hundred and fifty thousand people in its neighborhood, and indirectly it supported half a million. It sent its products to every country in the civilized world, and it furnished the food for no less than thirty million people!

To all these things our friends would listen open mouthed—it seemed to them impossible of belief that anything so stupendous could have been devised by mortal man. That was why to Jurgis it seemed almost profanity to speak about the place as did Jokubas, sceptically; it was a thing as tremendous as the universe—the laws and ways of its working no more than the universe to be questioned or understood. All that a mere man could do, it seemed to Jurgis, was to take a thing like this as he found it, and do as he was told; to be given a place in it and to share in its wonderful activities was a blessing to be grateful for, as one was grateful for the sunshine and the rain. Jurgis was even glad that he had not seen the place before meeting with his triumph, for he felt that the size of it would have overwhelmed him. But now he had been admitted— he was a part of it all! He had the feeling that this whole huge establishment had taken him under his protection, and had become responsible for his welfare. So guileless was he, and ignorant of the nature of business, that he did not even realize that he had become an employee of Brown's and that Brown and Durham were supposed by all the world to be deadly rivals—were even required to be deadly rivals by the law of the land, and ordered to try to ruin each other under penalty of fine and imprisonment! * * *

And there were things ever stranger than this, according to the gossip of the men. The packers had secret mains, through which they stole billions of gallons of the city's water. The newspapers had been full of this scandal—and once there had been an investigation, and an actual uncovering of the pipes; but nobody had been punished, and the thing went right on. And then there was the condemned meat industry, with its endless horrors. The people of Chicago saw the government inspectors in Packingtown, and they all took that to mean that they were protected from diseased meat; they did not understand that these hundred and sixty-three inspectors had been appointed at the request of the packers, and that they were paid by the United States government to certify that all the diseased meat was kept in the state. They had no authority beyond that; for the inspection of meat to be sold in the city and state the whole force in Packingtown consisted of three henchmen of the local political machine! And shortly afterward one of these, a physician, made the discovery that the carcasses of steers which had been condemned as tubercular by the government inspectors, and which therefore contained ptomaines, which are deadly poisons, were left upon an open platform and carted away to be sold in the city; and he insisted that these carcasses be treated with an injection of kerosene—and was ordered to resign the same week! So indignant were the packers that they went farther, and compelled the mayor to abolish the whole bureau of inspection; so that since then there has not been even a pretence of any interference with the graft. There was said to be two thousand dollars a week hush-money from the tubercular steers alone; and as much again from the hogs which had died of cholera on the trains, and which you might see any day being loaded into box-cars and hauled away to a place called Globe, in Indiana, where they made a fancy grade of lard.

There were the men in the pickle-rooms, for instance, where old Antanas had gotten his death; scarce a one of these that had not some spot of horror on his person. Let a man so much as scrape his finger pushing a truck in the pickle-rooms, and he might have a sore that would put him out of the world; all the joints in his fingers might be eaten by the acid, one by one. Of the butchers and floorsmen, the beef-boners and trimmers, and all those who used knives, you could scarcely find a person who had the use of his thumb; time and time again the base of it had been slashed, till it was a mere lump of flesh against which the man pressed the knife to hold it. The hands of these men would be criss-crossed with cuts, until you could no longer pretend to count them or to trace them. They would have no nails,—they had worn them off pulling hides; their knuckles were swollen so that their fingers spread out like a fan. There were men who worked in the cooking-rooms, in the midst of steam and sickening odors, by artificial light; in these rooms the germs of tuberculosis might live for two years, but the supply was renewed every hour. There were the beef-luggers, who carried two-hundred-pound quarters into the refrigerator-cars; a fearful kind of work, that began at four o'clock in the morning, and that wore out the most powerful men in a few years. There were those who worked in the chilling-rooms, and whose special disease was rheumatism; the time-limit that a man could work in the chilling-rooms was said to be five years. There were the wool-pluckers, whose hands went to pieces even sooner than the hands of the pickle-men; for the pelts of the sheep had to be painted with acid to loosen the wool, and then the pluckers had to pull out this wool with their bare hands, till the acid had eaten their fingers off. There were those who made the tins for the canned-meat; and their hands, too, were a maze of cuts, and each cut represented a chance for blood-poisoning. Some worked at the stamping-machines, and it was very seldom that one could work long there at the pace that was set, and not give out and forget himself, and have a part of his hand chopped off. There were the "hoisters," as they were called, whose task it was to press the lever which lifted the dead cattle off the floor. They ran along upon a rafter, peering down through the damp and the steam; and as old Durham's architects had not built the killing-room for the convenience of the hoisters, at every few feet they would have to stoop under a beam, say four feet above the one they ran on; which got them into the habit of stooping, so that in a few years they would be walking like chimpanzees. Worst of any, however, were the fertilizer-men, and those who served in the cooking-rooms. These people could not be shown to the visitor,—for the odor of a fertilizer-man would scare any ordinary visitor at a hundred yards, and as for the other men, who worked in tank-rooms full of steam, and in some of which there were open vats near the level of the floor, their peculiar trouble was that they fell into the vats; and when they were fished out, there was never enough of them left to be worth exhibiting,—sometimes they would be overlooked for days, till all but the bones of them had gone out to the world as Durham's Pure Leaf Lard! * * *

With one member trimming beef in a cannery, and another working in a sausage factory, the family had a first-hand knowledge of the great majority of Packingtown swindles. For it was the custom, as they found, whenever meat was so spoiled that it could not be used for anything else, either to can it or else to chop it up into sausage. With what had been told them by Jonas, who had worked in the pickle-rooms, they could now study the whole of the spoiled-meat industry on the inside, and read a new and grim meaning into that old Packingtown jest,—that they used everything of the pig except the squeal.

Jonas had told them how the meat that was taken out of pickle would often be found sour, and how they would rub it up with soda to take away the smell, and sell it to be eaten on free-lunch counters; also of all the miracles of chemistry which they performed, giving to any sort of meat, fresh or salted, whole or chopped, any color and any flavor and any odor they chose. In the pickling of hams they had an ingenious apparatus, by which they saved time and increased the capacity of the plant—a machine consisting of a hollow needle attached to a pump; by plunging this needle into the meat and working with his foot, a man could fill a ham with pickle in a few seconds. And yet, in spite of this, there would be hams found spoiled, some of them with an odor so bad that a man could hardly bear to be in the room with them. To pump into these the packers had a second and much stronger pickle which destroyed the odor—a process known to the workers as "giving them thirty per cent." Also, after the hams had been smoked, there would be found some that had gone to the bad. Formerly these had been sold as "Number Three Grade," but later on some ingenious person had hit upon a new device, and now they would extract the bone, about which the bad part generally lay, and insert in the hole a white-hot iron. After this invention there was no longer Number One, Two and Three Grade—there was only Number One Grade. The packers were always originating such schemes—they had what they called "boneless hams," which were all the odds and ends of pork stuffed into casings; and "California hams," which were the shoulders, with big knuckle-joints, and nearly all the meat cut out; and fancy "skinned hams," which were made of the oldest hogs, whose skin were so heavy and coarse that no one would buy them—that is, until they had been cooked and chopped fine and labelled "head cheese"!

It was only when the whole ham was spoiled that it came into the department of Elzbieta. Cut up by the two-thousand-revolutions-a-minute flyers, and mixed with half a ton of other meat, no odor that ever was in a ham could make any difference. There was never the least attention paid to what was cut up for sausage; there would come all the way back from Europe old sausage that had been rejected, and that was moldy and white—it would be dosed with borax and glycerine, and dumped into the hoppers, and made over again for home consumption. There would be meat that had tumbled out on the floor, in the dirt and sawdust, where the workers had tramped and spit uncounted billions of consumption germs.

There would be meat stored in great piles in rooms; and the water from leaky roofs would drip over it, and thousands of rats would race about on it. It was too dark in these storage places to see well, but a man could run his hand over these piles of meat and sweep off handfuls of dried dung of rats. These rats were nuisances, and the packers would put poisoned bread out for them; they would die, and then rats, bread, and meat would go into the hoppers together. This is no fairy story and no joke; the meat would be shovelled into carts, and the man who did the shovelling would not trouble to lift out a rat even when he saw one—there were things that went into the sausage in comparison with which a poisoned rat was a tidbit. There was no place for the men to wash their hands before they ate their dinner, and so they made a practice of washing them in the water that was to be ladled into the sausage. There were the butt-ends of smoked meat, and the scraps of corned beef, and all the odds and ends of the waste of the plants, that would be dumped into old barrels in the cellar and left there. Under the system of rigid economy which the packers enforced, there were some jobs that it only paid to do once in a long time, and among these was the cleaning out of the waste-barrels. Every spring they did it, and in the barrels would be dirt and rust and old nails and stale water—and cart load after cart load of it would be taken up and dumped into the hoppers with fresh meat, and sent out to the public's breakfast. Some of it they would make into "smoked" sausage—but as the smoking took time, and was therefore expensive, they would call upon their chemistry department, and preserve it with borax and color it with gelatine to make it brown. All of their sausage came out of the same bowl, but when they came to wrap it they would stamp some of it "special," and for this they would charge two cents more a pound.

Such were the new surroundings in which Elzbieta was placed, and such was the work she was compelled to do. It was stupefying, brutalizing work; it left her no time to think, no strength for anything. She was part of the machine she tended, and every faculty that was not needed for the machine was doomed to be crushed out of existence. There was only one mercy about the cruel grind—that it gave her the gift of insensibility. Little by little she sank into a torpor—she fell silent. She would meet Jurgis and Ona in the evening, and the three would walk home together, often without saying a word. Ona, too, was falling into a habit of silence—Ona, who had once gone about singing like a bird. She was sick and miserable, and often she would barely have strength enough to drag herself home. And there they would eat what they had to eat, and afterwards, because there was only their misery to talk of, they would crawl into bed and fall into a stupor and never stir until it was time to get up again, and dress by candlelight, and go back to the machines. They were so numbed that they did not even suffer much from hunger, now; only the children continued to fret when the food ran short.

Yet the soul of Ona was not dead—the souls of none of them were dead, but only sleeping; and now and then they would waken, and these were cruel times. The gates of memory would roll open—old joys would stretch out their arms to them, old hopes and dreams would call to them, and they would stir beneath the burden that lay upon them, and feel its forever immeasurable weight. They could not even cry out beneath it; but anguish would seize them, more dreadful than agony of death. It was a thing scarcely to be spoken—a thing never spoken by all the world, that will not know its own defeat.

They were beaten; they had lost the game, they were swept aside. It was not less tragic because it was so sordid, because it had to do with wages and grocery bills and rents. They had dreamed of freedom; of a chance to look about them and learn something; to be decent and clean, to see their child grow up to be strong. And now it was all gone—it would never be! They had played the game and they had lost. Six years more of toil they had to face before they could expect the least respite, the cessation of the payments upon the house; and how cruelly certain it was that they could never stand six years of such a life as they were living! They were lost, they were going down—and there was no deliverance for them, no hope; for all the help it gave them the vast city in which they lived might have been an ocean waste, a wilderness, a desert, a tomb. So often this mood would come to Ona, in the night-time, when something wakened her; she would lie, afraid of the beating of her own heart, fronting the blood-red eyes of the old primeval terror of life. Once she cried aloud, and woke Jurgis, who was tired and cross. After that she learned to weep silently—their moods so seldom came together now! It was as if their hopes were buried in separate graves. * * *

Until long after midnight Jurgis sat lost in the conversation of his new acquaintance. It was a most wonderful experience to him—an almost supernatural experience. It was like encountering an inhabitant of the fourth dimension of space, a being who was free from all one's own limitations. For four years now, Jurgis had been wandering and blundering in the depths of a wilderness; and here, suddenly, a hand reached down and seized him, and lifted him out of it, and set him upon a mountain top, from which he could survey it all,—could see the paths from which he had wandered, the morasses into which he had stumbled, the hiding-places of the beasts of prey that had fallen upon him. There were his Packingtown experiences, for instance—what was there about Packingtown that Ostrinski could not explain! To Jurgis the packers had been equivalent to fate; Ostrinski showed him that they were the Beef Trust. They were a gigantic combination of capital, which had crushed all opposition, and overthrown the laws of the land, and was preying upon the people. Jurgis recollected how, when he had first come to Packingtown, he had stood and watched the hog-killing, and thought how cruel and savage it was, and come away congratulating himself that he was not a hog; now his new acquaintance showed him that a hog was just what he had been—one of the packers' hogs. What they wanted from a hog was all the profits that could be got out of him; and that was what they wanted from the working-man, and also that was what they wanted from the public. What the hog thought of it, and what he suffered, were not considered; and no more was it with labor, and no more with the chaser of meat. That was true everywhere in the world, but it was especially true in Packingtown; there seemed to be something about the work of slaughtering that tended to ruthlessness and ferocity—it was literally the fact that in the methods of the packers a hundred human lives did not balance a penny of profit. When Jurgis had made himself familiar with the Socialist literature, as he would very quickly, he would get glimpses of the Beef Trust from all sorts of aspects, and he would find it everywhere the same; it was the incarnation of the blind and insensate Greed. It was a monster devouring with a thousand mouths, trampling with a thousand hoofs; it was the Great Butcher—it was the spirit of Capitalism made flesh. Upon the ocean of commerce it sailed as a pirate ship; it had hoisted the black flag and declared war upon civilization. Bribery and corruption were its everyday methods. In Chicago the city government was simply one of its branch-offices; it stole billions of gallons of city water openly, it dictated to the courts the sentences of disorderly strikers, it forbade the mayor to enforce the building laws against it. In the national capital it had power to prevent inspection of its product, and to falsify government reports; it violated the rebate laws, and when an investigation was threatened it burned its books and sent its criminal agents out of the country. In the commercial world it was a Juggernaut car; it wiped out thousands of businesses every year, it drove men to madness and suicide. It had forced the price of cattle so low as to destroy the stock-raising industry, an occupation upon which whole states existed; it had ruined thousands of butchers who had refused to handle its products. It divided the country into districts, and fixed the price of meat in all of them; and it owned all the refrigerator cars, and levied an enormous tribute upon all poultry and eggs and fruit and vegetables. With the millions of dollars a week that poured in upon it, it was reaching out for the control of other interests, railroads and trolley lines, gas and electric light franchises—it already owned the leather and the grain business of the country. The people were tremendously stirred up over its encroachments, but nobody had any remedy to suggest; it was the task of Socialists to teach and organize them, and prepare them for the time when they were to seize the huge machine called the Beef Trust, and use it to produce food for human beings and not to heap up fortunes for a band of pirates.—It was long after midnight when Jurgis lay down upon the floor of Ostrinski's kitchen; and yet it was an hour before he could get to sleep, for the glory of that joyful vision of the people of Packingtown marching in and taking possession of the Union Stockyards!

MONSIGNOR JOHN RYAN

A Living Wage (1906)

One of the most important religious figures in the Progressive movement
was Monsignor John Ryan (1869–1945). A Minnesota farm boy or-
dained as a Catholic priest in 1898, Ryan spent most of his career as a
teacher at Catholic University. He published the influential A Living
Wage in 1906. In it, he argued that Catholic doctrine required that each
person be guaranteed a proper share of the social product via a mini-
mum wage. Many of his proposals, as set forth in this selection from A
Living Wage and his other writings early in the century, would be en-
acted in New Deal legislation.

Intelligent students and workers in the field of charitable effort no
longer impute all pauperism and poverty to deficiencies in the individual. They realize that a considerable proportion of dependency occurs despite the utmost efforts of the individual, despite the absence of unusual
sickness, accidents or other misfortunes, despite the presence of individual capacities that are fully up to the average. The true cause of such dependency is to be sought in insufficient incomes and insufficient
standards of living. * * *

Possessing this knowledge, the members of charity organizations, and
all who speak or write on the problem of dependency, can accomplish a
splendid work of education. They can bring home to well-meaning but
thoughtless employers some idea of the amount of poverty that is due to
their failure to pay living wages; they can help very materially to bring
upon employers who are not well-meaning the condemnation of public
opinion; they can contribute to the enactment of laws which directly or
indirectly will enforce an adequate standard of compensation and of living; they can educate the whole public into a more accurate conception
of the proportion of poverty that is due to social causes, and out of the
complacent notion, which is still all too common, that the poverty
stricken have only themselves to blame.

The State, and only the State, can prevent a large part, probably the larger
part, of the social distress which is due primarily to environment. In the physical order it can and ought to provide suitable economic conditions, by en-

forcing reasonable minimum standards of labor and livelihood. Specifically, it should prohibit the employment of any worker of average capacity at less than living wages, or for a longer day than is consistent with the material and moral health of the individual and the race, or in unsafe and unsanitary work places. It should also forbid child labor, and interdict the employment of women and young persons at tasks that are harmful to health or morals. Insofar as the wage earners are unable to protect themselves against the unfavorable contingencies of life and employment by adequate savings or insurance, the State should supply the deficiency. Hence the need in many communities of workmen's compensation laws, labor exchanges, insurance against sickness, accidents, unemployment, and disability, and a system of old age pensions. In a word, the State ought to provide and enforce all those economic and industrial conditions which are necessary and sufficient for normal and reasonable human life. This will not injure individual initiative, or individual freedom, or the individual desire to excel. It will merely lift the plane of competition, and confine these qualities within reasonable and healthy limits. * * *

By way of conclusion, then, we observe that the sphere of the State in dealing with social distress is by no means small. Neither is it indefinitely large. It is confined within fairly definite limits by certain clear and fundamental principles. Neither in the field of prevention nor in that of relief is it wise or right for the State to do anything that can be done as well by voluntary agencies; and wherever practicable it should subsidize, cooperate with and supplement private effort.

JANE ADDAMS

The Spirit of Youth and the City Streets (1909)

Jane Addams (1860–1935) championed juvenile justice, housing reform, municipal reform, workplace safety, women's suffrage, and an eight-hour workday for women. In 1889 Addams and her friend Ellen Gates Starr founded Hull House, which offered college-level courses and a variety of social, cultural, and health-care services to poorer residents of Chicago. A strong supporter of research on the causes of crime and poverty, Addams believed that the public provision of recreation and cultural activities could inhibit antisocial behavior and even rejuvenate morals among urban youth.

Nothing is more certain than that each generation longs for a reassurance as to the value and charm of life, and is secretly afraid lest it lose its sense of the youth of the earth. This is doubtless one reason why it so passionately cherishes its poets and artists who have been able to explore for themselves and to reveal to others the perpetual springs of life's self-renewal.

And yet the average man cannot obtain this desired reassurance through literature, nor yet through glimpses of earth and sky. It can come to him only through the chance embodiment of joy and youth which life itself may throw in his way. It is doubtless true that for the mass of men the message is never so unchallenged and so invincible as when embodied in youth itself. One generation after another has depended upon its young to equip it with gaiety and enthusiasm, to persuade it that living is a pleasure, until men everywhere have anxiously provided channels through which this wine of life might flow, and be preserved for their delight. The classical city promoted play with careful solicitude, building the theater and stadium as it built the market place and the temple. The Greeks held their games so integral a part of religion and patriotism that they came to expect from their poets the highest utterances at the very moments when the sense of pleasure released the national life. In the medieval city the knights held their tourneys, the guilds their pageants, the people their dances, and the church made festival for its most cherished saints with gay street processions, and presented a drama in which no less a theme than the history of creation became a matter of thrilling interest. Only in the modern city have men concluded that it is no longer necessary for the municipality to provide for the insatiable desire for play. In so far as they have acted upon this conclusion, they have entered upon a most difficult and dangerous experiment; and this at the very moment when the city has become distinctly industrial, and daily labor is continually more monotonous and subdivided. We forget how new the modern city is, and how short the span of time in which we have assumed that we can eliminate public provision for recreation.

A further difficulty lies in the fact that this industrialism has gathered together multitudes of eager young creatures from all quarters of the earth as a labor supply for the countless factories and workshops, upon which the present industrial city is based. Never before in civilization have such numbers of young girls been suddenly released from the protection of the home and permitted to walk unattended upon city streets and to work under alien roofs; for the first time they are being prized more for their labor power than for their innocence, their tender beauty, their ephemeral gaiety. Society cares more for the products they manufacture than for their immemorial ability to reaffirm the charm of existence. Never before have such numbers of young boys earned money independently of the family life, and felt themselves free to spend it as they choose in the midst of vice deliberately disguised as pleasure.

This stupid experiment of organizing work and failing to organize play has, of course, brought about a fine revenge. The love of pleasure will not be denied, and when it has turned into all sorts of malignant and vicious appetites, then we, the middle aged, grow quite distracted and resort to all sorts of restrictive measures. We even try to dam up the sweet fountain itself because we are affrighted by these neglected streams; but almost worse than the restrictive measures is our apparent belief that the city itself has no obligation in the matter, an assumption upon which the modern city turns over to commercialism practically all the provisions for public recreation.

Quite as one set of men has organized the young people into industrial enterprises in order to profit from their toil, so another set of men and also of women, I am sorry to say, have entered the neglected field of recreation and have organized enterprises which make profit out of this invincible love of pleasure.

In every city arise so-called "places"—"gin-palaces," they are called in fiction; in Chicago we euphemistically say merely "places,"—in which alcohol is dispensed, not to allay thirst, but, ostensibly to stimulate gaiety, it is sold really in order to empty pockets. Huge dance halls are opened to which hundreds of young people are attracted, many of whom stand wistfully outside a roped circle, for it requires five cents to procure within it for five minutes the sense of allurement and intoxication which is sold in lieu of innocent pleasure. These coarse and illicit merrymakings remind one of the unrestrained jollities of Restoration London, and they are indeed their direct descendants, properly commercialized, still confusing joy with lust, and gaiety with debauchery. Since the soldiers of Cromwell shut up the people's playhouses and destroyed their pleasure fields, the Anglo-Saxon city has turned over the provision for public recreation to the most evil-minded and the most unscrupulous members of the community. We see thousands of girls walking up and down the streets on a pleasant evening with no chance to catch a sight of pleasure even through a lighted window, save as these lurid places provide it. Apparently the modern city sees in these girls only two possibilities, both of them commercial: first, a chance to utilize by day their new and tender labor power in its factories and shops, and then another chance in the evening to extract from them their petty wages by pandering to their love of pleasure.

As these overworked girls stream along the street, the rest of us see only the self-conscious walk, the giggling speech, the preposterous clothing. And yet through the huge hat, with its wilderness of bedraggled feathers, the girl announces to the world that she is here. She demands attention to the fact of her existence, she states that she is ready to live, to take her place in the world. The most precious moment in human development is the young creature's assertion that he is unlike any other human being, and has an individual contribution to make to the world. The variation from the established type is at the root of all change, the only possible basis for progress, all that keeps life from growing unprofitably stale and repetitious. * * *

But quite as the modern city wastes this most valuable moment in the life of the girl, and drives into all sorts of absurd and obscure expressions her love and yearning towards the world in which she forecasts her destiny, so it often drives the boy into gambling and drinking in order to find his adventure. * * *

We cannot afford to be ungenerous to the city in which we live without suffering the penalty which lack of fair interpretation always entails. Let us know the modern city in its weakness and wickedness, and then seek to rectify and purify it until it shall be free at least from the grosser temptations which now beset the young people who are living in its tenement houses and working in its factories. The mass of these young people are possessed of good intentions and they are equipped with a certain understanding of city life. This itself could be made a most valuable social instrument toward securing innocent recreation and better social organization. They are already serving the city in so far as it is honeycombed with mutual benefit societies, with "pleasure clubs," with organizations connected with churches and factories which are filling a genuine social need. And yet the whole apparatus for supplying pleasure is wretchedly inadequate and full of danger to whomsoever may approach it. Who is responsible for its inadequacy and dangers? We certainly cannot expect the fathers and mothers who have come to the city from farms or who have emigrated from other lands to appreciate or rectify these dangers. We cannot expect the young people themselves to cling to conventions which are totally unsuited to modern city conditions, nor yet to be equal to the task of forming new conventions through which this more agglomerate social life may express itself. Above all we cannot hope that they will understand the emotional force which seizes them and which, when it does not find the traditional line of domesticity, serves as a cancer in the very tissues of society and as a disrupter of the securest social bonds. No attempt is made to treat the manifestations of this fundamental instinct with dignity or to give it possible social utility. The spontaneous joy, the clamor for pleasure, the desire of the young people to appear finer and better and altogether more lovely than they really are, the idealization not only of each other but of the whole earth which they regard but as a theater for their noble exploits, the unworldly ambitions, the romantic hopes, the make-believe world in which they live, if properly utilized, what might they not do to make our sordid cities more beautiful, more companionable? And yet at the present moment every city is full of young people who are utterly bewildered and uninstructed in regard to the basic experience which must inevitably come to them, and which has varied, remote, and indirect expressions. * * *

We are informed by high authority that there is nothing in the environment to which youth so keenly responds as to music, and yet the streets, the vaudeville shows, the five-cent theaters are full of the most blatant and vulgar songs. The trivial and obscene words, the meaningless and flippant airs run through the heads of hundreds of young people for hours at a time while they are engaged in monotonous factory work. We totally ignore that ancient connection between music and morals which was so long insisted upon by philosophers as well as poets. The street music has quite broken away from all control, both of the educator and the patriot, and we have grown singularly careless in regard to its influence upon young people. Although we legislate against it in saloons because of its dangerous influence there, we constantly permit music on the street to incite that which should be controlled, to degrade that which should be exalted, to make sensuous that which might be lifted into the realm of the higher imagination.

Our attitude towards music is typical of our carelessness towards all those things which make for common joy and for the restraints of higher civilization on the streets. It is as if our cities had not yet developed a sense of responsibility in regard to the life of the streets, and continually forget that recreation is stronger than vice, and that recreation alone can stifle the lust for vice.

Perhaps we need to take a page from the philosophy of the Greeks to whom the world of fact was also the world of the ideal, and to whom the realization of what ought to be, involved not the destruction of what was, but merely its perfecting upon its own lines. To the Greeks virtue was not a hard conformity to a law felt as alien to the natural character, but a free expression of the inner life. To treat thus the fundamental susceptibility of sex which now so bewilders the street life and drives young people themselves into all sorts of difficulties, would mean to loosen it from the things of sense and to link it to the affairs of the imagination. It would mean to fit to this gross and heavy stuff the wings of the mind, to scatter from it "the clinging mud of banality and vulgarity," and to speed it on through our city streets amid spontaneous laughter, snatches of lyric song, the recovered forms of old dances, and the traditional rondels of merry games. It would thus bring charm and beauty to the prosaic city and connect it subtly with the arts of the past as well as with the vigor and renewed life of the future.

WALTER RAUSCHENBUSCH

Christianity and the Social Crisis (1909)

A Baptist minister and professor of church history at the Rochester Theological Seminary, Walter Rauschenbusch (1861–1918) was a leader of the Social Gospel movement. Rauschenbusch became interested in social reforms after he was exposed to urban conditions in poorer neighborhoods in New York City. As these passages from his first book indicate, the minister believed that the church should work with the state to improve social conditions in order "to transform humanity into the kingdom of God."

The spiritual force of Christianity should be turned against the materialism and mammonism of our industrial and social order.

If a man sacrifices his human dignity and self-respect to increase his income, or stunts his intellectual growth and his human affections to swell his bank account, he is to that extent serving mammon and denying God. Likewise if he uses up and injures the life of his fellow-men to make money for himself, he serves mammon and denies God. But our industrial order does both. It makes property the end, and man the means to produce it.

Man is treated as a *thing* to produce more things. Men are hired as hands and not as men. They are paid only enough to maintain their working capacity and not enough to develop their manhood. When their working force is exhausted, they are flung aside without consideration of their human needs. Jesus asked, "Is not a man more than a sheep?" Our industry says "No." It is careful of its live stock and machinery, and careless of its human working force. It keeps its electrical engines immaculate in burnished cleanliness and lets its human dynamos sicken in dirt. In the 15th Assembly District in New York City, between 10th and 11th avenues, 1321 families in 1896 had three bathtubs between them. Our industrial establishments are institutions for the creation of dividends, and not for the fostering of human life. In all our public life the question of profit is put first. Pastor Stöcker, in a speech on child and female labor in the German Reichstag, said: "We have put the question the wrong way. We have asked: How much child and female labor does industry need in order to flourish, to pay dividends, and to sell goods abroad? Whereas we ought to have asked: How ought industry to be organized in order to protect and foster the family, the human individual, and the Christian life?" That simple reversal of the question marks the difference between the Christian conception of life and property and the mammonistic.

"Life is more than food and raiment." More, too, than the apparatus which makes food and raiment. What is all the machinery of our industrial organization worth if it does not make human life healthful and happy? But is it doing that? Men are first of all men, folks, members of our human family. To view them first of all as labor force is civilized barbarism. It is the attitude of the exploiter. Yet unconsciously we have all been taught to take that attitude and talk of men as if they were horsepowers or volts. Our commercialism has tainted our sense of fundamental human verities and values. We measure our national prosperity by pig-iron and steel instead of by the welfare of the people. In city affairs the property owners have more influence than the family owners. For instance, the pall of coal smoke hanging over our industrial cities is injurious to the eyes; it predisposes to diseases of the respiratory organs; it depresses the joy of living; it multiplies the labor of housewives in cleaning and washing. But it continues because it would impose expense on business to install smoke consumers or pay skilled stokers. If an agitation is begun to abolish the smoke nuisance, the telling argument is not that it inflicts injury on the mass of human life, but that the smoke "hurts business," and that it really "pays" to consume the wasted carbon. In political life one can constantly see the cause of human life pleading long and vainly for redress, like the widow before the unjust judge. Then suddenly comes the bass voice of Property, and all men stand with hat in hand.

Our scientific political economy has long been an oracle of the false god. It has taught us to approach economic questions from the point of view of goods and not of man. It tells us how wealth is produced and divided and consumed by man, and not how man's life and development can best be fostered by material wealth. It is significant that the discussion of "Consumption" of wealth has been most neglected in political economy; yet that is humanly the most important of all. Theology must become christocentric; political economy must become anthropocentric. Man is Christianized when he puts God before self; political economy will be Christianized when it puts man before wealth. Socialistic political economy does that. It is materialistic in its theory of human life and history, but it is humane in its aims, and to that extent is closer to Christianity than the orthodox science has been.

It is the function of religion to teach the individual to value his soul more than his body, and his moral integrity more than his income. In the same way it is the function of religion to teach society to value human life more than property, and to value property only in so far as it forms the material basis for the higher development of human life. When life and property are in apparent collision, life must take precedence. This is not only Christian but prudent. When commercialism in its headlong greed deteriorates the mass of human life, it defeats its own covetousness by killing the goose that lays the golden egg. Humanity is that goose—in more senses than one. It takes faith in the moral law to believe that this penny-wise craft is really suicidal folly, and to assert that wealth which uses up the people paves the way to beggary. Religious men have been cowed by the prevailing materialism and arrogant selfishness of our business world. They should have the courage of religious faith and assert that "man liveth not by bread alone," but by doing the will of God, and that the life of a nation "consisteth not in the abundance of things" which it produces, but in the way men live justly with one another and humbly with their God. * * *

But we have an exaggerated idea of the importance of laws. Our legislative bodies are the greatest law factories the world has ever seen. Our zest for legislation blinds us to the subtle forces behind and beyond the law. Those influences which really make and mar human happiness and greatness are beyond the reach of the law. The law can compel a man to support his wife, but it cannot compel him to love her, and what are ten dollars a week to a woman whose love lies in broken shards at her feet? The law can compel a father to provide for his children and can interfere if he maltreats them, but it cannot compel him to give them that loving fatherly intercourse which puts backbone into a child forever. The law can keep neighbors from trespassing, but it cannot put neighborly courtesy and good-will into their relations. The State can establish public schools and hire teachers, but it cannot put enthusiasm and moral power into their work; yet those are the qualities which distinguish the few true teachers to whom we look back in after years as the real makers of our lives. The highest qualities and influences are beyond the law and must be created elsewhere.

The law is a moral agency, as effective and as rough as a policeman's club, sweeping in its operation and unable to adjust itself to individual needs and the finer shadings of moral life. It furnishes the stiff skeleton of public morality which supports the finer tissues, but these tissues must be deposited by other forces. The State is the outer court of the moral law; within stands the sanctuary of the Spirit. Religion creates morality, and morality then deposits a small part of its contents in written laws.

The State can protect the existing morality and promote the coming morality, but the vital creative force of morality lies deeper.

The law becomes impotent if it is not supported by a diffused, spontaneous moral impulse in the community. If religion implants love, mutual helpfulness, and respect for the life and rights of others, there will be little left to do for the law and its physical force. The stronger the silent moral compulsion of the community, the less need for the physical compulsion of the State. If parents have to resort to physical punishment constantly, it furnishes presumptive evidence that their training has been defective in its moral factors. If we have to order out the militia frequently to quell riots and protect property, it constitutes a charge of inefficiency against the religious and educational institutions of the community.

Thus it is clear that the Church has a large field for social activity before touching legislation. It cannot make laws, but it can make customs, and "*quid leges sine moribus?*" Of what avail are laws without customs? Our two words, "morals" and "ethics," the one from the Latin and the other from the Greek, both mean that which is customary. There is a singular lack of appreciation in American thought for the importance of custom; possibly because in our new and plastic life customs are less rigid and formative than anywhere on earth. Yet our life, too, is ruled largely by unenacted laws. Our helpfulness toward children and old people, our respect for womanhood and the consequent unparalleled freedom of woman's social intercourse, the comparative disappearance of profanity and obscenity from conversation—all this rests on custom and not on law, and these customs are in large part the product of purified modern religion. The disappearance of alcoholic liquors from the homes of great strata of our people is in most localities due to custom rather than law. Religion first demanded it, and educational, scientific, and economic motives have since reenforced the custom. Religion first created the custom of Sunday rest and the law then protected it. The weekly rest day is a gift of religion to the people. If it was not already so firmly established in our life, it would be almost impossible to wrest one full day from the whirl of modern commercialism. The law did not create Sunday rest; neither is it able to maintain its finer qualities. It can prohibit work, but it cannot prescribe how the day shall be spent.

It is entirely feasible for the Church to mitigate the social hardships of the working classes by lending force to humane customs. Its help would make the Saturday half holiday in summer practicable. It could ease the strain of the Christmas shopping season. It could secure seats and rest rooms for the girls in the department stores. It could counteract the tendency of tenement owners to crowd the people. It could encourage employers in making a place for their aged employees and discourage the early exploitation of children. A single frank and prayerful discussion of one of these questions in a social meeting of the church or its societies would create more social morality and good custom than many columns in the newspapers. Such an activity would not solve the fundamental questions of capitalism, but it would ease the pressure a little and would save the people from deterioration, while the social movement is moving toward the larger solution.

Good customs are perpetually in danger, and the Church can act as a conservative influence in guarding them against hostile inroads. For instance, the custom which barred alcoholic drinks from respectable and educated homes is now being undermined by the influence of the idle upper class which needs stimulants and copies their use from foreign society, and the Church should undertake a new temperance crusade with all the resources of advanced physiological and sociological science. The head of an important Eastern institution a few years ago proposed to introduce beer in the social gatherings of students in order to make them more sociable. Such an innovation would not merely create the habit of moderate drinking in many young men, but would introduce a foreign custom into American life. Many of our public dinners are now wholly free from the flush of wine or beer. The excellence of American after-dinner speaking, and the prevalence of real humor and fun at our public dinners, are mainly due to the fact that both speaker and audience are in full control of their critical faculties and therefore demand fine intellectual work and are in condition to appreciate it. The alcoholic paralysis begins with the brain and lessens the capacity for self-scrutiny and self-restraint. An alcoholized audience will howl at anything unseemly and be too dull for anything really witty. Even if the students of that institution should all stop drinking when they graduated, a lasting damage would be done to American college life if it became customary for the college community to pass into partial narcosis as a preparation for social enjoyment. Against all such corruptions of good custom the Church should do sentinel duty.

Any permanent and useful advance in legislation is dependent on the previous creation of moral conviction and custom. It is a commonplace that a law cannot be enforced without the support of public opinion, and that an unenforced law breaks down the usefulness of all related laws and the reverence for law in general. If the law advances faster than the average moral sense, it becomes inoperative and harmful. The real advance, therefore, will have to come through those social forces which create and train the sense of right. The religious and educational forces in their totality are the real power that runs the cart uphill; the State can merely push a billet of wood under the wheels to keep it from rolling down again. Some of the gravest evils of our day are either not covered by enacted law or the law against them does not work. In such cases the forces which create active moral conviction are under accusation for neglect of duty.

The process of guarding, creating, or strengthening useful institutions is similar to the process of creating good customs. It is a function in which religious sentiment and the organized Church can work freely. For instance, our public parks are an institution of the highest value to the physical and moral life of the cities. About fifty years ago no city in the United States had purchased an acre of land for park purposes. Mainly through the influence of public-spirited men, supported by enlightened moral sentiment, parks have been created and are now not only increasing their acreage and their beauty, but their usefulness. They are beginning to offer sand-hills for the little children, swimming baths in summer, skating in winter, music on holidays, gymnastic apparatus, and open-air games. Instead of warning the people to "keep off the grass," they are bidding for the inflow of the people. Yet it is safe to say that every one of these advances cost some struggle and effort, and at every such moment of struggle a lift from the powerful shoulders of the organized religious community would be practically decisive. * * *

Such a coöperation of the religious and political forces of the community furnishes the positive solution of the problem of Church and State. Historical experience has compelled us to separate Church and State because each can accomplish its special task best without the interference of the other. But they are not unrelated. Our life is not a mechanical duality, built in two air-tight compartments. Church and State both minister to something greater and larger than either, and they find their true relation in this unity of aim and service. When the State supports morality by legal constraint, it coöperates with the voluntary moral power of the Church; but if it should seek to control the organization and influence of the Church by appointing its officers or interfering with its teaching, it would tamper with the seedplot of moral progress. When the Church implants religious impulses toward righteousness and trains the moral convictions of the people, it coöperates with the State by creating the most delicate and valuable elements of social welfare and progress; but if it should enter into politics to get funds from the public treasury or police support for its doctrine and ritual, it would inject a divisive and corrosive force into political life. The machinery of Church and State must be kept separate, but the output of each must mingle with the other to make social life increasingly wholesome and normal. Church and State are alike but partial organizations of humanity for special ends. Together they serve what is greater than either: humanity. Their common aim is to transform humanity into the kingdom of God.

THORSTEIN VEBLEN

The Theory of the Leisure Class (1899)

The economist and social scientist Thorstein Bunde Veblen (1857–1929) taught at several American universities and edited both the academic Journal of Political Economy *and the literary magazine* The Dial. *Veblen developed an evolutionary institutional approach to the study of economic life in his first book,* The Theory of the Leisure Class, *a popular work in which he coined the phrase "conspicuous consumption." In an age when industrial tycoons raked Europe for the paintings to hang in their palatial Fifth Avenue mansions, where they outdid each other with sumptuous dinners at Delmonico's, Veblen analyzed the way conspicuous consumption, "pecuniary emulation," and other acquisitive practices undermined productive activity and workmanship in modern economic life.*

The quasi-peaceable gentleman of leisure, then, not only consumes of the staff of life beyond the minimum required for subsistence and physical efficiency, but his consumption also undergoes a specialization as regards the quality of the goods consumed. He consumes freely and of the best in food, drink, narcotics, shelter, services, ornaments, apparel, weapons and accoutrements, amusements, amulets, and idols or divinities. In the process of gradual amelioration which takes place in the articles of his consumption, the motive principle and the proximate aim of innovation is no doubt the higher efficiency of the improved and more elaborate products for personal comfort and well-being. But that does not remain the sole purpose of their consumption. The canon of reputability is at hand and seizes upon such innovations as are, according to its standard, fit to survive. Since the consumption of these more excellent goods is an evidence of wealth, it becomes honorific; and conversely, the failure to consume in due quantity and quality becomes a mark of inferiority and demerit.

This growth of punctilious discrimination as to qualitative excellence in eating, drinking, etc., presently affects not only the manner of life, but also the training and intellectual activity of the gentleman of leisure. He is no longer simply the successful, aggressive male—the man of strength, resource, and intrepidity. In order to avoid stultification he must also cultivate his tastes, for it now becomes incumbent on him to discriminate with some nicety between the noble and the ignoble in consumable goods. He becomes a connoisseur in creditable viands of various degrees of merit, in manly beverages and trinkets, in seemly apparel and architecture, in weapons, games, dances, and the narcotics. This cultivation of the aesthetic faculty requires time and application, and the demands made upon the gentleman in this direction therefore tend to change his life of leisure into a more or less arduous application to the business of learning how to live a life of ostensible leisure in a becoming way. Closely related to the requirement that the gentleman must consume freely and of the right kind of goods, there is the requirement that he must know how to consume them in a seemly manner. His life of leisure must be conducted in due form. Hence arise good manners in the way pointed out in an earlier chapter. Highbred manners and ways of living are items of conformity to the norm of conspicuous leisure and conspicuous consumption.

Conspicuous consumption of valuable goods is a means of reputability to the gentleman of leisure. As wealth accumulates on his hands, his own unaided effort will not avail to sufficiently put his opulence in evidence by this method. The aid of friends and competitors is therefore brought in by resorting to the giving of valuable presents and expensive feasts and entertainments. Presents and feasts had probably another origin than that of naive ostentation, but they acquired their utility for this purpose very early, and they have retained that character to the present; so that their utility in this respect has now long been the substantial ground on which these usages rest. Costly entertainments, such as the potlatch or the ball, are peculiarly adapted to serve this end. The competitor with whom the entertainer wishes to institute a comparison is, by this method, made to serve as a means to the end. He consumes vicariously for his host at the same time that he is a witness to the consumption of that excess of good things which his host is unable to dispose of singlehanded, and he is also made to witness his host's facility in etiquette.

In the giving of costly entertainments other motives, of a more genial kind, are of course also present. The custom of festive gatherings probably originated in motives of conviviality and religion; these motives are also present in the later development, but they do not continue to be the sole motives. The latter-day leisure-class festivities and entertainments may continue in some slight degree to serve the religious need and in a higher degree the needs of recreation and conviviality, but they also serve an invidious purpose; and they serve it none the less effectually for having a colorable noninvidious ground in these more avowable motives. But the economic effect of these social amenities is not therefore lessened, either in the vicarious consumption of goods or in the exhibition of difficult and costly achievements in etiquette.

As wealth accumulates, the leisure class develops further in function and structure and there arises a differentiation within the class. There is a more or less elaborate system of rank and grades. This differentiation is furthered by the inheritance of wealth and the consequent inheritance of gentility. With the inheritance of gentility goes the inheritance of obligatory leisure; and gentility of a sufficient potency to entail a life of leisure may be inherited without the complement of wealth required to maintain a dignified leisure. Gentle blood may be transmitted without goods enough to afford a reputably free consumption at one's ease. Hence results a class of impecunious gentlemen of leisure, incidentally referred to already. These half-caste gentlemen of leisure fall into a system of hierarchical gradations. Those who stand near the higher and the highest grades of the wealthy leisure class, in point of birth, or in point of wealth, or both, outrank the remoter-born and the pecuniarily weaker. These lower grades, especially the impecunious, or marginal, gentlemen of leisure, affiliate themselves by a system of dependence or fealty to the great ones; by so doing they gain an increment of repute, or of the means with which to lead a life of leisure, from their patron. They become his courtiers or retainers, servants; and being fed and countenanced by their patron they are indices of his rank and vicarious consumers of his superfluous wealth. Many of these affiliated gentlemen of leisure are at the same time lesser men of substance in their own right so that some of them are scarcely at all, others only partially, to be rated as vicarious consumers. So many of them, however, as make up the retainers and hangers-on of the patron may be classed as vicarious consumers without qualification. Many of these again, and also many of the other aristocracy of less degree, have in turn attached to their persons a more or less comprehensive group of vicarious consumers in the persons of their wives and children, their servants, retainers, etc. * * *

The early ascendency of leisure as a means of reputability is traceable to the archaic distinction between noble and ignoble employments. Leisure is honourable and becomes imperative partly because it shows exemption from ignoble labour. The archaic differentiation into noble and ignoble classes is based on an invidious distinction between employments as honorific or debasing; and this traditional distinction grows into an imperative canon of decency during the early quasi-peaceable stage. Its ascendency is furthered by the fact that leisure is still fully as effective an evidence of wealth as consumption. Indeed, so effective is it

in the relatively small and stable human environment to which the individual is exposed at that cultural stage, that, with the aid of the archaic
tradition which deprecates all productive labour, it gives rise to a large
impecunious leisure class, and it even tends to limit the production of
the community's industry to the subsistence minimum. This extreme inhibition of industry is avoided because slave labour, working under a
compulsion more rigorous than that of reputability, is forced to turn out
a product in excess of the subsistence minimum of the working class.
The subsequent relative decline in the use of conspicuous leisure as a
basis of repute is due partly to an increasing relative effectiveness of
consumption as an evidence of wealth; but in part it is traceable to another force, alien, and in some degree antagonistic, to the usage of conspicuous waste.

This alien factor is the instinct of workmanship. Other circumstances
permitting, that instinct disposes men to look with favour upon productive efficiency and on whatever is of human use. It disposes them to deprecate waste of substance or effort. The instinct of workmanship is
present in all men, and asserts itself even under very adverse circumstances. So that however wasteful a given expenditure may be in reality,
it must at least have some colourable excuse in the way of an ostensible
purpose. The manner in which, under special circumstances, the instinct eventuates in a taste for exploit and an invidious discrimination
between noble and ignoble classes has been indicated in an earlier chapter. In so far as it comes into conflict with the law of conspicuous waste,
the instinct of workmanship expresses itself not so much in insistence on
substantial usefulness as in an abiding sense of the odiousness and aesthetic impossibility of what is obviously futile. Being of the nature of an
instinctive affection, its guidance touches chiefly and immediately the
obvious and apparent violations of its requirements. It is only less
promptly and with less constraining force that it reaches such substantial violations of its requirements as are appreciated only upon reflection.

So long as all labour continues to be performed exclusively or usually
by slaves, the baseness of all productive effort is too constantly and de-
terrently present in the mind of men to allow the instinct of workmanship seriously to take effect in the direction of industrial usefulness;
but when the quasi-peaceable stage (with slavery and status) passes
into the peaceable stage of industry (with wage labour and cash payment) the instinct comes more effectively into play. It then begins ag-
gressively to shape men's views of what is meritorious, and asserts itself
at least as an auxiliary canon of self-complacency. All extraneous considerations apart, those persons (adults) are but a vanishing minority to-

day who harbour no inclination to the accomplishment of some end, or who are not impelled of their own motion to shape some object or fact or relation for human use. The propensity may in large measure be overborne by the more immediately constraining incentive to a reputable leisure and an avoidance of indecorous usefulness, and it may therefore work itself out in make-believe only; as for instance in "social duties," and in quasi-artistic or quasi-scholarly accomplishments, in the care and decoration of the house, in sewing-circle activity or dress reform, in proficiency at dress, cards, yachting, golf, and various sports. But the fact that it may under stress of circumstances eventuate in inanities no more disproves the presence of the instinct than the reality of the brooding instinct is disproved by inducing a hen to sit on a nestful of china eggs.

CHARLES A. BEARD

The Economic Basis of Politics (1922)

The historian and social scientist Charles Austin Beard (1874–1948) taught political science at Columbia University from 1904 to 1917, cofounded the New School for Social Research in 1919, and served as the president of both the American Historical Association and the American Political Science Association. Best known for his revisionist study An Economic Interpretation of the Constitution of the United States *(1913), Beard used his scholarship to draw attention to socioeconomic motivations as sources of political conflict and historical change. First published in 1922,* The Economic Basis of Politics *outlines Beard's view that property interests formed the foundation of American politics from its very beginnings.*

An examination of the first American state constitutions reveals no abandonment of the Old-World notion that government rests upon property. Take, for instance, the Massachusetts Constitution of 1780 drawn by John Adams and adopted after long and serious deliberation. In this document we discover that no man could vote for members of the legislature or for governor, unless he had a freehold estate of the annual value of three pounds, or some estate of the value of sixty pounds. Here is a distinct recognition of two classes of property interests in the government,—real property and personalty. To add further security to the two orders or "estates" the constitution provided that no one could be elected governor who did not possess a freehold of the value of one thousand pounds, and furthermore, that the senators should be distributed among the respective districts of the state on the score of the amount of taxes paid in each of them. It was in defence of this last provision that Daniel Webster made his famous speech in the Massachusetts convention of 1820, defending the economic basis of government. If the Massachusetts constitution proved to be rather democratic in its operations, that was, as Webster pointed out, due to the wide distribution of property, not to any desire of the Massachusetts Fathers to sacrifice the security of property to a political shibboleth. * * *

Admitting the plain evidence of the first state constitutions, that the wise founders of this Republic recognized the place of property interests in political processes, it may be said that the Constitution of the United States, drawn in that period, nowhere takes into account the existence of economic divisions. This is true, if we read merely the language of the instrument and not the records of the convention which drafted it. In the document itself there are no provisions similar to those which appear in the first state constitutions, placing landed- and personal-property qualifications on the suffrage and office holding; but the omission was not made because the framers of that immortal instrument were indifferent to the rights of property or unaware of the influence wielded by economic groups upon the course of government. Neither was it because they disapproved of property qualifications, for such existed in nearly every state in the Union. In fact property qualifications for officers and for voters were proposed in the convention, but it was impossible to agree on their precise form. Inasmuch as many of the troubles under the Articles of the Confederation had arisen from attacks on capital by state legislatures elected by freeholders, and inasmuch as the convention was especially eager to safeguard the rights of personal property, a freehold qualification did not seem to offer an adequate remedy. On the other hand, to impose a large personal-property qualification on voters would have meant the defeat of the Constitution by the farmers who were, of necessity, called upon to ratify it. Under the circumstances the framers of the Constitution relied, not upon direct economic qualifications, but upon checks and balances to secure the rights of property—particularly personal property—against the assaults of the farmers and the proletariat. * * *

The great political philosophers, with few exceptions, have regarded property as the fundamental element in political power, and have looked upon a constitution as a balance of economic groups. The governments founded and developed before the nineteenth century were in fact complexes of group interests. Nowhere was the representative system, in its origin, designed to reflect the opinions of mere numerical aggregations of human beings considered in the abstract apart from property and employment. On the contrary, it reflected the sentiments and views of different sorts and conditions of men, estates or orders: clergy, nobility, burghers, and peasants.

In the United States where there was no clerical estate or established nobility to be represented in the government, the existence of the two fundamental property groups—the owners of realty and the owners of personalty—was taken into account either in positive constitutional law or in the check and balance system provided by the separation of powers. If the first American constitutions were more democratic than those of Europe, the fact is not to be attributed to radical changes in human nature, induced by a voyage across the Atlantic, but, as the great Webster pointed out, to a very wide distribution of property, due mainly to cheap land.

So things stood in the closing years of the old régime. Then suddenly came two great revolutions, one in economic fact, and the other in political theory. The first was brought about by the invention of the steam engine and machinery, creating an immense amount of property which had hitherto existed only as a minor element in economic life, namely, industrial and mercantile capital. So rapidly did this new form of property accumulate that even in the United States, by the middle of the nineteenth century, it exceeded in value the agricultural land of the country.

Being more mobile and more easily concentrated than land, a vast portion of it quickly fell into the hands of, relatively speaking, a small portion of society. As land was the great stabilizer of the old order, so capital became the great disturber in the new order. Like a mighty giant tossing to and fro in a fever, in its quest for profits, it tore masses of men from the land, from their sleepy villages and hamlets, and hurled them here and there all over the globe. Under its influence the old sharp class differences were disarranged. The peasant might become a successful cotton spinner, a financial magnate, a contributor to party war-chests, a peer of the realm. The Manchester individualists, Cobden and Bright, looking upon the new order which they had helped to create, pronounced it good and declared that because any hustling individual might rise from poverty to wealth, the era of *individual* equality had arrived. Instead of studying the new groups, the new class divisions, more subtle and complex than ever before, they proclaimed the glad day of equality.

While James Watt was experimenting in Glasgow with the steam engine, and thus preparing to blow up the old economic order in the realm of fact, a French philosopher, Jean Jacques Rousseau, was experimenting with ideas scarcely less dangerous to the *ancien régime* than the operations of the Scotch mechanic. Unlike his distinguished predecessor in political science, Montesquieu, Rousseau did not search assiduously among the institutions and habits of mankind to find a basis for his political philosophy. Rousseau was not a man of science or a detached scholar. He was a passionate propagandist. He formulated the sentiments and views of the third estate in France then beginning to thunder against the monarchy, which was buttressed by the special privileges of the clergy and the nobility. In his *Social Contract* he set forth the moral and philosophic justification for the revolt of the third estate. * * *

Having found the origin of society in a general agreement of free and equal men, Rousseau naturally places sovereign power by moral right in "the people"—a collectivity of all the individual members of the state. The law of the state is therefore not the will of some class (like the landed gentry) imposed upon all others, or a compromise rule produced by a balance of conflicting group interests, but is, according to Rousseau, an expression of "the general will." This alone is its justification. * * *

But Rousseau is face to face with the fact that unanimity among citizens is impossible and that the general will cannot be the will of the whole ten thousand or the whole hundred thousand, as the case may be, but must, perforce, be the will of a certain fraction of the citizens. He boldly meets the problem, and following the old philosophers he holds that the exercise of sovereignty is by the majority. The *general will* of which he makes so much, is in practice, the will of a majority. With fine confidence he contends that the will of the majority is right and works for the good of the state. * * *

But it may be asked, how did this levelling doctrine of universal political equality find a foothold in the United States where there were no official clergy and nobility to be overthrown by the third estate? Well, some writers have laboured hard to show that it is a French creation utterly at variance with Anglo-Saxon tradition—whatever that may mean. In the interest of truth, however, it should be said that the free-and-equal doctrine is not French, but English in origin. Its beginnings among English-speaking peoples may be traced to the flood of speculation that broke loose in England during the seventeenth century when the merchants and gentry were engaged in a revolt against the crown and aristocracy—the clergy having been broken a century earlier by the bluff king, Henry VIII, who confiscated much of their property. It was from English defenders of revolution, like John Locke, rather than from French authors, that Jefferson derived the gospel of the Declaration of Independence. Moreover the economic circumstances in the United States were on the whole favorable to the propaganda of that word. There was no established clergy here. There was no titled aristocracy. There was no such proletariat as formed the "mob" of Paris. Land was the chief form of property and its wide distribution among the whites (leaving the slaves out of account) brought about in fact a considerable economic equality to correspond to the theory of political equality.

Moreover, at the time that America was committed to the theory of political equality, the people were engaged in a revolt against the government imposed on them under the authority of Great Britain. Like the third estate in France they needed some effective and compelling justification for their extraordinary conduct. Of course the leaders of the American Revolution could have said coldly: "We are fighting for the plantation owners of the South, the merchants and landed gentry of the North, and the free farmers in both sections, in order that they may govern themselves."

Obviously, such a chilly declaration of fact would not have thrilled the masses, especially the mechanics of the towns who enjoyed no political rights under either system, the old or the new. It was necessary to have something that would ring throughout the country. Hence the grand words of the Declaration of Independence: "All men are created equal" and "governments derive their just powers from the consent of the governed." There were critics ready to point out that these high principles did not square with slavery, indentured servitude, and political disfranchisement, but they did not prevail. In the fervour of the moment, Jefferson, while bent on justifying the revolt against George III, in fact challenged the rule of property which was guaranteed by the state constitutions drafted by his fellow revolutionists in that very epoch. Even Jeffersonians, when confronted, like Rousseau's followers, with the logical consequences of their doctrine shrank from applying it. Nevertheless the grand words stood for all time, and advocates of manhood suffrage and woman suffrage afterward appealed to them with great effect in attacking property and sex qualifications on the right to vote.

When once the free-and-equal doctrine had been let loose in the New World and the Old, it was impossible to check its course. Steadily it made headway against governments founded upon a class basis. Steadily it supplanted the old philosophy of politics which gave to property and to estates a place in the process of government. Within seventy years after the Declaration of Independence the battle for white manhood suffrage was virtually won in the United States. Some remnants of the old system of class privilege in politics remained, but they were regarded as anachronisms. Time was to dispose of them. America was committed to the great doctrine that in politics all heads are equal and all are entitled to the same share of power in the government. * * *

The logical application of Rousseau's doctrine of complete and abstract human equality is clear. It means that the number of members in any legislature shall be apportioned among geographical districts approximately according to the number of inhabitants without reference to their wealth, occupations, or interests. It means that all high public officers shall be elected by majorities or pluralities. Man is to be regarded as a "political" animal. No account is to be taken of those sentiments and views which, as Madison says, arise from the possession of different degrees and kinds of property. All heads are equal and, from the point of view of politics, alike. The statesman is a mathematician concerned with counting heads. The rule of numbers is enthroned. The homage once paid to kings is to be paid to the statistics of election returns. Surely, in all the history of thought, there is nothing more wonderful than this.

While this political revolution has been going on, have the economic groups once recognized by statesmen and political philosophers disappeared? The answer is emphatic. It is to be found in the census returns, which, as certainly as the doomsday book of William the Conqueror, record the perdurance of group and class interests despite the rhetoric of political equality. It is to be found in practical politics day by day. Does any one think that a thousand farmers or labourers, going on about their tasks, have the same influence in the formation of a protective tariff bill as a thousand manufacturers represented by spokesmen in the lobbies and committee rooms of the Congress of the United States? Does any one suppose that the exemption of trade unions from the provisions of the Sherman Anti-Trust Law was the result of the platonic wishes of "the people," rather than the determined and persistent activity of The American Federation of Labor?

We are therefore confronted by an inherent antagonism between our generally accepted political doctrines, and the actual facts of political life. In the world of natural science men do not tarry long with hypotheses that will not square with observed phenomena. Shall we in the field of political science cling to a delusion that we have to deal only with an abstract man divorced from all economic interests and group sentiments?

Nevertheless, the democratic device of universal suffrage does not destroy economic classes or economic inequalities. It ignores them. Herein lies the paradox, the most astounding political contradiction that the world has ever witnessed. Hence the question arises: Has political democracy solved the problem of the ages, wrung the answer from the sphinx? Is it a guarantee against the storms of revolution? Does it make impossible such social conflicts as those which tore ancient societies asunder? Does it afford to mankind a mastery over its social destiny?

To ask these questions is to answer them. Nothing was more obvious in the thinking of western civilization before the outbreak of the World War than dissatisfaction with political democracy. Equally obvious was the discontent with representative government based on the doctrine of abstract numbers and civic equality. Whether one went into the country-side of Oregon or strolled along Quai d'Orsay, one heard lively debates over "the failure of representative government." The initiative and refer-endum and recall—direct government—more head counting on the the-ory of numbers and abstract equality, such was the answer of the Far West to the riddle. * * *

The upshot of all this seems to be that in a modern industrial society, the problem of property, so vital in politics, is not as simple as it was in old agricultural societies. It was one thing for peasants to destroy their land-lords and go on tilling the soil as they had long been wont to do. It is an-other thing for workingmen to destroy capitalists as a class and assume all the complex and staggering burdens of management and exchange. It is also clear that, as efficient production depends to a great extent upon skill, skill itself is a form of property even if property in capital is abolished.

In short a great society, whether capitalist or communist, must possess different kinds and grades of skill and talent and carry on widely diversi-fied industries. There must be miners, machinists, electricians, engi-neers, accountants, transport workers, draftsmen, managers, and a hundred other kinds of specialists. They may be temporarily welded to-gether in a conflict with their capitalist employers, but they will be di-vided over the distribution of wealth among themselves after the capitalists have been disposed of. Conceivably a highly militarist govern-ment might destroy their organizations and level them down, but the re-sult would be ruin of production and of the state itself. Even a communist could hardly defend his system on the theory that all must choose between military despotism and utter ruin.

The grand conclusion, therefore, seems to be exactly that advanced by our own James Madison in the Tenth Number of the Federalist. To express his thought in modern terms: a landed interest, a transport interest, a rail-way interest, a shipping interest, an engineering interest, a manufacturing interest, a public-official interest, with many lesser interests, grow up of necessity in all great societies and divide them into different classes actu-ated by different sentiments and views. The regulation of these various and interfering interests, whatever may be the formula for the ownership of property, constitutes the principal task of modern statesmen and in-volves the spirit of party in the necessary and ordinary operations of gov-ernment. In other words, there is no rest for mankind, no final solution of eternal contradictions. Such is the design of the universe. The recognition of this fact is the beginning of wisdom—and of statesmanship.

WILLIAM JAMES

Pragmatism: A New Name for Old Ways of Thinking (1907)

William James (1842–1910) revolutionized the study of psychology as a teacher at Harvard. He wrote several acclaimed works on religion and further developed the ideas of pragmatism, earlier introduced by the philosopher Charles Sanders Pierce. Pragmatism, which emphasized the practical, instrumental value of ideas and principles based on experience and observation, was resolutely opposed to philosophical absolutism and dogmatism. Progressive intellectuals and activists found pragmatism's results-oriented focus congenial to a politics of reform. James explained the major principles of pragmatism in the Lowell Lectures, delivered in Boston in 1906 and published the following year in book form.

Truth, as any dictionary will tell you, is a property of certain of our ideas. It means their 'agreement,' as falsity means their disagreement, with 'reality.' Pragmatists and intellectualists both accept this definition as a matter of course. They begin to quarrel only after the question is raised as to what may precisely be meant by the term 'agreement,' and what by the term 'reality,' when reality is taken as something for our ideas to agree with.

In answering these questions the pragmatists are more analytic and painstaking, the intellectualists more offhand and irreflective. The popular notion is that a true idea must copy its reality. Like other popular views, this one follows the analogy of the most usual experience. Our true ideas of sensible things do indeed copy them. Shut your eyes and think of yonder clock on the wall, and you get just such a true picture or copy of its dial. But your idea of its 'works' (unless you are a clock-maker) is much less of a copy, yet it passes muster, for it in no way clashes with the reality. Even tho it should shrink to the mere word 'works,' that word still serves you truly; and when you speak of the 'time-keeping function' of the clock, or of its spring's 'elasticity,' it is hard to see exactly what your ideas can copy.

You perceive that there is a problem here. Where our ideas cannot copy definitely their object, what does agreement with that object mean? Some idealists seem to say that they are true whenever they are what God means that we ought to think about that object. Others hold the copy-view all through, and speak as if our ideas possessed truth just in proportion as they approach to being copies of the Absolute's eternal way of thinking.

These views, you see, invite pragmatistic discussion. But the great assumption of the intellectualists is that truth means essentially an inert static relation. When you've got your true idea of anything, there's an end of the matter. You're in possession; you *know*; you have fulfilled your thinking destiny. You are where you ought to be mentally; you have obeyed your categorical imperative; and nothing more need follow on that climax of your rational destiny. Epistemologically you are in stable equilibrium.

Pragmatism, on the other hand, asks its usual question. "Grant an idea or belief to be true," it says, "what concrete difference will its being true make in anyone's actual life? How will the truth be realized? What experiences will be different from those which would obtain if the belief were false? What, in short, is the truth's cash-value in experiential terms?"

The moment pragmatism asks this question, it sees the answer: *True ideas are those that we can assimilate, validate, corroborate and verify. False ideas are those that we cannot.* That is the practical difference it makes to us to have true ideas; that, therefore, is the meaning of truth, for it is all that truth is known as.

This thesis is what I have to defend. The truth of an idea is not a stagnant property inherent in it. Truth *happens* to an idea. It *becomes* true, is *made* true by events. Its verity *is* in fact an event, a process: the process namely of its verifying itself, its veri-*fication*. Its validity is the process of its valid-*action*.

* * *

Our account of truth is an account of truths in the plural, of processes of leading, realized *in rebus,* and having only this quality in common, that they *pay*. They pay by guiding us into or towards some part of a system that dips at numerous points into sense-percepts, which we may copy mentally or not, but with which at any rate we are now in the kind of commerce vaguely designated as verification. Truth for us is simply a collective name for verification-processes, just as health, wealth, strength, etc., are names for other processes connected with life, and also pursued because it pays to pursue them. Truth is *made*, just as health, wealth and strength are made, in the course of experience.

Here rationalism is instantaneously up in arms against us. I can imagine a rationalist to talk as follows:

"Truth is not made," he will say; "it absolutely obtains, being a unique relation that does not wait upon any process, but shoots straight over the head of experience, and hits its reality every time. Our belief that yon thing on the wall is a clock is true already, altho no one in the whole history of the world should verify it. The bare quality of standing in that transcendent relation is what makes any thought true that possesses it, whether or not there be verification. You pragmatists put the cart before the horse in making truth's being reside in verification-processes. These are merely signs of its being, merely our lame ways of ascertaining after the fact, which of our ideas already has possessed the wondrous quality. The quality itself is timeless, like all essences and natures. Thoughts partake of it directly, as they partake of falsity or of irrelevancy. It can't be analyzed away into pragmatic consequences."

The whole plausibility of this rationalist tirade is due to the fact to which we have already paid so much attention. In our world, namely, abounding as it does in things of similar kinds and similarly associated, one verification serves for others of its kind, and one great use of knowing things is to be led not so much to them as to their associates, especially to human talk about them. The quality of truth, obtaining *ante rem*, pragmatically means, then, the fact that in such a world innumerable ideas work better by their indirect or possible than by their direct and actual verification. Truth *ante rem* means only verifiability, then; or else it is a case of the stock rationalist trick of treating the *name* of a concrete phenomenal reality as an independent prior entity, and placing it behind the reality as its explanation. * * *

In the case of 'wealth' we all see the fallacy. We know that wealth is but a name for concrete processes that certain men's lives play a part in, and not a natural excellence found in Messrs. Rockefeller and Carnegie, but not in the rest of us.

Like wealth, health also lives *in rebus*. It is a name for processes, as digestion, circulation, sleep, etc., that go on happily, tho in this instance we are more inclined to think of it as a principle and to say the man digests and sleeps so well *because* he is so healthy.

With 'strength' we are, I think, more rationalistic still, and decidedly inclined to treat it as an excellence pre-existing in the man and explanatory of the herculean performances of his muscles.

With 'truth' most people go over the border entirely, and treat the rationalistic account as self-evident. But really all these words in *th* are exactly similar. Truth exists *ante rem* just as much and as little as the other things do.

The scholastics, following Aristotle, made much of the distinction between habit and act. Health *in actu* means, among other things, good sleeping and digesting. But a healthy man need not always be sleeping, or always digesting, any more than a wealthy man need be always handling money, or a strong man always lifting weights. All such qualities sink to the status of 'habits' between their times of exercise; and similarly truth becomes a habit of certain of our ideas and beliefs in their intervals of rest from their verifying activities. But those activities are the root of the whole matter, and the condition of there being any habit to exist in the intervals.

'*The true,*' *to put it very briefly, is only the expedient in the way of our thinking, just as '*the right*' is only the expedient in the way of our behaving.* Expedient in almost any fashion; and expedient in the long run and on the whole of course; for what meets expediently all the experience in sight won't necessarily meet all farther experiences equally satisfactorily. Experience, as we know, has ways of *boiling over,* and making us correct our present formulas.

The 'absolutely' true, meaning what no farther experience will ever alter, is that ideal vanishing-point towards which we imagine that all our temporary truths will some day converge. It runs on all fours with the perfectly wise man, and with the absolutely complete experience; and, if these ideals are ever realized, they will all be realized together. Meanwhile we have to live to-day by what truth we can get to-day, and be ready to-morrow to call it falsehood. Ptolemaic astronomy, euclidean space, aristotelian logic, scholastic metaphysics, were expedient for centuries, but human experience has boiled over those limits, and we now call these things only relatively true, or true within those borders of experience. 'Absolutely' they are false; for we know that those limits were casual, and might have been transcended by past theorists just as they are by present thinkers.

When new experiences lead to retrospective judgments, using the past tense, what these judgments utter *was* true, even tho no past thinker had been led there. We live forwards, a Danish thinker has said, but we understand backwards. The present sheds a backward light on the world's previous processes. They may have been truth-processes for the actors in them. They are not so for one who knows the later revelations of the story.

This regulative notion of a potential better truth to be established later, possibly to be established some day absolutely, and having powers of retroactive legislation, turns its face, like all pragmatist notions, towards concreteness of fact, and towards the future. Like the half-truths, the absolute truth will have to be *made,* made as a relation incidental to the growth of a mass of verification-experience, to which the half-true ideas are all along contributing their quota.

I have already insisted on the fact that truth is made largely out of previous truths. Men's beliefs at any time are so much experience *funded*. But the beliefs are themselves parts of the sum total of the world's experience, and become matter, therefore, for the next day's funding operations. So far as reality means experienceable reality, both it and the truths men gain about it are everlastingly in process of mutation—mutation towards a definite goal, it may be—but still mutation.

Mathematicians can solve problems with two variables. On the Newtonian theory, for instance, acceleration varies with distance, but distance also varies with acceleration. In the realm of truth-processes facts come independently and determine our beliefs provisionally. But these beliefs make us act, and as fast as they do so, they bring into sight or into existence new facts which re-determine the beliefs accordingly. So the whole coil and ball of truth, as it rolls up, is the product of a double influence. Truths emerge from facts; but they dip forward into facts again and add to them; which facts again create or reveal new truth (the word is indifferent) and so on indefinitely. The 'facts' themselves meanwhile are not *true*. They simply *are*. Truth is the function of the beliefs that start and terminate among them.

The case is like a snowball's growth, due as it is to the distribution of the snow on the one hand, and to the successive pushes of the boys on the other, with these factors co-determining each other incessantly.

The most fateful point of difference between being a rationalist and being a pragmatist is now fully in sight. Experience is in mutation, and our psychological ascertainments of truth are in mutation—so much rationalism will allow; but never that either reality itself or truth itself is mutable. Reality stands complete and ready-made from all eternity, rationalism insists, and the agreement of our ideas with it is that unique unanalyzable virtue in them of which she has already told us. As that intrinsic excellence, their truth has nothing to do with our experiences. It adds nothing to the content of experience. It makes no difference to reality itself; it is supervenient, inert, static, a reflexion merely. It doesn't *exist*, it *holds* or *obtains*, it belongs to another dimension from that of either facts or fact-relations, belongs, in short, to the epistemological dimension—and with that big word rationalism closes the discussion.

Thus, just as pragmatism faces forward to the future, so does rationalism here again face backward to a past eternity. True to her inveterate habit, rationalism reverts to 'principles,' and thinks that when an abstraction once is named, we own an oracular solution.

The tremendous pregnancy in the way of consequences for life of this radical difference of outlook will only become apparent in my later lectures. I wish meanwhile to close this lecture by showing that rationalism's sublimity does not save it from inanity.

When, namely, you ask rationalists, instead of accusing pragmatism of desecrating the notion of truth, to define it themselves by saying exactly what *they* understand by it, the only positive attempts I can think of are these two:

1. "Truth is just the system of propositions which have an unconditional claim to be recognized as valid."

2. Truth is a name for all those judgments which we find ourselves under obligation to make by a kind of imperative duty.

The first thing that strikes one in such definitions is their unutterable triviality. They are absolutely true, of course, but absolutely insignificant until you handle them pragmatically. What do you mean by 'claim' here, and what do you mean by 'duty'? As summary names for the concrete reasons why thinking in true ways is overwhelmingly expedient and good for mortal men, it is all right to talk of claims on reality's part to be agreed with, and of obligations on our part to agree. We feel both the claims and the obligations, and we feel them for just those reasons.

But the rationalists who talk of claim and obligation *expressly say that they have nothing to do with our practical interests or personal reasons.* Our reasons for agreeing are psychological facts, they say, relative to each thinker, and to the accidents of his life. They are his evidence merely, they are no part of the life of truth itself. That life transacts itself in a purely logical or epistemological, as distinguished from a psychological, dimension, and its claims antedate and exceed all personal motivations whatsoever. Tho neither man nor God should ever ascertain truth, the word would still have to be defined as that which *ought* to be ascertained and recognized.

There never was a more exquisite example of an idea abstracted from the concretes of experience and then used to oppose and negate what it was abstracted from.

Philosophy and common life abound in similar instances. The 'sentimentalist fallacy' is to shed tears over abstract justice and generosity, beauty, etc., and never to know these qualities when you meet them in the street, because there the circumstances make them vulgar. Thus I read in the privately printed biography of an eminently rationalistic mind: "It was strange that with such admiration for beauty in the abstract, my brother had no enthusiasm for fine architecture, for beautiful painting, or for flowers." And in almost the last philosophic work I have read, I find such passages as the following: "Justice is ideal, solely ideal. Reason conceives that it ought to exist, but experience shows that it cannot. . . . Truth, which ought to be, cannot be. . . . Reason is deformed by experience. As soon as reason enters experience, it becomes contrary to reason."

The rationalist's fallacy here is exactly like the sentimentalist's. Both extract a quality from the muddy particulars of experience, and find it so pure when extracted that they contrast it with each and all its muddy instances as an opposite and higher nature. All the while it is *their* nature. It is the nature of truths to be validated, verified. It pays for our ideas to be validated. Our obligation to seek truth is part of our general obligation to do what pays. The payments true ideas bring are the sole why of our duty to follow them.

JOHN DEWEY

The Influence of Darwin on Philosophy (1910)

The pragmatist philosopher and educator John Dewey (1859–1952) was a leading progressive public intellectual and reformer. Over a long career Dewey taught philosophy and related fields at the universities of Michigan, Minnesota, and Chicago, and held a chair in philosophy at Columbia University while publishing hundreds of scholarly works on a wide range of subjects. An active participant in contemporary political debates, Dewey helped found the American Civil Liberties Union, contributed regularly to liberal periodicals such as the New Republic, and held various positions in the Liberal Party of New York, the League for Industrial Democracy, the People's Lobby, and other liberal political organizations. Although Dewey's early philosophical interests focused on the rationalistic and dogmatic idealism of Hegelian thought, he turned to the experimental, instrumentalist orientation of pragmatism during his time at the University of Chicago. In this piece Dewey uses Darwinism to make the pragmatist's case against finding ideal values in the "remote and transcendent" or in "unknowable absolutes" rather than in "demonstration of experience" and "experimental tests."

There are, indeed, but two alternative courses. We must either find the appropriate objects and organs of knowledge in the mutual interactions of changing things; or else, to escape the infection of change, we *must* seek them in some transcendent and supernal region. The human mind, deliberately as it were, exhausted the logic of the changeless, the final, and the transcendent, before it essayed adventure on the pathless wastes of generation and transformation. We dispose all too easily of the efforts of the schoolmen to interpret nature and mind in terms of real essences, hidden forms, and occult faculties, forgetful of the seriousness and dignity of the ideas that lay behind. We dispose of them by laughing at the famous gentleman who accounted for the fact that opium put people to sleep on the ground it had a dormitive faculty. But the doctrine, held in our own day, that knowledge of the plant that yields the poppy consists in referring the peculiarities of an individual to a type, to a universal form, a doctrine so firmly established that any other method of knowing was conceived to be unphilosophical and unscientific, is a survival of precisely the same logic. This identity of conception in the scholastic and anti-Darwinian theory may well suggest greater sympathy for what has become unfamiliar as well as greater humility regarding the further unfamiliarities that history has in store.

Darwin was not, of course, the first to question the classic philosophy of nature and of knowledge. The beginnings of the revolution are in the physical science of the sixteenth and seventeenth centuries. When Galileo said: "It is my opinion that the earth is very noble and admirable by reason of so many and so different alterations and generations which are incessantly made therein," he expressed the changed temper that was coming over the world; the transfer of interest from the permanent to the changing. When Descartes said: "The nature of physical things is much more easily conceived when they are beheld coming gradually into existence, than when they are only considered as produced at once in a finished and perfect state," the modern world became self-conscious of the logic that was henceforth to control it, the logic of which Darwin's "Origin of Species" is the latest scientific achievement. Without the methods of Copernicus, Kepler, Galileo, and their successors in astronomy, physics, and chemistry, Darwin would have been helpless in the organic sciences. But prior to Darwin the impact of the new scientific method upon life, mind, and politics, had been arrested, because between these ideal or moral interests and the inorganic world intervened the kingdom of plants and animals. The gates of the garden of life were barred to the new ideas; and only through this garden was there access to mind and politics. The influence of Darwin upon philosophy resides in his having conquered the phenomena of life for the principle of transition, and thereby freed the new logic for application to mind and morals and life.

The exact bearings upon philosophy of the new logical outlook are, of course, as yet, uncertain and inchoate. We live in the twilight of intellectual transition. One must add the rashness of the prophet to the stubbornness of the partizan to venture a systematic exposition of the influence upon philosophy of the Darwinian method. At best, we can but inquire as to its general bearing—the effect upon mental temper and complexion, upon that body of half-conscious, half-instinctive intellectual aversions and preferences which determine, after all, our more deliberate intellectual enterprises. In this vague inquiry there happens to exist as a kind of touchstone a problem of long historic currency that has also been much discussed in Darwinian literature. I refer to the old problem of design *versus* chance, mind *versus* matter, as the causal explanation, first or final, of things.

As we have already seen, the classic notion of species carried with it the idea of purpose. In all living forms, a specific type is present directing the earlier stages of growth to the realization of its own perfection. Since this purposive regulative principle is not visible to the senses, it follows that it must be an ideal or rational force. Since, however, the perfect form is gradually approximated through the sensible changes, it also follows that in and through a sensible realm a rational ideal force is working out its own ultimate manifestation. These inferences were extended to nature: (*a*) She does nothing in vain; but all for an ulterior purpose. (*b*) Within natural sensible events there is therefore contained a spiritual causal force, which as spiritual escapes perception, but is apprehended by an enlightened reason. (*c*) The manifestation of this principle brings about a subordination of matter and sense to its own realization, and this ultimate fulfilment is the goal of nature and of man. The design argument thus operated in two directions. Purposefulness accounted for the intelligibility of nature and the possibility of science, while the absolute or cosmic character of this purposefulness gave sanction and worth to the moral and religious endeavors of man. Science was underpinned and morals authorized by one and the same principle, and their mutual agreement was eternally guaranteed. * * *

The Darwinian principle of natural selection cut straight under this philosophy. If all organic adaptations are due simply to constant variation and the elimination of those variations which are harmful in the struggle for existence that is brought about by excessive reproduction, there is no call for a prior intelligent causal force to plant and preordain them. Hostile critics charged Darwin with materialism and with making chance the cause of the universe. * * *

So much for some of the more obvious facts of the discussion of design *versus* chance, as causal principles of nature and of life as a whole. We brought up this discussion, you recall, as a crucial instance. What does our touchstone indicate as to the bearing of Darwinian ideas upon philosophy? In the first place, the new logic outlaws, flanks, dismisses—

what you will—one type of problems and substitutes for it another type. Philosophy forswears inquiry after absolute origins and absolute finalities in order to explore specific values and the specific conditions that generate them.

Darwin concluded that the impossibility of assigning the world to chance as a whole and to design in its parts indicated the insolubility of the question. Two radically different reasons, however, may be given as to why a problem is insoluble. One reason is that the problem is too high for intelligence; the other is that the question in its very asking makes assumptions that render the question meaningless. The latter alternative is unerringly pointed to in the celebrated case of design *versus* chance. Once admit that the sole verifiable or fruitful object of knowledge is the particular set of changes that generate the object of study together with the consequences that then flow from it, and no intelligible question can be asked about what, by assumption, lies outside. To assert—as is often asserted—that specific values of particular truth, social bonds and forms of beauty, if they can be shown to be generated by concretely knowable conditions, are meaningless and in vain; to assert that they are justified only when they and their particular causes and effects have all at once been gathered up into some inclusive first cause and some exhaustive final goal, is intellectual atavism. Such argumentation is reversion to the logic that explained the extinction of fire by water through the formal essence of aqueousness and the quenching of thirst by water through the final cause of aqueousness. Whether used in the case of the special event or that of life as a whole, such logic only abstracts some aspect of the existing course of events in order to reduplicate it as a petrified eternal principle by which to explain the very changes of which it is the formalization. * * *

Interest shifts from the wholesale essence back of special changes to the question of how special changes serve and defeat concrete purposes; shifts from an intelligence that shaped things once for all to the particular intelligences which things are even now shaping; shifts from an ultimate goal of good to the direct increments of justice and happiness that intelligent administration of existent conditions may beget and that present carelessness or stupidity will destroy or forego.

* * *

In the second place, the classic type of logic inevitably set philosophy upon proving that life *must* have certain qualities and values—no matter how experience presents the matter—because of some remote cause and eventual goal. The duty of wholesale justification inevitably accompanies all thinking that makes the meaning of special occurrences depend upon something that once and for all lies behind them. The habit of derogating from present meanings and uses prevents our looking the facts of experience in the face; it prevents serious acknowledgement of the evils they present and serious concern with the goods they promise but do not as yet fulfil. It turns thought to the business of finding a wholesale transcendent remedy for the one and guarantee for the other. One is reminded of the way many moralists and theologians greeted Herbert Spencer's recognition of an unknowable energy from which welled up the phenomenal physical processes without and the conscious operations within. Merely because Spencer labeled his unknowable energy "God," this faded piece of metaphysical goods was greeted as an important and grateful concession to the reality of the spiritual realm. Were it not for the deep hold of the habit of seeking justification for ideal values in the remote and transcendent, surely this reference of them to an unknowable absolute would be despised in comparison with the demonstrations of experience that knowable energies are daily generating about us precious values.

The displacing of this wholesale type of philosophy will doubtless not arrive by sheer logical disproof, but rather by growing recognition of its futility. Were it a thousand times true that opium produces sleep because of its dormitive energy, yet the inducing of sleep in the tired, and the recovery to waking life of the poisoned, would not be thereby one least step forwarded. And were it a thousand times dialectically demonstrated that life as a whole is regulated by a transcendent principle to a final inclusive goal, none the less truth and error, health and disease, good and evil, hope and fear in the concrete, would remain just what and where they now are. To improve our education, to ameliorate our manners, to advance our politics, we must have recourse to specific conditions of generation.

Finally, the new logic introduces responsibility into the intellectual life. To idealize and rationalize the universe at large is after all a confession of inability to master the courses of things that specifically concern us. As long as mankind suffered from this impotency, it naturally shifted a burden of responsibility that it could not carry over to the more competent shoulders of the transcendent cause. But if insight into specific conditions of value and into specific consequences of ideas is possible, philosophy must in time become a method of locating and interpreting the more serious of the conflicts that occur in life, and a method of projecting ways for dealing with them: a method of moral and political diagnosis and prognosis.

The claim to formulate *a priori* the legislative constitution of the universe is by its nature a claim that may lead to elaborate dialectic developments. But it is also one that removes these very conclusions from subjection to experimental test, for, by definition, these results make no differences in the detailed course of events. But a philosophy that humbles its pretensions to the work of projecting hypotheses for the education and conduct of mind, individual and social, is thereby subjected to test by the way in which the ideas it propounds work out in practice. In having modesty forced upon it, philosophy also acquires responsibility.

Doubtless I seem to have violated the implied promise of my earlier remarks and to have turned both prophet and partisan. But in anticipating the direction of the transformations in philosophy to be wrought by the Darwinian genetic and experimental logic, I do not profess to speak for any save those who yield themselves consciously or unconsciously to this logic. No one can fairly deny that at present there are two effects of the Darwinian mode of thinking. On the one hand, there are many making sincere and vital efforts to revise our traditional philosophic conceptions in accordance with its demands. On the other hand, there is as definitely a recrudescence of absolutistic philosophies; an assertion of a type of philosophic knowing distinct from that of the sciences, one which opens to us another kind of reality from that to which the sciences give access; an appeal through experience to something that essentially goes beyond experience. This reaction affects popular creeds and religious movements as well as technical philosophies. The very conquest of the biological sciences by the new ideas has led many to proclaim an explicit and rigid separation of philosophy from science.

Old Ideas give way slowly; for they are more than abstract logical forms and categories. They are habits, predispositions, deeply engrained attitudes of aversion and preference. Moreover, the conviction persists— though history shows it to be a hallucination—that all the questions that the human mind has asked are questions that can be answered in terms of the alternatives that the questions themselves present. But in fact intellectual progress usually occurs through sheer abandonment of questions together with both of the alternatives they assume—an abandonment that results from their decreasing vitality and a change of urgent interest. We do not solve them: we get over them. Old questions are solved by disappearing, evaporating, while new questions corresponding to the changed attitude of endeavor and preference take their place. Doubtless the greatest dissolvent in contemporary thought of old questions, the greatest precipitant of new methods, new intentions, new problems, is the one effected by the scientific revolution that found its climax in the "Origin of Species."

JOHN DEWEY

The Public and Its Problems (1927)

One of the major theorists of democracy in American political thought, Dewey emphasized the centrality of community in his conception of democracy. This progressive thinker believed that democratic habits had to permeate all human associations or else the community would never become a "democratically effective Public." His book The Public and Its Problems *underscored the importance to democracy of a scientifically informed and critical public opinion.*

We have had occasion to refer in passing to the distinction between democracy as a social idea and political democracy as a system of government. The two are, of course, connected. The idea remains barren and empty save as it is incarnated in human relationships. Yet in discussion they must be distinguished. The idea of democracy is a wider and fuller idea than can be exemplified in the state even at its best. To be realized it must affect all modes of human association, the family, the school, industry, religion. And even as far as political arrangements are concerned, governmental institutions are but a mechanism for securing to an idea channels of effective operation. It will hardly do to say that criticisms of the political machinery leave the believer in the idea untouched. For, as far as they are justified—and no candid believer can deny that many of them are only too well grounded—they arouse him to bestir himself in order that the idea may find a more adequate machinery through which to work. What the faithful insist upon, however, is that the idea and its external organs and structures are not to be identified. We object to the common supposition of the foes of existing democratic government that the accusations against it touch the social and moral aspirations and ideas which underlie the political forms. The old saying that the cure for the ills of democracy is more democracy is not apt if it means that the evils may be remedied by introducing more machinery of the same kind as that which already exists, or by refining and perfecting that machinery. But the phrase may also indicate the need of returning to the idea itself, of clarifying and deepening our apprehension of it, and of employing our sense of its meaning to criticize and remake its political manifestations.

Confining ourselves, for the moment, to political democracy, we must, in any case, renew our protest against the assumption that the idea has itself produced the governmental practices which obtain in democratic states; General suffrage, elected representatives, majority rule, and so on. The idea has influenced the concrete political movement, but it has not caused it. The transition from family and dynastic government supported by the loyalties of tradition to popular government was the outcome primarily of technological discoveries and inventions working a change in the customs by which men had been bound together. It was not due to the doctrines of doctrinaires. The forms to which we are accustomed in democratic governments represent the cumulative effect of a multitude of events, unpremeditated as far as political effects were concerned and having unpredictable consequences. There is no sanctity in universal suffrage, frequent elections, majority rule, congressional and cabinet government. These things are devices evolved in the direction in which the current was moving, each wave of which involved at the time of its impulsion a minimum of departure from antecedent custom and law. The devices served a purpose; but the purpose was rather that of meeting existing needs which had become too intense to be ignored, than that of forwarding the democratic idea. In spite of all defects, they served their own purpose well. * * *

Nevertheless the current has set steadily in one direction: toward democratic forms. That government exists to serve its community, and that this purpose cannot be achieved unless the community itself shares in selecting its governors and determining their policies, are a deposit of fact left, as far as we can see, permanently in the wake of doctrines and forms, however transitory the latter. They are not the whole of the democratic idea, but they express it in its political phase. Belief in this political aspect is not a mystic faith as if in some overruling providence that cares for children, drunkards and others unable to help themselves. It marks a well-attested conclusion from historic facts. We have every reason to think that whatever changes may take place in existing democratic machinery, they will be of a sort to make the interest of the public a more supreme guide and criterion of governmental activity, and to enable the public to form and manifest its purposes still more authoritatively. In this sense the cure for the ailments of democracy is more democracy. The prime difficulty, as we have seen, is that of discovering the means by which a scattered, mobile and manifold public may so recognize itself as to define and express its interests. This discovery is necessarily precedent to any fundamental change in the machinery. We are not concerned therefore to set forth counsels as to advisable improvements in the political forms of democracy. Many have been suggested. It is no derogation of their relative worth to say that consideration of these changes is not at present an affair of primary importance. The problem lies deeper; it is in the first instance an intellectual problem: the search for conditions under which the Great Society may become the Great Community. When these conditions are brought into being they will make their own forms. Until they have come about, it is somewhat futile to consider what political machinery will suit them.

In a search for the conditions under which the inchoate public now extant may function democratically, we may proceed from a statement of the nature of the democratic idea in its generic social sense. From the standpoint of the individual, it consists in having a responsible share according to capacity in forming and directing the activities of the groups to which one belongs and in participating according to need in the values which the groups sustain. From the standpoint of the groups, it demands liberation of the potentialities of members of a group in harmony with the interests and goods which are common. Since every individual is a member of many groups, this specification cannot be fulfilled except when different groups interact flexibly and fully in connection with other groups. A member of a robber band may express his powers in a way consonant with belonging to that group and be directed by the interest common to its members. But he does so only at the cost of repression of those of his potentialities which can be realized only through membership in other groups. The robber band cannot interact flexibly with other groups; it can act only through isolating itself. It must prevent the operation of all interests save those which circumscribe it in its separateness. But a good citizen finds his conduct as a member of a political group enriching and enriched by his participation in family life, industry, scientific and artistic associations. There is a free give-and-take: fullness of integrated personality is therefore possible of achievement, since the pulls and responses of different groups reinforce one another and their values accord.

Regarded as an idea, democracy is not an alternative to other principles of associated life. It is the idea of community life itself. It is an ideal in the only intelligible sense of an ideal: namely, the tendency and movement of some thing which exists carried to its final limit, viewed as completed, perfected. Since things do not attain such fulfillment but are in actuality distracted and interfered with, democracy in this sense is not a fact and never will be. But neither in this sense is there or has there ever been anything which is a community in its full measure, a community unalloyed by alien elements. The idea or ideal of a community presents, however, actual phases of associated life as they are freed from restrictive and disturbing elements, and are contemplated as having attained their limit of development. Wherever there is conjoint activity whose consequences are appreciated as good by all singular persons who take part in it, and where the realization of the good is such as to effect an energetic desire and effort to sustain it in being just because it is a good shared by all, there is in so far a community. The clear consciousness of a communal life, in all its implications, constitutes the idea of democracy.

Only when we start from a community as a fact, grasp the fact in thought so as to clarify and enhance its constituent elements, can we reach an idea of democracy which is not utopian. The conceptions and shibboleths which are traditionally associated with the idea of democracy take on a veridical and directive meaning only when they are construed as marks and traits of an association which realizes the defining characteristics of a community. Fraternity, liberty and equality isolated from communal life are hopeless abstractions. Their separate assertion leads to mushy sentimentalism or else to extravagant and fanatical violence which in the end defeats its own aims. Equality then becomes a creed of mechanical identity which is false to facts and impossible of realization. Effort to attain it is divisive of the vital bonds which hold men together; as far as it puts forth issue, the outcome is a mediocrity in which good is common only in the sense of being average and vulgar. Liberty is then thought of as independence of social ties, and ends in dissolution and anarchy. It is more difficult to sever the idea of brotherhood from that of a community, and hence it is either practically ignored in the movements which identify democracy with Individualism, or else it is a sentimentally appended tag. In its just connection with communal experience, fraternity is another name for the consciously appreciated goods which accrue from an association in which all share, and which give direction to the conduct of each. Liberty is that secure release and fulfillment of personal potentialities which take place only in rich and manifold association with others: the power to be an individualized self making a distinctive contribution and enjoying in its own way the fruits of association. Equality denotes the unhampered share which each individual member of the community has in the consequences of associated action. It is equitable because it is measured only by need and capacity to utilize, not by extraneous factors which deprive one in order that another may take and have.

* * *

It denotes effective regard for whatever is distinctive and unique in each, irrespective of physical and psychological inequalities. It is not a natural possession but is a fruit of the community when its action is directed by its character as a community.

Associated or joint activity is a condition of the creation of a community. But association itself is physical and organic, while communal life is moral, that is emotionally, intellectually, consciously sustained.

* * * Human associations may be ever so organic in origin and firm in operation, but they develop into societies in a human sense only as their consequences, being known, are esteemed and sought for. Even if "society" were as much an organism as some writers have held, it would not on that account be society. Interactions, transactions, occur *de facto* and the results of interdependence follow. But participation in activities and sharing in results are additive concerns. They demand *communication* as a prerequisite. * * *

The work of conversion of the physical and organic phase of associated behavior into a community of action saturated and regulated by mutual interest in shared meanings, consequences, which are translated into ideas and desired objects by means of symbols, does not occur all at once nor completely. At any given time, it sets a problem rather than marks a settled achievement. We are born organic beings associated with others, but we are not born members of a community. The young have to be brought within the traditions, outlook and interests which characterize a community by means of education: by unremitting instruction and by learning in connection with the phenomena of overt association. Everything which is distinctively human is learned, not native, even though it could not be learned without native structures which mark man off from other animals. To learn in a human way and to human effect is not just to acquire added skill through refinement of original capacities. * * *

This is the meaning of the statement that the problem is a moral one dependent upon intelligence and education. We have in our prior account sufficiently emphasized the role of technological and industrial factors in creating the Great Society. What was said may even have seemed to imply acceptance to the deterministic version of an economic interpretation of history and institutions. It is silly and futile to ignore and deny economic facts. They do not cease to operate because we refuse to note them, or because we smear them over with sentimental idealizations. As we have also noted, they generate as their result overt and external conditions of action and these are known with various degrees of adequacy. What actually happens in consequence of industrial forces is dependent upon the presence or absence of perception and communication of consequences, upon foresight and its effect upon desire and endeavor. Economic agencies produce one result when they are left to work themselves out on the merely physical level, or on that level modified only as the knowledge, skill and technique which the community has accumulated are transmitted to its members unequally and by chance. They have a different outcome in the degree in which knowledge of consequences is equitably distributed, and action is animated by an informed and lively sense of a shared interest. The doctrine of economic interpretation as usually stated ignores the transformation which meanings may effect; it passes over the new medium which communication may interpose between industry and its eventual consequences. It is obsessed by the illusion which vitiated the "natural economy": an illusion due to failure to note the difference made in action by perception and publication of its consequences, actual and possible. It thinks in terms of antecedents, not of the eventual; of origins, not fruits.

We have returned, through this apparent excursion, to the question in which our earlier discussion culminated: What are the conditions under which it is possible for the Great Society to approach more closely and vitally the status of a Great Community, and thus take form in genuinely democratic societies and state? What are the conditions under which we may reasonably picture the Public emerging from its eclipse?

* * * The object of the analysis will be to show that *unless* ascertained specifications are realized, the Community cannot be organized as a democratically effective Public. It is not claimed that the conditions which will be noted will suffice, but only that at least they are indispensable. In other words, we shall endeavor to frame a hypothesis regarding the democratic state to stand in contrast with the earlier doctrine which has been nullified by the course of events.

Two essential constituents in that older theory, as will be recalled, were the notions that each individual is of himself equipped with the intelligence needed, under the operation of self-interest, to engage in political affairs; and that general suffrage, frequent elections of officials and majority rule are sufficient to ensure the responsibility of elected rulers to the desires and interests of the public. As we shall see, the second conception is logically bound up with the first and stands or falls with it. At the basis of the scheme lies what Lippmann has well called the idea of the "omnicompetent" individual: competent to frame policies, to judge their results; competent to know in all situations demanding political action what is for his own good, and competent to enforce his idea of good and the will to effect it against contrary forces. Subsequent history has proved that the assumption involved illusion. Had it not been for the misleading influence of a false psychology, the illusion might have been detected in advance. But current philosophy held that ideas and knowledge were functions of a mind or consciousness which originated in individuals by means of isolated contact with objects. But in fact, knowledge is a function of association and communication; it depends upon tradition, upon tools and methods socially transmitted, developed and sanctioned. Faculties of effectual observation, reflection and desire are habits acquired under the influence of the culture and institutions of society, not ready-made inherent powers. The fact that man acts from crudely intelligized emotion and from habit rather than from rational consideration, is now so familiar that it is not easy to appreciate that the other idea was taken seriously as the basis of economic and political philosophy. The measure of truth which it contains was derived from observation of a relatively small group of shrewd business men who regulated their enterprises by calculation and accounting, and of citizens of small and stable local communities who were so intimately acquainted with the persons and affairs of their locality that they could pass competent judgment upon the bearing of proposed measures upon their own concerns.

Habit is the mainspring of human action, and habits are formed for the most part under the influence of the customs of a group. The organic structure of man entails the formation of habit, for, whether we wish it or not, whether we are aware of it or not, every act effects a modification of attitude and set which directs future behavior. The dependence of habit-forming upon those habits of a group which constitute customs and institutions is a natural consequence of the helplessness of infancy. * * *

The influence of habit is decisive because all distinctively human action has to be learned, and the very heart, blood and sinews of learning is creation of habitudes. Habits bind us to orderly and established ways of action because they generate ease, skill and interest in things to which we have grown used and because they instigate fear to walk in different ways, and because they leave us incapacitated for the trial of them. Habit does not preclude the use of thought, but it determines the channels within which it operates. Thinking is secreted in the interstices of habits.

* * * Thinking itself becomes habitual along certain lines; a specialized occupation. Scientific men, philosophers, literary persons, are not men and women who have so broken the bonds of habits that pure reason and emotion undefiled by use and wont speak through them. They are persons of a specialized infrequent habit. Hence the idea that men are moved by an intelligent and calculated regard for their own good is pure mythology. Even if the principle of self-love actuated behavior, it would still be true that the *objects* in which men find their love manifested, the objects which they take as constituting their peculiar interests, are set by habits reflecting social customs.

These facts explain why the social doctrinaires of the new industrial movement had so little prescience of what was to follow in consequence of it. These facts explain why the more things changed, the more they were the same; they account, that is, for the fact that instead of the sweeping revolution which was expected to result from democratic political machinery, there was in the main but a transfer of vested power from one class to another. A few men, whether or not they were good judges of their own true interest and good, were competent judges of the conduct of business for pecuniary profit, and of how the new governmental machinery could be made to serve their ends. It would have taken a new race of human beings to escape, in the use made of political forms, from the influence of deeply engrained habits, of old institutions and customary social status, with their in-wrought limitations of expectation, desire and demand. And such a race, unless of disembodied angelic constitution, would simply have taken up the task where human beings assumed it upon emergency from the condition of anthropoid apes. In spite of sudden and catastrophic revolutions, the essential continuity of history is doubly guaranteed. Not only are personal desire and belief functions of habit and custom, but the objective conditions which provide the resources and tools of action, together with its limitations, obstructions and traps, are precipitates of the past, perpetuating, willy-nilly, its hold and power. The creation of a *tabula rasa* in order to permit the creation of a new order is so impossible as to set at naught both the hope of buoyant revolutionaries and the timidity of scared conservatives.

Nevertheless, changes take place and are cumulative in character. Observation of them in the light of their recognized consequences arouses reflection, discovery, invention, experimentation. When a certain state of accumulated knowledge, of techniques and instrumentalities is attained, the process of change is so accelerated, that, as to-day, it appears externally to be the dominant trait. But there is a marked lag in any corresponding change of ideas and desires. Habits of opinion are the toughest of all habits; when they have become second nature, and are supposedly thrown out of the door, they creep in again as stealthily and surely as does first nature. And as they are modified, the alteration first shows itself negatively, in the disintegration of old beliefs, to be replaced by floating, volatile and accidentally snatched up opinions. Of course there has been an enormous increase in the amount of knowledge possessed by mankind, but it does not equal, probably, the increase in the amount of errors and half-truths which have got into circulation. In social and human matters, especially, the development of a critical sense and methods of discriminating judgment has not kept pace with the growth of careless reports and of motives for positive misrepresentation. * * *

Why should the public and its officers, even if the latter are termed statesmen, be wiser and more effective? The prime condition of a democratically organized public is a kind of knowledge and insight which does not yet exist. In its absence, it would be the height of absurdity to try to tell what it would be like if it existed. But some of the conditions which must be fulfilled if it is to exist can be indicated. We can borrow that much from the spirit and method of science even if we are ignorant of it as a specialized apparatus. An obvious requirement is freedom of social inquiry and of distribution of its conclusions. The notion that men may be free in their thought even when they are not in its expression and dissemination has been sedulously propagated. It had its origin in the idea of a mind complete in itself, apart from action and from objects. Such a conciousness presents in fact the spectacle of mind deprived of its normal functioning, because it is baffled by the actualities in connection with which alone it is truly mind, and is driven back in secluded and impotent revery.

There can be no public without full publicity in respect to all consequences which concern it. Whatever obstructs and restricts publicity, limits and distorts public opinion and checks and distorts thinking on social affairs. Without freedom of expression, not even methods of social inquiry can be developed. For tools can be evolved and perfected only in operation; in application to observing, reporting and organizing actual subject-matter; and this application cannot occur save through free and systematic communication. The early history of physical knowledge, of Greek conceptions of natural phenomena, proves how inept become the conceptions of the best endowed minds when those ideas are elaborated apart from the closest contact with the events which they purport to state and explain. The ruling ideas and methods of the human sciences are in much the same condition today. They are also evolved on the basis of past gross observations, remote from constant use in regulation of the material of new observations.

The belief that thought and its communication are now free simply because legal restrictions which once obtained have been done away with is absurd. Its currency perpetuates the infantile state of social knowledge. For it blurs recognition of our central need to possess conceptions which are used as tools of directed inquiry and which are tested, rectified and caused to grow in actual use. No man and no mind was ever emancipated merely by being left alone. Removal of formal limitations is but a negative condition; positive freedom is not a state but an act which involves methods and instrumentalities for control of conditions. Experience shows that sometimes the sense of external oppression, as by censorship, acts as a challenge and arouses intellectual energy and excites courage. But a belief in intellectual freedom where it does not exist contributes only to complacency in virtual enslavement, to sloppiness, superficiality and recourse to sensations as a substitute for ideas: marked traits of our present estate with respect to social knowledge. On one hand, thinking deprived of its normal course takes refuge in academic specialism, comparable in its way to what is called scholasticism. On the other hand, the physical agencies of publicity which exist in such abundance are utilized in ways which constitute a large part of the present meaning of publicity: advertising, propaganda, invasion of private life, the "featuring" of passing incidents in a way which violates all the moving logic of continuity, and which leaves us with those isolated intrusions and shocks which are the essence of "sensations."

It would be a mistake to identify the conditions which limit free communication and circulation of facts and ideas, and which thereby arrest and pervert social thought or inquiry, merely with overt forces which are obstructive. It is true that those who have ability to manipulate social relations for their own advantage have to be reckoned with. They have an uncanny instinct for detecting whatever intellectual tendencies even remotely threaten to encroach upon their control. They have developed an extraordinary facility in enlisting upon their side the inertia, prejudices and emotional partisanship of the masses by use of a technique which impedes free inquiry and expression. We seem to be approaching a state of government by hired promoters of opinion called publicity agents. But the more serious enemy is deeply concealed in hidden entrenchments.

Emotional habituations and intellectual habitudes on the part of the mass of men create the conditions of which the exploiters of sentiment and opinion only take advantage. Men have got used to an experimental method in physical and technical matters. They are still afraid of it in human concerns. The fear is the more efficacious because like all deeplying fears it is covered up and disguised by all kinds of rationalizations. One of its commonest forms is a truly religious idealization of, and reverence for, established institutions; for example in our own politics, the Constitution, the Supreme Court, private property, free contract and so on. The words "sacred" and "sanctity" come readily to our lips when such things come under discussion. They testify to the religious aureole which protects the institutions. If "holy" means that which is not to be approached nor touched, save with ceremonial precautions and by specially anointed officials, then such things are holy in contemporary political life. As supernatural matters have progressively been left high and dry upon a secluded beach, the actuality of religious taboos has more and more gathered about secular institutions, especially those connected with the nationalistic state. Psychiatrists have discovered that one of the commonest causes of mental disturbance is an underlying fear of which the subject is not aware, but which leads to withdrawal from reality and to unwillingness to think things through. There is a social pathology which leads to withdrawal from reality and to unwillingness to think things through. There is a social pathology which works powerfully against effective inquiry into social institutions and conditions. It manifests itself in a thousand ways; in querulousness, in impotent drifting, in uneasy snatching at distractions, in idealization of the long established, in a facile optimism assumed as a cloak, in riotous glorification of things "as they are," in intimidation of all dissenters—ways which depress and dissipate thought all the more effectually because they operate with subtle and unconscious pervasiveness. * * *

Nevertheless the course of development has left us of this age in a plight. When we say that a subject of science is technically specialized, or that it is highly "abstract," what we practically mean is that it is not conceived in terms of its bearing upon human life. All *merely* physical knowledge is technical, couched in a technical vocabulary communicable only to the few. Even physical knowledge which does affect human conduct, which does modify what we do and undergo, is also technical and remote in the degree in which its bearings are not understood and used. The sunlight, rain, air, and soil have always entered in visible ways into human experience; atoms and molecules and cells and most other things with which the sciences are occupied affect us, but not visibly. Because they enter life and modify experience in imperceptible ways, and their consequences are not realized, speech about them is technical; communication is by means of peculiar symbols. One would think, then, that a fundamental and ever-operating aim would be to translate knowledge of the subject-matter of physical conditions into terms which are generally understood, into signs denoting human consequences of services and disservices rendered. For ultimately all consequences which enter human life depend upon physical conditions; they can be understood and mastered only as the latter are taken into account. One would think, then, that any state of affairs which tends to render the things of the environment unknown and incommunicable by human beings in terms of their own activities and sufferings would be deplored as a disaster; that it would be felt to be intolerable, and to be put up with only as far as it is, at any given time, inevitable.

But the facts are to the contrary. Matter and the material are words which in the minds of many convey a note of disparagement. They are taken to be foes of whatever is of ideal value in life, instead of as conditions of its manifestation and sustained being. In consequence of this division, they do become in fact enemies, for whatever is consistently kept apart from human values depresses thought and renders values sparse and precarious in fact. There are even some who regard the materialism and dominance of commercialism of modern life as fruits of undue devotion to physical science, not seeing that the split between man and nature, artificially made by the tradition which originated before there was understanding of the physical conditions that are the medium of human activities, is the benumbing factor. The most influential form of the divorce is separation between pure and applied science. Since "application" signifies recognized bearing upon human experience and well-being, honor of what is "pure" and contempt for what is "applied" has for its outcome a science which is remote and technical, communicable only to specialists, and a conduct of human affairs which is haphazard, biased, unfair in distribution of values. What is applied and employed as the alternative to knowledge in regulation of society is ignorance, prejudice, class interest and accident. Science is converted into knowledge in its honorable and emphatic sense *only* in application. Otherwise it is truncated, blind, distorted. When it is then applied, it is in ways which explain the unfavorable sense so often attached to "application" and the "utilitarian": namely, use for pecuniary ends to the profit of a few.

At present, the application of physical science is rather *to* human concerns than *in* them. That is, it is external, made in the interests of its consequences for a possessing and acquisitive class. Application *in* life would signify that science was absorbed and distributed: that it was the instrumentality of that common understanding and thorough communication which is the precondition of the existence of a genuine and effective public. The use of science to regulate industry and trade has gone on steadily. The scientific revolution of the seventeenth century was the precursor of the industrial revolution of the eighteenth and nineteenth. In consequence, man has suffered the impact of an enormously enlarged control of physical energies without any corresponding ability to control himself and his own affairs. Knowledge divided against itself, a science to whose incompleteness is added an artificial split, has played its part in generating enslavement of men, women and children in factories in which they are animated machines to tend inanimate machines. It has maintained sordid slums, flurried and discontented careers, grinding poverty and luxurious wealth, brutal exploitation of nature and man in times of peace and high explosives and noxious gases in times of war. Man, a child in understanding of himself, has placed in his hands physical tools of incalculable power. He plays with them like a child, and whether they work harm or good is largely a matter of accident. The instrumentality becomes a master and works fatally as if possessed of a will of its own—not because it has a will but because man has not.

The glorification of "pure" science under such conditions is a rationalization of an escape; it marks a construction of an asylum of refuge, a shirking of responsibility. The true purity of knowledge exists not when it is uncontaminated by contact with use and service. It is wholly a moral matter, an affair of honesty, impartiality and generous breadth of intent in search and communication. The adulteration of knowledge is due not to its use, but to vested bias and prejudice, to one-sidedness of outlook, to vanity, to conceit of possession and authority, to contempt or disregard of human concern in its use. Humanity is not, as was once thought, the end for which all things were formed; it is but a slight and feeble thing, perhaps an episodic one, in the vast stretch of the universe. But for man, man is the center of interest and the measure of importance. The magnifying of the physical realm at the cost of man is but an abdication and a flight. To make physical science a rival of human interests is bad enough, for it forms a diversion of energy which can ill be afforded. But the evil does not stop there. The ultimate harm is that the understanding by man of his own affairs and his ability to direct them are sapped at their root when knowledge of nature is disconnected from its human function.

It has been implied throughout that knowledge is communication as well as understanding. I well remember the saying of a man, uneducated from the standpoint of the schools, in speaking of certain matters: "Sometime they will be found out and not only found out, but they will be known." The schools may suppose that a thing is known when it is found out. My old friend was aware that a thing is fully known only when it is published, shared, socially accessible. Record and communication are indispensable to knowledge. Knowledge cooped up in a private consciousness is a myth, and knowledge of social phenomena is peculiarly dependent upon dissemination, for only by distribution can such knowledge be either obtained or tested. A fact of community life which is not spread abroad so as to be a common possession is a contradiction in terms. Dissemination is something other than scattering at large. Seeds are sown, not by virtue of being thrown out at random, but by being so distributed as to take root and have a chance of growth. Communication of the results of social inquiry is the same thing as the formation of public opinion. This marks one of the first ideas framed in the growth of political democracy as it will be one of the last to be fulfilled. For public opinion is judgment which is formed and entertained by those who constitute the public and is about public affairs. Each of the two phases imposes for its realization conditions hard to meet.

Opinions and beliefs concerning the public presuppose effective and organized inquiry. Unless there are methods for detecting the energies which are at work and tracing them through an intricate network of interactions to their consequences, what passes as public opinion will be "opinion" in its derogatory sense rather than truly public, no matter how widespread the opinion is. The number who share error as to fact and who partake of a false belief measures power for harm. Opinion casually formed and formed under the direction of those who have something at stake in having a lie believed can be *public* opinion only in name. Calling it by this name, acceptance of the name as a kind of warrant, magnifies its capacity to lead action astray. The more who share it, the more injurious its influence. Public opinion, even if it happens to be correct, is intermittent when it is not the product of methods of investigation and reporting constantly at work. It appears only in crises. Hence its "rightness" concerns only an immediate emergency. Its lack of continuity makes it wrong from the standpoint of the course of events. It is as if a physician were able to deal for the moment with an emergency in disease but could not adapt his treatment of it to the underlying conditions which brought it about. He may then "cure" the disease—that is, cause its present alarming symptoms to subside—but he does not modify its causes; his treatment may even affect them for the worse. Only continuous inquiry, continuous in the sense of being connected as well as persistent, can provide the material of enduring opinion about public matters.

There is a sense in which "opinion" rather than knowledge, even under the most favorable circumstances, is the proper term to use—namely, in the sense of judgment, estimate. For in its strict sense, knowledge can refer only to what *has* happened and been done. What is still *to be* done involves a forecast of a future liability to error in judgment involved in all anticipation of probabilities. There may well be honest divergence as to policies to be pursued, even when plans spring from knowledge of the same facts. But genuinely public policy cannot be generated unless it be informed by knowledge, and this knowledge does not exist except when there is systematic, thorough, and well-equipped search and record.

Moreover, inquiry must be as nearly contemporaneous as possible; otherwise it is only of antiquarian interest. Knowledge of history is evidently necessary for connectedness of knowledge. But history which is not brought down close to the actual scene of events leaves a gap and exercises influence upon the formation of judgments about the public interest only by guess-work about intervening events. Here, only too conspicuously, is a limitation of the existing social sciences. Their material comes too late, too far after the event, to enter effectively into the formation of public opinion about the immediate public concern and what is to be done about it.

A glance at the situation shows that the physical and external means of collecting information in regard to what is happening in the world have far outrun the intellectual phase of inquiry and organization of its results. Telegraph, telephone, and now the radio, cheap and quick mails, the printing press, capable of swift reduplication of materials at low cost, have attained a remarkable development. But when we ask what sort of material is recorded and how it is organized, when we ask about the intellectual form in which the material is presented, the tale to be told is very different. "News" signifies something which has just happened, and which is new just because it deviates from the old and regular. But its *meaning* depends upon relation to what it imports, to what its social consequences are. This import cannot be determined unless the new is placed in relation to the old, to what has happened and been integrated into the course of events. Without coordination and consecutiveness, events are not events, but mere occurrences, intrusions; an event implies that out of which a happening proceeds. Hence even if we discount the influence of private interests in procuring suppression, secrecy and misrepresentation, we have here an explanation of the triviality and "sensational" quality of so much of what passes as news. The catastrophic, namely, crime, accident, family rows, personal clashes and conflicts, are the most obvious forms of breaches of continuity; they supply the element of shock which is the strictest meaning of sensation; they are the *new* par excellence, even though only the date of the newspaper could inform us whether they happened last year or this, so completely are they isolated from their connections.

So accustomed are we to this method of collecting, recording and presenting social changes, that it may well sound ridiculous to say that a genuine social science would manifest its reality in the daily press, while learned books and articles supply and polish tools of inquiry. But the inquiry which alone can furnish knowledge as a precondition of public judgments must be contemporary and quotidian. Even if social sciences as a specialized apparatus of inquiry were more advanced than they are, they would be comparatively impotent in the office of directing opinion on matters of concern to the public as long as they are remote from application in the daily and unremitting assembly and interpretation of "news." On the other hand, the tools of social inquiry will be clumsy as long as they are forged in places and under conditions remote from contemporary events.

What has been said about the formation of ideas and judgments concerning the public apply as well to the distribution of the knowledge which makes it an effective possession of the members of the public. Any separation between the two sides of the problem is artificial. The discussion of propaganda and propagandism would alone, however, demand a volume, and could be written only by one much more experienced than the present writer. Propaganda can accordingly only be mentioned, with the remark that the present situation is one unprecedented in history. The political forms of democracy and quasi-democratic habits of thought on social matters have compelled a certain amount of public discussion and at least the simulation of general consultation in arriving at political decisions. Representative government must at least seem to be founded on public interests as they are revealed to public belief. The days are past when government can be carried on without any pretense of ascertaining the wishes of the governed. In theory, their assent must be secured. Under the older forms, there was no need to muddy the sources of opinion on political matters. No current of energy flowed from them. To-day the judgments popularly formed on political matters are so important, in spite of all factors to the contrary, that there is an enormous premium upon all methods which affect their formation.

The smoothest road to control of political conduct is by control of opinion. As long as interests of pecuniary profit are powerful, and a public has not located and identified itself, those who have this interest will have an unresisted motive for tampering with the springs of political action in all that affects them. Just as in the conduct of industry and exchange generally the technological factor is obscured, deflected and defeated by "business," so specifically in the management of publicity. The gathering and sale of subject-matter having a public import is part of the existing pecuniary system. Just as industry conducted by engineers on a factual technological basis would be a very different thing from what it actually is, so the assembling and reporting of news would be a very different thing if the genuine interests of reporters were permitted to work freely.

One aspect of the matter concerns particularly the side of dissemination. It is often said, and with a great appearance of truth, that the freeing and perfecting of inquiry would not have any especial effect. For, it is argued, the mass of the reading public is not interested in learning and assimilating the results of accurate investigation. Unless these are read, they cannot seriously affect the thought and action of members of the public; they remain in secluded library alcoves, and are studied and understood only by a few intellectuals. The objection is well taken save as the potency of art is taken into account. A technical high-brow presentation would appeal only to those technically high-brow; it would not be news to the masses. Presentation is fundamentally important, and presentation is a question of art. A newspaper which was only a daily edition of a quarterly journal of sociology or political science would undoubtedly possess a limited circulation and a narrow influence. Even at that, however, the mere existence and accessibility of such material would have some regulative effect. But we can look much further than that. The material would have such an enormous and widespread human bearing that its bare existence would be an irresistible invitation to a presentation of it which would have a direct popular appeal. The freeing of the artist in literary presentation, in other words, is as much a precondition of the desirable creation of adequate opinion on public matters as is the freeing of social inquiry. Men's conscious life of opinion and judgment often proceeds on a superficial and trivial plane. But their lives reach a deeper level. The function of art has always been to break through the crust of conventionalized and routine consciousness. Common things, a flower, a gleam of moonlight, the song of a bird, not things rare and remote, are means with which the deeper levels of life are touched so that they spring up as desire and thought. This process is art. Poetry, the drama, the novel, are proofs that the problem of presentation is not insoluble. Artists have always been the real purveyors of news, for it is not the outward happening in itself which is new, but the kindling by it of emotion, perception and appreciation.

We have but touched lightly and in passing upon the conditions which must be fulfilled if the Great Society is to become a Great Community; a society in which the ever-expanding and intricately ramifying consequences of associated activities shall be known in the full sense of that word, so that an organized, articulate Public comes into being. The highest and most difficult kind of inquiry and a subtle, delicate, vivid and responsive art of communication must take possession of the physical machinery of transmission and circulation and breathe life into it. When the machine age has thus perfected its machinery it will be a means of life and not its despotic master. Democracy will come into its own, for democracy is a name for a life of free and enriching communion. It had its seer in Walt Whitman. It will have its consummation when free social inquiry is indissolubly wedded to the art of full and moving communication.

OLIVER WENDELL HOLMES, JR.

Dissent in *Lochner v. New York* (1905)

Oliver Wendell Holmes, Jr. (1841–1935), taught at Harvard Law School and served as a judge on the Supreme Judicial Court of Massachusetts before he became a justice of the U.S. Supreme Court in 1902. A persistent advocate of judicial restraint, the philosophically skeptical Holmes believed that popular majorities have the right to express their opinions in law. In his dissent from the majority opinion in Lochner v. New York, Holmes argued that judges should not read particular social or economic theories into the Constitution in order to prevent states from passing laws, such as the one under question that limited the working hours of bakers.

This case is decided upon an economic theory which a large part of the country does not entertain. If it were a question whether I agreed with that theory, I should desire to study it further and long before making up my mind. But I do not conceive that to be my duty, because I strongly believe that my agreement or disagreement has nothing to do with the right of a majority to embody their opinions in law. It is settled by various decisions of this court that state constitutions and state laws may regulate life in many ways which we as legislators might think as injudicious or if you like as tyrannical as this, and which equally with this interfere with the liberty to contract. Sunday laws and usury laws are ancient examples. A more modern one is the prohibition of lotteries. The liberty of the citizen to do as he likes so long as he does not interfere with the liberty of others to do the same, which has been a shibboleth for some well-known writers, is interfered with by school laws, by the Post Office, by every state or municipal institution which takes his money for purposes thought desirable, whether he likes it or not. The Fourteenth Amendment does not enact Mr. Herbert Spencer's Social Statics. * * * United States and state statutes and decisions cutting down the liberty to contract by way of combination are familiar to this court. * * * Some of these laws embody convictions or prejudices which judges are likely to share. Some may not. But a constitution is not intended to embody a particular economic theory, whether of paternalism and the organic relation of the citizen to the State or of *laissez faire*. It is made for people of fundamentally differing views, and the accident of our finding certain opinions natural and familiar or novel and even shocking ought not to conclude our judgement upon the question whether statutes embodying them conflict with the Constitution of the United States.

General propositions do not decide concrete cases. The decision will depend on a judgement or intuition more subtle than any articulate major premise. But I think that the proposition just stated, if it is accepted, will carry us far toward the end. Every opinion tends to become a law. I think that the word liberty in the Fourteenth Amendment is perverted when it is held to prevent the natural outcome of a dominant opinion, unless it can be said that a rational and fair man necessarily would admit that the statute proposed would infringe fundamental principles as they have been understood by the traditions of our people and our law. It does not need research to show that no such sweeping condemnation can be passed upon the statute before us. A reasonable man might think it a proper measure on the score of health. Men whom I certainly could not pronounce unreasonable would uphold it as a first instalment of a general regulation of the hours of work. Whether in the latter aspect it would be open to the charge of inequality I think it unnecessary to discuss.

OLIVER WENDELL HOLMES, JR.

Natural Law (1918)

Influenced by pragmatism and Darwinism, Justice Holmes doubted that philosophy could establish either absolute truth or the existence of fundamental rights grounded in natural law. But as Holmes explained in a Harvard Law Review article published at the end of the First World War, the fact that personal beliefs are based on arbitrary conventions does not mean that political—or military—action becomes impossible.

It is not enough for the knight of romance that you agree that his lady is a very nice girl—if you do not admit that she is the best that God ever made or will make, you must fight. There is in all men a demand for the superlative, so much so that the poor devil who has no other way of reaching it attains it by getting drunk. It seems to me that this demand is at the bottom of the philosopher's effort to prove that truth is absolute and of the jurist's search for criteria of universal validity which he collects under the head of natural law.

I used to say, when I was young, that truth was the majority vote of that nation that could lick all others. Certainly we may expect that the received opinion about the present war will depend a good deal upon which side wins, (I hope with all my soul it will be mine), and I think that the statement was correct in so far as it implied that our test of truth is a reference to either a present or an imagined future majority in favor of our view. If, as I have suggested elsewhere, the truth may be defined as the system of my (intellectual) limitations, what gives it objectivity is the fact that I find my fellow man to a greater or less extent (never wholly) subject to the same *Can't Helps*. If I think that I am sitting at a table I find that the other persons present agree with me; so if I say that the sum of the angles of a triangle is equal to two right angles. If I am in a minority of one they send for a doctor or lock me up; and I am so far able to transcend the to me convincing testimony of my senses or my reason as to recognize that if I am alone probably something is wrong with my works.

Certitude is not the test of certainty. We have been cock-sure of many things that were not so. If I may quote myself again, property, friendship, and truth have a common root in time. One can not be wrenched from the rocky crevices into which one has grown for many years without feeling that one is attacked in one's life. What we most love and revere generally is determined by early associations. I love granite rocks and barberry bushes, no doubt because with them were my earliest joys that reach back through the past eternity of my life. But while one's experience thus makes certain preferences dogmatic for oneself, recognition of how they came to be so leaves one able to see that others, poor souls, may be equally dogmatic about something else. And this again means scepticism. Not that one's belief or love does not remain. Not that we would not fight and die for it if important—we all, whether we know it or not, are fighting to make the kind of a world that we should like—but that we have learned to recognize that others will fight and die to make a different world, with equal sincerity or belief. Deep-seated preferences can not be argued about—you can not argue a man into liking a glass of beer—and therefore, when differences are sufficiently far reaching, we try to kill the other man rather than let him have his way. But that is perfectly consistent with admitting that, so far as appears, his grounds are just as good as ours.

The jurists who believe in natural law seem to me to be in that naïve state of mind that accepts what has been familiar and accepted by them and their neighbors as something that must be accepted by all men everywhere. No doubt it is true that, so far as we can see ahead, some arrangements and the rudiments of familiar institutions seem to be necessary elements in any society that may spring from our own and that would seem to us to be civilized—some form of permanent association between the sexes—some residue of property individually owned—some mode of binding oneself to specified future conduct—at the bottom of all, some protection for the person. But without speculating whether a group is imaginable in which all but the last of these might disappear and the last be subject to qualifications that most of us would abhor, the question remains as to the *Ought* of natural law.

It is true that beliefs and wishes have a transcendental basis in the sense that their foundation is arbitrary. You can not help entertaining and feeling them, and there is an end of it. As an arbitrary fact people wish to live, and we say with various degrees of certainty that they can do so only on certain conditions. To do it they must eat and drink. That necessity is absolute. It is a necessity of less degree but practically general that they should live in society. If they live in society, so far as we can see, there are further conditions. Reason working on experience does tell us, no doubt, that if our wish to live continues, we can do it only on those terms. But that seems to me the whole of the matter. I see no *a priori* duty to live with others and in that way, but simply a statement of what I must do if I wish to remain alive. If I do live with others they tell me that I must do and abstain from doing various things or they will put the screws on to me. I believe that they will, and being of the same mind as to their conduct I not only accept the rules but come in time to accept them with sympathy and emotional affirmation and begin to talk about duties and rights. But for legal purposes a right is only the hypostasis of a prophecy—the imagination of a substance supporting the fact that the public force will be brought to bear upon those who do things said to contravene it— just as we talk of the force of gravitation accounting for the conduct of bodies in space. One phrase adds no more than the other to what we know without it. No doubt behind these legal rights is the fighting will of the subject to maintain them, and the spread of his emotions to the general rules by which they are maintained; but that does not seem to me the same thing as the supposed *a priori* discernment of a duty or the assertion of a preëxisting right. A dog will fight for his bone.

The most fundamental of the supposed preëxisting rights—the right to life—is sacrificed without a scruple not only in war, but whenever the interest of society, that is, of the predominant power in the community, is thought to demand it.

* * * I remember a very tender-hearted judge being of opinion that closing a hatch to stop a fire and the destruction of a cargo was justified even if it was known that doing so would stifle a man below. It is idle to illustrate further, because to those who agree with me I am uttering commonplaces and to those who disagree I am ignoring the necessary foundations of thought. The *a priori* men generally call the dissentients superficial. But I do agree with them in believing that one's attitude on these matters is closely connected with one's general attitude toward the universe. Proximately, as has been suggested, it is determined largely by early associations and temperament, coupled with the desire to have an absolute guide. Men to a great extent believe what they want to— although I see in that no basis for a philosophy that tells us what we should want to want.

Now when we come to our attitude toward the universe I do not see any rational ground for demanding the superlative—for being dissatisfied unless we are assured that our truth is cosmic truth, if there is such a thing—that the ultimates of a little creature on this little earth are the last word of the unimaginable whole. If a man sees no reason for believing that significance, consciousness and ideals are more than marks of the finite, that does not justify what has been familiar in French sceptics; getting upon a pedestal and professing to look with haughty scorn upon a world in ruins. The real conclusion is that the part can not swallow the whole—that our categories are not, or may not be, adequate to formulate what we can not know. If we believe that we come out of the universe, not it out of us, we must admit that we do not know what we are talking about when we speak of brute matter. We do know that a certain complex of energies can wag its tail and another can make syllogisms. These are among the powers of the unknown, and if, as maybe, it has still greater powers that we can not understand, as Fabre in his studies of instinct would have us believe, studies that gave Bergson one of the strongest strands for his philosophy and enabled Maeterlinck to make us fancy for a moment that we heard a clang from behind phenomena—if this be true, why should we not be content? Why should we employ the energy that is furnished to us by the cosmos to defy it and shake our fist at the sky? It seems to me silly.

That the universe has in it more than we understand, that the private soldiers have not been told the plan of campaign, or even that there is one, rather than some vaster unthinkable to which every predicate is an impertinence, has no bearing upon our conduct. We still shall fight—all of us because we want to live, some, at least, because we want to realize our spontaneity and prove our powers, for the joy of it, and we may leave to the unknown the supposed final valuation of that which in any event has value to us. It is enough for us that the universe has produced us and has within it, as less than it, all that we believe and love. If we think of our existence not as that of a little god outside, but as that of a ganglion within, we have the infinite behind us. It gives us our only but our adequate significance. A grain of sand has the same, but what competent person supposes that he understands a grain of sand? That is as much beyond our grasp as man. If our imagination is strong enough to accept the vision of ourselves as parts inseverable from the rest, and to extend our final interest beyond the boundary of our skins, it justifies the sacrifice even of our lives for ends outside of ourselves. The motive, to be sure, is the common wants and ideals that we find in man. Philosophy does not furnish motives, but it shows men that they are not fools for doing what they already want to do. It opens to the forlorn hopes on which we throw ourselves away, the vista of the farthest stretch of human thought, the chords of a harmony that breathes from the unknown.

WALTER LIPPMANN

Public Opinion (1922)

The political writer Walter Lippmann (1889–1974) was an assistant ed-itor of the New Republic, *an editorial writer for the* World, *and finally a widely read syndicated columnist for the* New York Herald Tribune. *The one-time Progressive became one of America's leading public intellectu-als in the middle of the century. His widely read book* Public Opinion, *which first appeared in 1922 and was reissued in 1956, addressed the difficulties of democracy in the age of modern mass communications. In it, Lippmann suggested that the "manufacture of consent" by political leaders had made uncoordinated and spontaneous "mass action" obso-lete.*

There is an island in the ocean where in 1914 a few Englishmen, Frenchmen, and Germans lived. No cable reaches that island, and the British mail steamer comes but once in sixty days. In September it had not yet come, and the islanders were still talking about the latest newspaper which told about the approaching trial of Madame Caillaux for the shooting of Gaston Calmette. It was, therefore, with more than usual eagerness that the whole colony assembled at the quay on a day in mid-September to hear from the captain what the verdict had been. They learned that for over six weeks now those of them who were En-glish and those of them who were French had been fighting in behalf of the sanctity of treaties against those of them who were Germans. For six strange weeks they had acted as if they were friends, when in fact they were enemies.

But their plight was not so different from that of most of the popula-tion of Europe. They had been mistaken for six weeks, on the continent the interval may have been only six days or six hours. There was an inter-val. There was a moment when the picture of Europe on which men were conducting their business as usual, did not in any way correspond to the Europe which was about to make a jumble of their lives. There was a time for each man when he was still adjusted to an environment that no longer existed. All over the world as late as July 25th men were making goods that they would not be able to ship, buying goods they would not be able to import, careers were being planned, enterprises contemplated, hopes and expectations entertained, all in the belief that the world as known was the world as it was. Men were writing books describing that world. They trusted the picture in their heads. And then over four years later, on a Thursday morning, came the news of an armistice, and people gave vent to their unutterable relief that the slaughter was over. Yet in the five days before the real armistice came, though the end of the war had been celebrated, several thousand young men died on the battlefields.

Looking back we can see how indirectly we know the environment in which nevertheless we live. We can see that the news of it comes to us now fast, now slowly; but that whatever we believe to be a true picture, we treat as if it were the environment itself. * * *

For the real environment is altogether too big, too complex, and too fleeting for direct acquaintance. We are not equipped to deal with so much subtlety, so much variety, so many permutations and combinations. And although we have to act in that environment, we have to reconstruct it on a simpler model before we can manage with it. To traverse the world men must have maps of the world. Their persistent difficulty is to secure maps on which their own need, or someone else's need, has not sketched in the coast of Bohemia.

The analyst of public opinion must begin then, by recognizing the triangular relationship between the scene of action, the human picture of that scene, and the human response to that picture working itself out upon the scene of action. * * *

The world that we have to deal with politically is out of reach, out of sight, out of mind. It has to be explored, reported, and imagined. Man is no Aristotelian god contemplating all existence at one glance. He is the creature of an evolution who can just about span a sufficient portion of reality to manage his survival, and snatch what on the scale of time are but a few moments of insight and happiness. Yet this same creature has invented ways of seeing what no naked eye could see, of hearing what no ear could hear, of weighing immense masses and infinitesimal ones, of counting and separating more items than he can individually remember. He is learning to see with his mind vast portions of the world that he could never see, touch, smell, hear, or remember. Gradually he makes for himself a trustworthy picture inside his head of the world beyond his reach.

Those features of the world outside which have to do with the behavior of other human beings, in so far as that behavior crosses ours, is dependent upon us, or is interesting to us, we call roughly public affairs. The pictures inside the heads of these human beings, the pictures of themselves, of others, of their needs, purposes, and relationship, are their public opinions. Those pictures which are acted upon by groups of people, or by individuals acting in the name of groups, are Public Opinion with capital letters. * * *

This goes to show that there are many variables in each man's impressions of the invisible world. The points of contact vary, the stereotyped expectations vary, the interest enlisted varies most subtly of all. The living impressions of a large number of people are to an immeasurable degree personal in each of them, and unmanageably complex in the mass. How, then, is any practical relationship established between what is in people's heads and what is out there beyond their ken in the environment? How in the language of democratic theory, do great numbers of people feeling each so privately about so abstract a picture, develop any common will? How does a simple and constant idea emerge from this complex of variables? How are those things known as the Will of the People, or the National Purpose, or Public Opinion crystallized out of such fleeting and casual imagery? * * *

The priest, the lord of the manor, the captains and the kings, the party leaders, the merchant, the boss, however these men are chosen, whether by birth, inheritance, conquest or election, they and their organized following administer human affairs. They are the officers, and although the same man may be field marshal at home, second lieutenant at the office, and scrub private in politics, although in many institutions the hierarchy of rank is vague or concealed, yet in every institution that requires the coöperation of many persons, some such hierarchy exists. In American politics we call it a machine, or "the organization."

There are a number of important distinctions between the members of the machine and the rank and file. The leaders, the steering committee and the inner circle, are in direct contact with their environment. They may, to be sure, have a very limited notion of what they ought to define as the environment, but they are not dealing almost wholly with abstractions. There are particular men they hope to see elected, particular balance sheets they wish to see improved, concrete objectives that must be attained. I do not mean that they escape the human propensity to stereotyped vision. Their stereotypes often make them absurd routineers. But whatever their limitations, the chiefs are in actual contact with some crucial part of that larger environment. They decide. They give orders. They bargain. And something definite, perhaps not at all what they imagined, actually happens.

Their subordinates are not tied to them by a common conviction. That is to say the lesser members of a machine do not dispose their loyalty according to independent judgment about the wisdom of the leaders. In the hierarchy each is dependent upon a superior and is in turn superior to some class of his dependents. What holds the machine together is a system of privileges. These may vary according to the opportunities and the tastes of those who seek them, from nepotism and patronage in all their aspects to clannishness, hero-worship or a fixed idea. They vary from military rank in armies, through land and services in a feudal system, to jobs and publicity in a modern democracy. That is why you can break up a particular machine by abolishing its privileges. But the machine in every coherent group is, I believe, certain to reappear. For privilege is entirely relative, and uniformity is impossible. Imagine the most absolute communism of which your mind is capable, where no one possessed any object that everyone else did not possess, and still, if the communist group had to take any action whatever, the mere pleasure of being the friend of the man who was going to make the speech that secured the most votes, would, I am convinced, be enough to crystallize an organization of insiders around him.

It is not necessary, then, to invent a collective intelligence in order to explain why the judgments of a group are usually more coherent, and often more true to form than the remarks of the man in the street. One mind, or a few can pursue a train of thought, but a group trying to think in concert can as a group do little more than assent or dissent. The members of a hierarchy can have a corporate tradition. As apprentices they learn the trade from the masters, who in turn learned it when they were apprentices, and in any enduring society, the change of personnel within the governing hierarchies is slow enough to permit the transmission of certain great stereotypes and patterns of behavior. From father to son, from prelate to novice, from veteran to cadet, certain ways of seeing and doing are taught. These ways become familiar, and are recognized as such by the mass of outsiders.

Distance alone lends enchantment to the view that masses of human beings ever coöperate in any complex affair without a central machine managed by a very few people. "No one," says Bryce, "can have had some years' experience of the conduct of affairs in a legislature or an administration without observing how extremely small is the number of persons by whom the world is governed." He is referring, of course, to affairs of state. To be sure if you consider all the affairs of mankind the number of people who govern is considerable, but if you take any particular institution, be it a legislature, a party, a trade union, a nationalist movement, a factory, or a club, the number of those who govern is a very small percentage of those who are theoretically supposed to govern.

Landslides can turn one machine out and put another in; revolutions sometimes abolish a particular machine altogether. The democratic revolution set up two alternating machines, each of which in the course of a few years reaps the advantage from the mistakes of the other. But nowhere does the machine disappear. Nowhere is the idyllic theory of democracy realized. Certainly not in trades unions, nor in socialist parties, nor in communist governments. There is an inner circle, surrounded by concentric circles which fade out gradually into the disinterested or uninterested rank and file.

Democrats have never come to terms with this commonplace of group life. They have invariably regarded it as perverse. For there are two visions of democracy: one presupposes the self-sufficient individual; the other an Oversoul regulating everything. Of the two the Oversoul has some advantage because it does at least recognize that the mass makes decisions that are not spontaneously born in the breast of every member. But the Oversoul as presiding genius in corporate behavior is a superfluous mystery if we fix our attention upon the machine. The machine is a quite prosaic reality. It consists of human beings who wear clothes and live in houses, who can be named and described. They perform all the duties usually assigned to the Oversoul.

The reason for the machine is not the perversity of human nature. It is that out of the private notions of any group no common idea emerges by itself. For the number of ways is limited in which a multitude of people can act directly upon a situation beyond their reach. Some of them can migrate, in one form or another, they can strike or boycott, they can applaud or hiss. They can by these means occasionally resist what they do not like, or coerce those who obstruct what they desire. But by mass action nothing can be constructed, devised, negotiated, or administered. * * *

Because of their transcendent practical importance, no successful leader has ever been too busy to cultivate the symbols which organize his following. What privileges do within the hierarchy, symbols do for the rank and file. They conserve unity. From the totem pole to the national flag, from the wooden idol to God the Invisible King, from the magic word to some diluted version of Adam Smith or Bentham, symbols have been cherished by leaders, many of whom were themselves unbelievers, because they were focal points where differences merged. The detached observer may scorn the "star-spangled" ritual which hedges the symbol, perhaps as much as the king who told himself that Paris was worth a few masses. But the leader knows by experience that only when symbols have done their work is there a handle he can use to move a crowd. In the symbol emotion is discharged at a common target, and the idiosyncrasy of real ideas blotted out. No wonder he hates what he calls destructive criticism, sometimes called by free spirits the elimination of buncombe. "Above all things," says Bagehot, "our royalty is to be reverenced, and if you begin to poke about it you cannot reverence it." For poking about with clear definitions and candid statements serves all high purposes known to man, except the easy conservation of a common will. Poking about, as every responsible leader suspects, tends to break the transference of emotion from the individual mind to the institutional symbol. And the first result of that is, as he rightly says, a chaos of individualism and warring sects. The disintegration of a symbol, like Holy Russia, or the Iron Diaz, is always the beginning of a long upheaval.

These great symbols possess by transference all the minute and detailed loyalties of an ancient and stereotyped society. They evoke the feeling that each individual has for the landscape, the furniture, the faces, the memories that are his first, and in a static society, his only reality. That core of images and devotions without which he is unthinkable to himself, is nationality. The great symbols take up these devotions, and can arouse them without calling forth the primitive images. The lesser symbols of public debate, the more casual chatter of politics, are always referred back to these proto-symbols, and if possible associated with them. The question of a proper fare on a municipal subway is symbolized as an issue between the People and the Interests, and then the People is inserted in the symbol American, so that finally in the heat of a campaign, an eight cent fare becomes unAmerican. The Revolutionary fathers died to prevent it. Lincoln suffered that it might not come to pass, resistance to it was implied in the death of those who sleep in France.

Because of its power to siphon emotion out of distinct ideas, the symbol is both a mechanism of solidarity, and a mechanism of exploitation. It enables people to work for a common end, but just because the few who are strategically placed must choose the concrete objectives, the symbol is also an instrument by which a few can fatten on many, deflect criticism, and seduce men into facing agony for objects they do not understand. * * *

Leaders often pretend that they have merely uncovered a program which existed in the minds of their public. When they believe it, they are usually deceiving themselves. Programs do not invent themselves synchronously in a multitude of minds. That is not because a multitude of minds is necessarily inferior to that of the leaders, but because thought is the function of an organism, and a mass is not an organism.

This fact is obscured because the mass is constantly exposed to suggestion. It reads not the news, but the news with an aura of suggestion about it, indicating the line of action to be taken. It hears reports, not objective as the facts are, but already stereotyped to a certain pattern of behavior. * * *

The established leaders of any organization have great natural advantages. They are believed to have better sources of information. The books and papers are in their offices. They took part in the important conferences.

They met the important people. They have responsibility. It is, therefore, easier for them to secure attention and to speak in a convincing tone. But also they have a very great deal of control over the access to the facts. Every official is in some degree a censor. And since no one can suppress information, either by concealing it or forgetting to mention it, without some notion of what he wishes the public to know, every leader is in some degree a propagandist. Strategically placed, and compelled often to choose even at the best between the equally cogent though conflicting ideals of safety for the institution, and candor to his public, the official finds himself deciding more and more consciously what facts, in what setting, in what guise he shall permit the public to know.

That the manufacture of consent is capable of great refinements no one, I think, denies. The process by which public opinions arise is certainly no less intricate than it has appeared in these pages, and the opportunities for manipulation open to anyone who understands the process are plain enough.

The creation of consent is not a new art. It is a very old one which was supposed to have died out with the appearance of democracy. But it has not died out. It has, in fact, improved enormously in technic, because it is now based on analysis rather than on rule of thumb. And so, as a result of psychological research, coupled with the modern means of communication, the practice of democracy has turned a corner. A revolution is taking place, infinitely more significant than any shifting of economic power.

Within the life of the generation now in control of affairs, persuasion has become a self-conscious art and a regular organ of popular government. None of us begins to understand the consequences, but it is no daring prophecy to say that the knowledge of how to create consent will alter every political calculation and modify every political premise. Under the impact of propaganda, not necessarily in the sinister meaning of the word alone, the old constants of our thinking have become variables. It is no longer possible, for example, to believe in the original dogma of democracy; that the knowledge needed for the management of human affairs comes up spontaneously from the human heart. Where we act on that theory we expose ourselves to self-deception, and to forms of persuasion that we cannot verify. It has been demonstrated that we cannot rely upon intuition, conscience, or the accidents of casual opinion if we are to deal with the world beyond our reach.

HERBERT CROLY

The Promise of American Life (1909)

The Progressive public intellectual Herbert David Croly (1869–1930) was the editor of the important Progressive weekly The New Republic, *which he helped found in 1914. Croly advocated the use of interventionist Hamiltonian means of big government through national industrial, labor, and business regulation to achieve the Jeffersonian ends of greater democracy and equality for the less privileged. Croly's ideas about the proper role of the state in the modern world provided the intellectual foundation for Theodore Roosevelt's "New Nationalism." In his most influential book,* The Promise of American Life, *which considers the various meanings of democracy, Croly argued that "positive and aggressive" state action was necessary to promote the democratic welfare of the "whole community."*

The best method of approaching a critical reconstruction of American political ideas will be by means of an analysis of the meaning of democracy. A clear popular understanding of the contents of the democratic principle is obviously of the utmost practical political importance to the American people. Their loyalty to the idea of democracy, as they understand it, cannot be questioned. Nothing of any considerable political importance is done or left undone in the United States, unless such action or inaction can be plausibly defended on democratic grounds; and the only way to secure for the American people the benefit of a comprehensive and consistent political policy will be to derive it from a comprehensive and consistent conception of democracy.

Democracy as most frequently understood is essentially and exhaustively defined as a matter of popular government; and such a definition raises at once a multitude of time-honored, but by no means superannuated, controversies. The constitutional liberals in England, in France, and in this country have always objected to democracy as so understood, because of the possible sanction it affords for the substitution of a popular despotism in the place of the former royal or oligarchic despotisms. From their point of view individual liberty is the greatest blessing which can be secured to a people by a government; and individual liberty can be permanently guaranteed only in case political liberties are in theory and practice subordinated to civil liberties. Popular political institutions constitute a good servant, but a bad master. When introduced in moderation they keep the government of a country in close relation with well-informed public opinion, which is a necessary condition of political sanitation; but if carried too far, such institutions compromise the security of the individual and the integrity of the state. They erect a power in the state, which in theory is unlimited and which constantly tends in practice to dispense with restrictions. A power which is theoretically absolute is under no obligation to respect the rights either of individuals or minorities; and sooner or later such power will be used for the purpose of oppressing the individual. The only way to secure individual liberty is, consequently, to organize a state in which the Sovereign power is deprived of any rational excuse or legal opportunity of violating certain essential individual rights. * * *

To be sure, a democracy may impose rules of action upon itself—as the American democracy did in accepting the Federal Constitution. But in adopting the Federal Constitution the American people did not abandon either its responsibilities or rights as Sovereign. Difficult as it may be to escape from the legal framework defined in the Constitution, that body of law in theory remains merely an instrument which was made for the people and which if necessary can and will be modified. A people, to whom was denied the ultimate responsibility for its welfare, would not have obtained the prime condition of genuine liberty. Individual freedom is important, but more important still is the freedom of a whole people to dispose of its own destiny; and I do not see how the existence of such an ultimate popular political freedom and responsibility can be denied by any one who has rejected the theory of a divinely appointed political order. The fallibility of human nature being what it is, the practical application of this theory will have its grave dangers; but these dangers are only evaded and postponed by a failure to place ultimate political responsibility where it belongs.

* * * Democracy may mean something more than a theoretically absolute popular government, but it assuredly cannot mean anything less.

If, however, democracy does not mean anything less than popular Sovereignty, it assuredly does mean something more. It must at least mean an expression of the Sovereign will, which will not contradict and destroy the continuous existence of its own Sovereign power. * * * A particular group of political institutions or course of political action may, then, be representative of the popular will, and yet may be undemocratic. Popular Sovereignty is self-contradictory, unless it is expressed in a manner favorable to its own perpetuity and integrity.

The assertion of the doctrine of popular Sovereignty is, consequently, rather the beginning than the end of democracy. There can be no democracy where the people do not rule; but government by the people is not necessarily democratic. The popular will must in a democratic state be expressed somehow in the interest of democracy itself; and we have not traveled very far towards a satisfactory conception of democracy until this democratic purpose has received some definition. In what way must a democratic state behave in order to contribute to its own integrity?

The ordinary American answer to this question is contained in the assertion of Lincoln, that our government is "dedicated to the proposition that all men are created equal." Lincoln's phrasing of the principle was due to the fact that the obnoxious and undemocratic system of Negro slavery was uppermost in his mind when he made his Gettysburg address; but he meant by his assertion of the principle of equality substantially what is meant today by the principle of "equal rights for all and special privileges for none." Government by the people has its natural and logical complement in government for the people. Every state with a legal framework must grant certain rights to individuals; and every state, in so far as it is efficient, must guarantee to the individual that his rights, as legally defined are secure. But an essentially democratic state consists in the circumstance that all citizens enjoy these rights equally. If any citizen or any group of citizens enjoys by virtue of the law any advantage over their fellow-citizens, then the most sacred principle of democracy is violated. On the other hand, a community in which no man or no group of men are granted by law any advantage over their fellow-citizens is the type of the perfect and fruitful democratic state. Society is organized politically for the benefit of all the people. Such an organization may permit radical differences among individuals in the opportunities and possessions they actually enjoy; but no man would be able to impute his own success or failure to the legal framework of society. Every citizen would be getting a "Square Deal."

Such is the idea of the democratic state, which the majority of good Americans believe to be entirely satisfactory. It should endure indefinitely, because it seeks to satisfy every interest essential to associated life. The interest of the individual is protected, because of the liberties he securely enjoys. The general social interest is equally well protected, because the liberties enjoyed by one or by a few are enjoyed by all. Thus the individual and the social interests are automatically harmonized. The virile democrat in pursuing his own interest "under the law" is contributing effectively to the interest of society, while the social interest consists precisely in the promotion of these individual interests, in so far as they can be equally exercised. The divergent demands of the individual and the social interest can be reconciled by grafting the principle of equality on the thrifty tree of individual rights, and the ripe fruit thereof can be gathered merely by shaking the tree.

It must be immediately admitted, also, that the principle of equal rights, like the principle of ultimate popular political responsibility is the expression of an essential aspect of democracy. There is no room for permanent legal privileges in a democratic state. Such privileges may be and frequently are defended on many excellent grounds. They may unquestionably contribute for a time to social and economic efficiency and to individual independence. But whatever advantage may be derived from such permanent discriminations must be abandoned by a democracy. It cannot afford to give any one class of its citizens a permanent advantage or to others a permanent grievance. It ceases to be a democracy, just as soon as any permanent privileges are conferred by its institutions or its laws; and this equality of right and absence of permanent privilege is the expression of a fundamental social interest.

But the principle of equal rights, like the principle of ultimate popular political responsibility, is not sufficient; and because of its insufficiency results in certain dangerous ambiguities and self-contradictions. American political thinkers have always repudiated the idea that by equality of rights they meant anything like equality of performance or power. The utmost varieties of individual power and ability are bound to exist and are bound to bring about many different levels of individual achievement. Democracy both recognizes the right of the individual to use his powers to the utmost, and encourages him to do so by offering a fair field and, in case of success, an abundant reward. The democratic principle requires an equal start in the race, while expecting at the same time an unequal finish. But Americans who talk in this way seem wholly blind to the fact that under a legal system which holds private property sacred there may be equal rights, but there cannot possibly be any equal opportunities for exercising such rights. The chance which the individual has to compete with his fellows and take a prize in the race is vitally affected by material conditions over which he has no control. It is as if the competitor in a Marathon cross country run were denied proper nourishment or proper training, and was obliged to toe the mark against rivals who had every benefit of food and discipline. Under such conditions he is not as badly off as if he were entirely excluded from the race. With the aid of exceptional strength and intelligence he may overcome the odds against him and win out. But it would be absurd to claim that, because all the rivals toed the same mark, a man's victory or defeat depended exclusively on his own efforts. Those who have enjoyed the benefits of wealth and thorough education start with an advantage which can be overcome only by very exceptional men,—men so exceptional, in fact, that the average competitor without such benefits feels himself disqualified for the contest.

Because of the ambiguity indicated above, different people with different interests, all of them good patriotic Americans, draw very different inferences from the doctrine of equal rights. The man of conservative ideas and interests means by the rights, which are to be equally exercised, only those rights which are defined and protected by the law—the more fundamental of which are the rights to personal freedom and to private property. The man of radical ideas, on the other hand, observing, as he may very clearly, that these equal rights cannot possibly be made really equivalent to equal opportunities, bases upon the same doctrine a more or less drastic criticism of the existing economic and social order and sometimes of the motives of its beneficiaries and conservators. The same principle, differently interpreted, is the foundation of American political orthodoxy and American political heterodoxy. * * * Privileges and discriminations seem to lurk in every political and economic corner. The "people" are appealing to the state to protect them against the usurpations of the corporations and the Bosses. The government is appealing to the courts to protect the shippers against the railroads. The corporations are appealing to the Federal courts to protect them from the unfair treatment of state legislatures. Employers are fighting trades-unionism, because it denies equal rights to their employes. The unionists are entreating public opinion to protect them against the unfairness of "government by injunction." To the free trader the whole protectionist system seems a flagrant discrimination on behalf of a certain portion of the community. Everybody seems to be clamoring for a "Square Deal" but nobody seems to be getting it.

The ambiguity of the principle of equal rights and the resulting confusion of counsel are so obvious that there must be some good reason for their apparently unsuspected existence. The truth is that Americans have not readjusted their political ideas to the teaching of their political and economic experience. For a couple of generations after Jefferson had established the doctrine of equal rights as the fundamental principle of the American democracy, the ambiguity resident in the application of the doctrine ws concealed. The Jacksonian Democrats, for instance, who were constantly nosing the ground for a scent of unfair treatment, could discover no example of political privileges, except the continued retention of their offices by experienced public servants; and the only case of economic privilege of which they were certain was that of the National Bank. The fact is, of course, that the great majority of Americans were getting a "Square Deal" as long as the economic opportunities of a new country had not been developed and appropriated. Individual and social interest did substantially coincide as long as so many opportunities were open to the poor and untrained man, and as long as the public interest demanded first of all the utmost celerity of economic development. But, as we have seen in a preceding chapter, the economic development of the country resulted inevitably in a condition which demanded on the part of the successful competitor either increasing capital, improved training, or a larger amount of ability and energy. With the advent of comparative economic and social maturity, the exercise of certain legal rights became substantially equivalent to the exercise of a privilege; and if equality of opportunity was to be maintained, it could not be done by virtue of non-interference. * * *

Hence it is that continued loyalty to a contradictory principle is destructive of a wholesome public sentiment and opinion. A wholesome public opinion in a democracy is one which keeps a democracy sound and whole: and it cannot prevail unless the individuals composing it recognize mutualties and responsibilities which lie deeper than any differences of interest and idea. No formula whose effect on public opinion is not binding and healing and unifying has any substantial claim to consideration as the essential and formative democratic idea. Belief in the principle of equal rights does not bind, heal, and unify public opinion. Its effect rather is confusing, distracting, and at worst, disintegrating. A democratic political organization has no immunity from grievances. They are a necessary result of a complicated and changing industrial and social organism. What is good for one generation will often be followed by consequences that spell deprivation for the next. What is good for one man or one class of men will bring ills to other men or classes of men. What is good for the community as a whole may mean temporary loss and a sense of injustice to a minority. All grievances from any cause should receive full expression in a democracy, but, inasmuch as the righteously discontented must be always with us, the fundamental democratic principle should, above all, counsel mutual forbearance and loyalty. The principle of equal rights encourages mutual suspicion and disloyalty. It tends to attribute individual and social ills, for which general moral, economic, and social causes are usually in large measure responsible, to individual wrong-doing; and in this way it arouses and intensifies that personal and class hatred, which never in any society lies far below the surface. Men who have grievances are inflamed into anger and resentment. In claiming what they believe to be their rights, they are in their own opinion acting on behalf not merely of their interests, but of an absolute democratic principle. Their angry resentment becomes transformed in their own minds into righteous indignation; and there may be turned loose upon the community a horde of self-seeking fanatics—like unto those soldiers in the religious wars who robbed and slaughtered their opponents in the service of God.

* * * The principle of equal rights has always appealed to its more patriotic and sensible adherents as essentially an impartial rule of political action—one that held a perfectly fair balance between the individual and society, and between different and hostile individual and class interests. But as a fundamental principle of democratic policy it is as ambiguous in this respect as it is in other respects. In its traditional form and expression it has concealed an extremely partial interest under a formal proclamation of impartiality. The political thinker who popularized it in this country was not concerned fundamentally with harmonizing the essential interest of the individual with the essential popular or social interest. Jefferson's political system was intended for the benefit only of a special class of individuals, viz., those average people who would not be helped by any really formative rule or method of discrimination. In practice it has proved to be inimical to individual liberty, efficiency, and distinction. An insistent demand for equality, even in the form of a demand for equal rights, inevitably has a negative and limiting effect upon the free and able exercise of individual opportunities. From the Jeffersonian point of view democracy would incur a graver danger from a violation of equality than it would profit from a triumphant assertion of individual liberty. Every opportunity for the edifying exercise of power, on the part either of an individual, a group of individuals, or the state is by its very nature also an opportunity for its evil exercise.

* * * The advocate of equal rights is preoccupied by these opportunities for the abusive exercise of power, because from his point of view rights exercised in the interest of inequality have ceased to be righteous.

* * *

A democracy of equal rights may tend to encourage certain expressions of individual liberty; but they are few in number and limited in scope. It rejoices in the freedom of its citizens, provided this freedom receives certain ordinary expressions. It will follow a political leader, like Jefferson or Jackson, with a blind confidence of which a really free democracy would not be capable, because such leaders are, or claim to be in every respect, except their prominence, one of the "people." Distinction of this kind does not separate a leader from the majority. It only ties them together more firmly. It is an acceptable assertion of individual liberty, because it is liberty converted by its exercise into a kind of equality. In the same way the American democracy most cordially admired for a long time men, who pursued more energetically and successfully than their fellows, ordinary business occupations, because they believed that such familiar expressions of individual liberty really tended towards social and industrial homogeneity. Herein they were mistaken; but the supposition was made in good faith, and it constitutes the basis of the Jeffersonian Democrat's illusion in reference to his own interest in liberty. He dislikes or ignores liberty, only when it looks in the direction of moral and intellectual emancipation. In so far as his influence has prevailed, Americans have been encouraged to think those thoughts and to perform those acts which everybody else is thinking and performing.

The effect of a belief in the principle of "equal rights" on freedom is, however, most clearly shown by its attitude toward Democratic political organization and policy. A people jealous of their rights are not sufficiently afraid of special individual efficiency and distinction to take very many precautions against it. They greet it oftener with neglect than with positive coercion. Jeffersonian Democracy is, however, very much afraid of any examples of associated efficiency. Equality of rights is most in danger of being violated when the exercise of rights is associated with power, and any unusual amount of power is usually derived from the association of a number of individuals for a common purpose. The most dangerous example of such association is not, however, a huge corporation or a labor union; it is the state.

∗ ∗ ∗ The power to legislate implies the power to discriminate; and the best way consequently for a good democracy of equal rights to avoid the danger of discrimination will be to organize the state so that its power for ill will be rigidly restricted. The possible preferential interference on the part of a strong and efficient government must be checked by making the government feeble and devoid of independence. The less independent and efficient the several departments of the government are permitted to become, the less likely that the government as a whole will use its power for anything but a really popular purpose. ∗ ∗ ∗ Even the meager social interest which Jefferson concealed under cover of his demand for equal rights could not be promoted without some effective organ of social responsibility; and the Democrats of to-day are obliged, as we have seen, to invoke the action of the central government to destroy those economic discriminations which its former inaction had encouraged. But even so the traditional democracy still retains its dislike of centralized and socialized responsibility. It consents to use the machinery of the government only for a negative or destructive object. Such must always be the case as long as it remains true to its fundamental principle. That principle defines the social interest merely in the terms of an indiscriminate individualism—which is the one kind of individualism murderous to both the essential individual and the essential social interest.

The net result has been that wherever the attempt to discriminate in favor of the average or indiscriminate individual has succeeded, it has succeeded at the expense of individual liberty, efficiency, and distinction; but it has more often failed than succeeded. Whenever the exceptional individual has been given any genuine liberty, he has inevitably conquered. That is the whole meaning of the process of economic and social development traced in certain preceding chapters. The strong and capable men not only conquer, but they seek to perpetuate their conquests by occupying all the strategic points in the economic and political battlefield—whereby they obtain certain more or less permanent advantages over their fellow-democrats. Thus in so far as the equal rights are freely exercised, they are bound to result in inequalities; and these inequalities are bound to make for their own perpetuation, and so to provoke still further discrimination. * * *

The only way in which the thoroughgoing adherent of the principle of equal rights can treat these tendencies to discrimination, when they develop, is rigidly to repress them; and this tendency to repression is now beginning to take possession of those Americans who represent the pure Democratic tradition. They propose to crush out the chief examples of effective individual and associated action, which their system of democracy has encouraged to develop. They propose frankly to destroy, as far as possible, the economic organization which has been built up under stress of competitive conditions; and by assuming such an attitude they have fallen away even from the pretense of impartiality, and have come out as frankly representative of a class interest. But even to assert this class interest efficiently they have been obliged to abandon, in fact if not in word, their correlative principle of national irresponsibility. Whatever the national interest may be, it is not to be asserted by the political practice of noninterference. The hope of automatic democratic fulfillment must be abandoned. The national government must step in and discriminate; but it must discriminate, not on behalf of liberty and the special individual, but on behalf of equality and the average man.

Thus the Jeffersonian principle of national irresponsibility can no longer be maintained by those Democrats who sincerely believe that the inequalities of power generated in the American economic and political system are dangerous to the integrity of the democratic state. To this extent really sincere followers of Jefferson are obliged to admit the superior political wisdom of Hamilton's principle of national responsibility, and once they have made this admission, they have implicitly abandoned their contention that the doctrine of equal rights is a sufficient principle of democratic political action. They have implicitly accepted the idea that the public interest is to be asserted, not merely by equalizing individual rights, but by controlling individuals in the exercise of those rights. The national public interest has to be affirmed by positive and aggressive action. The nation has to have a will and a policy as well as the individual; and this policy can no longer be confined to the merely negative task of keeping individual rights from becoming in any way privileged.

The arduous and responsible political task which a nation in its collective capacity must seek to perform is that of selecting among the various prevailing ways of exercising individual rights those which contribute to national perpetuity and integrity. Such selection implies some interference with the natural course of popular action; and that interference is always costly and may be harmful either to the individual or the social interest must be frankly admitted. He would be a foolish Hamiltonian who would claim that a state, no matter how efficiently organized and ably managed, will not make serious and perhaps enduring mistakes; but he can answer that inaction and irresponsibility are more costly and dangerous than intelligent and responsible interference. The practice of non-interference is just as selective in its effects as the practice of state interference. It means merely that the nation is willing to accept the results of natural selection instead of preferring to substitute the results of artificial selection. In one way or another a nation is bound to recognize the results of selection. The Hamiltonian principle of national responsibility recognizes the inevitability of selection; and since it is inevitable, is not afraid to interfere on behalf of the selection of the really fittest. If a selective policy is pursued in good faith and with sufficient intelligence, the nation will at least be learning from its mistakes. It should find out gradually the kind and method of selection, which is most desirable, and how far selection by non-interference is to be preferred to active selection.

As a matter of fact the American democracy both in its central and in its local governments has always practiced both methods of selection. The state governments have sedulously indulged in a kind of interference conspicuous both for its activity and its inefficiency. The Federal government, on the other hand, has been permitted to interfere very much less; but even during the palmiest days of national irresponsibility it did not altogether escape active intervention. A protective tariff is, of course, a plain case of preferential class legislation, and so was the original Interstate Commerce Act. They were designed to substitute artificial preferences for those effected by unregulated individual action, on the ground that the proposed modification of the natural course of trade would contribute to the general economic prosperity. * * * But whether in any particular case the state takes sides or remains impartial, it most assuredly has a positive function to perform on the premises. If it remains impartial, it simply agrees to abide by the results of natural selection. If it interferes, it seeks to replace natural with artificial discrimination. In both cases it authorizes discriminations which in their effect violate the doctrines of "equal rights." Of course, a reformer can always claim that any particular measure of reform proposes merely to restore to the people a "Square Deal"; but that is simply an easy and thoughtless way of concealing novel purposes under familiar formulas. Any genuine measure of economic or political reform will, of course, give certain individuals better opportunities than those they have been recently enjoying, but it will reach this result only by depriving other individuals of advantages which they have earned.

Impartiality is the duty of the judge rather than the statesman, of the courts rather than the government. The state which proposes to draw a ring around the conflicting interests of its citizens and interfere only on behalf of a fair fight will be obliged to interfere constantly and will never accomplish its purpose. In economic warfare, the fighting can never be fair for long, and it is the business of the state to see that its own friends are victorious. It holds, if you please, itself a hand in the game. The several players are playing, not merely with one another, but with the political and social bank. The security and perpetuity of the state, and of the individual in so far as he is a social animal, depend upon the victory of the national interest—as represented both in the assurance of the national profit and in the domination of the nation's friends. It is in the position of the bank at Monte Carlo, which does pretend to play fair, but which frankly promulgates rules advantageous to itself. Considering the percentage in its favor and the length of its purse, it cannot possibly lose. It is not really gambling; and it does not propose to take any unnecessary risks. Neither can a state, democratic or otherwise, which believes in its own purpose. While preserving at times an appearance of impartiality so that its citizens may enjoy for a while a sense of the reality of their private game, it must on the whole make the rules in its own interest. It must help those men to win who are most capable of using their winnings for the benefit of society.

* * * Assuming, then, that a democracy cannot avoid the constant assertion of national responsibility for the national welfare, an all-important question remains as to the way in which and the purpose for which this interference should be exercised. Should it be exercised on behalf of individual liberty? Should it be exercised on behalf of social equality? Is there any way in which it can be exercised on behalf of both liberty and equality?

Hamilton and the constitutional liberals asserted that the state should interfere exclusively on behalf of individual liberty; but Hamilton was no democrat and was not outlining the policy of a democratic state. In point of fact democracies have never been satisfied with a definition of democratic policy in terms of liberty. Not only have the particular friends of liberty usually been hostile to democracy, but democracies both in idea and behavior have frequently been hostile to liberty; and they have been justified in distrusting a political regime organized wholly or even chiefly for its benefit. * * *

The desirable democratic object, implied in the traditional democratic demand for equality, consists precisely in that of bestowing a share of the responsibility and the benefits, derived from political and economic association, upon the whole community. Democracies have assumed and have been right in assuming that a proper diffusion of effective responsibility and substantial benefits is the one means whereby a community can be supplied with an ultimate and sufficient bond of union. The American democracy has attempted to manufacture a sufficient bond out of the equalization of rights: but such a bond is, as we have seen, either a rope of sand or a link of chains. A similar object must be achieved in some other way; and the ultimate success of democracy depends upon its achievement.

The fundamental political and social problem of a democracy may be summarized in the following terms. A democracy, like every political and social group, is composed of individuals, and must be organized for the benefit of its constituent members. But the individual has no chance of effective personal power except by means of the secure exercise of certain personal rights. Such rights, then, must be secured and exercised; yet when they are exercised, their tendency is to divide the community into divergent classes. Even if enjoyed with some equality in the beginning, they do not continue to be equally enjoyed, but make towards discriminations advantageous to a minority. The state, as representing the common interest, is obliged to admit the inevitability of such classifications and divisions, and has itself no alternative but to exercise a decisive preference on behalf of one side or the other. A well-governed state will use its power to promote edifying and desirable discriminations. But if discriminations tend to divide the community, and the state itself cannot do more than select among the various possible cases of discrimination those which it has some reason to prefer, how is the solidarity of the community to be preserved? And above all, how is a democratic community, which necessarily includes everybody in its benefits and responsibilities, to be kept well united? Such a community must retain an ultimate bond of union which counteracts the divergent effect of the discriminations, yet which at the same time is not fundamentally hostile to individual liberties.

The clew to the best available solution of the problem is supplied by a consideration of the precise manner, in which the advantages derived from the efficient exercise of liberties become inimical to a wholesome social condition. The hostility depends, not upon the existence of such advantageous discriminations for a time, but upon their persistance for too long a time. When, either from natural or artificial causes, they are properly selected, they contribute at the time of their selection both to individual and to social efficiency. They have been earned, and it is both just and edifying that, in so far as they have been earned, they should be freely enjoyed. On the other hand, they should not, so far as possible, be allowed to outlast their own utility. They must continue to be earned. It is power and opportunity enjoyed without being earned which help to damage the individual—both the individuals who benefit and the individuals who consent—and which tend to loosen the ultimate social bond. A democracy, no less than a monarchy or an aristocracy, must recognize political, economic, and social discriminations, but it must also manage to withdraw its consent whenever these discriminations show any tendency to excessive endurance. The essential wholeness of the community depends absolutely on the ceaseless creation of a political, economic, and social aristocracy and their equally incessant replacement.

Both in its organization and in its policy a democratic state has consequently to seek two different but supplementary objects. It is the function of such a state to represent the whole community; and the whole community includes the individual as well as the mass, the many as well as the few. The individual is merged in the mass, unless he is enabled to exercise efficiently and independently his own private and special purposes. He must not only be permitted, he must be encouraged to earn distinction; and the best way in which he can be encouraged to earn distinction is to reward distinction both by abundant opportunity and cordial appreciation. Individual distinction, resulting from the efficient performance of special work, is not only the foundation of all genuine individuality, but is usually of the utmost social value. In so far as it is efficient, it has a tendency to be constructive. It both inserts some member into the social edifice which forms for the time being a desirable part of the whole structure, but it tends to establish a standard of achievement which may well form a permanent contribution to social amelioration. It is useful to the whole community, not because it is derived from popular sources or conforms to popular standards, but because it is formative and so helps to convert the community into a well-formed whole.

* * * But American statesmen have not always been obliged to choose between Hamilton's unpopular integrity and Henry Clay's unprincipled bidding for popular favor. The greatest American political leaders have been popular without any personal capitulation; and their success is indicative of what is theoretically the most wholesome relation between individual political liberty and a democratic distribution of effective political power. The highest and most profitable individual political distinction is that which is won from a large field and from a whole people.

Political, even more than other kinds of distinction, should not be the fruit of a limited area of selection. It must be open to everybody, and it must be acceptable to the community as a whole. * * *

Taking American political traditions, ideals, institutions, and practices as a whole, there is no reason to believe that the American democracy cannot and will not combine sufficient opportunities for individual political distinction with an effective ultimate popular political responsibility. The manner in which the combination has been made hitherto is far from flawless, and the American democracy has much to learn before it reaches an organization adequate to its own proper purposes. It must learn, above all, that the state, and the individuals who are temporarily responsible for the action of the state, must be granted all the power necessary to redeem that responsibility. Individual opportunity and social welfare both depend upon the learning of this lesson; and while it is still very far from being learned, the obstacles in the way are not of a disheartening nature.

With the economic liberty of the individual the case is different. The Federalists refrained from protecting individual political rights by incorporating in the Constitution any limitation of the suffrage; but they sought to protect the property rights of the individual by the most absolute constitutional guarantees. Moreover, American practice has allowed the individual a far larger measure of economic liberty than is required by the Constitution; and this liberty was granted in the expectation that it would benefit, not the individual as such, but the great mass of the American people. It has undoubtedly benefited the great mass of the American people; but it has been of far more benefit to a comparatively few individuals. Americans are just beginning to learn that the great freedom which the individual property-owner has enjoyed is having the inevitable result of all unrestrained exercise of freedom. It has tended to create a powerful but limited class whose chief object it is to hold and to increase the power which they have gained; and this unexpected result has presented the American democracy with the most difficult and radical of its problems. Is it to the interest of the American people as a democracy to permit the increase or the perpetuation of the power gained by this aristocracy of money?

A candid consideration of the foregoing question will, I believe, result in a negative answer. A democracy has as much interest in regulating for its own benefit the distribution of economic power as it has the distribution of political power, and the consequences of ignoring this interest would be as fatal in one case as in the other. In both instances regulation in the democratic interest is as far as possible from meaning the annihilation of individual liberty; but in both instances individual liberty should be subjected to conditions which will continue to keep it efficient and generally serviceable. Individual economic power is not any more dangerous than individual political power—provided it is not held too absolutely and for too long a time. But in both cases the interest of the community as a whole should be dominant; and the interest of the whole community demands a considerable concentration of economic power and responsibility, but only for the ultimate purpose of its more efficient exercise and the better distribution of its fruits. * * *

No doubt the institution of private property, necessitating, as it does, the transmission to one person of the possessions and earnings of another, always involves the inheritance of unearned power and opportunity. But the point is that in the case of very large fortunes the inherited power goes far beyond any legitimate individual needs, and in the course of time can hardly fail to corrupt its possessors. The creator of a large fortune may well be its master; but its inheritor will, except in the case of exceptionally able individuals, become its victim, and most assuredly the evil social effects are as bad as the evil individual effects. The political bond which a democracy seeks to create depends for its higher value upon an effective social bond. Gross inequalities in wealth, wholly divorced from economic efficiency on the part of the rich, as effectively loosen the social bond as do gross inequalities of political and social standing. A wholesome social condition in a democracy does not imply uniformity of wealth any more than it implies uniformity of ability and purpose, but it does imply the association of great individual economic distinction with responsibility and efficiency. It does imply that economic leaders, no less than political ones, should have conditions imposed upon them which will force them to recognize the responsibilities attached to so much power. Mutual association and confidence between the leaders and followers is as much a part of democratic economic organization as it is of democratic political organization; and in the long run the inheritance of vast fortunes destroys any such relation. They breed class envy on one side, and class contempt on the other; and the community is either divided irremediably by differences of interest and outlook, or united, if at all, by snobbish servility.

If the integrity of a democracy is injured by the perpetuation of unearned economic distinctions, it is also injured by extreme poverty, whether deserved or not. A democracy which attempted to equalize wealth would incur the same disastrous fate as a democracy which attempted to equalize political power; but a democracy can no more be indifferent to the distribution of wealth than it can to the distribution of the suffrage. In a wholesome democracy every male adult should participate in the ultimate political responsibility, partly because of the political danger of refusing participation to the people, and partly because of the advantages to be derived from the political union of the whole people. So a wholesome democracy should seek to guarantee to every male adult a certain minimum of economic power and responsibility. No doubt it is much easier to confer the suffrage on the people than it is to make poverty a negligible social factor; but the difficulty of the task does not make it the less necessary. It stands to reason that in the long run the people who possess the political power will want a substantial share of the economic fruits. A prudent democracy should anticipate this demand. Not only does any considerable amount of grinding poverty constitute a grave social danger in a democratic state, but so, in general, does a widespread condition of partial economic privation. The individuals constituting a democracy lack the first essential of individual freedom when they cannot escape from a condition of economic dependence.

The American democracy has confidently believed in the fatal prosperity enjoyed by the people under the American system. In the confidence of that belief it has promised to Americans a substantial satisfaction of their economic needs; and it has made that promise an essential part of the American national idea. The promise has been measurably fulfilled hitherto, because the prodigious natural resources of a new continent were thrown open to anybody with the energy to appropriate them. But those natural resources have in no large measure passed into the possession of individuals, and American statesmen can no longer count upon them to satisfy the popular hunger for economic independence. An even larger proportion of the total population of the country is taking to industrial occupations, and an industrial system brings with it much more definite social and economic classes, and a diminution of the earlier social homogeneity. The contemporary wage-earner is no longer satisfied with the economic results of being merely an American citizen. His union is usually of more obvious use to him than the state, and he is tending to make his allegiance to his union paramount to his allegiance to the state. This is only one of many illustrations that the traditional American system has broken down. The American state can regain the loyal adhesion of the economically less independent class only by positive service. What the wage-earner needs, and what it is to the interest of a democratic state he should obtain, is a constantly higher standard of living. The state can help him to conquer a higher standard of living without doing any necessary injury to his employers and with a positive benefit to general economic and social efficiency. If it is to earn the loyalty of the wage-earners, it must recognize the legitimacy of his demand, and make the satisfaction of it an essential part of its public policy.

The American state is dedicated to such a duty, not only by its democratic purpose, but by its national tradition. So far as the former is concerned, it is absurd and fatal to ask a popular majority to respect the rights of a minority, when those rights are interpreted so as to seriously hamper, if not to forbid, the majority from obtaining the essential condition of individual freedom and development—viz. The highest possible standard of living. But this absurdity becomes really critical and dangerous, in view of the fact that the American people, particularly those of alien birth and descent, have been explicitly promised economic freedom and prosperity. The promise was made on the strength of what was believed to be an inexhaustible store of natural opportunities; and it will have to be kept even when those natural resources are no longer to be had for the asking. It is entirely possible, of course, that the promise can never be kept,—that its redemption will prove to be beyond the patience, the power, and the wisdom of the American people and their leaders; but if it is not kept, the American commonwealth will no longer continue to be a democracy.

* * * We are now prepared, I hope, to venture upon a more fruitful definition of democracy. The popular definitions err in describing it in terms of its machinery or of some partial political or economic object. Democracy does not mean merely government by the people, or majority rule, or universal suffrage. All of these political forms or devices are a part of its necessary organization; but the chief advantage such methods of organization have is their tendency to promote some salutary and formative purpose. The really formative purpose is not exclusively a matter of individual liberty, although it must give individual liberty abundant scope. Neither is it a matter of equal rights alone, although it must always cherish the social bond which the principle represents. The salutary and formative democratic purpose consists in using the democratic organization for the joint benefit of individual distinction and social improvement.

To define the really democratic organization as one which makes expressly and intentionally for individual distinction and social improvement is nothing more than a translation of the statement that such an organization should make expressly and intentionally for the welfare of the whole people. The whole people will always consist of individuals, constituting small classes, who demand special opportunities, and the mass of the population who demand for their improvement more generalized opportunities. At any particular time or in any particular case, the improvement of the smaller classes may conflict with that of the larger class, but the conflict becomes permanent and irreconcilable only when it is intensified by the lack of a really binding and edifying public policy, and by the consequent stimulation of class and factional prejudices and purposes. A policy, intelligently informed by the desire to maintain a joint process of individual and social amelioration, should be able to keep a democracy sound and whole both in sentiment and in idea. Such a democracy would not be dedicated either to liberty or to equality in their abstract expressions, but to liberty and equality, in so far as they made for human brotherhood. * * * The two subordinate principles, that is, one representing the individual and the other the social interest, can by their subordination to the principle of human brotherhood, be made in the long run mutually helpful.

The foregoing definition of the democratic purpose is the only one which can entitle democracy to an essential superiority to other forms of political organization. Democrats have always tended to claim some such superiority for their methods and purposes, but in case democracy is to be considered merely as a piece of political machinery, or a partial political idea, the claim has no validity. Its superiority must be based upon the fact that democracy is the best possible translation into political and social terms of an authoritative and comprehensive moral idea; and, provided a democratic state honestly seeks to make its organization and policy contribute to a better quality of individuality and a higher level of associated life, it can within certain limits claim the allegiance of mankind on rational moral grounds.

The proposed definition may seem to be both vague and commonplace; but it none the less brings with it practical consequences of paramount importance. The subordination of the machinery of democracy to its purpose, and the comprehension within that purpose of the higher interests both of the individual and society, is not only exclusive of many partial and erroneous ideas, but demands both a reconstructive programme and an efficient organization. A government by the people, which seeks an organization and a policy beneficial to the individual and to society, is confronted by a task as responsible and difficult as you please; but it is a specific task which demands the adoption of certain specific and positive means. Moreover it is a task which the American democracy has never sought consciously to achieve. American democrats have always hoped for individual and social amelioration as the result of the operation of their democratic system; but if any such result was to follow, its achievement was to be a happy accident. The organization and policy of a democracy should leave the individual and society to seek their own amelioration. The democratic state should never discriminate in favor of anything or anybody. It should only discriminate against all sorts of privilege. Under the proposed definition, on the other hand, popular government is to make itself expressly and permanently responsible for the amelioration of the individual and society; and a necessary consequence of this responsibility is an adequate organization and a reconstructive policy.

The majority of good Americans will doubtless consider that the reconstructive policy, already indicated, is flagrantly socialistic both in its methods and its objects; and if any critic likes to fasten the stigma of socialism upon the foregoing conception of democracy, I am not concerned with dodging the odium of the word. The proposed definition of democracy is socialistic, if it is socialistic to consider democracy inseparable from a candid, patient, and courageous attempt to advance the social problem towards a satisfactory solution. It is also socialistic in case socialism cannot be divorced from the use, wherever necessary, of the political organization in all its forms to realize the proposed democratic purpose. On the other hand, there are some doctrines frequently associated with socialism, to which the proposed conception of democracy is wholly inimical; and it should be characterized not so much socialistic, as unscrupulously and loyally nationalistic.

A democracy dedicated to individual and social betterment is necessarily individualistic as well as socialist. It has little interest in the mere multiplication of average individuals, except in so far as such multiplication is necessary to economic and political efficiency; but it has the deepest interest in the development of a higher quality of individual self-expression. There are two indispensable economic conditions of qualitative individual self-expression. One is the preservation of the institution of private property in some form, and the other is the radical transformation of its existing nature and influence. A democracy certainly cannot fulfill its mission without the eventual assumption by the state of many functions now performed by individuals, and without becoming expressly responsible for an improved distribution of wealth; but if any attempt is made to accomplish these results by violent means, it will most assuredly prove to be a failure. An improvement in the distribution of wealth or in economic efficiency which cannot be accomplished by purchase on the part of the state or by a legitimate use of the power of taxation, must be left to the action of time, assisted, of course, by such arrangements as are immediately practical. But the amount of actual good to the individual and society which can be effected *at any one time* by an alteration in the distribution of wealth is extremely small; and the same statement is true of any proposed state action in the interest of the democratic purpose. Consequently, while responsible state action is an essential condition of any steady approach to the democratic consummation, such action will be wholly vain unless accompanied by a larger measure of spontaneous individual amelioration. In fact, one of the strongest arguments on behalf of a higher and larger conception of state responsibilities in a democracy is that the candid, courageous, patient, and intelligent attempt to redeem those responsibilities provides one of the highest types of individuality—viz. the public-spirited man with a personal opportunity and a task which should be enormously stimulating and edifying.

The great weakness of the most popular form of socialism consists, however, in its mixture of a revolutionary purpose with an international scope. It seeks the abolition of national distinctions by revolutionary revolts of the wage-earner against the capitalist; and in so far as its proposes to undermine the principle of national cohesion and to substitute for it an international organization of a single class, it is headed absolutely in the wrong direction. Revolutions may at times be necessary and on the whole helpful, but not in case there is any other practicable method of removing grave obstacles to human amelioration; and in any event their tendency is socially disintegrating. The destruction or the weakening of nationalities for the ostensible benefit of an international socialism would in truth gravely imperil the bond upon which actual human association is based. The peoples who have inherited any share in Christian civilization are effectively united chiefly by national habits, traditions, and purposes; and perhaps the most effective way of bringing about an irretrievable division of purpose among them would be the adoption by the class of wage-earners of the programme of international socialism. It is not too much to say that no permanent good can, under existing conditions, come to the individual and society except through the preservation and the development of the existing system of nationalized states.

Radical and enthusiastic democrats have usually failed to attach sufficient importance to the ties whereby civilized men are at the present time actually united. Inasmuch as national traditions are usually associated with all sorts of political, economic, and social privileges and abuses, they have sought to identify the higher social relation with the destruction of the national tradition and the substitution of an ideal bond. In so doing they are committing a disastrous error; and democracy will never become really constructive until this error is recognized and democracy abandons its former alliance with revolution. The higher human relation must be brought about chiefly by the improvement and the intensification of existing human relations.

* * * The only possible foundation for a better social structure is the existing social order, of which the contemporary system of nationalized states forms the foundation.

Loyalty to the existing system of nationalized states does not necessarily mean loyalty to an existing government merely because it exists. There have been, and still are, governments whose ruin is a necessary condition of popular liberation; and revolution doubtless still has a subordinate part to play in the process of human amelioration. The loyalty which a citizen owes to a government is dependent upon the extent to which the government is representative of national traditions and is organized in the interest of valid national purposes. National traditions and purposes always contain a large infusion of dubious ingredients; but loyalty to them does not necessarily mean the uncritical and unprotesting acceptance of the national limitations and abuses. Nationality is a political and social idea as well as the great contemporary political fact. Loyalty to the national interest implies devotion to a progressive principle. It demands, to be sure, that the progressive principle be realized without any violation of fundamental national ties. It demands that any national action taken for the benefit of the progressive principle be approved by the official national organization. But it also serves as a ferment quite as much as a bond. It bids the loyal national servants to fashion their fellow-countrymen into more of a nation; and the attempt to perform this bidding constitutes a very powerful and wholesome source of political development. It constitutes, indeed, a source of political development which is of decisive importance for a satisfactory theory of political and social progress, because a people which becomes more of a nation has a tendency to become for that very reason more of a democracy.

* * *

If a people, in becoming more of a nation, become for that very reason more of a democracy, the realization of the democratic purpose is not rendered any easier, but democracy is provided with a simplified, a consistent, and a practicable programme. An alliance is established thereby between the two dominant political and social forces in modern life. The suspicion with which aggressive advocates of the national principle have sometimes regarded democracy would be shown to have only a conditional justification; and the suspicion with which many ardent democrats have regarded aggressive nationalism would be similarly disarmed. A democrat, so far as the statement is true, could trust the fate of his cause in each particular state to the friends of national progress. Democracy would not need for its consummation the ruin of the traditional political fabrics, but so far as those political bodies were informed by genuinely national ideas and aspirations, it could await confidently the process of national development. In fact, the first duty of a good democrat would be that of rendering to his country loyal patriotic service. Democrats would abandon the task of making over the world to suit their own purposes, until they had come to a better understanding with their own countrymen. One's democracy, that is, would begin at home and it would for the most part stay at home; and the cause of national well-being would derive invaluable assistance from the loyal cooperation of good democrats. * * *

Americans have always been both patriotic and democratic, just as they have always been friendly both to liberty and equality, but in neither case have they brought the two ideas or aspirations into mutually helpful relations. As democrats they have often regarded nationalism with distrust, and have consequently deprived their patriotism of any sufficient substance and organization. As nationalists they have frequently regarded essential aspects of democracy with a wholly unnecessary and embarrassing suspicion. They have been after a fashion Hamiltonian, and Jeffersonian after more of a fashion; but they have never recovered from the initial disagreement between Hamilton and Jefferson. If there is any truth in the idea of a constructive relation between democracy and nationality this disagreement must be healed. They must accept both principles loyally and unreservedly; and by such acceptance their "noble national theory" will obtain a wholly unaccustomed energy and integrity. The alliance between the two principles will not leave either of them intact; but it will necessarily do more harm to the Jeffersonian group of political ideas than it will to the Hamiltonian. The latter's nationalism can be adapted to democracy without an essential injury to itself, but the former's democracy cannot be nationalized without being transformed.

* * * It must cease to be a democracy of indiscriminate individualism, and become one of selected individuals who are obliged constantly to justify their selection; and its members must be united not by a sense of joint irresponsibility, but by a sense of joint responsibility for the success of their political and social ideal. They must become, that is, a democracy devoted to the welfare of the whole people by means of a conscious labor of individual and social improvement; and that is precisely the sort of democracy which demands for its realization the aid of the Hamiltonian nationalistic organization and principle.

THEODORE ROOSEVELT

New Nationalism (1910)

As president of the United States, Roosevelt strengthened the powers of the office, promoted environmental conservation, and earned a reputation as a progressive reformer for his support of consumer protection, his promotion of a more regulatory state, and his "trust-busting" efforts. Although he left the White House after being elected to and

serving a second term, Roosevelt reentered politics in 1912 as the
presidential nominee of the Progressive ("Bull Moose") Party. In a
speech he delivered at Ossawatomie, Kansas, Roosevelt outlined the
main themes of his "New Nationalism," his commitment to greater use
of the national government to solve national problems.

Our interest is primarily in the application to-day of the lessons taught by the contest of half a century ago. It is of little use for us to pay lip loyalty to the mighty men of the past unless we sincerely endeavor to apply to the problems of the present precisely the qualities which in other crises enabled the men of that day to meet those crises. It is half melancholy and half amusing to see the way in which well-meaning people gather to do honor to the men who, in company with John Brown, and under the lead of Abraham Lincoln, faced and solved the great problems of the nineteenth century, while, at the same time, these same good people nervously shrink from, or frantically denounce, those who are trying to meet the problems of the twentieth century in the spirit which was accountable for the successful solution of the problems of Lincoln's time.

Of that generation of men to whom we owe so much, the man to whom we owe most is, of course, Lincoln. Part of our debt to him is because he forecast our present struggle and saw the way out. He said:—

> I hold that while man exists it is his duty to improve not only his own condition, but to assist in ameliorating mankind.

And again:—

> Labor is prior to, and independent of, capital. Capital is only the fruit of labor, and could never have existed if labor had not first existed. Labor is the superior of capital, and deserves much the higher consideration.

If that remark was original with me, I should be even more strongly denounced as a communist agitator than I shall be anyhow. It is Lincoln's. I am only quoting it; and that is one side; that is the side the capitalist should hear. Now, let the workingman hear his side.

> Capital has its rights, which are as worthy of protection as any other rights. . . . Nor should this lead to a war upon the owners of property. Property is the fruit of labor; . . . property is desirable; is a positive good in the world.

And then comes a thoroughly Lincolnlike sentence:—

Let not him who is houseless pull down the house of another, but let him work diligently and build one for himself, thus by example assuring that his own shall be safe from violence when built.

It seems to me that, in these words, Lincoln took substantially the attitude that we ought to take; he showed the proper sense of proportion in his relative estimates of capital and labor, of human rights and property rights. Above all, in this speech, as in many others, he taught a lesson in wise kindliness and charity; an indispensable lesson to us of to-day. But this wise kindliness and charity never weakened his arm or numbed his heart. We cannot afford weakly to blind ourselves to the actual conflict which faces us to-day. The issue is joined, and we must fight or fail.

In every wise struggle for human betterment one of the main objects, and often the only object, has been to achieve in large measure equality of opportunity. In the struggle for this great end, nations rise from barbarism to civilization, and through it people press forward from one stage of enlightenment to the next. One of the chief factors in progress is the destruction of special privilege. The essence of any struggle for healthy liberty has always been, and must always be, to take from some one man or class of men the right to enjoy power, or wealth, or position, or immunity, which has not been earned by service to his or their fellows. That is what you fought for in the Civil War, and that is what we strive for now.

At many stages in the advance of humanity, this conflict between the men who possess more than they have earned and the men who have earned more than they possess is the central condition of progress. In our day it appears as the struggle of free men to gain and hold the right of self-government as against the special interests, who twist the methods of free government into machinery for defeating the popular will. At every stage, and under all circumstances, the essence of the struggle is to equalize opportunity, destroy privilege, and give to the life and citizenship of every individual the highest possible value both to himself and to the commonwealth. That is nothing new. All I ask in civil life is what you fought for in the Civil War. I ask that civil life be carried on according to the spirit in which the army was carried on. You never get perfect justice, but the effort in handling the army was to bring to the front the men who could do the job. Nobody grudged promotion to Grant, or Sherman, or Thomas, or Sheridan, because they earned it. The only complaint was when a man got promotion which he did not earn.

Practical equality of opportunity for all citizens, when we achieve it, will have two great results. First, every man will have a fair chance to make of himself all that in him lies; to reach the highest point to which his capacities, unassisted by special privilege of his own and unhampered by the special privilege of others, can carry him, and to get for himself and his family substantially what he has earned. Second, equality of opportunity means that the commonwealth will get from every citizen the highest service of which he is capable. No man who carries the burden of the special privileges of another can give to the commonwealth that service to which it is fairly entitled.

I stand for the square deal. But when I say that I am for the square deal, I mean not merely that I stand for fair play under the present rules of the game, but that I stand for having those rules changed so as to work for a more substantial equality of opportunity and of reward for equally good service. One word of warning, which, I think, is hardly necessary in Kansas. When I say I want a square deal for the poor man, I do not mean that I want a square deal for the man who remains poor because he has not got the energy to work for himself. If a man who has had a chance will not make good, then he has got to quit. And you men of the Grand Army, you want justice for the brave man who fought, and punishment for the coward who shirked his work. Is not that so?

Now, this means that our government, national and state, must be freed from the sinister influence or control of special interests. Exactly as the special interests of cotton and slavery threatened our political integrity before the Civil War, so now the great special business interests too often control and corrupt the men and methods of government for their own profit. We must drive the special interests out of politics. That is one of our tasks to-day. Every special interest is entitled to justice— full, fair, and complete,—and, now, mind you, if there were any attempt by mob violence to plunder and work harm to the special interest, whatever it may be, that I most dislike, and the wealthy man, whomsoever he may be, for whom I have the greatest contempt, I would fight for him, and you would if you were worth your salt. He should have justice. For every special interest is entitled to justice, but not one is entitled to a vote in Congress, to a voice on the bench, or to representation in any public office. The Constitution guarantees protection to property, and we must make that promise good. But it does not give the right of suffrage to any corporation.

The true friend of property, the true conservative, is he who insists that property shall be the servant and not the master of the commonwealth; who insists that the creature of man's making shall be the servant and not the master of the man who made it. The citizens of the United States must effectively control the mighty commercial forces which they have themselves called into being.

There can be no effective control of corporations while their political activity remains. To put an end to it will be neither a short nor an easy task, but it can be done.

We must have complete and effective publicity of corporate affairs, so that the people may know beyond peradventure whether the corporations obey the law and whether their management entitles them to the confidence of the public. It is necessary that laws should be passed to prohibit the use of corporate funds directly or indirectly for political purposes; it is still more necessary that such laws should be thoroughly enforced. Corporate expenditures for political purposes, and especially such expenditures by public service corporations, have supplied one of the principal sources of corruption in our political affairs.

It has become entirely clear that we must have government supervision of the capitalization, not only of public service corporations, including, particularly, railways, but of all corporations doing an interstate business. I do not wish to see the nation forced into the ownership of the railways if it can possibly be avoided, and the only alternative is thoroughgoing and effective regulation, which shall be based on a full knowledge of all the facts, including a physical valuation of property. This physical valuation is not needed, or, at least, is very rarely needed, for fixing rates; but it is needed as the basis of honest capitalization.

We have come to recognize that franchises should never be granted except for a limited time, and never without proper provision for compensation to the public. It is my personal belief that the same kind and degree of control and supervision which should be exercised over public service corporations should be extended also to combinations which control necessaries of life, such as meat, oil, and coal, or which deal in them on an important scale. I have no doubt that the ordinary man who has control of them is much like ourselves. I have no doubt he would like to do well, but I want to have enough supervision to help him realize that desire to do well.

I believe that the officers, and, especially, the directors, of corporations should be held personally responsible when any corporation breaks the law.

Combinations in industry are the result of an imperative economic law which cannot be repealed by political legislation. The effort at prohibiting all combination has substantially failed. The way out lies, not in attempting to prevent such combinations, but in completely controlling them in the interest of the public welfare. For that purpose the Federal Bureau of Corporations is an agency of first importance. Its powers, and, therefore, its efficiency, as well as that of the Interstate Commerce Commission, should be largely increased. We have a right to expect from the

Bureau of Corporations and from the Interstate Commerce Commission a very high grade of public service. We should be as sure of the proper conduct of the interstate railways and the proper management of interstate business as we are now sure of the conduct and management of the national banks, and we should have as effective supervision in one case as in the other. The Hepburn Act, and the amendment to the Act in the shape in which it finally passed Congress at the last session, represent a long step in advance, and we must go yet further.

There is a widespread belief among our people that, under the methods of making tariffs which have hitherto obtained, the special interests are too influential. Probably this is true of both the big special interests and the little special interests. These methods have put a premium on selfishness, and, naturally, the selfish big interests have gotten more than their smaller, though equally selfish, brothers. The duty of Congress is to provide a method by which the interest of the whole people shall be all that receives consideration. To this end there must be an expert tariff commission, wholly removed from the possibility of political pressure or of improper business influence. Such a commission can find the real difference between cost of production, which is mainly the difference of labor cost here and abroad. As fast as its recommendations are made, I believe in revising one schedule at a time. A general revision of the tariff almost inevitably leads to log-rolling and the subordination of the general public interest to local and special interests.

The absence of effective state, and, especially, national, restraint upon unfair money getting has tended to create a small class of enormously wealthy and economically powerful men, whose chief object is to hold and increase their power. The prime need is to change the conditions which enable these men to accumulate power which it is not for the general welfare that they should hold or exercise. We grudge no man a fortune which represents his own power and sagacity, when exercised with entire regard to the welfare of his fellows. Again, comrades over there, take the lesson from your own experience. Not only did you not grudge, but you gloried in the promotion of the great generals who gained their promotion by leading the army to victory. So it is with us. We grudge no man a fortune in civil life if it is honorably obtained and well used. It is not even enough that it should have been gained without doing damage to the community. We should permit it to be gained only so long as the gaining represents benefit to the community. This, I know, implies a policy of a far more active governmental interference with social and economic conditions in this country than we have yet had, but I think we have got to face the fact that such an increase in governmental control is now necessary.

No man should receive a dollar unless that dollar has been fairly earned. Every dollar received should represent a dollar's worth of service rendered—not gambling in stocks, but service rendered. The really big fortune, the swollen fortune, by the mere fact of its size acquires qualities which differentiate it in kind as well as in degree from what is possessed by men of relatively small means. Therefore, I believe in a graduated income tax on big fortunes, and in another tax which is far more easily collected and far more effective—a graduated inheritance tax on big fortunes, properly safeguarded against evasion and increasing rapidly in amount with the size of the estate. * * *

Moreover, I believe that the natural resources must be used for the benefit of all our people, and not monopolized for the benefit of the few, and here again is another case in which I am accused of taking a revolutionary attitude. People forget now that one hundred years ago there were public men of good character who advocated the nation selling its public lands in great quantities, so that the nation could get the most money out of it, and giving it to the men who could cultivate it for their own uses. We took the proper democratic ground that the land should be granted in small sections to the men who were actually to till it and live on it. Now, with the water power, with the forests, with the mines, we are brought face to face with the fact that there are many people who will go with us in conserving the resources only if they are to be allowed to exploit them for their benefit. That is one of the fundamental reasons why the special interests should be driven out of politics. Of all the questions which can come before this nation, short of the actual preservation of its existence in a great war, there is none which compares in importance with the great central task of leaving this land even a better land for our descendants than it is for us, and training them into a better race to inhabit the land and pass it on. Conservation is a great moral issue, for it involves the patriotic duty of insuring the safety and continuance of the nation. Let me add that the health and vitality of our people are at least as well worth conserving as their forests, waters, lands, and minerals, and in this great work the national government must bear a most important part.

* * *

Nothing is more true than that excess of every kind is followed by reaction; a fact which should be pondered by reformer and reactionary alike. We are face to face with new conceptions of the relations of property to human welfare, chiefly because certain advocates of the rights of property as against the rights of men have been pushing their claims too far. The man who wrongly holds that every human right is secondary to his profit must now give way to the advocate of human welfare, who rightly maintains that every man holds his property subject to the general right of the community to regulate its use to whatever degree the public welfare may require it.

But I think we may go still further. The right to regulate the use of wealth in the public interest is universally admitted. Let us admit also the right to regulate the terms and conditions of labor, which is the chief element of wealth, directly in the interest of the common good. The fundamental thing to do for every man is to give him a chance to reach a place in which he will make the greatest possible contribution to the public welfare. Understand what I say there. Give him a chance, not push him up if he will not be pushed. Help any man who stumbles; if he lies down, it is a poor job to try to carry him; but if he is a worthy man, try your best to see that he gets a chance to show the worth that is in him. No man can be a good citizen unless he has a wage more than sufficient to cover the bare cost of living, and hours of labor short enough so that after his day's work is done he will have time and energy to bear his share in the management of the community, to help in carrying the general load. We keep countless men from being good citizens by the conditions of life with which we surround them. We need comprehensive workmen's compensation acts, both state and national laws to regulate child labor and work for women, and, especially, we need in our common schools not merely education in book learning, but also practical training for daily life and work. We need to enforce better sanitary conditions for our workers and to extend the use of safety appliances for our workers in industry and commerce, both within and between the states. Also, friends, in the interest of the workingman himself we need to set our faces like flint against mob violence just as against corporate greed; against violence and injustice and lawlessness by wage workers just as much as against lawless cunning and greed and selfish arrogance of employers. If I could ask but one thing of my fellow countrymen, my request would be that, whenever they go in for reform, they remember the two sides, and that they always exact justice from one side as much as from the other. I have small use for the public servant who can always see and denounce the corruption of the capitalist, but who cannot persuade himself, especially before election, to say a word about lawless mob violence. And I have equally small use for the man, be he a judge on the bench, or editor of a great paper, or wealthy and influential private citizen, who can see clearly enough and denounce the lawlessness of mob violence, but whose eyes are closed so that he is blind when the question is one of corruption in business on a gigantic scale. Also remember what I said about excess in reformer and reactionary alike. If the reactionary man, who thinks of nothing but the rights of property, could have his way, he would bring about a revolution; and one of my chief fears in connection with progress comes because I do not want to see our people, for lack of proper leadership, compelled to follow men whose intentions are excellent, but whose eyes are a little too wild to make it really safe to trust them. Here in Kansas there is one paper which habitually denounces me as the tool of Wall Street, and at the same time frantically repudiates the statement that I am a Socialist on the ground that that is an unwarranted slander of the Socialists.

National efficiency has many factors. It is a necessary result of the principle of conservation widely applied. In the end it will determine our failure or success as a nation. National efficiency has to do, not only with natural resources and with men, but it is equally concerned with institutions. The state must be made efficient for the work which concerns only the people of the state; and the nation for that which concerns all the people. There must remain no neutral ground to serve as a refuge for lawbreakers, and especially for lawbreakers of great wealth, who can hire the vulpine legal cunning which will teach them how to avoid both jurisdictions. It is a misfortune when the national legislature fails to do its duty in providing a national remedy, so that the only national activity is the purely negative activity of the judiciary in forbidding the state to exercise power in the premises.

I do not ask for overcentralization; but I do ask that we work in a spirit of broad and far-reaching nationalism when we work for what concerns our people as a whole. We are all Americans. Our common interests are as broad as the continent. I speak to you here in Kansas exactly as I would speak in New York or Georgia, for the most vital problems are those which affect us all alike. The national government belongs to the whole American people, and where the whole American people are interested, that interest can be guarded effectively only by the national government. The betterment which we seek must be accomplished, I believe, mainly through the national government.

The American people are right in demanding that New Nationalism, without which we cannot hope to deal with new problems. The New Nationalism puts the national need before sectional or personal advantage. It is impatient of the utter confusion that results from local legislatures attempting to treat national issues as local issues. It is still more impatient of the impotence which springs from overdivision of governmental powers, the impotence which makes it possible for local selfishness or for legal cunning, hired by wealthy special interests, to bring national activities to a deadlock. This New Nationalism regards the executive power as the steward of the public welfare. It demands of the judiciary that it shall be interested primarily in human welfare rather than in property, just as it demands that the representative body shall represent all the people rather than any one class or section of the people.

I believe in shaping the ends of government to protect property as well as human welfare. Normally, and in the long run, the ends are the same; but whenever the alternative must be faced, I am for men and not for property, as you were in the Civil War. I am far from underestimating the importance of dividends; but I rank dividends below human character. Again, I do not have any sympathy with the reformer who says he does not care for dividends. Of course, economic welfare is necessary, for a man must pull his own weight and be able to support his family. I know well that the reformers must not bring upon the people economic ruin, or the reforms themselves will go down in the ruin. But we must be ready to face temporary disaster, whether or not brought on by those who will war against us to the knife. Those who oppose all reform will do well to remember that ruin in its worst form is inevitable if our national life brings us nothing better than swollen fortunes for the few and the triumph in both politics and business of a sordid and selfish materialism.

LOUIS D. BRANDEIS

The Living Law (1915)

The Progressive lawyer and social reformer Louis Dembitz Brandeis (1856–1941) was the first to use economic and sociological data in legal briefs in his defense of various state laws that promoted the health and welfare of laborers. His efforts against monopolies and other anticompetitive business practices contributed to the passage of the Clayton Anti-Trust Act in 1914. In 1916 he was appointed to the Supreme Court by President Woodrow Wilson, becoming the first Jewish justice. In an address to the Chicago Bar Association reprinted in the Illinois Law Review, Brandeis sounded a theme common among progressives: the need for the law to keep up with the rapid pace of social and economic changes. The best way to do this, he suggested, was to broaden legal education in order to offset the negative effects of ever-increasing specialization.

The history of the United States, since the adoption of the constitution, covers less than 128 years. Yet in that short period the American ideal of government has been greatly modified. At first our ideal was expressed as 'A government of laws and not of men.' Then it became 'A government of the people, by the people, for the people.' Now it is 'Democracy and social justice.'

In the last half century our democracy has deepened. Coincidentally there has been a shifting of our longing from legal justice to social justice, and—it must be admitted—also a waning respect for law. Is there any casual connection between the shifting of our longing from legal justice to social justice and waning respect for law? If so, was that result unavoidable. * * *

Has not the recent dissatisfaction with our law as administered been due, in large measure, to the fact that it had not kept pace with the rapid development of our political, economic and social ideals? In other words, is not the challenge of legal justice due to its failure to conform to contemporary conceptions of social justice?

Since the adoption of the federal constitution, and notably within the last fifty years, we have passed through an economic and social revolution which affected the life of the people more fundamentally than any political revolution known to history. Widespread substitution of machinery for hand labor (thus multiplying a hundredfold man's productivity), and the annihilation of space through steam and electricity, have wrought changes in the conditions of life which are in many respects greater than those which had occurred in civilized countries during thousands of years preceding. The end was put to legalized human slavery—an institution which had existed since the dawn of history. But of vastly greater influence upon the lives of the great majority of all civilized peoples was the possibility which invention and discovery created of emancipating women and of liberating men called free from the excessive toil theretofore required to secure food, clothing and shelter. Yet, while invention and discovery created the possibility of releasing men and women from the thraldom of drudgery, there actually came, with the introduction of the factory system and the development of the business corporation, new dangers to liberty. Large publicly owned corporations replaced small privately owned concerns. Ownership of the instruments of production passed from the workman to the employer. Individual personal relations between the proprietor and his help ceased. The individual contract of service lost its character, because of the inequality in position between employer and employee. The group relation of employee to employer with collective bargaining became common, for it was essential to the workers' protection.

Political as well as economic and social science noted these revolutionary changes. But legal science—the unwritten or judge-made laws as distinguished from legislation—was largely deaf and blind to them. Courts continued to ignore newly arisen social needs. They applied complacently

18th century conceptions of the liberty of the individual and of the sacredness of private property. Early 19th century scientific half-truths, like 'The survival of the fittest,' which translated into practice meant 'The devil take the hindmost,' were erected by judicial sanction into a moral law. Where statutes giving expression to the new social spirit were clearly constitutional, judges, imbued with the relentless spirit of individualism, often construed them away. Where any doubt as to the constitutionality of such statutes could find lodgment, courts all too frequently declared the acts void. Also in other countries the strain upon the law has been great during the last generation, because there also the period has been one of rapid transformation; and the law has everywhere a tendency to lag behind the facts of life. But in America the strain became dangerous, because constitutional limitations were invoked to stop the natural vent of legislation. In the course of relatively few years hundreds of statutes which embodied attempts (often very crude) to adjust legal rights to the demands of social justice were nullified by the courts, on the grounds that the statutes violated the constitutional guaranties of liberty or property. Small wonder that there arose a clamor for the recall of judges and of judicial decisions and that demand was made for amendment of the constitutions and even for their complete abolition.

* * *

The challenge of existing law does not * * * come only from the working classes. Criticism of the law is widespread among business men. The tone of their criticism is more courteous than that of the working classes, and the specific objections raised by business men are different. Business men do not demand recall of judges or of judicial decisions. Business men do not ordinarily seek constitutional amendments. They are more apt to desire repeal of statutes than enactment. But both business men and working men insist that courts lack understanding of contemporary industrial conditions. Both insist that the law is not 'up to date.' Both insist that the lack of familiarity with the facts of business life results in erroneous decisions. * * * Both business men and working men have given further evidence of their distrust of the courts and of lawyers by their efforts to establish non-legal tribunals or commissions to exercise functions which are judicial (even where not legal) in their nature, and by their insistence that the commissions shall be manned with business and working men instead of lawyers. And business men have been active in devising other means of escape from the domain of the courts, as is evidenced by the widesread tendency to arbitrate controversies through committees of business organizations. * * *

The remedy so sought is not adequate, and may prove a mischievous one. What we need is not to displace the courts, but to make them efficient instruments of justice; not to displace the lawyer, but to fit him for his official or judicial task. And indeed the task of fitting the lawyer and the judge to perform adequately the functions of harmonizing law with life is a task far easier of accomplishment than that of endowing men, who lack legal training, with the necessary qualifications. * * *

The pursuit of the legal profession involves a happy combination of the intellectual with the practical life. The intellectual tends to breadth of view; the practical to that realization of limitations which are essential to the wise conduct of life. Formerly the lawyer secured breadth of view largely through wide professional experience. Being a general practitioner, he was brought into contact with all phases of contemporary life. His education was not legal only, because his diversified clientage brought him, by the mere practice of his profession, an economic and social education. The relative smallness of the communities tended to make his practice diversified not only in the character of matters dealt with, but also in the character or standing of his clients. For the same lawyer was apt to serve at one time or another both rich and poor, both employer and employee. Furthermore—nearly every lawyer of ability took some part in political life. Our greatest judges, Marshall, Kent, Story, Shaw, had secured this training. * * *

The last fifty years have wrought a great change in professional life. Industrial development and the consequent growth of cities have led to a high degree of specialization—specialization not only in the nature and class of questions dealt with, but also specialization in the character of clientage. The term 'corporation lawyer' is significant in this connection. The growing intensity of professional life tended also to discourage participation in public affairs, and thus the broadening of view which comes from political life was lost. The deepening of knowledge in certain subjects was purchased at the cost of vast areas of ignorance and grave danger of resultant distortion of judgment.

The effect of this contraction of the lawyers' intimate relation to contemporary life was doubly serious, because it came at a time when the rapidity of our economic and social transformation made accurate and broad knowledge of present-day problems essential to the administration of justice.

The judge came to the bench unequipped with the necessary knowledge of economic and social science, and his judgment suffered likewise through lack of equipment in the lawyers who presented the cases to him. For a judge rarely performs his functions adequately unless the case before him is adequately presented. Thus were the blind led by the blind. It is not surprising that under such conditions the laws as administered failed to meet contemporary economic and social demands.

We are powerless to restore the general practitioner and general participation in public life. Intense specialization must continue. But we can correct its distorting effects by broader education—by study undertaken preparatory to practice—and continued by lawyer and judge throughout life: study of economics and sociology and politics which embody the facts and present the problems of today.

'Every beneficent change in legislation,' Professor Henderson said, 'comes from a fresh study of social conditions, and social ends, and from such rejection of obsolete laws to make room for a rule which fits the new facts. One can hardly escape from the conclusion that a lawyer who has not studied economics and sociology is very apt to become a public enemy.'

LOUIS D. BRANDEIS

Industrial Absolutism and Democracy (1915)

In testimony before the United States Commission on Industrial Relations, Brandeis, who was then an advisor to President Wilson, explained that huge concentrations of power in corporations had created a tension between "political liberty" and "industrial absolutism." He suggested that employees should share decision-making responsibility with management as part of broader workplace democracy. Brandeis's warnings about the threat large corporate institutions posed to democracy became a distinctive hallmark of Wilsonian progressivism.

My observation leads me to believe that while there are many contributing causes to unrest, that there is one case which is fundamental. That is the necessary conflict—the contrast between our political liberty and our industrial absolutism. We are as free politically, perhaps, as free as it is possible for us to be. Every male has his voice and vote; and the law has endeavored to enable, and has succeeded practically, in enabling him to exercise his political franchise without fear. He therefore has his part; and certainly can secure an adequate part in the government of the country in all of its political relations; that is, in all relations which are determined directly by legislation or governmental administration.

On the other hand, in dealing with industrial problems the position of the ordinary worker is exactly the reverse. The individual employee has no effective voice or vote. And the main objection, as I see it, to the very large corporation is, that it makes possible—and in many cases makes inevitable—the exercise of industrial absolutism. It is not merely the case of the individual worker against the employer which, even if he is a reasonably sized employer, presents a serious situation calling for the interposition of a union to protect the individual. But we have the situation of an employer so potent, so well organized, with such concentrated forces and with such extraordinary powers of reserve and the ability to endure against strikes and other efforts of a union, that the relatively loosely organized masses of even strong unions are unable to cope with the situation. We are dealing here with a question, not of motive, but of condition. Now, the large corporation and the managers of the powerful corporation are probably in large part actuated by motives just the same as the employer of a tenth of their size. Neither of them, as a rule, wishes to have his liberty abridged; but the smaller concern usually comes to the conclusion that it is necessary that it should be, where an important union must be dealt with. But when a great financial power has developed—when there exists these powerful organizations, which can successfully summon forces from all parts of the country, which can afford to use tremendous amounts of money in any conflict to carry out what they deem to be their business principle, and can also afford to suffer large losses—you have necessarily a condition of inequality between the two contending forces. Such contests, though undertaken with the best motives and with strong conviction on the part of the corporate managers that they are seeking what is for the best interests not only of the company but of the community, lead to absolutism. The result, in the cases of these large corporation, may be to develop a benevolent absolutism, but it is an absolutism all the same; and it is that which makes the great corporation so dangerous. There develops within the State a state so powerful that the ordinary social and industrial forces existing are insufficient to cope with it.

I noted * * * that the question * * * put to me concerning the employees of these large corporations related to their physical condition. Their mental condition is certainly equally important. Unrest, to my mind, never can be removed—and fortunately never can be removed—by mere improvement of the physical and material condition of the workingman. If it were possible we should run great risk of improving their material condition and reducing their manhood. We must bear in mind all the time, that however much we may desire material improvement and must desire it for the comfort of the individual, that the United States is a democracy, and that we must have above all things, men. It is the development of manhood to which any industrial and social system should be directed. We Americans are committed not only to social justice in the sense of avoiding things which bring suffering and harm, like unjust distribution of wealth; but we are committed primarily to democracy. The social justice for which we are striving is an incident of our democracy, not the main end. It is rather the result of democracy—perhaps its finest expression—but it rests upon democracy, which implies the rule by the people. And therefore the end for which we must strive is the attainment of rule by the people, and that involves industrial democracy as well as political democracy. That means that the problem of a trade should be no longer the problems of the employer alone. The problems of his business, and it is not the employer's business alone, are the problem of all in it. The union cannot shift upon the employer the responsibility for conditions, not can the employer insist upon determining, according to his will, the conditions which shall exist. The problems which exist are the problems of the trade; they are the problems of employer and employee. Profit sharing, however liberal, cannot meet the situation. That would mean merely dividing the profits of business. Such a division may do harm or it might do good, dependent on how it is applied.

There must be a division not only of profits, but a division also of responsibilities. The employees must have the opportunity of participating in the decisions as to what shall be their condition and how the business shall be run. They must learn also in sharing that responsibility that they, too, must bear the suffering arising from grave mistakes, just as the employer must. But the right to assist in making the decisions, the right of making their own mistakes, if mistakes there must be, is a privilege which should not be denied to labor. We must insist upon labor sharing the responsibilities for the result of the business.

Now, to a certain extent we are gradually getting it—in smaller business. The grave objection to the large business is that, almost inevitably, the form of organisation, the absentee stockholdings and its remote directorship prevent participation, ordinarily, of the employees in such management. The executive officials become stewards in charge of the details of the operation of the business, they alone coming into direct relation with labor. Thus we lose that necessary co-operation which naturally flows from contact between employers and employees—and which the American aspirations for democracy demand. It is in the resultant absolutism that you will find the fundamental cause of prevailing unrest; no matter what is done with the superstructure, no matter how it may be improved in one way or the other, unless we eradicate that fundamental difficulty, unrest will not only continue, but, in my opinion, will grow worse. * * *

In dealing with the problem of industrial democracy there underlies all of the difficulties the question of the concentration of power. This factor so important in connection with the subject of credit and in connection with the subject of trusts and monopolies is no less important in treating the labor problem. As long as there is such concentration of power no effort of the workingmen to secure democratization will be effective. The statement that size is not a crime is entirely correct when you speak of it from the point of motive. But size may become such a danger in its results to the community that the community may have to set limits. A large part of our protective legislation consists of prohibiting things which we find are dangerous, according to common experience. Concentration of power has been shown to be dangerous in a democracy, even though that power may be used beneficently. For instance, on our public highways we put a limit on the size of an autotruck, no matter how well it is run. It may have the most skillful and considerate driver, but its mere size may make it something which the community cannot tolerate, in view of the other uses of the highway and the danger inherent in its occupation to so large an extent by a single vehicle.

WOODROW WILSON

The New Freedom (1913)

The moralistic Princeton University professor and president Woodrow Thomas Wilson (1856–1924) became governor of New Jersey in 1910 with the support of Progressives. Two years later Wilson, a Democrat, successfully ran for president of the United States against the Republican incumbent William Howard Taft and the Bull Moose candidate Teddy Roosevelt. In his campaign speeches for the presidency, Wilson called his comprehensive proposals for political and economic reform the "New Freedom," a program that resembled Roosevelt's "New Nationalism" in its vision of a new role for the government. In a book based on those speeches and called The New Freedom, *Wilson argued that dramatic social and economic changes made it necessary to establish a new legal and political order. But as this selection shows, Wilson disagreed with Roosevelt's enthusiasm for bigness because it tended to create a "heartless" and "impersonal" system that threatened individuality. He disagreed with Croly's reading of Hamilton and Jefferson, as well, though he, too, insisted that "freedom today is something more than being let alone."*

There is one great basic fact which underlies all the questions that are discussed on the political platform at the present moment. That singular fact is that nothing is done in this country as it was done twenty years ago.

We are in the presence of a new organization of society. Our life has broken away from the past. The life of America is not the life that it was twenty years ago. We have changed our economic conditions, absolutely, from top to bottom; and, with our economic society, the organization of our life. The old political formulas do not fit the present problems; they read now like documents taken out of a forgotten age. The older cries sound as if they belonged to a past age which men have almost forgotten. Things which used to be put into the party platforms of ten years ago would sound antiquated if put into a platform now. We are facing the necessity of fitting a new social organization, as we did once fit the old organization, to the happiness and prosperity of the great body of citizens; for we are conscious that the new order of society has not been made to fit and provide the convenience or prosperity of the average man. The life of the nation has grown infinitely varied. It does not centre now upon questions of governmental structure or of the distribution of governmental powers. It centres upon questions of the very structure and operation of society itself, of which government is only the instrument. Our development has run so fast and so far along the lines sketched in the earlier day of constitutional definition, has so crossed and interlaced those lines, has piled upon them such novel structures of trust and combination, has elaborated within them a life so manifold, so full of forces which transcend the boundaries of the country itself and fill the eyes of the world, that a new nation seems to have been created which the old formulas do not fit or afford a vital interpretation of.

We have come upon a very different age from any that preceded us. We have come upon an age when we do not do business in the way in which we used to do business,—when we do not carry on any of the operations of manufacture, sale, transportation, or communication as men used to carry them on. There is a sense in which in our day the individual has been submerged. In most parts of our country men work, not for themselves, not as partners in the old way in which they used to work, but generally as employees,—in a higher or lower grade,—of great corporations. There was a time when corporations played a very minor part in our business affairs, but now they play the chief part, and most men are the servants of corporations.

You know what happens when you are the servant of a corporation. You have in no instance access to the men who are really determining the policy of the corporation. If the corporation is doing the things that it ought not to do, you really have no voice in the matter and must obey the orders, and you have oftentimes with deep mortification to co-operate in the doing of things which you know are against the public interest. Your individuality is swallowed up in the individuality and purpose of a great organization.

It is true that, while most men are thus submerged in the corporation, a few, a very few, are exalted to a power which as individuals they could never have wielded. Through the great organizations of which they are the heads, a few are enabled to play a part unprecedented by anything in history in the control of the business operations of the country and in the determination of the happiness of great numbers of people.

Yesterday, and ever since history began, men were related to one another as individuals. To be sure there were the family, the Church, and the State, institutions which associated men in certain wide circles of relationship. But in the ordinary concerns of life, in the ordinary work, in the daily round, men dealt freely and directly with one another. To-day, the everyday relationships of men are largely with great impersonal concerns, with organizations, not with other individual men.

Now this is nothing short of a new social age, a new era of human relationships, a new stage-setting for the drama of life.

In this new age we find, for instance, that our laws with regard to the relations of employer and employee are in many respects wholly antiquated and impossible. They were framed for another age, which nobody now living remembers, which is, indeed, so remote from our life that it would be difficult for many of us to understand it if it were described to us. The employer is now generally a corporation or a huge company of some kind; the employee is one of hundreds or of thousands brought together, not by individual masters whom they know and with whom they have personal relations, but by agents of one sort or another. Workingmen are marshaled in great numbers for the performance of a multitude of particular tasks under a common discipline. They generally use dangerous and powerful machinery, over whose repair and renewal they have no control. New rules must be devised with regard to their obligations and their rights, their obligations to their employers and their responsibilities to one another. Rules must be devised for their protection, for their compensation when injured, for their support when disabled.

There is something very new and very big and very complex about these new relations of capital and labor. A new economic society has sprung up, and we must effect a new set of adjustments. We must not pit power against weakness. The employer is generally, in our day, as I have said, not an individual, but a powerful group; and yet the workingman when deal-ing with his employer is still, under our existing law, an individual.

Why is it that we have a labor question at all? It is for the simple and very sufficient reason that the laboring man and the employer are not in-timate associates now as they used to be in time past. Most of our laws were formed in the age when employer and employees knew each other, knew each other's characters, were associates with each other, dealt with each other as man with man. That is no longer the case. You not only do not come into personal contact with the men who have the supreme com-mand in those corporations, but it would be out of the question for you to do it. Our modern corporations employ thousands, and in some instances hundreds of thousands, of men. The only persons whom you see or deal with are local superintendents or local representatives of a vast organiza-tion, which is not like anything that the workingmen of the time in which our laws were framed knew anything about. A little group of workingmen, seeing their employer every day, dealing with him in a personal way, is one thing, and the modern body of labor engaged as employees of the huge enterprises that spread all over the country, dealing with men of whom they can form no personal conception, is another thing. A very dif-ferent thing. You never saw a corporation, any more than you ever saw a government. Many a workingman to-day never saw the body of men who are conducting the industry in which he is employed. And they never saw him. What they know about him is written in ledgers and books and let-ters, in the correspondence of the office, in the reports of the superin-tendents. He is a long way off from them.

So what we have to discuss is, not wrongs which individuals intention-ally do,—I do not believe there are a great many of those,—but the wrongs of a system. I want to record my protest against any discussion of this matter which would seem to indicate that there are bodies of our fellow-citizens who are trying to grind us down and do us injustice. There are some men of that sort. I don't know how they sleep o' nights, but there are men of that kind. Thank God, they are not numerous. The truth is, we are all caught in a great economic system which is heartless. The modern corporation is not engaged in business as an individual. When we deal with it, we deal with an impersonal element, an immaterial piece of society. A modern corporation is a means of co-operation in the con-duct of an enterprise which is so big that no one man can conduct it, and which the resources of no one man are sufficient to finance. A company is formed; that company puts out a prospectus; the promoters expect to raise a certain fund as capital stock. Well, how are they going to raise it? They are going to raise it from the public in general, some of whom will buy their stock. The moment that begins, there is formed—what? A joint stock corporation. Men begin to pool their earnings, little piles, big piles. A certain number of men are elected by the stockholders to be directors, and these directors elect a president. This president is the head of the undertaking, and the directors are its managers.

Now, do the workingmen employed by that stock corporation deal with that president and those directors? Not at all. Does the public deal with that president and that board of directors? It does not. Can anybody bring them to account? It is next to impossible to do so. If you undertake it you will find it a game of hide and seek, with the objects of your search taking refuge now behind the tree of their individual personality, now behind that of their corporate irresponsibility.

And do our laws take note of this curious state of things? Do they even attempt to distinguish between a man's act as a corporation director and as an individual? They do not. Our laws still deal with us on the basis of the old system. The law is still living in the dead past which we have left behind. This is evident, for instance, with regard to the matter of employers' liability for workingmen's injuries. Suppose that a superintendent wants a workman to use a certain piece of machinery which it is not safe for him to use, and that the workman is injured by that piece of machinery. Some of our courts have held that the superintendent is a fellow-servant, or, as the law states it, a fellow-employee, and that, therefore, the man cannot recover damages for his injury. The superintendent who probably engaged the man is not his employer. Who is his employer? And whose negligence could conceivably come in there? The board of directors did not tell the employee to use that piece of machinery; and the president of the corporation did not tell him to use that piece of machinery. And so forth. Don't you see by that theory that a man never can get redress for negligence on the part of the employer? When I hear judges reason upon the analogy of the relationships that used to exist between workmen and their employers a generation ago, I wonder if they have not opened their eyes to the modern world. You know, we have a right to expect that judges will have their eyes open, even though the law which they administer hasn't awakened.

Yet that is but a single small detail illustrative of the difficulties we are in because we have not adjusted the law to the facts of the new order.

Since I entered politics, I have chiefly had men's views confided to me privately. Some of the biggest men in the United States, in the field of commerce and manufacture, are afraid of somebody, are afraid of something. They know that there is power somewhere so organized, so subtle, so watchful, so interlocked, so complete, so pervasive, that they had better not speak above their breath when they speak in condemnation of it.

They know that America is not a place of which it can be said, as it used to be, that a man may choose his own calling and pursue it just as far as his abilities enable him to pursue it; because to-day, if he enters certain fields, there are organizations which will use means against him that will prevent his building up a business which they do not want to have built up; organizations that will see to it that the ground is cut from under him and the markets shut against him. For if he begins to sell to certain retail dealers, to any retail dealers, the monopoly will refuse to sell to those dealers, and those dealers, afraid, will not buy the new man's wares.

And this is the country which has lifted to the admiration of the world its ideals of absolutely free opportunity, where no man is supposed to be under any limitation except the limitations of his character and of his mind; where there is supposed to be no distinction of class, no distinction of blood, no distinction of social status, but where men win or lose on their merits.

I lay it very close to my own conscience as a public man whether we can any longer stand at our doors and welcome all newcomers upon those terms. American industry is not free, as once it was free; American enterprise is not free; the man with only a little capital is finding it harder to get into the field, more and more impossible to compete with the big fellow. Why? Because the laws of this country do not prevent the strong from crushing the weak. That is the reason, and because the strong have crushed the weak the strong dominate the industry and the economic life of this country. No man can deny that the lines of endeavor have more and more narrowed and stiffened; no man who knows anything about the development of industry in this country can have failed to observe that the larger kinds of credit are more and more difficult to obtain, unless you obtain them upon the terms of uniting your efforts with those who already control the industries of the country; and nobody can fail to observe that any man who tries to set himself up in competition with any process of manufacture which has been taken under the control of large combinations of capital will presently find himself either squeezed out or obliged to sell and allow himself to be absorbed.

There is a great deal that needs reconstruction in the United States. I should like to take a census of the business men,—I mean the rank and file of the business men,—as to whether they think that conditions in this country, or rather whether the organization of business in this country, is satisfactory or not. I know what they would say if they dared. If they could vote secretly they would vote overwhelmingly that the present organization of business was meant for the big fellows and was not meant for the little fellows; that it was meant for those who are at the top and was meant to exclude those who were at the bottom; that it was meant to shut out beginners, to prevent new entries in the race, to prevent the building up of competitive enterprises that would interfere with the monopolies which the great trusts have built up.

What this country needs above everything else is a body of laws which will look after the men who are on the make rather than the men who are already made. Because the men who are already made are not going to live indefinitely, and they are not always kind enough to leave sons as able and as honest as they are.

The originative part of America, the part of America that makes new enterprises, the part into which the ambitious and gifted workingman makes his way up, the class that saves, that plans, that organizes, that presently spreads its enterprises until they have a national scope and character,—that middle class is being more and more squeezed out by the processes which we have been taught to call processes of prosperity. Its members are sharing prosperity, no doubt; but what alarms me is that they are not *originating* prosperity. No country can afford to have its prosperity originated by a small controlling class. The treasury of America does not lie in the brains of the small body of men now in control of the great enterprises that have been concentrated under the direction of a very small number of persons. The treasury of America lies in those ambitions, those energies, that cannot be restricted to a special favored class. It depends upon the inventions of unknown men, upon the originations of unknown men, upon the ambitions of unknown men. Every country is renewed out of the ranks of the unknown, not out of the ranks of those already famous and powerful and in control.

There has come over the land that un-American set of conditions which enables a small number of men who control the government to get favors from the government; by those favors to exclude their fellows from equal business opportunity; by those favors to extend a network of control that will presently dominate every industry in the country, and so make men forget the ancient time when America lay in every hamlet, when America was to be seen in every fair valley, when America displayed her great forces on the broad prairies, ran her fine fires of enterprise up over the mountainsides and down into the bowels of the earth, and eager men were everywhere captains of industry, not employees; not looking to a distant city to find out what they might do, but looking about among their neighbors, finding credit according to their character, not according to their connections, finding credit in proportion to what was known to be in them and behind them, not in proportion to the securities they held that were approved where they were not known. In order to start an enterprise now, you have to be authenticated, in a perfectly impersonal way, not according to yourself, but according to what you own that somebody else approves of your owning. You cannot begin such an enterprise as those that have made America until you are so authenticated, until you have succeeded in obtaining the good-will of large allied capitalists. Is that freedom? That is dependence, not freedom.

We used to think in the old-fashioned days when life was very simple that all government had to do was to put on a policeman's uniform, and say, "Now don't anybody hurt anybody else." We used to say that the ideal of government was for every man to be left alone and not interfered with, except when he interfered with somebody else; and that the best government was the government that did as little governing as possible. That was the idea that obtained in Jefferson's time. But we are coming now to realize that life is so complicated that we are not dealing with the old conditions, and that the law has to step in and create new conditions under which we may live, the conditions which will make it tolerable for us to live.

One of the most alarming phenomena of the time,—or rather it would be alarming if the nation had not awakened to it and shown its determination to control it,—one of the most significant signs of the new social era is the degree to which government has become associated with business. I speak, for the moment, of the control over the government exercised by Big Business. Behind the whole subject, of course, is the truth that, in the new order, government and business must be associated closely. But that association is at present of a nature absolutely intolerable; the precedence is wrong, the association is upside down. Our government has been for the past few years under the control of heads of great allied corporations with special interests. It has not controlled these interests and assigned them a proper place in the whole system of business; it has submitted itself to their control. As a result, there have grown up vicious systems and schemes of governmental favoritism (the most obvious being the extravagant tariff), far-reaching in effect upon the whole fabric of life, touching to his injury every inhabitant of the land, laying unfair and impossible handicaps upon competitors, imposing taxes in every direction, stifling everywhere the free spirit of American enterprise.

Now this has come about naturally; as we go on we shall see how very naturally. It is no use denouncing anybody, or anything, except human nature. Nevertheless, it is an intolerable thing that the government of the republic should have got so far out of the hands of the people; should have been captured by interests which are special and not general. In the train of this capture follow the troops of scandals, wrongs, indecencies, with which our politics swarm.

* * *

All over the Union people are coming to feel that they have no control over the course of affairs. I live in one of the greatest States in the union, which was at one time in slavery. Until two years ago we had witnessed with increasing concern the growth in New Jersey of a spirit of almost cynical despair. Men said: "We vote; we are offered the platform we want; we elect the men who stand on that platform, and we get absolutely nothing." So they began to ask: "What is the use of voting? We know that the machines of both parties are subsidized by the same persons, and therefore it is useless to turn in either direction."

This is not confined to some of the state governments and those of some of the towns and cities. We know that something intervenes between the people of the United States and the control of their own affairs at Washington. It is not the people who have been ruling there of late.

* * *

We are upon the eve of a great reconstruction. It calls for creative statesmanship as no age has done since that great age in which we set up the government under which we live, that government which was the admiration of the world until it suffered wrongs to grow up under it which have made many of our own compatriots question the freedom of our institutions and preach revolution against them. I do not fear revolution. I have unshaken faith in the power of America to keep its self-possession. Revolution will come in peaceful guise, as it came when we put aside the crude government of the Confederation and created the great Federal Union which governs individuals, not States, and which has been these hundred and thirty years our vehicle of progress. Some radical changes we must make in our law and practice. Some reconstructions we must push forward, which a new age and new circumstances impose upon us. But we can do it all in calm and sober fashion, like statesmen and patriots. * * *

There are two theories of government that have been contending with each other ever since government began. One of them is the theory which in America is associated with the name of a very great man, Alexander Hamilton. A great man, but, in my judgment, not a great American. He did not think in terms of American life. Hamilton believed that the only people who could understand government, and therefore the only people who were qualified to conduct it, were the men who had the biggest financial stake in the commercial and industrial enterprises of the country.

That theory, though few have now the hardihood to profess it openly, has been the working theory upon which our government has lately been conducted. It is astonishing how persistent it is. It is amazing how quickly the political party which had Lincoln for its first leader,—Lincoln, who

not only denied, but in his own person so completely disproved the aristocratic theory,—it is amazing how quickly that party, founded on faith in
the people, forgot the precepts of Lincoln and fell under the delusion that
the 'masses' needed the guardianship of 'men of affairs.'

For indeed, if you stop to think about it, nothing could be a greater departure from original Americanism, from faith in the ability of a confident,
resourceful, and independent people, than the discouraging doctrine that
somebody has got to provide prosperity for the rest of us. And yet that is
exactly the doctrine on which the government of the United States has
been conducted lately. * * * The gentlemen whose ideas have been sought
are the big manufacturers, the bankers, and the heads of the great railroad combinations. The masters of the government of the United States
are the combined capitalists and manufacturers of the United States. It is
written over every intimate page of the records of Congress, it is written
all through the history of conferences at the White House, that the suggestions of economic policy in this country have come from one source,
not from many sources. The benevolent guardians, the kind-hearted
trustees who have taken the troubles of government off our hands, have
become so conspicuous that almost anybody can write out a list of them.
They have become so conspicuous that their names are mentioned upon
almost every political platform. The men who have undertaken the interesting job of taking care of us do not force us to requite them with anony-
mously directed gratitude. We know them by name. * * *

The government of our country cannot be lodged in any special class.
The policy of a great nation cannot be tied up with any particular set of
interests. I want to say, again and again, that my arguments do not touch
the character of the men to whom I am opposed. I believe that the very
wealthy men who have got their money by certain kinds of corporate enterprise have closed in their horizon, and that they do not see and do not
understand the rank and file of the people. It is for that reason that I
want to break up the little coterie that has determined what the government of the nation should do. * * *

No group of men less than the majority has a right to tell me how I
have got to live in America. I will submit to the majority, because I have
been trained to do it,—though I may sometimes have my private opinion
even of the majority. I do not care how wise, how patriotic, the trustees
may be, I have never heard of any group of men in whose hands I am willing to lodge the liberties of America in trust. * * *

If I thought that the American people were reckless, were ignorant,
were vindictive, I might shrink from putting the government into their
hands. But the beauty of democracy is that when you are reckless you destroy your own established conditions of life; when you are vindictive,

you wreak vengeance upon yourself; the whole stability of a democratic polity rests upon the fact that every interest is every man's interest.

The theory that the men of biggest affairs, whose field of operation is the widest, are the proper men to advise the government is, I am willing to admit, rather a plausible theory. If my business covers the United States not only, but covers the world, it is to be presumed that I have a pretty wide scope in my vision of business. But the flaw is that it is my own business that I have a vision of, and not the business of the men who lie outside of the scope of the plans I have made for a profit out of the particular transactions I am connected with. And you can't, by putting together a large number of men who understand their own business, no matter how large it is, make up a body of men who will understand the business of the nation as contrasted with their own interest. * * *

I have long had an image in my mind of what constitutes liberty. Suppose that I were building a great piece of powerful machinery, and suppose that I should so awkwardly and unskilfully assemble the parts of it that every time one part tried to move it would be interfered with by the others, and the whole thing would buckle up and be checked. Liberty for the several parts would consist in the best possible assembling and adjustment of them all, would it not? If you want the great piston of the engine to run with absolute freedom, give it absolutely perfect alignment and adjustment with the other parts of the machine, so that it is free, not because it is let alone or isolated, but because it has been associated most skillfully and carefully with the other parts of the great structure.

What is liberty? You say of the locomotive that it runs free. What do you mean? You mean that its parts are so assembled and adjusted that friction is reduced to a minimum, and that it has perfect adjustment. * * * Human freedom consists in perfect adjustments of human interests and human activities and human energies.

Now, the adjustments necessary between individuals, between individuals and the complex institutions amidst which they live, and between those institutions and the government, are infinitely more intricate to-day than ever before. * * * Life has become complex; there are many more elements, more parts, to it than ever before. And, therefore, it is harder to keep everything adjusted,—and harder to find out where the trouble lies when the machine gets out of order.

You know that one of the interesting things that Mr. Jefferson said in those early days of simplicity which marked the beginnings of our government was that the best government consisted in as little governing as possible. And there is still a sense in which that is true. It is still intolerable for the government to interfere with our individual activities except where it is necessary to interfere with them in order to free them. But I feel confident that if Jefferson were living in our day he would see what we see: that the individual is caught in a great confused nexus of all sorts of complicated circumstances, and that to let him alone is to leave him helpless as against the obstacles with which he has to contend, and that, therefore, law in our day must come to the assistance of the individual. It must come to his assistance to see that he gets fair play; that is all, but that is much. Without the watchful interference, the resolute interference, of the government, there can be no fair play between individuals and such powerful institutions as the trusts. Freedom to-day is something more than being let alone. The program of a government of freedom must in these days be positive, not negative merely. * * *

I believe in human liberty as I believe in the wine of life. There is no salvation for men in the pitiful condescensions of industrial masters. Guardians have no place in a land of freemen. Prosperity guaranteed by trustees has no prospect of endurance. Monopoly means the atrophy of enterprise. If monopoly persists, monopoly will always sit at the helm of the government. I do not expect to see monopoly restrain itself. If there are men in this country big enough to own the government of the United States, they are going to own it; what we have to determine now is whether we are big enough, whether we are men enough, whether we are free enough, to take possession again of the government which is our own. * * *

I do not believe that America is securely great because she has great men in her now. America is great in proportion as she can make sure of having great men in the next generation. She is rich in her unborn children; rich, that is to say, if those unborn children see the sun in a day of opportunity, see the sun when they are free to exercise their energies as they will. If they open their eyes in a land where there is no special privilege, then we shall come into a new era of American greatness and American liberty; but if they open their eyes in a country where they must be employees or nothing, if they open their eyes in a land of merely regulated monopoly, where all the conditions of industry are determined by small groups of men, then they will see an America such as the founders of this Republic would have wept to think of. * * *

Since their day the meaning of liberty has deepened. But it has not ceased to be a fundamental demand of the human spirit, a fundamental necessity for the life of the soul. And the day is at hand when it shall be realized on this consecrated soil,—a New Freedom,—a Liberty widened and deepened to match the broadened life of man in modern America.

PART V

LEVIATHAN

AND LIBERALISM

1932 TO THE

PRESENT

The new American state of the mid-twentieth century, the colossal Leviathan state, did not spring forth all at once. There was no revolution with a specific, long-term vision. Like jazz, the Roosevelt revolution was revolution by improvisation. Franklin Delano Roosevelt and the political and intellectual leaders around him in the early years of the Great Depression were rich in ideas but had little certainty about what they were doing—except that they had to do something quickly. On October 15, 1929, stock prices had earned a record high, which was embraced as a "permanent plateau," with more growth to come. Less than two weeks later, on the 24th, there was a "great crash," immortalized as Black Thursday. Within one month most of the paper values accrued in the decade of the twenties were wiped out. Yet no reputable economist disputed President Hoover's assurance the following March that "the worst effect of the crash . . . will have passed during the next sixty days." Two months later he called it a depression, while claiming "[W]e have now passed the worst." Disagree as they might, the worthiest economists would not fully recognize its impact and call it the Great Depression until many years later. In 1929, 1.5 million workers (3 percent of the total workforce) were unemployed; by 1933, over 13 million (25 percent) of the workforce was idle. Reality defined itself with the presence of unprecedented bread lines, a 200 percent increase in the number of families on relief, and hordes of farmers refusing to market their now-unprofitable products, dumping their milk and destroying shipments from nonstriking farmers. Signs of rebellion and fears of revolution were widespread. In the spring of 1933, as the famous "One Hundred Days" were just beginning (the presidential inauguration was still on March 4, not January 20 as it is today), one of the White House intellectuals, Adolf Berle, urged labor secretary Frances Perkins to leave Washington before summer in order to be safe from certain violence in the streets of the capital.

Roosevelt, although not an intellectual himself, had very good taste in intellectuals, and his advisers came to be known—often with fear and envy—as the Brain Trust. And much like American society itself, they brought to the White House a smorgasbord of ideas, with Roosevelt the policy entrepreneur, picking and choosing among their proposals. He managed and used his advisers without requiring that they come to him with a single voice. It is therefore not his speeches nor his fireside chats but his special kind of policy leadership that makes Franklin D. Roosevelt our first signature character of this era. For the post–New Deal period there will be two rather than one signature character because, for the first time in American history, we had developed an international as well as a domestic regime. Our choices for that period will be George Kennan and Martin Luther King, Jr.

FDR: Policy Entrepreneurship and Political Economy

Roosevelt, the policy entrepreneur, was a mover, not a shaper. He shared the faith generated by science and fueled by the early twentieth century progressives that human beings, especially American human beings, had the capacity to control the socioeconomic environment as well as the natural environment. That belief was strong enough to fulfill Archimedes's promise with the discovery of the lever: "Give me a firm place to stand, and I will move the earth." And any earth moving in the 1930s was going to take a lot of leverage, considering the state of the old Democratic party, half northern progressive and half southern conservative—with the latter controlling the House and Senate through control of the chairmanships of virtually all key legislative committees.

To complicate matters further, the Brain Trust was composed of proponents of several different theories of political economy. The first in importance was Keynesianism. The Harvard Professor Alvin Hansen had imported the ideas of John Maynard Keynes from Cambridge, England, to Cambridge, Massachusetts, and sent Keynesianism on to Washington through the many Harvard graduates who were committed to the "new economics." But when asked after a lecture to a large audience of business leaders in 1940, "In your opinion, is the basic principle of the New Deal economically sound?" Professor Hansen replied, "I really do not know what the basic principle of the New Deal is."

This was the brutal truth. Though progressivism was to become the dominant element in the theory of the new American state, its victory was slow to come. Roosevelt met with the British economist Keynes only once, in 1934, and, according to Secretary of Labor Frances Perkins, dismissed his presentation as a "rigmarole of figures . . . [by] a mathematician rather than a political economist." Keynes, in turn, brushed Roosevelt aside with a remark that he had "supposed the President was more literate, economically speaking." Keynes's view was confirmed by many American intellectuals. The writer Edmund Wilson painted FDR as "a kind of amicable boy scout," and the political commentator Walter Lippmann judged him "an amiable man with many philanthropic impulses but with neither a firm grasp on public affairs nor very strong convictions." The aging Oliver Wendell Holmes, Jr., confided to a friend that FDR was "a second-class intellect, but a first-class temperament."

Other political economists had their own theories to guide the New Deal. Some, following Adolph Berle, were concerned for the crisis of capitalism itself. Thurman Arnold wrote cleverly about *The Folklore of Capitalism*, Charles Beard about "The Myth of American Rugged Individualism," Rexford Tugwell in *The Stricken Land* about the failure of economics to deal with the shortcomings of the private market system. Other authors, equally equipped, wrote for particular sectors of the economy, either as the key to the larger puzzle or unabashedly as the spokespeople of the interest groups representing those particular sectors of the economy. One of the more successful was George Peek for organized agriculture. Another was Henry Wallace, who spoke for working-class agriculture effectively enough to be brought into the Roosevelt cabinet and then elevated to vice president (1941–1945). And Raymond Moley, one of Roosevelt's most confidential advisers, helped formulate the rationale connecting the First to the Second New Deal, the former characterized as recovery, the latter best characterized as reconstruction.

It was the Second New Deal, following Roosevelt's reelection in 1936, that brought all the ideas together with an embrace of the national government's permanent presence in the modern capitalist economy. No single work of political economy formulated such a synthesis, although Tugwell, Moley, and Wallace intimated that the national government must develop a capacity for planning. "Planning" carried a strong socialist coloration in the United States, despite the fact that Lenin and other real socialist planners were imitating American corporations with their "Five Year Plans" and other such programs. Yet, no single American author and no single government commission drafted anything like a synthesis for a new regime, a modern national state.

For Roosevelt and most of his brain trust, state theory was political economy, a discourse dominated by economists. This conglomeration of ideas, interests, and ideologies only emerged when Keynesian economics achieved hegemony. Although Keynes himself had passed from the scene, there was a growing hunger for a consensus political economy. The minimovement of Keynesianism out of Cambridge, Massachusetts, into Washington was just the beginning of its conquest of the American Economics Association and then the hearts and the heads of New Deal policy makers, including Roosevelt.

The story of the Keynesian capture of Roosevelt, the New Deal, and of American liberalism can best be told through Paul Samuelson, a Harvard PhD and a junior member of the MIT faculty who did not join the the Cambridge professors' march on Washington. It is impossible to determine whether Samuelson's story was a cause or a consequence of the victory of Keynesianism. Either way, it is significant. Samuelson would go on to win the Nobel Prize in economics in recognition of his contribution to the pure, mathematized science of economics, but his most important contribution to the history of political thought was his undergraduate Keynesian textbook bearing the simple title *Economics*. Published in 1948, it sold over 2 million copies in its first twenty-five years. Using a conservative multiple of 2, or a generous multiple of 3, to estimate the number of secondhand copies sold, the scale of the exposure of college student minds to Keynesian theory has been astronomical in the United States alone, not counting the world influence of *Economics*, which has been translated in at least forty languages.

From the perspective of political thought, the Keynesian consensus from at least the Second New Deal through the 1960s can be reduced to a few sentences. First, Keynes confirmed with scientific, mathematical exactitude that Adam Smith's magnificent conception of a self-regulating market system can produce the wealth of a nation to a far greater extent than any deliberate, benevolent government effort can produce. Second, however, Keynes turned pure economic theory into political economy by including cases of market imperfection—"market failures" such as the Great Depression and, far more frequently, cases where markets reach their "natural equilibrium" too far below an acceptable level of employment, basic demands, and human needs. Third, as capitalist markets grow through specialization and interdependence, they become more vulnerable, needing outside help from governments for stability. Fourth, strange as it may seem, Keynesian economics (truly political economy) is strongly procapitalist. Except in the view of those who embrace the market economy as an object of worship, it shows that there are moderate and proven ways that ordinary governments can meet fundamental needs of the economy that cannot be provided by market mechanisms alone. For example: law and order; protection of property rights; enforcement of contracts; credible, uniform currency; uniform standards of weights and measures; and the provision of certain "public goods" that are deemed necessary but are beyond the capacity of any one company or entrepreneur to provide for itself alone—such as its own transportation or communication, a fund of workers who can read and write, and independent umpires who can settle disputes peacefully. But beyond these infrastructural requirements for capitalism, many of which even Adam Smith had written of, it was, Keynes argued, necessary for capitalist governments to spend money and run deficits in order to put people back to work during depressions.

Finally, Keynesianism is not only procapitalist but also prodemocracy in its reinforcement of the faith that citizens need not be slaves to the system, waiting and working dutifully for the system to right itself "in the long run." The Keynes reply was, "In the long run, we are all dead."

In a very important sense, Roosevelt discovered Keynesianism by trial and error. It gave his New Deal a rationale that helped restore American confidence in capitalism and the American system even though it went through a second recession in 1937 and did not put depression behind until the war. With these new economic methods, economic reasoning and economic discourse, economics displaced law as the language of the state. This not only helped restore optimism; it helped the Roosevelt revolution circumvent and postpone dealing with the two other fundamental concerns that the new American state would eventually have to confront: issues of world politics and domestic justice.

Its economic preoccupations led the New Deal to turn its back on a world that was rejecting democracy and embracing totalitarianism, with the most powerful totalitarian countries seeking to solve their internal problems by mobilizing for war. Even more pressing during the 1930s, economics was used to finesse the most profound internal contradiction of the now hegemonic Democratic party: half northern liberalism and half southern feudalism. The Faustian bargain, described in our introductory essay, took hold. The southern Democrats supported regulatory programs through Congress because, as true conservatives, they had doubts about free-wheeling capitalism. They accepted Social Security and other redistributive programs because those programs relieved them of some of the burden on their hard-pressed employers. In return, the federal government did not meddle with race, class, and gender, and gave discretion in each statute as to how the programs would be locally implemented. Under the great banner of states' rights, the South would then be able to take care of its own folk, preserving order and basic values by keeping everyone in their proper place. That is true conservatism. And that postponed the promise of the Fourteenth Amendment of 1868 for another thirty years.

George Kennan: The Cold War and Containment

The Japanese attack on Pearl Harbor definitively ended the new American state's avoidance of world politics. And in February 1946, when the dust of war had not yet settled, Joseph Stalin made a rare public address, in which he revived, with special vehemence, the principle of the inherent incompatibility of communism and capitalism. It was received as a rhetorical atom bomb in Washington— as a "declaration of World War III." All the while, the career diplomat George Kennan, only a few blocks away from the Kremlin in the U.S. embassy, had been sending messages to Washington critical of the policy of U.S.-Soviet cooperation arising out of the successful experience as allies during World War II.

Within two weeks of Stalin's speech Kennan received a request for more information, and he responded with an eight-thousand-word cable (about thirty-two typewritten pages) laying out his "theory of Soviet conduct" and what should be done about it. He opened his report on a point of agreement with Stalin:

> There could never be on Moscow's side any sincere assumption of a community of interest between the Soviet Union and powers which are regarded as capitalist.

He then followed with the warning that

> We should not be misled by tactical maneuvers . . . [and] it is clear that the main element of any U.S. policy toward the Soviet Union must be that of a long-term, patient but firm and vigilant containment of Russian expansive tendencies.

The response in Washington was sensational. The State Department sent Kennan a letter of commendation while forwarding his telegram to President Truman, who was new to his office and in great need of principles and doctrines for guidance in foreign affairs.

The secretary of the navy, James Forrestal (who the following year was to become America's first secretary of defense) had the telegram reproduced and circulated as required reading for all high-ranking military officers. The telegram was deliberately leaked to a leading journal, *Foreign Affairs*, where it was published for a broader public under the pseudonym "X" (1947).

Although the article was not at first greeted with universal approval outside the Truman administration, it became the hegemonic doctrine. By 1950, following consolidation of all military services in the new Department of Defense and the creation of a supercabinet National Security Council (NSC), the Kennan theory was overtaken as doctrine by an official foreign policy guideline known as NSC-68, one of the most important documents produced by the government during the cold war. It goes well beyond Kennan's 1946–1947 formulation but Kennan's hand was in it, in his new capacity as State Department counselor and director of the newly created Policy Planning Staff.

The following excerpt captures the relevant portion of NSC-68:

> The fundamental design of those who control the Soviet Union and the International Communist movement . . . calls for complete subversion or forcible destruction of the machinery of government and structure of society in the countries of the non-Soviet world and their replacement by an apparatus and structure subservient to and controlled from the Kremlin. . . . The Soviet Union is developing the military capacity to support its design for world domination. . . . [T]he cold war is in fact a real war in which the survival of the free world is at stake.

The significance of Kennan's contribution is difficult to overemphasize. The name *cold war* was coined by Herbert Bayard Swope, a publicist and ghostwriter for the famous wealthy amateur philosopher and presidential adviser Bernard Baruch, to meet a need felt by almost everyone: how to distinguish "hot war" and "shooting war" from the warlike hostilities between the United States and the USSR in the late 1940s. The concept of the cold war seemed to satisfy the need so well that few ever bothered to give it a definition. But the essential factor was the term emphasized in Kennan's cable from Moscow: *containment*. Containment became the all-encompassing strategic posture of U.S. foreign policy during the cold war, and it went well beyond strategy and policy: It produced a cold war culture, mobilizing all Americans to the fullest extent possible.

All aspects of containment were driven by Kennan's theory that Soviet world communism would expand wherever and whenever there was a sign of weakness in the United States and its allies. Every act of political violence anywhere in the world confirmed the theory according to its proponents. And when there were no signs of communist expansion, the theory of containment was also confirmed. The theory is, in effect, self-confirming.

Some would call this perspective paranoia. But this suggests that the events and nonevents are illusory. The cold war mentality is far better understood as a culture, in which the communist threat is an accepted reality. Culture is "a way of life," a "design for living" acquired through learning. The Cold War culture was an all-encompassing, society-wide mobilization because the threat was deemed to be not only worldwide but within our own country—"the enemy within." The fear of a domestic communist threat came to be called McCarthyism, but this term is misleading if taken for the cultural phenomenon itself. McCarthy was a single—albeit effective—voice in domestic mobilization and the silencing of dissent. But the necessary conditions for the cold war culture ran far deeper and broader than a few voices. The farther we extended our iron curtain of international containment, the more we had to strengthen the theory of certain attack by the world communist conspiracy.

The first step was to make permanent the war apparatus of domestic intelligence. The FBI's broad discretionary wartime surveillance powers were remobilized and extended explicitly from Nazi to communist subversion. Congress's spectacular investigatory intervention into the entertainment industry featured such tactics as stigmatizing as "Fifth Amendment communists" any witnesses seeking the Fifth Amendment protections against having to be witnesses against themselves, the blacklisting of thousands of government employees, actors, writers, and other intellectuals, and holding all who dared remain silent rather than testify in criminal contempt of Congress. These were just a few of the elements of cultural mobilization. Americans in jeopardy of suspicion and investigation extended to as many as 20 percent of all government employees at national, state, and local levels and to employees of all companies doing business with any of those governmental entities. As of October 1947, over 2 million persons employed by the federal government alone were subjected to investigations to determine their loyalty. In 1952, this broad jurisdiction established by presidential edict was further extended and confirmed by law. And the popular formulation was "Americanism," a cultural concept unique to the United States; "un-American" described a person who displayed insufficient embrace of the American creed, as defined by the accuser. "Un-American" implied "disloyal," a well-defined capital offense called treason.

Cold war culture was internal containment policy, with the same objectives, procedures, and apparatus as international containment policy. Moreover, this culture was entirely bipartisan, with the liberal Democrats leading the way. President Truman directed the Justice Department to go beyond the 2 million government employees to the civil society at large and compile a list of organizations considered to be "totalitarian" or "subversive" and to compile and publish an attorney general's List of Subversive Organizations. "Considered" is the crucial term because the decision to list an organization was entirely at the discretion of the attorney general; membership in a listed organization was *prima facie* evidence for summary discharge. This was denounced as a "bill of attainder" under Article I, Section 9 of the Constitution (prohibiting direct punishment by legislation or executive order without trial), but the issue was rendered moot by the bipartisan passage of the Communist Control Act of 1954, declaring the Communist party an agent of a hostile foreign power and "a clear and present danger to the security of the United States [which] should be outlawed." This act clearly violated the First and Fifth Amendments as well as the bill of attainder provision, but it never came to full adjudication because it was never seriously implemented. It was a symbolic act, a cultural coup d'état.

The cold war persisted through the 1970s. Although President Jimmy Carter was a moderate cold warrior, he still found sufficient ground to argue "that when violence occurred in almost any place on earth, the Soviets or their proxies were most likely to be at the root of it." President Reagan revitalized the cold war for the 1980s with his very simple shibboleth, "the evil empire." But by then, it was a crumbling empire. The 1990s ushered in the post-Soviet era and the end of the cold war.

Martin Luther King, Jr.: Equality and the Law

The second issue avoided and postponed by the new Leviathan American state was domestic justice and here we encounter the signature role of Martin Luther King, Jr. It has often been asserted that Mahatma Gandhi and his campaign of nonviolent resistance would never have succeeded if the colonial power had been any other than Great Britain. Can the same be said of Martin Luther King, Jr., confronting America? He did not begin as a Gandhian. His biographer David Garrow informs us that early during the Montgomery bus boycott, in response to a question about Gandhi from an admiring visitor, King confessed that "I know who the man is. I have read some statements by him . . . but I will have to say that I know very little about the man."

As King became more prominent, references to Gandhi increased, possibly because he had done more reading and was more confident that his followers would appreciate combining "Gandhian precepts with Christian principles." But this combining of the "passive resistance" of Gandhi with the "non-violence in the Gospel of Jesus" was also a very practical matter as southern white opposition became increasingly intense, ideological, and violent. Even the revered Billy Graham as late as 1960 could preach that "the Bible . . . recognizes that each individual has the right to choose his own friendships and social relations" and that "[F]orced integration will never work." Graham also censured clergymen of both races who made the "race issue" their gospel, when they should have been concerned with saving souls. Intimidation, terror, and a number of racially inspired assassinations climaxed with the Alabama governor George Wallace's infamous proclamation at his January 1963 inaugural address, in defiance of the court-ordered desegregation of the University of Alabama: "I draw the line in the dust . . . and I say, Segregation now! Segregation tomorrow! Segregation forever!"

The climactic year for Martin Luther King, Jr., and George Wallace probably began September 30, 1962, and ended November 22, 1963. It began at the all-white University of Mississippi with the enrollment of James Meredith, enforced by a squadron of five hundred federal marshals. Ordered by Attorney General Robert Kennedy, this was the first involvement of any sort by the Kennedy administration in the civil rights controversy, but this incident convinced King that confrontation, albeit nonviolent, was necessary. And the place for it was Birmingham, reputedly the most segregated city in the United States, whose mayor, the former public safety commissioner Eugene "Bull" Connor, was demonstrably an unreconstructed racist.

The confrontation started the morning of Wednesday, April 3, 1963, with sit-ins, pickets, arrests, and police dogs, which would become a symbol of southern white resistance. After a week's standoff, King was served with a state court injunction, and his defiance earned him solitary confinement in a Birmingham jail. In a public statement eight local religious leaders chastised King and the protesters. In response, King wrote his now historic "Letter from Birmingham Jail" literally with purloined pen on scraps of paper. On release, King found himself confronting loyal black adult supporters suffering from fatigue and discouragement, which turned him to younger reinforcements. Mayhem returned with more dogs, nightsticks, and fire hoses. Quiet came only after President Kennedy stationed three thousand army troops just outside the city, coupled with an unprecedented presidential threat to nationalize the Alabama National Guard.

The Birmingham drama fueled plans already afoot to nationalize the movement with a March on Washington, but there was no response from the White House until June 11, when two black students sought admission to the University of Alabama and found the door of the admissions office blocked by the governor, George Wallace. This spectacle, with worldwide press and TV coverage, brought President Kennedy to his first and only confrontation with racial discrimination as "a moral issue." But that speech, coupled with a promise to make civil rights legislation high priority did not, as hoped, obviate the August 28 March on Washington.

The culminating moment of the civil rights movement should have been that August 28, 1963, in Washington, the largest such gathering in American history. But it turned out instead to be in Dallas three months later, on November 22. The Kennedy assassination and its traumatic impact made it easier for Lyndon Johnson to wrest national standards of civil rights from Congress, even though the legislative committees, the workhorses of legislation, were still dominated by conservative southerners.

King, like most influential Americans, made his mark in action, not in thought. His oratory was his form of action. His ideas were derivative, but he gave them life and relevance. In this respect, we could just as well be here describing Winthrop or Jefferson. King's rhetoric was inspirational, not philosophic. His crowning moment, the "I Have a Dream" valedictory to the Washington marchers, came in an impromptu postscript to his prepared speech, when, as he was gathering his notes and preparing to take his seat, Mahalia Jackson called out to him, "Tell them about your dream, Martin! Tell them about the dream!"

Yet King played an important role in late-twentieth-century political thought not only because of his actions but because some of his arguments, derivative or not, do have bearing, especially in joining Gandhian principles to the Christian message and putting them to work in a genuine American communal radicalism as old as the seventeenth century. In his book *Hellfire Nation*, the political scientist James Morone argues:

King's Social Gospel . . . begins modestly enough by bringing religion down to earth. But it goes on to embrace that other Puritan ideal [that] the people collectively share moral responsibility for their community. . . . The communal faith does not fit easily with a competitive, highly individualist America.

Another closely related element of political thought came through in King's "Letter from Birmingham Jail." And his argument is best appreciated by comparison with the argument of the young Abraham Lincoln in his 1838 Lyceum speech, "The Perpetuation of Our Political Institutions."

King:

One may well ask, "How can you advocate breaking some laws and obeying others?" The answer is found in the fact that there are two types of laws: There are just laws and there are unjust laws. One has not only a legal but a moral responsibility to obey just laws. . . . An unjust law is a code that a majority inflicts on a minority that is not binding on itself.

Lincoln:

Let every American, every lover of liberty . . . swear by the blood of the Revolution never to violate in the least particular the laws of the country; . . . in short, let it become the 'political religion' of the nation. . . .

[L]et me not be understood as saying there are no bad laws. . . . But I do mean to say that, . . . while they continue in force, for the sake of example they should be religiously observed.

Lincoln's was a mainstream, constitutionalist, and positivist vision of a proper state and regime. It was also antirevolutionary. In his closing Lyceum comment, he argued that the American Revolution tended to create a man who "disdains a beaten path;" but "This state of feeling *must fade* . . . with the circumstances that produced it" (emphasis in original). In contrast, King's was a radical, natural-law posture, with rights existing before and beyond the state, resting with the people in civil society. For King, there was a right of resistance passing through Jesus and Thomas Paine to Gandhi and the civil rights movement, in the form of the right to nonviolent protest.

King did in fact try to participate in lawmaking as well as law protesting. King's joining the March on Washington was in largest part a product of frustration with Kennedy's avoidance of civil rights laws until his New Frontier economic plans to complete Roosevelt's revolution were in place. Because of the part he played in the March on Washington, King was not included in Kennedy's funeral ceremony. He paid his respects from an obscure spot on the crowded curbside as the caisson passed by. Immediately after the assassination, however, with President Johnson's leadership, lawmaking opportunities opened. Johnson kept King and several other prominent black leaders close to the White House in 1964 and 1965, and they made no secret of their cooperation with Johnson and their pleasure with the civil rights record Johnson was compiling. They were also impressed with Johnson's courage in the face of recognition that pursuit of civil rights laws would deliver the South to the Republican party.

As "white backlash" mounted, King returned to his movement role, rejoining his Southern Christian Leadership Conference (SCLC) in the South and then setting up new headquarters in Chicago to confront white backlash in northern, hitherto liberal states. With organized and spontaneous violence spreading and with southern state officials joining in "interposition" against school desegregation and black registration and voting, King's passive resistance was augmented by more radical groups, ranging from student groups to "black power" groups, to those still more confrontational and separationist such as Malcolm X, the Nation of Islam, and the Black Panthers. Meanwhile, King himself was moving left, breaking with Johnson over Vietnam. King insisted that civil rights and opposition to the war were "very compatible" concerns, especially in light of the highly disproportionate participation of young blacks in that war.

King's singular role in the quest for equality under law was facilitated in part by the Supreme Court's *Brown v. Board of Education* desegregation decision in 1954, holding that the "civil rights" covered by the Fourteenth Amendment's equal protection clause imposed an obligation on government (national or state) to take "affirmative action" to see to it that any service or privilege "offered to the public" by government *and also* by private entities must be offered *on an equal basis* to all persons. President Johnson's response eleven years later in his commencement address to Howard University committed the Federal Government to a policy of affirmative action. To legitimize this radically new initiative Johnson sanctified it with the ever-recurring metaphor of the American liberal race of life.

You do not take a person, who for years has been hobbled by chains and liberate him, bring him up to the starting line of a race and then say "you are free to compete with the others," and still justly believe you have been completely fair.

Beyond Civil Rights: The Philosophical Turn

The last third of the twentieth century saw a flowering of philosophical readings of politics in America. John Rawls, one of the few American philosophers ever to be accepted among philosophers as "world class," sought an original way to build a just society from the bottom up. Rawls bypassed the mythology of a "state of nature" and built his just society on the basis of a hypothesis that he called the "original position." It characterized life as beginning in a state of innocence, behind a "veil of ignorance," in which rational individuals would choose general rules of fairness because it is in their rational self-interest to do so. In an important sense, Rawls was reinventing the rules of war, in which it is in the interest of each belligerent to stay within some humane limits in the hope and expectation that it would be in the rational interest also of the adversary. Rawls turned slightly to the left of classical liberalism with his "difference principle," to deal with liberalism's most agonizing problem: inequality. His difference principle is actually two principles, first holding that inequalities can be tolerated as long as the benefits of inequality go to "the least advantaged," and, second, that the inequalities be "attached to positions and offices . . . [that are] open to all." Despite the extreme abstraction of his writing—in the tradition of analytic philosophy and distinctly not in the American tradition of thought and action—Rawls contributed to a flourishing of genuine political theory in late-twentieth-century America.

In addition to Rawls and partly in critical response to his interventionist message the liberalism of Adam Smith was revived. As the liberal label came to be associated with the New Deal progressive liberals (or state-centered liberals), the more appropriate label for this revival of Adam Smith and classical liberal economics is libertarianism. The most famous and surely the most influential figure in this libertarian movement was Milton Friedman, a Nobel Prize–winning economist and a radical political ideologist. Friedman eagerly took on the role of lead critic of Roosevelt and Keynes. However, the more important philosophical libertarian authors of political thought in this epoch are generally considered to be Friedrich von Hayek and Robert Nozick.

Hayek, an Austrian aristocrat who took refuge first in Britain and then in the United States (who then promptly dropped the *von* from his name), became, like Samuelson and Friedman, a Nobel Prize–winning economist who had a dual career as a political theorist and an ideologist. His 1944 book *The Road to Serfdom* laid the foundation for the revival of classical economics—a remarkable fact given the depth to which it had sunk because of the depression. Hayek set out to prove the impossibility of the centrally planned political economy associated with socialism, although he never embraced the pure, radical, antistate libertarianism to which his work contributed. That position was most systematically presented by Robert Nozick, whose work is so radically antistate as to suggest that income tax is "on a par with forced labor." The revival of libertarianism as state theory saw its best chance with the election of President Ronald Reagan in 1980. It was somewhat oddly classified as a category of conservatism, even by such astute public intellectuals as William F. Buckley, Jr., and Harvey Mansfield, Jr., who were themselves genuine conservatives for whom all liberals, definitely including libertarians, lacked what the conservative political scientist James Q. Wilson termed "the moral sense."

This links directly to the other important revival of political thought in the late decades of the twentieth century: the genuine conservatism of the secular Burkeans, the religious right, and the neoconservatives. Despite many differences, they came together around a vision of an organic society, a morally ordered community, to which the individual is subordinated. Conservatives never fail to castigate both kinds of liberalism, even though they have accepted the relabeling of libertarianism as a "category" of conservatism for at least one reason: that it helped make possible the coalition of conservatism and libertarianism within a revived Republican Party that came into full control of the American national policy agenda after the "Gingrich revolution" of 1994. From 1932 until the 1990s, there had been two liberal parties in America—one the Roosevelt liberal-progressive Democratic Party and the other a libertarian derivation from the original Lincoln nationalist–free market Republican Party. But during the first decade of the twenty-first century, the Republican Party became a genuine conservative party with a libertarian minority wing. The arena of political action, electoral politics and winning elections, cleared the air. Once again American political thought and public philosophy would be closely linked to political action, as they were in the beginning and have most often been.

BIBLIOGRAPHY

Auden, W. H. *The Age of Anxiety*. New York: Random House, 1946.

Brinkley, Alan. "The New Deal and the Idea of the State." In *The Rise and Fall of the New Deal Order, 1930–1980*, edited by Steven Fraser and Gary Gersh. Princeton: Princeton University Press, 1989.

Burns, James MacGregor. *Roosevelt: The Lion and the Fox*. New York: Harcourt, 1956.

Fite, Gilbert C. *George Peek and the Fight for Farm Parity*. Norman: University of Oklahoma Press, 1954.

Freidel, Frank. *FDR: Launching the New Deal*. Boston: Little, Brown, 1973.

Galbraith, John Kenneth. *Money: Where It Came, Where It Went*. New York: Bantam Books, 1975.

Garrow, David, *Bearing the Cross*. New York: William Morrow, 1986.

Hession, Charles, and Hyman Sardy. *Ascent to Affluence: A History of American Economic Development*. Boston: Allyn & Bacon, 1969.

Hofstadter, Richard. *The American Political Tradition   And the Men Who Made It*. New York: Vintage–Random House, 1948.

Kennan, George ("X"). "The Sources of Soviet Conduct." *Foreign Affairs*, July 1949.

Lincoln, Abraham. "The Perpetuation of Our Political Institutions." In *Collected Works of Abraham Lincoln*, Vol.1, edited by Roy P. Beslar. New Brunswick: Rutgers University Press, 1953.

Morone, James. *Hellfire Nation*. New Haven: Yale University Press, 2003.

Samuelson, Paul A. *Economics*. New York: McGraw Hill, 1948.

Weisbrot, Robert. *Freedom Bound: A History of America's Civil Rights Movement*. New York: Penguin, 1991.

The New Deal and Its Critics

HERBERT HOOVER

American Individualism (1922)

The political thought of the New Deal must be read as a response to pre-
vailing ideas of laissez-faire that dominated the 1920s. The Stanford-
trained engineer Herbert Clark Hoover (1874–1964) served as the head
of Allied relief operations in Europe during and after World War I. He
then became secretary of commerce under President Warren Harding
and was elected the thirty-first president in 1928. Hoover believed that
the solution to the depression should not involve government intrusion
into economic life, which would violate individual freedom and lead to
waste, corruption, and socialism. As the following selection from his
1922 book American Individualism *demonstrates, Hoover was convinced*
that American "individualism" and protecting the ideal of equal opportu-
nity was the surest—and most proven—basis for progress.

For myself, let me say at the very outset that my faith in the essential truth, strength, and vitality of the developing creed by which we have hitherto lived in this country of ours has been confirmed and deepened by the searching experiences of seven years of service in the backwash and misery of war. Seven years of contending with economic degeneration, with social disintegration, with incessant political dislocation, with all of its seething and ferment of individual and class conflict, could but impress me with the primary motivation of social forces, and the necessity for broader thought upon their great issues to humanity. And from it all I emerge an individualist—an unashamed individualist. But let me say also that I am an American individualist. For America has been steadily developing the ideals that constitute progressive individualism.

No doubt, individualism run riot, with no tempering principle, would provide a long category of inequalities, of tyrannies, dominations, and injustices. America, however, has tempered the whole conception of individualism by the injection of a definite principle, and from this principle it follows that attempts at domination, whether in government or in the processes of industry and commerce, are under an insistent curb. If we would have the values of individualism, their stimulation to initiative, to the development of hand and intellect, to the high development of thought and spirituality, they must be tempered with that firm and fixed ideal of American individualism—*an equality of opportunity*. If we would have these values we must soften its hardness and stimulate progress through that sense of service that lies in our people.

Therefore, it is not the individualism of other countries for which I would speak, but the individualism of America. Our individualism differs from all others because it embraces these great ideals: *that while we build our society upon the attainment of the individual, we shall safeguard to every individual an equality of opportunity to take that position in the community to which his intelligence, character, ability, and ambition entitle him; that we keep the social solution free from frozen strata of classes; that we shall stimulate effort of each individual to achievement; that through an enlarging sense of responsibility and understanding we shall assist him to this attainment; while he in turn must stand up to the emery wheel of competition.*

Individualism cannot be maintained as the foundation of a society based upon contracts, property, and political equality. Such legalistic safeguards are themselves not enough. In our individualism we have long since abandoned the laissez faire of the 18th Century—the notion that it is "every man for himself and the devil take the hindmost." We abandoned that when we adopted the ideal of equality of opportunity—the fair chance of Abraham Lincoln. We have confirmed its abandonment in terms of legislation, of social and economic justice,—in part because we have learned that it is the hindmost who throws the bricks at our social edifice, in part because we have learned that the foremost are not always the best nor the hindmost the worst—and in part because we have learned that social injustice is the destruction of justice itself. We have learned that the impulse to production can only be maintained at a high pitch if there is a fair division of the product. We have also learned that fair division can only be obtained by certain restrictions on the strong and the dominant. We have indeed gone even further in the 20th Century with the embracement of the necessity of a greater and broader sense of service and responsibility to others as a part of individualism.

Whatever may be the case with regard to Old World individualism (and we have given more back to Europe than we received from her) the truth that is important for us to grasp today is that there is a world of difference between the principles and spirit of Old World individualism and that which we have developed in our own country.

We have, in fact, a special social system of our own. We have made it ourselves from materials brought in revolt from conditions in Europe. We have lived it; we constantly improve it; we have seldom tried to define it. It abhors autocracy and does not argue with it, but fights it. It is not capitalism, or socialism, or syndicalism, nor a cross breed of them. Like most Americans, I refuse to be damned by anybody's word-classification of it, such as "capitalism," "plutocracy," "proletariat," or "middle class," or any other, or to any kind of compartment that is based on the assumption of some group dominating somebody else.

The social force in which I am interested is far higher and far more precious a thing than all these. It springs from something infinitely more enduring; it springs from the one source of human progress—that each individual shall be given the chance and stimulation for development of the best with which he has been endowed in heart and mind; it is the sole source of progress; it is American individualism.

The rightfulness of our individualism can rest either on philosophic, political, economic, or spiritual grounds. It can rest on the ground of being the only safe avenue to further human progress. * * *

Individualism has been the primary force of American civilization for three centuries. It is our sort of individualism that has supplied the motivation of America's political, economic, and spiritual institutions in all these years. It has proved its ability to develop its institutions with the changing scene. Our very form of government is the product of the individualism of our people, the demand for an equal opportunity, for a fair chance.

The American pioneer is the epic expression of that individualism, and the pioneer spirit is the response to the challenge of opportunity, to the challenge of nature, to the challenge of life, to the call of the frontier. That spirit need never die for lack of something for it to achieve. There will always be a frontier to conquer or to hold as long as men think, plan, and dare. Our American individualism has received much of its character from our contacts with the forces of nature on a new continent. It evolved government without official emissaries to show the way; it plowed and sowed two score of great states; it built roads, bridges, railways, cities; it carried forward every attribute of high civilization over a continent. The days of the pioneer are not over. There are continents of human welfare of which we have penetrated only the coastal plain. The great continent of science is as yet explored only on its borders, and it is only the pioneer who will penetrate the frontier in the quest for new worlds to conquer. The very genius of our institutions has been given to them by the pioneer spirit. Our individualism is rooted in our very nature. It is based on conviction born of experience. Equal opportunity, the demand for a fair chance, became the formula of American individualism because it is the method of American achievement.

After the absorption of the great plains of the West came the era of industrial development with the new complex of forces that it has brought us. Now haltingly, but with more surety and precision than ever before and with a more conscious understanding of our mission, we are finding solution of these problems arising from new conditions, for the forces of our social system can compass and comprise these.

Our individualism is no middle ground between autocracy—whether of birth, economic or class origin—and socialism. Socialism of different varieties may have something to recommend it as an intellectual stop-look-and-listen sign, more especially for Old World societies. But it contains only destruction to the forces that make progress in our social system. Nor does salvation come by any device for concentration of power, whether political or economic, for both are equally reversions to Old World autocracy in new garments.

Salvation will not come to us out of the wreckage of individualism. What we need today is steady devotion to a better, brighter, broader individualism—an individualism that carries increasing responsibility and service to our fellows. Our need is not for a way out but for a way forward. We found our way out three centuries ago when our forefathers left Europe for these shores, to set up here a commonwealth conceived in liberty and dedicated to the development of individuality.

* * *

The primary safeguard of American individualism is an understanding of it; of faith that it is the most precious possession of American civilization, and a willingness courageously to test every process of national life upon the touchstone of this basic social premise. Development of the human institutions and of science and of industry have been long chains of trial and error. Our public relations to them and to other phases of our national life can be advanced in no other way than by a willingness to experiment in the remedy of our social faults. The failures and unsolved problems of economic and social life can be corrected; they can be solved within our social theme and under no other system. The solution is a matter of will to find solution; of a sense of duty as well as of a sense of right and citizenship. No one who buys "bootleg" whiskey can complain of gunmen and hoodlumism.

Humanity has a long road to perfection, but we of America can make sure progress if we will preserve our individualism, if we will preserve and stimulate the initiative of our people, if we will build up our insistence and safeguards to equality of opportunity, if we will glorify service as a part of our national character. Progress will march if we hold an abiding faith in the intelligence, the initiative, the character, the courage, and the divine touch in the individual. We can safeguard these ends if we give to each individual that opportunity for which the spirit of America stands. We can make a social system as perfect as our generation merits and one that will be received in gratitude by our children.

HERBERT HOOVER

Rugged Individualism (1928)

In an optimistic campaign speech delivered in New York, the presidential hopeful articulated a theory of liberal individualism that valued self-government and liberty rather than what he saw as the destructive doctrines of socialism, paternalism, and bureaucracy.

After the war, when the Republican Party assumed administration of the country, we were faced with the problem of determination of the very nature of our national life. During 150 years we have builded up a form of self-government and a social system which is peculiarly our own. It differs essentially from all others in the world. It is the American system. It is just as definite and positive a political and social system as has ever been developed on earth. It is founded upon a particular conception of self-government in which decentralized local responsibility is the very base. Further than this, it is founded upon the conception that only through ordered liberty, freedom and equal opportunity to the individual will his initiative and enterprise spur on the march of progress. And in our insistence upon equality of opportunity has our system advanced beyond all the world.

During the war we necessarily turned to the Government to solve every difficult economic problem. The Government having absorbed every energy of our people for war, there was no other solution. For the preservation of the State the Federal Government became a centralized despotism which undertook unprecedented responsibilities, assumed autocratic powers, and took over the business of citizens. To a large degree we regimented our whole people temporarily into a socialistic state. However justified in time of war if continued in peace time it would destroy not only our American system but with it our progress and freedom as well.

When the war closed, the most vital of all issues both in our own country and throughout the world was whether Governments should continue their wartime ownership and operation of many instrumentalities of production and distribution. We were challenged with a peace-time choice between the American system of rugged individualism and a European philosophy of diametrically opposed doctrines—doctrines of paternalism and state socialism. The acceptance of these ideas would have meant the destruction of self-government through centralization of government. It would have meant the undermining of the individual initiative and enterprise through which our people have grown to unparalleled greatness.

The Republican Party from the beginning resolutely turned its face away from these ideas and these war practices. * * * When the Republican Party came into full power it went at once resolutely back to our fundamental conception of the State and the rights and responsibilities of the individual. Thereby it restored confidence and hope in the American people, it freed and stimulated enterprise, it restored the Government to its position as an umpire instead of a player in the economic game. For these reasons the American people have gone forward in progress while the rest of the world has halted, and some countries have even gone backwards. If anyone will study the causes of retarded recuperation in Europe, he will find much of it due to the stifling of private initiative on one hand, and overloading of the Government with business on the other.

There has been revived in this campaign, however, a series of proposals which, if adopted, would be a long step toward the abandonment of our American system and a surrender to the destructive operation of governmental conduct of commercial business. Because the country is faced with difficulty and doubt over certain national problems—that is, prohibition, farm relief and electrical power—our opponents propose that we must thrust government a long way into the businesses which give rise to these problems. In effect, they abandon the tenets of their own party and turn to State socialism as a solution for the difficulties presented by all three. It is proposed that we shall change from prohibition to the State purchase and sale of liquor. If their agricultural relief program means anything, it means that the Government shall directly or indirectly buy and sell and fix prices of agricultural products. And we are to go into the hydro-electric-power business. In other words, we are confronted with a huge program of government in business.

There is, therefore, submitted to the American people a question of fundamental principle. That is: shall we depart from the principles of our

American political and economic system, upon which we have advanced beyond all the rest of the world, in order to adopt methods based on principles destructive of its very foundations? And I wish to emphasize the seriousness of these proposals. I wish to make my position clear; for this goes to the very roots of American life and progress.

I should like to state to you the effect that this projection of government in business would have upon our system of self-government and our economic system. That effect would reach to the daily life of every man and woman. It would impair the very basis of liberty and freedom not only for those left outside the fold of expanded bureaucracy but for those embraced within it.

Let us first see the effect upon self-government. When the Federal Government undertakes to go into commercial business it must at once set up the organization and administration of that business, and it immediately finds itself in a labyrinth, every alley of which leads to the destruction of self-government.

Commercial business requires a concentration of responsibility. Self-government requires decentralization and many checks and balances to safeguard liberty. Our Government to succeed in business would need become in effect a despotism. There at once begins the destruction of self-government. * * *

It is a false liberalism that interprets itself into the Government operation of commercial business. Every step of bureaucratizing of the business of our country poisons the very roots of liberalism—that is, political equality, free speech, free assembly, free press, and equality of opportunity. It is the road not to more liberty, but to less liberty. Liberalism should be found not striving to spread bureaucracy but striving to set bounds to it. True liberalism seeks all legitimate freedom, first in the confident belief that without such freedom the pursuit of all other blessings and benefits is vain. That belief is the foundation of all American progress, political as well as economic.

Liberalism is a force truly of the spirit, a force proceeding from the deep realization that economic freedom cannot be sacrificed if political freedom is to be preserved. Even if Governmental conduct of business could give us more efficiency instead of less efficiency, the fundamental objection to it would remain unaltered and unabated. It would destroy political equality. It would increase rather than decrease abuse and corruption. It would stifle initiative and invention. It would undermine the development of leadership. It would cramp and cripple the mental and spiritual energies of our people. It would extinguish equality and opportunity. It would dry up the spirit of liberty and progress. For these reasons primarily it must be resisted. For a hundred and fifty years liberalism has found its true spirit in the American system, not in the European systems.

I do not wish to be misunderstood in this statement. I am defining a general policy. It does not mean that our Government is to part with one iota of its national resources without complete protection to the public interest. * * *

Nor do I wish to be misinterpreted as believing that the United States is free-for-all and devil-take-the-hindmost. The very essence of equality of opportunity and of American individualism is that there shall be no domination by any group or combination in this Republic, whether it be business or political. On the contrary, it demands economic justice as well as political and social justice. It is no system of laissez faire.

I feel deeply on this subject because during the war I had some practical experience with governmental operation and control. I have witnessed not only at home but abroad the many failures of Government in business. I have seen its tyrannies, its injustices, its destructions of self-government, its undermining of the very instincts which carry our people forward to progress. I have witnessed the lack of advance, the lowered standards of living, the depressed spirits of people working under such a system. My objection is based not upon theory or upon a failure to recognize wrong or abuse, but I know the adoption of such methods would strike at the very roots of American life and would destroy the very basis of American progress.

Our people have the right to know whether we can continue to solve our great problems without abandonment of our American system. I know we can. * * *

And what have been the results of our American system? Our country has become the land of opportunity to those born without inheritance, not merely because of the wealth of its resources and industry, but because of this freedom of initiative and enterprise. Russia has natural resources equal to ours. Her people are equally industrious, but she has not had the blessings of 150 years of our form of government and of our social system.

By adherence to the principles of decentralized self-government, ordered liberty, equal opportunity and freedom to the individual, our American experiment in human welfare has yielded a degree of well-being unparalleled in all the world. It has come nearer to the abolition of poverty, to the abolition of fear of want, than humanity has ever reached before. Progress of the past seven years is the proof of it. This alone furnishes the answer to our opponents who ask us to introduce destructive elements into the system by which this has been accomplished. * * *

I have endeavored to present to you that the greatness of America has grown out of a political and social system and a method of control of economic forces distinctly its own—our American system—which has carried this great experiment in human welfare further than ever before in all history. We are nearer today to the ideal of the abolition of poverty and fear from the lives of men and women than ever before in any land. And I again repeat that the departure from our American system by injecting principles destructive to it which our opponents propose will jeopardize the very liberty and freedom of our people, will destroy equality of opportunity, not alone to ourselves but to our children.

HERBERT HOOVER

The Challenge to Liberty (1936)

Once he left office, Hoover became an outspoken critic of the New Deal. In this speech, delivered in Denver, Colorado, Hoover warned that the bureaucratic centralization and redistributive policies of the New Deal would make "millions of citizens dependent upon the government" and destroy the freedom and self-reliance of Americans.

I gave the warning against this philosophy of government four years ago from a heart heavy with anxiety for the future of our country. It was born from many years' experience of the forces moving in the world which would weaken the vitality of American freedom. It grew in four years of battle as President to uphold the banner of free men.

And that warning was based on sure ground from my knowledge of the ideas that Mr. Roosevelt and his bosom colleagues had covertly embraced despite the Democratic Platform.

Those ideas were not new. Most of them had been urged upon me.

During my four years powerful groups thundered at the White House with these same ideas. Some were honest, some promising votes, most of them threatening reprisals, and all of them yelling "reactionary" at us.

I rejected the notion of great trade monopolies and price fixing through codes. That could only stifle the little business man by regimenting him under his big brother. That idea was born of certain American Big Business and grew up to be the NRA.

I rejected the schemes of "economic planning" to regiment and coerce the farmer. That was born of a Roman despot fourteen hundred years ago and grew up into the AAA.

I refused national plans to put the government into business in competition with its citizens. That was born of Karl Marx.

I vetoed the idea of recovery through stupendous spending to prime the pump. That was born of a British professor.

I threw out attempts to centralize relief in Washington for politics and social experimentation. I defeated other plans to invade State rights, to centralize power in Washington. Those ideas were born of American radicals.

I stopped attempts at currency inflation and repudiation of government obligation. That was robbery of insurance-policy holders, savings-banks depositors and wage earners. That was born of the early Brain Trusters.

I rejected all these things because they would not only delay recovery but because I knew that in the end they would shackle free men.

Rejecting these ideas we Republicans had erected agencies of government which did start our country to prosperity without the loss of a single atom of American freedom.

All the ardent peddlers of these Trojan horses received sympathetic hearings from Mr. Roosevelt and joined vociferously in his election. Men are to be judged by the company they keep.

Our people did not recognize the gravity of the issue when I stated it four years ago. That is no wonder, for the day Mr. Roosevelt was elected Recovery was in progress, the Constitution was untrampled, the integrity of the government and the institutions of freedom were intact. It was not until after the election that the people began to awake. Then the realization of intended tinkering with the currency drove bank depositors into the panic that greeted Mr. Roosevelt's inauguration. Recovery was set back for two years, and hysteria was used as the bridge to reach the goal of personal government. * * *

I am proud to have carried the banner of free men to the last hour of the term my countrymen entrusted it to me. It matters nothing in the history of a race what happens to those who in their time have carried the banner of free men. What matters is that the battle shall go on.

The people know now the aims of this New Deal philosophy of government.

We propose instead leadership and authority in government within the moral and economic framework of the American System.

We propose to hold to the Constitutional safeguards of free men.

We propose to relieve men from fear, coercion and spite that are inevitable in personal government.

We propose to demobilize and decentralize all this spending upon which vast personal power is being built. We propose to amend the tax laws so as not to defeat free men and free enterprise.

We propose to turn the whole direction of this country toward liberty, not away from it.

The New Dealers say that all this that we propose is a worn-out System; that this machine age requires new measures for which we must sacrifice some part of the freedom of men. Men have lost their way with a confused idea that governments should run machines. Man-made machines cannot be of more worth than men themselves. Free men made these machines. Only free spirits can master them to their proper use.

The relation of our government with all these questions is complicated and difficult. They rise into the very highest ranges of economics, statesmanship, and morals.

And do not mistake. Free government is the most difficult of all government. But it is everlastingly true that the plain people will make fewer mistakes than any group of men no matter how powerful. But free government implies vigilant thinking and courageous living and self-reliance in a people.

Let me say to you that any measure which breaks our dykes of freedom will flood the land with misery. * * *

We must have government that builds stamina into communities and men. That makes men instead of mendicants. We must stop this softening of thrift, self-reliance and self-respect through dependence on government. We must stop telling youth that the country is going to the devil and they haven't a chance. We must stop this dissipating the initiative and aspirations of our people. We must revive the courage of men and women and their faith in American liberty. We must recover these spiritual heritages of America.

All this clatter of class and class hate should end. Thieves will get into high places as well as low places and they should both be given economic security—in jail. But they are not a class. This is a classless country. If we hold to our unique American ideal of equal opportunity there can never be classes or masses in our country. To preach these class ideas from the White House is new in American life. There is no employing class, no working class, no farming class. You may pigeonhole a man or woman as a farmer or a worker or a professional man or an employer or even a banker. But the son of the farmer will be a doctor or a worker or even a banker, and his daughter a teacher. The son of a worker will be an employer—or maybe President. And certainly the sons of even economic royalists have a bad time holding the title of nobility.

The glory of our country has been that every mother could look at the babe in her arms with confidence that the highest position in the world was open to it.

The transcendent issue before us today is free men and women. How do we test freedom? It is not a catalogue of political rights. It is a thing of the spirit. Men must be free to worship, to think, to hold opinions, to speak without fear. They must be free to challenge wrong and oppression with surety of justice. Freedom conceives that the mind and spirit of man can be free only if he be free to pattern his own life, to develop his own talents, free to earn, to spend, to save, to acquire property as the security of his old age and his family.

Freedom demands that these rights and ideals shall be protected from infringement by others, whether men or groups, corporations or governments.

The conviction of our fathers was that all these freedoms come from the Creator and that they can be denied by no man or no government or no New Deal. They were spiritual rights of men. The prime purpose of liberal government is to enlarge and not to destroy these freedoms. It was for that purpose that the Constitution of the United States was enacted. For that reason we demand that the safeguards of freedom shall be upheld. It is for this reason that we demand that this country should turn its direction from a system of personal centralized government to the ideals of liberty.

And again I repeat that statement of four years ago—"This campaign is more than a contest between two men. It is a contest between two philosophies of government."

Whatever the outcome of this election that issue is set. We shall battle it out until the soul of America is saved.

HERBERT HOOVER

The Fifth Freedom (1941)

In response to Franklin Roosevelt's speech on the four freedoms (of speech and expression, of religion, from fear, and from want), Hoover made the case for a fifth, economic freedom. Fearing that bureaucratic regulations of economic life eventually lead to tyranny, the former president argued, in this widely reprinted speech, that protecting the threatened fifth freedom was essential to the preservation of all other freedoms.

The President of the United States on January 6, 1941, stated that we seek 'everywhere in the world' the four old freedoms: freedom of speech and expression, freedom of religion, freedom from fear, freedom from want.

Soon thereafter I called attention to the fact that there is a Fifth Freedom—economic freedom—without which none of the other four freedoms will be realized.

I have stated many times over the years that to be free, men must choose their jobs and callings, bargain for their own wages and salaries, save and provide by private property for their families and old age. And they must be free to engage in enterprise so long as each does not injure his fellowmen. And that requires laws to prevent abuse. And when I use the term 'Fifth Freedom,' I use it in this sense only, not in the sense of laissez-faire or economic exploitation. Exploitation is the negation of freedom. The Fifth Freedom does not mean going back to abuses.

Laws to prevent men doing economic injury to their fellows were universal in civilized countries long before the First World War. In the United States, for example, the State and Federal Governments had established regulation of banks, railroads, utilities, coinage; prevention of combinations to restrain trade; government support to credit in times of stress; public works; tariffs; limitations on hours of labor and in other directions.

The key of such government action to economic freedom is that government must not destroy but promote freedom. When governments exert regulation of economic life, they must do so by definite statutory rules of conduct imposed by legislative bodies that all men may read as they run and in which they may have at all times the protection of the courts. No final judicial or legislative authority must be delegated to bureaucrats, or at once tyranny begins.

When Government violates these principles, it sooner or later weakens constitutional safeguards of personal liberty and representative government.

When Government goes into business in competition with citizens, bureaucracy always relies upon tyranny to win. And bureaucracy never develops that competence in management which comes from the mills of competition. Its conduct of business inevitably lowers the living standards of the people. Nor does bureaucracy ever discover or invent. A Millikan, Ford, or Edison never came from a bureaucracy.

And inherent in bureaucracy is the grasping spirit of more and more power. It always resents criticism and sooner or later begins directly or indirectly to limit free speech and free press. Intellectual and spiritual freedom will not long survive the passing of economic freedom. One of the illusions of our time is that we can have totalitarian economics and the personal freedoms. Ten nations on the Continent of Europe tried it and wound up with dictators and no liberty.

The first trench in the battle for the five freedoms is to maintain them in America. That rests upon fidelity not only to the letter, but to the spirit of constitutional government. Failure of Congress to assert its responsibilities or for the Executive to take steps beyond the authority of Congress is a direct destruction of the safeguards of freedom. We badly need a complete overhaul of our governmental relations to the Fifth Freedom if it is to be preserved.

The Fifth Freedom in no way inhibits social reforms and social advancement. In fact, it furnishes the increasing resources upon which such progress can be built. And itself flourishes upon the advancing social aspirations of our people. Social advancement was part of the whole American concept during the whole of our national life. The greatest of all social advances was free education. Next came concern for public health. We have always held it an obligation to prevent suffering from misfortune, to care for widows, orphans, and old age, and those upon whom disaster falls.

The methods have gradually improved from the ancient work-house, the asylum, and the county hospital to more systematic and more inclusive action. And that more inclusive action has only been possible with the growing wealth born from the Fifth Freedom. For many years in the United States our States and the nation have been gradually developing protection to children, to women, limitation of hours, and safeguards of health in industry. From these forty-eight laboratories we have seen the development of such actions as public health control, hospitalization, care of children, workmen's compensation, unemployment and health insurance, old-age, widows', and orphans' pensions. They are not new ideas. As we expand in these purposes, there are safeguards to liberty that can and must be preserved.

One of these safeguards is where personal insurance for any purpose is given by the Government it must be contributory. Even where subsidized by the Federal Government it should be administered by the States to limit the growth of centralized bureaucracy and political action.

Liberty has its greatest protection from local not centralized government.

Another concept in all social insurance or pensions must be that the responsibility of the people as a whole is to provide only a reasonable subsistence basis. Beyond that the citizen must look after himself if initiative and self-respect are to be maintained. Today our measures in these matters badly need vigorous overhauling to make them comport with these fundamental principles; to put them upon a 'pay-as-you-go' basis; to make them inclusive of everybody; and to make them synchronize and not destroy private institutions and efforts.

A system devoted to development of individuality and personal freedom is a complicated business. It can destroy its own purposes by foolish action.

Today we are faced with the relation of personal liberty to total war. Our people must be mobilized for that immediate purpose.

We must sacrifice much economic freedom to win the war. That is economic Fascism, for Fascist economics were born of just these measures in the last war. But there are two vast differences in the application of this sort of economic system at the hands of democracies or at the hands of dictators. First, in democracies we strive to keep free speech, free press, free worship, trial by jury, and other personal liberties alive. And, second, we want so to design our actions that these Fascist economic measures are not frozen into life, but shall thaw out after the war.

Even the temporary suspension of economic liberty creates grave dangers because liberty rapidly atrophies from disuse. Vested interests and vested habits grow around its restrictions. It would be a vain thing to fight the war and lose our own liberties. If we would have them return, we must hold furiously to the ideals of economic liberty. We must challenge every departure from them. There are just two tests: 'Is this departure necessary to win the war?' 'How are we going to restore these freedoms after the war?' * * *

Under the stress of reconstruction after the war, our liberties will be slow in coming back, but the essential thing in this sort of question is the direction in which we travel. We must establish the direction now.

CHARLES A. BEARD

The Myth of Rugged American Individualism (1931)

In addition to his historical research, Beard was deeply concerned with contemporary political issues. He resigned in protest from Columbia University, for example, over the dismissal of faculty members accused of disloyalty to the government during World War I. In this selection from his 1931 book The Myth of Rugged American Individualism, *Beard argued that state regulation of the economy had occurred principally at the prompting of businesses, which then use the myth of rugged individualism to prevent positive governmental action that interfered with their material interests. Planning, he argues, must replace the "anarchy celebrated in the name of individualism."*

There are] many straws in the wind indicating a movement to exalt rugged individualism into a national taboo beyond the reach of inquiring minds. From day to day it becomes increasingly evident that some of our economic leaders (by no means all of them) are using the phrase as an excuse for avoiding responsibility, for laying the present depression on "Government interference," and for seeking to escape from certain forms of taxation and regulation which they do not find to their interest. If a smoke screen big enough can be laid on the land, our commercial prestidigitators may work wonders—for themselves.

Still more direct evidence confirms this view. For example, in the autumn of 1930, a New York bank published, as a kind of revelation from on high, a slashing attack on "Government interference with business," written by that stanch English Whig, Macaulay, a hundred years ago; and a few weeks later one of the leading advertising firms took a whole page in the *New York Times* to blazon forth the creed anew under the captivating head: "Cheer Up! Our Best Times Are Still Ahead of Us!" And the whole gospel was summed up in these words from Macaulay: "Our rulers will best promote the improvement of the people by strictly confining themselves to their own legitimate duties—by leaving capital to find its most lucrative course, commodities their fair price, industry and intelligence their natural reward, idleness and folly their natural punishment—by maintaining peace, by defending property, by diminishing the price of law, and by observing strict economy in every department of the State. Let the Government do this—the people will assuredly do the rest." In other words, here was put forth in the name of American business, with all the pontifical assurance that characterized Macaulay's shallowest sophistry, the pure creed of historic individualism, and here was served on the Government and people of the United States a warning revelation of confident expectations.

A year later, in a release to the press, Mr. Otto Kahn discussed the subject of planning and intimated that the fortunate position of France to-day is to be ascribed to the fact that the French Government interferes less with business than does the Government of Germany or Great Britain, with the implication that the United States might profit from this experience. About the same time the Honorable Newton D. Baker made a long address at Williamstown which was evidently designed to show that nothing important could be done in the present crisis by the Federal Government, except perhaps in the way of tariff reduction by international agreement. And now comes from Chicago the announcement that a number of rugged business men are forming a national association to combat Government in business, to break up this unholy alliance. There is not a professional lunching-and-dining fellowship in America that is not now applauding to the echo such ringing cries as "Let Us Alone," "Take Government Out of Business," "Hands Off," "Unburden Capital." With an eye on such straws in the wind, President Hoover publicly states that all notions about planned economy come out of Russia, thus placing such distinguished men as Gerard Swope and Owen D. Young under the horrible Red ban. As one of the high-powered utility propagandists recently explained, the best way to discredit an opponent is to pin a Red tag on him—without reference to his deserts, of course.

Hence it is important to ask, calmly and without reference to election heats, just what all this means. In what way is the Government "in business" and how did it get there? Here we climb down out of the muggy atmosphere of controversy and face a few stubborn facts. They are entered in the indubitable records of the Government of the United States and are as evident as the hills to them that have eyes to see. Let us catalogue a few of them *seriatim* for the first time in the history of this adventure in logomachy.

1. Government Regulation of Railways, from 1887 to the last Act of Congress. How did the Government get into this business? The general cause was the conduct of railway corporations under the rule of rugged individualism—rebates, pools, stock watering, bankruptcy-juggling, all the traffic will bear, savage rate slashing, merciless competition, and the rest of it. If any one wants to know the facts, let him read the history of railroading in the sixties, seventies, and early eighties, or, if time is limited, the charming illustrations presented in Charles Francis Adams' "A Chapter of Erie." And what was the immediate cause of the Government's intervention? The insistence of business men, that is, shippers, who were harassed and sometimes ruined by railway tactics, and of farmers, the most rugged of all the rugged individualists the broad land of America has produced. * * *

2. Waterways. Since its foundation the Government has poured hundreds of millions into rivers, harbors, canals, and other internal improvements. It is still pouring in millions. Some of our best economists have denounced it as wasteful and have demonstrated that most of it does not pay in any sense of the word. But President Hoover, instead of leaving this work to private enterprise, insists on projecting and executing the most elaborate undertakings, in spite of the fact that some of them are

unfair if not ruinous to railways. Who is back of all this? Business men and farmers who want lower freight rates.

3. The United States Barge Corporation. Who got the Government into the job of running barges on some of its improved waterways? Certainly not the Socialists, but good Republicans and Democrats. * * *

4. The Shipping Business. The World War was the occasion, but not the cause of this departure. For more than half a century the politicians of America fought ship subsidies against business men engaged in the shipbuilding and allied industries. At last, under the cover of war necessities, the Government went into the shipping business, with cheers from business. Who is back of the huge expenditures for the merchant marine? Business men. * * *

5. Aviation. The Government is "in" this business. It provides costly airway services free of charge and subsidizes air mail. Who is behind this form of Government enterprise? Gentlemen engaged in aviation and the manufacture of planes and dirigibles. * * *

6. Canals. Who zealously supported the construction of the Panama Canal? Shippers on the Pacific Coast who did not like the railway rates. Also certain important shipping interests on both coasts—all controlled by business men. * * *

7. Highway Building. Who has supported Federal highway aid—the expenditures of hundreds of millions on roads, involving the taxation of railways to pay for ruinous competition? Everybody apparently, but specifically business men engaged in the manufacture and sale of automobiles and trucks. * * *

8. The Department of Commerce. Who is responsible for loading on the Government the job of big drummer at large for business? Why shouldn't these rugged individualists do their own drumming instead of asking the taxpayers to do it for them? Business men have been behind this enormous-expansion, and Mr. Hoover, as Secretary of Commerce, outdid every predecessor in the range of his activities and the expenditure of public money. * * *

9. The Big Pork Barrel—appropriations for public buildings, navy yards, and army posts. An interesting enterprise for the United States Chamber of Commerce would be to discover a single piece of pork in a hundred years that has not been approved by local business men as beneficiaries. * * *

10. The Bureau of Standards. Besides its general services, it renders valuable aid to business undertakings. Why shouldn't they do their own investigating at their own expense, instead of turning to the Government?

11. The Federal Trade Commission. Who runs there for rulings on "fair practices"? Weary consumers? Not often. Principally, business men

who do not like to be outwitted or cheated by their competitors. If we are rugged individualists, why not let every individualist do as he pleases, without invoking Government intervention at public expense?

12. The Anti-Trust Acts. Business men are complaining against these laws on the ground that they cannot do any large-scale planning without incurring the risk of prosecution. The contention is sound, but who put these laws on the books and on what theory were they based? They were the product of a clamor on the part of farmers and business men against the practices of great corporations. Farmers wanted lower prices. Business men of the smaller variety objected to being undersold, beaten by clever tricks, or crushed to the wall by competitors with immense capital. * * * And what was the philosophy behind the Sherman Act and the Clayton Act? Individualism, pure and undefiled. "The New Freedom" as President Wilson phrased it in literary language. "Break up the trusts and let each tub stand on its own bottom." That was the cry among little business men. As lawyers put it in their somber way, "the natural person's liberty should not be destroyed by artificial persons known as corporations created under the auspices of the State." Whether any particular business man is for or against the anti-trust laws depends upon his particular business and the state of his earnings.

13. The Tariff. On this tender subject it is scarcely possible to speak soberly. It seems safe to say, however, that if all the business men who demand this kind of "interference"—with the right of capital to find its most lucrative course, industry and intelligence their natural reward, commodities their fair price, and idleness and folly their natural punishment—were to withdraw their support for protection, cease their insistence on it, then the politicians would probably reduce the levy or go over to free trade; with what effect on business no one can correctly predict. At all events there are thousands of business men who want to keep the Government in the business of protecting their business against foreign competition. If competition is good, why not stand up and take it?

* * *

In this survey of a few leading economic activities of the Federal Government the emphasis is not critical; so far as the present argument is concerned, any or all of these functions may be justified with respect to national interest. Indeed it is difficult to find any undertaking of the Government which is not supported by some business men on the ground of national defense. In the early days of our history even those statesmen who generally espoused free trade or low tariffs were willing to concede the importance of making the nation independent in the manufacture of munitions of war. And in the latest hour, subsidies to the merchant marine, to aviation, and to waterways development are stoutly defended in the name of preparedness. Transforming a creek into a river navigable by outboard motor boats can be supported by military engineers on the theory that it gives them practice in their art. No; the emphasis here is not critical. The point is that the Federal Government does not operate in a vacuum, but under impulsion from without; and all of the measures which put the Government into business have been supported by rugged individualists—business men or farmers or both. The current tendency to describe the Government as a meddling busybody, prying around and regulating for the mere pleasure of taking the joy out of somebody's life, betrays an ignorance of the facts in the case. The Government of the United States operates continually in the midst of the most powerful assembly of lobbyists the world has ever seen—the representatives of every business interest that has arisen above the level of a corner grocery; and there is not a single form of Government interference with business that does not have the approval of one or more of these interests—except perhaps the taxation of incomes for the purpose, among other things, of paying the expenses of subsidizing and regulating business.

For forty years or more there has not been a President, Republican or Democratic, who has not talked against Government interference and then supported measures adding more interference to the huge collection already accumulated. Take, for instance, President Wilson. He made his campaign in 1912 on the classical doctrine of individualism; he blew mighty blasts in the name of his new freedom against the control of the Government by corporate wealth and promised to separate business and Government, thus setting little fellows free to make money out of little business. The heir of the Jeffersonian tradition, he decried paternalism of every kind. Yet look at the statutes enacted under his benign administration: the trainmen's law virtually fixing wages on interstate railways for certain classes of employees; the shipping board law; the Farm Loan Act; Federal aid for highway construction; the Alaskan railway; the Federal Reserve Act; the Water Power Act; and all the rest of the bills passed during his régime. Only the Clayton anti-trust law can be called individualistic. No wonder Mr. E. L. Doheny exclaimed to Mr. C. W. Barron that President Wilson was a college professor gone Bolshevist! And why did Democrats who had been saying "the less government the better" operate on the theory that the more government the better? Simply because their mouths were worked by ancient memories and their actions were shaped by inexorable realities.

Then the Republicans came along in 1921 and informed the country that they were going back to normalcy, were determined to take the

Government out of business. Well, did they repeal a single one of the important measures enacted during the eight years of President Wilson's rule? It would be entertaining to see the sanhedrim of the United States Chamber of Commerce trying to make out a list of laws repealed in the name of normalcy and still more entertaining to watch that august body compiling a list of additional laws interfering with "the natural course of business" enacted since 1921. Heirs of the Hamiltonian tradition, the Republicans were not entitled to talk about separating the Government from business. Their great spiritual teacher, Daniel Webster, a pupil of Hamilton, had spoken truly when he said that one of the great reasons for framing the Constitution was the creation of a government that could regulate commerce. They came honestly by subsidies, bounties, internal improvements, tariffs, and other aids to business. What was the trouble with them in the age of normalcy? Nothing; they just wanted their kind of Government intervention in the "natural course of industry." Evidently, then, there is some confusion on this subject of individualism, and it ought to be examined dispassionately in the light of its history with a view to discovering its significance and its limitations; for there is moral danger in saying one thing and doing another—at all events too long.

Historically speaking, there are two schools of individualism: one American, associated with the name of Jefferson, and the other English, associated with the name of Cobden. The former was agrarian in interest, the latter capitalistic. Jefferson wanted America to be a land of free, upstanding farmers with just enough government to keep order among them; his creed was an agrarian creed nicely fitted to a civilization of sailing ships, ox carts, stagecoaches, wooden plows, tallow dips, and home-made bacon and sausages; and since most of the people in the United States, during the first century of their independence, were engaged in agriculture, they thought highly of Jefferson's praise of agriculture and his doctrine of anarchy plus the police constable. Cobden's individualism was adapted to capitalist England at the middle of the nineteenth century—early industrial England. At that moment his country was the workshop of the world, was mistress of the world market in manufactured commodities, and feared no competition from any foreign country. English capitalists thus needed no protective tariffs and subsidies and, therefore, wanted none. Hence they exalted free trade to the level of a Mosaic law, fixed and eternal. They wanted to employ labor on their own terms and turn working people out to starve when no profitable business was at hand; so they quite naturally believed that any Government interference with their right to do as they pleased was "bad." Their literary apologist, Macaulay, clothed their articles of faith in such magnificent rhetoric that even the tiredest business man could keep awake reading it at night.

Closely examined, what is this creed of individualism? Macaulay defines it beautifully in the passage which the New York Bank and our happy advertising agency quoted so joyously. Let the Government maintain peace, defend property, reduce the cost of litigation, and observe economy in expenditure—that is all. Do American business men want peace all the time, in Nicaragua, for instance, when their undertakings are disturbed? Or in Haiti or Santo Domingo? Property must be defended, of course. But whose property? And what about the cost of litigation and economy in expenditures? If they would tell their hired men in law offices to cut the costs of law, something might happen. As for expenditures, do they really mean to abolish subsidies, bounties, and appropriations-in-aid from which they benefit? Speaking brutally, they do not. That is not the kind of economy in expenditures which they demand; they prefer to cut off a few dollars from the Children's Bureau.

Then comes Macaulay's system of private economy: let capital find its most lucrative course alone, unaided: no Government tariffs, subsidies, bounties, and special privileges. That is the first item. Do American business men who shout for individualism believe in that? Certainly not. So that much is blown out of the water. Macaulay's next item is: let commodities find their fair price. Do the gentlemen who consolidate, merge, and make price understandings want to allow prices to take their "natural course"? By no means; they are trying to effect combinations that will hold prices up to the point of the largest possible profit. Macaulay's third item is: let industry and intelligence receive their natural reward. Whose industry and intelligence and what industry and intelligence? When these questions are asked all that was clear and simple dissolves in mist.

Then there is Macaulay's last item: let idleness and folly reap their natural punishment. That was a fundamental specification in the bill of Manchesterism. Malthus made it a law for the economists: the poor are poor because they have so many babies and are improvident; nothing can be done about it, at least by any Government, even though it enforces drastic measures against the spread of information on birth control. Darwin made a natural science of it: biology sanctified the tooth and claw struggle of business by proclaiming the eternal tooth and claw struggle of the jungle. If the Government will do nothing whatever, all people will rise or sink to the level which their industry or idleness, their intelligence or folly commands. No distinction was made between those who were idle because they could find no work and those who just loved idleness for its own sake—either in slums or mansions. Those who hit bottom and starved simply deserved it. That is the good, sound, logical creed of simon-pure individualism which Herbert Spencer embedded in fifty pounds of printed matter. To him and all his devotees, even public schools and public libraries were anathema: let the poor educate themselves at their own expense; to educate them at public expense is robbery of the taxpayer—that industrious, intelligent, provident person who is entitled to keep his "natural reward."

* * *

There is another side to this stalwart individualism that also deserves consideration. Great things have been done in its name, no doubt, and it will always have its place in any reasoned scheme of thinking. Individual initiative and energy are absolutely indispensable to the successful conduct of any enterprise, and there is ample ground for fearing the tyranny and ineptitude of Governments. In the days of pioneering industry in England, in our pioneering days when forests were to be cut and mountain fastnesses explored, individualism was the great dynamic which drove enterprise forward. But on other pages of the doom book other entries must be made. In the minds of most people who shout for individualism vociferously, the creed, stripped of all flashy rhetoric, means getting money, simply that and nothing more. And to this creed may be laid most of the shame that has cursed our cities and most of the scandals that have smirched our Federal Government.

* * *

The cold truth is that the individualist creed of everybody for himself and the devil take the hindmost is principally responsible for the distress in which Western civilization finds itself—with investment racketeering at one end and labor racketeering at the other. Whatever merits the creed may have had in days of primitive agriculture and industry, it is not applicable in an age of technology, science, and rationalized economy. Once useful, it has become a danger to society. Every thoughtful business man who is engaged in management as distinguished from stock speculation knows that stabilization, planning, orderly procedure, prudence, and the adjustment of production to demand are necessary to keep the economic machine running steadily and efficiently. Some of our most distinguished citizens—Owen D. Young, Gerard Swope, Nicholas Murray Butler, and Otto Kahn, for example—have, in effect, warned the country that only by planning can industry avoid the kind of disaster from which we are now suffering; on all sides are signs of its coming—perhaps soon, perhaps late, but inevitably.

And all of them know that this means severe restraints on the anarchy celebrated in the name of individualism. The task before us, then, is not to furbish up an old slogan, but to get rid of it, to discover how much planning is necessary, by whom it can best be done, and what limitations must be imposed on the historic doctrine of Manchesterism. And to paraphrase Milton, methinks puissant America, mewing her mighty youth, will yet kindle her undazzled eyes at the full midday beam, purge and unscale her long abused sight, while timorous and flocking birds, with those that love the twilight, flutter about, amazed at what she means, and in their envious gabble would prognosticate a year of sects and schisms.

JOHN DEWEY

Liberalism and Social Action (1935)

In his book Liberalism and Social Action, *Dewey sought to radicalize liberalism while still remaining true to its traditional values of liberty, individualism, and free thought. He suggested that liberals abandon their commitment to laissez-faire and use "scientific" and "experimental intelligence" to reorder society in terms of agreed-upon social purposes.*

Civilization existed for most human history in a state of scarcity in the material basis for a humane life. Our ways of thinking, planning and working have been attuned to this fact. Thanks to science and technology we now live in an age of potential plenty. The immediate effect of the emergence of the new possibility was simply to stimulate, to a point of incredible exaggeration, the striving for the material resources, called wealth, opened to men in the new vista. It is a characteristic of all development, physiological and mental, that when a new force and factor appears, it is first pushed to an extreme. Only when its possibilities have been exhausted (at least relatively) does it take its place in the life perspective. The economic-material phase of life, which belongs in the basal ganglia of society, has usurped for more than a century the cortex of the social body. The habits of desire and effort that were bred in the age of scarcity do not readily subordinate themselves and take the place of the matter-of-course routine that becomes appropriate to them when machines and impersonal power have the capacity to liberate man from bondage to the strivings that were once needed to make secure his physical basis. Even now when there is a vision of an age of abundance and when the vision is supported by hard fact, it is material security as an end that appeals to most rather than the way of living which this security makes possible. Men's minds are still pathetically held in the clutch of old habits and haunted by old memories.

For, in the second place, insecurity is the natural child and the foster child, too, of scarcity. Early liberalism emphasized the importance of insecurity as a fundamentally necessary economic motive, holding that without this goad men would not work, abstain or accumulate. Formulation of this conception was new. But the fact that was formulated was nothing new. It was deeply rooted in the habits that were formed in the long struggle against material scarcity. The system that goes by the name of capitalism is a systematic manifestation of desires and purposes built up in an age of ever threatening want and now carried over into a time of ever increasing potential plenty. The conditions that generate insecurity for the many no longer spring from nature. They are found in institutions and arrangements that are within deliberate human control. Surely this change marks one of the greatest revolutions that has taken place in all human history. Because of it, insecurity is not now the motive to work and sacrifice but to despair. It is not an instigation to put forth energy but to an impotency that can be converted from death into endurance only by charity. But the habits of mind and action that modify institutions to make potential abundance an actuality are still so inchoate that most of us discuss labels like individualism, socialism and communism instead of even perceiving the possibility, much less the necessity for realizing what can and should be.

In the third place, the patterns of belief and purpose that still dominate economic institutions were formed when individuals produced with their hands, alone or in small groups. The notion that society in general is served by the unplanned coincidence of the consequences of a vast multitude of efforts put forth by isolated individuals without reference to any social end, was also something new as a formulation. But it also formulated the working principle of an epoch which the advent of new forces of production was to bring to an end. It demands no great power of intelligence to see that under present conditions the isolated individual is well-nigh helpless. Concentration and corporate organization are the rule. But the concentration and corporate organization are still controlled in their operation by ideas that were institutionalized in eons of separate individual effort. The attempts at coöperation for mutual benefit that are put forth are precious as experimental moves. But that society itself should see to it that a coöperative industrial order be instituted, one that is consonant with the realities of production enforced by an era of machinery and power, is so novel an idea to the general mind that its mere suggestion is hailed with abusive epithets— sometimes with imprisonment.

When, then, I say that the first object of a renascent liberalism is education, I mean that its task is to aid in producing the habits of mind and character, the intellectual and moral patterns, that are somewhere near even with the actual movements of events. It is, I repeat, the split between the latter as they have externally occurred and the ways of desiring, thinking, and of putting emotion and purpose into execution that is the basic cause of present confusion in mind and paralysis in action. The educational task cannot be accomplished merely by working upon men's minds, without action that effects actual change in institutions. The idea that dispositions and attitudes can be altered by merely "moral" means conceived of as something that goes on wholly inside of persons is itself one of the old patterns that has to be changed. Thought, desire and purpose exist in a constant give and take of interaction with environing conditions. But resolute thought is the first step in that change of action that will itself carry further the needed change in patterns of mind and character.

In short, liberalism must now become radical, meaning by "radical" perception of the necessity of thorough-going changes in the set-up of institutions and corresponding activity to bring the changes to pass. For the gulf between what the actual situation makes possible and the actual state itself is so great that it cannot be bridged by piecemeal policies undertaken *ad hoc*. The process of producing the changes will be, in any case, a gradual one. But "reforms" that deal now with this abuse and now with that without having a social goal based upon an inclusive plan, differ entirely from effort at re-forming, in its literal sense, the institutional scheme of things. The liberals of more than a century ago were denounced in their time as subversive radicals, and only when the new economic order was established did they become apologists for the *status quo* or else content with social patchwork. If radicalism be defined as perception of need for radical change, then today any liberalism which is not also radicalism is irrelevant and doomed. * * *

The crisis in democracy demands the substitution of the intelligence that is exemplified in scientific procedure for the kind of intelligence that is now accepted. The need for this change is not exhausted in the demand for greater honesty and impartiality, even though these qualities be now corrupted by discussion carried on mainly for purposes of party supremacy and for imposition of some special but concealed interest. These qualities need to be restored. But the need goes further. The social use of intelligence would remain deficient even if these moral traits were exalted, and yet intelligence continued to be identified simply with discussion and persuasion, necessary as are these things. Approximation to use of scientific method in investigation and of the engineering mind in the invention and projection of far-reaching social plans is demanded. The

habit of considering social realities in terms of cause and effect and social policies in terms of means and consequences is still inchoate. The
contrast between the state of intelligence in politics and in the physical
control of nature is to be taken literally. What has happened in this latter
is the outstanding demonstration of the meaning of organized intelligence. The combined effect of science and technology has released more
productive energies in a bare hundred years than stands to the credit of
prior human history in its entirety. Productively it has multiplied nine
million times in the last generation alone. The prophetic vision of Francis
Bacon of subjugation of the energies of nature through change in methods of inquiry has well-nigh been realized. The stationary engine, the locomotive, the dynamo, the motor car, turbine, telegraph, telephone, radio
and moving picture are not the products of either isolated individual
minds nor of the particular economic régime called capitalism. They are
the fruit of methods that first penetrated to the working causalities of
nature and then utilized the resulting knowledge in bold imaginative ventures of invention and construction. * * *

When I say that scientific method and technology have been the active
force in producing the revolutionary transformations society is undergo-
ing, I do not imply no other forces have been at work to arrest, deflect and
corrupt their operation. Rather this fact is positively implied. At this point,
indeed, is located the conflict that underlies the confusions and uncertainties of the present scene. The conflict is between institutions and
habits originating in the pre-scientific and pre-technological age and the
new forces generated by science and technology. The application of science, to a considerable degree, even its own growth, has been conditioned
by the system to which the name of capitalism is given, a rough designation of a complex of political and legal arrangements centering about a
particular mode of economic relations. Because of the conditioning of science and technology by this setting, the second and humanly most important part of Bacon's prediction has so far largely missed realization. The
conquest of natural energies has not accrued to the betterment of the
common human estate in anything like the degree he anticipated.

Because of conditions that were set by the legal institutions and the
moral ideas existing when the scientific and industrial revolutions came
into being, the chief usufruct of the latter has been appropriated by a relatively small class. Industrial entrepreneurs have reaped out of all proportion to what they sowed. By obtaining private ownership of the means
of production and exchange they deflected a considerable share of the results of increased productivity to their private pockets. This appropriation
was not the fruit of criminal conspiracy or of sinister intent. It was sanctioned not only by legal institutions of age-long standing but by the entire

prevailing moral code. The institution of private property long antedated feudal times. It is the institution with which men have lived, with few exceptions, since the dawn of civilization. Its existence has deeply impressed itself upon mankind's moral conceptions. Moreover, the new industrial forces tended to break down many of the rigid class barriers that had been in force, and to give to millions a new outlook and inspire a new hope;—especially in this country with no feudal background and no fixed class system.

Since the legal institutions and the patterns of mind characteristic of ages of civilization still endure, there exists the conflict that brings confusion into every phase of present life. The problem of bringing into being a new social orientation and organization is, when reduced to its ultimates, the problem of using the new resources of production, made possible by the advance of physical science, for social ends, for what Bentham called the greatest good of the greatest number. Institutional relationships fixed in the pre-scientific age stand in the way of accomplishing this great transformation. Lag in mental and moral patterns provides the bulwark of the older institutions; in expressing the past they still express present beliefs, outlooks and purposes. Here is the place where the problem of liberalism centers today. * * *

It is frequently asserted that the method of experimental intelligence can be applied to physical facts because physical nature does not present conflicts of class interests, while it is inapplicable to society because the latter is so deeply marked by incompatible interests. It is then assumed that the "experimentalist" is one who has chosen to ignore the uncomfortable fact of conflicting interests. Of course, there *are* conflicting interests; otherwise there would be no social problems. The problem under discussion is precisely *how* conflicting claims are to be settled in the interest of the widest possible contribution to the interests of all—or at least of the great majority. The method of democracy—inasfar as it is that of organized intelligence—is to bring these conflicts out into the open where their special claims can be seen and appraised, where they can be discussed and judged in the light of more inclusive interests than are represented by either of them separately. There is, for example, a clash of interests between munition manufacturers and most of the rest of the population. The more the respective claims of the two are publicly and scientifically weighed, the more likely it is that the public interest will be disclosed and be made effective. There is an undoubted objective clash of interests between finance-capitalism that controls the means of production and whose profit is served by maintaining relative scarcity, and idle workers and hungry consumers. But what generates violent strife is failure to bring the conflict into the light of intelligence where the conflicting interests can be adjudicated in behalf of the interest of the great majority. Those most committed to the dogma of inevitable force recognize the need for intelligently discovering and expressing the dominant social interest up to a certain point and then draw back. The "experimentalist" is one who would see to it that the method depended upon by all in some degree in every democratic community be followed through to completion. * * *

The argument, drawn from history, that great social changes have been effected only by violent means, needs considerable qualification, in view of the vast scope of changes that are taking place without the use of violence. But even if it be admitted to hold of the past, the conclusion that violence is the method now to be depended upon does not follow— unless one is committed to a dogmatic philosophy of history. The radical who insists that the future method of change must be like that of the past has much in common with the hide-bound reactionary who holds to the past as an ultimate fact. Both overlook the *fact that history in being a process of change generates change not only in details but also in the method of directing social change.* I recur to what I said at the beginning of this chapter. It is true that the social order is largely conditioned by the use of coercive force, bursting at times into open violence. But what is also true is that mankind now has in its possession a new method, that of coöperative and experimental science which expresses the method of intelligence. I should be meeting dogmatism with dogmatism if I asserted that the existence of this historically new factor completely invalidates all arguments drawn from the effect of force in the past. But it is within the bounds of reason to assert that the presence of this social factor demands that the present situation be analyzed on its own terms, and not be rigidly subsumed under fixed conceptions drawn from the past.

Any analysis made in terms of the present situation will not fail to note one fact that militates powerfully against arguments drawn from past use of violence. Modern warfare is destructive beyond anything known in older times. This increased destructiveness is due primarily, of course, to the fact that science has raised to a new pitch of destructive power all the agencies of armed hostility. But it is also due to the much greater interdependence of all the elements of society. The bonds that hold modern communities and states together are as delicate as they are numerous. The self-sufficiency and independence of a local community, characteristic of more primitive societies, have disappeared in every highly industrialized country. The gulf that once separated the civilian population from the military has virtually gone. War involves paralysis of all normal social activities, and not merely the meeting of armed forces in the field. The Communist Manifesto presented two alternatives: *either* the revolutionary change and transfer of power to the proletariat, *or* the common ruin of the contending parties. Today, the civil war that would be adequate to effect transfer of power and a reconstitution of society at large, as understood by official Communists, would seem to present but one possible consequence: the ruin of all parties and the destruction of civilized life. This fact alone is enough to lead us to consider the potentialities of the method of intelligence. * * *

It is true that in this country, because of the interpretations made by courts of a written constitution, our political institutions are unusually inflexible. It is also true, as well as even more important (because it is a factor in causing this rigidity) that our institutions, democratic in form, tend to favor in substance a privileged plutocracy. Nevertheless, it is sheer defeatism to assume in advance of actual trial that democratic political institutions are incapable either of further development or of constructive social application. Even as they now exist, the forms of representative government are potentially capable of expressing the public will when that assumes anything like unification. And there is nothing inherent in them that forbids their supplementation by political agencies that represent definitely economic social interests, like those of producers and consumers.

The final argument in behalf of the use of intelligence is that as are the means used so are the actual ends achieved—that is, the consequences. I know of no greater fallacy than the claim of those who hold to the dogma of the necessity of brute force that this use will be the method of calling genuine democracy into existence—of which they profess themselves the simon-pure adherents. It requires an unusually credulous faith in the Hegelian dialectic of opposites to think that all of a sudden the use of force by a class will be transmuted into a democratic classless society. Force breeds counterforce; the Newtonian law of action and reaction still holds in physics, and violence is physical. * * *

The alternatives are continuation of drift with attendant improvisations to meet special emergencies; dependence upon violence; dependence upon socially organized intelligence. The first two alternatives, however, are not mutually exclusive, for if things are allowed to drift the result may be some sort of social change effected by the use of force, whether so planned or not. Upon the whole, the recent policy of liberalism has been to further "social legislation"; that is, measures which add performance of social services to the older functions of government. The value of this addition is not to be despised. It marks a decided move away from *laissez faire* liberalism, and has considerable importance in educating the public mind to a realization of the possibilities of organized social control. It has helped to develop some of the techniques that in any case will be needed in a socialized economy. But the cause of liberalism will be

lost for a considerable period if it is not prepared to go further and so-
cialize the forces of production, now at hand, so that the liberty of individuals will be supported by the very structure of economic organization.

The ultimate place of economic organization in human life is to assure
the secure basis for an ordered expression of individual capacity and for the
satisfaction of the needs of man in non-economic directions. The effort of
mankind in connection with material production belongs, as I said earlier,
among interests and activities that are, relatively speaking, routine in character, "routine" being defined as that which, without absorbing attention
and energy, provides a constant basis for liberation of the values of intellectual, esthetic and companionship life. Every significant religious and moral
teacher and prophet has asserted that the material is instrumental to the
good life. Nominally at least, this idea is accepted by every civilized community. The transfer of the burden of material production from human
muscles and brain to steam, electricity and chemical processes now makes
possible the effective actualization of this ideal. Needs, wants and desires
are always the moving force in generating creative action. When these
wants are compelled by force of conditions to be directed for the most part,
among the mass of mankind, into obtaining the means of subsistence,
what should be a means becomes perforce an end in itself. Up to the present the new mechanical forces of production, which are the means of
emancipation from this state of affairs, have been employed to intensify
and exaggerate the reversal of the true relation between means and ends.
Humanly speaking, I do not see how it would have been possible to avoid
an epoch having this character. But its perpetuation is the cause of the
continually growing social chaos and strife. Its termination cannot be effected by preaching to individuals that they should place spiritual ends
above material means. It can be brought about by organized social reconstruction that puts the results of the mechanism of abundance at the free
disposal of individuals. The actual corrosive "materialism" of our times
does not proceed from science. It springs from the notion, sedulously cultivated by the class in power, that the creative capacities of individuals can
be evoked and developed only in a struggle for material possessions and
material gain. We either should surrender our professed belief in the supremacy of ideal and spiritual values and accommodate our beliefs to the
predominant material orientation, or we should through organized endeavor institute the socialized economy of material security and plenty that
will release human energy for pursuit of higher values.

Since liberation of the capacities of individuals for free, self-initiated
expression is an essential part of the creed of liberalism, liberalism that is
sincere must will the means that condition the achieving of its ends. Regimentation of material and mechanical forces is the only way by which

the mass of individuals can be released from regimentation and consequent suppression of their cultural possibilities. The eclipse of liberalism is due to the fact that it has not faced the alternatives and adopted the means upon which realization of its professed aims depends. Liberalism can be true to its ideals only as it takes the course that leads to their attainment. The notion that organized social control of economic forces lies outside the historic path of liberalism shows that liberalism is still impeded by remnants of its earlier *laissez faire* phase, with its opposition of society and the individual. The thing which now dampens liberal ardor and paralyzes its efforts is the conception that liberty and development of individuality as ends exclude the use of organized social effort as means. Earlier liberalism regarded the separate and competing economic action of individuals as the means to social well-being as the end. We must reverse the perspective and see that socialized economy is the means of free individual development as the end.

That liberals are divided in outlook and endeavor while reactionaries are held together by community of interests and the ties of custom is well-nigh a commonplace. Organization of standpoint and belief among liberals can be achieved only in and by unity of endeavor. Organized unity of action attended by consensus of beliefs will come about in the degree in which social control of economic forces is made the goal of liberal action. The greatest educational power, the greatest force in shaping the dispositions and attitudes of individuals, is the social medium in which they live. The medium that now lies closest to us is that of unified action for the inclusive end of a socialized economy. The attainment of a state of society in which a basis of material security will release the powers of individuals for cultural expression is not the work of a day. But by concentrating upon the task of securing a socialized economy as the ground and medium for release of the impulses and capacities men agree to call ideal, the now scattered and often conflicting activities of liberals can be brought to effective unity.

FRANKLIN DELANO ROOSEVELT

Speech at Oglethorpe University (1932)

Franklin Delano Roosevelt (1882–1945) developed an impressive political résumé before becoming president in 1933: New York state senator,

assistant secretary of the navy during World War I, and New York gover-
nor. FDR's political experimentation grew out of a pragmatic approach
to politics that placed actual results above theoretical principles. Even
though he lacked the overarching philosophical framework of the pro-
gressive presidents, his vision of a more active American government re-
sulted in America's approximation of a welfare state. In a commencement
address he delivered at Oglethorpe University, Roosevelt sounded
themes that would recur throughout his presidency. Blaming the na-
tion's economic woes on the lack of planning and foresight by individu-
als in government and business, FDR called for greater controls and
planning in the distribution of industrial products. More generally, he
insisted on the importance of real leadership, immediate action, and
"bold, persistent experimentation."

The year 1928 does not seem far in the past, but since that time, as all of us are aware, the world about us has experienced significant changes. Four years ago, if you heard and believed the tidings of the time, you could expect to take your place in a society well supplied with material things and could look forward to the not too distant time when you would be living in your own homes, each (if you believed the politicians) with a two-car garage; and, without great effort, would be providing yourselves and your families with all the necessities and amenities of life, and perhaps in addition, assure by your savings their security and your own in the future. Indeed, if you were observant, you would have seen that many of your elders had discovered a still easier road to material success. They had found that once they had accumulated a few dollars they needed only to put them in the proper place and then sit back and read in comfort the hieroglyphics called stock quotations which proclaimed that their wealth was mounting miraculously without any work or effort on their part. Many who were called and who are still pleased to call themselves the leaders of finance celebrated and assured us of an eternal future for this easy-chair mode of living. And to the stimulation of belief in this dazzling chimera were lent not only the voices of some of our public men in high office, but their influence and the material aid of the very instruments of Government which they controlled.

How sadly different is the picture which we see around us today! If only the mirage had vanished, we should not complain, for we should all be better off. But with it have vanished, not only the easy gains of speculation, but much of the savings of thrifty and prudent men and women, put by for their old age and for the education of their children. With these savings has gone, among millions of our fellow citizens, that sense of security to which they have rightly felt they are entitled in a land abundantly endowed with natural resources and with productive facilities to convert them into the necessities of life for all of our population. More calamitous still, there has vanished with the expectation of future security the certainty of today's bread and clothing and shelter.

Some of you—I hope not many—are wondering today how and where you will be able to earn your living a few weeks or a few months hence. Much has been written about the hope of youth. I prefer to emphasize another quality. I hope that you who have spent four years in an institution whose fundamental purpose, I take it, is to train us to pursue truths relentlessly and to look at them courageously, will face the unfortunate state of the world about you with greater clarity of vision than many of your elders.

As you have viewed this world of which you are about to become a more active part, I have no doubt that you have been impressed by its chaos, its lack of plan. Perhaps some of you have used stronger language. And stronger language is justified. Even had you been graduating, instead of matriculating, in these rose-colored days of 1928, you would, I believe, have perceived this condition. For beneath all the happy optimism of those days there existed lack of plan and a great waste.

This failure to measure true values and to look ahead extended to almost every industry, every profession, every walk of life. Take, for example, the vocation of higher education itself.

If you had been intending to enter the profession of teaching, you would have found that the universities, the colleges, the normal schools of our country were turning out annually far more trained teachers than the schools of the country could possibly use or absorb. You and I know that the number of teachers needed in the Nation is a relatively stable figure, little affected by the depression and capable of fairly accurate estimate in advance with due consideration for our increase in population. And yet, we have continued to add teaching courses, to accept every young man or young woman in those courses without any thought or regard for the law of supply and demand. In the State of New York alone, for example, there are at least seven thousand qualified teachers who are out of work, unable to earn a livelihood in their chosen profession just because nobody had the wit or the forethought to tell them in their younger days that the profession of teaching was gravely oversupplied.

Take, again, the profession of the law. Our common sense tells us that we have too many lawyers and that thousands of them, thoroughly trained, are either eking out a bare existence or being compelled to work with their hands, or are turning to some other business in order to keep themselves from becoming objects of charity. The universities, the bar, the courts themselves have done little to bring this situation to the knowledge of young men who are considering entering any one of our multitude of law schools. Here again foresight and planning have been notable for their complete absence.

In the same way we cannot review carefully the history of our industrial advance without being struck with its haphazardness, the gigantic waste with which it has been accomplished, the superfluous duplication of productive facilities, the continual scrapping of still useful equipment, the tremendous mortality in industrial and commercial undertakings, the thousands of dead-end trails into which enterprise has been lured, the profligate waste of natural resources. Much of this waste is the inevitable by-product of progress in a society which values individual endeavor and which is susceptible to the changing tastes and customs of the people of which it is composed. But much of it, I believe, could have been prevented by greater foresight and by a larger measure of social planning. Such controlling and directive forces as have been developed in recent years reside to a dangerous degree in groups having special interests in our economic order, interests which do not coincide with the interests of the Nation as a whole. I believe that the recent course of our history has demonstrated that, while we may utilize their expert knowledge of certain problems and the special facilities with which they are familiar, we cannot allow our economic life to be controlled by that small group of men whose chief outlook upon the social welfare is tinctured by the fact that they can make huge profits from the lending of money and the marketing of securities—an outlook which deserves the adjectives "selfish" and "opportunist."

You have been struck, I know, by the tragic irony of our economic situation today. We have not been brought to our present state by any natural calamity—by drought or floods or earthquakes or by the destruction of our productive machine or our man power. Indeed, we have a superabundance of raw materials, a more than ample supply of equipment for manufacturing these materials into the goods which we need, and transportation and commercial facilities for making them available to all who need them. But raw materials stand unused, factories stand idle, railroad traffic continues to dwindle, merchants sell less and less, while millions of able-bodied men and women, in dire need, are clamoring for the opportunity to work. This is the awful paradox with which we are confronted, a stinging rebuke that challenges our power to operate the economic machine which we have created.

We are presented with a multitude of views as to how we may again set into motion that economic machine. Some hold to the theory that the periodic slowing down of our economic machine is one of its inherent peculiarities—a peculiarity which we must grin, if we can, and bear

because if we attempt to tamper with it we shall cause even worse ailments. According to this theory, as I see it, if we grin and bear long
enough, the economic machine will eventually begin to pick up speed
and in the course of an indefinite number of years will again attain that
maximum number of revolutions which signifies what we have been
wont to miscall prosperity, but which, alas, is but a last ostentatious twirl
of the economic machine before it again succumbs to that mysterious
impulse to slow down again. This attitude toward our economic machine
requires not only greater stoicism, but greater faith in immutable economic law and less faith in the ability of man to control what he has created than I, for one, have. Whatever elements of truth lie in it, it is an
invitation to sit back and do nothing; and all of us are suffering today, I
believe, because this comfortable theory was too thoroughly implanted
in the minds of some of our leaders, both in finance and in public affairs.

* * *

Of these other phases [of our problem], that which seems most important to me in the long run is the problem of controlling by adequate planning the creation and distribution of those products which our vast
economic machine is capable of yielding. It is true that capital, whether
public or private, is needed in the creation of new enterprise and that
such capital gives employment.

But think carefully of the vast sums of capital or credit which in the
past decade have been devoted to unjustified enterprises—to the development of unessentials and to the multiplying of many products far
beyond the capacity of the Nation to absorb. It is the same story as the
thoughtless turning out of too many school teachers and too many
lawyers.

Here again, in the field of industry and business many of those whose
primary solicitude is confined to the welfare of what they call capital
have failed to read the lessons of the past few years and have been moved
less by calm analysis of the needs of the Nation as a whole than by a
blind determination to preserve their own special stakes in the economic
order. I do not mean to intimate that we have come to the end of this
period of expansion. We shall continue to need capital for the production
of newly-invented devices, for the replacement of equipment worn out or
rendered obsolete by our technical progress; we need better housing in
many of our cities and we still need in many parts of the country more
good roads, canals, parks and other improvements.

But it seems to me probable that our physical economic plant will not
expand in the future at the same rate at which it has expanded in the
past. We may build more factories, but the fact remains that we have
enough now to supply all of our domestic needs, and more, if they are

used. With these factories we can now make more shoes, more textiles, more steel, more radios, more automobiles, more of almost everything than we can use.

No, our basic trouble was not an insufficiency of capital. It was an insufficient distribution of buying power coupled with an oversufficient speculation in production. While wages rose in many of our industries, they did not as a whole rise proportionately to the reward to capital, and at the same time the purchasing power of other great groups of our population was permitted to shrink. We accumulated such a superabundance of capital that our great bankers were vying with each other, some of them employing questionable methods, in their efforts to lend this capital at home and abroad.

I believe that we are at the threshold of a fundamental change in our popular economic thought, that in the future we are going to think less about the producer and more about the consumer. Do what we may have to do to inject life into our ailing economic order, we cannot make it endure for long unless we can bring about a wiser, more equitable distribution of the national income.

It is well within the inventive capacity of man, who has built up this great social and economic machine capable of satisfying the wants of all, to insure that all who are willing and able to work receive from it at least the necessities of life. In such a system, the reward for a day's work will have to be greater, on the average, than it has been, and the reward to capital, especially capital which is speculative, will have to be less. But I believe that after the experience of the last three years, the average citizen would rather receive a smaller return upon his savings in return for greater security for the principal, than experience for a moment the thrill or the prospect of being a millionaire only to find the next moment that his fortune, actual or expected, has withered in his hand because the economic machine has again broken down.

It is toward that objective that we must move if we are to profit by our recent experiences. Probably few will disagree that the goal is desirable. Yet many, of faint heart, fearful of change, sitting tightly on the roof-tops in the flood, will sternly resist striking out for it, lest they fail to attain it. Even among those who are ready to attempt the journey there will be violent differences of opinion as to how it should be made. So complex, so widely distributed over our whole society are the problems which confront us that men and women of common aim do not agree upon the method of attacking them. Such disagreement leads to doing nothing, to drifting. Agreement may come too late.

Let us not confuse objectives with methods. Too many so-called leaders of the Nation fail to see the forest because of the trees. Too many of them fail to recognize the vital necessity of planning for definite objectives. True leadership calls for the setting forth of the objectives and the rallying of public opinion in support of these objectives.

Do not confuse objectives with methods. When the Nation becomes substantially united in favor of planning the broad objectives of civilization, then true leadership must unite thought behind definite methods.

The country needs and, unless I mistake its temper, the country demands bold, persistent experimentation. It is common sense to take a method and try it: If it fails, admit it frankly and try another. But above all, try something. The millions who are in want will not stand by silently forever while the things to satisfy their needs are within easy reach.

We need enthusiasm, imagination and the ability to face facts, even unpleasant ones, bravely. We need to correct, by drastic means if necessary, the faults in our economic system from which we now suffer. We need the courage of the young.

FRANKLIN DELANO ROOSEVELT

Commonwealth Club Speech (1932)

Like most of Roosevelt's presidential campaign speeches in 1932, his speech in San Francisco to the Commonwealth Club of California was drafted by his aides Adolf Berle and Rexford Guy Tugwell. Since Roosevelt did not have a chance to revise the speech before he actually delivered it, it was uncommonly dour for the usually optimistic New Yorker. Nevertheless, the speech did express Roosevelt's view that genuine statesmanship requires government to play a more active and innovative role in the economy. In contrast to Hoover and his economic individualism, the presidential challenger stressed that business has certain responsibilities to the community since "private economic power" is "a public trust."

I want to speak not of politics but of Government. I want to speak not of parties, but of universal principles. They are not political, except in that larger sense in which a great American once expressed a definition of politics, that nothing in all of human life is foreign to the science of politics. * * *

The issue of Government has always been whether individual men and women will have to serve some system of Government or economics, or whether a system of Government and economics exists to serve individual men and women. This question has persistently dominated the discussion of Government for many generations. On questions relating to these things men have differed, and for time immemorial it is probable that honest men will continue to differ.

The final word belongs to no man; yet we can still believe in change and in progress. Democracy * * * is a quest, a never-ending seeking for better things, and in the seeking for these things and the striving for them, there are many roads to follow. But, if we map the course of these roads, we find that there are only two general directions.

When we look about us, we are likely to forget how hard people have worked to win the privilege of Government. The growth of the national Governments of Europe was a struggle for the development of a centralized force in the Nation, strong enough to impose peace upon ruling barons. In many instances the victory of the central Government, the creation of a strong central Government, was a haven of refuge to the individual. The people preferred the master far away to the exploitation and cruelty of the smaller master near at hand.

But the creators of national Government were perforce ruthless men. They were often cruel in their methods, but they did strive steadily toward something that society needed and very much wanted, a strong central State able to keep the peace, to stamp out civil war, to put the unruly nobleman in his place, and to permit the bulk of individuals to live safely. The man of ruthless force had his place in developing a pioneer country, just as he did in fixing the power of the central Government in the development of Nations. Society paid him well for his services and its development. When the development among the Nations of Europe, however, had been completed, ambition and ruthlessness, having served their term, tended to overstep their mark.

There came a growing feeling that Government was conducted for the benefit of a few who thrived unduly at the expense of all. The people sought a balancing—a limiting force. There came gradually, through town councils, trade guilds, national parliaments, by constitution and by popular participation and control, limitations on arbitrary power.

Another factor that tended to limit the power of those who ruled, was the rise of the ethical conception that a ruler bore a responsibility for the welfare of his subjects.

The American colonies were born in this struggle. The American Revolution was a turning point in it. After the Revolution the struggle continued and shaped itself in the public life of the country. There were those who because they had seen the confusion which attended the years of war for American independence surrendered to the belief that popular Government was essentially dangerous and essentially unworkable. They were honest people, my friends, and we cannot deny that their experience had warranted some measure of fear. The most brilliant, honest and able exponent of this point of view was Hamilton. He was too impatient of slow-moving methods. Fundamentally he believed that the safety of the republic lay in the autocratic strength of its Government, that the destiny of individuals was to serve that Government, and that fundamentally a great and strong group of central institutions, guided by a small group of able and public-spirited citizens, could best direct all Government.

But Mr. Jefferson, in the summer of 1776, after drafting the Declaration of Independence turned his mind to the same problem and took a different view. He did not deceive himself with outward forms. Government to him was means to an end, not an end in itself; it might be either a refuge and a help or a threat and a danger, depending on the circumstances. We find him carefully analyzing the society for which he was to organize a Government. "We have no paupers. The great mass of our population is of laborers, our rich who cannot live without labor, either manual or professional, being few and of moderate wealth. Most of the laboring class possess property, cultivate their own lands, have families and from the demand for their labor, are enabled to exact from the rich and the competent such prices as enable them to feed abundantly, clothe above mere decency, to labor moderately and raise their families."

These people, he considered, had two sets of rights, those of "personal competency" and those involved in acquiring and possessing property. By "personal competency" he meant the right of free thinking, freedom of forming and expressing opinions, and freedom of personal living, each man according to his own lights. To insure the first set of rights, a Government must so order its functions as not to interfere with the individual. But even Jefferson realized that the exercise of the property rights might so interfere with the rights of the individual that the Government, without whose assistance the property rights could not exist, must intervene, not to destroy individualism, but to protect it.

You are familiar with the great political duel which followed; and how Hamilton, and his friends, building toward a dominant centralized power were at length defeated in the great election of 1800, by Mr. Jefferson's party. Out of that duel came the two parties, Republican and Democratic, as we know them today.

So began, in American political life, the new day, the day of the individual against the system, the day in which individualism was made the great watchword of American life. The happiest of economic conditions made that day long and splendid. On the Western frontier, land was substantially free. No one, who did not shirk the task of earning a living, was entirely without opportunity to do so. Depressions could, and did, come and go; but they could not alter the fundamental fact that most of the people lived partly by selling their labor and partly by extracting their livelihood from the soil, so that starvation and dislocation were practically impossible. At the very worst there was always the possibility of climbing into a covered wagon and moving west where the untilled prairies afforded a haven for men to whom the East did not provide a place. So great were our natural resources that we could offer this relief not only to our own people, but to the distressed of all the world; we could invite immigration from Europe, and welcome it with open arms. Traditionally, when a depression came a new section of land was opened in the West; and even our temporary misfortune served our manifest destiny.

It was in the middle of the nineteenth century that a new force was released and a new dream created. The force was what is called the industrial revolution, the advance of steam and machinery and the rise of the forerunners of the modern industrial plant. The dream was the dream of an economic machine, able to raise the standard of living for everyone; to bring luxury within the reach of the humblest; to annihilate distance by steam power and later by electricity, and to release everyone from the drudgery of the heaviest manual toil. It was to be expected that this would necessarily affect Government. Heretofore, Government had merely been called upon to produce conditions within which people could live happily, labor peacefully, and rest secure. Now it was called upon to aid in the consummation of this new dream. There was, however, a shadow over the dream. To be made real, it required use of the talents of men of tremendous will and tremendous ambition, since by no other force could the problems of financing and engineering and new developments be brought to a consummation.

So manifest were the advantages of the machine age, however, that the United States fearlessly, cheerfully, and, I think, rightly, accepted the bitter with the sweet. It was thought that no price was too high to pay for the advantages which we could draw from a finished industrial system. The history of the last half century is accordingly in large measure a history of a group of financial Titans, whose methods were not scrutinized with too much care, and who were honored in proportion as they produced the results, irrespective of the means they used. The financiers who pushed the railroads to the Pacific were always ruthless, often wasteful, and frequently corrupt; but they did build railroads, and we have them today. It has been estimated that the American investor paid for the

American railway system more than three times over in the process; but despite this fact the net advantage was to the United States. As long as we had free land; as long as population was growing by leaps and bounds; as long as our industrial plants were insufficient to supply our own needs, society chose to give the ambitious man free play and unlimited reward provided only that he produced the economic plant so much desired.

During this period of expansion, there was equal opportunity for all and the business of Government was not to interfere but to assist in the development of industry. This was done at the request of business men themselves. The tariff was originally imposed for the purpose of "fostering our infant industry," a phrase I think the older among you will remember as a political issue not so long ago. The railroads were subsidized, sometimes by grants of money, oftener by grants of land; some of the most valuable oil lands in the United States were granted to assist the financing of the railroad which pushed through the Southwest. A nascent merchant marine was assisted by grants of money, or by mail subsidies, so that our steam shipping might ply the seven seas. Some of my friends tell me that they do not want the Government in business. With this I agree; but I wonder whether they realize the implications of the past. For while it has been American doctrine that the Government must not go into business in competition with private enterprises, still it has been traditional, particularly in Republican administrations, for business urgently to ask the Government to put at private disposal all kinds of Government assistance. The same man who tells you that he does not want to see the Government interfere in business—and he means it, and has plenty of good reasons for saying so—is the first to go to Washington and ask the Government for a prohibitory tariff on his product. When things get just bad enough, as they did two years ago, he will go with equal speed to the United States Government and ask for a loan; and the Reconstruction Finance Corporation is the outcome of it. Each group has sought protection from the Government for its own special interests, without realizing that the function of Government must be to favor no small group at the expense of its duty to protect the rights of personal freedom and of private property of all its citizens.

In retrospect we can now see that the turn of the tide came with the turn of the century. We were reaching our last frontier; there was no more free land and our industrial combinations had become great uncontrolled and irresponsible units of power within the State. Clearsighted men saw with fear the danger that opportunity would no longer be equal; that the growing corporation, like the feudal baron of old, might threaten the economic freedom of individuals to earn a living. In that hour, our antitrust laws were born. The cry was raised against the great corporations. Theodore Roosevelt, the first great Republican Progressive, fought a Presidential campaign on the issue of "trust busting" and talked freely about malefactors of great wealth. If the Government had a policy it was rather to turn the clock back, to destroy the large combinations and to return to the time when every man owned his individual small business.

This was impossible; Theodore Roosevelt, abandoning the idea of "trust busting," was forced to work out a difference between "good" trusts and "bad" trusts. The Supreme Court set forth the famous "rule of reason" by which it seems to have meant that a concentration of industrial power was permissible if the method by which it got its power, and the use it made of that power, were reasonable.

Woodrow Wilson, elected in 1912, saw the situation more clearly. Where Jefferson had feared the encroachment of political power on the lives of individuals, Wilson knew that the new power was financial. He saw, in the highly centralized economic system, the despot of the twentieth century, on whom great masses of individuals relied for their safety and their livelihood, and whose irresponsibility and greed (if they were not controlled) would reduce them to starvation and penury. The concentration of financial power had not proceeded so far in 1912 as it has today; but it had grown far enough for Mr. Wilson to realize fully its implications. * * *

A glance at the situation today only too clearly indicates that equality of opportunity as we have known it no longer exists. Our industrial plant is built; the problem just now is whether under existing conditions it is not overbuilt. Our last frontier has long since been reached, and there is practically no more free land. More than half of our people do not live on the farms or on lands and cannot derive a living by cultivating their own property. There is no safety valve in the form of a Western prairie to which those thrown out of work by the Eastern economic machines can go for a new start. We are not able to invite the immigration from Europe to share our endless plenty. We are now providing a drab living for our own people.

* * *

Just as freedom to farm has ceased, so also the opportunity in business has narrowed. It still is true that men can start small enterprises, trusting to native shrewdness and ability to keep abreast of competitors; but area after area has been preempted altogether by the great corporations, and even in the fields which still have no great concerns, the small man starts under a handicap. The unfeeling statistics of the past three decades show that the independent business man is running a losing race. Perhaps he is forced to the wall; perhaps he cannot command credit; perhaps he is "squeezed out," in Mr. Wilson's words, by highly organized corporate competitors, as your corner grocery man can tell you. Recently a careful study was made of the concentration of business in the United States. It showed that our economic life was dominated by some six hundred odd corporations who controlled two-thirds of American industry. Ten million small business men divided the other third. More striking still, it appeared that if the process of concentration goes on at the same rate, at the end of another century we shall have all American industry controlled by a dozen corporations, and run by perhaps a hundred men. Put plainly, we are steering a steady course toward economic oligarchy, if we are not there already.

Clearly, all this calls for a re-appraisal of values. A mere builder of more industrial plants, a creator of more railroad systems, an organizer of more corporations, is as likely to be a danger as a help. The day of the great promoter or the financial Titan, to whom we granted anything if only he would build, or develop, is over. Our task now is not discovery or exploitation of natural resources, or necessarily producing more goods. It is the soberer, less dramatic business of administering resources and plants already in hand, of seeking to reestablish foreign markets for our surplus production, of meeting the problem of underconsumption, of adjusting production to consumption, of distributing wealth and products more equitably, of adapting existing economic organizations to the service of the people. The day of enlightened administration has come.

Just as in older times the central Government was first a haven of refuge, and then a threat, so now in a closer economic system the central and ambitious financial unit is no longer a servant of national desire, but a danger. I would draw the parallel one step farther. We did not think because national Government had become a threat in the 18th century that therefore we should abandon the principle of national Government. Nor today should we abandon the principle of strong economic units called corporations, merely because their power is susceptible of easy abuse. In other times we dealt with the problem of an unduly ambitious central Government by modifying it gradually into a constitutional democratic Government. So today we are modifying and controlling our economic units.

As I see it, the task of Government in its relation to business is to assist the development of an economic declaration of rights, an economic constitutional order. This is the common task of statesman and business man. It is the minimum requirement of a more permanently safe order of things.

Happily, the times indicate that to create such an order not only is the proper policy of Government, but it is the only line of safety for our economic structures as well. We know, now, that these economic units cannot exist unless prosperity is uniform, that is, unless purchasing power is well distributed throughout every group in the Nation. That is why even the most selfish of corporations for its own interest would be glad to see wages restored and unemployment ended and to bring the Western farmer back to his accustomed level of prosperity and to assure a permanent safety to both groups. That is why some enlightened industries themselves endeavor to limit the freedom of action of each man and business group within the industry in the common interest of all; why business men everywhere are asking a form of organization which will bring the scheme of things into balance, even though it may in some measure qualify the freedom of action of individual units within the business.

The exposition need not further be elaborated. It is brief and incomplete, but you will be able to expand it in terms of your own business or occupation without difficulty. I think everyone who has actually entered the economic struggle—which means everyone who was not born to safe wealth—knows in his own experience and his own life that we have now to apply the earlier concepts of American Government to the conditions of today.

The Declaration of Independence discusses the problem of Government in terms of a contract. Government is a relation of give and take, a contract, perforce, if we would follow the thinking out of which it grew. Under such a contract rulers were accorded power, and the people consented to that power on consideration that they be accorded certain rights. The task of statesmanship has always been the re-definition of these rights in terms of a changing and growing social order. New conditions impose new requirements upon Government and those who conduct Government.

* * *

I feel that we are coming to a view through the drift of our legislation and our public thinking in the past quarter century that private economic power is, to enlarge an old phrase, a public trust as well. I hold that continued enjoyment of that power by any individual or group must depend upon the fulfillment of that trust. The men who have reached the summit of American business life know this best; happily, many of these urge the binding quality of this greater social contract.

The terms of that contract are as old as the Republic, and as new as the new economic order.

Every man has a right to life; and this means that he has also a right to make a comfortable living. He may by sloth or crime decline to exercise that right; but it may not be denied him. We have no actual famine or dearth; our industrial and agricultural mechanism can produce enough and to spare. Our Government formal and informal, political and economic, owes to everyone an avenue to possess himself of a portion of that plenty sufficient for his needs, through his own work.

Every man has a right to his own property; which means a right to be assured, to the fullest extent attainable, in the safety of his savings. By no other means can men carry the burdens of those parts of life which, in the nature of things, afford no chance of labor; childhood, sickness, old age. In all thought of property this right is paramount; all other property rights must yield to it. If, in accord with this principle, we must restrict the operations of the speculator, the manipulator, even the financier, I believe we must accept the restriction as needful, not to hamper individualism but to protect it.

These two requirements must be satisfied, in the main, by the individuals who claim and hold control of the great industrial and financial combinations which dominate so large a part of our industrial life. They have undertaken to be, not business men, but princes of property. I am not prepared to say that the system which produces them is wrong. I am very clear that they must fearlessly and competently assume the responsibility which goes with the power. So many enlightened business men know this that the statement would be little more than a platitude, were it not for an added implication.

This implication is, briefly, that the responsible heads of finance and industry instead of acting each for himself, must work together to achieve the common end. They must, where necessary, sacrifice this or that private advantage; and in reciprocal self-denial must seek a general advantage. It is here that formal Government—political Government, if you chose—comes in. Whenever in the pursuit of this objective the lone wolf, the unethical competitor, the reckless promoter, the Ishmael or Insull whose hand is against every man's, declines to join in achieving an end recognized as being for the public welfare, and threatens to drag the industry back to a state of anarchy, the Government may properly be asked to apply restraint. Likewise, should the group ever use its collective power contrary to the public welfare, the Government must be swift to enter and protect the public interest.

The Government should assume the function of economic regulation only as a last resort, to be tried only when private initiative, inspired by high responsibility, with such assistance and balance as Government can give, has finally failed. As yet there has been no final failure, because there has been no attempt; and I decline to assume that this Nation is unable to meet the situation.

The final term of the high contract was for liberty and the pursuit of happiness. We have learned a great deal of both in the past century. We know that individual liberty and individual happiness mean nothing unless both are ordered in the sense that one man's meat is not another man's poison. We know that the old "rights of personal competency," the right to read, to think, to speak, to choose and live a mode of life, must be respected at all hazards. We know that liberty to do anything which deprives others of those elemental rights is outside the protection of any compact; and that Government in this regard is the maintenance of a balance, within which every individual may have a place if he will take it; in which every individual may find safety if he wishes it; in which every individual may attain such power as his ability permits, consistent with his assuming the accompanying responsibility.

All this is a long, slow talk. Nothing is more striking than the simple innocence of the men who insist, whenever an objective is present, on the prompt production of a patent scheme guaranteed to produce a result. Human endeavor is not so simple as that. Government includes the art of formulating a policy, and using the political technique to attain so much of that policy as will receive general support; persuading, leading, sacrificing, teaching always, because the greatest duty of a statesman is to educate. But in the matters of which I have spoken we are learning rapidly, in a severe school. The lessons so learned must not be forgotten, even in the mental lethargy of a speculative upturn. We must build toward the time when a major depression cannot occur again; and if this means sacrificing the easy profits of inflationist booms, then let them go; and good riddance.

Faith in America, faith in our tradition of personal responsibility, faith in our institutions, faith in ourselves demand that we recognize the new terms of the old social contract. We shall fulfill them, as we fulfilled the obligation of the apparent Utopia which Jefferson imagined for us in 1776, and which Jefferson, Roosevelt and Wilson sought to bring to realization. We must do so, lest a rising tide of misery, engendered by our common failure, engulf us all. But failure is not an American habit; and in the strength of great hope we must all shoulder our common load.

FRANKLIN DELANO ROOSEVELT

First Inaugural Address (1933)

Unlike most of his presidential campaign speeches, Roosevelt drafted his first inaugural himself. The most memorable line in the speech, "the only thing we have to fear is fear itself," was likely inspired by Henry

David Thoreau's remark that "Nothing is so much to be feared as fear,"
which Roosevelt had came across only a few days before the inaugura-
tion. The address, which was broadcast live on radio, expressed the new
president's optimistic vision for the future and his promise of action and
bold leadership in dealing with the nation's economic crisis.

I am certain that my fellow Americans expect that on my induction into
the Presidency I will address them with a candor and a decision which
the present situation of our Nation impels. This is preeminently the time
to speak the truth, the whole truth, frankly and boldly. Nor need we
shrink from honestly facing conditions in our country today. This great
Nation will endure as it has endured, will revive and will prosper. So, first
of all, let me assert my firm belief that the only thing we have to fear is
fear itself—nameless, unreasoning, unjustified terror which paralyzes
needed efforts to convert retreat into advance. In every dark hour of our
national life a leadership of frankness and vigor has met with that understanding and support of the people themselves which is essential to victory. I am convinced that you will again give that support to leadership in
these critical days.

In such a spirit on my part and on yours we face our common difficulties. They concern, thank God, only material things. Values have shrunken
to fantastic levels; taxes have risen; our ability to pay has fallen; government of all kinds is faced by serious curtailment of income; the means of
exchange are frozen in the currents of trade; the withered leaves of industrial enterprise lie on every side; farmers find no markets for their produce; the savings of many years in thousands of families are gone.

More important, a host of unemployed citizens face the grim problem
of existence, and an equally great number toil with little return. Only a
foolish optimist can deny the dark realities of the moment.

Yet our distress comes from no failure of substance. We are stricken by
no plague of locusts. Compared with the perils which our forefathers
conquered because they believed and were not afraid, we have still much
to be thankful for. Nature still offers her bounty and human efforts have
multiplied it. Plenty is at our doorstep, but a generous use of it languishes
in the very sight of the supply. Primarily this is because rulers of the exchange of mankind's goods have failed through their own stubbornness
and their own incompetence, have admitted their failure, and have abdicated. Practices of the unscrupulous money changers stand indicted in
the court of public opinion, rejected by the hearts and minds of men.

True they have tried, but their efforts have been cast in the pattern of
an outworn tradition. Faced by failure of credit they have proposed only
the lending of more money. Stripped of the lure of profit by which to

induce our people to follow their false leadership, they have resorted to exhortations, pleading tearfully for restored confidence. They know only the rules of a generation of self-seekers. They have no vision, and when there is no vision the people perish.

The money changers have fled from their high seats in the temple of our civilization. We may now restore that temple to the ancient truths. The measure of the restoration lies in the extent to which we apply social values more noble than mere monetary profit.

Happiness lies not in the mere possession of money; it lies in the joy of achievement, in the thrill of creative effort. The joy and moral stimulation of work no longer must be forgotten in the mad chase of evanescent profits. These dark days will be worth all they cost us if they teach us that our true destiny is not to be ministered unto but to minister to ourselves and to our fellow men.

Recognition of the falsity of material wealth as the standard of success goes hand in hand with the abandonment of the false belief that public office and high political position are to be valued only by the standards of pride of place and personal profit; and there must be an end to a conduct in banking and in business which too often has given to a sacred trust the likeness of callous and selfish wrongdoing. Small wonder that confidence languishes, for it thrives only on honesty, on honor, on the sacredness of obligations, on faithful protection, on unselfish performance; without them it cannot live.

Restoration calls, however, not for changes in ethics alone. This Nation asks for action, and action now.

Our greatest primary task is to put people to work. This is no unsolvable problem if we face it wisely and courageously. It can be accomplished in part by direct recruiting by the government itself, treating the task as we would treat the emergency of a war, but at the same time, through this employment, accomplishing greatly needed projects to stimulate and reorganize the use of our natural resources.

Hand in hand with this we must frankly recognize the overbalance of population in our industrial centers and, by engaging on a national scale in a redistribution, endeavor to provide a better use of the land for those best fitted for the land. The task can be helped by definite efforts to raise the values of agricultural products and with this the power to purchase the output of our cities. It can be helped by preventing realistically the tragedy of the growing loss through foreclosure of our small homes and our farms. It can be helped by insistence that the Federal, State, and local governments act forthwith on the demand that their cost be drastically reduced. It can be helped by the unifying of relief activities which today are often scattered, uneconomical, and unequal. It can be helped by national planning for and supervision of all forms of transportation and of communications and other utilities which have a definitely public character. There are many ways in which it can be helped, but it can never be helped merely by talking about it. We must act and act quickly.

Finally, in our progress toward a resumption of work we require two safeguards against a return of the evils of the old order: there must be a strict supervision of all banking and credits and investments, so that there will be an end to speculation with other people's money; and there must be provision for an adequate but sound currency.

These are the lines of attack. I shall presently urge upon a new Congress, in special session, detailed measures for their fulfillment, and I shall seek the immediate assistance of the several States.

Through this program of action we address ourselves to putting our own national house in order and making income balance outgo. Our international trade relations, though vastly important, are in point of time and necessity secondary to the establishment of a sound national economy. I favor as a practical policy the putting of first things first. I shall spare no effort to restore world trade by international economic readjustment, but the emergency at home cannot wait on that accomplishment.

The basic thought that guides these specific means of national recovery is not narrowly nationalistic. It is the insistence, as a first consideration, upon the interdependence of the various elements in and parts of the United States—a recognition of the old and permanently important manifestation of the American spirit of the pioneer. It is the way to recovery. It is the immediate way. It is the strongest assurance that the recovery will endure.

In the field of world policy I would dedicate this Nation to the policy of the good neighbor—the neighbor who resolutely respects himself and, because he does so, respects the rights of others—the neighbor who respects his obligations and respects the sanctity of his agreements in and with a world of neighbors.

If I read the temper of our people correctly, we now realize as we have never realized before our interdependence on each other; that we cannot merely take but we must give as well; that if we are to go forward, we must move as a trained and loyal army willing to sacrifice for the good of a common discipline, because without such discipline no progress is made, no leadership becomes effective. We are, I know, ready and willing to submit our lives and property to such discipline, because it makes possible a leadership which aims at a larger good. This I propose to offer, pledging that the larger purposes will bind upon us all as a sacred obligation with a unity of duty hitherto evoked only in time of armed strife.

With this pledge taken, I assume unhesitatingly the leadership of this great army of our people dedicated to a disciplined attack upon our common problems.

Action in this image and to this end is feasible under the form of government which we have inherited from our ancestors. Our Constitution is so simple and practical that it is possible always to meet extraordinary needs by changes in emphasis and arrangement without loss of essential form. That is why our constitutional system has proved itself the most superbly enduring political mechanism the modern world has produced. It has met every stress of vast expansion of territory, of foreign wars, of bitter internal strife, of world relations.

It is to be hoped that the normal balance of Executive and legislative authority may be wholly adequate to meet the unprecedented task before us. But it may be that an unprecedented demand and need for undelayed action may call for temporary departure from that normal balance of public procedure.

I am prepared under my constitutional duty to recommend the measures that a stricken Nation in the midst of a stricken world may require. These measures, or such other measures as the Congress may build out of its experience and wisdom, I shall seek, within my constitutional authority, to bring to speedy adoption.

But in the event that the Congress shall fail to take one of these two courses, and in the event that the national emergency is still critical, I shall not evade the clear course of duty that will then confront me. I shall ask the Congress for the one remaining instrument to meet the crisis— broad Executive power to wage a war against the emergency, as great as the power that would be given to me if we were in fact invaded by a foreign foe.

For the trust reposed in me I will return the courage and the devotion that befit the time. I can do no less.

We face the arduous days that lie before us in the warm courage of national unity; with the clear consciousness of seeking old and precious moral values; with the clean satisfaction that comes from the stern performance of duty by old and young alike. We aim at the assurance of a rounded and permanent national life.

We do not distrust the future of essential democracy. The people of the United States have not failed. In their need they have registered a mandate that they want direct, vigorous action. They have asked for discipline and direction under leadership. They have made me the present instrument of their wishes. In the spirit of the gift, I take it.

In this dedication of a Nation we humbly ask the blessing of God. May He protect each and every one of us. May He guide me in the days to come.

FRANKLIN DELANO ROOSEVELT

Annual Message to Congress (1936)

Roosevelt's annual message to Congress in January 1936 was a harsh indictment of businessmen who, he argued, pursued their own interests at the expense of the public interest. FDR likened the economic domination of special interests in America to that of the autocrats who threatened peace throughout the world.

Within democratic nations the chief concern of the people is to prevent the continuation or the rise of autocratic institutions that beget slavery at home and aggression abroad. Within our borders, as in the world at large, popular opinion is at war with a power-seeking minority.

This is no new thing. It was fought out in the Constitutional Convention of 1787. From time to time since then the battle has been continued, under Thomas Jefferson, Andrew Jackson, Theodore Roosevelt and Woodrow Wilson.

In these latter years we have witnessed the domination of government by financial and industrial groups, numerically small but politically dominant in the twelve years that succeeded the World War. The present group of which I speak is indeed numerically small and, while it exercises a large influence and has much to say in the world of business, it does not, I am confident, speak the true sentiments of the less articulate, but more important elements that constitute real American business.

In March, 1933, I appealed to the Congress and to the people * * * in a new effort to restore power to those to whom it rightfully belonged. The response to that appeal resulted in the writing of a new chapter in the history of popular government. You, the members of the legislative branch, and I, the Executive, contended for an established new relationship between government and people.

What were the terms of that new relationship? They were an appeal from the clamor of many private and selfish interests, yes, an appeal from the clamor of partisan interest, to the ideal of public interest. Government became the representative and the trustee of the public interest. Our aim was to build upon essentially democratic institutions, seeking all the while the adjustment of burdens, the help of the needy, the protection of the weak, the liberation of the exploited and the genuine protection of the people's property.

It goes without saying that to create such an economic constitutional order more than a single legislative enactment was called for. We had to build, you in the Congress and I, as the Executive, upon a broad base. Now, after thirty-four months of work, we contemplate a fairly rounded whole. We have returned the control of the Federal Government to the city of Washington.

To be sure, in so doing, we have invited battle. We have earned the hatred of entrenched greed. The very nature of the problem that we faced made it necessary to drive some people from power and strictly to regulate others. I made that plain when I took the oath of office in March, 1933. I spoke of the practices of the unscrupulous money-changers who stood indicted in the court of public opinion. I spoke of the rulers of the exchanges of mankind's goods, who failed through their own stubbornness and their own incompetence. I said that they had admitted their failure and had abdicated.

Abdicated? Yes, in 1933, but now with the passing of danger they forget their damaging admissions and withdraw their abdication.

They seek the restoration of their selfish power. They offer to lead us back round the same old corner into the same old dreary street.

Yes, there are still determined groups that are intent upon that very thing. Rigorously held up to popular examination, their true character reveals itself. They steal the livery of great national constitutional ideals to serve discredited special interests. As guardians and trustees for great groups of individual stockholders, they wrongfully seek to carry the property and the interest entrusted to them into the arena of partisan politics. They seek—this minority in business and industry—to control and often do control and use for their own purposes legitimate and highly honored business associations; they engage in vast propaganda to spread fear and discord among the people—they would 'gang up' against the people's liberties.

The principle that they would instill into government if they succeed in seizing power is well shown by the principles which many of them have instilled into their own affairs: Autocracy toward labor, toward stockholders, toward consumers, toward public sentiment. Autocrats in smaller things, they seek autocracy in bigger things. 'By their fruits ye shall know them.'

If these gentlemen believe, as they say they believe, that the measures adopted by this Congress and its predecessor, and carried out by this administration, have hindered rather than promoted recovery, let them be consistent. Let them propose to this Congress the complete repeal of these measures. The way is open to such a proposal.

Let action be positive and not negative. The way is open in the Congress of the United States for an expression of opinion by yeas and nays. Shall we say that values are restored and that the Congress will, therefore, repeal the laws under which we have been bringing them back? Shall we say that because national income has grown with rising prosperity, we shall repeal existing taxes and thereby put off the day of approaching a balanced budget and of starting to reduce the national debt? Shall we abandon the reasonable support and regulation of banking? Shall we restore the dollar to its former gold content?

Shall we say to the farmer—'The prices for your products are in part restored, now go and hoe your own row'?

Shall we say to the home owners—'We have reduced your rates of interest. We have no further concern with how you keep your home or what you pay for your money. That is your affair'?

Shall we say to the several millions of unemployed citizens who face the very problem of existence—yes, of getting enough to eat—'We will withdraw from giving you work we will turn you back to the charity of your communities and to those men of selfish power who tell you that perhaps they will employ you if the government leaves them strictly alone'?

Shall we say to the needy unemployed—'Your problem is a local one except that perhaps the Federal Government, as an act of mere generosity, will be willing to pay to your city or to your county a few grudging dollars to help maintain your soup kitchens'? * * *

We have been specific in our affirmative action. Let them be specific in their negative attack.

But the challenge faced by this Congress is more menacing than merely a return to the past—bad as that would be. Our resplendent economic autocracy does not want to return to that individualism of which they prate, even though the advantages under that system went to the ruthless and the strong. They realize that in thirty-four months we have built up new instruments of public power. In the hands of a people's government this power is wholesome and proper. But in the hands of political puppets of an economic autocracy such power would provide shackles for the liberties of the people. Give them their way and they will take the course of every autocracy of the past—power for themselves, enslavement for the public.

Their weapon is the weapon of fear. I have said—'The only thing we have to fear is fear itself,' and that is as true today as it was in 1933. But such fear as they instill today is not natural fear, a normal fear; it is a synthetic, manufactured, poisonous fear that is being spread subtly, expensively and cleverly by the same people who cried in those other days—'Save us, save us, else we perish.' * * *

In the light of our substantial material progress, in the light of the increasing effectiveness of the restoration of popular rule, I recommend to the Congress that we advance and that we do not retreat.

FRANKLIN DELANO ROOSEVELT

The Four Freedoms (1941)

In his annual address to Congress in 1941, FDR stated the aspirations and objectives of American foreign policy in the face of grave threats to democracy and freedom around the world. He looked forward "to a world founded upon four essential human freedoms."

I address you, the Members of the Seventy-seventh Congress, at a moment unprecedented in the history of the Union. I use the word 'unprecedented,' because at no previous time has American security been as seriously threatened from without as it is today.

Since the permanent formation of our Government under the Constitution, in 1789, most of the periods of crisis in our history have related to our domestic affairs. Fortunately, only one of these—the four-year War Between the States—ever threatened our national unity. Today, thank God, one hundred and thirty million Americans, in forty-eight States, have forgotten points of the compass in our national unity. * * *

Every realist knows that the democratic way of life is at this moment being directly assailed in every part of the world—assailed either by arms, or by secret spreading of poisonous propaganda by those who seek to destroy unity and promote discord in nations that are still at peace.

During sixteen long months this assault has blotted out the whole pattern of democratic life in an appalling number of independent nations, great and small. The assailants are still on the march, threatening other nations, great and small. * * *

Armed defense of democratic existence is now being gallantly waged in four continents. If that defense fails, all the population and all the resources of Europe, Asia, Africa and Australasia will be dominated by the conquerors. * * *

No realistic American can expect from a dictator's peace international generosity, or return of true independence, or world disarmament, or freedom of expression, or freedom of religion—or even good business. * * *

Just as our national policy in internal affairs has been based upon a decent respect for the rights and the dignity of all our fellow men within our gates, so our national policy in foreign affairs has been based on a decent respect for the rights and dignity of all nations, large and small. And the justice of morality must and will win in the end.

Our national policy is this:

First, by an impressive expression of the public will and without regard to partisanship, we are committed to all-inclusive national defense.

Second, by an impressive expression of the public will and without regard to partisanship, we are committed to full support of all those resolute peoples, everywhere, who are resisting aggression and are thereby keeping war away from our Hemisphere. By this support, we express our determination that the democratic cause shall prevail; and we strengthen the defense and the security of our own nation.

Third, by an impressive expression of the public will and without regard to partisanship, we are committed to the proposition that principles of morality and considerations for our own security will never permit us to acquiesce in a peace dictated by aggressors and sponsored by appeasers. We know that enduring peace cannot be bought at the cost of other people's freedom. * * *

In fulfillment of this purpose we will not be intimidated by the threats of dictators that they will regard as a breach of international law or as an act of war our aid to the democracies which dare to resist their aggression. Such aid is not an act of war, even if a dictator should unilaterally proclaim it so to be. * * *

The happiness of future generations of Americans may well depend upon how effective and how immediate we can make our aid felt. No one can tell the exact character of the emergency situations that we may be called upon to meet. The Nation's hands must not be tied when the Nation's life is in danger.

We must all prepare to make the sacrifices that the emergency— almost as serious as war itself—demands. Whatever stands in the way of speed and efficiency in defense preparations must give way to the national need. * * *

As men do not live by bread alone, they do not fight by armaments alone. Those who man our defenses, and those behind them who build our defenses, must have the stamina and the courage which come from unshakable belief in the manner of life which they are defending. The mighty action that we are calling for cannot be based on a disregard of all things worth fighting for.

The Nation takes great satisfaction and much strength from the things which have been done to make its people conscious of their individual stake in the preservation of democratic life in America. Those things have toughened the fibre of our people, have renewed their faith and strengthened their devotion to the institutions we make ready to protect.

Certainly this is no time for any of us to stop thinking about the social and economic problems which are the root cause of the social revolution which is today a supreme factor in the world.

For there is nothing mysterious about the foundations of a healthy and strong democracy. The basic things expected by our people of their political and economic systems are simple. They are:

Equality of opportunity for youth and for others.

Jobs for those who can work.

Security for those who need it.

The ending of special privilege for the few.

The preservation of civil liberties for all.

The enjoyment of the fruits of scientific progress in a wider and constantly rising standard of living. * * *

Many subjects connected with our social economy call for immediate improvement.

As examples:

We should bring more citizens under the coverage of old-age pensions and unemployment insurance.

We should widen the opportunities for adequate medical care.

We should plan a better system by which persons deserving or needing gainful employment may obtain it. * * *

In the future days, which we seek to make secure, we look forward to a world founded upon four essential human freedoms.

The first is freedom of speech and expression—everywhere in the world.

The second is freedom of every person to worship God in his own way—everywhere in the world.

The third is freedom from want—which, translated into world terms, means economic understandings which will secure to every nation a healthy peacetime life for its inhabitants—everywhere in the world.

The fourth is freedom from fear—which, translated into world terms, means a world-wide reduction of armaments to such a point and in such a thorough fashion that no nation will be in a position to commit an act of physical aggression against any neighbor—anywhere in the world.

That is no vision of a distant millennium. It is a definite basis for a kind of world attainable in our own time and generation. That kind of world is the very antithesis of the so-called new order of tyranny which the dictators seek to create with the crash of a bomb. * * *

Since the beginning of our American history we have been engaged in change, in a perpetual, peaceful revolution, a revolution which goes on steadily, quietly, adjusting itself to changing conditions without the concentration camp or the quick-lime in the ditch. The world order which we seek is the co-operation of free countries, working together in a friendly, civilized society.

This nation has placed its destiny in the hands, heads and hearts of its millions of free men and women, and its faith in freedom under the guidance of God. Freedom means the supremacy of human rights everywhere. Our support goes to those who struggle to gain those rights and keep them. Our strength is in our unity of purpose.

To that high concept there can be no end save victory.

FRANKLIN DELANO ROOSEVELT

A Second Bill of Rights (1944)

In his January 11, 1944, State of the Union message to Congress, Roosevelt reflected on the importance of economic security and independence to "true individual freedom." He described "a second Bill of Rights," a set of "self-evident" economic rights.

This Republic had its beginning, and grew to its present strength, under the protection of certain inalienable political rights—among them the right of free speech, free press, free worship, trial by jury, freedom from unreasonable searches and seizures. They were our rights to life and liberty.

As our Nation has grown in size and stature, however—as our industrial economy expanded—these political rights proved inadequate to assure us equality in the pursuit of happiness.

We have come to a dear realization of the fact that true individual freedom cannot exist without economic security and independence. 'Necessitous men are not free men.' People who are hungry and out of a job are the stuff of which dictatorships are made.

In our day these economic truths have become accepted as self-evident. We have accepted, so to speak, a second Bill of Rights under which a new basis of security and prosperity can be established for all—regardless of station, race, or creed. Among these are:

The right to a useful and remunerative job in the industries or ships or farms or mines of the Nation:

The right to earn enough to provide adequate food and clothing and recreation:

The right of every farmer to raise and sell his products at a return which will give him and his family a decent living:

The right of every businessman, large and small, to trade in an atmosphere of freedom from unfair competition and domination by monopolies at home or abroad:

The right of every family to a decent home:

The right to adequate medical care and the opportunity to achieve and enjoy good health;

The right to adequate protection from the economic fears of old age, sickness, accident, and unemployment:

The right to a good education.

All of these rights spell security. And after this war is won we must be prepared to move forward, in the implementation of these rights, to new goals of human happiness and well-being.

R. G. TUGWELL

The Principle of Planning and the Institution of Laissez Faire (1932)

A member of Roosevelt's Brain Trust, the Columbia University economist Rexford Guy Tugwell (1891–1979) was a campaign adviser during the 1932 presidential election and helped formulate important New Deal policies as assistant secretary and then undersecretary of agriculture in Roosevelt's first administration. The most radical of the intellectuals Roosevelt brought to Washington, Tugwell was a strong advocate of central planning by government. In this 1932 American Economic

Review article, he argued that "order and reason are superior to adventuresome competition."

There can be no secure peace in the world so long as its peoples are divided among absolute sovereignties. The divergencies of purpose among them will always cause irritations which sometimes must fail to stop short of the ultimate compromise of war. Sovereign nationalities function in a wider field than industries do; there is, for all that, a useful analogy between them. For industry is also organized in independent units which possess many of the attributes of nations. They have a purpose which they pursue with zeal and foresight; they may pursue it in all essentials, and provided they can reach agreement quietly among themselves, with no governance save of their own making. These purposes, being exclusive and single minded, and being carried out at the expense of competitors, frequently involve recourse to ultimate measures. These begin in the subtle fashions of diplomacy but often end in appeals to force. All this is of the essence of laissez faire.

War in industry is just as ruinous as war among nations; and equally strenuous measures are taken to prevent it. The difficulty in the one case is precisely the difficulty in the other; so long as nations and industries are organized for conflict, wars will follow, and no elaboration of machinery for compromise will be altogether successful. There are vast, well-meaning endeavors being made in both fields which must necessarily be wasted. The disasters of recent years have caused us to ask again how the ancient paradox of business—conflict to produce order—can be resolved; the interest of the liberals among us in the institutions of the new Russia of the Soviets, spreading gradually among puzzled business men, has created wide popular interest in "planning" as a possible refuge from persistent insecurity; by many people it is now regarded as a kind of economic Geneva where all sorts of compromises may be had and where peace and prosperity may be insured.

* * *

* * *[I]t would certainly be one of the characteristics of any planned economy that the few who fare so well as things are now, would be required to give up nearly all the exclusive perquisites they have come to consider theirs of right, and that these should be in some sense socialized. In a romantic, risky, adventurous economy the business of managing industry can be treated as a game; the spoils can be thought of as belonging to the victor as spoils have always belonged to victors. But a mature and rational economy which considered its purposes and sought reasonable ways to attain them would certainly not present many of the characteristics of the present—its violent contrasts of well-being, its irrational allotments of individual liberty, its unconsidered exploitation of human and natural resources. It is better that these things be recognized early rather than late.

National planning can be thought of—in a technical rather than a political sense—merely as normal extension and development of the kind of planning which is a familiar feature of contemporary business. It is not as a technical problem that the idea gives us pause; it is that the implications for other institutions, which we may suddenly see too late, are likely to cause us finally to hesitate and to turn aside from the severe logic of events. * * *

It is impossible to pursue a discussion of planning beyond the most elementary considerations without raising the question of motive. Most economists, even today, believe that Adam Smith laid his finger on a profound truth when he said that not benevolent feelings but rather self-interest actuated the butchers and bakers of this world; most of them believe, furthermore, that this self-interestedness requires an economy in which profit is the reward for characteristic virtue and lack of it the penalty of sin. This belief must appear, from even an amateurish contact with modern psychology, to be so obviously an instance of wishful borrowing, as to give its persistence something of a stubborn and determined air. For persons with the usual intellectual contacts of our time to go on harboring these views, there has to be some violent rationalization. Surely they must be aware of the growing average size of our industrial organizations; and from this it is a simple conclusion that fewer persons all the time are profit-receivers in any direct sense. Surely they must be aware of the growing separation of ownership and control; and from this it seems a fairly simple inference that since profits go only to owners, control is effectively separated from its assumed motive. As a matter of fact, how many railway men, steel workers, or even central office employees, have any stake in company earnings? We know that there are almost none; and that this is true from workman to superintendent in most industries. Yet in defiance of such well-known and obviously relevant facts we go on treating motives quite as though our knowledge of men and of industry had been derived from a few eigteenth century books rather than from any contemporary knowledge of the world and of men. The truth is that if industry could not run without this incentive it would have stopped running long ago.

It is even arguable that profits, instead of furnishing an indispensable actuating principle, tend to inject into industry many of those elements of uncertainty which we as economists unanimously deplore. For, being at the disposal of directorates largely divorced from productive operations, they are set aside as surplus reserves. These are intended as dividend insurance, though the intention may not result in accomplishment. But at the same time, they clearly produce insecurity everywhere else. They are optimistically used for creating overcapacity in every profitable line; they are injected into money market operations in such ways as to contribute to inflation; they are used, most absurdly of all, as investments in the securities of other industries.

If profits are really the actuating motive in modern enterprise, why is it that so great a proportion of them go to those who have no share in the control of operations; and why is it that industry continues to run even when those who run it have no major stake in its gains? But, most important of all, if profits are so important to our system, why do we allow them to be used in such ways as not only to destroy the source of future earnings, but to create unemployment and hardship amongst millions of people whose only contact with them in any form has been through reading about them in the newspapers?

It is clear that this institution does not, in any real sense, actuate our productive equipment. Furthermore its malign influence is reasonably obvious. Why is it, then, that we protect and argue for it with a violence and persistence out of all proportion to the gains we may expect? Because, it seems to me, we are not genuinely interested in security, order, or rationality. Profits, in the sense in which we use the term, belong to a speculative age, one in which huge gambles are taken, and in which the rewards for success may be outstanding. When we speak of them as motives, we do not mean that the hope of making 4 per cent induces us to undertake an operation; we mean that we hope for some fabulous story-book success. These vast gambling operations are closer to the spirit of American business even yet, with all the hard lessons we have had, than are the contrasting ideas which have to do with constructive restraint and social control. In fact our business men have only a rudimentary conception of industry as a social function, as carrying a heavy responsibility of provision. Industry is thought of rather as a field for adventure, in which the creation of goods is a minor matter. Who among our millions of Wall Street amateurs hopes merely for dividends on his investment? Or who thinks of the securities he buys and sells as having anything to do with an economic function?

The truth is that profits persuade us to speculate; they induce us to allocate funds where we believe the future price situation will be favorable; they therefore have a considerable effect on the distribution of capital among various enterprises—an effect which seems clearly enough inefficient so that other methods might easily be better; but they have little effect in actually inducing or in supporting productive enterprises. All this appears merely from examination of the evidence available to us as economists; if we look into the evidence from the field of psychology, one of the first things we discover is that this main supporting generalization—that the only effective motive for enterprise is money-getting—appears in the psychologists' works as a standard humorous reference to the psychological ideas of laymen.

* * *

It ought rather to be a source of wonder that a society could operate at all when profits are allowed to be earned and disposed of as we do it. The hope of making them induces dangerous adventures, more speculative than productive; and the uses to which they are put are a constant menace to general security. These conclusions only become clearer as time goes on, yet no movement to limit them or to control their uses has made headway among us. If there had been a more widespread suspicion of this sort over some period of time there would be more reason to expect success for proposals looking toward a profitless régime. The universal confidence in profits, still unshaken in the Western World, is quite likely to hinder measurably the advance of planning.

A central group of experts charged with the duty of planning the country's economic life, but existing as a suggestive or consultative body only, without power, has been advocated by numerous persons and organizations. * * * The deadliest and most subtle enemy of speculative profit-making which could be devised would be an implemented scheme for planning production. For such a scheme would quiet conflict and inject into economic affairs an order and regularity which no large speculation could survive. Every depression period wearies us with insecurity; the majority of us seem all to be whipped at once; and what we long for temporarily is safety rather than adventure. Planning seems at first to offer this safety and so gains a good deal of unconsidered support. But when it is discovered that planning for production means planning for consumption too; that something more is involved than simple limitation to amounts which can be sold at any price producers temporarily happen to find best for themselves; that profits must be limited and their uses controlled; that what really is implied is something not unlike an integrated group of enterprises run for its consumers rather than for its owners—when all this gradually appears, there is likely to be a great changing of sides.

Strange as it may seem—directly antithetical to the interests of business and unlikely to be allowed freedom of speech, to say nothing of action—it seems altogether likely that we shall set up, and soon, such a consultative body. When the Chamber of Commerce of the United States is brought to consent, realization cannot be far off. It seems to me quite possible to argue that, in spite of its innocuous nature, the day on which it comes into existence will be a dangerous one for business, just as the founding day of the League of Nations was a dangerous one for nationalism. There may be a long and lingering death, but it must be regarded as inevitable. Any new economic council will be hampered on every side; it will be pressed for favors and undermined by political jobbery. It will not dare call its soul its own, nor speak its mind in any emergency. But it will be a clear recognition, one that can never be undone, that order and reason are superior to adventurous competition. It will demonstrate these day by day and year by year in the personnel of a civil service devoted to disinterested thinking rather than romantic hopes of individual gain. Let it be as poor a thing as it may, still it will be a constant reminder that once business was sick to death and that it will be again; that once the expert is applied for, his advice must be taken or refuted. Even if it does so little, and that so badly, as hardly to exist at all, it will still have had a different purpose: the achieving of order. And not improbably it will have been demonstrably wiser than the powers which will be creating the events surrounding it.

These will, however, be the only ways in which the qualities of a planning body will be able to show themselves. It will be unable to act and therefore unable to eliminate uncertainties; uncertainties make prediction impossible; and planning is a process of predicting and making it come true, not merely a matter of advising voluntary groups. Mr. Slichter is quite justified in pointing out that no scheme we are likely to adopt would be able to do its work effectively. He asks for instance: "Could it prevent depressions? Could it prevent the great overdevelopment of industries? If a council had been in existence as early as 1920, could it have checked the great overdevelopment of the textile industry, the shoe industry, the coal industry, the petroleum industry, the automobile industry, and others? Could it have solved the farm problem? Could it have prevented the depression of 1930 or substantially reduced the severity of the depression? Could it have prevented our foreign trade from being injured by a general upward revision of the tariff in 1930?" And he is certain that the answer to all these questions is "no."

The answer has to be "no" because the necessary conditions of planning are not established by any "purely advisory National Economic Council." An advisory council might guess but it could not plan; and the difference between guessing and planning is the difference between laissez faire and social control. Under the institutions of laissez faire the sole uses of such a body will be to lead us slowly, by precept and demonstration, toward a less uncertain future. It seems improbable that this will be other than a very reluctant and grudging change.

* * *

It is necessary to realize quite finally that everything will be changed if the linking of industry can finally be brought to completion in a "plan." It was a reluctant and half blind step which led one executive after another to complete the serialization of his machines. And even then he was sometimes astonished at the results. This new undertaking is vaster; it requires a new and complicated technology which is not yet wholly invented; and it follows not from one executive's decision, but from a thousand preliminary consents, abdications, and acceptances of responsibility. Yet to enter upon it would be to take but a single short step from where we are; the most momentous and final, but still a short one. We have traveled a long road to this threshold we now consider crossing.

The setting up of even an emasculated and ineffective central coordinating body in Washington will form a focus about which recognition may gradually gather. It will be an action as significant as the first observations of Taylor; and it can lead eventually to the completion and crowning of that genius' work. The major subject matter of economics during the next few years might well be a particularizing of the implications of this. For we have a century and more of development to undo. The institutions of laissez faire have become so much a part of the fabric of modern life that the untangling and removing of their tissues will be almost like dispensing with civilization itself. We shall all of us be made unhappy in one way or another; for things we love as well as things that are only privileges will have to go. The protective vine makes the ruined wall seem beautiful; we dislike abandoning it for something different. But we shall have to see, no doubt, a wholesale sacrifice of such things, like it as little as we may.

The first series of changes will have to do with statutes, with constitutions, and with government. The intention of eighteenth and nineteenth century law was to install and protect the principle of conflict; this, if we begin to plan, we shall be changing once for all, and it will require the laying of rough, unholy hands on many a sacred precedent, doubtless calling on an enlarged and nationalized police power for enforcement. We shall also have to give up a distinction of great consequence, and very dear to many a legalistic heart, but economically quite absurd, between private and public or quasi-public employments. There is no private business, if by that we mean one of no consequence to anyone but its proprietors; and so none exempt from compulsion to serve a planned public interest. Furthermore we shall have to progress sufficiently far in elementary realism to recognize that only the federal area, and often not even that, is large enough to be coextensive with modern industry; and that consequently the states are wholly ineffective instruments for control. All three of these wholesale changes are required by even a limited acceptance of the planning idea.

Planning is by definition the opposite of conflict; its meaning is aligned to co-ordination, to rationality, to publicly defined and expertly approached aims; but not to private money-making ventures; and not to the guidance of a hidden hand. It is equally true that planning in any social sense cannot leave out of its calculations any industry or group of industries and still remain planning. To do so would be to expose the scheme to the very uncertainty which is sought to be eliminated and to concentrate its advantages in the hands of the nonco-operators. It would be easy for any free industry to erect an empire if all or even many of the others were restricted. It will be required, furthermore, in any successful attempt to plan, that the agency which imposes its disinterested will on industry, must equal, in the area of its jurisdiction, the spread of the industry. Planning will necessarily become a function of the federal government; either that or the planning agency will supersede that government, which is why, of course, such a scheme will eventually be assimilated to the state, rather than possess some of its powers without its responsibilities.

The next series of changes will have to do with industry itself. It has already been suggested that business will logically be required to disappear. This is not an overstatement for the sake of emphasis; it is literally meant. The essence of business is its free venture for profits in an unregulated economy. Planning implies guidance of capital uses; this would limit entrance into or expansion of operations. Planning also implies adjustment of production to consumption; and there is no way of accomplishing this except through a control of prices and of profit margins. It would never be sufficient to plan production for an estimated demand if that demand were likely to fail for lack of purchasing power. The insurance of adequate buying capacity would be a first and most essential task of any plan which was expected to work. To take away from business its freedom of venture and of expansion, and to limit the profits it may acquire, is to destroy it as business and to make of it something else. That something else has no name; we can only wonder what it may be like and whether all the fearsome predictions concerning it will come true. The traditional incentives, hope of money-making, and fear of money-loss, will be weakened; and a kind of civil-service loyalty and fervor will need to grow gradually into acceptance. New industries will not just happen as the automobile industry did; they will have to be foreseen, to be argued for, to seem probably desirable features of the whole economy before they can be entered upon.

This sweeping statement of the logic of planning is simply an attempt to foresee what our economic institutions will be like if we adopt the planning principle. We shall not, we never do, proceed to the changes here suggested all at once. Little by little, however, we may be driven the whole length of this road; once the first step is taken, which we seem about to take, that road will begin to suggest itself as the way to a civilized industry. For it will become more and more clear, as thinking and discussion centers on industrial and economic rather than business problems, that not very much is to be gained until the last step has been taken. What seems to be indicated now is years of gradual modification, accompanied by agonies and recriminations, without much visible gain; then, suddenly, as it was with the serialization of machines, the last link will almost imperceptibly find its place and suddenly we shall discover that we have a new world, as, some years ago, we suddenly discovered that we had unconsciously created a new industry.

These struggles and changes may seem to the future historian who looks backward, like the purposive journey of a seedling toward the light. The seedling could not see or feel that light; it merely obeyed its nature. If only society had a greater and more widely diffused power to comprehend and pursue the purposes of its nature we should save ourselves the great waste of energy which goes into opposing and regretting change. The difficulty with this is that society is not an organism; that it has no discoverable nature to obey; that there are no natural requirements for its development. We are not going anywhere; we are merely on the way. For this lack of the purpose, which nature kindly supplies to her lower organisms, society must substitute plans born of intellectual effort, and imposed by awkward democratic devices. This is a hard condition for human nature. We have no great gift for shaping our behavior in accordance with large aims, and no great gift either for tolerating the necessary disciplines. It has been by a series of seeming miracles that we have acquired the technique of control and the industrial basis for economic planning. The still further, perhaps greater, miracle of discipline is needed.

It is perhaps no accident that planning has recently become a center of discussion in economic affairs in substitution for laissez faire. Changes in contemporary philosophy have prepared the way. Chance has substituted itself for the anthropomorphic interpretation of history as a causal sequence. Even the evolutionary principle has the defect, in social history, of making the present seem to have been what we were struggling for. Of course we were not trying to attain any of the institutions we have. They resulted from the chance conjunction of changes. Only the backward look, determined by the view from some contemporary hillock, gives history a meaning. We have, nevertheless, as we are just now dimly beginning to see, the possibility, in a world of discontinuous development and chance combination, of producing a new history guided quite consciously toward foreseen ends.

There is something hostile to mankind in the cold notion of a world which progresses toward unseen ends, regardless of human desires. So long as it was possible we tried to delude ourselves, in one way or another, that purpose existed and that it had a definite reference to mankind. All that comfort is torn away now; and we remain poor, inconsequent creatures exposed to chance developments which are neither kind nor unkind with reference to ourselves, but simply impersonal. It is perhaps characteristic of human nature that we should reject such a view until it became intellectually impossible to cherish our delusions further; and that we should then turn to the only alternative. If there is no order and sequence in events, if the world is indifferent to man, we still remain men. It is perhaps the most magnificent of all human gestures to accept inconsequence and to set out determinedly to bring order out of chaos. I do not regard it as settled that the world is ready, yet, for creating its future according to a determined purpose. But we are at the point where discussion of this possible mastering of future history is beginning to assume practical aspects; and there is undoubtedly some need for haste if change is to come peaceably. It is my view that the prospective discussion ought to be carried out with a clear view of its philosophical implications and of its institutional requirements. If we accept the principle of planning we must accept its implied destruction of the structure of a laissez faire industry.

It is, in other words, a logical impossibility to have a planned economy and to have businesses operating its industries, just as it is also impossible to have one within our present constitutional and statutory structure. Modifications in both, so serious as to mean destruction and rebeginning, are required. It is strange, in a way, that we should have come so long a journey to the very threshold of this new economic order with so little change as is yet visible either in our institutions or our intentions. The reason must be that in this, as in so many instances, only the last steps become conscious. We are incorrigibly averse to any estimate of the logic of our acts; and we are also, somewhat paradoxically, fonder of our systems of theory than might be expected, reluctant to expose them to the tests of reality. Consequently we begin with small unnoticed changes and end by not being able to resist vast and spectacular ones—at which time our systems of theory tumble unwept into the grave along with the outworn techniques they accompanied. When this kind of thing follows a relatively unimpeded course there is rapid industrial change such as once happened in England; when politicians, theorists, and vested interests resist too strenuously, there is a revolution on the French model. How rapidly the pressures rise to explosive proportions depends both upon the visibility of a better future and upon the hardships of the present.

There is no denying that the contemporary situation in the United States has explosive possibilities. The future is becoming visible in Russia; the present is bitterly in contrast; politicians, theorists, and vested interests seem to conspire ideally for the provocation to violence of a long-patient people. No one can pretend to know how the release of this pressure is likely to come. Perhaps our statesmen will give way or be more or less gently removed from duty; perhaps our constitutions and statutes will be revised; perhaps our vested interests will submit to control without too violent resistance. It is difficult to believe that any of these will happen; it seems just as incredible that we may have a revolution. Yet the new kind of economic machinery we have in prospect cannot function in our present economy. The contemporary situation is one in which all the choices are hard; yet one of them has to be made.

HENRY A. WALLACE

New Frontiers (1934)

The agricultural expert and writer Henry Agard Wallace (1888–1965) served as secretary of agriculture during the first two Franklin Roosevelt administrations and as vice president during the third. The liberal Iowan helped formulate New Deal agricultural policy. This excerpt from Wallace's book New Frontiers, *which he wrote in 1934 during Roosevelt's first term in office, captures the pragmatic and populist spirit of the New Deal.*

Two aspects of the problem stand out clearly. One has to do with planning in the physical sense of the term. The other has to do with changing the rules of the game—with laws governing tariffs, money, the regulation of corporations, taxation, and railroad and public utility rates.

We must control that part of our individualism which produces anarchy and widespread misery. If the majority of us are to have automobiles, we must obey the traffic lights and observe certain rules of common decency in order to get speedily and safely from one place to another. In the process our individuality has been curbed, but once certain habits of mutual consideration are established, we discover that the advantages outweigh the handicaps. The range of individual expression has really been widened.

Insofar as the process of production and distribution operates on a large scale over wide territories, it will be absolutely necessary for the state to assume its true functions of "directing, watching, stimulating and restraining as circumstances suggest or necessity demands." The words quoted are from no less a radical than Pope Pius XI, who has also stated that there should be "a reasonable relationship between the prices obtained for the products of the various economic groups, agrarian, industrial, etc." Most broadminded people will further agree that it is a function of the state to promulgate such a spirit of justice as will bring about that harmonious proportion in which "men's various economic activities combine and unite into one single organism and become members of a common body, lending each other mutual help and services."

Obviously, certain limits must be placed on competition and individualism. These limits should be placed by a state in the justice of whose acts there is absolute confidence. The limits should not deal with irritating particulars but with broad outlines. On these broad outlines there should be substantial unanimity of opinion among thinking people in both the Republican and Democratic parties, and among leaders of labor, industry and agriculture. If such agreement can be reached there will be infinite opportunities for the 125 million individuals of the United States to develop their ruggedness to mutual advantage instead of to their competitive disadvantage.

It is important for all, and for younger people especially, to realize that the New Deal spirit ebbs and flows. Ordinarily, the progressive liberals get a real opportunity to change the rules only about once in a generation. Human nature is such that complacency prevails and conservatives stay in the saddle until things get pretty bad. From a logical point of view the leadership of the United States from 1920 to 1930 was bad. But the conservatives stayed in power. Most people resolutely refuse to think politically if they have jobs, a place to sleep and something to eat and wear. The economic well-being of the moment was pumped up by a false statesmanship. It took ten years and an economic smash before the people would heed the warnings of those who said, "This thing is built on sand."

Most of the so-called young liberals of today received their first political inspiration between 1906 and 1915 from Woodrow Wilson and Theodore Roosevelt. They saw liberalism go out of date in the '20's and wondered if the American people had permanently accepted a Belly-God. The young men who today are between eighteen and thirty years of age and who are anxious to see America built over fundamentally and completely in line with their dreams, will perhaps also have an opportunity to watch the conservatives get back into power. This may not come for eight, twelve or sixteen years, but it will come almost as surely as prosperity returns. People like to be comfortable and "let alone." The conservative is bound to triumph fully half the time.

But it must also be remembered that there is something inherently inadequate and often rotting about comfort. The conservative type of mind is constitutionally incapable of understanding the inevitability of certain changes. * * *

I am not suggesting that all our younger people be liberals. There are many who should be conservatives. I am deeply concerned, however, that the leadership of the future, whether liberal or conservative, should grapple more definitely and clearly with the facts and forces involved. It seems a pity that the liberals and conservatives, the Democrats and the Republicans, as we call them now, should spend so much time calling each other names. There are tremendously important problems to be put before the people. It may not be good politics to conduct this education, but it is absolutely vital if our democracy is to survive.

* * *

I am hoping we can advance by means of an aroused, educated Democracy. Socialism, Communism, and Fascism, it is true, have the advantage of certain precise rules not available to Democracy. They make the path to the land of tomorrow seem straight and short. The only rules a democracy can rely upon make the path seem by comparison long and tortuous. But the point is that most Americans think less rigid rules and the clash of free opinion allowed by Democracy will in the long run take us farther than will the precise, decisive dogma of Communism or Fascism. So do I.

There is nothing novel or sensational about the rules of the game I have in mind. Until recently, however, the full significance of such rules has been obscured, and the rules have been manipulated more or less secretly for the benefit of the few at the expense of the many. Now the time seems ripe for a change in behalf of the many.

The first step is to understand these rules in all their significance. They have to do with such devices as the tariff, the balance of international payments, monetary policy, subsidies, taxation, price and production policies, and railroad rate regulations. Their significance lies in the fact that by their manipulation it is possible to direct, stimulate, restrain, and balance those forces which have to do with proportioning the national income. All governments that have advanced beyond the pioneer stage find it necessary to use such controls, in lieu of free competition. In using them, a democracy worthy of the name must be guided by concern for social justice and social charity—in other words, the greatest good for the greatest number.

Reliance upon such devices to redistribute income and opportunity, is not the way of Socialism, of Communism or of Fascism. Neither is it the way of the free-booter capitalists of the neo-Manchester school of economics. With their devotion to unlimited competition, these people seem to think the traffic lights should be removed so motorists and pedestrians might illustrate the doctrine of the survival of the fittest at every street corner. It is necessary in a democracy to furnish the red and green lights to guide the traffic, but not to supply drivers for every car on the road.

Long before the World War, competition was limited by rules, both public and private. Since then, it has been limited increasingly. The vital question is: In whose behalf is competition limited? Is the limitation making the rich richer and the poor poorer? If so, there is danger that a day may come when the extreme left will join hands with the extreme right to bring about that most dangerous of all forms of government, a corrupt oligarchy, maintaining itself in power by pandering to the vices and prejudices of a bitter, materialistic, perennially unemployed multitude.

An enduring democracy can be had only by promoting a balance among all our major producing groups, and in such a way as does not build up a small, inordinately wealthy class. The danger in democracies, as we have known them in the past, is this: All too easily, under pressure of changing conditions, they play into the hands of either the extreme left or the extreme right. The same legislators will allow themselves to be stampeded by scared capitalists toward the extreme right, and by the unemployed toward the extreme left. The complexities and the confusion of modern civilization are such that legislators quickly forget objectives of social and economic balance, and give way to the special pressures of the moment.

There is no likelihood of a dictatorship in this country, whether of the proletariat, of the technicians, or of the financiers, unless our middle class is wiped out. If we get into a really big war, the after-effect might include something of this sort; but without such a catastrophe it would seem that we have much better than an even chance to use our democratic powers and escape such regimentation by government as has been invoked in the totalitarian or autarchic states of Europe.

* * *

I see no reason as yet why we in the United States should go into precise detailed planning except, perhaps, with respect to natural resources and to certain rather small segments of our national life on an emergency basis. With the situation that exists and is likely to exist in the United States for the next ten years, the chief objective of our democracy should be so to manage the tariff, and the money system, to control railroad interest rates; and to encourage price and production policies that will maintain a continually balanced relationship between the income of agriculture, labor, and industry.

* * *

We of this administration are not committed indefinitely to crop control or to NRA codes. We are committed to getting the farmer, the laborer, and the industrialist such share of the national income as will put each in a balanced relationship with the other. Without such balance the foundation of the state sags. * * *

The hard but necessary first lesson we all must learn is that we cannot prosper separately. Even individual pressure groups must catch the idea that pressure on behalf of any individual group makes necessary, sooner or later, compensating pressure in behalf of other groups. In our march to a real democracy, governmental powers should not be loaned too lightly to any group. For the ultimate security of that loan, there must be clear-cut evidence that the power will be used to advance a harmonious relationship between forces now contending. The degree to which this principle can be grasped and applied by business men, laborers, and farmers reared in a freebooter tradition remains to be seen. That, as it develops, will set the pracital limits of "self-governing industry" and "self-governing agriculture."

* * *

The old frontier was real. There were Indians and fear of foreign conquest. People in the older Colonies or States had to stand together against actual perils on the edge of a new civilization.

* * * For a hundred and fifty years we felt it was manifest destiny to push onward, until the Pacific Coast was reached, until all the fertile lands between had been plowed and bound together by railroads and paved highways.

The obvious physical task to which we set ourselves has been accomplished; and in so doing, we have destroyed in large measure the thing which gave us hope and unity as a people.

We now demand a new unity, a new hope. There are many spiritual and mental frontiers yet to be conquered, but they lead in many different directions and our hearts have not yet fully warmed to any one of them. They do not point in an obvious single direction as did that downright physical challenge which, for so many generations, existed on the Western edge of our life. Now we have come to the time when we must search our souls and the relationship of our souls and bodies to those of other human beings.

* * *

The keynote of the new frontier is cooperation just as that of the old frontier was individualistic competition. The mechanism of progress of the new frontier is social invention, whereas that of the old frontier was mechanical invention and the competitive seizure of opportunities for wealth. Power and wealth were worshiped in the old days. Beauty and justice and joy of spirit must be worshiped in the new.

* * *

In the old days, we could not trust ourselves with joy and beauty because they ran counter to our competitive search for wealth and power. * * * The men of the new day must have their social discipline comparable in its power with that of the inner drive toward the hard-working, competitive frugality of the old frontier. People may actually work harder than they did on the old frontier, but their motive will be different. * * *

But their efforts will, of necessity, be continually moved by the spirit of cooperative achievement. They will devise way in which the monetary mechanism can be modified to distribute the rewards of labor more uniformly. They will work with disinterested spirit to modify the governmental and political machinery so that there is a balanced relationship between prices, an even flow of employment, and a far-wider possibility of social justice and social charity.

So enlisted, men may rightfully feel that they are serving a function as high as that of any minister of the Gospel. They will not be Socialists, Communists or Fascists, but plain men trying to gain by democratic methods the professed objectives of the Communists, Socialists and Fascists: security, peace, and the good life for all.

WALTER LIPPMANN

Planning in an Economy of Abundance (1937)

One of the most common criticisms of the New Deal was that it would lead to a Soviet-style planned economy. In an essay published in the Atlantic Monthly magazine, the journalist and former Progressive Walter Lippmann (1889–1974) argued that planning was impossible in a complex economy during peacetime. It also demanded too many restrictions on freedom of choice. Ominously, he also warned that planning requires a degree of control over economic life that would lead to an oligarchic despotism.

The difficulty of planning production to satisfy many choices is the rock on which the whole conception founders. We have seen that in military planning this difficulty does not exist. It is the insurmountable difficulty of civilian planning, and although advocates like Mr. Mumford, Mr. Chase, and Mr. Soule have never, I think, faced it squarely, they are not unaware that it exists. They show that they are troubled because they denounce so vehemently the tastes of the people and the advertising which helps to form those tastes. They insist that the people have foolish and vulgar desires, which may be true enough, and that altogether better standards, simpler, more vital, more æsthetic, and more hygienic, ought to replace them. I agree. But I do not see how the purification of the public taste is to be worked out by a government commission. I can see how and why the general staff can decide how soldiers should live under martial discipline; but I cannot see how any group of officials can decide how a civilian population shall live nobly and abundantly.

For the fundamental characteristic of a rising standard of life is that an increasing portion of each man's income is spent on unessentials; it is applied, in other words, to things in which preference rather than necessity is the criterion. If all income had to be spent on the absolute necessities of life, the goods required would be few in number and their production could readily be standardized into a routine. Now it should be noted that all known examples of planned economy have flourished under conditions of scarcity. * * * But as productivity rises above the level of necessity the variety of choice is multiplied; and as choice is multiplied the possibility of an overhead calculation of the relation between demand and supply diminishes.

We may approximate an idea of the order of magnitudes in this field by remembering that during the year 1929 the American people spent approximately ninety billion dollars. I have sought in vain to find even a loose estimate of how many different kinds of goods and services they bought. But one can obtain some sense of their infinite variety by thinking of the goods offered for sale in a big department store, by glancing at the names of the corporations listed on the stock exchanges, by thumbing through a city directory and a telephone book, by looking at mail-order catalogues and the help-wanted columns and the advertisements in the newspapers. The variety of goods and services offered in the markets of America defies description. Now, of the ninety billions spent, some twenty billions went into the purchase of food. This meant a highly varied diet. But even assuming that food is the most nearly calculable of human necessities, the one that can, by simplifying the public bill of fare, be rationed successfully among large bodies of men, there would have remained in 1929 variable expenditures of about seventy billions.

By what formula could a planning authority determine which goods to provide against the purchases of thirty million families with seventy billions of free spendable income? The calculation is not even theoretically possible. For, unless the people are to be deprived of the right to dispose of their incomes voluntarily, anyone who sets out to plan American production must first forecast how many units of each commodity the people would buy, not only at varying prices for that commodity, but in all possible combinations of prices for all commodities.

* * *

Out of all the possible plans of production some schedule would have to be selected arbitrarily. There is absolutely no objective and universal criterion by which to decide between better houses and more automobiles, between pork and beef, between the radio and the movies. In military planning one criterion exists: to mobilize the most powerful army that national resources will support. That criterion can be defined by the general staff as so many men with such and such equipment, and the economy can be planned accordingly. But civilian planning for a more abundant life has no definable criterion. It can have none. The necessary calculations cannot, therefore, be made, and the concept of a civilian planned economy is not merely administratively impracticable; it is not even theoretically conceivable. The conception is totally devoid of meaning, and there is, speaking literally, nothing in it.

The primary factor which makes civilian planning incalculable is the freedom of the people to spend their income. Planning is theoretically possible only if consumption is rationed. For a plan of production is a plan of consumption. If the authority is to decide what shall be produced, it has already decided what shall be consumed. In military planning that is precisely what takes place: the authorities decide what the army shall consume and what of the national product shall be left for the civilians. No economy can, therefore, be planned for civilians unless there is such scarcity that the necessities of existence can be rationed. As productivity rises above the subsistence level, free spending becomes possible. A planned production to meet a free demand is a contradiction in terms and as meaningless as a square circle.

It follows, too, that a plan of production is incompatible with voluntary labor, with freedom to choose an occupation. A plan of production is not only a plan of consumption, but a plan of how long and where the people shall work, and what they shall work at. By no possible manipulation of wage rates could the planners attract to the various jobs precisely the right number of workers. Under voluntary labor, particularly with consumption rationed and standardized, the unpleasant jobs would be avoided and the good jobs overcrowded. Therefore the inevitable and necessary complement of the rationing of consumption is the conscription of labor, either by overt act of law or by driving workers into the undesirable jobs by offering them starvation as the alternative. This is, of course, exactly what happens in a thoroughly militarized state.

The conscription of labor and the rationing of consumption are not to be regarded as transitional or as accidental devices in a planned economy. They are the very substance of it. To make a five-year plan of what a whole nation shall produce is to determine how it shall labor and what it shall receive. It can receive only what the plan provides. It can obtain what the plan provides only by doing the work which the plan calls for. It must do that work or the plan is a failure; it must accept what the plan yields in the way of goods or it must do without.

* * *

There is, in short, no way by which the objectives of a planned economy can be made to depend upon popular decision. They must be imposed by an oligarchy of some sort, and that oligarchy must, if the plan is to be carried through, be without responsibility in matters of policy. Individual oligarchs might, of course, be held accountable for breaches of the law just as generals can be court-martialed. But their policy can no more be made a matter of continuous accountability to the voters than the strategic arrangements of the generals can be determined by the rank and file. The planning board or their superiors have to determine what the life and labor of the people shall be.

Not only is it impossible for the people to control the plan, but, what is more, the planners must control the people. They must be despots who tolerate no effective challenge to their authority. Therefore civilian planning is compelled to presuppose that somehow the despots who climb to power will be benevolent—that is to say, will know and desire the supreme good of their subjects. This is the implicit premise of all the books which recommend the establishment of a planned economy in a civilian society. They paint an entrancing vision of what a benevolent despotism could do. They ask—never very clearly, to be sure—that somehow the people should surrender the planning of their existence to 'engineers,' 'experts,' and 'technologists,' to leaders, saviors, heroes. This is the political premise of the whole collectivist philosophy: that the dictators will be patriotic or class-conscious, whichever term seems the more eulogistic to the orator. It is the premise, too, of the whole philosophy of regulation by the state, currently regarded as progressivism. Though it is disguised by the illusion that a bureaucracy accountable to a majority of voters, and susceptible to the pressure of organized minorities, is not exercising compulsion, it is evident that the more varied and comprehensive the regulation becomes, the more the state becomes a despotic power as against the individual. For the fragment of control over the government that one man exercises through his vote is in no effective sense proportionate to the authority exercised over him by the government.

Benevolent despots might indeed be found. On the other hand, they might not be. They may appear at one time; they may not appear at another. The people, unless they choose to face the machine guns on the barricades, can take no steps to see to it that benevolent despots are selected and the malevolent cashiered. They cannot select their despots. The despots must select themselves, and, no matter whether they are good or bad, they will continue in office so long as they can suppress rebellion and escape assassination.

Thus, by a kind of tragic irony, the search for security and a rational society, if it seeks salvation through political authority, ends in the most irrational form of government imaginable—in the dictatorship of casual oligarchs, who have no hereditary title, no constitutional origin or responsibility, who cannot be replaced except by violence. The reformers who are staking their hopes on good despots, because they are so eager to plan the future, leave unplanned that on which all their hopes depend. Because a planned society must be one in which the people obey their rulers, there can be no plan to find the planners: the selection of the despots who are to make society so rational and so secure has to be left to the insecurity of irrational chance.

The Cold War

REINHOLD NIEBUHR

The Children of Light and the Children of Darkness: A Vindication of Democracy and a Critique of Its Traditional Defense (1944)

For over thirty years the Protestant theologian Reinhold Niebuhr (1892–1971) taught at New York's Union Theological Seminary, where he developed a brand of Christian realism that emphasized the capacity for evil that was part of humanity's mixed nature. A former socialist and pacifist, Niebuhr persuaded many Christians to support the war against nazism and was a founder of the liberal anticommunist group Americans for Democratic Action. In this excerpt from his important 1944 book The Children of Light and the Children of Darkness, *Niebuhr offered a pessimistic reading of human nature to temper democratic enthusiasm.*

Democracy, as every other historic ideal and institution, contains both ephemeral and more permanently valid elements. Democracy is on the one hand the characteristic fruit of a bourgeois civilization; on the other hand it is a perennially valuable form of social organization in which freedom and order are made to support, and not to contradict, each other.

Democracy is a "bourgeois ideology" in so far as it expresses the typical viewpoints of the middle classes who have risen to power in European civilization in the past three or four centuries. Most of the democratic ideals, as we know them, were weapons of the commercial classes who engaged in stubborn, and ultimately victorious, conflict with the ecclesiastical and aristocratic rulers of the feudal-medieval world. The ideal of equality, unknown in the democratic life of the Greek city states and derived partly from Christian and partly from Stoic sources, gave the bourgeois classes a

sense of self-respect in overcoming the aristocratic pretension and conde-
scension of the feudal overlords of medieval society. The middle classes
defeated the combination of economic and political power of mercantil-
ism by stressing economic liberty; and, through the principles of political
liberty, they added the political power of suffrage to their growing economic power. The implicit assumptions, as well as the explicit ideals, of
democratic civilization were also largely the fruit of middle-class existence. The social and historical optimism of democratic life, for instance,
represents the typical illusion of an advancing class which mistook its own
progress for the progress of the world.

Since bourgeois civilization, which came to birth in the sixteenth to
eighteenth centuries and reached its zenith in the nineteenth century, is
now obviously in grave peril, if not actually in *rigor mortis* in the twentieth century, it must be obvious that democracy, in so far as it is a middle-
class ideology, also faces its doom.

This fate of democracy might be viewed with equanimity, but for the
fact that it has a deeper dimension and broader validity than its middle-
class character. Ideally democracy is a permanantly valid form of social
and political organization which does justice to two dimensions of human
existence: to man's spiritual stature and his social character; to the
uniqueness and variety of life, as well as to the common necessities of all
men. Bourgeois democracy frequently exalted the individual at the expense of the community; but its emphasis upon liberty contained a valid
element, which transcended its excessive individualism. The community
requires liberty as much as does the individual; and the individual requires community more than bourgeois thought comprehended. Democracy can therefore not be equated with freedom. An ideal democratic
order seeks unity within the conditions of freedom; and maintains freedom within the framework of order.

Man requires freedom in his social organization because he is "essentially" free, which is to say, that he has the capacity for indeterminate
transcendence over the processes and limitations of nature. This freedom
enables him to make history and to elaborate communal organizations in
boundless variety and in endless breadth and extent. But he also requires
community because he is by nature social. He cannot fulfill his life within
himself but only in responsible and mutual relations with his fellows.

Bourgeois democrats are inclined to believe that freedom is primarily a
necessity for the individual, and that community and social order are necessary only because there are many individuals in a small world, so that
minimal restrictions are required to prevent confusion. Actually the community requires freedom as much as the individual; and the individual requires order as much as does the community.

Both the individual and the community require freedom so that neither communal nor historical restraints may prematurely arrest the po-
tencies which inhere in man's essential freedom and which express
themselves collectively as well as individually. It is true that individuals
are usually the initiators of new insights and the proponents of novel
methods. Yet there are collective forces at work in society which are not
the conscious contrivance of individuals. In any event society is as much
the beneficiary of freedom as the individual. In a free society new forces
may enter into competition with the old and gradually establish themselves. In a traditional or tyrannical form of social organization new
forces are either suppressed, or they establish themselves at the price of
social convulsion and upheaval.

The order of a community is, on the other hand, a boon to the individual as well as to the community. The individual cannot be a true self in
isolation. Nor can he live within the confines of the community which
"nature" establishes in the minimal cohesion of family and herd. His
freedom transcends these limits of nature, and therefore makes larger
and larger social units both possible and necessary. It is precisely because
of the essential freedom of man that he requires a contrived order in his
community.

The democratic ideal is thus more valid than the libertarian and individualistic version of it which bourgeois civilization elaborated. Since the
bourgeois version has been discredited by the events of contemporary
history and since, in any event, bourgeois civilization is in process of disintegration, it becomes important to distinguish and save what is permanently valid from what is ephemeral in the democratic order.

If democracy is to survive it must find a more adequate cultural basis
than the philosophy which has informed the building of the bourgeois
world. The inadequacy of the presuppositions upon which the democratic experiment rests does not consist merely in the excessive individualism and libertarianism of the bourgeois world view; though it must
be noted that this excessive individualism prompted a civil war in the
whole western world in which the rising proletarian classes pitted an
excessive collectivism against the false individualism of middle-class
life. This civil conflict contributed to the weakness of democratic civilization when faced with the threat of barbarism. Neither the individualism nor the collectivism did justice to all the requirements of man's
social life, and the conflict between half-truth and half-truth divided
the civilized world in such a way that the barbarians were able to claim
first one side and then the other in this civil conflict as their provisional
allies.

But there is a more fundamental error in the social philosophy of democratic civilization than the individualism of bourgeois democracy and the collectivism of Marxism. It is the confidence of both bourgeois and proletarian idealists in the possibility of achieving an easy resolution of the tension and conflict between self-interest and the general interest. Modern bourgeois civilization is not, as Catholic philosophers and medievalists generally assert, a rebellion against universal law, or a defiance of universal standards of justice, or a war against the historic institutions which sought to achieve and preserve some general social and international harmony. Modern secularism is not, as religious idealists usually aver, merely a rationalization of self-interest, either individual or collective. Bourgeois individualism may be excessive and it may destroy the individual's organic relation to the community; but it was not intended to destroy either the national or the international order. On the contrary the social idealism which informs our democratic civilization had a touching faith in the possibility of achieving a simple harmony between self-interest and the general welfare on every level. * * *

Our modern civilization, on the other hand, was ushered in on a wave of boundless social optimism. Modern secularism is divided into many schools. But all the various schools agreed in rejecting the Christian doctrine of original sin. It is not possible to explain the subtleties or to measure the profundity of this doctrine in this connection. But it is necessary to point out that the doctrine makes an important contribution to any adequate social and political theory the lack of which has robbed bourgeois theory of real wisdom; for it emphasizes a fact which every page of human history attests. Through it one may understand that no matter how wide the perspectives which the human mind may reach, how broad the loyalties which the human imagination may conceive, how universal the community which human statecraft may organize, or how pure the aspirations of the saintliest idealists may be, there is no level of human moral or social achievement in which there is not some corruption of inordinate self-love.

This sober and true view of the human situation was neatly rejected by modern culture. That is why it conceived so many fatuous and futile plans for resolving the conflict between the self and the community; and between the national and the world community. Whenever modern idealists are confronted with the divisive and corrosive effects of man's self-love, they look for some immediate cause of this perennial tendency, usually in some specific form of social organization. One school holds that men would be good if only political institutions would not corrupt them; another believes that they would be good if the prior evil of a faulty economic organization could be eliminated. Or another school thinks of this evil as no more than ignorance, and therefore waits for a more perfect educational process to redeem man from his partial and particular loyalties. But no school asks how it is that an essentially good man could have produced corrupting and tyrannical political organizations or exploiting economic organizations, or fanatical and superstitious religious organizations. * * *

The democratic idealists of practically all schools of thought have managed to remain remarkably oblivious to the obvious facts. Democratic theory therefore has not squared with the facts of history. This grave defect in democratic theory was comparatively innocuous in the heyday of the bourgeois period, when the youth and the power of democratic civilization surmounted all errors of judgment and confusions of mind. But in this latter day, when it has become important to save what is valuable in democratic life from the destruction of what is false in bourgeois civilization, it has also become necessary to distinguish what is false in democratic theory from what is true in democratic life. * * *

A free society is justified by the fact that the indeterminate possibilities of human vitality may be creative. Every definition of the restraints which must be placed upon these vitalities must be tentative; because all such definitions, which are themselves the products of specific historical insights, may prematurely arrest or suppress a legitimate vitality, if they are made absolute and fixed. The community must constantly re-examine the presuppositions upon which it orders its life, because no age can fully anticipate or predict the legitimate and creative vitalities which may arise in subsequent ages.

The limitations upon freedom in a society are justified, on the other hand, by the fact that the vitalities may be destructive. We have already noted that the justification of classical *laissez-faire* theories was the mistaken belief that human passions were naturally ordinate and limited. It must be added that there are also some types of social theory, which understand the boundless character of man's vitalities and yet advocate unlimited freedom. In the nineteenth century Darwinian, rather than physiocratic, presuppositions frequently furnished the *rationale* of *laissez-faire* social theory. The physiocrats trusted the pre-established harmony of nature. The Darwinians attributed a moral historical significance to the struggles of nature. They failed to understand that human society is a vast moral and historical artifact, which would be destroyed if natural conflicts and contests between various vitalities were not mitigated, managed and arbitrated. * * *

The final question to confront the proponent of a democratic and free society is whether the freedom of a society should extend to the point of allowing these principles to be called into question. Should they not stand above criticism or amendment? If they are themselves subjected to the democratic process and if they are made dependent upon the moods and vagaries of various communities and epochs, have we not sacrificed the final criterion of justice and order, by which we might set bounds to what is inordinate in both individual and collective impulses?

It is on this question that Catholic Christianity has its final difficulties with the presuppositions of a democratic society in the modern, liberal sense, fearing, in the words of a recent pronouncement of the American bishops, that questions of "right and wrong" may be subjected to the caprice of majority decisions. For Catholicism believes that the principles of natural law are fixed and immutable, a faith which the secular physiocrats of the eighteenth century shared. It believes that the freedom of a democratic society must stop short of calling these principles of natural law in question.

The liberal democratic tradition of our era gave a different answer to this question. It did not have very plausible reasons for its answer; but history has provided better ones. The truth is that the bourgeois democratic theory held to the idea of absolute and unrestricted liberty, partly because it assumed the unlimited right of private judgment to be one of the "inalienable" rights which were guaranteed by the liberal version of the natural law. Its adherence to the principle of complete liberty of private judgment was also partly derived from its simple confidence in human reason. It was certain that reason would, when properly enlightened, affirm the "self-evident" truths of the natural law. Both the Catholic and the liberal confidence in the dictates of the natural law, thus rest upon a "non-existential" description of human reason. Both fail to appreciate the perennial corruptions of interest and passion which are introduced into any historical definition of even the most ideal and abstract moral principles. The Catholic confidence in the reason of common men was rightly less complete than that of the Enlightenment. Yet it wrongly sought to preserve some realm of institutional religious authority which would protect the uncorrupted truths of the natural law. The Enlightenment erroneously hoped for a general diffusion of intelligence which would make the truths of the natural law universally acceptable. Yet it rightly refused to reserve any area of authority which would not be subject to democratic criticism.

The reason this final democratic freedom is right, though the reasons given for it in the modern period are wrong, is that there is no historical reality, whether it be church or government, whether it be the reason of wise men or specialists, which is not involved in the flux and relativity of human existence; which is not subject to error and sin, and which is not tempted to exaggerate its errors and sins when they are made immune to criticism.

Every society needs working principles of justice, as criteria for its positive law and system of restraints. The profoundest of these actually transcend reason and lie rooted in religious conceptions of the meaning of existence. But every historical statement of them is subject to amendment. If it becomes fixed it will destroy some of the potentialities of a higher justice, which the mind of one generation is unable to anticipate in the life of subsequent eras.

GEORGE KENNAN

The Sources of Soviet Conduct (1947)

After entering the foreign service in 1925, George Frost Kennan (1904–2005), who later became a diplomat and a Pulitzer Prize–winning historian, spent several years in Europe studying the Russian language and Soviet ideology. As counselor of the American embassy in Moscow, Kennan formulated the containment doctrine, which advocated the selective use of counterpressure to oppose Soviet expansionism during the cold war. In a highly influential Foreign Affairs article signed "X," Kennan argued that "the adroit and vigilant application of counter-force" would either force the Soviet Union to cooperate with the United States or lead to an eventual internal Soviet collapse.

Of the original [Soviet] ideology, nothing has been officially junked. Belief is maintained in the basic badness of capitalism, in the inevitability of its destruction, in the obligation of the proletariat to assist in that destruction and to take power into its own hands. But stress has come to be laid primarily on those concepts which relate most specifically to the Soviet régime itself: to its position as the sole truly Socialist régime in a dark and misguided world, and to the relationships of power within it.

The first of these concepts is that of the innate antagonism between capitalism and Socialism. We have seen how deeply that concept has become imbedded in foundations of Soviet power. It has profound implications for Russia's conduct as a member of international society. It means that there can never be on Moscow's side any sincere assumption of a community of aims between the Soviet Union and powers which are regarded as capitalist. It must invariably be assumed in Moscow that the aims of the capitalist world are antagonistic to the Soviet régime, and therefore to the interests of the peoples it controls. If the Soviet Government occasionally sets its signature to documents which would indicate the contrary, this is to be regarded as a tactical manœuvre permissible in dealing with the enemy (who is without honor) and should be taken in the spirit of *caveat emptor*. Basically, the antagonism remains. It is postulated. And from it flow many of the phenomena which we find disturbing in the Kremlin's conduct of foreign policy: the secretiveness, the lack of frankness, the duplicity, the wary suspiciousness, and the basic unfriendliness of purpose. These phenomena are there to stay, for the foreseeable future. There can be variations of degree and of emphasis. When there is something the Russians want from us, one or the other of these features of their policy may be thrust temporarily into the background; and when that happens there will always be Americans who will leap forward with gleeful announcements that "the Russians have changed," and some who will even try to take credit for having brought about such "changes." But we should not be misled by tactical manœuvres. These characteristics of Soviet policy, like the postulate from which they flow, are basic to the internal nature of Soviet power, and will be with us, whether in the foreground or the background, until the internal nature of Soviet power is changed.

This means that we are going to continue for a long time to find the Russians difficult to deal with. It does not mean that they should be considered as embarked upon a do-or-die program to overthrow our society by a given date. The theory of the inevitability of the eventual fall of capitalism has the fortunate connotation that there is no hurry about it. The forces of progress can take their time in preparing the final *coup de grâce*. Meanwhile, what is vital is that the "Socialist fatherland"—that oasis of power which has been already won for Socialism in the person of the Soviet Union—should be cherished and defended by all good Communists at home and abroad, its fortunes promoted, its enemies badgered and confounded. The promotion of premature, "adventuristic" revolutionary projects abroad which might embarrass Soviet power in any way would be an inexcusable, even a counter-revolutionary act. The cause of Socialism is the support and promotion of Soviet power, as defined in Moscow.

This brings us to the second of the concepts important to contemporary Soviet outlook. That is the infallibility of the Kremlin. The Soviet concept of power, which permits no focal points of organization outside the Party itself, requires that the Party leadership remain in theory the sole repository of truth. For if truth were to be found elsewhere, there would be justification for its expression in organized activity. But it is precisely that which the Kremlin cannot and will not permit.

The leadership of the Communist Party is therefore always right, and has been always right ever since in 1929 Stalin formalized his personal power by announcing that decisions of the Politburo were being taken unanimously.

* * *

But we have seen that the Kremlin is under no ideological compulsion to accomplish its purposes in a hurry. Like the Church, it is dealing in ideological concepts which are of long-term validity, and it can afford to be patient. It has no right to risk the existing achievements of the revolution for the sake of vain baubles of the future. The very teachings of Lenin himself require great caution and flexibility in the pursuit of Communist purposes. Again, these precepts are fortified by the lessons of Russian history: of centuries of obscure battles between nomadic forces over the stretches of a vast unfortified plain. Here caution, circumspection, flexibility and deception are the valuable qualities; and their value finds natural appreciation in the Russian or the oriental mind. Thus the Kremlin has no compunction about retreating in the face of superior force. And being under the compulsion of no timetable, it does not get panicky under the necessity for such retreat. * * *

These considerations make Soviet diplomacy at once easier and more difficult to deal with than the diplomacy of individual aggressive leaders like Napoleon and Hitler. On the one hand it is more sensitive to contrary force, more ready to yield on individual sectors of the diplomatic front when that force is felt to be too strong, and thus more rational in the logic and rhetoric of power. On the other hand it cannot be easily defeated or discouraged by a single victory on the part of its opponents. And the patient persistence by which it is animated means that it can be effectively countered not by sporadic acts which represent the momentary whims of democratic opinion but only by intelligent long-range policies on the part of Russia's adversaries—policies no less steady in their purpose, and no less variegated and resourceful in their application, than those of the Soviet Union itself.

In these circumstances it is clear that the main element of any United States policy toward the Soviet Union must be that of a long-term, patient but firm and vigilant containment of Russian expansive tendencies. It is important to note, however, that such a policy has nothing to do with outward histrionics: with threats or blustering or superfluous gestures of outward "toughness." While the Kremlin is basically flexible in its reaction to political realities, it is by no means unamenable to considerations of prestige. Like almost any other government, it can be placed by tactless and threatening gestures in a position where it cannot afford to yield even though this might be dictated by its sense of realism. The Russian leaders are keen judges of human psychology, and as such they are highly conscious that loss of temper and of self-control is never a source of strength in political affairs. They are quick to exploit such evidences of weakness. For these reasons, it is a *sine qua non* of successful dealing with Russia that the foreign government in question should remain at all times cool and collected and that its demands on Russian policy should be put forward in such a manner as to leave the way open for a compliance not too detrimental to Russian prestige.

In the light of the above, it will be clearly seen that the Soviet pressure against the free institutions of the western world is something that can be contained by the adroit and vigilant application of counter-force at a series of constantly shifting geographical and political points, corresponding to the shifts and manœuvres of Soviet policy, but which cannot be charmed or talked out of existence. The Russians look forward to a duel of infinite duration, and they see that already they have scored great successes. It must be borne in mind that there was a time when the Communist Party represented far more of a minority in the sphere of Russian national life than Soviet power today represents in the world community.

* * *

Thus the future of Soviet power may not be by any means as secure as Russian capacity for self-delusion would make it appear to the men in the Kremlin. That they can keep power themselves, they have demonstrated. That they can quietly and easily turn it over to others remains to be proved. Meanwhile, the hardships of their rule and the vicissitudes of international life have taken a heavy toll of the strength and hopes of the great people on whom their power rests. It is curious to note that the ideological power of Soviet authority is strongest today in areas beyond the frontiers of Russia, beyond the reach of its police power. This phenomenon brings to mind a comparison used by Thomas Mann in his great novel "Buddenbrooks." Observing that human institutions often show the greatest outward brilliance at a moment when inner decay is in reality farthest advanced, he compared the Buddenbrook family, in the days of its greatest glamour, to one of those stars whose light shines most brightly on this world when in reality it has long since ceased to exist. And who can say with assurance that the strong light still cast by the Kremlin on the dissatisfied peoples of the western world is not the powerful afterglow of a constellation which is in actuality on the wane? This cannot be proved. And it cannot be disproved. But the possibility remains (and in the opinion of this writer it is a strong one) that Soviet power, like the capitalist world of its conception, bears within it the seeds of its own decay, and that the sprouting of these seeds is well advanced.

It is clear that the United States cannot expect in the foreseeable future to enjoy political intimacy with the Soviet régime. It must continue to regard the Soviet Union as a rival, not a partner, in the political arena. It must continue to expect that Soviet policies will reflect no abstract love of peace and stability, no real faith in the possibility of a permanent happy coexistence of the Socialist and capitalist worlds, but rather a cautious, persistent pressure toward the disruption and weakening of all rival influence and rival power.

Balanced against this are the facts that Russia, as opposed to the western world in general, is still by far the weaker party, that Soviet policy is highly flexible, and that Soviet society may well contain deficiencies which will eventually weaken its own total potential. This would of itself warrant the United States entering with reasonable confidence upon a policy of firm containment, designed to confront the Russians with unalterable counter-force at every point where they show signs of encroaching upon the interests of a peaceful and stable world.

But in actuality the possibilities for American policy are by no means limited to holding the line and hoping for the best. It is entirely possible for the United States to influence by its actions the internal developments, both within Russia and throughout the international Communist movement, by which Russian policy is largely determined. This is not only a question of the modest measure of informational activity which this government can conduct in the Soviet Union and elsewhere, although that, too, is important. It is rather a question of the degree to which the United States can create among the peoples of the world generally the impression of a country which knows what it wants, which is coping successfully with the problems of its internal life and with the responsibilities of a World Power, and which has a spiritual vitality capable of holding its own among the major ideological currents of the time. To the extent that such an impression can be created and maintained, the aims of Russian Communism must appear sterile and quixotic, the hopes and enthusiasm of Moscow's supporters must wane, and added strain must be imposed on the Kremlin's foreign policies. For the palsied decrepitude of the capitalist world is the keystone of Communist philosophy. Even the failure of the United States to experience the early economic depression which the ravens of the Red Square have been predicting with such complacent confidence since hostilities ceased would have deep and important repercussions throughout the Communist world.

By the same token, exhibitions of indecision, disunity and internal dis-integration within this country have an exhilarating effect on the whole Communist movement. At each evidence of these tendencies, a thrill of hope and excitement goes through the Communist world; a new jaunti-ness can be noted in the Moscow tread; new groups of foreign supporters climb on to what they can only view as the band wagon of international politics; and Russian pressure increases all along the line in international affairs.

It would be an exaggeration to say that American behavior unassisted and alone could exercise a power of life and death over the Communist movement and bring about the early fall of Soviet power in Russia. But the United States has it in its power to increase enormously the strains under which Soviet policy must operate, to force upon the Kremlin a far greater degree of moderation and circumspection than it has had to ob-serve in recent years, and in this way to promote tendencies which must eventually find their outlet in either the break-up or the gradual mellow-ing of Soviet power. For no mystical, Messianic movement—and particu-larly not that of the Kremlin—can face frustration indefinitely without eventually adjusting itself in one way or another to the logic of that state of affairs.

Thus the decision will really fall in large measure in this country itself. The issue of Soviet-American relations is in essence a test of the over-all worth of the United States as a nation among nations. To avoid destruc-tion the United States need only measure up to its own best traditions and prove itself worthy of preservation as a great nation.

ARTHUR M. SCHLESINGER, JR.

What Is Loyalty? A Difficult Question (1947)

Arthur Meier Schlesinger, Jr. (1917–2007), was a liberal American his-torian and public intellectual who served in the Office of War Infor-mation, the Office of Strategic Services, and the U.S. Army during World War II. The youngest historian to win the Pulitzer Prize, this self-described New Dealer later became a professor of history at Harvard, a founder of the Americans for Democratic Action, and a presidential assistant to John F. Kennedy. In the midst of the growing

*anticommunist hysteria that led to widespread accusations of disloy-
alty to America, Schlesinger believed it was necessary for liberals and
conservatives alike to moderate their positions. In a New York Times
Magazine article published November 2, 1947, he urged Americans to
reject Communism without trampling on civil liberties.*

We have heard a good deal in recent months about loyalty and
Americanism. Spokesmen on one side proclaim that the American way of life is in imminent danger from any one who questions the
eternal rightness of the capitalist system. Spokesmen on the other side
proclaim that a sinister witch-hunt is already transforming the United
States into a totalitarian police state.

The situation cries out for a little less hysteria and a little more calm
sense. A calm survey surely reveals two propositions on which we can all
agree: (1) that Americanism is not a totalitarian faith, which can impose
a single economic or political dogma or require a uniformity in observance from all its devotees; but (2) that a serious problem for national security has been created by that fanatical group which rejects all American
interests in favor of those of the Soviet Union.

In other words, the disciples of the Un-American Activities Committee
and the leadership of the American Legion must be reminded that Americanism means something far richer and deeper than submission to their
own collection of petty prejudices; and civil libertarians who honestly
fear a witch-hunt must be reminded that in an imperfect world of spies
and traitors a Government must be conceded the right of self-protection.
We see here an inescapable conflict between civil liberty and national security, and we must face up to the problem of resolving the conflict.

What is Americanism? To get quickly to what its loudest exponents
seem to regard as its basic point—private enterprise—there is nothing
un-American about criticizing the capitalist system. Let us reveal the
hideous secret: capitalism was not handed down with the Ten Commandments at Sinai. The Constitution of the United States does not ordain the
economic status quo. It can well be argued that there is nothing in our
fundamental law to prevent Congress from socializing all basic industry
tomorrow; there is certainly nothing in our state laws to prevent public
ownership.

Are we to assume that revelations concerning the sacrosanctity of private
capitalism have been vouchsafed to the NAM [National Association of
Manufacturers] and to the Republican Party which were denied to the
Founding Fathers? More than this, the basic tradition in American
democracy—the tradition associated with such names as Jefferson, Jackson,

Wilson and the two Roosevelts—has been a fight on behalf of the broad masses against the economic excesses of capitalism and against the political aspirations of the business community.

* * *

This insistence on the infailibility of capitalism and on the heresy of change finds no sanction in the usages of the American democratic tradition. It reaches its pinnacle of imbecility in such episodes as the attack on the film "The Best Years of Our Lives" as Communist-minded because it makes fun of the American business man, or in the standards employed by the Un-American Committee in their current Hollywood investigation. What havoc the rigid identification of Americanism with business worship would wreak upon the history and traditions of our country! Yet this very identification pervades altogether too much of the popular campaign against communism. Many conservatives are happily pouncing upon the Communist scare as an excuse for silencing all critics of business supremacy.

* * *

Experience by now must have exposed the illusion that it is possible to work with Communists or fellow-travelers—with persons whose loyalties are signed, sealed and delivered elsewhere. President Gonzales Videla of Chile and Joe Curran of the National Maritime Union have presented only the most recent case histories. One may still wonder perhaps whether the divergence of political loyalties really goes to the length of espionage. Again the record is clear. Herbert Morrison, hardly a reactionary, has borne testimony, for example, to the cases of Communist espionage which came to him as British Home Secretary at a time when Britain and Russia were fighting allies.

"It may be said that all countries spy, and it may be that they do," Morrison observed. "But there is a grave difference between the ordinary spying of the professional spy . . . and espionage through a political organization." The documents of the Canadian spy case report the techniques of Communist political corruption in fascinating and indisputable detail—in particular, the use of the "study group" as a way of feeling out the degrees of political fanaticism.

* * *

It would be rash to assume that Moscow has its intelligence networks operating in every country except the one it has repeatedly named as its chief enemy—the United States. Certainly the American Communist party has made no secret of its belief that the United States should always follow the Soviet lead. As recently as September, 1947, *Political Affairs*, the American Communist theological organ, made its usual references to the "fact" that "the policies of the Soviet Union before, during and since the anti-Axis war, have corresponded to the best interest of the American people."

In view of such repeated declarations, it becomes increasingly difficult to see how even Henry Wallace can continue saying, "The very few Communists I have met have been very good Americans." The presumption becomes overwhelming that the U.S.S.R. through the NKVD, its underground Communist cells and its front organizations, is commissioning agents to penetrate the "sensitive" branches of the Government, particularly the State Department, the Department of National Defense and the Atomic Energy Commission.

Let us then admit that a real danger exists. But the solution is surely not, on the one hand, to fire every one suspected of liberal leanings, nor, on the other, to fire only avowed and open Communists. The solution is rather to construct some means of ridding the security agencies of questionable characters, while at the same time retaining enough safeguards to insure against indiscriminate purges.

Discharge in advance of an overt act may seem a rough policy. Yet the failure to discharge suspicious persons may well imperil national security; it certainly would lead to the use of precautionary measures, such as wire-tapping and constant shadowing, which would bring the police state much nearer. Let us recall for a moment the situation in 1938. Obviously Nazis, their conscious fellow-travelers and soft-headed Americans who conceived Germany to be a much misunderstood nation had no business in the State Department; and liberals were correct in demanding their dismissal in advance of overt acts. I cannot see why this same principle does not apply today to the fellow-travelers of a rival totalitarianism.

Have we, in fact, a witch-hunt today? We must first discriminate between the wishes of some members of Congress and the intentions of the Executive. The most shocking actions of the Administration—notably the President's executive order, the State Department's loyalty code and some of the recent firings—have doubtless been motivated in great part by a desire to head off more extreme action from Congress. Yet, this very process of appeasing the worst element in Congress has led to the compromise of principles which cannot be properly compromised in a democracy. Appeasement has produced throughout the Executive Branch an atmosphere of apprehension and anxiety that is fatal to boldness in government.

* * *

Yet the executive order and the State Department code are inexcusably defective. In particular, the recent action of the State Department in denying most of those discharged both the right to a hearing and the right to resignation without prejudice betrays a state of mind going beyond the requirements of security and entering the realm of persecution. The department must be able to terminate employment on suspicion: this can be done in a number of ways; but the department cannot be allowed to stigmatize individuals and wreck lives on suspicion.

* * * The final result can only be to enthrone the narrow, bureaucratic conformist at the expense of the belief in human dignity which purports to be the main objective of our foreign policy.

Still, honest civil libertarians might better devote themselves, not to blanket abuse of any attempts to meet the problem but to the construction of alternatives which would better secure individual rights while still permitting the Government to deal effectively with the grim dangers of foreign espionage. * * *

The first constructive step, perhaps, would be to make a clear distinction between the citizen and the rights of a government employee in a security agency. The private political views of a Hollywood writer, for example, hardly seem to be the proper consideration of the United States Government or a committee of Congress. An American citizen clearly must be protected in his right to think and speak freely—as a Communist, a Fascist or whatever he wants; but no rule of the Constitution or of common sense requires the State Department to employ him.

* * *

The second step would be to hedge round the process of dismissal from security agencies with much firmer procedural safeguards. At some point in the process' full power to summon witnesses and to weigh evidence must be concentrated. That point plainly must be, not the investigative agency, but a government review board to which all persons dismissed on security grounds can appeal. That board must acquaint the accused with the charges and permit him the protection of counsel. It must be able to obtain from the FBI full data concerning the reliability of the evidence: the situation is intolerable where the administrator must act on the basis of statements from informants identified only by letters, numbers or FBI code-names.

The board must have the further power to interrogate these informants. The problem of permitting the accused to confront the informants, however, is not so simple as it sounds. Espionage breeds counter-espionage; and government counter-espionage agencies simply cannot unveil their agents at every demand of a defense attorney. Where the evidence by itself is substantial, the review board cannot be expected to require confrontation. But, where the evidence is tenuous, the board must have the power on confronting the accused with the accuser. If the FBI does not think the case important enough to risk blowing a counter-espionage chain, it must choose between the chain and the conviction.

* * *

The situation imposes a special responsibility, too, I think, upon the American left. Liberals who complain when Parnell Thomas fails to distinguish between liberals and Communists should remember that too often they have failed to make that distinction themselves. History by now has surely documented that distinction to the point of surfeit; the attack on the free Socialist parties in the recent Belgrade manifesto is only the most recent example of the deadly Soviet hostility to the non-Communist left.

The liberal movement in this country must reject the Communists as forthrightly as the British Labor party has rejected them; it must not squander its energy and influence in covering up for them. This is the dictate of strategy as well as principle. Whatever conservatism may say about Wilson Wyatt or Leon Henderson and Americans for Democratic Action or about such labor leaders as Walter Reuther and David Dubinsky, it cannot combat them by smearing them as fellow-travelers.

But the situation imposes just as grave a responsibility upon American conservatives. They must remember that the only criterion for disloyalty is superior loyalty to another country, and that reservations about the capitalist system or skepticism concerning the wisdom of the business community are by themselves no evidence at all of external loyalties. The essential fight in Europe today, for example, is between socialism and communism; and socialism has many supporters and sympathizers in this country who are resolutely anti-totalitarian. If the leadership of this country were to be confined to men endorsed by the business community, then the United States would be doomed once more to that morass of confusion and failure into which business rule has invariably plunged us through our history.

There is no easy answer to this conflict of principles between civil liberty and national security. The practical results thus must depend too much for comfort upon the restraint and wisdom of individuals. This responsibility becomes only one aspect of the great moral challenge which confronts us. If we cannot handle this conflict of principle soberly and responsibly, if we cannot rise to the world crisis, then we lack the qualities of greatness as a nation, and we can expect to pay the price of hysteria or of paralysis.

WILLIAM F. BUCKLEY, JR.

God and Man at Yale (1951)

The conservative public intellectual William Frank Buckley, Jr. (1925–2008), founded and edited the influential conservative magazine National Review, *hosted the weekly political interview program* Firing Line, *and has written numerous political books and spy novels. Written in 1951 shortly after his graduation from Yale University, Buckley's* God and Man at Yale *linked two strands of thought that would define conservatism for a generation. Attacking "the superstitions of academic freedom" as nothing more than an excuse to propagate atheism and socialism, Buckley argued that Yale had an obligation to teach the values of religion and free-market individualism.*

During the years 1946 to 1950, I was an undergraduate at Yale University. I arrived in New Haven fresh from a two-year stint in the Army, and I brought with me a firm belief in Christianity and a profound respect for American institutions and traditions. I had always been taught, and experience had fortified the teachings, that an active faith in God and a rigid adherence to Christian principles are the most powerful influences toward the good life. I also believed, with only a scanty knowledge of economics, that free enterprise and limited government had served this country well and would probably continue to do so in the future.

These two attitudes were basic to my general outlook. One concerned the role of man in the universe; the other, in all its implications, the role of man in his society. I knew, of course, of the existence of many persons who had no faith in God and even less in the individual's capacity to work out his own destiny without recourse to the state. I therefore looked eagerly to Yale University for allies against secularism and collectivism.

I am one of a small group of students who fought, during undergraduate days, in the columns of the newspaper, in the Political Union, in debates and seminars, against those who seek to subvert religion and individualism. The fight we waged continues even though little headway was made. The struggle was never more bitter than when the issue concerned educational policy.

As opportunity afforded, some of us advanced the viewpoint that the faculty of Yale is morally and constitutionally responsible to the trustees of Yale, who are in turn responsible to the alumni, and thus duty bound to transmit to their students the wisdom, insight, and value judgments which in the trustees' opinion will enable the American citizen to make the optimum adjustment to the community and to the world. I contended that the trustees of Yale, along with the vast majority of the alumni, are committed to the desirability of fostering both a belief in God, and a recognition of the merits of our economic system. I therefore concluded that as our educational overseers, it was the clear responsibility of the trustees to guide the teaching at Yale toward those ends.

The reaction to this point of view has been violent. A number of persons affiliated with the University, all the way from President-emeritus Charles Seymour to a host of students, have upheld what they call "academic freedom," by which they mean the freedom of the faculty member to teach what he sees fit as he sees fit—provided, of course, he is "honest" and "professionally competent." Here the argument rested when I left Yale.

A number of persons sympathetic to this point of view have urged me to deal at greater length with the problem. I was not disposed to do this, in part because I lack the scholarly equipment to deal with it adequately, in part because I was unwilling to spend the necessary time. I finally decided to make an attempt, largely because I fell victim to arguments I have so often utilized myself: that the so-called conservative, uncomfortably disdainful of controversy, seldom has the energy to fight his battles, while the radical, so often a member of the minority, exerts disproportionate influence because of his dedication to his cause.

I *am* dedicated to my cause. At the same time, I cannot claim to have approached this project with the diligence and patience of a professional scholar. As far as pure scholarship is concerned, it is best said of me that I have the profoundest respect for it, and no pretension to it. As witness to this, I propose, in the nontheoretical portion of this book, to confine myself to Yale. Ideally, my observations would be based on an exhaustive study of the curricula and attitudes of a number of colleges and universities. Instead, I have confined myself to the university that I know first hand. * * *

I propose, simply, to expose what I regard as an extraordinarily irresponsible educational attitude that, under the protective label "academic freedom," has produced one of the most extraordinary incongruities of our time: the institution that derives its moral and financial support from Christian individualists and then addresses itself to the task of persuading the sons of these supporters to be atheistic socialists. * * *

I have some notion of the bitter opposition that this book will inspire. But I am through worrying about it. My concern over present-day educational practice stems from my conviction that, after each side has had its say, we are right and they are wrong; and my greatest anguish is not in contemplation of the antagonism that this essay will evoke from many quarters, but rather from the knowledge that they are winning and we are losing.

I shall insert here what may seem obvious: I consider this battle of educational theory important and worth time and thought even in the context of a world-situation that seems to render totally irrelevant any fight except the power struggle against Communism. I myself believe that the duel between Christianity and atheism is the most important in the world. I further believe that the struggle between individualism and collectivism is the same struggle reproduced on another level. I believe that if and when the menace of Communism is gone, other vital battles, at present subordinated, will emerge to the foreground. And the winner must have help from the classroom.

I should also like to state that I am not here concerned with writing an *apologia* either for Christianity or for individualism. That is to say, this essay will not attempt to prove either the divinity of Christ or to defend the advantages of conducting our lives with reference to divine sanctions. Nor shall I attempt to demonstrate the contemporary applicability of the principal theses of Adam Smith.

Rather, I will proceed on the assumption that Christianity and freedom are "good," without ever worrying that by so doing, I am being presumptuous.

The first duty, of course, is to arrive at a judgment as to whether or not there exists at Yale an atmosphere of detached impartiality with respect to the great value-alternatives of the day, that is, Christianity *versus* agnosticism and atheism, and individualism *versus* collectivism. My belief is that such impartiality does not exist. I shall document this opinion. What is more, for practical reasons I have restricted my survey to the undergraduate school, even though some of the graduate departments, the Yale Law School in particular, would provide far more flamboyant copy.

The question then arises: If there is a bias does it coincide with the bias of the educational trustees of Yale? In other words, if there is not impartiality, does the net impact of Yale education encourage those values probably held by the alumni? My opinion is that on the contrary, the emphases at Yale are directly opposed to those of her alumni.

I shall then ask if impartiality—assuming it to be possible—is desirable in classroom treatment of conflicting ideologies. I shall go on to question what so many persons consider axiomatic, namely the proposition that "all sides should be presented impartially," that the student should be encouraged to select the side that pleases him most. I hope to point out that this attitude, acknowledged in theory by the University, has never been practiced, and in fact, can never and ought never to be practiced.

WHITTAKER CHAMBERS

Witness (1952)

A former Russian agent and member of the American Communist party, Whittaker Chambers (1901–1961) was a senior editor at Time magazine in 1948 when he accused Alger Hiss, a State Department official, of spying for the Soviets during the 1930s. Chambers's sensational testimony before the House Un-American Activities Committee seemed to bolster claims made by such anticommunists as Senator Joseph McCarthy that communists had infiltrated the highest levels of the American government. In the prologue to his autobiographical bestseller, Chambers described the crisis of the cold war as a deadly struggle between the empty materialism of communism and the spiritual fulfillment of God-given freedom.

Much more than Alger Hiss or Whittaker Chambers was on trial in the trials of Alger Hiss. Two faiths were on trial. Human societies, like human beings, live by faith and die when faith dies. At issue in the Hiss Case was the question whether this sick society, which we call Western civilization, could in its extremity still cast up a man whose faith in it was so great that he would voluntarily abandon those things which men hold good, including life, to defend it. At issue was the question whether this man's faith could prevail against a man whose equal faith it was that this society is sick beyond saving, and that mercy itself pleads for its swift extinction and replacement by another. At issue was the question whether, in the desperately divided society, there still remained the will to recognize the issues in time to offset the immense rally of public power to distort and pervert the facts.

At heart, the Great Case was this critical conflict of faiths; that is why it was a great case. On a scale personal enough to be felt by all, but big

enough to be symbolic, the two irreconcilable faiths of our time—
Communism and Freedom—came to grips in the persons of two conscious and resolute men. Indeed, it would have been hard, in a world still
only dimly aware of what the conflict is about, to find two other men who
knew so clearly. Both had been schooled in the same view of history (the
Marxist view). Both were trained by the same party in the same selfless,
semisoldierly discipline. Neither would nor could yield without betraying,
not himself, but his faith; and the different character of these faiths was
shown by the different conduct of the two men toward each other
throughout the struggle. For, with dark certitude, both knew, almost from
the beginning, that the Great Case could end only in the destruction of
one or both of the contending figures, just as the history of our times
(both men had been taught) can end only in the destruction of one or
both of the contending forces. * * *

I was a witness. I do not mean a witness for the Government or against
Alger Hiss and the others. Nor do I mean the short, squat, solitary figure,
trudging through the impersonal halls of public buildings to testify before
Congressional committees, grand juries, loyalty boards, courts of law.
A man is not primarily a witness *against* something. That is only incidental to the fact that he is a witness *for* something. A witness, in the sense
that I am using the word, is a man whose life and faith are so completely
one that when the challenge comes to step out and testify for his faith, he
does so, disregarding all risks, accepting all consequences.

* * *

I see in Communism the focus of the concentrated evil of our time. You
will ask: Why, then, do men become Communists? How did it happen that
you, our gentle and loved father, were once a Communist? Were you simply stupid? No, I was not stupid. Were you morally depraved? No, I was
not morally depraved. Indeed, educated men become Communists chiefly
for moral reasons. Did you not know that the crimes and horrors of Communism are inherent in Communism? Yes, I knew that fact. Then why did
you become a Communist? It would help more to ask: How did it happen
that this movement, once a mere muttering of political outcasts, became
this immense force that now contests the mastery of mankind? Even when
all the chances and mistakes of history are allowed for, the answer must
be: Communism makes some profound appeal to the human mind. You
will not find out what it is by calling Communism names. That will not
help much to explain why Communism whose horrors, on a scale unparalleled in history, are now public knowledge, still recruits its thousands and
holds its millions—among them some of the best minds alive. Look at
Klaus Fuchs, standing in the London dock, quiet, doomed, destroyed, and
say whether it is possible to answer in that way the simple question: Why?

First, let me try to say what Communism is not. It is not simply a vicious plot hatched by wicked men in a sub-cellar. It is not just the writings of Marx and Lenin, dialectical materialism, the Politburo, the labor theory of value, the theory of the general strike, the Red Army, secret police, labor camps, underground conspiracy, the dictatorship of the proletariat, the technique of the coup d'état. It is not even those chanting, bannered millions that stream periodically, like disorganized armies, through the heart of the world's capitals: Moscow, New York, Tokyo, Paris, Rome. These are expressions of Communism, but they are not what Communism is about.

In the Hiss trials, where Communism was a haunting specter, but which did little or nothing to explain Communism, Communists were assumed to be criminals, pariahs, clandestine men who lead double lives under false names, travel on false passports, deny traditional religion, morality, the sanctity of oaths, preach violence and practice treason. These things are true about Communists, but they are not what Communism is about.

The revolutionary heart of Communism is not the theatrical appeal: "Workers of the world, unite. You have nothing to lose but your chains. You have a world to gain." It is a simple statement of Karl Marx, further simplified for handy use: "Philosophers have explained the world; it is necessary to change the world." Communists are bound together by no secret oath. The tie that binds them across the frontiers of nations, across barriers of language and differences of class and education, in defiance of religion, morality, truth, law, honor, the weaknesses of the body and the irresolutions of the mind, even unto death, is a simple conviction: It is necessary to change the world. Their power, whose nature baffles the rest of the world, because in a large measure the rest of the world has lost that power, is the power to hold convictions and to act on them. It is the same power that moves mountains; it is also an unfailing power to move men. Communists are that part of mankind which has recovered the power to live or die—to bear witness—for its faith. And it is a simple, rational faith that inspires men to live or die for it.

It is not new. It is, in fact, man's second oldest faith. Its promise was whispered in the first days of the Creation under the Tree of the Knowledge of Good and Evil: "Ye shall be as gods." It is the great alternative faith of mankind. Like all great faiths, its force derives from a simple vision. Other ages have had great visions. They have always been different versions of the same vision: the vision of God and man's relationship to God. The Communist vision is the vision of Man without God.

It is the vision of man's mind displacing God as the creative intelligence of the world. It is the vision of man's liberated mind, by the sole force of its rational intelligence, redirecting man's destiny and reorganizing man's life and the world. It is the vision of man, once more the central figure of the Creation, not because God made man in His image, but because man's mind makes him the most intelligent of the animals. Copernicus and his successors displaced man as the central fact of the universe by proving that the earth was not the central star of the universe. Communism restores man to his sovereignty by the simple method of denying God.

* * *

Hence the Communist Party is quite justified in calling itself the most revolutionary party in history. It has posed in practical form the most revolutionary question in history: God or Man? It has taken the logical next step which three hundred years of rationalism hesitated to take, and said what millions of modern minds think, but do not dare or care to say: If man's mind is the decisive force in the world, what need is there for God? Henceforth man's mind is man's fate.

This vision is the Communist revolution, which, like all great revolutions, occurs in man's mind before it takes form in man's acts. Insurrection and conspiracy are merely methods of realizing the vision; they are merely part of the politics of Communism. Without its vision, they, like Communism, would have no meaning and could not rally a parcel of pickpockets. Communism does not summon men to crime or to utopia, as its easy critics like to think. On the plane of faith, it summons mankind to turn its vision into practical reality. On the plane of action, it summons men to struggle against the inertia of the past which, embodied in social, political and economic forms, Communism claims, is blocking the will of mankind to make its next great forward stride. It summons men to overcome the crisis, which, Communism claims, is in effect a crisis of rending frustration, with the world, unable to stand still, but unwilling to go forward along the road that the logic of a technological civilization points out—Communism.

This is Communism's moral sanction, which is twofold. Its vision points the way to the future: its faith labors to turn the future into present reality. It says to every man who joins it: the vision is a practical problem of history; the way to achieve it is a practical problem of politics, which is the present tense of history. Have you the moral strength to take upon yourself the crimes of history so that man at last may close his chronicle of age-old, senseless suffering, and replace it with purpose and a plan? The answer a man makes to this question is the difference between the Communist and those miscellaneous socialists, liberals, fellow travelers, unclassified progressives and men of good will, all of whom share a similar vision, but do not share the faith because they will not take upon themselves the penalties of the faith. The answer is the root of that sense of moral superiority which makes Communists, though caught in crime, berate their opponents with withering self-righteousness.

* * *

The vision inspires. The crisis impels. The workingman is chiefly moved by the crisis. The educated man is chiefly moved by the vision. The workingman, living upon a mean margin of life, can afford few visions—even practical visions. An educated man, peering from the Harvard Yard, or any college campus, upon a world in chaos, finds in the vision the two certainties for which the mind of man tirelessly seeks: a reason to live and a reason to die. No other faith of our time presents them with the same practical intensity. That is why Communism is the central experience of the first half of the 20th century, and may be its final experience—will be, unless the free world, in the agony of its struggle with Communism, overcomes its crisis by discovering, in suffering and pain, a power of faith which will provide man's mind, at the same intensity, with the same two certainties: a reason to live and a reason to die. If it fails, this will be the century of the great social wars. If it succeeds, this will be the century of the great wars of faith.

* * *

One thing most ex-Communists could agree upon: they broke because they wanted to be free. They do not all mean the same thing by "free." Freedom is a need of the soul, and nothing else. It is in striving toward God that the soul strives continually after a condition of freedom. God alone is the inciter and guarantor of freedom. He is the only guarantor. External freedom is only an aspect of interior freedom. Political freedom, as the Western world has known it, is only a political reading of the Bible. Religion and freedom are indivisible. Without freedom the soul dies. Without the soul there is no justification for freedom. Necessity is the only ultimate justification known to the mind. Hence every sincere break with Communism is a religious experience, though the Communist fail to identify its true nature, though he fail to go to the end of the experience. His break is the political expression of the perpetual need of the soul whose first faint stirring he has felt within him, years, months or days before he breaks. A Communist breaks because he must choose at last between irreconcilable opposites—God or Man, Soul or Mind, Freedom or Communism.

Communism is what happens when, in the name of Mind, men free themselves from God. But its view of God, its knowledge of God, its experience of God, is what alone gives character to a society or a nation, and meaning to its destiny. Its culture, the voice of this character, is merely that view, knowledge, experience, of God, fixed by its most intense spirits in terms intelligible to the mass of men. There has never been a society or a nation without God. But history is cluttered with the wreckage of nations that became indifferent to God and died.

LEARNED HAND

A Plea for the Freedom of Dissent (1955)

The distinguished federal judge Billings Learned Hand (1872–1961) served on the Second Circuit of the U.S. Court of Appeals from 1924 until his retirement in 1951. Although he sometimes sustained the convictions of communist dissenters and other radicals, Hand developed a relatively libertarian test in cases dealing with seditious speech against the government. In an address given at the annual meeting of the American Jewish Committee in January 1955 and later published in the New York Times Magazine, *the former judge defended the values of dissent and nonconformity and the habits of toleration that preserve civil liberties.*

What do we mean by "principles of civil liberties and human rights"? We cannot go far in that inquiry until we have achieved some notion of what we mean by Liberty; and that has always proved a hard concept to define. The natural, though naïve, opinion is that it means no more than that each individual shall be allowed to pursue his own desires without let or hindrance; and that, although it is true that this is practically impossible, still it does remain the goal, approach to which measures our success. Why, then, is not a beehive or an anthill a perfect example of a free society? Surely you have been a curious and amused watcher beside one of these.

In and out of their crowded pueblo the denizens pass in great number, each bent upon his own urgent mission, quite oblivious of all the rest except as he must bend his path to avoid them. It is a scene of strenuous, purposeful endeavor in which each appears to be, and no doubt in fact is, accomplishing his own purpose; and yet he is at the same time accomplishing the purpose of the group as a whole. As I have gazed at it, the sentence from the Collect of the Episcopal prayerbook has come to me: "Whose service is perfect freedom."

Why is it, then, that we so positively rebel against the hive and the hill as a specimen of a free society? Why is it that such prototypes of totalitarianisms arouse our deepest hostility? Unhappily it is not because they cannot be realized, or at least because they cannot be approached, for a substantial period. Who can be sure that such appalling forecasts as Aldous Huxley's "Brave New World" or Orwell's "1984" are not prophetic? Indeed, there have often been near approaches to such an order.

Germany at the end of 1940 was probably not far removed from one, and who of us knows that there are not countless persons today living within the boundaries of Russia and perhaps of China who are not willing partners, accepting as their personal aspirations the official definitions of the good, the true and the beautiful? Indeed, there have been, and still are, in our own United States large and powerful groups who, if we are to judge their purposes by their conduct, see treason in all dissidence and would welcome an era in which all of us should think, feel and live in consonance with duly prescribed patterns.

Human nature is malleable, especially if you can indoctrinate the disiple with indefectible principles before anyone else reaches him. (I fancy that the Janissaries were as fervent Mohammedans as the authentic Turks.) Indeed, we hear from those who are entitled to an opinion that at times the abject confessions made in Russia by victims who know that they are already marked for slaughter are not wrung from them by torture or threats against their families. Rather, they come from partisans, so obsessed with the faith that when they are told that the occasion calls for scapegoats and that they have been selected, recognize and assent to the propriety of the demand and cooperate in its satisfaction. It is as though, when the right time comes, the drones agreed to their extinction in the interest of the hive.

Nor need we be surprised that men so often embrace almost any doctrines, if they are proclaimed with a voice of absolute assurance. In a universe that we do not understand, but with which we must in one way or another somehow manage to deal, and aware of the conflicting desires that clamorously beset us, between which we must choose and which we must therefore manage to weigh, we turn in our bewilderment to those who tell us that they have found a path out of the thickets and possess the scales by which to appraise our needs.

Over and over again such prophets succeed in converting us to unquestioning acceptance; there is scarcely a monstrous belief that has not had its day and its passionate adherents, so eager are we for safe footholds in our dubious course. How certain is any one of us that he, too, might not be content to follow any fantastic creed, if he was satisfied that nothing would ever wake him from the dream? And, indeed, if there were nothing to wake him, how should he distinguish its articles from the authentic dictates of verity?

Remember, too, that it is by no means clear that we are happier in the faith we do profess than we should be under the spell of an orthodoxy that was safe against all heresy. Cruel and savage as orthodoxies have always proved to be, the faithful seem able to convince themselves that the heretics, as they continue to crop up, get nothing worse than their due, and to rest with an easy conscience.

In any event, my thesis is that the best answer to such systems is not so much in their immoral quality—immoral though they be—as in the fact that they are inherently unstable, because they are at war with our only trustworthy way of living in accord with the facts. For I submit that it is only by trial and error, by insistent scrutiny and by readiness to re-examine presently accredited conclusions that we have risen, so far as in fact we have risen, from our brutish ancestors, and I believe that in our loyalty to these habits lies our only chance, not merely of progress, but even of survival.

They were not indeed a part of our aboriginal endowment: Man, as he emerged, was not prodigally equipped to master the infinite diversity of his environment. Obviously, enough of us did manage to get through; but it has been a statistical survival, for the individual's native powers of adjustment are by no means enough for his personal safety any more than are those of other creatures. The precipitate of our experience is far from absolute verity, and our exasperated resentment at all dissent is a sure index of our doubts. Take, for instance, our constant recourse to the word, "subversive," as a touchstone of impermissible deviation from accepted canons.

All discussion, all debate, all dissidence tends to question and in consequence to upset existing convictions: that is precisely its purpose and its justification. He is, indeed, a "subversive" who disputes those precepts that I most treasure and seeks to persuade me to substitute his own. He may have no shadow of desire to resort to anything but persuasion; he may be of those to whom any forcible sanction of conformity is anathema; yet it remains true that he is trying to bring about my apostasy, and I hate him just in proportion as I fear his success.

Contrast this protective resentment with the assumption that lies at the base of our whole system that the best chance for truth to emerge is a fair field for all ideas. Nothing, I submit, more completely betrays our latent disloyalty to this premise to all that we pretend to believe than the increasingly common resort to this and other question-begging words. Their imprecision comforts us by enabling us to suppress arguments that disturb our complacency and yet to continue to congratulate ourselves on keeping the faith as we have received it from the Founding Fathers.

Heretics have been hateful from the beginning of recorded time; they have been ostracized, exiled, tortured, maimed and butchered; but it has generally proved impossible to smother them, and when it has not, the society that has succeeded has always declined. Facades of authority, however imposing, do not survive after it has appeared that they rest upon the sands of human conjecture and compromise.

And so, if I am to say what are "the principles of civil liberties and human rights," I answer that they lie in habits, customs—conventions, if you will—that tolerate dissent and can live without irrefragable certainties; that are ready to overhaul existing assumptions; that recognize that we never see save through a glass, darkly, and that at long last we shall succeed only so far as we continue to undertake "the intolerable labor of thought"—that most distasteful of all our activities.

If such a habit and such a temper pervade a society, it will not need institutions to protect its "civil liberties and human rights"; so far as they do not, I venture to doubt how far anything else can protect them: whether it be Bills of Rights, or courts that must in the name of interpretation read their meaning into them.

This may seem to you a bleak and cheerless conclusion, too alien to our nature to be practical. "We must live from day to day"—you will say—"to live is to act, and to act is to choose and decide. How can we carry on at all without some principles, some patterns to meet the conflicts in which each day involves us?" Indeed, we cannot, nor am I suggesting that we should try; but I *am* suggesting that it makes a vital difference—*the* vital difference—whether we deem our principles and our patterns to be eternal verities, rather than the best postulates so far attainable.

* * *

By some happy fortuity man is a projector, a designer, a builder, a craftsman; it is among his most dependable joys to impose upon the flux that passes before him some mark of himself, aware though he always must be of the odds against him. His reward is not so much in the work as in its making; not so much in the prize as in the race. We may win when we lose, if we have done what we can; for by so doing we have made real at least some part of that finished product in whose fabrication we are most concerned—ourselves.

* * *

It is still in the lap of the gods whether a society can succeed, based on "civil liberties and human rights," conceived as I have tried to describe them; but of one thing at least we may be sure: the alternatives that have so far appeared have been immeasurably worse, and so, whatever the outcome, I submit to you that we must press along.

WALTER LIPPMANN

The Public Philosophy (1955)

In his analysis of the crisis of modern democracy in the aftermath of World War II, Lippmann called for a renewed commitment to the principles of Western society in the face of emerging threats to freedom at home and abroad. To restore faith in the "public philosophy of a free society," Lippmann argued that it was necessary to distinguish transcendent public values from "private interests and desires." In his 1955 book The Public Philosophy, *Lippmann offers a Platonic defense of absolute standards of good and right and a renewed belief in natural law that would in the decades to follow become a core conservative argument against liberal ethical relativism.*

How is the public interest discerned and judged? From what we have been saying we know that we cannot answer the question by attempting to forecast what the invisible community, with all its unborn constituents, will, would, or might say if and when it ever had a chance to vote. There is no point in toying with any notion of an imaginary plebiscite to discover the public interest. We cannot know what we ourselves will be thinking five years hence, much less what infants now in the cradle will be thinking when they go into the polling booth.

Yet their interests, as we observe them today, are within the public interest. Living adults share, we must believe, the same public interest. For them, however, the public interest is mixed with, and is often at odds with, their private and special interests. Put this way, we can say, I suggest, that the public interest may be presumed to be what men would choose if they saw clearly, thought rationally, acted disinterestedly and benevolently.

* * *

The public philosophy is known as *natural law*, a name which, alas, causes great semantic confusion. This philosophy is the premise of the institutions of the Western society, and they are, I believe, unworkable in communities that do not adhere to it. Except on the premises of this philosophy, it is impossible to reach intelligible and workable conceptions of popular election, majority rule, representative assemblies, free speech, loyalty, property, corporations, and voluntary associations. The founders of these institutions, which the recently enfranchised democracies have inherited, were all of them adherents of some one of the various schools of natural law. * * *

To speak of a public philosophy is, I am well aware, to raise dangerous questions, rather like opening Pandora's box.

Within the Western nations, as Father Murray has put it, there is "a plurality of incompatible faiths"; there is also a multitude of secularized and agnostic people. Since there is so little prospect of agreement, and such certainty of dissension, on the content of the public philosophy, it seems expedient not to raise the issues by talking about them. It is easier to follow the rule that each person's beliefs are private and that only overt conduct is a public matter.

One might say that this prudent rule reflects and registers the terms of settlement of the religious wars and of the long struggle against exclusive authority in the realm of the spirit by "thrones or dominations, or principalities or powers."

Freedom of religion and of thought and of speech were achieved by denying both to the state and to the established church a sovereign monopoly in the field of religion, philosophy, morals, science, learning, opinion, and conscience. The liberal constitutions, with their bills of rights, fixed the boundaries past which the sovereign—the King, the Parliament, the Congress, the voters—were forbidden to go.

Yet the men of the seventeenth and eighteenth centuries who established these great salutary rules would certainly have denied that a community could do without a general public philosophy. They were themselves the adherents of a public philosophy—of the doctrine of natural law, which held that there was law "above the ruler and the sovereign people . . . above the whole community of mortals."

The traditions of civility spring from this principle, which was first worked out by the Stoics. * * *

These traditions were expounded in the treatises of philosophers, were developed in the tracts of the publicists, were absorbed by the lawyers and applied in the courts. At times of great stress some of the endangered traditions were committed to writing, as in the Magna Carta and the Declaration of Independence. For the guidance of judges and lawyers, large portions were described—as in Lord Coke's examination of the common law. The public philosophy was in part expounded in the Bill of Rights of 1689. It was re-enacted in the first ten amendments of the Constitution of the United States. The largest part of the public philosophy was never explicitly stated. Being the wisdom of a great society over the generations, it can never be stated in any single document. But the traditions of civility permeated the peoples of the West and provided a standard of public and private action which promoted, facilitated, and protected the institutions of freedom and the growth of democracy.

The founders of our free institutions were themselves adherents of this public philosophy. When they insisted upon excluding the temporal power from the realm of the mind and the spirit, it was not that they had no public philosophy. It was because experience had taught them that as power corrupts, it corrupts the public philosophy. It was, therefore, a practical rule of politics that the government should not be given sovereignty and proprietorship over the public philosophy.

* * *

As time went on, there fell out of fashion the public philosophy of the founders of Western institutions. The rule that the temporal power should be excluded from the realm of the mind and of the spirit was then subtly transformed. It became the rule that ideas and principles are private—with only subjective relevance and significance. Only when there is "a clear and present danger" to public order are the acts of speaking and publishing in the public domain. All the first and last things were removed from the public domain. All that has to do with what man is and should be, or how he should hold himself in the scheme of things, what are his rightful ends and the legitimate means, became private and subjective and publicly unaccountable. And so the liberal democracies of the West became the first great society to treat as a private concern the formative beliefs that shape the character of its citizens.

This has brought about a radical change in the meaning of freedom. Originally it was founded on the postulate that there was a universal order on which all reasonable men were agreed; within that public agreement on the fundamentals and on the ultimates, it was safe to permit and it would be desirable to encourage, dissent, and dispute. But with the disappearance of the public philosophy—and of a consensus on the first and last things—there was opened up a great vacuum in the public mind, yawning to be filled.

As long as it worked, there was an obvious practical advantage in treating the struggle for the ultimate allegiance of men as not within the sphere of the public interest. It was a way of not having to open the Pandora's box of theological, moral, and ideological issues which divide the Western society. But in this century, when the hard decisions have had to be made, this rule of prudence has ceased to work. The expedient worked only as long as the general mass of the people were not seriously dissatisfied with things as they were. It was an expedient that looked toward reforms and improvement. But it assumed a society which was secure, progressive, expanding, and unchallenged. That is why it was only in the fine Victorian weather, before the storm clouds of the great wars began to gather, that the liberal democratic policy of public agnosticism and practical neutrality in ultimate issues was possible.

We come, then, to a crucial question. If the discussion of public philosophy has been, so to speak, tabled in the liberal democracies, can we assume that, though it is not being discussed, there is a public philosophy? Is there a body of positive principles and precepts which a good citizen cannot deny or ignore? I am writing this book in the conviction that there is. It is a conviction which I have acquired gradually, not so much from a theoretical education, but rather from the practical experience of seeing how hard it is for our generation to make democracy work. I believe there is a public philosophy. Indeed there is such a thing as the public philosophy of civility. It does not have to be discovered or invented. It is known. But it does have to be revived and renewed. * * *

In our time the institutions built upon the foundations of the public philosophy still stand. But they are used by a public who are not being taught, and no longer adhere to, the philosophy. Increasingly, the people are alienated from the inner principles of their institutions. The question is whether and how this alienation can be overcome, and the rupture of the traditions of civility repaired.

* * *

Yet when we have demonstrated the need for the public philosophy, how do we prove that the need can be satisfied? Not, we may be sure, by exhortation, however eloquent, to rise to the enormity of the present danger, still less by lamentations about the glory and the grandeur that are past. Modern men, to whom the argument is addressed, have a low capacity to believe in the invisible, the intangible, and the imponderable.

Exhortation can capture the will to believe. But of the will to believe there is no lack. The modern trouble is in a low capacity to believe in precepts which restrict and restrain private interests and desire. Conviction of the need of these restraints is difficult to restore once it has been radically impaired. Public principles can, of course, be imposed by a despotic government. But the public philosophy of a free society cannot be restored by fiat and by force. To come to grips with the unbelief which underlies the condition of anomy, we must find a way to reestablish confidence in the validity of public standards. We must renew the convictions from which our political morality springs.

In the prevailing popular culture all philosophies are the instruments of some man's purpose, all truths are self-centered and self-regarding, and all principles are the rationalizations of some special interest. There is no public criterion of the true and the false, of the right and the wrong, beyond that which the preponderant mass of voters, consumers, readers, and listeners happen at the moment to be supposed to want.

There is no reason to think that this condition of mind can be changed until it can be proved to the modern skeptic that there are certain principles which, when they have been demonstrated, only the willfully irrational can deny, that there are certain obligations binding on all men who are committed to a free society, and that only the willfully subversive can reject them.

*　*　*

We come now to the problem of communicating the public philosophy to the modern democracies. The problem has been, to be sure, only too obvious from the beginning. For * * * the public philosophy is in a deep contradiction with the Jacobin ideology, which is, in fact, the popular doctrine of the mass democracies. The public philosophy is addressed to the government of our appetites and passions by the reasons of a second, civilized, and, therefore, acquired nature. Therefore, the public philosophy cannot be popular. For it aims to resist and to regulate those very desires and opinions which are most popular. The warrant of the public philosophy is that while the regime it imposes is hard, the results of rational and disciplined government will be good. And so, while the right but hard decisions are not likely to be popular when they are taken, the wrong and soft decisions will, if they are frequent and big enough, bring on a disorder in which freedom and democracy are destroyed.

If we ask whether the public philosophy can be communicated to the democracies, the answer must begin with the acknowledgment that there must be a doctrine to communicate. The philosophy must first be made clear and pertinent to our modern anxieties. Our reconnaissance has been addressed to that first need.

But beyond it lies the problem of the capacity and the willingness of modern men to receive this kind of philosphy. The concepts and the principles of the public philosophy have their being in the realm of immaterial entities. They cannot be experienced by our sense organs or even, strictly speaking, imagined in visual or tangible terms. Yet these essences, these abstractions which are out of sight and out of touch, are to have and to hold men's highest loyalties.

The problem of communication is posed because in the modern world, as it is today, most men—not all men, to be sure, but most active and influential men—are in practice positivists who hold that the only world which has reality is the physical world. Only seeing is believing. Nothing is real enough to be taken seriously, nothing can be a matter of deep concern, which cannot, or at least might not, somewhere and sometime, be seen, heard, tasted, smelled, or touched.

*　*　*

The crucial point, however, is not where the naturalists and supernaturalists disagreed. It is that they did agree that there was a valid law which, whether it was the commandment of God or the reason of things, was transcendent. They did agree that it was not something decided upon by certain men and then proclaimed by them. It was not someone's fancy, someone's prejudice, someone's wish or rationalization, a psychological experience and no more. It is there objectively, not subjectively. It can be discovered. It has to be obeyed.

* * *

At the end, then, the questions are how we conceive of ourselves and the public world beyond our private selves. Much depends upon the philosophers. For though they are not kings, they are, we may say, the teachers of the teachers. "In the history of Western governments," says Francis G. Wilson, "the transition of society can be marked by the changing character of the intellectuals," who have served the government as lawyers, advisers, administrators, who have been teachers in the schools, who have been members of professions like medicine and theology. It is through them that doctrines are made to operate in practical affairs. And their doctrine, which they, themselves, have learned in the schools and universities, will have the shape and the reference and the direction which the prevailing philosophy gives it.

That is how and why philosophy and theology are the ultimate and decisive studies in which we engage. In them are defined the main characteristics of the images of man which will be acted upon in the arts and sciences of the epoch. The role of philosophers is rarely, no doubt, creative. But it is critical, so that they have a deciding influence in determining what may be believed, how it can be believed, and what cannot be believed. The philosophers, one might say, stand at the crossroads. While they may not cause the traffic to move, they can stop it and start it, they can direct it one way or the other.

I do not contend, though I hope, that the decline of Western society will be arrested if the teachers in our schools and universities come back to the great tradition of the public philosophy. But I do contend that the decline, which is already far advanced, cannot be arrested if the prevailing philosophers oppose this restoration and revival, if they impugn rather than support the validity of an order which is superior to the values that Sartre tells each man "to invent."

* * *

I have been arguing, hopefully and wishfully, that it may be possible to alter the terms of discourse if a convincing demonstration can be made that the principles of the good society are not, in Sartre's phrase, invented and chosen—that the conditions which must be met if there is to be a good society are there, outside our wishes, where they can be discovered by rational inquiry, and developed and adapted and refined by rational discussion.

If eventually this were demonstrated successfully, it would I believe, rearm all those who are concerned with the anomy of our society, with its progressive barbarization, and with its descent into violence and tyranny. Amidst the quagmire of moral impressionism they would stand again on hard intellectual ground where there are significant objects that are given and are not merely projected, that are compelling and are not merely wished. Their hope would be re-established that there is a public world, sovereign above the infinite number of contradictory and competing private worlds. Without this certainty their struggle must be unavailing.

As the defenders of civility, they cannot do without the signs and seals of legitimacy, of rightness and of truth. For it is a practical rule, well known to experienced men, that the relation is very close between our capacity to act at all and our conviction that the action we are taking is right. This does not mean, of course, that the action *is* necessarily right. What is necessary to continuous action is that it shall be *believed* to be right. Without that belief, most men will not have the energy and will to persevere in the action. Thus satanism, which prefers evil as such, is present in some men and perhaps potential in many. Yet, except in a condition of the profoundest hysteria, as in a lynching, satanism cannot be preached to multitudes. Even Hitler, who was enormously satanic and delighted in monstrous evil, did nevertheless need, it would seem, to be reassured that he was not only a great man but, in a mysterious way a righteous one.

William Jennings Bryan once said that to be clad in the armor of righteousness will make the humblest citizen of all the land stronger than all the hosts of error. That is not quite true. But the reason the humblest citizen is not stronger than the hosts of error is that the latter also are clad in an armor which they at least believe is the armor of righteousness. Had they not been issued the armor of righteousness, they would not, as a matter of fact, be a host at all. For political ideas acquire operative force in human affairs when, as we have seen, they acquire legitimacy, when they have the title of being right which binds men's consciences. Then they possess, as the Confucian doctrine has it, "the mandate of heaven."

In the crisis within the Western society, there is at issue now the mandate of heaven.

LOUIS HARTZ

The Concept of a Liberal Society (1955)

Few interpretations of American political thought were as influential in the second half of the twentieth century as that offered by Louis Hartz (1919–1986) in his seminal book, The Liberal Tradition in America. *A professor of government at Harvard, Hartz insisted that Lockean individualist ideas had a stranglehold on the American mind. This "irrational" Lockeanism could flourish because America had no feudal or aristocratic past, which Hartz saw as also explaining America's lack of a real socialist tradition. Hartz argued that this produced America's "conformitarian spirit," which other intellectuals during the cold war labeled America's "consensus" politics. This excerpt is from the first chapter of* The Liberal Tradition in America.

The analysis which this book contains is based on what might be called the storybook truth about American history: that America was settled by men who fled from the feudal and clerical oppressions of the Old World. If there is anything in this view, as old as the national folklore itself, then the outstanding thing about the American community in Western history ought to be the nonexistence of those oppressions, or since the reaction against them was in the broadest sense liberal, that the American community is a liberal community. We are confronted, as it were, with a kind of inverted Trotskyite law of combined development, America skipping the feudal stage of history as Russia presumably skipped the liberal stage. I know that I am using broad terms broadly here. "Feudalism" refers technically to the institutions of the medieval era, and it is well known that aspects of the decadent feudalism of the later period, such as primogeniture, entail, and quitrents, were present in America even in the eighteenth century. "Liberalism" is an even vaguer term, clouded as it is by all sorts of modern social reform connotations, and even when one insists on using it in the classic Lockian sense, as I shall insist here, there are aspects of our original life in the Puritan colonies and the South which hardly fit its meaning. But these are the liabilities of any large generalization, danger points but not insuperable barriers. What in the end is more interesting is the curious failure of

American historians, after repeating endlessly that America was grounded in escape from the European past, to interpret our history in the light of that fact. There are a number of reasons for this which we shall encounter before we are through, but one is obvious at the outset: the separation of the study of American from European history and politics. Any attempt to uncover the nature of an American society without feudalism can only be accomplished by studying it in conjunction with a European society where the feudal structure and the feudal ethos did in fact survive. This is not to deny our national uniqueness, one of the reasons curiously given for studying America alone, but actually to affirm it. How can we know the uniqueness of anything except by contrasting it with what is not unique? The rationale for a separate American study, once you begin to think about it, explodes the study itself.

In the end, however, it is not logic but experience, to use a Holmesian phrase, which exposes the traditional approach. We could use our uniqueness as an excuse for evading its study so long as our world position did not really require us to know much about it. Now that a whole series of alien cultures have crashed in upon the American world, shattering the peaceful landscape of Bancroft and Beard, the old non sequitur simply will not do. When we need desperately to know the idiosyncrasies which interfere with our understanding of Europe, we can hardly break away from "European schemes" of analysis, as J. Franklin Jameson urged American historians to do in 1891 (not that they ever really used them in the first place) on the ground that we are idiosyncratic. But the issue is deeper than foreign policy, for the world involvement has also brought to the surface of American life great new domestic forces which must remain inexplicable without comparative study. It has redefined, as Communism shows, the issue of our internal freedom in terms of our external life. So in fact it is the entire crisis of our time which compels us to make that journey to Europe and back which ends in the discovery of the American liberal world. * * *

One of the central characteristics of a nonfeudal society is that it lacks a genuine revolutionary tradition, the tradition which in Europe has been linked with the Puritan and French revolutions: that it is "born equal," as Tocqueville said. And this being the case, it lacks also a tradition of reaction: lacking Robespierre it lacks Maistre, lacking Sydney it lacks Charles II. Its liberalism is what Santayana called, referring to American democracy, a "natural" phenomenon. But the matter is curiously broader than this, for a society which begins with Locke, and thus transforms him, stays with Locke, by virtue of an absolute and irrational attachment it develops for him, and becomes as indifferent to the challenge of socialism in the later era as it was unfamiliar with the heritage of feudalism in the earlier one. It has within it, as it were, a kind of self-completing mechanism, which insures the universality of the liberal idea. Here, we shall see, is one of the places where Marx went wrong in his historical analysis, attributing as he did the emergence of the socialist ideology to the objective movement of economic forces. Actually socialism is largely an ideological phenomenon, arising out of the principles of class and the revolutionary liberal revolt against them which the old European order inspired. It is not accidental that America which has uniquely lacked a feudal tradition has uniquely lacked also a socialist tradition. The hidden origin of socialist thought everywhere in the West is to be found in the feudal ethos. The *ancien régime* inspires Rousseau; both inspire Marx.

Which brings us to the substantive quality of the natural liberal mind. And this poses no easy problem. For when the words of Locke are used and a prior Filmer is absent, how are we to delineate the significance of the latter fact? In politics men who make speeches do not go out of their way to explain how differently they would speak if the enemies they had were larger in size or different in character. On the contrary whatever enemies they fight they paint in satanic terms, so that a problem sufficiently difficult to begin with in a liberal society becomes complicated further by the inevitable perspectives of political battle. Take the American Revolution. With John Adams identifying the Stamp Act with the worst of the historic European oppressions, how can we distinguish the man from Lilburne or the philosophers of the French Enlightenment? And yet if we study the American liberal language in terms of intensity and emphasis, if we look for silent omissions as well as explicit inclusions, we begin to see a pattern emerging that smacks distinctively of the New World. It has a quiet, matter of fact quality, it does not understand the meaning of sovereign power, the bourgeois class passion is scarcely present, the sense of the past is altered, and there is about it all, as compared with the European pattern, a vast and almost charming innocence of mind. Twain's "Innocents Abroad" is a pretty relevant concept, for the psyche that springs from social war and social revolution is given to far suspicions and sidelong glances that the American liberal cannot easily understand. Possibly this is what people mean when they say that European thought is "deeper" than American, though anyone who tries to grapple with America in Western terms will wonder whether the term "depth" is the proper one to use. There can be an appalling complexity to innocence, especially if your point of departure is guilt.

Now if the *ancien régime* is not present to begin with, one thing follows automatically: it does not return in a blaze of glory. It does not flower in the nineteenth century in a Disraeli or a Ballanche, however different from each other these men may be. I do not mean to imply that no trace of the feudal urge, no shadow whatsoever of Sir Walter Scott, has been found on the hills and plains of the New World. One can get into a lot of useless argument if he affirms the liberalness of a liberal society in absolute mathematical fashion. The top strata of the American community, from the time of Peggy Hutchinson to the time of Margaret Kennedy, have yearned for the aristocratic ethos. But instead of exemplifying the typical Western situation, these yearnings represent an inversion of it. America has presented the world with the peculiar phenomenon, not of a frustrated middle class, but of a "frustrated aristocracy"—of men, Aristotelian-like, trying to break out of the egalitarian confines of middle class life but suffering guilt and failure in the process. The South before the Civil War is the case par excellence of this, though New England of course exemplifies it also. Driven away from Jefferson by abolitionism, the Fitzhughs of the ante-bellum era actually dared to ape the doctrinal patterns of the Western reaction, of Disraeli and Bonald. But when Jefferson is traditional, European traditionalism is a curious thing indeed. The Southerners were thrown into fantastic contradictions by their iconoclastic conservatism, by what I have called the "Reactionary Enlightenment," and after the Civil War for good historical reasons they fell quickly into oblivion. The South, as John Crowe Ransom has said, has been the part of America closest to Old World Europe, but it has never really been Europe. It has been an alien child in a liberal family, tortured and confused, driven to a fantasy life which, instead of disproving the power of Locke in America, portrays more poignantly than anything else the tyranny he has had.

But is not the problem of Fitzhugh at once the problem of De Leon? Here we have one of the great and neglected relationships in American history: the common fecklessness of the Southern "feudalists" and the modern socialists. It is not accidental, but something rooted in the logic of all of Western history, that they should fail alike to leave a dent in the American liberal intelligence. For if the concept of class was meaningless in its Disraelian form, and if American liberalism had never acquired it in its bourgeois form, why should it be any more meaningful in its Marxian form? This secret process of ideological transmission is not, however, the only thing involved. Socialism arises not only to fight capitalism but remnants of feudalism itself, so that the failure of the Southern Filmerians, in addition to setting the pattern for the failure of the later Marxists, robbed them in the process of a normal ground for growth. Could De Leon take over the liberal goal of extended suffrage as Lasalle did in Germany or the crusade against the House of Lords as the Labor Party did in England? Marx himself noted the absence of an American feudalism, but since he misinterpreted the complex origins of European socialism in the European *ancien régime*, he did not grasp the significance of it.

Surely, then, it is a remarkable force: this fixed, dogmatic liberalism of a liberal way of life. It is the secret root from which have sprung many of the most puzzling of American cultural phenomena. Take the unusual power of the Supreme Court and the cult of constitution worship on which it rests. Federal factors apart, judicial review as it has worked in America would be inconceivable without the national acceptance of the Lockian creed, ultimately enshrined in the Constitution, since the removal of high policy to the realm of adjudication implies a prior recognition of the principles to be legally interpreted. At the very moment that Senator Benton was hailing the rise of America's constitutional fetishism, in France Royer Collard and the Doctrinaires were desperately trying to build precisely the same atmosphere around the Restoration Charter of 1814, but being a patchwork of Maistre and Rousseau, that constitutional document exploded in their faces in the July Revolution. *Inter arma leges silent.* If in England a marvelous organic cohesion has held together the feudal, liberal, and socialist ideas, it would still be unthinkable there that the largest issues of public policy should be put before nine Talmudic judges examining a single text. But this is merely another way of saying that law has flourished on the corpse of philosophy in America, for the settlement of the ultimate moral question is the end of speculation upon it. Pragmatism, interestingly enough America's great contribution to the philosophic tradition, does not alter this, since it feeds itself on the Lockian settlement. It is only when you take your ethics for granted that all problems emerge as problems of technique. Not that this is a bar in America to institutional innovations of highly non-Lockian kind. Indeed, as the New Deal shows, when you simply "solve problems" on the basis of a submerged and absolute liberal faith, you can depart from Locke with a kind of inventive freedom that European Liberal reformers and even European socialists, dominated by ideological systems, cannot duplicate. But the main point remains: if Fitzhugh and De Leon were crucified by the American general will, John Marshall and John Dewey flourished in consequence of their crucifixion. The moral unanimity of a liberal society reaches out in many directions.

At bottom it is riddled with paradox. Here is a Lockian doctrine which in the West as a whole is the symbol of rationalism, yet in America the devotion to it has been so irrational that it has not even been recognized for what it is: liberalism. There has never been a "liberal movement" or a real "liberal party" in America: we have only had the American Way of Life, a nationalist articulation of Locke which usually does not know that Locke himself is involved; and we did not even get that until after the Civil War when the Whigs of the nation, deserting the Hamiltonian tradition, saw the capital that could be made out of it. This is why even critics who have noticed America's moral unity have usually missed its substance. Ironically, "liberalism" is a stranger in the land of its greatest realization and fulfillment. But this is not all. Here is a doctrine which everywhere in the West has been a glorious symbol of individual liberty, yet in America its compulsive power has been so great that it has posed a threat to liberty itself. Actually Locke has a hidden conformitarian germ to begin with, since natural law tells equal people equal things, but when this germ is fed by the explosive power of modern nationalism, it mushrooms into something pretty remarkable. One can reasonably wonder about the liberty one finds in Burke.

I believe that this is the basic ethical problem of a liberal society: not the danger of the majority which has been its conscious fear, but the danger of unanimity, which has slumbered unconsciously behind it: the "tyranny of opinion" that Tocqueville saw unfolding as even the pathetic social distinctions of the Federalist era collapsed before his eyes. But in recent times this manifestation of irrational Lockianism, or of "Americanism," to use a favorite term of the American Legion, one of the best expounders of the national spirit that Whiggery discovered after the Civil War, has neither slumbered nor been unconscious. It has been very much awake in a red scare hysteria which no other nation in the West has really been able to understand. And this suggests a very significant principle: that when a liberal community faces military and ideological pressure from without it transforms eccentricity into sin, and the irritating figure of the bourgeois gossip flowers into the frightening figure of an A. Mitchell Palmer or a Senator McCarthy. Do we not find here, hidden away at the base of the American mind, one of the reasons why its legalism has been so imperfect a barrier against the violent moods of its mass Lockianism? If the latter is nourished by the former, how can we expect it to be strong? We say of the Supreme Court that it is courageous when it challenges Jefferson, but since in a liberal society the individualism of Hamilton is also a secret part of the Jeffersonian psyche, we make too much of this. The real test of the Court is when it faces the excitement both of Jefferson and Hamilton, when the Talmudic text is itself at stake, when the general will on which it feeds rises to the surface in anger. And here, brave as the Court has been at moments, its record has been no more heroic than the logic of the situation would suggest.

The decisive domestic issue of our time may well lie in the counter resources a liberal society can muster against this deep and unwritten tyrannical compulsion it contains. They exist. Given the individualist nature of the Lockian doctrine, there is always a logical impulse within it to transcend the very conformitarian spirit it breeds in a Lockian society: witness the spirit of Holmes and Hand. Given the fact, which we shall study at length later, that "Americanism" oddly disadvantages the

Progressive despite the fact that he shares it to the full, there is always a strategic impulse within him to transcend it: witness the spirit of Brandeis, Roosevelt, and Stevenson. In some sense the tragedy of these movements has lain in the imperfect knowledge they have had of the enemy they face, above all in their failure to see their own unwitting contribution to his strength. The record of Brandeis was good on civil liberties, but anyone who studies his Progressive thought will see that he was, for good or bad, on that score a vital part of the compulsive "Americanism" which bred the hysteria he fought. The Progressive tradition, if it is to transcend the national general will, has got to realize, as it has not yet done, how deeply its own Jacksonian heroes have been rooted in it.

But the most powerful force working to shatter the American absolutism is, paradoxically enough, the very international involvement which tensifies it. This involvement is complex in its implications. If in the context of the Russian Revolution it elicits a domestic red scare, in the context of diplomacy it elicits an impulse to impose Locke everywhere. The way in which "Americanism" brings McCarthy together with Wilson is of great significance and it is, needless to say, another one of Progressivism's neglected roots in the Rousseauan tide it often seeks to stem. Thus to say that world politics shatters "Americanism" at the moment it intensifies it is to say a lot: it is to say that the basic horizons of the nation both at home and abroad are drastically widened by it. But has this not been the obvious experience of the recent past? Along with the fetish that has been made of Locke at peace conferences and at Congressional investigations has not Locke suffered a relativistic beating at the same time? You can turn the issue of Wilsonianism upside down: when has the nation appreciated more keenly the limits of its own cultural pattern as applied to the rest of the world? You can turn the issue of McCarthyism upside down: when has the meaning of civil liberties been more ardently understood than now? A dialectic process is at work, evil eliciting the challenge of a conscious good, so that in difficult moments progress is made. The outcome of the battle between intensified "Americanism" and new enlightenment is still an open question.

Historically the issue here is one for which we have little precedent. It raises the question of whether a nation can compensate for the uniformity of its domestic life by contact with alien cultures outside it. It asks whether American liberalism can acquire through external experience that sense of relativity, that spark of philosophy which European liberalism acquired through an internal experience of social diversity and social conflict. But if the final problem posed by the American liberal community is bizarre, this is merely a continuation of its historic record. That community has always been a place where the common issues of the West have taken strange and singular shape. * * *

So far I have spoken of natural liberalism as a psychological whole, embracing the nation and inspiring unanimous decisions. We must not assume, however, that this is to obscure or to minimize the nature of the internal conflicts which have characterized American political life. We can hardly choose between an event and its context, though in the study of history and politics there will always be some who will ask us to do so. What we learn from the concept of a liberal society, lacking feudalism and therefore socialism and governed by an irrational Lockianism, is that the domestic struggles of such a society have all been projected with the setting of Western liberal alignments. And here there begin to emerge, not a set of negative European correlations, but a set of very positive ones which have been almost completely neglected.

We can thus say of the right in America that it exemplifies the tradition of big propertied liberalism in Europe, a tradition familiar enough though, as I shall suggest in a moment, much still remains to be done in studying it along transnational lines. It is the tradition which embraces loosely the English Presbyterian and the English Whig, the French Girondin and the French Liberal: a tradition which hates the *ancien régime* up to a certain point, loves capitalism, and fears democracy. Occasionally, as a matter of fact, American Hamiltonianism has been called by the English term "Whiggery," though no effort has been made to pursue the comparative analysis which this label suggests. Similarly the European "petit-bourgeois" tradition is the starting point for an understanding of the American left. Here, to be sure, there are critical problems of identification, since one of the main things America did was to expand and transform the European "petit-bourgeois" by absorbing both the peasantry and the proletariat into the structure of his personality. It is only the beginning of comparative analysis to link up American Progressivism with the tradition of the French Jacobins and to counterparts elsewhere in Europe. But even though agrarian and proletarian factors complicate this issue enormously, bringing us for all practical purposes out of the petit-bourgeois world of Europe, the basic correlation remains a sound one.

One of the reasons these European liberal correlations have gone neglected is quite obvious once you try to make them. America represents the liberal mechanism of Europe functioning without the European social antagonisms, but the truth is, it is only through these antagonisms that we recognize the mechanism. We know the European liberal, as it were, by the enemies he has made: take them away in American fashion and he does not seem like the same man at all. This is true even of the Whig who prior to 1840 poses the easiest problem in this respect. Remove Wellington from Macaulay, and you have in essence Alexander Hamilton, but the link between the latter two is not at first easy to see. After 1840, when the American Whig gives up his Hamiltonian elitism and discovers the Horatio Alger ethos of a liberal society, discovers "Americanism," the task of identification is even harder. For while it is true that the liberals of England and France ultimately accepted political democracy, Algerism and "Americanism" were social ideologies they could hardly exploit. So that the continuing problem of a missing Toryism, which is enough to separate the American Republicans from the reactionary liberals of Victorian England and the Neo-Girondins of the Third Republic, is complicated further by the unique ideological shape that the Whig tradition is destined to take in a liberal society.

The American democrat, that "petit-bourgeois" hybrid of the American world, raises even more intricate questions. To take away the Social Republic from the French Montagnards changes their appearance just about as much as taking away the feudal right from the English Whigs. But the American democrat, alas, deviated sharply from the Montagnards to begin with, since in addition to being "petit-bourgeois" in their sense he was a liberal peasant and a liberal proletarian as well: indeed the whole of the nation apart from the Whig, a condition hardly vouchsafed to the Montagnards. And yet even in the face of such tremendous variations, comparative analysis can continue. We have to tear the giant figure of Jackson apart, sorting out not only the "petit-bourgeois" element of the man but those rural and urban elements which the American liberal community has transformed. Ultimately, as with the Whigs, for all of the magical chemistry of American liberal society, we are dealing with social materials common to the Western world.

That society has been a triumph for the liberal idea, but we must not assume that this ideological victory was not helped forward by the magnificent material setting it found in the New World. The agrarian and proletarian strands of the American democratic personality, which in some sense typify the whole of American uniqueness, reveal a remarkable collusion between Locke and the New World. Had it been merely the liberal spirit alone which inspired the American farmer to become capitalistically oriented, to repudiate save for a few early remnants the village organization of Europe, to produce for a market and even to enter capitalist occupations on the side such as logging and railroad building, then the difficulties he encountered would have been greater than they were. But where land was abundant and the voyage to the New World itself a claim to independence, the spirit which repudiated peasantry and tenantry flourished with remarkable ease. Similarly, had it merely been an aspect of irrational Lockianism which inspired the American worker to think in terms of the capitalist setup, the task would have been harder than it was.

But social fluidity was peculiarly fortified by the riches of a rich land, so that there was no small amount of meaning to Lincoln's claim in 1861 that the American laborer, instead of "being fixed to that condition for life," works for "a while," then "saves," then "hires another beginner" as he himself becomes an entrepreneur. And even when factory industrialism gained sway after the Civil War, and the old artisan and cottage-and-mill mentality was definitely gone, it was still a Lockian idea fortified by material resources which inspired the triumph of the job mentality of Gompers rather than the class mentality of the European worker. The "petit-bourgeois" giant of America, though ultimately a triumph for the liberal idea, could hardly have chosen a better material setting in which to flourish.

BARRY GOLDWATER

The Conscience of a Conservative (1960)

The conservative Arizona Republican Barry Morris Goldwater (1909–1998) served several terms in the U.S. Senate and ran unsuccessfully for president in 1964. A sharp critic of the personal dependency that he believed the welfare state and bureaucratic centralization engendered, the anticommunist Goldwater became a leading spokesman for small government and the leader of the conservative wing of the Republican party during the 1960s. His Conscience of a Conservative (1960) was a manifesto calling for the return of power and autonomy to state and local governments in the interest of individual freedom. Actually ghost-written by William Buckley's brother-in-law L. Brent Bozell, the book sold over 100,000 copies in its first year and enhanced Goldwater's reputation among conservatives.

This book is not written with the idea of adding to or improving on the Conservative philosophy. Or of "bringing it up to date." The ancient and tested truths that guided our Republic through its early days will do equally well for us. The challenge to Conservatives today is quite simply to demonstrate the bearing of a proven philosophy on the problems of our own time.

I should explain the considerations that led me to join in this effort. I am a politician, a United States Senator. As such, I have had an opportunity to learn somthing about the political instincts of the American people, I have crossed the length and breadth of this great land hundreds of times and talked with tens of thousands of people, with Democrats and Republicans, with farmers and laborers and businessmen. I find that America is fundamentally a Conservative nation. The preponderant judgment of the American people, especially of the young people, is that the radical, or Liberal, approach has not worked and is not working. They yearn for a return to Conservative principles.

At the same time, I have been in a position to observe first hand how Conservatism is faring in Washington. And it is all too clear that in spite of a Conservative revival among the people the radical ideas that were promoted by the New and Fair Deals under the guise of Liberalism still dominate the councils of our national government.

In a country where it is now generally understood and proclaimed that the people's welfare depends on individual self reliance rather than on state paternalism, Congress annually deliberates over whether the *increase* in government welfarism should be small or large.

In a country where it is now generally understood and proclaimed that the federal government spends too much, Congress annually deliberates over whether to raise the federal budget by a few billion dollars or by many billion.

In a country where it is now generally understood and proclaimed that individual liberty depends on decentralized government, Congress annually deliberates over whether vigorous or halting steps should be taken to bring state government into line with federal policy.

In a country where it is now generally understood and proclaimed that Communism is an enemy bound to destroy us, Congress annually deliberates over means of "co-existing" with the Soviet Union.

And so the question arises: Why have American people been unable to translate their views into appropriate political action? Why should the nation's underlying allegiance to Conservative principles have failed to produce corresponding deeds in Washington?

I do not blame my brethren in government, all of whom work hard and conscientiously at their jobs. I blame Conservatives—ourselves—myself. Our failure, as one Conservative writer has put it, is the failure of the Conservative demonstration. Though we Conservatives are deeply persuaded that our society is ailing, and know that Conservatism holds the key to national salvation—and feel sure the country agrees with us—we seem unable to demonstrate the practical relevance of Conservative principles to the needs of the day. We sit by impotently while Congress seeks to improvise solutions to problems that are not the real problems facing the country, while the government attempts to assuage imagined concerns and ignores the real concerns and real needs of the people.

Perhaps we suffer from an over-sensitivity to the judgments of those who rule the mass communications media. We are daily consigned by "enlightened" commentators to political oblivion: Conservatism, we are told, is out-of-date. The charge is preposterous and we ought boldly to say so. The laws of God, and of nature, have no dateline. The principles on which the Conservative political position is based have been established by a process that has nothing to do with the social, economic and political landscape that changes from decade to decade and from century to century. These principles are derived from the nature of man, and from the truths that God has revealed about His creation. Circumstances do change. So do the problems that are shaped by circumstances. But the principles that govern the solution of the problems do not. To suggest that the Conservative philosophy is out of date is akin to saying that the Golden Rule, or the Ten Commandments or Aristotle's *Politics* are out of date. The Conservative approach is nothing more or less than an attempt to apply the wisdom and experience and the revealed truths of the past to the problems of today. The challenge is not to find new or different truths, but to learn how to apply established truths to the problems of the contemporary world. My hope is that one more Conservative voice will be helpful in meeting this challenge.

* * *

I have been much concerned that so many people today with Conservative instincts feel compelled to apologize for them. Or if not to apologize directly, to qualify their commitment in a way that amounts to breast-beating. "Republican candidates," Vice President Nixon has said, "should be economic conservatives, but conservatives with a heart." President Eisenhower announced during his first term, "I am conservative when it comes to economic problems but liberal when it comes to human problems." Still other Republican leaders have insisted on calling themselves "progressive" Conservatives. These formulations are tantamount to an admission that Conservatism is a narrow, mechanistic *economic* theory that may work very well as a bookkeeper's guide, but cannot be relied upon as a comprehensive political philosophy.

The same judgment, though in the form of an attack rather than an admission, is advanced by the radical camp. "We liberals," they say, "are interested in *people*. Our concern is with human beings, while you Conservatives are preoccupied with the preservation of economic privilege and status." Take them a step further, and the Liberals will turn the accusations into a class argument: it is the little people that concern us, not the "malefactors of great wealth."

Such statements, from friend and foe alike, do great injustice to the Conservative point of view. Conservatism is *not* an economic theory, though it has economic implications. The shoe is precisely on the other foot: it is Socialism that subordinates all other considerations to man's material well-being. It is Conservatism that puts material things in their proper place—that has a structured view of the human being and of human society, in which economics plays only a subsidiary role.

The root difference between the Conservatives and the Liberals of today is that Conservatives take account of the *whole* man, while the Liberals tend to look only at the material side of man's nature. The Conservative believes that man is, in part, an economic, an animal creature; but that he is also a spiritual creature with spiritual needs and spiritual desires. What is more, these needs and desires reflect the *superior* side of man's nature, and thus take precedence over his economic wants. Conservatism therefore looks upon the enhancement of man's spiritual nature as the primary concern of political philosophy. Liberals, on the other hand,—in the name of a concern for "human beings"—regard the satisfaction of economic wants as the dominant mission of society. They are, moreover, in a hurry. So that their characteristic approach is to harness the society's political and economic forces into a collective effort to *compel* "progress." In this approach, I believe they fight against Nature.

Surely the first obligation of a political thinker is to understand the nature of man. The Conservative does not claim special powers of perception on this point, but he does claim a familiarity with the accumulated wisdom and experience of history, and he is not too proud to learn from the great minds of the past.

The first thing he has learned about man is that each member of the species is a unique creature. Man's most sacred possession is his individual soul—which has an immortal side, but also a mortal one. The mortal side establishes his absolute differentness from every other human being. *Only a philosophy that takes into account the essential differences between men, and, accordingly, makes provision for developing the different potentialities of each man can claim to be in accord with Nature.* We have heard much in our time about "the common man." It is a concept that pays little attention to the history of a nation that grew great through the initiative and ambition of uncommon men. The Conservative knows that to regard man as part of an undifferentiated mass is to consign him to ultimate slavery.

Secondly, the Conservative has learned that the economic and spiritual aspects of man's nature are inextricably intertwined. He cannot be economically free, or even economically efficient, if he is enslaved politically; conversely, man's political freedom is illusory if he is dependent for his economic needs on the State.

The Conservative realizes, thirdly, that man's development, in both its spiritual and material aspects, is not something that can be directed by outside forces. Every man, for his individual good and for the good of his society, is responsible for his *own* development. The choices that govern his life are choices that *he* must make: they cannot be made by any other human being, or by a collectivity of human beings. If the Conservative is less anxious than his Liberal brethren to increase Social Security "benefits," it is because he is more anxious than his Liberal brethren that people be free throughout their lives to spend their earnings when and as they see fit.

So it is that Conservatism, throughout history, has regarded man neither as a potential pawn of other men, nor as a part of a general collectivity in which the sacredness and the separate identity of individual human beings are ignored. Throughout history, true Conservatism has been at war equally with autocrats and with "democratic" Jacobins. The true Conservative was sympathetic with the plight of the hapless peasant under the tyranny of the French monarchy. And he was equally revolted at the attempt to solve that problem by a mob tyranny that paraded under the banner of egalitarianism. The conscience of the Conservative is pricked by *anyone* who would debase the dignity of the individual human being. Today, therefore, he is at odds with dictators who rule by terror, and equally with those gentler collectivists who ask our permission to play God with the human race.

With this view of the nature of man, it is understandable that the Conservative looks upon politics as the art of achieving the maximum amount of freedom for individuals that is consistent with the maintenance of social order. The Conservative is the first to understand that the practice of freedom requires the establishment of order: it is impossible for one man to be free if another is able to deny him the exercise of his freedom. But the Conservative also recognizes that the political power on which order is based is a self-aggrandizing force; that its appetite grows with eating. He knows that the utmost vigilance and care are required to keep political power within its proper bounds.

In our day, order is pretty well taken care of. The delicate balance that ideally exists between freedom and order has long since tipped against freedom practically everywhere on earth. In some countries, freedom is altogether down and order holds absolute sway. In our country the trend is less far advanced, but it is well along and gathering momentum every day. Thus, for the American Conservative, there is no difficulty in identifying the day's overriding political challenge: it is *to preserve and extend freedom.* As he surveys the various attitudes and institutions and laws that currently prevail in America, many questions will occur to him, but the Conservative's first concern will always be: *Are we maximizing free-*

dom? I suggest we examine some of the critical issues facing us today with this question in mind.

* * *

The New Deal, Dean Acheson wrote approvingly in a book called *A Democrat Looks At His Party*, "conceived of the federal government as the whole people organized to do what had to be done." A year later Mr. Larson wrote *A Republican Looks At His Party*, and made much the same claim in his book for Modern Republicans. The "underlying philosophy" of the New Republicanism, said Mr. Larson, is that "if a job has to be done to meet the needs of the people, and no one else can do it, then it is the proper function of the federal government."

Here we have, by prominent spokesmen of both political parties, an unqualified repudiation of the principle of limited government. There is no reference by either of them to the Constitution, or any attempt to define the legitimate functions of government. The government can do whatever *needs* to be done; note, too, the implicit but necessary assumption that it is the government itself that determines *what* needs to be done. We must not, I think underrate the importance of these statements. They reflect the view of a majority of the leaders of one of our parties, and of a strong minority among the leaders of the other, and they propound the first principle of totalitarianism: that the State is competent to do all things and is limited in what it actually does only by the will of those who control the State.

It is clear that this view is in direct conflict with the Constitution which is an instrument, above all, for *limiting* the functions of government, and which is as binding today as when it was written. But we are advised to go a step further and ask why the Constitution's framers restricted the scope of government. Conservatives are often charged, and in a sense rightly so, with having an overly mechanistic view of the Constitution: "It is America's enabling document; we are American citizens; therefore," the Conservatives' theme runs, "we are morally and legally obliged to comply with the document." All true. But the Constitution has a broader claim on our loyalty than that. The founding fathers had a *reason* for endorsing the principle of limited government; and this reason recommends defense of the constitutional scheme even to those who take their citizenship obligations lightly. The reason is simple, and it lies at the heart of the Conservative philosophy.

Throughout history, government has proved to be the chief instrument for thwarting man's liberty. Government represents power in the hands of some men to control and regulate the lives of other men. And power, as Lord Acton said, *corrupts* men. "Absolute power," he added, "corrupts absolutely."

State power, considered in the abstract, need not restrict freedom: but absolute state power always does. The *legitimate* functions of government are actually conducive to freedom. Maintaining internal order, keeping foreign foes at bay, administering justice, removing obstacles to the free interchange of goods—the exercise of these powers makes it possible for men to follow their chosen pursuits with maximum freedom. But note that the very instrument by which these desirable ends are achieved *can* be the instrument for achieving undesirable ends—that government can, instead of extending freedom, restrict freedom. And note, secondly, that the "can" quickly becomes "will" the moment the holders of government power are left to their own devices. This is because of the corrupting influence of power, the natural tendency of men who possess *some* power to take unto themselves *more* power. The tendency leads eventually to the acquisition of *all* power—whether in the hands of one or many makes little difference to the freedom of those left on the outside.

Such, then, is history's lesson, which Messrs. Acheson and Larson evidently did not read: release the holders of state power from any restraints other than those they wish to impose upon themselves, and you are swinging down the well-travelled road to absolutism.

The framers of the Constitution had learned the lesson. They were not only students of history, but victims of it: they knew from vivid, personal experience that freedom depends on effective restraints against the accumulation of power in a single authority. And that is what the Constitution is: *a system of restraints against the natural tendency of government to expand in the direction of absolutism.* We all know the main components of the system. The first is the limitation of the federal government's authority to specific, delegated powers. The second, a corollary of the first, is the reservation to the States and the people of all power not delegated to the federal government. The third is a careful division of the federal government's power among three separate branches. The fourth is a prohibition against impetuous alteration of the system—namely, Article V's tortuous, but wise, amendment procedures.

Was it then a *Democracy* the framers created? Hardly. The system of restraints, on the face of it, was directed not only against individual tyrants, but also against a tyranny of the masses. The framers were well aware of the danger posed by self-seeking demagogues—that they might persuade a majority of the people to confer on government vast powers in return for deceptive promises of economic gain. And so they forbade such a transfer of power—first by declaring, in effect, that certain activities are outside the natural and legitimate scope of the public authority, and secondly by dispersing public authority among several levels and branches of government in the hope that each seat of authority, jealous of its own prerogatives, would have a natural incentive to resist aggression by the others.

But the framers were not visionaries. They knew that rules of government, however brilliantly calculated to cope with the imperfect nature of man, however carefully designed to avoid the pitfalls of power, would be no match for men who were determined to disregard them. In the last analysis their system of government would prosper only if the governed were sufficiently determined that it should. "What have you given us?" a woman asked Ben Franklin toward the close of the Constitutional Convention. "A Republic," he said, *"if you can keep it!"*

We have not kept it. The Achesons and Larsons have had their way. The system of restraints has fallen into disrepair. The federal government has moved into every field in which it believes its services are needed. The state governments are either excluded from their rightful functions by federal preemption, or they are allowed to act at the sufferance of the federal government. Inside the federal government both the executive and judicial branches have roamed far outside their constitutional boundary lines. And all of these things have come to pass without regard to the amendment procedures prescribed by Article V. The result is a Leviathan, a vast national authority out of touch with the people, and out of their control. This monolith of power is bounded only by the will of those who sit in high places.

* * *

I am convinced that most Americans now want to reverse the trend. I think that concern for our vanishing freedoms is genuine. I think that the people's uneasiness in the stifling omnipresence of government has turned into something approaching alarm. But bemoaning the evil will not drive it back, and accusing fingers will not shrink government.

The turn will come when we entrust the conduct of our affairs to men who understand that their first duty as public officials is to divest themselves of the power they have been given. It will come when Americans, in hundreds of communities throughout the nation, decide to put the man in office who is pledged to enforce the Constitution and restore the Republic. Who will proclaim in a campaign speech: "I have little interest in streamlining government or in making it more efficient, for I mean to reduce its size. I do not undertake to promote welfare, for I propose to extend freedom. My aim is not to pass laws, but to repeal them. It is not to inaugurate new programs, but to cancel old ones that do violence to the Constitution, or that have failed in their purpose, or that impose on the people an unwarranted financial burden. I will not attempt to discover whether legislation is 'needed' before I have first determined whether it is constitutionally permissible. And if I should later be attacked for neglecting my constituents' 'interests,' I shall reply that I was informed their main interest is liberty and that in that cause I am doing the very best I can."

The 1960s

C. WRIGHT MILLS

The Power Elite (1956)

*Charles Wright Mills (1916–1962) was a professor of sociology at Co-
lumbia University whose writings would profoundly influence 1960s
radicalism. In his 1956 book* The Power Elite, *Mills argued that a small
group from government, business, and the military run the country. This
excerpt insists that the power of these elites is based in a set of interrelated and centralized institutions of power.*

The powers of ordinary men are circumscribed by the everyday
worlds in which they live, yet even in these rounds of job, family,
and neighborhood they often seem driven by forces they can neither understand nor govern. 'Great changes' are beyond their control, but affect
their conduct and outlook none the less. The very framework of modern
society confines them to projects not their own, but from every side, such
changes now press upon the men and women of the mass society, who accordingly feel that they are without purpose in an epoch in which they
are without power.

But not all men are in this sense ordinary. As the means of information and of power are centralized, some men come to occupy positions
in American society from which they can look down upon, so to speak,
and by their decisions mightily affect, the everyday worlds of ordinary
men and women. They are not made by their jobs; they set up and break
down jobs for thousands of others; they are not confined by simple family responsibilities; they can escape. They may live in many hotels and
houses, but they are bound by no one community. They need not merely
'meet the demands of the day and hour'; in some part, they create these
demands, and cause others to meet them. Whether or not they profess
their power, their technical and political experience of it far transcends
that of the underlying population. What Jacob Burckhardt said of 'great

men,' most Americans might well say of their elite: 'They are all that we are not.'

The power elite is composed of men whose positions enable them to transcend the ordinary environments of ordinary men and women; they are in positions to make decisions having major consequences. Whether they do or do not make such decisions is less important than the fact that they do occupy such pivotal positions: their failure to act, their failure to make decisions, is itself an act that is often of greater consequence than the decisions they do make. For they are in command of the major hierarchies and organizations of modern society. They rule the big corporations. They run the machinery of the state and claim its prerogatives. They direct the military establishment. They occupy the strategic command posts of the social structure, in which are now centered the effective means of the power and the wealth and the celebrity which they enjoy.

The power elite are not solitary rulers. Advisers and consultants, spokesmen and opinion-makers are often the captains of their higher thought and decision. Immediately below the elite are the professional politicians of the middle levels of power, in the Congress and in the pressure groups, as well as among the new and old upper classes of town and city and region. Mingling with them, in curious ways which we shall explore, are those professional celebrities who live by being continually displayed but are never, so long as they remain celebrities, displayed enough. If such celebrities are not at the head of any dominating hierarchy, they do often have the power to distract the attention of the public or afford sensations to the masses, or, more directly, to gain the ear of those who do occupy positions of direct power. More or less unattached, as critics of morality and technicians of power, as spokesmen of God and creators of mass sensibility, such celebrities and consultants are part of the immediate scene in which the drama of the elite is enacted. But that drama itself is centered in the command posts of the major institutional hierarchies.

The truth about the nature and the power of the elite is not some secret which men of affairs know but will not tell. Such men hold quite various theories about their own roles in the sequence of event and decision. Often they are uncertain about their roles, and even more often they allow their fears and their hopes to affect their assessment of their own power. No matter how great their actual power, they tend to be less acutely aware of it than of the resistances of others to its use. Moreover, most American men of affairs have learned well the rhetoric of public relations, in some cases even to the point of using it when they are alone, and thus coming to believe it. The personal awareness of the actors is only one of the several sources one must examine in order to understand the higher circles. Yet many who believe that there is no elite, or at any rate none of any consequence, rest their argument upon what men of affairs believe about themselves, or at least assert in public.

There is, however, another view: those who feel, even if vaguely, that a compact and powerful elite of great importance does now prevail in America often base that feeling upon the historical trend of our time. They have felt, for example, the domination of the military event, and from this they infer that generals and admirals, as well as other men of decision influenced by them, must be enormously powerful. They hear that the Congress has again abdicated to a handful of men decisions clearly related to the issue of war or peace. They know that the bomb was dropped over Japan in the name of the United States of America, although they were at no time consulted about the matter. They feel that they live in a time of big decisions; they know that they are not making any. Accordingly, as they consider the present as history, they infer that at its center, making decisions or failing to make them, there must be an elite of power.

On the one hand, those who share this feeling about big historical events assume that there is an elite and that its power is great. On the other hand, those who listen carefully to the reports of men apparently involved in the great decisions often do not believe that there is an elite whose powers are of decisive consequence.

Both views must be taken into account, but neither is adequate. The way to understand the power of the American elite lies neither solely in recognizing the historic scale of events nor in accepting the personal awareness reported by men of apparent decision. Behind such men and behind the events of history, linking the two, are the major institutions of modern society. These hierarchies of state and corporation and army constitute the means of power; as such they are now of a consequence not before equaled in human history—and at their summits, there are now those command posts of modern society which offer us the sociological key to an understanding of the role of the higher circles in America.

Within American society, major national power now resides in the economic, the political, and the military domains. Other institutions seem off to the side of modern history, and, on occasion, duly subordinated to these. No family is as directly powerful in national affairs as any major corporation; no church is as directly powerful in the external biographies of young men in America today as the military establishment; no college is as powerful in the shaping of momentous events as the National Security Council. Religious, educational, and family institutions are not autonomous centers of national power; on the contrary, these decentralized areas are increasingly shaped by the big three, in which developments of decisive and immediate consequence now occur.

Families and churches and schools adapt to modern life; governments and armies and corporations shape it; and, as they do so, they turn these lesser institutions into means for their ends. Religious institutions provide chaplains to the armed forces where they are used as a means of increasing the effectiveness of its morale to kill. Schools select and train men for their jobs in corporations and their specialized tasks in the armed forces. The extended family has, of course, long been broken up by the industrial revolution, and now the son and the father are removed from the family, by compulsion if need be, whenever the army of the state sends out the call. And the symbols of all these lesser institutions are used to legitimate the power and the decisions of the big three.

The life-fate of the modern individual depends not only upon the family into which he was born or which he enters by marriage, but increasingly upon the corporation in which he spends the most alert hours of his best years; not only upon the school where he is educated as a child and adolescent, but also upon the state which touches him throughout his life; not only upon the church in which on occasion he hears the word of God, but also upon the army in which he is disciplined.

If the centralized state could not rely upon the inculcation of nationalist loyalties in public and private schools, its leaders would promptly seek to modify the decentralized educational system. If the bankruptcy rate among the top five hundred corporations were as high as the general divorce rate among the thirty-seven million married couples, there would be economic catastrophe on an international scale. If members of armies gave to them no more of their lives than do believers to the churches to which they belong, there would be a military crisis.

Within each of the big three, the typical institutional unit has become enlarged, has become administrative, and, in the power of its decisions, has become centralized. Behind these developments there is a fabulous technology, for as institutions, they have incorporated this technology and guide it, even as it shapes and paces their developments.

The economy—once a great scatter of small productive units in autonomous balance—has become dominated by two or three hundred giant corporations, administratively and politically interrelated, which together hold the keys to economic decisions.

The political order, once a decentralized set of several dozen states with a weak spinal cord, has become a centralized, executive establishment which has taken up into itself many powers previously scattered, and now enters into each and every cranny of the social structure.

The military order, once a slim establishment in a context of distrust fed by state militia, has become the largest and most expensive feature of government, and, although well versed in smiling public relations, now has all the grim and clumsy efficiency of a sprawling bureaucratic domain.

In each of these institutional areas, the means of power at the disposal of decision makers have increased enormously; their central executive powers have been enhanced; within each of them modern administrative routines have been elaborated and tightened up.

As each of these domains becomes enlarged and centralized, the consequences of its activities become greater, and its traffic with the others increases. The decisions of a handful of corporations bear upon military and political as well as upon economic developments around the world. The decisions of the military establishment rest upon and grievously affect political life as well as the very level of economic activity. The decisions made within the political domain determine economic activities and military programs. There is no longer, on the one hand, an economy, and, on the other hand, a political order containing a military establishment unimportant to politics and to money-making. There is a political economy linked, in a thousand ways, with military institutions and decisions. On each side of the world-split running through central Europe and around the Asiatic rimlands, there is an ever-increasing interlocking of economic, military, and political structures. If there is government intervention in the corporate economy, so is there corporate intervention in the governmental process. In the structural sense, this triangle of power is the source of the interlocking directorate that is most important for the historical structure of the present.

The fact of the interlocking is clearly revealed at each of the points of crisis of modern capitalist society—slump, war, and boom. In each, men of decision are led to an awareness of the interdependence of the major institutional orders. In the nineteenth century, when the scale of all institutions was smaller, their liberal integration was achieved in the automatic economy, by an autonomous play of market forces, and in the automatic political domain, by the bargain and the vote. It was then assumed that out of the imbalance and friction that followed the limited decisions then possible a new equilibrium would in due course emerge.

That can no longer be assumed, and it is not assumed by the men at the top of each of the three dominant hierarchies.

For given the scope of their consequences, decisions—and indecisions— in any one of these ramify into the others, and hence top decisions tend either to become co-ordinated or to lead to a commanding indecision. It has not always been like this. When numerous small entrepreneurs made up the economy, for example, many of them could fail and the consequences still remain local; political and military authorities did not intervene. But now, given political expectations and military commitments, can they afford to allow key units of the private corporate economy to break down in slump? Increasingly, they do intervene in economic affairs, and as they do so, the controlling decisions in each order are inspected by agents of the other two, and economic, military, and political structures are interlocked.

At the pinnacle of each of the three enlarged and centralized domains, there have arisen those higher circles which make up the economic, the political, and the military elites. At the top of the economy, among the corporate rich, there are the chief executives; at the top of the political order, the members of the political directorate; at the top of the military establishment, the elite of soldier-statesmen clustered in and around the Joint Chiefs of Staff and the upper echelon. As each of these domains has coincided with the others, as decisions tend to become total in their consequence, the leading men in each of the three domains of power— the warlords, the corporation chieftains, the political directorate—tend to come together, to form the power elite of America.

The higher circles in and around these command posts are often thought of in terms of what their members possess: they have a greater share than other people of the things and experiences that are most highly valued. From this point of view, the elite are simply those who have the most of what there is to have, which is generally held to include money, power, and prestige—as well as all the ways of life to which these lead. But the elite are not simply those who have the most, for they could not 'have the most' were it not for their positions in the great institutions. For such institutions are the necessary bases of power, of wealth, and of prestige, and at the same time, the chief means of exercising power, of acquiring and retaining wealth, and of cashing in the higher claims for prestige.

By the powerful we mean, of course, those who are able to realize their will, even if others resist it. No one, accordingly, can be truly powerful unless he has access to the command of major institutions, for it is over these institutional means of power that the truly powerful are, in the first instance, powerful. Higher politicians and key officials of government command such institutional power; so do admirals and generals, and so do the major owners and executives of the larger corporations. Not all power, it is true, is anchored in and exercised by means of such institutions, but only within and through them can power be more or less continuous and important.

Wealth also is acquired and held in and through institutions. The pyramid of wealth cannot be understood merely in terms of the very rich; for the great inheriting families, as we shall see, are now supplemented by the corporate institutions of modern society: every one of the very rich families has been and is closely connected—always legally and frequently managerially as well—with one of the multi-million dollar corporations.

The modern corporation is the prime source of wealth, but, in latter-day capitalism, the political apparatus also opens and closes many avenues to wealth. The amount as well as the source of income, the power over consumer's goods as well as over productive capital, are determined by position within the political economy. If our interest in the very rich goes beyond their lavish or their miserly consumption, we must examine their relations to modern forms of corporate property as well as to the state; for such relations now determine the chances of men to secure big property and to receive high income.

Great prestige increasingly follows the major institutional units of the social structure. It is obvious that prestige depends, often quite decisively, upon access to the publicity machines that are now a central and normal feature of all the big institutions of modern America. Moreover, one feature of these hierarchies of corporation, state, and military establishment is that their top positions are increasingly interchangeable. One result of this is the accumulative nature of prestige. Claims for prestige, for example, may be initially based on military roles, then expressed in and augmented by an educational institution run by corporate executives, and cashed in, finally, in the political order, where, for General Eisenhower and those he represents, power and prestige finally meet at the very peak. Like wealth and power, prestige tends to be cumulative: the more of it you have, the more you can get. These values also tend to be translatable into one another: the wealthy find it easier than the poor to gain power; those with status find it easier than those without it to control opportunities for wealth.

If we took the one hundred most powerful men in America, the one hundred wealthiest, and the one hundred most celebrated away from the institutional positions they now occupy, away from their resources of men and women and money, away from the media of mass communication that are now focused upon them—then they would be powerless and poor and uncelebrated. For power is not of a man. Wealth does not center in the person of the wealthy. Celebrity is not inherent in any personality. To be celebrated, to be wealthy, to have power requires access to major institutions, for the institutional positions men occupy determine in large part their chances to have and to hold these valued experiences.

The people of the higher circles may also be conceived as members of a top social stratum, as a set of groups whose members know one another, see one another socially and at business, and so, in making decisions, take one another into account. The elite, according to this conception, feel themselves to be, and are felt by others to be, the inner circle of 'the upper social classes.' They form a more or less compact social and psychological entity; they have become self-conscious members of a social class. People are either accepted into this class or they are not, and there is a qualitative split, rather than merely a numerical scale, separating them from those who are not elite. They are more or less aware of themselves as a social class and they behave toward one another differently from the way they do toward members of other classes. They accept one another, understand one another, marry one another, tend to work and to think if not together at least alike.

Now, we do not want by our definition to prejudge whether the elite of the command posts are conscious members of such a socially recognized class, or whether considerable proportions of the elite derive from such a clear and distinct class. These are matters to be investigated. Yet in order to be able to recognize what we intend to investigate, we must note something that all biographies and memoirs of the wealthy and the powerful and the eminent make clear: no matter what else they may be, the people of these higher circles are involved in a set of overlapping 'crowds' and intricately connected 'cliques.' There is a kind of mutual attraction among those who 'sit on the same terrace'—although this often becomes clear to them, as well as to others, only at the point at which they feel the need to draw the line; only when, in their common defense, they come to understand what they have in common, and so close their ranks against outsiders.

The idea of such ruling stratum implies that most of its members have similar social origins, that throughout their lives they maintain a network of informal connections, and that to some degree there is an interchangeability of position between the various hierarchies of money and power and celebrity. We must, of course, note at once that if such an elite stratum does exist, its social visibility and its form, for very solid historical reasons, are quite different from those of the noble cousinhoods that once ruled various European nations.

That American society has never passed through a feudal epoch is of decisive importance to the nature of the American elite, as well as to American society as a historic whole. For it means that no nobility or aristocracy, established before the capitalist era, has stood in tense opposition to the higher bourgeoisie. It means that this bourgeoisie has monopolized not only wealth but prestige and power as well. It means that no set of noble families has commanded the top positions and monopolized the values that are generally held in high esteem; and certainly that no set has done so explicitly by inherited right. It means that no high church dignitaries or court nobilities, no entrenched landlords with honorific accouterments, no monopolists of high army posts have opposed the enriched bourgeoisie and in the name of birth and prerogative successfully resisted its self-making.

But this does *not* mean that there are no upper strata in the United States. That they emerged from a 'middle class' that had no recognized aristocratic superiors does not mean they remained middle class when enormous increases in wealth made their own superiority possible. Their origins and their newness may have made the upper strata less visible in America than elsewhere. But in America today there are in fact tiers and ranges of wealth and power of which people in the middle and lower ranks know very little and may not even dream. There are families who, in their well-being, are quite insulated from the economic jolts and lurches felt by the merely prosperous and those farther down the scale. There are also men of power who in quite small groups make decisions of enormous consequence for the underlying population.

* * *

To say that there are obvious gradations of power and of opportunities to decide within modern society is not to say that the powerful are united, that they fully know what they do, or that they are consciously joined in conspiracy. Such issues are best faced if we concern ourselves, in the first instance, more with the structural position of the high and mighty, and with the consequences of their decisions, than with the extent of their awareness or the purity of their motives.

C. WRIGHT MILLS

Letter to the New Left (1960)

*A leftist advocate of change, Mills was convinced, along with other rad-
ical intellectuals, that the working class could no longer be counted on
as the agent of historical transformation that Marxist theory had predicted. In an influential article written in the fall of 1960 that appeared
in the recently established journal* New Left Review, *Mills anticipated
social and political developments in the 1960s by suggesting that young
intellectuals and students could become the prime agents of political
change. In doing so, Mills helped define the social and intellectual mission of the emerging New Left.*

The most important issue of political reflection—and of political
action—in our time [is]: the problem of the historical agency of
change, of the social and institutional means of structural change. There
are several points about this problem I would like to put to you.

First, the historic agencies of change for liberals of the capitalist societies
have been an array of voluntary associations, coming to a political climax
in a parliamentary or congressional system. For socialists of almost all varieties, the historic agency has been the working class—and later the
peasantry; also parties and unions variously composed of members of the
working class or (to blur, for now, a great problem) of political parties acting in its name—"representing its interests."

I cannot avoid the view that in both cases, the historic agency (in the
advanced capitalist countries) has either collapsed or become most ambiguous: so far as structural change is concerned, *these* don't seem to be
at once available and effective as *our* agency any more. I know this is a
debatable point among us, and among many others as well; I am by no
means certain about it. But surely the fact of it—if it be that—ought not
to be taken as an excuse for moaning and withdrawal (as it is by some of
those who have become involved with the end-of-ideology); it ought not
to be bypassed (as it is by many Soviet scholars and publicists, who in
their reflections upon the course of advanced capitalist societies simply
refuse to admit the political condition and attitudes of the working class).

Is anything more certain than that in 1970—indeed this time next year—our situation will be quite different, and—the chances are high—decisively so? But of course, that isn't saying much. The seeming collapse of our historic agencies of change ought to be taken as a problem, an issue, a trouble—in fact, as *the* political problem which *we* must turn into issue and trouble.

Second, is it not obvious that when we talk about the collapse of agencies of change, we cannot seriously mean that such agencies do not exist. On the contrary, the means of history-making—of decision and of the enforcement of decision—have never in world history been so enlarged and so available to such small circles of men on both sides of The Curtains as they now are. My own conception of the shape of power—the theory of the power elite—I feel no need to argue here. This theory has been fortunate in its critics, from the most diverse points of political view, and I have learned from several of these critics. But I have not seen, as of this date, any analysis of the idea that causes me to modify any of its essential features.

The point that is immediately relevant does seem obvious: what is utopian for us is not at all utopian for the presidium of the Central Committee in Moscow, or the higher circles of the Presidency in Washington, or—recent events make evident—for the men of SAC and CIA. The historic agencies of change that have collapsed are those which were at least thought to be open to *the left* inside the advanced Western nations: those who have wished for structural changes of these societies. Many things follow from this obvious fact; of many of them, I am sure, we are not yet adequately aware.

Third, what I do not quite understand about some New-Left writers is why they cling so mightily to "the working class" of the advanced capitalist societies as *the* historic agency, or even as the most important agency, in the face of the really impressive historical evidence that now stands against this expectation.

Such a labour metaphysic, I think, is a legacy from Victorian Marxism that is now quite unrealistic.

It is an historically specific idea that has been turned into an a-historical and unspecific hope.

The social and historical conditions under which industrial workers tend to become a-class-for-themselves, and a decisive political force, must be fully and precisely elaborated. There have been, there are, there will be such conditions; of course these conditions vary according to national social structure and the exact phase of their economic and political development. Of course we can't "write off the working class." But we must *study* all that, and freshly. Where labour exists as an agency, of course we must work with it, but we must not treat it as The Necessary Lever—as nice old Labour Gentlemen in your country and elsewhere tend to do.

Although I have not yet completed my own comparative studies of working classes, generally it would seem that only at certain (earlier) stages of industrialisation, and in a political context of autocracy, etc., do wage-workers tend to become a class-for-themselves, etc. The "etcs." mean that I can here merely raise the question.

It is with this problem of agency in mind that I have been studying, for several years now, the cultural apparatus, the intellectuals—as a possible, immediate, radical agency of change. For a long time, I was not much happier with this idea than were many of you; but it turns out now, in the spring of 1960, that it may be a very relevant idea indeed.

In the first place, is it not clear that if we try to be realistic in our utopianism—and that is no fruitless contradiction—a writer in our countries on the Left today *must* begin there? For that is what we are, that is where we stand.

In the second place, the problem of the intelligentsia is an extremely complicated set of problems on which rather little factual work has been done. In doing this work, we must—above all—not confuse the problems of the intellectuals of West Europe and North America with those of the Soviet Bloc or with those of the underdeveloped worlds. In each of the three major components of the world's social structure today, the character and the role of the intelligentsia is distinct and historically specific. Only by detailed comparative studies of them in all their human variety can we hope to understand any one of them.

In the third place, who is it that is getting fed up? Who is it that is getting disgusted with what Marx called "all the old crap"? Who is it that is thinking and acting in radical ways? All over the world—in the bloc, outside the bloc and in between—the answer's the same: it is the young intelligentsia.

I cannot resist copying out for you, with a few changes, some materials I've just prepared for a 1960 paperback edition of a book of mine on war:

"In the spring and early summer of 1960—more of the returns from the American decision and default are coming in. In Turkey, after student riots, a military junta takes over the state, of late run by Communist Container Menderes. In South Korea too, students and others knock over the corrupt American-puppet regime of Syngman Rhee. In Cuba, a genuinely left-wing revolution begins full-scale economic reorganisation— without the domination of US corporations. Average age of its leaders:

about 30—and certainly a revolution without any Labour As Agency. On Taiwan, the eight million Taiwanese under the American-imposed dictatorship of Chiang Kai-shek, with his two million Chinese, grow increasingly restive. On Okinawa—a US military base—the people get their first chance since World War II ended to demonstrate against US seizure of their island: and some students take that chance, snake-dancing and chanting angrily to the visiting President: "Go home, go home—take away your missiles." (Don't worry, 12,000 US troops easily handled the generally grateful crowds; also the President was "spirited out the rear end of the United States compound"—and so by helicopter to the airport). In Great Britain, from Aldermaston to London, young—but you were there. In Japan, weeks of student rioting succeed in rejecting the President's visit, jeopardise a new treaty with the USA, displace the big-business, pro-American Prime Minister, Kishi. And even in our own pleasant Southland, Negro and white students are—but let us keep that quiet: it really *is* disgraceful.

"That is by no means the complete list; that was yesterday; see today's newspaper. Tomorrow, in varying degree, the returns will be more evident. Will they be evident enough? They will have to be very obvious to attract real American attention: sweet complaints and the voice of reason—these are not enough. In the slum countries of the world today, what are they saying? The rich Americans, they pay attention only to violence—and to money. You don't care what they say, American? Good for you. Still, they may insist; things are no longer under the old control; you're not getting it straight, American: your country—it would seem— may well become the target of a world hatred the like of which the easy-going Americans have never dreamed. Neutralists and Pacifists and Unilateralists and that confusing variety of Leftists around the world—all those tens of millions of people, of course they are misguided, absolutely controlled by small conspiratorial groups of trouble-makers, under direct orders straight from Moscow and Peking. Diabolically omnipotent, it is *they* who create all this messy unrest. It is *they* who have given the tens of millions the absurd idea that they shouldn't want to remain, or to become, the seat of American nuclear bases—those gay little outposts of American civilisation. So now they don't want U-2's on their territory; so now they want to contract out of the American military machine; they want to be neutral among the crazy big antagonists. And they don't want their own societies to be militarised.

"But take heart, American: you won't have time to get really bored with your friends abroad: they won't be your friends much longer. You don't need *them*; it will all go away; don't let them confuse you."

* * *

Add to that: In the Soviet bloc, who is it that has been breaking out of apathy? It has been students and young professors and writers; it has been the young intelligentsia of Poland and Hungary, and of Russia too. Never mind that they've not won; never mind that there are other social and moral types among them. First of all, it has been these types. But the point is clear—isn't it?

That's why we've got to study these new generations of intellectuals around the world as real live agencies of historic change. Forget Victorian Marxism, except whenever you need it; and read Lenin again (be careful)—Rosa Luxemburg, too.

"But it's just some kind of moral upsurge, isn't it?" Correct. But under it: no apathy. Much of it is direct non-violent action, and it seems to be working, here and there. Now we must learn from their practice and work out with them new forms of action.

"But it's all so ambiguous. Turkey, for instance. Cuba, for instance." Of course it is; history-making is always ambiguous; wait a bit; in the meantime, *help* them to focus their moral upsurge in less ambiguous political ways; work out with them the ideologies, the strategies, the theories that will help them consolidate their efforts: new theories of structural changes of and by human societies in our epoch.

DANIEL BELL

The End of Ideology (1960)

The sociologist Daniel Bell (1919–) was the managing editor of the New Leader and an editor at Fortune magazine before he went on to teach sociology at Columbia and Harvard universities and to cofound the journal Public Interest. Much of Bell's research reflected his interest in the way political and economic institutions shape individual identity and consciousness. In this selection from his important 1960 book The End of Ideology: On the Exhaustion of Political Ideas in the Fifties, Bell announced "the end of ideology" as a driving force for social action and the emergence of a new consensus on the value of pluralistic liberal democracy.

Ideology is the conversion of ideas into social levers. Without irony, Max Lerner once entitled a book "Ideas Are Weapons." This is the

language of ideology. It is more. It is the commitment to the consequences of ideas. * * *

What gives ideology its force is its passion. Abstract philosophical inquiry has always sought to eliminate passion, and the person, to rationalize all ideas. For the ideologue truth arises in action, and meaning is
given to experience by the "transforming moment." He comes alive not in
contemplation, but in "the deed." One might say, in fact, that the most
important, latent, function of ideology is to tap emotion. Other than religion (and war and nationalism), there have been few forms of channeliz-
ing emotional energy. Religion symbolized, drained away, dispersed
emotional energy from the world onto the litany, the liturgy, the sacra-
ments, the edifices, the arts. Ideology fuses these energies and channels
them into politics.

* * *

A social movement can rouse people when it can do three things: simplify ideas, establish a claim to truth, and, in the union of the two, demand a commitment to action. Thus, not only does ideology transform
ideas, it transforms people as well. The nineteenth-century ideologies, by
emphasizing inevitability and by infusing passion into their followers,
could compete with religion. By identifying inevitability with progress,
they linked up with the positive values of science. But more important,
these ideologies were linked, too, with the rising class of intellectuals,
which was seeking to assert a place in society.

The differences between the intellectual and the scholar, without
being invidious, are important to understand. The scholar has a bounded
field of knowledge, a tradition, and seeks to find his place in it, adding to
the accumulated, tested knowledge of the past as to a mosaic. The
scholar, qua scholar, is less involved with his "self." The intellectual
begins with *his* experience, *his* individual perceptions of the world, *his*
privileges and deprivations, and judges the world by these sensibilities.
Since his own status is of high value, his judgments of the society reflect
the treatment accorded him. In a business civilization, the intellectual
felt that the wrong values were being honored, and rejected the society.
Thus there was a "built-in" compulsion for the free-floating intellectual
to become political. The ideologies, therefore, which emerged from the
nineteenth century had the force of the intellectuals behind them. They
embarked upon what William James called "the faith ladder," which in its
vision of the future cannot distinguish possibilities from probabilities,
and converts the latter into certainties.

Today, these ideologies are exhausted. The events behind this important sociological change are complex and varied. Such calamities as the

Moscow Trials, the Nazi-Soviet pact, the concentration camps, the suppression of the Hungarian workers, form one chain; such social changes as the modification of capitalism, the rise of the Welfare State, another. In philosophy, one can trace the decline of simplistic, rationalistic beliefs and the emergence of new stoic-theological images of man, e.g. Freud, Tillich, Jaspers, etc. This is not to say that such ideologies as communism in France and Italy do not have a political weight, or a driving momentum from other sources. But out of all this history, one simple fact emerges: for the radical intelligentzia, the old ideologies have lost their "truth" and their power to persuade.

Few serious minds believe any longer that one can set down "blueprints" and through "social engineering" bring about a new utopia of social harmony. At the same time, the older "counter-beliefs" have lost their intellectual force as well. Few "classic" liberals insist that the State should play no role in the economy, and few serious conservatives, at least in England and on the Continent, believe that the Welfare State is "the road to serfdom." In the Western world, therefore, there is today a rough consensus among intellectuals on political issues: the acceptance of a Welfare State; the desirability of decentralized power; a system of mixed economy and of political pluralism. In that sense, too, the ideological age has ended.

And yet, the extraordinary fact is that while the old nineteenth-century ideologies and intellectual debates have become exhausted, the rising states of Asia and Africa are fashioning new ideologies with a different appeal for their own people. These are the ideologies of industrialization, modernization, Pan-Arabism, color, and nationalism. In the distinctive difference between the two kinds of ideologies lies the great political and social problems of the second half of the twentieth century. The ideologies of the nineteenth century were universalistic, humanistic, and fashioned by intellectuals. The mass ideologies of Asia and Africa are parochial, instrumental, and created by political leaders. The driving forces of the old ideologies were social equality and, in the largest sense, freedom. The impulsions of the new ideologies are economic development and national power.

* * *

Thus one finds, at the end of the fifties, a disconcerting caesura. In the West, among the intellectuals, the old passions are spent. The new generation, with no meaningful memory of these old debates, and no secure tradition to build upon, finds itself seeking new purposes within a framework of political society that has rejected, intellectually speaking, the old apocalyptic and chiliastic visions. In the search for a "cause," there is a deep, desperate, almost pathetic anger. The theme runs through a remarkable book, *Convictions*, by a dozen of the sharpest young Left Wing intellectuals in Britain. They cannot define the content of the "cause" they seek, but the yearning is clear. In the U.S. too there is a restless search for a new intellectual radicalism. Richard Chase, in his thoughtful assessment of American society, *The Democratic Vista,* insists that the greatness of nineteenth-century America for the rest of the world consisted in its radical vision of man (such a vision as Whitman's), and calls for a new radical criticism today. But the problem is that the old politico-economic radicalism (pre-occupied with such matters as the socialization of industry) has lost its meaning, while the stultifying aspects of contemporary culture (e.g., television) cannot be redressed in political terms. At the same time, American culture has almost completely accepted the avant-garde, particularly in art, and the older academic styles have been driven out completely. The irony, further, for those who seek "causes" is that the workers, whose grievances were once the driving energy for social change, are more satisfied with the society than the intellectuals. The workers have not achieved utopia, but their expectations were less than those of the intellectuals, and the gains correspondingly larger.

The young intellectual is unhappy because the "middle way" is for the middle-aged, not for him; it is without passion and is deadening. Ideology, which by its nature is an all-or-none affair, and temperamentally the thing he wants, is intellectually devitalized, and few issues can be formulated any more, intellectually, in ideological terms. The emotional energies—and needs—exist, and the question of how one mobilizes these energies is a difficult one. Politics offers little excitement. Some of the younger intellectuals have found an outlet in science or university pursuits, but often at the expense of narrowing their talent into mere technique; others have sought self-expression in the arts, but in the wasteland the lack of content has meant, too, the lack of the necessary tension that creates new forms and styles.

Whether the intellectuals in the West can find passions outside of politics is moot. Unfortunately, social reform does not have any unifying appeal, nor does it give a younger generation the outlet for "self-expression" and "self-definition" that it wants. The trajectory of enthusiasm has curved East, where, in the new ecstasies for economic utopia, the "future" is all that counts.

YOUNG AMERICANS FOR FREEDOM

The Sharon Statement (1960)

Young Americans for Freedom, a conservative student organization, was established in the fall of 1960 at a conference held at the estate of William F. Buckley, Jr., in Sharon, Connecticut. Staunchly anticommunist, the group also reflected its mentor's commitment to limited government and economic freedom.

IN THIS TIME of moral and political crises, it is the responsibility of the youth of America to affirm certain eternal truths.

WE, as young conservatives believe:

THAT foremost among the transcendent values is the individual's use of his God-given free will, whence derives his right to be free from the restrictions of arbitrary force;

THAT liberty is indivisible, and that political freedom cannot long exist without economic freedom;

THAT the purpose of government is to protect those freedoms through the preservation of internal order, the provision of national defense, and the administration of justice;

THAT when government ventures beyond these rightful functions, it accumulates power, which tends to diminish order and liberty;

THAT the Constitution of the United States is the best arrangement yet devised for empowering government to fulfill its proper role, while restraining it from the concentration and abuse of power;

THAT the genius of the Constitution—the division of powers—is summed up in the clause that reserves primacy to the several states, or to the people in those spheres not specifically delegated to the Federal government;

THAT the market economy, allocating resources by the free play of supply and demand, is the single economic system compatible with the requirements of personal freedom and constitutional government, and that it is at the same time the most productive supplier of human needs;

THAT when government interferes with the work of the market economy, it tends to reduce the moral and physical strength of the nation, that when it takes from one to bestow on another, it diminishes the incentive of the first, the integrity of the second, and the moral autonomy of both;

THAT we will be free only so long as the national sovereignty of the United States is secure; that history shows periods of freedom are rare, and can exist only when free citizens concertedly defend their rights against all enemies * * *

THAT the forces of international Communism are, at present, the greatest single threat to these liberties;

THAT the United States should stress victory over, rather than coexistence with this menace; and

THAT American foreign policy must be judged by this criterion: does it serve the just interests of the United States?

ROBERT A. DAHL

Who Governs? Democracy and Power in an American City (1961)

The Yale political scientist Robert Dahl (1915–) is the foremost theorist of the pluralist reading of democracy. In his 1961 book Who Governs?, *Dahl's study of political power and influence in New Haven, Connecticut, the political scientist demonstrates that power in a pluralist system tends to be so dispersed that no single group or individual is capable of dominating across political issues. This excerpt from Dahl's discussion of the ambiguous relation between leaders and their constituents illustrates his view that influence is fluid and dispersed in a pluralistic democracy.*

Now it has always been held that if equality of power among citizens is possible at all—a point on which many political philosophers have had grave doubts—then surely considerable equality of social conditions is a necessary prerequisite. But if, even in America, with its universal creed of democracy and equality, there are great inequalities in the conditions of different citizens, must there not also be great inequalities in the capacities of different citizens to influence the decisions of their various governments? And if, because they are unequal in other conditions, citizens of a democracy are unequal in power to control their government, then who in fact does govern? How does a "democratic" system work amid inequality of resources? These are the questions I want to explore by examining one urban American community, New Haven, Connecticut.

* * *

In the course of the past two centuries, New Haven has gradually changed from oligarchy to pluralism. Accompanying and probably causing this change—one might properly call it a revolution—appears to be a profound alteration in the way political resources are distributed among the citizens of New Haven. This silent socioeconomic revolution has not substituted equality for inequality so much as it has involved a shift from cumulative inequalities in political resources * * * to noncumulative or dispersed inequalities. This point will grow clearer as we proceed.

The main evidence for the shift from oligarchy to pluralism is found in changes in the social characteristics of elected officials in New Haven since 1784, the year the city was first incorporated after a century and a half as colony and town.

* * *

In the political system of the patrician oligarchy, political resources were marked by a cumulative inequality: when one individual was much better off than another in one resource, such as wealth, he was usually better off in almost every other resource—social standing, legitimacy, control over religious and educational institutions, knowledge, office. In the political system of today, inequalities in political resources remain, but they tend to be *noncumulative*. The political system of New Haven, then, is one of *dispersed inequalities*.

* * *

Within a century a political system dominated by one cohesive set of leaders had given way to a system dominated by many different sets of leaders, each having access to a different combination of political resources. It was, in short, a pluralist system. If the pluralist system was very far from being an oligarchy, it was also a long way from achieving the goal of political equality advocated by the philosophers of democracy and incorporated into the creed of democracy and equality practically every American professes to uphold.

An elite no longer rules New Haven. But in the strict democratic sense, the disappearance of elite rule has not led to the emergence of rule by the people. Who, then, rules in a pluralist democracy?

* * *

One of the difficulties that confronts anyone who attempts to answer the question, "Who rules in a pluralist democracy?" is the ambiguous relationship of leaders to citizens.

Viewed from one position, leaders are enormously influential—so influential that if they are seen only in this perspective they might well be considered a kind of ruling elite. Viewed from another position, however, many influential leaders seem to be captives of their constituents. Like the blind men with the elephant, different analysts have meticulously examined different aspects of the body politic and arrived at radically different conclusions. To some, a pluralistic democracy with dispersed inequalities is all head and no body; to others it is all body and no head.

Ambiguity in the relations of leaders and constituents is generated by several closely connected obstacles both to observation and to clear conceptualization. To begin with, the American creed of democracy and equality prescribes many forms and procedures from which the actual practices of leaders diverge. Consequently, to gain legitimacy for their actions leaders frequently surround their covert behavior with democratic rituals. These rituals not only serve to disguise reality and thus to complicate the task of observation and analysis, but—more important—in complex ways the very existence of democratic rituals, norms, and requirements of legitimacy based on a widely shared creed actually influences the behavior of both leaders and constituents even when democratic norms are violated. Thus the distinction between the rituals of power and the realities of power is frequently obscure.

Two additional factors help to account for this obscurity. First, among all the persons who influence a decision, some do so more directly than others in the sense that they are closer to the stage where concrete alternatives are initiated or vetoed in an explicit and immediate way. Indirect influence might be very great but comparatively difficult to observe and weigh. Yet to ignore indirect influence in analysis of the distribution of influence would be to exclude what might well prove to be a highly significant process of control in a pluralistic democracy.

Second, the relationship between leaders and citizens in a pluralistic democracy is frequently reciprocal: leaders influence the decisions of constituents, but the decisions of leaders are also determined in part by what they think are, will be, or have been the preferences of their constituents. Ordinarily it is much easier to observe and describe the distribution of influence in a political system where the flow of influence is strongly in one direction (an asymmetrical or unilateral system, as it is sometimes called) than in a system marked by strong reciprocal relations. In a political system with competitive elections, such as New Haven's, it is not unreasonable to expect that relationships between leaders and constituents would normally be reciprocal.

* * *

In New Haven, as in other political systems, a small stratum of individuals is much more highly involved in political thought, discussion, and action than the rest of the population. These citizens constitute the political stratum.

Members of this stratum live in a political subculture that is partly but not wholly shared by the great majority of citizens. Just as artists and intellectuals are the principal bearers of the artistic, literary, and scientific skills of a society, so the members of the political stratum are the main bearers of political skills. If intellectuals were to vanish overnight, a society would be reduced to artistic, literary, and scientific poverty. If the political stratum were destroyed, the previous political institutions of the society would temporarily stop functioning. In both cases, the speed with which the loss could be overcome would depend on the extent to which the elementary knowledge and basic attitudes of the elite had been diffused. In an open society with widespread education and training in civic attitudes, many citizens hitherto in the apolitical strata could doubtless step into roles that had been filled by members of the political stratum. However, sharp discontinuities and important changes in the operation of the political system almost certainly would occur.

In New Haven, as in the United States, and indeed perhaps in all pluralistic democracies, differences in the subcultures of the political and the apolitical strata are marked, particularly at the extremes. In the political stratum, politics is highly salient; among the apolitical strata, it is remote. In the political stratum, individuals tend to be rather calculating in their choice of strategies; members of the political stratum are, in a sense, relatively rational political beings. In the apolitical strata, people are notably less calculating; their political choices are more strongly influenced by inertia, habit, unexamined loyalties, personal attachments, emotions, transient impulses. In the political stratum, an individual's political beliefs tend to fall into patterns that have a relatively high degree of coherence and internal consistency; in the apolitical strata, political orientations are disorganized, disconnected, and unideological. In the political stratum, information about politics and the issues of the day is extensive; the apolitical strata are poorly informed. Individuals in the political stratum tend to participate rather actively in politics; in the apolitical strata citizens rarely go beyond voting and many do not even vote. Individuals in the political stratum exert a good deal of steady, direct, and active influence on government policy; in fact some individuals have a quite extraordinary amount of influence. Individuals in the apolitical strata, on the other hand, have much less direct or active influence on policies.

* * *

In many pluralistic systems, however, the political stratum is far from being a closed or static group. In the United States the political stratum does not constitute a homogeneous class with well-defined class interests. In New Haven, in fact, the political stratum is easily penetrated by anyone whose interests and concerns attract him to the distinctive political culture of the stratum. It is easily penetrated because (among other reasons) elections and competitive parties give politicians a powerful motive for expanding their coalitions and increasing their electoral followings.

In an open pluralistic system, where movement into the political stratum is easy, the stratum embodies many of the most widely shared values and goals in the society. If popular values are strongly pragmatic, then the political stratum is likely to be pragmatic; if popular values prescribe reverence toward the past, then the political stratum probably shares that reverence; if popular values are oriented toward material gain and personal advancement, then the political stratum probably reflects these values; if popular values are particularly favorable to political, social, or economic equality, then the political stratum is likely to emphasize equality. The apolitical strata can be said to "govern" as much through the sharing of common values and goals with members of the political stratum as by other means. However, if it were not for elections and competitive parties, this sharing would—other things remaining the same—rapidly decline.

Not only is the political stratum in New Haven not a closed group, but its "members" are far from united in their orientations and strategies. There are many lines of cleavage. The most apparent and probably the most durable are symbolized by affiliations with different political parties. Political parties are rival coalitions of leaders and subleaders drawn from the members of the political stratum. Leaders in a party coalition seek to win elections, capture the chief elective offices of government, and insure that government officials will legalize and enforce policies on which the coalition leaders can agree.

In any given period of time, various issues are salient within the political stratum. Indeed, a political issue can hardly be said to exist unless and until it commands the attention of a significant segment of the political stratum. Out of all the manifold possibilities, members of the political stratum seize upon some issues as important or profitable; these then become the subject of attention within the political stratum. To be sure, all the members of the political stratum may not initially agree that a particular issue is worthy of attention. But whenever a sizable minority of the legitimate elements in the political stratum is determined to bring some question to the force, the chances are high that the rest of the political stratum will soon begin to pay attention.

* * *

In any durable association of more than a handful of individuals, typically a relatively small proportion of the people exercises relatively great direct influence over all the important choices bearing on the life of the association—its survival, for example, or its share in such community resources as wealth, power, and esteem, or the way these resources are shared within the association, or changes in the structure, activities, and dominant goals of the association, and so on. These persons are, by definition, the leaders. * * *

The goals and motives that animate leaders are evidently as varied as the dreams of men. They include greater income, wealth, economic security, power, social standing, fame, respect, affection, love, knowledge, curiosity, fun, the pleasure of exercising skill, delight in winning, esthetic satisfaction, morality, salvation, heroism, self-sacrifice, envy, jealousy, revenge, hate—whatever the whole wide range may be. Popular beliefs and folklore to the contrary, there is no convincing evidence at present that any single common denominator of motives can be singled out in leaders of associations. We are not compelled, therefore, to accept the simple view that Moses, Jesus, Caligula, Savanarola, St. Ignatius, Abraham Lincoln, Boss Tweed, Mahatma Ghandi, Carrie Chapman Catt, Huey Long, and Joseph Stalin all acted from essentially the same motives.

To achieve their goals, leaders develop plans of action, or strategies. But actions take place in a universe of change and uncertainty; goals themselves emerge, take shape, and shift with new experiences. Hence a choice among strategies is necessarily based more on hunch, guesswork, impulse, and the assessment of imponderables than on scientific predictions. Adopting a strategy is a little bit like deciding how to look for a fuse box in a strange house on a dark night after all the lights have blown.

Ordinarily the goals and strategies of leaders require services from other individuals. (Both Christ and Lenin needed disciples to increase and rally their followers.) To perform these services more or less regularly, reliably, and skillfully, auxiliaries or subleaders are needed. The tasks of subleaders include aid in formulating strategies and policies; carrying out the dull, routine, time-consuming or highly specialized work of the eternal spear bearers, the doorbell ringers, the file clerks;

recruiting and mobilizing the following; and, in a country like the United States where there exists a strong democratic ethos, helping by their very existence to furnish legitimacy to the actions of the leaders by providing a democratic façade.

To secure the services of subleaders, leaders must reward them in some fashion. Here too the range of rewards seems to be as broad as the spectrum of human motives. However, some kinds of rewards are easier to manipulate than others. In business organizations, the rewards are mainly financial ones, which are probably the easiest of all to manipulate. In many other kinds of associations—and evidently to some extent even in business—either financial rewards are too low to attract and hold subleaders capable of performing the tasks at the minimum levels required by the leaders, or within a certain range other kinds of rewards are more important to the auxiliaries than financial ones. Leaders may therefore contrive to pay off their auxiliaries with nonfinancial rewards like social standing, prestige, fun, conviviality, the hope of salvation, and so on.

Thus the survival of an association of leaders and subleaders depends on frequent transactions between the two groups in which the leaders pay off the subleaders in return for their services. To pay off the subleaders, leaders usually have to draw on resources available only outside the association. Sometimes leaders can obtain these resources from outside by coercion, particularly if they happen to control the single most effective institution for coercion: the government. This is one reason—but by no means the only one—why government is always such an important pawn in struggles among leaders. Ordinarily, however, the association must produce something that will appeal to outsiders, who then contribute resources that serve, directly or indirectly, to maintain the association. Probably the most important direct contribution of these outsiders—let us call them constituents—is money; their most important indirect contribution is votes, which can be converted into office and thus into various other resources.

* * *

It is easy to see why observers have often pessimistically concluded that the internal dynamics of political associations create forces alien to popular control and hence to democratic institutions. Yet the characteristics I have described are not necessarily dysfunctional to a pluralistic democracy in which there exists a considerable measure of popular control over the policies of leaders, for minority control by leaders within associations is not necessarily inconsistent with popular control over leaders through electoral processes.

For example, suppose that (1) a leader of a political association feels a strong incentive for winning an election; (2) his constituents comprise most of the adult population of the community; (3) nearly all of his constituents are expected to vote; (4) voters cast their ballot without receiving covert rewards or punishments as a direct consequence of the way they vote; (5) voters give heavy weight to the overt policies of a candidate in making their decision as to how they will vote; (6) there are rival candidates offering alternative policies; and (7) voters have a good deal of information about the policies of the candidates. In these circumstances, it is almost certain that leaders of political associations would tend to choose overt policies they believed most likely to win the support of a majority of adults in the community. Even if the policies of political associations were usually controlled by a tiny minority of leaders in each association, the policies of the leaders who won elections to the chief elective offices in local government would tend to reflect the preferences of the populace. I do not mean to suggest that any political system actually fulfills all these conditions, but to the extent that it does the leaders who directly control the decisions of political associations are themselves influenced in their own choices of policies by their assumptions as to what the voting populace wants.

* * * We shall discover that in each of a number of key sectors of public policy, a few persons have great *direct* influence on the choices that are made; most citizens, by contrast, seem to have rather little direct influence. Yet it would be unwise to underestimate the extent to which voters may exert *indirect* influence on the decisions of leaders by means of elections.

In a political system where key offices are won by elections, where legality and constitutionality are highly valued in the political culture, and where nearly everyone in the political stratum publicly adheres to a doctrine of democracy, it is likely that the political culture, the prevailing attitudes of the political stratum, and the operation of the political system itself will be shaped by the role of elections. Leaders who in one context are enormously influential and even rather free from demands by their constituents may reveal themselves in another context to be involved in tireless efforts to adapt their policies to what they think their constituents want.

To be sure, in a pluralistic system with dispersed inequalities, the direct influence of leaders on policies extends well beyond the norms implied in the classical models of democracy developed by political philosophers. But if the leaders lead, they are also led. Thus the relations between leaders, subleaders, and constituents produce in the distribution of influence a stubborn and pervasive ambiguity that permeates the entire political system.

STUDENTS FOR A DEMOCRATIC
SOCIETY (SDS)

The Port Huron Statement (1962)

Founded in 1960 by college students, SDS was the leading New Left or-
ganization for student activism during much of the 1960s. At its 1962
convention in Port Huron, Michigan, SDS issued a statement that of-
fered a comprehensive critique of what it characterized as the apathy
and depersonalization pervading American society. Written mostly by
the anti–Vietnam War activist Tom Hayden, the Port Huron statement
expressed the anxiety and estrangement that many young Americans
felt in spite of American prosperity. SDS sought to reduce the domi-
nance of economic institutions and the materialism of American culture
by increasing democratic participation and individual responsibility.

INTRODUCTION: AGENDA FOR A GENERATION

We are people of this generation, bred in at least modest comfort, housed now in universities, looking uncomfortably to the world we inherit.

When we were kids the United States was the wealthiest and strongest country in the world; the only one with the atom bomb, the least scarred by modern war, an initiator of the United Nations that we thought would distribute Western influence throughout the world. Freedom and equality for each individual, government of, by, and for the people—these American values we found good, principles by which we could live as men. Many of us began maturing in complacency.

As we grew, however, our comfort was penetrated by events too troubling to dismiss. First, the permeating and victimizing fact of human degradation, symbolized by the Southern struggle against racial bigotry, compelled most of us from silence to activism. Second, the enclosing fact of the Cold War, symbolized by the presence of the Bomb, brought awareness that we ourselves, and our friends, and millions of abstract "others" we knew more directly because of our common peril, might die at any time. We might deliberately ignore, or avoid, or fail to feel all other human problems, but not these two, for these were too immediate and crushing in their impact, too challenging in the demand that we as individuals take the responsibility for encounter and resolution.

While these and other problems either directly oppressed us or rankled our consciences and became our own subjective concerns, we began to see complicated and disturbing paradoxes in our surrounding America. The declaration "all men are created equal . . ." rang hollow before the facts of Negro life in the South and the big cities of the North. The proclaimed peaceful intentions of the United States contradicted its economic and military investments in the Cold War status quo.

We witnessed, and continue to witness, other paradoxes. With nuclear energy whole cities can easily be powered, yet the dominant nation-states seem more likely to unleash destruction greater than that incurred in all wars of human history. Although our own technology is destroying old and creating new forms of social organization, men still tolerate meaningless work and idleness. While two-thirds of mankind suffers undernourishment, our own upper classes revel amidst superfluous abundance. Although world population is expected to double in forty years, the nations still tolerate anarchy as a major principle of international conduct and uncontrolled exploitation governs the sapping of the earth's physical resources. Although mankind desperately needs revolutionary leadership, America rests in national stalemate, its goals ambiguous and tradition-bound instead of informed and clear, its democratic system apathetic and manipulated rather than "of, by, and for the people."

Not only did tarnish appear on our image of American virtue, not only did disillusion occur when the hypocrisy of American ideals was discovered, but we began to sense that what we had originally seen as the American Golden Age was actually the decline of an era. The worldwide outbreak of revolution against colonialism and imperialism, the entrenchment of totalitarian states, the menace of war, overpopulation, international disorder, supertechnology—these trends were testing the tenacity of our own commitment to democracy and freedom and our abilities to visualize their application to a world in upheaval.

Our work is guided by the sense that we may be the last generation in the experiment with living. But we are a minority—the vast majority of our people regard the temporary equilibriums of our society and world as eternally-functional parts. In this is perhaps the outstanding paradox: we ourselves are imbued with urgency, yet the message of our society is that there is no viable alternative to the present. Beneath the reassuring tones of the politicians, beneath the common opinion that America will "muddle through," beneath the stagnation of those who have closed their minds to the future, is the pervading feeling that there simply are no alternatives, that our times have witnessed the exhaustion not only of Utopias, but of any new departures as well. Feeling the press of complexity upon the emptiness of life, people are fearful of the thought that at any moment things might be thrust out of control. They fear change itself, since change might smash whatever invisible framework seems to hold back chaos for them now. For most Americans, all crusades are suspect, threatening. The fact that each individual sees apathy in his fellows perpetuates the common reluctance to organize for change. The dominant institutions are complex enough to blunt the minds of their potential critics, and entrenched enough to swiftly dissipate or entirely repel the energies of protest and reform, thus limiting human expectancies. Then, too, we are a materially improved society, and by our own improvements we seem to have weakened the case for further change.

Some would have us believe that Americans feel contentment amidst prosperity—but might it not better be called a glaze above deeply-felt anxieties about their role in the new world? And if these anxieties produce a developed indifference to human affairs, do they not as well produce a yearning to believe there *is* an alternative to the present, that something *can* be done to change circumstances in the school, the workplaces, the bureaucracies, the government? It is to this latter yearning, at once the spark and engine of change, that we direct our present appeal. The search for truly democratic alternatives to the present, and a commitment to social experimentation with them, is a worthy and fulfilling human enterprise, one which moves us and, we hope, others today. On such a basis do we offer this document of our convictions and analysis: as an effort in understanding and changing the conditions of humanity in the late twentieth century, an effort rooted in the ancient, still unfulfilled conception of man attaining determining influence over his circumstances of life.

VALUES

Making values explicit—an initial task in establishing alternatives—is an activity that has been devalued and corrupted. The conventional moral terms of the age, the politician moralities—"free world," "people's democracies"—reflect realities poorly, if at all, and seem to function more as ruling myths than as descriptive principles. But neither has our experience in the universities brought us moral enlightenment. Our professors and administrators sacrifice controversy to public relations; their curriculums change more slowly than the living events of the world; their skills and silence are purchased by investors in the arms race; passion is called unscholastic. The questions we might want raised—what is really important? can we live in a different and better way? if we wanted to change society, how would we do it?—are not thought to be questions of a "fruitful, empirical nature," and thus are brushed aside.

Unlike youth in other countries we are used to moral leadership being exercised and moral dimensions being clarified by our elders. But today, for us, not even the liberal and socialist preachments of the past seem adequate to the forms of the present. Consider the old slogans: Capitalism Cannot Reform Itself, United Front Against Fascism, General Strike, All Out on May Day. Or, more recently, No Cooperation with Commies and Fellow Travellers, Ideologies are Exhausted, Bipartisanship, No Utopias. These are incomplete, and there are few new prophets. It has been said that our liberal and socialist predecessors were plagued by vision without program, while our own generation is plagued by program without vision. All around us there is astute grasp of method, technique—the committee, the ad hoc group, the lobbyist, the hard and soft sell, the make, the projected image—but, if pressed critically, such expertise is incompetent to explain its implicit ideals. It is highly fashionable to identify oneself by old categories, or by naming a respected political figure, or by explaining "how we would vote" on various issues.

Theoretic chaos has replaced the idealistic thinking of old—and, unable to reconstitute theoretic order, men have condemned idealism itself. Doubt has replaced hopefulness—and men act out a defeatism that is labelled realistic. The decline of utopia and hope is in fact one of the defining features of social life today. The reasons are various: the dreams of the older left were perverted by Stalinism and never recreated; the congressional stalemate makes men narrow their view of the possible; the specialization of human activity leaves little room for sweeping thought; the horrors of the twentieth century, symbolized in the gas-ovens and concentration camps and atom bombs, have blasted hopefulness. To be idealistic is to be considered apocalyptic, deluded. To have no serious aspirations, on the contrary, is to be "toughminded."

In suggesting social goals and values, therefore, we are aware of entering a sphere of some disrepute. Perhaps matured by the past, we have no sure formulas, no closed theories—but that does not mean values are beyond discussion and tentative determination. A first task of any social movement is to convince people that the search for orienting theories and the creation of human values is complex but worthwhile. We are aware that to avoid platitudes we must analyze the concrete conditions of social order. But to direct such an analysis we must use the guideposts of basic principles. Our own social values involve conceptions of human beings, human relationships, and social systems.

We regard *men* as infinitely precious and possessed of unfulfilled capacities for reason, freedom, and love. In affirming these principles we are
aware of countering perhaps the dominant conceptions of man in the
twentieth century: that he is a thing to be manipulated, and that he is inherently incapable of directing his own affairs. We oppose the depersonalization that reduces human beings to the status of things—if anything, the
brutalities of the twentieth century teach that means and ends are intimately related, that vague appeals to "posterity" cannot justify the mutila-
tions of the present. We oppose, too, the doctrine of human incompetence
because it rests essentially on the modern fact that men have been "competently" manipulated into incompetence—we see little reason why men
cannot meet with increasing skill the complexities and responsibilities of
their situation, if society is organized not for minority, but for majority,
participation in decision-making.

Men have unrealized potential for self-cultivation, self-direction, self-
understanding, and creativity. It is this potential that we regard as crucial
and to which we appeal, not to the human potentiality for violence, un-
reason, and submission to authority. The goal of man and society should
be human independence: a concern not with image of popularity but with
finding a meaning in life that is personally authentic; a quality of mind
not compulsively driven by a sense of powerlessness, nor one which unthinkingly adopts status values, nor one which represses all threats to its
habits, but one which has full, spontaneous access to present and past experiences, one which easily unites the fragmented parts of personal history, one which openly faces problems which are troubling and unresolved;
one with an intuitive awareness of possibilities, an active sense of curiosity, an ability and willingness to learn.

This kind of independence does not mean egotistic individualism—the
object is not to have one's way so much as it is to have a way that is one's
own. Nor do we deify man—we merely have faith in his potential.

Human relationships should involve fraternity and honesty. Human interdependence is contemporary fact; human brotherhood must be willed,
however, as a condition of future survival and as the most appropriate
form of social relations. Personal links between man and man are
needed, especially to go beyond the partial and fragmentary bonds of
function that bind men only as worker to worker, employer to employee,
teacher to student, American to Russian.

Lonelinesss, estrangement, isolation describe the vast distance between man and man today. These dominant tendencies cannot be overcome by better personnel management, nor by improved gadgets, but
only when a love of man overcomes the idolotrous worship of things by
man. As the individualism we affirm is not egoism, the selflessness we af-

firm is not self-elimination. On the contrary, we believe in generosity of a kind that imprints one's unique individual qualities in the relation to other men, and to all human activity. Further, to dislike isolation is not to favor the abolition of privacy; the latter differs from isolation in that it occurs or is abolished according to individual will.

We would replace power rooted in possession, privilege, or circumstance by power and uniqueness rooted in love, reflectiveness, reason, and creativity. As a *social system* we seek the establishment of a democracy of individual participation, governed by two central aims: that the individual share in those social decisions determining the quality and direction of his life; that society be organized to encourage independence in men and provide the media for their common participation.

In a participatory democracy, the political life would be based in several root principles:

that decision-making of basic social consequence be carried on by public groupings;

that politics be seen positively, as the art of collectively creating an acceptable pattern of social relations;

that politics has the function of bringing people out of isolation and into community, thus being a necessary, though not sufficient, means of finding meaning in personal life;

that the political order should serve to clarify problems in a way instrumental to their solution; it should provide outlets for the expression of personal grievance and aspiration; opposing views should be organized so as to illuminate choices and facilitate the attainment of goals; channels should be commonly available to relate men to knowledge and to power so that private problems—from bad recreation facilities to personal alienation—are formulated as general issues.

The economic sphere would have as its basis the principles:

that work should involve incentives worthier than money or survival. It should be educative, not stultifying; creative, not mechanical; self-directed, not manipulated, encouraging independence, a respect for others, a sense of dignity and a willingness to accept social responsibility, since it is this experience that has crucial influence on habits, perceptions and individual ethics;

that the economic experience is so personally decisive that the individual must share in its full determination;

that the economy itself is of such social importance that its major resources and means of production should be open to democratic participation and subject to democratic social regulation.

Like the political and economic ones, major social institutions—cultural, educational, rehabilitative, and others—should be generally organized with the well-being and dignity of man as the essential measure of success.

In social change or interchange, we find violence to be abhorrent because it requires generally the transformation of the target, be it a human being or a community of people, into a depersonalized object of hate. It is imperative that the means of violence be abolished and the institutions—local, national, international—that encourage nonviolence as a condition of conflict be developed.

These are our central values, in skeletal form. It remains vital to understand their denial or attainment in the context of the modern world.

* * *

POLITICS WITHOUT PUBLICS

The American political system is not the democratic model of which its glorifiers speak. In actuality it frustrates democracy by confusing the individual citizen, paralyzing policy discussion, and consolidating the irresponsible power of military and business interests.

* * *

What emerges from the party contradiction and insulation of privately-held power is the organized political stalemate: calcification dominates flexibility as the principle of parliamentary organization, frustration is the expectancy of legislators intending liberal reform, and Congress becomes less and less central to national decision-making, especially in the area of foreign policy. In this context, confusion and blurring is built into the formulation of issues, long-range priorities are not discussed in the rational manner needed for policy-making, the politics of personality and "image" become a more important mechanism than the construction of issues in a way that affords each voter a challenging and real option. The American voter is buffeted from all directions by pseudo-problems, by the structurally-initiated sense that nothing political is subject to human mastery. Worried by his mundane problems which never get solved, but constrained by the common belief that politics is an agonizingly slow accommodation of views, he quits all pretense of bothering.

A most alarming fact is that few, if any, politicians are calling for changes in these conditions. Only a handful even are calling on the President to "live up to" platform pledges; no one is demanding structural changes, such as the shuttling of Southern Democrats out of the Democratic Party. Rather than protesting the state of politics, most politicians are reinforcing and aggravating that state. While in practice they rig public opinion to suit their own interests, in word and ritual they enshrine "the sovereign public" and call for more and more letters. Their speeches and campaign actions are banal, based on a degrading conception of what people want to hear. They respond not to dialogue, but to pressure: and knowing this, the ordinary citizen sees even greater inclination to shun the political sphere. The politician is usually a trumpeter to "citizenship" and "service to the nation," but since he is unwilling to seriously rearrange power relationships, his trumpetings only increase apathy by creating no outlets. Much of the time the call to "service" is justified not in idealistic terms, but in the crasser terms of "defending the free world from communism"—thus making future idealistic impulses harder to justify in anything but Cold War terms.

* * *

Towards American Democracy

Every effort to end the Cold War and expand the process of world industrialization is an effort hostile to people and institutions whose interests lie in perpetuation of the East-West military threat and the postponement of change in the "have not" nations of the world. Every such effort, too, is bound to establish greater democracy in America. The major goals of a domestic effort would be:

1 *America must abolish its political party stalemate.*

* * *

2 *Mechanisms of voluntary association must be created through which political information can be imparted and political participation encouraged.*

* * *

3 *Institutions and practices which stifle dissent should be abolished, and the promotion of peaceful dissent should be actively promoted.*

* * *

4 *Corporations must be made publicly responsible.*

* * *

5 *The allocation of resources must be based on social needs. A truly "public sector" must be established, and its nature debated and planned.*

* * *

6 *America should concentrate on its genuine social priorities: abolish squalor, terminate neglect, and establish an environment for people to live in with dignity and creativeness.*

* * *

ALTERNATIVES TO HELPLESSNESS

The goals we have set are not realizable next month, or even next election—but that fact justifies neither giving up altogether nor a determination to work only on immediate, direct, tangible problems. Both responses are a sign of helplessness, fearfulness of visions, refusal to hope, and tend to bring on the very conditions to be avoided. Fearing vision, we justify rhetoric or myopia. Fearing hope, we reinforce despair.

The first effort, then, should be to state a vision: what is the perimeter of human possibility in this epoch? This we have tried to do. The second effort, if we are to be politically responsible, is to evaluate the prospects for obtaining at least a substantial part of that vision in our epoch: what are the social forces that exist, or that must exist, if we are to be at all successful? And what role have we ourselves to play as a social force?

1. In exploring the existing social forces, note must be taken of the Southern civil rights movement as the most heartening beacuse of the justice it insists upon, exemplary because it indicates that there can be a passage out of apathy.

* * *

2. The broadest movement for *peace* in several years emerged in 1961–62. In its political orientation and goals it is much less identifiable than the movement for civil rights: it includes socialists, pacifists, liberals, scholars, militant activists, middle-class women, some professionals, many students, a few unionists. Some have been emotionally single-issue: Ban the Bomb. Some have been academically obscurantist. Some have rejected the System (sometimes both systems). Some have attempted, also, to "work within" the system. Amidst these conflicting streams of emphasis, however, certain basic qualities appear. The most important is that the "peace movement" has operated almost exclusively through peripheral institutions—almost never through mainstream institutions. Similarly, individuals interested in peace have nonpolitical social roles that cannot be turned to the support of peace activity. Concretely, liberal religious societies, anti-war groups, voluntary associations and ad hoc committees have been the political unit of the peace movement; and its human movers have been students, teachers, housewives, secretaries, lawyers, doctors, clergy. The units have not been located in spots of major social influence; the people have not been able to turn their resources fully to the issues that concern them. The results are political ineffectiveness and personal alienation.

* * *

3. Central to any analysis of the potential for change must be an appraisal of *organized labor*. It would be ahistorical to disregard the immense influence of labor in making modern America a decent place in which to live. It would be confused to fail to note labor's presence today as the most liberal of mainstream institutions. But it would be irresponsible not to criticize labor for losing much of the idealism that once made it a driving movement. Those who expected a labor upsurge after the 1955 AFL-CIO merger can only be dismayed that one year later, in the Stevenson-Eisenhower campaign, the AFL-CIO Committee on Political Education was able to obtain solicited $1.00 contributions from only one of every 24 unionists, and prompt only 40 percent of the rank-and-file to vote.

* * *

A new politics must include a revitalized labor movement: a movement which sees itself, and is regarded by others, as a major leader of the breakthrough to a politics of hope and vision. Labor's role is no less unique or important in the needs of the future than it was in the past; its numbers and potential political strength, its natural interest in the abolition of explotation, its reach to the grass roots of American society, combine to make it the best candidate for the synthesis of the civil rights, peace, and economic reform movements.

* * *

THE UNIVERSITY AND SOCIAL CHANGE

* * * But the civil rights, peace, and student movements are too poor and socially slighted, and the labor movement too quiescent, to be counted with enthusiasm. From where else can power and vision be summoned? We believe that the universities are an overlooked seat of influence.

First, the university is located in a permanent position of social influence. Its educational function makes it indispensable and automatically makes it a crucial institution in the formation of social attitudes. Second, in an unbelievably complicated world, it is the central institution for organizing, evaluating, and transmitting knowledge. Third, the extent to which academic resources presently are used to butress immoral social practice is revealed first, by the extent to which defense contracts make the universities engineers of the arms race. Too, the use of modern social science as a manipulative tool reveals itself in the "human relations" consultants to the modern corporations, who introduce trivial sops to give laborers feelings of "participation" or "belonging," while actually deluding them in order to further exploit their labor. And, of course, the use of motivational research is already infamous as a manipulative aspect of American politics. But these social uses of the universities' resources also demonstrate the unchangeable reliance by men of power on the men and storehouses of knowledge: this makes the university functionally tied to society in new ways, revealing new potentialities, new levers for change. Fourth, the university is the only mainstream institution that is open to participation by individuals of nearly any viewpoint.

These, at least, are facts, no matter how dull the teaching, how paternalistic the rules, how irrelevant the research that goes on. Social relevance, the accessibility to knowledge, and internal openness—these together make the university a potential base and agency in a movement of social change.

1. Any new left in America must be, in large measure, a left with real intellectual skills, committed to deliberativeness, honesty, reflection as working tools. The university permits the political life to be an adjunct to the academic one, and action to be informed by reason.

2. A new left must be distributed in significant social roles throughout the country. The universities are distributed in such a manner.

3. A new left must consist of younger people who matured in the postwar world, and partially be directed to the recruitment of younger people. The university is an obvious beginning point.

4. A new left must include liberals and socialists, the former for their relevance, the latter for their sense of thoroughgoing reforms in the system. The university is a more sensible place than a political party for these two traditions to begin to discuss their differences and look for political synthesis.

5. A new left must start controversy across the land, if national policies and national apathy are to be reversed. The ideal university is a community of controversy, within itself and in its effects on communities beyond.

6. A new left must transform modern complexity into issues that can be understood and felt close-up by every human being. It must give form to the feelings of helplessness and indifference, so that people may see the political, social, and economic sources of their private troubles and organize to change society. In a time of supposed prosperity, moral complacency, and political manipulation, a new left cannot rely on only aching stomachs to be the engine force of social reform. The case for change, for alternatives that will involve uncomfortable personal efforts, must be argued as never before. The university is a relevant place for all of these activities.

But we need not indulge in illusions: the university system cannot complete a movement of ordinary people making demands for a better life. From its schools and colleges across the nation, a militant left might awaken its allies, and by beginning the process towards peace, civil rights, and labor struggles, reinsert theory and idealism where too often reign confusion and political barter. The power of students and faculty united is not only potential; it has shown its actuality in the South, and in the reform movements of the North.

The bridge to political power, though, will be built through genuine cooperation, locally, nationally, and internationally, between a new left of young people, and an awakening community of allies. In each community we must look within the university and act with confidence that we can be powerful, but we must look outwards to the less exotic but more lasting struggles for justice.

To turn these possibilities into realities will involve national efforts at university reform by an alliance of students and faculty. They must wrest control of the educational process from the administrative bureaucracy. They must make fraternal and functional contact with allies in labor, civil rights, and other liberal forces outside the campus. They must import major public issues into the curriculum—research and teaching on problems of war and peace is an outstanding example. They must make debate and controversy, not dull pedantic cant, the common style for educational life. They must consciously *build a base* for their assault upon the loci of power.

As students for a democratic society, we are committed to stimulating this kind of social movement, this kind of vision and program in campus and community across the country. If we appear to seek the unattainable, as it has been said, then let it be known that we do so to avoid the unimaginable.

MARIO SAVIO

An End to History (1964)

The social reformer and civil rights activist Mario Robert Savio (1942–1996) became the de facto leader of the free speech movement at the University of California at Berkeley after the administration prohibited students from distributing political literature on campus property.

Although Savio and other students were arrested for occupying the administration building, the university's Board of Regents eventually recognized the First Amendment rights of students. In a speech delivered on the steps of the administration building at Berkeley in 1964, Savio compared the injustices faced by the civil rights and students movements and criticized the cold, alienating effects of bureaucracy in America, especially in the university.

L ast summer I went to Mississippi to join the struggle there for civil rights. This fall I am engaged in another phase of the same struggle, this time in Berkeley. The two battlefields may seem quite different to some observers, but this is not the case. The same rights are at stake in both places—the right to participate as citizens in democratic society and the right to due process of law. Further, it is a struggle against the same enemy. In Mississippi an autocratic and powerful minority rules, through organized violence, to suppress the vast, virtually powerless, majority. In California, the privileged minority manipulates the University bureaucracy to suppress the students' political expression. That "respectable" bureaucracy masks the financial plutocrats; that impersonal bureaucracy is the efficient enemy in a "Brave New World."

In our free speech fight at the University of California, we have come up against what may emerge as the greatest problem of our nation— depersonalized, unresponsive bureaucracy. We have encountered the organized status quo in Mississippi, but it is the same in Berkeley. Here we find it impossible usually to meet with anyone but secretaries. Beyond that, we find functionaries who cannot make policy but can only hide behind the rules. We have discovered total lack of response on the part of the policy makers. To grasp a situation which is truly Kafkesque, it is necessary to understand the bureaucratic mentality. And we have learned quite a bit about it this fall, more outside the classroom than in.

As bureaucrat, an administrator believes that nothing new happens. He occupies an a-historical point of view. In September, to get the attention of this bureaucracy which had issued arbitrary edicts suppressing student political expression and refused to discuss its action, we held a sit-in on the campus. We sat around a police car and kept it immobilized for over thirty-two hours. At last, the administrative bureaucracy agreed to negotiate. But instead, on the following Monday, we discovered that a committee had been appointed, in accordance with usual regulations, to resolve the dispute. Our attempt to convince any of the administrators that an event had occurred, that something new had happened, failed. They saw this simply as something to be handled by normal University procedures.

The same is true of all bureaucracies. They begin as tools, means to certain legitimate goals, and they end up feeding their own existence. The conception that bureaucrats have is that history has in fact come to an end. No events can occur now that the Second World War is over which can change American society substantially. We proceed by standard procedures as we are.

The most crucial problems facing the United States today are the problem of automation and the problem of racial injustice. Most people who will be put out of jobs by machines will not accept an end to events, this historical plateau, as the point beyond which no change occurs. Negroes will not accept an end to history here. All of us must refuse to accept history's final judgment that in America there is no place in society for people whose skins are dark. On campus students are not about to accept it as fact that the University has ceased evolving and is in its final state of perfection, that students and faculty are respectively raw material and employees, or that the University is to be autocratically run by unresponsive bureaucrats.

Here is the real contradiction: the bureaucrats hold history as ended. As a result significant parts of the population both on campus and off are dispossessed, and these dispossessed are not about to accept this a-historical point of view. It is out of this that the conflict has occurred with the University bureaucracy and will continue to occur until that bureaucracy becomes responsive or until it is clear the University can not function.

The things we are asking for in our civil rights protests have a deceptively quaint ring. We are asking for the due process of law. We are asking for our actions to be judged by committees of our peers. We are asking that regulations ought to be considered as arrived at legitimately only from the consensus of the governed. These phrases are all pretty old, but they are not being taken seriously in America today, nor are they being taken seriously on the Berkeley campus.

I have just come from a meeting with the Dean of Students. She notified us that she was aware of certain violations of University regulations by certain organizations. University friends of SNCC, which I represent, was one of these. We tried to draw from her some statement on these great principles, consent of the governed, jury of one's peers, due process. The best she could do was to evade or to present the administration party line. It is very hard to make any contact with the human being who is behind these organizations.

The university is the place where people begin seriously to question the conditions of their existence and raise the issue of whether they can be committed to the society they have been born into. After a long period of apathy during the 50's, students have begun not only to question but,

having arrived at answers, to act on those answers. This is part of a growing understanding among many people in America that history has not
ended, that a better society is possible, and that it is worth dying for.

This free speech fight points up a fascinating aspect of contemporary
campus life. Students are permitted to talk all they want so long as their
speech has no consequences.

One conception of the university, suggested by a classical Christian
formulation, is that it be in the world but not of the world. The conception of Clark Kerr by contrast is that the university is part and parcel of
this particular stage in the history of American society; it stands to serve
the need of American industry; it is a factory that turns out a certain
product needed by industry or government. Because speech does often
have consequences which might alter this perversion of higher education, the university must put itself in a position of censorship. It can permit two kinds of speech, speech which encourages continuation of the
status quo, and speech which advocates changes in it so radical as to be
irrelevant in the foreseeable future. Someone may advocate radical
change in all aspects of American society, and this I am sure he can do
with impunity. But if someone advocates sit-ins to bring about changes in
discriminatory hiring practices, this can not be permitted because it goes
against the status quo of which the university is a part. And that is how
the fight began here.

The Administration of the Berkeley campus has admitted that external, extra-legal groups have pressured the university not to permit students on campus to organize picket lines, not to permit on campus any
speech with consequences. And the bureaucracy went along. Speech
with consequences, speech in the area of civil rights, speech which some
might regard as illegal, must stop.

Many students here at the university, many people in society, are wandering aimlessly about. Strangers in their own lives, there is no place for
them. They are people who have not learned to compromise, who for example have come to the university to learn to question, to grow, to
learn—all the standard things that sound like cliches because no one
takes them seriously. And they find at one point or other that for them to
become part of society, to become lawyers, ministers, business men, people in government, that very often they must compromise those principles
which were most dear to them. They must suppress the most creative impulses that they have; this is a prior condition for being part of the system. The university is well structured, well tooled, to turn out people
with all the sharp edges worn off, the well-rounded person. The university is well equipped to produce that sort of person, and this means that
the best among the people who enter must for four years wander aim-

lessly much of the time questioning why they are on campus at all, doubting whether there is any point in what they are doing, and looking toward a very bleak existence afterward in a game in which all of the rules have been made up, which one can not really amend.

It is a bleak scene, but it is all a lot of us have to look forward to. Society provides no challenge. American society in the standard conception it has of itself is simply no longer exciting. The most exciting things going on in America today are movements to change America. America is becoming ever more the utopia of sterilized, automated contentment. The "futures" and "careers" for which American students now prepare are for the most part intellectual and moral wastelands. This chrome-plated consumers paradise would have us grow up to be well-behaved children. But an important minority of men and women coming to the front today have shown that they will die rather than be standardized, replaceable and irrelevant.

MARTIN LUTHER KING, JR.

The Power of Nonviolence (1957)

The charismatic black Baptist minister Martin Luther King, Jr. (1929–1968), led the civil rights movement as the founder and president of the Southern Christian Leadership Conference. From 1955 until his assassination in Memphis, Tennessee, in 1968, King organized a number of nonviolent boycotts, demonstrations, and marches against segregation and other forms of racial injustice, for which he won the Nobel Peace Prize in 1964. King's eloquent appeals to the Christian values of brotherly love and the American principles of freedom and equality elicited the support of many whites. His commitment to nonviolent resistance contributed to his reputation as a moderate civil rights leader. In this excerpt from a 1957 speech to students at the University of California, Berkeley, King explained that nonviolent direct action was the most effective way to combat evil.

From the very beginning there was a philosophy undergirding the Montgomery boycott, the philosophy of nonviolent resistance. There was always the problem of getting this method over because it didn't make sense to most of the people in the beginning. We had to use our mass meetings to explain nonviolence to a community of people who had never heard of the philosophy and in many instances were not sympathetic with it. We had meetings twice a week on Mondays and on Thursdays, and we had an institute on nonviolence and social change. We had to make it clear that nonviolent resistance is not a method of cowardice. It does resist. It is not a method of stagnant passivity and deadening complacency. The nonviolent resister is just as opposed to the evil that he is standing against as the violent resister but he resists without violence. This method is nonaggressive physically but strongly aggressive spiritually.

* * *

Another thing that we had to get over was the fact that the nonviolent resister does not seek to humiliate or defeat the opponent but to win his friendship and understanding. This was always a cry that we had to set before people that our aim is not to defeat the white community, not to humiliate the white community, but to win the friendship of all of the persons who had perpetrated this system in the past. The end of violence or the aftermath of violence is bitterness. The aftermath of nonviolence is reconciliation and the creation of a beloved community. A boycott is never an end within itself. It is merely a means to awaken a sense of shame within the oppressor but the end is reconciliation, the end is redemption.

Then we had to make it clear also that the nonviolent resister seeks to attack the evil system rather than individuals who happen to be caught up in the system. And this is why I say from time to time that the struggle in the South is not so much the tension between white people and Negro people. The struggle is rather between justice and injustice, between the forces of light and the forces of darkness. And if there is a victory it will not be a victory merely for fifty thousand Negroes. But it will be a victory for justice, a victory for good will, a victory for democracy.

Another basic thing we had to get over is that nonviolent resistance is also an internal matter. It not only avoids external violence or external physical violence but also internal violence of spirit. And so at the center of our movement stood the philosophy of love. The attitude that the only way to ultimately change humanity and make for the society that we all long for is to keep love at the center of our lives. Now people used to ask me from the beginning what do you mean by love and how is it that you can tell us to love those persons who seek to defeat us and those persons who stand against us; how can you love such persons? And I had to make it clear all along that love in its highest sense is not a sentimental sort of thing, not even an affectionate sort of thing.

* * *

The Greek language uses three words for love. It talks about *eros*. *Eros* is a sort of aesthetic love. It has come to us to be a sort of romantic love and it stands with all of its beauty. But when we speak of loving those who oppose us we're not talking about *eros*. The Greek language talks about *philia* and this is a sort of reciprocal love between personal friends. This is a vital, valuable love. But when we talk of loving those who oppose you and those who seek to defeat you we are not talking about *eros* or *philia*. The Greek language comes out with another word and it is *agape*. *Agape* is understanding, creative, redemptive good will for all men. Biblical theologians would say it is the love of God working in the minds of men. It is an overflowing love which seeks nothing in return. And when you come to love on this level you begin to love men not because they are likable, not because they do things that attract us, but because God loves them and here we love the person who does the evil deed while hating the deed that the person does. It is the type of love that stands at the center of the movement that we are trying to carry on in the Southland—*agape*.

* * *

I am quite aware of the fact that there are persons who believe firmly in nonviolence who do not believe in a personal God, but I think every person who believes in nonviolent resistance believes somehow that the universe in some form is on the side of justice. That there is something unfolding in the universe whether one speaks of it as an unconscious process, or whether one speaks of it as some unmoved mover, or whether someone speaks of it as a personal God. There is something in the universe that unfolds for justice and so in Montgomery we felt somehow that as we struggled we had cosmic companionship. And this was one of the things that kept the people together, the belief that the universe is on the side of justice.

God grant that as men and women all over the world struggle against evil systems they will struggle with love in their hearts, with understanding good will. *Agape* says you must go on with wise restraint and calm reasonableness but you must keep moving. We have a great opportunity in America to build here a great nation, a nation where all men live together as brothers and respect the dignity and worth of all human personality. We must keep moving toward that goal. I know that some people are saying we must slow up. They are writing letters to the North and they are appealing to white people of good will and to the Negroes saying slow up, you're pushing too fast. They are saying we must adopt a policy of moderation. Now if moderation means moving on with wise restraint and calm reasonableness, then moderation is a great virtue that all men of good will must seek to achieve in this tense period of transition. But if moderation means slowing up in the move for justice and capitulating to the whims and caprices of the guardians of the deadening status quo, then moderation is a tragic vice which all men of good will must condemn. We must continue to move on. Our self-respect is at stake; the prestige of our nation is at stake. Civil rights is an eternal moral issue which may well determine the destiny of our civilization in the ideological struggle with communism. We must keep moving with wise restraint and love and with proper discipline and dignity.

* * *

Modern psychology has a word that is probably used more than any other word. It is the word "maladjusted." Now we all should seek to live a well adjusted life in order to avoid neurotic and schizophrenic personalities. But there are some things within our social order to which I am proud to be maladjusted and to which I call upon you to be maladjusted. I never intend to adjust myself to segregation and discrimination. I never intend to adjust myself to mob rule. I never intend to adjust myself to the tragic effects of the methods of physical violence and to tragic militarism. I call upon you to be maladjusted to such things. I call upon you to be as mal-adjusted as Amos who in the midst of the injustices of his day cried out in words that echo across the generation, "Let judgment run down like wa-ters and righteousness like a mighty stream." As maladjusted as Abraham Lincoln who had the vision to see that this nation could not exist half slave and half free. As maladjusted as Jefferson, who in the midst of an age amazingly adjusted to slavery could cry out, "All men are created equal and are endowed by their Creator with certain inalienable rights and that among these are life, liberty and the pursuit of happiness." As maladjusted as Jesus of Nazareth who dreamed a dream of the father-hood of God and the brotherhood of man. God grant that we will be so maladjusted that we will be able to go out and change our world and our civilization. And then we will be able to move from the bleak and desolate midnight of man's inhumanity to man to the bright and glittering day-break of freedom and justice.

MARTIN LUTHER KING, JR.

Letter from Birmingham Jail (1963)

After one of his many arrests for peacefully demonstrating against racial injustice in the South, King responded in April 1963 to criti-cisms from fellow clergymen in a moving letter that rejected their pleas for patience and accused them of impeding the path to progress.

King's sense of the urgent need for "constructive nonviolent tension"
against unjust laws leads to a powerful defense of civil disobedience,
rooted in the Christian natural-law tradition and its distinction be-
tween just and unjust laws.

My dear Fellow Clergymen,

While confined here in the Birmingham city jail, I came across your recent statement calling our present activities "unwise and untimely." Seldom, if ever, do I pause to answer criticism of my work and ideas. If I sought to answer all of the criticisms that cross my desk, my secretaries would be engaged in little else in the course of the day, and I would have no time for constructive work. But since I feel that you are men of genuine good will and your criticisms are sincerely set forth, I would like to answer your statement in what I hope will be patient and reasonable terms.

I think I should give the reason for my being in Birmingham, since you have been influenced by the argument of "outsiders coming in." I have the honor of serving as president of the Southern Christian Leadership Conference, an organization operating in every southern state, with headquarters in Atlanta, Georgia. * * * Several months ago our local affiliate here in Birmingham invited us to be on call to engage in a nonviolent direct-action program if such were deemed necessary. We readily consented and when the hour came we lived up to our promises. So I am here, along with several members of my staff, because we were invited here. I am here because I have basic organizational ties here.

Beyond this, I am in Birmingham because injustice is here. Just as the eighth century prophets left their little villages and carried their "thus saith the Lord" far beyond the boundaries of their hometowns; and just as the Apostle Paul left his little village of Tarsus and carried the gospel of Jesus Christ to practically every hamlet and city of the Graeco-Roman world, I too am compelled to carry the gospel of freedom beyond my particular hometown. Like Paul, I must constantly respond to the Macedonian call for aid.

* * *

You deplore the demonstrations that are presently taking place in Birmingham. But I am sorry that your statement did not express a similar concern for the conditions that brought the demonstrations into being. I am sure that each of you would want to go beyond the superficial social analyst who looks merely at effects, and does not grapple with underlying causes. I would not hesitate to say that it is unfortunate that so-called demonstrations are taking place in Birmingham at this time, but I would say in more emphatic terms that it is even more unfortunate that the white power structure of this city left the Negro community with no other alternative.

In any nonviolent campaign there are four basic steps: (1) collection of the facts to determine whether injustices are alive, (2) negotiation, (3) self-purification, and (4) direct action. We have gone through all of these steps in Birmingham. There can be no gainsaying of the fact that racial injustice engulfs this community.

Birmingham is probably the most thoroughly segregated city in the United States. Its ugly record of police brutality is known in every section of this country. Its injust treatment of Negroes in the courts is a notorious reality. There have been more unsolved bombings of Negro homes and churches in Birmingham than any city in this nation. These are the hard, brutal and unbelievable facts. On the basis of these conditions Negro leaders sought to negotiate with the city fathers. But the political leaders consistently refused to engage in good faith negotiation.

* * *

You may well ask, "Why direct action? Why sit-ins, marches, etc.? Isn't negotiation a better path?" You are exactly right in your call for negotiation. Indeed, this is the purpose of direct action. Nonviolent direct action seeks to create such a crisis and establish such creative tension that a community that has constantly refused to negotiate is forced to confront the issue. It seeks so to dramatize the issue that it can no longer be ignored. I just referred to the creation of tension as a part of the work of the nonviolent resister. This may sound rather shocking. But I must confess that I am not afraid of the word tension. I have earnestly worked and preached against violent tension, but there is a type of constructive nonviolent tension that is necessary for growth. Just as Socrates felt that it was necessary to create a tension in the mind so that individuals could rise from the bondage of myths and half-truths to the unfettered realm of creative analysis and objective appraisal, we must see the need of having nonviolent gadflies to create the kind of tension in society that will help men to rise from the dark depths of prejudice and racism to the majestic heights of understanding and brotherhood. So the purpose of the direct action is to create a situation so crisis-packed that it will inevitably open the door to negotiation. We, therefore, concur with you in your call for negotiation. Too long has our beloved Southland been bogged down in the tragic attempt to live in monologue rather than dialogue.

* * * My friends, I must say to you that we have not made a single gain in civil rights without determined legal and nonviolent pressure. History is the long and tragic story of the fact that privileged groups seldom give up their privileges voluntarily. Individuals may see the moral light and voluntarily give up their unjust posture; but as Reinhold Niebuhr has reminded us, groups are more immoral than individuals.

We know through painful experience that freedom is never voluntarily given by the oppressor; it must be demanded by the oppressed. Frankly, I have never yet engaged in a direct action movement that was "well-timed," according to the timetable of those who have not suffered unduly from the disease of segregation. For years now I have heard the words "Wait!" It rings in the ear of every Negro with a piercing familiarity. This "Wait" has almost always meant "Never." It has been a tranquilizing thalidomide, relieving the emotional stress for a moment, only to give birth to an ill-formed infant of frustration. We must come to see with the distinguished jurist of yesterday that "justice too long delayed is justice denied." We have waited for more than 340 years for our constitutional and God-given rights. The nations of Asia and Africa are moving with jetlike speed toward the goal of political independence, and we still creep at horse and buggy pace toward the gaining of a cup of coffee at a lunch counter. I guess it is easy for those who have never felt the stinging darts of segregation to say, "Wait." But when you have seen vicious mobs lynch your mothers and fathers at will and drown your sisters and brothers at whim; when you have seen hate-filled policemen curse, kick, brutalize and even kill your black brothers and sisters with impunity; when you see the vast majority of your twenty million Negro brothers smothering in an airtight cage of poverty in the midst of an affluent society; when you suddenly find your tongue twisted and your speech stammering as you seek to explain to your six-year-old daughter why she can't go to the public amusement park that has just been advertised on television, and see tears welling up in her little eyes when she is told that Funtown is closed to colored children, and see the depressing clouds of inferiority begin to form in her little mental sky, and see her begin to distort her little personality by unconsciously developing a bitterness toward white people; when you have to concoct an answer for a five-year-old son asking in agonizing pathos: "Daddy, why do white people treat colored people so mean?"; when you take a cross-country drive and find it necessary to sleep night after night in the uncomfortable corners of your automobile because no motel will accept you; when you are humiliated day in and day out by nagging signs reading "white" and "colored"; when your first name becomes "nigger" and your middle name becomes "boy" (however old you are) and your last name becomes "John," and when your wife and mother are never given the respected title "Mrs."; when you are harried by day and haunted by night by the fact that you are a Negro, living constantly at tiptoe stance never quite knowing what to expect next, and plagued with inner fears and outer resentments; when you are forever fighting a degenerating sense of "nobodiness"; then you will understand why we find it difficult to wait.

There comes a time when the cup of endurance runs over, and men are no longer willing to be plunged into an abyss of injustice where they experience the blackness of corroding despair. I hope, sirs, you can understand our legitimate and unavoidable impatience.

You express a great deal of anxiety over our willingness to break laws. This is certainly a legitimate concern. Since we so diligently urge people to obey the Supreme Court's decision of 1954 outlawing segregation in the public schools, it is rather strange and paradoxical to find us consciously breaking laws. One may well ask, "How can you advocate breaking some laws and obeying others?" The answer is found in the fact that there are two types of laws: there are *just* and there are *unjust* laws. I would agree with Saint Augustine that "An unjust law is no law at all." Now what is the difference between the two? How does one determine when a law is just or unjust? A just law is a man-made code that squares with the moral law or the law of God. An unjust law is a code that is out of harmony with the moral law. To put it in the terms of Saint Thomas Aquinas, an unjust law is a human law that is not rooted in eternal and natural law. Any law that uplifts human personality is just. Any law that degrades human personality is unjust. All segregation statutes are unjust because segregation distorts the soul and damages the personality. It gives the segregator a false sense of superiority, and the segregated a false sense of inferiority. To use the words of Martin Buber, the great Jewish philosopher, segregation substitutes an "I-it" relationship for the "I-thou" relationship, and ends up relegating persons to the status of things. So segregation is not only politically, economically and sociologically unsound, but it is morally wrong and sinful. Paul Tillich has said that sin is separation. Isn't segregation an existential expression of man's tragic separation, an expression of his awful estrangement, his terrible sinfulness? So I can urge men to disobey segregation ordinances because they are morally wrong.

Let us turn to a more concrete example of just and unjust laws. An unjust law is a code that a majority inflicts on a minority that is not binding on itself. This is difference made legal. On the other hand a just law is a code that a majority compels a minority to follow that it is willing to follow itself. This is sameness made legal.

Let me give another explanation. An unjust law is a code inflicted upon a minority which that minority had no part in enacting or creating because they did not have the unhampered right to vote. Who can say that the legislature of Alabama which set up the segregation laws was democratically elected? Throughout the state of Alabama all types of conniving methods are used to prevent Negroes from becoming registered voters and there are some counties without a single Negro registered to vote despite the fact that the Negro constitutes a majority of the population. Can any law set up in such a state be considered democratically structured?

These are just a few examples of unjust and just laws. There are some instances when a law is just on its face and unjust in its application. For instance, I was arrested Friday on a charge of parading without a permit. Now there is nothing wrong with an ordinance which requires a permit for a parade, but when the ordinance is used to preserve segregation and to deny citizens the First Amendment privilege of peaceful assembly and peaceful protest, then it becomes unjust.

I hope you can see the distinction I am trying to point out. In no sense do I advocate evading or defying the law as the rabid segregationist would do. This would lead to anarchy. One who breaks an unjust law must do it *openly*, *lovingly* (not hatefully as the white mothers did in New Orleans when they were seen on television screaming, "nigger, nigger, nigger"), and with a willingness to accept the penalty. I submit that an individual who breaks a law that conscience tells him is unjust, and willingly accepts the penalty by staying in jail to arouse the conscience of the community over its injustice, is in reality expressing the very highest respect for law.

Of course, there is nothing new about this kind of civil disobedience. It was seen sublimely in the refusal of Shadrach, Meshach and Abednego to obey the laws of Nebuchadnezzar because a higher moral law was involved. It was practiced superbly by the early Christians who were willing to face hungry lions and the excruciating pain of chopping blocks, before submitting to certain unjust laws of the Roman Empire. To a degree academic freedom is a reality today because Socrates practiced civil disobedience.

We can never forget that everything Hitler did in Germany was "legal" and everything the Hungarian freedom fighters did in Hungary was "illegal." It was "illegal" to aid and comfort a Jew in Hitler's Germany. But I am sure that if I had lived in Germany during that time I would have aided and comforted my Jewish brothers even though it was illegal. If I lived in a Communist country today where certain principles dear to the Christian faith are suppressed, I believe I would openly advocate disobeying these anti-religious laws. I must make two honest confessions to you, my Christian and Jewish brothers. First, I must confess that over the last few years I have been gravely disappointed with the white moderate. I have almost reached the regrettable conclusion that the Negro's great stumbling block in the stride toward freedom is not the White Citizen's Counciler or the Ku Klux Klanner, but the white moderate who is more devoted to "order" than to justice; who prefers a negative peace which is the absence of tension to a positive peace which is the presence of justice; who constantly says, "I agree with you in the goal you seek, but I can't agree with your methods of direct action"; who paternalistically feels that he can set the timetable for another man's freedom; who lives by the myth of time and who constantly advised the Negro to wait until a "more convenient season." Shallow understanding from people of good will is more frustrating than absolute misunderstanding from people of ill will. Lukewarm acceptance is much more bewildering than outright rejection.

I had hoped that the white moderate would understand that law and order exist for the purpose of establishing justice, and that when they fail to do this they become dangerously structured dams that block the flow of social progress. I had hoped that the white moderate would understand that the present tension of the South is merely a necessary phase of the transition from an obnoxious negative peace, where the Negro passively accepted his unjust plight, to a substance-filled positive peace, where all men will respect the dignity and worth of human personality. Actually, we who engage in nonviolent direct action are not the creators of tension. We merely bring to the surface the hidden tension that is already alive. We bring it out in the open where it can be seen and dealt with. Like a boil that can never be cured as long as it is covered up but must be opened with all its pus-flowing ugliness to the natural medicines of air and light, injustice must likewise be exposed, with all of the tension its exposing creates, to the light of human conscience and the air of national opinion before it can be cured.

In your statement you asserted that our actions, even though peaceful must be condemned because they precipitate violence. But can this assertion be logically made? Isn't this like condemning the robbed man because his possession of money precipitated the evil act of robbery? Isn't this like condemning Socrates because his unswerving commitment to truth and his philosophical delvings precipitated the misguided popular mind to make him drink the hemlock? Isn't this like condemning Jesus because His unique God-consciousness and never-ceasing devotion to his will precipitated the evil act of crucifixion? We must come to see, as federal courts have consistently affirmed, that it is immoral to urge an individual to withdraw his efforts to gain his basic constitutional rights because the quest precipitates violence. Society must protect the robbed and punish the robber.

I had also hoped that the white moderate would reject the myth of time. I received a letter this morning from a white brother in Texas which said: "All Christians know that the colored people will receive equal rights eventually, but it is possible that you are in too great of a religious hurry. It has taken Christianity almost two thousand years to accomplish what it has. The teachings of Christ take time to come to earth." All that is said here grows out of a tragic misconception of time. It is the strangely irrational notion that there is something in the very flow of time that will inevitably cure all ills. Actually time is neutral. It can be used either destructively or constructively. I am coming to feel that the people of ill will have used time much more effectively than the people of good will. We will have to repent in this generation not merely for the vitriolic words and actions of the bad people, but for the appalling silence of the good people. We must come to see that human progress never rolls in on wheels of inevitability. It comes through the tireless efforts and persistent work of men willing to be co-workers with God, and without this hard word time itself becomes an ally of the forces of social stagnation. We must use time creatively, and forever realize that the time is always ripe to do right. Now is the time to make real the promise of democracy, and transform our pending national clegy into a creative psalm of brotherhood. Now is the time to lift our national policy from the quicksand of racial injustice to the solid rock of human dignity.

You spoke of our activity in Birmingham as extreme. At first I was rather disappointed that fellow clergymen would see my nonviolent efforts as those of the extremist. I started thinking about the fact that I stand in the middle of two opposing forces in the Negro community. One is a force of complacency made up of Negroes who, as a result of long years of oppression, have been so completely drained of self-respect and a sense of "somebodiness" that they have adjusted to segregation, and, of a few Negroes in the middle class who, because of a degree of academic and economic security, and because at points they profit by segregation, have unconsciously become insensitive to the problems of the masses. The other force is one of bitterness and hatred, and comes perilously close to advocating violence. It is expressed in the various black nationalist groups that are springing up over the nation, the largest and best known being Elijah Muhammad's Muslim movement. This movement is nourished by the contemporary frustration over the continued existence of racial discrimination. It is made up of people who have lost faith in America, who have absolutely repudiated Christianity, and who have concluded that the white man is an incurable "devil." I have tried to stand between these two forces, saying that we need not follow the "do-nothingism" of the complacent or the hatred and despair of the black nationalist. There is the more excellent way of love and nonviolent protest. I'm grateful to God that, through the Negro church, the dimension of nonviolence entered our struggle. If this philosophy had not emerged, I am convinced that by now many streets of the South would be flowing with floods of blood. And I am further convinced that if our white brothers dismiss us as "rabble-rousers" and "outside agitators"—those of us who are working through the channels of nonviolent direct action—and refuse to support our nonviolent efforts, millions of Negroes, out of frustration and despair, will seek solace and security in black nationalist ideologies, a development that will lead inevitably to a frightening racial nightmare.

Oppressed people cannot remain oppressed forever. The urge for freedom will eventually come. This is what happened to the American Negro. Something within has reminded him of his birthright of freedom; something without has reminded him that he can gain it. Consciously and unconsciously, he has been swept in by what the Germans call the *Zeitgeist*, and with his black brothers of Africa, and his brown and yellow brothers of Asia, South America and the Caribbean, he is moving with a sense of cosmic urgency toward the promised land of racial justice. Recognizing this vital urge that has engulfed the Negro community, one should readily understand public demonstrations. The Negro has many pent-up resentments and latent frustrations. He has to get them out. So let him march sometime; let him have his prayer pilgrimages to the city hall; understand why he must have sit-ins and freedom rides. If his repressed emotions do not come out in these nonviolent ways, they will come out in ominous expressions of violence. This is not a threat; it is a fact of history. So I have not said to my people "get rid of your discontent." But I have tried to say that this normal and healthy discontent can be channelized through the creative outlet of nonviolent direct action. Now this approach is being dismissed as extremist. I must admit that I was initially disappointed in being so categorized.

But as I continued to think about the matter I gradually gained a bit of satisfaction from being considered an extremist. Was not Jesus an extremist in love—"Love your enemies, bless them that curse you, pray for them that despitefully use you." Was not Amos an extremist for justice—"Let justice roll down like waters and righteousness like a mighty stream." Was not Paul an extremist for the gospel of Jesus Christ—"I bear in my body the marks of the Lord Jesus." Was not Martin Luther an extremist—"Here I stand; I can do none other so help me God." Was not John Bunyan an extremist—"I will stay in jail to the end of my days before I make a butchery of my conscience." Was not Abraham Lincoln an extremist—"This nation cannot survive half slave and half free." Was not Thomas Jefferson an extremist—"We hold these truths to be self-evident, that all men are created equal." So the question is not whether we will be extremist but what kind of extremist will we be. Will we be extremists for hate or will we be extremists for love? Will we be extremists for the preservation of injustice—or will we be extremists for the cause of justice? In that dramatic scene on Calvary's hill, three men were crucified. We must not forget that all three were crucified for the same crime—the crime of extremism. Two were extremists for immorality, and thusly fell below their environment. The other, Jesus Christ, was an extremist for love, truth and goodness, and thereby rose above his environment. So, after all, maybe the South, the nation and the world are in dire need of creative extremists.

* * *

I wish you had commended the Negro sit-inners and demonstrators of Birmingham for their sublime courage, their willingness to suffer and their amazing discipline in the midst of the most inhuman provocation. One day the South will recognize its real heroes. They will be the James Merediths, courageously and with a majestic sense of purpose facing jeering and hostile mobs and the agonizing loneliness that characterizes the life of the pioneer. They will be old, oppressed, battered Negro women, symbolized in a seventy-two-year-old woman of Montgomenery Alabama, who rose up with a sense of dignity and with her people de-cided not to ride the segregated buses, and responded to one who in-quired about her tiredness with ungrammatical profundity: "My feet is tired, but my soul is rested." They will be the young high school and col-lege students, young ministers of the gospel and a host of their elders courageously and nonviolently sitting-in at lunch counters and willingly going to jail for conscience's sake. One day the South will know that when these disinherited children of God sat down at lunch counters they were in reality standing up for the best in the American dream and the most sacred values in our Judeo-Christian heritage, and thusly, carrying our whole nation back to those great wells of democracy which were dug deep by the Founding Fathers in the formulation of the Constitution and the Declaration of Independence.

* * *

Yours for the cause of Peace and Brotherhood,
Martin Luther King, Jr.

MARTIN LUTHER KING, JR.

I Have a Dream (1963)

In his most memorable speech, which was televised live from the steps of the Lincoln Memorial as the keynote address of the March on Wash-ington on August 28, 1963, King eloquently stated the hopes and aspi-rations of the civil rights movement as he called on the nation to fulfill its promise of freedom and justice for black Americans.

I am happy to join with you today in what will go down in history as the greatest demonstration for freedom in the history of our nation.

Fivescore years ago, a great American, in whose symbolic shadow we stand today, signed the Emancipation Proclamation. This momentous decree came as a great beacon light of hope to millions of Negro slaves who had been seared in the flames of withering injustice. It came as a joyous daybreak to end the long night of their captivity.

But one hundred years later, the Negro still is not free; one hundred years later, the life of the Negro is still sadly crippled by the manacles of segregation and the chains of discrimination; one hundred years later, the Negro lives on a lonely island of poverty in the midst of a vast ocean of material prosperity; one hundred years later, the Negro is still languished in the corners of American society and finds himself in exile in his own land.

So we've come here today to dramatize a shameful condition. In a sense we've come to our nation's capital to cash a check. When the architects of our republic wrote the magnificent words of the Constitution and the Declaration of Independence, they were signing a promissory note to which every American was to fall heir. This note was the promise that all men, yes, black men as well as white men, would be guaranteed the unalienable rights of life, liberty, and the pursuit of happiness.

It is obvious today that America has defaulted on this promissory note in so far as her citizens of color are concerned. Instead of honoring this sacred obligation, America has given the Negro people a bad check; a check which has come back marked "insufficient funds." We refuse to believe that there are insufficient funds in the great vaults of opportunity of this nation. And so we've come to cash this check, a check that will give us upon demand the riches of freedom and the security of justice.

We have also come to this hallowed spot to remind America of the fierce urgency of now. This is no time to engage in the luxury of cooling off or to take the tranquilizing drug of gradualism. Now is the time to make real the promises of democracy; now is the time to rise from the dark and desolate valley of segregation to the sunlit path of racial justice; now is the time to lift our nation from the quicksands of racial injustice to the solid rock of brotherhood; now is the time to make justice a reality for all God's children. It would be fatal for the nation to overlook the urgency of the moment. This sweltering summer of the Negro's legitimate discontent will not pass until there is an invigorating autumn of freedom and equality.

Nineteen sixty-three is not an end, but a beginning. And those who hope that the Negro needed to blow off steam and will now be content, will have a rude awakening if the nation returns to business as usual.

There will be neither rest nor tranquility in America until the Negro is granted his citizenship rights. The whirlwinds of revolt will continue to shake the foundations of our nation until the bright day of justice emerges.

But there is something that I must say to my people who stand on the warm threshold which leads into the palace of justice. In the process of gaining our rightful place we must not be guilty of wrongful deeds.

Let us not seek to satisfy our thirst for freedom by drinking from the cup of bitterness and hatred. We must forever conduct our struggle on the high plane of dignity and discipline. We must not allow our creative protest to degenerate into physical violence. Again and again we must rise to the majestic heights of meeting physical force with soul force.

The marvelous new militancy which has engulfed the Negro community must not lead us to a distrust of all white people, for many of our white brothers, as evidenced by their presence here today, have come to realize that their destiny is tied up with our destiny and they have come to realize that their freedom is inextricably bound to our freedom. This offense we share mounted to storm the battlements of injustice must be carried forth by a biracial army. We cannot walk alone.

And as we walk, we must make the pledge that we shall always march ahead. We cannot turn back. There are those who are asking the devotees of civil rights, "When will you be satisfied?" We can never be satisfied as long as the Negro is the victim of the unspeakable horrors of police brutality.

We can never be satisfied as long as our bodies, heavy with fatigue of travel, cannot gain lodging in the motels of the highways and the hotels of the cities. We cannot be satisfied as long as the Negro's basic mobility is from a smaller ghetto to a larger one.

We can never be satisfied as long as our children are stripped of their selfhood and robbed of their dignity by signs stating "for whites only." We cannot be satisfied as long as a Negro in Mississippi cannot vote and a Negro in New York believes he has nothing for which to vote. No, we are not satisfied, and we will not be satisfied until justice rolls down like waters and righteousness like a mighty stream.

I am not unmindful that some of you have come here out of excessive trials and tribulation. Some of you have come fresh from narrow jail cells. Some of you have come from areas where your quest for freedom left you battered by the storms of persecution and staggered by the winds of police brutality. You have been the veterans of creative suffering. Continue to work with the faith that unearned suffering is redemptive.

Go back to Mississippi; go back to Alabama; go back to South Carolina; go back to Georgia; go back to Louisiana; go back to the slums and ghettos of the northern cities, knowing that somehow this situation can, and will be changed. Let us not wallow in the valley of despair.

So I say to you, my friends, that even though we must face the difficulties of today and tomorrow, I still have a dream. It is a dream deeply rooted in the American dream that one day this nation will rise up and live out the true meaning of its creed—we hold these truths to be self-evident, that all men are created equal.

I have a dream that one day on the red hills of Georgia, sons of former slaves and sons of former slave-owners will be able to sit down together at the table of brotherhood.

I have a dream that one day, even the state of Mississippi, a state sweltering with the heat of injustice, sweltering with the heat of oppression, will be transformed into an oasis of freedom and justice.

I have a dream my four little children will one day live in a nation where they will not be judged by the color of their skin but by content of their character. I have a dream today!

I have a dream that one day, down in Alabama, with its vicious racists, with its governor having his lips dripping with the words of interposition and nullification, that one day, right there in Alabama, little black boys and black girls will be able to join hands with little white boys and white girls as sisters and brothers. I have a dream today!

I have a dream that one day every valley shall be exalted, every hill and mountain shall be made low, the rough places shall be made plain, and the crooked places shall be made straight and the glory of the Lord will be revealed and all flesh shall see it together.

This is our hope. This is the faith that I go back to the South with.

With this faith we will be able to hear out of the mountain of despair a stone of hope. With this faith we will be able to transform the jangling discords of our nation into a beautiful symphony of brotherhood.

With this faith we will be able to work together, to pray together, to struggle together, to go to jail together, to stand up for freedom together, knowing that we will be free one day. This will be the day when all of God's children will be able to sing with new meaning—"my country 'tis of thee; sweet land of liberty; of thee I sing; land where my fathers died, land of the pilgrim's pride; from every mountain side, let freedom ring"— and if America is to be a great nation, this must become true.

So let freedom ring from the prodigious hilltops of New Hampshire.

Let freedom ring from the mighty mountains of New York.

Let freedom ring from the heightening Alleghenies of Pennsylvania.

Let freedom ring from the snow-capped Rockies of Colorado.

Let freedom ring from the curvaceous slopes of California.

But not only that.

Let freedom ring from Stone Mountain of Georgia.

Let freedom ring from Lookout Mountain of Tennessee.

Let freedom ring from every hill and molehill of Mississippi, from every mountainside, let freedom ring.

And when we allow freedom to ring, when we let it ring from every village and hamlet, from every state and city, we will be able to speed up that day when all of God's children—black men and white men, Jews and Gentiles, Catholics and Protestants—will be able to join hands and to sing in the words of the old Negro spiritual, "Free at last, free at last; thank God Almighty, we are free at last."

STUDENT NONVIOLENT COORDINATING COMMITTEE (SNCC)

Statement of Purpose (1960)

In 1960, a group of college students dedicated to the civil rights cause and to Martin Luther King, Jr.'s, philosophy of nonviolence formed the Student Nonviolent Coordinating Committee in order to coordinate ongoing demonstrations and sit-ins against segregation. Although SNCC's statement of purpose contained no blueprint for action or list of objectives, it did express the idealistic commitments of most black student leaders at this stage of the civil rights movement.

We affirm the philosophical or religious ideal of nonviolence as the foundation of our purpose, the pre-supposition of our faith, and the manner of our action. Nonviolence as it grows from Judaic-Christian traditions seeks a social order of justice permeated by love. Integration of human endeavor represents the crucial first step towards such a society.

Through nonviolence, courage displaces fear; love transforms hate. Acceptance dissipates prejudice; hope ends despair. Peace dominates war; faith reconciles doubt. Mutual regards cancel enmity. Justice for all overthrows injustice. The redemptive community supercedes [sic] systems of gross social immorality.

Love is the central motif of nonviolence. Love is the force by which God binds man to himself and man to man. Such love goes to the extreme; it remains loving and forgiving even in the midst of hostility. It matches the capacity of evil to inflict suffering with an even more enduring capacity to absorb evil, all the while persisting in love.

By appealing to conscience and standing on the moral nature of human existence, nonviolence nurtures the atmosphere in which reconciliation and justice become actual possibilities.

MALCOLM X

The Ballot or the Bullet (1964)

In a speech he gave at Cleveland's Cory Methodist Church in April 1964, Malcolm X explained the political and economic philosophy of black nationalism and clarified his views on the use of defensive violence to fight racial oppression.

M r. Moderator, Brother Lomax, brothers and sisters, friends and enemies: I just can't believe everyone in here is a friend and I don't want to leave anybody out. The question tonight, as I understand it, is "The Negro Revolt, and Where Do We Go From Here?" or "What Next?" In my little humble way of understanding it, it points toward either the ballot or the bullet.

* * *

If we don't do something real soon, I think you'll have to agree that we're going to be forced either to use the ballot or the bullet. It's one or the other in 1964. It isn't that time is running out—time has run out! 1964 threatens to be the most explosive year America has ever witnessed. The most explosive year. Why? It's also a political year. It's the year when all of the white politicians will be back in the so-called Negro community jiving you and me for some votes. The year when all of the white political crooks will be right back in your and my community with their false promises, building up our hopes for a letdown, with their trickery and their treachery, with their false promises which they don't intend to keep. As they nourish these dissatisfactions, it can only lead to one thing, an explosion; and now we have the type of black man on the scene in America today—I'm sorry, Brother Lomax—who just doesn't intend to turn the other cheek any longer.

* * *

It was the black man's vote that put the present administration in Washington, D.C. Your vote, your dumb vote, your ignorant vote, your wasted vote put in an administration in Washington, D.C., that has seen fit to pass every kind of legislation imaginable, saving you until last, then filibustering on top of that. And your and my leaders have the audacity to run around clapping their hands and talk about how much progress we're making. And what a good president we have. If he wasn't good in Texas, he sure can't be good in Washington, D.C. Because Texas is a lynch state. It is in the same breath as Mississippi, no different; only they lynch you in Texas with a Texas accent and lynch you in Mississippi with a Mississippi accent. And these Negro leaders have the audacity to go and have some coffee in the White House with a Texan, a Southern cracker—that's all he is—and then come out and tell you and me that he's going to be better for us because, since he's from the South, he knows how to deal with the Southerners. What kind of logic is that? Let Eastland be president, he's from the South too. He should be better able to deal with them than Johnson.

In this present administration they have in the House of Representatives 257 Democrats to only 177 Republicans. They control two-thirds of the House vote. Why can't they pass something that will help you and me? In the Senate, there are 67 senators who are of the Democratic Party. Only 33 of them are Republicans. Why, the Democrats have got the government sewed up, and you're the one who sewed it up for them. And what have they given you for it? Four years in office, and just now getting around to some civil-rights legislation. Just now, after everything else is gone, out of the way, they're going to sit down now and play with you all summer long—the same old giant con game that they call filibuster. All those are in cahoots together. Don't you ever think they're not in cahoots together, for the man that is heading the civil-rights filibuster is a man from Georgia named Richard Russell. When Johnson became president, the first man he asked for when he got back to Washington, D.C., was "Dicky"—that's how tight they are. That's his boy, that's his pal, that's his buddy. But they're playing that old con game. * * *

So, what I'm trying to impress upon you, in essence, is this: You and I in America are faced not with a segregationist conspiracy, we're faced with a government conspiracy. Everyone who's filibustering is a senator—that's the government. Everyone who's finagling in Washington, D.C., is a congressman—that's the government. You don't have anybody putting blocks in your path but people who are a part of the government. The same government that you go abroad to fight for and die for is the government that is in a conspiracy to deprive you of your voting rights, deprive you of your economic opportunities, deprive you of decent housing, deprive you of decent education. You don't need to go to the employer alone, it is the government itself, the government of America, that is responsible for the oppression and exploitation and degradation of black people in this country. And you should drop it in their lap. This government has failed the Negro. This so-called democracy has failed the Negro. And all these white liberals have definitely failed the Negro.

* * *

* * * A segregationist is a criminal. You can't label him as anything other than that. And when you demonstrate against segregation, the law is on your side. The Supreme Court is on your side.

Now, who is it that opposes you in carrying out the law? The police department itself. With police dogs and clubs. Whenever you demonstrate against segregation, whether it is segregated education, segregated housing, or anything else, the law is on your side, and anyone who stands in the way is not the law any longer. They are breaking the law, they are not representatives of the law. Any time you demonstrate against segregation and a man has the audacity to put a police dog on you, kill that dog, kill him, I'm telling you, kill that dog. I say it, if they put me in jail tomorrow, kill—that—dog. Then you'll put a stop to it. Now, if these white people in here don't want to see that kind of action, get down and tell the mayor to tell the police department to pull the dogs in. That's all you have to do. If you don't do it, someone else will.

If you don't take this kind of stand, your little children will grow up and look at you and think "shame." If you don't take an uncompromising stand—I don't mean go out and get violent; but at the same time you should never be nonviolent unless you run into some nonviolence. I'm nonviolent with those who are nonviolent with me. But when you drop that violence on me, then you've made me go insane, and I'm not responsible for what I do. And that's the way every Negro should get. Any time you know you're within the law, within your legal rights, within your moral rights, in accord with justice, then die for what you believe in. But don't die alone. Let your dying be reciprocal. This is what is meant by equality. What's good for the goose is good for the gander.

* * *

Let the world know how bloody [Uncle Sam's] hands are. Let the world know the hypocrisy that's practiced over here. Let it be the ballot or the bullet. Let him know that it must be the ballot or the bullet.

* * *

The political philosophy of black nationalism means that the black man should control the politics and the politicians in his own community; no more. The black man in the black community has to be re-educated into the science of politics so he will know what politics is supposed to bring him in return. Don't be throwing out any ballots. A ballot is like a bullet. You don't throw your ballots until you see a target, and if that target is not within your reach, keep your ballot in your pocket. The political philosophy of black nationalism is being taught in the Christian church. It's being taught in the NAACP. It's being taught in CORE meetings. It's being taught in SNCC [Student Nonviolent Co-ordinating Committee] meetings. It's being taught in Muslim meetings. It's being taught where nothing but atheists and agnostics come together. It's being taught everywhere. Black people are fed up with the dillydallying, pussyfooting, compromising approach that we've been using toward getting our freedom. We want freedom *now*, but we're not going to get it saying "We Shall Overcome." We've got to fight until we overcome.

The economic philosophy of black nationalism is pure and simple. It only means that we should control the economy of our community. Why should white people be running all the stores in our community? Why should white people be running the banks of our community? Why should the economy of our community be in the hands of the white man? Why? If a black man can't move his store into a white community, you tell me why a white man should move his store into a black community. The philosophy of black nationalism involves a re-education program in the black community in regards to economics. Our people have to be made to see that any time you take your dollar out of your community and spend it in a community where you don't live, the community where you live will get poorer and poorer, and the community where you spend your money will get richer and richer. Then you wonder why where you live is always a ghetto or a slum area. And where you and I are concerned, not only do we lose it when we spend it out of the community, but the white man has got all our stores in the community tied up; so that though we spend it in the community, at sundown the man who runs the store takes it over across town somewhere. He's got us in a vise.

So the economic philosophy of black nationalism means in every church, in every civic organization, in every fraternal order, it's time now for our people to become conscious of the importance of controlling the economy of our community. If we own the stores, if we operate the businesses, if we try and establish some industry in our own community, then we're developing to the position where we are creating employment for our own kind. Once you gain control of the economy of your own community, then you don't have to picket and boycott and beg some cracker downtown for a job in his business.

The social philosophy of black nationalism only means that we have to get together and remove the evils, the vices, alcoholism, drug addiction, and other evils that are destroying the moral fiber of our community. We ourselves have to lift the level of our community, the standard of our community to a higher level, make our own society beautiful so that we will be satisfied in our own social circles and won't be running around here trying to knock our way into a social circle where we're not wanted.

So I say, in spreading a gospel such as black nationalism, it is not designed to make the black man re-evaluate the white man—you know him already—but to make the black man re-evaluate himself. Don't change the white man's mind—you can't change his mind, and that whole thing about appealing to the moral conscience of America—America's conscience is bankrupt. She lost all conscience a long time ago. Uncle Sam has no conscience. They don't know what morals are. They don't try and eliminate an evil because it's evil, or because it's illegal, or because it's immoral; they eliminate it only when it threatens their existence. So you're wasting your time appealing to the moral conscience of a bankrupt man like Uncle Sam. If he had a conscience, he'd straighten this thing out with no more pressure being put upon him. So it is not necessary to change the white man's mind. We have to change our own mind. You can't change his mind about us. We've got to change our own minds about each other. We have to see each other with new eyes. We have to see each other as brothers and sisters. We have to come together with warmth so we can develop unity and harmony that's necessary to get this problem solved ourselves. * * *

We will work with anybody, anywhere, at any time, who is genuinely interested in tackling the problem head-on, nonviolently as long as the enemy is nonviolent, but violent when the enemy gets violent. We'll work with you on the voter-registration drive, we'll work with you on rent strikes, we'll work with you on school boycotts—I don't believe in any kind of integration; I'm not even worried about it because I know you're not going to get it anyway; you're not going to get it because you're afraid to die; you've got to be ready to die if you try and force yourself on the white man, because he'll get just as violent as those crackers in Mississippi, right here in Cleveland. But we will still work with you on the school boycotts because we're against a segregated school system. A segregated school system produces children who, when they graduate, graduate with crippled minds. But this does not mean that a school is segregated because it's all black. A segregated school means a school that is controlled by people who have no real interest in it whatsoever.

Let me explain what I mean. A segregated district or community is a community in which people live, but outsiders control the politics and the economy of that community. They never refer to the white section as a segregated community: It's the all-Negro section that's a segregated community. Why? The white man controls his own school, his own bank, his own economy, his own politics, his own everything, his own community—but he also controls yours. When you're under someone else's control, you're segregated. They'll always give you the lowest or the worst that there is to offer, but it doesn't mean you're segregated just because you have your own. You've got to *control* your own. Just like the white man has control of his, you need to control yours.

You know the best way to get rid of segregation? The white man is more afraid of separation than he is of integration. Segregation means that he puts you away from him, but not far enough for you to be out of his jurisdiction; separation means you're gone. And the white man will integrate faster than he'll let you separate. So we will work with you against the segregated school system because it's criminal, because it is absolutely destructive, in every way imaginable, to the minds of the children who have to be exposed to that type of crippling education.

Last but not least, I must say this concerning the great controversy over rifles and shotguns. The only thing that I've ever said is that in areas where the government has proven itself either unwilling or unable to defend the lives and the property of Negroes, it's time for Negroes to defend themselves. Article number two of the constitutional amendments provides you and me the right to own a rifle or a shotgun. It is constitutionally legal to own a shotgun or a rifle. This doesn't mean you're going to get a rifle and form battalions and go out looking for white folks, although you'd be within your rights—I mean, you'd be justified; but that would be illegal and we don't do anything illegal. If the white man doesn't want the black man buying rifles and shotguns, then let the government do its job. That's all. And don't let the white man come to you and ask you what you think about what Malcolm says—why, you old Uncle Tom. He would never ask you if he thought you were going to say, "Amen!" No, he is making a Tom out of you.

So, this doesn't mean forming rifle clubs and going out looking for people, but it is time, in 1964, if you are a man, to let that man know. If he's not going to do his job in running the government and providing you and me with the protection that our taxes are supposed to be for, since he spends all those billions for his defense budget, he certainly can't begrudge you and me spending $12 or $15 for a single-shot, or double-action. I hope you understand. Don't go out shooting people, but any time, brothers and sisters, and especially the men in this audience—some of you wearing Congressional Medals of Honor, with shoulders this wide, chests this big, muscles that big—any time you and I sit around and read where they bomb a church and murder in cold blood, not some grownups, but four little girls while they were praying to the same god the white man taught them to pray to, and you and I see the government go down and can't find who did it.

Why, this man—he can find Eichmann hiding down in Argentina somewhere. Let two or three American soldiers, who are minding somebody else's business way over in South Vietnam, get killed, and he'll send battleships, sticking his nose in their business. He wanted to send troops down to Cuba and make them have what he calls free elections—this old cracker who doesn't have free elections in his own country. No, if you never see me another time in your life, if I die in the morning, I'll die saying one thing: the ballot or the bullet, the ballot or the bullet.

If a Negro in 1964 has to sit around and wait for some cracker senator to filibuster when it comes to the rights of black people, why, you and I should hang our heads in shame. You talk about a march on Washington in 1963, you haven't seen anything. There's some more going down in '64. And this time they're not going like they went last year. They're not going singing "We Shall Overcome." They're not going with white friends. They're not going with placards already painted for them. They're not going with round-trip tickets. They're going with one-way tickets.

And if they don't want that non-nonviolent army going down there, tell them to bring the filibuster to a halt. The black nationalists aren't going to wait. Lyndon B. Johnson is the head of the Democratic Party. If he's for civil rights, let him go into the Senate next week and declare himself. Let him go in there right now and declare himself. Let him go in there and denounce the Southern branch of his party. Let him go in there right now and take a moral stand—right now, not later. Tell him, don't wait until election time. If he waits too long, brothers and sisters, he will be responsible for letting a condition develop in this country which will create a climate that will bring seeds up out of the ground with vegetation on the end of them looking like something these people never dreamed of. In 1964, it's the ballot or the bullet. Thank you.

BAYARD RUSTIN

From Protest to Politics: The Future of the Civil Rights Movement (1965)

The pacifist and moderate civil rights leader Bayard Rustin (1912–1987) began organizing civil rights demonstrations as early as the 1940s, when he joined the Congress of Racial Equality. Firmly com-

mitted to nonviolent civil disobedience, Rustin assisted Martin Luther King, Jr., in his boycott against the segregated bus system in Montgomery, Alabama, and organized the August 1963 March on Washington. Despite sharp criticism from more militant blacks, Rustin formed successful coalitions with white liberals, labor unions, and the Jewish-American community. In an essay that appeared in February 1965 in the journal Commentary, *Rustin recommended the formation of such coalitions as the most effective way for the civil rights movement to achieve the political power necessary to effect positive social and economic change.*

I

The decade spanned by the 1954 Supreme Court decision on school desegregation and the Civil Rights Act of 1964 will undoubtedly be recorded as the period in which the legal foundations of racism in America were destroyed. To be sure, pockets of resistance remain; but it would be hard to quarrel with the assertion that the elaborate legal structure of segregation and discrimination, particularly in relation to public accommodations, has virtually collapsed. On the other hand, without making light of the human sacrifices involved in the direct-action tactics (sit-ins, freedom rides, and the rest) that were so instrumental to this achievement, we must recognize that in desegregating public accommodations, we affected institutions which are relatively peripheral both to the American socio-economic order and to the fundamental conditions of life of the Negro people. In a highly industrialized, 20th-century civilization, we hit Jim Crow precisely where it was most anachronistic, dispensable, and vulnerable—in hotels, lunch counters, terminals, libraries, swimming pools, and the like. For in these forms, Jim Crow does impede the flow of commerce in the broadest sense: it is a nuisance in a society on the move (and on the make). Not surprisingly, therefore, it was the most mobility-conscious and relatively liberated groups in the Negro community—lower-middle-class college students—who launched the attack that brought down this imposing but hollow structure.

The term "classical" appears especially apt for this phase of the civil rights movement. But in the few years that have passed since the first flush of sit-ins, several developments have taken place that have complicated matters enormously. One is the shifting focus of the movement in the South, symbolized by Birmingham; another is the spread of the revolution to the North; and the third, common to the other two, is the expansion of the movement's base in the Negro community. * * *

Thus, the movement in the South began to attack areas of discrimination which were not so remote from the Northern experience as were Jim Crow lunch counters. At the same time, the interrelationship of these apparently distinct areas became increasingly evident. What is the value of winning access to public accommodations for those who lack money to use them? The minute the movement faced this question, it was compelled to expand its vision beyond race relations to economic relations, including the role of education in modern society. And what also became clear is that all these interrelated problems, by their very nature, are not soluble by private, voluntary efforts but require government action—or politics. Already Southern demonstrators had recognized that the most effective way to strike at the police brutality they suffered from was by getting rid of the local sheriff—and that meant political action, which in turn meant, and still means, political action within the Democratic party where the only meaningful primary contests in the South are fought.

And so, in Mississippi, thanks largely to the leadership of Bob Moses, a turn toward political action has been taken. More than voter registration is involved here. A conscious bid for *political power* is being made, and in the course of that effort a tactical shift is being effected: direct-action techniques are being subordinated to a strategy calling for the building of community institutions or power bases. Clearly, the implications of this shift reach far beyond Mississippi. What began as a protest movement is being challenged to translate itself into a political movement. Is this the right course? And if it is, can the transformation be accomplished?

II

The very decade which has witnessed the decline of legal Jim Crow has also seen the rise of *de facto* segregation in our most fundamental socio-economic institutions. More Negroes are unemployed today than in 1954, and the unemployment gap between the races is wider. The median income of Negroes has dropped from 57 per cent to 54 per cent of that of whites. A higher percentage of Negro workers is now concentrated in jobs vulnerable to automation than was the case ten years ago. More Negroes attend *de facto* segregated schools today than when the Supreme Court handed down its famous decision; while school integration proceeds at a snail's pace in the South, the number of Northern schools with an excessive proportion of minority youth proliferates. And behind this is the continuing growth of racial slums, spreading over our central cities and trapping Negro youth in a milieu which, whatever its legal definition, sows an unimaginable demoralization. Again, legal niceties aside, a resident of a racial ghetto lives in segregated housing, and more Negroes fall into this category than ever before.

These are the facts of life which generate frustration in the Negro community and challenge the civil rights movement. At issue, after all, is not *civil rights*, strictly speaking, but social and economic conditions. Last summer's riots were not race riots; they were outbursts of class aggression in a society where class and color definitions are converging disastrously. How can the (perhaps misnamed) civil rights movement deal with this problem?

Before trying to answer, let me first insist that the task of the movement is vastly complicated by the failure of many whites of good will to understand the nature of our problem. There is a widespread assumption that the removal of artificial racial barriers should result in the automatic integration of the Negro into all aspects of American life. This myth is fostered by facile analogies with the experience of various ethnic immigrant groups, particularly the Jews. But the analogies with the Jews do not hold for three simple but profound reasons. First, Jews have a long history as a literate people, a resource which has afforded them opportunities to advance in the academic and professional worlds, to achieve intellectual status even in the midst of economic hardship, and to evolve sustaining value systems in the context of ghetto life. Negroes, for the greater part of their presence in this country, were forbidden by law to read or write. Second, Jews have a long history of family stability, the importance of which in terms of aspiration and self-image is obvious. The Negro family structure was totally destroyed by slavery and with it the possibility of cultural transmission (the right of Negroes to marry and rear children is barely a century old). Third, Jews are white and have the *option* of relinquishing their cultural-religious identity, intermarrying, passing, etc. Negroes, or at least the overwhelming majority of them, do not have this option. There is also a fourth, vulgar reason. If the Jewish and Negro communities are not comparable in terms of education, family structure, and color, it is also true that their respective economic roles bear little resemblance.

This matter of economic role brings us to the greater problem—the fact that we are moving into an era in which the natural functioning of the market does not by itself ensure every man with will and ambition a place in the productive process. The immigrant who came to this country during the late 19th and early 20th centuries entered a society which was expanding territorially and/or economically. It was then possible to start at the bottom, as an unskilled or semi-skilled worker, and move up the ladder, acquiring new skills along the way. Especially was this true when industrial unionism was burgeoning, giving new dignity and higher wages to organized workers. Today the situation has changed. We are not expanding territorially, the western frontier is settled, labor organizing has leveled off, our rate of economic growth has been stagnant for a decade. And we are in the midst of a technological revolution which is altering the fundamental structure of the labor force, destroying unskilled and semi-skilled jobs—jobs in which Negroes are disproportionately concentrated.

Whatever the pace of this technological revolution may be, the *direction* is clear: the lower rungs of the economic ladder are being lopped off. This means that an individual will no longer be able to start at the bottom and work his way up; he will have to start in the middle or on top, and hold on tight. It will not even be enough to have certain specific skills, for many skilled jobs are also vulnerable to automation. A broad educational background, permitting vocational adaptability and flexibility, seems more imperative than ever. We live in a society where, as Secretary of Labor Willard Wirtz puts it, machines have the equivalent of a high school diploma. Yet the average educational attainment of American Negroes is 8.2 years.

Negroes, of course, are not the only people being affected by these developments. It is reported that there are now 50 per cent fewer unskilled and semi-skilled jobs than there are high school dropouts. Almost one-third of the 26 million young people entering the labor market in the 1960's will be dropouts. But the percentage of Negro dropouts nationally is 57 per cent, and in New York City, among Negroes 25 years of age or over, it is 68 per cent. They are without a future.

To what extent can the kind of self-help campaign recently prescribed by Eric Hoffer in the *New York Times Magazine* cope with such a situation? I would advise those who think that self-help is the answer to familiarize themselves with the long history of such efforts in the Negro community, and to consider why so many foundered on the shoals of ghetto life. It goes without saying that any effort to combat demoralization and apathy is desirable, but we must understand that demoralization in the Negro community is largely a common-sense response to an objective reality. Negro youths have no need of statistics to perceive, fairly accurately, what their odds are in American society. Indeed, from the point of view of motivation, some of the healthiest Negro youngsters I know are juvenile delinquents: vigorously pursuing the American Dream of material acquisition and status, yet finding the conventional means of attaining it blocked off, they do not yield to defeatism but resort to illegal (and often ingenious) methods. They are not alien to American culture. They are, in Gunnar Myrdal's phrase, "exaggerated Americans." To want a Cadillac is not un-American; to push a cart in the garment center is. If Negroes are to be persuaded that the conventional path (school, work, etc.) is superior, we had better provide evidence which is now sorely lacking. It is a double cruelty to harangue Negro youth about education and training when we do not know what jobs will be available for them. When a Negro youth can reasonably foresee a future free of slums, when the prospect of gainful employment is realistic, we will see motivation and self-help in abundant enough quantities.

Meanwhile, there is an ironic similarity between the self-help advocated by many liberals and the doctrines of the Black Muslims. Professional sociologists, psychiatrists, and social workers have expressed amazement at the Muslims' success in transforming prostitutes and dope addicts into respectable citizens. But every prostitute the Muslims convert to a model of Calvinist virtue is replaced by the ghetto with two more. Dedicated as they are to maintenance of the ghetto, the Muslims are powerless to affect substantial moral reform. So too with every other group or program which is not aimed at the destruction of slums, their causes and effects. Self-help efforts, directly or indirectly, must be geared to mobilizing people into power units capable of effecting social change. That is, their goal must be genuine self-help, not merely self-improvement. Obviously, where self-improvement activities succeed in imparting to their participants a feeling of some control over their environment, those involved may find their appetites for change whetted; they may move into the political arena.

III

Let me sum up what I have thus far been trying to say: the civil rights movement is evolving from a protest movement into a full-fledged *social movement*—an evolution calling its very name into question. It is now concerned not merely with removing the barriers to full *opportunity* but with achieving the fact of *equality*. From sit-ins and freedom rides we have gone into rent strikes, boycotts, community organization, and political action. As a consequence of this natural evolution, the Negro today finds himself stymied by obstacles of far greater magnitude than the legal barriers he was attacking before: automation, urban decay, *de facto* school segregation. These are problems which, while conditioned by Jim Crow, do not vanish upon its demise. They are more deeply rooted in our socio-economic order; they are the result of the total society's failure to meet not only the Negro's needs, but human needs generally.

These propositions have won increasing recognition and acceptance, but with a curious twist. They have formed the common premise of two apparently contradictory lines of thought which simultaneously nourish and antagonize each other. On the one hand, there is the reasoning of the New York *Times* moderate who says that the problems are so enormous and complicated that Negro militancy is a futile irritation, and that the need is for "intelligent moderation." Thus, during the first New York school boycott, the *Times* editorialized that Negro demands, while abstractly just, would necessitate massive reforms, the funds for which could not realistically be anticipated; therefore the just demands were also foolish demands and would only antagonize white people. Moderates of this stripe are often correct in perceiving the difficulty or impossibility of racial progress in the context of present social and economic policies. But they accept the context as fixed. They ignore (or perhaps see all too well) the potentialities inherent in linking Negro demands to broader pressures for radical revision of existing policies. They apparently see nothing strange in the fact that in the last twenty-five years we have spent nearly a trillion dollars fighting or preparing for wars, yet throw up our hands before the need for overhauling our schools, clearing the slums, and really abolishing poverty. My quarrel with these moderates is that they do not even envision radical changes; their admonitions of moderation are, for all practical purposes, admonitions to the Negro to adjust to the status quo, and are therefore immoral.

The more effectively the moderates argue their case, the more they convince Negroes that American society will not or cannot be reorganized for full racial equality. Michael Harrington has said that a successful war on poverty might well require the expenditure of a $100 billion. Where, the Negro wonders, are the forces now in motion to compel such a commitment? If the voices of the moderates were raised in an insistence upon a reallocation of national resources at levels that could not be confused with tokenism (that is, if the moderates stopped being moderates), Negroes would have greater grounds for hope. Meanwhile, the Negro movement cannot escape a sense of isolation.

It is precisely this sense of isolation that gives rise to the second line of thought I want to examine—the tendency within the civil rights movement which, despite its militancy, pursues what I call a "no-win" policy. Sharing with many moderates a recognition of the magnitude of the obstacles to freedom, spokesmen for this tendency survey the American scene and find no forces prepared to move toward radical solutions. From this they conclude that the only viable strategy is shock; above all, the hypocrisy of white liberals must be exposed. These spokesmen are often described as the radicals of the movement, but they are really its moralists. They seek to change white hearts—by traumatizing them. Frequently abetted by white self-flagellants, they may gleefully applaud (though not really agreeing with) Malcolm X because, while they admit he has no program, they think he can frighten white people into doing the right thing. To believe this, of course, you must be convinced, even if unconsciously, that at the core of the white man's heart lies a buried affection for Negroes—a proposition one may be permitted to doubt. But in any case, hearts are not relevant to the issue; neither racial affinities nor racial hostilities are rooted there. It is institutions—social, political, and economic institutions—which are the ultimate molders of collective sentiments. Let these institutions be reconstructed *today*, and let the ineluctable gradualism of history govern the formation of a new psychology.

My quarrel with the "no-win" tendency in the civil rights movement (and the reason I have so designated it) parallels my quarrel with the moderates outside the movement. As the latter lack the vision or will for fundamental change, the former lack a realistic strategy for achieving it. For such a strategy they substitute militancy. But militancy is a matter of posture and volume and not of effect.

I believe that the Negro's struggle for equality in America is essentially revolutionary. While most Negroes—in their hearts—unquestionably seek only to enjoy the fruits of American society as it now exists, their quest cannot *objectively* be satisfied within the framework of existing political and economic relations. The young Negro who would demonstrate his way into the labor market may be motivated by a thoroughly bourgeois ambition and thoroughly "capitalist" considerations, but he will end up having to favor a great expansion of the public sector of the economy. At any rate, that is the position the movement will be forced to take as it looks at the number of jobs being generated by the private economy, and if it is to remain true to the masses of Negroes.

The revolutionary character of the Negro's struggle is manifest in the fact that this struggle may have done more to democratize life for whites than for Negroes. Clearly, it was the sit-in movement of young Southern Negroes which, as it galvanized white students, banished the ugliest features of McCarthyism from the American campus and resurrected political debate. It was not until Negroes assaulted *de facto* school segregation in the urban centers that the issue of quality education for *all* children stirred into motion. Finally, it seems reasonably clear that the civil rights movement, directly and through the resurgence of social conscience it kindled, did more to initiate the war on poverty than any other single force.

It will be—it has been—argued that these by-products of the Negro struggle are not revolutionary. But the term revolutionary, as I am using it, does not connote violence; it refers to the qualitative transformation of fundamental institutions, more or less rapidly, to the point where the social and economic structure which they comprised can no longer be said to be the same. The Negro struggle has hardly run its course; and it will not stop moving until it has been utterly defeated or won substantial equality. But I fail to see how the movement can be victorious in the absence of radical programs for full employment, abolition of slums, the reconstruction of our educational system, new definitions of work and leisure. Adding up the cost of such programs, we can only conclude that we are talking about a refashioning of our political economy. It has been estimated, for example, that the price of replacing New York City's slums with public housing would be $17 billion. Again, a multi-billion dollar federal public-works program, dwarfing the currently proposed $2 billion program, is required to reabsorb unskilled and semi-skilled workers into the labor market—and this must be done if Negro workers in these categories are to be employed. "Preferential treatment" cannot help them.

I am not trying here to delineate a total program, only to suggest the scope of economic reforms which are most immediately related to the plight of the Negro community. One could speculate on their political implications—whether, for example, they do not indicate the obsolescence of state government and the superiority of regional structures as viable units of planning. Such speculations aside, it is clear that Negro needs cannot be satisfied unless we go beyond what has so far been placed on the agenda. How are these radical objectives to be achieved? The answer is simple, deceptively so: *through political power*.

There is a strong moralistic strain in the civil rights movement which would remind us that power corrupts, forgetting that the absence of power also corrupts. But this is not the view I want to debate here, for it is waning. Our problem is posed by those who accept the need for political power but do not understand the nature of the object and therefore lack sound strategies for achieving it; they tend to confuse political institutions with lunch counters.

A handful of Negroes, acting alone, could integrate a lunch counter by strategically locating their bodies so as *directly* to interrupt the operation of the proprietor's will; their numbers were relatively unimportant. In politics, however, such a confrontation is difficult because the interests involved are merely *represented*. In the execution of a political decision a direct confrontation may ensue (as when federal marshals escorted James Meredith into the University of Mississippi—to turn from an example of non-violent coercion to one of force backed up with the threat of violence). But in arriving at a political decision, numbers and organizations are crucial, especially for the economically disenfranchised. (Needless to say, I am assuming that the forms of political democracy exist in America, however imperfectly, that they are valued, and that elitist or putschist conceptions of exercising power are beyond the pale of discussion for the civil rights movement.)

Neither that movement nor the country's twenty million black people can win political power alone. We need allies. The future of the Negro struggle depends on whether the contradictions of this society can be resolved by a coalition of progressive forces which becomes the *effective* political majority in the United States. I speak of the coalition which staged the March on Washington, passed the Civil Rights Act, and laid the basis for the Johnson landslide—Negroes, trade unionists, liberals, and religious groups.

There are those who argue that a coalition strategy would force the Negro to surrender his political independence to white liberals, that he would be neutralized, deprived of his cutting edge, absorbed into the Establishment. Some who take this position urged last year that votes be withheld from the Johnson-Humphrey ticket as a demonstration of the Negro's political power. Curiously enough, these people who sought to demonstrate power through the non-exercise of it, also point to the Negro "swing vote" in crucial urban areas as the source of the Negro's independent political power. But here they are closer to being right: the urban Negro vote will grow in importance in the coming years. If there is anything positive in the spread of the ghetto, it is the potential political power base thus created, and to realize this potential is one of the most challenging and urgent tasks before the civil rights movement. If the movement can wrest leadership of the ghetto vote from the machines, it will have acquired an organized constituency such as other major groups in our society now have.

But we must also remember that the effectiveness of a swing vote depends solely on "other" votes. It derives its power from them. In that sense, it can never be "independent," but must opt for one candidate or the other, even if by default. Thus coalitions are inescapable, however tentative they may be. And this is the case in all but those few situations in which Negroes running on an independent ticket might conceivably win. "Independence," in other words, is not a value in itself. The issue is which coalition to join and how to make it responsive to your program. Necessarily there will be compromise. But the difference between expediency and morality in politics is the difference between selling out a principle and making smaller concessions to win larger ones. The leader who shrinks from this task reveals not his purity but his lack of political sense.

The task of molding a political movement out of the March on Washington coalition is not simple, but no alternatives have been advanced. We need to choose our allies on the basis of common political objectives. It has become fashionable in some no-win Negro circles to decry the white liberal as the main enemy (his hypocrisy is what sustains racism); by virtue of this reverse recitation of the reactionary's litany (liberalism leads to socialism, which leads to Communism) the Negro is left in majestic isolation, except for a tiny band of fervent white initiates. But the objective fact is that *Eastland and Goldwater* are the main enemies—they and the opponents of civil rights, of the war on poverty, of medicare, of social security, of federal aid to education, of unions, and so forth. The labor movement, despite its obvious faults, has been the largest single organized force in this country pushing for progressive social legislation. And where the Negro-labor-liberal axis is weak, as in the farm belt, it was the religious groups that were most influential in rallying support for the Civil Rights Bill.

The durability of the coalition was interestingly tested during the election. I do not believe that the Johnson landslide proved the "white backlash" to be a myth. It proved, rather, that economic interests are more fundamental than prejudice: the backlashers decided that loss of social security was, after all, too high a price to pay for a slap at the Negro. This lesson was a valuable first step in re-educating such people, and it must be kept alive, for the civil rights movement will be advanced only to the degree that social and economic welfare gets to be inextricably entangled with civil rights.

The 1964 elections marked a turning point in American politics. The Democratic landslide was not merely the result of a negative reaction to Goldwaterism; it was also the expression of a majority liberal consensus. The near unanimity with which Negro voters joined in that expression was, I am convinced, a vindication of the July 25th statement by Negro leaders calling for a strategic turn toward political action and a temporary curtailment of mass demonstrations. * * *

The role of the civil rights movement in the reorganization of American political life is programmatic as well as strategic. We are challenged now to broaden our social vision, to develop functional programs with concrete objectives. We need to propose alternatives to technological unemployment, urban decay, and the rest. We need to be calling for public works and training, for national economic planning, for federal aid to education, for attractive public housing—all this on a sufficiently massive scale to make a difference. We need to protest the notion that our integration into American life, so long delayed, must now proceed in an atmosphere of competitive scarcity instead of in the security of abundance which technology makes possible. We cannot claim to have answers to all the complex problems of modern society. That is too much to ask of a movement still battling barbarism in Mississippi. But we can agitate the right questions by probing at the contradictions which still stand in the way of the "Great Society." The questions having been asked, motion must begin in the larger society, for there is a limit to what Negroes can do alone.

STOKELY CARMICHAEL

Toward Black Liberation (1966)

Born in Trinidad, British West Indies, the civil rights activist Stokely Carmichael (1941–1998) participated in the freedom rides of 1961, formed the Lowndes County Freedom Organization in 1964 to register black voters in Mississippi, became chairman of the Student Nonviolent Coordinating Committee in 1966, and became prime minister of the Black Panther party in 1967. In a famous speech he gave during the March Against Fear in 1966 Carmichael popularized the phrase "black power" as a slogan for militant black self-determination. In this excerpt from an essay that appeared in the Massachusetts Review, Carmichael argued that blacks could not reclaim their cultural identity through integration until they affirmed what was valuable within the black community. He would himself assert his African identity by changing his name to Kwame Touré and becoming involved with pan-African parties.

One of the most pointed illustrations of the need for Black Power, as a positive and redemptive force in a society degenerating into a form of totalitarianism, is to be made by examining the history of distortion that the concept has received in national media of publicity. In this "debate," as in everything else that affects our lives, Negroes are dependent on, and at the discretion of, forces and institutions within the white society which have little interest in representing us honestly. * * *

Our concern for black power addresses itself directly to this problem, the necessity to reclaim our history and our identity from the cultural terrorism and depredation of self-justifying white guilt.

To do this we shall have to struggle for the right to create our own terms through which to define ourselves and our relationship to the society, and to have these terms recognized. This is the first necessity of a free people, and the first right that any oppressor must suspend. The white fathers of American racism knew this—instinctively it seems—as is indicated by the continuous record of the distortion and omission in their dealings with the red and black men. In the same way that southern apologists for the "Jim Crow" society have so obscured, muddied and misrepresented the record of the reconstruction period, until it is almost impossible to tell what really happened, their contemporary counterparts are busy doing the same thing with the recent history of the civil rights movement.

* * *

Traditionally, for each new ethnic group, the route to social and political integration into America's pluralistic society, has been through the organization of their own institutions with which to represent their communal needs within the larger society. This is simply stating what the advocates of black power are saying. The strident outcry, *particularly* from the liberal community, that has been evoked by this proposal can only be understood by examining the historic relationship between Negro and White power in this country.

Negroes are defined by two forces, their blackness and their powerlessness. There have been traditionally two communities in America. The White community, which controlled and defined the forms that all institutions within the society would take, and the Negro community which has been excluded from participation in the power decisions that shaped the society, and has traditionally been dependent upon, and subservient to the White community.

This has not been accidental. The history of every institution of this society indicates that a major concern in the ordering and structuring of the society has been the maintaining of the Negro community in its condition of dependence and oppression. This has not been on the level of individual acts of discrimination between individual whites against individual Negroes, but as total acts by the White community against the Negro community. This fact cannot be too strongly emphasized—that racist assumptions of white superiority have been so deeply ingrained in the structure of the society that it infuses its entire functioning, and is so much a part of the national subconscious that it is taken for granted and is frequently not even recognized.

* * *

It is more than a figure of speech to say that the Negro community in America is the victim of white imperialism and colonial exploitation. This is in practical economic and political terms true. There are over 20 million black people comprising ten percent of this nation. They for the most part live in well-defined areas of the country—in the shanty-towns and rural black belt areas of the South, and increasingly in the slums of northern and western industrial cities. If one goes into any Negro community, whether it be in Jackson, Miss., Cambridge, Md. or Harlem, N. Y., one will find that the same combination of political, economic, and social forces are at work. The people in the Negro community do not control the resources of that community, its political decisions, its law enforcement, its housing standards; and even the physical ownership of the land, houses, and stores *lie outside the community*.

It is white power that makes the laws, and it is violent white power in the form of armed white cops that enforces those laws with guns and nightsticks. The vast majority of Negroes in this country live in these captive communities and must endure these conditions of oppression because, and only because, *they are black and powerless.* * * *

In recent years the answer to these questions which has been given by most articulate groups of Negroes and their white allies, the "liberals" of all stripes, has been in terms of something called "integration." According to the advocates of integration, social justice will be accomplished by "integrating the Negro into the mainstream institutions of the society from which he has been traditionally excluded." It is very significant that each time I have heard this formulation it has been in terms of "the Negro," the individual Negro, rather than in terms of the community.

This concept of integration had to be based on the assumption that there was nothing of value in the Negro community and that little of value could be created among Negroes, so the thing to do was to siphon off the "acceptable" Negroes into the surrounding middle-class white community. Thus the goal of the movement for integration was simply to loosen up the restrictions barring the entry of Negroes into the white community. Goals around which the struggle took place, such as public accommodation, open housing, job opportunity on the executive level (which is easier to deal with than the problem of semi-skilled and blue collar jobs which involve more far-reaching economic adjustments), are quite simply middle-class goals, articulated by a tiny group of Negroes who had middle-class aspirations. It is true that the student demonstrations in the South during the early sixties, out of which SNCC came, had a similar orientation. But while it is hardly a concern of a black sharecropper, dishwasher, or welfare recipient whether a certain fifteen-dollar-a-day motel offers accommodations to Negroes, the overt symbols of white superiority and the imposed limitations on the Negro community had to be destroyed. Now, black people must look beyond these goals, to the issue of collective power.

Such a limited class orientation was reflected not only in the program and goals of the civil rights movement, but in its tactics and organization. It is very significant that the two oldest and most "respectable" civil rights organizations have constitutions which *specifically* prohibit partisan political activity. CORE once did, but changed that clause when it changed its orientation toward black power. But this is perfectly understandable in terms of the strategy and goals of the older organizations. The civil rights movement saw its role as a kind of liaison between the powerful white community and the dependent Negro one. The dependent status of the black community apparently was unimportant since—if the movement were successful—it was going to blend into the white community anyway. We made no pretense of organizing and developing institutions of community power in the Negro community, but appealed to the conscience of white institutions of power. The posture of the civil rights movement was that of the dependent, the suppliant. The theory was that without attempting to create any organized base of political strength itself, the civil rights movement could, by forming coalitions with various "liberal" pressure organizations in the white community—liberal reform clubs, labor unions, church groups, progressive civic groups—and at times one or other of the major political parties—influence national legislation and national social patterns.

* * *

The major limitation of this approach was that it tended to maintain the traditional dependence of Negroes, and of the movement. We depended upon the good-will and support of various groups within the white community whose interests were not always compatible with ours. To the extent that we depended on the financial support of other groups, we were vulnerable to their influence and domination.

Also the program that evolved out of this coalition was really limited and inadequate in the long term and one which affected only a small select group of Negroes. Its goal was to make the white community accessible to "qualified" Negroes and presumably each year a few more Negroes armed with their passport—a couple of university degrees—would escape into middle-class America and adopt the attitudes and life styles of that group; and one day the Harlems and the Watts would stand empty, a tribute to the success of integration. This is simply neither realistic nor particularly desirable. You can integrate communities, but you assimilate individuals. Even if such a program were possible its result would be, not to develop the black community as a functional and honorable segment of the total society, with its own cultural identity, life patterns, and institutions, but to abolish it—the final solution to the Negro problem. Marx said that the working class is the first class in history that ever wanted to abolish itself. If one listens to some of our "moderate" Negro leaders it appears that the American Negro is the first race that ever wished to abolish itself. The fact is that what must be abolished is not the black community, but the dependent colonial status that has been inflicted upon it. The racial and cultural personality of the black community must be preserved and the community must win its freedom while preserving its cultural integrity. This is the essential difference between integration as it is currently practised and the concept of black power.

* * *

SNCC proposes that it is now time for the black freedom movement to stop pandering to the fears and anxieties of the white middle class in the attempt to earn its "good-will," and to return to the ghetto to organize these communities to control themselves. This organization must be attempted in northern and southern urban areas as well as in the rural black belt counties of the South. The chief antagonist to this organization is, in the South, the overtly racist Democratic party, and in the North the equally corrupt big city machines.

* * *

We must organize black community power to end these abuses, and to give the Negro community a chance to have its needs expressed. A leadership which is truly "responsible"—not to the white press and power structure, but to the community—must be developed. Such leadership will recognize that its power lies in the unified and collective strength of that community. This will make it difficult for the white leadership group to conduct its dialogue with individuals in terms of patronage and prestige, and will force them to talk to the community's representatives in terms of real power.

The single aspect of the black power program that has encountered most criticism is this concept of independent organization. This is presented as third-partyism which has never worked, or a withdrawal into black nationalism and isolationism. If such a program is developed it will not have the effect of isolating the Negro community but the reverse. When the Negro community is able to control local office, and negotiate with other groups from a position of organized strength, the possibility of meaningful political alliances on specific issues will be increased. That is a rule of politics and there is no reason why it should not operate here. The only difference is that we will have the power to define the terms of these alliances.

BETTY FRIEDAN

The Feminine Mystique (1963)

The feminist writer Betty Naomi Goldstein Friedan (1921–2006) was the cofounder and first president of the National Organization for Women. Deeply dissatisfied with the emptiness of her life as a suburban housewife and mother of three, Friedan discovered (through a high-school reunion survey questionnaire she sent out to former classmates) that many other women could not find fulfillment in their prescribed domestic social roles as mothers and housewives. The Feminine Mystique, which gave poignant expression to the unhappiness of many women, became an instant classic when it was published in 1963. It revealed that "the problem that has no name" was widespread among white, middle-class, suburban women.

The problem lay buried, unspoken, for many years in the minds of American women. It was a strange stirring, a sense of dissatisfaction, a yearning that women suffered in the middle of the twentieth century in the United States. Each suburban wife struggled with it alone. As she made the beds, shopped for groceries, matched slipcover material, ate peanut butter sandwiches with her children, chauffeured Cub Scouts and Brownies, lay beside her husband at night—she was afraid to ask even of herself the silent question—"Is this all?"

For over fifteen years there was no word of this yearning in the millions of words written about women, for women, in all the columns, books and articles by experts telling women their role was to seek fulfillment as wives and mothers. Over and over women heard in voices of tradition and of Freudian sophistication that they could desire no greater destiny than to glory in their own femininity. Experts told them how to catch a man and keep him, how to breastfeed children and handle their toilet training, how to cope with sibling rivalry and adolescent rebellion; how to buy a dishwasher, bake bread, cook gourmet snails, and build a swimming pool with their own hands; how to dress, look, and act more feminine and make marriage more exciting; how to keep their husbands from dying young and their sons from growing into delinquents. They were taught to pity the neurotic, unfeminine, unhappy women who wanted to be poets or physicists or presidents. They learned that truly feminine women do not want careers, higher education, political rights— the independence and the opportunities that the old-fashioned feminists fought for. Some women, in their forties and fifties, still remembered painfully giving up those dreams, but most of the younger women no longer even thought about them. A thousand expert voices applauded their femininity, their adjustment, their new maturity. All they had to do was devote their lives from earliest girlhood to finding a husband and bearing children.

* * *

In the fifteen years after World War II, this mystique of feminine fulfillment became the cherished and self-perpetuating core of contemporary American culture. Millions of women lived their lives in the image of those pretty pictures of the American suburban housewife, kissing their husbands goodbye in front of the picture window, depositing their stationwagonsful of children at school, and smiling as they ran the new electric waxer over the spotless kitchen floor. They baked their own bread, sewed their own and their children's clothes, kept their new washing machines and dryers running all day. They changed the sheets on the beds twice a week instead of once, took the rug-hooking class in adult education, and pitied their poor frustrated mothers, who had dreamed of having a career. Their only dream was to be perfect wives and mothers; their highest ambition to have five children and a beautiful house, their only fight to get and keep their husbands. They had no thought for the unfeminine problems of the world outside the home; they wanted the men to make the major decisions. They gloried in their role as women, and wrote proudly on the census blank: "Occupation: housewife."

* * *

If a woman had a problem in the 1950's and 1960's, she knew that something must be wrong with her marriage, or with herself. Other women were satisfied with their lives, she thought. What kind of a woman was she if she did not feel this mysterious fulfillment waxing the kitchen floor? She was so ashamed to admit her dissatisfaction that she never knew how many other women shared it. If she tried to tell her husband, he didn't understand what she was talking about. She did not really understand it herself. For over fifteen years women in America found it harder to talk about this problem than about sex. Even the psychoanalysts had no name for it. When a woman went to a psychiatrist for help, as many women did, she would say, "I'm so ashamed," or "I must be hopelessly neurotic." "I don't know what's wrong with women today," a suburban psychiatrist said uneasily. "I only know something is wrong because most of my patients happen to be women. And their problem isn't sexual." Most women with this problem did not go to see a psychoanalyst, however. "There's nothing wrong really," they kept telling themselves. "There isn't any problem."

* * *

Gradually I came to realize that the problem that has no name was shared by countless women in America. As a magazine writer I often interviewed women about problems with their children, or their marriages, or their houses, or their communities. But after a while I began to recognize the telltale signs of this other problem. I saw the same signs in suburban ranch houses and split-levels on Long Island and in New Jersey and Westchester County; in colonial houses in a small Massachusetts town; on patios in Memphis; in suburban and city apartments; in living rooms in the Midwest. Sometimes I sensed the problem, not as a reporter, but as a suburban housewife, for during this time I was also bringing up my own three children in Rockland County, New York. I heard echoes of the problem in college dormitories and semiprivate maternity wards, at PTA meetings and luncheons of the League of Women Voters, at suburban cocktail parties, in station wagons waiting for trains, and in snatches of conversation overheard at Schrafft's. The groping words I heard from other women, on quiet afternoons when children were at school or on quiet evenings when husbands worked late, I think I understood first as a woman long before I understood their larger social and psychological implications.

Just what was this problem that has no name? What were the words women used when they tried to express it? Sometimes a woman would say "I feel empty somehow . . . incomplete." Or she would say, "I feel as if I don't exist." Sometimes she blotted out the feeling with a tranquilizer. Sometimes she thought the problem was with her husband, or her children, or that what she really needed was to redecorate her house, or move to a better neighborhood, or have an affair, or another baby. Sometimes, she went to a doctor with symptoms she could hardly describe: "A tired feeling . . . I get so angry with the children it scares me . . . I feel like crying without any reason." (A Cleveland doctor called it "the housewife's syndrome.") A number of women told me about great bleeding blisters that break out on their hands and arms. "I call it the housewife's blight," said a family doctor in Pennsylvania. "I see it so often lately in these young women with four, five and six children who bury themselves in their dishpans. But it isn't caused by detergent and it isn't cured by cortisone."

Sometimes a woman would tell me that the feeling gets so strong she runs out of the house and walks through the streets. Or she stays inside her house and cries. Or her children tell her a joke, and she doesn't laugh because she doesn't hear it. I talked to women who had spent years on the analyst's couch, working out their "adjustment to the feminine role," their blocks to "fulfillment as a wife and mother." But the desperate tone in these women's voices, and the look in their eyes, was the same as the tone and the look of other women, who were sure they had no problem, even though they did have a strange feeling of desperation.

* * *

In 1960, the problem that has no name burst like a boil through the image of the happy American housewife. In the television commercials the pretty housewives still beamed over their foaming dishpans and *Time*'s cover story on "The Suburban Wife, an American Phenomenon" protested: "Having too good a time . . . to believe that they should be unhappy." But the actual unhappiness of the American housewife was suddenly being reported—from the *New York Times* and *Newsweek* to *Good Housekeeping* and CBS Television. * * *

It is no longer possible to ignore that voice, to dismiss the desperation of so many American women. This is not what being a woman means, no matter what the experts say. For human suffering there is a reason; perhaps the reason has not been found because the right questions have not been asked, or pressed far enough. I do not accept the answer that there is no problem because American women have luxuries that women in other times and lands never dreamed of; part of the strange newness of the problem is that it cannot be understood in terms of the age-old material problems of man: poverty, sickness, hunger, cold. The women who suffer this problem have a hunger that food cannot fill. * * *

It is no longer possible today to blame the problem on loss of femininity: to say that education and independence and equality with men have made American women unfeminine. I have heard so many women try to deny this dissatisfied voice within themselves because it does not fit the pretty picture of femininity the experts have given them. I think, in fact, that this is the first clue to the mystery: the problem cannot be understood in the generally accepted terms by which scientists have studied women, doctors have treated them, counselors have advised them, and writers have written about them. Women who suffer this problem, in whom this voice is stirring, have lived their whole lives in the pursuit of feminine fulfillment. They are not career women (although career women may have other problems); they are women whose greatest ambition has been marriage and children. For the oldest of these women, these daughters of the American middle class, no other dream was possible. The ones in their forties and fifties who once had other dreams gave them up and threw themselves joyously into life as housewives. For the youngest, the new wives and mothers, this was the only dream. They are the ones who quit high school and college to marry, or marked time in some job in which they had no real interest until they married. These women are very "feminine" in the usual sense, and yet they still suffer the problem.

* * *

How can any woman see the whole truth within the bounds of her own life? How can she believe that voice inside herself, when it denies the conventional, accepted truths by which she has been living? And yet the women I have talked to, who are finally listening to that inner voice, seem in some incredible way to be groping through to a truth that has defied the experts.

I think the experts in a great many fields have been holding pieces of that truth under their microscopes for a long time without realizing it. I found pieces of it in certain new research and theoretical developments in psychological, social and biological science whose implications for women seem never to have been examined. I found many clues by talking to suburban doctors, gynecologists, obstetricians, child-guidance clinicians, pediatricians, high-school guidance counselors, college professors, marriage counselors, psychiatrists and ministers—questioning them not on their theories, but on their actual experience in treating American women. I became aware of a growing body of evidence, much of which has not been reported publicly because it does not fit current modes of thought about women—evidence which throws into question the standards of feminine normality, feminine adjustment, feminine fulfillment, and feminine maturity by which most women are still trying to live.

I began to see in a strange new light the American return to early marriage and the large families that are causing the population explosion; the recent movement to natural childbirth and breastfeeding; suburban conformity, and the new neuroses, character pathologies and sexual problems being reported by the doctors. I began to see new dimensions to old problems that have long been taken for granted among women: menstrual difficulties, sexual frigidity, promiscuity, pregnancy fears, childbirth depression, the high incidence of emotional breakdown and suicide among women in their twenties and thirties, the menopause crises, the so-called passivity and immaturity of American men, the discrepancy between women's tested intellectual abilities in childhood and their adult achievement, the changing incidence of adult sexual orgasm in American women, and persistent problems in psychotherapy and in women's education.

If I am right, the problem that has no name stirring in the minds of so many American women today is not a matter of loss of femininity or too much education, or the demands of domesticity. It is far more important than anyone recognizes. It is the key to these other new and old problems which have been torturing women and their husbands and children, and puzzling their doctors and educators for years. It may well be the key to our future as a nation and a culture. We can no longer ignore that voice within women that says: "I want something more than my husband and my children and my home."

* * *

It is my thesis that the core of the problem for women today is not sexual but a problem of identity—a stunting or evasion of growth that is perpetuated by the feminine mystique. It is my thesis that as the Victorian culture did not permit women to accept or gratify their basic sexual needs, our culture does not permit women to accept or gratify their basic need to grow and fulfill their potentialities as human beings, a need which is not solely defined by their sexual role.

* * *

There have been identity crises for man at all the crucial turning points in human history, though those who lived through them did not give them that name. It is only in recent years that the theorists of psychology, sociology and theology have isolated this problem, and given it a name. But it is considered a man's problem. It is defined, for man, as the crisis of growing up, of choosing his identity, "the decision as to what one is and is going to be," in the words of the brilliant psychoanalyst Erik H. Erikson. * * *

But why have theorists not recognized this same identity crisis in women? In terms of the old conventions and the new feminine mystique women are not expected to grow up to find out who they are, to choose their human identity. Anatomy is woman's destiny, say the theorists of femininity; the identity of women is determined by her biology.

But is it? More and more women are asking themselves this question. As if they were waking from a coma, they ask, "Where am I . . . what am I doing here?" For the first time in their history, women are becoming aware of an identity crisis in their own lives, a crisis which began many generations ago, has grown worse with each succeeding generation, and will not end until they, or their daughters, turn an unknown corner and make of themselves and their lives the new image that so many women now so desperately need.

In a sense that goes beyond any one woman's life, I think this is the crisis of women growing up—a turning point from an immaturity that has been called femininity to full human identity. I think women had to suffer this crisis of identity, which began a hundred years ago, and have to suffer it still today, simply to become fully human.

NATIONAL ORGANIZATION FOR WOMEN

Bill of Rights (1967)

Founded in 1967 by Betty Friedan and other feminists to pressure the Equal Employment Opportunity Commission to enforce ignored bans against sex discrimination in employment, the National Organization for Women (NOW) sought "to bring women into full participation in the mainstream of American society now." Although NOW faced some internal divisions over the equal rights amendment and abortion, there was wide support among its members for equal employment opportunities, equal educational opportunities, and federal aid for child-care services, as indicated in its Bill of Rights.

WE DEMAND:

I. That the U.S. Congress immediately pass the Equal Rights Amendment to the Constitution to provide that "Equality of rights under the law shall not be denied or abridged by the United States or by any State on account of sex," and that such then be immediately ratified by the several States.

II. That equal employment opportunity be guaranteed to all women, as well as men, by insisting that the Equal Employment Opportunity Commission enforces the prohibitions against racial discrimination.

III. That women be protected by law to ensure their rights to return to their jobs within a reasonable time after childbirth without loss of senority or other accrued benefits, and be paid maternity leave as a form of social security and/or employee benefit.

IV. Immediate revision of tax laws to permit the deduction of home and child-care expenses for working parents.

V. That child-care facilities be established by law on the same basis as parks, libraries, and public schools, adequate to the needs of children from the pre-school years through adolescence, as a community resource to be used by all citizens from all income levels.

VI. That the right of women to be educated to their full potential equally with men be secured by Federal and State legislation, eliminating all discrimination and segregation by sex, written and unwritten, at all levels of education, including colleges, graduate and professional schools, loans and fellowships, and Federal and State training programs such as the Job Corps.

VII. The right of women in poverty to secure job training, housing, and family allowances on equal terms with men, but without prejudice to a parent's right to remain at home to care for his or her children; revision of welfare legislation and poverty programs which deny women dignity, privacy, and self-respect.

VIII. The right of women to control their own reproducive lives by removing from the penal code laws limiting access to contraceptive information and devices, and by repealing penal laws governing abortion.

Redstockings Manifesto (1969)

Founded in 1969 by Shulamith Firestone, Ellen Willis, and other women's activists, the short-lived Redstockings were a group of militant feminists who conducted numerous "speakouts" and demonstrations against sexual discrimination. They achieved instant notice when they disrupted a New York state legislative hearing on abortion to call for immediate repeal—rather than reform—of existing abortion laws. Critical of the tendency of other feminists to blame impersonal institutions for the oppression of women, the Redstockings Manifesto, published in 1969, emphasized the need "to change men" and to seek collective solutions to male dominiation.

I After centuries of individual and preliminary political struggle, women are uniting to achieve their final liberation from male supremacy. Redstockings is dedicated to building this unity and winning our freedom.

II Women are an oppressed class. Our oppression is total, affecting every facet of our lives. We are exploited as sex objects, breeders, domestic servants, and cheap labor. We are considered inferior beings, whose only purpose is to enhance men's lives. Our humanity is denied. Our prescribed behavior is enforced by the threat of physical violence.

Because we have lived so intimately with our oppressors, in isolation from each other, we have been kept from seeing our personal suffering as a political condition. This creates the illusion that a woman's relationship with her man is a matter of interplay between two unique personalities, and can be worked out individually. In reality, every such relationship is a *class* relationship, and the conflicts between individual men and women are *political* conflicts that can only be solved collectively.

III We identify the agents of our oppression as men. Male supremacy is the oldest, most basic form of domination. All other forms of exploitation and oppression (racism, capitalism, imperialism, etc.) are extensions of male supremacy: men dominate women, a few men dominate the rest. All power structures throughout history have been male-dominated and male-oriented. Men have controlled all political, economic and cultural institutions and backed up this control with physical force. They have used their power to keep women in an inferior position. *All men* receive economic, sexual, and psychological benefits from male supremacy. *All men* have oppressed women.

IV Attempts have been made to shift the burden of responsibility from men to institutions or to women themselves. We condemn these arguments as evasions. Institutions alone do not oppress; they are merely tools of the oppressor. To blame institutions implies that men and women are equally victimized, obscures the fact that men benefit from the subordination of women, and gives men the excuse that they are forced to be oppressors. On the contrary, any man is free to renounce his superior position provided that he is willing to be treated like a woman by other men.

We also reject the idea that women consent to or are to blame for their own oppression. Women's submission is not the result of brainwashing, stupidity, or mental illness but of continual, daily pressure from men. We do not need to change ourselves, but to change men.

The most slanderous evasion of all is that women can oppress men. The basis for this illusion is the isolation of individual relationships from their political context and the tendency of men to see any legitimate challenge to their privileges as persecution.

V We regard our personal experience, and our feelings about that experience, as the basis for an analysis of our common situation. We cannot rely on existing ideologies as they are all products of male supremacist culture. We question every generalization and accept none that are not confirmed by our experience.

Our chief task at present is to develop female class consciousness through sharing experience and publicly exposing the sexist foundation of all our institutions. Consciousness-raising is not "therapy," which implies the existence of individual solutions and falsely assumes that the male-female relationship is purely personal, but the only method by which we can ensure that our program for liberation is based on the concrete realities of our lives.

The first requirement for raising class consciousness is honesty, in private and in public, with ourselves and other women.

VI We identify with all women. We define our best interest as that of the poorest, most brutally exploited woman.

We repudiate all economic, racial, educational or status privileges that divide us from other women. We are determined to recognize and eliminate any prejudices we may hold against other women.

We are committed to achieving internal democracy. We will do whatever is necessary to ensure that every woman in our movement has an equal chance to participate, assume responsibility, and develop her political potential.

VII We call on all our sisters to unite with us in struggle.

We call on all men to give up their male privileges and support women's liberation in the interest of our humanity and their own.

In fighting for our liberation we will always take the side of women against their oppressors. We will not ask what is "revolutionary" or "reformist," only what is good for women.

The time for individual skirmishes has passed. This time we are going all the way.

JERRY RUBIN

A Yippie Manifesto (1969)

After quitting his graduate program in sociology at the University of California at Berkeley, Jerry Rubin (1938–1994) participated in the Berkeley free speech movement and led a variety of protests during the 1960s. In 1968 the flamboyant Rubin was arrested for leading an antiwar protest at the tumultuous Democratic National Convention in Chicago. A classic example of the irreverence of 1960s youth counterculture, Rubin's 1969 Yippie (Youth International Party) Manifesto challenged young people to rebel against hierarchy and hypocrisy.

America and the West suffer from a great spiritual crisis. And so the yippies are a revolutionary religious movement.

We do not advocate political solutions that you can vote for. You are never going to be able to *vote* for the revolution. Get that hope out of your mind.

And you are not going to be able to buy the revolution in a supermarket, in the tradition of our consumer society. The revolution is not a can of goods.

Revolution only comes through personal transformation: finding God and changing your life. Then millions of converts will create a massive social upheaval.

The religion of the yippies is: "RISE UP AND ABANDON THE CREEPING MEATBALL!!"

That means anything you want it to mean. Which is why it is so powerful a revolutionary slogan. The best picket sign I ever saw was blank. Next best was: "We Protest ——!"

Slogans like "Get out of Vietnam" are informative, but they do not create myths. They don't ask you to do anything but carry them.

Political demonstrations should make people dream and fantasize. A religious-political movement is concerned with people's souls, with the creation of a magic world which we make real.

When the national media first heard our slogan, they reported that the "creeping meatball" was Lyndon Johnson. Which was weird and unfair, because we liked Lyndon Johnson.

We cried when LBJ dropped out. "LBJ, you took us too literally! We didn't mean YOU should drop out! Where would WE be if it weren't for you, LBJ?"

Is there any kid in America, or anywhere in the world, who wants to be like LBJ when he grows up?

As a society falls apart, its children reject their parents. The elders offer us Johnsons, Agnews, and Nixons, dead symbols of a dying past.

The war between THEM and US will be decided by the seven-year-olds.

We offer: sex, drugs, rebellion, heroism, brotherhood.

They offer: responsibility, fear, puritanism, repression.

* * *

"Don't trust anyone over 30!" say the yippies—a much-quoted warning.

I am four years old.

We are born twice. My first birth was in 1938, but I was reborn in Berkeley in 1964 in the Free Speech Movement.

When we say "Don't trust anyone over 30," we're talking about the second birth. I got 26 more years.

When people 40 years old come up to me and say, "Well, I guess I can't be part of your movement," I say, "What do you mean? You could have been born yesterday. Age exists in your head."

Bertrand Russell is our leader. He's 90 years old.

Another yippie saying is: "THE GROUND YOU STAND ON IS LIBERATED TERRITORY!"

Everybody in this society is a policeman. We all police ourselves. When we free ourselves, the real cops take over.

I don't smoke pot in public often, although I love to. I don't want to be arrested: that's the only reason.

I police myself.

We do not own our own bodies.

We fight to regain our bodies—to make love in the parks, say "fuck" on television, do what we want to do whenever we want to do it.

Prohibitions should be prohibited.

Rules are made to be broken.

Never say "no."

The yippies say: "PROPERTY IS THEFT."

What America got, she stole.

How was this country built? By the forced labor of slaves. America owes black people billions in compensation.

"Capitalism" is just a polite schoolbook way of saying: "Stealing."

Who deserves what they get in America? Do the Rockefellers deserve their wealth? HELL NO!

Do the poor deserve their poverty? HELL NO!!

America says that people work only for money. But check it out: those who don't have money work the hardest, and those who have money take very long lunch hours.

When I was born I had food on my table and a roof over my head. Most babies born in the world face hunger and cold. What is the difference between them and me?

Every well-off white American better ask himself that question or he will never understand why people hate America.

The enemy is this dollar bill right here in my hand.

Now if I get a match, I'll show you what I think of it.

This burning gets some political radicals very uptight. I don't know exactly why. They burn a lot of money putting out leaflets nobody reads.

I think it is more important today to burn a dollar bill than it is to burn a draft card.

(Hmmm, pretty resilient. Hard to burn. Anybody got a lighter?)

We go to the New York Stock Exchange, about 20 of us, our pockets stuffed with dollar bills. We want to throw real dollars down at all those people on the floor playing monopoly games with numbers.

An official stops us at the door and says, "You can't come in. You are hippies and you are coming to demonstrate."

With TV cameras flying away we reply: "Hippies? Demonstrate? We're Jews. And we're coming to see the stock market."

Well, that gets the guy uptight, and he lets us in. We get to the top, and the dollars start raining down on the floor below.

These guys deal in millions of dollars as a game, never connecting it to people starving. Have they ever seen a real dollar bill?

"This is what it is all about, you sonavabitches!!"

Look at them: wild animals chasing and fighting each other for the dollar bills thrown by the hippies!

And then the cops come. The cops are a necessary part of any demonstration theater. When you are planning a demonstration, always include a role for the cops. Cops legitimize demonstrations.

The cops throw us out.

It is noon. Wall Street. Businessmen with briefcases and suits and ties. Money freaks going to lunch. Important business deals. Time. Appointments.

And there we are in the middle of it, burning five-dollar bills. Burning their world. Burning their Christ.

"Don't! Don't!" some scream, grasping for the sacred paper. Several near fist-fights break out.

We escape with our lives.

Weeks later *The New York Times* publishes a short item revealing that the New York Stock Exchange is installing a bulletproof glass window between the visitors' platform and the floor, so that "nobody can shoot a stockbroker."

(In Chicago 5,000 yippies come, armed only with our skin. The cops bring tanks, dogs, guns, gas, long-range rifles, missiles. Is it South Vietnam or Chicago? America always overreacts.)

The American economy is doomed to collapse because it has no soul. Its stability is war and preparation for war. Consumer products are built to break, and advertising brainwashes us to consume new ones.

The rich feel guilty. The poor are taught to hate themselves. The guilty and the wretched are on a collision course.

If the men who control the technology used it for human needs and not profit and murder, every human being on the planet could be free from starvation. Machines could do most of the work: people would be free to do what they want.

We should be very realistic and demand the impossible. Food, housing, clothing, medicine, and color TV free for all!!

People would work because of love, creativity, and brotherhood. A new economic structure would produce a new man.

That new structure will be created by new men.

American society, because of its Western-Christian-Capitalist bag, is organized on the fundamental premise that man is bad, society evil, and that: People must be motivated and forced by external reward and punishment.

We are a new generation, species, race. We are bred on affluence, turned on by drugs, at home in our bodies, and excited by the future and its possibilities.

Everything for us is an experience, done for love or not done at all.

We live off the fat of society. Our fathers worked all-year-round for a two-week vacation. Our entire life is a vacation!

Every moment, every day we decide what we are going to do.

We do not groove with Christianity, the idea that people go to heaven after they are dead. We want HEAVEN NOW!

We do not believe in studying to obtain degrees in school. Degrees and grades are like money and credit, good only for burning.

There is a war going on in the Western world: a war of genocide by the old against the young.

The economy is closed. It does not need us. Everything is built.

So the purpose of universities is: to get us off the streets. Schools are baby-sitting agencies.

The purpose of the Vietnam war is: to get rid of blacks. They are a nuisance. America got the work she needed out of blacks, but now she has no use for them.

It is a psychological war. The old say, "We want you to die for us." The old send the young to die for the old.

Our response? Draft-card burning and draft dodging! We won't die for you.

Young whites are dropping out of white society. We are getting our heads straight, creating new identities. We're dropping out of middle-class institutions, leaving their schools, running away from their homes, and forming our own communities.

We are becoming the new niggers.

* * *

Our long hair communicates disrespect to America. A racist, short-hair society gets freaked by long hair. It blinds people. In Vietnam, America bombs the Vietnamese, but cannot see them because they are brown.

Long hair is vital to us because it enables us to recognize each other. We have white skin like our oppressors. Long hair ties us together into a visible counter-community.

* * *

From 1964 to 1968 the movement has been involved in the destruction of the old symbols of America. Through our actions we have redefined those symbols for the youth.

Kids growing up today expect school to be a place to demonstrate, sit-in, fight authority, and maybe get arrested.

Demonstrations become the initiation rites, rituals, and social celebrations of a new generation.

Remember the Pentagon, center of the military ego? We urinated on it. Thousands of stoned freaks stormed the place, carrying Che's picture and stuffing flowers in the rifles of the 82nd Airborne.

Remember the Democratic Convention? Who, after Chicago, can read schoolbook descriptions of national political conventions with a straight face anymore? The farce within the convention became clear because of the war between the yippies and the cops in the streets.

We are calling the bluff on the myths of America. Once the myth is exposed, the structure behind it crumbles like sand. Chaos results. People must create new realities.

In the process we create new myths, and these new myths forecast the future.

In America in 1969 old myths can be destroyed overnight, and new ones created overnight because of the power of television. By making communications instantaneous, television telescopes the revolution by centuries. What might have taken 100 years will now take 20. What used to happen in 10 years now happens in two. In a dying society, television becomes a revolutionary instrument.

For her own protection, the government is soon going to have to suppress freedom of the press and take direct control over what goes on television, especially the news.

TV has dramatized the longhair drop-out movement so well that virtually every young kid in the country wants to grow up and be a demonstrator.

What do you want to be when you grow up? A fireman? A cop? A professor?

"I want to grow up and make history."

Young kids watch TV's thrill-packed coverage of demonstrations— including the violence and excitement—and dream about being in them. They look like fun.

* * *

There is NO WORD that the Man has to turn off your youth, no scare word.

"They're for ANARCHY!"

Damn right, we're for anarchy! This country is fucking over-organized anyway.

"DON'T DO THIS, DON'T DO THAT, DON'T!"

Growing up in America is learning what NOT to do.

We say: "DO IT, DO IT. DO Whatever YOU WANT TO DO."

Our battlegrounds are the campuses of America. White middle-class youth are strategically located in the high schools and colleges of this country. They are our power bases.

If one day 100 campuses were closed in a nationally coordinated rebellion, we could force the President of the United States to sue for peace at the conference table.

As long as we are in school we are prisoners. Schools are voluntary jails. We must liberate ourselves.

Dig the geography of a university. You can always tell what the rulers have up their sleeves when you check out the physical environment they create. The buildings tell you how to behave. Then there is less need for burdensome rules and cops. They designed classrooms so that students sit in rows, one after the other, hierarchically, facing the professor who stands up front talking to all of them.

Classrooms say:

"Listen to the Professor.

"He teaches you.

"Keep your place.

"Don't stretch out.

"Don't lie on the floor.

"Don't relax.

"Don't speak out of turn.

"Don't take off your clothes.

"Don't get emotional.

"Let the mind rule the body.

"Let the needs of the classroom rule the mind."

Classrooms are totalitarian environments. The main purpose of school and education in America is to force you to accept and love authority, and to distrust your own spontaneity and emotions.

How can you grow in such an over-structured environment? You can't. Schools aren't for learning.

Classrooms should be organized in circles, with the professor one part of the circle. A circle is a democratic environment.

Try breaking up the environment. Scream "Fuck" in the middle of your prof's lecture.

* * *

We must bring psychological guerrilla war to the University.

The mind is programmed. Get in there and break that bloody program!

Can you imagine what a feeling a professor has standing in front of a class and looking at a room full of bright faces taking down every word he says, raising their hands and asking him questions? It really makes someone think he is God. And to top it off, he has the power to reward and punish you, to decide whether or not you are fit to advance in the academic rat race.

Is this environment the right one for teacher and student?

Socrates is turning in his grave.

* * *

There is anti-intellectualism in America because professors have created an artificial environment. That is why the average working guy does not respect professors.

The university is a protective and plastic scene, shielding people from the reality of life, the reality of suffering, of ecstasy, of struggle. The university converts the agony of life into the security of words and books.

You can't learn anything in school. Spend one hour in a jail or a courtroom and you will learn more than in five years spent in a university.

All I learned in school was how to beat the system, how to fake answers. But there are no answers. There are only more questions. Life is a long journey of questions, answered through the challenge of living. You would never know that, living in a university ruled by the "right" answers to the wrong questions.

Graffiti in school bathrooms tells you more about what's on people's minds than all the books in the library.

We must liberate ourselves. I dropped out. The shit got up to my neck and I stopped eating. I said: NO. NO. NO!! I'm dropping out.

People at Columbia found out what it felt like to learn when they seized buildings and lived in communes for days.

We have to redesign the environment and remake human relationships. But if you try it, you will be kicked out.

You know what professors and deans will say? "If you don't like it here, why don't you go back to Russia!"

A lot is demanded of white, middle-class youth in 1969. The whole thing about technological and bureaucratic society is that it is not made for heroes. We must become heroes.

* * *

The yippies asked that the presidential elections be canceled until the rules of the game were changed. We said that everyone in the world should vote in the American election because America controls the world.

Free elections are elections in which the people who vote are the people affected by the results. The Vietnamese have more right to vote in the American elections than some 80-year-old grandmother in Omaha. They're being bombed by America! They should have at least some choice about if, how, and by whom they are going to be bombed.

I have nothing in particular against 80-year-old grandmothers, but I am in favor of lowering the voting age to 12 or 14 years. And I am not sure whether people over 50 should vote.

It is the young kids who are going to live in this world in the next 50 years. They should choose what they want for themselves.

Most people over 50 don't think about the potentialities of the future: they are preoccupied with justifying their past.

The only people who can choose change without suffering blows to their egos are the young, and change is the rhythm of the universe.

* * *

The Vietnam war is an education for America. It is an expensive teaching experience, but the American people are the most brainwashed people in the world.

At least the youth are learning that this country is no paradise— America kills infants and children in Vietnam without blinking. Only professional killers can be so cool.

If you become hip to America in Vietnam, you can understand the reaction against the red-white-and-blue in Latin America, and you can feel why China hates us.

They are not irrational—America is.

Wallace is a left-wing agitator. Dig him. He speaks to the same anxiety and powerlessness that the New Left and yippies talk about.

Do you feel overwhelmed by bigness, including Big Government?

Do you lack control over your own life?

Are you distrustful of the politicians and bureaucrats in Washington?

Are you part of the "little people"?

Wallace stirs the masses. Revolutions should do that too.

When is the left going to produce an inflammatory and authentic voice of the people? A guy who reaches people's emotions? Who talks about revolution the way some of those nuts rap about Christ?

Wallace says: "We're against niggers, intellectuals, liberals, hippies."

Everybody! He puts us all together. He organizes us for us.

We must analyze how America keeps people down. Not by physical force, but by fear. From the second kids are hatched, we are taught fear.

If we can overcome fear, we will discover that we are Davids fighting Goliath.

KATE MILLETT

Sexual Politics (1970)

The radical feminist author and artist Katherine Murray Millett (1934–)
used literature to develop a comprehensive feminist critique of patri-
archy. One of the first to argue that "the personal is political," Millett ex-
plored the various sources of male power and dominance in her widely
read 1970 book Sexual Politics.

In introducing the term "sexual politics," one must first answer the inevitable question "Can the relationship between the sexes be viewed in a political light at all?" The answer depends on how one defines politics. This essay does not define the political as that relatively narrow and exclusive world of meetings, chairmen, and parties. The term "politics" shall refer to power-structured relationships, arrangements whereby one group of persons is controlled by another. By way of parenthesis one might add that although an ideal politics might simply be conceived of as the arrangement of human life on agreeable and rational principles from whence the entire notion of power *over* others should be banished, one must confess that this is not what constitutes the political as we know it, and it is to this that we must address ourselves.

The following sketch, which might be described as "notes toward a theory of patriarchy," will attempt to prove that sex is a status category with political implications. * * *

The word "politics" is enlisted here when speaking of the sexes primarily because such a word is eminently useful in outlining the real nature of their relative status, historically and at the present. It is opportune, perhaps today even mandatory, that we develop a more relevant psychology and philosophy of power relationships beyond the simple conceptual framework provided by our traditional formal politics. Indeed, it may be imperative that we give some attention to defining a theory of politics which treats of power relationships on grounds less conventional than those to which we are accustomed. I have therefore found it pertinent to define them on grounds of personal contact and interaction between members of well-defined and coherent groups: races, castes, classes, and sexes. For it is precisely because certain groups have no representation in a number of recognized political structures that their position tends to be so stable, their oppression so continuous.

In America, recent events have forced us to acknowledge at last that the relationship between the races is indeed a political one which involves the general control of one collectivity, defined by birth, over another collectivity, also defined by birth. Groups who rule by birthright are fast disappearing, yet there remains one ancient and universal scheme for the domination of one birth group by another—the scheme that prevails in the area of sex. The study of racism has convinced us that a truly political state of affairs operates between the races to perpetuate a series of oppressive circumstances. The subordinated group has inadequate redress through existing political institutions, and is deterred thereby from organizing into conventional political struggle and opposition.

Quite in the same manner, a disinterested examination of our system of sexual relationship must point out that the situation between the sexes now, and throughout history, is a case of that phenomenon Max Weber defined as *herrschaft*, a relationship of dominance and subordinance. What goes largely unexamined, often even unacknowledged (yet is institutionalized nonetheless) in our social order, is the birthright priority whereby males rule females. Through this system a most ingenious form of "interior colonization" has been achieved. It is one which tends moreover to be sturdier than any form of segregation, and more rigorous than class stratification, more uniform, certainly more enduring. However muted its present appearance may be, sexual dominion obtains nevertheless as perhaps the most pervasive ideology of our culture and provides its most fundamental concept of power.

This is so because our society, like all other historical civilizations, is a patriarchy. The fact is evident at once if one recalls that the military, industry, technology, universities, science, political office, and finance—in short, every avenue of power within the society, including the coercive force of the police, is entirely in male hands. As the essence of politics is power, such realization cannot fail to carry impact. What lingers of supernatural authority, the Deity, "His" ministry, together with the ethics and values, the philosophy and art of our culture—its very civilization—as T. S. Eliot once observed, is of male manufacture.

If one takes patriarchal government to be the institution whereby that half of the populace which is female is controlled by that half which is male, the principles of patriarchy appear to be two fold: male shall dominate female, elder male shall dominate younger. However, just as with any human institution, there is frequently a distance between the real and the ideal; contradictions and exceptions do exist within the system. While patriarchy as an institution is a social constant so deeply entrenched as to run through all other political, social, or economic forms, whether of caste or class, feudality or bureaucracy, just as it pervades all major religions, it also exhibits great variety in history and locale. In democracies, for example, females have often held no office or do so (as now) in such minuscule numbers as to be below even token representation. Aristocracy, on the other hand, with its emphasis upon the magic and dynastic properties of blood, may at times permit women to hold power. The principle of rule by elder males is violated even more frequently. Bearing in mind the variation and degree in patriarchy—as say between Saudi Arabia and Sweden, Indonesia and Red China—we also recognize our own form in the U.S. and Europe to be much altered and attenuated by the reforms described in the next chapter.

* * *

Hannah Arendt has observed that government is upheld by power supported either through consent or imposed through violence. Conditioning to an ideology amounts to the former. Sexual politics obtains consent through the "socialization" of both sexes to basic patriarchal polities with regard to temperament, role, and status. As to status, a pervasive assent to the prejudice of male superiority guarantees superior status in the male, inferior in the female. The first item, temperament, involves the formation of human personality along stereotyped lines of sex category ("masculine" and "feminine"), based on the needs and values of the dominant group and dictated by what its members cherish in themselves and find convenient in subordinates: aggression, intelligence, force, and efficacy in the male; passivity, ignorance, docility, "virtue," and ineffectuality in the female. This is complemented by a second factor, sex role, which decrees a consonant and highly elaborate code of conduct, gesture and attitude for each sex. In terms of activity, sex role assigns domestic service and attendance upon infants to the female, the rest of human achievement, interest, and ambition to the male. The limited role allotted the female tends to arrest her at the level of biological experience. Therefore, nearly all that can be described as distinctly human rather than animal activity (in their own way animals also give birth and care for their young) is largely reserved for the male. Of course, status again follows from such an assignment. Were one to analyze the three categories one might designate status as the political component, role as the sociological, and temperament as the psychological—yet their interdependence is unquestionable and they form a chain. Those awarded higher status tend to adopt roles of mastery, largely because they are first encouraged to develop temperaments of dominance. That this is true of caste and class as well is self-evident.

* * *

Patriarchal religion, popular attitude, and to some degree, science as well assumes these psycho-social distinctions to rest upon biological differences between the sexes, so that where culture is acknowledged as shaping behavior, it is said to do no more than cooperate with nature. Yet the temperamental distinctions created in patriarchy ("masculine" and "feminine" personality traits) do not appear to originate in human nature, those of role and status still less.

The heavier musculature of the male, a secondary sexual characteristic and common among mammals, is biological in origin but is also culturally encouraged through breeding, diet and exercise. Yet it is hardly an adequate category on which to base political relations *within civilization*. Male supremacy, like other political creeds, does not finally reside in physical strength but in the acceptance of a value system which is not biological. Superior physical strength is not a factor in political relations—vide those of race and class. Civilization has always been able to substitute other methods (technic, weaponry, knowledge) for those of physical strength, and contemporary civilization has no further need of it. At present, as in the past, physical exertion is very generally a class factor, those at the bottom performing the most strenuous tasks, whether they be strong or not.

* * *

So much for the evanescent delights afforded by the game of origins. The question of the historical origins of patriarchy—whether patriarchy originated primordially in the male's superior strength, or upon a later mobilization of such strength under certain circumstances—appears at the moment to be unanswerable. It is also probably irrelevant to contemporary patriarchy, where we are left with the realities of sexual politics, still grounded, we are often assured, on nature. Unfortunately, as the psycho-social distinctions made between the two sex groups which are said to justify their present political relationship are not the clear, specific, measurable and neutral ones of the physical sciences, but are instead of an entirely different character—vague, amorphous, often even quasi-religious in phrasing—it must be admitted that many of the generally understood distinctions between the sexes in the more significant areas of role and temperament, not to mention status, have in fact, essentially cultural, rather than biological, bases. Attempts to prove that temperamental dominance is inherent in the male (which for its advocates, would be tantamount to validating, logically as well as historically, the patriarchal situation regarding role and status) have been notably unsuccessful. Sources in the field are in hopeless disagreement about the nature of sexual differences, but the most reasonable among them have despaired of the ambition of any definite equation between temperament and biological nature. It appears that we are not soon to be enlightened as to the existence of any significant inherent differences between male and female beyond the bio-genital ones we already know. Endocrinology and genetics afford no definite evidence of determining mental-emotional differences.

Not only is there insufficient evidence for the thesis that the present social distinctions of patriarchy (status, role, temperament) are physical in origin, but we are hardly in a position to assess the existing differentiations, since distinctions which we know to be culturally induced at present so outweigh them. Whatever the "real" differences between the sexes may be, we are not likely to know them until the sexes are treated differently, that is alike. And this is very far from being the case at present. Important new research not only suggests that the possibilities of innate temperamental differences seem more remote than ever, but even raises questions as to the validity and permanence of psycho-sexual identity. In doing so it gives fairly concrete positive evidence of the overwhelmingly *cultural* character of gender, i.e. personality structure in terms of sexual category.

* * *

Because of our social circumstances, male and female are really two cultures and their life experiences are utterly different—and this is crucial. Implicit in all the gender identity development which takes place through childhood is the sum total of the parents', the peers', and the culture's notions of what is appropriate to each gender by way of temperament, character, interests, status, worth, gesture, and expression. Every moment of the child's life is a clue to how he or she must think and behave to attain or satisfy the demands which gender places upon one. In adolescence, the merciless task of conformity grows to crisis proportions, generally cooling and settling in maturity.

Since patriarchy's biological foundations appear to be so very insecure, one has some cause to admire the strength of a "socialization" which can continue a universal condition "on faith alone," as it were, or through an acquired value system exclusively. What does seem decisive in assuring the maintenance of the temperamental differences between the sexes is the conditioning of early childhood. Conditioning runs in a circle of self-perpetuation and self-fulfilling prophecy. To take a simple example: expectations the culture cherishes about his gender identity encourage the young male to develop aggressive impulses, and the female to thwart her own or turn them inward. The result is that the male tends to have aggression reinforced in his behavior, often with significant anti-social possibilities. Thereupon the culture consents to believe the possession of the male indicator, the testes, penis, and scrotum, in itself characterizes the aggressive impulse, and even vulgarly celebrates it in such encomiums as "that guy has balls." The same process of reinforcement is evident in producing the chief "feminine" virtue of passivity.

In contemporary terminology, the basic division of temperamental trait is marshaled along the line of "aggression is male" and "passivity is female." All other temperamental traits are somehow—often with the most dexterous ingenuity—aligned to correspond. If aggressiveness is the trait of the master class, docility must be the corresponding trait of a subject group. The usual hope of such line of reasoning is that "nature," by some impossible outside chance, might still be depended upon to rationalize the patriarchal system. An important consideration to be remembered here is that in patriarchy, the function of norm is unthinkingly delegated to the male—were it not, one might as plausibly speak of "feminine" behavior as active, and "masculine" behavior as hyperactive or hyperaggressive.

* * *

* * * Under patriarchy the female did not herself develop the symbols by which she is described. As both the primitive and the civilized worlds are male worlds, the ideas which shaped culture in regard to the female were also of male design. The image of women as we know it is an image created by men and fashioned to suit their needs. These needs spring from a fear of the "otherness" of woman. Yet this notion itself presupposes that patriarchy has already been established and the male has already set himself as the human norm, the subject and referent to which the female is "other" or alien. Whatever its origin, the function of the male's sexual antipathy is to provide a means of control over a subordinate group and a rationale which justifies the inferior station of those in a lower order, "explaining" the oppression of their lives.

* * *

Patriarchy has God on its side. One of its most effective agents of control is the powerfully expeditious character of its doctrines as to the nature and origin of the female and the attribution to her alone of the dangers and evils it imputes to sexuality. The Greek example is interesting here: when it wishes to exalt sexuality it celebrates fertility through the phallus; when it wishes to denigrate sexuality, it cites Pandora. Patriarchal religion and ethics tend to lump the female and sex together as if the whole burden of the onus and stigma it attaches to sex were the fault of the female alone. Thereby sex, which is known to be unclean, sinful, and debilitating, pertains to the female, and the male identity is preserved as a human, rather than a sexual one.

The Pandora myth is one of two important Western archetypes which condemn the female through her sexuality and explain her position as her well-deserved punishment for the primal sin under whose unfortunate consequences the race yet labors. Ethics have entered the scene, replacing the simplicities of ritual, taboo, and mana. The more sophisticated vehicle of myth also provides official explanations of sexual history. In Hesiod's tale, Zeus, a rancorous and arbitrary father figure, in sending Epimetheus evil in the form of female genitalia, is actually chastising him for adult heterosexual knowledge and activity. In opening the vessel she brings (the vulva or hymen, Pandora's "box") the male satisfies his curiosity but sustains the discovery only by punishing himself at the hands of the father god with death and the assorted calamities of postlapsarian life. The patriarchal trait of male rivalry across age or status line, particularly those of powerful father and rival son, is present as well as the ubiquitous maligning of the female.

The myth of the Fall is a highly finished version of the same themes. As the central myth of the Judeo-Christian imagination and therefore of our immediate cultural heritage, it is well that we appraise and acknowledge the enormous power it still holds over us even in a rationalist era which has long ago given up literal belief in it while maintaining its emotional assent intact. This mythic version of the female as the cause of human suffering, knowledge, and sin is still the foundation of sexual attitudes, for it represents the most crucial argument of the patriarchal tradition in the West.

* * *

The continual surveillance in which [woman] is held tends to perpetuate the infantilization of women even in situations such as those of higher education. The female is continually obliged to seek survival or advancement through the approval of males as those who hold power. She may do this either through appeasement or through the exchange of her sexuality for support and status. As the history of patriarchal culture and the representations of herself within all levels of its cultural media, past and present, have a devastating effect upon her self image, she is customarily deprived of any but the most trivial sources of dignity or self-respect. In many patriarchies, language, as well as cultural tradition, reserve the human condition for the male. With the Indo-European languages this is a nearly inescapable habit of mind, for despite all the customary pretense that "man" and "humanity" are terms which apply equally to both sexes, the fact is hardly obscured that in practice, general application favors the male far more often than the female as referent, or even sole referent, for such designations.

When in any group of persons, the ego is subjected to such invidious versions of itself through social beliefs, ideology, and tradition, the effect is bound to be pernicious. This coupled with the persistent though frequently subtle denigration women encounter daily through personal contacts, the impressions gathered from the images and media about them, and the discrimination in matters of behavior, employment, and education which they endure, should make it no very special cause for surprise that women develop group characteristics common to those who suffer minority status and a marginal existence. A witty experiment by Philip Goldberg proves what everyone knows, that having internalized the disesteem in which they are held, women despise both themselves and each other. This simple test consisted of asking women undergraduates to respond to the scholarship in an essay signed alternately by one John McKay and one Joan McKay. In making their assessments the students generally agreed that John was a remarkable thinker, Joan an unimpressive mind. Yet the articles were identical: the reaction was dependent on the sex of the supposed author.

* * *

The gnawing suspicion which plagues any minority member, that the myths propagated about his inferiority might after all be true often reaches remarkable proportions in the personal insecurities of women. Some find their subordinate position so hard to bear that they repress and deny its existence. But a large number will recognize and admit their circumstances when they are properly phrased. Of two studies which asked women if they would have preferred to be born male, one found that one fourth of the sample admitted as much, and in another sample, one half. When one inquires of children, who have not yet developed as serviceable techniques of evasion, what their choice might be, if they had one, the answers of female children in a large majority of cases clearly favor birth into the elite group, whereas boys overwhelmingly reject the option of being girls. The phenomenon of parents' prenatal preference for male issue is too common to require much elaboration. In the light of the imminent possibility of parents actually choosing the sex of their child, such a tendency is becoming the cause of some concern in scientific circles.

* * *

Perhaps patriarchy's greatest psychological weapon is simply its universality and longevity. A referent scarcely exists with which it might be contrasted or by which it might be confuted. While the same might be said of class, patriarchy has a still more tenacious or powerful hold through its successful habit of passing itself off as nature. Religion is also universal in human society and slavery was once nearly so; advocates of each were fond of arguing in terms of fatality, or irrevocable human "instinct"—even "biological origins." When a system of power is thoroughly in command, it has scarcely need to speak itself aloud; when its workings are exposed and questioned, it becomes not only subject to discussion, but even to change.

The Contemporary Discourse

JOHN RAWLS

A Theory of Justice (1971)

The liberal theorist John Rawls (1921–2002) was the James Bryant Conant University Professor at Harvard University, where he taught philosophy. Perhaps the most important twentieth-century work of American political philosophy, Rawls's Theory of Justice provides a philosophical justification of the modern welfare state based on the liberal egalitarian notion of "justice as fairness" as an alternative to the utilitarian idea that society should maximize the greatest good of the greatest number. Rawls argues that it is rationally possible for individuals to derive fundamental principles of justice by putting themselves in a hypothetical "original position," where they generate a social contract behind a "veil of ignorance" to ensure the fairness of those principles.

My aim is to present a conception of justice which generalizes and carries to a higher level of abstraction the familiar theory of the social contract as found, say, in Locke, Rousseau, and Kant. In order to do this we are not to think of the original contract as one to enter a particular society or to set up a particular form of government. Rather, the guiding idea is that the principles of justice for the basic structure of society are the object of the original agreement, They are the principles that free and rational persons concerned to further their own interests would accept in an initial position of equality as defining the fundamental terms of their association. These principles are to regulate all further agreements; they specify the kinds of social cooperation that can be entered into and the forms of government that can be established. This way of regarding the principles of justice I shall call justice as fairness.

Thus we are to imagine that those who engage in social cooperation choose together, in one joint act, the principles which are to assign basic rights and duties and to determine the division of social benefits. Men are to decide in advance how they are to regulate their claims against one another and what is to be the foundation charter of their society. Just as each person must decide by rational reflection what constitutes his good, that is, the system of ends which it is rational for him to pursue, so a group of persons must decide once and for all what is to count among them as just and unjust. The choice which rational men would make in this hypothetical situation of equal liberty, assuming for the present that this choice problem has a solution, determines the principles of justice.

In justice as fairness the original position of equality corresponds to the state of nature in the traditional theory of the social contract. This original position is not, of course, thought of as an actual historical state of affairs, much less as a primitive condition of culture. It is understood as a purely hypothetical situation characterized so as to lead to a certain conception of justice. Among the essential features of this situation is that no one knows his place in society, his class position or social status, nor does any one know his fortune in the distribution of natural assets and abilities, his intelligence, strength, and the like. I shall even assume that the parties do not know their conceptions of the good or their special psychological propensities. The principles of justice are chosen behind a veil of ignorance. This ensures that no one is advantaged or disadvantaged in the choice of principles by the outcome of natural chance or the contingency of social circumstances. Since all are similarly situated and no one is able to design principles to favor his particular condition, the principles of justice are the result of a fair agreement or bargain. For given the circumstances of the original position, the symmetry of everyone's relations to each other, this initial situation is fair between individuals as moral persons, that is, as rational beings with their own ends and capable, I shall assume, of a sense of justice. The original position is, one might say, the appropriate initial status quo, and thus the fundamental agreements reached in it are fair. This explains the propriety of the name "justice as fairness": it conveys the idea that the principles of justice are agreed to in an initial situation that is fair. The name does not mean that the concepts of justice and fairness are the same, any more than the phrase "poetry as metaphor" means that the concepts of poetry and metaphor are the same.

Justice as fairness begins, as I have said, with one of the most general of all choices which persons might make together, namely, with the choice of the first principles of a conception of justice which is to regulate all subsequent criticism and reform of institutions. Then, having chosen a conception of justice, we can suppose that they are to choose a constitution and a legislature to enact laws, and so on, all in accordance with the principles of justice initially agreed upon. Our social situation is just if it is such that by this sequence of hypothetical agreements we would have contracted into the general system of rules which defines it. Moreover, assuming that the original position does determine a set of principles (that is, that a particular conception of justice would be chosen), it will then be true that whenever social institutions satisfy these principles those engaged in them can say to one another that they are cooperating on terms to which they would agree if they were free and equal persons whose relations with respect to one another were fair. They could all view their arrangements as meeting the stipulations which they would acknowledge in an initial situation that embodies widely accepted and reasonable constraints on the choice of principles. The general recognition of this fact would provide the basis for a public acceptance of the corresponding principles of justice. No society can, of course, be a scheme of cooperation which men enter voluntarily in a literal sense; each person finds himself placed at birth in some particular position in some particular society, and the nature of this position materially affects his life prospects. Yet a society satisfying the principles of justice as fairness comes as close as a society can to being a voluntary scheme, for it meets the principles which free and equal persons would assent to under circumstances that are fair. In this sense its members are autonomous and the obligations they recognize self-imposed.

One feature of justice as fairness is to think of the parties in the initial situation as rational and mutually disinterested. This does not mean that the parties are egoists, that is, individuals with only certain kinds of interests, say in wealth, prestige, and domination. But they are conceived as not taking an interest in one another's interests. They are to presume that even their spiritual aims may be opposed, in the way that the aims of those of different religions may be opposed. Moreover, the concept of rationality must be interpreted as far as possible in the narrow sense, standard in economic theory, of taking the most effective means to given ends. * * *

In working out the conception of justice as fairness one main task clearly is to determine which principles of justice would be chosen in the original position. To do this we must describe this situation in some detail and formulate with care the problem of choice which it presents. These matters I shall take up in the immediately succeeding chapters. It may be observed, however, that once the principles of justice are thought of as arising from an original agreement in a situation of equality, it is an open question whether the principle of utility would be acknowledged. Offhand it hardly seems likely that persons who view themselves as equals, entitled to press their claims upon one another, would agree to a principle which may require lesser life prospects for some simply for the sake of a greater sum of advantages enjoyed by others. Since each desires to protect his interests, his capacity to advance his conception of the good, no one has a reason to acquiesce in an enduring loss for himself in order to bring about a greater net balance of satisfaction. In the absence of strong and lasting benevolent impulses, a rational man would not accept a basic structure merely because it maximized the algebraic sum of advantages irrespective of its permanent effects on his own basic rights and interests. Thus it seems that the principle of utility is incompatible with the conception of social cooperation among equals for mutual advantage. It appears to be inconsistent with the idea of reciprocity implicit in the notion of a well-ordered society. Or, at any rate, so I shall argue.

I shall maintain instead that the persons in the initial situation would choose two rather different principles: the first requires equality in the assignment of basic rights and duties, while the second holds that social and economic inequalities, for example inequalities of wealth and authority, are just only if they result in compensating benefits for everyone, and in particular for the least advantaged members of society. These principles rule out justifying institutions on the grounds that the hardships of some are offset by a greater good in the aggregate. It may be expedient but it is not just that some should have less in order that others may prosper. But there is no injustice in the greater benefits earned by a few provided that the situation of persons not so fortunate is thereby improved. The intuitive idea is that since everyone's well-being depends upon a scheme of cooperation without which no one could have a satisfactory life, the division of advantages should be such as to draw forth the willing cooperation of everyone taking part in it, including those less well situated. Yet this can be expected only if reasonable terms are proposed. The two principles mentioned seem to be a fair agreement on the basis of which those better endowed, or more fortunate in their social position, neither of which we can be said to deserve, could expect the willing cooperation of others when some workable scheme is a necessary condition of the welfare of all. Once we decide to look for a conception of justice that nullifies the accidents of natural endowment and the contingencies of social circumstance as counters in quest for political and economic advantage, we are led to these principles. They express the result of leaving aside those aspects of the social world that seem arbitrary from a moral point of view.

* * *

Justice as fairness is an example of what I have called a contract theory. Now there may be an objection to the term "contract" and related expressions, but I think it will serve reasonably well. * * *

The merit of the contract terminology is that it conveys the idea that principles of justice may be conceived as principles that would be chosen by rational persons, and that in this way conceptions of justice may be explained and justified. The theory of justice is a part, perhaps the most significant part, of the theory of rational choice. Furthermore, principles of justice deal with conflicting claims upon the advantages won by social cooperation; they apply to the relations among several persons or groups. The word "contract" suggests this plurality as well as the condition that the appropriate division of advantages must be in accordance with principles acceptable to all parties. The condition of publicity for principles of justice is also connoted by the contract phraseology. Thus, if these principles are the outcome of an agreement, citizens have a knowledge of the principles that others follow. It is characteristic of contract theories to stress the public nature of political principles. Finally there is the long tradition of the contract doctrine. Expressing the tie with this line of thought helps to define ideas and accords with natural piety. There are then several advantages in the use of the term "contract." With due precautions taken, it should not be misleading.

* * *

I shall now state in a provisional form the two principles of justice that I believe would be chosen in the original position. In this section I wish to make only the most general comments, and therefore the first formulation of these principles is tentative. As we go on I shall run through several formulations and approximate step by step the final statement to be given much later. I believe that doing this allows the exposition to proceed in a natural way.

The first statement of the two principles reads as follows.

First: each person is to have an equal right to the most extensive basic liberty compatible with a similar liberty for others.

Second: social and economic inequalities are to be arranged so that they are both (a) reasonably expected to be to everyone's advantage, and (b) attached to positions and offices open to all.

* * *

By way of general comment, these principles primarily apply, as I have said, to the basic structure of society. They are to govern the assignment of rights and duties and to regulate the distribution of social and economic advantages. As their formulation suggests, these principles presuppose that the social structure can be divided into two more or less distinct parts, the first principle applying to the one, the second to the other. They distinguish between those aspects of the social system that define and secure the equal liberties of citizenship and those that specify and establish social and economic inequalities. The basic liberties of citizens are, roughly speaking, political liberty (the right to vote and to be eligible for public office) together with freedom of speech and assembly; liberty of conscience and freedom of thought; freedom of the person along with the right to hold (personal) property; and freedom from arbitrary arrest and seizure as defined by the concept of the rule of law. These liberties are all required to be equal by the first principle, since citizens of a just society are to have the same basic rights.

The second principle applies, in the first approximation, to the distribution of income and wealth and to the design of organizations that make use of differences in authority and responsibility, or chains of command. While the distribution of wealth and income need not be equal, it must be to everyone's advantage, and at the same time, positions of authority and offices of command must be accessible to all. One applies the second principle by holding positions open, and then, subject to this constraint, arranges social and economic inequalities so that everyone benefits.

These principles are to be arranged in a serial order with the first principle prior to the second. This ordering means that a departure from the institutions of equal liberty required by the first principle cannot be justified by, or compensated for, by greater social and economic advantages. The distribution of wealth and income, and the hierarchies of authority, must be consistent with both the liberties of equal citizenship and equality of opportunity.

* * * For the present, it should be observed that the two principles (and this holds for all formulations) are a special case of a more general conception of justice that can be expressed as follows.

> All social values—liberty and opportunity, income and wealth, and the bases of self-respect—are to be distributed equally unless an unequal distribution of any, or all, of these values is to everyone's advantage.

Injustice, then, is simply inequalities that are not to the benefit of all. Of course, this conception is extremely vague and requires interpretation.

As a first step, suppose that the basic structure of society distributes certain primary goods, that is, things that every rational man is presumed to want. These goods normally have a use whatever a person's rational plan of life. For simplicity, assume that the chief primary goods at the disposition of society are rights and liberties, powers and opportunities, income and wealth. (Later on in Part Three the primary good of self-respect has a central place.) These are the social primary goods. Other primary goods such as health and vigor, intelligence and imagination, are natural goods; although their possession is influenced by the basic structure, they are not so directly under its control. Imagine, then, a hypothetical initial arrangement in which all the social primary goods are equally distributed: everyone has similar rights and duties, and income and wealth are evenly shared. This state of affairs provides a benchmark for judging improvements. If certain inequalities of wealth and organizational powers would make everyone better off than in this hypothetical starting situation, then they accord with the general conception.

Now it is possible, at least theoretically, that by giving up some of their fundamental liberties men are sufficiently compensated by the resulting social and economic gains. The general conception of justice imposes no restrictions on what sort of inequalities are permissible; it only requires that everyone's position be improved. We need not suppose anything so drastic as consenting to a condition of slavery. Imagine instead that men forego certain political rights when the economic returns are significant and their capacity to influence the course of policy by the exercise of these rights would be marginal in any case. It is this kind of exchange which the two principles as stated rule out; being arranged in serial order they do not permit exchanges between basic liberties and economic and social gains. The serial ordering of principles expresses an underlying preference among primary social goods. When this preference is rational so likewise is the choice of these principles in this order.

* * *

Now the second principle insists that each person benefit from permissible inequalities in the basic structure. This means that it must be reasonable for each relevant representative man defined by this structure, when he views it as a going concern, to prefer his prospects with the inequality to his prospects without it. One is not allowed to justify differences in income or organizational powers on the ground that the disadvantages of those in one position are outweighed by the greater advantages of those in another. Much less can infringements of liberty be counterbalanced in this way. Applied to the basic structure, the principle of utility would have us maximize the sum of expectations of representative men (weighted by the number of persons they represent, on the classical view); and this would permit us to compensate for the losses of some by the gains of others. Instead, the two principles require that everyone benefit from economic and social inequalities. * * *

To illustrate the difference principle, consider the distribution of income among social classes. Let us suppose that the various income groups correlate with representative individuals by reference to whose expectations we can judge the distribution. Now those starting out as members of the entrepreneurial class in property-owning democracy, say, have a better prospect than those who begin in the class of unskilled laborers. It seems likely that this will be true even when the social injustices which now exist are removed. What, then, can possibly justify this kind of initial inequality in life prospects? According to the difference principle, it is justifiable only if the difference in expectation is to the advantage of the representative man who is worse off, in this case the representative unskilled worker. The inequality in expectation is permissible only if lowering it would make the working class even more worse off. Supposedly, given the rider in the second principle concerning open positions, and the principle of liberty generally, the greater expectations allowed to entrepreneurs encourages them to do things which raise the long-term prospects of laboring class. Their better prospects act as incentives so that the economic process is more efficient, innovation proceeds at a faster pace, and so on. Eventually the resulting material benefits spread throughout the system and to the least advantaged. I shall not consider how far these things are true. The point is that something of this kind must be argued if these inequalities are to be just by the difference principle.

* * *

* * * We see then that the difference principle represents, in effect, an agreement to regard the distribution of natural talents as a common asset and to share in the benefits of this distribution whatever it turns out to be. Those who have been favored by nature, whoever they are, may gain from their good fortune only on terms that improve the situation of those who have lost out. The naturally advantaged are not to gain merely because they are more gifted, but only to cover the costs of training and education and for using their endowments in ways that help the less fortunate as well. No one deserves his greater natural capacity nor merits a more favorable starting place in society. But it does not follow that one should eliminate these distinctions. There is another way to deal with them. The basic structure can be arranged so that these contingencies work for the good of the least fortunate. Thus we are led to the difference principle if we wish to set up the social system so that no one gains or loses from his arbitrary place in the distribution of natural assets or his initial position in society without giving or receiving compensating advantages in return.

In view of these remarks we may reject the contention that the ordering of institutions is always defective because the distribution of natural talents and the contingencies of social circumstance are unjust, and this injustice must inevitably carry over to human arrangements. Occasionally this reflection is offered as an excuse for ignoring injustice, as if the refusal to acquiesce in injustice is on a par with being unable to accept death. The natural distribution is neither just nor unjust; nor is it unjust that persons are born into society at some particular position. These are simply natural facts. What is just and unjust is the way that institutions deal with these facts. Aristocratic and caste societies are unjust because they make these contingencies the ascriptive basis for belonging to more or less enclosed and privileged social classes. The basic structure of these societies incorporates the arbitrariness found in nature. But there is no necessity for men to resign themselves to these contingencies. The social system is not an unchangeable order beyond human control but a pattern of human action. In justice as fairness men agree to share one another's fate. In designing institutions they undertake to avail themselves of the accidents of nature and social circumstance only when doing so is for the common benefit. The two principles are a fair way of meeting the arbitrariness of fortune; and while no doubt imperfect in other ways, the institutions which satisfy these principles are just.

A further point is that the difference principle expresses a conception of reciprocity. It is a principle of mutual benefit. We have seen that, at least when chain connection holds, each representative man can accept the basic structure as designed to advance his interests. The social order can be justified to everyone, and in particular to those who are least favored; and in this sense it is egalitarian. But it seems necessary to consider in an intuitive way how the condition of mutual benefit is satisfied. Consider any two representative men A and B, and let B be the one who is less favored. Actually, since we are most interested in the comparison with the least favored man, let us assume that B is this individual. Now B can accept A's being better off since A's advantages have been gained in ways that improve B's prospects. If A were not allowed his better position, B would be even worse off than he is. The difficulty is to show that A has no grounds for complaint. Perhaps he is required to have less than he might since his having more would result in some loss to B. Now what can be said to the more favored man? To begin with, it is clear that the well-being of each depends on a scheme of social cooperation without which no one could have a satisfactory life. Secondly, we can ask for the willing cooperation of everyone only if the terms of the scheme are reasonable. The difference principle, then, seems to be a fair basis on which those better endowed, or more fortunate in their social circumstances, could expect others to collaborate with them when some workable arrangement is a necessary condition of the good of all.

There is a natural inclination to object that those better situated deserve their greater advantages whether or not they are to the benefit of others. At this point it is necessary to be clear about the notion of desert. It is perfectly true that given a just system of cooperation as a scheme of public rules and the expectations set up by it, those who, with the prospect of improving their condition, have done what the system announces that it will reward are entitled to their advantages. In this sense the more fortunate have a claim to their better situation; their claims are legitimate expectations established by social institutions, and the community is obligated to meet them. But this sense of desert presupposes the existence of the cooperative scheme; it is irrelevant to the question whether in the first place the scheme is to be designed in accordance with the difference principle or some other criterion.

Perhaps some will think that the person with greater natural endowments deserves those assets and the superior character that made their development possible. Because he is more worthy in this sense, he deserves the greater advantages that he could achieve with them. This view, however, is surely incorrect. It seems to be one of the fixed points of our considered judgments that no one deserves his place in the distribution of native endowments, any more than one deserves one's initial starting place in society. The assertion that a man deserves the superior character that enables him to make the effort to cultivate his abilities is equally problematic; for his character depends in large part upon fortunate family and social circumstances for which he can claim no credit. The notion of desert seems not to apply to these cases. Thus the more advantaged representative man cannot say that he deserves and therefore has a right to a scheme of cooperation in which he is permitted to acquire benefits in ways that do not contribute to the welfare of others. There is no basis for his making this claim. From the standpoint of common sense, then, the difference principle appears to be acceptable both to the more advantaged and to the less advantaged individual. Of course, none of this is strictly speaking an argument for the principle, since in a contract theory arguments are made from the point of view of the original position. But these intuitive considerations help to clarify the nature of the principle and the sense in which it is egalitarian.

* * *

It seems clear * * * that the two principles are at least a plausible conception of justice. The question, though, is how one is to argue for them more systematically. Now there are several things to do. One can work out their consequences for institutions and note their implications for fundamental social policy. In this way they are tested by a comparison with our considered judgments of justice. Part II is devoted to this. But one can also try to find arguments in their favor that are decisive from the standpoint of the original position. In order to see how this might be done, it is useful as a heuristic device to think of the two principles as the maximin solution to the problem of social justice. There is an analogy between the two principles and the maximin rule for choice under uncertainty. This is evident from the fact that the two principles are those a person would choose for the design of a society in which his enemy is to assign him his place. The maximin rule tells us to rank alternatives by their worst possible outcomes: we are to adopt the alternative the worst outcome of which is superior to the worst outcomes of the others. The persons in the original position do not, of course, assume that their initial place in society is decided by a malevolent opponent. As I note below, they should not reason from false premises. The veil of ignorance does not violate this idea, since an absence of information is not misinformation. But that the two principles of justice would be chosen if the parties were forced to protect themselves against such a contingency explains the sense in which this conception is the maximin solution. And this analogy suggests that if the original position has been described so that it is rational for the parties to adopt the conservative attitude expressed by this rule, a conclusive argument can indeed be constructed for these principles. Clearly the maximin rule is not, in general, a suitable guide for choices under uncertainty. But it is attractive in situations marked by certain special features. My aim, then, is to show that a good case can be made for the two principles based on the fact that the original position manifests these features to the fullest possible degree, carrying them to the limit, so to speak.

* * *

Now, as I have suggested, the original position has been defined so that it is a situation in which the maximin rule applies. In order to see this, let us review briefly the nature of this situation with these three special features in mind. To begin with, the veil of ignorance excludes all but the vaguest knowledge of likelihoods. The parties have no basis for determining the probable nature of their society, or their place in it. Thus they have strong reasons for being wary of probability calculations if any other course is open to them. They must also take into account the fact that their choice of principles should seem reasonable to others, in particular their descendants, whose rights will be deeply affected by it. * * * Not only are they unable to conjecture the likelihoods of the various possible circumstances, they cannot say much about what the possible circumstances are, much less enumerate them and foresee the outcome of each alternative available. * * *

Several kinds of arguments for the two principles of justice illustrate the second feature. Thus, if we can maintain that these principles provide a workable theory of social justice, and that they are compatible with reasonable demands of efficiency, then this conception guarantees a satisfactory minimum. There may be, on reflection, little reason for trying to do better. Thus much of the argument, especially in Part Two, is to show, by their application to the main questions of social justice, that the two principles are a satisfactory conception. These details have a philosophical purpose. Moreover, this line of thought is practically decisive if we can establish the priority of liberty, the lexical ordering of the two principles. For this priority implies that the persons in the original position have no desire to try for greater gains at the expense of the equal liberties. The minimum assured by the two principles in lexical order is not one that the parties wish to jeopardize for the sake of greater economic and social advantages. * * *

Finally, the third feature holds if we can assume that other conceptions of justice may lead to institutions that the parties would find intolerable. For example, it has sometimes been held that under some conditions the utility principle (in either form) justifies, if not slavery or serfdom, at any rate serious infractions of liberty for the sake of greater social benefits. We need not consider here the truth of this claim, or the likelihood that the requisite conditions obtain. For the moment, this contention is only to illustrate the way in which conceptions of justice may allow for outcomes which the parties may not be able to accept. And having the ready alternative of the two principles of justice which secure a satisfactory minimum, it seems unwise, if not irrational, for them to take a chance that these outcomes are not realized.

IRVING KRISTOL

Capitalism, Socialism, and Nihilism (1973)

The New York political writer and former professor Irving Kristol (1920–) has been the editor of periodicals including Encounter, Commentary, *and* The Public Interest *and is the author of many books on contemporary politics and ideology. A leftist during his days as a student at the City College of New York, Kristol later became one of the founding leaders of the neoconservative movement. He has been a sharp critic of what he sees as the moral relativism and lack of values in modern liberal society. In this essay, a spirited defense of the social significance of religion, which first appeared in* The Public Interest *in 1973, Kristol analyzed the implications of "thinking economically" for politics and morality in the modern liberal state.*

W henever and wherever defenders of "free enterprise," "individual liberty," and "a free society" assemble, these days, one senses a peculiar kind of nostalgia in the air. It is a nostalgia for that time when they were busily engaged in confronting their old and familiar enemies, the avowed proponents of a full-blown "collectivist" economic and social order. In the debate with these traditional enemies, advocates of "a free society" have, indeed, done extraordinarily well. It is therefore a source of considerable puzzlement to them that, though the other side seems to have lost the argument, their side seems somehow not to have won it.

* * *

As a result of the efforts of [Friedrich A.] Hayek, [Milton] Friedman, and the many others who * * * share their general outlook, the idea of a centrally-planned and centrally-administered economy, so popular in the 1930's and early 1940's, has been discredited. Even in the socialist nations, economists are more interested in reviving the market than in permanently burying it. Whether they can have a market economy without private property is, of course, an issue they will shortly have to face up to.

The question then naturally arises: If the traditional economics of socialism has been discredited, why has not the traditional economics of capitalism been vindicated? I should say that the reasons behind this state of affairs are quite obvious and easily comprehensible—only they are terribly difficult to explain to economists.

On "Thinking Economically"

The original appeal of the idea of central economic planning—like the traditional appeal of socialism itself—was cast primarily in economic terms. It was felt that such planning was necessary to (a) overcome the recurrent crises—i.e., depressions—of a market economy and (b) provide for steady economic growth and greater material prosperity for all. This importance which traditional socialism—the Old Left, as we would call it today—ascribed to economics was derived from Marxism, which in turn based itself on the later writings of Marx. But the socialist impulse always had other ideological strands in it, especially a yearning for "fraternity" and "community," and a revulsion against the "alienation" of the individual in liberal-bourgeois society. These ideological strands were prominent among the "utopian socialists," as Engels was to label them, and in the early thought of Karl Marx himself, in which economics received much less attention than religion and political philosophy. They are prominent again today, in the thinking of what is called the "New Left."

The Old Left has been intellectually defeated on its chosen battle-ground, i.e., economics. But the New Left is now launching an assault on liberal society from quite other directions. One of the most astonishing features of the New Left—astonishing, at least, to a middle-aged observer—is how little interest it really has in economics. I would put it even more strongly: The identifying marks of the New Left are its refusal *to think economically* and its contempt for bourgeois society precisely be-cause this is a society that does think economically.

What do I mean by "thinking economically"? I have found that it is very hard to convey this meaning to economists, who take it for granted that this is the only possible way for a sensible man to think—that, in-deed, thinking economically is the same thing as thinking rationally. Eco-nomics is the social science *par excellence* of modernity, and economists as a class find it close to impossible to detach themselves from the philo-sophical presuppositions of modernity. This would not be particularly significant—has until recently not been particularly significant—were it not for the fact that the New Left is in rebellion against these philosoph-ical presuppositions themselves.

Let me give you a simple illustration. One of the keystones of modern economic thought is that it is impossible to have an *a priori* knowledge of what constitutes happiness for other people; that such knowledge is in-corporated in an individual's "utility schedules"; and this knowledge, in turn, is revealed by the choices the individual makes in a free market. This is not merely the keystone of modern economic thought—it is also the keystone of modern, liberal, secular society itself. This belief is so deeply ingrained in us that we are inclined to explain any deviation from it as perverse and pathological. Yet it is a fact that for several millennia, until the advent of modernity, people did not believe any such thing—would, indeed, have found such a belief to be itself shockingly pathologi-cal and perverse. For all pre-modern thinkers, *a priori* knowledge of what constituted other people's happiness was not only possible, it was a fact. True, such knowledge was the property of a small elite—religious, philo-sophical, or political. But this was deemed to be altogether proper: Such uncommon knowledge could not be expected to be found among com-mon men. So you did not need a free market or a free society to maximize individual happiness; on the contrary, a free market, not being guided by the wisdom of the elite, was bound to be ultimately frustrating, since the common people could not possibly know what they *really* wanted or what would really yield them "true" happiness.

Now, we know from our experience of central economic planning that this pre-modern approach is fallacious—but if, and only if, you define "happiness" and "satisfaction" in terms of the material production and material consumption of commodities. If you do not define "happiness" or "satisfaction" in this way, if you refuse to "think economically," then the pre-modern view is more plausible than not. It is, after all, one thing to say that there is no authentically superior wisdom about people's tastes and preferences in commodities; it is quite another thing to deny that there is a superior wisdom about the spiritual dimensions of a good life. Even today, that last proposition does not sound entirely ridiculous to us. And if you believe that man's spiritual life is infinitely more important than his trivial and transient adventures in the marketplace, then you may tolerate a free market for practical reasons, within narrow limits, but you certainly will have no compunctions about overriding it if you think the free market is interfering with more important things.

THE SHAMEFACED COUNTERREVOLUTION

Modern economists are for the most part unaware that their habit of "thinking economically" only makes sense within a certain kind of world, based on certain peculiarly modern presuppositions. They insist that economics is a science—which is certainly true, but only if you accept the premises of modern economics. Thus, one of our most distinguished economists, Ludwig Von Mises, wrote:

> Economics is a theoretical science and as such abstains from any judgment of value. It is not its task to tell people what ends they should aim at. It is a science of the means to be applied for the attainment of ends chosen, not . . . a science of the choosing of ends.

* * *

Modern, liberal, secular society is based on the revolutionary premise that there is no superior, authoritative information available about the good life or the true nature of human happiness—that this information is implicit only in individual preferences, and that therefore the individual has to be free to develop and express these preferences. What we are witnessing in Western society today are the beginnings of a counterrevolution against this conception of man and society. It is a shamefaced counterrevolution, full of bad faith and paltry sophistry, because it feels compelled to define itself as some kind of progressive extension of modernity instead of, what it so clearly is, a reactionary revulsion against modernity. It is this failure in self-definition that gives rise to so much irrelevant controversy.

* * *

I think we can summarize our situation as follows: The Old Left accepted the idea of the common good proposed by bourgeois-liberal society. The essential ingredients of this idea were material prosperity and technological progress. Bourgeois liberalism insisted that individual liberty was a precondition of this common good; the Old Left insisted that centralized planning was a precondition—but that individual liberty would be an eventual consequence. The experience of the post–World War II decades has revealed that the Old Left simply could not compete with bourgeois liberalism in this ideological debate. The result has been the emergence of a New Left which implicitly rejects both the bourgeois-liberal and the Old Left idea of the common good, and which therefore rejects (again implicitly, for the most part) the ideological presuppositions of modernity itself. This movement, which seeks to end the sovereignty over our civilization of the common man, must begin by seeking the death of "economic man," because it is in the marketplace that this sovereignty is most firmly established. It thinks of itself as a "progressive" movement, whereas its import is regressive. This is one of the reasons why the New Left, every day and in every way, comes more and more to resemble the Old Right, which never did accept the liberal-bourgeois revolutions of the 18th and 19th centuries.

THE INADEQUACIES OF LIBERALISM

One is bound to wonder at the inadequacies of bourgeois liberalism that have made it so vulnerable, first to the Old Left, and now to the New. These inadequacies do not, in themselves, represent a final judgment upon it—every civilization has its necessary costs and benefits. But it does seem to be the case that, in certain periods, a civilization will have greater difficulty striking an acceptable balance than in others—and that sometimes it arrives at a state of permanent and precarious "tilt" for reasons it cannot quite comprehend. What it is important to realize, and what contemporary social science finds it so hard to perceive, is that such reasons are not necessarily new events or new conditions; they may merely be older inadequacies—long since recognized by some critics—that have achieved so cumulative an effect as to become, suddenly, and seemingly inexplicably, intolerable.

Certainly, one of the key problematic aspects of bourgeois-liberal society has long been known and announced. This is the fact that liberal society is of necessity a secular society, one in which religion is mainly a private affair. Such a disestablishment of religion, it was predicted by Catholic thinkers and others, would gradually lead to a diminution of religious faith and a growing skepticism about the traditional consolations of religion—especially the consolations offered by a life after death. That has unquestionably happened, and with significant consequences. One such consequence is that the demands placed upon liberal society, in the name of temporal "happiness," have become ever more urgent and ever more unreasonable. In every society, the overwhelming majority of the people lead lives of considerable frustration, and if society is to endure, it needs to be able to rely on a goodly measure of stoical resignation. In theory, this could be philosophical rather than religious; in fact, philosophical stoicism has never been found suitable for mass consumption. Philosophical stoicism has always been an aristocratic prerogative; it has never been able to give an acceptable rationale of "one's station and one's duties" to those whose stations are low and whose duties are onerous. So liberal civilization finds itself having spiritually expropriated the masses of its citizenry, whose demands for material compensation gradually become as infinite as the infinity they have lost. All of this was clearly foreseen by many of the anti-modern critics who witnessed the birth of modernity.

Another (and related) consequence of the disestablishment of religion as a publicly-sanctioned mythos has been the inability of liberal society ever to come up with a convincing and generally-accepted theory of political obligation. Liberal philosophers have proposed many versions of utilitarianism to this end, but these have remained academic exercises and have not had much popular impact. Nor is this surprising: No merely utilitarian definition of civic loyalty is going to convince anyone that it makes sense for him to die for his country. In actual fact, it has been the secular myth of nationalism which, for the past century and a half, has provided this rationale. But this secular myth, though it has evolved hand-in-hand with bourgeois society, is not intrinsically or necessarily bourgeois. Nationalism ends by establishing "equal sacrifice" as the criterion of justice; and this is no kind of bourgeois criterion. We have seen, in our own day, how the spirit of nationalism can be utterly contemptuous of bourgeois proprieties, and utterly subversive of the bourgeois order itself.

The Depletion of Moral Capital

Even the very principles of individual opportunity and social mobility, which originally made the bourgeois-liberal idea so attractive, end up— once the spirit of religion is weakened—by creating an enormous problem for bourgeois society. This is the problem of publicly establishing an acceptable set of rules of distributive justice. The problem does not arise so long as the bourgeois ethos is closely linked to what we call the Puritan or Protestant ethos, which prescribes a connection between personal merit—as represented by such bourgeois virtues as honesty, sobriety, diligence, and thrift—and worldly success. But from the very beginnings of modern capitalism there has been a different and equally influential definition of distributive justice. This definition, propagated by Mandeville and Hume, is purely positive and secular rather than philosophical or religious. It says that, under capitalism, whatever is, is just—that all the inequalities of liberal-bourgeois society must be necessary, or else the free market would not have created them, and therefore they must be justified. This point of view makes no distinction between the speculator and the bourgeois-entrepreneur: Both are selfish creatures who, in the exercise of their private vices (greed, selfishness, avarice), end up creating public benefits.

Let us leave aside the intellectual deficiencies of this conception of justice—I myself believe these deficiencies are radical—and ask ourselves the question which several contemporaries of Mandeville and Hume asked before us: Will this positive idea of distributive justice commend itself to the people? Will they accept it? Will they revere it? Will they defend it against its enemies? The answer, I submit, is as obvious as it is negative. Only a philosopher could be satisfied with an *ex post facto* theory of justice. Ordinary people will see it merely as a self-serving ideology; they insist on a more "metaphysical" justification of social and economic inequalities. In the absence of such a justification, they will see more sense in simple-minded egalitarianism than in the discourses of Mandeville or Hume. And so it has been: As the connection between the Protestant ethic and liberal-bourgeois society has withered away, the egalitarian temper has grown ever more powerful.

For well over a hundred and fifty years now, social critics have been warning us that bourgeois society was living off the accumulated moral capital of traditional religion and traditional moral philosophy, and that once this capital was depleted, bourgeois society would find its legitimacy ever more questionable. These critics were never, in their lifetime, either popular or persuasive. The educated classes of liberal-bourgeois society simply could not bring themselves to believe that religion or philosophy was that important to a polity. *They* could live with religion or morality as a purely private affair, and they could not see why everyone else—after a proper secular education, of course—could not do likewise. Well, I think it is becoming clear that religion, and a moral philosophy associated with religion, is far more important politically than the philosophy of liberal individualism admits. Indeed, I would go further and say that it is becoming clearer every day that even those who thought they were content with a religion that was a private affair are themselves discovering that such a religion is existentially unsatisfactory.

LIBERTARIANISM AND LIBERTINISM

But if the grave problems that secularization would inevitably produce for liberal-bourgeois society were foreseen, if only in general terms, not all the problems that our liberal society faces today were foreseen. While many critics predicted a dissolution of this society under certain stresses and strains, none predicted—none could have predicted—the blithe and mindless self-destruction of bourgeois society which we are witnessing today. *The enemy of liberal capitalism today is not so much socialism as nihilism.* Only liberal capitalism doesn't see nihilism as an enemy, but rather as just another splendid business opportunity.

One of the most extraordinary features of our civilization today is the way in which the "counterculture" of the New Left is being received and sanctioned as a "modern" culture appropriate to "modern" bourgeois society. Large corporations today happily publish books and magazines, or press and sell records, or make and distribute movies, or sponsor television shows which celebrate pornography, denounce the institution of the family, revile the "ethics of acquisitiveness," justify civil insurrection, and generally argue in favor of the expropriation of private industry and the "liquidation" of private industrialists. Some leaders of the New Left are sincerely persuaded that this is part of a nefarious conspiracy to emasculate them through "cooptation." In this, as in almost everything else, they are wrong. There is no such conspiracy—one is almost tempted to add, "alas." Our capitalists promote the ethos of the New Left for only one reason: They cannot think of any reason why they should not. For them, it is "business as usual."

And indeed, why shouldn't they seize this business opportunity? The prevailing philosophy of liberal capitalism gives them no argument against it. Though Milton Friedman's writings on this matter are not entirely clear—itself an odd and interesting fact, since he is usually the most pellucid of thinkers—one gathers that he is, in the name of "libertarianism," reluctant to impose any prohibition or inhibition on the libertine tendencies of modern bourgeois society. He seems to assume, as I read him, that one must not interfere with the dynamics of "self-realization" in a free society. He further seems to assume that these dynamics cannot, in the nature of things, be self-destructive—that "self-realization" in a free society can only lead to the creation of a self that is compatible with such a society. I don't think it has been sufficiently appreciated that Friedman is the heir, not only to Hume and Mandeville, but to modern romanticism too. In the end, you can maintain the belief that private vices, freely exercised, will lead to public benefits only if you are further persuaded that human nature can never be utterly corrupted by these vices, but rather will always transcend them. The idea of bourgeois virtue has been eliminated from Friedman's conception of bourgeois society, and has been replaced by the idea of individual liberty. The assumption is that, in "the nature of things," the latter will certainly lead to the former. There is much hidden metaphysics here, and of a dubious kind.

And Hayek, too, though obviously hostile in temperament and mood to the new nihilism, has no grounds for opposing it in principle. When Hayek criticizes "scientism," he does indeed write very much like a Burkean Whig, with a great emphasis on the superior wisdom implicit in tradition, and on the need for reverence toward traditional institutions that incorporate this wisdom. But when he turns to a direct contemplation of present-day society, he too has to fall back on a faith in the ultimate benefits of "self-realization"—a phrase he uses as infrequently as possible, but which he is nevertheless forced to use at crucial instances. And what if the "self" that is "realized" under the conditions of liberal capitalism is a self that despises liberal capitalism, and uses its liberty to subvert and abolish a free society? To this question, Hayek—like Friedman—has no answer.

And yet this is *the* question we now confront, as our society relentlessly breeds more and more such selves, whose private vices in no way provide public benefits to a bourgeois order. Perhaps one can say that the secular, "libertarian" tradition of capitalism—as distinct from the Protestant-bourgeois tradition—simply had too limited an imagination when it came to vice. It never really could believe that vice, when unconstrained by religion, morality, and law, might lead to viciousness. It never really could believe that self-destructive nihilism was an authentic and permanent possibility that any society had to guard against. It could refute Marx effectively, but it never thought it would be called upon to refute the Marquis de Sade and Nietzsche. It could demonstrate that the Marxist vision was utopian; but it could not demonstrate that the utopian vision of Fourier—the true ancestor of our New Left—was wrong. It was, in its own negligent way, very much a bourgeois tradition in that, while ignoring the bourgeois virtues, it could summon up only a bourgeois vision of vice.

THE HUNGER FOR LEGITIMACY

Today, the New Left is rushing in to fill the spiritual vacuum at the center of our free and capitalist society. For the most part, it proclaims itself as "socialist," since that is the only tradition available to it. It unquestionably feeds upon the old, socialist yearnings for community—for a pre-individualist society—and is therefore, if not collectivist, at least "communalist" in its economics and politics. But it is also nihilistic in its insistence that, under capitalism, the individual must be free to create his own morality. The New Left is best seen as a socialist heresy, in that it refuses to "think economically" in any serious way. One might say it is a socialist heresy that corresponds to the liberal heresy it is confronting: the heresy of a "free society" whose individuals are liberated from the bourgeois ethos that used to bind them together in a bourgeois-liberal community. And as the "free society" produces material affluence, but also moral and political anarchy, so the New Left—even as it pushes individual liberty beyond anarchy itself—longs for a moral and political community in which "thinking economically" will be left to our Helots, the machines. In all their imagined utopian communities, the free individual who contracts for "the good life" has to surrender both his individualism and his freedom.

It is in the nature of heresies to take a part for the whole. Thus, our version of the "free society" is dedicated to the proposition that to be free is to be good. The New Left, though it echoes this proposition when it is convenient for its purposes, is actually dedicated to the counter-belief—which is the pre-liberal proposition—that to be good is to be free. In the first case, the category of goodness is emptied of any specific meaning; in the second case, it is the category of freedom which is emptied of any specific meaning. In the war between these two heresies, the idea of a free society that is in some specific sense virtuous (the older "bourgeois" ideal) and the idea of a good community that is in some specific sense free (the older "socialist" ideal as represented, say, by European social democracy)—both are emasculated, and the very possibility of a society that can be simultaneously virtuous and free, i.e., that organically weds order to liberty, becomes ever more remote.

And yet no society that fails to celebrate the union of order and liberty, in some specific and meaningful way, can ever hope to be accepted as legitimate by its citizenry. The hunger for such legitimacy is, I should say, the dominant political fact in the world today—in the "free" nations and among the "socialist" countries as well.

* * *

I find even more pathetic the efforts of the governments of the "free world" and of the "socialist" nations to achieve some minimum legitimacy by imitating one another. The "free societies" move haltingly toward collectivism, in the hope that this will calm the turbulence that agitates them and threatens to tear them apart. The "socialist" nations take grudging steps toward "liberalization," for the same purpose. The results, in both cases, are perverse. Each such step, so far from pacifying the populace, further provokes them—since each such step appears as a moral justification of the turbulence that caused it.

What medicine does one prescribe for a social order that is sick because it has lost its soul? Our learned doctors, the social scientists, look askance at this kind of "imaginary" illness, which has dramatic physical symptoms but no apparent physical causes. Some, on what we conventionally call the "right," cannot resist the temptation to conclude that the patient is actually in robust health, and that only his symptoms are sick. Others, on what we conventionally call the "left," declare that the patient is indeed sick unto death and assert that it is his symptoms which are the causes of his malady. Such confusion, of course, is exactly what one would expect when both patient and doctors are suffering from the same mysterious disease.

ROBERT NOZICK

Anarchy, State, and Utopia (1974)

The philosopher Robert Nozick (1938–2002) was the Joseph Pellegrino University Professor at Harvard University. In his 1974 National Book Award–winning Anarchy, State, and Utopia, Nozick developed a libertarian critique of Rawls's theory of justice and other defenses of state redistribution. Nozick rejected "patterned" principles of distribution that emphasize the end result in favor of an entitlement theory of justice that focuses on the way that individual rights constrain the actions of others. Nozick's analysis led him to the conclusion that "the minimal state is the most extensive state that can be justified."

Individuals have rights, and there are things no person or group may do to them (without violating their rights). So strong and far-reaching are these rights that they raise the question of what, if anything, the state and its officials may do. How much room do individual rights leave for the state? The nature of the state, its legitimate functions and its justifications, if any, is the central concern of this book; a wide and diverse variety of topics intertwine in the course of our investigation.

Our main conclusions about the state are that a minimal state, limited to the narrow functions of protection against force, theft, fraud, enforcement of contracts, and so on, is justified; that any more extensive state will violate persons' rights not to be forced to do certain things, and is unjustified; and that the minimal state is inspiring as well as right. Two noteworthy implications are that the state may not use its coercive apparatus for the purpose of getting some citizens to aid others, or in order to prohibit activities to people for their *own* good or protection.

   Despite the fact that it is only coercive routes toward these goals that are excluded, while voluntary ones remain, many persons will reject our conclusions instantly, knowing they don't *want* to believe anything so apparently callous toward the needs and suffering of others. I know that reaction; it was mine when I first began to consider such views. With reluctance, I found myself becoming convinced of (as they are now often called) libertarian views, due to various considerations and arguments. This book contains little evidence of my earlier reluctance. Instead, it contains many of the considerations and arguments, which I present as forcefully as I can. Thereby, I run the risk of offending doubly: for the position expounded, and for the fact that I produce reasons to support this position.

* * *

The night-watchman state of classical liberal theory, limited to the functions of protecting all its citizens against violence, theft, and fraud, and to the enforcement of contracts, and so on, appears to be redistributive. We can imagine at least one social arrangement intermediate between the scheme of private protective associations and the night-watchman state. Since the night-watchman state is often called a minimal state, we shall call this other arrangement the *ultraminimal state*. An ultraminimal state maintains a monopoly over all use of force except that necessary in immediate self-defense, and so excludes private (or agency) retaliation for wrong and exaction of compensation; but it provides protection and enforcement services *only* to those who purchase its protection and enforcement policies. People who don't buy a protection contract from the monopoly don't get protected. The minimal (night-watchman) state is equivalent to the ultraminimal state conjoined with a (clearly redistributive) Friedmanesque voucher plan, financed from tax revenues. Under this plan all people, or some (for example, those in need), are given tax-funded vouchers that can be used only for their purchase of a protection policy from the ultraminimal state.

* * *

The minimal state is the most extensive state that can be justified. Any state more extensive violates people's rights. Yet many persons have put forth reasons purporting to justify a more extensive state. It is impossible within the compass of this book to examine all the reasons that have been put forth. Therefore, I shall focus upon those generally acknowledged to be most weighty and influential, to see precisely wherein they fail. In this chapter we consider the claim that a more extensive state is justified, because necessary (or the best instrument) to achieve distributive justice. * * *

The term "distributive justice" is not a neutral one. Hearing the term "distribution," most people presume that some thing or mechanism uses some principle or criterion to give out a supply of things. Into this process of distributing shares some error may have crept. So it is an open question, at least, whether redistribution should take place; whether we should do again what has already been done once, though poorly. However, we are not in the position of children who have been given portions of pie by someone who now makes last minute adjustments to rectify careless cutting. There is no *central* distribution, no person or group entitled to control all the resources, jointly deciding how they are to be doled out. What each person gets, he gets from others who give to him in exchange for something, or as a gift. In a free society, diverse persons control different resources, and new holdings arise out of the voluntary exchanges and actions of persons. There is no more a distributing or distribution of shares than there is a distributing of mates in a society in which persons choose whom they shall marry. The total result is the product of many individual decisions which the different individuals involved are entitled to make. Some uses of the term "distribution," it is true, do not imply a previous distributing appropriately judged by some criterion (for example, "probability distribution"); nevertheless, despite the title of this chapter [Distributive Justice], it would be best to use a terminology that clearly is neutral. We shall speak of people's holdings; a principle of justice in holdings describes (part of) what justice tells us (requires) about holdings. I shall state first what I take to be the correct view about justice in holdings, and then turn to the discussion of alternate views.

* * *

The subject of justice in holdings consists of three major topics. The first is the *original acquisition of holdings,* the appropriation of unheld things. This includes the issues of how unheld things may come to be held, the process, or processes, by which unheld things may come to be held, the things that may come to be held by these processes, the extent of what comes to be held by a particular process, and so on. We shall refer to the complicated truth about this topic, which we shall not formulate here, as the principle of justice in acquisition. The second topic concerns the *transfer of holdings*

from one person to another. By what processes may a person transfer holdings to another? How may a person acquire a holding from another who
holds it? Under this topic come general descriptions of voluntary exchange,
and gift and (on the other hand) fraud, as well as reference to particular
conventional details fixed upon in a given society. The complicated truth
about this subject (with placeholders for conventional details) we shall call
the principle of justice in transfer. (And we shall suppose it also includes
principles governing how a person may divest himself of a holding, passing
it into an unheld state.)

If the world were wholly just, the following inductive definition would
exhaustively cover the subject of justice in holdings.

1. A person who acquires a holding in accordance with the principle
   of justice in acquisition is entitled to that holding.
2. A person who acquires a holding in accordance with the principle
   of justice in transfer, from someone else entitled to the holding, is
   entitled to the holding.
3. No one is entitled to a holding except by (repeated) applications of
   1 and 2.

The complete principle of distributive justice would say simply that a distribution is just if everyone is entitled to the holdings they possess under
the distribution.

A distribution is just if it arises from another just distribution by legitimate means. The legitimate means of moving from one distribution
to another are specified by the principle of justice in transfer. The legitimate first "moves" are specified by the principle of justice in acquisition. Whatever arises from a just situation by just steps is itself just.
The means of change specified by the principle of justice in transfer
preserve justice. As correct rules of inference are truth-preserving, and
any conclusion deduced via repeated application of such rules from
only true premises is itself true, so the means of transition from one
situation to another specified by the principle of justice in transfer are
justice-preserving, and any situation actually arising from repeated
transitions in accordance with the principle from a just situation is itself just. The parallel between justice-preserving transformations and
truth-preserving transformations illuminates where it fails as well as
where it holds. That a conclusion could have been deduced by truth-
preserving means from premises that are true suffices to show its
truth. That from a just situation a situation *could* have arisen via
justice-preserving means does *not* suffice to show its justice. The fact
that a thief's victims voluntarily *could* have presented him with gifts

does not entitle the thief to his ill-gotten gains. Justice in holdings is historical; it depends upon what actually has happened. We shall return to this point later.

Not all actual situations are generated in accordance with the two principles of justice in holdings: the principle of justice in acquisition and the principle of justice in transfer. Some people steal from others, or defraud them, or enslave them, seizing their product and preventing them from living as they choose, or forcibly exclude others from competing in exchanges. None of these are permissible modes of transition from one situation to another. And some persons acquire holdings by means not sanctioned by the principle of justice in acquisition. The existence of past injustice (previous violations of the first two principles of justice in holdings) raises the third major topic under justice in holdings: the rectification of injustice in holdings. If past injustice has shaped present holdings in various ways, some identifiable and some not, what now, if anything, ought to be done to rectify these injustices? What obligations do the performers of injustice have toward those whose position is worse than it would have been had the injustice not been done? Or, than it would have been had compensation been paid promptly? How, if at all, do things change if the beneficiaries and those made worse off are not the direct parties in the act of injustice, but, for example, their descendants? Is an injustice done to someone whose holding was itself based upon an unrectified injustice? How far back must one go in wiping clean the historical slate of injustices? What may victims of injustice permissibly do in order to rectify the injustices being done to them, including the many injustices done by persons acting through their government? I do not know of a thorough or theoretically sophisticated treatment of such issues. Idealizing greatly, let us suppose theoretical investigation will produce a principle of rectification. This principle uses historical information about previous situations and injustices done in them (as defined by the first two principles of justice and rights against interference), and information about the actual course of events that flowed from these injustices, until the present, and it yields a description (or descriptions) of holdings in the society. The principle of rectification presumably will make use of its best estimate of subjunctive information about what would have occurred (or a probability distribution over what might have occurred, using the expected value) if the injustice had not taken place. If the actual description of holdings turns out not to be one of the descriptions yielded by the principle, then one of the descriptions yielded must be realized.

The general outlines of the theory of justice in holdings are that the holdings of a person are just if he is entitled to them by the principles of justice in acquisition and transfer, or by the principle of rectification of injustice (as specified by the first two principles). If each person's holdings are just, then the total set (distribution) of holdings is just. To turn these general outlines into a specific theory we would have to specify the details of each of the three principles of justice in holdings: the principle of acquisition of holdings, the principle of transfer of holdings, and the principle of rectification of violations of the first two principles. I shall not attempt that task here. * * *

* * *

The general outlines of the entitlement theory illuminate the nature and defects of other conceptions of distributive justice. The entitlement theory of justice in distribution is *historical*; whether a distribution is just depends upon how it came about. In contrast, *current time-slice principles* of justice hold that the justice of a distribution is determined by how things are distributed (who has what) as judged by some *structural* principle(s) of just distribution. A utilitarian who judges between any two distributions by seeing which has the greater sum of utility and, if the sums tie, applies some fixed equality criterion to choose the more equal distribution, would hold a current time-slice principle of justice. As would someone who had a fixed schedule of trade-offs between the sum of happiness and equality. According to a current time-slice principle, all that needs to be looked at, in judging the justice of a distribution, is who ends up with what; in comparing any two distributions one need look only at the matrix presenting the distributions. No further information need be fed into a principle of justice. It is a consequence of such principles of justice that any two structurally identical distributions are equally just. (Two distributions are structurally identical if they present the same profile, but perhaps have different persons occupying the particular slots. My having ten and your having five, and my having five and your having ten are structurally identical distributions.) Welfare economics is the theory of current time-slice principles of justice. * * *

Most persons do not accept current time-slice principles as constituting the whole story about distributive shares. They think it relevant in assessing the justice of a situation to consider not only the distribution it embodies, but also how that distribution came about. If some persons are in prison for murder or war crimes, we do not say that to assess the justice of the distribution in the society we must look only at what this person has, and that person has, and that person has, . . . at the current time. We think it relevant to ask whether someone did something so that he *deserved* to be punished, deserved to have a lower share. Most will agree to the relevance of further information with regard to punishments and penalties. Consider also desired things. One traditional socialist view is that workers are entitled to the product and full fruits of their labor; they have earned it; a distribution is unjust if it does not give the workers what they are entitled to. Such entitlements are based upon some past history. No socialist holding this view would find it comforting to be told that because the actual distribution A happens to coincide structurally with the one he desires D, A therefore is no less just than D; it differs only in that the "parasitic" owners of capital receive under A what the workers are entitled to under D, and the workers receive under A what the owners are entitled to under D, namely very little. This socialist rightly, in my view, holds onto the notions of earning, producing, entitlement, desert, and so forth, and he rejects current time-slice principles that look only to the structure of the resulting set of holdings. (The set of holdings resulting from what? Isn't it implausible that how holdings are produced and come to exist has no effect at all on who should hold what?) His mistake lies in his view of what entitlements arise out of what sorts of productive processes.

We construe the position we discuss too narrowly by speaking of *current* time-slice principles. Nothing is changed if structural principles operate upon a time sequence of current time-slice profiles and, for example, give someone more now to counterbalance the less he has had earlier. A utilitarian or an egalitarian or any mixture of the two over time will inherit the difficulties of his more myopic comrades. He is not helped by the fact that *some* of the information others consider relevant in assessing a distribution is reflected, unrecoverably, in past matrices. Henceforth, we shall refer to such unhistorical principles of distributive justice, including the current time-slice principles, as *end-result principles* or *end-state principles*.

In contrast to end-result principles of justice, *historical principles* of justice hold that past circumstances or actions of people can create differential entitlements or differential deserts to things. An injustice can be worked by moving from one distribution to another structurally identical one, for the second, in profile the same, may violate people's entitlements or deserts; it may not fit the actual history.

* * *

The entitlement principles of justice in holdings that we have sketched are historical principles of justice. To better understand their precise character, we shall distinguish them from another subclass of the historical principles. Consider, as an example, the principle of distribution according to moral merit. This principle requires that total distributive shares vary directly with moral merit; no person should have a greater share than anyone whose moral merit is greater. (If moral merit could be not merely ordered but measured on an interval or ratio scale, stronger principles could be formulated.) Or consider the principle that results by substituting "usefulness to society" for "moral merit" in the previous principle. Or instead of "distribute according to moral merit," or "distribute according to usefulness to society," we might consider "distribute according to the weighted sum of moral merit, usefulness to society, and need," with the weights of the different dimensions equal. Let us call a principle of distribution *patterned* if it specifies that a distribution is to vary along with some natural dimension, weighted sum of natural dimensions, or lexicographic ordering of natural dimensions. And let us say a distribution is patterned if it accords with some patterned principle. (I speak of natural dimensions, admittedly without a general criterion for them, because for any set of holdings some artificial dimensions can be gimmicked up to vary along with the distribution of the set.) The principle of distribution in accordance with moral merit is a patterned historical principle, which specifies a patterned distribution. "Distribute according to I.Q." is a patterned principle that looks to information not contained in distributional matrices. It is not historical, however, in that it does not look to any past actions creating differential entitlements to evaluate a distribution; it requires only distributional matrices whose columns are labeled by I.Q. scores. The distribution in a society, however, may be composed of such simple patterned distributions, without itself being simply patterned. Different sectors may operate different patterns, or some combination of patterns may operate in different proportions across a society. A distribution composed in this manner, from a small number of patterned distributions, we also shall term "patterned." And we extend the use of "pattern" to include the overall designs put forth by combinations of end-state principles.

Almost every suggested principle of distributive justice is patterned: to each according to his moral merit, or needs, or marginal product, or how hard he tries, or the weighted sum of the foregoing, and so on. The principle of entitlement we have sketched is *not* patterned. There is no one natural dimension or weighted sum or combination of a small number of natural dimensions that yields the distributions generated in accordance with the principle of entitlement. The set of holdings that results when some persons receive their marginal products, others win at gambling, others receive a share of their mate's income, others receive gifts from foundations, others receive interest on loans, others receive gifts from admirers, others receive returns on investment, others make for themselves much of what they have, others find things, and so on, will not be patterned. Heavy strands of patterns will run through it; significant portions of the variance in holdings will be accounted for by pattern-variables. If most people most of the time choose to transfer some of their entitlements to others only in exchange for something from them, then a large part of what many people hold will vary with what they held that others wanted. More details are provided by the theory of marginal productivity. But gifts to relatives, charitable donations, bequests to children, and the like, are not best conceived, in the first instance, in this manner. Ignoring the strands of pattern, let us suppose for the moment that a distribution actually arrived at by the operation of the principle of entitlement is random with respect to any pattern. Though the resulting set of holdings will be unpatterned, it will not be incomprehensible, for it can be seen as arising from the operation of a small number of principles. These principles specify how an initial distribution may arise (the principle of acquisition of holdings) and how distributions may be transformed into others (the principle of transfer of holdings). The process whereby the set of holdings is generated will be intelligible, though the set of holdings itself that results from this process will be unpatterned.

* * * Will people tolerate for long a system yielding distributions that they believe are unpatterned? No doubt people will not long accept a distribution they believe is *unjust*. People want their society to be and to look just. But must the look of justice reside in a resulting pattern rather than in the underlying generating principles? We are in no position to conclude that the inhabitants of a society embodying an entitlement conception of justice in holdings will find it unacceptable. Still, it must be granted that were people's reasons for transferring some of their holdings to others always irrational or arbitrary, we would find this disturbing. (Suppose people always determined what holdings they would transfer, and to whom, by using a random device.) We feel more comfortable upholding the justice of an entitlement system if most of the transfers under it are done for reasons. This does not mean necessarily that all deserve what holdings they receive. It means only that there is a purpose or point to someone's transferring a holding to one person rather than to another; that usually we can see what the transferrer thinks he's gaining, what cause he thinks he's serving, what goals he thinks he's helping to achieve, and so forth. Since in a capitalist society people often transfer holdings to others in accordance with how much they perceive these others benefiting them, the fabric constituted by the individual transactions and transfers is largely reasonable and intelligible. (Gifts to loved ones, bequests to children, charity to the needy also are nonarbitrary components of the fabric.) In stressing the large strand of distribution in accordance with benefit to others, Hayek shows the point of many transfers, and so shows that the system of transfer of entitlements is not just spinning its gears aimlessly. The system of entitlements is defensible when constituted by the individual aims of individual transactions. No overarching aim is needed, no distributional pattern is required.

To think that the task of a theory of distributive justice is to fill in the blank in "to each according to his ———" is to be predisposed to search for a pattern; and the separate treatment of "from each according to his ———" treats production and distribution as two separate and independent issues. On an entitlement view these are *not* two separate questions. Whoever makes something, having bought or contracted for all other held resources used in the process (transferring some of his holdings for these cooperating factors), is entitled to it. The situation is *not* one of something's getting made, and there being an open question of who is to get it. Things come into the world already attached to people having entitlements over them. From the point of view of the historical entitlement conception of justice in holdings, those who start afresh to complete "to each according to his ———" treat objects as if they appeared from nowhere, out of nothing. A complete theory of justice might cover this limit case as well; perhaps here is a use for the usual conceptions of distributive justice.

So entrenched are maxims of the usual form that perhaps we should present the entitlement conception as a competitor. Ignoring acquisition and rectification, we might say:

> From each according to what he chooses to do, to each according to what he makes for himself (perhaps with the contracted aid of others) and what others choose to do for him and choose to give him of what they've been given previously (under this maxim) and haven't yet expended or transferred.

This, the discerning reader will have noticed, has its defects as a slogan. So as a summary and great simplification (and not as a maxim with any independent meaning) we have:

> *From each as they choose, to each as they are chosen.*

* * *

It is not clear how those holding alternative conceptions of distributive justice can reject the entitlement conception of justice in holdings. For suppose a distribution favored by one of these nonentitlement conceptions is realized. Let us suppose it is your favorite one and let us call this distribution D_1; perhaps everyone has an equal share, perhaps shares vary in accordance with some dimension you treasure. Now suppose that Wilt Chamberlain is greatly in demand by basketball teams, being a great gate attraction. (Also suppose contracts run only for a year, with players being free agents.) He signs the following sort of contract with a team: In each home game, twenty-five cents from the price of each ticket of admission goes to him. (We ignore the question of whether he is "gouging" the owners, letting them look out for themselves.) The season starts, and people cheerfully attend his team's games; they buy their tickets, each time dropping a separate twenty-five cents of their admission price into a special box with Chamberlain's name on it. They are excited about seeing him play; it is worth the total admission price to them. Let us suppose that in one season one million persons attend his home games, and Wilt Chamberlain winds up with $250,000, a much larger sum than the average income and larger even than anyone else has. Is he entitled to this income? Is this new distribution D_2, unjust? If so, why? There is *no* question about whether each of the people was entitled to the control over the resources they held in D_1; because that was the distribution (your favorite) that (for the purposes of argument) we assumed was acceptable. Each of these persons *chose* to give twenty-five cents of their money to Chamberlain. They could have spent it on going to the movies, or on candy bars, or on copies of *Dissent* magazine, or of *Monthly Review*. But they all, at least one million of them, converged on giving it to Wilt Chamberlain in exchange for watching him play basketball. If D_1 was a just distribution, and people voluntarily moved from it to D_2, transferring parts of their shares they were given under D_1 (what was it for if not to do something with?), isn't D_2 also just? If the people were entitled to dispose of the resources to which they were entitled (under D_1), didn't this include their being entitled to give it to, or exchange it with, Wilt Chamberlain? Can anyone else complain on grounds of justice? Each other person already has his legitimate share under D_1. Under D_1, there is nothing that anyone has that anyone else has a claim of justice against. After someone transfers something to Wilt Chamberlain, third parties *still* have their legitimate shares; *their* shares are not changed. By what process could such a transfer among two persons give rise to a legitimate claim of distributive justice on a portion of what was transferred, by a third party who had no claim of justice on any holding of the others *before* the transfer? To cut off objections irrelevant here, we might imagine the exchanges occurring in a socialist society, after hours. After playing whatever basketball he does in his daily work, or doing whatever other daily work he does, Wilt Chamberlain decides to put in *overtime* to earn additional money. (First his work quota is set; he works time over that.) Or imagine it is a skilled juggler people like to see, who puts on shows after hours.

Why might someone work overtime in a society in which it is assumed their needs are satisfied? Perhaps because they care about things other than needs. I like to write in books that I read, and to have easy access to books for browsing at odd hours. It would be very pleasant and convenient to have the resources of Widener Library in my back yard. No society, I assume, will provide such resources close to each person who would like them as part of his regular allotment (under D_1). Thus, persons either must do without some extra things that they want, or be allowed to do something extra to get some of these things. On what basis could the inequalities that would eventuate be forbidden? Notice also that small factories would spring up in a socialist society, unless forbidden. I melt down some of my personal possessions (under D_1) and build a machine out of the material. I offer you, and others, a philosophy lecture once a week in exchange for your cranking the handle on my machine, whose products I exchange for yet other things, and so on. (The raw materials used by the machine are given to me by others who possess them under D_1, in exchange for hearing lectures.) Each person might participate to gain things over and above their allotment under D_1. Some persons even might want to leave their job in socialist industry and work full time in this private sector. I shall say something more about these issues in the next chapter. Here I wish merely to note how private property even in means of production would occur in a socialist society that did not forbid people to use as they wished some of the resources they are given under the socialist distribution D_1. The socialist society would have to forbid capitalist acts between consenting adults.

The general point illustrated by the Wilt Chamberlain example and the example of the entrepreneur in a socialist society is that no end-state principle or distributional patterned principle of justice can be continuously realized without continuous interference with people's lives. Any favored pattern would be transformed into one unfavored by the principle, by people choosing to act in various ways; for example, by people exchanging goods and services with other people, or giving things to other people, things the transferrers are entitled to under the favored distributional pattern. To maintain a pattern one must either continually interfere to stop people from transferring resources as they wish to, or continually (or periodically) interfere to take from some persons resources that others for some reason chose to transfer to them. (But if some time limit is to be set on how long people may keep resources others voluntarily transfer to them, why let them keep these resources for *any* period of time? Why not have immediate confiscation?) It might be objected that all persons voluntarily will choose to refrain from actions which would upset the pattern. This presupposes unrealistically (1) that all will most want to maintain the pattern (are those who don't, to be "reeducated" or forced to undergo "self-criticism"?), (2) that each can gather enough information about his own actions and the ongoing activities of others to discover which of his actions will upset the pattern, and (3) that diverse and far-flung persons can coordinate their actions to dovetail into the pattern. Compare the manner in which the market is neutral among persons' desires, as it reflects and transmits widely scattered information via prices, and coordinates persons' activities.

It puts things perhaps a bit too strongly to say that every patterned (or end-state) principle is liable to be thwarted by the voluntary actions of the individual parties transferring some of their shares they receive under the principle. For perhaps some *very* weak patterns are not so thwarted. Any distributional pattern with any egalitarian component is overturnable by the voluntary actions of individual persons over time; as is every patterned condition with sufficient content so as actually to have been proposed as presenting the central core of distributive justice.

* * *

Proponents of patterned principles of distributive justice focus upon criteria for determining who is to receive holdings; they consider the reasons for which someone should have something, and also the total picture of holdings. Whether or not it is better to give than to receive, proponents of patterned principles ignore giving altogether. In considering the distribution of goods, income, and so forth, their theories are theories of recipient justice; they completely ignore any right a person might have to give something to someone. Even in exchanges where each party is simultaneously giver and recipient, patterned principles of justice focus only upon the recipient role and its supposed rights. Thus discussions tend to focus on whether people (should) have a right to inherit, rather than on whether people (should) have a right to bequeath or on whether persons who have a right to hold also have a right to choose that others hold in their place. I lack a good explanation of why the usual theories of distributive justice are so recipient oriented; ignoring givers and transferrers and their rights is of a piece with ignoring producers and their entitlements. But why is it *all* ignored?

Patterned principles of distributive justice necessitate *re*distributive activities. The likelihood is small that any actual freely-arrived-at set of holdings fits a given pattern; and the likelihood is nil that it will continue to fit the pattern as people exchange and give. From the point of view of an entitlement theory, redistribution is a serious matter indeed, involving, as it does, the violation of people's rights. (An exception is those takings that fall under the principle of the rectification of injustices.) From other points of view, also, it is serious.

Taxation of earnings from labor is on a par with forced labor. Some persons find this claim obviously true: taking the earnings of *n* hours labor is like taking *n* hours from the person; it is like forcing the person to work *n* hours for another's purpose. Others find the claim absurd. But even these, *if* they object to forced labor, would oppose forcing unemployed hippies to work for the benefit of the needy. And they would also object to forcing each person to work five extra hours each week for the benefit of the needy. But a system that takes five hours' wages in taxes does not seem to them like one that forces someone to work five hours, since it offers the person forced a wider range of choice in activities than does taxation in kind with the particular labor specified. (But we can imagine a gradation of systems of forced labor, from one that specifies a particular activity, to one that gives a choice among two activities, to . . . ; and so on up.) Furthermore, people envisage a system with something like a proportional tax on everything above the amount necessary for basic needs. Some think this does not force someone to work extra hours, since there is no fixed number of extra hours he is forced to work, and since he can avoid the tax entirely by earning only enough to cover his basic needs. This is a very uncharacteristic view of forcing for those who *also* think people are forced to do something *whenever* the alternatives they face are considerably worse. However, *neither* view is correct. The fact that others intentionally intervene, in violation of a side constraint against aggression, to threaten force to limit the alternatives, in this case to paying taxes or (presumably the worse alternative) bare subsistence, makes the taxation system one of forced labor and distinguishes it from other cases of limited choices which are not forcings.

The man who chooses to work longer to gain an income more than sufficient for his basic needs prefers some extra goods or services to the leisure and activities he could perform during the possible nonworking hours; whereas the man who chooses not to work the extra time prefers the leisure activities to the extra goods or services he could acquire by working more. Given this, if it would be illegitimate for a tax system to seize some of a man's leisure (forced labor) for the purpose of serving the needy, how can it be legitimate for a tax system to seize some of a man's goods for that purpose? Why should we treat the man whose happiness requires certain material goods or services differently from the man whose preferences and desires make such goods unnecessary for his happiness? Why should the man who prefers seeing a movie (and who has to earn money for a ticket) be open to the required call to aid the needy, while the person who prefers looking at a sunset (and hence need earn no extra money) is not? Indeed, isn't it surprising that redistributionists choose to ignore the man whose pleasures are so easily attainable without extra labor, while adding yet another burden to the poor unfortunate who must work for his pleasures? If anything, one would have expected the reverse. * * *

What sort of right over others does a legally institutionalized end-state pattern give one? The central core of the notion of a property right in X, relative to which other parts of the notion are to be explained, is the right to determine what shall be done with X; the right to choose which of the constrained set of options concerning X shall be realized or attempted. The constraints are set by other principles or laws operating in the society; in our theory, by the Lockean rights people possess (under the minimal state). My property rights in my knife allow me to leave it where I will, but not in your chest. I may choose which of the acceptable options involving the knife is to be realized. This notion of property helps us to understand why earlier theorists spoke of people as having property in themselves and their labor. They viewed each person as having a right to decide what would become of himself and what he would do, and as having a right to reap the benefits of what he did.

* * *

When end-result principles of distributive justice are built into the legal structure of a society, they (as do most patterned principles) give each citizen an enforceable claim to some portion of the total social product; that is, to some portion of the sum total of the individually and jointly made products. This total product is produced by individuals laboring, using means of production others have saved to bring into existence, by people organizing production or creating means to produce new things or things in a new way. It is on this batch of individual activities that patterned distributional principles give each individual an enforceable claim. Each person has a claim to the activities and the products of other persons, independently of whether the other persons enter into particular relationships that give rise to these claims, and independently of whether they voluntarily take these claims upon themselves, in charity or in exchange for something.

   Whether it is done through taxation on wages or on wages over a certain amount, or through seizure of profits, or through there being a big *social pot* so that it's not clear what's coming from where and what's going where, patterned principles of distributive justice involve appropriating the actions of other persons. Seizing the results of someone's labor is equivalent to seizing hours from him and directing him to carry on various activities. If people force you to do certain work, or unrewarded work, for a certain period of time, they decide what you are to do and what purposes your work is to serve apart from your decisions. This process whereby they take this decision from you makes them a *part-owner* of you; it gives them a property right in you. Just as having such partial control and power of decision, by right, over an animal or inanimate object would be to have a property right in it.

PHYLLIS SCHLAFLY

The Power of the Positive Woman (1977)

The Republican columnist and radio commentator Phyllis Stewart Schlafly (1924–) is an outspoken opponent of the feminist movement and the founder of the conservative profamily organization Eagle Forum. In the 1970s she led the fight against the equal rights amendment because she believed it would destroy families and require unisex public facilities. Schlafly praised the values of motherhood, personal responsibility, and sexual difference in her 1977 book The Power of the Positive Woman, *a biting critique of what she perceived as the negativity and resentment characteristic of the women's liberation movement.*

The cry of "women's liberation" leaps out from the "lifestyle" sections of newspapers and the pages of slick magazines, from radio speakers and television screens. Cut loose from past patterns of behavior and expectations, women of all ages are searching for their identity—the college woman who has new alternatives thrust upon her via "women's studies" courses, the young woman whose routine is shattered by a chance encounter with a "consciousness-raising session," the woman in her middle years who suddenly finds herself in the "empty-nest syndrome," the woman of any age whose lover or lifetime partner departs for greener pastures (and a younger crop).

All of these women, thanks to the women's liberation movement, no longer see their predicament in terms of personal problems to be confronted and solved. They see their own difficulties as a little cog in the big machine of establishment restraints and stereotypical injustice in which they have lost their own equilibrium. Who am I? Why am I here? Why am I just another faceless victim of society's oppression, a nameless prisoner behind walls too high for me to climb alone?

If I were stymied by a slice in my golf drive, I would seek lessons from a pro rather than join the postmortems in the bar at the "nineteenth hole." If I found a lump on my breast, I would run, not walk, to the best available physician, rather than join rap sessions with other women who had recently made similar discoveries. If my business were sliding into bankruptcy, I would ask advice from those whose companies operate in the black rather than in the red.

Likewise, it would seem that, for a woman to find her identity in the modern world, the path should be sought from the Positive Women who have found the road and possess the map, rather than from those who have not. In this spirit, I share with you the thoughts of one who loves life as a woman and lives love as a woman, whose credentials are from the school of practical experience, and who has learned that fulfillment as a woman is a journey, not a destination.

Like every human being born into this world, the Positive Woman has her share of sorrows and sufferings, of unfulfilled desires and bitter defeats. But she will never be crushed by life's disappointments, because her positive mental attitude has built her an inner security that the actions of other people can never fracture. To the Positive Woman, her particular set of problems is not a conspiracy against her, but a challenge to her character and her capabilities.

* * *

The first requirement for the acquisition of power by the Positive Woman is to understand the differences between men and women. Your outlook on life, your faith, your behavior, your potential for fulfillment, all are determined by the parameters of your original premise. The Positive Woman starts with the assumption that the world is her oyster. She rejoices in the creative capability within her body and the power potential of her mind and spirit. She understands that men and women are different, and that those very differences provide the key to her success as a person and fulfillment as a woman.

The women's liberationist, on the other hand, is imprisoned by her own negative view of herself and of her place in the world around her. This view of women was most succinctly expressed in an advertisement designed by the principal women's liberationist organization, the National Organization for Women (NOW), and run in many magazines and newspapers and as spot announcements on many television stations. The advertisement showed a darling curlyheaded girl with the caption: "This healthy, normal baby has a handicap. She was born female."

This is the self-articulated dog-in-the-manger, chip-on-the-shoulder, fundamental dogma of the women's liberation movement. Someone—it is not clear who, perhaps God, perhaps the "Establishment," perhaps a conspiracy of male chauvinist pigs—dealt women a foul blow by making them female. It becomes necessary, therefore, for women to agitate and demonstrate and hurl demands on society in order to wrest from an oppressive male-dominated social structure the status that has been wrongfully denied to women through the centuries.

By its very nature, therefore, the women's liberation movement precipitates a series of conflict situations—in the legislatures, in the courts, in the schools, in industry—with man targeted as the enemy. Confrontation replaces cooperation as the watchword of all relationships. Women and men become adversaries instead of partners.

The second dogma of the women's liberationists is that, of all the injustices perpetrated upon women through the centuries, the most oppressive is the cruel fact that women have babies and men do not. Within the confines of the women's liberationist ideology, therefore, the abolition of this overriding inequality of women becomes the primary goal. This goal must be achieved at any and all costs—to the woman herself, to the baby, to the family, and to society. Women must be made equal to men in their ability *not* to become pregnant and *not* to be expected to care for babies they may bring into the world.

This is why women's liberationists are compulsively involved in the drive to make abortion and child-care centers for all women, regardless of religion or income, both socially acceptable and government-financed. Former Congresswoman Bella Abzug has defined the goal: "to enforce the constitutional right of females to terminate pregnancies that they do not wish to continue."

If man is targeted as the enemy, and the ultimate goal of women's liberation is independence from men and the avoidance of pregnancy and its consequences, then lesbianism is logically the highest form in the ritual of women's liberation. Many, such as Kate Millett, come to this conclusion, although many others do not.

The Positive Woman will never travel that dead-end road. It is self-evident to the Positive Woman that the female body with its baby-producing organs was not designed by a conspiracy of men but by the Divine Architect of the human race. Those who think it is unfair that women have babies, whereas men cannot, will have to take up their complaint with God because no other power is capable of changing that fundamental fact. On some college campuses, I have been assured that other methods of reproduction will be developed. But most of us must deal with the real world rather than with the imagination of dreamers.

Another feature of the woman's natural role is the obvious fact that women can breast-feed babies and men cannot. This functional role was not imposed by conspiratorial males seeking to burden women with confining chores, but must be recognized as part of the plan of the Divine Architect for the survival of the human race through the centuries and in the countries that know no pasteurization of milk or sterilization of bottles.

The Positive Woman looks upon her femaleness and her fertility as part of her purpose, her potential, and her power. She rejoices that she has a capability for creativity that men can never have.

The third basic dogma of the women's liberation movement is that there is no difference between male and female except the sex organs, and that all those physical, cognitive, and emotional differences you *think* are there, are merely the result of centuries of restraints imposed by a male-dominated society and sex-stereotyped schooling. The role imposed on women is, by definition, inferior, according to the women's liberationists.

The Positive Woman knows that, while there are some physical competitions in which women are better (and can command more money) than men, including those that put a premium on grace and beauty, such as figure skating, the superior physical strength of males over females in competitions of strength, speed, and short-term endurance is beyond rational dispute.

* * *

The Positive Woman recognizes the fact that, when it comes to sex, women are simply not the equal of men. The sexual drive of men is much stronger than that of women. That is how the human race was designed in order that it might perpetuate itself. The other side of the coin is that it is easier for women to control their sexual appetites. A Positive Woman cannot defeat a man in a wrestling or boxing match, but she can motivate him, inspire him, encourage him, teach him, restrain him, reward him, and have power over him that he can never achieve over her with all his muscle. How or whether a Positive Woman uses her power is determined solely by the way she alone defines her goals and develops her skills.

The differences between men and women are also emotional and psychological. Without woman's innate maternal instinct, the human race would have died out centuries ago. There is nothing so helpless in all earthly life as the newborn infant. It will die within hours if not cared for. Even in the most primitive, uneducated societies, women have always cared for their newborn babies. They didn't need any schooling to teach them how. They didn't need any welfare workers to tell them it is their social obligation. Even in societies to whom such concepts as "ought," "social responsibility," and "compassion for the helpless" were unknown, mothers cared for their new babies.

Why? Because caring for a baby serves the natural maternal need of a woman. Although not nearly so total as the baby's need, the woman's need is nonetheless real.

The overriding psychological need of a woman is to love something alive. A baby fulfills this need in the lives of most women. If a baby is not available to fill that need, women search for a baby-substitute. This is the reason why women have traditionally gone into teaching and nursing careers. They are doing what comes naturally to the female psyche. The schoolchild or the patient of any age provides an outlet for a woman to express her natural maternal need.

This maternal need in women is the reason why mothers whose children have grown up and flown from the nest are sometimes cut loose from their psychological moorings. The maternal need in women can show itself in love for grandchildren, nieces, nephews, or even neighbors' children. The maternal need in some women has even manifested itself in an extraordinary affection lavished on a dog, a cat, or a parakeet.

This is not to say that every woman must have a baby in order to be fulfilled. But it is to say that fulfillment for most women involves expressing their natural maternal urge by loving and caring for someone.

The women's liberation movement complains that traditional stereotyped roles assume that women are "passive" and that men are "aggressive." The anomaly is that a woman's most fundamental emotional need is not passive at all, but active. A woman naturally seeks to love affirmatively and to show that love in an active way by caring for the object of her affections.

The Positive Woman finds somebody on whom she can lavish her maternal love so that it doesn't well up inside her and cause psychological frustrations. Surely no woman is so isolated by geography or insulated by spirit that she cannot find someone worthy of her maternal love. All persons, men and women, gain by sharing something of themselves with their fellow humans, but women profit most of all because it is part of their very nature.

One of the strangest quirks of women's liberationists is their complaint that societal restraints prevent men from crying in public or showing their emotions, but permit women to do so, and that therefore we should "liberate" men to enable them, too, to cry in public. The public display of fear, sorrow, anger, and irritation reveals a lack of self-discipline that should be avoided by the Positive Woman just as much as by the Positive Man. Maternal love, however, is not a weakness but a manifestation of strength and, service, and it should be nurtured by the Positive Woman.

* * *

Finally, women are different from men in dealing with the fundamentals of life itself. Men are philosophers, women are practical, and 'twas ever thus. Men may philosophize about how life began and where we are heading; women are concerned about feeding the kids today. No woman would ever, as Karl Marx did, spend years reading political philosophy in the British Museum while her child starved to death. Women don't take naturally to a search for the intangible and the abstract. The Positive Woman knows who she is and where she is going, and she will reach her goal because the longest journey starts with a very practical first step.

MILTON FRIEDMAN AND ROSE D. FRIEDMAN

Free to Choose (1980)

The free-market economist and 1976 Nobel Prize winner in economics Milton Friedman (1912–2006) was the Paul Snowden Russell Distinguished Service Professor of Economics at the University of Chicago. There he led the Chicago School of Economics, which stresses the role of the government's monetary policy in the business cycle. Friedman was a member of various governmental advisory commissions on economics. With his wife, Rose (1911–), who served on the staffs of several governmental boards, he coauthored numerous books on the importance of preserving individual freedom in public policy. In Free to Choose, a book that accompanied a ten-part television series of the same name on PBS, the couple argued that government should limit itself to the minimal role of umpire in the economy because "economic freedom is an essential requisite for political freedom."

The story of the United States is the story of an economic miracle and a political miracle that was made possible by the translation into practice of two sets of ideas—both, by a curious coincidence, formulated in documents published in the same year, 1776.

One set of ideas was embodied in *The Wealth of Nations*, the masterpiece that established the Scotsman Adam Smith as the father of modern economics. It analyzed the way in which a market system could combine the freedom of individuals to pursue their own objectives with the extensive cooperation and collaboration needed in the economic field to produce our food, our clothing, our housing. Adam Smith's key insight was that both parties to an exchange can benefit and that, *so long as cooperation is strictly voluntary*, no exchange will take place unless both parties do benefit. No external force, no coercion, no violation of freedom is necessary to produce cooperation among individuals all of whom can benefit. That is why, as Adam Smith put it, an individual who "intends only his own gain" is "led by an invisible hand to promote an end which was no part of his intention. Nor is it always the worse for the society that it was no part of it. By pursuing his own interest he frequently promotes that of the society more effectually than when he really intends to promote it. I have never known much good done by those who affected to trade for the public good."

The second set of ideas was embodied in the Declaration of Independence, drafted by Thomas Jefferson to express the general sense of his fellow countrymen. It proclaimed a new nation, the first in history established on the principle that every person is entitled to pursue his own values: "We hold these truths to be self-evident, that all men are created equal, that they are endowed by their Creator with certain unalienable Rights; that among these are Life, Liberty, and the pursuit of Happiness."

Or, as stated in more extreme and unqualified form nearly a century later by John Stuart Mill,

The sole end for which mankind are warranted, individually or collectively, in interfering with the liberty of action of any of their number, is self protection. . . . [T]he only purpose for which power can be rightfully exercised over any member of a civilized community, against his will, is to prevent harm to others. His own good, either physical or moral, is not a sufficient warrant. . . . The only part of the conduct of any one, for which he is amenable to society, is that which concerns others. In the part which merely concerns himself, his independence is, of right, absolute. Over himself, over his own body and mind, the individual is sovereign.

Much of the history of the United States revolves about the attempt to translate the principles of the Declaration of Independence into practice—from the struggle over slavery, finally settled by a bloody civil war, to the subsequent attempt to promote equality of opportunity, to the more recent attempt to achieve equality of results.

Economic freedom is an essential requisite for political freedom. By enabling people to cooperate with one another without coercion or central direction, it reduces the area over which political power is exercised. In addition, by dispersing power, the free market provides an offset to whatever concentration of political power may arise. The combination of economic and political *power* in the same hands is a sure recipe for tyranny.

The combination of economic and political *freedom* produced a golden age in both Great Britain and the United States in the nineteenth century. The United States prospered even more than Britain. It started with a clean slate: fewer vestiges of class and status; fewer government restraints; a more fertile field for energy, drive, and innovation; and an empty continent to conquer.

The fecundity of freedom is demonstrated most dramatically and clearly in agriculture. When the Declaration of Independence was enacted, fewer than 3 million persons of European and African origin (i.e., omitting the native Indians) occupied a narrow fringe along the eastern coast. Agriculture was the main economic activity. It took nineteen out of twenty workers to feed the country's inhabitants and provide a surplus for export in exchange for foreign goods. Today it takes fewer than one out of twenty workers to feed the 220 million inhabitants and provide a surplus that makes the United States the largest single exporter of food in the world.

* * *

Smith and Jefferson alike had seen concentrated government power as a great danger to the ordinary man; they saw the protection of the citizen against the tyranny of government as the perpetual need. That was the aim of the Virginia Declaration of Rights (1776) and the United States Bill of Rights (1791); the purpose of the separation of powers in the U.S. Constitution; the moving force behind the changes in the British legal structure from the issuance of the Magna Carta in the thirteenth century to the end of the nineteenth century. To Smith and Jefferson, government's role was as an umpire, not a participant. Jefferson's Ideal, as he expressed it in his first inaugural address (1801), was "[a] wise and frugal government, which shall restrain men from injuring one another, which shall leave them otherwise free to regulate their own pursuits of industry and improvement."

Ironically, the very success of economic and political freedom reduced its appeal to later thinkers. The narrowly limited government of the late nineteenth century possessed little concentrated power that endangered the ordinary man. The other side of that coin was that it possessed little power that would enable good people to do good. And in an imperfect world there were still many evils. Indeed, the very progress of society made the residual evils seem all the more objectionable. As always, people took the favorable developments for granted. They forgot the danger to freedom from a strong government. Instead, they were attracted by the good that a stronger government could achieve—if only government power were in the "right" hands.

These ideas began to influence government policy in Great Britain by the beginning of the twentieth century. They gained increasing acceptance among intellectuals in the United States but had little effect on government policy until the Great Depression of the early 1930s. * * *

[T]he depression was produced by a failure of government in one area—money—where it had exercised authority ever since the beginning of the Republic. However, government's responsibility for the depression was not recognized—either then or now. Instead, the depression was widely interpreted as a failure of free market capitalism. That myth led the public to join the intellectuals in a changed view of the relative responsibilities of individuals and government. Emphasis on the responsibility of the individual for his own fate was replaced by emphasis on the individual as a pawn buffeted by forces beyond his control. The view that government's role is to serve as an umpire to prevent individuals from coercing one another was replaced by the view that government's role is to serve as a parent charged with the duty of coercing some to aid others.

These views have dominated developments in the United States during the past half-century. They have led to a growth in government at all levels, as well as to a transfer of power from local government and local control to central government and central control. The government has increasingly undertaken the task of taking from some to give to others in the name of security and equality. One government policy after another has been set up to "regulate" our "pursuits of industry and improvement," standing Jefferson's dictum on its head * * * .

These developments have been produced by good intentions with a major assist from self-interest. Even the strongest supporters of the welfare and paternal state agree that the results have been disappointing. In the government sphere, as in the market, there seems to be an invisible hand, but it operates in precisely the opposite direction from Adam Smith's: an individual who intends only to serve the public interest by fostering government intervention is "led by an invisible hand to promote" private interests, "which was no part of his intention." * * *

So far, in Adam Smith's words, "the uniform, constant, and uninterrupted effort of every man to better his condition, the principle from which public and national, as well as private opulence is originally derived," has been "powerful enough to maintain the natural progress of things toward improvement, in spite both of the extravagance of governments and of the greatest errors of administration. Like the unknown principle of animal life, it frequently restores health and vigour to the constitution, in spite, not only of the disease, but of the absurd prescriptions of the doctor." So far, that is, Adam Smith's invisible hand has been powerful enough to overcome the deadening effects of the invisible hand that operates in the political sphere.

The experience of recent years—slowing growth and declining productivity—raises a doubt whether private ingenuity can continue to overcome the deadening effects of government control if we continue to grant ever more power to government, to authorize a "new class" of civil servants to spend ever larger fractions of our income supposedly on our behalf. Sooner or later—and perhaps sooner than many of us expect—an ever bigger government would destroy both the prosperity that we owe to the free market and the human freedom proclaimed so eloquently in the Declaration of Independence.

We have not yet reached the point of no return. We are still free as a people to choose whether we shall continue speeding down the "road to serfdom," as Friedrich Hayek entitled his profound and influential book, or whether we shall set tighter limits on government and rely more heavily on voluntary cooperation among free individuals to achieve our several objectives. Will our golden age come to an end in a relapse into the tyranny and misery that has always been, and remains today, the state of most of mankind? Or shall we have the wisdom, the foresight, and the courage to change our course, to learn from experience, and to benefit from a "rebirth of freedom"?

* * *

Fortunately, the tide is turning. In the United States, in Great Britain, the countries of Western Europe, and in many other countries around the world, there is growing recognition of the dangers of big government, growing dissatisfaction with the policies that have been followed. This shift is being reflected not only in opinion, but also in the political sphere. It is becoming politically profitable for our representatives to sing a different tune—and perhaps even to act differently. We are experiencing another major change in public opinion. We have the opportunity to nudge the change in opinion toward greater reliance on individual initiative and voluntary cooperation, rather than toward the other extreme of total collectivism.

* * *

Every day each of us uses innumerable goods and services—to eat, to wear, to shelter us from the elements, or simply to enjoy. We take it for granted that they will be available when we want to buy them. We never stop to think how many people have played a part in one way or another in providing those goods and services. We never ask ourselves how it is that the corner grocery store—or nowadays, supermarket—has the items on its shelves that we want to buy, how it is that most of us are able to earn the money to buy those goods.

It is natural to assume that someone must give orders to make sure that the "right" products are produced in the "right" amounts and available at the "right" places. That is one method of coordinating the activities of a large number of people—the method of the army. The general gives orders to the colonel, the colonel to the major, the major to the lieu-tenant, the lieutenant to the sergeant, and the sergeant to the private.

But that command method can be the exclusive or even principal method of organization only in a very small group. Not even the most au-tocratic head of a family can control every act of other family members entirely by order. No sizable army can really be run entirely by command. The general cannot conceivably have the information necessary to direct every movement of the lowliest private. At every step in the chain of com-mand, the soldier, whether officer or private, must have discretion to take into account information about specific circumstances that his command-ing officer could not have. Commands must be supplemented by voluntary cooperation—a less obvious and more subtle, but far more fundamental, technique of coordinating the activities of large numbers of people.

Russia is the standard example of a large economy that is supposed to be organized by command—a centrally planned economy. But that is more fiction than fact. At every level of the economy, voluntary coopera-tion enters to supplement central planning or to offset its rigidities—sometimes legally, sometimes illegally.

In agriculture, full-time workers on government farms are permitted to grow food and raise animals on small private plots in their spare time for their own use or to sell in relatively free markets. These plots account for less than 1 percent of the agricultural land in the country, yet they are said to provide nearly a third of total farm output in the Soviet Union (are "said to" because it is likely that some products of government farms are clan-destinely marketed as if from private plots).

In the labor market individuals are seldom ordered to work at specific jobs; there is little actual direction of labor in this sense. Rather, wages are offered for various jobs, and individuals apply for them—much as in capitalist countries. Once hired, they may subsequently be fired or may leave for jobs they prefer. Numerous restrictions affect who may work where, and, of course, the laws prohibit anyone from setting up as an employer—although numerous clandestine workshops serve the extensive black market. Allocation of workers on a large scale primarily by compul-sion is just not feasible; and neither, apparently, is complete suppression of private entrepreneurial activity.

The attractiveness of different jobs in the Soviet Union often depends on the opportunities they offer for extralegal or illegal moonlighting. A resident of Moscow whose household equipment fails may have to wait months to have it repaired if he calls the state repair office. Instead, he may hire a moonlighter—very likely someone who works for the state re-pair office. The householder gets his equipment repaired promptly; the moonlighter gets some extra income. Both are happy.

These voluntary market elements flourish despite their inconsistency with official Marxist ideology because the cost of eliminating them would be too high. Private plots could be forbidden—but the famines of the 1930s are a stark reminder of the cost. The Soviet economy is hardly a model of efficiency now. Without the voluntary elements it would operate at an even lower level of effectiveness. Recent experience in Cambodia tragically illustrates the cost of trying to do without the market entirely.

Just as no society operates entirely on the command principle, so none operates entirely through voluntary cooperation. Every society has some command elements. These take many forms. They may be as straightforward as military conscription or forbidding the purchase and sale of heroin or cyclamates or court orders to named defendants to desist from or perform specified actions. Or, at the other extreme, they may be as subtle as imposing a heavy tax on cigarettes to discourage smoking—a hint, if not a command, by some of us to others of us.

It makes a vast difference what the mix is—whether voluntary exchange is primarily a clandestine activity that flourishes because of the rigidities of a dominant command element, or whether voluntary exchange is the dominant principle of organization, supplemented to a smaller or larger extent by command elements. Clandestine voluntary exchange may prevent a command economy from collapsing, may enable it to creak along and even achieve some progress. It can do little to undermine the tyranny on which a predominantly command economy rests. A predominantly voluntary exchange economy, on the other hand, has within it the potential to promote both prosperity and human freedom. It may not achieve its potential in either respect, but we know of no society that has ever achieved prosperity and freedom unless voluntary exchange has been its dominant principle of organization. We hasten to add that voluntary exchange is not a sufficient condition for prosperity and freedom. That, at least, is the lesson of history to date. Many societies organized predominantly by voluntary exchange have not achieved either prosperity or freedom, though they have achieved a far greater measure of both than authoritarian societies. But voluntary exchange is a necessary condition for both prosperity and freedom. * * *

* * *

The key insight of Adam Smith's *Wealth of Nations* is misleadingly simple: if an exchange between two parties is voluntary, it will not take place unless both believe they will benefit from it. Most economic fallacies derive from the neglect of this simple insight, from the tendency to assume that there is a fixed pie, that one party can gain only at the expense of another.

This key insight is obvious for a simple exchange between two individuals. It is far more difficult to understand how it can enable people living all over the world to cooperate to promote their separate interests.

The price system is the mechanism that performs this task without central direction, without requiring people to speak to one another or to like one another. When you buy your pencil or your daily bread, you don't know whether the pencil was made or the wheat was grown by a white man or a black man, by a Chinese or an Indian. As a result, the price system enables people to cooperate peacefully in one phase of their life while each one goes about his own business in respect of everything else.

Adam Smith's flash of genius was his recognition that the prices that emerged from voluntary transactions between buyers and sellers—for short, in a free market—could coordinate the activity of millions of people, each seeking his own interest, in such a way as to make everyone better off. It was a startling idea then, and it remains one today, that economic order can emerge as the unintended consequence of the actions of many people, each seeking his own interest. * * *

* * *

Where does government enter into the picture? To some extent government is a form of voluntary cooperation, a way in which people choose to achieve some of their objectives through governmental entities because they believe that is the most effective means of achieving them.

The clearest example is local government under conditions where people are free to choose where to live. You may decide to live in one community rather than another partly on the basis of the kind of services its government offers. If it engages in activities you object to or are unwilling to pay for, and these more than balance the activities you favor and are willing to pay for, you can vote with your feet by moving elsewhere. There is competition, limited but real, so long as there are available alternatives.

But government is more than that. It is also the agency that is widely regarded as having a monopoly on the legitimate use of force or the threat of force as the means through which some of us can legitimately impose restraints through force upon others of us. The role of government in that more basic sense has changed drastically over time in most societies and has differed widely among societies at any given time. Much of the rest of this book deals with how its role has changed in the United States in recent decades, and what the effects of its activities have been.

In this initial sketch we want to consider a very different question. In a society whose participants desire to achieve the greatest possible freedom to choose as individuals, as families, as members of voluntary groups, as citizens of an organized government, what role should be assigned to government?

It is not easy to improve on the answer that Adam Smith gave to this question two hundred years ago:

> All systems either of preference or of restraint, therefore, being thus completely taken away, the obvious and simple system of natural liberty establishes itself of its own accord. Every man, as long as he does not violate the laws of justice, is left perfectly free to pursue his own interest his own way, and to bring both his industry and capital into competition with those of any other man, or order of men. The sovereign is completely discharged from a duty, in the attempting to perform which he must always be exposed to innumerable delusions, and for the proper performance of which no human wisdom or knowledge could ever be sufficient; the duty of superintending the industry of private people, and of directing it towards the employments most suitable to the interest of the society. According to the system of natural liberty, the sovereign has only three duties to attend to; three duties of great importance, indeed, but plain and intelligible to common understandings: first, the duty of protecting the society from the violence and invasion of other independent societies; secondly, the duty of protecting, as far as possible, every member of the society from the injustice or oppression of every other member of it, or the duty of establishing an exact administration of justice; and, thirdly, the duty of erecting and maintaining certain public works and certain public institutions, which it can never be for the interest of any individual, or small number of individuals, to erect and maintain; because the profit could never repay the expence to any individual or small number of individuals, though it may frequently do much more than repay it to a great society.

The first two duties are clear and straightforward: the protection of individuals in the society from coercion whether it comes from outside or from their fellow citizens. Unless there is such protection, we are not really free to choose. The armed robber's "Your money or your life" offers me a choice, but no one would describe it as a free choice or the subsequent exchange as voluntary.

Of course, as we shall see repeatedly throughout this book, it is one thing to state the purpose that an institution, particularly a governmental institution, "ought" to serve; it is quite another to describe the purposes the institution actually serves. The intentions of the persons responsible for setting up the institution and of the persons who operate it often differ sharply. Equally important, the results achieved often differ widely from those intended.

Military and police forces are required to prevent coercion from without and within. They do not always succeed and the power they possess is sometimes used for very different purposes. A major problem in achieving and preserving a free society is precisely how to assure that coercive powers granted to government in order to preserve freedom are limited to that function and are kept from becoming a threat to freedom. The founders of our country wrestled with that problem in drawing up the Constitution. We have tended to neglect it.

Adam Smith's second duty goes beyond the narrow police function of protecting people from physical coercion; it includes "an exact administration of justice." No voluntary exchange that is at all complicated or extends over any considerable period of time can be free from ambiguity. There is not enough fine print in the world to specify in advance every contingency that might arise and to describe precisely the obligations of the various parties to the exchange in each case. There must be some way to mediate disputes. Such mediation itself can be voluntary and need not involve government. In the United States today, most disagreements that arise in connection with commercial contracts are settled by resort to private arbitrators chosen by a procedure specified in advance. In response to this demand an extensive private judicial system has grown up. But the court of last resort is provided by the governmental judicial system.

This role of government also includes facilitating voluntary exchanges by adopting general rules—the rules of the economic and social game that the citizens of a free society play. The most obvious example is the meaning to be attached to private property. I own a house. Are you "trespassing" on my private property if you fly your private airplane ten feet over my roof? One thousand feet? Thirty thousand feet? There is nothing "natural" about where my property rights end and yours begin. The major way that society has come to agree on the rules of property is through the growth of common law, though more recently legislation has played an increasing role.

Adam Smith's third duty raises the most troublesome issues. He himself regarded it as having a narrow application. It has since been used to justify an extremely wide range of government activities. In our view it describes a valid duty of a government directed to preserving and strengthening a free society; but it can also be interpreted to justify unlimited extensions of government power.

The valid element arises because of the cost of producing some goods or services through strictly voluntary exchanges. To take one simple example suggested directly by Smith's description of the third duty: city streets and general-access highways could be provided by private voluntary exchange, the costs being paid for by charging tolls. But the costs of collecting the tolls would often be very large compared to the cost of building and maintaining the streets or highways. This is a "public work" that it might not "be for the interest of any individual . . . to erect and maintain . . . though it" might be worthwhile for "a great society."

A more subtle example involves effects on "third parties," people who are not parties to the particular exchange—the classic "smoke nuisance" case. Your furnace pours forth sooty smoke that dirties a third party's shirt collar. You have unintentionally imposed costs on a third party. He would be willing to let you dirty his collar for a price—but it is simply not feasible for you to identify all of the people whom you affect or for them to discover who has dirtied their collars and to require you to indemnify them individually or reach individual agreements with them.

The effect of your actions on third parties may be to confer benefits rather than impose costs. You landscape your house beautifully, and all passersby enjoy the sight. They would be willing to pay something for the privilege but it is not feasible to charge them for looking at your lovely flowers.

To lapse into technical jargon, there is a "market failure" because of "external" or "neighborhood" effects for which it is not feasible (i.e., would cost too much) to compensate or charge the people affected; third parties have had involuntary exchanges imposed on them.

Almost everything we do has some third-party effects, however small and however remote. In consequence, Adam Smith's third duty may at first blush appear to justify almost any proposed government measure. But there is a fallacy. Government measures also have third-party effects. "Government failure" no less than "market failure" arises from "external" or "neighborhood" effects. And if such effects are important for a market transaction, they are likely also to be important for government measures intended to correct the "market failure." The primary source of significant third-party effects of private actions is the difficulty of identifying the external costs or benefits. When it is easy to identify who is hurt or who is benefited, and by how much, it is fairly straightforward to replace involuntary by voluntary exchange, or at least to require individual compensation. If your car hits someone else's because of your negligence, you can be made to pay him for damages even though the exchange was involuntary. If it were easy to know whose collars were going to be dirtied, it would be possible for you to compensate the people affected, or alternatively, for them to pay you to pour out less smoke.

If it is difficult for private parties to identify who imposes costs or benefits on whom, it is difficult for government to do so. As a result a government attempt to rectify the situation may very well end up making matters worse rather than better—imposing costs on innocent third parties or conferring benefits on lucky bystanders. To finance its activities it must collect taxes, which themselves affect what the taxpayers do—still another third-party effect. In addition, every accretion of government power for whatever purpose increases the danger that government, instead of serving the great majority of its citizens, will become a means whereby some of its citizens can take advantage of others. Every government measure bears, as it were, a smokestack on its back.

Voluntary arrangements can allow for third-party effects to a much greater extent than may at first appear. To take a trivial example, tipping at restaurants is a social custom that leads you to assure better service for people you may not know or ever meet and, in return, be assured better service by the actions of still another group of anonymous third parties. Nonetheless, third-party effects of private actions do occur that are sufficiently important to justify government action. The lesson to be drawn from the misuse of Smith's third duty is not that government intervention is never justified, but rather that the burden of proof should be on its proponents. We should develop the practice of examining both the benefits and the costs of proposed government interventions and require a very clear balance of benefits over costs before adopting them. This course of action is recommended not only by the difficulty of assessing the hidden costs of government intervention but also by another consideration. Experience shows that once government undertakes an activity, it is seldom terminated. The activity may not live up to expectation but that is more likely to lead to its expansion, to its being granted a larger budget, than to its curtailment or abolition.

A fourth duty of government that Adam Smith did not explicitly mention is the duty to protect members of the community who cannot be regarded as "responsible" individuals. Like Adam Smith's third duty, this one, too, is susceptible of great abuse. Yet it cannot be avoided.

Freedom is a tenable objective only for responsible individuals. We do not believe in freedom for madmen or children. We must somehow draw a line between responsible individuals and others, yet doing so introduces a fundamental ambiguity into our ultimate objective of freedom. We cannot categorically reject paternalism for those whom we consider as not responsible.

For children we assign responsibility in the first instance to parents. The family, rather than the individual, has always been and remains today the basic building block of our society, though its hold has clearly been weakening—one of the most unfortunate consequences of the growth of government paternalism. Yet the assignment of responsibility for children to their parents is largely a matter of expediency rather than principle. We believe, and with good reason, that parents have more interest in their children than anyone else and can be relied on to protect them and to assure their development into responsible adults. However, we do not believe in the right of the parents to do whatever they will with their children—to beat them, murder them, or sell them into slavery. Children are responsible individuals in embryo. They have ultimate rights of their own and are not simply the playthings of their parents.

Adam Smith's three duties, or our four duties of government, are indeed "of great importance," but they are far less "plain and intelligible to common understandings" than he supposed. Though we cannot decide the desirability or undesirability of any actual or proposed government intervention by mechanical reference to one or another of them, they provide a set of principles that we can use in casting up a balance sheet of pros and cons. Even on the loosest interpretation, they rule out much existing government intervention—all those "systems either of preference or of restraint" that Adam Smith fought against, that were subsequently destroyed, but have since reappeared in the form of today's tariffs, governmentally fixed prices and wages, restrictions on entry into various occupations, and numerous other departures from his "simple system of natural liberty." * * *

In today's world big government seems pervasive. We may well ask whether there exist any contemporaneous examples of societies that rely primarily on voluntary exchange through the market to organize their economic activity and in which government is limited to our four duties.

Perhaps the best example is Hong Kong—a speck of land next to mainland China containing less than 400 square miles with a population of roughly 4.5 million people. The density of population is almost unbelievable—14 times as many people per square mile as in Japan, 185 times as many as in the United States. Yet they enjoy one of the highest standards of living in all of Asia—second only to Japan and perhaps Singapore.

Hong Kong has no tariffs or other restraints on international trade (except for a few "voluntary" restraints imposed by the United States and some other major countries). It has no government direction of economic activity, no minimum wage laws, no fixing of prices. The residents are free to buy from whom they want, to sell to whom they want, to invest however they want, to hire whom they want, to work for whom they want.

Government plays an important role that is limited primarily to our four duties interpreted rather narrowly. It enforces law and order, provides a means for formulating the rules of conduct, adjudicates disputes, facilitates transportation and communication, and supervises the issuance of currency. It has provided public housing for arriving refugees from China. Though government spending has grown as the economy has grown, it remains among the lowest in the world as a fraction of the income of the people. As a result, low taxes preserve incentives. Businessmen can reap the benefits of their success but must also bear the costs of their mistakes.

It is somewhat ironic that Hong Kong, a Crown colony of Great Britain, should be the modern exemplar of free markets and limited government. The British officials who govern it have enabled Hong Kong to flourish by following policies radically at variance with the welfare state policies that have been adopted by the mother country.

Though Hong Kong is an excellent current example, it is by no means the most important example of limited government and free market societies in practice. For this we must go back in time to the nineteenth century. * * *

Two other examples are Great Britain and the United States. Adam Smith's *Wealth of Nations* was one of the early blows in the battle to end government restrictions on industry and trade. The final victory in that battle came seventy years later, in 1846, with the repeal of the so-called Corn Laws—laws that imposed tariffs and other restrictions on the importation of wheat and other grains, referred to collectively as "corn." That ushered in three-quarters of a century of complete free trade lasting until the outbreak of World War I and completed a transition that had begun decades earlier to a highly limited government, one that left every resident of Britain, in Adam Smith's words quoted earlier, "perfectly free to pursue his own interest his own way, and to bring both his industry and capital into competition with those of any other man, or order of men."

Economic growth was rapid. The standard of life of the ordinary citizen improved dramatically—making all the more visible the remaining areas of poverty and misery portrayed so movingly by Dickens and other contemporary novelists. Population increased along with the standard of life. Britain grew in power and influence around the world. All this while government spending fell as a fraction of national income—from close to one-quarter of the national income early in the nineteenth century to about one-tenth of national income at the time of Queen Victoria's Jubilee in 1897, when Britain was at the very apex of its power and glory.

The United States is another striking example. There were tariffs, justified by Alexander Hamilton in his famous *Report on Manufactures* in which he attempted—with a decided lack of success—to refute Adam Smith's arguments in favor of free trade. But they were modest, by modern standards, and few other government restrictions impeded free trade at home or abroad. Until after World War I immigration was almost completely free (there were restrictions on immigration from the Orient). As the Statue of Liberty inscription has it:

> Give me your tired, your poor,
> Your huddled masses yearning to breathe free,
> The wretched refuse of your teeming shore.
> Send these, the homeless, tempest-tossed to me:
> I lift my lamp beside the golden door.

They came by the millions, and by the millions they were absorbed. They prospered because they were left to their own devices.

A myth has grown up about the United States that paints the nineteenth century as the era of the robber baron, of rugged, unrestrained individualism. Heartless monopoly capitalists allegedly exploited the poor, encouraged immigration, and then fleeced the immigrants unmercifully. Wall Street is pictured as conning Main Street, as bleeding the sturdy farmers in the Middle West, who survived despite the widespread distress and misery inflicted on them.

The reality was very different. Immigrants kept coming. The early ones might have been fooled, but it is inconceivable that millions kept coming to the United States decade after decade to be exploited. They came because the hopes of those who had preceded them were largely realized. The streets of New York were not paved with gold, but hard work, thrift, and enterprise brought rewards that were not even imaginable in the Old World. The newcomers spread from east to west. As they spread, cities sprang up, ever more land was brought into cultivation. The country grew more prosperous and more productive, and the immigrants shared in the prosperity.

If farmers were exploited, why did their number increase? The prices of farm products did decline. But that was a sign of success, not of failure, reflecting the development of machinery, the bringing under cultivation of more land, and improvements in communication, all of which led to a rapid growth in farm output. The final proof is that the price of farmland rose steadily—hardly a sign that farming was a depressed industry!

The charge of heartlessness, epitomized in the remark that William H. Vanderbilt, a railroad tycoon, is said to have made to an inquiring reporter, "The public be damned," is belied by the flowering of charitable activity in the United States in the nineteenth century. Privately financed schools and colleges multiplied; foreign missionary activity exploded; nonprofit private hospitals, orphanages, and numerous other institutions sprang up like weeds. Almost every charitable or public service organization, from the Society for the Prevention of Cruelty to Animals to the

YMCA and YWCA, from the Indian Rights Association to the Salvation Army, dates from that period. Voluntary cooperation is no less effective in organizing charitable activity than in organizing production for profit.

The charitable activity was matched by a burst of cultural activity—art museums, opera houses, symphonies, museums, public libraries arose in big cities and frontier towns alike.

The size of government spending is one measure of government's role. Major wars aside, government spending from 1800 to 1929 did not exceed about 12 percent of the national income. Two-thirds of that was spent by state and local governments, mostly for schools and roads. As late as 1928, federal government spending amounted to about 3 percent of the national income.

The success of the United States is often attributed to its generous natural resources and wide open spaces. They certainly played a part—but then, if they were crucial, what explains the success of nineteenth-century Great Britain and Japan or twentieth-century Hong Kong?

It is often maintained that while a let-alone, limited government policy was feasible in sparsely settled nineteenth-century America, government must play a far larger, indeed dominant, role in a modern urbanized and industrial society. One hour in Hong Kong will dispose of that view.

Our society is what we make it. We can shape our institutions. Physical and human characteristics limit the alternatives available to us. But none prevents us, if we will, from building a society that relies primarily on voluntary cooperation to organize both economic and other activity, a society that preserves and expands human freedom, that keeps government in its place, keeping it our servant and not letting it become our master.

BELL HOOKS

Feminist Theory from Margin to Center (1984)

Born Gloria Watkins, bell hooks (1952–) is a leading black feminist professor who teaches English at the City College of New York. (She uses lower-case letters in her name to draw attention away from herself as author and toward her text, which she considers far more important.) Dedicated to ending what she calls "white supremacist capitalist patriarchy," hooks has explored the complex interconnections among class, race, and gender in a broad range of scholarly

works that draw connections between popular culture and theory. In
this excerpt from her second book, hooks argues that a "mass-based
feminist movement" is necessary to combat sexism and other systemic
forms of oppression.

Contemporary feminist movement in the United States called attention to the exploitation and oppression of women globally. This was
a major contribution to feminist struggle. In their eagerness to highlight
sexist injustice, women focused almost exclusively on the ideology and
practice of male domination. Unfortunately, this made it appear that
feminism was more a declaration of war between the sexes than a political struggle to end sexist oppression, a struggle that would imply change
on the part of women and men. Underlying much white women's liberationist rhetoric was the implication that men had nothing to gain by feminist movement, that its success would make them losers. Militant white
women were particularly eager to make feminist movement privilege
women over men. Their anger, hostility, and rage was so intense that they
were unable to resist turning the movement into a public forum for their
attacks. Although they sometimes considered themselves "radical feminists," their responses were reactionary. Fundamentally, they argued *that*
all men are the enemies of all women and proposed as solutions to this
problem a utopian woman nation, separatist communities, and even the
subjugation or extermination of all men. Their anger may have been a
catalyst for individual liberatory resistance and change. It may have encouraged bonding with other women to raise consciousness. It did not
strengthen public understanding of the significance of authentic feminist
movement.

Sexist discrimination, exploitation, and oppression have created the
war between the sexes. Traditionally the battleground has been the
home. In recent years, the battle ensues in any sphere, public or private,
inhabited by women and men, girls and boys. The significance of feminist movement (when it is not co-opted by opportunistic, reactionary
forces) is that it offers a new ideological meeting ground for the sexes, a
space for criticism, struggle, and transformation. Feminist movement
can end the war between the sexes. It can transform relationships so
that the alienation, competition, and dehumanization that characterize
human interaction can be replaced with feelings of intimacy, mutuality,
and camaraderie.

Ironically, these positive implications of feminist movement were often ignored by liberal organizers and participants. Since vocal bourgeois
white women were insisting that women repudiate the role of servant to
others, they were not interested in convincing men or even other women

that feminist movement was important for everyone. Narcissistically, they focused solely on the primacy of feminism in their lives, universalizing their own experiences. Building a mass-based women's movement was never the central issue on their agenda. After many organizations were established, leaders expressed a desire for greater participant diversity; they wanted women to join who were not white, materially privileged, middle class, or college-educated. It was never deemed necessary for feminist activists to explain to masses of women the significance of feminist movement. Believing their emphasis on social equality was a universal concern, they assumed the idea would carry its own appeal. Strategically the failure to emphasize the necessity for mass-based movement, grassroots organizing, and sharing with everyone the positive significance of feminist movement helped marginalize feminism by making it appear relevant only to those women who joined organizations.

* * *

Many contemporary feminist activists argue that eradicating sexist oppression is important because it is the primary contradiction, the basis of all other oppressions. Racism as well as class structure is perceived as stemming from sexism. Implicit in this line of analysis is the assumption that the eradication of sexism, "the oldest oppression," "the primary contradiction," is necessary before attention can be focused on racism or classism. Suggesting a hierarchy of oppression exists, with sexism in first place, evokes a sense of competing concerns that is unnecessary. While we know that sex role divisions existed in the earliest civilizations, not enough is known about these societies to conclusively document the assertion that women were exploited or oppressed. The earliest civilizations discovered so far have been in archaic black Africa where presumably there was no race problem and no class society as we know it today. The sexism, racism, and classism that exist in the West may resemble systems of domination globally but they are forms of oppression which have been primarily informed by Western philosophy. They can be best understood within a Western context, not via an evolutionary model of human development. Within our society, all forms of oppression are supported by traditional Western thinking. The primary contradiction in Western cultural thought is the belief that the superior should control the inferior. * * *

Sexist oppression is of primary importance not because it is the basis of all other oppression, but because it is the practice of domination most people experience, whether their role be that of discriminator or discriminated against, exploiter or exploited. It is the practice of domination most people are socialized to accept before they even know that other forms of group oppression exist. This does not mean that eradicating sexist oppression would eliminate other forms of oppression. Since all forms of oppression are linked in our society because they are supported by similar institutional and social structures, one system cannot be eradicated while the others remain intact. Challenging sexist oppression is a crucial step in the struggle to eliminate all forms of oppression.

* * *

Contemporary feminist analyses of family often implied that successful feminist movement would either begin with or lead to the abolition of family. This suggestion was terribly threatening to many women, especially non-white women. While there are white women activists who may experience family primarily as an oppressive institution, (it may be the social structure wherein they have experienced grave abuse and exploitation) many black women find the family the least oppressive institution. Despite sexism in the context of family, we may experience dignity, self-worth, and a humanization that is not experienced in the outside world wherein we confront all forms of oppression. We know from our lived experiences that families are not just households composed of husband, wife, and children or even blood relations; we also know that destructive patterns generated by belief in sexism abound in varied family structures. We wish to affirm the primacy of family life because we know that family ties are the only sustained support system for exploited and oppressed peoples. We wish to rid family life of the abusive dimensions created by sexist oppression without devaluing it.

Devaluation of family life in feminist discussion often reflects the class nature of the movement. Individuals from privileged classes rely on a number of institutional and social structures to affirm and protect their interests. The bourgeois woman can repudiate family without believing that by so doing she relinquishes the possibility of relationship, care, protection. If all else fails, she can buy care. Since many bourgeois women active in feminist movement were raised in the modern nuclear household, they were particularly subjected to the perversion of family life created by sexist oppression; they may have had material privilege and no experience of abiding family love and care. Their devaluation of family life alienated many women from feminist movement. Ironically, feminism is the one radical political movement that focuses on transforming family relationships. Feminist movement to end sexist oppression affirms family life by its insistence that the purpose of family structure is not to reinforce patterns of domination in the interest of the state. By challenging Western philosophical beliefs that impress on our consciousness a concept of family life that is essentially destructive, feminism would liberate family so that it could be an affirming, positive kinship structure with no oppressive dimensions based on sex differentiation, sexual preference, etc.

* * *

An important stage in the development of political consciousness is reached when individuals recognize the need to struggle against all forms of oppression. The fight against sexist oppression is of grave political significance—it is not for women only. Feminist movement is vital both in its power to liberate us from the terrible bonds of sexist oppression and in its potential to radicalize and renew other liberation struggles.

* * *

Today hardly anyone speaks of feminist revolution. Thinking that revolution would happen simply and quickly, militant feminist activists felt that the great surges of activity—protest, organizing, and consciousness-raising—which characterized the early contemporary feminist movement were all it would take to establish a new social order. Although feminist radicals have always recognized that society must be transformed if sexist oppression is to be eliminated, feminist successes have been mainly in the area of reforms (this is due primarily to the efforts and visions of radical groups like Bread and Roses and the Combahee River Collective, etc.). Such reforms have helped many women make significant strides towards social equality with men in a number of areas within the present white supremacist, patriarchal system but these reforms have not corresponded with decreased sexist exploitation and/or oppression. Prevailing sexist values and assumptions remain intact and it has been easy for politically conservative anti-feminists to undermine feminist reforms. Many politically progressive critics of feminist movement see the impulse towards reforms as counter-productive. * * *

Reforms can be a vital part of the movement towards revolution but what is important is the types of reforms that are initiated. Feminist focus on reforms to improve the social status of women within the existing social structure allowed women and men to lose sight of the need for total transformation of society. The ERA campaign, for example, diverted a great deal of money and human resources towards a reform effort that should have been a massive political campaign to build a feminist constituency. This constituency would have guaranteed the success of the ERA. Unfortunately, revolutionary reforms focused first and foremost on educating masses of women and men about feminist movement, showing them ways it would transform their lives for the better, were not initiated. Instead women involved with feminist reforms were inclined to think less about transforming society and more about fighting for equality and equal rights with men.

Many radical activists in the women's movement who were not interested in obtaining social equality with men in the existing social structure chose to attack exploitative and oppressive sexist behavior. Identifying men as the villains, the "enemy," they concentrated their attention on exposing male "evil." One example of this has been the critique and attack on pornography. It is obvious that pornography promotes degradation of women, sexism, and sexualized violence. It is also obvious that endless denunciations of pornography are fruitless if there is not greater emphasis on transforming society and by implication sexuality. This more significant struggle has not been seriously attended to by feminist movement. The focus on "men" and "male behavior" has overshadowed emphasis on women developing themselves politically so that we can begin making the cultural transformations that would pave the way for the establishment of a new social order. Much feminist consciousness-raising has centered on helping women to understand the nature of sexism in personal life, especially as it relates to male dominance. While this is a necessary task, it is not the only task for consciousness-raising.

Feminist consciousness-raising has not significantly pushed women in the direction of revolutionary politics. For the most part, it has not helped women understand capitalism: how it works, as a system that exploits female labor and its inter-connections with sexist oppression. It has not urged women to learn about different political systems like socialism or encouraged women to invent and envision new political systems. It has not attacked materialism and our society's addiction to over-consumption. It has not shown women how we benefit from the exploitation and oppression of women and men globally or shown us ways to oppose imperialism. Most importantly, is has not continually confronted women with the understanding that feminist movement to end sexist oppression can be successful only if we are committed to revolution, to the establishment of a new social order.

* * *

Although feminist rebellion has been a success it is not leading to further revolutionary development. Internally its progress is retarded by those feminist activists who do not feel that the movement exists for the advancement of all women and men, who seem to think it exists to advance individual participants, who are threatened by opinions and ideas that differ from the dominant feminist ideology, who seek to suppress and silence dissenting voices, who do not acknowledge the necessity for continued effort to create a liberatory ideology. These women resist efforts to critically examine prevailing feminist ideology and refuse to acknowledge its limitations. Externally the progress of feminist movement is retarded by organized anti-feminist activity and by the political indifference of masses of women and men who are not well enough acquainted with either side of the issue to take a stand.

To move beyond the stage of feminist rebellion, to move past the impasse that characterizes contemporary feminist movement, women must recognize the need for reorganization. Without dismissing the positive dimensions of feminist movement up to this point, we need to accept that there was never a strategy on the part of feminist organizers and participants to build mass awareness of the need for feminist movement through political education. Such a strategy is needed if feminism is to be a political movement impacting on society as a whole in a revolutionary and transformative way. We also need to face the fact that many of the dilemmas facing feminist movement today were created by bourgeois women who shaped the movement in ways that served their opportunistic class interests. We must now work to change its direction so that women of all classes can see that their interest in ending sexist oppression is served by feminist movement. Recognizing that bourgeois opportunists have exploited feminist movement should not be seen as an attack upon all bourgeois women. There are individual bourgeois women who are repudiating class privilege, who are politically progressive, who have given, are giving, or are willing to give of themselves in a revolutionary way to advance feminist movement. Reshaping the class politics of feminist movement is strategy that will lead women from all classes to join feminist struggle.

To build a mass-based feminist movement, we need to have a liberatory ideology that can be shared with everyone. That revolutionary ideology can be created only if the experiences of people on the margin who suffer sexist oppression and other forms of group oppression are understood, addressed, and incorporated. They must participate in feminist movement as makers of theory and as leaders of action. In past feminist practice, we have been satisfied with relying on self-appointed individuals, some of whom are more concerned about exercising authority and power than with communicating with people from various backgrounds and political perspectives. Such individuals do not choose to learn about collective female experience, but impose their own ideas and values. Leaders are needed, and should be individuals who acknowledge their relationship to the group and who are accountable to it. They should have the ability to show love and compassion, show this love through their actions, and be able to engage in successful dialogue. * * * Women must begin the work of feminist reorganization with the understanding that we have all (irrespective of our race, sex, or class) acted in complicity with the existing oppressive system. We all need to make a conscious break with the system. Some of us make this break sooner than others. The compassion we extend to ourselves, the recognition that our change in consciousness and action has been a process, must characterize our approach to those individuals who are politically unconscious. We cannot motivate them to join feminist struggle by asserting a political superiority that makes the movement just another oppressive hierarchy.

Before we can address the masses, we must recapture the attention, the support, the participation of the many women who were once active in feminist movement and who left disillusioned. Too many women have abandoned feminist movement because they cannot support the ideas of a small minority of women who have hegemonic control over feminist discourse—the development of the theory that informs practice. Too many women who have caring bonds with men have drifted away from feminist movement because they feel that identification of "man as enemy" is an unconstructive paradigm. Too many women have ceased to support feminist struggle because the ideology has been too dogmatic, too absolutist, too closed. Too many women have left feminist movement because they were identified as the "enemy." * * * To restore the revolutionary life force to feminist movement, women and men must begin to re-think and re-shape its direction. While we must recognize, acknowledge, and appreciate the significance of feminist rebellion and the women (and men) who made it happen, we must be willing to criticize, reexamine, and begin feminist work anew, a challenging task because we lack historical precedents. There are many ways to make revolution. Revolutions can be and usually are initiated by violent overthrow of an existing political structure. In the United States, women and men committed to feminist struggle know that we are far outpowered by our opponents, that they not only have access to every type of weaponry known to humankind, but they have both the learned consciousness to do and accept violence as well as the skill to perpetuate it. Therefore, this cannot be the basis for feminist revolution in this society. Our emphasis must be on cultural transformation: destroying dualism, eradicating systems of domination. Our struggle will be gradual and protracted. Any effort to make feminist revolution here can be aided by the example of liberation struggles led by oppressed peoples globally who resist formidable powers.

THURGOOD MARSHALL

The Constitution's Bicentennial: Commemorating the Wrong Document? (1987)

As legal director of the NAACP from 1940 to 1961, the civil rights activist Thurgood Marshall (1908–1993) successfully argued twenty-nine of his thirty-two cases before the Supreme Court prior to becoming the first black justice of the Supreme Court in 1967. Famous for his dissents in cases dealing with racial, economic, and sexual inequality, Marshall was an advocate for the rights of the underprivileged on and off the bench. In a 1987 speech, Marshall announced that he could not celebrate the bicentennial of a flawed Constitution that deliberately excluded women and racial minorities. But in explaining that the Constitution is a "living document," Marshall suggested it is possible to overcome its inherent defects.

1987 marks the 200th anniversary of the United States Constitution. A Commission has been established to coordinate the celebration. The official meetings, essay contests, and festivities have begun.

The planned commemoration will span three years, and I am told 1987 is "dedicated to the memory of the Founders and the document they drafted in Philadelphia." We are to "recall the achievements of our Founders and the knowledge and experience that inspired them, the nature of the government they established, its origins, its character, and its ends, and the rights and privileges of citizenship, as well as its attendant responsibilities."

Like many anniversary celebrations, the plan for 1987 takes particular events and holds them up as the source of all the very best that has followed. Patriotic feelings will surely swell, prompting proud proclamations of the wisdom, foresight, and sense of justice shared by the Framers and reflected in a written document now yellowed with age. This is unfortunate—not the patriotism itself, but the tendency for the celebration to oversimplify, and overlook the many other events that have been instrumental to our achievements as a nation. The focus of this celebration invites a complacent belief that the vision of those who debated and compromised in Philadelphia yielded the "more perfect Union" it is said we now enjoy.

I cannot accept this invitation, for I do not believe that the meaning of the Constitution was forever "fixed" at the Philadelphia Convention. Nor do I find the wisdom, foresight, and sense of justice exhibited by the Framers particularly profound. To the contrary, the government they devised was defective from the start, requiring several amendments, a civil war, and momentous social transformation to attain the system of constitutional government, and its respect for the individual freedoms and human rights, we hold as fundamental today. When contemporary Americans cite "The Constitution," they invoke a concept that is vastly different from what the Framers barely began to construct two centuries ago.

For a sense of the evolving nature of the Constitution we need look no further than the first three words of the document's preamble: "We the

People." When the Founding Fathers used this phrase in 1787, they did not have in mind the majority of America's citizens. "We the People" included, in the words of the Framers, "the whole Number of free Persons." On a matter so basic as the right to vote, for example, Negro slaves were excluded, although they were counted for representational purposes—at three-fifths each. Women did not gain the right to vote for over a hundred and thirty years.

These omissions were intentional. The record of the Framers' debates on the slave question is especially clear: The Southern States acceded to the demands of the New England States for giving Congress broad power to regulate commerce, in exchange for the right to continue the slave trade. The economic interests of the regions coalesced: New Englanders engaged in the "carrying trade" would profit from transporting slaves from Africa as well as goods produced in America by slave labor. The perpetuation of slavery ensured the primary source of wealth in the Southern States.

Despite this clear understanding of the role slavery would play in the new republic, use of the words "slaves" and "slavery" was carefully avoided in the original document. Political representation in the lower House of Congress was to be based on the population of "free Persons" in each State, plus three-fifths of all "other Persons." Moral principles against slavery, for those who had them, were compromised, with no explanation of the conflicting principles for which the American Revolutionary War had ostensibly been fought: the self-evident truths "that all men are created equal, that they are endowed by their Creator with certain unalienable Rights, that among these are Life, Liberty and the pursuit of Happiness."

It was not the first such compromise. Even these ringing phrases from the Declaration of Independence are filled with irony, for an early draft of what became that Declaration assailed the King of England for suppressing legislative attempts to end the slave trade and for encouraging slave rebellions. The final draft adopted in 1776 did not contain this criticism. And so again at the Constitutional Convention eloquent objections to the institution of slavery went unheeded, and its opponents eventually consented to a document which laid a foundation for the tragic events that were to follow.

Pennsylvania's Gouverneur Morris provides an example. He opposed slavery and the counting of slaves in determining the basis for representation in Congress. At the Convention he objected that

> the inhabitant of Georgia [or] South Carolina who goes to the coast of Africa, and in defiance of the most sacred laws of humanity tears away his fellow creatures from their dearest connections and damns them to

the most cruel bondages, shall have more votes in a Government instituted for protection of the rights of mankind, than the Citizen of Pennsylvania or New Jersey who views with a laudable horror, so nefarious a
practice.

And yet Gouverneur Morris eventually accepted the three-fifths accommodation. In fact, he wrote the final draft of the Constitution, the very
document the Bicentennial will commemorate.

As a result of compromise, the right of the Southern States to continue importing slaves was extended, officially, at least until 1808. We
know that it actually lasted a good deal longer, as the Framers possessed
no monopoly on the ability to trade moral principles for self-interest. But
they nevertheless set an unfortunate example. Slaves could be imported,
if the commercial interests of the North were protected. To make the
compromise even more palatable, customs duties would be imposed at up
to ten dollars per slave as a means of raising public revenues.

No doubt it will be said, when the unpleasant truth of the history of
slavery in America is mentioned during this Bicentennial year, that the
Constitution was a product of its times, and embodied a compromise
which, under other circumstances, would not have been made. But the
effects of the Framers' compromise have remained for generations. They
arose from the contradiction between guaranteeing liberty and justice to
all, and denying both to Negroes.

The original intent of the phrase, "We the People," was far too clear
for any ameliorating construction. Writing for the Supreme Court in
1857, Chief Justice Taney penned the following passage in the *Dred Scott*
case, on the issue whether, in the eyes of the Framers, slaves were "constituent members of the sovereignty," and were to be included among "We
the People":

> We think they are not, and that they are not included, and were not in-
> tended to be included. . . .
>
>   . . . .
>
> They had for more than a century before been regarded as beings of
> an inferior order; and altogether unfit to associate with the white
> race . . . ; and so far inferior, that they had no rights which the white
> man was bound to respect; and that the negro might justly and lawfully
> be reduced to slavery for his benefit.
>
>   . . . .
>
> [A]ccordingly, a negro of the African race was regarded . . . as an ar-
> ticle of property, and held, and bought and sold as such. . . . [N]o one
> seems to have doubted the correctness of the prevailing opinion of the
> time.

And so, nearly seven decades after the Constitutional Convention, the Supreme Court reaffirmed the prevailing opinion of the Framers regarding the rights of Negroes in America. It took a bloody civil war before the thirteenth amendment could be adopted to abolish slavery, though not the consequences slavery would have for future Americans.

While the Union survived the Civil War, the Constitution did not. In its place arose a new, more promising basis for justice and equality, the fourteenth amendment, ensuring protection of the life, liberty, and property of *all* persons against deprivations without due process, and guaranteeing equal protection of the laws. And yet almost another century would pass before any significant recognition was obtained of the rights of black Americans to share equally even in such basic opportunities as education, housing, and employment, and to have their votes counted, and counted equally. In the meantime, blacks joined America's military to fight its wars and invested untold hours working in its factories and on its farms, contributing to the development of this country's magnificent wealth and waiting to share in its prosperity.

What is striking is the role legal principles have played throughout America's history in determining the condition of Negroes. They were enslaved by law, emancipated by law, disenfranchised and segregated by law; and, finally, they have begun to win equality by law. Along the way, new constitutional principles have emerged to meet the challenges of a changing society. The progress has been dramatic, and it will continue.

The men who gathered in Philadelphia in 1787 could not have envisioned these changes. They could not have imagined, nor would they have accepted, that the document they were drafting would one day be construed by a Supreme Court to which had been appointed a woman and the descendent of an African slave. "We the People" no longer enslave, but the credit does not belong to the Framers. It belongs to those who refused to acquiesce in outdated notions of "liberty," "justice," and "equality," and who strived to better them.

And so we must be careful, when focusing on the events which took place in Philadelphia two centuries ago, that we not overlook the momentous events which followed, and thereby lose our proper sense of perspective. Otherwise, the odds are that for many Americans the Bicentennial celebration will be little more than a blind pilgrimage to the shrine of the original document now stored in a vault in the National Archives. If we seek, instead, a sensitive understanding of the Constitution's inherent defects, and its promising evolution through 200 years of history, the celebration of the "Miracle at Philadelphia" will, in my view, be a far more meaningful and humbling experience. We will see that the true miracle was not the birth of the Constitution, but its life, a life nurtured through two turbulent centuries of our own making, and a life embodying much good fortune that was not.

Thus, in this Bicentennial year, we may not all participate in the festivities with flag-waving fervor. Some may more quietly commemorate the suffering, struggle, and sacrifice that has triumphed over much of what was wrong with the original document, and observe the anniversary with hopes not realized and promises not fulfilled. I plan to celebrate the Bicentennial of the Constitution as a living document, including the Bill of Rights and the other amendments protecting individual freedoms and human rights.

ALLAN BLOOM

The Closing of the American Mind (1987)

The political philosopher Allan Bloom (1930–1992) taught at Yale, Cornell, the University of Toronto, Tel Aviv University, the University of Paris, and the University of Chicago, where he spent most of his career. Bloom promoted the careful study of the classics, or "great books," as the best way to acquire wisdom and insight into the problems of contemporary political and social life. Bloom's phenomenally bestselling Closing of the American Mind was one of the first books to attack what many conservatives regard as rampant political correctness, excessive multiculturalism, and declining standards in higher education. Bloom attributed the decay of liberal education to the spread of a 1960s-style anything-goes type of moral relativism that denies the existence of absolute standards of morality and truth.

What image does a first-rank college or university present today to a teen-ager leaving home for the first time, off to the adventure of a liberal education? He has four years of freedom to discover himself—a space between the intellectual wasteland he has left behind and the inevitable dreary professional training that awaits him after the baccalaureate. In this short time he must learn that there is a great world beyond the little one he knows, experience the exhilaration of it and digest enough of it to sustain himself in the intellectual deserts he is destined to traverse. He must do this, that is, if he is to have any hope of a higher life. These are the charmed years when he can, if he so chooses, become anything he wishes and when he has the opportunity to survey his alternatives, not merely those current in his time or provided by careers, but those available to him as a human being. The importance of these years for an American cannot be overestimated. They are civilization's only chance to get to him.

In looking at him we are forced to reflect on what he should learn if he is to be called educated; we must speculate on what the human potential to be fulfilled is. In the specialties we can avoid such speculation, and the avoidance of them is one of specialization's charms. But here it is a simple duty. What are we to teach this person? The answer may not be evident, but to attempt to answer the question is already to philosophize and to begin to educate. Such a concern in itself poses the question of the unity of man and the unity of the sciences. It is childishness to say, as some do, that everyone must be allowed to develop freely, that it is authoritarian to impose a point of view on the student. In that case, why have a university? If the response is "to provide an atmosphere for learning," we come back to our original questions at the second remove. Which atmosphere? Choices and reflection on the reasons for those choices are unavoidable. The university has to stand for something. The practical effects of unwillingness to think positively about the contents of a liberal education are, on the one hand, to ensure that all the vulgarities of the world outside the university will flourish within it, and, on the other, to impose a much harsher and more illiberal necessity on the student—the one given by the imperial and imperious demands of the specialized disciplines unfiltered by unifying thought.

The university now offers no distinctive visage to the young person. He finds a democracy of the disciplines—which are there either because they are autochthonous or because they wandered in recently to perform some job that was demanded of the university. This democracy is really an anarchy, because there are no recognized rules for citizenship and no legitimate titles to rule. In short there is no vision, nor is there a set of competing visions, of what an educated human being is. The question has disappeared, for to pose it would be a threat to the peace. There is no organization of the sciences, no tree of knowledge. Out of chaos emerges dispiritedness, because it is impossible to make a reasonable choice. Better to give up on liberal education and get on with a specialty in which there is at least a prescribed curriculum and a prospective career. On the way the student can pick up in elective courses a little of whatever is thought to make one cultured. The student gets no intimation that great mysteries might be revealed to him, that new and higher motives of action might be discovered within him, that a different and more human way of life can be harmoniously constructed by what he is going to learn.

Simply, the university is not distinctive. Equality for us seems to culminate in the unwillingness and incapacity to make claims of superiority, particularly in the domains in which such claims have always been made—art, religion and philosophy. When Weber found that he could not choose between certain high opposites—reason vs. revelation, Buddha vs. Jesus—he did not conclude that all things are equally good, that the distinction between high and low disappears. As a matter of fact he intended to revitalize the consideration of these great alternatives in showing the gravity and danger involved in choosing among them; they were to be heightened in contrast to the trivial considerations of modern life that threatened to overgrow and render indistinguishable the profound problems the confrontation with which makes the bow of the soul taut. The serious intellectual life was for him the battleground of the great decisions, all of which are spiritual or "value" choices. One can no longer present this or that particular view of the educated or civilized man as authoritative; therefore one must say that education consists in knowing, really knowing, the small number of such views in their integrity. This distinction between profound and superficial—which takes the place of good and bad, true and false—provided a focus for serious study, but it hardly held out against the naturally relaxed democratic tendency to say, "Oh, what's the use?" The first university disruptions at Berkeley were explicitly directed against the multiversity smorgasbord and, I must confess, momentarily and partially engaged my sympathies. It may have even been the case that there was some small element of longing for an education in the motivation of those students. But nothing was done to guide or inform their energy, and the result was merely to add multilife-styles to multidisciplines, the diversity of perversity to the diversity of specialization. What we see so often happening in general happened here too; the insistent demand for greater community ended in greater isolation. Old agreements, old habits, old traditions were not so easily replaced.

Thus, when a student arrives at the university, he finds a bewildering variety of departments and a bewildering variety of courses. And there is no official guidance, no university-wide agreement, about what he *should* study. Nor does he usually find readily available examples, either among students or professors, of a unified use of the university's resources. It is easiest simply to make a career choice and go about getting prepared for that career. The programs designed for those having made such a choice render their students immune to charms that might lead them out of the conventionally respectable. The sirens sing *sotto voce* these days, and the young already have enough wax in their ears to pass them by without danger. These specialties can provide enough courses to take up most of their time for four years in preparation for the inevitable graduate study. With the few remaining courses they can do what they please, taking a bit of this and a bit of that. No public career these days—not doctor nor lawyer nor politician nor journalist nor businessman nor entertainer—has much to do with humane learning. An education, other than purely professional or technical, can even seem to be an impediment. That is why a countervailing atmosphere in the university would be necessary for the students to gain a taste for intellectual pleasures and learn that they are viable.

The real problem is those students who come hoping to find out what career they want to have, or are simply looking for an adventure with themselves. There are plenty of things for them to do—courses and disciplines enough to spend many a lifetime on. Each department or great division of the university makes a pitch for itself, and each offers a course of study that will make the student an initiate. But how to choose among them? How do they relate to one another? The fact is they do not address one another. They are competing and contradictory, without being aware of it. The problem of the whole is urgently indicated by the very existence of the specialties, but it is never systematically posed. The net effect of the student's encounter with the college catalogue is bewilderment and very often demoralization. It is just a matter of chance whether he finds one or two professors who can give him an insight into one of the great visions of education that have been the distinguishing part of every civilized nation. Most professors are specialists, concerned only with their own fields, interested in the advancement of those fields in their own terms, or in their own personal advancement in a world where all the rewards are on the side of professional distinction. They have been entirely emancipated from the old structure of the university, which at least helped to indicate that they are incomplete, only parts of an unexamined and undiscovered whole. So the student must navigate among a collection of carnival barkers, each trying to lure him into a particular sideshow. This undecided student is an embarrassment to most universities, because he seems to be saying, "I am a whole human being. Help me to form myself in my wholeness and let me develop my real potential," and he is the one to whom they have nothing to say.

* * *

There are attempts to fill the vacuum painlessly with various kinds of fancy packaging of what is already there—study abroad options, individualized majors, etc. Then there are Black Studies and Women's or Gender Studies, along with Learn Another Culture. Peace Studies are on their way to a similar prevalence. All this is designed to show that the university is with it and has something in addition to its traditional specialties. The latest item is computer literacy, the full cheapness of which is evident only to those who think a bit about what literacy might mean. It would make some sense to promote literacy literacy, inasmuch as most high school graduates nowadays have difficulty reading and writing. And some institutions are quietly undertaking this worthwhile task. But they do not trumpet the fact, because this is merely a high school function that our current sad state of educational affairs has thrust upon them, about which they are not inclined to boast.

Now that the distractions of the sixties are over, and undergraduate education has become more important again (because the graduate departments, aside from the professional schools, are in trouble due to the shortage of academic jobs), university officials have had somehow to deal with the undeniable fact that the students who enter are uncivilized, and that the universities have some responsibility for civilizing them. If one were to give a base interpretation of the schools' motives, one could allege that their concern stems from shame and self-interest. It is becoming all too evident that liberal education—which is what the small band of prestigious institutions are supposed to provide, in contrast to the big state schools, which are thought simply to prepare specialists to meet the practical demands of a complex society—has no content, that a certain kind of fraud is being perpetrated. For a time the great moral consciousness alleged to have been fostered in students by the great universities, especially their vocation as gladiators who fight war and racism, seemed to fulfill the demands of the collective university conscience. They were doing something other than offering preliminary training for doctors and lawyers. Concern and compassion were thought to be the indefinable X that pervaded all the parts of the Arts and Sciences campus. But when that evanescent mist dissipated during the seventies, and the faculties found themselves face to face with ill-educated young people with no intellectual tastes—unaware that there even are such things, obsessed with getting on with their careers before having looked at life—and the universities offered no counterpoise, no alternative goals, a reaction set in.

Liberal education—since it has for so long been ill-defined, has none of the crisp clarity or institutionalized prestige of the professions, but nevertheless perseveres and has money and respectability connected with it—has always been a battleground for those who are somewhat eccentric in relation to the specialties. It is in something like the condition of churches as opposed to, say, hospitals. Nobody is quite certain of what the religious institutions are supposed to do anymore, but they do have some kind of role either responding to a real human need or as the vestige of what was once a need, and they invite the exploitation of quacks, adventurers, cranks and fanatics. But they also solicit the warmest and most valiant efforts of persons of peculiar gravity and depth. In liberal education, too, the worst and the best fight it out, fakers vs. authentics, sophists vs. philosophers, for the favor of public opinion and for control over the study of man in our times. The most conspicuous participants in the struggle are administrators who are formally responsible for presenting some kind of public image of the education their colleges offer, persons with a political agenda or vulgarizers of what the specialties know, and real teachers of the humane disciplines who actually see their relation to the whole and urgently wish to preserve the awareness of it in their students' consciousness.

So, just as in the sixties universities were devoted to removing requirements, in the eighties they are busy with attempts to put them back in, a much more difficult task. The word of the day is "core." It is generally agreed that "we went a bit far in the sixties," and that a little fine-tuning has now become clearly necessary.

There are two typical responses to the problem. The easiest and most administratively satisfying solution is to make use of what is already there in the autonomous departments and simply force the students to cover the fields, i.e., take one or more courses in each of the general divisions of the university: natural science, social science and the humanities. The reigning ideology here is *breadth,* as was *openness* in the age of laxity. The courses are almost always the already existing introductory courses, which are of least interest to the major professors and merely assume the worth and reality of that which is to be studied. It is general education, in the sense in which a jack-of-all-trades is a generalist. He knows a bit of everything and is inferior to the specialist in each area. Students may wish to sample a variety of fields, and it may be good to encourage them to look around and see if there is something that attracts them in one of which they have no experience. But this is not a liberal education and does not satisfy any longing they have for one. It just teaches that there is no high-level generalism, and that what they are doing is preliminary to the real stuff and part of the childhood they are leaving behind. Thus they desire to get it over with and get on with what their professors do seriously. Without recognition of important questions of common concern, there cannot be serious liberal education, and attempts to establish it will be but failed gestures.

It is a more or less precise awareness of the inadequacy of this approach to core curricula that motivates the second approach, which consists of what one might call composite courses. These are constructions developed especially for general-education purposes and usually require collaboration of professors drawn from several departments. These courses have titles like "Man in Nature," "War and Moral Responsibility,"

"The Arts and Creativity," "Culture and the Individual." Everything, of course, depends upon who plans them and who teaches them. They have the clear advantage of requiring some reflection on the general needs of students and force specialized professors to broaden their perspectives, at least for a moment. The dangers are trendiness, mere popularization and lack of substantive rigor. In general, the natural scientists do not collaborate in such endeavors, and hence these courses tend to be unbalanced. In short, they do not point beyond themselves and do not provide the student with independent means to pursue permanent questions independently, as, for example, the study of Aristotle or Kant as wholes once did. They tend to be bits of this and that. Liberal education should give the student the sense that learning must and can be both synoptic and precise. For this, a very small, detailed problem can be the best way, if it is framed so as to open out on the whole. Unless the course has the specific intention to lead to the permanent questions, to make the student aware of them and give him some competence in the important works that treat of them, it tends to be a pleasant diversion and a dead end—because it has nothing to do with any program of further study he can imagine. If such programs engage the best energies of the best people in the university, they can be beneficial and provide some of the missing intellectual excitement for both professors and students. But they rarely do, and they are too cut off from the top, from what the various faculties see as their real business. Where the power is determines the life of the whole body. And the intellectual problems unresolved at the top cannot be resolved administratively below. The problem is the lack of any unity of the sciences and the loss of the will or the means even to discuss the issue. The illness above is the cause of the illness below, to which all the good-willed efforts of honest liberal educationists can at best be palliatives.

Of course, the only serious solution is the one that is almost universally rejected: the good old Great Books approach, in which a liberal education means reading certain generally recognized classic texts, just reading them, letting them dictate what the questions are and the method of approaching them—not forcing them into categories we make up, not treating them as historical products, but trying to read them as their authors wished them to be read. I am perfectly well aware of, and actually agree with, the objections to the Great Books cult. It is amateurish; it encourages an autodidact's self-assurance without competence; one cannot read all of the Great Books carefully; if one only reads Great Books, one can never know what a great, as opposed to an ordinary, book is; there is no way of determining who is to decide what a Great Book or what the canon is; books are made the ends and not the means; the whole movement has a certain coarse evangelistic tone that is the opposite of good taste; it engenders a spurious intimacy with greatness; and so forth. But one thing is certain: wherever the Great Books make up a central part of the curriculum, the students are excited and satisfied, feel they are doing something that is independent and fulfilling, getting something from the university they cannot get elsewhere. The very fact of this special experience, which leads nowhere beyond itself, provides them with a new alternative and a respect for study itself. The advantage they get is an awareness of the classic—particularly important for our innocents; an acquaintance with what big questions were when there were still big questions; models, at the very least, of how to go about answering them; and, perhaps most important of all, a fund of shared experiences and thoughts on which to ground their friendships with one another. Programs based upon judicious use of great texts provide the royal road to students' hearts. Their gratitude at learning of Achilles or the categorical imperative is boundless. Alexandre Koyré, the late historian of science, told me that his appreciation for America was great when—in the first course he taught at the University of Chicago, in 1940 at the beginning of his exile—a student spoke in his paper of Mr. Aristotle, unaware that he was not a contemporary. Koyré said that only an American could have the naive profundity to take Aristotle as living thought, unthinkable for most scholars. A good program of liberal education feeds the student's love of truth and passion to live a good life. It is the easiest thing in the world to devise courses of study, adapted to the particular conditions of each university, which thrill those who take them. The difficulty is in getting them accepted by the faculty.

None of the three great parts of the contemporary university is enthusiastic about the Great Books approach to education. The natural scientists are benevolent toward other fields and toward liberal education, if it does not steal away their students and does not take too much time from their preparatory studies. But they themselves are interested primarily in the solution of the questions now important in their disciplines and are not particularly concerned with discussions of their foundations, inasmuch as they are so evidently successful. They are indifferent to Newton's conception of time or his disputes with Leibniz about calculus; Aristotle's teleology is an absurdity beneath consideration. Scientific progress, they believe, no longer depends on the kind of comprehensive reflection given to the nature of science by men like Bacon, Descartes, Hume, Kant and Marx. This is merely historical study, and for a long time now, even the greatest scientists have given up thinking about Galileo and Newton. Progress is undoubted. The difficulties about the truth of science raised by positivism, and those about the goodness of science raised by Rousseau and Nietzsche, have not really penetrated to the center of scientific consciousness. Hence, no Great Books, but incremental progress, is the theme for them.

Social scientists are in general hostile, because the classic texts tend to deal with the human things the social sciences deal with, and they are very proud of having freed themselves from the shackles of such earlier thought to become truly scientific. And, unlike the natural scientists, they are insecure enough about their achievement to feel threatened by the works of earlier thinkers, perhaps a bit afraid that students will be seduced and fall back into the bad old ways. Moreover, with the possible exception of Weber and Freud, there are no social science books that can be said to be classic. This may be interpreted favorably to the social sciences by comparing them to the natural sciences, which can be said to be a living organism developing by the addition of little cells, a veritable body of knowledge proving itself to be such by the very fact of this almost unconscious growth, with thousands of parts oblivious to the whole, nevertheless contributing to it. This is in opposition to a work of imagination or of philosophy, where a single creator makes and surveys an artificial whole. But whether one interprets the absence of the classic in the social sciences in ways flattering or unflattering to them, the fact causes social scientists discomfort. I remember the professor who taught the introductory graduate courses in social science methodology, a famous historian, responding scornfully and angrily to a question I naively put to him about Thucydides with "Thucydides was a fool!"

More difficult to explain is the tepid reaction of humanists to Great Books education, inasmuch as these books now belong almost exclusively to what are called the humanities. One would think that high esteem for the classic would reinforce the spiritual power of the humanities, at a time when their temporal power is at its lowest. And it is true that the most active proponents of liberal education and the study of classic texts are indeed usually humanists. But there is division among them. Some humanities disciplines are just crusty specialties that, although they depend on the status of classic books for their existence, are not really interested in them in their natural state—much philology, for example, is concerned with the languages but not what is said in them—and will and can do nothing to support their own infrastructure. Some humanities disciplines are eager to join the real sciences and transcend their roots in the now overcome mythic past. Some humanists make the legitimate complaints about lack of competence in the teaching and learning of Great Books, although their criticism is frequently undermined by the fact that they are only defending recent scholarly interpretation of the classics rather than a vital, authentic understanding. In their reaction there is a strong element of specialist's jealousy and narrowness. Finally, a large part of the story is just the general debilitation of the humanities, which is both symptom and cause of our present condition.

To repeat, the crisis of liberal education is a reflection of a crisis at the peaks of learning, an incoherence and incompatibility among the first principles with which we interpret the world, an intellectual crisis of the greatest magnitude, which constitutes the crisis of our civilization. But perhaps it would be true to say that the crisis consists not so much in this incoherence but in our incapacity to discuss or even recognize it. Liberal education flourished when it prepared the way for the discussion of a unified view of nature and man's place in it, which the best minds debated on the highest level. It decayed when what lay beyond it were only specialties, the premises of which do not lead to any such vision. The highest is the partial intellect; there is no synopsis.

* * *

These are the shadows cast by the peaks of the university over the entering undergraduate. Together they represent what the university has to say about man and his education, and they do not project a coherent image. The differences and the indifferences are too great. It is difficult to imagine that there is either the wherewithal or the energy within the university to constitute or reconstitute the idea of an educated human being and establish a liberal education again.

However, the contemplation of this scene is in itself a proper philosophic activity. The university's evident lack of wholeness in an enterprise that clearly demands it cannot help troubling some of its members. The questions are all there. They only need to be addressed continuously and seriously for liberal learning to exist; for it does not consist so much in answers as in the permanent dialogue. It is in such perplexed professors that at least the idea might persevere and help to guide some of the needy young persons at our doorstep. The matter is still present in the university; it is the form that has vanished. One cannot and should not hope for a general reform. The hope is that the embers do not die out.

Men may live more truly and fully in reading Plato and Shakespeare than at any other time, because then they are participating in essential being and are forgetting their accidental lives. The fact that this kind of humanity exists or existed, and that we can somehow still touch it with the tips of our outstretched fingers, makes our imperfect humanity, which we can no longer bear, tolerable. The books in their objective beauty are still there, and we must help protect and cultivate the delicate tendrils reaching out toward them through the unfriendly soil of students' souls. Human nature, it seems, remains the same in our very altered circumstances because we still face the same problems, if in different guises, and have the distinctively human need to solve them, even though our awareness and forces have become enfeebled.

After a reading of the *Symposium* a serious student came with deep melancholy and said it was impossible to imagine that magic Athenian atmosphere reproduced, in which friendly men, educated, lively, on a footing of equality, civilized but natural, came together and told wonderful stories about the meaning of their longing. But such experiences are always accessible. Actually, this playful discussion took place in the midst of a terrible war that Athens was destined to lose, and Aristophanes and Socrates at least could foresee that this meant the decline of Greek civilization. But they were not given to culture despair, and in these terrible political circumstances, their abandon to the joy of nature proved the viability of what is best in man, independent of accidents, of circumstance. We feel ourselves too dependent on history and culture. This student did not have Socrates, but he had Plato's book about him, which might even be better; he had brains, friends and a country happily free enough to let them gather and speak as they will. What is essential about that dialogue, or any of the Platonic dialogues, is reproducible in almost all times and places. He and his friends can think together. It requires much thought to learn that this thinking might be what it is all for. That's where we are beginning to fail. But it is right under our noses, improbable but always present.

Throughout this book I have referred to Plato's *Republic*, which is for me *the* book on education, because it really explains to me what I experience as a man and a teacher, and I have almost always used it to point out what we should not hope for, as a teaching of moderation and resignation. But all its impossibilities act as a filter to leave the residue of the highest and non-illusory possibility. The real community of man, in the midst of all the self-contradictory simulacra of community, is the community of those who seek the truth, of the potential knowers, that is, in principle, of all men to the extent they desire to know. But in fact this includes only a few, the true friends, as Plato was to Aristotle at the very moment they were disagreeing about the nature of the good. Their common concern for the good linked them; their disagreement about it proved they needed one another to understand it. They were absolutely one soul as they looked at the problem. This, according to Plato, is the only real friendship, the only real common good. It is here that the contact people so desperately seek is to be found. The other kinds of relatedness are only imperfect reflections of this one trying to be self-subsisting, gaining their only justification from their ultimate relation to this one. This is the meaning of the riddle of the improbable philosopher-kings. They have a true community that is exemplary for all other communities.

This is a radical teaching but perhaps one appropriate to our own radical time, in which proximate attachments have become so questionable and we know of no others. This age is not utterly insalubrious for philosophy. Our problems are so great and their sources so deep that to understand them we need philosophy more than ever, if we do not despair of it, and it faces the challenges on which it flourishes. I still believe that universities, rightly understood, are where community and friendship can exist in our times. Our thought and our politics have become inextricably bound up with the universities, and they have served us well, human things being what they are. But for all that, and even though they deserve our strenuous efforts, one should never forget that Socrates was not a professor, that he was put to death, and that the love of wisdom survived, partly because of his *individual* example. This is what really counts, and we must remember it in order to know how to defend the university.

This is the American moment in world history, the one for which we shall forever be judged. Just as in politics the responsibility for the fate of freedom in the world has devolved upon our regime, so the fate of philosophy in the world has devolved upon our universities, and the two are related as they have never been before. The gravity of our given task is great, and it is very much in doubt how the future will judge our stewardship.

MICHAEL WALZER

What Does It Mean to Be an "American"? (1990)

Michael L. Walzer (1935–), a professor of social science at Princeton's Institute for Advanced Studies and the editor of the political journal Dissent, *is one of America's leading liberal public intellectuals. He has written studies of just war, tolerance, justice and equality. In this essay, which appeared originally in the 1990 issue of the journal* Social Research, *Walzer enters the conversation about identity and citizenship that flourishes still in American political thought. His argument is developed in response to an important early-twentieth-century book on cultural pluralism by Horace Kallen,* Culture and Democracy in the United States.

There is no country called America. We live in the United States *of* America, and we have appropriated the adjective "American" even though we can claim no exclusive title to it. Canadians and Mexicans are also Americans, but they have adjectives more obviously their own, and we have none. Words like "unitarian" and "unionist" won't do; our sense of ourselves is not captured by the mere fact of our union, however important that is. Nor will "statist," even "united statist," serve our purposes; a good many of the citizens of the United States are antistatist. Other countries, wrote the "American" political theorist Horace Kallen, get their names from the people, or from one of the peoples, who inhabit them. "The United States, on the other hand, has a peculiar anonymity." It is a name that doesn't even pretend to tell us who lives here. Anybody can live here, and just about everybody does—men and women from all the world's peoples. (The *Harvard Encyclopedia of American Ethnic Groups* begins with Acadians and Afghans and ends with Zoroastrians.) It is peculiarly easy to become an American. The adjective provides no reliable information about the origins, histories, connections, or cultures of those whom it designates. What does it say, then, about their political allegiance?

American politicians engage periodically in a fierce competition to demonstrate their patriotism. This is an odd competition, surely, for in most countries the patriotism of politicians is not an issue. There are other issues, and this question of political identification and commitment rarely comes up; loyalty to the *patrie*, the fatherland (or motherland), is simply assumed. Perhaps it isn't assumed here because the United States isn't a *patrie*. Americans have never spoken of their country as a fatherland (or a motherland). The kind of natural or organic loyalty that we (rightly or wrongly) recognize in families doesn't seem to be a feature of our politics. When American politicians invoke the metaphor of family they are usually making an argument about our mutual responsibilities and welfarist obligations, and among Americans, that is a controversial argument. One can be an American patriot without believing in the mutual responsibilities of American citizens— indeed, for some Americans disbelief is a measure of one's patriotism.

Similarly, the United States isn't a "homeland" (where a national family might dwell), not, at least, as other countries are, in casual conversation and unreflective feeling. It is a country of immigrants who, however grateful they are for this new place, still remember the old places. And their children know, if only intermittently, that they have roots elsewhere. They, no doubt, are native grown, but some awkward sense of newness here, or of distant oldness, keeps the tongue from calling this land "home." The older political uses of the word "home," common in Great Britain, have never taken root here: home counties, home station, Home Office, home rule. To be "at home" in America is a personal matter: Americans have homesteads and homefolks and hometowns, and each of these is an endlessly interesting topic of conversation. But they don't have much to say about a common or communal home.

Nor is there a common *patrie*, but rather many different ones—a multitude of fatherlands (and motherlands). For the children, even the grandchildren, of the immigrant generation, one's *patrie*, the "native land of one's ancestors," is somewhere else. The term "Native Americans" designates the very first immigrants, who got here centuries before any of the others. At what point do the rest of us, native grown, become natives? The question has not been decided; for the moment, however, the language of nativism is mostly missing (it has never been dominant in American public life), even when the political reality is plain to see. Alternatively, nativist language can be used against the politics of nativism, as in these lines of Horace Kallen, the theorist of an anonymous America:

> Behind [the individual] in time and tremendously in him in quality are his ancestors; around him in space are his relatives and kin, carrying in common with him the inherited organic set from a remoter common ancestry. In all these he lives and moves and has his being. They constitute his, literally, *natio*, the inwardness of his nativity.

But since there are so many "organic sets" (language is deceptive here: Kallen's antinativist nativism is cultural, not biological), none of them can rightly be called "American." Americans have no inwardness of their own; they look inward only by looking backward.

According to Kallen, the United States is less importantly a union of states than it is a union of ethnic, racial, and religious groups—a union of otherwise unrelated "natives." What is the nature of this union? The Great Seal of the United States carries the motto *E pluribus unum*, "From many, one," which seems to suggest that manyness must be left behind for the sake of oneness. Once there were many, now the many have merged or, in Israel Zangwell's classic image, been melted down into one. But the Great Seal presents a different image: the "American" eagle holds a sheaf of arrows. Here there is no merger or fusion but only a fastening, a putting together: many-in-one. Perhaps the adjective "American" describes this kind of oneness. We might say, tentatively, that it points to the citizenship, not the nativity or nationality, of the men and women it designates. It is a political adjective, and its politics is liberal in the strict sense: generous, tolerant, ample, accommodating—it allows for the survival, even the enhancement and flourishing, of manyness.

On this view, appropriately called "pluralist," the word "from" on the Great Seal is a false preposition. There is no movement from many to one, but rather a simultaneity, a coexistence—once again, many-in-one. But I don't mean to suggest a mystery here, as in the Christian conception of a God who is three-in-one. The language of pluralism is sometimes a bit mysterious—thus Kallen's description of America as a "nation of nationalities" or John Rawls's account of the liberal state as a "social union of social unions"—but it lends itself to a rational unpacking. A sheaf of arrows is not, after all, a mysterious entity. We can find analogues in the earliest forms of social organization: tribes composed of many clans, clans composed of many families. The conflicts of loyalty and obligation, inevitable products of pluralism, must arise in these cases too. And yet, they are not exact analogues of the American case, for tribes and clans lack Kallen's "anonymity." American pluralism is, as we shall see, a peculiarly modern phenomenon—not mysterious but highly complex.

In fact, the United States is not a literal "nation of nationalities" or a "social union of social unions." At least, the singular nation or union is not constituted by, it is not a combination or fastening together of, the plural nationalities or unions. In some sense, it includes them; it provides a framework for their coexistence; but they are not its parts. Nor are the individual states, in any significant sense, the parts that make up the United States. The parts are individual men and women. The United States is an association of citizens. Its "anonymity" consists in the fact that these citizens don't transfer their collective name to the association. It never happened that a group of people called Americans came together to form a political society called America. The people are Americans only by virtue of having come together. And whatever identity they had before becoming Americans, they retain (or, better, they are free to retain) afterward. There is, to be sure, another view of Americanization, which holds that the process requires for its success the mental erasure of all previous identities—forgetfulness or even, as one enthusiast wrote in 1918, "absolute forgetfulness." But on the pluralist view, Americans are allowed to remember who they were and to insist, also, on *what else they are.*

They are not, however, bound to the remembrance or to the insistence. Just as their ancestors escaped the old country, so they can if they choose escape their old identities, the "inwardness" of their nativity. Kallen writes of the individual that "whatever else he changes, he cannot change his grandfather." Perhaps not; but he can call his grandfather a "greenhorn," reject his customs and convictions, give up the family name, move to a new neighborhood, adopt a new "life-style."

He doesn't become a better American by doing these things (though that is sometimes his purpose), but he may become an American simply, an American and nothing else, freeing himself from the hyphenation that pluralists regard as universal on this side, though not on the other side, of the Atlantic Ocean. But, free from hyphenation, he seems also free from ethnicity: "American" is not one of the ethnic groups recognized in the United States census. Someone who is only an American is, so far as our bureaucrats are concerned, ethnically anonymous. He has a right, however, to his anonymity; that is part of what it means to be an American.

* * *

Citizenship in the "new order" was not universally available, since blacks and women and Indians (Native Americans) were excluded, but it was never linked to a single nationality. "To be or to become an American," writes Philip Gleason, "a person did not have to be of any particular national, linguistic, religious, or ethnic background. All he had to do was to commit himself to the political ideology centered on the abstract ideals of liberty, equality, and republicanism." These abstract ideals made for a politics separated not only from religion but from culture itself or, better, from all the particular forms in which religious and national culture was, and is, expressed—hence a politics "anonymous" in Kallen's sense. Anonymity suggests autonomy too, though I don't want to claim that American politics was not qualified in important ways by British Protestantism, later by Irish Catholicism, later still by German, Italian, Polish, Jewish, African, and Hispanic religious commitments and political experience. But these qualifications never took what might be called a strong adjectival form, never became permanent or exclusive qualities of America's abstract politics and citizenship. The adjective "American" named, and still names, a politics that is relatively unqualified by religion or nationality or, alternatively, that is qualified by so many religions and nationalities as to be free from any one of them.

It is this freedom that makes it possible for America's oneness to encompass and protect its manyness. Nevertheless, the conflict between the one and the many is a pervasive feature of American life. Those Americans who attach great value to the oneness of citizenship and the centrality of political allegiance must seek to constrain the influence of cultural manyness; those who value the many must disparage the one. The conflict is evident from the earliest days of the republic, but I will begin my own account of it with the campaign to restrict immigration and naturalization in the 1850s. Commonly called "nativist" by historians, the campaign was probably closer in its politics to a Rousseauian republicanism. Anti-Irish and anti-Catholic bigotry played a large part in mobilizing support for the American (or American Republican) party, popularly called the Know-Nothings; and the political style of the party, like that of contemporary abolitionists and free-soilers, displayed many of the characteristics of Protestant moralism. But in its self-presentation, it was above all republican, more concerned about the civic virtue of the new immigrants than about their ethnic lineages, its religious critique focused on the ostensible connection between Catholicism and tyranny. The legislative program of the Know-Nothings had to do largely with questions of citizenship at the national level and of public education at the local level. In Congress, where the party had 75 representatives (and perhaps another 45 sympathizers, out of a total of 234) at the peak of its strength in 1855, it seemed more committed to restricting the suffrage than to cutting off immigration. Some of its members would have barred "paupers" from entering the United States, and others would have required an oath of allegiance from all immigrants immediately upon landing. But their energy was directed mostly toward revising the naturalization laws. It was not the elimination of manyness but its disenfranchisement that the Know-Nothings championed.

Something like this was probably the position of most American "nativists" until the last years of the nineteenth century. In 1845, when immigration rates were still fairly low, a group of "native Americans" meeting in Philadelphia declared that they would "kindly receive [all] persons who came to America, and give them every privilege except office and suffrage." I would guess that the nativist view of American blacks was roughly similar. Most of the northern Know-Nothings (the party's greatest strength was in New England) were strongly opposed to slavery, but it did not follow from that opposition that they were prepared to welcome former slaves as fellow citizens. The logic of events led to citizenship, after a bloody war, and the Know-Nothings, by then loyal Republicans, presumably supported that outcome. But the logic of republican principle, as they understood it, would have suggested some delay. Thus a resolution of the Massachusetts legislature in 1856 argued that "republican institutions were especially adapted to an educated and intelligent people, capable of *and accustomed to* self-government. Free institutions could be confined safely only to free men . . ." The legislators went on to urge a twenty-one-year residence requirement for naturalization. Since it was intended that disenfranchised residents should nonetheless be full members of civil society, another piece of Know-Nothing legislation would have provided that any alien free white person (this came from a Mississippi senator) should be entitled after twelve months residence "to all the protection of the government, and [should] be allowed to inherit, and hold, and transmit real estate . . . in the same manner as though he were a citizen."

Civil society, then, would include a great variety of ethnic and religious and perhaps even racial groups, but the members of these groups would acquire the "inestimable" good of citizenship only after a long period of practical education (but does one learn just by watching?) in democratic virtue. Meanwhile, their children would get a formal education. Despite their name, the Know-Nothings thought that citizenship was a subject about which a great deal had to be known. Some of them wanted to make attendance in public schools compulsory, but, faced with constitutional objections, they insisted only that no public funding should go to the support of parochial schools. It is worth emphasizing that the crucial principle here was not the separation of church and state. The Know-Nothing party did not oppose sabbatarian laws. Its members believed that tax money should not be used to underwrite social manyness—not in the case of religion, obviously, but also not in the case of language and culture. Political identity, singular in form, would be publicly inculcated and defended; the plurality of social identities would have to be sustained in private.

I don't doubt that most nativists hoped that plurality would not, in fact, be sustained. They had ideas, if not sociological theories, about the connection of politics and culture—specifically, as I have said, republican politics and British Protestant culture. I don't mean to underestimate the centrality of these ideas: this was presumably the knowledge that the Know-Nothings were concealing when they claimed to know nothing. Nonetheless, the logic of their position, as of any "American" republican position, pressed toward the creation of a politics independent of all the ethnicities and religions of civil society. Otherwise too many people would be excluded; the political world would look too much like Old England and not at all like the "new order of the ages," not at all like "America." Nor could American nativists challenge ethnic and religious pluralism directly, for both were protected (as the parochial schools were protected) by the constitution to which they claimed a passionate attachment. They could only insist that passionate attachment should be the mark of all citizens—and set forth the usual arguments against the seriousness of love at first sight and in favor of long engagements. They wanted what Rousseau wanted: that citizens should find the greater share of their happiness in public (political) rather than in private (social) activities. And they were prepared to deny citizenship to men and women who seemed to them especially unlikely to do that.

No doubt, again, public happiness came easily to the nativists because they felt so entirely at home in American public life. But we should not be too quick to attribute this feeling to the carry-over of ethnic consciousness into the political sphere. For American politics in the 1850s was already so open, egalitarian, and democratic (relative to European politics) that almost anyone could feel at home in it. Precisely because the United States was no one's *national* home, its politics was universally accessible. All that was necessary in principle was ideological commitment, in practice, a good line of talk. The Irish did very well and demonstrated as conclusively as one could wish that "British" and "Protestant" were not necessary adjectives for American politics. They attached to the many, not to the one.

For this reason, the symbols and ceremonies of American citizenship could not be drawn from the political culture or history of British-Americans. Our Congress is not a Commons; Guy Fawkes Day is not an American holiday; the Magna Carta has never been one of our sacred texts. American symbols and ceremonies are culturally anonymous, invented rather than inherited, voluntaristic in style, narrowly political in content: the flag, the Pledge, the Fourth, the Constitution. It is entirely appropriate that the Know-Nothing party had its origin in the Secret Society of the Star-Spangled Banner. And it is entirely understandable that the flag and the Pledge continue, even today to figure largely in political debate. With what reverence should the flag be treated? On what occasions must it be saluted? Should we require school children to recite the Pledge, teachers to lead the recitation? Questions like these are the tests of a political commitment that can't be assumed, because it isn't undergirded by the cultural and religious commonalities that make for mutual trust. The flag and the Pledge are, as it were, all we have. One could suggest, of course, alternative and more practical tests of loyalty—responsible participation in political life, for example. But the real historical alternative is the test proposed by the cultural pluralists: one proves one's Americanism, in their view, by living in peace with all the other "Americans," that is, by agreeing to respect social manyness rather than by pledging allegiance to the "one and indivisible" republic. And pluralists are led on by the logic of this argument to suggest that citizenship is something less than an "inestimable" good.

* * *

Good it certainly was to be an American citizen. Horace Kallen was prepared to call citizenship a "great vocation," but he clearly did not believe (in the 1910s and '20s, when he wrote his classic essays on cultural pluralism) that one could make a life there. Politics was a necessary, but not a spiritually sustaining activity. It was best understood in instrumental terms; it had to do with the arrangements that made it possible for groups of citizens to "realize and protect" their diverse cultures and "attain the excellence appropriate to their kind." These arrangements, Kallen thought, had to be democratic, and democracy required citizens of a certain sort—autonomous, self-disciplined, capable of cooperation and compromise. "Americanization" was entirely legitimate insofar as it aimed to develop these qualities; they made up Kallen's version of civic virtue, and he was willing to say that they should be common to all Americans. But, curiously perhaps, they did not touch the deeper self. "The common city-life, which depends upon like-mindedness, is not in-

ward, corporate, and inevitable, but external, inarticulate, and incidental . . . not the expression of a homogeneity of heritage, mentality, and
interest."

Hence Kallen's program: assimilation "in matters economic and political," dissimilation "in cultural consciousness." The hyphen joined these
two processes in one person, so that a Jewish-American (like Kallen) was
similar to other Americans in his economic and political activity, but similar only to other Jews at the deeper level of culture. It is clear that
Kallen's "hyphenates," whose spiritual life is located so emphatically to
the left of the hyphen, cannot derive the greater part of their happiness
from their citizenship. Nor, in a sense, should they, since culture, for the
cultural pluralists, is far more important than politics and promises a
more complete satisfaction. Pluralists, it seems, do not make good
republicans—for the same reason that republicans, Rousseau the classic
example, do not make good pluralists. The two attend to different sorts of
goods.

Kallen's hyphenated Americans can be attentive and conscientious citizens, but on a liberal, not a republican model. This means two things.
First, the various ethnic and religious groups can intervene in political life
only in order to defend themselves and advance their common interests—
as in the case of the NAACP or the Anti-Defamation League—but not in
order to impose their culture or their values. They have to recognize that
the state is anonymous (or, in the language of contemporary political theorists, neutral) at least in this sense: that it can't take on the character or
the name of any of the groups that it includes. It isn't a nation-state of a
particular kind and it isn't a Christian republic. Second, the primary political commitment of individual citizens is to protect their protection, to
uphold the democratic framework within which they pursue their more
substantive activities. This commitment is consistent with feelings of gratitude, loyalty, even patriotism of a certain sort, but it doesn't make for fellowship. There is indeed *union* in politics (and economics) but union of a
sort that precludes intimacy. "The political and economic life of the commonwealth," writes Kallen, "is a single unit and serves as the foundation
and background for the realization of the distinctive individuality of each
nation." Here pluralism is straightforwardly opposed to republicanism:
politics offers neither self-realization nor communion. All intensity lies, or
should lie, elsewhere.

Kallen believes, of course, that this "elsewhere" actually exists; his is
not a utopian vision; it's not a case of "elsewhere, perhaps." The "organic groups" that make up Kallen's America appear in public life as interest groups only, organized for the pursuit of material and social goods
that are universally desired but sometimes in short supply and often

unfairly distributed. That is the only appearance countenanced by a liberal and democratic political system. But behind it, concealed from public view, lies the true significance of ethnicity or religion: "It is the center at which [the individual] stands, the point of his most intimate social relations, therefore of his intensest emotional life." I am inclined to say that this is too radical a view of ethnic and religious identification, since it seems to rule out moral conflicts in which the individual's emotions are enlisted, as it were, on both sides. But Kallen's more important point is simply that there is space and opportunity *elsewhere* for the emotional satisfactions that politics can't (or shouldn't) provide. And because individuals really do find this satisfaction, the groups within which it is found are permanently sustainable: they won't melt down, not, at least, in any ordinary (noncoercive) social process. Perhaps they can be repressed, if the repression is sufficiently savage; even then, they will win out in the end.

Kallen wasn't entirely unaware of the powerful forces making for cultural meltdown, even without repression. He has some strong lines on the effectiveness of the mass media—though he knew these only in their infancy and at a time when newspapers were still a highly localized medium and the foreign-language press flourished. In his analysis and critique of the pressure to conform, he anticipated what became by the 1950s a distinctively American genre of social criticism. It isn't always clear whether he sees pluralism as a safeguard against or an antidote for the conformity of ethnic-Americans to that spiritless "Americanism" he so much disliked, a dull protective coloring that destroys all inner brightness. In any case, he is sure that inner brightness will survive, "for Nature is naturally pluralistic; her unities are eventual, not primary." Eventually, he means, the American union will prove to be a matter of "mutual accommodation," leaving intact the primacy of ethnic and religious identity. In the years since Kallen wrote, this view has gathered a great deal of ideological, but much less of empirical, support. "Pluralist principles . . . have been on the ascendancy," writes a contemporary critic of pluralism [Stephen Steinberg], "precisely at a time when ethnic differences have been on the wane." What if the "excellence" appropriate to our "kind" is, simply, an American excellence? Not necessarily civic virtue of the sort favored by nativists, republicans, and contemporary communitarians, but nonetheless some local color, a brightness of our own?

* * *

This local color is most visible, I suppose, in popular culture—which is entirely appropriate in the case of the world's first mass democracy. Consider, for example, the movie *American in Paris,* where the hero is an

American simply and not at all an Irish- or German- or Jewish-American. Do we drop our hyphens when we travel abroad? But what are we, then, without them? We carry with us cultural artifacts of a quite specific sort: *"une danse americaine,"* Gene Kelly tells the French children as he begins to tap dance. What else could he call it, this melted-down combination of Northern English clog dancing, the Irish jig and reel, and African rhythmic foot stamping, to which had been added, by Kelly's time, the influence of the French and Russian ballet? Creativity of this sort is both explained and celebrated by those writers and thinkers, heroes of the higher culture, that we are likely to recognize as distinctively American: thus Emerson's defense of the experimental life (I am not sure, though, that he would have admired tap dancing), or Whitman's democratic inclusiveness, or the pragmatism of Peirce and James.

"An American nationality," writes Gleason, "does in fact exist." Not just a political status, backed up by a set of political symbols and ceremonies, but a full-blooded nationality, reflecting a history and a culture—exactly like all the other nationalities from which Americans have been, and continue to be, recruited. The ongoing immigration makes it difficult to see the real success of Americanization in creating distinctive types, characters, styles, artifacts of all sorts which, were Gene Kelly to display them to his Parisian neighbors, they would rightly recognize as "American." More important, Americans recognize one another, take pride in the things that fellow Americans have made and done, identify with the national community. So, while there no doubt are people plausibly called Italian-Americans or Swedish-Americans, spiritual (as well as political) life—this is Gleason's view—is lived largely to the right of the hyphen: contrasted with real Italians and real Swedes, these are real Americans.

This view seems to me both right and wrong. It is right in its denial of Kallen's account of America as an anonymous nation of named nationalities. It is wrong in its insistence that America is a nation like all the others. But the truth does not lie, where we might naturally be led to look for it, somewhere between this rightness and this wrongness—as if we could locate America at some precise point along the continuum that stretches from the many to the one. I want to take the advice of that American song, another product of the popular culture, which tells us: "Don't mess with mister in-between." If there are cultural artifacts, songs and dances, styles of life and even philosophies, that are distinctively American, there is also an idea of America that is itself distinct, incorporating oneness and manyness in a "new order" that may or may not be "for the ages" but that is certainly for us, here and now.

The cultural pluralists come closer to getting the new order right than do the nativists and the nationalists and the American communitarians. Nonetheless, there is a nation and a national community and, by now, a very large number of native Americans. Even first- and second-generation Americans, as Gleason points out, have graves to visit and homes and neighborhoods to remember *in this country,* on this side of whatever waters their ancestors crossed to get here. What is distinctive about the nationality of these Americans is not its insubstantial character— substance is quickly acquired—but its nonexclusive character. Remembering the God of the Hebrew Bible, I want to argue that America is not a jealous nation. In this sense, at least, it is different from most of the others.

Consider, for example, a classic moment in the ethnic history of France: the debate over the emancipation of the Jews in 1790 and '91. It is not, by any means, a critical moment; there were fewer than 35,000 Jews in revolutionary France, only 500 in Paris. The Jews were not economically powerful or politically significant or even intellectually engaged in French life (all that could come only after emancipation). But the debate nonetheless was long and serious, for it dealt with the meaning of citizenship and nationality. When the Constituent Assembly voted for full emancipation in September 1791, its position was summed up by Clermont-Tonnerre, a deputy of the Center, in a famous sentence: "One must refuse everything to the Jews as a nation, and give everything to the Jews as individuals. . . . It would be repugnant to have . . . a nation within a nation." The Assembly's vote led to the disestablishment of Jewish corporate existence in France, which had been sanctioned and protected by the monarchy. "Refusing everything to the Jews as a nation" meant withdrawing the sanction, denying the protection. Henceforth Jewish communities would be voluntary associations, and individual Jews would have rights against the community as well as against the state: Clermont-Tonnerre was a good liberal.

But the Assembly debate also suggests that most of the deputies favoring emancipation would not have looked with favor even on the voluntary associations of the Jews, insofar as these reflected national sensibility or cultural difference. The future Girondin leader Brissot, defending emancipation, predicted that Jews who became French citizens would "lose their particular characteristics." I suspect that he could hardly imagine a greater triumph of French *civisme* than this—as if the secular Second Coming, like the religious version, awaited only the conversion of the Jews. Brissot thought the day was near: "Their eligibility [for citizenship] will regenerate them." Jews could be good citizens only insofar as they were regenerated, which meant, in effect, that they could be good citizens only insofar as they became French. (They must, after all, have some "particular characteristics," and if not their own, then whose?) Their emancipators had, no doubt, a generous view of their capacity to do that but would not have been generous in the face of resistance (from the Jews or from any other of the corporate groups of the old regime). The price of emancipation was assimilation.

This has been the French view of citizenship ever since. Though they have often been generous in granting the exalted status of citizen to foreigners, the successive republics have been suspicious of any form of ethnic pluralism. Each republic really has been "one and indivisible," and it has been established, as Rousseau thought it should be, on a strong national oneness. Oneness all the way down is, on this view, the only guarantee that the general will and the common good will triumph in French politics.

America is very different, and not only because of the eclipse of republicanism in the early nineteenth century. Indeed, republicanism has had a kind of afterlife as one of the legitimating ideologies of American politics. The Minute Man is a republican image of embodied citizenship. Reverence for the flag is a form of republican piety. The Pledge of Allegiance is a republican oath. But emphasis on this sort of thing reflects social disunity rather than unity; it is a straining after oneness where oneness doesn't exist. In fact, America has been, with severe but episodic exceptions, remarkably tolerant of ethnic pluralism (far less so of racial pluralism). I don't want to underestimate the human difficulties of adapting even to a hyphenated Americanism, nor to deny the bigotry and discrimination that particular groups have encountered. But tolerance has been the cultural norm.

Perhaps an immigrant society has no choice; tolerance is a way of muddling through when any alternative policy would be violent and dangerous. But I would argue that we have, mostly, made the best of this necessity, so that the virtues of toleration, in principle though by no means always in practice, have supplanted the singlemindedness of republican citizenship. We have made our peace with the "particular characteristics" of all the immigrant groups (though not, again, of all the racial groups) and have come to regard American nationality as an addition to rather than a replacement for ethnic consciousness. The hyphen works, when it is working, more like a plus sign. "American," then, is a name indeed, but unlike "French" or "German" or "Italian" or "Korean" or "Japanese" or "Cambodian," it can serve as a second name. And as in those modern marriages where two patronymics are joined, neither the first nor the second name is dominant: here the hyphen works more like a sign of equality.

We might go further than this: in the case of hyphenated Americans, it doesn't matter whether the first or the second name is dominant. We insist, most of the time, that the "particular characteristics" associated with the first name be sustained, as the Know-Nothings urged, without state help—and perhaps they will prove unsustainable on those terms. Still, an ethnic-American is someone who can, in principle, live his spiritual life as he chooses, *on either side of the hyphen.* In this sense, American citizenship is indeed anonymous, for it doesn't require a full commitment to American (or to any other) nationality. The distinctive national culture that Americans have created doesn't underpin, it exists alongside of, American politics. It follows, then, that the people I earlier called Americans simply, Americans and nothing else, have in fact a more complicated existence than those terms suggest. They are American-Americans, one more group of hyphenates (not quite the same as all the others), and one can imagine them attending to the cultural aspects of their Americanism and refusing the political commitment that republican ideology demands. They might still be good or bad citizens. And similarly, Orthodox Jews as well as secular (regenerate) Jews, Protestant fundamentalists as well as liberal Protestants, Irish republicans as well as Irish Democrats, black nationalists as well as black integrationists—all these can be good or bad citizens, given the American (liberal rather than republican) understanding of citizenship.

One step more is required before we have fully understood this strange America: it is not the case that Irish-Americans, say, are culturally Irish and politically American, as the pluralists claim (and as I have been assuming thus far for the sake of the argument). Rather, they are culturally Irish-American and politically Irish-American. Their culture has been significantly influenced by American culture; their politics is still, both in style and substance, significantly ethnic. With them, and with every ethnic and religious group except the American-Americans, hyphenation is doubled. It remains true, however, that what all the groups have in common is most importantly their citizenship and what most differentiates them, insofar as they are still differentiated, is their culture. Hence the alternation in American life of patriotic fevers and ethnic revivals, the first expressing a desire to heighten the commonality, the second a desire to reaffirm the difference.

At both ends of this peculiarly American alternation, the good that is defended is also exaggerated and distorted, so that pluralism itself is threatened by the sentiments it generates. The patriotic fevers are the symptoms of a republican pathology. At issue here is the all-important ideological commitment that, as Gleason says, is the sole prerequisite of American citizenship. Since citizenship isn't guaranteed by oneness all the way down, patriots or superpatriots seek to guarantee it by loyalty oaths and campaigns against "un-American" activities. The Know-Nothing party having failed to restrict naturalization, they resort instead to political purges and deportations. Ethnic revivals are less militant and less cruel, though not without their own pathology. What is at issue here is communal pride and power—a demand for political recognition without assimilation, an assertion of interest-group politics against republican ideology, an effort to distinguish this group (one's own) from all the others. American patriotism is always strained and nervous because hyphenation makes indeed for dual loyalty but seems, at the same time, entirely American. Ethnic revivalism is also strained and nervous, because the hyphenates are already Americans, on both sides of the hyphen.

In these circumstances, republicanism is a mirage, and American nationalism or communitarianism is not a plausible option; it doesn't reach to our complexity. A certain sort of communitarianism is available to each of the hyphenate groups—except, it would seem, the American-Americans, whose community, if it existed, would deny the Americanism of all the others. So Horace Kallen is best described as a Jewish (-American) communitarian and a (Jewish-) American liberal, and this kind of coexistence, more widely realized, would constitute the pattern he called cultural pluralism. But the different ethnic and religious communities are all of them far more precarious than he thought, for they have, in a liberal political system, no corporate form or legal structure or coercive power. And, without these supports, the "inherited organic set" seems to dissipate—the population lacks cohesion, cultural life lacks coherence. The resulting "groups" are best conceived, John Higham suggests, as a core of activists and believers and an expanding periphery of passive members or followers, lost, as it were, in a wider America. At the core, the left side of the (double) hyphen is stronger; along the periphery, the right side is stronger, though never fully dominant. Americans choose, as it were, their own location; and it appears that a growing number of them are choosing to fade into the peripheral distances. They become American-Americans, though without much passion invested in the becoming. But if the core doesn't hold, it also doesn't disappear; it is still capable of periodic revival.

At the same time, continued large-scale immigration reproduces a Kallenesque pluralism, creating new groups of hyphenate Americans and encouraging revivalism among activists and believers in the old groups. America is still a radically unfinished society, and for now, at least, it makes sense to say that this unfinishedness is one of its distinctive features. The country has a political center, but it remains in every other sense decentered. More than this, the political center, despite occasional patriotic fevers, doesn't work against decentering elsewhere. It neither requires nor demands the kind of commitment that would put the legitimacy of ethnic or religious identification in doubt. It doesn't aim at a finished or fully coherent Americanism. Indeed, American politics, itself pluralist in character, *needs* a certain sort of incoherence. A radical program of Americanization would really be unAmerican. It isn't inconceivable that America will one day become an American nation-state, the many giving way to the one, but that is not what it is now; nor is that its destiny. America has no singular national destiny—and to be an "American" is, finally, to know that and to be more or less content with it.

PAT ROBERTSON

A Portrait of America (1993)

Marion Gordon Robertson (1930–), known always as "Pat," is the leading Christian televangelist in America as host of the popular television show The 700 Club. The son of a U.S. Senator, Robertson graduated from Washington and Lee University and Yale Law School. He is the founder of the Christian Coalition and of Regent University in Virginia Beach, Virginia, which he serves as chancellor. A major figure in the Republican Party—a candidate, in fact, for its presidential nomination in 1988—Robertson is an outspoken defender of conservative and Christian values. He is also the author of fourteen books. In this excerpt from his 1993 The Turning Tide he blames "philosophical brainwashing" by university faculties for the social and moral decay he sees everywhere in America.

Unless we can get a firm grip on the ethical moorings of this country and stop its slide down the slippery slope of moral relativity and social decay, our entire culture will soon find itself on a high-speed ride to chaos and anarchy. We find ourselves caught between two views of reality and thrown into a battle over ideologies.

On one side of today's cultural divide are those who cling to traditional values and historic, republican virtues. On the other side are those fighting for some grand, opaque vision of a collectivist future with no absolutes. "The rules of morality," Scottish philosopher David Hume observed, "are not the conclusions of our reason." Rather, they are natural and eternal principles, the kind that make possible the vision of one nation, under God, with liberty and justice for all. A vision that could give a secure moral foundation for those men and women who desire a better world for themselves and their children is found in Robert Kennedy's much-quoted statement, "Some men see things as they are and ask, 'Why?' But I dream things that never were and I ask, 'Why not?'"

This clash over cultural ideals has raged for more than thirty years. There is no one today who is not engaged in one way or another in this monumental conflict.

* * * One side of this struggle is made up largely of everyday American workers and their families who want a simple, wholesome life, a better standard of living, and freedom from regulations and social distress. Pulling with them are the vast majority of small businesses, store owners and managers, and even a majority of large corporation leaders who perceive the benefits of a prosperous and unstressed society. The majority of clergy and established religious institutions are here as well, joined by conservative politicians and the leadership of the Republican party.

It is also noteworthy that most new Americans, including large numbers of Hispanic and Asian immigrants, are pulling for this side. For them the American dream means personal safety and the opportunity to compete in a free and open society. With it comes the promise of protection from the dangers of anarchy, social engineering, and immorality. It means limited government, lower taxes, and a healthy respect for individual rights *and* responsibilities. By and large, everyone on this side of the debate is pulling for a conservative and morally responsible society in an environment of mutual support and common sense. For twelve years this team also included the presidents of the United States, but now that has changed.

The opposite side of this debate fills its ranks with those who want to bring about massive changes in the form and focus of American culture. They would call themselves progressives. They want greater and greater liberties for smaller and smaller groups of people and sanctions that would restrict others from infringing upon their "social welfare." They do not want competition, equal access, or freedom of speech for all people. They want special status based on race, physical, mental, or social disabilities, and personal and sexual preferences.

This group is not nearly as large as the other, but it has enormous strength due to the support it receives from those in positions of power and influence in the world. There are some ordinary citizens among them, but the majority of these people are experts, bureaucrats, union leaders, journalists and publishers, media professionals, university professors, public school educators, and members of fringe industries that trade on permissiveness, self-indulgence, and vice. This group also includes the leadership of the Democratic party and all three branches of government—executive, legislative, and judicial—with few exceptions. This side has a large number of lawyers, those who profit from disturbances in society, along with large numbers of lawless people who thrive on anarchy and corruption.

Sexual liberation and all it entails is one of this side's loudest battle cries; public responsibility for personal choices is its creed. Liberals, socialists, and many libertarians are fully engaged on this side, while a number of socially active religious groups fill out the group. These spiritually and socially sensitive individuals are politically weak and contribute little, but they feed off the commotion and frenzy, and they do their best to offer aid and comfort to those actively involved in the struggle.

* * * One of the most challenging differences between these two groups is to be seen in their very different reactions to their adversaries. The first group is intolerant of crime and mischief, and they have little patience with those who habitually break the rules. But contrary to the claims of their enemies, they are remarkably tolerant of the natural philosophical differences between people. They believe in law and order, and consequently they expect the maximum sentence for offenders against the law, but they do not wish to punish people who disagree with them because of what they may think, say, or believe.

The other group, however, considers crime and public disorder to be political and philosophical issues, not moral concerns. Criminals, for example, need understanding and therapy. The only group these people wish to punish are their ideological opponents, and they punish them harshly and openly through public censure, ridicule, and imprisonment whenever possible. They are generally opposed to the death penalty for criminals, regardless of the crime, but they would no doubt harbor mixed feelings on this matter if the political and philosophical beliefs of their philosophical opponents could be included.

No doubt this illustration is overly simplistic, but I believe it illustrates the essential differences in the world-views of the principal opponents in today's culture war. * * *

The traditionalists have no argument with truth. Most accept a historic view of truth based on Judeo-Christian values, and they hold the belief that there are absolute standards of right and wrong in the world. These standards establish for them the terms of all debate and the priorities of individual behavior in all situations. * * * [T]hey have recognized the need to bring their desires into submission to the standards of truth.

The liberals, however, generally see rules and standards as euphemisms for imposing the will of one group upon the other groups. All laws are discriminatory, they hold, and traditional values are merely a codification of the prejudice and bigotry of a bygone era. Organized religions, many also claim, provide a pretext for enforcing the bias of the few upon the many. The only truth is the truth of the individual. Whatever works for one person is all the truth there is; there are no absolutes, no ultimate right and wrong, and no laws of importance except those the people voluntarily choose to obey for the good of the community. Truth must be shaped to accommodate one's personal desires.

* * * In his book *Why Johnny Can't Tell Right from Wrong,* William Kirk Kilpatrick describes the first view, which transforms desire to truth, as the "moral imagination." It is a world-view that seeks to interpret life on the basis of visible and perceived restraints. He describes the other view as the "idyllic imagination." It is a view that looks beyond reality to the ideal. It admits no restraints. "The moral imagination holds up an ideal that is attainable," writes Kilpatrick, "although only through hard work." But he adds:

> The idyllic imagination wants to escape from the harsh realities of ordinary life, either to a dream world, or to nature, or to a more primitive life. It follows mood rather than conscience, and rejects conventional morality in favor of a natural morality that will, it believes, emerge spontaneously in the absence of cultural restraints. When the idyllic imagination takes a spiritual turn, as it often does, it prefers a spirituality without morality or dogma?

The author goes on to say that the moral imagination understands the practical, the pedestrian, and the tragic elements of life. It accepts the view that much of life is ordinary, "daily," and sometimes desperate. But the idyllic imagination—especially that which blossomed in the 1960s and still makes up the core of modern liberalism—is idealistic and lacks a tragic sense.

Such people hold idealistic fantasies about the meaning of life; they have an existentialist view of reality that demands "engagement." They visualize popular movements, causes, and demonstrations on behalf of the oppressed peoples of the world, and they seek out relief efforts to save any endangered species of whatever variety happens to seize their imagination. It is not, after all, the species that fascinates them, but the idea of fighting tyranny. They are in love with rebellion, and they are, as Kilpatrick suggests, modern Romantics who share their beliefs not only with the hippies of Haight-Ashbury, but with the poets and dreamers of literature.

This idyllic, or Romantic, temperament makes them all the more easily defeated by harsh realities and real tragedies. They have difficulty dealing with life as it is actually lived. "Last year's Romantic idealist," writes Kilpatrick, "turns out to be this year's suicide. And because the Romantic is essentially naive about evil, he is less resistant to it." Writers such as T. S. Eliot and Russell Kirk have suggested that unless the idyllic imagination is tempered by morality, it can easily devolve into the "diabolical imagination." If you look at the Left's fascination with promiscuous sexuality, free speech, abortion rights, and legal protections for pornographers, it is not difficult to assume that this conversion has already taken place in our culture.

* * *

While most Americans hold on to some part of their religious convictions, they can see that these ideas are being assaulted by a highly articulate "cultural elite," supported by scientists and educators. Although statisticians report that 90 percent of Americans are affiliated with some religious group, most are leery about expressing their beliefs openly. * * *

* * *[T]here is good news from the culture wars. The death of the Religious Right has been greatly exaggerated, and common sense is making a dramatic comeback. The rule of experts is being challenged in all quarters, in part because the Democrats who control the White House, the Senate, the House of Representatives, and the bureaucracy have shown that they are not the moderates they claimed to be. They are firmly committed to leftist politics and the growth of big government. While they are stacking the cabinet, the courts, and the halls of state with the most radical women and men they can find, the public has lost patience with them and is beginning to lay out the hardware for a new attack.

What's more, government liberals and their cohorts in the media and the universities are coming under intense fire as well. The big news from the university campuses is that "PC" is no longer politically correct! Better yet, politically "incorrect" is in, and on more and more campuses the language of multicultural diversity is on its way out. A lead story in the lifestyle section of *USA Today* reported on the nationwide backlash against the PC movement, saying that "being perfectly PC may be passé. To the point that the scales are tipping backward." Early indicators of the change come from media personalities as diverse as radio talk show host Rush Limbaugh and liberal cartoonist Gary Trudeau. The latter's cartoon strip, "Doonesbury," has portrayed the vicissitudes of PC on the university campus and the bubbleheaded rhetoric of left-wing academics.

The problem is that each year more than 13 million students enroll in American colleges and universities. Of those, just under 20 percent, or about 2.5 million, are ethnic minorities. Most of these people begin the life-changing transition into the world of higher education with a combination of anxiety and hope. They undertake the changes with the understanding that they will be developing new friendships, new relationships, and taking a giant step toward adult independence and responsibility. Most of them will also be moving away from home and discovering a new world of ideas and new ways of dealing with the issues of daily life. But there are some surprises ahead.

Unfortunately, what they actually discover on many campuses today is not what they had expected. Instead of encouragement, enlightenment, and intellectual stimulation, they receive massive doses of indoctrination and a dark and somber vision of the future. Author Dinesh D'Souza says:

> By percent and example, universities have taught them that "all rules are unjust" and "all preferences are principled"; that justice is simply the will of the stronger party; that standards and values are arbitrary, and the ideal of the educated person is largely a figment of bourgeois white male ideology, which should be cast aside; . . . that all knowledge can be reduced to politics and should be pursued not for its own sake but for the political end of power; . . . that double standards are acceptable as long as they are enforced to the benefit of minority victims.

In other words, the reality of political correctness is no joke for students. Distorted though it is, it becomes a way of life and often the key to academic survival.

᙮ ᙮ ᙮ The best selling English author and historian Paul Johnson offers another apt assessment of the current state of affairs in British and American universities today. Writing in the London *Spectator*, he says:

> Universities are the most overrated institutions of our age. Of all the calamities which have befallen the 20th century, apart from the two world wars, the expansion of higher education in the 1950s and 1960s was the most enduring. It is a myth that universities are nurseries of reason. They are hothouses for every kind of extremism, irrationality, intolerance, and prejudice, where intellectual and social snobbery is almost purposefully instilled and where [faculty members] attempt to pass on to their students their own sins of pride. The wonder is that so many people emerge from these dens still employable, though a significant minority, as we have learned to our cost, go forth well equipped for a lifetime of public mischief-making.

In commenting on Johnson's analysis of the situation, Richard John Neuhaus, editor of the journal *First Things*, also cites the comments of the Heritage Foundation's Midge Decter, who has offered a brilliant formula for bringing university administrators back to their senses. She suggests, "If five or six major corporations would announce that they are no longer going to require a college degree, that they are going to train their own people, and that they will make provision for workers to learn Shakespeare and other good things in night school (which is more than they are learning in university now), the current system of higher education would collapse overnight." In plain business terms, they propose to break the monopoly of the universities. Make them compete for students like any other business and, miraculously, they will be forced to return to the real world for a change. Even if the universities should collapse, Neuhaus suggests, the truly gifted teachers would have no shortage of students. That is, after all, how the universities began some thousands of years ago.

Like the disaster of the public schools in this country—which also came about entirely as a result of empowering a state-run monopoly of public educators—the universities have transformed their mission of educating future leaders into a mandate for philosophical brainwashing. The perpetrators of PC on both British and American campuses—otherwise known as the academic "thought police"—are the same tenured radicals described in Roger Kimball's important 1991 book on the subject, entitled *Tenured Radicals*. They are, by and large, middle-aged hippies who have brought the idealism and anarchy of the sixties into the classroom, and they refuse to perceive the tortured logic of their position even when it is undeniable and distasteful to everyone else.

* * *

* * * Every human being has enormous potential to God, because all of this creation was meant for us. Now in light of this great truth, common sense would say that it is only natural for people to embrace the Judeo-Christian view of the dignity of men and women. According to the Bible, man is a little lower than the angels, destined to rule and reign with Christ. But the nihilists and the politically correct prefer to say that there is no God, there is no Jesus, there is no salvation, and there is no hope. That, very simply, is why their philosophy goes against the inner yearnings of all mankind and *why in a very short time liberalism is doomed to fall in America.*

Throughout history, the liberals have tried to reduce humanity to its lowest form and to identify humanity with the slime and the ooze of the earth, rather than identifying humanity as children of the living God and fellow heirs of the kingdom of heaven. The greatness of mankind is found in the dignity we achieve with God. When we see the accomplishments of Christian civilization, we have to recognize that those achievements have been nothing short of awesome.

But the incredible thing is that despite the attempts of the nihilists and the leftists, the tide is turning and we are seeing a movement of freedom. We are seeing a worldwide movement toward faith in God and its accompanying liberties—free enterprise and representative government all around the globe. From the darkest corners of the Third World to the mansions of Beverly Hills an awakening is taking place in the human heart that before long will sweep the land. There will be plenty of fierce challenges to overcome, but destiny is ours.

CORNEL WEST

Race Matters (1993)

Formerly a professor at Harvard University, the black theologian and public intellectual Cornel West (1953–) is now the Class of 1943 University Professor of Religion at Princeton University. A dynamic and popular speaker, West has written and lectured widely on pragmatic philosophy, religion, and race relations in America. In his best-selling book Race Matters, West reflects on the political, cultural, economic, and spiritual status of African Americans in the aftermath of the 1992 Los Angeles riots.

What happened in Los Angeles in April of 1992 was neither a race riot nor a class rebellion. Rather, this monumental upheaval was a multiracial, trans-class, and largely male display of justified social rage. For all its ugly, xenophobic resentment, its air of adolescent carnival, and its downright barbaric behavior, it signified the sense of powerlessness in American society. Glib attempts to reduce its meaning to the pathologies of the black underclass, the criminal actions of hoodlums, or the political revolt of the oppressed urban masses miss the mark. Of those arrested, only 36 percent were black, more than a third had full-time jobs, and most claimed to shun political affiliation. What we witnessed in Los Angeles was the consequence of a lethal linkage of economic decline, cultural decay, and political lethargy in American life. Race was the visible catalyst, not the underlying cause.

The meaning of the earthshaking events in Los Angeles is difficult to grasp because most of us remain trapped in the narrow framework of the dominant liberal and conservative views of race in America, which with its

worn-out vocabulary leaves us intellectually debilitated, morally disempow-
ered, and personally depressed. The astonishing disappearance of the event
from public dialogue is testimony to just how painful and distressing a serious engagement with race is. Our truncated public discussions of race suppress the best of who and what we are as a people because they fail to
confront the complexity of the issue in a candid and critical manner. The
predictable pitting of liberals against conservatives, Great Society Democrats against self-help Republicans, reinforces intellectual parochialism
and political paralysis.

The liberal notion that more government programs can solve racial
problems is simplistic—precisely because it focuses *solely* on the economic dimension. And the conservative idea that what is needed is a
change in the moral behavior of poor black urban dwellers (especially
poor black men, who, they say, should stay married, support their children, and stop committing so much crime) highlights immoral actions
while ignoring public responsibility for the immoral circumstances that
haunt our fellow citizens.

The common denominator of these views of race is that each still sees
black people as a "problem people," in the words of Dorothy I. Height,
president of the National Council of Negro Women, rather than as fellow
American citizens with problems. Her words echo the poignant "unasked
question" of W. E. B. Du Bois, who, in *The Souls of Black Folk* (1903),
wrote:

> They approach me in a half-hesitant sort of way, eye me curiously or
> compassionately, and then instead of saying directly, How does it feel
> to be a problem? they say, I know an excellent colored man in my
> town. . . . Do not these Southern outrages make your blood boil? At
> these I smile, or am interested, or reduce the boiling to a simmer, as the
> occasion may require. To the real question, How does it feel to be a
> problem? I answer seldom a word.

Nearly a century later, we confine discussions about race in America to
the "problems" black people pose for whites rather than consider what
this way of viewing black people reveals about us as a nation.

This paralyzing framework encourages liberals to relieve their guilty
consciences by supporting public funds directed at "the problems"; but at
the same time, reluctant to exercise principled criticism of black people,
liberals deny them the freedom to err. Similarly, conservatives blame the
"problems" on black people themselves—and thereby render black social
misery invisible or unworthy of public attention.

Hence, for liberals, black people are to be "included" and "integrated" into "our" society and culture, while for conservatives they are to be "well be-haved" and "worthy of acceptance" by "our" way of life. Both fail to see that the presence and predicaments of black people are neither additions to nor defections from American life, but rather *constitutive elements of that life*.

* * *

To engage in a serious discussion of race in America, we must begin not with the problems of black people but with the flaws of American society—flaws rooted in historic inequalities and longstanding cultural stereotypes. How we set up the terms for discussing racial issues shapes our perception and response to these issues. As long as black people are viewed as a "them," the burden falls on blacks to do all the "cultural" and "moral" work necessary for healthy race relations. The implication is that only certain Americans can define what it means to be American—and the rest must simply "fit in."

The emergence of strong black-nationalist sentiments among blacks, especially among young people, is a revolt against this sense of having to "fit in." The variety of black-nationalist ideologies, from the moderate views of Supreme Court Justice Clarence Thomas in his youth to those of Louis Farrakhan today, rest upon a fundamental truth: white America has been historically weak-willed in ensuring racial justice and has continued to resist fully accepting the humanity of blacks. As long as double stan-dards and differential treatment abound—as long as the rap performer Ice-T is harshly condemned while former Los Angeles Police Chief Daryl F. Gates's antiblack comments are received in polite silence, as long as Dr. Leonard Jeffries's anti-Semitic statements are met with vitriolic out-rage while presidential candidate Patrick J. Buchanan's anti-Semitism re-ceives a genteel response—black nationalisms will thrive.

Afrocentrism, a contemporary species of black nationalism, is a gal-lant yet misguided attempt to define an African identity in a white society perceived to be hostile. It is gallant because it puts black doings and suf-ferings, not white anxieties and fears, at the center of discussion. It is misguided because—out of fear of cultural hybridization and through si-lence on the issue of class, retrograde views on black women, gay men, and lesbians, and a reluctance to link race to the common good—it rein-forces the narrow discussions about race.

To establish a new framework, we need to begin with a frank acknow-ledgment of the basic humanness and Americanness of each of us. And we must acknowledge that as a people—*E Pluribus Unum*—we are on a slippery slope toward economic strife, social turmoil, and cultural chaos. If we go down, we go down together. The Los Angeles upheaval forced us to see not only that we are not connected in ways we would like to be but also, in a more profound sense, that this failure to connect binds us even more tightly together. The paradox of race in America is that our common destiny is more pronounced and imperiled precisely when our divisions are deeper. The Civil War and its legacy speak loudly here. And our divisions are growing deeper. Today, eighty-six percent of white suburban Americans live in neighborhoods that are less than 1 percent black, meaning that the prospects for the country depend largely on how its cities fare in the hands of a suburban electorate. There is no escape from our interracial interdependence, yet enforced racial hierarchy dooms us as a nation to collective paranoia and hysteria—the unmaking of any democratic order.

The verdict in the Rodney King case which sparked the incidents in Los Angeles was perceived to be wrong by the vast majority of Americans. But whites have often failed to acknowledge the widespread mistreatment of black people, especially black men, by law enforcement agencies, which helped ignite the spark. The verdict was merely the occasion for deep-seated rage to come to the surface. This rage is fed by the "silent" depression ravaging the country—in which real weekly wages of all American workers since 1973 have declined nearly 20 percent, while at the same time wealth has been upwardly distributed.

The exodus of stable industrial jobs from urban centers to cheaper labor markets here and abroad, housing policies that have created "chocolate cities and vanilla suburbs" (to use the popular musical artist George Clinton's memorable phrase), white fear of black crime, and the urban influx of poor Spanish-speaking and Asian immigrants—all have helped erode the tax base of American cities just as the federal government has cut its supports and programs. The result is unemployment, hunger, homelessness, and sickness for millions.

And a pervasive spiritual impoverishment grows. The collapse of meaning in life—the eclipse of hope and absence of love of self and others, the breakdown of family and neighborhood bonds—leads to the social deracination and cultural denudement of urban dwellers, especially children. We have created rootless, dangling people with little link to the supportive networks—family, friends, school—that sustain some sense of purpose in life. We have witnessed the collapse of the spiritual communities that in the past helped Americans face despair, disease, and death and that transmit through the generations dignity and decency, excellence and elegance.

The result is lives of what we might call "random nows," of fortuitous and fleeting moments preoccupied with "getting over"—with acquiring pleasure, property, and power by any means necessary. (This is not what Malcolm X meant by this famous phrase.) Post-modern culture is more and more a market culture dominated by gangster mentalities and self-destructive wantonness. This culture engulfs all of us—yet its impact on the disadvantaged is devastating, resulting in extreme violence in everyday life. Sexual violence against women and homicidal assaults by young black men on one another are only the most obvious signs of this empty quest for pleasure, property, and power.

Last, this rage is fueled by a political atmosphere in which images, not ideas, dominate, where politicians spend more time raising money than debating issues. The functions of parties have been displaced by public polls, and politicians behave less as thermostats that determine the climate of opinion than as thermometers registering the public mood. American politics has been rocked by an unleashing of greed among opportunistic public officials—who have followed the lead of their counterparts in the private sphere, where, as of 1989, 1 percent of the population owned 37 percent of the wealth and 10 percent of the population owned 86 percent of the wealth—leading to a profound cynicism and pessimism among the citizenry.

And given the way in which the Republican Party since 1968 has appealed to popular xenophobic images—playing the black, female, and homophobic cards to realign the electorate along race, sex, and sexual-orientation lines—it is no surprise that the notion that we are all part of one garment of destiny is discredited. Appeals to special interests rather than to public interests reinforce this polarization. The Los Angeles upheaval was an expression of utter fragmentation by a powerless citizenry that includes not just the poor but all of us.

What is to be done? How do we capture a new spirit and vision to meet the challenges of the post-industrial city, post-modern culture, and post-party politics?

First, we must admit that the most valuable sources for help, hope, and power consist of ourselves and our common history. As in the ages of Lincoln, Roosevelt, and King, we must look to new frameworks and languages to understand our multilayered crisis and overcome our deep malaise.

Second, we must focus our attention on the public square—the common good that undergirds our national and global destinies. The vitality of any public square ultimately depends on how much we *care* about the quality of our lives together. The neglect of our public infrastructure, for example—our water and sewage systems, bridges, tunnels, highways, subways, and streets—reflects not only our myopic economic policies, which impede productivity, but also the low priority we place on our common life.

The tragic plight of our children clearly reveals our deep disregard for public well-being. About one out of every five children in this country lives in poverty, including one out of every two black children and two out of every five Hispanic children. Most of our children—neglected by overburdened parents and bombarded by the market values of profit-hungry corporations—are ill-equipped to live lives of spiritual and cultural quality. Faced with these facts, how do we expect ever to constitute a vibrant society?

One essential step is some form of large-scale public intervention to ensure access to basic social goods—housing, food, health care, education, child care, and jobs. We must invigorate the common good with a mixture of government, business, and labor that does not follow any existing blueprint. After a period in which the private sphere has been sacralized and the public square gutted, the temptation is to make a fetish of the public square. We need to resist such dogmatic swings.

Last, the major challenge is to meet the need to generate new leadership. The paucity of courageous leaders—so apparent in the response to the events in Los Angeles—requires that we look beyond the same elites and voices that recycle the older frameworks. We need leaders—neither saints nor sparkling television personalities—who can situate themselves within a larger historical narrative of this country and our world, who can grasp the complex dynamics of our peoplehood and imagine a future grounded in the best of our past, yet who are attuned to the frightening obstacles that now perplex us. Our ideals of freedom, democracy, and equality must be invoked to invigorate all of us, especially the landless, propertyless, and luckless. Only a visionary leadership that can motivate "the better angels of our nature," as Lincoln said, and activate possibilities for a freer, more efficient, and stable America—only that leadership deserves cultivation and support.

This new leadership must be grounded in grass-roots organizing that highlights democratic accountability. Whoever *our* leaders will be as we approach the twenty-first century, their challenge will be to help Americans determine whether a genuine multiracial democracy can be created and sustained in an era of global economy and a moment of xenophobic frenzy.

Let us hope and pray that the vast intelligence, imagination, humor, and courage of Americans will not fail us. Either we learn a new language of empathy and compassion, or the fire this time will consume us all.

MICHAEL J. SANDEL

The Public Philosophy of
Contemporary Liberalism (1996)

The contemporary political philosopher Michael J. Sandel (1953–) is a professor of government at Harvard University. A popular teacher, he has emerged as a major critic of Rawls's theory of justice. In this essay, a chapter from his 1996 book, Democracy's Discontent: America in Search of a Public Philosophy, *Sandel argues that Americans should strive more for the normative ideals of republicanism than the procedural values enshrined in liberalism.*

LIBERAL AND REPUBLICAN FREEDOM

The political philosophy by which we live is a certain version of liberal political theory. Its central idea is that government should be neutral toward the moral and religious views its citizens espouse. Since people disagree about the best way to live, government should not affirm in law any particular vision of the good life. Instead, it should provide a framework of rights that respects persons as free and independent selves, capable of choosing their own values and ends. Since this liberalism asserts the priority of fair procedures over particular ends, the public life it informs might be called the procedural republic.

In describing the prevailing political philosophy as a version of liberal political theory, it is important to distinguish two different meanings of liberalism. In the common parlance of American politics, liberalism is the opposite of conservatism; it is the outlook of those who favor a more generous welfare state and a greater measure of social and economic equality. In the history of political theory, however, liberalism has a different, broader meaning. In this historical sense, liberalism describes a tradition of thought that emphasizes toleration and respect for individual rights and that runs from John Locke, Immanuel Kant, and John Stuart Mill to John Rawls. The public philosophy of contemporary American politics is a version of this liberal tradition of thought, and most of our debates proceed within its terms.

The idea that freedom consists in our capacity to choose our ends finds prominent expression in our politics and law. Its province is not limited to those known as liberals rather than conservatives in American politics; it can be found across the political spectrum. Republicans sometimes argue, for example, that taxing the rich to pay for welfare programs is a form of coerced charity that violates people's freedom to choose what to do with their own money. Democrats sometimes argue that government should assure all citizens a decent level of income, housing, and health, on the grounds that those who are crushed by economic necessity are not truly free to exercise choice in other domains. Although the two sides disagree about how government should act to respect individual choice, both assume that freedom consists in the capacity of persons to choose their values and ends.

So familiar is this vision of freedom that it seems a permanent feature of the American political and constitutional tradition. But Americans have not always understood freedom in this way. As a reigning public philosophy, the version of liberalism that informs our present debates is a recent arrival, a development of the last forty or fifty years. Its distinctive character can best be seen by contrast with a rival public philosophy that it gradually displaced. This rival public philosophy is a version of republican political theory.

Central to republican theory is the idea that liberty depends on sharing in self-government. This idea is not by itself inconsistent with liberal freedom. Participating in politics can be one among the ways in which people choose to pursue their ends. According to republican political theory, however, sharing in self-rule involves something more. It means deliberating with fellow citizens about the common good and helping to shape the destiny of the political community. But to deliberate well about the common good requires more than the capacity to choose one's ends and to respect others' rights to do the same. It requires a knowledge of public affairs and also a sense of belonging, a concern for the whole, a moral bond with the community whose fate is at stake. To share in self-rule therefore requires that citizens possess, or come to acquire, certain qualities of character, or civic virtues. But this means that republican politics cannot be neutral toward the values and ends its citizens espouse. The republican conception of freedom, unlike the liberal conception, requires a formative politics, a politics that cultivates in citizens the qualities of character self-government requires.

Both the liberal and republican conceptions of freedom have been present throughout our political experience, but in shifting measure and relative importance. Broadly speaking, republicanism predominated earlier in American history, liberalism later. In recent decades, the civic or formative aspect of our politics has largely given way to the liberalism that conceives persons as free and independent selves, unencumbered by moral or civic ties they have not chosen.

This shift sheds light on our present political predicament. For despite its appeal, the liberal vision of freedom lacks the civic resources to sustain self-government. This defect ill-equips it to address the sense of disempowerment that afflicts our public life. The public philosophy by which we live cannot secure the liberty it promises, because it cannot inspire the sense of community and civic engagement that liberty requires.

How the liberal conception of citizenship and freedom gradually crowded out the republican conception involves two intersecting tales. One traces the advent of the procedural republic from the first stirrings of American constitutionalism to recent debates about religious liberty, free speech, and privacy rights. Another traces the decline of the civic strand of American political discourse from Thomas Jefferson's day to the present.

These stories, taken together, bring to clarity the self-image that animates—and sometimes debilitates—our public life. They do not reveal a golden age when all was right with American democracy. The republican tradition coexisted with slavery, with the exclusion of women from the public realm, with property qualifications for voting, with nativist hostility to immigrants; indeed it sometimes provided the terms within which these practices were defended.

And yet, for all its episodes of darkness, the republican tradition, with its emphasis on community and self-government, may offer a corrective to our impoverished civic life. Recalling the republican conception of freedom as self-rule may prompt us to pose questions we have forgotten how to ask: What economic arrangements are hospitable to self-government? How might our political discourse engage rather than avoid the moral and religious convictions people bring to the public realm? And how might the public life of a pluralist society cultivate in citizens the expansive self-understandings that civic engagement requires? If the public philosophy of our day leaves little room for civic considerations, it may help to recall how earlier generations of Americans debated such questions, before the procedural republic took hold. But in order to identify the relevant strands of the story, we need to specify more fully the version of liberalism that informs our present politics.

THE ASPIRATION TO NEUTRALITY

The idea that government should be neutral on the question of the good life is distinctive to modern political thought. Ancient political theory held that the purpose of politics was to cultivate the virtue, or moral excellence,

of citizens. All associations aim at some good, Aristotle wrote, and the polis, or political association, aims at the highest, most comprehensive good:
"any polis which is truly so called, and is not merely one in name, must devote itself to the end of encouraging goodness. Otherwise, a political association sinks into a mere alliance, which only differs in space from other
forms of alliance where the members live at a distance from one another.
Otherwise, too, law becomes a mere covenant—or (in the phrase of the
Sophist Lycophron) 'a guarantor of men's rights against one another'—
instead of being, as it should be, a rule of life such as will make the members of a polis good and just."

According to Aristotle, political community is more than "an association for residence on a common site, or for the sake of preventing mutual
injustice and easing exchange." Although these are necessary conditions
for political community, they are not its purpose or ultimate justification.
"The end and purpose of a polis is the good life, and the institutions of
social life are means to that end." It is only as participants in political association that we can realize our nature and fulfill our highest ends.

Unlike the ancient conception, liberal political theory does not see political life as concerned with the highest human ends or with the moral
excellence of its citizens. Rather than promote a particular conception of
the good life, liberal political theory insists on toleration, fair procedures,
and respect for individual rights—values that respect people's freedom to
choose their own values. But this raises a difficult question. If liberal
ideals cannot be defended in the name of the highest human good, then
in what does their moral basis consist?

It is sometimes thought that liberal principles can be justified by a simple version of moral relativism. Government should not "legislate morality,"
because all morality is merely subjective, a matter of personal preference
not open to argument or rational debate. "Who is to say what is literature
and what is filth? That is a value judgment, and whose values should decide?" Relativism usually appears less as a claim than as a question: "Who
is to judge?" But the same question can be asked of the values that liberals
defend. Toleration and freedom and fairness are values too, and they can
hardly be defended by the claim that no values can be defended. So it is a
mistake to affirm liberal values by arguing that all values are merely subjective. The relativist defense of liberalism is no defense at all.

Utilitarianism versus Kantian Liberalism

What, then, is the case for the neutrality the liberal invokes? Recent political philosophy has offered two main alternatives—one utilitarian, the

other Kantian. The utilitarian view, following John Stuart Mill, defends liberal principles in the name of maximizing the general welfare. The state should not impose on its citizens a preferred way of life, even for their own good, because doing so will reduce the sum of human happiness, at least in the long run. It is better that people choose for themselves, even if, on occasion, they get it wrong.

"The only freedom which deserves the name," writes Mill in *On Liberty*, "is that of pursuing our own good in our own way, so long as we do not attempt to deprive others of theirs, or impede their efforts to obtain it." He adds that his argument does not depend on any notion of abstract right, only on the principle of the greatest good for the greatest number. "I regard utility as the ultimate appeal on all ethical questions; but it must be utility in the largest sense, grounded on the permanent interests of man as a progressive being."

Many objections have been raised against utilitarianism as a general doctrine of moral philosophy. Some have questioned the concept of utility and the assumption that all human goods are in principle commensurable. Others have objected that by reducing all values to preferences and desires, utilitarians are unable to admit qualitative distinctions of worth, unable to distinguish noble desires from base ones. But most recent debate has focused on whether utilitarianism offers a convincing basis for liberal principles, including respect for individual rights.

At first glance, utilitarianism seems well suited to liberal purposes. Seeking to maximize overall happiness does not require judging people's values, only aggregating them. And the willingness to aggregate preferences without judging them suggests a tolerant spirit, even a democratic one. When people go to the polls we count their votes, whatever they are.

But the utilitarian calculus is not always as liberal as it first appears. If enough cheering Romans pack the Coliseum to watch the lion devour the Christian, the collective pleasure of the Romans will surely outweigh the pain of the Christian, intense though it be. Or if a big majority abhors a small religion and wants it banned, the balance of preferences will favor suppression, not toleration. Utilitarians sometimes defend individual rights on the grounds that respecting them now will serve utility in the long run. But this calculation is precarious and contingent. It hardly secures the liberal promise not to impose on some the values of others.

The case against utilitarianism was made most powerfully by Immanuel Kant. He argued that empirical principles such as utility were unfit to serve as a basis for morality. A wholly instrumental defense of freedom and rights not only leaves rights vulnerable but fails to respect the inherent dignity of persons. The utilitarian calculus treats people as means to the happiness of others, not as ends in themselves, worthy of respect.

Contemporary liberals extend Kant's argument with the claim that utilitarianism fails to take seriously the distinction between persons. In seeking above all to maximize the general welfare, the utilitarian treats society as a whole as if it were a single person; it conflates our many, diverse desires into a single system of desires. It is indifferent to the distribution of satisfactions among persons, except insofar as this may affect the overall sum. But this fails to respect our plurality and distinctness. It uses some as means to the happiness of all, and so fails to respect each as an end in himself or herself.

In the view of modern-day Kantians, certain rights are so fundamental that even the general welfare cannot override them. As John Rawls writes in *A Theory of Justice,* "Each person possesses an inviolability founded on justice that even the welfare of society as a whole cannot override. . . . The rights secured by justice are not subject to political bargaining or to the calculus of social interests."

So Kantian liberals need an account of rights that does not depend on utilitarian considerations. More than this, they need an account that does not depend on any particular conception of the good, that does not presuppose the superiority of one way of life over others. Only a justification neutral among ends could preserve the liberal resolve not to favor any particular ends or to impose on its citizens a preferred way of life. But what sort of justification could this be? How is it possible to affirm certain liberties and rights as fundamental without embracing some vision of the good life, without endorsing some ends over others?

The solution proposed by Kantian liberals is to draw a distinction between the "right" and the "good"—between a framework of basic rights and liberties, and the conceptions of the good that people may choose to pursue within the framework. It is one thing for the state to support a fair framework, they argue, something else to affirm some particular ends. For example, it is one thing to defend the right to free speech so that people may be free to form their own opinions and choose their own ends, but something else to support it on grounds that a life of political discussion is inherently worthier than a life unconcerned with public affairs, or on the grounds that free speech will increase the general welfare. Only the first defense is available on the Kantian view, resting as it does on the ideal of a neutral framework.

Now the commitment to a framework neutral with respect to ends can be seen as a kind of value—in this sense the Kantian liberal is no relativist—but its value consists precisely in its refusal to affirm a preferred way of life or conception of the good. For Kantian liberals, then, the right is prior to the good, and in two senses. First, individual rights cannot be sacrificed for the sake of the general good; and second, the principles of justice that specify these rights cannot be premised on any particular vision of the good life. What justifies the rights is not that they maximize the general welfare or otherwise promote the good, but rather that they constitute a fair framework within which individuals and groups can choose their own values and ends, consistent with a similar liberty for others.

The claim for the priority of the right over the good connects the ideal of neutrality with the primacy of individual rights. For Kantian liberals, rights "function as trump cards held by individuals." They protect individuals from policies, even democratically enacted ones, that would impose a preferred conception of the good and so fail to respect people's freedom to choose their own conceptions.

Of course, proponents of the liberal ethic notoriously disagree about what rights are fundamental and what political arrangements the ideal of the neutral framework requires. Egalitarian liberals support the welfare state and favor a scheme of civil liberties together with certain social and economic rights—rights to welfare, education, health care, and so on. They argue that respecting the capacity of persons to pursue their own ends requires government to assure the minimal prerequisites of a dignified life. Libertarian liberals (usually called conservatives in contemporary politics) defend the market economy and claim that redistributive policies violate people's rights. They argue that respect for persons requires assuring to each the fruits of his or her own labor, and so favor a scheme of civil liberties combined with a strict regime of private property rights. Whether egalitarian or libertarian, Kantian liberalism begins with the claim that we are separate, individual persons, each with our own aims, interests, and conceptions of the good life. It seeks a framework of rights that will enable us to realize our capacity as free moral agents, consistent with a similar liberty for others.

THE LIBERAL SELF

The Kantian case against utilitarianism derives much of its force from its contrasting conception of the person, its view of what it means to be a moral agent. Where utilitarians conflate our many desires into a single system of desire, Kantian liberals insist on the separateness of persons. Where the utilitarian self is simply defined as the sum of its desires, the Kantian self is a choosing self, independent of the desires and ends it may have at any moment. Kant expressed this idea by attributing to human beings the capacity to act with an autonomous will. Contemporary liberals rely on the similar notion of a self given prior to and independent of its purposes and ends.

The claim for the priority of the right over the good, and the conception of the person that attends it, oppose Kantian liberalism not only to utilitarianism but also to any view that regards us as obligated to fulfill ends we have not chosen—ends given by nature or God, for example, or by our identities as members of families, peoples, cultures, or traditions. Encumbered identities such as these are at odds with the liberal conception of the person as free and independent selves, unbound by prior moral ties, capable of choosing our ends for ourselves. This is the conception that finds expression in the ideal of the state as a neutral framework. For Kantian liberals, it is precisely because we are freely choosing, independent selves that we need a neutral framework, a framework of rights that refuses to choose among competing values and ends. For the liberal self, what matters above all, what is most essential to our personhood, is not the ends we choose but our capacity to choose them. "It is not our aims that primarily reveal our nature," but rather the framework of rights we would agree to if we could abstract from our aims. "For the self is prior to the ends which are affirmed by it; even a dominant end must be chosen from among numerous possibilities."

The liberal ethic derives much of its moral force from the appeal of the self-image that animates it. This appeal has at least two sources. First, the image of the self as free and independent, unencumbered by aims and attachments it does not choose for itself, offers a powerful liberating vision. Freed from the sanctions of custom and tradition and inherited status, unbound by moral ties antecedent to choice, the liberal self is installed as sovereign, cast as the author of the only obligations that constrain. More than the simple sum of circumstance, we become capable of the dignity that consists in being persons of our "own creating, making, choosing." We are agents and not just instruments of the purposes we pursue. We are "self-originating sources of valid claims."

A second appeal of the liberal self-image consists in the case it implies for equal respect. The idea that there is more to a person than the roles he plays or the customs she keeps or the faith he affirms suggests a basis for respect independent of life's contingencies. Liberal justice is blind to such differences between persons as race, religion, ethnicity, and gender, for in the liberal self-image, these features do not really define our identity in the first place. They are not constituents but merely attributes of the self, the sort of things the state should look beyond. "Our social position and class, our sex and race should not influence deliberations made from a moral point of view." Once these contingencies are seen as products of our situation rather than as aspects of our person, they cease to supply the familiar grounds for prejudice and discrimination.

Nor does it matter, from the standpoint of liberal justice, what virtues we display or what values we espouse. "That we have one conception of the good rather than another is not relevant from a moral standpoint. In acquiring it we are influenced by the same sort of contingencies that lead us to rule out a knowledge of our sex and class." Despite their many differences, libertarian and egalitarian liberals agree that people's entitlements should not be based on their merit or virtue or moral desert, for the qualities that make people virtuous or morally deserving depend on factors "arbitrary from a moral point of view." The liberal state therefore does not discriminate; none of its policies or laws may presuppose that any person or way of life is intrinsically more virtuous than any other. It respects persons as persons, and secures their equal right to live the lives they choose.

CRITIQUE OF KANTIAN LIBERALISM

Kantian liberals thus avoid affirming a conception of the good by affirming instead the priority of the right, which depends in turn on a picture of the self given prior to its ends. But how plausible is this self-conception? Despite its powerful appeal, the image of the unencumbered self is flawed. It cannot make sense of our moral experience, because it cannot account for certain moral and political obligations that we commonly recognize, even prize. These include obligations of solidarity, religious duties, and other moral ties that may claim us for reasons unrelated to a choice. Such obligations are difficult to account for if we understand ourselves as free and independent selves, unbound by moral ties we have not chosen. Unless we think of ourselves as encumbered selves, already claimed by certain projects and commitments, we cannot make sense of these indispensable aspects of our moral and political experience.

Consider the limited scope of obligation on the liberal view. According to Rawls, obligations can arise in only one of two ways, as "natural duties" we owe to human beings as such or as voluntary obligations we incur by consent. The natural duties are those we owe persons *qua* persons—to do justice, to avoid cruelty, and so on. All other obligations, the ones we owe to particular others, are founded in consent and arise only in virtue of agreements we make, be they tacit or explicit.

Conceived as unencumbered selves, we must respect the dignity of all persons, but beyond this, we owe only what we agree to owe. Liberal justice requires that we respect people's rights (as defined by the neutral framework), not that we advance their good. Whether we must concern ourselves with other people's good depends on whether, and with whom, and on what terms, we have agreed to do so.

One striking consequence of this view is that "there is no political obligation, strictly speaking, for citizens generally." Although those who run for office voluntarily incur a political obligation (that is, to serve their country if elected), the ordinary citizen does not. "It is not clear what is the requisite binding action or who has performed it." The average citizen is therefore without any special obligations to his or her fellow citizens, apart from the universal, natural duty not to commit injustice.

The liberal attempt to construe all obligation in terms of duties universally owed or obligations voluntarily incurred makes it difficult to account for civic obligations and other moral and political ties that we commonly recognize. It fails to capture those loyalties and responsibilities whose moral force consists partly in the fact that living by them is inseparable from understanding ourselves as the particular persons we are—as members of this family or city or nation or people, as bearers of that history, as citizens of this republic. Loyalties such as these can be more than values I happen to have, and to hold, at a certain distance. The moral responsibilities they entail may go beyond the obligations I voluntarily incur and the "natural duties" I owe to human beings as such.

Some of the special responsibilities that flow from the particular communities I inhabit I may owe to fellow members, such as obligations of solidarity. Others I may owe to members of those communities with which my own community has some morally relevant history, such as the morally burdened relations of Germans to Jews, of American whites to American blacks, or of England and France to their former colonies. Whether they look inward or outward, obligations of membership presuppose that we are capable of moral ties antecedent to choice. To the extent that we are, the meaning of our membership resists redescription in contractarian terms.

It is sometimes argued, in defense of the liberal view, that loyalties and allegiances not grounded in consent, however psychologically compelling, are matters of sentiment, not of morality, and so do not suggest an obligation unavailable to unencumbered selves. But it is difficult to make sense of certain familiar moral and political dilemmas without acknowledging obligations of solidarity and the thickly constituted, encumbered selves that they imply.

Consider the case of Robert E. Lee on the eve of the Civil War. Lee, then an officer in the Union army, opposed secession, in fact regarded it as treason. And yet when war loomed, Lee concluded that his obligation to Virginia outweighed his obligation to the Union and also his reported opposition to slavery. "With all my devotion to the Union," he wrote, "I have not been able to make up my mind to raise my hand against my relatives, my children, my home. . . . If the Union is dissolved, and the Government disrupted, I shall return to my native State and share the miseries of my people. Save in her defense, I will draw my sword no more."

One can appreciate the poignance of Lee's predicament without necessarily approving of the choice he made. But one cannot make sense of his dilemma as a *moral* dilemma without acknowledging that the call to stand with his people, even to lead them in a cause he opposed, was a claim of moral and not merely sentimental import, capable at least of weighing in the balance against other duties and obligations. Otherwise, Lee's predicament was not really a moral dilemma at all, but simply a conflict between morality on the one hand and mere sentiment or prejudice on the other.

A merely psychological reading of Lee's predicament misses the fact that we not only sympathize with people such as Lee but often admire them, not necessarily for the choices they make but for the quality of character their deliberation reflects. The quality at stake is the disposition to see and bear one's life circumstance as a reflectively situated being—claimed by the history that implicates me in a particular life, but self-conscious of its particularity, and so alive to other ways, wider horizons. But this is precisely the quality that is lacking in those who would think of themselves as unencumbered selves, bound only by the obligations they choose to incur.

As the Lee example illustrates, the liberal conception of the person is too thin to account for the full range of moral and political obligations we commonly recognize, such as obligations of solidarity. This counts against its plausibility generally. But it may even be too weak to support the less strenuous communal obligations expected of citizens in the modern welfare state. Some stronger conception of community may be required, not only to make sense of tragic-heroic dilemmas such as Lee's, but even to sustain the rights that many liberals defend.

While libertarian liberals ask little of citizens, more generous expressions of the liberal ethic support various policies of public provision and redistribution. Egalitarian liberals defend social and economic rights as well as civil and political rights, and so demand of their fellow citizens a high measure of mutual engagement. They insist on the "plurality and distinctness" of individuals but also require that we "share one another's fate" and regard the distribution of natural talents as "a common asset."

Liberalism as an ethic of sharing emphasizes the arbitrariness of fortune and the importance of certain material prerequisites for the meaningful exercise of equal liberties. Since "necessitous men are not free men," and since in any case the distribution of assets and endowments that make for success is "arbitrary from a moral point of view," egalitarian liberals would tax the rich to help the poor secure the prerequisites of a dignified life. Thus the liberal case for the welfare state depends not on a theory of the common good or on some strong notion of communal obligation, but instead on the rights we would agree to respect if we could abstract from our interests and ends.

The liberal case for public provision seems well suited to conditions in which strong communal ties cannot be relied on, and this is one source of its appeal. But it lies vulnerable nonetheless to the libertarian objection that redistributive policies use some people as means to others' ends, and so offend the "plurality and distinctness" of individuals that liberalism seeks above all to secure. In the contractual vision of community alone, it is unclear how the libertarian objection can be met. If those whose fate I am required to share really are, morally speaking, *others*, rather than fellow participants in a way of life with which my identity is bound, then liberalism as an ethic of sharing seems open to the same objections as utilitarianism. Its claim on me is not the claim of a community with which I identify, but rather the claim of an arbitrarily defined collectivity whose aims I may or may not share.

If the egalitarian replies that social and economic rights are required as a matter of equal respect for persons, the question remains why *these* persons, the ones who happen to live in my country, have a claim on my concern that others do not. Tying the mutual responsibilities of citizenship to the idea of respect for persons *qua* persons puts the moral case for welfare on a par with the case for foreign aid—a duty we owe strangers with whom we share a common humanity but possibly little else. Given its conception of the person, it is unclear how liberalism can defend the particular boundaries of concern its own ethic of sharing must presuppose.

What egalitarian liberalism requires, but cannot within its own terms provide, is some way of defining the relevant community of sharing, some way of seeing the participants as mutually indebted and morally engaged to begin with. It needs a way of answering Emerson's challenge to the man who solicited his contribution to the poor—"Are they *my* poor?" Since liberal social and economic rights cannot be justified as expressing or advancing a common life of shared pursuits, the basis and bounds of communal concern become difficult to defend. For as we have seen, the strong notion of community or membership that would save and situate

the sharing is precisely the one denied to the liberal self. The moral encumbrances and antecedent obligations it implies would undercut the
priority of right.

MINIMALIST LIBERALISM

If we are not the freely choosing, unencumbered selves that Kantian liberals imagine us to be, does it follow that government need not be neutral, that politics should cultivate the virtue of its citizens after all? Some
political philosophers argue that the case for neutrality can be detached
from the Kantian conception of the person. The case for liberalism, they
argue, is political, not philosophical or metaphysical, and so does not depend on controversial claims about the nature of the self. The priority of
the right over the good is not the application to politics of Kantian moral
philosophy, but a practical response to the familiar fact that people in
modern democratic societies typically disagree about the good. Since this
defense of neutrality does not depend on a Kantian conception of the
person but instead "stays on the surface, philosophically speaking," it
might be described as minimalist liberalism.

Minimalist liberals acknowledge that we may sometimes be claimed by
moral or religious obligations unrelated to a choice. But they insist that
we set these obligations aside when we enter the public realm, that we
bracket our moral and religious convictions when deliberating about politics and law. In our personal lives, we may regard it as unthinkable to
view ourselves "apart from certain religious, philosophical, and moral
convictions, or from certain enduring attachments and loyalties." But we
should draw a distinction between our personal and our political identities. However encumbered we may be in private, however claimed by
moral or religious convictions, we should bracket our encumbrances in
public and regard ourselves, *qua* public selves, as independent of any particular loyalties or conceptions of the good.

The insistence that we separate our identity as citizens from our identity as persons gives rise to an obvious challenge. Why should our political identities not express the moral and religious convictions we affirm in
our personal lives? Why, in deliberating about justice and rights, must we
set aside the moral judgments that inform the rest of our lives? Minimalist liberals reply that separating our identity as citizens from our identity
as persons honors an important fact about modern democratic life. In
traditional societies, people sought to shape political life in the image of
their own moral and religious ideals. But modern democratic societies
are marked by a plurality of moral and religious ideals. Moreover, this

pluralism is reasonable; it reflects the fact that, even after reasoned reflection, decent, intelligent people will come to different conceptions about the nature of the good life. Given the fact of reasonable pluralism, we should try to decide questions of justice and rights without affirming one conception of the good over others. Only in this way can we affirm the political value of social cooperation based on mutual respect.

Minimalist liberalism seeks to detach liberal principles from political controversy, including debates about the nature of the self. It presents itself "not as a conception of justice that is true," but as one that can serve as a basis for political agreement in a democratic society. It asserts "the priority of democracy over philosophy." It offers a political conception of justice, not a metaphysical or philosophical one.

The minimalist case for liberalism depends on the plausibility of separating politics from philosophy, of bracketing moral and religious questions where politics is concerned. But this raises the question why the practical interest in securing social cooperation and mutual respect is always so compelling as to defeat any competing moral interest that could arise from within a substantive moral or religious view. One way of assuring the priority of the practical is to deny that any of the moral or religious conceptions it brackets could be true. But this is precisely the sort of controversial metaphysical claim the minimalist liberal wants to avoid. If the liberal must therefore allow that some such conceptions might be true, then the question remains: What guarantees that no moral or religious doctrine can generate interests sufficiently compelling to burst the brackets, so to speak, and morally outweigh the practical interest in social cooperation?

CRITIQUE OF MINIMALIST LIBERALISM

Minimalist liberalism lacks a convincing answer to this question. For notwithstanding the importance of political values such as toleration, social cooperation, and mutual respect, it is not always reasonable to set aside competing values that may arise from substantive moral and religious doctrines. At least where grave moral questions are concerned, whether it is reasonable to bracket moral and religious controversies for the sake of political agreement partly depends on which of the contending moral or religious doctrines is true. Minimalist liberalism wants to separate the case for toleration from any judgment about the moral worth of the practices being tolerated. But this separation is not always defensible. We cannot determine whether toleration is justified in any given case without passing moral judgment on the practice in question.

This difficulty is illustrated by two political controversies that bear on grave moral and religious questions. One is the contemporary debate about abortion rights. The other is the famous debate in 1858 between Abraham Lincoln and Stephen Douglas over popular sovereignty and slavery.

The Abortion Debate

Given the intense disagreement over the moral permissibility of abortion, the case for seeking a political solution that brackets the moral and religious issues—that is neutral with respect to them—would seem especially strong. But whether it is reasonable to bracket, for political purposes, the moral and religious doctrines at stake depends largely on which of those doctrines is true. If the doctrine of the Catholic church is true, if human life in the relevant moral sense really does begin at conception, then bracketing the moral-theological question of when human life begins is far less reasonable than it would be on rival moral and religious assumptions. The more confident we are that fetuses are, in the relevant moral sense, *different* from babies, the more confident we can be in affirming a political conception of justice that sets aside the controversy about the moral status of fetuses.

As the contemporary debate over abortion reflects, even a political conception of justice presupposes a certain view of the controversies it would bracket. For the debate about abortion is not only a debate about when human life begins, but also a debate about how reasonable it is to abstract from that question for political purposes. Opponents of abortion resist the translation from moral to political terms because they know that more of their view will be lost in the translation; the neutral territory offered by minimalist liberalism is likely to be less hospitable to their religious convictions than to those of their opponents. For defenders of abortion, little comparable is at stake; there is little difference between believing that abortion is morally permissible and agreeing that, as a political matter, women should be free to decide the moral question for themselves. The moral price of political agreement is far higher if abortion is wrong than if it is permissible. How reasonable it is to bracket the contending moral and religious views depends partly on which of those views is more plausible.

The minimalist liberal might reply that the political values of toleration and equal citizenship for women are sufficient grounds for concluding that women should be free to choose for themselves whether to have an abortion; government should not take sides on the moral and religious controversy over when human life begins. But if the Catholic church is right about the moral status of the fetus, if abortion is morally tantamount to murder, then it is not clear why the political values of toleration and women's equality, important though they are, should prevail. If the Catholic doctrine is true, then the minimalist liberal's case for the priority of political values must become an instance of just-war theory; he or she would have to show why these values should prevail even at the cost of some 1.5 million civilian deaths each year.

Of course, to suggest the impossibility of bracketing the moral-theological question of when human life begins is not to argue against a right to abortion. It is simply to show that the case for abortion rights cannot be neutral with respect to the underlying moral and religious controversy. It must engage rather than avoid the substantive moral and religious doctrines at stake. Liberals often resist this engagement because it violates the priority of the right over the good. But the abortion debate shows that this priority cannot be sustained. The case for respecting a woman's right to decide for herself whether to have an abortion depends on showing that there is a relevant moral difference between aborting a fetus at a relatively early stage of development and killing a child.

The Lincoln-Douglas Debates

Perhaps the most famous case for bracketing a controversial moral question for the sake of political agreement was made by Stephen Douglas in his debates with Abraham Lincoln. Since people were bound to disagree about the morality of slavery, Douglas argued, national policy should be neutral on that question. The doctrine of popular sovereignty he defended did not judge slavery right or wrong but left the people of the territories free to make their own judgments. "To throw the weight of federal power into the scale, either in favor of the free or the slave states," would violate the fundamental principles of the Constitution and run the risk of civil war. The only hope of holding the country together, he argued, was to agree to disagree, to bracket the moral controversy over slavery and respect "the right of each state and each territory to decide these questions for themselves."

Lincoln argued against Douglas' case for a political conception of justice. Policy should express rather than avoid a substantive moral judgment about slavery, he maintained. Although Lincoln was not an abolitionist, he believed that government should treat slavery as the moral wrong it was and prohibit its extension to the territories. "The real issue in this controversy—pressing upon every mind—is the sentiment on the part of one class that looks upon the institution of slavery as a wrong, and of another class that does not look upon it as a wrong." Lincoln and the

Republican party viewed slavery as a wrong and insisted that it "be treated as a wrong, and one of the methods of treating it as a wrong is to make provision that it shall grow no larger."

Whatever his personal moral views, Douglas claimed that, for political purposes at least, he was agnostic on the question of slavery; he did not care whether slavery was "voted up or voted down." Lincoln replied that it was reasonable to bracket the question of the morality of slavery only on the assumption that it was not the moral evil he regarded it to be. Any man can advocate political neutrality "who does not see anything wrong in slavery, but no man can logically say it who does see a wrong in it; because no man can logically say he don't care whether a wrong is voted up or voted down."

The debate between Lincoln and Douglas was not primarily about the morality of slavery, but about whether to bracket a moral controversy for the sake of political agreement. In this respect, their debate over popular sovereignty is analogous to the contemporary debate over abortion rights. As some contemporary liberals argue that government should not take a stand one way or another on the morality of abortion, but let each woman decide the question for herself, so Douglas argued that national policy should not take a stand one way or the other on the morality of slavery, but let each territory decide the question for itself. There is of course the difference that in the case of abortion rights, those who would bracket the substantive moral question typically leave the choice to the individual, while in the case of slavery, Douglas' way of bracketing was to leave the choice to the territories.

But Lincoln's argument against Douglas was an argument about bracketing as such, at least where grave moral questions are at stake. Lincoln's point was that the political conception of justice defended by Douglas depended for its plausibility on a particular answer to the substantive moral question it sought to bracket. Even in the face of so dire a threat to social cooperation as the prospect of civil war, it made neither moral nor political sense to aspire to political neutrality. As Lincoln concluded in his final debate with Douglas, "Is it not a false statesmanship that undertakes to build up a system of policy upon the basis of caring nothing about the very thing that every body does care the most about?"

Present-day liberals will surely resist the company of Douglas and want national policy to oppose slavery, presumably on the grounds that slavery violates people's rights. But it is doubtful that liberalism conceived as a political conception of justice can make this claim without violating its own strictures against appeals to comprehensive moral ideals. For example, a Kantian liberal can oppose slavery as a failure to treat persons as ends in themselves, worthy of respect. But this argument, resting as it does on a Kantian conception of the person, is unavailable to minimalist liberalism. So too are the antislavery arguments of many American abolitionists in the 1830s and 1840s, who emphasized the sin of slavery and made their case in religious terms.

The debates over abortion and slavery show that a political conception of justice must sometimes presuppose an answer to the moral and religious questions it purports to bracket. At least where grave moral questions are at stake, it is not possible to detach politics and law from substantive moral judgment. But even in cases where it is possible to conduct political debate without reference to our moral and religious convictions, it may not always be desirable. The effort to banish moral and religious argument from the public realm for the sake of political agreement may end by impoverishing political discourse and eroding the moral and civic resources necessary to self-government.

    This tendency can be seen in our present public life. With a few notable exceptions, such as the civil rights movement of the 1950s and 1960s, our political discourse in recent decades has come to reflect the liberal resolve that government be neutral on moral and religious questions, that matters of policy and law be debated and decided without reference to any particular conception of the good life. But we are beginning to find that a politics that brackets morality and religion too completely soon generates its own disenchantment. A procedural republic cannot contain the moral energies of a vital democratic life. It creates a moral void that opens the way for narrow, intolerant moralisms. And it fails to cultivate the qualities of character that equip citizens to share in self-rule.

RICHARD RORTY

A Cultural Left (1998)

One of America's leading philosophers, Richard Rorty (1931–2007) taught at Stanford University. Alongside his formal philosophical writings on pragmatism, contingency, and objectivity, Rorty—the grandson of Walter Rauschenbusch—involved himself in political debate. Often he criticized fellow intellectuals whose erudite writings, he argued, do not serve a practical progressive agenda. In this excerpt Rorty offers two

*suggestions for the American left. It is from a series of lectures published
in 1998 in a volume entitled* Achieving Our Country: Leftist Thought in
Twentieth-Century America.

I t is often said that we Americans, at the end of the twentieth century,
no longer have a Left. Since nobody denies the existence of what I have
called the cultural Left, this amounts to an admission that that Left is unable to engage in national politics. It is not the sort of Left which can be
asked to deal with the consequences of globalization. To get the country to
deal with those consequences, the present cultural Left would have to
transform itself by opening relations with the residue of the old reformist
Left, and in particular with the labor unions. It would have to talk much
more about money, even at the cost of talking less about stigma.

I have two suggestions about how to effect this transition. The first is
that the Left should put a moratorium on theory. It should try to kick its
philosophy habit. The second is that the Left should try to mobilize what
remains of our pride in being Americans. It should ask the public to consider how the country of Lincoln and Whitman might be achieved.

In support of my first suggestion, let me cite a passage from Dewey's
Reconstruction in Philosophy in which he expresses his exasperation with
the sort of sterile debate now going on under the rubric of "individualism
versus communitarianism." Dewey thought that all discussions which
took this dichotomy seriously

> suffer from a common defect. They are all committed to the logic of
> general notions under which specific situations are to be brought.
> What we want is light upon this or that group of individuals, this or
> that concrete human being, this or that special institution or social
> arrangement. For such a logic of inquiry, the traditionally accepted
> logic substitutes discussion of the meaning of concepts and their di-
> alectical relationships with one another.

Dewey was right to be exasperated by sociopolitical theory conducted at
this level of abstraction. He was wrong when he went on to say that as-
cending to this level is typically a rightist maneuver, one which supplies
"the apparatus for intellectual justifications of the established order." For
such ascents are now more common on the Left than on the Right. The
contemporary academic Left seems to think that the higher your level of
abstraction, the more subversive of the established order you can be. The
more sweeping and novel your conceptual apparatus, the more radical
your critique.

When one of today's academic leftists says that some topic has been "inadequately theorized," you can be pretty certain that he or she is going to drag in either philosophy of language, or Lacanian psychoanalysis, or some neo-Marxist version of economic determinism. Theorists of the Left think that dissolving political agents into plays of differential subjectivity, or political initiatives into pursuits of Lacan's impossible object of desire, helps to subvert the established order. Such subversion, they say, is accomplished by "problematizing familiar concepts."

Recent attempts to subvert social institutions by problematizing concepts have produced a few very good books. They have also produced many thousands of books which represent scholastic philosophizing at its worst. The authors of these purportedly "subversive" books honestly believe that they are serving human liberty. But it is almost impossible to clamber back down from their books to a level of abstraction on which one might discuss the merits of a law, a treaty, a candidate, or a political strategy. Even though what these authors "theorize" is often something very concrete and near at hand—a current TV show, a media celebrity, a recent scandal—they offer the most abstract and barren explanations imaginable.

These futile attempts to philosophize one's way into political relevance are a symptom of what happens when a Left retreats from activism and adopts a spectatorial approach to the problems of its country. Disengagement from practice produces theoretical hallucinations. These result in an intellectual environment which is, as Mark Edmundson says in his book *Nightmare on Main Street,* Gothic. The cultural Left is haunted by ubiquitous specters, the most frightening of which is called "power." This is the name of what Edmundson calls Foucault's "haunting agency, which is everywhere and nowhere, as evanescent and insistent as a resourceful spook."

In its Foucauldian usage, the term "power" denotes an agency which has left an indelible stain on every word in our language and on every institution in our society. It is always already there, and cannot be spotted coming or going. One might spot a corporate bagman arriving at a congressman's office, and perhaps block his entrance. But one cannot block off power in the Foucauldian sense. Power is as much inside one as outside one. It is nearer than hands and feet. As Edmundson says: one cannot "confront power; one can only encounter its temporary and generally unwitting agents . . . [it] has capacities of motion and transformation that make it a *preternatural* force." Only interminable individual and social self-analysis, and perhaps not even that, can help us escape from the infinitely fine meshes of its invisible web.

The ubiquity of Foucauldian power is reminiscent of the ubiquity of Satan, and thus of the ubiquity of original sin—that diabolical stain on every human soul. I argued in my first lecture that the repudiation of the concept of sin was at the heart of Dewey and Whitman's civic religion. I also claimed that the American Left, in its horror at the Vietnam War, reinvented sin. It reinvented the old religious idea that some stains are ineradicable. I now wish to say that, in committing itself to what it calls "theory," this Left has gotten something which is entirely too much like religion. For the cultural Left has come to believe that we must place our country within a theoretical frame of reference, situate it within a vast quasi-cosmological perspective.

Stories about the webs of power and the insidious influence of a hegemonic ideology do for this Left what stories about the Lamanites did for Joseph Smith and what stories about Yakkub did for Elijah Muhammad. What stories about blue-eyed devils are to the Black Muslims, stories about hegemony and power are to many cultural leftists—the only thing they really want to hear. To step into the intellectual world which some of these leftists inhabit is to move out of a world in which the citizens of a democracy can join forces to resist sadism and selfishness into a Gothic world in which democratic politics has become a farce. It is a world in which all the daylit cheerfulness of Whitmanesque hypersecularism has been lost, and in which "liberalism" and "humanism" are synonyms for naiveté—for an inability to grasp the full horror of our situation.

I have argued in various books that the philosophers most often cited by cultural leftists—Nietzsche, Heidegger, Foucault, and Derrida—are largely right in their criticisms of Enlightenment rationalism. I have argued further that traditional liberalism and traditional humanism are entirely compatible with such criticisms. We can still be old-fashioned reformist liberals even if, like Dewey, we give up the correspondence theory of truth and start treating moral and scientific beliefs as tools for achieving greater human happiness, rather than as representations of the intrinsic nature of reality. We can be this kind of liberal even after we turn our backs on Descartes, linguistify subjectivity, and see everything around us and within us as one more replaceable social construction.

But I have also urged that insofar as these antimetaphysical, anti-Cartesian philosophers offer a quasi-religious form of spiritual pathos, they should be relegated to private life and not taken as guides to political deliberation. The notion of "infinite responsibility," formulated by Emmanuel Levinas and sometimes deployed by Derrida—as well as Derrida's own frequent discoveries of impossibility, unreachability, and unrepresentability—may be useful to some of us in our individual quests for private perfection. When we take up our public responsibilities, however, the infinite and the unrepresentable are merely nuisances. Thinking of our responsibilities in these terms is as much of a stumbling-block to effective political organization as is the sense of sin. Emphasizing the impossibility of meaning, or of justice, as Derrida sometimes does, is a temptation to Gothicize—to view democratic politics as ineffectual, because unable to cope with preternatural forces.

Whitman and Dewey, I have argued, gave us all the romance, and all the spiritual uplift, we Americans need to go about our public business. As Edmundson remarks, we should not allow Emerson, who was a precursor of both Whitman and Dewey, to be displaced by Poe, who was a precursor of Lacan. For purposes of thinking about how to achieve our country, we do not need to worry about the correspondence theory of truth, the grounds of normativity, the impossibility of justice, or the infinite distance which separates us from the other. For those purposes, we can give both religion and philosophy a pass. We can just get on with trying to solve what Dewey called "the problems of men."

To think about those problems means to refrain from thinking so much about otherness that we begin to acquiesce in what Todd Gitlin has called, in the title of a recent book, "the twilight of common dreams." It means deriving our moral identity, at least in part, from our citizenship in a democratic nation-state, and from leftist attempts to fulfill the promise of that nation.

The cultural Left often seems convinced that the nation-state is obsolete, and that there is therefore no point in attempting to revive national politics. The trouble with this claim is that the government of our nation-state will be, for the foreseeable future, the only agent capable of making any real difference in the amount of selfishness and sadism inflicted on Americans.

It is no comfort to those in danger of being immiserated by globalization to be told that, since national governments are now irrelevant, we must think up a replacement for such governments. The cosmopolitan super-rich do not think any replacements are needed, and they are likely to prevail. Bill Readings was right to say that "the nation-state [has ceased] to be the elemental unit of capitalism," but it remains the entity which makes decisions about social benefits, and thus about social justice. The current leftist habit of taking the long view and looking beyond nationhood to a global polity is as useless as was faith in Marx's philosophy of history, for which it has become a substitute. Both are equally irrelevant to the question of how to prevent the reemergence of hereditary castes, or of how to prevent right-wing populists from taking advantage of resentment at that reemergence.

When we think about these latter questions, we begin to realize that one of the essential transformations which the cultural Left will have to undergo is the shedding of its semiconscious anti-Americanism, which it carried over from the rage of the late Sixties. This Left will have to stop thinking up ever more abstract and abusive names for "the system" and start trying to construct inspiring images of the country. Only by doing so can it begin to form alliances with people outside the academy—and, specifically, with the labor unions. Outside the academy, Americans still want to feel patriotic. They still want to feel part of a nation which can take control of its destiny and make itself a better place.

If the Left forms no such alliances, it will never have any effect on the laws of the United States. To form them will require the cultural Left to forget about Baudrillard's account of America as Disneyland—as a country of simulacra—and to start proposing changes in the laws of a real country, inhabited by real people who are enduring unnecessary suffering, much of which can be cured by governmental action. Nothing would do more to resurrect the American Left than agreement on a concrete political platform, a People's Charter, a list of specific reforms. The existence of such a list— endlessly reprinted and debated, equally familiar to professors and production workers, imprinted on the memory both of professional people and of those who clean the professionals' toilets—might revitalize leftist politics.

The problems which can be cured by governmental action, and which such a list would canvass, are mostly those that stem from selfishness rather than sadism. But to bring about such cures it would help if the Left would change the tone in which it now discusses sadism. The pre-Sixties reformist Left, insofar as it concerned itself with oppressed minorities, did so by proclaiming that all of us—black, white, and brown—are Americans, and that we should respect one another as such. This strategy gave rise to the "platoon" movies, which showed Americans of various ethnic backgrounds fighting and dying side by side. By contrast, the contemporary cultural Left urges that America should not be a melting-pot, because we need to respect one another in our differences. This Left wants to preserve otherness rather than ignore it.

The distinction between the old strategy and the new is important. The choice between them makes the difference between what Todd Gitlin calls "common dreams" and what Arthur Schlesinger calls "disuniting America." To take pride in being black or gay is an entirely reasonable response to the sadistic humiliation to which one has been subjected. But insofar as this pride prevents someone from also taking pride in being an American citizen, from thinking of his or her country as capable of reform, or from being able to join with straights or whites in reformist initiatives, it is a political disaster.

The rhetorical question of the "platoon" movies—"What do our differences matter, compared with our commonality as fellow Americans?"—did not commend pride in difference, but neither did it condemn it. The intent of posing that question was to help us become a country in which a person's difference would be largely neglected by others, unless the person in question wished to call attention to it. If the cultural Left insists on its present strategy—on asking us to respect one another in our differences rather than asking us to cease noticing those differences—it will have to find a new way of creating a sense of commonality at the level of national politics. For only a rhetoric of commonality can forge a winning majority in national elections.

I doubt that any such new way will be found. Nobody has yet suggested a viable leftist alternative to the civic religion of which Whitman and Dewey were prophets. That civic religion centered around taking advantage of traditional pride in American citizenship by substituting social justice for individual freedom as our country's principal goal. We were supposed to love our country because it showed promise of being kinder and more generous than other countries. As the blacks and the gays, among others, were well aware, this was a counsel of perfection rather than description of fact. But you cannot urge national political renewal on the basis of descriptions of fact. You have to describe the country in terms of what you passionately hope it will become, as well as in terms of what you know it to be now. You have to be loyal to a dream country rather than to the one to which you wake up every morning. Unless such loyalty exists, the ideal has no chance of becoming actual.

But the country of one's dreams must be a country one can imagine being constructed, over the course of time, by human hands. One reason the cultural Left will have a hard time transforming itself into a political Left is that, like the Sixties Left, it still dreams of being rescued by an angelic power called "the people." In this sense, "the people" is the name of a redemptive preternatural force, a force whose demonic counterpart is named "power" or "the system." The cultural Left inherited the slogan "Power to the people" from the Sixties Left, whose members rarely asked about how the transference of power was supposed to work. This question still goes unasked.

Edmundson, Delbanco, and other cultural commentators have remarked that the contemporary United States is filled with visions of demons and angels. Stephen King and Tony Kushner have helped form a national collective unconscious which is "Gothic" in Edmundson's sense. It produces dreams not of political reforms but of inexplicable, magical transformations. The cultural Left has contributed to the formation of this politically useless unconscious not only by adopting "power" as the name of an invisible, ubiquitous, and malevolent presence, but by adopting ideals which nobody is yet able to imagine being actualized.

Among these ideals are participatory democracy and the end of capitalism. Power will pass to the people, the Sixties Left believed, only when decisions are made by all those who may be affected by their results. This means, for example, that economic decisions will be made by stakeholders rather than by shareholders, and that entrepreneurship and markets will cease to play their present role. When they do, capitalism as we know it will have ended, and something new will have taken its place.

But what this new thing will be, nobody knows. The Sixties did not ask how the various groups of stakeholders were to reach a consensus about when to remodel a factory rather than build a new one, what prices to pay for raw materials, and the like. Sixties leftists skipped lightly over all the questions which had been raised by the experience of nonmarket economies in the so-called socialist countries. They seemed to be suggesting that once we were rid of both bureaucrats and entrepreneurs, "the people" would know how to handle competition from steel mills or textile factories in the developing world, price hikes on imported oil, and so on. But they never told us how "the people" would learn how to do this.

The cultural Left still skips over such questions. Doing so is a consequence of its preference for talking about "the system" rather than about specific social practices and specific changes in those practices. The rhetoric of this Left remains revolutionary rather than reformist and pragmatic. Its insouciant use of terms like "late capitalism" suggests that we can just wait for capitalism to collapse, rather than figuring out what, in the absence of markets, will set prices and regulate distribution. The voting public, the public which must be won over if the Left is to emerge from the academy into the public square, sensibly wants to be told the details. It wants to know how things are going to work after markets are put behind us. It wants to know how participatory democracy is supposed to function.

The cultural Left offers no answers to such demands for further information, but until it confronts them it will not be able to be a political Left. The public, sensibly, has no interest in getting rid of capitalism until it is offered details about the alternatives. Nor should it be interested in participatory democracy—the liberation of the people from the power of the technocrats—until it is told how deliberative assemblies will acquire the same know-how which only the technocrats presently possess. Even someone like myself, whose admiration for John Dewey is almost unlimited, cannot take seriously his defense of participatory democracy against Walter Lippmann's insistence on the need for expertise.

The cultural Left has a vision of an America in which the white patriarchs have stopped voting and have left all the voting to be done by members of previously victimized groups, people who have somehow come

into possession of more foresight and imagination than the selfish subur-
banites. These formerly oppressed and newly powerful people are expected to be as angelic as the straight white males were diabolical. If I
shared this expectation, I too would want to live under this new dispensation. Since I see no reason to share it, I think that the Left should get
back into the business of piecemeal reform within the framework of a
market economy. This was the business the American Left was in during
the first two-thirds of the century.

Someday, perhaps, cumulative piecemeal reforms will be found to have
brought about revolutionary change. Such reforms might someday produce a presently unimaginable nonmarket economy, and much more
widely distributed powers of decisionmaking. They might also, given similar reforms in other countries, bring about an international federation, a
world government. In such a new world, American national pride would
become as quaint as pride in being from Nebraska or Kazakhstan or
Sicily. But in the meantime, we should not let the abstractly described
best be the enemy of the better. We should not let speculation about a totally changed system, and a totally different way of thinking about human
life and human affairs, replace step-by-step reform of the system we
presently have.

Let me return, yet again, to the theme with which I began: the contrast
between spectatorship and agency.

From the point of view of a detached cosmopolitan spectator, our
country may seem to have little to be proud of. The United States of
America finally freed its slaves, but it then invented segregation laws
which were as ingeniously cruel as Hitler's Nuremberg laws. It started to
create a welfare state, but quickly fell behind the rest of the industrial
democracies in providing equal medical care, education, and opportunity
to the children of the rich and of the poor. Its workers built a strong labor
movement, but then allowed this movement to be crushed by restrictive
legislation and by the gangsters whom they weakly allowed to take over
many locals. Its government perverted a justified crusade against an evil
empire into a conspiracy with right-wing oligarchs to suppress social
democratic movements.

I have been arguing that the appropriate response to such observations
is that we Americans should not take the point of view of a detached cosmopolitan spectator. We should face up to unpleasant truths about ourselves, but we should not take those truths to be the last word about our
chances for happiness, or about our national character. Our national
character is still in the making. Few in 1897 would have predicted the
Progressive Movement, the forty-hour week, Women's Suffrage, the New

Deal, the Civil Rights Movement, the successes of second-wave feminism, or the Gay Rights Movement. Nobody in 1997 can know that America will not, in the course of the next century, witness even greater moral progress.

Whitman and Dewey tried to substitute hope for knowledge. They wanted to put shared utopian dreams—dreams of an ideally decent and civilized society—in the place of knowledge of God's Will, Moral Law, the Laws of History, or the Facts of Science. Their party, the party of hope, made twentieth-century America more than just an economic and military giant. Without the American Left, we might still have been strong and brave, but nobody would have suggested that we were good. As long as we have a functioning political Left, we still have a chance to achieve our country, to make it the country of Whitman's and Dewey's dreams.

BILL McKIBBEN

The End of Nature (1999)

One of America's leading environmentalists, Bill McKibben (1960–) is Resident Scholar in Environmental Studies at Middlebury College in Vermont. A former staff writer for the New Yorker *and a frequent contributor to* Harper's Magazine, *he is the author of* Wandering Home: A Long Walk Across America's Most Hopeful Landscape. *This essay is the introduction to the tenth-anniversary republication of his* End of Nature, *in which he singles out global warming as the number-one ecological threat of our time.*

When I wrote *The End of Nature* in the late 1980s, I began with two observations. First, that we tell time badly—that we're used to thinking of the Earth as changing with infinite slowness, but that in fact it is now speeding up, changing in rapid, dangerous, and profound ways as a result of our alterations. And second, that our sense of scale is awry—that we're used to thinking of people as small and the world as large, but that in our lifetimes the opposite has become the truth.

In the winter of 1999, as I write this new introduction for the tenth anniversary edition of the book, those two thoughts still fill my mind. NASA has just announced that the twelve months of 1998 were the twelve warmest months since records have been kept. And 1998 beat 1997 by a record margin, which in turn topped 1995, and . . . in fact, seven of the ten warmest years that we know about have taken place since *The End of Nature* was first published in 1989. Those are the most important statistics of the decade just past, more important than the booming stock market, or the President's approval rating, or all the other numbers we paid more attention to. They underline the point that we live in the oddest moment since our species first stood upright, the moment when we are finally grown so big in numbers and in appetites that we alter everything around us. Those numbers demonstrate the end of nature as an independent force, something larger than us.

But if the cycles of the Earth now move more quickly—spring on average comes *a week earlier* across the Northern Hemisphere than it did just two decades ago—human society seems, at least on these most important of issues, to be paralyzed. Political and economic time has stood still for a decade: despite a few international conferences and grand declarations, we've done next to nothing to stem the flow of carbon dioxide that fuels the global warming. In fact, the United States alone now pours nearly 15 percent more CO_2 into the atmosphere than it did when this book was first published. In 1989, I said we needed to drive smaller cars and drive them less; in the intervening decade, average Americans have taken to piloting vehicles that would turn General Patton green with envy. We're not getting it.

It is the contrast between the pace at which the physical world is changing and the pace at which the human society is reacting that constitutes the key environmental fact of our time.

A decade ago, those of us who were convinced that the climate was warming fast were out on a limb. A sturdy limb—the fact that carbon dioxide trapped heat near the planet seemed irrefutable—but a limb nonetheless. All the studies and reports that catalogued the greenhouse effect fit neatly on my desk when I was writing this book; the science was still, in many ways, rudimentary. And so it was no surprise when that science, and the conclusions drawn from it, came under attack. That's how science works—each hypothesis tortured to find its weakness. By now, the studies on global warming would fill an airplane hangar. Postdocs have tapped into tundra, overflown rain forests, launched satellites, collected ancient pollen, counted tree rings, cored ice sheets, floated weather balloons, sent sound waves across entire oceans. Unlike the politicians, they really have worked overtime. And what have they learned? That the predictions of a decade ago were remarkably close to correct. We know a lot more about cloud formation and sulfur particles and sunspots than we did in 1989, but the expectation about how it will all sum out is essentially the same— human beings, with their cars and factories and burning rain forests, will increase the planet's temperature three or four degrees in the century to come.

Accidents of one kind or another helped speed the scientific work. Most notably, when Mount Pinatubo in the Philippines erupted with spectacular force in 1992, it filled the sky with an easily estimated quantity of various chemicals. The scientists running the various computer models of the planet's climate could plug those estimates right into their programs and forecast what would happen in the years ahead. NASA's James Hansen, who had already done more than anyone else to warn the world about the greenhouse effect, made the gutsiest call, issuing a precise prediction for how the planet's temperature would shift, month by month, in the next three years. At first he seemed to have missed, and greenhouse skeptics jumped all over the early results, using them to call the whole theory into question. But at a memorable scientific meeting in Hawaii, Hansen stood up and said, "I believe this is one case where the model is right and the world is wrong." And indeed, beginning with the very next month's readings, global temperatures began to match his predictions with eerie precision. The incident was one of many that made climatologists more confident of their complex models, and by 1995 the scientific jury had delivered its verdict. The International Panel on Climate Change, a collection of 1,500 scientists assembled by the United Nations, summarized all the data and concluded with this dry but historic understatement: "The balance of evidence suggests that there is a discernible human influence on global climate."

In other words, global warming no longer belonged in the category of distant and speculative threats. It was not like the danger of an asteroid strike. Instead, it was *under way*—we were in the rapids, not the smooth water above them. And, in fact, researchers increasingly insisted they could see its effects, even in these relatively early stages. As the air warms, it should evaporate more water from the surface, and it should then drop that extra water back on the planet—in other words, there should be an increase both in drought and in rainfall. One would expect events like the forest fires that turned day into night across Malaysia and Indonesia in 1997, or like the flooding that struck China, Bangladesh, Korea, Mexico, and a dozen other places in 1998. A study reported two years ago by Thomas Karl of the National Oceanic and Atmospheric Administration showed that "extreme precipitation events"—those storms that dump more than two inches of water in twenty-four hours—had increased 20 percent across our continent compared with 1900. That's an almost unbelievable surge. "If you look out your window, part of what you see in terms of weather is produced by ourselves," says Karl. "If you look out the window fifty years from now, we're going to be responsible for more of it."

So glaciers retreat around the world; the Arctic and Antarctic ice grows thinner and more unstable; the sea level rises imperceptibly but steadily. An increasing body of evidence indicates that if the temperatures increase past a certain threshold, it may well be enough to shut down the Gulf Stream, wreaking havoc on Europe. The world changes, changes dramatically, as we raise its temperature even slightly. That's what the last ten years have taught us.

But the message of the rainfall and the ice melt, and the dramatic findings of the scientific community, has been muted, thanks to a powerful campaign of disinformation launched and funded by those industries that can't imagine a future without fossil fuels. Next to my desk I have all of last year's reports on climate change from Greenwire, the *National Journal*'s daily e-mail update of environmental news. It covers all the new studies (polar bears weigh hundreds of pounds less than they did thirty years ago, because the ice fields where they hunt have shrunk; zooplankton decreased by 70 percent along the West Coast, thanks to warmer water). But just as importantly it provides short summaries of all the op-ed pieces and columns and essays that newspapers and magazines and TV shows have run on the issue. At least half, and in many weeks nearly all, of those essays and editorials seem to be coming from some other planet. The tiny squad of climate change skeptics, backed by lots of coal and oil money, never let up. Any tiny caveat in the deluge of studies—some scientist's admission that the computer forecasts are by their very nature "uncertain"—is seized upon as conclusive proof that the whole greenhouse theory is a sham. In 1998, during the warmest year in our history, a huge petition emerged, supposedly signed by thousands of scientists who think global warming won't occur; after widespread coverage, it turned out to be a worthless compilation of undocumented names collected over the Internet, including such luminaries as the Spice Girls.

I repeat—a decade ago such reactions were not only to be expected, they were necessary. It was part of the process; if journalists had not sought balance from the competing scientific camps, they would not have been doing their jobs. But by now it is an intellectual fraud to continue spreading the notion that global warming is one more theory that may or may not prove true.

The science, however, was only one part of the original book—and not its most important. What mattered most to me was the inference I drew from that science: that for the first time human beings had become so large that they altered everything around us. That we had ended nature as an independent force, that our appetites and habits and desires could now be read in every cubic meter of air, in every increment on the thermometer.

This doesn't make the consequences of global warming any worse in a practical sense, of course—we'd be in as tough a spot if the temperature was going up for entirely "natural" reasons. But to me it made this historical moment entirely different from any other, filled with implications for our philosophy, our theology, our sense of self. We are no longer able to think of ourselves as a species tossed about by larger forces—now we *are* those larger forces. Hurricanes and thunderstorms and tornadoes become not acts of God but acts of man. That was what I meant by the "end of nature."

Of course, everyone thinks they live at the hinge points of history. The academic debate that followed the book's release was, and continues to be, lively; many critics claimed that we weren't really "ending" nature because either we had been altering our surroundings for centuries, or we were a part of nature ourselves and hence couldn't destroy it.

Both objections, of course, are true. Emerging into the world hairless, slow, and relatively weak, we've had to use our one asset—our largish brains—to alter our surroundings. We've changed the places where we lived, the places where we grew our food, and even to some extent the wildernesses surrounding them. On this continent, for instance, the Indians would periodically burn sections of forest and prairie to improve the hunting. But always before our disruptions had some boundary to them; they were akin to the work of the beaver who lives next to me and manages to flood quite a large section of the lowland behind his dam. But there are plenty of places beyond the reach of his high water. Similarly, you could always find vast territory where human influence mattered not at all.

Beginning with the invisible releases of radiation, and then the toxic pollutants like DDT, and then the by-products of large-scale industrialization like acid rain, though, we began to alter even those places where we were not. Short of widescale nuclear war, global warming represents the largest imaginable such alteration: by changing the very temperature of the planet, we inexorably affect its flora, its fauna, its rainfall and evaporation, the decomposition of its soils. Every inch of the planet is different; indeed, the physics of climate means the most extreme changes are going on at the north and south poles, farthest from human beings. The byproducts—the pollutants—of one species have become the most powerful force for change on the planet. This change in quantity is so large that it becomes a change in quality. The story of our moment, of these few short decades when we happen to be alive, is the story of crossing that threshold.

And of course it is also true that we are part of nature—indeed, over the last few centuries we've forgotten, to our peril, how connected we actually are to the rest of the fabric of creation. But to me this does not make our blundering alteration of everything around us any more defensible or any less sad. Imagine that you have hiked to the edge of a pond in the forest and stand there admiring the sunset. If you should happen to look down and see a Coke can that someone has tossed there in the rushes, it will affect you differently than if you see a pile of deer droppings. And the reason, or at least one reason, is our intuitive understanding that the person who dropped the Coke can didn't need to, any more than we need to go on raising the temperature of the planet. We *are* different from the rest of the natural order, for the single reason that we possess the possibility of self-restraint, of choosing some other way.

Which brings us to politics, to the realm where we will make the collective decision on whether or not to restrain ourselves. Ten years ago, I said I thought real change would be extremely difficult, because addressing the issue meant altering the fundamentals of our lives. In important ways, modern human beings are machines for burning fossil fuels. Therefore, to level off fossil fuel consumption, much less reduce it the 70 percent the scientists say is necessary, involves tinkering with virtually every facet of our daily lives. We would need to change the ways we move ourselves around, the spaces we live in, the jobs we perform, the food we eat.

It's not that it *can't* be done. I've spent much of the last decade looking for ways out, for places that work. In a book called *Hope, Human and Wild*, I've written about the city of Curitiba in Brazil, where the bus system is so marvelous that its citizens use a third less fuel than other Brazilians. I've spent time in the Indian state of Kerala, where on an annual income of $300 and hence with minimal environmental impact on the globe, people have life expectancies, birthrates, and literacy rates that rival our own.

But such examples run completely counter to the trend of the past decade. In 1989, when I wrote *The End of Nature*, we still fretted about what would happen to the environment *if* China became a consumer nation; in the past ten years, it has annually added electric generating capacity equal to all of Southern California's, and now its auto industry is exploding. And China is merely symptomatic of the entire globe. With the Cold War over, the most powerful ideology by far is consumerism—there is no place on the planet now that does not fall under the enchantment of our images of the good life. One human being in five sees *Baywatch* each week, more than bow to Mecca or take communion or do any of the other things that theoretically shape our souls.

Even in our own sated nation, despite the advent of some individual shifts in the direction of voluntary simplicity, our sense of who and what we are becomes ever more linked to money and to goods. Bill Clinton, who dominated the decade, rose to power on the slogan "It's the economy, stupid," and boy was he right. We live in a buoyant and optimistic moment, with the stock market racing ever higher; the only things that truly scare us, like the Y2K computer bug or the Asian financial meltdown, are direct and immediate threats to that prosperity.

So it is no wonder that we haven't taken any steps at all toward dealing with global warming. In some sense, the physical world is no longer as real to us as the economic world—we cosset and succor the economy; our politicians gear every decision to speeding its further growth. So if someone says, "Ending our reliance on fossil fuels will harm the economy," that settles the issue. By contrast, if someone says, "Relying on fossil fuels is wrecking the planet," it seems an almost irrelevant objection—the Earth has become abstract, and the economy concrete, to us.

Some environmentalists have tried to argue, therefore, that weaning ourselves away from fossil fuels will in fact trigger an economic boom— that the transition to benign sources of energy will spur the next great technical revolution. In the long run, they are likely right. But in the short run, it presents the most wrenching changes, so wrenching that even environmentally minded politicians like Al Gore have instinctively shied away from making us face them. Gasoline now costs a quarter of the price of bottled water, and everyone knows that fact lies at the heart of our problems. But who will say so?

Other environmentalists have pinned their hopes on the idea that the consequences of global warming will become so unmistakable and terrifying that we will be roused from our consumer enchantment and moved to take action. In the late 1980s, for instance, NASA's Hansen predicted that climate change would be easily visible to the man in the street by the late 1990s. And he was dead-on. Most ordinary people think something's funny with the weather. How could they not? The price tag for 1998's round of natural disasters alone topped the bill for the entire 1980s.

So far, though, these floods and forest fires and heat waves don't seem to be spurring much demand for change. One reason may be the intuitive sense that in some ways it's too late to do anything about it all—that the physical forces we've unleashed are so large and terrifying that raising the gas tax a dime or even a dollar seems almost comically puny in comparison. In a way, this intuition is completely correct: it's far too late to stop global warming. All we can do is make it less bad than it will otherwise be. Our crusade, if we ever mount it, will be on behalf of a relatively livable world, not on behalf of the world that we were born into.

The scariest part of the chemistry of global warming involves "feedback loops"—the idea that as you raise the temperature you cause changes that will raise the temperature even more. If you warm the Arctic, for instance, thawing tundra may release huge amounts of carbon that will in turn accelerate the warming.

But feedback loops operate in other realms, too. A few years after *The End of Nature*, I wrote a book called *The Age of Missing Information*. To write it, I watched everything that came across the largest cable TV system on Earth for a single day—2,400 hours of videotape, a snapshot of our age. If you boiled down all that chatter to its most essential message, it would be this: you are the center of the world, the most important item in all creation. For environmentalists (as for preachers, and for those interested in social justice) no idea could be more dangerous. Not only do we need to see that we are part of something much larger, we need to feel the claims of that larger order. If our environmental problem is that we've gotten too large, then we need to figure out how to make ourselves smaller, *less* central.

But in ending nature, in finishing off that separate realm that has always served to make us feel smaller, we've completed a feedback loop of our own. It's harder to go to the forest now, or to the mountains, or to the ocean, or even to a patch of wildflowers and feel the same kind of wonderful smallness. Those Coke cans are everywhere. We're everywhere.

I have had the great luxury of living in the Adirondack Mountains of upstate New York these past ten years—one of the few places on the planet that gets more wild with each passing season. Thanks to the wisdom of the people of New York, it is a vast protected wilderness, one where people live in and among the rest of creation. You can still feel small here sometimes, which is for me the great antidote to despair. My daughter, now six years old, has grown up with an abiding sense of nature's size and peace and meaning. But even its untouched wildernesses are threatened by climate change and by the myriad of other human excesses. Its winters grow shorter, its summers hotter, its forests less stable. In the past decade, a great windstorm and an epic ice storm have passed through here, leveling thousands of square miles of forest. By the old way of reckoning, these were not disasters, just extreme incidences of the powerful forces that made this place. But now who knows what mixture of "nature" and of "us" they embody? Who knows what they mean?

So people sometimes ask: How should I cope with the sadness of watching nature end in our lifetimes, and with the guilt of knowing that each of us is in some measure responsible. The answer to the second part is easier: at the very least, we have to put up a good fight. I've worked on and written about materialism, population, and planning in the last decade, knowing that how well we control our numbers, our appetites, and the efficiency with which we satisfy those appetites will ordain just how desperate the situation becomes. They are the battles for our time, as morally compulsory as the battles for civil rights or against totalitarianism.

But even with that work, the sadness that drove me to write this book in the first place has not really lifted. This home of ours, the blessed hunk of rock and sky and biology that we were born onto, becomes each day a less complex and a more violent place; its rhythms of season and storm shifted and shattered. We didn't create this world, but we are busy decreating it. Still the sun rises; still the moon wanes and waxes; but they look down on a planet that means something different than it used to. Something less than it used to. This buzzing, blooming, mysterious, cruel, lovely globe of mountain, sea, city, forest; of fish and wolf and bug and man; of carbon and hydrogen and nitrogen—it has come unbalanced in our short moment on it. It's mostly us now.

AMITAI ETZIONI

Communitarianism and the Moral Dimension (2000)

The first University Professor of the George Washington University and the founding editor of the communitarian quarterly Responsive Community, *Amitai Etzioni (1929–) is a leading academic in the communitarian movement. The author of numerous scholarly works, Etzioni also writes frequently for major national newspapers on public policy issues that affect communities. In the following essay Etzioni contributes to current debates about the importance of "civil society" in America by distinguishing it from the more expansive and value-laden concept of the "good society," which he promotes as a communitarian moral ideal.*

A recent, very tempered debate between William A. Galston and Robert P. George brought into relief the importance of a concept neither employed, that of the good society. Galston argued, drawing on Aristotle, that we ought to differentiate between the good *citizen* and the good *person*. The preliberal state, he added, was concerned with the good person; the liberal state is one that limits itself to the cultivation of the good citizen. George, true to his social conservative position, countered that he does not see a great need or compelling merit in drawing a sharp distinction between the good citizen and the good person. Before I suggest a third position, a few more words of background.

Galston is representative of a communitarian variation of classical liberal thinking. Liberals limit themselves to ensuring that individuals develop those *personal* virtues that they need to be good citizens of the liberal state, for instance the ability to think critically. In contrast, social conservatives maintain that it is the role of the state to promote not merely citizenship but also the good person, not only skills needed to participate in the polity, but also *social* virtues—those that make the society a good one.

George Will champions this position, arguing that people are self-indulgent by nature: left to their own devices, they will abuse their liberties, becoming profligate and indolent as a result. People need a "strong national government" that will be a "shaper" of citizens, and help them cope with the weaker angles of their nature. William Kristol and David Brooks argue that anti-government themes provide too narrow a base for constructing a winning ideological political agenda. Conservatives, they conclude, need to build on the virtue of America, on the ideal of national greatness.

Religious social conservatives have long been willing to rely on the powers of the state to foster behavior they consider virtuous. The measures they favor include banning abortion, banning most kinds of porn, making divorce more difficult, curbing homosexual activities, and institutionalizing prayers in public schools. Additionally, both religious and secular social conservatives have strongly advocated longer, more arduous prison terms for more individuals, for more kinds of crime, favoring especially life-sentences without the possibility of parole and death sentences. These penalties often are applied to people of whose business and consumption the state disapproves (a large proportion of those in jail are there for nonviolent, drug-related crimes) rather than for failing to discharge their citizen duties or actually endangering public safety. These are, on the face of it, not citizen issues but good-person issues.

The term "good state" appropriately summarizes this position because far from being viewed as an institution that if extended inevitably would diminish or corrupt people, the state is treated as an institution that can be entrusted with the task of making people good. That is, while it is not at all suggested that the state is good in itself, it is indicated that the state can be good—provided it acts to foster virtue.

Before moving on, it should be noted that among social conservatives, as among all such large and encompassing schools of thought and belief, there are important differences of opinion. It is relevant for the discussion at hand to note that there are many social conservatives who are less state- and more society-minded, such as Michael Oakeshott and a group associated with the Heritage Foundation called the National Foundation for Civic Renewal. That there are strong and less-strong social conservatives does not, however, invalidate their defining characteristic. To put it differently, thinkers who would rely mainly on the society and on persuasion to promote virtue by my definition are not social conservatives, but rather have one of the defining attributes of communitarians.

Both the liberal and social conservative positions have rich, well-known histories and profound roots in social philosophy and political theory. While I will not retrace their often-reviewed intellectual foundations here, I refer to one item of the sociology of knowledge: Each of these two positions can be viewed as addressing a particular historical constellation. The liberal position speaks to both the authoritarian and dogmatic environments in which it was first formulated by Locke, Smith, and Mill, as well as the totalitarian experiences of the twentieth century. At its core is a profound concern with the overpowering state and established church, especially if these institutions muster not merely superior and encompassing force but also actually succeed in acquiring an ideological mantle of virtue. The liberal position, which arose as a rejection of the good state, tended to reject all social formulations of the good.

Contemporary social conservative positions, by contrast, address the loss of virtue that modernization and populism have engendered, and reflect a profound concern with rising moral anarchy. While such concerns have been raised since the beginning of industrialization (if not before), they have particularly reintensified since the 1970s. It is this condition that religious fundamentalism seeks to correct, whether the fundamentalists in question are Muslims, Orthodox Jews, or some members of the religious right in the United States.

The third position, the communitarian one, which focuses on the good society, addresses the same sociohistorical conditions that motivate contemporary social conservatives, but provides a fundamentally different response. Much like its liberal cousin, the communitarian position rejects state regulation of moral behavior. Liberals, however, typically take this position because they favor moral pluralism; that is, they hold a broad conception of tolerance that includes the "right to do wrong." In the words of Michael Sandel, they "take pride in defending what they oppose." Communitarians, by contrast, advocate state restraint because they believe that the society should be the agent responsible for promoting moral behavior. Thus, while the communitarian alternative I outline here may seem similar in certain limited respects to both social conservative and liberal positions, it nonetheless should be clear that its focus on the good society is conceptually distinct from both of these.

The Core, not The Whole

A good society formulates and promotes shared moral understanding rather than merely pluralism, and hence is far from value-neutral. This does not mean, however, that a good society sets an all-encompassing or even "thick" moral agenda. I discuss first the special nature of the formulation of the good by a communitarian society and then its limited scope.

Much has been written about whether or not there are sociological needs and moral justifications for social formulations of the good. The discussion, it has been stressed, concerns the public realm, namely the formulations that guide the state, which in turn may impose them on those who do not see the goodness of these formulations. I refer here to shared formulations that arise out of moral dialogues among the members of the society, initiated by secular and religious intellectuals and moral authorities, community leaders, other opinion makers, and nourished by the media.

Developing and sustaining a good society does require reaching into what is considered the private realm, the realm of the person. (Indeed, it might be said, that this "is" where the society is in the first place.) A good society, for instance, fosters trust among its members not solely or even primarily to enhance their trust in the government or to reduce burdens on the general public (for example, the problem of litigiousness), but rather to foster what is considered a *better* society. (What is "better" can be accounted for in utilitarian terms—for instance, by observing that in a society with a higher level of trust among its members there will be less white-collar crime—as well as in deontological ones, a notion I do not pursue further in this article.) Other examples: a good society may extol substantive values such as stewardship toward the environment, charity for those who are vulnerable, marriage over singlehood, having children, and showing special consideration to the young and elderly. These are all specific goods with regard to which the society, through its various social mechanisms, prefers *one* basic form of conduct over all others. For instance, contemporary American society considers commitment to the well-being of the environment a significant good. While differences regarding what exactly this commitment entails are considered legitimate, this is not the case for normative positions that are neglectful of, not to mention hostile to, the needs of the environment.

To suggest that the scope of the private realm needs to be reduced; however, does not mean that all or even most private matters need to be subject to societal scrutiny and control. Indeed, one major way the communitarian position differs from its totalitarian, authoritarian, theocratic, and social conservative counterparts (referred to from here on as holistic governments) is that while the good society reaches the person, it seeks to cultivate only a limited set of *core* virtues rather than to be more expansive or holistic. A good society does not seek to ban moral pluralism on many secondary matters. For example, American society favors being religious over being atheist, but is rather "neutral" with regard to what religion a person follows. Similarly, American society expects that its members will show a measure of commitment to the American creed, but is quite accepting of people who cherish their divergent ethnic heritages, as long as such appreciation does not conflict with national loyalties. Unlike totalitarian regimes, American society does not foster one kind of music over others (both Nazis and communists tried to suppress jazz). There are no prescribed dress codes (e.g., no spartan Mao shirts), correct number of children to have, places one is expected to live, and so forth. In short, one key defining characteristic of the good society is that it defines shared formulations of the good, in contrast to the liberal state, while the scope of the good is much smaller than that advanced by holistic governments.

Reliance on Culture; its Agencies

Aside from limiting the scope of its moral agenda, the good society differs from its alternatives in the principal means by which it nurtures virtue. The basic dilemma that the concept of the good society seeks to resolve is how to cultivate virtue if one views the state as an essentially inappropriate and coercive entity.

In addressing this question, it is important to note that reference is not merely or even mainly to obeying the relevant laws, but rather to those large areas of personal and social conduct that are not governed by law, as well as to those that must be largely voluntarily carried out even if covered by laws, if law enforcement is not to be overwhelmed. At issue are such questions as what obligations parents owe to their children, children to their elderly parents, neighbors to one another, members of communities to other members and to other communities.

The means of nurturing virtue that good societies chiefly rely upon often are subsumed under the term "culture." Specifically, these means include (a) agencies of *socialization* (family, schools, some peer groups, places of worship, and some voluntary associations) that instill values into new members of the society, resulting in an internal moral voice (or conscience) that guides people toward goodness. (b) Agencies of *social reinforcement* that support, in the social psychosocial sense of the term, the values members already have acquired (especially interpersonal bonds, peer relations, communal bonds, public visibility and leadership). These provide an external moral voice. And (c) values fostered because they are built into *societal institutions* (for instance, into marriage). I explore first the moral voice (internal and external) and ask whether it is compatible with liberty, and then the question of how the role societal institutions play in the good society differs from that which they play in the civil society.

THE MORAL VOICE AND LIBERTY

One main instrument of the good society, the mainstay of "culture," is the moral voice, which urges people to behave in prosocial ways. While there is a tendency to stress the importance of the inner voice, and hence good parenting and moral or character education, communitarians recognize the basic fact that without continual external reinforcement, the conscience tends to deteriorate. The opinion of fellow human beings, especially those to whom a person is attached through familial or communal bonds, carries a considerable weight because of a profound human need to win and sustain the approval of others.

The question has arisen whether compliance with the moral voice is compatible with free choice, whether one's right to be let (or left) alone includes a right to be free not only from state controls but also social pressure. This issue is highlighted by different interpretations assigned to an often-cited line by John Stuart Mill. In *On Liberty*, Mill writes, "The object of this Essay is to assert one very simple principle, as entitled to govern absolutely the dealings of society with the individual in the way of compulsion and control, whether the means used be physical force in the form of legal penalties, or the moral coercion of public opinion." Some have interpreted this statement to suggest on its face that the moral voice is just as coercive as the government. Similarly, Alexis de Tocqueville, years earlier, wrote that "The multitude require no laws to coerce those who do not think like themselves: public disapprobation is enough; a sense of their loneliness and impotence overtakes them and drives them to despair." If one takes these lines as written, the difference between reinforcement by the community and that by the state becomes a distinction without a difference. One notes, though, that de Tocqueville is also known for having highlighted the importance of communal associations in holding the state at bay. As I see it, it is essential to recognize not only that there is a profound difference between the moral voice of the community and coercion, but also that up to a point, the moral voice is the best antidote to an oppressive state.

At the heart of the matter are the assumptions one makes about human nature. If one believes that people are good by nature, and external forces merely serve to pervert them, one correctly rejects all social input. It follows that the freer people are from all pressures, the better their individual and collective condition. If one assumes that people possess frailties that lead to behavior that is damaging not only to self but also others, the question arises of how to foster prosocial behavior (or the "social order"). Classical liberals tend to solve this tension between liberty and order by assuming that rational individuals whose interests are mutually complementary will voluntarily agree to arrangements that provide for the needed order. Communitarians suggest that reasonable individuals cannot be conceived of outside a social order; that the ability to make rational choices, to be free, presumes that the person is embedded in a social fabric. Moreover, communitarians posit that there is an inverse relation between the social order and state coercion: tyrannies arise when the social fabric frays. The moral voice speaks for the social fabric, thereby helping to keep it in good order.

Aside from being an essential prerequisite of social order and hence liberty, the moral voice is much more compatible with free choice than state coercion. The internal moral voice is as much a part of the person's self as the other parts of the self that drive his or her choices, the various tastes that specify the person's pleasures. The external moral voice, that of the community, leaves the final judgment and determination of how to proceed to the acting person—an element that is notably absent when coercion is applied. The society persuades, cajoles, censures, and educates, but that final decision remains the actor's. The state may also persuade, cajole, and censure, but actors realize *a priori* that when the state is not heeded, it will seek to force the actors to comply.

Some have questioned whether the moral voice is never coercive. In part, this is a definitional matter. When the moral voice is backed up by legal or economic sanctions, one must take care to note that it is not the moral voice per se, but rather these added elements that are coercive. Also, it is true in the West that in earlier historical periods, when people were confined to a single village and the community voice was all-powerful, a unified chorus of moral voices could be quite overwhelming even if it is not technically coercive, as physical force is not used or threatened. (It clearly can still be so in some limited parts of the West, and most assuredly in other parts of the world.) However, most people in contemporary free societies are able to choose, to a significant extent, the communities to which they are psychologically committed, and can often draw on one to limit the persuasive power of another. And the voices are far from monolithic. Indeed, it is a principal communitarian thesis that, in Western societies, moral voices often are, by and large, far from overwhelming. In fact, more often than not, they are too conflicted, hesitant, and weak to provide for a good society. In short, highly powerful moral voices exist(ed) largely in other places and eras.

A comparison of the way the United States government fights the use of controlled substances and the way American society fosters parents' responsibilities for their children highlights this issue. The war against drugs depends heavily upon coercive agents; the treatment of children, by contrast, relies primarily upon the moral voice of members of the immediate and extended family, friends, neighbors, and others in the community. Admittedly, the state occasionally steps in. Yet most parents discharge their responsibilities not because they fear jail, but rather because they believe this to be the right way to conduct themselves, notions that are reinforced by the social fabric of their lives.

The difference between the ways societies and states foster values is further highlighted by comparing transferring wealth via charity to taxes; between volunteering to serve one's country and being drafted; and between attending Alcoholics Anonymous meetings and being jailed for alcohol abuse.

The basically voluntaristic nature of the moral voice is the profound reason the good society can, to a large extent, be reconciled with liberty, while a state that fosters good persons cannot. It is the reason the good society requires a clear moral voice, speaking for a set of shared core values, which a civic society and a liberal state do not.

VIRTUES IN SOCIAL INSTITUTIONS

The other main instrument of the good society are social institutions. While the moral voice often is correctly referred to as "informal," because it is not encoded in law, and is integrated into one's personality and interactions with others, societal institutions are formal and structured. Institutions are societal patterns that embody the values of the particular society or community. A large volume of interactions and transactions are greatly facilitated in that they are predated by social forms upon which actors draw. Contracts are a case in point. Not only can actors often build in whole or in part on texts of contracts prepared by others, but the actors find the very concept of a contract and what this entails in terms of mutual obligations and the moral notion that "contracts ought to be observed" ready-made in their culture. While these institutions change over time, at any one point in time many of them stand by to guide social life, especially in well-functioning societies.

Social institutions are important for the characterization of the difference between the good society and others, because most institutions are neither merely procedural nor value-neutral; in effect, most are the embodiment of particular values. For instance, the family, a major societal institution, is never value-neutral, but always reflects a particular set of values. This reality is highlighted by the reluctance of the Catholic Church to marry divorced people, attempts by several organized religions to encourage people to prepare better for their marriage (e.g., through *pre*marital counseling), and to strengthen their marriages (e.g., by means of counseling, retreats, and renewal of vows). All these institutionalized endeavors reflect the value of marriage—and a particular kind of marriage—that society seeks to uphold.

Similarly, societies do not merely provide public schools as neutral agencies for the purpose of imparting knowledge and skills. Public schools typically foster, despite recent tendencies to deny this fact, a long list of values, including empathy for the poor, interracial and interethnic and other forms of mutual respect (beyond merely tolerance), high regard for science, secularism, patriotism, and stewardship toward the environment. That societies foster specific values, through their institutions, is crucial for the understanding of the limits of conceptions of the civic society.

A CIVIL AND GOOD SOCIETY

A comparison of the good society with the civil society provides a clearer delineation of both concepts. It should be noted at the outset that these terms are by no means oppositional. The good society is simply a more expansive concept. Thus, far from being uncivil, it fosters additional virtues beyond the merely civil. To put it differently, the two concepts are like concentric circles, with the smaller circle representing the domain of civil society, and the larger that of the good society.

While there is no single, agreed-upon definition of civil society, most usages of the term reflect two institutional features and the values they embody. One is a rich array of voluntary associations that countervails the state and that provides the citizens with the skills and practices that democratic government requires. Another is holding of passions at bay and enhancing deliberative, reasoned democracy by maintaining the civility of discourse.

In a special issue of the *Brookings Review* dedicated to the civil society, editor E. J. Dionne Jr. characterizes the civil society as (a) "a society where people treat each other with kindness and respect, avoiding the nastiness we have come to associate with 30-second political ads and a certain kind of televised brawl." And (b) a collection of voluntary associations that includes Boy and Girl Scouts, Little League, veterans groups, book clubs, Lions and Elks, churches, and neighborhood crime watch groups. Most discussions stress the second feature. "Bowling alone" has become somewhat of a symbol for this line of thinking. Robert Putnam argues that bowling with one's friends (which he terms alone) is less sustaining of civil society than bowling as members of a bowling league because such leagues are part and parcel of the voluntary associations that civil society requires.

From the viewpoint of the discussion at hand, the most important aspect of these characterizations of civil society is that they draw *no difference among voluntary associations with regard to any substantive values* that are fostered by bowling leagues, book clubs, Little Leagues, or any other such voluntary associations. I am not suggesting that these associations are actually without specific normative dispositions. Little Leagues, for instance, may cherish a healthy body and sporting behavior (or—winning at all costs); book clubs foster respect for learning and culture, and so on. But from the viewpoint of their contribution to civil society they all are treated by champions of civil society as basically equivalent; none is, normatively speaking, inherently morally superior to the other. In this particular sense, they are treated as normatively neutral.

Certainly champions of civil society do recognize some differences among voluntary associations, but these are limited to their functions as elements of the civil society rather than their normative content. For instance, voluntary associations that are more effective in developing citizen skills are preferred over those that are less so. But the actual values to which these people apply their skills is not under review nor are other substantive values the associations embody. Thus, the civil society does affirm some values, but only a thin layer of procedural and/or tautological ones; it basically affirms itself. Hence, the civil society (and the associations that constitute its backbone) cherishes reasoned (rather then value-laden) discourse, mutual tolerance, participatory skills, and, of course, volunteerism. Yet these values, upon closer examination, do not entail any particular social formulations of the good. They do not suggest what one best participates in or for, what one should volunteer to support, or which normative conclusions of a public discourse one ought to promote or find troubling.

Particularly telling are recent calls to find *a* common ground and to deliberate in a civil manner—two contentless elements of civility often evoked whenever civil society is discussed. Commonality is celebrated on any grounds as long as it is common. And the proponents of civility seem satisfied as long as one adheres to the rules of engagements (not to demonize the other side, not raise one's voice, etc.), and as long as the dialogue itself is civil, regardless of what actually is being discussed.

For the civil society, an association that facilitates people joining to play bridge has the same basic standing as NARAL or Operation Rescue; members of the Elks share the same status as those of the Promise Keepers; and bowling leagues are indistinguishable from NAMBLA, whose members meet to exchange tips on how to seduce boys who are younger than eight. Indeed, beyond league bowling (and bridge playing), other mainstays of "social capital" that Putnam found in those parts of Italy that are more soundly civil and democratic than others were bird-watching groups and choral societies. Bird-watching groups may enhance respect for nature and choirs may cherish culture (or certain kinds of culture over others), but this is not the reason Putnam praises them. As Putnam puts it, he extols them because "[t]aking part in a choral society or a bird-watching club can teach self-discipline and an appreciation for the joys of successful collaboration." So could most if not all other voluntary associations.

In short, from the basic standpoint of the civil society, one voluntary association is, in principle, as good as any another. They differ greatly, however, from the perspective of the good society, precisely because they embody different values. Thus, to the extent that American society cherishes the notion of interracial integration, it views the Urban League and NAACP as much more in line with its values than the Nation of Islam, and the Ripon Society more so than the Aryan groups—all voluntary associations.

The concept of the good society differs from that of the civil one in that while the former also strongly favors voluntary associations—a rich and strong social fabric, and civility of discourse—it formulates and seeks to uphold some *particular* social conceptions of the good. The good society is, as I have already suggested, centered around a core of substantive, particularistic values. For instance, different societies foster different values or at least give much more normative weight to some values than other societies that exhibit a commitment to the same values. Thus, Austria, Holland, and Switzerland place special value on social harmony, acting only after profound and encompassing shared understandings are achieved. Many continental societies value the welfare state, lower inequality, and social amenities more than American and British societies do, and also put less emphasis upon economic achievements.

Similarly, the question of whether or not religion is disestablished is far from a procedural matter. Many democratic societies that establish one church (e.g., Anglican in the United Kingdom, Lutheran in Scandinavia) also allow much greater and more open inclusion of a specific religion into their institutionalized life than does American society. The presence of crucifixes in Bavarian public schools and the routine pronouncement of Christian prayers in UK schools both illustrate this point. Promoting these religious values is deemed an integral part of what is considered a good society.

I digress to note that none of the societies mentioned are "good" in some perfected sense; they are societies that aspire to promote specific social virtues, and in this sense aspire to be good societies. The extent to which they are successful, and the normative evaluation of the specific virtues one society promotes as compared to others, are subjects not studied here because this would requires an extensive treatment that I have provided elsewhere. All that I argue here is that good societies promote particularistic, substantive formations of the good; that these are limited sets of core values that are promoted largely by the moral voice and not by state coercion. The conditions under which the particular values fostered earn our acclaim is not studied here.

To summarize the difference between a good and a civil society regarding the core institution of voluntary association, one notes that while both kinds of society draw on these associations, these play different roles within these two societies. In civil societies, voluntary associations serve as mediating institutions between the citizen and the state, and help cultivate citizen skills (ways to gain knowledge about public affairs, form associations, gain a political voice, and so on); they develop and exercise the democratic muscles, so to speak. In the good society, voluntary associations *also* serve to introduce members to particularistic values, and to reinforce individuals' normative commitments. Thus, while from the perspective of a civil society a voluntary association is a voluntary association, *from the view of a good society, no two voluntary associations are equivalent.* The regard in which voluntary associations are held ranges from those that are celebrated (because they foster the social virtues the good society seeks to cultivate), to those that are neutral, to those that— while voluntary—sustain values divergent from or even contradictory to those the society seeks to foster.

ACKNOWLEDGMENTS

Abigail Adams: "Letter to John Adams, Braintree, MA, March 31, 1776." Reprinted with permission of the publisher from *The Adams Papers: Adams Family Correspondence, Volume 1*: December 1761–May 1776, edited by L. H. Butterfield, Cambridge, Mass.: The Belknap Press of Harvard University Press, Copyright © 1963 by the Massachusetts Historical Society.

Charles A. Beard: "The Myth of Rugged American Individualism." Copyright © 1931 by Harper's Magazine. All rights reserved. Reproduced from the October issue by special permission.

Daniel Bell: From *The End of Ideology* (Free Press of Glencoe: 1960), pp. 370–375. Reprinted by permission of the author.

Allan Bloom: "Liberal Education" and "Conclusion." Reprinted with the permission of Simon & Schuster Adult Publishing Group from *The Closing of the American Mind* by Allan Bloom. Copyright © 1987 by Allan Bloom.

William F. Buckley, Jr.: From the book *God & Man at Yale* by William F. Buckley, Jr. Copyright © 1951. Published by Regnery Publishing, Inc. All rights reserved. Reprinted by special permission of Regnery Publishing, Inc., Washington, D.C.

Stokely Carmichael: "Toward Black Liberation," *The Massachusetts Review*, August 1966, pp. 639–640; 642–651. Reprinted with permission of The Massachusetts Review.

Whittaker Chambers: From *Witness* by Whittaker Chambers, copyright © 1952 by Whittaker Chambers. Used by permission of Random House, Inc.

Robert A. Dahl: From *Who Governs? Democracy and Power in an American City* (1961), pp. 1–3, 11, 85–86, 89–92, 95–97, 100–102. Copyright © 1961 Yale University Press. Reprinted with permission.

John Dewey: From *Liberalism and Social Action* by John Dewey, copyright 1935 by John Dewey, renewed 1962 by Roberta L. Dewey. Used by permission of G.P. Putnam's Sons, a division of Penguin Group (USA) Inc. "The Public and Its Problems" from *The Collected Works of John Dewey, The Later Works, 1925–1953 Volume 2: 1925–1927 Essays, Reviews, Miscellany, and The Public and Its Problems*. Copyright © 1988 by the Board of Trustees, Southern Illinois University, reproduced by permission of the publisher.

Amitai Etzioni: "Communitarianism and the Moral Dimension," *The Essential Civil Society Reader*, ed. Don E. Eberly, pp. 123–133. Reprinted with permission of Rowman & Littlefield Publishers, Inc.

Hiram W. Evans: "The Klan's Fight for Americanism," *North American Review*, Volume 223, No. 1, 1926. Reprinted with permission of the North American Review. This selection is a historical document and does not reflect the current language, opinions, or priorities of the North American Review or the University of Northern Iowa.

Betty Friedan: From *The Feminine Mystique* by Betty Friedan. Copyright © 1983, 1974, 1973, 1963 by Betty Friedan. Used by permission of W.W. Norton & Company, Inc.

Milton Friedman and Rose D. Friedman: Excerpts from *Free to Choose: A Personal Statement*, copyright © 1980 by Milton Friedman and Rose D. Friedman, reprinted by permission of Harcourt, Inc.

Barry M. Goldwater: pp. 5–7, 9–20, 22–23 from *The Conscience of a Conservative.* © 1960 by Victor Publishing Co., Inc., General Editor's Intro. © 2007 by Sean Wilentz. Published by Princeton University Press. Reprinted by permission of Princeton University Press.

Learned Hand: "A Plea for the Freedom of Dissent" from *The New York Times Magazine*, February 6, 1955, pp. 12, 33, 35. Reprinted by permission of the Estate of Learned Hand.

Louis Hartz: "The Concept of a Liberal Society." Excerpts from *The Liberal Tradition in America: An Interpretation of American Political Thought Since the Revolution*, copyright © 1955 and renewed 1983 by Louis Hartz, reprinted by permission of Harcourt, Inc.

bell hooks: From *Feminist Theory: From Margin to Center*, pp. 33–35, 37, 40–41, 157–163. Reprinted by permission of South End Press.

Herbert Hoover: "The Fifth Freedom" from *The Rotarian Magazine*, April, 1943 and "The Challenge to Liberty" from a speech delivered before the Young Republicans League of Colorado, Denver, Colorado, October 30, 1936. Reprinted by permission of the Herbert Hoover Presidential Library.

Langston Hughes: "Let America Be America Again" from *The Collected Poems of Langston Hughes* by Langston Hughes, edited by Arnold Rampersad with David Roessel, Associate Editor, copyright © 1994 by The Estate of Langston Hughes. Used by permission of Alfred A. Knopf, a division of Random House, Inc.

George Kennan: "The Sources of Soviet Conduct," *Foreign Affairs*. Reprinted by permission of Foreign Affairs (25, July 1947). Copyright © 1947 by the Council on Foreign Relations, Inc.

Martin Luther King Jr.: "I Have a Dream" and "Letter from Birmingham Jail," Reprinted by arrangement with The Heirs to the Estate of Martin Luther King Jr., c/o Writers House as agent for the proprietor, New York, NY. Copyright © 1963 Martin Luther King Jr.; Copyright © renewed 1991 Coretta Scott King.

Irving Kristol: "Capitalism, Socialism, and Nihilism," *The Public Interest*, No. 31, Spring 1973, pp. 3–7, 9–16. Reprinted by permission of the author.

Walter Lippmann: From *The Public Philosophy* by Walter Lippmann. Copyright © 1955 by Walter Lippmann. Reprinted by permission of Little, Brown and Co. "Planning in an Economy of Abundance," *Atlantic Monthly*, Vol. 159, Jan.–June 1937, pp. 42–46. Walter Lippmann Papers, Manuscripts and Archives, Yale University Library. Reprinted with the permission of the Yale University Library.

Malcolm X: "The Ballot or the Bullet" from *The Autobiography of Malcolm X* by Malcolm X and Alex Haley, copyright © 1964 by Alex Haley and Malcolm X. Copyright © 1965 by Alex Haley and Betty Shabazz. Used by permission of Random House, Inc.

Thurgood Marshall: "The Constitution's Bicentennial," *Vanderbilt Law Review*, Vol. 40, 1987, pp. 1337–1342. Reprinted with permission from Vanderbilt Law Review.

Bill McKibben: "Introduction," from *The End of Nature* by William McKibben, copyright © 1989, 2006 by William McKibben. Used by permission of Random House, Inc.

Kate Millett: From *Sexual Politics* by Kate Millett. Copyright © 1969, 1970, 1990, 2000 by Kate Millett. (University of Illinois Press). Reprinted by permission of Georges Borchardt, Inc., for Kate Millett.

C. Wright Mills: "Letter to the New Left," *New Left Review* I/5, pp. 21–23. Reprinted by permission. From *The Power Elite*, pp. 3–12, 18. Copyright © 1956 by Oxford University Press, Inc. Reprinted by permission of Oxford University Press, Inc.

NOW: National Organization for Women's 1967 Bill of Rights. Reproduced with permission of the National Organization for Women. The NOW Bill of Rights is a historical document and may not reflect the current language or priorities of the organization.

Reinhold Niebuhr: From *The Children of Light and the Children of Darkness*, pp. 1–7, 16–17, 40, 63–65, 68–71. Reprinted with permission of the Estate of Reinhold Niebuhr.

Robert Nozick: *Anarchy, State, and Utopia*, pp. ix, 26–27, 149–164, 168–170, 172. Copyright © 1974 by Basic Books, Inc. Reprinted with permission of Perseus Books Group.

John Rawls: Reprinted by permission of the publisher from *A Theory of Justice* by John Rawls, pp. 11–16, 60–65, 78, 101–104, 152–153, 155–156, Cambridge, Mass.: The Belknap Press of Harvard University Press, Copyright © 1971, 1999 by the President and Fellows of Harvard College.

Redstockings of the Women's Liberation Movement: "The Redstockings Manifesto." Reprinted with the permission of Archives for Action. Further information about the Manifesto and other materials from the 1960's rebirth years of feminism is available from the Redstockings Women's Liberation Archives for Action at www.redstockings.org or PO Box 744, Stuyvesant Station, New York, NY 10009.

Pat Robertson: "A Portrait of America" from *The Turning Tide* by Pat Robertson, pp. 245–249, 251, 253–255, 267. Reprinted by permission of the author.

Richard Rorty: Reprinted by permission of the publisher from "A Cultural Left" in *Achieving Our Country: Leftist Thought in Twentieth-Century America* by Richard Rorty, pp. 91–107, Cambridge, Mass.: Harvard University Press, Copyright © 1998 by the President and Fellows of Harvard College.

Jerry Rubin: "A Yippie Manifesto," *The Evergreen Review*, Vol. 13, No. 6, 1969, pp. 41–43, 83–86, 88–90, 92. Reprinted with permission of Evergreen Review, Inc.

Bayard Rustin: "From Protest to Politics," *Commentary*, Volume 39, No. 2, 1965. Reprinted from Commentary, February 1965, by permission; all rights reserved.

Michael J. Sandel: "The Public Philosophy of Contemporary Liberalism" reprinted by permission of the publisher from *Democracy's Discontent: America in Search of a Public Philosophy* by Michael J. Sandel, pp. 4–24, Cambridge, Mass.: The Belknap Press of Harvard University Press, Copyright © 1996 by Michael J. Sandel.

Mario Savio: "An End to History" from *Humanity: An Arena of Critique and Commitment*, No. 2, Dec. 1964. Used with permission of Lynne Hollander Savio.

Phyllis Schlafly: From *The Power of the Positive Woman* by Phyllis Schlafly. Copyright © 1977 by Phyllis Schlafly. Reprinted by permission.

Arthur M. Schlesinger, Jr.: "What Is Loyalty? A Difficult Question." First published in *The New York Times*, November 2, 1947. Copyright © 1947 by Arthur Schlesinger. Reprinted by permission of The Wylie Agency.

Student Nonviolent Coordinating Committee: "Statement of Purpose" from *The Student Voice 1960–1965: Periodical of the Student Nonviolent Coordinating Committee*, ed. Clayborne Carson, p. 2. Copyright © 1990 Martin Luther King, Jr. Papers Project. Reproduced with permission of Greenwood Publishing Group, Inc., Westport, CT.

Students for a Democratic Society: The Port Huron Statement, 1962, pp. 3–8, 13–14, 46–48, 50. Reprinted by permission of Tom Hayden.

R. G. Tugwell: "The Principle of Planning and the Institution of Laissez Faire," *The American Economic Review*, Vol. 22, No. 1, March 1932, p. 75–80, 82–85, 88–92. Reprinted with permission of the American Economic Association.

Twelve Southerners: From *I'll Take My Stand: The South and Agrarian Tradition*. Copyright © 1930 by Harper & Brothers. Copyright renewed 1958 by Donald Davidson. Introduction copyright © 1962, 1977 by Louis D. Rubin, Jr. Biographical essays copyright © 1962, 1977 by Virginia Rock. Reprinted with permission from Louisiana State University Press.

Henry A. Wallace: Excerpts from *New Frontiers*, copyright © 1934 by Henry A. Wallace, reprinted by permission of Harcourt, Inc.

Michael Walzer: "What Does It Mean to Be an 'American'?" *Social Research: An International Quarterly of the Social Sciences*. 57:3 (Fall 1990): 591–614. www.socres.org. Reprinted by permission.

Cornel West: *Race Matters* by Cornel West, pp 1–8. Copyright © 1993, 2001 by Cornel West. Reprinted by permission of Beacon Press, Boston.

Young Americans for Freedom: The Sharon Statement, *National Review*, September 24, 1960. Reprinted by permission of Young Americans for Freedom/YAF Foundation.

Every effort has been made to contact the copyright holder of each of the selections. Rights holders of any selections not credited should contact Permissions Department, W. W. Norton & Company, Inc., 500 Fifth Avenue, New York, NY 10110, in order for a correction to be made in the next reprinting of our work.

INDEX